Nineteenth-Century Literature Criticism

Guide to Gale Literary Criticism Series

For criticism on	Consult these Gale series
Authors now living or who died after December 31, 1999	*CONTEMPORARY LITERARY CRITICISM (CLC)*
Authors who died between 1900 and 1999	*TWENTIETH-CENTURY LITERARY CRITICISM (TCLC)*
Authors who died between 1800 and 1899	*NINETEENTH-CENTURY LITERATURE CRITICISM (NCLC)*
Authors who died between 1400 and 1799	*LITERATURE CRITICISM FROM 1400 TO 1800 (LC)* *SHAKESPEAREAN CRITICISM (SC)*
Authors who died before 1400	*CLASSICAL AND MEDIEVAL LITERATURE CRITICISM (CMLC)*
Authors of books for children and young adults	*CHILDREN'S LITERATURE REVIEW (CLR)*
Dramatists	*DRAMA CRITICISM (DC)*
Poets	*POETRY CRITICISM (PC)*
Short story writers	*SHORT STORY CRITICISM (SSC)*
Black writers of the past two hundred years	*BLACK LITERATURE CRITICISM (BLC)* *BLACK LITERATURE CRITICISM SUPPLEMENT (BLCS)*
Hispanic writers of the late nineteenth and twentieth centuries	*HISPANIC LITERATURE CRITICISM (HLC)* *HISPANIC LITERATURE CRITICISM SUPPLEMENT (HLCS)*
Native North American writers and orators of the eighteenth, nineteenth, and twentieth centuries	*NATIVE NORTH AMERICAN LITERATURE (NNAL)*
Major authors from the Renaissance to the present	*WORLD LITERATURE CRITICISM, 1500 TO THE PRESENT (WLC)* *WORLD LITERATURE CRITICISM SUPPLEMENT (WLCS)*

ISSN 0732-1864

Volume 91

Nineteenth-Century Literature Criticism

Excerpts from Criticism of the
Works of Novelists, Philosophers, and Other
Creative Writers Who Died between 1800
and 1899, from the First Published Critical
Appraisals to Current Evaluations

Juliet Byington
Editor

GALE GROUP

Detroit
New York
San Francisco
London
Boston
Woodbridge, CT

STAFF

Lynn M. Spampinato, Janet Witalec, *Managing Editors, Literature Product*
Kathy D. Darrow, *Product Liaison*
Juliet Byington, Suzanne Dewsbury, *Editors*
Mark W. Scott, *Publisher, Literature Product*

Mary Ruby, Patti A. Tippett, *Technical Training Specialists*
Deborah J. Morad, Kathleen Lopez Nolan, *Managing Editors, Literature Content*
Susan M. Trosky, *Director, Literature Content*

Maria L. Franklin, *Permissions Manager*
Edna Hedblad, *Permissions Specialist*
Shalice Shah, *Permissions Assistant*

Victoria B. Cariappa, *Research Manager*
Tracie A. Richardson, *Project Coordinator*
Andrew Guy Malonis, Barbara McNeil, Gary J. Oudersluys, Maureen Richards, Cheryl L. Warnock, *Research Specialists*
Tamara C. Nott, *Research Associate*
Tim Lehnerer, Ron Morelli, *Research Assistants*

Dorothy Maki, *Manufacturing Manager*
Stacy L. Melson, *Buyer*

Mary Beth Trimper, *Composition and Prepress Manager*
Carolyn Roney, *Composition Specialist*

Randy Bassett, *Image Database Supervisor*
Robert Duncan, *Imaging Specialist*
Michael Logusz, *Graphic Artist*
Pamela A. Reed, *Imaging Coordinator*
Kelly A. Quin, *Imaging Editor*

Library of Congress Catalog Card Number
ISBN 0-7876-4546-X
ISSN 0732-1864
Printed in the United States of America

10 9 8 7 6 5 4 3 2 1

Contents

Preface vii

Acknowledgments xi

Herman Melville 1819-1891 1
American novelist and short-story writer
Entry devoted to Pierre, or, The Ambiguities

Richard Brinsley Sheridan 1751-1816 229
Irish playwright, librettist, and poet

Anne Louise Germaine Necker, Baronne de Staël-Holstein 1766-1817 290
French critic, novelist, historian, and playwright

Literary Criticism Series Cumulative Author Index 369

Literary Criticism Series Cumulative Topic Index 443

NCLC Cumulative Nationality Index 451

NCLC-91 Title Index 455

Preface

S ince its inception in 1981, *Nineteeth-Century Literature Criticism* (*NCLC*) has been a valuable resource for students and librarians seeking critical commentary on writers of this transitional period in world history. Designated an "Outstanding Reference Source" by the American Library Association with the publication of is first volume, *NCLC* has since been purchased by over 6,000 school, public, and university libraries. The series has covered more than 300 authors representing 29 nationalities and over 17,000 titles. No other reference source has surveyed the critical reaction to nineteenth-century authors and literature as thoroughly as *NCLC*.

Scope of the Series

NCLC is designed to introduce students and advanced readers to the authors of the nineteenth century and to the most significant interpretations of these authors' works. The great poets, novelists, short story writers, playwrights, and philosophers of this period are frequently studied in high school and college literature courses. By organizing and reprinting commentary written on these authors, *NCLC* helps students develop valuable insight into literary history, promotes a better understanding of the texts, and sparks ideas for papers and assignments. Each entry in *NCLC* presents a comprehensive survey of an author's career or an individual work of literature and provides the user with a multiplicity of interpretations and assessments. Such variety allows students to pursue their own interests; furthermore, it fosters an awareness that literature is dynamic and responsive to many different opinions.

Every fourth volume of *NCLC* is devoted to literary topics that cannot be covered under the author approach used in the rest of the series. Such topics include literary movements, prominent themes in nineteenth-century literature, literary reaction to political and historical events, significant eras in literary history, prominent literary anniversaries, and the literatures of cultures that are often overlooked by English-speaking readers.

NCLC continues the survey of criticism of world literature begun by Gale's *Contemporary Literary Criticism* (*CLC*) and *Twentieth-Century Literary Criticism* (*TCLC*).

Organization of the Book

An *NCLC* entry consists of the following elements:

- The **Author Heading** cites the name under which the author most commonly wrote, followed by birth and death dates. Also located here are any name variations under which an author wrote, including transliterated forms for authors whose native languages use nonroman alphabets. If the author wrote consistently under a pseudonym, the pseudonym will be listed in the author heading and the author's actual name given in parenthesis on the first line of the biographical and critical information. Uncertain birth or death dates are indicated by question marks. Single-work entries are preceded by a heading that consists of the most common form of the title in English translation (if applicable) and the original date of composition.

- The **Introduction** contains background information that introduces the reader to the author, work, or topic that is the subject of the entry.

- A **Portrait of the Author** is included when available.

- The list of **Principal Works** is ordered chronologically by date of first publication and lists the most important works by the author. The genre and publication date of each work is given. In the case of foreign authors whose works have been translated into English, the list will focus primarily on twentieth-century translations, selecting those works most commonly considered the best by critics. Unless otherwise indicated, dramas are dated by first performance, not first publication. Lists of **Representative Works** by different authors appear with topic entries.

- Reprinted **Criticism** is arranged chronologically in each entry to provide a useful perspective on changes in critical evaluation over time. The critic's name and the date of composition or publication of the critical work are given at the beginning of each piece of criticism. Unsigned criticism is preceded by the title of the source in which it appeared. All titles by the author featured in the text are printed in boldface type. Footnotes are reprinted at the end of each essay or excerpt. In the case of excerpted criticism, only those footnotes that pertain to the excerpted texts are included. Criticism in topic entries is arranged chronologically under a variety of subheadings to facilitate the study of different aspects of the topic.

- A complete **Bibliographical Citation** of the original essay or book precedes each piece of criticism.

- Critical essays are prefaced by brief **Annotations** explicating each piece.

- An annotated bibliography of **Further Reading** appears at the end of each entry and suggests resources for additional study. In some cases, significant essays for which the editors could not obtain reprint rights are included here. Boxed material following the further reading list provides references to other biographical and critical sources on the author in series published by Gale.

Indexes

Each volume of *NCLC* contains a **Cumulative Author Index** listing all authors who have appeared in a wide variety of reference sources published by the Gale Group, including *NCLC*. A complete list of these sources is found facing the first page of the Author Index. The index also includes birth and death dates and cross references between pseudonyms and actual names.

A **Cumulative Nationality Index** lists all authors featured in *NCLC* by nationality, followed by the number of the *NCLC* volume in which their entry appears.

A **Cumulative Topic Index** lists the literary themes and topics treated in the series as well as in *Classical and Medieval Literature Criticism, Literature Criticism from 1400 to 1800, Twentieth-Century Literary Criticism,* and the *Contemporary Literary Criticism* Yearbook, which was discontinued in 1998.

An alphabetical **Title Index** accompanies each volume of *NCLC*, with the exception of the Topics volumes. Listings of titles by authors covered in the given volume are followed by the author's name and the corresponding page numbers where the titles are discussed. English translations of foreign titles and variations of titles are cross-referenced to the title under which a work was originally published. Titles of novels, dramas, nonfiction books, and poetry, short story, or essay collections are printed in italics, while individual poems, short stories, and essays are printed in roman type within quotation marks.

In response to numerous suggestions from librarians, Gale also produces an annual paperbound edition of the *NCLC* cumulative title index. This annual cumulation, which alphabetically lists all titles reviewed in the series, is available to all customers. Additional copies of this index are available upon request. Librarians and patrons will welcome this separate index; it saves shelf space, is easy to use, and is recyclable upon receipt of the next edition.

Citing *Nineteenth-Century Literature Criticism*

When writing papers, students who quote directly from any volume in the Literary Criticism Series may use the following general format to footnote reprinted criticism. The first example pertains to material drawn from periodicals, the second to material reprinted from books.

Kim McQuaid, "William Apes, Pequot: An Indian Reformer in the Jackson Era," *The New England Quarterly,* 50 (December 1977): 605-25; excerpted and reprinted in *Nineteenth-Century Literature Criticism,* vol. 73, ed. Janet Witalec (Farmington Hills, Mich.: The Gale Group, 1999), 3-4.

Richard Harter Fogle, *The Imagery of Keats and Shelley: A Comparative Study* (Archon Books, 1949), 211-51; excerpted and reprinted in *Nineteenth-Century Literature Criticism,* vol. 73, ed. Janet Witalec (Farmington Hills, Mich.: The Gale Group, 1999), 157-69.

Suggestions are Welcome

Readers who wish to suggest new features, topics, or authors to appear in future volumes, or who have other suggestions or comments are cordially invited to call, write, or fax the Managing Editor:

Managing Editor, Literary Criticism Series
The Gale Group
27500 Drake Road
Farmington Hills, MI 48331-3535
1-800-347-4253 (GALE)
Fax: 248-699-8054

Acknowledgments

The editors wish to thank the copyright holders of the excerpted criticism included in this volume and the permissions managers of many book and magazine publishing companies for assisting us in securing reproduction rights. We are also grateful to the staffs of the Detroit Public Library, the Library of Congress, the University of Detroit Mercy Library, Wayne State University Purdy/Kresge Library Complex, and the University of Michigan Libraries for making their resources available to us. Following is a list of the copyright holders who have granted us permission to reproduce material in this volume of *NCLC*. Every effort has been made to trace copyright, but if omissions have been made, please let us know.

COPYRIGHTED EXCERPTS IN *NCLC*, VOLUME 91, WERE REPRODUCED FROM THE FOLLOWING PERIODICALS:

American Literature, v. XLVIII, November, 1976; v. 69, December, 1997. Copyright © 1976, 1997 by Duke University Press, Durham, NC. Reproduced by permission.—*American Transcendental Quarterly,* no. 7, Summer, 1970; v. 1, September, 1987; v. 1, September, 1987. Copyright © 1970, 1987 by Kenneth Walter Cameron. Reproduced by permission.—*The Arizona Quarterly,* v. 31, Spring, 1975. Copyright © 1975 by the Regents of the University of Arizona. Reproduced by permission of the publisher and the author.—*Atlantis,* v. 7, Autumn, 1981. Reproduced by permission.—*Ball State University Forum,* Summer, 1986. Copyright © 1986 by Ball State University. Reproduced by permission.—*boundary 2,* v. 17, Spring, 1990. Copyright © 1990 by Duke University Press, Durham, NC. Reproduced by permission.—*Bulletin of Research in the Humanities,* v. 86, 1985. Reproduced by permission of The New York Public Library, Astor, Lennox, and Tilden Foundations.—*Eighteenth-Century Fiction,* v. 7, July, 1995. Reproduced by permission.—*The Emerson Society Quarterly,* no. 48, Third Quarter, 1967. Reproduced by permission.—*Esquire,* no. 60, Summer, 1970; v. 33, 3rd Quarter, 1987. Copyright © 1970, 1987 by Esquire Associates. Reproduced by permission.—*L'Esprit Créateur,* v. XXXIV, Fall, 1994. Copyright © 1994 by L'Esprit Créateur. Reproduced by permission.—*Literature and Medicine,* v. 16, Fall, 1997. Reproduced by permission.—*The New Criterion,* v. 16, May, 1998. Copyright © 1998 by The Foundation for Cultural Review. Reproduced by permission of the author.—*Papers on Language & Literature,* v. V, Winter, 1969; v. 26, 1990. Copyright © 1969, 1990 by The Board of Trustees, Southern Illinois University at Edwardsville. Reproduced by permission.—*The Romanic Review,* v. 87, January, 1996. © The Trustees of Columbia University. Reproduced by permission.—*The Southern Humanities Review,* v. XV, Summer, 1981. Copyright © 1981 by Auburn University. Reproduced by permission of the author.—*Studies in Eighteenth-Century Culture,* v. 24, 1995. Reproduced by permission.—*Studies in the Novel,* v. VI, Summer, 1974; v. XV, Fall, 1983; v. XVI, Winter, 1984; v. XVIII, Winter, 1986. Copyright © 1974, 1983, 1984, 1986 by North Texas State University. Reproduced by permission.—*Texas Studies in Literature and Language,* v. 38, Winter, 1996. Reproduced by permission.—*The Theatre Annual,* v. XXXVIII, 1983. Reproduced by permission.

COPYRIGHTED EXCERPTS IN *NCLC*, VOLUME 91, WERE REPRODUCED FROM THE FOLLOWING BOOKS:

Besser, Gretchen R. From "Forays into Fiction: Delphine," in *Germaine de Stael Revisited.* Twayne Publishers, 1994. Copyright © The Gale Group. Reproduced by permission.—Bowman, Frank P. From "Communication and Power in Germaine de Stäel: Transparency and Obstacle," in *Germaine de Stäel: Crossing the Borders.* Edited by Madelyn Gutwirth, Avriel Goldberger, and Karyna Szmurlo. Rutgers University Press, 1991. Copyright © 1991 by Rutgers, The State University. All rights reserved. Reproduced by permission.—Brown, Gillian. From "Anti-Sentimentalism and Authorship in Pierre," in *Domestic Individualism: Imagining Self in Nineteenth-Century America.* University of California Press, 1990. Copyright © 1990 by The Regents of the University of California. Reproduced by permission of the publisher and author.—Clayton, Christopher. From "The Political Career of Richard Brinsley Sheridan," in *Sheridan Studies.* Cambridge University Press, 1995. Copyright © Cambridge University Press 1995. Reproduced by permission of the author and the publisher.—Creech, James. From "Pierre, or The Ambiguities: A Camp Reading," in *Closet Writing/Gay Reading: The Case of Melville's "Pierre."* The University of Chicago Press, 1993. Copyright © 1993 by The University of Chicago. Reproduced by permission.—Durant, Jack D. From "Poet," in *Richard Brinsley Sheridan.* Twayne Publishers, 1975. Copyright © 1975 by Twayne Publishers, Inc. Reproduced by permission of the author.—Gray, Richard. "'All's o'er and ye know him not': A Reading of Pierre," in *Herman Melville: Reassessments.* Edited by A. Robert Lee. Vision and Barnes & Noble, 1984. Copyright © 1984 (London) Vision Press. Reproduced by permission.—Higgins, Brian and Hershel Parker.

PHOTOGRAPHS AND ILLUSTRATIONS APPEARING IN *NCLC*, VOLUME 91, WERE RECEIVED FROM THE FOLLOWING SOURCES:

Pierre, or, The Ambiguities

Herman Melville

The following entry presents criticism of Melville's novel *Pierre* (1852). For information on Melville's complete career, see *NCLC*, Volume 3; for discussion of the novel *Moby-Dick*, see *NCLC*, Volume 12; for discussion of the novel *Billy Budd*, see *NCLC*, Volume 29; for discussion of the novel *Typee*, see *NCLC*, Volume 45; and for discussion of the short story "Bartleby, the Scrivener," see *NCLC*, Volume 49.

INTRODUCTION

Many critics have deemed *Pierre* the most puzzling, and—alongside *Moby-Dick* (1851)—the most structurally and thematically complex work of Melville's career. Denigrated by most contemporary reviewers for its main themes of fornication, incest, and illegitimacy, *Pierre* was praised by some as a successful sentimental romance. The history of *Pierre* criticism has been controversial, with critics agreeing on very little, in part because the novel itself seems to contain and encompass two sides of every critical argument. For example, it is a romance that also parodies the genre of romance, a philosophical work that satirizes philosophers and philosophizing, and the story of an idealist who consistently undermines his own good intentions and ultimately commits suicide. *Pierre* has become increasingly popular in the latter part of the twentieth century, with many readers speculating about its psychosexual themes, Melville's intentions in the work, and the novel's place in Melville's corpus.

BIOGRAPHICAL INFORMATION

By the time he began writing *Pierre* in late 1851, Melville had already published seven novels—*Typee* (1846), *The Story of Toby* (1846), *Omoo* (1847), *Mardi* (1849), *Redburn* (1849), *White Jacket* (1850), and *Moby-Dick*—and was well-established in his literary career. His earlier narratives of exotic sea voyages appealed to the reading public, but *Moby-Dick* received mixed assessments. While some reviewers recognized and lauded Melville's technical and thematic accomplishment in that novel, many others found the work inscrutable. Most important to Melville himself was the enthusiastic praise of the novel by fellow novelist Nathaniel Hawthorne, whom Melville considered a soulmate. In a letter written in 1851, Melville conveyed his heartfelt "content" with Hawthorne's response to *Moby-Dick,* but also expressed the continued pressure of his creative impulse and the need to move on: "So, now let us

add *Moby-Dick* to our blessing, and step from that. Leviathan is not the biggest fish;—I have heard of Krakens." Melville was feeling impatient with his past achievements, and also vulnerable as a result of harsh criticism of *Moby-Dick.* By Christmas, according to his family, he was so "engaged in a new work as frequently not to leave his room until quite dark . . . under a state of morbid excitement which will soon injure his health." The new work was *Pierre.* The book, which grew from an estimated 360 pages to 500, was published by Harper and Brothers in the United States, but Melville's English publisher, Bentley, declined to publish it despite Melville's description of the work as "calculated for popularity . . . being a regular romance, with a mysterious plot to it, and stirring passions." The advance proofs Melville had sent to Bentley clearly told a different story. Emotionally and physically exhausted, and unsure of what was expected of him any more as a novelist in the United States, after the publication of *Pierre* Melville decided to abandon novel writing and instead focused on short fiction.

PLOT AND MAJOR CHARACTERS

A superficial plot outline of *Pierre* does indeed read like a typical sentimental novel of its day, but its dark psychological undercurrents manifest themselves soon enough. The novel's protagonist, Pierre Glendenning, the only son of a wealthy widow, grows up on a fine estate, Saddle Meadows, in bucolic upstate New York, and receives the best education available to a young man of his station. In addition, he is brought up to honor the near-saintly image of his dead father. In time, Pierre becomes engaged to Lucy Tartan, the daughter of another prominent New York family. His life changes drastically, however, when he meets Isabel and learns that she is his father's illegitimate daughter, and, therefore, his half-sister. Pierre's mother, leery of family scandal, does her utmost to hide the facts of the situation by controlling Pierre, but Pierre rebels and comes to believe that it is his duty and newfound mission in life to protect Isabel from his mother and from the world at large. He realizes that acknowledging Isabel as his sister would disgrace his father's memory, so he pretends to marry her and they elope to New York City. Now poor and friendless, Pierre pursues a career as an author, working on a book that no publisher will accept. Lucy, who is still in love with Pierre, follows him to New York, and in turn is followed by her brother and Pierre's cousin. The two threaten Pierre with discovery and Pierre kills the cousin. Lucy and Mrs. Glendenning die of grief when they hear the news, and Pierre and Isabel, who are now in love with each other, commit suicide together in his prison cell.

MAJOR THEMES

The major theme of *Pierre,* as its subtitle suggests, is ambiguity, and this idea is played out on many different levels of the novel. Melville was interested in the idea of exploring human psychology, especially repressed sexual urges, and in seeing how good can turn into evil in unpredictable ways. Pierre believes that conventional Christianity does not offer a high enough standard of conduct, and he sets for himself the goal of true Christ-like behavior. When Pierre and Isabel, in a pivotal chapter, are escaping to New York, he finds by chance a "philosophical lecture" on "Chronometricals and Horologicals." The author of this discourse on time argues that the perfection of the chronometer makes it an imperfect timepiece for ordinary purposes and people ("Christ was a chronometer"). A horologue, which is adjustable to local standards, is more practical. Pierre aspires to follow chronometric time but, despite his high moral principles, ends in destroying those around him as well as himself. Melville develops the theme of the ambiguous nature of good and evil through Pierre, but also through the story of Isabel's childhood, and

through Pierre's relationship with his manipulative mother. Again and again, Melville focuses on the mixed motives and the murky reasoning of the major characters of the novel. Even the treatment of nature proves problematic: Pierre rhapsodizes about the scenery of his native upstate New York and in part derives his optimistic philosophy from it, but discussions of nature often turn into satire and result in self-parody. The structure of *Pierre* also supports the idea of ambiguity. There are numerous shifts in tone and style, characters take on different roles with each other, narrative voices change over the course of the work, and there is a sharp change in the novel as the locale moves from rural upstate New York to the wasteland of New York City. Many critics have also pointed out an autobiographical dimension to the novel. Pierre, like Melville, is a novelist without a reading public who is trying to determine what is expected of him and to what extent he can comply with those expectations.

CRITICAL RECEPTION

Pierre failed on both the critical and popular fronts and it did not bring Melville even the private satisfaction that *Moby-Dick* had offered. His popularity as an author, already seriously damaged by the publication of *Moby-Dick,* was completely destroyed by *Pierre.* The reading public, who preferred the entertainment of *Typee* and *Omoo,* were confused by the novel's metaphysical questionings and offended by its theme of incest. The book does contain conventional Romantic material, such as the beautiful blonde sweetheart and the mysterious dark lady with whom Pierre elopes, and the melodrama with its sexual tensions, murder, and suicide is not far off from the potboilers of the day. Contemporary readers rejected it probably for what they perceived as a lack of direction and good taste, but critics point out that they were probably also distressed by its acerbic treatment of the New York cultural scene, its undercutting of transcendental optimism and genteel conduct, and its subversion of religious doctrine embodied in the ironic outcome of Pierre's attempt to model his behavior on received Christian principles. Many critics, including Lewis Mumford, Hershel Parker, Gillian Brown, John Carlos Rowe, and Wyn Kelly have written about the autobiographical aspect of *Pierre,* often focusing on Melville's evolving view of himself as a writer and on his questioning of the validity of the profession of authorship in America. Broadening this discussion, Steve Gowler and Nicola Nixon have emphasized the pertinence of the American social context in the mid-nineteenth century to *Pierre* and to Melville's dilemma regarding his own choice of career. Other scholars, including R. K. Gupta and Nicholas Canaday, for example, have paid close attention to Melville's literary style in *Pierre,* discussing narrative stance, characterization, and Melville's borrowings from other genres. There is still an ongoing debate about the unity of *Pierre* as a novel; recently Bert C. Bach and Carol Colclough Strickland, among others, have argued for the novel's unity based on levels of narration and imagery, respectively. Perhaps most intriguing of all for late-twentieth-century critics has been exploration of Melville's treatment of human psychology, especially sexuality; R. Scott Kellner, James Creech, and Stephen Rachman have offered varied and controversial approaches to this field of study. Critical interest in *Pierre* has grown exponentially since the 1920s and the novel has provided a fertile field for research. Most Melville scholars now agree with Brian Higgins and Hershel Parker in their assessment of *Pierre* as perhaps "the best psychological novel that had yet been written in English."

PRINCIPAL WORKS

Typee: A Peep at Polynesian Life. During a Four Months' Residence in a Valley of the Marquesas (novel) 1846

The Story of Toby (novel) 1846

Omoo: A Narrative of Adventures in the South Seas (novel) 1847

Mardi: And a Voyage Thither (novel) 1849

Redburn: His First Voyage (novel) 1849

White-Jacket; or, The World in a Man-of-War (novel) 1850

Moby-Dick; or, The Whale (novel) 1851; also published as *The Whale* (novel) 1851

Pierre; or, The Ambiguities (novel) 1852

Israel Potter: His Fifty Years in Exile (novel) 1855

The Piazza Tales (short stories) 1856

The Confidence-Man: His Masquerade (novel) 1857

Battle-Pieces and Aspects of the War (poetry) 1866

Clarel: A Poem and Pilgrimage in the Holy Land (poetry) 1876

John Marr and Other Sailors (poetry) 1888

Timoleon (poetry) 1891

Billy Budd and Other Prose Pieces (novel and short stories) 1924

CRITICISM

Lewis Mumford (essay date 1929)

SOURCE: "From 'Amor, Threatening,'" in *Critical Essays on Herman Melville's* Pierre; or, The Ambiguities, edited by Brian Higgins and Hershel Parker, G. K. Hall & Co., 1983, pp. 135-49.

[*In the following excerpt from an essay originally published in 1929, Mumford links the themes of* Pierre *with events in Melville's life while he was writing the novel, concluding that "*Pierre *disclosed a lesion that never entirely healed."*]

Moby-Dick was done. In the fall of 1851 it appeared, first in England, then, a few weeks later, in America. Melville was exhausted, exhausted and overwrought. In the prodigious orchestration of **Moby-Dick,** Melville had drained his energies, and, participating in Ahab's own pursuit and defiance, he had reached a point of spiritual exasperation which, like Ahab's illness after Moby-Dick had amputated him, was increased by his lowered physical tone, by his weak eyes. Books like this are written out of health and energy, but they do not leave health and energy behind. On the contrary, the aftermath of such an effort is irritation, debility, impotence.

Melville was worked up, in the writing of **Moby-Dick,** to the highest pitch of effort; and he was harried, no doubt, by his ever-present necessity to keep his public and add to his income. The spiritual momentum remained, but the force behind it dwindled away. With no time for recuperation, he plunged into his new work: an unwise decision. Melville was not without his weaknesses, and they rose to the surface in his new book, **Pierre, or The Ambiguities. Moby-Dick,** had disintegrated him: by some interior electrolysis, its sanative salt was broken up into baneful chemical elements. In this disintegration, **Pierre** rises at times as high as **Moby-Dick,** and sinks lower than any of Melville's other books. It contains passages that are the finest utterances of his spirit; it also has passages that would scarcely honour Laura Jean Libbey.

What caused this break-up? What value has **Pierre** in the sum of Melville's work? Neither of these questions admits of a quick and facile answer. One cannot dismiss the novel high-handedly as Melville's contemporaries did; and since the relation of the personal life of the artist to his art is still one of the major ambiguities in psychology, one cannot give a decisive or confident answer to the first question.

2

Melville's situation at the time of writing **Pierre** might have upset him even in a period of completer poise and more abundant health. He had written a great book: of that he could not possibly have had any doubt. Minor writers may think their rhinestones are diamonds, but rarely does a Shakespeare, a Swift, a Melville make the contrary mistake: if he speak lightly of his own work, or affect to disregard it, it is only for the reason that once he has reached the utmost depths of consciousness and realizes that vast and myriad interior which can never be fully reported, he begins to realize that diamonds, too, are only another kind of rhinestone: they are mined too cheaply.

Melville knew that **Moby-Dick** was bound to be his chief title to fame. In 1849 he had written to Mr. Duyckinck: "Would that a man could do something and then say It is finished—not that one thing only, but all others—that he has reached his uttermost and can never exceed it." Melville had done this: he had mined and tunnelled through every part of his experience to produce this book. "There is a sure, though secret sign in some works," he wrote in 1850, "which proves the culmination of the powers . . . that produced them," and he recognized this secret sign in *Moby-Dick*: his letters to Hawthorne announce it. Mid all the tribulations and vexations of his life, there was, as in the heart of the whale Armada, a quiet place of calm and inward peace; within that spot, he had no reason to doubt or be dissatisfied with his work.

Still, what a writer articulates is always, though his words stay in a private diary, an effort at communication; the very nature of language makes this inevitable. Melville was necessarily not without his curiosity as to how the world would greet this magnificent product of his maturity, the first book in which he was in full command of his powers. And what was the world's answer?

The world's answer was no doubt what was to be expected; but it was no less discouraging for this reason. The *Literary World* indeed treated *Moby-Dick* with respect, and with as much understanding as a purely bookish man, like Mr. Duyckinck, could be expected to show: though it wasted most of the first review telling about the parallel fate of the Ann Alexander, it made up for this adventitious journalism by a second article which acknowledged *Moby-Dick*'s manifold powers and excellences. "An intellectual chowder of romance, philosophy, natural history, fine writing, good feeling, bad sayings . . . over which, in spite of all uncertainties, and in spite of the author himself, predominates his keen perceptive faculties, exhibited in vivid narration." In the light of other contemporary reviews, this was fairly handsome. The *Dublin University Magazine,* with steady opacity, said *Moby-Dick* was quite as eccentric and monstrously extravagant in many of its incidents as even *Mardi,* but was a valuable book because it contained an unparalleled mass of information about the whale. As for the *Athenaeum,* it righteously reminded Mr. Melville that he "has to thank himself only if his horrors and his heroics are flung aside by the general reader as so much trash"—criticism which reached a pinnacle in the *New Monthly Magazine,* which described the style of *Moby-Dick* as "maniacal—mad as a March hare—mowing, gibbering, screaming, like an incurable Bedlamite, reckless of keeper or strait-waistcoat." [July 1853. Ed. Note.]

One need not go into all the forms under which the contemporary critic disclosed his insensitiveness to great prose and his servile compliance with the idola of the market; but one must note a singular fact: from Fitz-James O'Brien's first criticism of Melville's work as a whole in 1853 down to Mr. Vernon Parrington's commentary in 1927, *Moby-Dick,* the keystone of Melville's work, has frequently been left out of account. The book that triumphantly smothers all the contradictory opinions about Melville—that he was a romantic, that he could only portray external scenes, that he was a pure introvert, that he was an adventurous ne'er-do-well, never happy or at home in a settled community, that he was irresponsive to the life around him, that he was a sheer realist who could only record what he had seen—the book that makes these generalizations silly suffered something worse than antagonis-

tic criticism: it met with complete neglect. It is only since 1914 in America that this neglect has been even partly atoned for.

Such obtuseness, such flat stupidity, must have had a dismaying effect upon Melville. The writer begins to doubt the possibility of literature in a world that so flagrantly misunderstands or ignores its higher manifestations. Faced with such contemporaries, the artist may retire within himself, as Bach or Ryder or Cézanne did; but it will only be a miracle that will keep him from taking into his retirement a deep contempt for the people around him. That contempt is worse than isolation; it brings isolation without hope. "I write to please myself," exclaimed Melville in one passage in *Pierre.* In that mood of wilful defiance, a man may revolt from the good sense of his contemporaries as well as from their deficiencies. There was nothing in the reception of *Moby-Dick* that would have lessened Melville's scorn, or helped him to fortify himself against his own weaknesses. Quite the contrary. Like Pierre himself he was to learn "and very bitterly learn, that though the world worship mediocrity and commonplace, yet hath it fire and sword for contemporary grandeur."

Moby-Dick was too much for them, was it? Well: it was a mere pencilling of the ultimate blackness that was his to paint: if one were going to tell the truth at all, one could go much further and be much plainer. "Henceforth," proclaimed Pierre, "I will know nothing but Truth; Glad Truth or Sad Truth; I will know what *is,* and do what my deepest angel dictates." And again: "I am more frank with Pierre than the best men are with themselves. I am all unguarded and magnanimous with Pierre: therefore you see his weakness, and therefore only. In reserves, men build imposing characters; not in revelations. He who shall be wholly honest, though nobler than Ethan Allen that man shall stand in danger of the meanest mortal's scorn."

It was in some such mood of defeat, foreboding, defiant candour, that *Pierre* was conceived and written. Meanwhile, in November, 1851, the Hawthorne family had moved away from the Berkshires and Melville settled to his work, in the spring of 1852, on the north porch that faced Mt. Monadnock [actually, in the fall of 1851, indoors, facing Mount Greylock. Ed. Note.], with an intense feeling of human isolation which brought the mountain closer to him, as his only friend. The one possibility of a friendly, rapturous union of spirits was behind him: no longer could he write to Hawthorne, as he had done just a few months before: "Whence came you, Hawthorne? By what right do you drink from my flagon of life? And when I put it to my lips—lo, they are yours, and not mine. I feel that the Godhead is broken up like the bread at the Supper, and that we are the pieces. Hence this infinite fraternity of feeling." No: already that was over: dead. If the spirit burned now, it burned as ice does to the human touch. It was not altogether in irony, or in wild whimsy, that Melville dedicated his next book, *Pierre,* to his one solitary and steadfast companion, Mt. Monadnock. [Actually, Mount Greylock. Ed. Note.]

3

There is a sense in which *Pierre* is an abortive complement to *Moby-Dick. Moby-Dick,* great fable that it is, contains a good part of human life under one figure or another; but it does not contain everything. I would claim
much for it; I would claim much for Melville's work as a
whole; but there is still a great segment that remained unexplored till Melville wrote *Pierre,* and that, to the end, he
never satisfactorily penetrated or freely brooded upon.

All Melville's books about the sea have the one anomaly
and defect of the sea from the central, human point of
view: one-half of the race, woman, is left out of it.
Melville's world, all too literally, is a man-of-war's world.
Woman neither charms nor nurtures nor threatens: she neither robs man of his strength nor rouses him to heroic
frenzy: she is not Circe: she is not Rosalind or Francesca
or even the Wife of Bath—she simply does not exist. When
the *Pequod* spreads sail, woman is left behind: she is the
phantom of home for Ahab and Starbuck. The whales dally
in *Moby-Dick* and beget offspring; but all the trouble,
beauty, madness, delight of human love, all that vast range
of experience from the mere touch of the flesh to the most
enduring spiritual loyalty, all that is absent. One looks for
some understanding of woman's lot and woman's life in
Moby-Dick; and one looks in vain. One looks for it again
in *Pierre,* and one is disappointed, although its ambiguities are concerned with nothing else. With experience of
woman in every relationship, daughter, girl, sister, wife,
mother, matron, he described her in only one aspect—that
of the remote and idealized mistress of romantic courtship.
Mother, sister, sweetheart, all appeared to Melville's hero
in this brief and peculiar aspect.

There was, one is driven to believe, something in Herman
Melville's life that caused him to dissociate woman from
his account of man's deepest experience. Mr. Waldo Frank
has suggested, in general social terms, that the quest of
power, which has preoccupied Western man since the Renaissance, has incapacitated him as a lover and kept him
from understanding woman and all her essential concerns.
If that is true, Melville pushed his aberration to a logical
extremity; and he, who captured to the full the poetry of
the sea, became as bashful as a boy when he beheld Ve-
nus, born of its foam, rising from the waters he knew so
well, the most unexpected of monsters, and the only denizen of the sea he dared neither snare nor harpoon nor otherwise dispose of, except by flight. . . .

5

This story of *Pierre,* hard to accept in bald summary, is no
less difficult to accept in detail. The plot is forced: the
situations are undeveloped: the dominant colours are as
crude as the lithograph advertisements of a melodrama, although there are subordinate parts which are as delicately
graded as a landscape by Corot. There is no passage between the various planes of action and mood, as there is in
Moby-Dick: Melville slips from prose into poetry, from realism into fantasy, from the mood of high tragedy into that
of the penny dreadful.

For the moment, Melville had lost the power to fuse these
discordant elements, to reject what could not be fully absorbed: he was at the mercy of his material. All that lives
with a vital unity in *Moby-Dick* has become a corpse in
Pierre: there is life in the dead members, but it does not
pertain to the body as a whole. The fragments of *Pierre*
are sometimes marvellous, as the broken leg or arm of a
great piece of sculpture may be: but the whole is lost.
From the moment the story opens to the fatal lines that
bring it to a close, one is in an atmosphere of unreality. I
do not mean that the facts are untrue to life; I mean that
the work as a whole is untrue to the imagination. One accepts Ahab as a demi-god: one cannot accept Pierre as a
human being, although Pierres are plentiful, while one
might dredge the five seas without bringing up the carcass
of another Ahab.

The style itself is witness to this psychal disruption, quite
as much as the fable. *Pierre* is quarried out of the same
quarry as *Moby-Dick*; but whereas there the texture is
even and firm, here it is full of flaws and intrusive granu-
lations. *Moby-Dick,* to use another figure, slides down a
long runway before it plunges into its poetic passages: by
the time one reaches Ahab's great apostrophes, one is all
prepared for the immersion; one's imagination has reached
the same pitch of intensity and concentration, and nothing
but the most rhythmic patterns will satisfy the mood itself.
The common prose in *Moby-Dick* is but an interval for
breathing: it sustains and carries forward the movement of
the more expressive passages; and as for the words themselves, they are the exact equivalent for the mood and purpose: distended though the envelope may be, they never
burst outside it.

In language, *Pierre* is just the opposite of this: from the
first pages, it is perfervid and poetical in a mawkish way.
With the disclosure of the two lovers, Pierre and Lucy, in
the opening chapter, the style becomes a perfumed silk,
taken from an Elizabethan chamber romance: it sounds exactly like Melville's first effusion in the *Lansingburgh Advertiser:* "'Truly,' thought the youth, with a still gaze of
inexpressible fondness, 'truly the skies do ope: and this invoking angel looks down. I would return these manifold
good-mornings, Lucy, did not that presume thou hadst
lived through the night; and by heaven, thou belongst to
the regions of an infinite day!'" This is a fair sample of
what happens in *Pierre* whenever Melville approaches romantic passion; his reflections were tied with the same ribbons and furbelows, as in his description of love as "a volume bound in rose-leaves, clasped with violets, and by the
beaks of humming-birds printed with peach juice on the
leaves of lilies." In style, Melville had suddenly lost both
taste and discretion. He opened on a note that could not be
carried through. Lovers may indeed once have used such
silly rhetoric, but it would take a more careful hand than
Melville's to persuade us that the rest of the world adopted
these affectations: when scene after scene is conducted in

the same tone, the style becomes tedious, intolerable, ridiculous. It would be bad if the characters were in the Renaissance costume of Daphnis and Chloe: it is even worse in a novel that contains realistic caricatures of the slums of New York and satiric commentaries upon the bizarre habits of the transcendentalists. Occasionally, by some happy concentration of emotion, Melville either drops these flabby phrases or permits the reader to forget them, and there are passages which, when read as poetry, are almost as fine as Whitman's verses. But these intervals of good writing do not overcome the main impression; and the main impression is of hectic and overwrought language. With the powerful control he had over *Moby-Dick,* Melville could never have written in the style that characterizes a large part of *Pierre.* In *Pierre* he was no longer the cool rider of words, but the flayed and foaming horse, running away.

There is still another unfortunate lapse in *Pierre*; and that is the disproportion between stimulus and effect. When Pierre is first beheld by Isabel, then completely a stranger to him, she shrieks and faints away. Her own action was not improbable; but there is no reason why Pierre, healthy, robust, ignorant, should be so profoundly disturbed by this exhibition. The same is true of Pierre's heroic resolution to shield Isabel under the form of wedlock: it is a wild and dangerous leap out of a much less pressing difficulty. When Pierre finally comes to town, the disproportion is so broad it is grotesque, almost comical: his cousin's turning upon him and cutting him, before a group of strangers, with a frigid stare and a command to take that fellow away, does not belong to anything but the pages of crude melodrama. The turning against Pierre is not the subtle, devious series of rebukes and frigidities he would actually receive: such an affront as Melville pictures occurs only in raw dream.

In *Moby-Dick,* Melville carefully prepared, a hundred pages in advance, for the final effect: Mr. E. M. Forster has even suggested that the emphasis upon "delight" in Father Mapple's sermon is related to the encountering of a ship called the Delight just before the final catastrophe. In *Pierre* all this subtle preparation is lacking: Melville's impatience turned a genuine theme, the conflict of adolescent purity of purpose with the apologetic compromises and sordid motives of the world, into a crude melodrama. Melville was so immersed in the dilemma of his hero that he did not observe how often he failed to satisfy the demands of art, which require that the very incoherencies of life somehow hang together and be acceptable to the mind.

Finally, Pierre's emotional reaction to Isabel is entirely out of proportion to the fact that he has found a sister whose existence he had never before suspected. For a young man, filially tied to his mother, and by active courtship to Lucy, the entrance of another young woman should not have had such a volcanic effect, since, under the most ancient of social taboos, the relationship between them precludes further intimacy. Kindness and fellow feeling might easily arise there: but what Melville pictures is sudden and violent passion. "Fate," he observes, "had separated the

brother and sister, till to each they seemed so not at all. Sisters shrink not from their brother's kisses. And Pierre felt that never, never would he be able to embrace Isabel with the mere brotherly embrace; while the thought of any other caress, which took hold of any domesticness, was entirely vacant from his uncontaminated soul, for it had never consciously intruded there. Therefore, forever unsistered for him by the stroke of Fate, and apparently for ever, and twice removed from the remotest possibility of that love which had drawn him to his Lucy; yet still the object of the ardentest and deepest emotions of his soul; therefore, to him, Isabel soared out of the realm of mortalness and for him became transfigured in the highest heaven of uncorrupted love."

The ambiguity that Melville finally brought his hero to confront in *Pierre* is that this highest heaven is not necessarily a heaven at all: such a transcendental displacement of earthly emotions and experiences is not the way of "willing, waking love": it is the mood of dream, and by continuous dissociation, it may eventually become the mood of madness. The highest heaven of love does not come with such romantic fixation upon an unapproachable deity: it comes rather with diffusion, when all men are brothers, when all women are sisters, when all children are just as dear as one's own issue. The fixation on a remote figure or symbol is in fact just the opposite of this generous suffusion of love, and of all love's corruptions it is possibly the most dangerous. In the thirteenth century, the Queen of Heaven had such a place, and her almost exclusive worship is perhaps as much a sign of the breakup of the mediaeval synthesis as any more obvious emblem of disintegration.

Man's roots are in the earth; and the effort to concentrate upon an ideal experience, that seeks no nourishment through these roots, may be quite as disastrous to spiritual growth as the failure to push upwards and to rise above the physical bed in which these roots are laid. In *Pierre,* Melville explored and followed such a fixation to its conclusion: disintegration and suicide. Had this been Melville's purpose in writing the book, *Pierre* might, in a decisive figure, have ended an epoch—the epoch of the romantic hero; for he had probed that hero's nobility and virtue and disclosed their deeper ambiguities, their conflicts, their irreconcilabilities. Pierre might have been a sort of anti-Werther. Unfortunately, this is just what it is not; for Melville identified himself with Pierre and defended his immaturity. How this came about we will inquire later; for we have not yet done justice to *Pierre* as a work of art.

6

What did Melville consciously set himself to do when he wrote *Pierre*? He sought, I think, to arrive at the same sort of psychological truth that he had achieved, in metaphysics, in *Moby-Dick.* His subject was, not the universe, but the ego; and again, not the obvious ego of the superficial novelist, but those implicated and related layers of self which reach from the outer appearances of physique and carriage down to the recesses of the unconscious personality. "The novel will find the way to our interiors, one day," he wrote in *Pierre*, "and will not always be a novel of costume merely." [Unlocated. Ed. Note.] Melville, to use his own words, had dropped his angle into the well of his childhood, to find out what fish might be there: before *Mardi*, he had sought for fish in the outer world, where swim the golden perch and pickerel: but now he had learned to dredge his unconscious, and to draw out of it, not the white whale, but motives, desires, hopes for which there had been no exit in his actual life. Men had been afraid to face the cold white malignity of the universe; they were even more reluctant to face their own unkempt, bewrayed selves. Even Shakespeare, deep as he was, had had reserves: Melville would set an example.

Melville was not concerned to portray "real life," for the unconscious is not for most people part of this reality: in a later book he gave an explanation of his own literary method. He describes readers after his own heart who read a novel as they might sit down to a play, with much the same expectation and feeling. "They look that fancy shall evoke scenes different from those of the same old crowd round the Custom House counter, and the same old dishes on the boarding house table, with characters unlike those of the same old acquaintances they meet in the same old way every day in the same old street. And as, in real life, the proprieties will not allow people to set out themselves with that unreserve permitted to the stage, so in books of fiction, they look not only for more entertainment, but, at bottom, for more reality, than real life itself can show. Thus, though they want novelty, they want nature, too; but nature unfettered, exhilarated, in effect transformed. In this way of thinking, the people in a fiction, like the people in a play, must dress as nobody exactly dresses, talk as nobody exactly talks, act as nobody exactly acts. It is with fiction as with religion: it should present another world, and yet one to which we feel the tie." For this conception of literary method, there is much to be said, and had *Pierre* carried it out with plausibility and consistency it might have made an even more important contribution to the art of the novel than George Meredith and Henry James were to make. If Melville met failure here, it was not because he had chosen a poor method, but because he lacked adeptness in using it.

As concerns his psychological purpose, however, *Pierre* for all its weaknesses will stand comparison with the pioneer works of its period. *Pierre* is one of the first novels in which the self is treated as anything but a unit, whose parts consist of the same material, with the grain, as it were, running the same way. Pierre's double relation towards his father's image and towards his mother's actual presence, his mixed attitudes towards Lucy and Isabel, the conflict between his latent interests and his actions and rationalizations, all these things are presented with remarkable penetration: if there is slag at the entrance of this mine, there is a vein of exceptionally rich ore running through it. Pierre's identification of his mother's love with

a supreme form of egotism, Pierre being the mirror in which she beholds her own proud grimace, is no less penetrating than Melville's account of the relation between Pierre and his cousin, which runs from romantic love into apathy and enmity. While the action of *Pierre* is full of harsh and even absurd contrasts, the psychological mood is portrayed with infinite retirement and with relentless surgical skill: Melville does not hold the pulse of his characters: he X-rays their very organs.

The supreme quality of *Pierre* is its candour. Like Pierre, the more Melville wrote, "and the deeper and deeper that he dived, [he] saw that everlasting elusiveness of Truth: the universal insincerity of even the greatest and purest written thoughts. Like knavish cards, the leaves of all great books were covertly packed." Melville did his best to avoid playing a foul hand: he dealt his cards as they slipped from the fingers of Fate, Chance, Necessity, Truth; and in this grave honesty of his the greatest of thinkers seemed little better than fictioneers. "Plato, Spinoza, and Goethe, and many more belong to this guild of self-impostors, with a preposterous rabble of muggletonian Scots and Yankees whose vile brogue still the more bestreaks the stripedness of their Greek or German Neoplatonic originals." Not exactly a kind criticism; but, in Melville's exacerbated state, he went even further: not merely did the "compensationists" or the "optimists" seem shallow: literature itself was a hollow business, too. The ultimate, the final truth was inexpressible, and even the mere hinting of it was inadequate: the intensest light of reason did not shed such blazonings upon the deeper truths in man as the profoundest gloom. Utter darkness is the wise man's light; silence his highest utterance. Catlike, one sees in the dark distinctly objects that are erased by blatant sunshine; indeed, one calls to one's aid senses and instincts that are dormant when one can move and see. "Not to know Gloom and Grief," said Melville, in the midst of this illumination, "is not to know aught that an heroic man should learn."

But if the gold of the transcendentalists was pewter and brass, Melville was equally honest about his own treasures. "By vast pains we mine into the pyramid; by horrible gaspings we come to the central room; with joy we espy the sarcophagus; but we lift the lid—and nobody is there!—appallingly vacant, as vast as the soul of man." One threw away literature and philosophy, yes, language itself, only to find oneself without visible support. One eliminated not merely the debris and muck: one got rid of the miner, and the very purpose of his occupation. "In those hyperborean regions to which enthusiastic Truth and Earnestness and Independence will invariably lead a mind fitted by nature for profound and fearless thoughts all objects are seen in a dubious uncertain and refracting light. Viewed through the rarefied atmosphere, the most immemorially admitted maxims of men begin to slide and fluctuate and finally become wholly inverted. . . . But the example of many minds forever lost, like undiscoverable Arctic explorers, amid those treacherous regions, warns us entirely away from them and we learn that it is not for man to follow the trail of truth too far, since by so doing he entirely loses the directing compass of his mind, for, arrived at the Pole, to whose barrenness only it points, there, the needle indifferently respects all points of the horizon alike."

Within the heap of fragments in **Pierre** that mark the thrust and power of Melville's mind, there is one fragment, fallen at random in the mass, that remains embedded in the memory. It is the message of the pamphlet that comes by accident into Pierre's hand when he is making his escape to New York: in his overwrought state, the words have a peculiar significance for his own purposes; and they are remarkable enough, in their enigmatic quality, to consider by themselves. The title of the pamphlet is *Chronometricals and Horologicals:* in it the fictitious lecturer purports to set forth his own heretical philosophy. The moral is embroidered in a single trope: the notion that there are two kinds of time in the world, that which is established at Greenwich and kept by chronometers, and that which prevails in other longitudes, recorded by the local watches. It is a parallel of the philosophic and practical aspects of life, or rather, of ideal and working morality; and I know no better exposure of the identity, yet dualism, of thought and action, ideal and practice.

The philosophic or religious minds are always correcting their watches by Greenwich time; and, by continuous observation of the heavens, they are always trying to make Greenwich time itself more correct. They know that the compromises and conveniences of society are useful: but they also know that these things have no ultimate reason for existence, and that one's employment of them must always be modified by reference to a scale of values alongside which they are false or meaningless. Shallow people never make such a correction: they believe in "dress" or "family" or "prestige" or "success" as if these were the vestments of eternity. Melville's error, at least Pierre's error, was just the opposite of this: he did not see that watches and local time are necessary, too, that there is no truth so cruelly meaningless as to give a person Greenwich time without telling him his longitude and enabling him to make his correction: that way lies disaster, confusion, shipwreck. A belief in ideal standards and values with no *via media* is scarcely better than a superficial life with no standards or insights at all.

The passage from the universal perception to the common life is difficult to make: it is the point at which religions and philosophies perpetually flounder. Melville saw this paradox; and he was plagued and puzzled by it; he even attributes it to Plotinus Plinlimmon, the leader of the transcendentalist sect, who drinks wine he forbids to his disciples, and, following supernal ideas, seems to prize cigars and food far more; Plinlimmon, whose non-benevolent stare seems to tell Pierre that all that he does is done in vain; Plinlimmon, the very embodiment of these ambiguities. Melville tended, with Pierre, to regard horologicals as a dubious frailty instead of what it actually is—the way that Greenwich time is universalized and incorporated in

local practice. Human ideals are, as Melville saw, like the points of the compass: one does not seek the north by going northward: one seeks to reach a humanly important part of the earth, like Pekin or Paris; and ideals are the means by which a life that more fully satisfies our human potentialities can be lived. To observe this paradox without falling into the rôle of Mr. Worldly Wiseman is the essence of an active morality. Melville confronted the paradox; but the point of it eluded him. He idealized ideals as he idealized sexual passion: he wished both to remain for him in that adolescent state in which they are pure, remote, untouchable—forgetting that life is impossible in that sterile and clarified medium. Though Melville had anatomized many human impulses and probed in many sore and hidden places, one part of the personality remained sacred to him in Pierre: the sanctum of adolescence. All the values in the book are distorted, its very purpose is deflected, by Melville's unconscious assumption that the romantic purity of adolescence, the purity that arises not through experience and fulfilment, that is, through continuous purification, but through an ignorance and stagnation within sealed vials—that this purity is central to all the other values. That chronometer was correct enough at nineteen: at thirty-three it was no longer accurate, for a single reason—it had stopped. That, we shall see, was the chief ambiguity of Melville's personal life.

Melville was not alone in parading these fundamental ambiguities. In the dissociation of society in America, the American writer was able to examine all the premises and established truths which a European ordinarily takes so much for granted that he is not aware of taking them at all; and he could separate the essence of our human institutions from their conventional overlayers. Emerson, in "Uriel," gives pithy expression to the same insidious ideas one finds in **Pierre**: but in Melville's novel they are on every page. His mother's love for her son is self-love and her admiration for him is vanity. His father's rectitude leads to a cold marriage, where an unclerked love had shown him a little radiant and a little finer at the core. Pierre's purest love is a disguised incest; his nobility is a worldly crime—while a lack of generous impulses would have led to wealth and honour. Melville's whole life, indeed, had taught him these ambiguities: Jack Chase was the real captain of the ship, not Captain Claret: the surgeon who amputated a living man, Surgeon Cuticle, with his glass eye, his false teeth, his wig, was more dead than the flesh he carved into: the cannibals of the South Seas were civilized, and the civilization of the New York slums was lower than cannibal gluttony: the missionary of Christ inflicted servitude, and the chief goods introduced by the trader were diseases: finally, the one civilization which thoroughly disregards the precepts of Christian morality is that of the Western world, which professes it.

These paradoxes were disturbing enough; but the fundamental ones were even worse. "The uttermost ideal of moral perfection in man is wide of the mark. The demigods trample on trash, and Virtue and Vice are trash!" Vice might lead to virtue; virtue might beget vice: the prostitute may teach purity and the holy man blasphemy! Where is one left when Melville and Emerson are through? One is left amid a debris of institutions and habits. Nothing is safe; nothing is secure: one no longer looks for the outer label, or believes in it. If north be the direction of one's ideal, the virtuous captain may have to tack back and forth from east to west in order to reach that destination: for no chart or compass ever enabled a ship to steer blindly for its port without paying close attention to wind and weather.

Had *Pierre,* as an imaginative work, been a more sufficient demonstration of these ambiguities, the book would have had a high destiny. But although the ideas are clear enough, they remain a potentiality in *Pierre,* since the story itself lacks integrity of form. The book is a precious crystal smashed out of its natural geometrical shape. Only by a chemical analysis of its elements do we discover what its primal character might have been.

7

The failure of *Pierre* as a work of art gives us a certain licence to deal with it as biography, all the more because Melville identified himself with the hero, giving him the initials and the Christian name of his beloved grandfather, Peter Gransevoort, and attaching him to objects like the portrait of his father which correspond to things about whose existence there is no doubt. If, as a work of art, *Pierre* was whole, we should have no good reason to suspect Melville's wholeness. It is the failure of *Pierre* as literature that draws our attention to Melville's predicament as a man; for in this particular way, he had not erred before. The young Melville who wrote *Typee* is not in *Pierre;* instead, a much younger self is there, a self erotically immature, expressing itself in unconscious incest fantasies, and capable of extravagant rationalizations in its effort to sustain them. *Pierre* is not a demonstration because it is a betrayal—and the person it betrays is Melville. In *Pierre,* he was an Iago, driven by his own frustration to betray the Othello who had been such a valiant captain in all his previous battles.

The significant question for us is what event, or series of occurrences, caused a hiatus in Melville's emotional and sexual development; and this question cannot be lightly answered by pointing to the obvious symbols in *Pierre*— for a symbol describes a tendency, rather than an objective event. We know that Melville's earliest associations of sex had been with vice and sexual disease; and in a sensitive lad, this introduction to passion may place bit and bridle on his own development. We know, too, that sexual relations in the United States among respectable people in the fifties were in a starved and stunted state: Stanley Hall, a boy in this very decade, recalled that he had never witnessed the slightest passage of affection between his father and his mother. It may be that Elizabeth, patient as a wife, was timid and irresponsive as a lover: in short, there are a dozen possible circumstances occurring long after childhood, which may have contributed to Melville's regres-

sion: and the incest-attachment, so far from being the cause of this, may in *Pierre* only serve as its emotional equivalent. Wherever sex is mentioned in other passages in Melville's books, it is referred to in a mood of disillusion. In *Clarel,* for example, he says:

> May love's nice balance, finely slight,
> Take tremor from fulfilled delight?
> Can nature such a doom dispense
> As, after ardor's tender glow,
> To make the rapture more than pall
> With evil secrets in the sense,
> And guile whose bud is innocence—
> Sweet blossom of the flower of gall?

And in one of the few passages in *Moby-Dick* where sex is referred to, the Sicilian sailor implies that sexual joy is in swayings, touchings, cozenings, and that when one tastes it directly, satiety comes. That, I submit, is not the experience of a healthy and well-mated man, or of a mature erotic state: to long for the pre-nuptial condition, to wish for fixation in courtship, is the mark of an immature, or at least an incomplete, attachment.

When one says that Melville longed for the pre-nuptial state one does not merely imply that he found his sexual relations difficult or unsatisfactory: this earlier condition meant something more: it meant irresponsibility, freedom to roam, carelessness about health and daily bread, the opportunity to do his work without foreboding and anxiety. Sex had brought disillusion not merely because the first ardour and glow had vanished suddenly with the first physical contact: it had increased all his burdens and threatened to curtail that inner development which he had come to prize above all things—even more than the robust outer experience that had produced *Typee.* Sex meant marriage; marriage meant a household and a tired wife and children and debts. No wonder he retreated: no wonder his fantasy attached him to a mother who could not surrender, to a half-sister who could not bear children! The ardent impulse remained; he sought only to make it innocuous to his own spiritual life.

In view of the terrific pressure upon Melville, one can sympathize with his retreat; but one sees that, so far from aiding his spiritual development, it halted a good part of it at a critical point: for he did not carry over into his thought and his work the experiences of a husband and a father and a happy lover. He does not speak about these experiences as a mature man: he speaks as an adolescent. At this point, his self did not grow and expand; rather, it became ingrown and withdrawn; and the symbol of incest is perhaps the symbol of this shrinkage, this defeat, and the ultimate blackness of mood that resulted from it. He associated his career with the deep well of adolescent purity, instead of with the running stream of maturity, turbid perhaps, but open to the sunlight, and swift. Doing so, he blocked his own development instead of releasing it: towards later experience he said No: No: and again No. For almost a decade after this, Melville's principal characters are tired, defeated, harassed, tormented, lonely men; and to the end of his days children, the last symbol of maturity, do not, directly or indirectly, enter his imaginative life.

So closely were Melville's sexual impulses and his intellectual career bound up that I am tempted to reverse the more obvious analysis of *Pierre,* and to see in its sexual symbols the unconscious revelation of his dilemmas as a writer. Lucy, then, may signify the naïve writings of his youth, which promised him happiness, and Isabel, the mysterious child of a foreign mother, lost in an obscure youth, may stand for that darker consciousness in himself that goads him to all his most heroic efforts, that goads him and baffles him, leaving him balked and sterile, incapable of going further in literature, and yet unable to retreat to the older and safer relations with Lucy—the Lucy of *Typee* and *Omoo.* We must recall that in writing *Moby-Dick* Melville had premonitions of his own final flowering and of his sudden falling into mould; and if this prospect haunted him, the relationship with Isabel would be a perfect symbol of it, since it showed him making an effort to go on with his literary career, living under the form of marriage with Isabel, but unable, through the very nature of their relationship, to enjoy the fruits of marriage. In spite of his confidence in *Moby-Dick,* a doubt might still lurk: suppose Isabel were an impostor! He had given up everything for her: he had abandoned the prospects of a happy literary career, such a career as his family, Elizabeth's family, all his friends and relatives, and the reviewers and society generally would approve of—abandoned it for a mad, chivalrous espousal of his inner life. He had defied the world for this dark mysterious girl; and what she was ready to give him in return the world regarded as an abominable sin. Very well: so much the worse for virtue, if virtue meant Mrs. Glendinning's pride or Lucy's lovely shallowness. Melville was not without hopes that success might join the unsanctified household, that Lucy and Isabel might live side by side; but when the reviewers told him, upon his publishing *Mardi* and *Moby-Dick,* that he had epoused a girl of the streets and seduced a virtuous maiden, he saw that there was no way out, except to shoot them and take the consequences.

Pierre itself, then, was a blow, aimed at his family with their cold pride, and at the critics, with their low standards, their failure to see where Melville's true vocation lay, and their hearty recommendation of "virtuous" courses that promised so little. Melville anticipated defeat: Lucy dies of shock, and Pierre and Isabel make away with themselves by poison; for he saw no way to go on with his deepest self, and still continue obedient to the conventions of society and the responsibilities of a married man. His failure to mature with his actual marriage contributed, I think, to his failure to go further with his spiritual union; but how much it contributed, and by what means the injury was done, we can still only speculate. There is no doubt about the final result. The mood of *Pierre,* the work of art, became the mood of Herman Melville, the man, for almost a decade. Before another year was over, he recovered his grip in writing, and his art became whole and suf-

ficient once more: but his life suffered, and his vision as a whole suffered: *Pierre* disclosed a lesion that never entirely healed.

R. K. Gupta (essay date 1967)

SOURCE: "Melville's Use of Non-Novelistic Conventions in *Pierre,*" in *The Emerson Society Quarterly,* No. 48, 3rd Quarter, 1967, pp. 141-45.

[*In the following essay, Gupta maintains that in writing* Pierre *Melville felt that the conventions of the novel were inadequate and restrictive, and thus he borrowed specific literary devices from the dramatic and epic genres.*]

In his essay "Melville's Search for Form" James E. Miller, Jr., says that Melville "was not content to accept without question the dominant form of his day—the novel. Instead, he adopted the outward shape but constantly pushed beyond the apparent limits. There is hardly a kind of literature he did not sample or assimilate: travel book, sea yarn, sociological study, philosophical tract, allegory, epic, domestic or historical romance, tragedy or comedy."[1] In *Pierre* Melville perhaps came closer to the form of the traditional novel than he did in any other work. At the same time, however, he found the conventions of the novel inadequate and unduly restrictive and, therefore, "pushed beyond the apparent limits" of his form and made use of certain specific devices derived from such literary genres as the epic and the drama. In *Pierre* Melville achieved some important artistic effects through epic and dramatic conventions, and hence my study of the ways in which they are used will, I hope, throw varied lights upon his art and technique.

The three epic devices repeatedly used in *Pierre* are invocation, apostrophe, and Homeric simile. Melville uses them functionally—to heighten an effect, to clarify a situation, or to illuminate a mental or emotional state. The invocation and the apostrophe are generally used by Pierre himself, and always in some tense, significant situation which they serve to clarify. For example, take his apostrophe to grief:

> Grief;—thou art a legend to me. I have known some fiery broils of glorious frenzy; I have oft tasted of revery; whence comes pensiveness; whence comes sadness; whence all delicious poetic presentiments;—but thou, Grief! art still a ghost-story to me. I know thee not,—do half disbelieve in thee. Not that I would be without my too little cherished fits of sadness now and then; but God keep me from thee, thou other shape of far profounder gloom! I shudder at thee![2]

This apostrophe, and the one to the mysterious face which immediately follows it, forcefully dramatize the naivete and immaturity of a Pierre to whom grief has been a pleasing fiction (a "ghost-story") rather than a painful reality. Then comes the invocation in which he calls upon the "sovereign powers" to "lift the veil":

Tread I on a mine, warn me; advance I on a precipice, hold me back; but abandon me to an unknown misery, that it shall suddenly seize me, and possess me, wholly—that ye will never do; else, Pierre's fond faith in ye—now clean, untouched—may clean depart; and give me up to be a railing atheist. (p. 56)

At the moment of this utterance, Pierre is in an emotionally distraught state, torn between contending thoughts, racked by doubt and despair. This is the first time that evil has intruded into his idyllic world, and the extremely complex, often conflicting, feelings aroused in him are aptly rendered in this soliloquy and highlighted by the use of the epic conventions. The concluding portion of the invocation foreshadows the heretical mood which comes upon him toward the end.

In the most elaborate of all the invocations—the one addressed to the Terror Stone—Pierre's despondency and the various ramifications of the dilemma which confronts him are admirably brought out:

If the miseries of the undisclosable things in me, shall ever unhorse me from my manhood's seat; if to vow myself all Virtue's and all Truth's, be but to make a trembling, distrusted slave of me; if Life is to prove a burden I cannot bear without ignominious cringings; if indeed our actions are all fore-ordained, and we are Russian serfs to Fate; if invisible devils do titter at us when we most nobly strive; if Life be a cheating dream, and virtue as unmeaning and unsequelled with any blessing as the midnight mirth of wine; if by sacrificing myself for Duty's sake, my own mother re-sacrifices me; if Duty's self be but a bugbear, and all things are allowable and unpunishable to man;—then do thou, Mute Massiveness, fall on me! Ages thou hast waited; and if these things be thus, then wait no more; for whom better canst thou crush than him who now lies here invoking thee? (p. 189)

Somewhat like the Joycean epiphanies, the apostrophes and invocations in the novel are flashes of illumination, moments of revelation and insight, bringing out the agony of Pierre's spiritual turmoil with an immediacy and intensity seldom attained in passages of authorial analysis.

Homeric similes also are used in *Pierre* with complete appropriateness. Not only does their scope for endless expansion and modification enable Melville to bring in considerable tangential detail and thus provide the reader with a kind of poetic relaxation, but they also have subtler implications and satisfy the imagination through implied comparisons relevant to the context. Consider, for example, the passage in which Lucy Tartan's yearning for the countryside is depicted:

It was very strange, but most eloquently significant of her own natural angelhood that, though born among brick and mortar in a sea-port, she still pined for un-baked earth and inland grass. So the sweet linnet, though born inside of wires in a lady's chamber on the ocean coast, and ignorant all its life of any other spot; yet, when spring-time comes, it is seized with flutter-

ings and vague impatiences; it cannot eat or drink for these wild longings. Though unlearned by any experience, still the inspired linnet divinely knows that the inland migrating time has come. And just so with Lucy in her first longings for the verdure. (pp. 33-34)

In these lines Melville, on the most obvious plane, is referring to Lucy's preference for rural life. But the simile goes further than that. Whereas the implied comparison between Lucy and the linnet brings out Lucy's sweetness and gentleness of disposition, words like "inspired" and "divinely" draw attention to her "angelic" qualities which Melville seeks to emphasize in his characterization of her. Again:

Weary with the invariable earth, the restless sailor breaks from every enfolding arm, and puts to sea in height of tempest that blows off shore. But in long night-watches at the antipodes, how heavily that ocean gloom lies in vast bales upon the deck; thinking that that very moment in his deserted hamlet-home the household sun is high, and many a sun-eyed maiden meridian as the sun. He curses Fate; himself he curses; his senseless madness, which is himself. For whoso once has known this sweet knowledge, and then fled it; in absence, to him the avenging dream will come.

Pierre was now this . . . self-upbraiding sailor: this dreamer of the avenging dream. (pp. 252-253)

This simile occurs immediately after Pierre has resolved to leave Saddle Meadows to befriend and protect Isabel, and it brings out, more suggestively than comments by the author possibly could, the pathos of Pierre's situation and his agonized awareness of all that he has irretrievably lost in rending his family bonds.

The Homeric similes in *Pierre*,[3] then, serve two important functions. On the one hand, by their luxuriance and amplitude they provide the imagination with moments of poetic beauty and contribute volume and variety to the narrative; on the other, they are an important and valuable aid to the analysis of characters.

Pierre is a dramatic novel not only in its structure and characterization but also because Melville employs in it certain techniques (foreshadowing, dramatic irony, soliloquy) which are specifically dramatic.

F. L. Lucas says that in tragedy suspense is a more effective and powerful weapon than surprise. According to him, "it is the power to create the tense, overcharged atmosphere before the storm, to 'pile the dim outlines of the coming doom,'" that forms a major part of the impressiveness of the great tragic dramatists.[4] In *Pierre* Melville prefers suspense to surprise and by a skilful use of foreshadowing creates an atmosphere of restlessness and foreboding. The authorial comments on fate and destiny which figure so prominently in the early sections of the novel are not satirical, as they are sometimes taken to be, but premonitory, a foreshadowing of the evil to come. In order to create a "tense, overcharged atmosphere," Melville as omniscient narrator inserts, in his portrayal of Pierre's early felicity, premonitory remarks such as the following:

> Thus loftily, in the days of his circumscribed youth, did Pierre glance along the background of his race, little recking of that maturer and larger interior development, which should forever deprive these things of their full power of pride in his soul. (p. 5)

> But while thus alive to the beauty and poesy of his father's faith, Pierre little foresaw that this world hath a secret deeper than beauty, and Life some burdens heavier than death. (p. 6)

> Now Pierre stands on this noble pedestal; we shall see if he keeps that fine footing; we shall see if Fate hath not just a little bit of a small word or two to say in this world. (p. 14)

These anticipatory comments help to create an atmosphere of gloom and suspense which is in harmony with the tragic action of the novel.

In *Pierre* Melville also uses several devices for creating suspense which are rooted in the action rather than in the narrator's commentary. Some of these—like the paraphernalia of mysterious faces, unearthly shrieks, and prophetic portraits—are Gothic rather than truly dramatic. But when Mrs. Glendinning unwittingly and in unrepressed fury stabs her own portrait (p. 183) and says that she feels as though in Pierre she had "borne the last of a swiftly to be extinguished race" (p. 184), or when Pierre proleptically falls over his threshold as though "jeeringly hurled from beneath his own ancestral roof" (p. 258), or when Lucy in her letter to Pierre expresses her misgiving that he may become involved in "some terrible jeopardy" (p. 433), the effect is essentially that of dramatic foreshadowing without any suggestion of contrivance or artificiality.

The tragic irony in *Pierre* not only governs the plot but also throws light on the characters. Throughout the novel there are statements in which the reader is made to see an ironic meaning of which the speaker may be wholly unconscious. Two kinds of tragic irony are found in *Pierre*: one in which the reader *immediately* grasps the ironic meaning underlying an apparently innocent statement; the other in which this meaning dawns upon him only gradually and *retrospectively*. The best example of the first kind occurs in the famous breakfast scene, at the moment when Mrs. Glendinning, sitting in judgment on the adulterous Ned and Delly, characterizes Ned's conduct as the "sheerest and most gratuitous profligacy" and remarks that men like him are to her way of thinking "more detestable than murderers":

> . . . is not the man, who has sinned like that Ned, worse than a murderer? Has he not sacrificed one woman completely, and given infamy to another—to both of them—for their portion. If his own legitimate boy should now hate him, I could hardly blame him. (p. 140)

As she glibly censures the conduct of the guilty lovers, she is unaware of the fact that her own situation is similar, and that her husband, whom she has always deified and idolized, may not have been any better than Ned. The reader, however, is conscious of the subtle overtones of the situation.

Melville's forte in *Pierre,* however, is the other kind of irony in which the reader does not see the ironic meaning underlying a statement at the time it is made as in Mrs. Glendinning's repeated admonitions to her son to follow the path of his "extremely gentlemanly" father:

> Never rave, Pierre; and never rant. Your father never did either; nor is it written of Socrates; and both were very wise men. Your father was profoundly in love— that I know to my certain knowledge—but I never heard him rant about it. He was always extremely gentlemanly: and gentlemen never rant. Milksops and Muggletonians rant, but gentlemen never. (p. 24)

> Bless you!—God bless you, my dear son! always think of him and you can never err; yes, always think of your dear perfect father, Pierre. (p. 25)

Later, when the reader discovers the details about the father's youth, his mind is thrown back to these early panegyrics and his reaction is intensified. The whole passage in which Mrs. Glendinning expresses her thoughts about Pierre and Lucy is charged with dramatic irony of the finest and subtlest kind:

> "A noble boy, and docile"—she murmured—"he has all the frolicsomeness of youth, with little of its giddiness. And he does not grow vain-glorious in sophomorean wisdom. I thank heaven I sent him not to college. A noble boy, and docile. A fine, proud, loving, docile, vigorous boy. Pray God, he never becomes otherwise to me. His little wife, that is to be, will not estrange him from me; for she too is docile—beautiful and reverential, and most docile. Seldom yet have I known such blue eyes as hers, that were not docile, and would not follow a bold black one, as two meek blue-ribboned ewes, follow their martial leader. How glad am I that Pierre loves her so, and not some dark-eyed haughtiness, with whom I could never live in peace; but who would be ever setting her young married state before my elderly widowed one, and claiming all the homage of my dear boy!—the fine, proud, loving, docile, vigorous boy!—the lofty-minded, well-born, noble boy; and with such sweet docilities!" (p. 25)

At the moment this soliloquy is uttered, the reader, of course, does not know any more than Mrs. Glendinning does that some "dark-eyed haughtiness" is soon to come between Pierre and his mother and divide irrevocably the "pure joined current" of their lives into "two unmixing streams" (p. 4). But later, when Pierre breaks his family ties for the sake of Isabel, the reader becomes aware of the deep irony implicit in Mrs. Glendinning's soliloquy, especially in her repeated application of the word "docile" to both Pierre and Lucy. The effect of the reiteration, at the time when Pierre is on the verge of defying her and hurting her in a sore spot, is to intensify the irony of the situation. Subsequently we discover that Lucy also is the very reverse of "docile," however timid and shrinking she may appear on the surface.

The cumulative effect of the use of dramatic foreshadowing and tragic irony in *Pierre* is to create a tense and portentous atmosphere which is an important component of that satisfying sense of unity which we find in the novel.

One may also mention at this point Melville's highly skilful use of the dramatic soliloquy in *Pierre* at crucial moments in the story. The soliloquy is used by several characters—by Pierre (pp. 55-57, 90-91, 189, 259, 273, 445), by Mrs. Glendinning (pp. 25, 26, 183-185, 268-269, 271, 272), by Charlie Millthorpe (pp. 499, 505), even by the innkeeper (pp. 282-283), the jailor (p. 503), and Delly Ulver (p. 447). When uttered by a major character, it gives us insight into his innermost thoughts and feelings. The most notable example is the great soliloquy, too long to be quoted, in Book II (pp. 55-57) in which all the twists of thought and fluctuations of feeling in Pierre are appropriately rendered in broken and tortured language. When used by a minor character like Charlie Millthorpe or the innkeeper, it on the one hand sharpens the pathos and irony of a particular event and, on the other, serves a choric function—presentation of an objective, detached point of view on a specific situation or character. A memorable example is the soliloquy of the landlord of the Black Swan Inn after Pierre's pretended marriage with Isabel and his departure for New York:

> I have kept this house, now, three-and-thirty years, and have had plenty of bridal-parties come and go; in their long train of wagons, break-downs, buggies, gigs—a gay and giggling train—Ha!—there's a pun! popped out like a cork—ay, and once, the merry bride was bedded on a load of sweet-scented new-cut clover. But such a bridal-party as this morning's—why, it's as sad as funerals. And brave Master Pierre Glendinning is the groom! Well, well, wonders is all the go. I thought I had done with wondering when I passed fifty; but I keep wondering still. Ah, somehow, now, I feel as though I had just come from lowering some old friend beneath the sod, and yet felt the grating cord-marks in my palms.—'Tis early, but I'll drink. Let's see; cider,—a mug of cider;—'tis sharp, and pricks like a game-cock's spur,—cider's the drink for grief. Oh, Lord! that fat men should be so thin-skinned, and suffer in pure sympathy on others' account. A thin-skinned, thin man, he don't suffer so, because there ain't so much stuff in him for his thin skin to cover. Well, well, well, well, well; of all colics, save me from melloncholics; green melons is the greenest thing!

Both in diction and effect, this soliloquy can be likened to those low-comedy interludes in Shakespeare (the porter scene in *Macbeth* and the grave-diggers' scene in *Hamlet*) in which, as Edward Rosenberry says, "a blood-curdling irony is achieved through characters in ignorance of the tragic issue of the business they are being droll about."[5] In general, then, the soliloquy is an important part of Melville's technique in *Pierre* and gives his characters complexity, subtlety, and dramatic immediacy. His use of

epic and dramatic conventions renders him vulnerable to the charge of having violated the integrity of the novelistic form. By relying on non-novelistic conventions, however, he succeeded in clarifying his themes and characters, in broadening and diversifying his range of effects, and in giving his work depth of meaning and richness of texture.

Notes

1. In *Bucknell Review,* VIII (1959), 276.

2. *Pierre: or The Ambiguities* (New York: E. P. Dutton & Co., Inc., Evergreen Books, Grove Press Edition, 1957), pp. 55-56. All subsequent references to *Pierre* will be to this edition and will be parenthetically incorporated in the text.

3. For more examples of the Homeric simile in the novel, see pp. 120, and 252-253.

4. *Tragedy* (New York, 1928), p. 88.

5. *Melville and the Comic Spirit* (Cambridge, Mass., 1955), p. 129.

Nicholas Canaday, Jr. (essay date 1969)

SOURCE: "Melville's *Pierre*: At War with Social Convention," in *Papers on Language and Literature,* Vol. V, No. 1, Winter, 1969, pp. 51-62.

[*In the following essay, Canaday explores Melville's treatment of the individual's need to follow his or her moral imperative—even at the cost of defying social convention—and describes the writer's attitude toward the problem as ambivalent.*]

The elements in Pierre Glendinning's vision of himself as Enceladus, when late in the novel Melville's hero contemplates the ruin of his life "with prophetic discomfiture and woe," provide by analogy a significant comment on Pierre's career in its penultimate moment.[1] Like Enceladus he is a rebel, and the "doubly incestuous" (408) Titan prefigures Pierre in his relationship with his mother and Isabel. But another element in the Enceladus myth has not received sufficient attention: he was an armed giant, not an Olympian god, and his war was with a society of gods. Enceladus's fate was to be buried in the earth. Although in spirit he was similar to Prometheus, another Titan, the general assault of Enceladus differed from the single, daring act of defiance against a single god. Pierre's spirit is akin to Ahab's but his immediate quarrel is with society.[2] His fate is to be buried alive in the social environment, until in a wild moment he destroys himself: scorned as an author by a Philistine publisher, trapped by poverty in a household of three dependent women, and assaulted by an outraged social convention represented by Glendinning Stanly and Frederic Tartan—the conventional lover and brother.

What Melville later calls "conventionalness" is the key to an understanding of the opening idyllic scenes of the novel.

The picture is ironic. William Braswell has written about the early love scenes: "Instead of showing an inexplicable loss of taste, or the debilitating influence of cheap, sentimental fiction he is known to have thought ridiculous, his style reveals a satirical purpose."[3] Braswell observes that extravagance and overstatement are the principal devices that reveal the irony. Conventionally conceived, Pierre's early world is a rural Eden. Yet convention, the enforcing arm of social authority, can be a relentless coercing power.

The environment of Saddle Meadows, locale of Pierre's youth, brings immediately to the novel an element of social authority. The feudal atmosphere makes great demands of the Glendinnings. They are looked to as examples of good conduct by those socially inferior to them, and their peers expect them to maintain at least the reputation for goodness so that their class may not be betrayed. As a member of the landed gentry, Pierre has an obligation to society, "for the country is not only the most poetical and philosophical, but it is the most aristocratic part of this earth" (13). Mrs. Glendinning sees it as her duty to be the biggest contributor to the church of the community, to provide for the poor and the sick, and to organize and oversee community functions. Such activities, of course, are the warrant for her authority as arbiter of manners and morals for the entire area. Her training of Pierre is designed to fix in him this same sense of what she conceives to be social responsibility.

The Glendinning family history, recited with grand extravagance by Melville, is another element in the novel that creates and enforces the social pressure on its hero. Pierre's paternal great-grandfather, General Pierre Glendinning, had fought an Indian battle in the meadows that slope away from the rear of the manor house. Mortally wounded in the encounter, the general had sat unhorsed upon his saddle in the grass, cheering his men in the fray. From that incident had been derived the name Saddle Meadows for the house, the village, and the area. A short distance away, Pierre's grandfather, also a general, had defended a rude stockade for several months against Tories, Indians, and Regulars during the War of the Revolution. With an exaggeration of detail verging on burlesque, Melville portrays Pierre's mother as the daughter of a general, and Pierre's duty to uphold the traditions of two families is constantly brought to his attention. Since his father's untimely death by a fever, Pierre has been the sole remaining male Glendinning. Reared in an atmosphere devoted to proud family memories and surrounded by trophies reminiscent of a glorious family history, Pierre is deeply imbued with an aristocratic sense of duty. Thus from his youth he has been subjected to a form of social pressure exerted by his illustrious ancestors.

Mary Glendinning, the proud matriarch of Saddle Meadows, is the chief exponent of the social pressure that is applied to her son Pierre. Her world is exclusively the shallow world of social status grandly conceived. She is described as "an affluent, and haughty widow; a lady who externally furnished a singular example of the preservative and beautifying influences of unfluctuating rank, health, and wealth, when joined to a fine mind of medium culture, uncankered by any inconsolable grief, and never worn by sordid cares" (2-3). Melville's emphasis on externals characterizes Mary Glendinning as a hollow woman concerned only with forms and social usages. She never felt deeply the premature death of her husband, nor troubled her mind with serious thoughts on any subject. Despite the affectionate veneer of their relationship, her joy in Pierre is simply "triumphant maternal pride" combined with a narcissistic self-love, because she sees in him "her own graces strangely translated into the opposite sex" (3). Mary Glendinning's life is summarized by Melville's statement that "in a life of nearly fifty years" the ordinary qualities of womanhood "had never betrayed her into a single published impropriety, or caused her one known pang at the heart" (15). Her obsession with conduct that is socially correct has always concealed her true inner feelings, if, indeed, she has any. If she was not entirely satisfied with her late husband's conduct, if he caused her any slight pang at the heart, her frigidly correct outward demeanor was all that showed itself to the world. She constantly admonishes Pierre to think of his "dear perfect father" (20). Whether she believes Pierre's father was perfect or not, her one concern is that he be considered so in the eyes of her son and society.

Still another form of social pressure is exerted on Pierre by Lucy's family. Mrs. Tartan is described as the "mistress of an ample fortune," aware of her wealth and position, and "inclined to force it upon the notice of other people, nowise interested in the matter" (29). The irony of Melville's description of Mrs. Tartan's world is immediately apparent: "Nevertheless, Mrs. Tartan was an excellent sort of lady, as this lady-like world goes. She subscribed to charities, and owned five pews in as many churches, and went about trying to promote the general felicity of the world, by making all the handsome young people of her acquaintance marry one another" (29-30). Mrs. Tartan, of course, is pleased with the marriage match she fancies she has made for her daughter, although her efforts, Melville wryly adds, were about as helpful as "match-making between the steel and the magnet" (31). Thus in Lucy's family the notions of propriety held by Mrs. Glendinning have their counterpart. In the seemingly idyllic community of Saddle Meadows inexorable forces are at work. The feudal environment, the proud Glendinning family background, the unsullied reputations of three Pierre Glendinnings, the two mothers so conscious of social status—these elements are the forces of society that surround and coerce the unfortunate Pierre.

Pierre is a "conventional" hero in two senses of the word. In the first place, he is a conventional romantic hero. The faceless young men in the romances so popular in Melville's day all had similar character traits and ideals. Melville begins the novel with an appropriately exaggerated setting of rural bliss. Pierre is first seen walking across a green and golden meadow to make a morning call upon his ideal young lady, whom he finds peering out of an upper casement surrounded by flowered vines. After an ex-change of compliments and sentiments, Pierre proceeds on his way, marching under her colors, as he says, because he has plucked a flower from her hedge and pinned it con-spicuously in his bosom. This first scene sets the tone for the first part of the book. Pierre's upbringing has molded a passive youth, a product of an ideal world far removed from ordinary facts of life. He had, in fact, spent long summer afternoons in his father's library, "where the Spenserian nymphs had early led him into many a maze of all-bewildering beauty" and had inspired "imaginative flames in his heart" (5). If Pierre fancies himself a modern version of the Red Cross Knight, it is because he cherishes the same ideals (and lives by the same conventions) as his literary predecessor.

Pierre's ideality is best revealed in his attitude toward women. Melville pictures the early Pierre-Lucy relation-ship as having all the characteristics found in popular ro-mantic fiction, and Pierre reveres his mother with the "pro-foundest filial respect" (14). Pierre lacks only a sister, the one omission in his seemingly idyllic world: "Oh, had my father but had a daughter! . . . some one whom I might love, and protect, and fight for, if need be. It must be a glorious thing to engage in a mortal quarrel on a sweet sister's behalf!" (6). Melville's specific irony in this pas-sage, which is only revealed later, indicates his attitude to-ward Pierre's entire romantic world. Pierre will find that the real fight in his sister's behalf will be the very oppo-site of glorious. Whatever villainous foe Pierre has in mind here can be nothing like the sordid enemy he soon finds himself pitted against. It is obvious that Pierre is ill-equipped to wage the battle into which he thrusts himself.

The young Pierre is also a "conventional" hero because of the oppressive conventions of society that have shaped him in his youth and that now bind and obligate him. Pierre's plight is that the very conventions that have so in-exorably molded him will be of no use to him in his struggle. In fact he will be forced to take a stand against the very social conventions that have been given so much emphasis in his life. His education has stressed sentiment, sensibility, and the appreciation of beauty, and his fore-bears have exemplified martial courage in the face of dan-ger or even death. Such values and examples are not suffi-cient: "Pierre little foresaw that this world hath a secret deeper than beauty, and life some burdens heavier than death" (6). Had Pierre been allowed to live out his days in the ideality of Saddle Meadows, the conventions of soci-ety would have served him as an adequate guide to life. This was not to be: "Now Pierre stands on this noble ped-estal; we shall see if he keeps that fine footing; we shall see if Fate hath not just a little bit of a small word or two to say in this world" (11). When Fate steps into Pierre's life, he soon finds that the social conventions offer no ad-equate solution to his dilemma.

Before Pierre makes his decision to leave Saddle Mead-ows but after he has heard of the existence of Isabel, he is permitted to witness a sample of the conventional response

to the affair of Delly Ulver, "forever ruined through the cruel arts of Ned" (130). His mother personifies that re-sponse and indeed dictates what is to be done about Delly. Pierre himself assents to the notion that Delly "is forever ruined" and that seduction is a "cruel art" practiced by the male on the unwitting, innocent female. The conventional response is to banish the offending female from the com-munity despite the fact that her sin springs from weakness rather than cruelty. Pierre is present when his mother indi-cates to the village clergyman, the Reverend Mr. Fals-grave, that her attitude toward Delly is uncompromisingly severe. Because it is relevant to Isabel's unhappy state and to his memory of his father, Pierre asks Mr. Falsgrave about the attitude he would have had toward Delly and her child if it had lived. Mrs. Glendinning interrupts to say that sinners deserve to be miserable, but Mr. Falsgrave seems more humane: "'The sins of the fathers shall be vis-ited upon the children to the third generation,' . . . But Madam, that does not mean, that the community is in any way to take the infamy of the children into their own vol-untary hands, as the conscious delegated stewards of God's inscrutable dispensations" (118). Mrs. Glendinning then speaks as the voice of social authority: "But if we entirely forget the parentage of the child, and every way receive the child as we would any other, feel for it in all respects the same, and attach no sign of ignominy to it—how then is the Bible dispensation to be fulfilled?" (118). Mr. Fals-grave is silenced by this question. The force of society also coerces the man of God, who dares not offend a prominent patroness.

In case there was any doubt in Pierre's mind, Mrs. Glendinning's reaction to the affair of Ned and Delly dem-onstrates to her son the futility of appealing to her in be-half of Isabel, and of course her maternal vindictiveness would increase when in addition her own pride is at stake. While Mrs. Glendinning serves notice that she is prepared to enforce vigorously Old Testament injunctions, Melville portrays Mr. Falsgrave somewhat more sympathetically. The minister's unassuming opinion that members of a community should not appoint themselves stewards of God's inscrutable dispensations is sound enough, but it is timidly expressed at a time when timidity is no virtue. Still Pierre agrees readily with Falsgrave's little sermon on the foolishness of adopting universal maxims to embrace all moral contingencies—a point relevant to the absolutism of the chronometrical man introduced later in the novel. Pierre is disappointed in Falsgrave, or perhaps more spe-cifically the institutional church as represented by Fals-grave, but later he comes to the conclusion that not too much can be expected of one who "is unavoidably en-tangled by all fleshly alliances, and can not move with godly freedom in a world of benefices" (193). Thus the church is buried in the social environment, and the minis-ter cannot directly reproach his chief contributor with her lack of Christian charity. The result is that the society of Saddle Meadows heartlessly expels its wayward members. The force of social authority operates on Delly and Ned just as later it is to coerce Pierre and Isabel.

When Melville entitles the chapter of Pierre's decision to leave Saddle Meadows "The Unprecedented Final Resolution of Pierre" (202), he is referring to a decision that has no precedent in the annals of romance or in the mind of conventionalness. Pierre's decision to leave with his supposed sister and to tell the world that she is his wife is an unconventional solution to a problem faced by a conventional hero. Yet Pierre's character clearly shapes the resolution. His decision is "not only strange and extraordinary in its novelty of mere aspect," but also it is "wonderful in its unequaled renunciation of himself" (202). Romantic heroes are noted for their self-sacrifice, and thus it appeals to his ideal nature. Unprecedented as this resolution is, it derives in this respect from his early upbringing.

Pierre's new knowledge of his father's transgression and his new experience with the harshness of what had seemed an ideal world has a profound effect on him, but he is not left totally without moral resources. Pierre no longer believes that he exists in a perfect society, and once he finds that the authority of his society is based neither on truth or right, he cannot continue to believe in it or obey it. Pierre's secluded, rural nurturing has protected him from that "darker, though truer aspect of things" (80). Unsettling as this new awareness is, still "he seemed to feel that in his deepest soul, lurked an indefinite but potential faith, which could rule in the interregnum of all hereditary beliefs, and circumstantial persuasions" (102). Pierre's unprecedented decision, consciously setting aside hereditary beliefs yet unconsciously shaped by them because it is romantically self-sacrificing, derives ultimately from an indefinite faith in his own ability to perceive right and to act upon it.

Although Pierre's obligations to his father's memory and to Isabel are important in his decision to flee Saddle Meadows, he is mainly concerned with his mother's pride. He wishes to spare his mother because he does not believe that she is to blame for the way she is made: "He too plainly saw, that not his mother had made his mother, but the Infinite Haughtiness had first fashioned her; and then the haughty world had further molded her; nor had a haughty Ritual omitted to finish her" (105). God, society, and conventional religiosity have thus created his mother and confirmed her in haughtiness. Pierre joins Ishmael in perceiving the powerful, mysterious authority of God the Creator. Melville makes the identification conclusive when he writes that at the moment of this perception Pierre feels "entirely lonesome, and orphan-like," as if he were "driven out an infant Ishmael into the desert, with no maternal Hagar to accompany and comfort him" (105). This loneliness is the price Pierre must pay for alienating himself from his mother and her society.

After Pierre leaves Saddle Meadows, the elements of the novel combine to portray Pierre as a social delinquent; he is a rebel against social forms. Pierre has not violated any standard of morality or the law. He has outraged his mother by eloping with an unknown girl, and later when Lucy joins his New York household Pierre is charged with exercising an undue influence over her. But he is not charged with immorality with Lucy—she thinks he is married to Isabel. And there is no evidence that there is a physical consummation of the love between Pierre and Isabel. In his study of **Pierre** and *Manfred*, Joseph J. Mogan expresses what seems to be the critical consensus that in the case of Pierre the "actual incest itself remains ambiguous."[4] Floyd C. Watkins is less tentative: ". . . the relationship between mother and son verges on the latently incestuous; this is a foreshadowing, perhaps, of the potential incest that probably becomes real between Isabel and Pierre."[5] John Bernstein maintains that "it is clearly indicated—or at least as clearly as the mores of the time would permit—that on one occasion the love between Pierre and Isabel is consummated."[6] On the other hand, in the introduction to the Hendricks House Edition of the novel Henry A. Murray thoroughly elaborates Pierre's double incestuous relationship but concludes that the love for Isabel is not consummated: "With this in mind [that a sister is the proper object of love in the courtly love tradition] we might guess that one of Pierre's secret motives was to avoid marriage, 'that climax which is so fatal to ordinary love,' and to commit himself forever to a wholly spiritual relationship. This hypothesis would explain Pierre's declaration that he has resolved 'to follow Virtue to her uttermost vista, where common souls never go,' and his apprehension lest 'the uttermost virtue, after all, provide a betraying pander to the monstrousest vice.'"[7] Such seems to be Pierre's conscious motivation, and it may be, as Nathalia Wright suggests, that there are hints of repressed homosexuality in Pierre's relationship with Glen Stanly and that a retarded sexual development "is partly responsible for his decision to abandon Lucy and to assume the relationship of brother and the masquerade of husband to Isabel."[8]

For Pierre to pursue the wildly unnatural, unprecedented, and self-sacrificing course of living with Isabel continently is perfectly in character. The motif of incest runs through the book, of course; it gives a flavor of unique folly to Pierre's action. He enjoys it while he despairs of it. Pierre is obviously attracted sexually by the dark Isabel, and he expresses doubts that he would so readily commit himself to the rescue of a supposed sister who lacks her appeal. Isabel's caresses in their darkened New York apartment stir him to a wild excitement, and Isabel definitely shows a sexual jealousy of Lucy when Pierre receives the letter announcing her arrival in the city. Yet in this same conversation it is made clear that the Pierre-Isabel relationship has not included sexual intercourse:

> "Oh, I want none in the world but thee, my brother—but thee, but thee! and, oh God! am I not enough for thee? . . ."

> Pierre spoke not; but he listened; a terrible burning curiosity was in him, that made him as heartless. But still all that she had said thus far was ambiguous. (367-68.)

In this conversation Pierre recognizes an invitation in her wild questionings, however ambiguous. A "terrible burning curiosity" is aroused about her sexual favors; lust makes him heartless. The temptation is clear, but equally clear is the fact that he has resisted it in the past and continues to do so. The conversation here does not result in physical consummation, and proof of past celibacy follows immediately. Isabel asks Pierre if Lucy is to sleep with her in her room, and Pierre answers: "On thy account; wishful for thy sake; to leave thee incommoded; and—and—not knowing precisely how things really are;—she probably anticipates and desires otherwise, my sister" (369). Thus late in the novel Pierre reminds Isabel that Lucy does not know precisely how things are, that their intimacy is only apparent, not real.[9] The story then moves rapidly to its conclusion, and there is no reason to believe that their relationship changes.

In his new social environment in New York Pierre still remains an outcast. He does not, then, substitute the mores of one society for another. He does not seek to adapt himself to the rough democratic society of his poor tenement house. He treats his fellow tenants like servants; he is rudely condescending to those who befriend him, even after Glendinning Stanly has given him the same treatment. He appeals to Charlie Millthorpe for help, and this son of a Saddle Meadows farmer, who is now apparently a successful lawyer in the city, responds with aid and the offer of friendship. But Pierre is "startled by his exceedingly frank and familiar manner" and shocked by his lack of "old manorial deference" (329). In the eyes of his new acquaintances in the city Pierre has defied his mother's authority to break off his engagement to a rich girl and has married a poor orphaned servant girl. No one knows, of course, not even Delly Ulver, that Isabel may be his half-sister. In the Bohemian society of the tenement there are many who would have respected his independent attitude had he desired to make friends with them.

There is no Ishmael to view Pierre's career and tell his story, but despite Melville's obvious sympathy for Pierre (he is a deep diver, a box of treasure that sinks, and Charlie Millthorpe a weightless floating bladder) one part of the author also judges his hero.[10] Pierre is quite capable of supporting himself financially while he is writing his book: the practical Charlie Millthorpe suggests that people will pay to hear Pierre lecture on Kantian philosophy. Three young women—Isabel, Delly, and later Lucy—are willing to aid him in any way they can, but he makes no effort to direct their energies toward some financial return. The practical, the expedient cannot be completely ignored. One recalls the lessons learned by Wellingborough Redburn and not learned by his English friend Harry Bolton.[11] The same impulse that brings Pierre away from Saddle Meadows, an impetuous pursuit of the heart, results in his isolation and ultimate death in the city. Yet on the grounds that "all the world does never gregariously advance to Truth" (195) Pierre stubbornly justifies his attitude and behavior.

Melville enlarges Pierre's struggle against society so that it gains cosmic significance. He learns about the vast mystery of life, that "all the world . . . was steeped a million fathoms in a mysteriousness wholly hopeless of solution"

(150). Pierre concludes, like Ishmael, that "human life . . . partakes of the unravelable inscrutableness of God" (166). One specific aspect of the problem of life is set out by the pamphlet that Pierre finds in the coach carrying him to New York, the chronometrical and horological argument of Plotinus Plinlimmon. Pierre has already discovered and identified the horological pressures as the conventions of society. The chronometrical man is assaulted by social forces: ". . . the never-entirely repulsed hosts of Commonness, and Conventionalness, and Worldly Prudent-mindedness return to the charge; press hard on the faltering soul; and with inhuman hootings deride all its nobleness as mere eccentricity, which further wisdom and experience shall assuredly cure" (197). The pamphlet warns that man must not do precisely what Pierre has done: man must "by no means make a complete unconditional sacrifice of himself in behalf of any other being, or any cause, or any conceit" (251). The chronometrical man will "array all men's earthly time-keepers against him, and thereby work himself woe and death," become involved in "strange, *unique* follies and sins, unimagined before," and commit "a sort of suicide as to the practical things of this world" (249-50). Pierre fulfills precisely these predictions.

Plinlimmon's dichotomy is a form of absolutism which Melville does not approve.[12] Two characters in the novel have been notably conquered by the hosts of commonness, prudent-mindedness, and conventionality—Mr. Falsgrave and Glendinning Stanly. They and their horological solutions are not sympathetically treated. Charles Millthorpe seems less objectionable, but because of his intellectual limitations and his humble origin he may have less obligation. Pierre's chronometrical soul, like Ahab's higher perception, does not receive Melville's unqualified approval either. As Melville says directly to the reader, the pamphlet "seems more the excellently illustrated restatement of a problem, than the solution of the problem itself" (246).

The cause of Pierre's social rebellion is his obedience to a moral imperative, "the loftiest behest of his soul" (244), which happens to be contrary to the dictates of social authority. The sanctions of society in the end have more force than the mere strength of moral right. This is the pessimism of Melville's **Pierre.** And the personal tragedy of Pierre Glendinning has as its cause the fact that though he rebels against the authority of his former society, nevertheless its shaping influence is precisely the reason for his downfall. Melville's attitude is ambivalent. On the one hand, he is sympathetically drawn to the war of his Encela-dus. Yet Pierre is a "fool of Truth, . . . fool of Virtue, . . . fool of Fate" (422), noble and foolish (the concept is ambiguous) to pursue such abstractions in wanton disregard of reason and the demands of this world. These, then, are the ambiguities promised by Melville's subtitle to the novel. Out of Pierre's obedience to a moral imperative in defiance of society have come heroism and foolishness, knowledge and grief, independence and death.

Notes

1. Herman Melville, *Pierre: Or, The Ambiguities,* ed. Henry A. Murray (New York, 1949), p. 407. Subse-

quent page references to this edition will be made parenthetically in the text.

2. John Bernstein, *Pacifism and Rebellion in the Writings of Herman Melville* (The Hague, 1964), p. 144, sees Pierre's rebellion as beginning in an attempt to right social injustice but ending with an Ahablike Pierre at war against God.

3. "The Early Love Scenes in Melville's *Pierre*," AL, [*American Literature: A Journal of Literary History, Criticism, and Bibliography*] XXII (1950), 285. In this article there is also a good summary of the views of earlier critics who had accused Melville of a lapse of taste in the opening scenes introducing the youthful Pierre and Lucy in love. Perhaps the most recent commentator on this point has been Floyd C. Watkins, who writes that in the opening of the novel Melville mocks pride, religion, triteness, and ideality. See "Melville's Plotinus Plinlimmon and Pierre," *Reality and Myth: Essays in American Literature in Memory of Richard Croom Beatty* (Nashville, Tenn., 1964), pp. 39-51, *passim*.

4. "*Pierre* and *Manfred*: Melville's Study of the Byronic Hero," PELL, I (Summer 1965), 239.

5. Watkins, p. 47.

6. Bernstein, p. 131.

7. P. lvii.

8. "*Pierre*: Herman Melville's *Inferno*," AL, XXXII (1960), 180.

9. The arrival of Lucy's letter and their conversation takes place some time after the scene that John Bernstein cites as the one occasion when Pierre and Isabel consummate their love.

10. Watkins suggests that Plinlimmon is Pierre's Ishmael, "the passive observer of his fate, the character who is exactly antithetical to him" (p. 40). Aside from the obvious difference that Ahab's entire story filters through Ishmael's consciousness, Ishmael's intellectual and emotional posture is somewhat different from but not antithetical to Ahab's.

11. Redburn's voyage to Liverpool as ordinary seaman aboard the merchantman *Highlander* serves as the initiation of a gentleman's son into the discipline of seafaring life; he survives because of his practical self-reliant shrewdness. His English counterpart, Harry Bolton, who signs aboard for the return voyage to New York, lacks the adaptability of the young American democrat and thus becomes the target of the "worst jibes and jeers" of the sailors and in fact "a hunted hare to the merciless crew" (*Redburn*, Constable Edition [London: 1922-24], p. 333).

12. That Melville does not approve Plinlimmon's pamphlet has long been noted. See, for example, Willard Thorp ed., *Herman Melville, Representative Selections* (New York, 1938), p. lxxvii; Tyrus Hillway, "Pierre, The Fool of Virtue," *AL*, XXI (1949), 202; Charles Moorman, "Melville's Pierre in the City," *AL*, XXVII (1956), 572-73.

Bert C. Bach (essay date 1970)

SOURCE: "Narrative Technique and Structure in *Pierre*," in *American Transcendental Quarterly*, No. 7, Part I, Summer, 1970, pp. 5-8.

[*In the following essay, Bach discusses the various levels of narration in* Pierre *and suggests that the alternating narrative voices help to unify the work.*]

In late 1851 Herman Melville, weary from his struggles to see **Moby-Dick** through publication, had no burning ambition for his next fictional production. **Pierre** would be a pastoral romance with a touch of the gothic and would, he hoped, regain some of the money and reputation with publishers that he had lost by his two previous publications, **Mardi** and **Moby-Dick.** In a letter written to his publisher Bentley on April 16, 1852, he indicated his assumption that his new book would prove agreeable to public taste: "And more especially am I impelled to decline those overtures upon the ground that my new book possessing unquestionable novelty, as regards my former ones,—treating of utterly new scenes & characters;—and, as I beleive [*sic*], very much more calculated for popularity than anything you have yet published of mine—being a regular romance, with a mysterious plot to it, & stirring passions at work, and withall, representing a new & elevated aspect of American life—all these considerations warrant me strongly in not closing with terms greatly inferior to those upon which our previous negotiations have proceeded. . . . If nothing has been made on the old books, may not something be made out of the new?"[1]

Whatever Melville considered a "regular romance" to be, he certainly knew that the symbolic and allegorical patterns employed in **Mardi** and **Moby-Dick** were not "calculated for popularity." He was also aware that they created a situation in which misreading and over-interpretation could easily take place. On January 8, 1852, he wrote Sophia Hawthorne, suggesting that her interpretations of certain symbolic sections of **Moby-Dick** had gone beyond his symbolic intention. In the same letter he asserted that **Pierre** would not be open to such over-interpretation, the implication being that the book would not be heavily symbolic: "But, my Dear Lady, I shall not again send you a bowl of salt water. The next chalice I shall commend, will be a rural bowl of milk."[2] How, we may ask, did Melville alter this original intention? The answer to the question rests principally in his use of narrative and structural devices that had not previously been a part of his aesthetic repertoire.

Almost every critic of **Pierre** has assumed both that it is related in the third person and that the third-person narrator is omniscient. Actually, neither of these assumptions is entirely true. On numerous occasions the narrator employs first person, and on other occasions he indicates existing limitations on his narrating powers. It is relevant, then, to clarify the exceptions to these general assumptions. A second cause for difficulty arises from the necessity to distinguish between levels of narration in the novel. Besides the semi-omniscient first narrator who relates most of the novel in the third person, there is also a second level of narration, represented by the character Pierre, who serves as the principal recorder or reflector of experience. Throughout the novel there is alternation from first to second level of narration, thus constituting a rhythmical quality which unifies the work. Moreover, the functions of the two levels of narration differ. The first is concerned with observation and imparting of knowledge; the second is concerned with the recording of experience.

Since the alternating modes of narration constitute Melville's principal structural devices in this novel, it is imperative to evaluate the first narrator's changing attitudes toward Pierre. The arcadian imagery of the first part of the novel is soon abandoned, and the narrator warns the reader to distinguish between Pierre's own thoughts and those thoughts which simply relate to him: "But the thoughts we here indite as Pierre's are to be very carefully discriminated from those we indite concerning him."[3] In *The Modern Psychological Novel,* Leon Edel cites a comparable situation in *The Turn of the Screw,* where there are actually three narrators, but the second is not really independent "since his account is at first being quoted or summarized by the First Narrator."[4] Melville's method is clearly not so systematic as James's; thus, from the first narrator's warning, one must conceive of his narration and that of the character Pierre as separate entities. Pierre is, of course, the catalyst for the novel's narrative progression; the principal pattern of the novel is constituted by his attempt to find a course of action, his finding it and meeting its results, and his continuous evaluation of the motives for which he has made his choice. Throughout the novel this threefold pattern is subservient to the rhythm of the juxtaposed narrative voices. Although R. P. Blackmur is incorrect in recognizing but three situations in the novel for which Pierre is not the sole register,[5] he is correct in assuming that such episodes are extremely rare. For this reason, if one accepts E. M. Forster's definition of plot as "a narrative of events, the emphasis falling on causality,"[6] he must also assert that Pierre, as principal catalyst and register, is central to all structural devices employed in the novel. A brief description of the spiral form of the novel, emphasizing a near perfect balance of imagery and character relationship, is therefore relevant. *Pierre* is made up of twenty-six books, each of different length and an unequal number of subsections. As the narrator says, "This history goes forward and goes backward, as occasion calls. Nimble center, circumference elastic you must have" (p. 62). Thus, while most of the books deal with the present and Pierre's actions in it, others are flashbacks or are devoted to narrative commentary not necessarily continuing the action which has taken place in the previous book.

Books I-XIII are set in or near Saddle Meadows, a rural estate which is described by highly romantic and arcadian imagery. In time, the thirteen books consume five summer days, and events are arranged in each of these days so that the reader recognizes movement from morning to evening.

This first setting serves as a background for introducing Pierre, Mrs. Glendinning, Lucy Tartan, Isabel Banford, Delly Ulver, and the ineffectual Reverend Falsgrave. The principal events include the close relation of Pierre and Mrs. Glendinning, the relation of Pierre to the "white" Lucy Tartan, Pierre's recounting the vision of a face and his receiving from Isabel the letter which claims she is his sister, Isabel's two narratives of her past life, Pierre's decision to abandon his past and present in order to fulfill his supposed sister's need of him, and his actual break with Lucy Tartan and his mother. Three significant image patterns are established: (1) Mrs. Glendinning is associated with past ideals and contemporary situations which suggest falsity of position; (2) Lucy Tartan is associated with images of whiteness, of purity, and of angelic qualities; and (3) Isabel Banford is associated with images of mystery, of uncertainty, and of darkness. Book XIV is the structural point of the spiral. In time, it constitutes a part of one day, beginning at 4 a.m. and extending for an unspecified time until Pierre has completed one act. It is set in a coach which is taking Pierre, Isabel, and Delly from Saddle Meadows to the city, and the one act related involves Pierre's finding, reading, and meditating on a piece of a pamphlet left in the coach by some previous occupant.

Books XV-XXVI are set in the city. They introduce three new characters: Plotinus Plinlimmon, the author of the document which Pierre had read in the coach and whom the reader deduces to be the counterpart of the Reverend Falsgrave in the first section, and Glendinning Stanly and Charlie Millthorpe, both of whom are associated with Pierre's past at Saddle Meadows and who demonstrate the various moral poles of that past. The principal events related are Pierre and Isabel's taking quarters in an old church called the Apostles, Pierre's varying success in attempting to write a book by which he could earn his livelihood, Pierre's rejection by his cousin Glen Stanly and the latter's inheriting of Saddle Meadows and courting of Lucy Tartan after the reported death of Mrs. Glendinning, Pierre's renewal of association with Charlie Millthorpe, Lucy's decision to come to the city to live with Pierre and Isabel, and the deaths of Lucy, Pierre, and Isabel. Books I-XIII, then, present a situation, offer a choice to the hero, and picture the making of that choice. Book XIV offers another view, an alternative emotional and intellectual position which could have been assumed by the hero. And Books XV-XXVI demonstrate the hero's facing the results of his choice and his eventual destruction by it.

Excluding the occasional use of the editorial "we," there are six major episodes which demonstrate the self-conscious narrator's breaking from third into first person. In each he is serving to impart knowledge, to clarify his position and method as narrator, or to foretell the final results of an action already begun. The first of these occurs in Book V: Pierre's "grand enthusiast resolution," his decision to abandon all that has previously constituted happiness, is "foetally forming in him" (p. 125). In a prayer, he employs a metaphor which likens his own potential sacrifice to that of Christ. The narrator, clarifying the ambiguity of the scene and anticipating the almost blasphemous nature of this facet of Pierre's character; comments: "How shall I steal yet further into Pierre, and show how this heavenly fire was helped to be contained in him, by mere contingent things, and things that he knew not. But I shall follow the endless, winding way,—the flowing river in the cave of man; careless whither I be led, reckless where I land. . . . I am more frank with Pierre than the best men are with themselves. I am all unguarded and magnanimous with Pierre; therefore you saw his weakness, and therefore only. In reserves men build imposing characters; not in revelations. He who shall be wholly honest, though nobler than Ethan Allen; that man shall stand in danger of the meanest mortal's scorn" (pp. 126-127).

The second commentary occurs in Book XIV. As Pierre is described reading a "curious paper-rag" written by Plotinus Plinlimmon, the narrator intervenes to present his reasons for inserting the document itself into the chapter. The reasons are that "Pierre may not in the end be entirely uninfluenced in his conduct by the torn pamphlet, when afterwards perhaps by some means he shall come to understand it; or, peradventure, come to know that he, in the first place, did . . ." (p. 246); and that Pierre will come to know the author of the pamphlet by reputation and be greatly influenced by seeing him from a distance. Following this the narrator shifts to the first person, commenting on the dubious authenticity of the views presented in the document: "For all these reasons I account sufficient apology for inserting in the following chapters the initial part of what seems to me a very fanciful and mystical, rather than philosophical lecture, from which, I confess, that I myself can derive no conclusion which permanently satisfies those peculiar motions in my soul, to which that lecture seems most particularly addressed. For to me it seems more the excellently illustrated re-statement of a problem, than the solution of the problem itself. But as such mere illustrations are almost universally taken for solutions (and perhaps they are the only possible human solutions), therefore it may help to the temporary quiet of some inquiring mind; and so not be wholly without use" (p. 246).

The third and fourth first-person intrusions appear in Books XVII and XVIII. These two books comprise narrative commentary relative to Pierre's ability as a writer. The first, ironic in tone, commends in Pierre everything which the narrator apparently considers despicable in a writer. The second, in an authoritative tone, evaluates seriously Pierre's potential as a writer. In both books the "I" narrator is an advocate of a type of literature antithetical to the pastoral optimism favored by an audience which he ironically says is constituted of Pierre's "more intimate acquaintances" and of "the less partial applauses of the always intelligent, and extremely discriminating public" (p. 288).

The fifth intrusion comments on the spirit of the dwellers at the Apostles, suggesting later that Charlie Millthorpe exemplifies the essential charity of the group. Almost all the dwellers are artists of various sorts who have attempted to ground their lives on somewhat mystical bases. The narrator mocks their efforts, yet recognizes that in their charity they will not resent such mocking: "Yet let me here offer up three locks of my hair, to the memory of all such glorious paupers who have lived and died in this world. Surely, and truly I honor them—noblemen often at bottom—and for that very reason I make bold to be gamesome about them; for where fundamental nobleness is, and fundamental honor is due, merriment is never accounted irreverent. The fools and pretenders of humanity, and the imposters and baboons among the gods, these only are offended with raillery; since both those gods and men whose titles to eminence are secure, seldom worry themselves about the seditious gossip of old apple-women, and the skylarkings of funny little boys in the street" (p. 314).

The last of these intrusions, most significant because it clarifies the theme of the novel, occurs in Book XXI. Pierre sees at a distance the face of Plinlimmon, which seems to tell him to desist from his present course of action, to refrain from a vain quest. Pierre then looks for Plinlimmon's pamphlet which he had read in the coach. Ironically he carries it in the lining of his coat but is unable to find it, and he curses himself that he had never understood the document. The narrator enters to question the truth of this assumption: "I think that, regarded in one light, the final career of Pierre will seem to show, that he did understand it. And here it may be randomly suggested, by way of bagatelle, whether some things that men think they do not know, are not for all that thoroughly comprehended by them; and yet, so to speak, though contained in themselves, are kept a secret from themselves?" (p. 346)

To summarize, Melville's use of the first-person narrative voice on a basically third-person frame serves to intensify the series of intrusions by contributing a definitive tone. The first intrusion patterns with the sixth, since the subject of each is the vanity of Pierre's quest and the depths of human motivations. The second anticipates Pierre's later recognition of the distinction between "horological" and "chronometrical" reality, while the third and fourth demonstrate the effect of self-confident enthusiasm in clouding that distinction. The fifth emphasizes the ironic ambiguity of the protagonist's role, for Pierre also has followed the "mystical" course of the Apostles. One may perhaps strain a point to say that Melville consciously patterns intensified narrative intrusions. However, he may say that the effect of intensity gained by the use of the first-person intrusion demonstrates in *Pierre* an interesting artistic innovation which is not observed in the author's earlier novels.

The degree of the first narrator's omniscience must also be clarified. While his comments are generally forceful, he often reveals a lack of knowledge of incidental details. For instance, after the second narrative of Isabel's past, Pierre kisses her and leaves. Walking back to Saddle Meadows he stops to seek advice from the Reverend Falsgrave, and on the walk he obviously is attempting to assimilate the significance of Isabel's story for his own life. Of these thoughts the narrator says: "We know not Pierre Glendinning's thoughts as he gained the village and passed on beneath its often shrouding trees . . ." (p. 191). While examples of narrative limitation such as this are numerous, on more revealing occasions the narrator admits that his interpretation of Pierre's motives, as well as any interpretations of them, has possibility of error: "Ofttimes it is very wonderful to trace the rarest and profoundest things, and find their probable origin in something extremely trite or trivial. Yet so strange and complicate is the human soul; so much is confusedly evolved from out itself, and such vast and varied accessions come to it from abroad, and so impossible is it always to distinguish between these two, that the wisest man were rash, positively to assign the precise and incipient origination of his final thoughts and acts. Far as we blind moles can see, man's life seems but an acting upon mysterious hints; it is somehow hinted to us, to do thus or thus. For surely no mere mortal who has at all gone down into himself will ever pretend that his slightest thought or act solely originates in his own defined identity" (p. 207). One may easily overestimate the omniscience of the overriding narrative voice, and the novel's subtitle, "The Ambiguities," further emphasizes this possibility. Perhaps, then, as the narrator later says, we cannot definitively find the basis of Pierre's choice or the motives on which he makes that choice; we can only continue to restate the problem (p. 246).

Notes

1. *The Letters of Herman Melville,* ed. Merrell R. Davis and William H. Gilman (New Haven, 1960), p. 150.

2. *Ibid.,* p. 146.

3. *Pierre; or, The Ambiguities,* ed. Henry A. Murray (N. Y., 1949), p. 196. Subsequent references to this edition appear in the text.

4. N. Y., 1955, pp. 39-40.

5. "The Craft of Herman Melville: A Putative Statement," in *Melville: A Collection of Critical Essays,* ed. Richard Chase (Englewood Cliffs, N.J., 1962), p. 82.

6. *Aspects of the Novel* (N. Y., 1954), p. 86.

Alan Holder (essay date 1970)

SOURCE: "Style and Tone in Melville's *Pierre,*" in *ESQ: A Journal of the American Renaissance,* No. 60, Summer, 1970, pp. 76-86.

[In the following essay, Holder discusses the shifts in narrative tone, attitude, and mood in Pierre, *conceding that, in the end, there is little to account for the novel's contradictions and fragments.]*

"It is hard always to be sure of its intention. . . ."

F. O. Matthiessen on *Pierre*

The stylistic variety of *Moby Dick* has generally been regarded as one of that book's glories, a source of wonder and delight. If critics have differed in their interpretations, they have at least shared a common admiration for *Moby Dick*'s richness. With *Pierre,* however, the shifts in style[1] have occasioned not only radical disagreements among Melville critics, but unhappy bewilderment and irritation as well. In addition to the puzzlement over the novel's stylistic changes, there exists considerable doubt about what Melville is up to when using a single style at a given moment in the book. Depending on which critic one is reading, or sometimes on which passage in a particular commentary one is looking at, Melville is seen as wallowing in literary sentimentality or parodying it, assenting to Pierre's speeches or regarding them as rant, presenting his protagonist as a tragic hero or as a repulsive egoist, writing with detached amusement or showing a desperation equal to that of Pierre. Melville's first use throughout an entire work of the omniscient narrator technique resulted, ironically, not in the relative poise and consistency of attitude we might expect but in astonishing tonal discontinuities. Through the close scrutiny of various portions of the novel that will be undertaken here, an attempt will be made to establish a clear auctorial intention when such can be textually supported, but there will also be an effort to indicate how the style (or styles) creates the tonal breaks and ambiguities that bulk so large in this thoroughly interesting but, finally, thoroughly exasperating book.

We need go no further than the book's first sections to find ourselves in disputed territory. These describe Pierre's privileged, carefree existence at Saddle Meadows, his family estate, and his relationship with the girl he plans to marry, Lucy Tartan. Lewis Mumford contends that the opening passage appears as though it were "taken from an Elizabethan chamber romance; it sounds exactly like Melville's first effusion in the *Lansingburgh Advertiser* . . ."[2] Mumford apparently accepts the following declaration, which is part of a supposed hymn to Love, and which has become a *locus classicus* of *Pierre* criticism, as a serious, sincere statement on Melville's part: ". . . Love is god of all. Man or woman who has never loved, nor once looked deep down into their own lover's eyes, they know not the sweetest and the loftiest religion of this earth. Love is both Creator's and Saviour's gospel to mankind; a volume bound in rose-leaves clasped with violets and by the beaks of humming-birds printed with peach-juice on the leaves of lilies."[3] F. O. Matthiessen gloomily observes that this "impotent echo of the Lady's Book" is presented "without undercutting. . . ."[4] Newton Arvin says, "It would be charitable to attribute such mannerism to the intention of parody; unhappily, the context makes such an interpretation impossible."[5] Lawrance Thompson, however, argues that "The early chapters of *Pierre* are easily misunderstood if they are not recognized as stylistic parodies of the saccharine domestic-sentimental fiction which was so popular in America in the middle of the nineteenth century. . . ." He then cites the humming-bird passage, saying that "Unless forewarned and on guard, anyone may read almost straight through such a passage—without suspecting that this is all parody. . . ."⁶ Thompson is right here, and none other than Melville himself has put us on guard.

On the very first page of the book we get this presentation of the "pastoral" scene into which Pierre enters: "The verdant trance lay far and wide; and through it nothing came but brindled kine, dreamily wandering to their pastures, followed, not driven, by ruddy-cheeked, white-footed boys." The very concentration of pastoral clichés, the eighteenth-century epithetic quality—"verdant trance," "brindled kine," "dreamily wandering," "ruddy-cheeked"—should give us pause, but if these do not, then the thrusting into the sentence of the qualifier, "not driven," certainly will. The *insistence* on lack of compulsion in this scene, an insistence focused on cows, is clearly evidence of a parodic intention.

The treatment of animals elsewhere in the early pages of the novel reinforces this conclusion. Much is made of the horses on the Glendinning estate. Those belonging to Pierre are described as "a sort of family cousins to Pierre . . . they were splendid young cousins . . ." (p. 23). This in itself constitutes a kind of joke on Melville's part, picking up as it does his comic use of simile some pages earlier when he described Nature as having blown "her windclarion from the blue hills . . . Pierre neighed out lyrical thoughts, as at the trumpet-blast, a war-horse paws himself into a lyric of foam" (p. 14). The exchange here between man and animal, effected by the use of a two-fold simile ("neighs" and "lyric") is surely a *jou d'esprit* on Melville's part and one that creates a ludicrous effect. Continuing his description of Pierre's horses he said, "These young cousins never permitted themselves to run from Pierre; they were impatient in their paces, but very patient in the halt. They were full of good-humor too, and kind as kittens" (pp. 23-24). The cadence and content of this last sentence surely smacks of children's literature, and should be taken as a mocking portrait of a pastoral relationship to animals.

The same holds true for the description of Pierre's colts as he steps between them. They turn their heads toward Lucy "as much to say—We understand young master; we understand him, Miss . . . why, bless your delicious little heart, we played with Pierre before you ever did" (p. 24). A little after this, the horse of Pierre's grandfather is depicted as responding to his master's death by refusing to be petted: "plain as horse can speak, the old gray steed says—'I smell not the wonted hand; where is grand old Pierre? Grain me not, and groom me not;—where is grand old Pierre?'" (p. 35). The horses who made motion "as much to say" have been succeeded by one who actually does talk, and if this were not dubious enough, Melville has given him a talent for alliteration (pointed up by the narrator's own use of alliteration in the preceding paragraph). Here is a gifted horse whose mouth heeds looking into. What we are viewing is a parody of sentimental portraits of animal devotion.

Helping to sustain the parodic effect of *Pierre*'s early pages is the use of extravagance. Describing Lucy,

Melville takes the cliché-ridden description of a beautiful girl and transforms it by going too far: "Her eyes some god brought down from heaven; her hair was Danae's, spangled with Jove's shower; her teeth were dived for in the Persian Sea" (p. 26). The sentence holds up until its last clause, at which point it takes a pratfall. After rendering the "poetic" properties of Lucy's eyes and hair, Melville implicitly refers to the image of "teeth like pearls," but extends this, bringing to it an effortfulness that renders it ludicrous. The sentence itself has gone diving in search of the poetic, but ends up drowning.

That such a comic effect was Melville's intention and not unwitting is indicated by his obvious self-consciousness in portraying Lucy. He asks: "By immemorial usage, am I not bound to celebrate this Lucy Tartan? Is she not my hero's own affianced? . . . Never shall I get down the vile inventory! . . . Who shall put down the charms of Lucy Tartan on paper?" (p. 28). Plainly, Melville is showing some good-humored resentment at the *a priori* demands made on the novelist, turning the supposed fulfillments of those demands into comic occasions.

His description of Lucy's teeth is immediately followed by another piece of extravagance that produces this burlesque of chivalric ideals in a supposed paean to female beauty: "A true gentleman in Kentucky would cheerfully die for a beautiful woman in Hindostan, though he never saw her" (p. 26). The sentence immediately collapses under the weight of its own absurdity. These findings are at variance with Edward Rosenberry's contention that "Melville almost certainly intended his worst writing in *Pierre* for satire, but there is no way of proving it by the test of exaggeration."⁷

The element of exaggeration should be borne in mind when we come to the hymn to love section and its notorious humming-bird image. A strain of comic hyperbole runs through this supposed hymn, beginning with the assertion that on the morning the narrative is speaking of, the sailors out at sea (presumably all sailors) "tied love-knots on every spangled spar" instead of bowline-knots (p. 36). Evidence of the power of love is found in the absence of wolves from Britain, of panthers and pards from Virginia: "the fierce things of this earth [are] daily, hourly going out . . ." (p. 38). Italy, we are assured, "hath not a sight before the beauty of a Yankee girl . . ." (p. 39). (What we have here perhaps is not only a parody of the sentimental glorification of love and female beauty but of the Emersonian habits of viewing the material world as infused and dominated by spirit, of seeing the supposedly large and imposing crumble into insignificance when confronted by the small, the personal, the individual.) Coming as it does between extravagant statements about love-stupefied sailors and fierce animals driven out by Love's power, the humming-bird passage most certainly is undercut, Matthiessen notwithstanding. And if we look at the sentences immediately preceding the humming-bird passage quoted above, we find: "The eye is Love's own magic glass, where all things that are not of earth, glide in supernatural light. There are not so many fishes in the sea, as there are sweet images in lovers' eyes. In those miraculous translucencies swim the strange eye-fish with wings, that sometimes leap out, instinct with joy; moist fish-wings wet the lover's cheek" (p. 38). This is surely a blatant parody of the treatment of eyes in literary portrayals of love. Melville has produced a preposterous conceit; "moist fish-wings wet the lover's cheek" evokes a picture of fin-covered faces that is grotesque. To view him as not knowing this is highly questionable.

What can account for critics so fine as Matthiessen and Arvin taking Melville's humming-bird seriously? For not only is there the evidence of a humorous intention in the materials immediately preceding and following the passage in question, there is the larger fact of the *distance* from his materials that Melville has already shown in Book I of *Pierre* (the hymn to love is found in Book II). In Book I, Melville explicitly indicates the gap between the apparently ideal condition of Pierre, together with his assumptions of future happiness, and the woe that is actually to befall him. The omniscient narrator reveals a painful knowledge of his protagonist's fate that renders the later, lyrical effusions on the power of Love impossible to take at face value. There are no fewer than four paragraphs in the second section of Book I that are given a parallel structure which provides an overview of Pierre plainly at variance with his own expectations. In each of these paragraphs, a picture of Pierre's happy life terminates with an indication of dire things to come (pp. 3-6).

In showing Melville's distance from his materials, one could cite as well the third section of Book I, which mocks the pride that members of the English peerage take in their long pedigrees. While the narrator advances the seemingly superior claims of Americans to such pedigrees, he derides the latter group as well, saying of the descendants of the Dutch patroons: "Unimaginable audacity of a worm that but crawls through the soil he so imperially claims!" (p. 10). The section that follows this deflation of "aristocracy," European and American, begins, "In general terms we have been thus decided in asserting the great genealogical and real-estate dignity of some families in America, because in so doing we poetically establish the richly aristocratic condition of Master Pierre Glendinning . . ." (p. 11). The mocking incongruity of the phrase "real-estate dignity" affects, of course, the way in which "poetically" should be taken, and should affect our reception of the "poetic treatment of Pierre, Lucy, and Love that we get in Book II.

Given all this, the assumption by such critics as Mumford, Matthiessen, and Arvin that Melville offers his humming-birds without irony would appear extremely puzzling. Matthiessen does see an element of mockery in the early sections of *Pierre,* and Arvin observes that an effect of "angry parody" dominates the whole of the book.[8] But neither extends these observations to the humming-birds. We are apparently faced here with examples of critical schizophrenia. But it should be said at once that such a condition is almost forced upon the reader of *Pierre.* It derives in part from finding in the book, along with the parodic, instances of sentimentality untouched by irony, for example, the following description of Pierre's entry into Lucy's bedroom (which anticipates Kenyon's reverent entry into Hilda's chamber in *The Marble Faun*): "So he advanced, and with a fond and gentle joyfulness, his eye now fell upon the spotless bed itself, and fastened on a snow-white roll that lay beside the pillow. Now he started; Lucy seemed coming in upon him; but no—'tis only the foot of one of her little slippers, just peeping into view from under the narrow nether curtains of the bed. Then again his glance fixed itself upon the slender, snow-white ruffled roll; and he stood as one enchanted. Never precious parchment of the Greek was half so precious in his eyes. Never trembling scholar longed more to unroll the mystic vellum, than Pierre longed to unroll the sacred secrets of that snow-white, ruffled thing" (p. 45). "If this, then why not humming birds?" critics like Matthiessen and Arvin could ask. For *here* there is nothing, either in the passage, or in what follows or precedes it, unmistakably to suggest undercutting. But more than such instances of unabashed sentimentality, the general movement in the book from the parody, satire, humor and distanced quality of its early chapters to the melodramatic, agonized, involved mode of much of the remainder of the story might account for critics' failing to find parody in a given passage.[9]

If such critics sometimes read the early parts of *Pierre* too much in the light of the later portions, a critic like Lawrance Thompson does just the reverse, extending the spirit of the opening chapters to the whole of the book. He claims that "Parody, parody, parody . . . will be found throughout the context which Melville builds around the central narrative of Pierre's pilgrim-like progress to defeat and damnation."[10] This assertion does not take account of the shift in the novel just described (there is certainly little, in the bulk of the book, of the humor one normally associates with parody). The same might be said of William Braswell's stress on the "satirical temper" of *Pierre.*[11] Such a characterization suggests a removal from his materials on Melville's part which is often not there.

The overall shift in the tone of the book is signalled by the initial reference to Isabel, occurring in a conversation between Pierre and Lucy, "Tell me [says Lucy] once more the story of that face, Pierre,—that mysterious, haunting face, which thou once told'st me, thou didst thrice vainly try to shun . . . tell me the story of the face.—the dark-eyed, lustrous, imploring, mournful face, that so mystically paled, and shrunk at thine. . . . Tell me, tell me, Pierre;—as a fixed basilisk, with eyes of steady, flaming mournfulness, that face this instant fastens me" (p. 42). The portentousness of this adjective-ridden, stylized speech is only too characteristic of the tone that will prevail in the treatment of Isabel. Here is a sample of Pierre's response to Isabel's face: "The terrors of the face were not those of Gorgon; not by repelling hideousness did it smite him so; but bewilderingly allured him, by its nameless beauty, and its long-suffering, hopeless anguish" (p. 56). This reaction is not jeered at by Melville as the product of an over-heated sensibility, of a too-ready inclination to Gothic *frissons,* but is, rather, an extension of Melville's own feeling. In the voice of the omniscient narrator we are told that Isabel's is "One of those faces, which now and then appear to man, and without one word of speech, still reveal glimpses of some fearful gospel. In natural guise, but lit by supernatural light; palpable to the senses, but inscrutable to the soul; in their perfectest impression on us, ever hovering between Tartarean misery and Paradisaic beauty; such faces, compounded so of hell and heaven, overthrow in us all foregone persuasions, and make us wondering children in this world again" (p. 49). The periodic sentence here, with its parallel clauses, its conjunction of opposites, its diction denoting extreme conditions, lends weight to Pierre's response to Isabel. It authenticates Pierre's reaction rather than making it seem headlong and excessive. No parody operates here.

Without such auctorial statement we might dismiss the grandiose, hysterical and stagey apostrophes of Pierre, the orotund conditionals he flings before the universe, as insufferable mouthings which are being laughed at by Melville. Such a dismissal would be the response of most readers encountering:

> "Now, never into the soul of Pierre, stole there before, a muffledness like this! If aught really lurks in it, ye sovereign powers that claim all my leal worshipings, I conjure ye to lift the veil; I must see it face to face. Tread I on a mine, warn me; advance I on a precipice, hold me back; but abandon me to an unknown misery, that it shall suddenly seize me, and possess me, wholly,—that ye will never do; else, Pierre's fond faith in ye—now clean, untouched—may clean depart; and give me up to be a railing atheist" (pp. 47-48).

> "On my strong faith in ye Invisibles, I stake three whole felicities, and three whole lives this day. If ye forsake me now,—farewell to Faith, farewell to Truth, farewell to God; exiled for aye from God and man, I shall declare myself an equal power with both; free to make war on Night and Day, and all thoughts and things of mind and matter, which the upper and the nether firmaments do clasp!" (p. 126).

> ". . . if Life be a cheating dream, and virtue as unmeaning and unsequeled with any blessing as the midnight mirth of wine; if by sacrificing myself for Duty's sake, my own mother re-sacrifices me; if Duty's self be but a bug-bear, and all things are allowable and unpunishable to man;—then do thou, Mute Massiveness, fall on me!" (p. 158).

These statements by Pierre, the outpourings of an Ahab *manqué,* are hard to take in a narrative where so little in the way of external events (up to the point of the last quotation) has occurred. The rhetoric is not floated by any tremendous actions (as it is in *Moby Dick*) but, rather, attempts to substitute itself for them. A wonderful opportunity for humor exists in such a situation, but humor runs in short supply for most of that portion of the book following Isabel's appearance. As Pierre confronts the fact of

Isabel and endures his fall into knowledge, Melville draws close to him and gives him a kind of license to declaim in the manner exemplified above. His suffering sanctions his style.

Isabel's entry into the book renders **Pierre** hospitable not only to the Gothic and the declamatory, but to the melodramatic as well (a category which often overlaps with the other two). This is particularly true in the story's treatment of sexual matters. Referring to a young man who has seduced and gotten pregnant one of the girls living on the Glendinning estate, Pierre's mother says "'My mind is made up concerning Ned; no such profligate shall pollute this place; nor shall the disgraceful Dolly'" (p. 113). Later, she refers to "'that vile fellow, Ned,'" and says "'Such men' . . . 'are to my way of thinking more detestable than murderers'" (p. 117). Mrs. Glendinning is seen by the novel as being unduly harsh towards Dolly. Her attitude is set in sharp opposition to that of Pierre, who decides to give the girl shelter. But his *style* of response to the situation is at one with that of his mother, both partaking of the crudest nineteenth-century renderings of sexual waywardness. When told of Dolly's seduction, her giving birth to a dead baby, and falling into despair, Pierre cries (in another of the book's *loci classici*), "'Curses, wasp-like, cohere on that villain, Ned, and sting him to his death!' . . ." (p. 183). Worse, Melville's *own* sensibility appears to be given expression here, for immediately following on Pierre's statement are the words "cried Pierre, smit by this most piteous tale" (p. 183). The auctorial voice joins with that of the protagonist to form a continuum of outraged, gushing feeling. Earlier, the narrator had referred to ". . . Dolly, forever ruined through the cruel arts of Ned" (p. 130).[12]

Melville and Pierre seem at one also in their response to New York, conceived of by both as the Wicked City, that wickedness largely defined in terms of sexual dangers. Says Pierre to Isabel as they ride into New York, "'Milk dropped from the milkman's can in December, freezes not more quickly on those stones, than does snow-white innocence, if in poverty, it chance to fall in these streets'" (p. 270). Melville stages Pierre's encounter with a prostitute as follows: ". . . in the flashing, sinister, evil cross-lights of a druggist's window, his eye caught the person of a wonderfully beautifully-featured girl; scarlet-cheeked, glaringly-arrayed, and of a figure all natural grace but unnatural vivacity. Her whole form, however, was horribly lit by the green and yellow rays from the druggist's. 'My God!' shuddered Pierre, hurrying forward, 'the town's first welcome to youth!'" (p. 278). The garish lighting Melville has provided is the perfect complement to Pierre's reaction. Shortly after this, we have the scene in the police station, done in the purest of melodramatic terms. Describing the people brought there by the police, Melville writes: "The thieves'-quarters, and all the brothels, Lock-and-Sin hospitals for incurables, and infirmaries and infernoes of hell seemed to have made one combined sortie, and poured out upon earth through the vile vomitory of some unmentionable cellar" (p. 283). Returning to the station, after having left Isabel and Dolly there in the supposed safe-keeping of the police, Pierre finds Isabel "struggling from the delirious reaching arms of a half-clad, reeling whiskerando. With an immense blow of his mailed fist, he sent the wretch humming . . ." (p. 283). His "mailed fist"—Pierre is clearly a knight in armor, rescuing his damsel in distress from a fate worse than death, as the story treats us to a bit of chivalric melodrama.

Melodramatic as well is Pierre's confrontation in New York with his cousin Glen Stanly, who pretends not to know him and who, in the face of Pierre's obviously distraught condition, plays the role of the cool cosmopolitan to the hilt. Pierre, outraged, terms his cousin a "'Hound, and base blot upon the general humanity!'" and flees from his house (p. 281). The quality of this scene between the cousins, which is placed in Book XVI along with the incidents of the prostitute and the melee at the police station, stands out all the more strongly because of the nature of the earlier treatment of the two. Melville had given over all of Book XV to tracing the relationship of Glen and Pierre. That book, done in a narrative and expository mode, is one of highly refined, even intricate analysis of motive and response, sometimes moving into generalizations about human behavior. Nothing could be in sharper contrast than the thoughtful, ruminating, analytic voice of this section, together with the subtle responses of Glen and Pierre that it describes, and the brief, sharp, melodramatic encounter of the two cousins in the next section. The abrupt change in style makes it hard for us to believe in the scene between Pierre and Glen, makes it hard to believe that Books XV and XVI are parts of the same story.

But the sudden change in style and tone that we have here is all too frequent in **Pierre,** and sometimes makes for great difficulty in discerning Melville's intention and his attitude toward his chief character. We find, for example, the melodrama and garishness of Book XVI giving way to a light, frolicsome caricature of contemporary literary standards and manners in Book XVII, entitled "Young America in Literature." There, we are told that on the basis of some trivial poems he had published, Pierre had been invited to lecture on "Human Destiny" to the "Urquhartian Club for the Immediate Extension of the Limits of all Knowledge, both Human and Divine," a club located in Zadockprattsville (p. 296). He had been urged by several men to allow them to write his biography: "'. . . how would his last hours be embittered by the thought [they contended], that he was about to depart forever, leaving the world utterly unprovided with the knowledge of what were the precise texture and hue of the first trowsers he wore. These representations did certainly touch him in a very tender spot, not previously unknown to the schoolmaster" (p. 299). Reading this, it is as though the encounters with Glen, the prostitute, and the "reeling whiskerando" had never occurred. We now view Pierre's situation with amusement rather than with the strong sense of horror, pity and indignation Melville apparently intended us to feel in reading of those events.

The humorous caricature and satire of "Young America in Literature" gives way, in turn, to a commentary (in Book XVIII) on the pains of serious authorship, a commentary full of bitterness and a sense of futility. And as though this change were not confusing enough, we find, sandwiched between remarks on Pierre's desertion by the gods and his heroic labors on his book, some wonderful satire on the asceticism of the "Apostles," the men who inhabit the building in which Pierre has taken up residence. We are told of their "Flesh-Brush Philosophy" and "Apple-Paring Dialectics." But such satire, very funny and engaging in itself, does not consort well with the depiction of Pierre who, at this time, is writing himself into exhaustion. Once again the impression arises of pages of different books having been pasted together.

The switching of styles and the consequent generation of very different tones may be said to be habitual with the book, a characteristic in evidence from the very start. The parody of the pastoral with which the novel opens is succeeded by the description of Pierre's relationship with his mother and his position *vis à vis* his family heritage, a description marked by a somberness of tone coming out of the narrator's awareness of the downward turn Pierre's fortunes will take. That somberness has hardly been anticipated by the parody. A little later on, Melville stresses the fact that Pierre has been brought up in the country, and, apparently without irony, draws a contrast between the country and the city with the former seen as the more desirable locale: ". . . the country, like any Queen, is ever attended by scrupulous lady's maids in the guise of the seasons, and the town hath but one dress of brick turned up with stone; but the country hath a brave dress for every week in the year; sometimes she changes her dress twenty-four times in the twenty-four hours; and the country weareth her sun by day as a diamond on a Queen's brow; and the stars by night as necklaces of gold beads; whereas the town's sun is smoky paste, and no diamond, and the town's stars are pinchbeck and not gold" (p. 13). This is followed immediately by a paragraph which tells us that Nature planted Pierre in the country because she ". . . intended a rare and original development in Pierre. Never mind if hereby she proved ambiguous to him in the end; nevertheless, in the beginning she did bravely. She blew her wind-clarion from the blue hills, and Pierre neighed out lyrical thoughts, as at the trumpet-blast, a war-horse paws himself into a lyric of foam. . . . She lifted her spangled crest of a thickly-starred night, and forth at that glimpse of their divine Captain and Lord, ten thousand mailed thoughts of heroicness started up in Pierre's soul, and glared round for some insulted good cause to defend" (pp. 13-14). We find here irony and humor at Pierre's expense. Noting this, what are we to think of the preceding passage, where the country seemed to be given genuine praise? Are the metaphors there to be regarded as parodic, an example of the saccharine used once again to mock the pastoral? And is the reference to lady's maids undercut by the scene that follows, in which Pierre plays at being "'First Lady in waiting to the Dowager Duchess Glendinning' . . ." (p. 14)? It would seem so but one cannot be sure. For if there is mockery here, how does it square with the apparent celebration later on of Lucy's aversion to the city and love of the country, a passage where no traces of irony can be found (pp. 28-29).

Another example of how Melville's tonal changes can puzzle us is found in his comment on Pierre's night visit to the Reverend Falsgrave, whom he routs out of bed to ask what the clergyman and Mrs. Glendinning have decided to do about the dishonored Dolly. Melville opens the chapter in question with a consideration of fearless thinkers who advance beyond the conventional boundaries of thought. Such minds, he says, are likely to be feared and hated. "What wonder, then, that those advanced minds, which in spite of advance, happen still to remain, for the time, ill-regulated, should now and then be goaded into turning round in acts of wanton aggression upon sentiments and opinions now forever left in their rear" (p. 195). Pierre, we are told, had been visited by such aggressiveness in going to Falsgrave. "Yielding to that unwarrantable mood, he had invaded the profound midnight slumbers of the Reverend Mr. Falsgrave, and most discourteously made war upon that really amiable and estimable person" (p. 195). This is surely a trivial and humorous instance of the aggressiveness Melville is talking about (think of that fatal aggressiveness Pierre will show later as he seeks out Glen to murder him). Humorous, too, is the sly metaphoric comment on Falsgrave's condition—his "profound midnight slumbers" are of the spirit as well as the body. We are forced to ask why Melville has inserted a comic touch in a serious context. The triviality of the occasion tends to deflate what had been put forward as a weighty and straightforward observation on the societal position of radical minds.

A similar clash of materials and tones occurs late in the book, when Pierre receives a truculent letter from his publishers, "Steel, Flint & Asbestos" (p. 420). This amusing naming of the firm comes at the end of a letter that is crucial to Pierre, rejecting as it does the manuscript he has slaved over. The letter is accompanied by one from Glen and Lucy's brother Frederick, which calls Pierre "'a villainous and perjured liar'" (p. 420). Pierre places the two letters under his heels, delivers one of his grand apostrophes, and goes out to meet his fate. If the general intention of the scene is serious, and it undoubtedly is, what purpose is served by the momentary slipping into the comic "Steel, Flint & Asbestos?" What we find, then, in the various instances we have been examining, is a kind of pressure exerted on a given passage by materials sharply different in tone and sometimes immediately adjacent to it. This pressure leaves us confused as to how the original passage should be taken.

A similar difficulty, perhaps even more perplexing, arises from Melville's use of dramatic irony, if, indeed, that is what he is using. Pierre thinks at one point that Fortune has endowed him "with all the beauty of a man," only that she might hide from him "all the truth of a man. Now I see that in his beauty a man is snared, and made stone-

blind. . . . Welcome then be Ugliness and Poverty and Infamy, and all ye other crafty ministers of Truth . . ." (p. 106). But the fact is that not Ugliness but Beauty, in the form of Isabel, will come to be associated with Poverty, Infamy and Truth. Yet, Pierre's statement has in it a local force which commands our assent at the time. Did Melville intend us to think of the statement as a piece of dramatic irony, or wish us to take it as being the case? The same question can be asked of Pierre's justification for burning his father's portrait. He says (the statement coming at the end of a long speech): "Of old Greek times, before man's brain went into doting bondage, and bleached and beaten in Baconian fulling-mills, his four limbs lost their barbaric tan and beauty; when the round world was fresh, and rosy, and spicy, as a new-plucked apple; all's wilted now!—in those bold times, the great dead were not, turkey-like dished in trenchers, and set down all garnished in the ground, to glut the damned Cyclop like a cannibal; but nobly envious Life cheated the glutton worm, and gloriously burned the corpse; so that the spirit up-pointed, and visibly forked to heaven!" Pierre proceeds to burn the portrait, declaring he now has no past and is free to do his own will. Pierre's assertion is proved wrong in the course of events, which present him as fated rather than free. But Melville has invested Pierre's speech justifying the burning with considerable rhetorical power. In retrospect, is that speech to be taken as a splendid disavowal of the burden of the past or a piece of empty bombast? Later in the book, Pierre, addressing Glen and Frederick, who are trying to keep Lucy from joining him, says "'I render no accounts: I am what I am'" (p. 382). This echo of Jehovah in the Old Testament would seem at first glance an insufferable piece of self-glorification, and one undermined by Pierre's all-too-mortal end. But shortly after his statement, Melville tells us that Glen and Frederick began to be affected by Pierre's manner at the time, "for any social unusualness or greatness is sometimes most impressive in the retrospect" (p. 384). Rather than mocking Pierre as having a grossly exaggerated conception of himself, this would seem to confirm him in his self-image.

As confounding a passage as any in the book is the one where Pierre says to Isabel: "'. . . we will love with the pure and perfect love of angel to angel.'" Such is plainly not the case with these two. Before long they will come together in a sexual embrace. The difficulty here is that Melville has prepared for Pierre's assertion by saying, "He leaped to his feet, and stood before her with such warm, god-like majesty of love and tenderness, that the girl gazed up at him as though he were the one benignant star in all her general night" (p. 181). Might we have here (and elsewhere) a piece of *auctorial* dramatic irony? That is, might Melville himself, rather than a character, be formulating a judgment that will turn out to be very far from the facts? Might the omniscient narrator be not so all-knowing after all? It is hard to believe that Melville is not aware at this point of what the future relationship of Pierre and Isabel will be, *but he writes as though he were not.* Observing this (and the other instances of presumable dramatic irony), one is reminded of what R. P. Blackmur once said of Melville: "He was without knowing it in the habit of succumbing to the greatest insincerity of all, the intoxicating insincerity of cadence and rhythm and apt image, or, to put it on another plane, the insincerity of surrendering to the force of a single insight, which sometimes amounts to a kind of self-violation."[13]

The questions that arise in looking at the nature of the dramatic irony that gets into *Pierre* are parts of a larger question: What is the novel's underlying attitude toward its central character? Relevant in a crucial way to that question is the matter of the tone assumed towards Plinlimmon's pamphlet, "Chronometricals and Horologicals," which is, plainly, a commentary upon and judgment of precisely the kind of moral career Pierre has chosen to pursue. William Ellery Sedgewick calls the pamphlet, with its advancement of horological (relative, moderate) moral standards, as opposed to chronometrical (absolute, ideal) standards, "an admirable critique upon Pierre's conduct. . . ." It "opens the doors of love and salvation to all kinds and conditions of men. . . ."[14] Sedgewick adds that "For all its good sense, its kindness and tolerance . . ." Melville has "no more stomach" for it than does Pierre.[15] Matthiessen finds Melville, in introducing the pamphlet, counseling a policy of "moderation," though his heart is not in the distinction he makes between the two kinds of moral standards.[16] Arvin says that Melville saw "what was harsh, egoistic, inhumane and destructive" in the kind of "virtuous enthusiasm" shown by Pierre. Arvin goes on to state: "Many readers of *Pierre* have imagined that Melville's simple purpose in this whole passage [the one reproducing Plinlimmon's pamphlet] was to deride the preachers of a low, expedient comfortable morality of compromise and adjustment; but surely this was not at all his conscious intention. On the intellectual level, the level of deliberate reflection, "Chronologicals and Horologicals" means just what it says. . . . The whole drift of the action of *Pierre* is intended to demonstrate that the hero's tragic error lay in his not distinguishing early enough between absolute, ideal Good and the good that is possible, achievable, consistent with other goods, and therefore genuinely human."[17] Arvin adds that Melville was not at one with himself in writing the book and that *Pierre*'s center does not lie in "Plinlimmon's mature sagacity. . . ."[18]

The three critics cited here appear to agree that the pamphlet *per se* holds up as a moral directive, while suggesting that other elements in the book go counter to it. Milton Stern, on the other hand, questions the pamphlet itself, saying that, from Melville's point of view, it is correct "Insofar as it makes God to be the impossibility. . . . In its reasons for rejecting the absolute, and because it swings to a polar denial of human aspiration . . . it is wrong."[19]

One must agree with Stern that Melville is not assenting to the pamphlet even temporarily, for, in addition to other considerations, the pamphlet is so written as to make us reject it. (We are prepared for that rejection by the narrator's noting that it was written on "miserable, sleazy paper-rag" which was "dried-fish-like . . ." (p. 242). The pam-

phlet's language is, at a crucial point, self-damning: "To give *all* that thou hast to the poor, this . . . is chronometrical; hence no average son of man ever did such a thing. Nevertheless, if a man gives with a certain self-considerate generosity to the poor; abstains from doing downright ill to any man; does his convenient best in a general way to do good to his whole race; takes watchful loving care of his wife and children, relatives, and friends; is perfectly tolerant to all other men's opinions, whatever they may be; is an honest dealer, an honest citizen, and all that; and more especially if he believe that there is a God for infidels, as well as for believers, and acts upon that belief . . . such a man need never lastingly despond, because he is guilty of some minor offense. . . ." (pp. 250-251). There is much here to seduce us into thinking that this is an admirable statement. But notice the formulation of a good part of the ethical directives. Generosity to the poor is strongly qualified by "self-considerate." The ill we are not to do is "downright"—something less direct or evident is apparently permitted. But what is really striking is the vagueness of the language: "convenient best in a general way," "his whole race," and, most revealing, "an honest dealer, an honest citizen, and all that. . . ." "And all that"—there is in this phrasing almost an impatience on the part of the pamphlet with the ethical content it is supposed to be dealing with. Surely, this is the point—that the stress falls on what a man need *not* do in the way of moral action rather than on what he should do. And when the pamphlet goes on to argue that a man should not make a sacrifice of himself for any cause or other being, it does so on the basis that nothing sacrifices itself for him, that the sun does not abate its heat for one who is swooning from it—a dubious analogy. Thus, the pamphlet, apart from the criticism implicitly brought to bear upon it in other parts of the novel (particularly in the treatment of Plinlimmon) subverts itself.

Does the novel, then, advocate the chronometrical course pursued so intensely by Pierre? What *is* its attitude toward him? Lawrance Thompson says Pierre's idealism is "ridiculous," but adds that it is made so by God and society.[20] William Braswell at one time formulated an extreme position when he said that "Pierre . . . is presented in a more or less ridiculous light throughout the novel."[21] But in a later comment on the book he asked: "Is it fitting that a novelist go so far in mocking a hero to whom he is obviously devoted and for whom he ultimately desires the reader's deepest sympathy?"[22] Stern's close study of *Pierre*[23] presents Melville as firmly rejecting Pierre's idealism, divorced as it is from time, history, and human limitation. Hungering for the inhuman absolute, he becomes inhuman himself. Stern does say that the book "indicates sympathy, perhaps love, for Pierre," but adds that "one must reject an identification between Melville and Pierre, for the tone always works hard to enable the narrative to show the reader that Pierre's goal is pathetically hopeless and foolish and murderous."[24] Stern's exhibition of the network of interlocking details and images in *Pierre* is impressive, testimony to the book's considerable art. But Stern is able to maintain his implicit view that *Pierre* displays a consistency of attitude only by failing to consider the problems of tone that this essay has concerned itself with (he refers to the matter of tone for the space of only two or three sentences). If the tone "works hard," it works hard to confound us. Also, one can hardly speak of "the" tone of Pierre, as has been demonstrated, nor can one call the book's narrator "reliable" as Stern does.[25]

Moreover, Stern's approach to the book does not begin to take adequate account of the many occasions when Pierre is admired for his sensitivity, sincerity, profundity, nobility, charity, purity, fearlessness or grandeur (all these are the narrator's terms). Can anybody, besides Stern, doubt that Melville is drawn to Pierre as Enceladus, as the Titan, hurtling himself upon the unattainable? It is true that Stern could point to passages where Melville warns against taking the path of Pierre, saying, "it is not for man to follow the trail of truth too far, since by so doing he entirely loses the directing compass of his mind . . ." (p. 194), or noting that "ultimate Truth . . . consumes all, and only consumes" (p. 258). He could point to the distinction Melville draws between the "steady philosophic mind [which] reaches forth and draws to itself, in their collective entirety, the objects of its contemplation," and the "young enthusiast" (the latter a term repeatedly applied to Pierre) whose perception distorts (p. 206). But to counter this, there is the passage where, after observing the wild humor in which Pierre's troubled feelings are released, Melville says, "The cool censoriousness of the mere philosopher would denominate such conduct as nothing short of temporary madness; and perhaps it is, since, in the inexorable and inhuman eyes of mere undiluted reason, all grief, whether on our own account, or that of others, is the sheerest unreason and insanity" (p. 219). Undoubtedly, it is such passages as this which make most critics, *e.g.,* Matthiessen, Arvin, and Leslie Fiedler, find a strong sense of identification on Melville's part with his hero. Stern's is a minority position.

Yet, imbalanced as it is, that position does focus attention on the challenge to Pierre's Titanism present in the book. There is, for one thing, the nature of Pierre's actions. In taking leave of Isabel and Lucy to seek out Glen, he wishes death upon them. He obviously wants to murder Glen and to bring about his own end. His idealism has brought him to the destruction of self and of others. Apart from this, there is the literary manner in which Melville renders Pierre's Titanism. That aspect of him is dramatized, to a large extent, through his labors on a momentous book (his dream of Enceladus comes during a state of trance following on his attempt to continue with the book despite severe troubles with his eyes). Melville calls on a grand metaphor to describe Pierre's dogged literary efforts, from which he takes no rest, even on holidays. "In the midst of the merriments of the mutations of Time, Pierre hath ringed himself in with the grief of Eternity. Pierre is a peak inflexible in the heart of Time, as the isle-peak, Pico, stands unassaultable in the midst of waves" (p. 358). But in the paragraph that follows we view Pierre through Isabel who, in the adjoining room, overhears "the long lonely scratch

of his pen. It is, as if she heard the busy claw of some midnight mole in the ground" (p. 358). The heroic image of Pierre has been swiftly supplanted by something very different, and we are made to stand between the two images, uncertain, confronting one more of the book's ambiguities. In Pierre's vision of Enceladus, Melville describes the Titan as writhing out of the earth and eternally assailing a majestic mountain which repels him and "deridingly [leaves] him to bay out his ineffectual howl" (p. 406). Up till the last phrase the picture of Enceladus has been one of superb defiance, but "ineffectual howl" tends to deflate this. Another example of tonal uncertainty in the novel's relating of Pierre to Enceladus occurs when Pierre is seen as a mixture of "heavenliness and earthliness"—his "reckless sky-assaulting mood . . . was . . . on one side the grandson of the sky. For it is according to eternal fitness, that the precipitated Titan should still seek to regain this paternal birthright even by fierce escalade" (p. 408). Yet, on the preceding page, Enceladus is seen as "wreaking his immitigable hate . . ." in assaulting the mountain (p. 407). This characterization hardly elicits the admiration drawn forth by the later formulation, and places the focus on the destructive violence of Pierre's Titanism. Melville seems distinctly unable to make up his mind about the desirability of that Titanism, and does not adequately acknowledge his ambivalence. Is Titanism noble aspiration or self-deluding, murderous self-aggrandizement? These two elements are not brought into synthesis through a tragic view. First one is put forth, then the other.

Looking at the book as a whole, one can reconcile the basically humorous and satiric treatment of Pierre in the early chapters with his later, more respectful presentation by saying that Melville mocks him only so long as he enjoys the protection afforded by Saddle Meadows and believes in the illusions it has fostered. Once he begins to know and to suffer, Melville shows sympathy and admiration for him. However, as has been demonstrated, there are major inconsistencies in Melville's handling of his materials even after the break in Pierre's life has occurred. These cannot be resolved. Time and again the book undermines itself.

Explanations for the novel's collapse into contradictions and fragments abound, and have been advanced by various critics. Perhaps, it has been suggested, the sexual and familial feelings of Pierre were too close to those of Melville himself, too powerful for him to have rendered in a controlled way. Perhaps the failure of *Moby Dick* to achieve a popular success comparable to that of his early works had plunged him into despair, and his labors on that book had induced the kind of exhaustion he describes in *Pierre.* It may have been that he was at once trying to satisfy genteel literary taste and to satirize it. It may have been that his contemplation of the ambiguity of human motives made him doubt the possibility of ever knowing or judging anything. Possibly, too, he had come to regard literary form as a falsifying instrument, questioning the thing under his hand in the very act of fashioning it. Whatever the explanation, the result is before us. In writing *Pierre,*

Melville did not land the Kraken, bigger than Leviathan, that he had hoped for,[26] but a very different kind of catch. For, like many creatures of the deep, **Pierre** fascinates but also repels.

Notes

1. Lewis Mumford, in his *Herman Melville* (N.Y. 1929), observes that in *Pierre*, ". . . Melville slips from prose into poetry, from realism into fantasy, from the mood of high tragedy into that of the penny dreadful," p. 206.

2. *Ibid.,* p. 207.

3. All quotations from *Pierre* have been taken from the Hendricks House edition, by Henry A. Murray, (N.Y., 1949). The quotation above is found on p. 38 of that edition. Subsequent quotations from *Pierre* will be followed by the relevant page numbers in the text of the essay itself.

4. Matthiessen, *American Renaissance,* (N.Y., 1941), p. 486.

5. Arvin, *Herman Melville,* (N.Y., 1957), pp. 230-231.

6. Thompson, in his "Foreword" to the Signet Classic edition of *Pierre,* (N.Y., 1964), p. xix.

7. Rosenberry, *Melville and the Comic Spirit,* (Cambridge, 1955), p. 160.

8. Arvin, *op. cit.,* p. 231.

9. This failure might also stem from the tonal changes found *within* the early chapters, changes which will be discussed later in the essay.

10. Thompson, *op. cit.,* p. xix.

11. Braswell, "The Satirical Temper of Melville's *Pierre," American Literature,* VII, (Jan., 1936), 424-438.

12. Milton Stern, who appears to believe that Pierre's "Curses" statement is an example of speech used for "a comic revelation of the speaker" ignores the continuity of Melville's style with Pierre's. See Stern, *The Fine Hammered Steel of Herman Melville,* (Urbana, 1957), p. 161.

13. Blackmur, "The Craft of Herman Melville: A Putative Statement," in *Melville: A Collection of Critical Essays,* ed. Richard Chase, (N.Y., 1962), p. 79.

14. Sedgewick, *Herman Melville: The Tragedy of Mind,* (Cambridge, 1945), p. 161.

15. *Ibid.,* p. 162.

16. Matthiessen, *op. cit.,* p. 471.

17. Arvin, *op. cit.,* p. 221.

18. *Ibid.,* p. 222.

19. Stern, *op. cit.,* p. 190.

20. Thompson, *Melville's Quarrel with God,* (Princeton, 1952), p. 278.

21. Braswell, *op. cit.,* 431.

22. Braswell, "The Early Love Scenes in Melville's *Pierre," American Literature,* XXII, (Nov., 1950), 289.

23. In Stern, *op. cit.,* pp. 15-205.

24. *Ibid.,* p. 163.

25. *Ibid.,* p. 154. I hope it has been made clear that this unreliability is not, wherever it occurs, an intended effect. In general, the narrator in the earlier portions of the story (*i.e.,* before the appearance of Isabel) is frequently unreliable because Melville is working in an ironic or parodic mode. But in the later part of the story, the narrator is unreliable in the sense of displaying inconsistencies of tone without showing awareness of those inconsistencies. It should be added that my assumption in the course of the essay has been that there is no significant distinction to be made between the narrator in the later portion of the book and Melville himself.

26. In a letter to Hawthorne, written in November, 1851, Melville said: "Let us add Moby Dick to our blessing, and step from that. Leviathan is not the biggest fish;—I have heard of Krakens." *The Melville Log,* ed. Jay Leyda, (N.Y., 1951), I, 435.

Robert Milder (essay date 1974)

SOURCE: "Melville's 'Intentions' in *Pierre," in Studies in the Novel,* Vol. VI, No. 2, Summer, 1974, pp. 186-99.

[*In the following essay, Milder suggests that in* Pierre *Melville set out to write a parody of the romance novel that would reveal the depravity of which mankind is capable.*]

With the publication of the Northwestern-Newberry edition of **Pierre** with its historical note by Leon Howard and Hershel Parker, an orthodox interpretation of the novel has begun to emerge, an interpretation not so much of the meaning of the book as of Melville's complex intentions in writing it. The essence of this interpretation, first presented by Professor Howard in his biography of Melville and modified only slightly in his section of the historical note, is that when Melville "began to write the book which was to become **Pierre,** he was planning to turn out a genuinely popular story, touched by the strange mystery of the Gothic romance yet full of the 'genialities' he had so admired in *The House of the Seven Gables.*"[1] In **Moby-Dick,** so the argument runs, Melville had exhausted the last remaining portion of his nautical experience, his twenty-six months as a whaleman, but more than that he had exhausted the patience and attention of his audience. By November 25, 1851, roughly two weeks after the publication of **Moby-Dick,** he was still over four hundred dollars in debt to Harper's and "needed a new book which would sell well enough to carry him over the next winter."[2] It was imperative that he "do something new,"[3] and with a shrewd appreciation of the popular taste he turned "toward the feminine audience which formed the largest novel-reading public in his time,"[4] hoping to regain a measure of his popularity through the tried-and-true formula of a romance. As it proved, he could not resist the "inner compulsion" to write as he pleased,[5] producing a book far less genial than appalling; yet his initial motive was pure: he genuinely conceived *Pierre* as a popular romance, and long after the book was completed he remained "curiously unwilling to face the fact of what he had done and persistently thought of the book he had intended rather than the book he had written."[6]

Though this theory has much to recommend it, it involves us in a highly controversial reading of *Pierre*, particularly of the early books, and relies heavily on two of Melville's letters of the period. As Merrell Davis has shown in his study of *Mardi*, the letters can be a valuable tool in elucidating Melville's literary purposes.[7] The difficulty here is, first, that the letters Howard cites are far from conclusive and require a good deal of interpretation themselves, and, second, that the implications he finds in them are not always compatible with the evidence of the text. *Pierre* is an overwrought book, even a "mad" one, but from the outset there is an unrelenting method to its madness which precludes the idea that Melville was writing a genial romance. Whatever its excesses, *Pierre* is an intensely deliberate book and, as I hope to suggest in my final section, an intensely personal one.

I

Before addressing myself to the problem of Melville's intentions in *Pierre*, I should like to consider the two pieces of biographical evidence which seem to support Howard's thesis—Melville's brief allusion to *Pierre* in a letter to Sophia Hawthorne and his more extended remarks in a letter to his English publisher, Richard Bentley. Responding to Mrs. Hawthorne's praise of *Moby-Dick*, Melville promised that his next offering would not be "a bowl of salt water" but "a rural bowl of milk,"[8] a reference which prompted Howard to conclude that Melville "had clearly made a distinction in his own mind between the tastes of masculine and feminine readers and was planning, when he wrote Mrs. Hawthorne, . . . to address his book to the latter."[9]

Possibly Melville did have this distinction in mind, though his comment might as easily have referred to the settings of the two books. Nor should we overlook the possibility of irony here. Like virtually all Melville's letters to women—those to Sarah Morewood, for example—the letter to Mrs. Hawthorne is written with a playfulness and mock-heroic gallantry which seem almost to parody the meaning of its words. "My Dear Lady," the allusion to *Pierre* reads in full, "I shall not again send you a bowl of salt water. The next chalice I shall commend, will be a rural bowl of milk" (*L* [*The Letters of Herman Melville*, edited by William H. Gilman and Merrell R. Davis, 1960], 146). Whether from awkwardness or from a certain genuine but embarrassed chivalry, this was Melville's charac-

teristic stance toward women, and while it may have produced much delight among Melville's female correspondents, it presents a serious problem of tone for the critic.

Howard's second and more persuasive piece of evidence is Melville's description of *Pierre* to Richard Bentley as "treating of utterly new scenes and characters:—and, as I beleive [*sic*], very much more calculated for popularity than anything you have yet published of mine—being a regular romance, with a mysterious plot to it, & stirring passions at work, and withall, representing a new & elevated aspect of American life" (*L,* 150). "Mysterious," passionate, and "new" we may accept as a truthful, if euphemistic, description of *Pierre*, but to believe that Melville intended his book as "a regular romance" "calculated for popularity"—or, more to the point, that he continued to regard it in this way after he had completed it—requires a considerable act of faith. If nothing else, the poor sales of *Mardi* and *Moby-Dick* should have taught Melville what was and what was not "calculated for popularity," so that he could hardly have recognized *Pierre* for what it was and at the same time have anticipated its favorable reception. Either he was so deceived in his new book that he drastically misjudged its popular appeal or, as Harrison Hayford has unflatteringly put it, "the whole letter to Bentley is to be shrugged off as an utterly insincere sales promotion designed to dupe and mulct his publisher."[10]

Howard inclines toward the first alternative, finding it "difficult to believe that Melville was either being facetious or trying to fool a shrewd and friendly publisher."[11] But a look at the context of Melville's remark suggests that this was precisely what he was trying to do. Bentley had declined to pay a flat sum for *Pierre*, citing his consistent losses on the four Melville works he had published and offering instead the safer and, from Melville's point of view, more dubious prospect of half-profits. Melville's answering letter is a patent attempt to overcome these reservations, and his claim for the probable success of the book is sandwiched between an appeal to Bentley's self-interest (an edition of *Pierre* would stimulate sales of the four previous books) and a plea for his indulgence ("Besides,—if you please, Mr. Bentley—let bygones be bygones; let those previous books, for the present, take care of themselves" [*L,* 150]). "Dupe" and "mulct" are strong words to apply to an author negotiating with his publisher, but it is far more plausible to believe that Melville was engaged in an urgent "sales promotion" than to imagine him wholly deceived in the tastes of his audience or the character of his new book.

A further problem arises when we look more closely at Melville's correspondence with Bentley. In declining to purchase *Pierre*, Bentley had complained that Melville's works were produced in too rapid a succession to be profitable, an objection which Melville attempted to answer by suggesting that his new book be published "anonymously, or under an assumed name" (*L,* 151). Though Bentley was not convinced by Melville's proposal, he did change his offer after reading through the proofs of *Pierre*: he would publish the book on the basis of half-profits, he now wrote Melville, but only "If you will give me permission to make or have made by a judicious literary friend such alterations as are absolutely necessary to **'Pierre'** being properly appreciated here."[12] Bentley did not specify his criticisms, and it is possible that he had nothing more in mind than those occasional indelicacies and flights of rhetoric which, in his own words, had "sometimes offended the feelings of many sensitive readers."[13] In any case, Melville refused. The American sheets of *Pierre* were bound and distributed in England by Harper's London affiliate, an event which proved costly to Melville, since "it lost *Pierre* at one stroke the chance to be widely reviewed in England and the chance to be sold to the English circulating libraries in the customary three-decker form."[14]

From his experience with past books Melville must have known the advantages of an English imprint, even at the price of bowdlerization, yet despite his pressing financial needs he refused to allow any tampering with *Pierre.* From his offer of anonymity it is apparent that he cared little for whatever fame the book might bring him. Why then did he insist upon publishing an unexpurgated *Pierre*? And why, more particularly, did he insist upon it if the book was conceived and written primarily as a money-making venture, another variation on the popular romance?

The explanation for this, I would argue, is that Melville's intentions in *Pierre* were much like Pierre's own when, his illusions shattered by experience, he resolved to pour forth his new understanding of life in the form of an autobiographical novel—in his own words, to "gospelize the world anew, and show them deeper secrets than the Apocalypse!"[15] Somewhere in the months between *Moby-Dick* and *Pierre* Melville himself discovered such "deeper secrets," and *Pierre* was his attempt to deliver them evangelically to an ignorant and maddeningly complacent world. It did not matter whether or not these truths went forth under his name; it did not even matter finally whether they brought him an appreciable profit. What mattered was that they be delivered whole in all their moral and metaphysical subversiveness, all their latent horror.

II

At this point it might be helpful to sketch my own interpretation of *Pierre.* To those few contemporary reviewers who managed to make sense of the book at all, the meaning of *Pierre* lay in its exploration of chronometricals and horologicals. "The purpose of the *Ambiguities*," wrote the reviewer of *The Southern Literary Messenger*, ". . . we should take to be the illustration of this fact—that it is quite possible for a young and fiery soul, *acting strictly from a sense of duty,* to erect itself in direct hostility to all the universally received rules of moral and social order."[16] The Duyckincks in *The Literary World* were even more blunt: "The most immoral *moral* of *Pierre,* if it has any

moral at all, seems to be the impracticability of virtue" and the "loathsome suggestion" that "virtue and religion are only for gods and not to be attempted by man."[17]

Yet for all the indignation it aroused, the problem of chronometricals and horologicals is by no means the most disturbing of *Pierre*'s morals, or the most profound. The central theme of *Pierre,* as of each of Melville's major works, is the problem of knowledge, knowledge of the external world and knowledge of the self. Like **Mardi, Pierre** explores these questions through the vehicle of a *bildungsroman;* but where **Mardi** had been a genuine attempt on Melville's part to order the chaotic thoughts which had begun to swarm through his mind, *Pierre* was written and conceived as what might be termed a "negative *bildungsroman,*" a deliberate *reductio ad absurdum* of all metaphysics, all ethics, and all psychology, founded on the proposition that nothing can be known, least of all the knower himself. After placing his hero amidst the certainties of Saddle Meadows, Melville leads him unsparingly from one dark insight to another, with each successive episode enmeshing him further in ambiguity and doubt. Plinlimmon's pamphlet marks one way station along this route, but what is of most importance in *Pierre* is the journey in its entirety—its direction and its inevitable goal.

The journey begins early in the narrative with the appearance of Isabel. To Pierre, comfortably at home in the world of Lucy and his mother, Isabel supplies the first hint that life may be a larger, sadder, more mysterious, and infinitely more terrible affair than he has previously imagined;[18] and when she reveals to him that she is his half-sister, that his father has sinned, and consequently that "the before undistrusted moral beauty of the world" is an illusion (p. 65), she precipitates his decision to "know nothing but Truth" (p. 65) and begins him on his fatal quest.

In much the same way it is through Isabel that Pierre is led to explore the recesses of his own soul. In devoting himself to Isabel, Pierre had gloried in the loftiness of his sacrifice and the heroic, "Christ-like feeling" it engendered in him (p. 106). Plinlimmon's pamphlet offers him a radically different view, and one which he eventually comes to accept. But what disposes Pierre toward Plinlimmon's skepticism is less an awareness of the disparity between Christ's law and the world's than a recognition of the highly *un*-Christlike character of his own motives.[19] The critical scene occurs in Book XII just prior to his departure from the Meadows and his reading of Plinlimmon, when, alone with Isabel, Pierre first discovers the incestuous nature of his love for her and "a terrible self-revelation" shoots across his face (p. 192). The effect of this insight is to destroy for him the moral beauty of the *inner* world and plunge him into the second and more psychological phase of his development. From this moment on Pierre's quest for Truth is complicated by an increasing self-distrust, as the mind comes to doubt not only the substance of its beliefs but the motives underlying them.

This point is underscored through a revealing metaphor in which Melville compares "the heart of a man" to "a spiral stair in a shaft, without any end, and where that endlessness is only concealed by the spiralness of the stair, and the blackness of the shaft" (pp. 288-89). Were we to take this metaphor further and apply it to the whole of *Pierre* we would find ourselves with two such spiral stairs winding infinitely in opposite directions, one descending inward to the depths of the heart, the other ascending outward to the furthest reaches of Absolute Truth. The further Pierre ascends the stair of Absolute Truth, or tries to, the more clearly he sees the hopeless immensity before him, while at the same time a dawning awareness of his own unconscious motives pulls him ever more deeply down the stairway of his self, away from the certainty he seeks. Book by book the distance between Pierre and his object increases until finally, having resolved to "gospelize the world anew," Pierre arrives at the most appalling realization of all: "the everlasting elusiveness of Truth" and "the universal lurking insincerity of even the greatest and purest written thoughts" (p. 339). From the assurance of his early life Pierre has been reduced to an epistemological nihilism and moral prostration; his twofold journey—outward toward Truth, inward toward the depths of his soul—is virtually complete.

III

The *Pierre* I have outlined here is a far more terrifying book than *Moby-Dick,* less tragic in the classical sense of the word yet more insistent in its vision of utter nothingness. Few students of Melville would deny that the author of *Pierre* was a deeper, if more chastened, thinker than the man who had written *Moby-Dick*; the point of dispute is whether this development took place before or during the composition of *Pierre.* We know from the letter to Bentley that *Pierre* grew to be "a larger book, by 150 pages & more," than Melville had originally planned (*L,* 150). Comparing this earlier version with the published text, Howard finds that the first eight books of *Pierre* "would have constituted two-thirds" of this initial volume and that there is "no incompatibility" between these eight books and the "rural bowl of milk" Melville described to Sophia Hawthorne.[20] His inference is that Melville began *Pierre* as a "regular romance," became caught up in the logic of his unfolding thought, and, commencing with Book IX, gradually transformed his narrative into a psychological melodrama.

Such a process, of course, would have ample precedent in *Mardi,* whose flaws of structure and theme bear witness to the several distinct stages of composition through which it passed. In *Pierre,* however, there is no evidence of such a discontinuity, and the impending tragedy of its young hero is foreshadowed from the very start. Scarcely has Melville introduced us to Pierre when these intimations begin—the allusions to "that maturer and larger development" which shall "forever deprive" Pierre of the "full power" of his family pride (p. 6); to that "period of remorseless insight" when the "delicate warmths" of his father's library "should seem frigid to him, and he should madly demand more ardent fires" (p. 6); and to the bitter realizations that "this

world hath a deeper secret than beauty, and Life some burdens heavier than Death" (p. 7). Not only does Melville know from the outset what he will do with Pierre, but he insists that the reader know as well. In some strange fashion, we are told, "Nature intended a rare and original development in Pierre" (p. 13), and though the particulars of this development are deliberately left obscure, we are made to feel that it will be something ghastly and unnerving, hardly the material of "a regular romance."[21]

This feeling is reinforced by the rhapsodical tone of the early books, which serves as a correlate to Pierre's saccharine view of the world and prepares us for its inevitable collapse. One passage seems particularly grotesque, the famous hymn to Love in Book II:

> Endless is the account of Love. Time and space cannot contain Love's story. . . . Love made not the Arctic zones, but Love is ever reclaiming them. Say, are not the fierce things of this earth daily, hourly going out? Where are now your wolves in Britain? Where in Virginia now, find you the panther and the Pard? Oh, Love is busy everywhere. Everywhere Love hath Moravian missionaries. No propagandist like to Love . . . (p. 34).

Not only is the optimism of this passage incompatible with the previous dark allusions to Pierre's fate,[22] but it is immediately juxtaposed to and qualified by an alternative vision of life, the "nameless sadness" evoked by the "lustrous, imploring, mournful face" of Isabel (p. 37). Even the title of the book is instructive—"Love, Delight, and Alarm"—for it indicates that this juxtaposition is highly deliberate, an attempt to foreshadow the two visions of life which will contend for Pierre's soul and the two figures, Lucy and Isabel, who will embody them. Here, as throughout the early books, the apparent sweetness of Melville's tone is belied by a latent and savage irony.

The conclusion to be drawn from all this is that Melville was in command of his material from the very start—in command of his plot, which did not change substantially as he labored on it, and in command of his complex and ironic attitude toward Pierre, which also did not change.[23] The book Melville published, "loathsome" as it seemed to many of its first readers, is the book he set out to write. It is as if he were determined to take the trappings of the popular romance—the light and dark heroines, the melodrama, the "elevated" style—and bend them to his purpose, producing a book which, "far from being a regular romance," would be a diabolical parody of the romance, "a vicious perversion of a formula so universally worshipped as to be sacrosanct."[24]

IV

Since I have suggested Melville's "intentions" in *Pierre,* let me close by trying to account for them—no small problem in itself, since there is little in Melville's outward situation that would seem to warrant the perverse evangelicalism of the book. From all appearances the summer and early fall of 1851 were among the happiest months in Melville's life, certainly among the most satisfying.[25] Hawthorne had understood and appreciated *Moby-Dick,* and for Melville the praise of such a discerning critic was reward enough. Moreover, Melville seems to have felt that his latest book was only the prelude to a greater and deeper book to come. "Lord, when shall we be done growing?" he wrote Hawthorne in November, 1851: "As long as we have anything more to do, we have done nothing. So, now, let us add Moby Dick to our blessing, and step from that. Leviathan is not the biggest fish;—I have heard of Krakens" (*L,* 143).

Though Melville's words are buoyant, implying an infinite reservoir of energy and an eagerness to venture on, there are indications that his confidence was by no means as well-founded as his letter suggests. For one thing, "Melville's strength had been thoroughly depleted by the terrific creative strain of writing *Moby-Dick*"[26] more so perhaps than he knew at the time—yet the burden of past debts, coupled with the poor sales of *Moby-Dick,* required that he begin a new work almost at once, his seventh in six years. No less important, Hawthorne had moved from Lenox to Concord in November, 1851, ending the brief but intense friendship so vital to Melville's development and leaving Melville once again profoundly alone.

Few facts are known about Melville's life during the winter of 1851-52, the months when he wrote *Pierre*; but Sarah Morewood, who hosted the Melvilles on Christmas Eve and who was as close to Melville as anyone, described him as "more quiet than usual" and given to "irreverent language" and unsettling religious opinions. "I hear that he is now so engaged in a new book," she added, "as frequently not to leave his room till dark in the evening when he for the first time during the whole day partakes of solid food—he must therefore write under a state of morbid excitement which will soon injure his health.—I laughed at him somewhat and told him that the recluse life he was leading made his city friends think he was slightly insane—he replied that long ago he came to the same conclusion himself but that if he left home to look after Hungary the cause in hungery would suffer."[27] Though it would be unwise to extrapolate too broadly from these remarks, we cannot help feeling that Melville was under a considerable strain during these months, a feeling that is strengthened by his granddaughter's hints of a mental and physical breakdown.

Nonetheless, there is more to the debacle of *Pierre* than Melville's exhaustion or frayed nerves. Even as he was completing *Moby-Dick,* more conscious of his creative strength than ever before, Melville confided to Hawthorne that strange premonition of decay so central to an understanding of his mind: "My development has all been within a few years past." He wrote:

> I am like one of those seeds taken out of the Egyptian pyramids, which, after being three thousand years a seed and nothing but a seed, being planted in English soil, it developed itself, grew to greenness, and then

fell to mould. So I. Until I was twenty-five, I had no development at all. From my twenty-fifth year I date my life. Three weeks have scarcely passed, at any time between then and now, that I have not unfolded within myself. But I feel that I am now come to the inmost leaf of the bulb, and that shortly the flower must fall to the mould (*L,* 130).

Why, a brief six years after his awakening in *Typee,* Melville felt so despondent, so utterly played out, we can only speculate; but one answer seems particularly convincing. As his flower image suggests, Melville tended to regard his development as organic—germinating from a seed planted belatedly in a fertile soil, sprouting and unfolding outward through fixed laws of growth, flourishing for a brief season, and then decaying and dying as all life must. Applying this metaphor to his own life, Melville seems to have felt that the same process of development which had brought him to the tragic vision of *Moby-Dick* would carry him irresistibly onward, beyond tragedy, to a debilitating skepticism. As he wrote in *Pierre,*

> it is only the miraculous vanity of man which ever persuades him, that even for the most richly gifted mind, there ever arrives an earthly period, where it can truly say to itself, I have come to the Ultimate of Human Speculative Knowledge; hereafter, at this present point I will abide. Sudden onsets of new truth will assail him, and overturn him as the Tartars did China; for there is no China wall that man can build in his soul, which shall permanently stay the irruptions of those barbarous hordes which Truth ever nourishes in the loins of her frozen, yet teeming North . . . (p. 167).

The thought that final knowledge is unattainable is scarcely a new one, even for Melville; what is significant here is Melville's language: "Sudden onsets," "assail," "overturn," "Tartars," "irruptions," "barbarous hordes," and "frozen, yet teeming North."[28] The implication is not only that new truth will force itself upon the individual whether he is willing or not, but that this new truth will be terrible, unwelcome, deeply chaotic, and unmanning.

What "new truth" precipitated Melville's decline, or sense of decline, we cannot say with certainty, but given the profoundly associational nature of Melville's letters we may conjecture a source in the perception which immediately follows his reference to the "inmost leaf." "It seems to me now," he told Hawthorne, "that Solomon was the truest man who ever spoke, and yet that he a little *managed* the truth with a view to popular conservatism" (*L,* 130).[29] We may recall that in *Moby-Dick* Solomon had represented a wisdom which, while recognizing the vanity of all things, had incorporated that knowledge into a larger affirmation of life and so had returned from "the congregation of the dead." What Melville appears to be saying here is that even Solomon's truth is a partial one, mitigated for reasons of expediency, and that the full truth involves a recognition of the irredeemable meaninglessness of life and of the shallowness of any philosophy that pretends to offer consolation.

Melville had touched on this idea himself almost a year earlier in **"Hawthorne and His Mosses"** when he had spoken of those "things, which we feel to be terrifically true, that it were all but madness for any good man, in his proper character, to utter, or even hint of them."[30] Though at that time, under the combined tutelage of Hawthorne and Shakespeare, he had begun to discover the "great power of blackness,"[31] it was not until the final month or two of **Moby-Dick** that he realized for himself the full meaning of his **"Mosses"** remark: that the truth, if told unsparingly, *was* terrible and subversive, madness to utter and madness even to think. It was then that he sensed where his thought was leading him and confided that sense to Hawthorne, though he understood full well (as he wrote of Pierre) that knowing his fatal condition did not enable him to change it (p. 303).

The perception of a moral darkness beyond Solomon was the first insight that assailed Melville, but no less important for **Pierre** was his growing awareness of the ambiguities of the self. In **Moby-Dick** Melville had shown what modern critics have since reaffirmed: that tragedy can exist with a context of metaphysical doubt, even of nihilism, as long as author and audience retain a common belief in man's potential heroism.[32] Yet as Melville's thought deepened and he began to concern himself more critically with the workings of the mind, it was precisely this potential heroism that he came to question. In Ahab he had created a hero worthy of his divine antagonist in every respect, but he had done so only through an extreme psychological reticence. He wrote in **Pierre**: "In reserves men build characters; not in revelations. He who shall be wholly honest, though nobler than Ethan Allen; that man shall stand in danger of the meanest mortal's scorn" (p. 108).

In **Pierre** the "reserves" of **Moby-Dick** give way to a scrupulous and almost indecent "revelation," with all the predictable consequences. No sooner does Pierre arrive at his "grand enthusiast resolution" to renounce his world for Isabel than Melville beings to scrutinize the motives for his choice. "Save me from being bound to Truth," he writes, and as if to dramatize the point: "How shall I steal yet further into Pierre, and show how this heavenly fire was helped to be contained in him, by mere contingent things, and things that he knew not. But I shall follow the endless, winding way,—the flowing river in the cave of man; careless whither I be led, reckless where I land" (p. 107). What follows is the suggestion of Pierre's incestuous love for Isabel with its implication that not even the noblest and seemingly most altruistic of resolves can ever be free from the taint of human clay. It is as though Melville discovered that on the deepest level all men were hypocrites, assigning motives to their behavior but propelled nonetheless "by mere contingent things" and "things [they] knew not." "Appalling is the soul of a man!" he wrote in **Pierre** (p. 284), appallingly "vast" and appallingly "vacant" (p. 285): layer upon layer in an infinite regression of rationalizations and half-truths, with no ascertainable core of being, no final and integral self, no "I." In short, the inner world was too immense and unknown to admit of "sovereign natures" like Ahab; there would be no more **Moby-Dick**s in Melville's fiction.

The effect of this discovery, as of his growing skepticism toward the wisdom of Solomon, was to lead Melville beyond the limits of conventional tragedy. Like Pierre he had followed "the trail of truth too far," and though he had not quite lost "the directing compass of his mind" (p. 165), he had come to doubt the most fundamental premises of moral and religious belief, not least of them the integrity of the individual soul. To his own mind there was an inevitable logic to this development, but an appreciation of that logic was scant consolation. His will to believe—in God and Truth, if it were possible; in himself, if it were not—balked at this revelation of nothingness, and from the disparity between the conclusions of his intellect and the requirements of his soul came the peculiar self-lacerating humor of **Pierre**. His mind had been "overturned" by a "sudden onset of new truth," and, driven as always by his fierce earnestness, he set out to deliver this truth, unmitigated, to the world—to "gospelize the world anew, and show them deeper secrets than the Apocalypse!"

Notes

1. Leon Howard, *Herman Melville* (Berkeley: Univ. of California Press, 1951), p. 184. See also Howard, "Historical Note" to *Pierre; or the Ambiguities* (Evanston and Chicago: Northwestern Univ. Press and the Newberry Library, 1971), p. 369.

2. Howard, "Historical Note," p. 365.

3. Ibid.

4. Ibid., p. 366.

5. Ibid., p. 372.

6. Howard, *Herman Melville*, p. 193.

7. See Merrell R. Davis, *Melville's MARDI: A Chartless Voyage* (New Haven: Yale Univ. Press, 1952).

8. *The Letters of Herman Melville,* ed. William H. Gilman and Merrell R. Davis (New Haven: Yale Univ. Press, 1960), p. 146. Subsequent references to the *Letters* are included in the text and abbreviated *L*.

9. Howard, "Historical Note," p. 365.

10. Harrison Hayford, "The Significance of Melville's 'Agatha' Letters," *ELH,* 13 (1946), 307.

11. Howard, "Historical Note," p. 365.

12. Richard Bentley, quoted in Bernard Jerman's "'With Real Admiration': More Correspondence Between Melville and Bentley," *AL* [*American Literature: A Journal of Literary History, Criticism, and Biography*], 25 (1953), 313.

13. Ibid., p. 312.

14. Howard, "Historical Note," p. 380.

15. Herman Melville, *Pierre; or the Ambiguities* (Evanston and Chicago: Northwestern Univ. Press and the Newberry Library, 1971), p. 273. Subsequent references to *Pierre* are included in the text.

16. Rev. of *Pierre* in *The Southern Literary Messenger,* quoted by Hugh W. Hetherington in *Melville's Re-*

viewers (Chapel Hill: Univ. of North Carolina Press, 1961), p. 233.

17. Rev. of *Pierre* in *The Literary World,* 11 (21 Aug. 1852), 119. The review is generally attributed to George and/or Evert Duyckinck.

18. See particularly Book II, vii (pp. 40-42) and Book III, ii (pp. 48-54).

19. A central paradox in *Pierre* and a cause for much of the critical confusion which surrounds the book is the fact that Pierre's deepest miseries do not result from his being "too chronometrical," but from his not being chronometrical enough. Plinlimmon is correct in claiming that the man who attempts to live chronometrically will almost invariably entangle himself in "unique follies and sins." The reason for this, however, is not primarily the incongruence between Christ's law and the world's, as many have asserted, but the element of human imperfection which mixes itself into all men's actions so that even the highest are impure—and hence un-Christlike, unchronometrical—from the first. Pierre's failure proves that he is not a Christ; it does not imply the failure of a true Christ. Thus, while Plinlimmon's pamphlet has an experiential relevance to "the mass of men," it should not be taken as a metaphysical absolute. Like "all our so-called wisdom," it too has only a "provisional" truth.

20. Howard, "Historical Note," pp. 369, 368.

21. Conscious perhaps of the difficulties raised by these early pages, Howard concedes that "There is no evidence that Melville . . . planned to be pellucid or merry in his . . . romance. Ambiguities and tragic implications were in *Pierre* from the beginning" ("Historical Note," p. 378). But Howard insists that these "ambiguities" were compatible with Melville's description of the book to Bentley and Mrs. Hawthorne, and that the changes which transformed *Pierre* occurred "not in the plot of [Melville's] romance but in his attitude toward it" ("Historical Note," p. 372). In other words, he implies, Melville was planning not only to write a popular story, but to write one which would contain such seemingly discordant elements as "the appearance of Plinlimmon and his pamphlet, the arrival of Lucy, and the events leading up to a final catastrophe" ("Historical Note," p. 372).

That Melville was aiming his novel toward a feminine audience is questionable enough; that he would found such a novel upon a suggestion of incest or include in it a pamphlet which held, without authorial refutation, that the Christian doctrine of forgiveness was a horologically "false one" (p. 215) seems extremely doubtful. If the plot of *Pierre* is all of a piece—and I strongly agree with Howard that it is—then clearly, given the demonic implications of that plot, Melville could scarcely have intended his book for a popular audience.

22. See Alan Holder, "Style and Tone in Melville's *Pierre,*" *ESQ* [*A Journal of the American Renaissance*], No. 60 (1970), 78.

23. This is an essential point in view of Howard's claim that Melville's irony toward Pierre does not fully emerge until Book IX, when he begins "to scold his hero in the manner of Carlyle" ("Historical Note," p. 372). The tone of the early books is one argument against Howard's theory; another is the fact that though Pierre does not become conscious of his deeper motives until Book XII, Melville alerts the reader to them as early as Book V—a clear indication that irony was central to Melville's intent from the very first.

24. Perry Miller, "The Romance and the Novel," *Nature's Nation* (Cambridge: Harvard Univ. Press, 1967), p. 243.

25. For an account of Melville's life during these months, see *Letters,* pp. 126-44. See also the letters of Hawthorne, Mrs. Melville, and Evert Duyckinck included in Elizabeth Melville Metcalf's *Herman Melville: Cycle and Epicycle* (Cambridge: Harvard Univ. Press, 1953), pp. 113-23, and the letters of Evert Duyckinck published in Luther S. Mansfield's "Glimpses of Herman Melville's Life in Pittsfield, 1850-51: Some Unpublished Letters of Evert A. Duyckinck," *AL,* 9 (1937), 26-48.

26. Metcalf, p. 135.

27. Sarah Morewood to George Duyckinck, quoted in Metcalf, p. 133.

28. A likely source of Melville's imagery here is Milton's description of the throng of fallen angels in *Paradise Lost* (Book I, ll. 351-55):

> A multitude, like which the populous North
> Pour'd never from her frozen loins, to pass
> *Rhene* or the *Danaw,* when her barbarous Sons
> Came like a Deluge on the South, and spread
> Beneath *Gibraltar* to the *Lybian* sands.

The association of these "sudden onsets of new truth" with Milton's devils underscores the havoc they wreak on the mind and suggests, much as Azzageddi did in *Mardi,* the demonic nature of Truth.

29. For Melville, as for many nineteenth-century readers of the Bible, Solomon was the author of Ecclesiastes, and it is in this capacity that Melville alludes to him both here and in "The Try-Works" in *Moby-Dick.*

30. Melville, "Hawthorne and His Mosses" included in *Moby-Dick,* ed. Harrison Hayford and Hershel Parker (New York: W. W. Norton, 1967), p. 541.

31. Ibid., p. 540.

32. See Murray Krieger, *The Tragic Vision* (Chicago: Univ. of Chicago Press, 1960); Susan Sontag, "The Death of Tragedy," *Against Interpretation* (New York: Farrar, Strauss, Giroux, 1966); and Northrop Frye, *Anatomy of Criticism* (Princeton: Princeton Univ. Press, 1957).

R. Scott Kellner (essay date 1975)

SOURCE: "Sex, Toads, and Scorpions: A Study of the Psychological Themes in Melville's *Pierre*," in *The Arizona Quarterly*, Vol. 31, No. 1, Spring, 1975, pp. 5-20.

[In the following essay, Kellner explores Melville's treatment of several psychological themes in Pierre, *focusing on the relationship between ideal love and instinctive sex, and between sex and death.]*

Although Melville was aware of the difficulties in pursuing half-conscious thoughts, he nevertheless persisted with psychological inquiries in his novels, probing "the endless, winding way,—the flowing river in the cave of man."[1] Melville saw the difference between man's conscious behavior and his unconscious desires as the difference between an open plain and a dark thicket. He believed his job as novelist was equal to the pioneer-explorers of his time, that an author was a scout "following the Indian trail" (p. 84) leading into the thickets of the mind. He was aware, though, of the dangers involved in such scouting. "It is not for man to follow the trail of truth too far," he writes halfway through *Pierre.* There are some truths that even the most avid truthseeker cannot bear to face, precipices at the end of that Indian trail, and thickets so dense that the prober "entirely loses the directing compass of his mind" (p. 165). Ironically enough, in the case of *Pierre,* the truth for Melville turns out to be his own fears—and the accompanying abhorrence—of sex.

The main character in *Pierre,* for whom the book is titled, undergoes a sexual awakening which eventually leads to disgust with, and an attempt to reject, the libido. Pierre is just emerging from his teens, still an adolescent; he is in late puberty perhaps, and inexperienced in love. That he is still a virgin is implied when Melville writes "as yet he had not seen so far and deep as Dante;" he has had no "sensational presentiment or experience" (p. 54) with which to understand his sexual emotions.

Pierre sublimates his sexual energy, releasing it in strenuous physical activity. He rides, walks, swims, and even vaults in order that he might "invigorate and embrawn himself." His outward concern is with becoming muscular and manly. Yet it is in *retreat* from masculinity that he seeks this "noble muscular manliness" (p. 50). All his robustness and athletic prowess, felling hemlock trees and fencing and boxing, are manifestations of an inward fear about his masculinity. Pierre is burdened with doubts of his manhood and seeks to hide these fears by a manly outward appearance: "It had always been one of the lesser ambitions of Pierre, to sport a flowing beard, which he deemed the most noble corporeal badge of the man" (p. 253).

There are a number of reasons for Pierre's insecurity. To begin with, his relationship with his mother has confused and stymied his sexual identity. Unfortunately for him, he sees himself both as his mother's platonic lover and as her "First Lady in waiting" (p. 14). This femininity in Pierre's nature is expressed in homosexual overtones in his relations with Glen Stanley and Lucy's brothers. Melville's description of Pierre and Glen's early association borders on homosexual love. Pierre's passionate embrace of Lucy's brothers understandably startles and offends them, just as Glen later refuses to acknowledge any love for Pierre. While other men outgrow their boyhood sexual confusion, Pierre retains his.

Most important though is Pierre's fear of impotency, which has resulted from these identity problems. He is under heavy pressure, sexually, as one of the last male Glendinnings. Pierre's mother has made his responsibility painfully clear—he must produce a son. Pierre has to live up to the image of his father and grandfather in this regard. He is unable to do so. He tries on his grandfather's vest and later, after he has run off with Isabel, gazes at his grandfather's old bedstead: "It seemed powerfully symbolical to him" (p. 270). And well it should—Pierre will not be furthering the line of Glendinning. By choosing his half-sister Isabel, a union which could not lead to any normal offspring, he has chosen extinction. This suicidal aspect of his sexual nature is again symbolized when he murders Glen Stanley, the last living male cousin: "Spatterings of his own kindred blood were upon the pavement; his own hand had extinguished his house" (p. 360). This is an extension for Pierre of his self-castration. "Pierre is neuter now!" (p. 360), he ultimately says.

Pierre's fears for himself are again evident in his Enceladus dream: the Titan is amputated, impotent, "without one serviceable ball-and-socket above the thigh" (p. 346). Pierre sees his own face on the Titan's armless and phallic trunk. Melville uses this image to depict Pierre's impotency and fears of being unable to fulfill his masculine function. The armless giant,

> despairing of any other mode of wreaking his immitigable hate, turned his vast trunk into a battering-ram, and hurled his own arched-out ribs again and yet again against the invulnerable steep. (p. 346)

This emphasizes Pierre's inability to have a normal sexual union, one that would lead to offspring and the fulfillment of his ancestral responsibility. He must have unusual stimulation, an incestuous love, simply to be potent. By so doing, though, he cuts himself off from his past and from society's laws, a past and laws which twisted his sexual desires in the first place.

The roots of Pierre's feelings of sexual inadequacy lie in his unusual relationship with his mother. Pierre is more a lover than a son to her. He addresses his mother as "sister" and she calls him "brother," a foreshadowing of the eventual relationship Pierre has with his real sister.

Pierre's confusion about his filial role is understandable. His mother is attractive to young men and is used to their attentions. She uses her son as she might use one of those younger suitors, to wait upon her and flatter her and feed her ego. Only when she is angry with him or in doubt of his attention does she call him son and put him in his place. She is so successful in her dual role that Pierre has threatened "with a playful malice" to make anyone who tried to marry her and take her away from him "immediately disappear from the earth" (p. 5).

The mother has her own overt sexual problems. She exhibits them when she likens adulterers to murderers. She views sex darkly, quite probably in reaction from her own true desires. She loathes Delly when she hears of that girl's untimely pregnancy; she even hates (fears would be more exact) the girl Pierre "marries." The girl, to her way of thinking, must be a bastard and vile (p. 131). Pierre's union with such a girl destroys "at one gross sensual dash, the fair succession of an honorable race! Mixing the choicest wine with filthy water from the plebeian pool" (p. 194).

Mrs. Glendinning does not want to believe that Pierre is ready for women. In a distinction she makes between the angelically sexless Lucy and herself—Lucy is "Pale Sherry" while she is "potent Port!"—she pictures Pierre only with pale sherry. Her son isn't quite ready for port, she says. Or she isn't ready to admit the physical side of Pierre's nature, particularly as it relates to her and her own latent desires. Her mistaken judgment about her son's libido becomes painfully clear to her when Pierre finally rejects Lucy for Isabel. He is ready for port after all.

His mother plays on his sympathies:

> Could you unalarmed see me sitting all alone here with this decanter, like any old nurse, Pierre; some solitary, forlorn old nurse, Pierre, deserted by her last friend, and therefore forced to embrace her flask? (p. 55)

If he marries Lucy, a compliant girl, he will not be leaving her all alone; he will still be under her dominance, still be hers. For Pierre, though, staying with his mother means being her surrogate lover; it means desiring her at least to some extent. By running off with Isabel, who is like his mother (and even related to Pierre by blood), he can break free from his mother's dominance and satisfy his Oedipal wishes at the same time.

The Oedipal aspect of this story is brought directly to the reader in three separate analogies: Pierre is compared to Hamlet on more than one occasion; he identifies himself with the Titan, the son of an incestuous union who later married his mother, compounding the incest; and in a vivid scene toward the end of the story, Pierre is struck blind (although only momentarily)—the fate of Oedipus. "He knew not where he was; he did not have any ordinary life-feeling at all. He could not see; though instinctively putting his hand to his eyes, he seemed to feel that the lids were open" (p. 341). Symbolically, he then falls into the gutter and is covered with mud and slime.

It is in keeping with the situation that Mrs. Glendinning becomes more like an angry mistress than a disappointed mother when she first suspects Pierre is keeping something from her. Her violent outrage upon learning of his "marriage" to Isabel is a logical extension of her sexual frustration. By not marrying Lucy and refusing to allow Mrs. Glendinning continued control over his libido, Pierre is threatening his mother's mental stability. She cannot stand the thought of his being with a "slut"—with "potent Port"—it brings out her own unconscious desires for her son. She is driven into insanity and finally death by the union between Pierre and Isabel: "How agonizedly now did it hint of her mortally-wounded love for her only and best-loved Pierre!" (p. 285).

His mother likes Lucy because she is docile. And so, she thinks, is Pierre. But Pierre needs a woman like his mother, somebody—in nineteenth-century metaphorical terms—with "the jettiest hair" (p. 118). Mrs. Glendinning has twisted Pierre's libido out of shape. Lucy is not the girl to stir his essential passions. She is "transcendent beauty." She is a blonde angel, sexless. Isabel, described as a dark angel, is quite different from Lucy's transcendence.

Lucy is Pierre's heaven. She is not made for sexual embraces. She is unearthly: "Her flowing, white, blue-ribboned dress, fleecily invested her." She has for him an "unearthly evanescence" (p. 58). Pierre is caught between this ideal love for Lucy and the forces of his more earthy libido. The subtitle of the novel, "The Ambiguities," is this dualistic aspect of his nature. On the one hand, Pierre desires sex, he certainly thinks of it—he sees a pillow that belongs to Lucy, "a snow-white glossy pillow reposes, and a trailing shrub has softly rested a rich, crimson flower against it" (pp. 3-4). But when he actually enters her bedroom he does so with "reverentialness," and the carpet to him seems "as holy ground" (p. 39). There is no crimson flower for him on the girl's bed. On the contrary, the bed is "spotless" (p. 39). And when he catches a glimpse of it in the mirror, he envisions two separate beds, symbolic of his inability to consummate a marriage with her.

Part of Pierre's incestuous longings stem from a breast fixation that manifests itself on several occasions in the book. Pierre fawns over his mother, helping her to dress and fix her hair; he passes a ribbon around her neck, crossing the ends in front across her breasts and then offers to "tack it with a kiss" (p. 14). It is only a few pages later when Melville injects the rather funny pun: "Don't be a milk-sop, Pierre!"

Isabel is included in this fixation when she tells Pierre, "the lips that do now speak to thee, never touched a woman's breast" (p. 114). Isabel claims that the sight of an infant feeding at its mother's breast saved her from insanity. She describes it as "that white and smiling breast" (p. 122).

Pierre's mother, motherhood, Isabel, and sexuality are all connected to this fixation. And the last dramatic scene in the story tragically underlines the consequences of this fixation. Pierre seizes Isabel and reaches into her bodice with these words: "wife or sister, saint or fiend! . . . in thy breasts, life for infants lodgeth not, but death-milk for thee and me" (p. 360). Hidden between her breasts is a vial filled with poison.

Another traumatic stage in Pierre's early development is explored by Melville. Pierre disassociates his father and mother from sexuality. He represses any such knowledge; thinking of his father's sexual nature reminds him of his own and verifies his worst fears about himself. Particularly as they regard his unconscious wish to take his father's place with his mother. When his father rages in his dying moments about his adultery, young Pierre refuses to examine the issue. "Into Pierre's awe-stricken, childish soul, there entered a kindred, though still more nebulous conceit. But it belonged to the spheres of the impalpable ether: and the child soon threw other and sweeter remembrances over it, and covered it up" (p. 71). When he is finally forced by the presence of Isabel to admit his father's sexuality, he must also face that side of his mother's nature: "Not even his lovely, immaculate mother, remained entirely untouched, unaltered by the shock" (p. 88). His parents are no longer saints; love cannot be viewed as ideal, existing above and apart from the corporeal person. Revelations about his father's sexuality shatter the young man's existence because it mocks the sexless love toward which he is aspiring.

The pressures of being the last male heir are not wholly depressing. There is a certain challenge in this that appeals on occasion to Pierre's pride. In a very phallic passage Melville writes:

> But in his more wonted natural mood, this thought was not wholly sad to him. Nay, sometimes it mounted into an exultant swell. For in the ruddiness, and flushfulness, and vaingloriousness of his youthful soul, he fondly hoped to have a monopoly of glory in capping the fame-column, whose tall shaft had been erected by his noble sires. (p. 8)

Phallic symbols abound in this novel. Outdoing the symbol of Moby-Dick, the book is dedicated to the mountain Greylock, which gives off "unstinted fertilizations." Images of sex and sexual organs pervade the entire structure of the story. Pierre goes out for a walk to search for Isabel; he takes his cane along. Melville cannot resist writing: "let thy cane stay still, good Pierre. Seek not to mystify the mystery so" (p. 53). And on another occasion the "mystery" deepens; Pierre burns his hand. When Isabel touches his hand she comments about the soot it leaves on her own: "I would catch the plague from thee, so that it should make me share thee" (p. 202). There is in this last image a contradiction of the positive aspects of "unstinted fertilizations." Sexual energy can be destructive as well as procreative.[2]

The unifying force of these somewhat disparate symbols is the character of Isabel. In almost every instance, the symbols are associated with her. Isabel's guitar becomes a womb and a phallic symbol, the very shape of the instru-

ment lending itself to this ambiguity. Isabel plays upon the guitar and Pierre feels strangely drawn to it and her. Its music is described as "supersensuous and all-confounding intimations" (p. 282), and its power "not only seemed irresistibly to draw him toward Isabel, but to draw him away from another quarter—wantonly as it were" (p. 151). Melville's choice of words here, "supersensuous" and "wantonly," are clear guides to his meaning in these passages.

Pierre's sexual longings for Isabel are represented in yet another phallic symbol, a "primeval pine-tree" alone in a meadow, which "drops melodious mournfulness" (p. 40). Sitting beneath this tree Pierre sees the face of Isabel. The face and the tree are connected in his mind and when the face disappears, he says: "Pray heaven it hath not only stolen back, and hidden again in thy high secrecies, oh tree! But 'tis gone—gone—entirely gone . . . Thou pine-tree!—henceforth I will resist thy too treacherous persuasiveness" (pp. 41-42).

More obvious is the use to which Melville puts the stove pipe in Pierre's apartments, the last phallic symbol we will discuss in this paper, but certainly not the last one in the novel. Isabel wants Lucy to get the warmth from the stove and suggests that Pierre redirect the pipe to Lucy's room. "'Pierre, there is no stove in the room. She will be very cold. The pipe—can we not send it this way?' And she looked more intently at him, than the question seemed to warrant" (p. 322). Pierre must choose between Lucy and Isabel. He chooses Isabel for the expression of his passions, and the pipe remains where it is. "It shall not be done, Isabel. Doth not that pipe and that warmth go into thy room? Shall I rob my wife . . . to benefit my most devoted and true-hearted cousin?" (p. 323).

Although Pierre is aroused by Isabel, his real wish is to transcend sex altogether. He wants to be like Christ, with "no unmanly, mean temptation" (p. 106) to come between him and his ideals. He would like to be an angel, sexless. In Plinlimmon's terms, Pierre would like to be governed by ideas chronometrical, celestial, rather than horological, terrestrial desires. Pierre strives to be noble; nobility to him means being beyond the stirrings of the libido. Such nobility, as it is made clear in the Plinlimmon pamphlet, is not really possible on earth. And Pierre, "though charged with the fire of all divineness, his containing thing was made of clay" (p. 107).

It remains clear then throughout the novel that there is a difference in relationship between Pierre and the two girls. As for Lucy, "he was never alone with her; though, as before, at times alone with Isabel" (p. 337). In context, being "alone" with Isabel means having had intercourse with her. In comparison, Lucy remains chaste and pure, representative of Pierre's now unattainable Ideal Love. While Lucy is the pure one, Isabel represents abandoned sex for Pierre. A description of her playing the guitar bears this out:

> with every syllable the hair-shrouded form of Isabel swayed to and fro with a like abandonment, and sud-

denness, and wantonness:—then it seemed not like any song; seemed not issuing from any mouth; but it came forth from beneath the same vail concealing the guitar. (pp. 126-27)

Watching her, "a strange wild heat burned" (p. 127) upon Pierre's brow, a reaction not evoked by Lucy.

Isabel is not a jezebel though, not out to seduce Pierre. Her attractiveness seduces him, but only as a result of his own confused inclinations. Isabel is "all plastic" (p. 189) in Pierre's hands, transferring her love for her father onto Pierre. "But it was most the sweet, inquisitive, kindly interested aspect of thy face," she tells Pierre, "so strangely like thy father's, too—the one only being that I first did love—it was that which stirred the distracting storm in me" (p. 158). Isabel longs to be a part of Pierre's existence, a longing for a family she never had. She does not feel at peace with herself alone. "I feel that there can be no perfect peace in individualness" (p. 119). She wants to become part of all things, including a union with Pierre. But her response to him was sexual only after he first embraced her. She gave him at first "no gesture of common and customary sisterly affection. Nay, from his embrace had she not struggled? nor kissed him once; nor had he kissed her, except when the salute was solely sought by him" (p. 142). Far from pursuing sex, Isabel actually fears it in her nature and deliberately withholds herself—or tries to.

But Isabel is schizoid in part. After playing the guitar abandonedly, she becomes gentle again, confusing Pierre:

. . . it seemed well nigh impossible that this unassuming maid should be the same dark, regal being who had but just now bade Pierre be silent in so imperious a tone, and around whose wondrous temples the strange electric glory had been playing. (p. 152)

She is capable of, and is continually expressing, the qualities of passion and frigidity. Whether it is schizophrenia or manic-depression (it is not plain guile), Isabel goes forth "into the places of delight," but only, according to her words, that she "might return more braced to minister in the haunts of woe" (p. 156).

Pierre is not prepared for the excitations Isabel arouses in him. He is too caught up in his own idealized versions of love; he has tried to repress his feelings about the "secret deeper than beauty" (p. 7). When he thinks about the mystery face, before he finds out Isabel's identity, his thoughts and feelings are accompanied by a touch "of unhealthiness" (p. 53). His repressed sexuality is expressed whenever Lucy asks him about the face of Isabel. He becomes vehemently impassioned and imagines devils taunting him and mocking his love for Lucy. He feels that his "whole previous moral being was overturned" (p. 87) after learning about Isabel.

Pierre's introduction to Isabel is noteworthy. He receives a message from her, delivered by "a hooded and obscure-

looking figure, whose half-averted countenance he could but indistinctly discern" (p. 61), the personification of his id, his own unconscious thoughts breaking through and mirrored in the world about him. When Pierre returns to his room with Isabel's letter and sees himself in the mirror, the image is understandably "strangely filled with features transformed, and unfamiliar to him" (p. 62). This evocation by Melville of the unfamiliar and distorted qualities of our unconscious thoughts is one of the strongest themes throughout the book. When Pierre first sees Isabel, before getting the message from her:

The emotions he experienced seemed to have taken hold of the deepest roots and subtlest fibres of his being. And so much the more that it was so subterranean in him, so much the more did he feel its weird inscrutableness. (pp. 48-49)

Pierre's feelings for Isabel are "mixed and mystical" (p. 226); until he ultimately possesses her and satisfies the demands of his id, his "subterranean" feelings will remain mystical.

Pierre's sexual interest in Isabel is evident right away. She reminds him of Francesca in Dante's *Inferno,* who committed the Unpardonable Sin of premarital intercourse with Paolo. When he looks at Isabel "his eyes fixed upon the girl's wonderfully beautiful ear, which, chancing to peep forth from among her abundant tresses, nestled in that blackness like a transparent sea-shell of pearl" (p. 119). Isabel's features and darkness transfix him. "Thy all-abounding hair falls upon me with some spell which dismisses all ordinary considerations from me" (p. 145). From their first embrace Pierre knows that he will never be able to embrace her with a brotherly attitude. Despite all his protestations of his glorious ideal love, when he first takes Isabel in his arms:

Over the face of Pierre there shot a terrible self-revelation; he imprinted repeated burning kisses upon her; pressed hard her hand; would not let go her sweet and awful passiveness . . . they coiled together, and entangledly stood mute. (p. 192)

However ambiguous Melville wishes to leave the question regarding ultimate contact between the brother and half-sister, one thing is certain: Pierre is very ardent with Isabel, eager to hold her in his arms. The problem for him is one of ambivalence rather than ambiguousness. He is torn between two different emotions for the girl. He is capable of feeling reverence for her, she soars "out of the realms of mortalness" for him and becomes "transfigured in the highest heaven of uncorrupted Love" (p. 142); and he suffers from "strange wild heat" which she produces in him as well.

Pierre's idea to pretend to be Isabel's husband is a form of wish-fulfillment on his part, a way of dealing with the wild heat she stirs in him. This enables him to succeed in another sense, to complete the transposition he had been trying to make with his mother. "Possibly the latent germ of Pierre's . . . conversion of a sister into a wife—might have been found in the previous conversational conversion of a mother into a sister" (pp. 176-77). There is a decided change of role for both Pierre and Isabel in their union with each other. Isabel becomes his mother, and he fulfills Isabel's unconscious wish for her father. Isabel unblushingly contrasts her mother's love for her father with her own love for Pierre. "But I saw *thee,* Pierre; and, more than ever filled my mother toward thy father, Pierre, then upheaved in me" (p. 155). Her father was the first person she loved, and Pierre takes his place. Only by his becoming her father does the later comparison Melville makes with the Cenci portrait hold together. Besides reinforcing the theme of incest, the comparison of Isabel and Beatrice works to clarify some of the ambiguity of the story. It is evident finally that Pierre and Isabel have consummated their relationship in sexual union.

There are several clues in the book to help the reader resolve the ambiguity of Pierre's sexual relationship with his half-sister. Their willingness to aid Delly, for instance, shows their liberalness in the affairs of sex—their uninhibitedness perhaps, which will prefigure their own sexual union. Delly's trouble, in Isabel's words, is not an "unpardonable shame" (p. 155), and therefore Pierre and Isabel's union will also be pardonable.

When Pierre and Isabel are alone in his room they make love.[3] But Melville disguises it. They sit on the camp-bed in the dark. "Sit close to me," says Isabel. "Each felt the other's throbbing." Pierre puts his arm around her and holds her tight. He trembles and calls out her name "in a low tone of wonderful intensity" (p. 272). His tremor passes over to her as she puts her arm around him. Pierre initially fights against his desire, but he gives in and tells her not to call him brother. He makes love to her on the pretense that she is not his sister. They both choose to ignore reality. In a very imagistic sentence, Isabel says: "I would boldly swim a starless sea, and be buoy to thee, there, when thou the strong swimmer shouldst faint" (p. 274). He will rest his body upon hers. This brings to mind Pierre's earlier comments about lying upon Lucy, about his body being too heavy for her. He has no such reservations with Isabel. "How can one sin in a dream?" he asks her.

> And so, on the third night, when the twilight was gone, and no lamp was lit, within the lofty window of that beggarly room, sat Pierre and Isabel hushed. (p. 274)

Substitution of the word "lay" for "sat" seems in order in the above quote.

Their sexual union is harmful to their love. Isabel sees herself as "a vile clog" (p. 355) and tries to kill herself. As an illegitimate child she was "dirty" to the old couple taking care of her (they throw away a loaf of bread because she has touched it); she is considered a slut by Pierre's mother; and the girls at the sewing club refer to her as "some other ruined Delly, run away;—minx" (p. 157). With so many accusing fingers being pointed at her, her

association with Pierre must lead to guilt and self-abuse. "Heard ye ever yet of a good angel with dark eyes, Pierre?" (p. 314), she asks him, comparing herself to the still chaste Lucy. She can no longer abide Lucy, who symbolizes what she herself has lost through sexual contact with Pierre. Isabel determines to keep Lucy in her place, purposely arranging to be in Pierre's embrace while the door adjoining their rooms opens to Lucy's view. She becomes as jealous of Lucy as Pierre's mother had been of her. "One look from me shall murder her, Pierre!" (p. 313). The cycle for Pierre is complete.

Once his passions are satisfied, once Isabel is no longer a mystery for him, Pierre becomes embarrassed whenever he finds himself alone with her. It is quite obvious that Pierre's desire for her has faded: "involuntarily he started a little back from her self-proffering form" (p. 332). He no longer wants Isabel to touch him. His love, based on libidinal desires, is gone once those desires are satisfied. Also, he is shocked by what he has done. Pierre accepts the anger Lucy's brother directs at him for having violated (as the brother mistakenly believes) Lucy's honor. Pierre is "thoroughly alive to the supernaturalism of that mad frothing hate which a spirited brother forks forth at the insulter of a sister's honor—beyond doubt the most uncompromising of all the social passions known to man" (p. 336). As the violator of his own sister, Pierre is frothing with hate at himself. So much so that he seeks death. That he finds death at the hands of his sister is symbolically fitting.

Pierre's greatest anguish is caused by his inability to remain pure. The discovery of his father's sexual liaison with Isabel's mother shatters his idolization of his father, and also corrupts his own intentions of living a Christ-like sexless existence. He is initially resolved to help Isabel purely "to assuage a fellow-being's grief" (p. 104), not to exploit her sexually. The discovery that his motives are other than philanthropic is not easy for him to accept. We can see in Plinlimmon's description of the man who tries to be like Christ, Pierre's situation:

> in his despair, he is too apt to run clean away into all manner of moral abandonment, self-deceit, and hypocrisy (cloaked, however, mostly under an aspect of the most respectable devotion). (p. 215)

Pierre has sought to make an unconditional sacrifice of himself, a noble act which calls for the rejection of his past and his passions. His inability to do so is underscored by the leering face (or so it seems to Pierre) of Plinlimmon, who is looking down at him from the tower. Plinlimmon becomes the personification of Pierre's guilt feelings. The position on morality taken by Plinlimmon is exactly opposite the high standards Pierre wishes to follow. It is quite right then for Pierre to feel that Plinlimmon is mocking him. The inner torment he feels frightens him, and he fears it will break loose, that everyone will be able to see through him. When a photographer wishes to take his picture, Pierre predictably reacts violently. "To the devil with you and your Daguerreotype!" (p. 254) he tells the insistent photographer. He is afraid that his real self will be exposed in the photograph, as was his father's in the portrait that his mother hated.

In summation, Pierre's rather distorted love for his mother is a retreat from normal love. Pierre and his mother have a presex love, anticipatory love, not to be ruined by sex. Their love is "not to be limited in duration by that climax which is so fatal to ordinary love" (p. 16). Their relationship gives Pierre a closeness with femininity which he needs, but a safe closeness. Their love is "etherealized from all drosses and stains" (p. 16). This helps explain Pierre's reactions to Isabel after they have intimate relations. He and Isabel are not able to love as he and his mother. Despite Isabel's assurance that "there is no sex in our immaculateness" (p. 149), Pierre feels that there is no immaculateness in their sex.

Melville regards sex in this novel as a necessary evil. Pierre "seemed gifted with loftiness, merely that it might be dragged down to the mud" (p. 339). Man aspires to love, while his body clamors for lust. The design on the clergyman's cameo brooch emphasizes this: "the allegorical union of the serpent and dove" (p. 102). That's what marriage and sex are to Melville—the union of lust and love. In another snake image in *Pierre*, Melville writes: "I felt that all good, harmless men and women were human things, placed at cross-purposes, in a world of snakes and lightnings" (p. 122). These cross-purposes, we must surmise, are the clash of ideal love and instinctive sex.

Sex is man's downfall. Man "stoops" to sex. Pierre insists "I do not stoop to thee, nor thou to me; but we both reach up alike to a glorious ideal!" (p. 192). This is a vision he is not able to maintain. In the end, the chivalrous knight Pierre wishes both Lucy and Isabel dead. "For ye two, my most undiluted prayer is now, that from your here unseen and frozen chairs ye may never stir alive" (p. 358). He has been ruined by his conflicting feelings about sex and women. It is only justice, in Melville's mind, that in a world where sex is the cause of the hero's ruin, all the heroines should be killed off with him.

The equation that Melville makes in *Pierre* between sex and death is not a very pleasant one, nor does it seem in keeping with the otherwise fearless questioning of restrictive social norms usually associated with this author. But the final statement is a clear one: man is pulled downward, away from the realm of the angels, away from all noble acts and aspirations, by his own sexual nature. Love between a man and a woman might seem a wonderful thing, but to Melville the reality is as "haunting toads and scorpions" (p. 91).

Notes

1. *Pierre, or The Ambiguities* (Evanston and Chicago: Northwestern University Press and the Newberry Library, 1971), p. 107. Subsequent references to this edition, volume seven of the Northwestern-Newberry edition of *The Works of Herman Melville* edited by Harrison Hayford, Hershel Parker, and G. Thomas Tanselle, will be placed in parentheses in the text.

2. Martin Leonard Pops in *The Melville Archetype* (Kent: The Kent State University Press, 1970), p. 83, writes: "In *Pierre* and in such later works as "Benito Cereno" and *The Confidence-Man* possession and use of the phallic weapon suggests that sexual energy is unfailingly destructive." This is an overstatement, but Pops's discussion is well worth reading.

3. This view is in opposition to the more prevalent one, which insists that Isabel remained "physically unattainable." The most impressive of these critics remains Henry A. Murray. See his Introduction to *Pierre* (New York: Hendricks House, Farrar Straus, 1949), p. xcii.

Hershel Parker (essay date 1976)

SOURCE: "Why *Pierre* Went Wrong," in *Studies in the Novel*, Vol. VIII, No. 1, Spring, 1976, pp. 7-23.

[*In the following essay, Parker examines documentary evidence such as Melville's correspondence with his publishers and reviews of* Moby-Dick *to suggest reasons why the author's focus on Pierre's psyche was diverted to self-analysis of his own literary career.*]

Melville's intentions in writing *Pierre* have been debated with intermittent energy for several decades, but many basic questions remain unanswered.[1] When and in what mood did Melville conceive it and write it? Did he conceive and begin it in one mood and finish it in another? Did he intend it to be a popular romance and only inadvertently or recklessly alter its course so that it was foredoomed to failure? Did he intend all along that it be simultaneously a profounder book than *Moby-Dick* and a book most readers could appreciate at a superficial level? How much had he written when he broke off work at the end of 1851 to make a two-or-three-week trip to New York City? Why did he make that trip, anyway? When did Melville first know that the Harpers would insist on less generous terms for *Pierre* than for any of his earlier books they had published? Did the negotiations for the contract take place early enough to have affected the composition of *Pierre*? What effect, if any, did the reviews of *Moby-Dick* have upon the composition of *Pierre,* and when did any such effects occur? If Melville was angered by his friend Evert Duyckinck's review in November 1851, why did he apparently wait until February 1852 before breaking the friendship? How can one explain the discrepancy between the low page-estimate in the contract, signed 20 February 1852, and the much longer manuscript which may well have been handed over to the publishers that day? The answers to some of these questions depend partly on aesthetic judgments and are beyond the scope of this paper, but the answers to others lie in documentary evidence, some of it overlooked until now or not previously sorted out in meaningful ways.

We do not know precisely when Melville began planning *Pierre.* Leon Howard suspected that he had it in mind as early as September 1851, when he wrote his Pittsfield neighbor, Sarah Morewood, that the Fates had plunged him "into certain silly thoughts and wayward speculations" which would keep him for a time from reading two books she had sent him. Whether Melville was thinking about *Pierre* that soon or not, Mrs. Morewood very likely figured more largely in the conception of *Pierre* than we can now establish. The archness of Melville's special language in his letters to her is so clearly related to the diction of certain passages early in his book that one suspects they were partly written with her in mind as one potential reader, just as passages in *Typee* were obviously written as a way of teasing his household of sisters. Demonstrably, Mrs. Morewood's inveterate socializing is related to the composition of *Pierre.*[2] Reclusive as Melville later seemed to many people, he at this time sought occasions for "vagabondism" (as he wrote Hawthorne on 22 July 1851). After a notably sociable August, when Evert and George Duyckinck, the joint editors of the New York *Literary World,* were exhilarated but exhausted guests, Melville took several outings with members of the Morewood and Melville families into the Berkshire hills during Elizabeth Melville's confinement before the birth of Stanwix on October 22. Many scenes in the first half of *Pierre* record the hero's perambulations about a landscape obviously based on the stretch of the Berkshires from Mount Greylock to Lenox. There is no need to imagine that Melville took field notes during these excursions, but the fictional scenes do derive from his immediate experiences: in dedicating *Pierre* to "Greylock's Most Excellent Majesty," he declared that he had received from that sovereign "most bounteous and unstinted fertilizations." One such fertilization was soon clear to many in the Berkshire area. Some time in 1851 (more likely during the August feting of city friends than during the family excursions of the fall), Melville and his party had picnicked at the local curiosity, the Balanced Rock, where Mrs. Morewood had placed a music box far under the overhanging stone, so as to make it breathe "mysterious and enchanting music." Melville himself thereupon inscribed "MEMNON" on the rock, and J. E. A. Smith coyly hinted that this act was linked to the abandonment of a broken champagne bottle at its foot.[3] It certainly was linked to the creation of the "Memnon Stone" in *Pierre.* Such verifiable use of the Berkshire scenery, while gossip-worthy to Melville's acquaintances, is insignificant compared to the profounder fertilizations manifested in the interior landscape of the hero's mind early in the book, as well as in the later vision of Enceladus.[4]

Probably some weeks elapsed between the fertilizing excursions and their springing forth in Melville's new manuscript. On 6 November, two weeks after Stanwix's birth, Melville received from Duyckinck a clipping about the sinking of the *Ann Alexander* by a whale. In his reply on the seventh Melville wrote: "For some days past being engaged in the woods with axe, wedge, & beetle, the Whale had almost completely slipped me for the time (& I was the merrier for it) when Crash! comes Moby Dick himself

(as you justly say) & reminds me of what I have been about for part of the last year or two." Melville's 17(?) November letter in response to Hawthorne's praise of *Moby-Dick* speaks anticipatorially about the next book, but not in terms of specific work already underway: "Lord, when shall we be done growing? As long as we have anything more to do, we have done nothing. So, now, let us add Moby Dick to our blessing, and step from that. Leviathan is not the biggest fish;—I have heard of Krakens." All in all, these two letters offer only negative evidence: Melville did not take advantage of two conspicuous opportunities to make casual mention of a new work in progress. However, any new book was to be more ambitious than *Moby-Dick*: "I have heard of Krakens."[5]

The actual book as he began it was remarkably well-plotted, the story of Pierre Glendinning, the young master of the great country estate of Saddle Meadows (evidently in the patroon region of New York)—a high-minded American enthusiast in search of a cause to champion. The cause, when it patly came, involved him in extraordinary mental, moral, and sexual ambiguities and allowed Melville the chance to demonstrate his mastery of many novelistic techniques even while subtly training his readers to be discontent with the superficial perplexities the "brisk novelist" regularly served up. It was the most objective and tightly controlled piece of writing Melville had yet achieved: for the first time his hero (whether putatively himself as in *Typee, Omoo,* and *White-Jacket,* or plainly a fictional character as in *Mardi, Redburn,* or *Moby-Dick*) was not telling his own story in the first person, and for the first time in one of his novels (*Mardi, Redburn,* and *Moby-Dick*) the voice of the narrator-hero was not dissolving at times into that of the author. The writing went steadily and intensely, as we know from a letter Mrs. Morewood wrote George Duyckinck three days after the Melvilles had eaten Christmas dinner at her house. This is the first definite mention of *Pierre:*[6]

> I hear that he is now so engaged in a new work as frequently not to leave his room till dark in the evening when he for the first time during the whole day partakes of solid food—he must therefore write under a state of morbid excitement which will soon injure his health.—I laughed at him somewhat and told him that the recluse life he was leading made his city friends think he was slightly insane—he replied that long ago he came to the same conclusion himself but that if he left home to look after Hungary the cause in hungery would suffer.

Certain facts stand out, though the claims in this letter must be weighed against other evidence. By the end of 1851 Melville was deeply engaged on the manuscript of *Pierre,* not merely entertaining silly thoughts and wayward speculations of one sort or another, for this rehearsal of his working habits implies a considerable duration. Mrs. Morewood could hardly have described him as so engaged that he "frequently" worked through till dark if he had just begun the routine a week or two earlier. The routine had gone on long enough for her to think he would "soon" injure his health if he continued in it, not the sort of thing one says about a healthy farmer-writer of thirty-two when he has only briefly been laboring under extreme conditions. Melville had been working on *Pierre* for at least several weeks, from about the time of the American publication of *Moby-Dick* in mid-November, if not still earlier, establishing a pattern of incessant application from which he was not deflected by any farm or household obligations or any reviews of *Moby-Dick* which he inevitably saw (such as the two-part review in the Duyckincks' *Literary World*, to which he subscribed) or any which his friends and relatives passed on to him.

Mrs. Morewood's account forms the basis for speculation about how much of the book was written by the end of 1851. When working at top speed, as he had done in the summer of 1849, Melville could write the equivalent of fifty Harper pages a week. If he began *Pierre* as late as mid-November, he could have written 250 pages, more or less, before he interrupted his schedule for the trip to New York. This guess gains some support from the letter he wrote Mrs. Hawthorne from New York on 8 January 1852. Although mainly concerned with her earlier praise of *Moby-Dick,* it contains Melville's first reference to the work in progress: "But, My Dear Lady, I shall not again send you a bowl of salt water. The next chalice I shall commend, will be a rural bowl of milk." Melville was having wry fun in echoing that fellow Scotch nobleman, Macbeth, and being archly condescending to an intellectual woman, but a question suggests itself: why did he not say, "a rural bowl of milk and a city vial of hebenon"? One reason is that he was setting up an ironically cheery and familiar contrast to his whaling book, but another may simply be that he had not yet written any or very many of the city scenes. Internal evidence makes it certain that he had planned from the outset to have Pierre and Isabel come to the city, but if he had already drafted many of the city chapters it is unlikely he would have written to Mrs. Hawthorne just as he did, even allowing for playfulness: actual bulky and messy manuscript pages have a reality which scenes yet to be written rarely have. As evidence about the composition, this reference to "a rural bowl of milk" is far from conclusive, but it interlocks with Mrs. Morewood's description of Melville's pre-Christmas labor and with later evidence, internal and external. A reasonable assumption is that when Melville interrupted his work on the manuscript at Christmas time in order to go to New York City he had reached or nearly reached the end of the Saddle Meadows section but had not gotten very far, if at all, into the city section, which he then thought would consist of about a hundred pages, at most.[7]

This trip has been puzzling to biographers, especially since it seems to have been hastily arranged (otherwise Sarah Morewood would have had no reason for writing George Duyckinck as she did on 4 January 1852: "Were you not surprised to see Herman Melville in Town?")[8] and since it lasted so long (from the last days of December through the second week of January or into the third). Leon Howard handled the dates and the motive in gingerly fashion, as-

suming that Melville's rural household routine was upset because Elizabeth had decided that "she needed to go 'home' in order fully to recuperate from her confinement," but that before seeing her off to Boston Melville had "escorted her to New York" and "spent a few days" with Allan Melville, his brother and his lawyer. Howard continued: "He was too busy to see as much of Duyckinck as he usually did on his visits; but he probably took time to check up on a few city scenes he planned to use in *Pierre* and certainly talked over his literary business with Allan."[9] This is educated guessing. What drew Melville to New York, almost certainly, was the fact that he thought himself nearly enough finished with the manuscript of *Pierre* to negotiate a contract with the Harpers for a book of 360 pages and perhaps even get an advance on it. The evidence is in the letter Allan wrote to the Harpers on 21 January 1852, presumably several days after Melville had left for home:[10]

> My brother would like to have his account with your house to the 1st Feby made up and ready to render to me, as near that date as will be convenient to you[.]
>
> Respecting '**Pierre**' the contract provides that if the book exceeded 360 pages a corresponding addition should be made to the number of copies required to liquidate the cost of the stereotype plates &c for a book of that size[.] As the book exceeds that number of pages it will of course be necessary to ascertain how many more copies are to be allowed than provided by the contract for a book of 360 pages. The retail price of the book has been also raised beyond the price fixed by the agreement, which was one dollar & of course a corresponding increase per copy should be made to the author.

This letter, hitherto known only in the portion of the first paragraph printed in the *Log,* has complex ramifications, and requires going backwards before going forwards.

The previous April, the Harpers had refused Melville an advance on *Moby-Dick,* alleging two reasons, first "an extensive and expensive addition to our establishment" and, second, the fact that Melville already owed them "nearly seven hundred dollars" ($695.65, to be precise). Late in the summer Melville had come to terms with Richard Bentley on *The Whale,* receiving less of an advance against half-profits than he had been given for *Mardi* and *White-Jacket,* though more than for *Redburn.* The Harper contract for *Moby-Dick* signed on 12 September contained no provision for an advance, unlike those for the three previous books, and when the 25 November 1851 statement reached Melville it showed that he still owed the Harpers $422.82, despite the sale of 1,535 copies of *Moby-Dick* and fewer copies of the older books.[11] The contract for *Pierre* which Herman and Allan worked out with the publishers during the early days of the post-Christmas trip could not have pleased the brothers, since the Harpers had been more cautious than ever before, stipulating that for the first 1,190 copies sold, the number required to pay for the plates of the projected 360-page book, the author was to receive no royalties. During the interval between the drawing up of the contract and his return to Pittsfield (that is, apparently between early and mid-January), Melville reconceived the unwritten part of *Pierre* and saw that 360 would be too low an estimate to accommodate the new material he would introduce. Allan's letter either means that Melville had *already* written enough new pages (presumably while in New York City) to drive the book beyond the initial estimate, or, less likely, that Melville had made up his mind to write passages which he knew would undoubtedly drive the book well beyond that length. The letter gives no clue as to why Melville's intentions had altered so suddenly and drastically, but it makes plain his unusual concern to know the precise status of his account. Despite this concern there was no money forthcoming until 20 February 1852, the day the contract was signed, when the Harpers paid him $500, of which just over $200 was already earned (mainly from *Moby-Dick*), while only $298.71 was technically an advance. On or soon after the day the contract was signed, the Harpers were given the manuscript, which proved to contain not the 360 pages which the final contract still called for but 495 pages of text, exclusive of the preliminary pages in roman numerals. There was no sudden, inexplicable composition of roughly 150 pages of unplanned material after the contract was signed: the additions not in the original plan had probably all been completed by 20 February. At that time the 360 estimate was some six or seven weeks old and already more than a month out of date, but there was no legal necessity for altering it since the contract provided for adjusting the number of copies that had to be sold before Melville's royalties began, depending on the length of the book.[12]

Although Allan's letter removes the problem of how Melville managed to write 150 pages after the contract was signed, a major question remains, for the disappointing negotiations with the Harpers do not fully account for the drastic differences in subject matter and authorial attitude between the parts of *Pierre* presumably written before Melville's trip to New York and those surely written either during the trip or after he arrived home. Melville's experiences in New York had profoundly altered his feelings about his career as a whole as well as the manuscript at hand. For months he had been talking aloofly about fame, saying calmly that if he wrote the Gospels in his century he would die in the gutter. Hawthorne's approval of *Moby-Dick* had confirmed him in that mood, as Melville's response shows:

> People think that if a man has undergone any hardship, he should have a reward. . . . My peace and my supper are my reward, my dear Hawthorne. So your joy-giving and exultation-breeding letter is not my reward for my ditcher's work with that book, but is the good goddess's bonus over and above what was stipulated for—for not one man in five cycles, who is wise, will expect appreciative recognition from his fellows, or any one of them. Appreciation! Recognition! Is love appreciated? Why, ever since Adam, who has got to the meaning of this great allegory—the world? Then we pygmies must be content to have our paper allegories but ill comprehended. I say your appreciation is my glorious gratuity. In my proud, humble way,—a shepherd-king,—I was lord of a little vale in the solitary Crimea; but you have now given me the crown of India.

Judging from Books 17 and 18 of *Pierre,* what broke Melville's exalted mood was the sudden exposure to a large number of reviews of *Moby-Dick* before, during, and after his disappointing negotiations with the Harpers. At Christmas he may have focused for the first time on reviews which had been accumulating around the house, but more likely he gained access to a number of earlier reviews once he reached New York, at just the time of month when the January magazines were appearing with reviews, including some of the most scathing of all. In the aftermath of his abnormal work pattern, which must have left him psychologically and physically vulnerable, and with his hazardously ambitious literary experiment still incomplete, Melville was in no position to content himself with the lavish praise which he must also have seen, especially not after his dealings with the Harpers enforced upon him the realization that he might have to abandon the hope of earning a living as a writer just when he had become a great one.

Melville's reaction to the contract discussions and to the reviews soon found a convenient outlet in the manuscript, which he surely had at hand in New York for showing to the Harpers. Instead of pursuing the consequences of Pierre's unprecedented resolution, Melville struck out in Book 17 against the reviewers who had offered him perfunctory and irrelevant praise as well as those who had condemned him or grudgingly praised him for what he knew should have entitled him to profoundest homage. In his new mood Melville began writing passages which could have relevance only to himself, not to the Pierre he had so consistently characterized in the Saddle Meadows section: "And in the inferior instances of an immediate literary success, in very young writers, it will be almost invariably observable, that for that instant success they were chiefly indebted to some rich and peculiar experience in life, embodied in a book, which because, for that cause, containing original matter, the author himself, forsooth, is to be considered original; in this way, many very original books, being the product of very unoriginal minds." This section from the end of Book 18 is extraordinary as self-analysis, as Melville's own objective understanding of why *Typee* had become so popular and what its ultimate worth was, but it is wholly irrelevant to Pierre, who had had no such rich and peculiar experience in life and who (we are belatedly and distractingly told) had embodied whatever experiences he had had in magazines, not in a book. Whether or not Melville had intended all along to make Pierre turn writer once he reached the city cannot be established, but he surely had not intended to make Pierre's career distortedly mirror whatever the reviewers would be saying about *Moby-Dick* through the year's end and the start of 1852.[13] Planning and writing Books 17 and 18 disturbed Melville's judicious narrative distance from his hero so thoroughly that he never fully regained it, and destroyed the intended proportion of longer rural section to shorter city section.

The evidence, which is mainly in Book 17, has been read with an imperfect sense of the chronology of Melville's work on **Pierre**. One of the commonest (and obviously correct) assumptions about the book is that in portraying the asinine critics of young Pierre, Melville was taking satirical revenge on his own critics. (Since the 1930s it has been known that Evert Duyckinck himself was the model for the impudently aggressive joint editor of the *Captain Kidd Monthly*.) Aware that Melville was recalling aspects of his own literary career in this Book and the next, many critics, myself among them, have taken for granted that what the reviewers say of Pierre is either very like or else patently the opposite of what real reviewers had said of Melville's **Typee, Omoo, Mardi, Redburn, White-Jacket,** and **Moby-Dick.** That turns out not to be altogether accurate. When the phrases attributed to Pierre's critics are compared with the known reviews of Melville's first six books, it becomes obvious that in Book 17 Melville was not reacting *generally* to the reviews of all six of these books (or to a certain segment of them, such as those in religious periodicals).[14] Rather, he was reacting *specifically* to the reviews of his latest book, **Moby-Dick.** Lewis Mumford's impression in 1929 was partly right: it *was* the reviews of **Moby-Dick** which Melville was reacting to, but *not* at the time he conceived and began **Pierre**; rather, his reaction came only during or after his trip to New York, when at least half and probably more of the book was already completed. One cannot safely point to particular reviews which Melville must have read before he wrote Book 17, but among the most conspicuous American reviews of **Moby-Dick** and those British reviews of **The Whale** most likely to have reached New York by early January, Melville could have seen many examples of the phrases which he satirizes in **Pierre**. He twists them one way or another for his immediate satirical ends, but the words are readily found in the reviews of **Moby-Dick** as they are *not* found in reviews of his earlier books.[15]

When Pierre was complimented for *his surprising command of language,* Melville had just been praised for his "mastery over language and its resources" (the London *Examiner*), condemned for ravings "meant for eloquent declamation" (the Charleston *Southern Quarterly Review*), and denounced for his "rhetorical artifice," "bad rhetoric," and "incoherent English" (the New York *Democratic Review*). Where Pierre was commended for *his euphonious construction of sentences,* a reviewer had just condemned Melville for his "involved syntax" (the *Democratic Review*). Where Pierre was praised for *the pervading symmetry of his general style,* Melville had just been praised for his "bold and impulsive style" (the New York *Harper's New Monthly Magazine*), tolerated for his "happy carelessness of style" (the Hartford *Daily Courant*) and his "quaint though interesting style" (the Springfield *Republican*), blamed for a style "disfigured by mad (rather than bad) English" (the London *Athenaeum*), for his "unbridled extravagance" (the London *Atlas*), and for his "eccentricity"

in style (the London *Britannia*). There is a bare possibility that by mid-January Melville might have seen a reproach for his not adhering to "the unchanging principles of the truthful and the symmetrical" (the London *Morning Chronicle*). While Pierre's writings were praised for *highly judicious smoothness and genteelness of the sentiments and fancies,* Melville had just been condemned for his "forced," "inflated," and "stilted" sentiment (the *Democratic Review*) and for allowing his fancy "not only to run riot, but absolutely to run amuck" (the London *Atlas*). Where Pierre was *characterized throughout by Perfect Taste,* Melville had just been condemned for "harassing manifestations of bad taste" (the *Athenaeum*) and for "many violations of good taste and delicacy" (the New York *Churchman*), and called (by Evert Duyckinck) "reckless at times of taste and propriety" (the New York *Literary World*) and called also the author of scenes which neither "good taste nor good morals can approve" (the Washington *National Intelligencer*). A reviewer said that Pierre *never permits himself to astonish; is never betrayed into any thing coarse or new; as assured that whatever astonishes is vulgar, and whatever is new must be crude.* Reviewers had just praised Melville himself for his "original genius" and "wildness of conception" (the London *Atlas*), for "genuine" evidence of "originality" (the London *Leader*), and for his "lawless flights, which put all regular criticism at defiance" (the New York *Daily Tribune*). A critic had just found Melville's materials "uncouth" and the Americanisms of **The Whale** charming, although the book might not fall within "the ordinary canons of beauty" (the London *John Bull*). A reviewer also had found that Melville evinced "originality and freshness in his matter" (the Worcester *Palladium*). A critic declared that *vulgarity and vigor—two inseparable adjuncts—were equally removed* from Pierre. Reviewers had just condemned Melville for "'a too much vigour,' as Dryden has it" in the earlier books but unsurpassed "vigour, originality, and interest" in **The Whale** (the London *Morning Herald*), or praised him for "vigor of style" (the *National Intelligencer*), even while condemning him for "vulgar immoralities" (the New York *Methodist Quarterly Review*). A clerical reviewer declared that Pierre was *blameless in morals, and harmless throughout,* while real critics had just condemned Melville's "irreverence" (the Albany *Argus*), his "irreverence and profane jesting" (the Worcester *Palladium*), his frequent "profaneness" and occasional "indelicacies" (the Boston *Daily Evening Traveller*), and his "insinuating licentiousness" (the *Democratic Review*), or else deplored his "primitive formation of profanity and indecency" (the New York *Independent*). A religious critic declared that *the predominant end and aim* of Pierre *was evangelical piety.* Melville had just been denounced by clerical critics or pious lay reviewers for his "heathenish talk" and "occasional thrusts against revealed religion" (*John Bull*), for "sneering at the truths of revealed religion" (New York *Commercial Advertiser*), for "a number of flings at religion" (the *Methodist Quarterly Review*), and for "irreligion and profanity" and "sneers at revealed religion and the burlesquing of sacred passages of Holy Writ" (the *Churchman*).[16] Similar parallels abound: these are offered as readily available comments from the reviews and not necessarily the particular comments which Melville read, though he certainly read some of them.

This theory that Melville lost his once-superb control over his manuscript and began farcing it out with disastrously inappropriate scenes goes far toward explaining one of the most baffling aspects of the period of composition, the contradiction between Melville's apparent amity with Evert Duyckinck while in New York[17] and his cold letter on 14 February 1852 to the "Editors of the Literary World":[18]

> You will please discontinue the two copies of your paper sent to J. M. Fly at Battleboro' (or Greenbush), and to H. Melville at Pittsfield.
>
> Whatever charges there may be outstanding for either or both copies, please send them to me, & they will receive attention.

Nothing in the recent issues of the magazine seems adequate to account for Melville's extraordinary rudeness, and no private communication between Melville and the Duyckincks at this time has been preserved, aside from Melville's hasty note while he was in town. We have tended to look for some public cause, as in Leon Howard's proposal that the February letter was "a delayed petulant reaction against parts of his friend Evert A. Duyckinck's review of *Moby-Dick* in the *Literary World*."[19] Even the hedging "delayed" and "parts of" (after all, the review implicitly compared him to Shakespeare) do not account for the timing and the abruptness of Melville's simultaneous cancellation of subscription and friendship. Melville's action may have been caused by an event much more recent than the review, but discussing it requires another look backward.

Melville's resentment against the Duyckincks might never have surfaced so plainly without the combination of events in late 1851 and early 1852, but it had long been building. In a late (and presumably late-written) section of *Mardi* (chap. 180), Melville had first declared his independence of the Duyckinck circle, implying in the process just how much he must have resented Duyckinck's treating him not as potentially a great writer but as a sailor-author always on call to review nautical books or books of inland travel. On 12 February 1851, almost precisely a year before he cancelled his subscription to the *Literary World,* Melville had (not for the first time) refused a request from Evert:

> How shall a man go about refusing a man?—Best be roundabout, or plumb on the mark?—I can not write the thing you want. I am in the humor to lend a hand to a friend, if I can;—but I am not in the humor to write the kind of thing you need—and I am not in the humor to write for Holden's Magazine. If I were to go on to give you all my reasons—you would pronounce me a bore, so I will not do that. You must be content to believe that I *have* reasons, or else I would not refuse so small a thing.—As for the Daguerreotype (I spell the word right from your sheet) that's what I can not send you, because I have none. And if I had, I would not send it for such a purpose, even to you.—Pshaw!

you cry—& so cry I.—"This is intensified vanity, not true modesty or anything of that sort!"—Again, I say so too. But if it be so, how can I help it. The fact is, almost everybody is having his "mug" engraved nowadays; so that this test of distinction is getting to be reversed; and therefore, to see one's "mug" in a magazine, is presumptive evidence that he's a nobody. So being as vain a man as ever lived; & beleiving that my illustrious name is famous throughout the world—I respectfully decline being oblivionated by a Daguerretype (what a devel of an unspellable word!)

Then Melville had gone on to say, "I trust you take me aright. If you dont' I shall be sorry—that's all." Knowing in early 1852 that he still could not and would not scramble for attention in the magazines, Melville foresaw that literary tit-men like Duyckinck could destroy his career. Their olympian criticisms had retarded sales of *Moby-Dick,* and Melville must have had irrepressible inklings that his new manuscript contained passages more explosive than any in his earlier books, for all his desire to persuade himself that it would pass for "a regular romance." But the event which impelled his Valentine's Day letter may have been less a reaction to the review of *Moby-Dick* in the *Literary World* than to Melville's own act of writing Duyckinck into Book 17 as the joint editor of the *Captain Kidd Monthly,* out to pirate Pierre's daguerreotype. Having written (or even come to the point of writing) the passage ridiculing Duyckinck, Melville may have felt that honesty demanded that he break the friendship. However, if this happened with no further explanation than a cancelled pair of subscriptions, the Duyckincks must have remained puzzled until they read *Pierre.* (They reviewed it with horror, especially at the hints of incest and the apparently atheistic moral of the Plinlimmon pamphlet, but wrote not a word of Books 17 and 18.) Although some mystery still remains, in our speculations we should remember that the event which caused Melville to break the friendship need not have been a new action of Evert Duyckinck's or even a delayed reaction on Melville's part to the November review: the planning, the writing, and the aftermath of writing Books 17 and 18 were momentous psychological events to Melville.

The aesthetic implications of this arraying of old and new evidence are analyzed in the collaborative Higgins-Parker study. For now, suffice it to say that by Christmas of 1851 Melville thought himself at least two-thirds through his dramatic analysis of the way an explosive tragic revelation may impel an exceptional human being into sudden and ambiguous mental growth; and he had pretty much convinced himself that the book would pass as sensational fiction even while embodying tragic profundities forbidden in the marketplace.[20] Had he continued in the same vein, *Pierre* would have been one of the world's masterpieces, although it would probably have been scorned by the critics and readers of 1852. But during an interruption of his intense labor at least two demoralizing events occurred to compound the disruption of his work schedule: the Harpers refused to grant him a contract on terms as good as those for his earlier books, and Melville in his wrought-up state read many of the reviews of **Moby-Dick,** including some of the most hostile. Stung by the reviews and by the realization of his impotence against them, and very likely stung by the suspicion that, after all, his book could not succeed on the two levels as he had hoped, Melville was diverted from the exploration of Pierre's psyche into a psychological analysis of his own literary career. What he wrote either in New York or after his return to Pittsfield was often superb of its kind (Books 17 and 18 are masterpieces of literary satire, for instance) but disastrous for the book he had first conceived and had brought far on the way to completion in one sustained period of composition. The book as finished was much longer and much less unified than it would have been if Melville had retained his initial purpose and intensity of concentration.

Earlier critics and scholars have often been very near the truth. Lewis Mumford was wrong in saying that **Pierre** was both "conceived and written" in a "mood of defeat, foreboding, defiant candour";[21] in fact, only certain parts among those composed after early January are products of such a mood. Leon Howard is right in believing that Melville "conceived" the book in "unusually good spirits,"[22] although he may be wrong in suspecting that Melville was seriously planning or writing it as early as September and October 1851. Howard was almost right in thinking that Melville's plans altered after ("during and after" is the safe formulation) his return from New York, but in my judgment wrong in thinking that the new mood led to more powerful writing than that before the trip. Howard was misled into thinking that Melville gave Allan instructions for the contract about Valentine's Day: in fact, Melville had discussed the contract with Allan and the Harpers well over a month before that. Howard was also misled into thinking that the unanticipated pages were added after the contract was signed: most of them, if not all, were written by then; but he was right in thinking that most of these pages had to do with Pierre as an author. The conjunction of old but inadequately-studied evidence (such as the relation of the reviews of **Moby-Dick** to **Pierre**) and new evidence (especially Allan Melville's letter of 21 January 1852) allows the story to be told with much greater accuracy than ever before. As an account of a writer at work, this is a poignant story enough, but its full significance cannot be comprehended until Melville's achievement in the first half of the book receives the sort of criticism it deserves. After Higgins and I have converted all skeptics to our sense of the novel's literary stature there will be ample time to claim that the greatest single tragedy in American literature is that Melville broke off work on his manuscript when he did in order to make a routine business trip to New York City.

Notes

1. For a review of the controversy (in which Raymond Weaver, Lewis Mumford, Robert S. Forsythe, William Braswell, Harrison Hayford, and Leon Howard were the main participants) see my part of the "Historical Note" in the Northwestern-Newberry edition of *Pierre,* eds., Harrison Hayford, Hershel Parker, and G. Thomas Tanselle (Evanston and Chicago: Northwestern Univ. Press and the Newberry Library, 1971), pp. 396-403. The only serious recent contribution to the debate is Robert Milder, "Melville's 'Intentions' in *Pierre,*" *Studies in the Novel,* 6 (1974), 186-99. I disagree with most of Milder's conclusions, but we start with several of the same questions.

For freedom to work out this new telling of an often-told story, I am grateful to the John Simon Guggenheim Memorial Foundation. Merton M. Sealts, Jr., generously criticized an early draft. Over the last seven years Brian Higgins and I have been teaching *Pierre* to each other, and now we are writing a book about where and why it is good and where and how it fails. Our demonstration proceeds mainly by close reading of the text, but the aesthetic judgments from internal evidence are supported by the external evidence adduced in this article.

2. There are good accounts of what Evert Duyckinck called Mrs. Morewood's maelstrom of hospitality. See especially Luther S. Mansfield, "Glimpses of Herman Melville's Life in Pittsfield, 1850-1851," *American Literature,* 9 (1937), 26-48; Leon Howard, *Herman Melville: A Biography* (Berkeley and Los Angeles: Univ. of California Press, 1951), chaps. 7 and 8; and Eleanor Melville Metcalf, *Herman Melville, Cycle and Epicycle* (Cambridge: Harvard Univ. Press, 1953), chap. 8. Good coverage of Melville's socializing in October and November 1851, before and after the birth of his son Stanwix, is in Metcalf, pp. 125-26.

3. Godfrey Greylock [J. E. A. Smith], *Taghconic; or Letters and Legends about Our Summer Home* (Boston, 1852), as printed in Merton M. Sealts, Jr., *The Early Lives of Melville* (Madison: Univ. of Wisconsin Press, 1974), p. 195. Published about the end of September, 1852, Smith's account was written before he read *Pierre;* otherwise having mentioned Melville's use of the Pittsfield Elm in *Moby-Dick* he would surely have mentioned the use of the Balanced Rock in Book 7, as he did in the short biography he wrote for the Pittsfield *Sun* after Melville's death. See *Early Lives,* 145-47.

4. A striking instance of the fusion of outer and inner landscape is the start of Book 6, "Isabel, and the First Part of the Story of Isabel."

5. *The Letters of Herman Melville,* eds., Merrell R. Davis and William H. Gilman (New Haven: Yale Univ. Press, 1960), p. 139 (7 November) and p. 143 (17[?] November). Hereafter letters are quoted from this edition but normally cited only by their dates. Caution requires the reminder that Melville had expressed a very similar ambitiousness between the publication of *Mardi* and the decision to write the unambitious *Redburn.* See *Letters,* p. 83, especially the image of putting one leg forward ten miles, then having the other distance it.

Several weeks later, on 8 January 1852, Melville claimed that Hawthorne's letter, by revealing to him "the part-&-part allegoricalness of the whole," had altered the way he thought about *Moby-Dick*. As Harrison Hayford pointed out in "The Significance of Melville's 'Agatha' Letters," *ELH*, 13 (1946), 299-310, Melville had already developed a theory that great works of literature could be simultaneously popular and profound, appealing to the masses while being truly understood only by a select few. Still, Hawthorne's special insight into *Moby-Dick* may have affected Melville's attitude toward *Pierre*: the book would—this time by conscious design—work on dual levels, being comprehensible and salable as a regular romance with stirring passions awork yet susceptible of profounder interpretation by readers such as Hawthorne, whose understanding of *Moby-Dick* had given Melville a "sense of unspeakable security."

6. This letter is in Jay Leyda, *The Melville Log* (New York: Harcourt, Brace, 1951; rpt. with a Supplement, New York: Gordian Press, 1969), p. 441, and in Metcalf, *Herman Melville*, p. 133. The passage is quoted here from Metcalf, since the *Log* wrongly omits "so" before "engaged." Later Melville might fairly have been described as a recluse, but the raillery in this letter can be comprehended only if one keeps in mind Sarah Morewood's compulsive socializing. As for the pun, involved as he had been with the manuscript, Melville had not escaped the triumphal progress through the country made by the Hungarian patriot Kossuth, an event which had all but monopolized space in American newspapers that month.

Earlier in this letter is a passage which ominously parallels the response many reviewers had had and were to have toward *Moby-Dick* and which suggests that the climate of opinion in the Berkshires may have triggered Melville's aggressiveness toward conventional Christianity in *Pierre*: "Mr. Herman was more quiet than usual—still he is a pleasant companion at all times and I like him very much—Mr. Morewood now that he knows him better likes him the more—still he dislikes many of Mr. Hermans opinions and religious views—It is a pity that Mr. Melville so often in conversation uses irreverent language—he will not be popular in society here on that account—but this will not trouble him—I think he cares very little as to what others may think of him or his books so long as they sell well—"

7. For proof of how short Melville then thought the city section would be, see the following paragraph. In visualizing the proportions of *Pierre* it helps to recall that in the Harper edition "The Journey and the Pamphlet" starts on p. 277 and the last page of the text is p. 495, with preliminary pages, including the preface, in roman numerals. I am assuming that the Saddle Meadows section was composed pretty much in the final order, or at least that Melville made few or no additions to it during the last weeks of his

work on the book. In our longer study Higgins and I will examine the evidence for thinking that some of the sections set in the city may well have been juggled about before attaining their final positions.

8. Metcalf, p. 134. The *Log*, p. 443, erroneously prints "Were you surprised. . . ." For checking this variant and the one mentioned in footnote 6, I am much indebted to Paul R. Rugen, Keeper of Manuscripts, the New York Public Library.

9. Howard, p. 186. The best attempt to trace Melville's movements in late December 1851 and January 1852 is in the *Letters*, pp. 347-48, the note to Melville's letter to Evert Duyckinck conjecturally dated 9 January 1852. Normally precise, Davis and Gilman were not proof against the complexities of this period in Melville's life. The Morewoods did not return to New York on 29 December, as the editors say; they stayed on at Pittsfield for the New Year and returned on Monday, 5 January. (Mr. Rugen pointed out to me that Mrs. Morewood altered the date of her letter to George Duyckinck from 4 to 5 January. Perhaps she began it in Pittsfield and completed it in New York.) Mrs. Morewood did not expect to see Elizabeth Melville in New York on 5 January, as Davis and Gilman say. Knowing Mrs. Morewood's need for company, one can guess that her mention of remaining "quietly indoors" ever since her arrival might have taken her to midweek: probably the following "evening" she hoped to pass with Elizabeth was the eighth or ninth, which would still allow Elizabeth time to reach Boston by the tenth. Also, it is not Elizabeth's brother who recorded her presence with her children in Boston, but her sister-in-law. Furthermore, Melville's saying to Duyckinck that he was "engaged to go out of town tomorrow" does not mean he left for Pittsfield at the same time his wife went to Boston: the note specifies that he was going out of town only for the day. (Maybe he accompanied her and the boys to Boston, then returned immediately to New York.) Finally, "9 December" is a typo for "9 January," and 21 January 1852 fell on a Wednesday, not a Friday! Although its terseness is appealing, one had better scrap the account in the *Letters* and make do with the less concise version offered here.

We still know very little of what Melville did in town aside from the crucial business dealings discussed below. He gave a copy of *Moby-Dick* to his friend Dr. Robert Tomes on the fifth (see the Supplement to the revised edition of the *Log*, p. 930), wrote Mrs. Hawthorne on the eighth, and wrote Evert Duyckinck on the ninth, apparently, to say that he would be out of town all the next day: "I will be glad to call though at some other time—not very remote in the future, either." It is quite possible that Melville ensconced himself to work on *Pierre* in the same third-story room (presumably at Allan's) where he had labored on *Moby-Dick* a few months before.

10. Leyda describes this letter in *Log*, p. 445, as Allan Melville's "adjusting the details of the contract for

Pierre," and quotes the opening words about rendering an account as of 1 February. Leyda may not fully have realized the letter's significance in dating the composition of *Pierre,* and Howard and I in preparing the "Historical Note" neglected to question Leyda's description of it or to obtain a copy. The letter is quoted with the kind permission of the Harvard College Library. I am indebted to Carolyn Jakeman for help in obtaining and transcribing the letter and to W. H. Bond for permission to quote it here.

11. The April statement is in *Log,* p. 410; the November statement in *Log,* p. 438. For details of the earlier contracts see the various "Historical Notes" in the Northwestern-Newberry Edition as well as Harrison Hayford, "Contract: *Moby-Dick,* by Herman Melville," *Proof,* 1 (1971), iii-vi, 1-7. For a detailed analysis of the contract for *Pierre* (including the surviving draft passages) see Hershel Parker, "Contract: *Pierre,* by Herman Melville," forthcoming in *Proof,* 5 (1976); the draft indicates that Allan's first impression was that the book was more likely to run shorter than 360 pages rather than longer.

12. Of course, it is misleading to speak of 150 unexpected pages. Melville did not simply write the amount he had planned from the first, then write 150 pages more for insertion at various points. He must have failed to write certain scenes he had projected—and had prepared the reader to expect—and have failed to elaborate certain scenes as fully as he had intended. Therefore along with the parts not planned from the outset, the book, or the second half of it, also contains the condensed presentation of some scenes which had been in Melville's mind all along.

Melville's compulsion to work his new preoccupations into the manuscript at the cost of lengthening it was at war with his best pecuniary interests. He had reason for thinking that every few pages he added beyond 360 would cause the Harpers to add several copies to the number they had to sell before he began accruing royalties. If the Harpers were to hold him to the letter of the contract, Melville probably realized, the more he wrote the more he would lose. As it turned out, they did not do so. In *Pierre,* the "Historical Note," p. 378, Leon Howard explains: "Although the contract provided for an increase or decrease in the number of copies required to pay the cost of stereotyping if the book was not of the estimated length, and although a large number of copies (150) were given away, the publishers only claimed the first 1,190 for costs. It was probably a just claim in view of the increased retail price, but, within the terms of the contract, they could have claimed the proceeds from 400 more. . . ."

13. There is some internal evidence that Books 17 and 18 (possibly even the whole plan to have Pierre become an author) were not part of the original plan for the book but were added under the new, autobiographical impulse. Certain passages in "Young America in Literature" and elsewhere indicate that

Melville had been away from his manuscript (physically or psychologically or both) long enough simply to have *forgotten* what he had earlier written, a distressing sort of lapse in what had begun as his most thoroughly plotted book. Higgins and I will elaborate on these internal contradictions; Higgins's forthcoming study of "The Author and Hero in Melville's *Pierre*" painstakingly considers that judicious distance and what happened to narrow it.

One more point: I do not mean to imply that Books 17 and 18 were necessarily written before all the subsequent Books. They probably were not, but their inclusion led Melville to damage the unity of passages which were already drafted.

14. Melville might seem to be recalling the Protestant clerical and lay attacks on *Typee* and *Omoo* in satirizing the clerical compliments paid to Pierre's effusions, and perhaps he is; but even here the language attributed to the fictional reviewers is best seen as precisely the reverse of what was being said of *Moby-Dick.*

For quotations from the reviews of Melville's first five books we are still dependent on the *Log* and, especially, Hugh W. Hetherington's unreliable *Melville's Reviewers* (Chapel Hill: Univ. of North Carolina Press, 1961), though certain reviews have been reprinted in my *Recognition of Herman Melville* (Ann Arbor: Univ. of Michigan Press, 1967) and still more in Watson G. Branch's *Melville: The Critical Heritage* (London and Boston: Routledge & Kegan Paul, 1974). Melville's contemporary reception is also discussed in each of the Northwestern-Newberry "Historical Notes." Before this article appears the Melville Society will have published a booklet by Steven Mailloux and Hershel Parker, *Checklist of Melville Reviews,* which is based on new research as well as dozens of older reports of reviews.

15. The quotations in the next paragraph are representative of many that Melville could have seen during his stay in New York City. They do *not* constitute a representative sampling of the range of commentary on *Moby-Dick,* however; Melville was ignoring many points the reviewers were making, especially anything said in praise. The quotations may readily be located in MOBY-DICK *as Doubloon,* eds., Hershel Parker and Harrison Hayford (New York: W. W. Norton, 1970), or (in the case of the quotations from the New York *Independent* and New York *Churchman*) in Hershel Parker, "Five Reviews not in MOBY-DICK *as Doubloon,*" *ELN* [*English Language Notes*], 9 (1972), 182-85. The quotation from *Harper's New Monthly Magazine* is not from the review in the December issue but the commentary on the British reception in the January issue. A melancholy addendum: The reviews in the *Athenaeum* and the *Spectator* were probably the two British reviews most widely distributed in this country (mainly through reprintings). As bad luck had it, they were among the most hostile, and in a final ironic twist their justifi-

able complaints about the bungled catastrophe influenced opinion in the United States, where they did not apply at all to the text being sold and read. (No one knows why there was no "Epilogue" in *The Whale,* but I am convinced that its absence was not deliberate. Maybe the American proof stuck to the wrapping paper, being at the bottom of the bundle sent to England, and got lost.)

16. These accusations, however well grounded, would probably have caused anguish in any household in the country. The anguish in the Melville household may have been intensified by the memory that Elizabeth's father, Lemuel Shaw, the Chief Justice of the Massachusetts Supreme Court, had become the last judge to sentence a man to jail for blasphemy in that state. At the sentencing of Abner Kneeland in 1836 Shaw had offered this as the legal definition of blasphemy: "speaking evil of the Deity with an impious purpose to derogate from the divine majesty, and to alienate the minds of others from the love and reverence of God. It is purposely using words concerning God, calculated and designed to impair and destroy the reverence, respect, and confidence due to him. . . . It is a wilful and malicious attempt to lessen men's reverence of God" (See Leonard W. Levy, *The Law of the Commonwealth and Chief Justice Shaw* [Cambridge: Harvard Univ. Press, 1957], p. 52).

17. As long as we thought the unexpected pages (including Books 17 and 18) were added after 20 February, we were not wholly free to look for any motive for the Valentine's Day letter other than the much earlier (and basically laudatory) review.

18. See *Letters,* pp. 122-23, for why Melville should have been uncertain of the address of his old friend Fly.

19. *Pierre,* "Historical Note," p. 376.

20. Melville probably did not admit to himself until late in the composition that he might fail in making the book both popular and profound, but in Book 26 the accusatory letter from Pierre's publishers, Steel, Flint, & Asbestos, can hardly be construed as anything but Melville's self-accusation: "Sir:—You are a swindler. Upon the pretense of writing a popular novel for us, you have been receiving cash advances from us, while passing through our press the sheets of a blasphemous rhapsody, filched from the vile Atheists, Lucian and Voltaire."

It is important to remember that Melville's mood of "lamentable rearward aggressiveness" (his own term in Book 9 for Pierre's behavior toward Falsgrave) may have lasted a relatively short time. He may have passed out of that particular mood well before he finished the book, though the damage had been done. In the months between the completion of the book and its publication nothing in his recorded behavior suggests that he was weighed down by a sense of guilt and trepidation. Both his reckless behavior and his self-accusatory mood may have been brief indeed, so

brief that he all but forgot that he had anything to feel guilty about.

21. Lewis Mumford, *Herman Melville* (New York: Harcourt, Brace, 1929), p. 200.

22. Ibid., p. 183.

Carol Colclough Strickland (essay date 1976)

SOURCE: "Coherence and Ambivalence in Melville's *Pierre,*" in *American Literature,* Vol. XLVIII, No. 3, November, 1976, pp. 302-11.

[*In the following essay, Strickland asserts that, while Melville's handling of imagery in* Pierre *provides a kind of coherence for the work, the novel remains ultimately "inconsistent and incomplete."*]

Readers familiar with the mastery of **Moby Dick** have often been perplexed by the mystery of Herman Melville's succeeding novel, **Pierre.** The mystery lies in the contrast between the artfully controlled style and structure of the earlier book, published in 1851, and the sophomoric fustian of **Pierre,** which appeared just one year later. Critics have attempted to explain this apparent regression in craftsmanship by noting in **Pierre** Melville's satiric purposes in the outbursts of juvenile overwriting, which reflect the hero's immaturity, and by detailing Melville's intentional parody of the style and substance of conventional romanticism.[1] But there is further evidence of authorial control in the novel: the recurrence of certain motifs of imagery lends a degree of unity and coherence which shows that the hand of the master, though shaky, is still operating to shape **Pierre.**

This recurrent imagery is often manifested dichotomously, a technique which is completely appropriate to the theme of the novel, since its hero's vision is polarized. Pierre's journey through the course of the novel is from one extreme position to another, from optimism to pessimism, faith to cynicism, dependence to autonomy, joy to despair. Melville embodies these shifts of stance in the imagery of opposites: summer and winter, light and dark, country and city,[2] meadow and mountain, morning and evening.[3] But there is one further opposition and one apposition which enhance the complexity of Melville's design in **Pierre.** He consistently counterpoises the green fertility of vegetation with the arid intractability of stone.[4] And, apposite to the novel's central theme, the imagery of marble permeates **Pierre,** linking many of the oppositions and illustrating Melville's message which so agonizingly eludes Pierre: that the dualities such as light and dark, good and evil, Lucy and Isabel, as well as the perpetual strife between the human heart and head, are not irreconcilable at all but are inseparable parts of the whole continuum of life.

Pierre's two paramours, Lucy and Isabel, illustrate Melville's tactic of presenting two apparent opposites which are fused to make one whole through the marble imagery. No two characters could seem more opposite. The ethereal, sexless Lucy, who is said to belong "to the regions of an infinite day,"[5] is associated with everything light, bright, and angelical. Her name suggests "lucid," and Pierre's initial relation with her is as clear and unclouded as Melville's depiction of Lucy herself, bathed "in golden loveliness and light" (p. 83). In contrast, the sensual Isabel, who possesses "extraordinary physical magnetism" (p. 180), is described as literally and figuratively dark; her scenes with Pierre take place at night or twilight. Isabel is the very opposite of Lucy's transparent lucidity, for her origins and the thoughts and emotions she arouses in Pierre are veiled in mystery, just as Isabel is veiled by her ebony hair.

Melville describes a vision Pierre has of the two girls which both reveals their antithetical symbolism and foreshadows their synthesis: "For an instant, the fond, all-understood blue eyes of Lucy displaced the as tender, but mournful and inscrutable dark glance of Isabel. He seemed placed between them, to choose one or the other; then both seemed his; but into Lucy's eyes there stole half of the mournfulness of Isabel's, without diminishing hers" (p. 157). The "all-understood" world which Lucy represents is the fertile lowland world of Saddle Meadows, of joy and serene summer mornings, of repose and rural sunshine. It is the realm of rationality about which the immature Pierre naively rhapsodizes at the beginning of the novel: "It is a flawless, speckless, fleckless beautiful world throughout; joy now, and joy forever!" (p. 85).

In the "inscrutable" world to which Isabel introduces Pierre, dark, unknown forces of the unconscious and the undecipherable mysteries of metaphysics reign. It is Isabel's letter which first impels Pierre to look for the dark truth beneath the "flawless" surface of his life at Saddle Meadows and to discover his father's, his mother's, and his own weaknesses. Thus, as opposed to Lucy, Isabel is associated with the arid, stony, urban environment, with the bitter winter, the dark night, and with Pierre's intellectual anguish.

Yet, as different as Isabel and Lucy appear to be, they are linked through Melville's use of stone and marble imagery. Lucy represents the whiteness of the marble. She is variously described as a "snowy, marble statue" (p. 233), "marble-white" (p. 370), a "marble girl" (p. 400), "transparently immaculate, without shadow of flaw or vein" (p. 357). But Pierre needs a lesson in petrology. Just as he must learn that the world is not "flawless, speckless, fleckless," he must recognize the painful truth of Melville's cry: "Why in the noblest marble pillar that stands beneath the all-comprising vault, ever should we descry the sinister vein?" (p. 135).

Just as the purest marble contains traces of other minerals, giving marble its distinctive coloration of contrasts, so Isabel represents the black vein in the white marble. Pierre's friend, Charlie Millthorpe, notes just such a dark vein in Pierre: "There was ever a black vein in this Glendinning;

and now that vein is swelled . . ." (p. 400). His prophecy is fulfilled when he comments on Pierre's suicide at the book's conclusion, "The dark vein's burst . . ." (p. 405). Isabel's identification with the dark vein is made clear, for it is her black hair which envelops Pierre as she pronounces the final words over him: "'All's o'er, and ye know him not!' . . . and her whole form sloped sideways, and she fell upon Pierre's heart, and her long hair ran over him, and arbored him in ebon vines" (p. 405).

The symmetry of Isabel's mirror-image relationship with Lucy is also revealed in this passage, for Lucy, in the naive ignorance of Saddle Meadows, had longed to be able to say to others, "They know him not;—I only know my Pierre" (p. 61). And, contrary to Isabel's "ebon vines" which now enclose Pierre, Lucy is associated with green vines, called by Pierre "green heart-strings" (p. 359), wreathing her easel. The fact that these "green heart-strings" are stripped from Lucy's easel when she comes to the city and that Isabel's black vines encircle his heart demonstrates Pierre's failure to keep the forces that Lucy and Isabel represent in equilibrium and his inability to perceive their inextricability.

This dualism is portrayed in the depiction of the mountain which is simultaneously the appealing Delectable Mountain and, from another perspective, the terrifying Mount of the Titans. Lucy and Isabel, the Delectable Mountain and Mount of the Titans, as well as all the other polarities of the novel, are like the "two mutually absorbing shapes" Pierre cites from Dante's *Inferno,* neither "double now, / Nor only one!" (p. 111). Thus, too, can the forces which contend for loyalty in the human soul neither resolve into complete separateness nor fuse homogeneously into one. Both the catnip and the amaranth compete for dominion on the mountain. Lucy, who represents the light of the heart, domestic tranquillity, and knowledge that is readily comprehensible to man, is the green catnip, "man's earthly household peace" (p. 386). Isabel, the girl of dark mystery who spurs Pierre to his recondite speculations, is the sterile amaranth, emblem of man's "ever-encroaching appetite for God" (p. 386).

The fact that Isabel is now associated with the whiteness of the amaranth, the color previously ascribed to Lucy, shows that Melville finally conceives of the two as one entity. Indeed, white is here invested with all the ambiguity and complexity of "the whiteness of the whale" in *Moby Dick.* For white, besides its prior association with the spotless Lucy, also describes flawed characters, such as Pierre's father, the equivocating Reverend Falsgrave, and Plotinus Plinlimmon, the advocate of expediency.[6]

Thus, it appears overly simplistic to assume that white is the color of purity and black its opposite, just as Pierre errs in facilely terming Lucy and Isabel his "Good Angel and Bad Angel" (p. 403). The separate attitudes associated with both Isabel and Lucy provide an incomplete outlook; only together do they make a whole. The title of Book IX reveals this indissoluble synthesis of the forces represented by the two girls: "More Light, and the Gloom of That Light. More Gloom, and the Light of That Gloom" (p. 195). Lucy Tartan's name also hints of this truth, for, like marble, a tartan always consists of more than one color.

It is Pierre's ignorance of the mixed elements in himself and all humanity which causes his career of grief. His conception of his father, who is consistently characterized in terms of stone and marble imagery, is an example. And, since Pierre's name means "stone" in French, the implications associated with his father's character should apply to Pierre also.

Pierre, in the ignorance of immaturity, first conceives of his dead father as a perfect saint. In Pierre's heart is enshrined "the perfect marble form of his departed father; without blemish, unclouded, snow-white, and serene . . ." (p. 93). When Pierre discovers his father's alleged iniquity, however, he completely reverses this idealized image of his father and of the world of Saddle Meadows. Pierre is incapable of moderation in his appraisals, and the violence of his reaction against his father is at the other pole from his former adulation.

The two extreme versions of Pierre's father are represented by the two differing portraits, which should have earlier given Pierre an inkling of the two sides of his father's personality. But Pierre is unable to affirm simultaneously these inseparable light and dark elements of human nature.[7] Pierre had failed to see the dark veins of sin and human weakness beneath the "snow-white" surface of his father's memory. After rejecting the saintly image of his father, he then sees him as completely blackened with sin.

At the end of the novel Pierre has allowed the darkness to supplant entirely the whiteness in his outlook on life, to the point that his eyes literally no longer can tolerate the light. He refuses to live in the holistic world of black and white mankind; he cannot view his father and himself as both black-and-white but insists on judging conduct through the perspective of either / or extremes. Pierre cannot admit that the white, idealized version of his father, symbolized by the world of Lucy and light, is valid only when fused with, not replaced by, the darker knowledge of human sin represented by Isabel, and vice versa.

The parable of the mythical Enceladus makes clear this mixed heritage of all humanity. Enceladus, whose fate and aspirations are identical with Pierre's, was the offspring of both heaven and earth. His claim to divine parentage made him assault the heavens for admission "to regain his paternal birthright" (p. 389), but the taint of his terrestrial mother kept him in bondage on earth. His fate, as well as Pierre's, was adumbrated by Melville in the very beginning of the book in the description of the ruins of Palmyra: "the proud stone that should have stood among the clouds, Time left abased beneath the soil" (p. 28).

Pierre, too, feels himself prompted by inner divinity, when he undertakes his course of Christ-like self-sacrifice for Isabel. But he, too, fails to escape his earthly manacles and ends paralyzed in a stony prison. Pierre must acknowledge that, "though charged with the fire of all divineness, his containing thing was made of clay" (pp. 134-135) when he realizes that his heavenly aspirations, his struggle to be completely virtuous, are partially motivated by incestuous desire for Isabel. Striving to be god-like, Pierre finds himself all too humanly fallible.

Yet, to the end, he resists capitulating to the knowledge of the inextricable good and evil, divinity and mortality, in himself and all humanity. In a final effort to escape the ignominious bonds of his mortal body, Pierre commits suicide, even at the point of death refusing to admit that he is an underling to God's decrees.

Pierre's assumption of a god-like role, first by attempting to practice the dictates of Christ without compromise, and then by seeking to penetrate the mysteries of existence, puts him in direct opposition to the recommendations of Plinlimmon's pamphlet. This tract raises the central philosophical question expounded by this allegory of the human soul, caught between the warring claims of its heavenly father, God, and its terrestrial mother, the world. The pamphlet urges man to accept the limitations imposed by the fact of his mortality.

The imagery Melville employs throughout the novel which shows opposites not as eternally separate and mutually exclusive but as linked points on a single continuum may appear to indicate that Melville feels such relativism to be the solution for Pierre's dipolar oscillation between extremes. But the difficulty here lies in the fact that Plinlimmon ignores the "heaven-aspiring" component in man and capitulates wholly to the "terrestrial taint" (p. 389), to borrow terms from the Enceladus analogy again. Melville insists upon "the organic *blended* heavenliness and earthliness of Pierre, another mixed, uncertain, heaven-aspiring, but still not wholly earth-emancipated mood" (p. 389; italics mine).

In the description of Enceladus Melville offers Pierre only two extreme alternatives and ignores the possibility of the compromising, middle way espoused by Plinlimmon: "Wherefore whoso storms the sky gives best proof he came from thither! But whatso crawls contented in the moat before that crystal fort, shows it was born within that slime, and there forever will abide" (p. 389). Pierre as the soul of man has only two choices: to be a stolid, ignoble creature (denoted by "it," "whatso") in the slime of earth or to be a human being (characterized by the words "whoso," "he") perpetually trying, and perpetually failing, to escape his humanity and gain full divinity. Henry Murray is correct in saying that the moral of this book "is that there is *no* moral. . . ."[8]

Thus, like Plinlimmon's pamphlet, Melville's book "seems more the excellently illustrated re-statement of a problem, than the solution of the problem itself" (p. 243). And perhaps this sense of incompleteness is one source of many readers' and critics' dissatisfaction with the novel. While it is true that the eddying complexities of *Pierre* approximate the ambiguities of life with a vengeance, one expects internal clarity and order from a carefully crafted work of art.

Melville seems of two minds about *Pierre*; he has made it half comedy and half tragedy, half parody and half serious philosophy.[9] Finally, Melville stubbornly refuses to deliver any answers to the reader, though the carefully constructed framework of imagery permeating the book implies a Hawthornian answer of acceptance of the mixed nature of humanity, where good is never absolute and evil never absent. The synthetic fusion, as in variegated marble, of the dichotomous images of the novel implies that good and evil, man's heavenly aspirations and mortal weaknesses, can viably co-exist in human nature.

The fused dichotomous imagery of fertility and aridity also demonstrates how the imagery of the novel implies what its denouement denies. The green vegetation of vines and flowers represented by Lucy and the summery, rural milieu of Saddle Meadows is opposed to the sterile stone represented by Pierre's devotion to Isabel in an urban, wintery environment. Isabel's face is often compared to Gorgon's (pp. 73, 91), though Pierre denies the correspondence when she asks him directly, "'Tell me, do I blast where I look? is my face Gorgon's?'" (p. 222). Pierre replies: "'Nay, sweet Isabel; but it hath a more sovereign power; that turned to stone; thine might turn white marble into mother's milk'" (p. 222). This prediction is ironically negated in the end of the book, however, when Pierre wrests the poison from Isabel's bosom with which he kills himself. He then concludes that Isabel's "mother's milk" is instead "death-milk" (p. 403). And Isabel's face does indeed turn Pierre to stone, for his dedication to her, and thence to the mysteries of existence, turns him against the glad joys of life and isolates him from common humanity until, as Melville had predicted after Pierre read Isabel's letter, "his petrifying heart dropped hollowly within him, as a pebble down Carisbrooke well" (p. 198).

Thus, Pierre's devotion to the forces Isabel represents, his antitheodicean speculations, necessitate his total denial of the forces of vitality symbolized by Lucy. He must give up *l'allegro* for *il penseroso,* the country for the city, Lucy's transparency for Isabel's mystery. And this preoccupation with the dark rather than the light is a life-negating process. For Pierre, extreme alternatives are mutually exclusive rather than symbiotic.

But Melville unites, as Pierre is unable to, the imagery of the two opposites, green growth and sterile stone, when he describes the rocks on the Mount of the Titans: ". . . for the rocks, so barren in themselves, distilled a subtle moisture, which fed with greenness all things that grew about their igneous marge" (p. 385). Melville had noted in the beginning of the book that "green is the peculiar signet of all-fertile Nature herself. . . . For the most mighty of nature's laws is this, that out of Death she brings Life" (p.

29). Such imagery suggests that it is possible to live with the wisdom that is woe, to unite the antagonistic facets of human nature.

For, even in Pierre's stone prison of his egotism and pride, "the stone cheeks of the walls were trickling" (p. 402). Could this moisture, too, yield life in inhospitable stone? Melville describes the Enceladus rock itself as "turbaned with upborne moss" (p. 387). The implication of the union of stone and vegetation imagery is that man can live as a hybrid of opposites, of "organic blended heavenliness and earthliness." Chastening self-knowledge could yield new growth rather than result in self-destruction. But Melville undercuts this possibility when he says Pierre was unable to gain comfort and caution from the Enceladus myth, unable to "leap the final barrier of gloom . . . flog this stubborn rock as Moses his, and force even aridity itself to quench his painful thirst" (p. 388).

Perhaps the thirst-quenching moisture would have been "chill as the last dews of death" (p. 385), as was the water on the Mount of the Titans. But perhaps the painful awareness Pierre gained of his human limitations would permit him to live and grow with true self-knowledge, recognizing that he is neither completely good nor completely evil but capable of both. The stony Mount of the Titans exhibited such a renewal of life out of death when it "put forth a thousand flowers [both amaranth and catnip], whose fragile smiles disguised his [Enceladus'] ponderous load" (p. 389). But in the world of Pierre's mind, as in Eliot's waste land, stone yields no fructifying water but only despair.

Though the imagery of marble combines light and dark elements and Melville fuses the opposites of fertility and aridity, Pierre cannot similarly unite the antithetical forces which compete for his allegiance. Unable to cope with his divergent desires, he is sundered by their opposite attractions. Herman Melville's novel *Pierre* exhibits a similar bifurcation; the meshed imagery of opposites implies a hopeful acceptance of imperfect reality, while the hero's bombastic defiance urges continued futile rebellion against the ignoble fact of checkered human nature. Thus, *Pierre* looks both forward and backward in the Melville canon: backward to Captain Ahab's "ungodly, god-like" usurpation of divine prerogative in *Moby Dick* and forward to Captain Vere's awareness in *Billy Budd*[10] of the impossibility of perfect human justice and his faith in ultimate acquittal by divine judgment. In *Pierre* Melville can neither laud nor condemn wholeheartedly Ahab's indomitable questing spirit or Vere's resolute and resonant humanity. And there is no Starbuck, no Ishmael to perceive the hero's valiance while lamenting his error.

"Pierre's world is gone," as F. O. Matthiessen notes, "but, contrary to Shakespeare's method, nothing rises to take its place and assert continuity."[11] The kindly, complacent, pompous Charlie Millthorpe hardly qualifies as Horatio or Fortinbras. Melville's unwillingness to take a positive stand *for* some character or solution, rather than merely *against* the opposite extremes of Pierre and Plinlimmon, may account for the reader's frequent failure to recognize the novel's satiric intentions. True satire is basically optimistic. Its end is to expose folly as a first step toward improvement. But Melville dooms Pierre to failure. He never allows his hero even the possibility of merging the extreme alternatives which split him, although Melville accomplishes this feat himself in the marble and stone/ verdure imagery.

Thus, the novel provides no hope for the future and no proposed philosophic solution. Pierre's suffering, without the possibility of amelioration, is pathetic rather than satiric. Pierre's failure cannot even be presumed to be Melville's unequivocal recommendation of how *not* to live, for often Melville seems to share Pierre's sense of his own superior vocation and scorn for the other characters.

The imagistic patterns of **Pierre** provide a framework of coherence which shows the extent of Melville's effort in the book, but his ambivalence toward the hero undercuts this accomplishment. Melville's book, like Pierre's, is inconsistent and incomplete. It portrays the catastrophe of perpetual vacillation between resistance and resignation while never resolving its own vacillations.

Notes

1. For example, William Braswell, in "The Satirical Temper of Melville's *Pierre*," *American Literature,* VII (Jan., 1936), 424-438 and "The Early Love Scenes of Melville's *Pierre*," *American Literature,* XXII. (Nov., 1950), 283-289, discusses the novel as satire. Raymond J. Nelson, "The Art of Herman Melville: The Author of *Pierre*," *Yale Review,* LIX (Winter, 1970), 197-214, cites specific objects of parody in *Pierre*.

2. See James Polk, "Melville and the Idea of the City," *University of Toronto Quarterly,* XLI (Summer, 1972), 277-292, on the country-city thematic opposition.

3. Michael Davitt Bell, in "The Glendinning Heritage: Melville's Literary Borrowings in *Pierre*," *Studies in Romanticism,* XII (Fall, 1973), 746, notes, "*Pierre* is built, thematically and structurally, upon a series of interrelated dichotomies. . . ." Richard Chase, "An Approach to Melville," in *Psychoanalysis and American Fiction,* ed. Irving Malin (New York, 1965), pp. 111-120, also mentions the novel's thematic oppositions. R. K. Gupta, "Imagery in Melville's *Pierre*," *Kyushu American Literature,* No. 10 (Dec., 1967), 41-49, presents a salient discussion of imagery.

4. H. Bruce Franklin's chapter on *Pierre,* in *The Wake of the Gods: Melville's Mythology* (Stanford, Calif., 1963), contains the most thorough discussion of stone imagery. Saburo Yamaya, in "The Stone Image in Melville's *Pierre*," *Studies in English Literature* (Japan), XXXIV (1957), 31-57, argues that Pierre's identification with a stone implies his gradual transcendence of earthly concerns and attainment of Nirvana.

5. Herman Melville, *Pierre; or, The Ambiguities,* with a Foreword by Lawrance Thompson (New York, 1949; rpt., 1964), p. 24. Subsequent citations refer to this edition and appear in parentheses in the text.

6. James Kissane, in "Imagery, Myth, and Melville's *Pierre*," *American Literature,* XXVI (Jan., 1955), 569, believes that the image of whiteness, associated with both the spotless Lucy and Pierre's sinning father, symbolizes the ambiguity and relativism of good and evil.

7. Merlin Bowen, *The Long Encounter: Self and Experience in the Writings of Herman Melville* (Chicago, 1960), p. 161.

8. Henry A. Murray, introduction to *Pierre; or, The Ambiguities* (New York, 1949), p. xvi. (Italics in original.)

9. Newton Arvin, *Herman Melville* (New York, 1950), p. 231, though denying Melville's intentional parody in *Pierre,* notes, "there is something in the violence, the overheatedness, the hysterical forcing of now one note, now another, in the novel, that inescapably suggests a doubleness in the mind of the man who wrote it, a bitter distaste of and disbelief in his own book in the very process of writing it. . . ." One senses Melville's ambivalence in the fact that Pierre is depicted alternately as ludicrous and heroic, the object of Melville's ridicule and grudging admiration.

10. *Billy Budd* was begun in the 1880's. It was unfinished at Melville's death in 1891 and not published until 1924.

11. F. O. Matthiessen, *American Renaissance: Art and Expression in the Age of Emerson and Whitman* (New York, 1941), p. 469.

Brian Higgins and Hershel Parker (essay date 1978)

SOURCE: "The Flawed Grandeur of Melville's *Pierre*," in *New Perspectives on Melville,* edited by Faith Pullin, Kent State University Press, 1978, pp. 162-96.

[*In the following essay, Higgins and Parker consider the various ways in which* Pierre *fails as a novel, at the same time proclaiming it the best psychological novel that had been written in English by the middle of the Nineteenth Century.*]

Pierre was not conceived as a lesser effort, a pot-boiler like **Redburn,** which Melville disparaged as something he wrote to buy tobacco with. Judging from his response to Hawthorne's praise of **Moby-Dick** in mid-November, 1851, Melville intended his next book to be as much grander than his last as the legendary Krakens are bigger than whales.[1] Never a novelist or romancer within the ordinary definitions, Melville in **Moby-Dick** had attempted to convert the whaling narrative, a flourishing division of nautical literature, into a vehicle for the philosophical and psychological speculations a pondering man like him was compelled toward. *Pierre* is his comparable attempt to convert the gothic romance (in one of its late permutations as sensational fiction primarily for female readers) into a vehicle for his psychological and philosophical speculations (now in this order of importance). The technical sea-knots he untied in *Moby-Dick* are grappled with again in the lacy toils of *Pierre*. In the earlier book, certain obligatory scenes, the staple of any whaling story, had to be converted into chapters which would retain their sturdy informativeness while advancing Melville's higher purposes. At best, as in 'The Try-Works', routine exposition was transformed into intense philosophical drama. Much the same way, Melville in *Pierre* inherited a Gothic toybox stuffed almost as full as Poe's with mysterious family relationships, enigmatical recollections of long-past events, suspenseful unravelling of dark, long-kept secrets, and landscapes symbolical of mental states, but once again in the best passages the trivial subgenre bore up under the weight of intense psychological and philosophical drama.

While *Moby-Dick* succeeded for many of its first readers, even if only as a reliable source of cetological information, *Pierre* failed disastrously on all levels. Yet Melville's basic preoccupations and aesthetic strategies are almost identical in both, except that in *Pierre* he shifted considerably from metaphysics toward psychology. Many of the themes of *Moby-Dick* recur, among them the determinant power of wayward moods over human destiny and the tragic necessity that loftier souls hurl themselves against the unresponsive gods in order to assert their own godhood; many of the images recur, especially the sliding, gliding aboriginal phantoms which link Fedallah and Isabel as embodiments of the Unconscious.[2] Stirred by these or other powerful elements, whether or not related to *Moby-Dick,* the best readers of *Pierre* have paid tribute to the heroic intellectual tasks Melville undertook in it. Yet of them only E. L. Grant Watson thought those heroic tasks had been successfully accomplished,[3] while others more often admired the endeavour, whatever they construed it to be, but praised only one aspect or another of the performance. This critical ambivalence toward *Pierre* is captured in the concluding assessment of the Historical Note in the Northwestern-Newberry Edition: 'none of Melville's other "secondary" works has so regularly evoked from its most thorough critics the sense that they are in the presence of grandeur, however flawed'.[4] But scholars and critics have not been able to define the precise nature of the book's grandeur or the precise nature of the flaws which prevent it from being the masterpiece which *Moby-Dick* indisputably is. The problem of how *Pierre* fails can be answered only by rigorous attention to both biographical and aesthetic evidence. Our answers derived from documentary evidence are presented elsewhere; here we focus on evidence from within the book itself.[5]

To understand Melville's achievements and failures in *Pierre,* especially the unusual complexity of its plottedness, the air it initially breathes of being all worked out in advance, requires going backwards beyond *Moby-Dick.*

Though real-life adventure dictated the simple, suspenseful outline of *Typee,* the book is marred by confusing shifts in narrative attitude, and several late-written chapters betray Melville's pragmatic necessity to overlay useful information onto his slim set of personal actions and perceptions. *Omoo* is much more of a piece, but its secure point of view does not wholly disguise the tinkering process by which Melville added chapters or parts of chapters as he gained access to certain sourcebooks or became absorbed with a particular topic. The first chapters of *Mardi* reveal far greater literary control than *Typee* and *Omoo,* but much of the book is notoriously 'chartless'. Far from being written consecutively according to a well-designed plan, the book reflects Melville's altering interests, as when the lengthy section of political satire was plumped down into a manuscript already thought of as completed. The latter half of *Redburn* is less unified than the first, despite the power of individual scenes. Most critics agree that an alteration in the point of view blurs the distance between Melville and his narrator and between the narrator and his younger self. As with *Mardi,* Melville seems to have drafted an ending of *Redburn* before inserting lengthy sections of new material, possibly even adding a major character. In *White-Jacket* Melville skilfully deals out through the book little sets of chapters concerning the Jacket, flogging, places visited or passed in the voyage, and chapters anatomizing the man-of-war and its inhabitants. His narrator this time is close enough akin to himself to speak the most profound thoughts Melville could think on subjects such as human societies, and even shares his own lesser crotchets and compulsions. Still more ambitious than *White-Jacket,* with epic and tragic drama the models rather than a somewhat perfunctorily allegorical anatomy, *Moby-Dick* triumphs over its grabbag qualities. Melville's narrator is once again all but indistinguishable from the author in his patterns of thought, and as much more complex than White Jacket as Melville himself had become during the intervening year or two. Still, Melville's letters to Hawthorne show that however strong the 'pervading thought that impelled the book', the completion of *Moby-Dick* involved last-minute patchwork. After the first half or so had gone to press, chapters or parts of chapters were inserted here and there in the latter parts of the manuscript. Unlike his first three books, *Moby-Dick* triumphantly sustains its power to the end. By *Moby-Dick,* however, an ominous pattern had emerged: when Melville failed, it was not at the outset of a book, but later on, when the initial impulse had faded.

We are convinced that in *Pierre* Melville knew what he wanted to do when he set out to write and that for many chapters (and entire 'Books') he did very much what he had planned, exhibiting an intellectual power and artistic control which before this he had manifested only in *Moby-Dick.* Leon Howard thought that *Pierre* was 'possibly the most carefully planned' of all Melville's novels, even though he also thought that Melville's attitude toward his plot changed after the eighth Book and that he subsequently made unexpected enlargements.[6] But we believe the evidence shows that what changed first was not

Melville's attitude toward his plot but toward his literary career: his unsuccessful efforts to peddle his manuscript on the good terms he had previously enjoyed coincided with his reading some of the most condemnatory reviews of *Moby-Dick,* so that he had good reason to feel that his career might well be brought to an abrupt end. Swiftly reconceiving the plot, Melville used the unfinished manuscript as an outlet for his all-absorbing preoccupation with authorship, not only introducing unplanned-for elements but also condensing or otherwise altering parts already written or projected. Still, signs of Melville's careful planning undeniably remain evident everywhere throughout the first half of *Pierre* and survive even later, especially at the level of plot details, just where he had never manifested anything approaching a compulsive tidiness.[7] A few awkwardnesses can be adduced,[8] but by and large the plotting in *Pierre* (at least in the first half) is intricate and accurate, and of a novelistic kind new to Melville. To the end of Book XIV, 'The Journey and the Pamphlet', action taking place in the novel's present occupies just four days, with Pierre and his companions leaving Saddle Meadows early on the morning of the fifth; lengthy flashbacks to different periods in the past illuminate and explain developments in the present. Care in plotting is also obvious— indeed, deliberately over-obvious—both in the elaborate predictions of events to come and in the complex set of cross references which lace parts of the book together.

The predictions come thick and fast at the outset, where one would expect them if they were going to come at all. We are led to expect that the lives of Pierre and his mother will divide (5), and that after Pierre's interior development he will not prize his ancestry so much (6). His aspirations clearly will be thwarted by Time (8), and his 'special family distinction' will be important to his singularly developed character and life career (12). Fate will very likely knock him off his pedestal (12), he will become philosophical (13), and will become a thoroughgoing democrat, even a Radical one (13). The predictions continue: Nature will prove ambiguous to Pierre in the end (13); Lucy will long afterwards experience far different 'flutterings' from those at Saddle Meadows (26); Pierre will never regain his lost sense of an undisturbed moral beauty in the world (65); his crawling under the Memnon Stone will later hold immense significance for him (135); in aftertimes with Isabel, Pierre will often recall his first magnetic night with her (151); Pierre, Isabel, and Delly will never return to Saddle Meadows once they leave (203). After the departure from Saddle Meadows the predictions diminish, as they naturally would past the middle of the book, when predictions are being fulfilled, not made. The pamphlet which Pierre reads in the coach may influence his conduct (210); he will later understand the utility of Machiavellian policy though not have the heart to use it (222); his ties to Glen will involve in the end the most serious consequences (224); and he will learn that the world has fire and sword for contemporary grandeur (264). On reflective scrutiny a few of these predictions seem a trifle misleading, as when the reader may gather (5) that Pierre's and his mother's lives will divide then continue apart for longer than actu-

ally happens. Still other predictions (such as those at page 135 and page 151) seem to promise a more patient following of Pierre's river of mind than occurs after he arrives at the city and becomes settled at the Apostles'. But the predictions usually come true in unambiguous fashion. If the early chapters now stand roughly in order of their composition, they indicate that Melville had much of the basic plot well outlined from the beginning. The rather thick-strewn predictions do not, however, prove that no radical new elements were introduced into the plot. Curiously enough, despite all the fulfilled predictions there is nothing which conclusively proves that Melville intended from the outset to have Pierre become a writer once he was exiled from his home. In fact, the pattern of predictions makes it seem most likely that if Melville had had any such plan he would have signalled it at intervals throughout the Saddle Meadows section. Moreover, Melville may not have elaborated the city episodes in the ways he had once intended. These limitations aside, the predictions do furnish at least some evidence as to the unusual degree of Melville's control over his material.

Equal care in plotting is revealed in the way much of the book is tied together by cross references such as those to Nature's bounty toward Pierre (13-14, 257); what Pierre and Lucy believe about lovers' secrecies (37, 81, 309); Lucy's easel (39, 318); the will of Pierre's father (55, 179); the first paragraph of Isabel's letter (63, 175); Pierre's promise to protect Isabel (66, 113, 205); the chair portrait in the chintz-covered chest (87, 196); Isabel's one outburst of aggressive enthusiasm (160, 174); Lucy's fainting words (183, 206, 308); Mrs Glendinning's words of banishment (185, 206); the military cloaks which Dates packs (187, 301); the fire at the Black Swan Inn (198, 217, 255-6); Pierre's interest in the pamphlet attributed to Plotinus Plinlimmon (209, 293); Pierre's youthful sonnet 'The Tropical Summer' (245, 263, 306); and Pierre as a toddler (296, 305). The number and aptness of most of the cross references indicate that sometimes Melville was planning ahead for such details with what was, for him, remarkable thoroughness, while at other times he was making an unusual effort to tie some of what he was writing to particular passages already written; and while writing some passages he may even have gone back to introduce forward-looking references.

Unusual though it was for Melville, control of such details obviously does not of itself lead to great fiction. Indeed the excessive emphasis on predictions early in *Pierre* reflects Melville's satirical playing with one of the routine conventions of popular fiction. His real triumph of control in *Pierre* is the way he leads the reader into fascinated engagement with his remarkable thematic preoccupations. At the outset he risks failing to achieve any such engagement at all, for he strangely idealizes the social rank and superior natures of the characters, who feel extraordinary emotions and speak an extraordinary language. In Book I, 'Pierre Just Emerging from His Teens', the first words of dialogue are ludicrous, by realistic standards, and there seems some fairy-tale quality about the whole situation.

The style is often pseudo-Elizabethan bombast, often near the cloying romanticism of female novels of Melville's own time. Yet rapidly the reader begins to feel the tension created between the idealization of the characters and the constant predictions of disaster: the novel is to be a grand experiment in which Fate will take a hand in the life history of a rare specimen of mankind. With daring and often outrageous stylistic improvising Melville is in fact mocking Pierre's adolescent heroics, his unearned sense of security, and his unwillingness to face those dark truths that are to be the burden of the novel. The reader is led to view Pierre with amused, objective condescension and even slight contempt at the same time that he feels concern for the approaching crash of Pierre's illusions. After the early sense of impending calamity, Melville moves into another way of engaging his readers, by giving his hero unbidden inklings of a darker side of life. Events within and without impel Pierre toward maturer thought, yet he is reluctant to become philosophic (which in this novel means to awaken to a tragic sense). At the end of Book II, 'Love, Delight, and Alarm', Grief is still only a 'ghost-story' to Pierre (41). He resists the 'treacherous persuasiveness' (42) of the mournful pine tree and curses his reading in Dante (42), rejecting even imagined, not felt, experience of the darker aspects of reality, thinking, in juvenile pugnaciousness, that deprived of joy he would find cause for deadly feuds with things invisible.

In Book III, 'The Presentiment and the Verification', as Melville begins to develop Pierre's deeper side, his narrative voice becomes more restrained and sombre. He portrays the first stirrings of Pierre's long-dormant Unconscious from which 'bannered armies of hooded phantoms' (49) attack and board his conscious mind. Yet Pierre still shrinks 'abhorringly from the infernal catacombs of thought' when beckoned by a 'fœtal fancy' (51); he fights against his new sensations as a 'sort of unhealthiness' (53) when stirred 'in his deepest moral being' (as he thinks) by the sight of Isabel's face (49). But after receiving Isabel's letter his reluctance to face Truth when he does not know what he is evading changes into overeagerness to face Truth when he does not know what he is inviting (65). Hereafter Melville continues to trace the process of Pierre's mental growth, so that the reader becomes privy to the seemingly 'boundless expansion' (66) of the young hero's life. Previously engrossed and perhaps intermittently baffled by the stylistic virtuosity with which Melville reveals Pierre's absurdities, the reader is now impelled to follow the murky courses of Pierre's mind through all the ambiguous consequences of his absolute behaviour.

Book IV, 'Retrospective', as the title suggests, interrupts Melville's analysis of Pierre's current mental state. Now Melville announces explicitly a major theme present from the beginning but not emphasized before: that of the supersubtle complexity of psychological motivations and indeed of all psychological processes. We had been told (7) that tracing out 'precisely the absolute motives' which prompted Pierre to partake of the Holy Sacraments at the age of sixteen would be needless as well as difficult;

merely, Pierre seemed to have inherited his ancestors' religion 'by the same insensible sliding process' that he inherited their other noble personal qualities and their forests and farms. But the stress had been more on Pierre's immaturity than on the subtlety of the processes by which he behaved as he did. Post-adolescent love-extravagancies are associated with 'subterranean sprites and gnomes' (34), but Melville does not then reveal that these quaint monstrosities emerge from the same Unconscious whence hooded phantoms are soon to embark (49). Early in the novel various images of mental processes as gliding and sliding prefigure Melville's full portrayal of the oblique workings of the mind, but not until the first chapter of 'Retrospective' does he confront the theme directly: 'In their precise tracings-out and subtle causations, the strongest and fieriest emotions of life defy all analytical insight. . . . The metaphysical writers confess, that the most impressive, sudden, and overwhelming event, as well as the minutest, is but the product of an infinite series of infinitely involved and untraceable foregoing occurrences. Just so with every motion of the heart' (67). The rest of Book IV uncovers the extremely complex combination of suddenly recalled events and stories and unbidden night-thoughts which leads to Pierre's immediate conviction that Isabel is his father's daughter. Hereafter, treatment of Pierre's inward development is inseparable from the theme of the shadowiness of all human motivation, the 'ever-elastic regions of evanescent invention' through which the mind roams up and down (82).

Moreover, by the end of Book IV Melville has gone beyond the supersubtlety of all human psychology to assert the *autonomy* of those subtler elements of man, as we first see in the description of the adolescent Pierre sometimes standing before the chair portrait of his father, 'unconsciously throwing himself open to all those ineffable hints and ambiguities, and undefined half-suggestions, which now and then people the soul's atmosphere, as thickly as in a soft, steady snow-storm, the snow-flakes people the air' (84). The imagery suggests an evanescence of thought which the individual no more controls than he does the snow-storm, and Melville distinguishes these 'reveries and trances' from the 'assured element of consciously bidden and self-propelled thought' (84). With similar intimations of forces beyond Pierre's control, Melville refers to the 'streams' of Pierre's reveries over the chair portrait of his father which did not seem 'to leave any conscious sediment in his mind; they were so light and so rapid, that they rolled their own alluvial along; and seemed to leave all Pierre's thought-channels as clean and dry as though never any alluvial stream had rolled there at all' (85). In Book V, 'Misgivings and Preparatives', Fate irresistibly gives Pierre an 'electric insight' into 'the vital character of his mother' so that he now sees her as unalterably dominated by 'hereditary forms and world-usages' (89). As Melville says, 'in these flashing revelations of grief's wonderful fire, we see all things as they are' (88). Such use of images of natural phenomena to suggest the involuntary character of thought continues with added intensity after

Pierre has had time to reflect on the letter from Isabel, when the thought of Lucy 'serpent-like . . . overlayingly crawled in upon his other shuddering imaginings' (104). These other thoughts, we are told, would often 'upheave' and absorb the thought of Lucy into themselves, 'so that it would in that way soon disappear from his cotemporary apprehension' (104). The serpent image and the image of upheaval imply, once again, an independent vitality in the thought, free of Pierre's conscious control. Natural imagery now becomes more complexly elaborated as Melville portrays an expansion of Pierre's interior dimensions during the mental turmoil into which his reading of the letter has plunged him: 'Standing half-befogged upon the mountain of his Fate, all that part of the wide panorama was wrapped in clouds to him; but anon those concealings slid aside, or rather, a quick rent was made in them' (105). Through the 'swift cloud-rent' Pierre catches one glimpse of Lucy's 'expectant and angelic face', but 'the next instant the stormy pinions of the clouds locked themselves over it again; and all was hidden as before; and all went confused in whirling rack and vapor as before'. Yet while thus 'for the most part wrapped from his consciousness and vision', the condition of Lucy 'was still more and more disentangling and defining itself from out its nether mist,' and even beneath the general upper fog' (105). This passage portrays a rapidly expanded mental terrain but still a chaotic and uncontrollable one.

What Melville has achieved is an extraordinary conversion of gothic sensationalism into profound psychological exploration. Isabel, Pierre's presumed half-sister, is identified either as his Unconscious or as a product of it, so that his closer involvement with her parallels his gradual opening to incursions from the Unconscious. His after-reveries on her face (41) are associated with his dawning half-admission that Grief may be more than merely a 'ghost-story'. Without 'one word of speech', her face had revealed 'glimpses of some fearful gospel' (43). Within an hour of first seeing Isabel, Pierre felt that 'what he had always before considered the solid land of veritable reality, was now being audaciously encroached upon by bannered armies of hooded phantoms, disembarking in his soul, as from flotillas of specter-boats' (49). After reading Isabel's letter, Pierre 'saw all preceding ambiguities, all mysteries ripped open as if with a keen sword, and forth trooped thickening phantoms of an infinite gloom' (85). Prior to his first interview with her in Book VI, 'Isabel, and the First Part of the Story of Isabel', Pierre gives himself up to 'long wanderings in the primeval woods of Saddle Meadows' (109); formerly sunny and Arcadian, the landscape now mirrors his new sense of the world: in the 'wet and misty eve the scattered, shivering pasture elms seemed standing in a world inhospitable'. The landscape also mirrors the depths and terrors Isabel has opened up in Pierre's psyche:

> On both sides, in the remoter distance, and also far beyond the mild lake's further shore, rose the long, mysterious mountain masses; shaggy with pines and hemlocks, mystical with nameless, vapory exhalations, and in that dim air black with dread and gloom. At their

base, profoundest forests lay entranced, and from their far owl-haunted depths of caves and rotted leaves, and unused and unregarded inland overgrowth of decaying wood—for smallest sticks of which, in other climes many a pauper was that moment perishing; from out the infinite inhumanities of those profoundest forests, came a moaning, muttering, roaring, intermitted, changeful sound: rain-shakings of the palsied trees, slidings of rocks undermined, final crashings of long-riven boughs, and devilish gibberish of the forest-ghosts. (109-110)

When Pierre at last meets Isabel at the red farmhouse, what she recounts concerns her childhood process of individuation, a process Pierre is undergoing only now, after first seeing her. She reveals that her constant psychological state is one in which the Unconscious impinges upon the Conscious: 'Always in me, the solidest things melt into dreams, and dreams into solidities' (117); only now has Pierre's own soul begun to be opened to the same integrative and disintegrative mental processes. But Isabel embodies the Unconscious in ways still alien from the awakening Pierre, even to the point of learning 'new things' from the thoughts which 'well up' in her and come forth on her tongue without the intervention of any conscious process, so that the speech is 'sometimes before the thought' (123). Bursting from the 'sorceries' of the interview (128), Pierre at the beginning of Book VII, 'Intermediate between Pierre's Two Interviews with Isabel at the Farm-house', for 'an instant' almost wishes for a reversion to his earlier vision of a simpler, unmysterious world and to ignorance of his own newly-opened, threatening depths: 'he almost could have prayed Isabel back into the wonder-world from which she had so slidingly emerged' (129). Yet the lure of these new depths is more powerful than their threats, for he again withdraws to a forest where his eye pursues 'its ever-shifting shadowy vistas' and where there come into his mind 'thoughts and fancies never imbibed within the gates of towns; but only given forth by the atmosphere of primeval forests' (139). Formerly the unconscious processes of Pierre's mind were imaged as a stream; now, indicative of his greater depths, from the 'thoughtful river' of his mind run 'unending, ever-flowing', thoughts of Isabel (141). But Pierre's process of yielding ground in his soul to the invading Unconscious continues to involve occasional checks or reversals. In the interval after his second interview with Isabel, during which he had made the most binding pledges, there comes a moment when, fain to disown his memory and mind, Pierre dashes himself against a wall and falls 'dabbling in the vomit of his loathed identity' (171). As the narrator warns, the human soul is 'strange and complicate' (176). Pierre's final resolution to champion Isabel by pretending to have married her is arrived at only by 'nameless struggles of the soul' (181).

Moreover, Pierre's 'infinite magnanimities' (177) from the outset are inextricably linked with appalling self-delusion. From the opening pages Melville has set forth, in scenes which initially baffle the reader, the chivalric artifice of Pierre's ideals and intimate relationships—a habit of mind that makes him uniquely vulnerable to the particular appeal Isabel makes. In our first glimpse of Pierre with Lucy he idealizes her as an 'invoking angel' while idealizing himself as a soldier marching under her 'colors'. She participates in the role-playing, crying '"Bravissimo! oh, my only recruit!"' when he fastens her flower to his bosom (4), and both of them speak in what seems an absurdly heightened rhetoric. From this depiction of Pierre as romantic cavalier Melville immediately moves to the depiction of 'romantic filial love', Pierre's benignly presented but ultimately unhealthy habit of treating 'his pedastaled mother' with a 'strange license' under which 'they were wont to call each other brother and sister' (5). Any suitor who might dare to propose marriage to this youthful-appearing widow 'would by some peremptory unrevealed agency immediately disappear from the earth', dispatched by her jealous chivalric protector (5). Pierre's dead father, we learn, had left him a legacy of idealistic maxims, one of which was that no one could claim to be a gentleman unless he 'could also rightfully assume the meek, but kingly style of Christian' (6). Thus at sixteen Pierre, playing the role of young Christian gentleman, partakes of the Holy Sacraments. In Pierre's exalted view 'the complete polished steel of the gentleman' was thereby 'girded with Religion's silken sash' (7). In this atmosphere of ideality he longs for a sister, someone whom he 'might love, and protect, and fight for, if need be' (7). He repeatedly images himself as would-be champion: 'It must be a glorious thing to engage in a mortal quarrel on a sweet sister's behalf!' (7). Predisposed toward such a self-image by both his parents, Pierre finds another source of chivalric notions in Nature herself, who in the beginning did 'bravely' by him (13): 'She lifted her spangled crest of a thickly-starred night, and forth at that glimpse of their divine Captain and Lord, ten thousand mailed thoughts of heroicness started up in Pierre's soul, and glared round for some insulted good cause to defend' (14).

For none of these chivalric impulses is there a normal outlet. There is no real likelihood that Pierre will need to fend off suitors from his mother, despite his playful-earnest role of her knight in waiting. With Lucy, Pierre's chivalric notions must be reduced merely to the courtesies of courtship, since she hardly needs his defence, what with two youthful brothers themselves overeager to fulfil their own chivalric obligations toward her. The first true appeal to his chivalry comes with his earliest glimpse of Isabel's face, on which 'he seemed to see the fair ground where Anguish had contended with Beauty, and neither being conqueror, both had laid down on the field' (47). The narrator's language reveals the intensity of Pierre's chivalric obsession. Beyond the bewildering allure of the beauty and the anguish of the face, Pierre is aware of a special effect, 'the face somehow mystically appealing to his own private and individual affections; and by a silent and tyrannic call, challenging him in his deepest moral being, and summoning Truth, Love, Pity, Conscience, to the stand' (49). Until he receives Isabel's letter, Pierre resists this appeal to his heroism, since his other chivalric obligations, his duty to his mother and his fiancée, forbid any re-

sponse and since there is no reasonable course of action he can take. Her letter finally gives him the heroic good cause he has been looking for: suddenly he has the sister on whose behalf he can engage in a mortal quarrel. After the first devastating shock, the letter arouses all his would-be heroic, chivalric impulses: he will 'comfort', 'stand by', and 'fight for' Isabel (66).

Yet Pierre is woefully ill-equipped to set out as a Christian Knight-Champion, most obviously because the pattern of chivalric, romantic idealization has developed simultaneously with dangerous sublimation of his sexual feelings. His glide toward physical maturity, we are told at the outset, was accompanied by ambiguous feelings aroused during his reading in 'his father's fastidiously picked and decorous library' (6). There the 'Spenserian nymphs had early led him into many a maze of all-bewildering beauty' that created 'a graceful glow on his limbs, and soft, imaginative flames in his heart' (6). When first mentioned these nymphs seem to be summoning courtly, aesthetic impulses, but later it becomes clear that Pierre is unconsciously responding to them with the stirrings of puberty. For most of the novel, in fact, Pierre idealizes his sexual impulses, failing to recognize them for what they are. Latently incestuous, his courtly 'lover-like adoration' of his mother (16) is deceptively suffused with religious sentiment: the spell which wheeled mother and son in one orbit of joy seemed 'almost to realize here below the sweet dreams of those religious enthusiasts, who paint to us a Paradise to come, when etherealized from all drosses and stains, the holiest passion of man shall unite all kindreds and climes in one circle of pure and unimpairable delight' (16). At the time the novel opens, Pierre is still unprepared to recognize his sexual feelings, despite his engagement to Lucy. During their outing in the phaeton he alternates between mysticalness and merriment, unaware of the strength of his own sexuality, for he does not acknowledge the erotic nature of the 'subterranean sprites and gnomes' and 'naiads' that surround him (34). Lucy instinctively shrinks from him in 'Fear and Wonder' (35) when he bursts 'forth in some screaming shout of joy', the 'striped tigers of his chestnut eyes' leaping 'in their lashed cages with a fierce delight'. But even after holding Lucy's hand, 'feeling, softly feeling of its soft tinglingness', Pierre still idealizes his sexuality, diffusing it into an exalted response to nature, so that he seems like someone 'in linked correspondence with the summer lightnings', by 'sweet shock on shock, receiving intimating foretastes of the etherealest delights of earth' (36). Later, as he fetches a portfolio from Lucy's chamber, we learn of more mental contortions which he undergoes in order to sublimate and generalize the feelings aroused in him:

> He never had entered that chamber but with feelings of a wonderful reverentialness. The carpet seemed as holy ground. Every chair seemed sanctified by some departed saint, there once seated long ago. Here his book of Love was all a rubric, and said—Bow now, Pierre, bow. But this extreme loyalty to the piety of love, called from him by such glimpses of its most secret inner shrine, was not unrelieved betimes by such quickenings

of all his pulses, that in fantasy he pressed the wide beauty of the world in his embracing arms; for all his world resolved itself into his heart's best love for Lucy. (39)

Thus predisposed, Pierre's mental processes twist themselves anew at the sewing circle in order to let him feel that the mysterious face he has glimpsed is somehow tyrannically challenging him 'in his deepest moral being' (49). Characteristically, he manages to tame and prettify the profound experience, safely Spenserizing it into a 'delicious sadness' so that some 'hazy fairy swam above him in the heavenly ether, and showered down upon him the sweetest pearls of pensiveness' (54).

One immediate aftereffect of reading Isabel's letter is that Pierre suddenly sees his father as morally corrupt, although he had always idolized him to the point of sacrilege (68), and the narrator emphasizes that the extreme of Pierre's idealization was possible only because at the age of nineteen he 'had never yet become so thoroughly initiated into that darker, though truer aspect of things, which an entire residence in the city from the earliest period of life, almost inevitably engraves upon the mind of any keenly observant and reflective youth' (69). To be sure, during the four years that he had possessed the chair portrait of his father, Pierre had felt 'ever new conceits come vaporing up' in him (83), so that the portrait seemed to speak with his father's voice: 'I am thy father, boy. There was once a certain, oh, but too lovely young Frenchwoman, Pierre'. Then, 'starting from these reveries and trances, Pierre would regain the assured element of consciously bidden and self-propelled thought' (84), promising never again to fall into such midnight reveries, suppressing suspicions of his father even as he begins to diffuse his own sexual feelings. In his agonized hours following the reading of Isabel's letter, Pierre feels that 'his whole previous moral being' (87) has been overturned. But though he is no longer free to worship his father, he still does not apply to himself the lesson earlier intimated by the chair portrait and apparently confirmed by Isabel's letter, that 'Youth is hot, and temptation strong', that beneath seeming innocence sexual impulses may be stirring (83). His sense of his own immaculateness is chronic. In sublime delusion he feels Christlike, as if 'deep in him lurked a divine unidentifiableness, that owned no earthly kith or kin' (89). While the narrator offers us 'hell-glimpses' (107), reminding us that Pierre was championing 'womanly beauty, and not womanly ugliness', Pierre himself is asking heaven to confirm him in his 'Christ-like feeling' (106).

More mental contortions follow as the deluded Christian knight begins to respond to Isabel's attractiveness. Accustomed from adolescence to a certain falseness in the relationship of mother-son, and more recently exposed to the new artifice by which Mrs Glendinning had converted Lucy into her little sister, Pierre blames Fate for his bewildered feelings about Isabel: 'Fate had done this thing for them. Fate had separated the brother and the sister, till to

each other they somehow seemed so not at all. Sisters shrink not from their brother's kisses' (142). Pierre begins 'to seem to see the mere imaginariness of the so supposed solidest principle of human association'—an incipient discrediting of the taboo against incest—yet feels 'that never, never would he be able to embrace Isabel with the mere brotherly embrace; while the thought of any other caress, which took hold of any domesticness, was entirely vacant from his uncontaminated soul, for it had never consciously intruded there' (142). In this state of mind, and just because his latent incestuous feelings are now stirring, Pierre is compelled, all ignorantly, to sublimate: 'Isabel wholly soared out of the realms of mortalness, and for him became transfigured in the highest heaven of uncorrupted Love' (142). Even as Lucy's bedroom had represented Love's 'secret inner shrine' for Pierre, at his second interview with Isabel the 'deep oaken recess of the double-casement' seems to him the 'vestibule of some awful shrine' (149), though Isabel's power over him is by now more obviously erotic: Pierre feels himself (150) 'surrounded by ten thousand sprites and gnomes, and his whole soul was swayed and tossed by supernatural tides'. (Here the narrator's word 'soul' merely reflects Pierre's own self-protective instinct toward sublimation.) Aware of an 'extraordinary physical magnetism' in Isabel, Pierre nevertheless generalizes his sexual attraction by associating it with a 'Pantheistic master-spell, which eternally locks in mystery and in muteness the universal subject world' (151). Reminiscent of his pledge to Lucy of 'the immutable eternities of joyfulness' (36), Pierre makes extravagant lover-like declarations to Isabel, wishing that his kisses on her hand 'were on the heart itself, and dropt the seeds of eternal joy and comfort there' (154). In egregious delusion of immaculate magnanimity, his pledges to Isabel become as extravagant as his recurrent threats to the gods: 'we will love with the pure and perfect love of angel to an angel. If ever I fall from thee, dear Isabel, may Pierre fall from himself; fall back forever into vacant nothingness and night!' (154). By reinforcing his sense of his own Christlikeness, calling him a 'visible token' of the 'invisible angel-hoods', and praising the 'gospel' of his acts (156), Isabel aids Pierre in sublimating the passion increasingly evident in his words.

Yet both Isabel and Pierre use the licence of their supposed brother-and-sister, champion-and-damsel, relationship to indulge in verbal love-making. In language that appeals to Pierre's religious-chivalric impulses, Isabel describes her reluctant surrender to him at the sewing circle: 'Once having met thy fixed regardful glance; once having seen the full angelicalness in thee, my whole soul was undone by thee . . . till I knew, that utterly decay and die away I must, unless pride let me go, and I, with the one little trumpet of a pen, blew my heart's shrillest blast, and called dear Pierre to me' (159). In his own imagination Pierre still sees himself as Christlike knight. When Isabel fears that he might be hurt by any public or secret relationship with her, he lies—denies what he has so recently learned about his father—in order to keep his heroic cause from slipping away: 'Is Love a harm? Can Truth betray to pain? Sweet Isabel, how can hurt come in the path to God?' (159-60). He swears by heaven that he 'will crush the disdainful world down on its knees' to Isabel (160). As she exultingly responds, her 'long scornful hair' trails out like a 'disheveled banner' before the would-be knight, who acknowledges 'that irrespective, darting majesty of humanity, which can be majestical and menacing in woman as in man' (160). (A part of Isabel's allure for Pierre is her fleeting resemblance to his mother, whose 'stately beauty had ever somewhat martial in it' [20].) As a culmination to the emotional self-indulgence which increases throughout this interview, Pierre and Isabel partake of what Pierre blasphemously calls 'the real sacrament of the supper' (162).

Miserably deluded, Pierre thinks, even after his second interview with Isabel, that he is responding to 'the unsuppressible and unmistakable cry of the godhead through her soul', a cry which commands him 'to fly to her, and do his highest and most glorious duty in the world' (174). By the time he has reached his final resolution his formula, sublimated once again, has become: 'Lucy or God?' (181), though soon afterward Pierre speciously claims that he and Isabel will act deceitfully for the 'united good' of themselves and those they deceive (190). Just after insisting that he is 'pure' (191) and claiming that he and Isabel reach up alike to a 'glorious ideal' (192), Pierre whispers his plan as 'his mouth wet her ear' (192). Then comes an immediate and appalling descent from the exaltation: 'The girl moved not; was done with all her tremblings; leaned closer to him, with an inexpressible strangeness of an intense love, new and inexplicable. Over the face of Pierre there shot a terrible self-revelation; he imprinted repeated burning kisses upon her; pressed hard her hand; would not let go her sweet and awful passiveness. Then they changed; they coiled together, and entangledly stood mute' (192). For the first time in the book Melville's deluded idealist acts—and knows that he acts—out of undisguised sexual passion.

But Pierre's capacity for evading unpleasant self-knowledge is far from exhausted. Shortly afterwards, at the Black Swan Inn, he decides that his memorial gold pieces must be spent now 'in this sacred cause' (196), an obvious denial that Isabel had 'become a thing of intense and fearful love for him' (197)—fearful precisely because of his terrible self-revelation at the dairy. Yet that sundown at the Inn Pierre burns the chair portrait of his father out of an unconscious need to free himself of the strongest visible reminder that his passion for Isabel, whatever else it is, is incestuous. In the coach next morning his 'still imperfectly conscious, incipient, new-mingled emotion toward this mysterious being' (206) appalls him, to the point that he feels 'threatened by the possibility of a sin anomalous and accursed'—perhaps the unpardonable sin itself. Though he has learned much about his mother's and his father's character, he is still in the first stages of reluctantly learning about his own. Just as he had destroyed the reminder of Isabel's paternity the night before, now in the coach Pierre refuses to recognize the applicability of the

strange pamphlet on 'Chronometricals and Horologicals' either to his own situation or to Christianity in general: he can neither admit that an absolute attempt to obey Christ is apt to involve ordinary mortals 'in strange, *unique* follies and sins, unimagined before' (213) nor that Christianity has flourished for two millennia only by systematically diluting the edicts of its founder, rather than taking them literally, as he has tried to do.

Nowhere in the book, moreover, does Pierre see that for all his efforts to be Christlike he has never been a true Christian. Despite his partaking with his mother of the Holy Sacraments, he has in fact been only nominally a Christian, drawn to the Church as a family responsibility laid down by his father, whose maxim linked gentlemanhood and Christianity. The superhuman powers Pierre invokes are ill-sortedly Christian or pagan; consistently he images his relationship with such powers as an antagonistic one: demons or gods, they are to be threatened and, especially, bargained with. The language he uses again and again threatens what he will do 'if' the powers do not act as he wishes. He conjures the 'sovereign powers' that claim all his 'leal worshipings' to lift the veil between him and the mysterious face; if they abandon him to 'an unknown misery', his faith 'may clean depart' and leave him 'a railing atheist' (41). If 'deprived of joy', he feels he would 'find cause for deadly feuds with things invisible' (41). He feels he has a 'choice quarrel' with the Fate which had led him to think the world was one of Joy, if in fact the night which wraps his soul after he reads Isabel's letter is genuine (65). In the interval before his first interview with Isabel he prays that heaven 'new-string' his soul (106), confirming in him 'the Christ-like feeling' he first felt on reading her letter; yet in the same speech he simultaneously invokes and threatens the 'sovereign powers' (106-7) if they betray his faith in them:

> I cast my eternal die this day, ye powers. On my strong faith in ye Invisibles, I stake three whole felicities, and three whole lives this day. If ye forsake me now,—farewell to Faith, farewell to Truth, farewell to God; exiled for aye from God and man, I shall declare myself an equal power with both; free to make war on Night and Day, and all thoughts and things of mind and matter, which the upper and the nether firmaments do clasp! (107)

Pierre's new Christlikeness is a most ambiguous one, since it leads instantly to threats against God. Then, between the two interviews with Isabel, Pierre slides under 'the very brow of the beetlings and the menacings of the Terror Stone', named by him for the temple of Memnon. Not threatening the Stone, he nevertheless promulgates a series of conditions in which the 'Mute Massiveness' is invited to fall on him (134). When the Stone fails to act on the implied challenge, he adolescently assumes a new haughtiness and goes his 'moody way' as though he 'owed thanks to none' (135).

The threats and bargains with the gods culminate in the scene with Pierre and Isabel at the Apostles' the third night after their arrival in the city. Once again Pierre makes pledges, inviting the 'high gods' to join the devils against him if he deceives Isabel (272). Once again he invites instant punishment if he fails in Virtue: 'then close in and crush me, ye stony walls, and into one gulf let all things tumble together!' (273). Once again he warns the gods, this time to 'look after their own combustibles': 'If they have put powder-casks in me—let them look to it! let them look to it!' (273). But in a crucial difference from earlier scenes Pierre now suspects that man himself, instead of the gods, may be a 'vile juggler and cheat' (272). Incapable now in Isabel's presence of denying to himself her erotic appeal, he fears that 'uttermost virtue, after all' may prove 'but a betraying pander to the monstrousest vice', and finally declares that the 'demigods trample on trash, and Virtue and Vice are trash!' (273). Declaring that Virtue and Vice are both nothing, and having already rid himself of the chair portrait, the most tangible reminder of Isabel's link to his father, Pierre is now free to commit incest, though whether or not actual sexual intercourse occurs that night at the Apostles' remains ambiguous but hideously possible.

Up to Pierre's arrival in the city with Isabel and Delly, everything has worked together to enhance the attentive reader's sense that he is in the hands of a profound thinker and innovative craftsman who will convey him through yet more hazardous regions of psychological and aesthetic experience. Melville has not only managed to put sensational gothic plot elements to the service of an acute analysis of a tortuously complex mind; he has also managed to convert analysis into very vivid action, repeatedly portraying Pierre's psychological states and processes in extended metaphors and images, passages that are short, graphic, and frequently intense narratives in themselves.[10] In these highly-charged passages, Melville combines penetrating analysis of his hero's states of mind with the enunciation of general truths, so that the record of Pierre's particular experience is continually expanding to include human experience at large.[11] By the beginning of Book XVI, 'First Night of Their Arrival in the City', the reader wants nothing more than to follow 'the thoughtful river' of Pierre's mind through all the ambiguous consequences of his sublimely absolute and miserably deluded behaviour. Yet despite the brilliance of the scene on the third night at the Apostles', the wish goes mainly unfulfilled. Melville's primary concerns in the first half of the novel only intermittently engage his attention in the second half, and at times he seems lamentably unaware of the direction the first half was taking.

Symptomatic is the flaw in the first paragraph of Book XVII, 'Young America in Literature':

> Among the various conflicting modes of writing history, there would seem to be two grand practical distinctions, under which all the rest must subordinately range. By the one mode, all contemporaneous circumstances, facts, and events must be set down contemporaneously; by the other, they are only to be set down as the general stream of the narrative shall dictate; for

matters which are kindred in time, may be very irrelative in themselves. I elect neither of these; I am careless of either; both are well enough in their way; I write precisely as I please. (244)

Earlier Melville had talked bluntly about his demands on the reader: 'This history goes forward and goes backward, as occasion calls. Nimble center, circumference elastic you must have' (54). He had called attention to his apparent disregard of rules in a passage that might strike the reader as 'rather irregular sort of writing' (25), and had announced that he followed 'the flowing river in the cave of man' careless whither he be led, reckless where he land (107). In these instances he had been in superb control, knowing exactly what he was doing with his stylistic absurdities in Books I and II, then knowing that his simultaneous exploration of Pierre's mind and his own might lead him into unknown winding passages (even as he kept to the outline of his plot), but confident that he could bravely follow that flowing river wherever it ran. Not recking where he landed was a way of proclaiming his determination to tell everything 'in this book of sacred truth' (107); he was not abandoning a point of view but asserting his determination to hold to it. The beginning of 'Young America in Literature' marks a drastic change in Melville's authorial purpose, a deep draining off of his control over the relationship between narrator and reader. The change is due to what happened in Melville's life between the last days of 1851 and the first days of 1852, but our concern here is with the effects on the manuscript, not the biographical causes.

After his claim to write precisely as he pleased, Melville continues with this remarkably inexact passage: 'In the earlier chapters of this volume, it has somewhere been passingly intimated, that Pierre was not only a reader of the poets and other fine writers, but likewise—and what is a very different thing from the other—a thorough allegorical understander of them, a profound emotional sympathizer with them' (244). On the contrary, we had been told, by Pierre himself in a moment of insight, that he had *not* been that sort of reader: 'Oh, hitherto I have but piled up words; bought books, and bought some small experiences, and built me in libraries; now I sit down and read' (91). Furthermore, Melville had also asserted that before Pierre was enlightened by flashing revelations of Grief's wonderful fire, he had *not* been a thorough allegorical understander of the poets:

> Fortunately for the felicity of the Dilletante in Literature, the horrible allegorical meanings of the Inferno, lie not on the surface; but unfortunately for the earnest and youthful piercers into truth and reality, those horrible meanings, when first discovered, infuse their poison into a spot previously unprovided with that sovereign antidote of a sense of uncapitulatable security, which is only the possession of the furthest advanced and profoundest souls. (169)

When he began Book XVII, Melville had simply forgotten this crucial aspect of his characterization of Pierre.[12] But even in the process of crediting Pierre with being 'a thorough allegorical understander' of and 'a profound emotional sympathizer' with poets and other fine writers, Melville seems to have recognized his blunder and attempted an immediate recovery:

> Not that as yet his young and immature soul had been accosted by the Wonderful Mutes, and through the vast halls of Silent Truth, had been ushered into the full, secret, eternally inviolable Sanhedrim, where the Poetic Magi discuss, in glorious gibberish, the Alpha and Omega of the Universe. But among the beautiful imaginings of the second and third degree of poets, he freely and comprehendingly ranged. (244-5)

In these rapid second thoughts Melville ends up saying quite another thing from what he had just said: in fact, he reverts to saying something very like what he had denied at the outset of the paragraph, that Pierre was no more than a normally alert reader. The bitter fun Melville has with his mockery of the rules of writing comes at the considerable cost of jeopardizing the reader's trust in the narrative voice.

Deflected into preoccupation with his own literary career, Melville in Books XVII and XVIII let absurdities intrude upon what he wrote of Pierre, as in his analysis of the phenomenon of young writers who win instant success with a book original in subject matter although not the product of a genuinely original mind. In this passage (259) Melville plainly has begun to write about the reception of his own *Typee* six years before, not about Pierre. From his new vantage point Melville was honest in his self-assessment, sure that *Typee* was, after all, original—the first eyewitness account of Polynesian life with the readability of fiction—although he had unoriginally cannibalized his source-books and employed a second or third hand style. The satire in Books XVII and XVIII is acute, but only as applied to Melville and his own critics, not to Pierre, in whose history it is distractingly out of place. Pierre, of course, has never 'embodied' any experiences at all in a book, much less 'some rich and peculiar experience' (259), although the reader is belatedly apprised of his authorship of 'little sonnets, brief meditative poems, and moral essays' (248). In suddenly determining to take satiric revenge upon his own reviewers and his literary competitors, Melville is indulging in a 'lamentable rearward aggressiveness' at least as unwarrantable and foolish as Pierre's toward the Rev. Mr Falsgrave (166). The reader was well prepared for Pierre's folly, but the narrator's own mature wisdom throughout the Saddle Meadows section, especially his cautious distance from his hero, had left the reader unprepared for authorial recklessness.

Even before the disastrous Books on literature in America ('before' in final placement though not necessarily so in order of composition), Melville had begun dissipating much of the accumulated tension by introducing lengthy narrative and expository passages largely or wholly irrelevant to the central concern of Pierre's commitment to Isabel. Book XV, 'The Cousins', which is devoted to the intense adolescent love-friendship between Pierre and Glen, might be defended as an essential part of this ruthlessly honest history of the soul in which no taboo in Melville's society can be left unviolated, and indeed the analysis of the stages in that relationship are interesting in themselves. However, the Book seems too long and distinctly anticlimactic, coming immediately after the pamphlet: it is not focused on major issues and the analysis does not impel the book forward, does not tell the reader things he needs to know or prepare him for highly significant things to come. Even the most comparable passage in the early part of the novel, the account of Aunt Dorothea's reminiscences, does not seem so relaxed, because there the reader is in suspense, actively putting things together as he absorbs and meditates upon her story rather faster than she tells it. Books XVII and XVIII have even less to do with the central issues of the first fourteen Books. By contrast, in Book XIX, 'The Church of the Apostles', the history of the building and its inhabitants is potentially relevant, since the Apostles can be seen as versions of Pierre, thwarted idealists, and since the building itself at least casually symbolizes the transfer of power from Christianity to something akin to Transcendentalism. Not enough is made of these points, and the 'gamesome' banter which Melville adopts (267) is distinctly out of keeping with the high seriousness of most of the early part of the novel. The satiric grotesquerie of these pages goes, if not for naught, at least for less than it might have gone in another novel, where other expectations had been set up. Book XX, 'Charlie Millthorpe', seems even more extraneous, since it begins by explaining something which had already been accepted without explanation—Pierre's being at the Apostles'. Now, after the fact, and after the intense scene between Pierre and Isabel which hints at actual physical incest, the reader is told much more than he wants to know about details which are not strictly relevant. Unlike the earlier Books ('Presentiment and Verification' makes a good contrast), Book XX does not significantly add to our knowledge of Pierre's motivation or to our understanding of the main themes. There is considerable verve in the portrait of Charles Millthorpe, just as there had been in the account of the Apostles, but none of the intensity the reader had come to expect. Later, the jocular account of the Apostles' eccentricities (298-301) is jarring, especially when the narrator is led into this commentary upon idealistic behaviour:

> Among all the innate, hyena-like repellants to the reception of any set form of a spiritually-minded and pure archetypical faith, there is nothing so potent in its skeptical tendencies, as that inevitable perverse ridiculousness, which so often bestreaks some of the essentially finest and noblest aspirations of those men, who disgusted with the common conventional quackeries, strive, in their clogged terrestrial humanities, after some imperfectly discerned, but heavenly ideals: ideals, not only imperfectly discerned in themselves, but the path to them so little traceable, that no two minds will entirely agree upon it.

These observations, offered as if they had just occurred to the narrator, had already formed some of the darkest implications of the pamphlet.[13]

Throughout the second half of the book Melville continues this sort of generalizing tendency, making observations on such subjects as 'boy-love' and the change to love of the opposite sex (216-17), the advisability of converting 'some well-wishers into foes' (221-2), the advantages of simplicity (224-5), the need for 'utter gladiatorianism' in dealing with some reversals of fortune (226-7), the 'dread of tautology' (227), the nature of coach-drivers (232), and 'the *povertiresque* in the social landscape' (276-7). Earlier in the novel Melville's generalizing commentary had been a major source of power, dealing as it had with the motivation and states of mind of Pierre and the social, moral, and metaphysical problems he exemplified. In the second half the authorial commentary largely creates the impression of improvisation and redundancy, an impression emphasized when the narrator compares himself to one of the 'strolling improvisatores of Italy' (259) and when he carelessly concludes one Book with the mention of something 'by way of bagatelle' (294). The reader who has paid alert attention can only feel cheated by this casualness and laxity in authorial commentary.

Bad as these lapses are, by far the worst failure lies in Melville's altered treatment of Pierre. In the first half of the book, one of the most remarkable features had been the scrupulous and often brilliant presentation of the hero's motives and states of mind. In the last Books, Melville not only fails to provide certain contemplative scenes which were earlier implied if not directly promised (such as scenes in which Pierre thinks about the episode of the Memnon Stone after reaching the city or in which he remembers his first evening with Isabel), he also neglects to analyze sufficiently Pierre's present states of mind, especially as they involve Isabel. Pierre had vowed to cherish and protect her, to treat her as an artisan handles 'the most exquisite, and fragile filagree of Genoa' (189). But he fails to carry out his pledges; instead, in a few days after reaching the city he becomes almost entirely preoccupied with the book he is writing. Isabel is not allowed to participate in his labours (except much later to read aloud proofs to him) and is no longer at the centre of his thoughts. After the arrival in the city, in fact, Isabel is absent from the narrative for long periods. Apart from the scene on the third night at the Apostles' (271-4), she scarcely figures in the story at all until the reintroduction of Lucy. Henry A. Murray aptly comments: 'Pierre, having devoured what Isabel had to give him, is withdrawing libido (interest, love) from her as a person and using it to fold, and warm, and egg round embryoes of thought and to feed a precipitant ambition'.[14] Such an outcome is perhaps credible enough, considering the trauma and the 'widely explosive' mental development Pierre has experienced; even so, Melville appears to have seized upon Pierre's authorship, the pretext for dramatizing his own precarious literary career, as a way to avoid tracing any minute shiftings in the relationship between Pierre and Isabel.[15]

Markedly, what we do learn of Pierre and Isabel—sexual arousal, deceit, insincerity, and unease on his part, suspicion, jealousy, and hysteria on hers—is presented dramatically for the most part, without the earlier omniscient commentary. We are told that, on the news of his mother's death and Glen Stanly's inheritance of Saddle Meadows and rumoured courtship of Lucy, Pierre curses himself for an 'idiot fool' because 'he had himself, as it were, resigned his noble birthright to a cunning kinsman for a mess of pottage, which now proved all but ashes in his mouth' (289). We also learn that he feels that these are 'unworthy pangs' and resolves to hide them from Isabel (289). But otherwise Pierre's feelings for her are scarcely explored. His awareness or unawareness of the extent to which the relationship has deteriorated, his attitude toward that change, are not examined. Pierre's incestuous passion, once central to the book, becomes the subject of offhand allusion: 'Not to speak of his being devoured by the all-exacting theme of his book, there were sinister preoccupations in him of a still subtler and more fearful sort, of which some inklings have already been given' (308). When late in the novel we learn of Pierre that the 'most tremendous displacing and revolutionizing thoughts were upheaving in him, with reference to Isabel' (353), the only such thought we actually learn about is the question of whether she is truly his half-sister. The crucial information that Pierre's virtuous enthusiasm in behalf of Isabel has declined comes in an aside; his 'transcendental persuasions' that she was his sister, we learn, were 'originally born, as he now seemed to feel, purely of an intense procreative enthusiasm:—an enthusiasm no longer so all-potential with him as of yore' (353). Melville's exploration of Pierre's problems as an author tends to disguise his failure to explore Pierre's changing attitude toward Isabel, but the careful reader cannot help but be aware of it.

The more emotionally involved Melville becomes in his portrayal of Pierre as author, the more he loses his grasp on the implications of other parts of his narrative. As Pierre's suffering and degradation in his attempt to be a profound writer worsen, Melville's rhetoric starts to exalt him: 'In the midst of the merriments of the mutations of Time, Pierre hath ringed himself in with the grief of Eternity. Pierre is a peak inflexible in the heart of Time, as the isle-peak, Piko, stands unassaultable in the midst of waves' (304). Implicitly approving Pierre's commitment, in spite of the self-destructiveness of his attempt to write a great book, Melville speaks of the 'devouring profundities' that have opened up in his hero: 'would he, he could not now be entertainingly and profitably shallow in some pellucid and merry romance' (305). In the next passage on Pierre as author, it is in his 'deepest, highest part' that he is 'utterly without sympathy from any thing divine, human, brute, or vegetable' (338). The mental distance between author and character diminishes appreciably: 'the deeper and the deeper' that he dives, Pierre perceives the 'everlasting elusiveness of Truth' (339), an elusiveness that Melville as narrator had postulated earlier (at page 165 and page 285). Pierre's scorn of the critics now is clearly Melville's: 'beforehand he felt the pyramidical scorn of the genuine loftiness for the whole infinite company of in-finitesimal critics' (339). As the distance between author and hero narrows, the hero is increasingly exalted, and Melville speaks of Pierre in the same terms as Pierre sees himself. Pierre begins to feel 'that in him, the thews of a Titan were forestallingly cut by the scissors of Fate' (339); Melville comments: 'Against the breaking heart, and the bursting head; against all the dismal lassitude, and death-ful faintness and sleeplessness, and whirlingness, and cra-ziness, still he like a demigod bore up' (339). Shortly af-terwards Melville writes that the 'very blood' in Pierre's body 'had in vain rebelled against his Titanic soul' (341). In focusing on his hero as author, Melville loses sight of Pierre the young man attempting to be Christlike but un-done by human flaws. Now he portrays Pierre the em-battled demi-god, whose degradation is an inevitable part of his Titanic greatness: 'gifted with loftiness' he is 'dragged down to the mud' (339), even literally (341). Pierre is identified with Enceladus, 'the most potent of all the giants', one with 'unconquerable front' and 'unabas-able face' (345). Melville approves the 'reckless sky-assaulting mood' of both Enceladus and Pierre: 'For it is according to eternal fitness, that the precipitated Titan should still seek to regain his paternal birthright even by fierce escalade. Wherefore whoso storms the sky gives best proof he came from thither! But whatso crawls con-tented in the moat before that crystal fort, shows it was born within that slime, and there forever will abide' (347).

But Pierre's increased stature as 'deep-diving' author and admirable 'sky-assaulting' demigod works against the logic of much of the novel's development. For despite Melville's preoccupation with the hardship and misery of Pierre's at-tempt to write profoundly, the last Books still bring to a climax the disaster entailed in his attempt to be Christlike. A number of events forcefully recall the pamphlet's warn-ings of calamity for the chronometrical idealist. Lucy writes to Pierre that she intends to join him, that she is commanded by God (311), and that in her 'long swoon' (after Pierre told her he was married) 'heaven' was prepar-ing her for a 'superhuman office', wholly estranging her from 'this earth' and fitting her 'for a celestial mission in terrestrial elements' (310). Pierre is 'sacrificing' himself, she writes, and she is hastening to 're-tie' herself to him (309). Obeying this impulse, she arrives at the Apostles' imitating Pierre's chronometrical self-sacrifice, thereby compounding the possibilities for disaster. In these last Books we are reminded more than once that Pierre is sexu-ally attracted to Isabel, that he may have committed incest with her (308, 337, 351). But after the arrival of Lucy's letter, his relationship with Isabel is seen to deteriorate rapidly and his relationship with Lucy becomes danger-ously ambiguous. In the final pages, Pierre bitterly rejects both Isabel and Lucy, and murders Glen; in his prison-cell Lucy dies on hearing Isabel call herself Pierre's sister; Pierre and Isabel commit suicide. Melville does not com-ment directly on much of the action in the last four Books of the novel, but these events clearly appear to illustrate the pamphlet's lesson that 'strange, *unique* follies and sins' are to be expected from one, like Pierre, attempting

'to live in this world according to the strict letter of the chronometricals' (213).

Yet for all Pierre's status as a profound, deep-diving au-thor, he never consciously understands the relevance of the pamphlet to his life, though he has glimmerings of under-standing (and Melville says that unconsciously he under-stood its application by the end of his life). He does not recognize the danger of Lucy's imitation of his sacrifice of self for another, in spite of his own experience. He reads Lucy's letter and is certain that 'whatever her enigmatical delusion' she 'remained transparently immaculate' in her heart (317), without even recognizing the possibility of a sexual motive in her decision to join him, as in his own deluded resolve to protect Isabel by living with her. He naively admires Lucy as 'an angel' (311), unmindful of the insidious sexual element in his earlier worship of Isabel as 'angel'. He later feels that 'some strange heavenly influ-ence was near him, to keep him from some uttermost harm' (337-8), once Lucy is ensconced at the Apostles', though to Isabel's 'covertly watchful eye' he 'would seem to look upon Lucy with an expression illy befitting their singular and so-supposed merely cousinly relation' (337). Even in the death-cell he sees his predicament as merely the result of his refusal to disown and portion off Isabel (360), just as earlier he tries to accept his grief at the news of his mother's death as a part of the cost at which 'the more exalted virtues are gained' (286). After belatedly rec-ognizing the incestuous nature of his attraction to Isabel, Pierre copes with the knowledge by shutting it out of his consciousness and continuing to deceive himself about his motives. In earlier Books Melville frequently comments on and analyzes Pierre's lack of awareness and his self-deception; now in the last four Books such commentary is notably lacking. Instead, Melville exalts his hero as con-sumed with devouring profundities, the result of his recent momentous experiences, even while Pierre is revealing a lack of profundity, a lack of perception, and an inability to face the truth of what he has actually experienced—limita-tions that are as dangerous as ever. While earlier Melville had commented incisively on Pierre's 'strange oversights and inconsistencies', he now fails to recognize a major contradiction in his characterization. He also forgets the origin of Pierre's book. Pierre announces to Isabel that he will 'gospelize the world anew' (273), but his new gospel is delusive, merely the result of his inability to accept himself as anything less than immaculate. Rather than rec-ognizing that he is no longer virtuous, he proclaims that 'Virtue and Vice are trash!' (273). Melville makes no at-tempt to reconcile Pierre's initial evasion of truth as an au-thor with his later supposed profundity. Nor does he make any attempt to explain the incongruity of Pierre's writing a blasphemous new gospel yet feeling protected by 'some strange heavenly influence' when Lucy joins him, though the incongruity makes Pierre seem more a simpleton than a man of profundity.

Still other parts of the novel are in conflict with the end-ing. In *Pierre* Melville sets out to demonstrate, among other things, that chronometrical altruism leads inevitably to catastrophe. His self-renouncing hero, as the pamphlet predicts, arrays 'men's earthly time-keepers against him' (212), falls into a 'fatal despair of becoming all good' (215), and works himself 'woe and death' (212). Yet near the end of this progression Melville endorses his hero's 'Titanism'. Thus, in *Pierre* Melville is sceptical of a world-rejecting Christian ethic because it destroys the individual who holds to it, but finally advocates a world-rejecting Titanism equally destructive of the individual who holds to it. Through many Books he prepares the reader to expect a catastrophic ending, a disaster that will be the inevitable result of Pierre's chronometrical sacrifice for Isabel and of his being merely human. But when the disastrous end comes, Pierre's state of mind is a 'reckless sky-assaulting mood' that Melville admires as evidence of demi-godliness. As he goes out to meet Glen and Fred, Pierre proclaims: '"I defy all world's bread and breath. Here I step out before the drawn-up worlds in widest space, and challenge one and all of them to battle!"' (357). In the prison-cell after the murder of Glen, Pierre is like Encela-dus with the mountain thrown down upon him: 'The cumbersome stone ceiling almost rested on his brow; so that the long tiers of massive cell-galleries above seemed partly piled on him'; Pierre's 'immortal, immovable, bleached cheek was dry' (360). His defiance in the prison-cell is again Enceladus-like, again implicitly approved, it would seem, by Melville: 'Well, be it hell. I will mold a trumpet of the flames, and, with my breath of flame, breathe back my defiance!' (360). In a sudden reversal, the chivalric posturing ('challenge one and all of them to battle', 'mold a trumpet of the flames', 'breathe back my defiance'), earlier indicative of Pierre's adolescent delusions, is now associated with a 'heaven-aspiring' nobility (347).

These conflicting attitudes toward Pierre's behaviour are not final, meaningful ambiguities Melville has carefully worked towards, but abrupt, confusing contradictions, the ultimate results of his excessively personal sympathy for Pierre's frustrations as an author. The decision to make the hero an author, whenever it was made, led to some powerful writing in the second half of *Pierre,* particularly in the Enceladus vision. It also deprived Melville of a full sense of what he was doing, in the second half and in the novel as a whole. 'Two books are being writ', said Melville (304), referring to the bungled one Pierre is putting on paper to offer to the world's eyes and the 'larger, and the infinitely better' one 'for Pierre's own private shelf', the one being written in his soul as the other is written on paper. In *Pierre* itself two books were also written, the one up through Book XIV (and intermittently thereafter) which examined the growth of a deluded but idealistic soul when confronted with the world's conventionality, and the later one which expressed Melville's sometimes sardonic, sometimes embittered reflections on his own career. There was no successful fusion of the two. As the new obsession drained off Melville's psychic and creative energies, the original purpose was blighted. Under the circumstances, it may be wrong to think of what *Pierre* might have been: behind Melville there was no educated literary milieu, no available models, no shoptalk with other literary masters,

no rigorously critical friend, no one to assure him of ultimate glory—nothing, in short, to help him hold to the pervading idea that impelled the first half of the book. Yet he had accomplished so much in this book that one becomes anguished as Melville's genius goes tragically to waste. The great epic of metaphysical whaling came tormentingly close to being succeeded within a few months by a Kraken-book, one of the finest psychological novels in world literature rather than merely the best psychological novel that had yet been written in English.

Notes

1. When he wrote this letter to Hawthorne, Melville had just begun work on *Pierre* or else was at the point of beginning it. The fullest timetable of the composition of the book is in Hershel Parker, 'Why *Pierre* Went Wrong', *Studies in the Novel,* vol. 8 (Spring 1976) 7-23.

2. Furthermore, ways of conceiving and organizing passages recur, as in Book IV, where Melville as narrator announces the ultimate futility of 'all analytical insight' (67) and instead resorts to subtler conjurations to convey his meaning, just as he has Ishmael do in 'The Whiteness of the Whale'.

3. 'Melville's *Pierre*', *New England Quarterly,* vol. 3 (April 1930) 195-234.

4. 'Historical Note', p. 407, in *Pierre,* ed. Harrison Hayford, Hershel Parker, and G. Thomas Tanselle (Evanston and Chicago: Northwestern University Press and the Newberry Library 1971). Page references are to this edition. The 'Historical Note' is by Leon Howard (365-79) and Hershel Parker (379-407).

5. See 'Why *Pierre* Went Wrong', cited in footnote one, and Hershel Parker's 'Contract: *Pierre,* by Herman Melville', *Proof,* vol. 5 (1977). Briefly, after several weeks' intense work on the manuscript, Melville went to New York City in the last days of 1851 to arrange a contract with the Harpers for publication of *Pierre,* then seen as a shortish book of around 360 pages, not the much longer book of some 500 pages which the Harpers eventually published. Not only did the Harpers fail to give Melville an advance, they also insisted upon less favourable terms than ever before. Distressed by his contract negotiations, and further exacerbated by scathing reviews of *Moby-Dick* which were appearing in the January periodicals, Melville immediately began writing his own literary frustrations into the manuscript. Before he left New York City (apparently in the third week of January 1852), Melville had enlarged the book beyond the size he had stipulated to the publisher and had instructed his lawyer-brother Allan Melville to alter the contract accordingly. Allan's letter to the Harpers on 21 January 1852 establishes the rapidity with which Melville's conception of the book changed and locates that change as occurring between the very end of 1851 and the first week or so of 1852.

6. 'Historical Note', pp. 366 and 372.

7. Melville had recently concluded in fact that 'There are some enterprises in which a careful disorderliness is the true method' (*Moby-Dick,* chapter 82, 'The Honor and Glory of Whaling').

8. In 'Retrospective' Pierre may be portrayed as rather more infantile than a lad of twelve or more should be, for instance. Some apparent awkwardnesses, such as the uncertain age of Isabel, may well be deliberate ambiguities.

9. The word 'nether' is Parker's recent emendation for the first edition's 'nearer'. The emendation will be incorporated in subsequent printings of the Northwestern-Newberry edition.

10. Page 65 provides a clear example: 'now, for the first time, Pierre, Truth rolls a black billow through thy soul! Ah, miserable thou, to whom Truth, in her first tides, bears nothing but wrecks!' The passage continues: 'as the mariner, shipwrecked and cast on the beach, has much ado to escape the recoil of the wave that hurled him there; so Pierre long struggled, and struggled, to escape the recoil of that anguish, which had dashed him out of itself, upon the beach of his swoon'. See also the accounts of the 'shrine in the fresh-foliaged heart of Pierre' (68); the 'choice fountain, in the filial breast of a tender-hearted and intellectually appreciative child' (68); the 'charred landscape' within Pierre (86); the 'billow' that had 'so profoundly whelmed Pierre' (104); the things 'fœtally forming' in Pierre (106); the 'electric fluid' in which Isabel seems to swim (151-2); the 'Hyperborean regions' into which strongest minds are led (165); and the 'vulnerable god' and 'self-upbraiding sailor' (180-1).

11. See, for example, the passages explaining that 'From without, no wonderful effect is wrought within ourselves, unless some interior, responding wonder meets it' (51); that 'in the warm halls of the heart one single, untestified memory's spark shall suffice to enkindle . . . a blaze of evidence' (71); that the 'inestimable compensation of the heavier woes' is 'a saddened truth' (88); that 'when suddenly encountering the shock of new and unanswerable relevations . . . man, at first, ever seeks to shun all conscious definitiveness in his thoughts and purposes' (92); that the soul of man 'can not, and does never intelligently confront the totality of its wretchedness' when 'on all sides assailed by prospects of disaster' (104); that the 'intensest light of reason and revelation combined, can not shed such blazonings upon the deeper truths in man, as will sometimes proceed from his own profoundest gloom' (169); that 'on the threshold of any wholly new and momentous devoted enterprise, the thousand ulterior intricacies and emperilings to which it must conduct . . . are mostly withheld from sight' (175); and that 'There is a dark, mad mystery in some human hearts' (180).

12. Also, the section of 'Young America in Literature' (250-1) on the flirtatious young ladies who entreat Pierre to 'grace their Albums with some nice little song' (and who live within easy walking or riding range, judging by the way his servants deliver the albums back to their owners) seems out of keeping with the portrayal of the maidens of Saddle Meadows in Book III (p. 46, especially). Until Book XVII there is no hint that Pierre has been sought out by any of the local girls, or that he has had social exchanges of any significance with any of them besides Lucy Tartan (who resides only part of the year in Saddle Meadows). Perhaps an even clearer example of Melville's forgetting his earlier characterization is in Book XXI, 'Plinlimmon', where he declares that a 'varied scope of reading, little suspected by his friends, and randomly acquired by a random but lynx-eyed mind' in the course of 'multifarious, incidental, bibliographic encounterings' as an 'inquirer after Truth' had 'poured one considerable contributary stream into that bottomless spring of original thought which the occasion and time had caused to burst out' in Pierre (283). But earlier Pierre's reading was said to have brought him 'into many a maze of all-bewildering beauty', not Truth (6). These examples are conspicuous; probably some other improvised passages are consistent enough with the rest of the book to escape notice.

13. There is always the possibility that this passage was written before the pamphlet and left uncancelled; similar redundancies were created by late additions in *Typee*. However, Melville's forgetting and improvising elsewhere in the second half of *Pierre* tends to cast doubt on this possibility.

14. *Pierre* (New York: Hendricks House, Inc. 1949) p. lxxxiii.

15. Melville's trip to New York probably coincided with his reaching a point beyond which it would have been difficult to proceed with a cautious enough development of the Pierre-Isabel relationship, for the inhibiting sexual mores of the time would hardly have allowed him to trace all the stages of an incestuous passion and still have his book published. Whatever comments the Harpers may have made on his work-in-progress, for practical purposes he had written himself into an impasse by the time he established Pierre's menage at the Apostles' and made his ambiguous suggestion that incestuous lust may have been consummated. The impasse would have encouraged his urge to explore his new preoccupation with authorship. It would also have encouraged the introduction of another character to facilitate some exploration of Pierre's relationship with Isabel without intensifying the suggestion of its incestuous nature. Melville's choice of Lucy as this agent had the further advantage of providing, through the involvement of Fred Tartan and Glendinning Stanly, the means of a tragic outcome.

Steve Gowler (essay date 1981)

SOURCE: "That Profound Silence: The Failure of Theodicy in *Pierre*," in *Southern Humanities Review,* Vol. XV, No. 3, Summer, 1981, pp. 243-54.

[*In the following essay, Gowler discusses the role of God and belief in* Pierre, *concluding that the novel portrays the breakdown of religious systems and "the absurdity of the human condition."*]

Herman Melville's *Pierre* is a story of unrelieved suffering, a devolution toward despair and suicide. In it Melville appears to have vented the bitter cynicism which infected him as he tried to consolidate his identity as artist, thinker, and husband. After completing *Moby-Dick,* Melville began the labyrinthine psychological probings of *Pierre* without respite. Though on the surface *Pierre* seems very unlike Melville's masterwork, some scholars believe it is the culminating work in a trilogy which includes *Mardi* as well as *Moby-Dick.*[1] With desperate urgency, *Pierre* presses the metaphysical questions introduced in these earlier works. Evil is no longer buffered by the unreality of *Mardi,* nor by the distancing of a healthy-minded narrator from a deranged psyche as in *Moby-Dick.* In *Pierre* evil appears as an immediate, inescapable power which rudely insinuates its way not only into the hero's thoughts and actions, but also into the anonymous narrator's ruminations.[2]

Pierre contains numerous thematic vectors which could be traced in isolation: the silence of God, the plight of the artist, the struggle of the idealist against social conventions, the destructiveness of pride, the conflict between sensuality and spirituality, the insulting indifference of Fate, the cruelty of the city, etc. However, it is the coalescence of themes like these that produces *Pierre*'s powerful statement of the absurdity of the human condition.[3] The meaning of *Pierre* is that meaning itself is ephemeral, devoid of discernible logic, beyond guarantee. *Pierre* portrays a young man of talent who sincerely desires some ordering principle, some defense against the onslaught of evil, but who is undermined in every attempt to construct a hedge of meaning.

Nathalia Wright has said that in *Pierre* Melville "came close to writing an anatomy of sin."[4] Pierre's plight is exaggerated, yet, in a sense, universal. Sin, suffering, and death inevitably intrude upon the lives of individuals and communities, raising disturbing questions about life's value and meaning. For most people, everyday reality has been so carefully constructed and is so massively reinforced by habit, tradition, ethos, and institutions that evil only infrequently subverts one's will to live, work, and love.[5] With *Pierre* Melville provides a test case, an example of an individual in close proximity to meaning structures which have proved effective for others, but which fail to supply him with the solace of meaning or an alternative to suicide.

Attempts to withstand the horrors of evil through the construction or appropriation of meaning structures are some-times called "theodicies." The term "theodicy," a combination of the Greek words "theos" (God) and "diké" (justice), customarily refers to the philosophical or theological justification of God in the face of evil. Often theodicy is seen as the academic equivalent of Milton's attempt to "justify the ways of God to men." But theodicy has accumulated more comprehensive connotations in this century. As sociologist Peter Berger points out, "the illiterate peasant who comments upon the death of a child by referring to the will of God is engaging in theodicy as much as the learned theologian who writes a treatise to demonstrate that the suffering of the innocent does not negate the conception of a God both all-good and all-powerful."[6] Here the term will be used in this broader sense as an attempt rationally and emotionally to circumvent despair, or, more specifically, as an attempt to explain and legitimate the continuation of life and action in spite of the jolting experience of evil and suffering. *Pierre* may be said to inhabit the realm of the absurd because it systematically depicts the failure of all available theodicies—secular as well as Christian—to provide the hero with a frame of meaning sturdy enough to withstand his increasing consciousness of evil. By Melville's time, Enlightenment scepticism had overturned the grand religio-philosophical attempts to reconcile the simultaneous existence of evil and of a good, powerful God. Thus, in this essay I will take up non-philosophical, practical, socially-available theodicies which were still operative for many people in Melville's day. In section I, I will deal with those arising out of the Biblical tradition, and in section II with those deriving from romanticism.

I

Although Pierre is allegedly a Christian, the Christianity found in his story is too enervated to serve as the sustaining element of his life. The two most prominent symbols of Christianity—the stammering clergyman Falsgrave, whose religious zeal was long before quenched by his desire to win the approbation of Saddle-Meadows' elite, and the husk of a church which houses a motley band of Kantian "apostles" in the city—both suggest that Christianity is a dessicated, worn-out institution irrelevant to present issues of vital importance.[7] The Church's inability to make sense of Pierre's situation dawns vividly upon the hero as he travels to the city:

> The imperishable monument of his holy Catholic Church; the imperishable record of his Holy Bible; the imperishable intuition of the innate truth of Christianity;—these were the indestructible anchors which still held the priest to his firm Faith's rock, when the sudden storm raised by the Evil One assailed him. But Pierre—where could *he* find the Church, the monument, the Bible, which unequivocally said to him—"Go on; thou art in the Right; I endorse thee all over; go on."[8]

Prior to Pierre's departure from Saddle-Meadows, there are scattered indications that Christianity might furnish the hero with a network of meaning capable of accommodating his subsequent sin and suffering. An integral part of

Pierre's heritage, Christianity was, in fact, a *sine qua non* of the Glendinning ideal of gentlemanliness. Pierre aligned himself with this family tradition by joining his mother in partaking of the Sacrament when he was sixteen. But Pierre's faith was an inheritance rather than a product of his own spirit. Christianity's power, if it ever existed, belonged to a former time, in this case a past time which was becoming increasingly unattractive to Pierre. Nevertheless, for a time, a genuine Christian idealism appears to motivate Pierre's decision to champion Isabel's cause while simultaneously sparing his father's honor and his mother's feelings. In a nocturnal confrontation with Falsgrave, Pierre seals his decision by suggesting that the clergyman's faith is specious and by invoking the true Christian spirit. Convinced that he is imbued with a unique sensitivity to the divine ("Pierre felt that deep in him lurked a divine unidentifiableness, that owned no earthly kith or kin" [p. 89]), Pierre embarks on a mission beyond the capacity of an ordinary man.

Thus, early in **Pierre,** the protagonist is apparently wholeheartedly devoted to the Christian ideal. However, he is also appallingly naive and inconsistent in his expression of faith. Despite his ostensible adoption of the Christian way, none of the Biblical theodicies shield him from the devastating effects of evil. In the first place, Pierre does not even entertain the possibility of a theodicy of retribution whereby good and evil are appropriately rewarded or punished by a just God, if not immediately, then in a life to come. The fact that Pierre never demonstrates a belief in life after death means that a retribution theodicy could only be salvaged if there were some evidence of a coherent distribution of justice in this life. Such a theodicy is extremely tenuous since it is subject to empirical falsification. Further, Pierre is so overwhelmed by his discovery of the anguishing reality of evil that a future harmony which might lend retroactive significance to his suffering is unimaginable.[9] The narrator comments explicitly on Pierre's doubt that things might be made understandable at some future date:

> By infallible presentiment he saw, that not always doth life's beginning gloom conclude in gladness; that wedding-bells peal not ever in the last scene of life's fifth act; that while the countless tribes of common novels laboriously spin vails of mystery, only to complacently clear them up at last; and while the countless tribe of common dramas do but repeat the same; yet the profounder emanations of the human mind, intended to illustrate all that can be humanly known of human life; these never unravel their own intricacies, and have no proper endings; but in imperfect, unanticipated, and disappointing sequels (as mutilated stumps), hurry to abrupt intermergings with the eternal tides of time and fate. (p. 141)

Even some of the Biblical writers recognized the problems of a theodicy of retribution. Job arose out of a countertradition which passionately objected to the idea that absolute justice holds sway in this world. Job's flirtation with blasphemy produces a theodicy totally unlike that of the retributionists. For Job, meaning arises from the fact that

his tenacious faith in the integrity of his life and in the inequity of his suffering earned him an audience with God. Even though God does not answer the question Job asked, the very fact that He responds in majesty renders all human confusion trivial but understandable. Pierre himself takes a Job-like stance when, in an audacious prayer, he challenges God to provide him with the strength to see his mission through to the end. His request ends in a tone of threatening defiance: "If ye forsake me now,—farewell to Faith, farewell to Truth, farewell to God . . ." (p. 107). But unlike Job's, Pierre's bold challenge provokes no response. No answering whirlwind greets Pierre, only silence, deafening in its profundity and absoluteness. The narrator, Pierre's keenest, most sympathetic observer, remarks: "Silence is at once the most harmless and the most awful thing in all nature. It speaks of the Reserved Forces of Fate. Silence is the only Voice of our God" (p. 204).

Christology is the strongest Christian theodicy. If Christ suffered as both God and man, evil and suffering no longer need be seen as discrepancies or injustices or intrusions; rather, they can be assimilated as unfortunate but essential aspects of the universe. God now needs no justification since even He is not immune to the pain and degradation of life's negativities.[10] Though this theodicy does not explain the "why" of evil, it does provide a powerful means of overcoming evil's paralyzing effects by allowing the individual to view God as a concerned co-sufferer instead of a capricious enemy. However, we have no indication that Pierre's suffering is alleviated by a consciousness of God as fellow-sufferer. In fact, Pierre's suffering is intensified by a radical aloneness; he shares his burden with no one.

Christological theodicy fails Pierre because he views Christ as exemplar only, never as savior. A brother-like fondness for Christ is merely Pierre's first tentative step toward Prometheanism. For Pierre, Christ provides no clue to the nature of the universe. Pierre is interested only in the strength of personality and radical devotion to calling which set Christ apart from the masses. Founded on a private, highly idiosyncratic interpretation of scripture and tradition, Pierre's strange version of Christianity is expressed through threats to God, gross inconsiderateness, and unabashed pride. Brian Higgins and Hershel Parker have commented upon Pierre's so-called "Christianity":

> Nowhere in the book, moreover, does Pierre see that for all his efforts to be Christlike he has never been a true Christian. Despite his partaking with his mother of the Holy Sacrament, he has in fact been only nominally a Christian, drawn to the Church as a family responsibility laid down by his father, whose maxim linked gentlemanhood and Christianity. The superhuman powers Pierre invokes are ill-sortedly Christian or pagan; consistently he images his relationship with such powers as an antagonistic one: demons or gods, they are to be threatened and, especially, bargained with.[11]

Clearly Pierre's Christianity is founded on a suspect, even heretical, theology. Yet the failure of faith is not exclusively Pierre's problem. Once Pierre moves to the city, references to Christianity cease, suggesting that the Church and her faith belong to the old ways of the country only. Pierre rejects Christian faith as an impotent holdover from a past which grows more disreputable the more he learns of it.

II

Pierre's break with his heritage dimly echoes the intellectual rumblings of the *Aufklärung*. Just as the most perceptive thinkers of the eighteenth century had recognized the inability of Christianity, in its traditional formulations, to answer the questions posed by their experience, so Melville, too, endured a crisis of faith. In a sense, Pierre is Melville's proxy as he looks outside his inherited faith for meaningful structures of existence. Melville was painfully aware of the fact that he lived in a post-Enlightenment world in which the hypothesis of a personal God who intervenes in the histories of individuals and societies was no longer tenable. The last thoroughgoing attempt at philosophical theodicy, Leibniz's grand exercise in monism, had been unceremoniously demolished by Voltaire, Kant, and others who made it abundantly clear that human experience denied, with absolute finality, that ours is "the best of all possible worlds."

The task of theodicy had been reformulated by the end of the eighteenth century. The idea of a benevolent God who needed to be justified in the face of the world's evil gave way to the idea of a distant and uninterested deity whom many held culpable for his indifference. For the majority of these thinkers, God's assumed indifference to the problems of humankind elicited a retaliatory indifference toward things divine. "To each realm its own" was the tacit supposition of most thinkers, with the proprietary rights to Christ the only matter to be settled. A God-man was unthinkable in the new scheme, so a de-hybridization of Christ was accomplished by appropriating him entirely into the human realm *sans* miracles.

This tidy solution of the God-problem left the evil-problem untouched. In Romanticism, which was constructed on the ruins of the old world order, men like Hegel, Goethe, and Kant tried to devise systems which could account for moral and historical fluctuations without relying on a *deus ex machina*. They, and their artistic counterparts, had somehow to incorporate evil and suffering meaningfully into a plot deprived of a divine whipping boy.

M. H. Abrams, in his *Natural Supernaturalism,* speaks at length about the theoretical treatment of evil in the early Romantic period. Simply put, the Romantics believed that individuals, and by extension all of humanity, are involved in a process of growth and education in which suffering and sin are necessary milestones on the journey toward maturity. Pain and sundry other evils serve to prick, sensitize, and heighten the consciousness of individuals-information. Rather than the Biblical *Heilsgeschichte,* or salvation history, the Romantics promulgated a *Bildungsgeschichte,* or formation history, a pattern of progress toward maturity in this world which accepts evil as its necessary concomitant.[12] In Abrams' words, "most Romantic versions of the educational journey, as we have seen, incorporate a displaced theodicy, in which error and suffering are justified as indispensable to the self-formation and self-realization of the mature individual, in a span of reference coterminous with his life in the world" (p. 244).

Melville had read widely in the works of the Romantics, and he was acutely aware of the various ways Romantic doctrines were being popularly translated by the transcendentalists and sentimentalists of his own day.[13] In fact, in *Pierre* Melville utilized many of the conventions of these traditions as well as the most characteristic Romantic narrative pattern, the *Bildungsroman.*[14] But just as he did with the Christian tradition, Melville portrays Romantic theodicies as failing to make sense of Pierre's life. *Pierre* blatantly parodies Romantic symbols and structures, gothic plot conventions, sentimental dialogue, and transcendental philosophy.[15] *Pierre* stands not as a recommendation, but as a rejection of the Romantic synthesis.

For the Romantics, nature is the individual's companion and mentor in the educational process. Abrams notes that "Wordsworth's argument, like Milton's, is a theodicy which locates the justification for human suffering in the restoration of a lost paradise" (p. 95). This Romantic paradise is not given from above, but is the result of the union of mind and nature. Pierre appears to live in such an integrated human-nature paradise when his story opens. The narrator composes psalms to express Pierre's relationship to the landscape: "Oh, praised be the beauty of this earth; the beauty, and the bloom, and the mirthfulness thereof" (p. 32). Pierre's singular life of love, security, and unity with his natural and social environments "seemed almost to realize here below the sweet dreams of those religious enthusiasts, who paint to us a Paradise to come" (p. 16).

But Saddle-Meadows as Paradise is only a vision of Pierre's dreaming, pre-conscious state, that period before Isabel appears with her shocking retinue of evil and suffering. After Pierre's "fall," nature offers no solace; in fact, Saddle-Meadows, with its unavoidable associations with a soured past, harbors so many terrors for Pierre that he flees to the city—precisely the opposite route of Wordsworth's escape to the country "From the vast city, where I long had pined / A discontented sojourner: now free" (*The Prelude,* Bk. I, ll. 7-8).

Pierre fares no better in the city. It becomes merely the harsh backdrop of his final days. Janis Stout calls *Pierre* "one of the strongest depictions of the Evil City in all American fiction."[16] However, the city is never set in opposition to the morally superior country left behind. Instead, the city, with its horrible loneliness, failed communication, and pervasive alienation, only completes a portrait of evil begun at Saddle-Meadows. Stout lists some of the ways Melville presents a tainted view of nature:

> He establishes an association of the country with a warlike aristocracy. . . . More devastating is the light

thrown on Pierre's country nurture by later events: the ominous overtures of incest in his relationship with his mother become more obvious as the incest motif with Isabel develops; concealed threats appear in the landscape itself; and Pierre comes to realize the fatuousness of his early literary effusions, which the narrator had pointedly linked to rural sensibility. (p. 165)

Moral country/evil city is an illusory dichotomy attributable simply to the fact that the natural landscape is better able to camouflage evil. Beneath the surface, however, country and city rest on a common dehumanizing base.

The narrator twice informs the reader, the second time with special emphasis, that "it had been the choice fate of Pierre to have been born and bred in the country" (pp. 5, 13) and that "Nature intended a rare and original development in Pierre" (p. 13). Subtly ironic, these words prove true in a way which belies their benevolent tone. Pierre's natural milieu wears a false face. Beneath its placid surface lie the seeds of Pierre's destruction. His experience directly contradicts the Emersonian idea that nature is the rich depository of commodity, beauty, discipline, and language, an expression of spirit which is both text and interpreter of the universe's essence and meaning. While he dreams of Enceladus, Pierre comes to the frightening realization that "say what some poets will, Nature is not so much her own ever-sweet interpreter, as the mere supplier of that cunning alphabet, whereby selecting and combining as he pleases, each man reads his own peculiar lesson according to his own peculiar mind and mood" (p. 342).

"To believe your own thought, to believe what is true for you in your private heart is true for all men,—that is genius. . . . Trust thyself: every heart vibrates to that iron string. . . . Society everywhere is conspiring against the manhood of every one of its members. . . . Whoso would be a man, must be a nonconformist." These maxims from Emerson's "Self-Reliance" embody the transcendentalist version of the Romantic notion of the surpassing excellence of the private life. Abrams speaks of the "theodicy of the private life" in addition to the "theodicy of the landscape." The growth and nurture of the individual soul "justifies sorrow and suffering as the necessary condition for achieving wisdom, resignation, and power of insight which are attributes of maturity" (Abrams, p. 132).

Pierre's awareness of his unique self-being and his desire to devote himself unreservedly to his own psychological and emotional development are mentioned repeatedly. The narrator speaks of Pierre's "singularly developed character and most singular life-career" (p. 12). Lucy "cherished a notion that Pierre bore a charmed life" (p. 22). Pierre himself "felt that deep in him lurked a divine unidentifiableness, that owned no earthly kith or kin" (p. 89). Pierre consistently acts and thinks as a self-reliant man. Giving his spirit its head, he accepts the dictates of his heart ("The heart! the heart! 'tis God's anointed; let me pursue the heart!" [p. 91]); he thrusts himself into actions which insure public censure; he breaks with family and society at large when they threaten his mission. He is the consum-

mate nonconformist. But close adherence to Emerson's maxims results in despair, not transcendental meaning. The theodicy of the private life fails Pierre because he realizes he is not an independent agent and because his exclusive attention to his own desires and development disintegrates into narcissism.

Even before quitting Saddle-Meadows, Pierre glimpses a sobering truth which would undermine any theodicy of personal progress: "Here, in imperfect inklings, tinglings, presentiments, Pierre began to feel—what all mature men, who are Magians, sooner or later know, and more or less assuredly—that not always in our actions, are we our own factors" (p. 51). In "Self-Reliance" Emerson warned that one should not court Chance, but should deal with Cause and Effect, the "chancellors of God." This is an impossible admonition for Pierre because, as the narrator informs the reader, he believed cause and effect are inscrutable, not only in the realm of physics, but also in the kingdom of the heart:

> Why this cheek kindles with a noble enthusiasm; why that lip curls in scorn; these are things not wholly imputable to the immediate apparent cause, which is only one link in the chain; but to a long line of dependencies whose further part is lost in the mid-regions of the impalpable air. (p. 67)

A theodicy of the private life is dependent upon the idea of free will; suffering can be interpreted as meaningful in a scheme of growth, development, and self-realization only if it is the result of a free decision-making process. If free choices succeed one another in a process of trial and error, even when the errors are genuinely and horribly painful, the whole process can be justified as an exercise in character-building. But if there is no connection between the free choices of the individual and the pain suffered, if the evil appears gratuitous, then a theodicy of the private life crumbles. As evil tightens its grasp on Pierre, he becomes less and less able to extricate himself by some free and self-reliant act. The futility of Pierre's situation is starkly summarized by the narrator: "Pierre was not arguing Fixed Fate and Free Will, now; Fixed Fate and Free Will were arguing him, and Fixed Fate got the better in the debate" (p. 182).[17]

Narcissism, as well as fate and chance, jeopardizes the theodicy of the private life. Pierre is so taken with his own talents and enthusiasm for duty that finally all of his actions result from motives which are perversely selfish. Pierre's ability to distinguish between the self and non-self breaks down; the world becomes an extension of himself. He tolerates no relationship which might perpetually remind him of his existence alongside others. Each woman with whom he desires a relationship is assigned a sibling equality; anything more (a mother) or less (an object of sensual desire) must be rejected as a serious threat to his carefully cultivated solipsism. Because he discounts everything but his own fluctuating desires, Pierre cannot find meaning even in love. His narcissistic sterility is evident in his abhorrence at the thought of consummating his love for Lucy and in his habit of flirting with members of his real or imagined family—his mother and Isabel—with whom sexual contact is unthinkable.

The private life also fails Pierre in its denial of the healing effects of community. Pierre breaks with every person and tradition that might provide him with a context of meaning as he attempts to deal with his perception of the depravity of the world. Even if community does not offer genuine love, it still yields a fresh perspective, a corrective to the necessarily limited point of view of the individual. Pierre turns inward and declares with frightening finality that he intends to live without the normal benefits of society. Unlike Ishmael, who could look back on his mixed experience aboard the *Pequod* and find refreshing intervals of shared purpose, Pierre, in an act of self-destructive pride, systematically severs his ties with family, fiancee, friends, and God.

The Romantic theodicies, then, fail Pierre as abysmally as those of Christianity. One after the other, traditional structures of meaning are shown to be inaccessible or irrelevant or impotent for Pierre. This record of empty theodicies bears some interesting affinities to a debunking work of the previous century, Voltaire's *Candide.* Helen Hauser contends that "the explicit moral of the book [*Pierre*] is very similar to that of *Candide,* a work which it resembles in some other particulars—cultivate your own garden, and do not seek to do the impossible."[18] Hauser's recognition of the similarity of the two works is instructive, but she goes too far when she suggests that they have similar morals. *Pierre* has no consoling coda of pleasant gardens; it ends in a body-strewn jail cell. In fact, *Pierre* explicitly rejects the notion that tending to one's own work is redeeming. Pierre's work as an author pushes him even more deeply into despair. It accelerates his awareness of the unendurable ubiquity of evil. Ishmael gained salvation by artistically arranging and rearranging his checkered history until discrepancies dissolved and a meaningful pattern emerged. Pierre is not so lucky; even art fails him in his quest for meaning.

Worse yet, Pierre is denied the terrifying, but quickening, meaning of defiant rebellion which is vouchsafed to Ahab. The minimal theodicy of rebellion is in some strange way the most satisfying, in that it represents the final, desperate attempt to retain one's humanity over against a universe which is perceived as hostile. In this theodicy suffering is welcomed as a sign of conflict with a superior foe, a black badge of courage which distinguishes its wearer as one who says "No! in thunder." But Pierre's "No!" does not thunder because it is uttered in an acoustical and metaphysical void. He has no Moby-Dick to ennoble his defiance. The final absurdity of *Pierre* is that the hero is forced to take his own life because the universe is left as blank and unaffected by his murderous passion as it was by his earlier idealism and docility.

By systematically demonstrating the impotence of common, socially and traditionally available theodicies,

Melville's work represents more than the anatomy of an ultimately tormented soul; it also serves as an indictment of life itself by portraying existence as a crucible of pain and evil which lacks any inherent means of amelioration. But this does not stand as Melville's final word. He did not accompany Pierre in suicide; he lived to write more fiction and poetry. Apparently he finally attained a degree of peace in his own life, but it came only after the struggle, after the jolting realization that life carries no guarantee of meaning. *Pierre* stands as a bleak picture of the breakdown of inherited structures of meaning, a sobering reminder of the inscrutability of life.

Notes

1. Melville's novels can be grouped thematically in various ways. Some scholars see *Pierre* as *sui generis,* a land-locked anomaly lying between the earlier sea trilogies and his final two novels, which return to a shipboard setting. I find a more helpful grouping the one suggested by Edward Wagenknecht in *Cavalcade of the American Novel* (New York: Henry Holt, 1952), pp. 59-72. He divides the works through *Pierre* into "romances of experience" (*Typee, Omoo, Redburn,* and *White-Jacket*) and "romances of imagination" (*Mardi, Moby-Dick,* and *Pierre*). George C. Homans, in "The Dark Angel: The Tragedy of Herman Melville," *The New England Quarterly,* 5 (1932), 699, advocates a scheme much like Wagenknecht's and maintains that *Mardi, Moby-Dick,* and *Pierre* "show a regularly developed action . . . completed with the catastrophe in the last."

2. This essay presupposes a close relationship between protagonist, narrator, and author. Even when describing Pierre's wildest actions and decisions, the narrator remains sympathetic and never adopts a condescending tone. The rhetorical evidence for an intimate relationship between Pierre and the narrator has led Raymond J. Nelson, in "The Art of Herman Melville: The Author of *Pierre,*" *Yale Review,* 59 (1970), 209, to posit Pierre himself as the narrator, and the book *Pierre* as the autobiographical work which we find the hero writing in the city. We can also assume some identification between Pierre and Melville because of their many biographical similarities. In his introduction to the Hendricks House edition of *Pierre* (New York, 1949), Henry A. Murray notes that "scarcely anyone denies that *Pierre* is, in some sense and in some degree, autobiographical" (p. xxi).

3. The idea that *Pierre* is a work of nihilism or absurdity has been suggested by many scholars. Joyce Carol Oates, in *The Edge of Impossibility* (Greenwich: Fawcett, 1972), p. 75, views *Pierre* as an important milestone in Melville's "apparent drift into nihilism." Margaret S. McCroskery, in "Melville's *Pierre:* The Inner Voyage," *Studies in the Humanities,* 2 (1971), 8, calls *Pierre* a "vanguard of the philosophy of the absurd" and a work which describes "the collapse of life-sustaining myths." Murray states that "the pervasive moral of the book . . .

is that there is *no* moral" (p. xvi). Nina Baym, in her recent "Melville's Quarrel with Fiction," *PMLA* [*Publications of the Modern Language Association of America*], 94 (1979), 909, aligns herself with those who believe Melville's writings betray a "sense of the absurdity of the universe, the meaninglessness of language, and, hence, the absurdity of writing." Robert Milder calls *Pierre* "a deliberate *reductio ad absurdum* of all metaphysics, all ethics, and all psychology" in his "Melville's 'Intentions' in *Pierre*," *Studies in the Novel*, 6 (1974), 186.

4. Nathalia Wright, "*Pierre:* Herman Melville's *Inferno*," *American Literature*, 32 (1960), 180.

5. The sociological theory lying behind this statement is derived from Peter L. Berger and Thomas Luckmann's *The Social Construction of Reality* (Garden City: Anchor Books, 1967).

The thesis of the present essay is akin to that of T. Walter Herbert's *Moby-Dick and Calvinism: A World Dismantled* (New Brunswick, N.J.: Rutgers University Press, 1977), a work which details Melville's reworking of his inherited theological meaning-structures in *Moby-Dick*. Herbert, too, uses Berger and Luckmann's "sociology of knowledge" in order to help shape his argument (see pp. 3-5).

6. Peter Berger, *The Sacred Canopy* (Garden City, N.Y.: Anchor Books, 1969), p. 53.

7. Another seemingly obvious negative comment on Christianity is Plinlimmon's pamphlet. I omit it from my discussion because of its equivocal meaning and role in the book. On the surface it seems to reinforce the idea of the impracticality of Christianity; however, its strong satirical tone and the unsavory appearance and personality of its author make it something less than a straight-forward argument against Christianity. For a cogent analysis of the pamphlet as satire see Brian Higgins, "Plinlimmon and the Pamphlet Again," *Studies in the Novel*, 4 (1972), 27-38.

8. Herman Melville, *Pierre*, ed. Harrison Hayford et al. (Evanston and Chicago: Northwestern Univ. Press and the Newberry Library, 1971), p. 205. All further references to *Pierre* will appear in the text and will be taken from this edition.

9. One of the most eloquent rejections of the theodicy of deferred justice is found in *The Brothers Karamazov*. Ivan challenges Alyosha with these words: "I must have justice, or I will destroy myself. And not justice in some remote infinite time and space, but here on earth. Justice that I can see myself. . . . I don't want harmony. From love for humanity I don't want it. . . . [T]oo high a price is asked for harmony; it's beyond our means to pay so much. And so I give back my entrance ticket . . ." Fyodor Dostoevsky, *The Brothers Karamazov*, trans. Constance Garnett (New York: Signet Classic, 1957), pp. 225-226.

10. The curious nature of a Christological theodicy has been powerfully summarized by Albert Camus in

The Rebel, trans. Anthony Bower (New York: Vintage, 1956), p. 34:

In that Christ had suffered, and had suffered voluntarily, suffering was no longer unjust and all pain was necessary. In one sense, Christianity's bitter intuition and legitimate pessimism concerning human behavior is based on the assumption that over-all injustice is as satisfying to man as total justice.. . . If everything, without exception, in heaven and earth is doomed to pain and suffering, then a strange form of happiness is possible.

11. Brian Higgins and Hershel Parker, "The Flawed Grandeur of Melville's *Pierre*," in *New Perspectives on Melville*, ed. Faith Pullin (Kent State Univ. Press, 1978), p. 180.

12. This comparison of *Heilsgeschichte* with *Bildungsgeschichte* is taken from M. H. Abrams, *Natural Supernaturalism* (New York: Norton, 1971), p. 188. All further references to this work appear in the text.

13. See William Braswell, *Melville's Religious Thought* (New York: Pageant Books, 1959) for a good discussion of Melville's reading.

14. *Pierre's* structural similarities to the *Bildungsroman* have been widely recognized in recent years. Joel Thomas, in "Melville's Use of Mysticism," *Philological Quarterly*, 57 (1974), 422, notes *Pierre's* "affinities with the *Bildungsroman*." Leon Howard and Hershel Parker, in their "Historical Note" in the Northwestern-Newberry edition of *Pierre*, say: "There is a great deal of Carlyle's *Bildungsroman* in the latter part of *Pierre*, as there had been in *Moby-Dick*, but none in the early part when Melville was firmly in control of his intentions" (p. 370). Robert Milder contends that the central idea of *Pierre* is the problem of knowledge in both its external and internal aspects and that this problem is explored "through the vehicle of a *bildungsroman*" (p. 186). Nina Baym calls *Pierre* "a domestic romance and *bildungsroman*" which Melville put to his own, unique use (p. 909).

15. That *Pierre* is a parody of romantic conventions has been discussed by too many scholars to mention. See Raymond Nelson, p. 203, for a catalogue of specific targets of parody.

16. Janis Stout, "The Encroaching Sodom: Melville's Urban Fiction," *Texas Studies in Literature and Language*, 17 (1975), 169. All further references to this work appear in the text.

17. *Pierre* promotes neither strict determinism nor predestination. Fate and free will are both aspects of human life according to Melville. R. E. Watters, in "Melville's Metaphysics of Evil," *University of Toronto Quarterly*, 9 (1947), 177, maintains that Melville's belief in both fate and free will, along with his inability to find any final purpose in the universe, resulted in a loose type of necessarianism. Though he never worked out a tight, systematic dis-

cussion of his position on freedom and fate, we can assume that these words of Ishmael reflect the interaction of the concepts as Melville saw it:

> . . . chance, free will, and necessity—no wise incompatible—all interweavingly working together. The straight warp of necessity, not to be swerved from its ultimate course—its every alternating vibration, indeed, only tending to that; free will still free to ply her shuttle between given threads; and chance, though restrained in its play within the right lines of necessity, and sideways in its motions modified by free will, though thus prescribed to by both, chance by turns rules either, and has the last featuring blow at events. *Moby-Dick* (New York: Norton Critical Edition, 1977), p. 185.

18. Helen Hauser, "Spinozan Philosophy in *Pierre*," *American Literature* 49 (1977), 51.

Paul Lewis (essay date 1983)

SOURCE: "Melville's *Pierre* and the Psychology of Incongruity," in *Studies in the Novel,* Vol. XV, No. 3, Fall, 1983, pp. 183-201.

[*In the following essay, Lewis explores* Pierre *in terms of the various characters' responses to the incongruous, suggesting that this theme contributes to the overall ambiguity of the work.*]

> That sort of wayward mood I am speaking of, comes over a man only in some time of extreme tribulation; it comes in the very midst of his earnestness, so that what just before might have seemed to him a thing momentous, now seems but a part of the general joke.
>
> Melville, *Moby-Dick*

> All of us are confronted with conflicts or problems that must be dealt with. By occasionally stepping back from the seriousness of the situation and approaching it with a sense of humor (sometimes called "looking on the light side"), we are presumably better able to deal with the source of the problem. If laughter does serve the tension-relief and impulse-control functions discussed, a person must be in a better position to cope with conflict after humor than before it.
>
> Paul E. McGhee, *Humor: Its Origin and Development*

Insights developed through research into the psychology of incongruity can be useful in understanding both Herman Melville's *Pierre; or, the Ambiguities* (1852) and the history of extreme responses to the novel. Although it has been widely regarded as a flawed, uncontrolled, and incongruous work, it is now possible to see *Pierre* as a valid analysis of the challenges and dangers of incongruity. The irony of *Pierre* criticism is that readers have often failed to understand the novel because they brought to the work the very ineptitude in dealing creatively with the incongruous that Melville's unamused hero brings to his life, in this way illustrating the importance of Melville's novel by reviling it.

In the past decade empirical psychologists have come to see the role of incongruity as a starting point for experiences of humor, fear, and creativity. An incongruous event (that is, one that contradicts our sense of the normal) can seem threatening, or amusing, or confusing, or all three in various sequences depending on the context in which it occurs, the nature of the event, and our ability to cope with its unexpected significance.[1] Such occurrences inevitably stimulate a higher level of arousal or tension, as the person affected attempts to deal with what is happening. If the occurrence seems threatening, fearful and defensive reactions may result. If the occurrence seems playful, smiling and laughing may result. And if the occurrence seems primarily puzzling, problem solving will be initiated.

The complexity of our response to the incongruous is easiest to see in the behavior of children, perhaps because they are most actively involved in the work of forming a world view.[2] Consider a two-year-old girl trying to figure out a Jack-in-the-box for the first time. Like other toys it is brightly colored, so she approaches it in a playful spirit. As she turns the crank and music surrounds her, she smiles in delight. But when Jack springs up the child's muscles tense, she lurches back, and starts to tremble. Between fear and humor, this is the crucial moment of incongruity. Because the child is startled, because nothing like this has ever happened to her, she may run away in terror, instinctively hoping to drive Jack's dreadful pop from her mind. Because the child is intrigued, she may stay to experiment with the toy, bobbing her own head in imitation of Jack's, laughing, and continuing to turn the crank as before. In the end, through this process of reality-assimilation, she may come to understand the toy, removing it from the category of the incongruous to that of the familiar.

As this example suggests, incongruous moments are important because, if richly experienced, they can challenge and expand our sense of the normal. If making a world out of fragments of perception is the business of consciousness, the incongruous is what keeps this process alive and growing. Only through an awareness of our inability to understand something are we motivated to stop and question ourselves. A seemingly odd but actually healthy combination of emotions can open us to the unknown. If we only laugh at the incongruous, we may dismiss it too lightly. If we only fear the incongruous, we may avoid or deny it. But if we can combine the relaxation of humor with the concentration of fear, we may be able to absorb and digest what we were not expecting and cannot easily assimilate. Opposing this rich and complex response to incongruity is a counterforce of denial, the measure of a person's inflexibility. We like to believe that we are at the center of a coherent world, that our experiences form a consistent whole. Because the incongruous presents an opportunity for self-expansion, it can threaten this sense of identity and control. But when we resist the incongruous, when we deny it, we remain locked into inappropriate and inadequate ideas and emotions.

As a stimulus, then, the incongruous is rich in potential especially when it seems most threatening or absurd. Appropriately, as the controlling force of a literary text, the in-congruous can frustrate aesthetic and moral norms and all too often inspire a harsh or limited critical response. Just as we resist the recognition of ideas and events that con-tradict our sense of the normal or possible, so works that uncompromisingly present us with incongruities are often greeted with the contempt of readers who are unwilling or unable to open themselves to the unexpected or the inex-plicable. This can be a problem for almost any narrative, insofar as all narratives originate in some form of action-generating conflict, difficulty, or incongruity. But this is es-pecially true of initial responses to texts that not only be-gin in incongruity but also wallow in it, using and abusing literary conventions to expose the limitations of accepted ideas.[3] The ridicule and mockery such texts often receive is too complacent not to be an instrument of self-satisfied repression.

Infamous in the history of such limited critical responses to incongruous texts is the case of Herman Melville's *Pierre,* a masterpiece of frustration. One need hardly dem-onstrate the presence of incongruities in *Pierre,* as this has been the universally accepted starting point for critics, various interpretations focusing on different patterns or groups of incongruities. It is impossible not to see ide-ational and emotional worlds colliding in this tale of sinful idealism, pastoral corruption, and expedient virtue. Ideas and relationships, even individual human identities, are protean in *Pierre,* as mothers become sisters, brothers hus-bands, madmen writers, and philosophers fools. In *Pierre,* Melville brings his white whale into drawing rooms and onto city streets, takes Moby Dick for country rides and to elegant breakfasts. Just as Ishmael is baffled by an un-knowable monster/deity, so, in *Pierre* it is impossible to arrive at any single view of the events and characters. Through a confusing world Melville follows a protagonist hell-bent on quickly labeling and understanding everything he sees. But *Pierre* is not simply a novel of incongruities; it is a novel about the psychology of the incongruous.

It is ironic that *Pierre,* a work about a person destroyed by his inability to accept the incongruous as a life principle, has often been misread or abused by critics unable to ac-cept incongruity as a principle in art. This critical failure is seen most clearly in contemporary reviews of the novel, although the nineteenth-century emphasis on the formal and philosophic confusion of the work, as I will show later, continues to color modern readings. From the start critics have concentrated on why *Pierre* the novel fails, themselves failing to see that a far more interesting and valid question is why Pierre the character fails.

The defensive, almost knee-jerk nature of the initial re-sponses of Melville's contemporaries to *Pierre* is obvious in their moral outrage, in their repudiation of thematic complexity, and in their failure to see anything funny about this hilariously painful book. Any novel published in 1852 that allowed its hero to contemplate incest would have earned the violent condemnation of most book reviewers. It is not surprising, then, in retrospect, to find *Pierre* re-viled within months of its publication for its "exceeding sinfulness."[4] What is revealing is the obvious nausea of Melville's contemporaries, a nausea based on their unwill-ingness to ponder the questions raised by the book's in-congruities. The tone of the reviewer for the *Athenaeum* is typical: "We take up novels to be amused—not bewil-dered—in search of pleasure for the mind—not in pursuit of cloudy metaphysics." Typical also is the reviewer writ-ing in the *Literary World* who snarled that "Mother and son, brother and sister are sacred facts not to be disturbed by any sacrilegious speculations" and asked rhetorically why Melville allowed his mind to "run riot amid remote analogies, where the chain of associations is invisible to mortal minds?" Most revealing, perhaps, is the self-limiting response of George Washington Peck writing in the *American Whig Review,* who concluded his long and vicious attack as follows: "We have dwelt long enough upon these 'Ambiguities.' We fear that if we were to con-tinue much longer, we should become ambiguous our-selves. . . . Mr. Melville is a man wholly unfitted for the task of writing wholesome fictions." What Melville clearly perceived is that such wholesomeness is a veil for self-righteous hypocrisy and that accepted intellectual "chains of association" are mind-forged manacles of convention.

The same critics who regarded *Pierre* with nausea and contempt and who scorned Melville's moral and meta-physical questioning often failed to appreciate the cruel humor of the book. Those who were aware of this comic line often saw it as a product of the author's insanity or lack of control. One reviewer who noted Melville's pa-rodic intention in the opening chapters absurdly burlesqued Melville's already satirical style:

> We have listened to its outbreathing of sweet-swarming sounds, and their melodious, mournful, wonderful, and unintelligible melodiousness has "dropped like pendu-lous, glittering icicles," with soft-ringing silveriness, upon our never-to-be-delighted-sufficiently organs of hearing; and, in the insignificant significancies of that deftly-stealing and wonderfully-serpentining melodi-ousness, we have found an infinite, unbounded, inex-pressible mysteriousness of nothingness.

This attempt to hoist Melville on his own petard ends by hoisting the hoister, a critic too comfortable in his world view to laugh at it. Like the toddler fleeing from the Jack-in-the-box, Melville's contemporaries turned the crank of *Pierre* until its incongruities popped up; and then, unable to laugh at and ponder them, they fled in righteous horror.

The irony is that what Melville's contemporaries did with *Pierre* the novel, Pierre the character does with life itself. Repeatedly Melville's adolescent hero reveals his immatu-rity by failing to accommodate startling experiences, fail-ing to learn from them. An anti-Bildungsroman, *Pierre* de-fines maturity inversely by showing us a character's inability to grow. With unsettling precision Melville traces this inability to its elements: a lack of humor and, in spite of Pierre's obvious intellectual depth, an unwillingness to entertain profound questions for long. The tension between our sense of how Pierre ought to respond to his experiences and how he actually does respond creates an unbearable fascination.

Pierre's reluctance to acknowledge the incongruous and his inability to see humor in those incongruities that briefly penetrate his defenses reduce him to what might be called an anti-comedic pattern of response. In a fascinating study Seymour Fisher and Rhoda L. Fisher demonstrate that a common personality trait of professional comedians is a lack of faith in conventional answers and ideals:

> The comic, in opening wide the door to surprise, intimates that anything is possible. He dramatizes the likelihood of the unpredictable. He conveys the view that we are surrounded by forces that are bound to lead us into unexpected trajectories. . . . He knows that inevitably the individual will be starkly surprised by the course of events. Comedy prepares the audience for novel intrusion by showing that customary and usually dependable rules are illusory. . . . In effect, the comic prepares his audience for chaos and half convinces it that the chaos can be fun.[5]

In *Pierre,* Melville follows the circular doom of a man who is unwilling or unable to cope with facts, ideas, or emotions that challenge his sense of reality. Unlike the comedians the Fishers studied who expect and celebrate the incongruous, Pierre recoils in horror from the unknown, the surprising, the mysterious.

Pierre's development is characterized by its dynamic stagnation, its psychic *plus ça change.* Buffeted by the incongruous way in which his ideals fail repeatedly to apply to his experiences, and unable to question the value of such ideals, Pierre moves from one useless absolute to another. His substitution of ideal Christianity for family pride and secular love, of absolute truth for ideal Christianity, and later of Satanic defiance for absolute truth is an evasion of any serious consideration of the confusion around him and the conflicts within, a way of remaining unchanged in the face of the incongruous. "I am Pierre and here I stand," he seems to shriek, unaware of the complexity of his identity and the quicksand into which he is sinking.

We first see Pierre as the chivalric, late adolescent suitor of the virginal Lucy Tartan. Projecting his passion onto the landscape, Pierre regards the whole earth as a "love-token"[6] and his Lucy as an angel belonging to "the regions of an infinite day" (p. 4). The problem with this rarefied view of love is that it cannot be reconciled with what Melville calls "uncelestial traits," our liability to the demands of the flesh. The fool of love, Pierre is the victim of a world view which defines his projected marriage with Lucy as an act of blasphemy: "*I* to wed this heavenly fleece? . . . I am of heavy earth, and she of airy light. By heaven, but marriage is an impious thing!" (p. 58).

Until circumstances force Pierre to abandon Lucy and his first notions about love, he refuses to allow his awareness of the incompatibility of heavenly and earthly love to alter his idealism. Unlike the narrator, who has his tongue planted in his cheek throughout the early chapters,[7] Pierre fails to see how funny the angelic view of love is. When Pierre gazes into Lucy's eyes, he sees "waves of infinite glee" (p. 35). But when the narrator discusses this experience, grotesque imagery and exaggerated assertions explode the ideal in laughter:

> There are not so many fishes in the sea, as there are sweet images in lovers' eyes. In those miraculous translucencies swim the strange eye-fish with wings, that sometimes leap out, instinct with joy; moist fish-wings wet the lover's cheek. (p. 33)

> All things that are sweet to see, or taste, or feel, or hear, all these things were made by Love; and none other things were made by Love. Love made not the Arctic zones, but Love is ever reclaiming them. Say, are not the fierce things of this earth daily, hourly going out? . . . Oh, Love is busy everywhere. (p. 34)

As the tone of these passages suggests, the problem with elevating a single principle or emotion to the level of supreme importance is that it will not be able to explain the many quirks and irregularities of life.

Pierre's addiction to the absolute (i.e., to undiluted emotions, pure morality, and clear abstractions) is a consequence of his aristocratic but unfortunate upbringing as a Glendinning male. The family fiction, inherited by virtue of a perverse psychic primogeniture, is that all of the Glendinning males have been perfect. His majestic grandfather, a hero of the Revolutionary War, lives in Pierre's mind as a "pure, cheerful, childlike, blue-eyed, divine old man; in whose meek, majestic soul, the lion and the lamb embraced—fit image of his God" (p. 30). His father, who died when Pierre was a toddler, is always spoken of as a gentleman and a Christian. Pierre's mother's remark early in the novel illustrates this paternal adulation: "God bless you, my dear son!—always think of him and you can never err; yes, always think of your dear perfect Father, Pierre" (p. 19). It is no wonder that when this son and grandson of supposed saints falls in love he should regard his relationship as a seraphic encounter.

Melville uses Pierre's relationship with his mother to separate the reader at the outset from Pierre's point of view. The first description of Mrs. Glendinning reveals both her attractions and her faults:

> Pierre was the only son of an affluent, and haughty widow; a lady who externally furnished a singular example of the preservative and beautifying influences of unfluctuating rank, health, and wealth, when joined to a fine mind of medium culture, uncankered by any inconsolable grief, and never worn by sordid cares. (p. 4)

Alluring as she is, Mrs. Glendinning is also vain, proud, conventional, and controlling, a "widow Bloom" (p. 5) with moral cankers. Pierre, however, at this point sees only her blossom, as eventually he will see only her pride and rigidity. Calling her "Sister Mary," he wallows unaware in an ambiguously "romantic filial love" (p. 5). She is his first angel for whom he feels (or thinks he feels) only a sweet and religious respect. But Melville explodes this simplistic domesticity by contrasting cloyingly incestuous scenes at the dressing mirror and dining table with inappropriate idealizations:

> In a detached and individual way, it [Pierre's relationship with his mother] seemed almost to realize here below the sweet dreams of those religious enthusiasts, who paint to us a Paradise to come, when etherialized from all drosses and stains, the holiest passion of man shall unite all kindreds and climes in one circle of pure and unimpairable delight. (p. 16)

If these are angels, Melville implies, God keep us from heaven.

Pierre's downfall can be seen as illustrating the necessity of coming to accept the fallibility of parents, their capacity for good and evil, inspiration and corruption.[8] It is certainly true that Pierre is eventually tormented by the realizations that his father was immoral and his mother cruel and inflexible. But the thematic unity of the novel becomes clearer if we think of Pierre's response to this unavoidable adolescent hurdle as one among several instances of his inability to cope with the incongruous. From this vantage point, Pierre's reactions to the "mystery of Isabel" is only the most fully developed episode in his repetitive emotional and intellectual collapse.

Pierre's response to Isabel's unexpected appearance in Saddle Meadows and to her claim that she is his illegitimate half sister reveals his unusual lack of preparation for such a shock. Although this response is divided into three stages (his response to her face, letter, and finally to her life story) and occupies about one-eighth of the book, it is distressingly circular, reflecting Melville's intuitive sense that being neurotic means doing the same things over and over again. Up to the moment of his first glance of Isabel, his life seemed to him a "perfect . . . scroll," a "sweetly-writ manuscript" (p. 7), but the shock of her sexuality and anguish unnerves him. Even before he receives her letter of appeal he is terrified and saddened by the mysterious sorrow of Isabel's face. Prior to this time Pierre's pensive interludes were always superficial, mixed with reverie, sweet sadness, and "delicious poetic presentiments" (p. 41). Now he is confronted with a mystery that threatens to overwhelm him largely because he refuses to fully engage it: "What, *who* art thou? Oh! wretched vagueness—too familiar to me, a yet inexplicable,—unknown, utterly unknown! I seem to founder in this perplexity" (p. 41). What Pierre most dreads, foundering in perplexity, is the stuff of human progress and development.[9]

Unable to laugh at Isabel and at himself—at the absurd collision of his inflated ideals and deflating counterappearances—Pierre is unwilling to think about what is happening. Afraid that he will become a "railing atheist," he withdraws from the incongruous and feverishly represses his memory of Isabel's face: "But 'tis gone—gone—entirely gone; and I thank God, and I feel joy again; joy, which I also feel to be my right as man; deprived of joy, I feel I should find cause for deadly feuds with things invisible" (p. 41). What Pierre does not realize, what he will never realize, is that simply deciding that you are happy or that you have understood your situation is inadequate. Such denial is a sign of desperation; the incongruous requires much more.

All of this emotional upheaval serves as a dress rehearsal for Pierre's full-blown reaction to Isabel's repulsive allure. When Isabel's letter reaches Pierre, we see his fatal addiction to moral absolutism at work. His "good angel" urges him to ignore self-interest and read the letter. His "bad angel" urges him to destroy the letter and be happy. But the contest is short and as he opens the envelope he feels "every vein in him pulsed to some heavenly swell" (p. 63). In spite of his conflicting feelings and in the face of Isabel's odd behavior, Pierre is already fitting the dark beauty into his ideal-mad world view as yet another angel—this one of pain and passion. His unwillingness to accept the fact that he is bewildered, or even confused, forces him to reach a familiar set of conclusions, conclusions that are both dubious and deadly.

The letter itself is rich enough and contradictory enough to inspire a wide range of emotions and ideas, a range of responses that Pierre is conspicuously incapable of achieving. Although it is bereft of factual evidence, the letter appeals to Pierre's moral sense, to his sense of guilt, and to his sense of familial pride. Like all of Isabel's acts, the letter is innocent but manipulative, childlike but passionate, self-sacrificing but self-absorbed. Her message is divided against itself, as the following passage shows: "No, I shall not, I will not implore thee.—Oh, my brother, my dear, dear Pierre,—help me, fly to me; see, I perish without thee;—pity, pity,—here I freeze in the wide, wide world;—no father, no mother, no sister, no brother, no living thing in the fair form of humanity, that holds me dear" (p. 64). What is extraordinary but also revealing is that for Pierre this melodramatic effusion is an emotional and intellectual dagger; it leaves him bleeding internally from a wound that never quite heals. His fear is understandable; he can feel his old world of parental respect careening out of its orbit. Humor would help him relax and reconsider, but he has no access to such profound laughter. He cannot, for instance, think to himself, following the passage just quoted, "I'm so *glad* she decided *not* to implore me!"

Pierre's inability to laugh here leaves him unable to speculate about what is, to say the least, a complex revelation, if it is a revelation at all. The amazing thing about Pierre's response to the letter is that, although it is the single most important event in his long and tortured decline, it occurs in just one paragraph. Struggling "to escape the recoil of anguish" (p. 65), Pierre vows to embrace "nothing but Truth . . . and do what my deepest angel dictates" (p. 65). Very briefly Pierre considers alternative explanations of Isabel's letter, that the whole episode is "some accursed dream" or that the letter itself is "a base and malicious forgery" (p. 65). However valid these conjectures may be (remember that Pierre has been in a walking dream since first seeing Isabel and that the letter offers no evidence whatsoever), Pierre finds it impossible to investigate them. As soon as these possibilities occur to him, he rejects them, preferring to curse his fate and to conclude that "This letter is not a forgery" (p. 66). With the logic of a child he babbles to himself: "Nothing but Truth can move me so" (p. 66). Fearing most of all the loss of a coherent identity, a position from which he can think, act, and emote, Pierre, by the end of the paragraph, is labelling himself Isabel's "Leapingly-acknowledging brother" (p. 66).

This leaping acknowledgment is an evasion of the problem solving and creativity called for by the incongruous. Pierre is devastated by the allegation that his father had an illegitimate child, devastated because this contradicts the view that his father was a saint on earth. The incongruity here has to do with the apparently irreconcilable belief in human perfection and the suggestion (accepted as a fact) that even the seemingly best of men are corrupt. Though disconcerting, this knot of ideas might lead in any number of interesting philosophic, psychological, and practical directions. Pierre has every reason to reject or at least defer accepting the view of his father suggested by the letter. But even after he accepts this revised family history, he might delay projecting it onto the world. Pierre immediately concludes that if his father was an imperfect Christian, Christianity as practiced by most people is a system of hypocritical vice. The implication for Pierre is that he must now become the perfect Christian. Although Pierre ignores them, there are many more open or speculative responses to this new "fact."

Pierre might reason that if his parents were not angels, angelic natures are not possible for human beings. Therefore, Isabel is no angel, Lucy is no angel, and even Pierre is flawed. Or he might suspect that it is impossible to understand human experience, that ultimate questions are a waste of time. Or he might simply decide to keep living and thinking until a coherent position evolves. But you cannot leap to action and assertion if you pause to think. And if such a pause terrifies you because it leaves your sense of who you are in suspension, then any conclusion, however poorly it fits all the discrepant pieces together, will be better than none.

Just as Pierre's sense of mystery should be expanding to allow him to cope with these new ideas and facts, it shrivels. Throughout his childhood Pierre's ideal image of his father had been poetically tinged by the mysteries of a portrait of Pierre Sr. smiling in an arch and unsettling way. This portrait, Pierre learned as a young boy, was painted at a time when Pierre's father was thought to be involved with a French woman. Also, Pierre has always wondered about his father's death, about the way the dying man called out for a daughter to hold his hand. These details, combined with Isabel's resemblance to the roguish portrait, destroy even the pleasant sense of doubt Pierre had

allowed himself to feel: "Pierre saw all preceding ambiguities, all mysteries ripped open as if with a keen sword" (p. 85). Refusing the "sordid scrutiny of small pros and cons" (p. 88), Pierre rejects his father and determines to fly to Isabel's side.

Like his earlier responses to the face and the letter and his later responses to other murky situations, Pierre's response to Isabel's story is a desperate denial and reduction of the incongruous. The tale of Isabel's youth is a Gothic set piece full of the heart-rending treatment she received at the hands of cruel or indifferent caretakers and from the inmates of an insane asylum. It is a tale of desperation and neglect, a Dickensian childhood without affection or belonging. Whether or not she is actually Pierre's half sister, what this bewildered and lonely young woman needs is protection and warmth, an effective helper and friend. What she gets is the ruin that results from Pierre's inability to treat her mysterious past as a mystery.

Melville divides Isabel's story into two parts, not because it is too long to tell in one sitting, but because he wants to concentrate on Pierre's reactions to the tale, not on the stimulus but the response. Book VII, "Intermediate between Pierre's Two Interviews with Isabel at the Farmhouse," shows us that Pierre reacts to Isabel's "enigmatical story" by beating "away all thoughts" (p. 129). After a sleepless night, Pierre plunges deep into a nearby wood, suggestive of the impending pathlessness of his life. Although Pierre has already resolved to follow "the inflexible rule of holy right" (p. 106), the narrator reminds us that the moral values of Pierre's new loyalty to Isabel are complex. Isabel is beautiful, but "How, if accosted in some squalid lane, a humped, and crippled, hideous girl should have snatched his garment's hem, with—'Save me, Pierre—love me, own me, brother; I am thy sister!'" (p. 107). It is just this sense of the mixed and mangled nature of man, of his own self, that Pierre finds it impossible to laugh at or accept. In the woods on the morning after the first part of Isabel's story, Pierre creeps under an enormous boulder and calls for his own death if he cannot live a morally perfect life. But the universe ignores his outcry; the boulder remains in place as only a bird lands on the rock and chirps down at the posturing youth.[10]

The seeds of Pierre's doom, germinating from the opening pages, take root in the interval between Isabel's narratives. The more Pierre resists the incongruous, the more it will torment and terrify him. Thus, at the very moment when he concludes that he is Isabel's brother, he senses unconsciously, disturbingly, that this may not be true, that her tale is incomplete, and that he is attracted to her with more than a brotherly love. Determined not to see his life as a set of "mysteries interpierced with mysteries" (p. 142), he reaffirms his habitual but by now idiotic belief in "uncorrupted Love" (p. 142). A smirking angel, Pierre hovers at the brink of yet another incestuous relationship.

Over this brink and into confusion Pierre tumbles when he arrives at the unprecedented idea of protecting his mother's pride, his family's honor, and Isabel by pretending to marry the girl and by actually eloping with her to a nearby city. On the practical level this plan is reckless: a penniless outcast, Pierre will not be able to keep Isabel from the poverty that has oppressed her. Apparently guilty of deceit and disloyalty himself (for abandoning Lucy and lying to his mother), Pierre cannot leave his family honor unbesmirched. But on the emotional level this plan is even worse because it leaves Pierre adrift. What more exquisite torture could a young man embrace than to live with a voluptuous and yielding woman whom it *might or might not* be a sin to touch? Pierre acts as though it would be worse to admit that he simply does not know what to make of Isabel, but the more he insists on maintaining a clear position, a coherent identity, the more he is endangered by the mysteries he denies.

The rest of Pierre's experiences extend and repeat the pattern we have been following, a circular process that begins with the disruption of Pierre's tenuous sense of absolute order and then moves too quickly to Pierre's reimposition of another set of inappropriate ideals. Attempts to define or deny the presence of thematic unity in *Pierre* often begin by asking whether Melville is writing to endorse either the absolutist (chronometrical) morality of Christ or the relative (horological) virtue of Plotinus Plinlimmon, the author of a pamphlet Pierre finds but then loses, as he always loses sight of ideas that challenge his world view. At times Melville seems to propose a synthesis of these competing value systems; at other times he seems to imply that man's divided nature (the supreme human incongruity of our middle state) makes such a synthesis a tragic impossibility.[11] In *Pierre,* however, Melville is far less interested in the answer to this question than in the psychology of questioning. When Melville's critics ask whether Melville is loyal to Christ or to Plinlimmon, they are asking in a calm way the same question that Pierre, "dabbling in the vomit of his loathed identity" (p. 171), asks about his decision to abandon his fiancée and elope with Isabel: "Then, for the time, all minor things were whelmed in him; his mother, Isabel, the whole wide world; and only one thing remained to him;—this all-including query—Lucy or God?" (p. 181).

What gives *Pierre* its thematic unity is not the advocacy of a coherent and universal morality but the intensity of its concentration on a single human experience: the incongruous moment. The critics who have seen a great rift in the novel at the point at which Pierre moves away from Saddle Meadows and becomes a writer have followed not Pierre's psychological development, the center of the work, but shifts in such things as plot, setting, and narrative tone.[12] But Pierre the writer is not very different from Pierre the son, Pierre the lover, or Pierre the brother. For Pierre, writing is just another way to take a stand, to broadcast the purity of his identity, or, as he puts it, "to gospelize the world anew" (p. 273). Those who argue that Melville's despair as a writer around the time when he was working on *Pierre* forced him to confuse his own dilemma with that of his protagonist mistake inspiration for obsession,

Melville's use of his own experiences for a surrender to them. It is true, as Hershel Parker demonstrates, that Melville draws on his own frustrations as a writer in the chapters dealing with Pierre's ill-fated literary career.[13] With some exceptions, however, this use of autobiographical materials is blended into the pattern, not of earlier references to Pierre as a writer, but of Pierre's general mind set. The inserted prose essays on an American literary scene divided between absolute integrity and expedient Philistinism provide an external parallel to Pierre's situation, and his uncompromising way of dealing with this scene recreates his earlier responses to other social conventions.

It is true, as several critics have noted, that there are many similarities between the book Pierre attempts to write and the one Melville succeeded in writing in *Pierre*.[14] Both are about young writers. Both deal with moral issues, examining the validity of the distinction between virtue and vice, the nature of Christian worship as a guide to action, and the possibility of achieving moral perfection. The differences between the two works, however, as seen in Melville's descriptions of Pierre as a writer and in the passages quoted from Pierre's book, are more significant. According to Melville, Pierre is attempting to write a mature book in an immature way. A "life amateur," Pierre allows his rage to warp his prose into a cry of despair and anger. The crucial difference is one of tone and distance. Like Pierre, Melville is enraged at the social hypocrisy of little sinners, but, unlike Pierre, Melville does not see himself as the apostle of absolute truth. To put it another way, the differences between Melville and Pierre are similar to the differences between Ishmael and Ahab, as is clear in the following passage describing Pierre as a writer:

> Ten million things were as yet uncovered to Pierre. The old mummy lies buried in cloth on cloth; it takes time to unwrap this Egyptian king. Yet now, forsooth, because Pierre began to see through the first superficiality of the world, he fondly weens he has come to the unlayered substance. But, far as any geologist has yet gone down into the world, it is found to consist of nothing but surface stratified on surface. (pp. 284-85)

For Melville, the awareness of the limits of human intelligence is both a curse and a salvation; for Pierre, the repression of this awareness is fatal.

The scraps from Pierre's manuscript that we are shown support the narrator's assertion that Pierre has plagiarized "from his own experiences to fill out the mood of his" author-hero, Vivia. Like Pierre, Vivia embraces a deep mournfulness and eschews all "humorous or indifferent disguises" (p. 302), that is, he decides to be always serious, always engaged by the injustice of the human condition. In all earnestness, Vivia, speaking for Pierre, scorns philosophy, acknowledges the reality of pain, denounces the body as a kind of jail, and reviles humor: "oh God, that men that call themselves men should still insist on a laugh! I hate the world, and could trample all lungs of mankind as grapes . . . to think of the woe and the cant,—to think of the Truth and the Lie! Oh! blessed be the twenty-first day of December, and cursed the twenty-first day of June!" (p. 303). What makes *Pierre* a more mature work than *Vivia* would have been is Melville's conviction that if you reject humor and embrace a single position, your caricatured self-reduction makes you a joke. So, when the vileness of the human body arises as a topic in *Pierre,* it is treated with the bantering seriousness that runs through the novel, not with Pierre's, or Vivia's dead-pan rage:

> Love me, love my dog, is only an adage for the old country-women who affectionately kiss their cows. The gods love the soul of a man; often, they will frankly accost it; but they abominate his body; and will forever cut it dead, both here and hereafter. So, if thou wouldst go to the gods, leave thy dog of a body behind thee. And most impotently thou strivest with thy purifying cold baths . . . to prepare it as a meet offering for their altar. (p. 299)

Even without the final pun that implies that human meat will never please the gods, this passage approaches Melville's obviously intense unease over the mind/body problem with a smile. In this way, it is possible to find darkly comic passages that comment on each of the problems that Pierre finds it impossible to laugh at or think about: God's silence (p. 204) and indifference (p. 139), the pain of poverty (pp. 267-68), and the comparative evil of great and small sinners (Satan and "yonder habadasher," pp. 177-78). And, of course, all of Pierre's rhetorically charged utterances (for instance, his "Guide me, gird me, guard me" speech on page 106) are at least in part jokes Melville enjoys at the expense of a character whose life and death are laughably sad.

A funny thing happens to Pierre on the way to his suicide: he has yet another humorless and ineffective revelation, this one teaching him that he has been a fool. Desperately pursuing clarity, Pierre has been tormented by the incongruities he has denied. The family he sought to protect is blasted when his mother dies in despair, leaving the Glendinning estate to a detested cousin. His efforts to live purely have been polluted by his lust for Isabel, and the moral significance of this lust keeps seeming to shift: is she his sister or not? Some occurrences support her story; some raise doubts—it is impossible to know for sure. And in the middle of all this and of Pierre's failing literary work, Lucy shows up at Pierre and Isabel's slum apartment. Another sordid angel, she comes ostensibly to help the perfect Pierre but in reality to compete for his love. The domestic scene is hilariously unpleasant. When Lucy volunteers to earn money by painting portraits, Isabel volunteers to sell her hair and teeth. And so it goes.

Finally rejecting both of his love-starved women, Pierre races toward his own annihilation:

> "For ye two, my most undiluted prayer is now, that from your here unseen and frozen chairs ye may never stir alive;—the fool of Truth, the fool of Virtue, the fool of Fate, now quits ye forever!" (p. 358)

The situation leading directly up to this speech is complex. Building toward an eruption, Pierre's misfortunes have just belched up two farcical letters of denunciation. The first letter, from Steel, Flint, and Asbestos, the outraged publishers of Pierre's aborted romance, lambastes Pierre as a swindler and vile atheist, bemoaning his substitution of a "blasphemous rhapsody" for the contracted "popular novel" (p. 356). The second letter, from the outraged Glen Stanley and Fred Tartan (Lucy's new suitor and brother) is so puffed up as to be comic: "Separately, and together, we brand thee, in thy every lung-cell, a liar;—liar, because that is the scornfullest and loathsomest title for a man; which in itself is the compend of all infamous things" (p. 357). Of course these letters remind us and Pierre of his complete failure as a social and economic being, but Melville has the contemptuous letter writers exaggerate to the point of foaming absurdity. Pierre should be laughing as he cries. Instead, true to his addiction to the absolute, he sees these rejections as yet two more "indices to all immensities," that is, as additional signs of the injustice of the universe.

On the morning of his final rejection of Lucy and Isabel, on his way to face his enemies, Pierre passes first Isabel, who shrieks and sits petrified, "glazed with an icy varnish" and then Lucy, who is sitting at her easel putting the finishing touches to a portrait. When Pierre stops to look at her work, he sees that it is a representation of himself as a skeleton. At this point—with the ludicrous percolating about him—Pierre has many emotional options. He might stop and say something like, "Oh, so that's what she thinks of me—hardly flattering," or "perhaps I have been losing too much weight lately," or "Well, boney hands do the devil's work." Instead of laughing, he gives the "fool of Truth" speech and rushes out to his doom.

What makes this speech so unsettling is that Pierre is foolish even in what he believes to be his moment of self-knowledge. There are more ways to be a fool than Pierre can see even now. As he insists, he has been destroyed by his foolish allegiance to absolute Truth and absolute Virtue in a world of subjective views and relative norms. What Pierre does not see is that he has also been destroyed by his failure to be either a low fool or a high fool. A low fool, that is someone who can see only the humorous side of experience, would never have been gripped by the tragic compulsion to identify evil and resist it. If the "whole world's a trick," as Charlie Millthorpe, the low fool in *Pierre* insists, then all we need to do is play along. As Charlie says, "Know the trick of it, all's right; don't know, all's wrong. Ha! Ha!" (p. 319). There is a higher folly as well, achieved by the narrator of *Pierre* but by none of the characters. This is the folly of Lear's fool and Beckett's tramps, of William Beckford and Edgar Allan Poe, of Charlie Chaplin and W. C. Fields, of Flannery O'Connor and William Faulkner, of Kurt Vonnegut and Nathanael West, of Alfred Hitchcock and Woody Allen, a folly that embraces the incongruous, allowing the mind to deal with it.

Readers have often observed that the narrator of *Pierre* is conspicuous for not providing an objective and consistent view. Instead, the perspective shifts abruptly from hysterical hyperbole to mock-tragic rage, from bitter condemnation to apparent support. Frequently the narrator attacks Pierre as an "infatuate": "Well may'st thou distrust thyself, and curse thyself . . . Oh! fool, blind fool, and a million times an ass! Go, go, thou poor and feeble one! High deeds are not for such blind grubs as thou" (p. 171). But just as often the narrator praises Pierre's nobility, as in the comparison between Pierre and the valiant if impotent Enceladus: "Wherefore whoso storms the sky gives best proof he came from thither! But whatso crawls contented in the moat before the crystal fort, shows it was born within that slime, and there forever will abide" (p. 347). It is not necessary (or possible) to demonstrate that every shift in narrative tone in this sprawling work develops a meaningful incongruity to see that this narrator is appropriately no more contradictory than the characters and ideas he discusses.

Pierre would be a far less unresolved novel if Melville, in exposing his protagonist's way of responding to life's oddities, contrasted Pierre's failure with a successful pattern of response. Such an alternative—embodied in a character or group of characters—would, however, undermine Melville's focus on the destructive consequences of arriving too quickly at intellectual and emotional conviction. Indeed, part of what can make *Pierre* unpleasant to read is that everyone in the book, the absolutists and the relativists, is unappealing. If Pierre, Lucy, and Isabel are constantly assuming ludicrously ideal postures of selfish sacrifice and beastly divinity, Mrs. Glendinning, the Rev. Mr. Falsgrave, Charlie Millthorpe, and Plotinus Plinlimmon are cold, evasive, superficial, or uncaring. True to his incongruous vision, Melville provides us with no resting place, no conclusion, only with a sense that all is not what we would have expected or can easily explain.[15]

Melville's interest in incongruity might be traced to any number of tensions in his personal or professional life, but one intellectual context seems preeminent.[16] If one impulse of romanticism is the yearning for an imaginative recovery of the numinous, another impulse, the basis of what has been called dark romanticism, insists on the impossibility of achieving satisfaction in this quest.[17] In the United States, where transcendentalists affirmed the congruence (Emerson's word was correspondence) between God, nature, and man at his best, serious writers of fiction before the Civil War often seem to be offering examples aimed at refuting this picture of the universe as a plant with God as root and man's mind and nature as corresponding offshoots. By focusing on the demonic, on the obsessive, and on the corrupt, Melville's contemporaries and immediate forebears—Hawthorne, Poe, and Brown—point to the thorns on Emerson's universal plant, to the diseases and imperfections that block correspondence. In both *Moby-Dick* and *Pierre,* Melville exposes the folly of trying to get at the root of things. Ahab and Ishmael are failing transcendentalists: Ahab, who controls his world but brings it to ruin, is a savage portrait of the Emersonian great man; Ishmael, after seemingly endless meditation and study, settles for "attainable felicity."

It is possible to see *Pierre* as an anti-*Walden,* a work in which transcendental yearning is the cause and not the cure of desperation.[18] Thoreau, seeking connections between the mundane and the ideal, casts his fishing lines down to earth and up toward heaven and, leaping in meditative reverie, catches two fish at once. Melville, who presented his own view of such a fishing expedition in *Moby-Dick,* allows Pierre to place the details of his life within various higher frameworks only to discover the lack of any but the most illusory alignment. For Melville the quest for ultimate meaning is doomed from the outset by the threefold evils of man's imperfection, God's silence, and nature's mystery. Emerson and Thoreau argue that an awareness of meaning blossoms in a life of careful observation and detailed thought, inspiration coming as the product of discipline. Using Pierre as a counterexample, Melville insists that the belief in such meaning can be sustained only by someone who is incapable of effective observation and thought. The less we think and see, Melville jeers, the easier it is to believe in absolute truths. For Emerson and Thoreau the undeveloped man has a mind cluttered with unconnected (that is, incongruous) ideas. For Melville, man is an incongruity in an incongruous world.

We often compare novel reading with the experience of entering another world, a world that may be more or less like our own but which has a clear set of operative norms. One of the joys of reading novels is this comfortable illusion that we are participating in the novelist's vision, that we are, to use a current phrase, entering the world according to Jane Austen, or Thomas Hardy, or, for that matter, John Irving. Novelists seeking to support this participation are careful to introduce us quickly to the rules and values that shape their fictions and that remain operative in the confrontation with, indeed are defined by how well they contain, the unexpected and the deviant. We are brought to an awareness of these controlling limits through the guidance of sympathetic characters, a clear narrative tone, and a sequence of meaningful events and emotions. Melville was one of the first novelists to realize that, in this sense, life is rarely like a good book. The easy-chair contentment that accompanies much novel reading, the sense of temporary absorption in another view of life, is exactly what Melville not only avoids but savagely frustrates in *Pierre.* In the absence of a consistent narrative perspective, of sympathetic characters, of meaningful events, the reader of *Pierre* is set adrift, like Pierre himself, in search of guiding principles.

Pierre's failure to achieve the balance, or sanity, or distance that humor can provide sours the novel, making its greatest joys bittersweet frustrations. All of the humor in the book is depressing, but, then, so is much of the humor that is most useful in life.[19] Because it is uncompromisingly true to the chaos of incongruous moments, *Pierre* has been attacked for what is seen as a lack of novelistic order and a distorted depiction of humanity. For Melville, such moments are not fleeting or aberrant; they express the undesirable truth that we will never understand the world in which we live. Offensive to all forms of piety and philosophic contentment, *Pierre* is heroic in its unflinching portrayal of the mind-boggling disorder of life.

Notes

1. For an overview of contemporary humor theory, see Anthony J. Chapman and Hugh C. Foot, eds., *Humour and Laughter: Theory Research and Application* (London: J. Wiley & Sons, 1976) and *It's A Funny Thing, Humour: International Conference on Humour and Laughter* (Oxford: Pergamon Press, 1977). I am drawing on Mary K. Rothbart's essay in *Humour and Laughter,* "Incongruity, Problem-Solving and Laughter," rather heavily in this paragraph.

2. For an extended discussion of humor in childhood, see Paul E. McGhee, *Humor: Its Origin and Development* (San Francisco: W. H. Freeman, 1979).

3. Literary texts that inspire both humor and fear are frequently discussed as examples of the grotesque, and defensive reader responses to such works have been probed by such critics of the grotesque as Wolfgang Kayser, Philip Thomson, and Michael Steig. In spite of some unavoidable overlapping, I am using the term "incongruous text" to emphasize the element of problem solving and to escape the element of physical abnormality that is a definitive characteristic of the grotesque.

4. This review and the succeeding ones quoted are included in Watson G. Branch, ed., *Melville: The Critical Heritage* (London: Routledge & Kegan Paul, 1974), pp. 292-322. For a review of criticism on *Pierre,* see Hugh W. Hetherington, *Melville's Reviewers, British and American: 1846-1891* (Chapel Hill: Univ. of North Carolina Press, 1961), pp. 227-46.

5. *Pretend the World is Funny and Forever: A Psychological Analysis of Comedians, Clowns, and Actors* (Hillsdale, N.J.: Lawrence Erlbaum Associates, 1981), p. 89.

6. Herman Melville, *Pierre, or the Ambiguities* (Chicago: Northwestern Univ. Press, 1971), p. 8. All references to *Pierre* are to this edition and will be cited parenthetically in the text.

7. There are three book-length studies of Melville's use of humor: Jane Mushabac, *Melville's Humor* (Hamden, Conn.: Archon Books, 1981); Joseph Flibbert, *Melville and the Art of the Burlesque* (Amsterdam: Rodopi N.V., 1974); Edward H. Rosenberry, *Melville and the Comic Spirit* (Cambridge: Harvard Univ. Press, 1955). For a discussion of humor in the early chapters of *Pierre,* see William Braswell, "The Satirical Temper of Melville's *Pierre,*" *American Literature,* 7 (1935), 424-38. An interesting overview of Melville's sense of the grotesque can be found in Richard M. Cook, "Evolving the Inscrutable: The Grotesque in Melville's Fiction," *American Literature,* 49 (1978), 544-49.

8. Arguing that Pierre's decline "squares with the demands of psychological realism," William Ellery Sedgwick, in *Herman Melville: The Tragedy of Mind* (Cambridge: Harvard Univ. Press, 1944), p. 142, notes that when Pierre throws his "lot in with Isabel, he spurns the props which surrounded him in adolescence." Sedgwick does not, however, see Pierre's behavior here as a part of a general pattern of response.

9. On the relation between incongruity, problem solving, and creativity, see Arthur Koestler's fascinating study, *The Act of Creation* (London: Hutchinson, 1964). For a summary of earlier theories of humor and their relation to modern insights, see the first section of this study, "The Jester," pp. 27-97.

10. Pierre's experience in the Terror Stone scene illustrates several of the most important differences between *Pierre* and *Moby-Dick.* Like Ahab, Pierre is constantly calling on God or the universe to appear before him and account for the nature of man's life. But whereas Ahab actually does fight his monstrous whale, Pierre is left waiting endlessly. Because there is no opponent worthy of Pierre's rage, because he refuses to see that he is his own worst enemy, Pierre reduces Ahab's heroic struggle to the level of ranting. By moving from external to internal conflict, Melville uses *Moby-Dick* to develop a metaphysics of the incongruous and *Pierre* to develop a psychology of incongruity.

11. In "Coherence and Ambivalence in Melville's *Pierre,*" *American Literature,* 48 (1976), 302-11, Carol Colclough Strickland discusses the lack of a clear morality in *Pierre.* Finding the novel unfortunately pathetic rather than satiric, Strickland concludes that *Pierre* "portrays the catastrophe of perpetual vacillation between resistance and resignation while never resolving its own vacillations" (p. 311).

12. A representative version of what has become a commonplace of *Pierre* criticism is offered by F. O. Matthiessen in *American Renaissance: Art and Expression in the Age of Emerson and Whitman* (Oxford: Oxford Univ. Press, 1970), pp. 480-81: "Melville insisted on that universality also in *Pierre.* . . . Yet he encountered great difficulty in objectifying his own sufferings. Especially when Pierre started to be an author, Melville could not keep the boy of nineteen separate from himself at thirty-two, from the man who, to judge from the texture of its thought and writing, was not only discouraged but nearly exhausted. . . . What Eliot has remarked about *Hamlet* might be applied to *Pierre,* that it gives the impression of being full of some 'intractable' stuff which its writer could not 'manipulate into art.'"

13. "Why *Pierre* Went Wrong," *Studies in the Novel,* 8 (1976), 7-23. See also Brian Higgins and Hershel Parker, "The Flawed Grandeur of Melville's *Pierre*" in *New Perspectives on Melville,* ed. Faith Pullin (Kent: Kent State Univ. Press, 1978), pp. 162-96, and Robert Milder, "Melville's 'Intentions' in *Pierre,*" *Studies in the Novel,* 6 (1974), 186-99.

14. See, for instance, Edward H. Rosenberry's comment in *Melville and the Comic Spirit* (p. 149), that "*Pierre*

is a Chinese puzzle about a man writing a bitter book about a man writing a bitter book. In the resultant mirror image the mood of Hamlet becomes the mood of *Pierre* the book as well as Pierre the man. The final effect is self-mockery, a spectacle that must embarrass any but the most morbid reader."

In "The Art of Herman Melville: The Author of *Pierre,*" *Yale Review,* 59 (Winter 1970), 197-214, Raymond J. Nelson defends *Pierre* from the familiar criticisms by arguing that *Pierre* is meant to be read as the actual book Pierre is trying to write at the Apostles. By way of this assumption, Nelson is able to explain many oddities of style and characterization, but this reading does not explain how Pierre could write a satire about himself. Even in his final self-hatred, Pierre lacks both the distance and humor that are preconditions of self-parody.

15. See Melville's extended treatment of "common" and "profound" novels in *Pierre* (pp. 141-42).

16. Psychoanalytic explanations of Melville's unconscious motivations have been offered by Dr. Henry A. Murray in his introduction to the Hendricks House edition of *Pierre* (New York, 1962) and by Charles J. Haberstroh, Jr. in *Melville and Male Identity* (Rutherford, N.J.: Associated Univ. Presses, 1980). Underestimating Melville's criticism of Pierre, Murray sees "the incongruities and failure of integration of *Pierre*" resulting from Melville's "inability to draw autobiographical materials together" (pp. xxiv-xxv). For Haberstroh, the novel is divided by "the tension between his [Melville's] hopeless and introverted sense of himself as a lost boy, and the desire to fulfill the extroverted traditions of male status, success, and assertiveness with which he grew up" (p. 29). See pages 108-11 for Haberstroh's fascinating discussion of the relation between Pierre, the narrator, and Melville.

A more fruitful psychological explanation of the apparent contradictions in *Pierre* might emerge from a comparative analysis of Melville, Pierre (the character), and the typical comedian described by the Fishers in *Pretend the World is Funny and Forever.* According to the Fishers, the professional comic is often someone whose sense of the incongruous nature of life originates in childhood when the not-yet-mature boy or girl is forced to assume inappropriate responsibilities. The resulting confusion about the parent/child or the adult/child distinction can engender a feeling that life is unpredictable, quirky, odd. It is possible to speculate that Melville's sometimes humorous sense of the "ungraspable phantom of life" originated in the burdens placed upon him by the untimely death of his father, and that in the pampered Pierre, whose mother's wealth and pride are both sheltering and infantalizing, Melville set out to create a foil for himself, a character so unprepared for life that he confuses lust with love, self-serving with idealism, and confusion with self-dissolution.

17. For a general treatment of Melville and American transcendentalism, see Matthiessen, *American Renaissance,* pp. 184-86, and Hershel Parker, "Melville's Satire of Emerson and Thoreau: An Evaluation of the Evidence" in *Studies in the Minor and Later Works of Melville,* ed. Ramona E. Hull (Hartford, Conn.: Transcendental Books, 1970), pp. 61-67. For a discussion of Melville's relation to dark romanticism, see Robert D. Hume, "Exuberant Gloom, Existential Agony, and Heroic Despair: Three Varieties of Negative Romanticism," in *The Gothic Imagination: Essays in Dark Romanticism,* ed. G. R. Thompson (Pullman: Washington State Univ. Press, 1974), pp. 109-27.

18. No possibility of direct influence exists here. *Walden* was published two years after *Pierre* appeared, and Thoreau was not interested in contemporary fiction. But it is impossible not to see these two works as opposing extremes on the same cultural continuum.

19. Melville's characteristic mingling of humor and fear is similar to Shakespeare's use of comic conventions within the great tragedies, although Shakespeare typically subverts comic expectations to intensify tragic effects while Melville holds comedy and tragedy in unresolved suspension. Fascinating discussions of this generic cross-fertilization can be found in G. Wilson Knight, "*King Lear* and the Comedy of the Grotesque," in *The Wheel of Fire,* 4th ed. (London: Methuen, 1949), pp. 160-76, and Susan Snyder, *The Comic Matrix of Shakespeare's Tragedies* (Princeton: Princeton Univ. Press, 1979).

Wai-chee Dimock (essay date 1984)

SOURCE: "*Pierre*: Domestic Confidence Game and the Drama of Knowledge," in *Studies in the Novel,* Vol. XVI, No. 4, Winter, 1984, pp. 396-409.

[*In the following essay, Dimock discusses the various characters' quests for knowledge in* Pierre *and concludes that, since the self proves to be unknowable in the novel, all the individual quests eventually degenerate into ambiguity.*]

> "They know him not;—I only know my Pierre;—none else beneath the circuit of yon sun."

> "All's o'er, and ye know him not!"

Lucy's and Isabel's pronouncements about Pierre, appearing near the beginning and at the very end of the book, both dwell on a single—and to them, presumably the most important—activity: "knowing" Pierre. **Pierre** has often been discussed as the protagonist's quest for knowledge. One tends to overlook the same obsession on the part of the three women, Mrs. Glendinning, Lucy, and Isabel. *Their* obsession, of course, is with knowledge of a rather special kind—not knowledge in the abstract, but knowledge of Pierre. What does it mean to "know" Pierre, why is this knowledge so crucial, and how do these women's quests for knowledge tally with Pierre's own? Is knowledge a psychological category—as it seems to be in the women's attempt to "know" Pierre—or is it an epistemological category, as it is in Pierre's vow to "know nothing but Truth"?[1] The book's drama, it seems to me, stems precisely from the interplay and interfusion of these two issues—epistemology on the one hand, psychology on the other—"knowledge" being, in both instances, the operative term. And the result, I will try to argue, is a book that undermines *both* psychology and epistemology.

The universal desire for knowledge in *Pierre* points to another important fact in the book, what we might call its climate of secrecy. Characters cannot help wanting to know, for they are surrounded by taunting secrets. Just as the desire for knowledge reigns as the natural desire in the book, secrecy reigns as the natural condition. The book's psychodrama consists, in fact, of a succession of secrets as well as a succession of "knowers"—since Pierre allies himself with different partners at different points. Each of the women tries to become Pierre's co-conspirator, for the advantage she enjoys over her rivals is measured precisely by her part in a secret, by the degree to which she is "in the know."

Lucy is the first to put in her request:

> "[C]ould I ever think, that thy heart hath yet one private nook or corner from me;—fatal disenchanting day for me, my Pierre, would that be. I tell thee, Pierre— and 'tis Love's own self that now speaks through me— only in unbounded confidence and interchangings of all subtlest secrets, can Love possibly endure. Love's self is a secret, and so feeds on secrets, Pierre. Did I only know of thee, what the whole common world may know—what then were Pierre to me?—Thou must be wholly a disclosed secret to me; Love is vain and proud; and when I walk the streets, and meet thy friends, I must still be laughing and hugging to myself the thought,—They know him not;—I only know my Pierre;—none else beneath the circuit of yon sun. Then, swear to me, dear Pierre, that thou wilt never keep a secret from me—no, never, never;—swear!" (p. 37)

Lucy's plea fails, but it is not to be lightly dismissed, for it defines not only what Lucy wants but also what each of the women subsequently wants. Lucy has interesting double standards about secrecy. Between Pierre and herself she will have no secrets at all: Pierre "must be wholly a disclosed secret" without "one privated nook or corner." She is not against secrecy on principle, however, and indeed she demands it, for secrecy alone ensures the value of that "unbounded confidence" between Pierre and herself. Common knowledge is no knowledge, and Lucy has only scorn for "what the whole common world may know." She takes pleasure not only in saying, "I know my Pierre," but also in saying, "They know him not."

To describe the unique privilege of knowing what no one else knows, Lucy chooses the word "confidence"—a word she uses not only in the sense of "confiding" (between

lovers), but also in the sense of "confidentiality" (with regard to everyone else). "Confidence," for most Melville readers, invariably brings to mind *The Confidence-Man.* The coincidence, I believe, is hardly fortuitous. Lucy does not specifically recommend "conning" as a part of confidence, although we do know, as the plot unfolds, that deception is unavoidable as a means of secrecy. "Confidence," then, embraces a number of meanings. Primarily it means: to confide (and, at the other end, to receive knowledge, to be confided in), but it can also mean: to keep a secret, to be confident, and, not the least, to con. Unknown to the petitioners and practitioners, "confidence" is already accruing sinister meanings and inscribing strange patterns of its own. Something else is at work in *Pierre* other than the human characters, and in this regard it is possible to think of *Pierre* as a prelude to *The Confidence-Man,* for even in *Pierre,* Melville is erecting a structure—built on the various senses of the word "confidence"—with a sardonic irony strikingly anticipatory of the later book. I have chosen the phrase "confidence game" to describe the quests for knowledge in the book, for provocative purposes— obviously—but also because the phrase reflects both the structure and the ambiguity I find central to *Pierre.*

The confidence game begins with the "perfect confidence" between Pierre and Mrs. Glendinning:

> In the playfulness of their unclouded love, and with that strange license which a perfect confidence and mutual understanding at all points, had long bred between them, they were wont to call each other brother and sister. Both in public and private this was their usage; nor when thrown among strangers, was this mode of address ever suspected for a sportful assumption; since the amaranthineness of Mrs. Glendinning fully sustained this youthful pretension. (p. 5)

Melville is supposedly talking about the "mutual understanding" between mother and son, and yet the only discernible "understanding" between them—either in this passage or indeed anywhere else in the book—seems to consist solely in the pretense they keep up. For lack of other evidence one must equate their "confidence" with their game of make-believe. This is not much of a confidence game, to be sure, although it does play a trick on innocent "strangers," to whom this "mode of address [is never] suspected for a sportful assumption."

Mrs. Glendinning is not destined to remain forever in Pierre's confidence, however, and she loses the privilege of knowing him at precisely the moment when Pierre first sets eyes on Isabel. The mother notices her son's strange transport and questions him directly, but to no avail. Later, when Pierre looks back on the incident, he sees that he has managed to "parry, nay, to evade, and in effect, to return something alarmingly like a fib, to an explicit question put to him by his mother," and he worries that he has become a "falsifyer—ay, a falsifyer and nothing else—to his own dearly-beloved, and confiding mother" (p. 51). Still, Pierre has no wish to make amends, and indeed, once he has taken his first step, he will never again be able to confide in his mother. No longer his accomplice in secrecy, she is about to become his first rejected confidante. This turn of events is not lost upon Mrs. Glendinning, and her immediate response is a demand for "confidence" from her son:

> "I feel, I know, that thou art deceiving me;—perhaps I erred in seeking to wrest thy secret from thee; but believe me, my son, I never thought thou hadst any secret thing from me, except thy first love for Lucy—and that, my own womanhood tells me, was most pardonable and right. But now, what can it be? Pierre, Pierre! consider well before thou determinest upon withholding confidence from me. I am thy mother. It may prove a fatal thing. Can that be good and virtuous, Pierre, which shrinks from a mother's knowledge? Let us not loose hands so, Pierre; thy confidence from me, mine goes from thee. . . ." (pp. 95-96)

In effect Mrs. Glendinning is making the same plea that Lucy has made earlier: that Pierre should never have "any secret thing from her," that he should never shrink "from a mother's knowledge." Ironically, on this occasion Pierre *is* giving her a species of "confidence": not the kind that she wants, to be sure, but the kind which makes him a "falsifyer." At the rupture between mother and son, one kind of confidence replaces another as Pierre withdraws his "perfect confidence" to become a "confidence man," embarked on what he calls an act of "pious imposture" (p. 173).

Mrs. Glendinning is the necessary casualty in the treacherous ambiguity of "confidence." The other casualty is, of course, Lucy, but at this point she is oddly invisible. Lucy's absence is worth noting since it gives us some inkling of the governing principle behind the plot. The battle of succession is a battle between two contenders, Mrs. Glendinning and Isabel, and *structural* purity dictates Lucy's absence. Thus for over a hundred pages, between the arrival of Isabel's letter and Pierre's decision to "marry" her (pp. 61-183), Lucy is neither heard from nor permitted to appear on the scene. With Mrs. Glendinning's defeat, Lucy is left somewhere in limbo, but she is not quite vanquished yet (her non-participation saves her from that). Her future return is virtually guaranteed by the book's configuration of principals, and, like her absence, attests to the centrality of structure in *Pierre.*

With the ousting of Mrs. Glendinning and the triumph of Isabel, the confidence game moves to a new phase. Once again, several senses of "confidence" come into play. Fond unreserve between the lovers, strict confidentiality toward the outside world, "pious imposture"—all these ingredients go into the making of Pierre's and Isabel's fictitious marriage. This is a more serious confidence game than the previous "sportful assumption" between mother and son. Like its predecessor, it too admits only two people. For the moment Isabel enjoys Pierre's exclusive "continual domestic confidence" (p. 192), but, with some justice, she is already worried about the day, as she tells Pierre, when "thou art minded to play deceivingly with me" (p. 189).

Isabel's fears are quickly realized in the final stage of the confidence game, when her nemesis appears, predictably enough, in the form of Lucy Tartan. Lucy's reemergence (in Book 23) completes *Pierre*'s structural symmetry, and it also puts the reigning confidante instantly on the defensive. When Isabel learns that Lucy is coming to stay, her immediate reaction is: "Either thou hast told thy secret, or she is not worth the commonest love of man! Speak Pierre—which?" To which Pierre replies, quite truthfully, that "the secret is still a secret" (p. 313). True enough, Lucy has no factual knowledge of the secret, but as she seems to have realized by now, there is more than one way of "knowing." Her new strategy is to disclaim any desire for knowledge. Lucy no longer makes the mistake of demanding confidence, as she once did. On the contrary, she now sweetly assures Pierre that she has no desire to know: "I will ask of thee nothing, Pierre; thou shalt tell me no secret. Very right wert thou, Pierre, when, in that ride to the hills, thou wouldst not swear the fond, foolish oath I demanded. Very right, very right; now I see it. . . . I solemnly vow, never to seek from thee any slightest thing which thou wouldst not willingly have me know" (p. 309). Lucy is being disingenuous, of course (and indeed, in the same breath, she also admits, "Yet something of thy secret I, as a seer, suspect" [p. 309]). In any case, she has managed to "slid[e] between" Pierre and Isabel, as the latter becomes "alive to some untraceable displacing agency" (pp. 337-38).

For all intents and purposes, Lucy has penetrated Pierre's and Isabel's secret. She must now, in her turn, introduce a new secret, one from which Isabel will be excluded. In this respect she is aided by a peculiar circumstance in the past. Either out of regard for Isabel's feelings, or for reasons considerably less admirable, Pierre has withheld from her one bit of knowledge—the fact that he has been engaged to Lucy. Intuitively Lucy senses this fact and uses it. Isabel is not the only one privileged with a secret, she points out. There is yet *another* secret, between Lucy herself and Pierre—"for thus far I am sure thou thyself hast never disclosed it to her what I once was to thee" (pp. 309-10). The important point for Lucy, we might notice, is not her former engagement to Pierre, but the fact that this engagement has "never [been] disclosed," that Isabel is ignorant of it. And Lucy means to keep Isabel ignorant. Her plan is to come to Pierre, but henceforth the two would assume perpetual "disguises": "Let it seem, as though I were some nun-like cousin immovably vowed to dwell with thee in thy strange exile" (p. 310). Lucy does not say that they will be deceiving Isabel (she settles for the euphemism "let it seem"), but deception clearly lies at the heart of her proposition, as it does in all the other bonds of confidence in the book. Oddly, for this deceitful conduct Lucy envisions the most extravagant celestial reward: "Our mortal lives, oh, my heavenly Pierre, shall henceforth be one mute wooing of each other; with no declaration, no bridal; till we meet in the pure realms of God's final blessedness for us . . . when, there, thy sweet heart, shall be openly and unreservedly mine" (p. 310). This is a very large claim to make on a married man, but Lucy is confident of it, presumably because the self-denying deception in this life entitles her to an eternity of flaunting conjugality.

The confidence game has run its course as Lucy, the former outsider, now comes to be in the know. And yet this structural completion leaves a great many questions unanswered. How does Lucy come to suspect Pierre's and Isabel's secret? What is it in her that makes her such a shrewd "seer," as she calls herself? And what are her reasons, anyway, for coming to Pierre? Is she innocent, guileless, angelical, as Pierre thinks, or is she possessive and calculating? We have no answers for these questions—just as we have no answers for similar questions about Lucy's predecessor, Isabel. Why does Isabel write to Pierre and reveal herself to him? What are her motives, and what does she want from him? Why does she acquiesce in the mock marriage? To ask these questions at all is to realize the huge gaps in Melville's domestic drama. Melville seems simply uninterested in the motives—and indeed, in the personalities—of his women characters.[2] It is only right, then, that we should ask what *does* interest him. If the women do not function as psychological presences, how do they in fact function? How important are they to the outcome of the confidence game? And furthermore, what gives this game its predictable shape and its particular flavor?

Just as there are strange negligences in the characterization of the women, there are also strange rigidities in the shape of the confidence game. There is no question of degree in the game, no question of texture, and no question of process. Melville seems to have no patience with the nitty-gritty of human attachments. New alliances become accomplished facts almost as soon as we first hear about them. Lucy has no trouble winning Pierre to her secret, just as Isabel, at an earlier stage, has no trouble winning Pierre to *hers*. In both cases the success is instantaneous and, it would seem, unearned. Why is Mrs. Glendinning defeated in a moment, and why does Isabel cease to intrigue Pierre even before Lucy's appearance on the scene?[3] These questions, once again, cannot be adequately answered, for there is something oddly preordained in the succession of confidantes—the logic of the succession being, in a rather chilling way, not a human logic at all.

Within the undeviating structure of the confidence game, the women function as abstract maneuverable parts. Thus, during the period of Isabel's ascendancy, "for the real Lucy [Pierre], in his scheming thoughts, had substituted but a sign—some empty x—and in the ultimate solution of the problem, that empty x still figured; not the real Lucy" (p. 181). Pierre's ability to reduce Lucy to a mathematical integer says something about him, but it also says something about the emotional logic of the book: a logic with the simplicity of a geometric equation. That equation, to put it most crudely, goes something like this: to those who seek, confidence will be given; from those who have, confidence will be taken away. The crucial factor in the confidence game is one's position, of which there are three well-defined ones: the aspirant, the incumbent, and the rejected, forming a clear linear progression.[4] The movement of any character from one position to another becomes something of a mechanical certainty. Mrs. Glendinning and Isabel are both casualties in the confidence game, not because they resemble each other, but because they both happen to occupy, at different points, the position of the incumbent. Their position alone makes their fate analogous.

One can argue, without too much exaggeration, that *Pierre* is a story centered, not on human personalities, but on "confidence" and its attendant structure.[5] Different characters serve as practitioners in confidence at different points, but it is "confidence," and not they, that dictates the plot and shapes the novel. "Confidence" lies at the heart of *Pierre*; its trajectory, its mode of operation, the shifting partnerships it engenders—these make up the scaffolding of the book. There are "stirring passions at work," to be sure, but these passions, too, seem to be exclusively passions for confidence.[6] The book that results is a book that is very much a skeleton of itself, a book strangely intent and mechanical. It is structure, and not texture, that makes the book what it is, just as it is characters-as-integers, and not characters-as-personalities, that carry on the evolving drama. In short, *Pierre* is a psychological novel that rejects, for the most part, psychological representation; it is a book of intimate ties that undermines the content of those ties; it is a book that begins with "stirring passions" and ends with a dispassionate structure.

Why is Melville impatient with human attachments? From the internal evidence of the novel, we can say only that he does not believe in them. In this regard he is working directly against the characters, who do believe in intimate ties, and who believe, furthermore, that they can seal these ties with confidence. The characters are mistaken, of course—or, we might say, they are conned—since none of the relations in the book turns out the way they think. To take an example we have already considered, the "perfect confidence" between Mrs. Glendinning and Pierre comes to nothing, as we might expect, but their *mode* of rupture is especially ironic and seems to reflect Melville's malicious cynicism toward human intimacy.

During that crisis, Mrs. Glendinning asks Pierre a seemingly trivial question—whether she should ring the bell to summon Dates. In effect, of course, she is giving Pierre the last chance to confide in her, and Pierre knows it:

> But though he knew all the significance of his mother's attitude, as she stood before him, intently eying him, with one hand upon the bell-cord; and though he felt that the same opening of the door that should now admit Dates, could not but give eternal exit to all confidence between him and his mother; and though he felt, too, that this was his mother's latent thought; nevertheless, he was girded up in his well-considered resolutions.
>
> "Pierre, Pierre! shall I touch the bell?"
>
> "Mother, stay!—yes do, sister."
>
> The bell was rung. . . . (p. 96)

The two words—"mother" and "sister"—present in close succession in Pierre's reply, rather heavy-handedly draw attention to the significance in Pierre's mode of address. Mrs. Glendinning remains "mother" as long as Pierre still thinks of confiding in her. Once he has made up his mind to "give eternal exit to all confidence" between them, however, she becomes "sister." In other words, their former term of endearment now serves as the signal for an irrevocable break. If Pierre once told a fond lie in calling his mother "sister," now, in reverting to the old habit, he is telling another kind of lie—a lie that repudiates rather than endears. The glaring falseness of the intimacy on this occasion cruelly parodies its former illusoriness. Confidence is, after all, a treacherous ideal; it works deviously and—unfortunately for its adherents—not always in the way they fancy.

Eventually all the bonds of confidence in the book turn out to be illusory. Presumably the women want to know Pierre because they love him, and yet love is hardly an expressible passion in the book. What prevails instead is a passion for knowledge, a passion so insistent and so final that it seems not so much a metaphor for love as a displacement of it. In other words, knowledge becomes, not a means to love, but an end in itself, and as an end it amounts merely to a mechanical compulsion. For if "knowing" can (at least in it biblical sense) mean consummation, in *Pierre* it is nonconsummation that poisons all the relations. After the deceit and intrigue of the book, none of the relations comes to fruition.[7] The women are really fighting a losing battle, a battle drained of its meaning from the very beginning and in its very definition of terms. In *Pierre* then, structure at once dictates the course of passion and usurps its place; for passion, like the human attachments it engenders, has lost its content and ground of being.

This brings us to the other side of "knowing." If knowledge fails as a means of intimacy, how successful is it as an epistemological exercise? Do any of the women "know" Pierre in this alternate sense of the word? Mrs. Glendinning assuredly does not, and Pierre has a rather shrewd insight into why she fails: "Me she loveth with pride's love; in me she thinks she seeth her own curled and haughty beauty; before my glass she stands,—pride's priestess—and to her mirrored image, not to me, she offers up her offering of kisses (p. 90). Perhaps Pierre exaggerates his mother's egotism, but he is certainly right to suspect that the Pierre she loves is in fact only an "image" of her own making. And her image of him is that of a "fine, proud, loving, docile, vigorous boy" (p. 20), a fitting complement to her own self-image as a proud, loving, idolized mother. This "Pierre" is the only one she knows—or accepts—and when Pierre deviates from that image, she understandably refuses to recognize the strange apparition "who was once Pierre Glendinning" (p. 185).

Image-making is, unfortunately, not confined to Mrs. Glendinning. Lucy and Isabel, too, make images, for each "knows" Pierre in her own way. He is Lucy's "shepherd-king" (p. 36), Isabel's brother-champion, and finally, the "noble and angelical Pierre" Lucy expects to marry in the "pure realms of God's final blessedness" (pp. 309-10).

"Knowing" Pierre means creating Pierre in a certain image, and each of the women knows Pierre only to that extent. Her "knowledge" is an epistemological illusion and evaporates as soon as Pierre trades images, as soon as he repudiates one identity to embrace a new one, tendered by another woman.

One side of the confidence game has proved itself completely futile. It is time now to consider the other side, for Pierre, too, has his own quest for knowledge to conduct. It is instructive to see how he fares against the women's poor showings. What does Pierre want to know, and how much does he end up knowing? On the surface of it, Pierre's passion seems no different from the women's. He, too, is driven by a desire to know, and the women appear, at least initially, to be the objects of his inquisitions. In the days of Isabel's ascendancy, for instance, she has seemed "inscrutable" (p. 129) and "unravelable" (p. 141), commanding "all the bewitchingness of the mysterious vault of night" (p. 142). Isabel seems to embody all that is unknown—all that is yet to be known—and Pierre is bewitched by her, although he has no trouble resisting Lucy, at that point too easily fathomable, too "fond, all-understood" (p. 129). By Book 26, however, Isabel's mystery has fallen into that class of "mysticisms and mysteries" of which Pierre has grown "uncompromisingly skeptical" (p. 354). A fresh mystery is called for to whet Pierre's appetite for knowledge, and Lucy supplies it. Her "inconceivable conduct," "enigmatical" resolve, "inexplicable motive," and "inscrutable divineness" all attest to her new-found allure for the "amazed" and "confounded" Pierre (pp. 315, 317).

A woman captivates Pierre to the degree that she mystifies him. And yet, Pierre does not primarily want to know her—at least not in the sense that the women want to know him—for the mystery that engrosses him is finally not her own. Beyond Isabel's mystery, even more important to Pierre is the fact that she "begat in him a certain condition of his being" (p. 53), that she "seemest to know somewhat of me, that I know not of myself" (p. 41). From her he hopes to wrest some explanation for his own "strange integral feeling": "Explain thou this strange integral feeling in me myself, he thought—turning upon the fancied face—and I will then renounce all other wonders, to gaze wonderingly at thee. But thou hast evoked in me profounder spells than the evoking one, thou face!" (pp. 51-52). Similarly, confronted with Lucy's surprising move, Pierre is elated by the thought that "the girl whose rare merits his intuitive soul had once so clearly and passionately discerned" should now acquit herself so well (p. 311). In other words, Lucy, like Isabel before her, fascinates precisely because she awakens Pierre to a new understanding of his own "intuitive soul." From her "inconceivable conduct" he derives a mystical knowledge: "there is a mysterious, inscrutable divineness in the world—a God—a Being positively present everywhere;—nay, He is now in this room; the air did part when I here sat down. I displaced the Spirit then—condensed it a little off from this spot" (p. 317).

There is something narcissistic in Pierre's attachment to the women, for the mystery that most obsesses him and the knowledge that he most eagerly seeks is the truth about himself. This mystery makes a rather graphic appearance when, upon reading Lucy's letter, Pierre "ran shuddering through hideous galleries of despair, in pursuit of some vague, white shape, and lo! two unfathomable dark eyes met his, and Isabel stood mutely and mournfully, yet all-ravishing before him" (p. 312). The "unfathomable," "vague, white shape" distinctly recalls the language of *Moby-Dick,* and indeed Pierre, like Ahab, is pursuing an "ungraspable phantom of life." This phantom, Henry A. Murray points out, lies—not without—but within Pierre himself.[8] It is the phantom of his own selfhood and, as the passage seems to suggest, it is compounded of *both* Lucy and Isabel, the "vague, white shape" of the one fusing into the "unfathomable dark eyes" of the other. Like Yillah and Hautia in *Mardi,* Lucy and Isabel are opposites, but at some level they too eventually merge and become one.[9] As vehicles for Pierre's self-realization, the two are analogous rather than antithetical, for both are elusive and eventually delusory.

Pierre's attempts at confidence are invariably attempts at *self*-confidence, a narcissistic variation on the women's endeavor, but no different, in essence, from theirs. The two versions of the confidence game, in fact, form a rather close parallel. If the women need to fabricate a "Pierre" in order to "know" Pierre, so Pierre, too, needs to fabricate a self in order to "know" himself. Pierre is a "self-made man"—of sorts—and there is something of the Emersonian bravado in his boast: "Henceforth, cast-out Pierre hath no paternity, and no past" (p. 199). And yet, a self that can be endlessly made over is also inescapably artificial. Docile son and solicitous brother, gallant champion and "grand victim" (p. 179), privileged scion and penniless genius—these are some of the indentities Pierre embraces, but they add up to no stable selfhood. There is something fictitious in the identities Pierre assumes, a fictitiousness that might have stemmed, as Melville suggests, from the "conversational conversion of a mother into a sister," which has long "habituated [Pierre] to a certain fictitiousness in one of the closest domestic relations of life" (p. 177). In any case, fictitiousness is a curse Pierre can rarely shake off. For the rest of the book, he is doomed to play, not just one part at a time, but a part within a part—not only as his mother's son but also as her brother, not only as Isabel's brother but also as her husband, and not only as Lucy's ex-fiancé but also as her cousin—the fake identities overshadowing and commingling with the "real" ones to such an extent that the latter themselves become all but meaningless.

The final difficulty, then, lies not so much in telling the real identities from the fake ones, but in demonstrating the "realness" of any identity at all. Knowing himself proves to be as much a losing battle for Pierre as knowing Pierre is for the women, because the "self" simply affords no ground for certitude. It is, in fact, nothing but layer upon layer of imposition and supposition, harnessed to no solid core of being. The central image in the book is therefore the image of an appalling and parodic inner void:

> Yet now, forsooth, because Pierre began to see through the first superficiality of the world, he fondly weens he has come to the unlayered substance. But, far as any geologist has yet gone down into the world, it is found to consist of nothing but surface stratified on surface. To the axis, the world being nothing but superinduced superficies. By vast pains we mine into the pyramid; by horrible gropings we come to the central room; with joy we espy the sarcophagus; but we lift the lid—and no body is there!—appallingly vacant as vast is the soul of a man! (p. 285)

For Melville, the self is unknowable, not because we do not try hard enough, but because there is nothing there to be known. Any attempt to know Pierre, whether by the women or by Pierre himself, is inherently doomed, for there is no "Pierre" to speak of, the only knowable Pierre being one fabricated for the occasion. All attempts to know oneself are vain exercises, and the point comes home to us when Pierre chances upon the imported portrait of a (possible fictitious) stranger, a stranger who might just as easily be Isabel's father. The very objective ground that anchors the self is now swept away. Since Pierre will never know who Isabel is, he will never know who he is. Just as she is "wife or sister, saint or fiend" (p. 360), so Pierre, too, is "husband or brother, hero or fool"—the tragedy residing precisely in that eternal "or."

Characters in *Pierre* compute their advantage by measuring what they know against what others know (or do not know). And yet this faith in knowledge, according to Melville, is a misguided faith—a false confidence, we might say. The little that we do know is partial, transient, and perhaps irrelevant. In one of his bitterest invectives against knowledge, Melville observes: "knowing his fatal condition does not one whit enable [Pierre] to change or better his condition. . . . For in tremendous extremities human souls are like drowning men, well enough they know they are in peril; well enough they know the causes of that peril;—nevertheless, the sea is the sea, and these drowning men do drown" (p. 303). Rather than being the key to our experience, knowledge is extraneous, a moot point. And it is not even just useless; it is downright cruel and mocking, for drowning must come all the more painfully to the drowning man because he knows it. One does not *attain* knowledge, then; one merely *succumbs* to it as one succumbs—in another striking metaphor of Melville's—to "the irruptions of those barbarous hordes which Truth ever nourishes in the loins of her frozen, yet teeming North" (p. 167). Any human faith in knowledge is a fatuous faith, for knowledge governs one and victimizes one, but rarely puts itself at one's service.

And after all the quests for knowledge, what happens when the reverse happens, when, instead of knowing, one is being known by someone else? Isabel, we have seen, anguishes over what Lucy may know, and even Pierre, for all his initial delight at being known, eventually finds the prospect insufferable. "Being known" is the underside of knowing, and not surprisingly it shadows forth many of its latent horrors. As *Pierre* progresses, knowledge appears increasingly in this externalized and menacing mode: as a threat rather than as an asset, as an alien imposition rather than as an experiential state of being. The darkening course of knowledge is marked by the sequence of two remarkably haunting faces, one appearing near the beginning, and the other toward the end of the book: "The face!—the face!—. . . Thou seemest to know somewhat of me, that I know not of myself,—what is it then? If thou hast a secret in thy eyes of mournful mystery, out with it" (p. 41).

> the face seemed to leer upon Pierre. And now it said to him—*Ass! ass! ass!* This expression was insufferable. . . . What was most terrible was the idea that by some magical means or other the face had got hold of his secret. "Ay," shuddered Pierre, "the face knows that Isabel is not my wife! And that seems the reason it leers." (p. 293)

The first face—Isabel's—is plaintive and alluring. It does not threaten, and it seems to promise some invaluable knowledge. Pierre's romantic hopes, however, turn out to be mistaken, for Isabel does not, in fact, know Pierre, and she tells him no hoped-for secrets. The face that is truly knowledgeable turns out to be Plinlimmon's. The trace of intelligence in such a man—a stranger, no kin of Pierre's, and not especially well-disposed toward him—cannot inspire anything but fear and loathing. The striking contrast between Isabel's face and Plinlimmon's marks the growing tyranny of knowledge and its evolution from enticement to terror. Plinlimmon's face revises Isabel's and parodies it. Indeed, there is nothing in common between Isabel's dark features and Plinlimmon's "ivory brow," his "steady observant blue-eyed countenance" "so clear and so mild" (pp. 291, 293). The only other character in the book that actually looks like Plinlimmon is Lucy, and this is where the true parallel lies. Lucy is to Isabel what Plinlimmon is to Pierre—alien presences with nonbenevolent knowing gaze. Ironically, knowledge can never be grasped as experiential reality; it comes to us only as *alienated* knowledge, only as encroaching threats from without.

If *Pierre* is indeed a psychological novel, as several critics have eloquently argued, in the long run it also undermines itself by destroying the premises of psychological inquiry.[10] In the course of the book Melville explodes the myth of selfhood, even as he reduces human relations to a mechanical structure of succession and displacement. Melville's psychology has, after all, much in common with his metaphysics. From *Moby-Dick* to *Pierre,* the question has changed from "How do I know the world?" to "How do I know Pierre?"—but the operating term, to "know," remains unchanged. Melville's psychology and epistemology both require the groundings of a sturdy selfhood, but since the self in *Pierre* is now "vacant," all attempts at knowledge—whether the women's attempt to know Pierre, or Pierre's attempt to know himself—degenerate into an empty confidence game, a game in which the trajectory of knowledge seems more important than the

human actors, and in which the confidence man and confidence women are their own victims. Isabel's last words, in this context, have an especially poignant ambiguity. "All's o'er, and ye know him not!" she says at the end of the book. Possibly these words are addressed to Fred and Millthorpe, impotent witnesses, or they may be addressed to the reader, just as they may be addressed to Isabel herself—or even to the dying Pierre. "Pierre" is not to be known, not by idle spectators and readers, and not by the women, and most certainly not by Pierre himself, for as Melville seems to have warned us in the title, Pierre *is* "The Ambiguities."

Notes

1. *Pierre, or, The Ambiguities* (Evanston and Chicago: Northwestern Univ. Press and the Newberry Library, 1971), p. 65. All further references to this edition will be included in the text.

2. For this reason, the women lend themselves especially to generalizations. An obvious generalization, for instance, identifies Lucy and Isabel as the light and dark ladies of the Gothic romance. But even sophisticated generalizations—such as Henry Murray's identifying Isabel with the Jungian Anima—attest to the simplicity of her being.

3. Hershel Parker and Brian Higgins have offered an interesting discussion of the abrupt termination of Isabel's influence. Parker and Higgins see a disjunction between the psychological drama in the first half of the book (of which Pierre's passion for Isabel plays an important part) and that of Pierre as a profound writer in the second half. Parker attributes this change in direction to a business trip Melville made to New York from December 1851 to January 1852. Disappointed over his contract with the Harpers and bitterly aggrieved by several newly-published, damning reviews of *Moby-Dick,* Melville jumped to his revenge, notably in Books 17 and 18, in which he satirizes *Pierre's* reading public in the form of "Miss Angelica Amabilia of Ambleside" and "Captain Kidd Monthly." See Brian Higgins and Hershel Parker, "The Flawed Grandeur of Melville's *Pierre,*" in *New Perspectives on Melville,* ed. Faith Pullin (Edinburgh: Edinburgh Univ. Press, 1978), pp. 162-96; also see Hershel Parker, "Why *Pierre* Went Wrong," *Studies in the Novel,* 8 (1976), 7-26. Parker and Higgins are right to point to the abrupt collapse of intimacy between Pierre and Isabel. However, as I will try to argue, the *collapsibility* of intimacy is not limited to Pierre and Isabel alone.

4. My positional analysis is inspired by Jacques Lacan's discussion of the three positions in Poe's "Purloined Letter." See "Seminar on 'The Purloined Letter,'" *Yale French Studies,* 48 (1976), 38-72.

5. In my sense of an underlying structure in *Pierre,* I am implicitly arguing against Hershel Parker's contention that Melville changed his course in the middle of the book. I do see Books 17 and 18 as digressions

from the rest of *Pierre*—for the biographical reasons that Parker convincingly demonstrates—but I do not see the entire second half of the novel as being independent of the first half.

6. In a letter to Bentley (April 1852), Melville characterized *Pierre* as a "regular romance, with a mysterious plot to it, & stirring passions at work." See *The Letters of Herman Melville,* ed. Merrell R. Davis and William H. Gilman (New Haven: Yale Univ. Press, 1960), p. 150.

7. It is possible to argue, of course, that Pierre and Isabel did consummate their relations in Book 19. But such a reading seems almost too sanguine to me. Melville plays with the idea of sexual consummation, but I think he makes a darker plot by leaving even that event uncertain.

8. Henry A. Murray, Introd., *Pierre* (New York: Hendricks House, 1949), p. lxxxiii.

9. For the kinship between Hautia and Yillah, see *Mardi* (Evanston and Chicago: Northwestern Univ. Press and the Newberry Library, 1970), p. 643.

10. For discussions of *Pierre* as a psychological novel, see the aforementioned articles by Hershel Parker and Brian Higgins, as well as Richard Brodhead's chapter on *Pierre* in *Hawthorne, Melville, and the Novel* (Chicago: Univ. of Chicago Press, 1976).

Richard Gray (essay date 1984)

SOURCE: "All's o'er and ye know him not': A Reading of *Pierre*," in *Herman Melville: Reassessments,* edited by A. Robert Lee, Vision and Barnes & Noble, 1984, pp. 116-34.

[*In the following essay, Gray explores* Pierre *as "an artifice that calls attention to its own artificiality" and suggests that the novel is a predecessor of Vladimir Nabokov's* Pale Fire *and Jorge Luis Borges's* Ficciones.]

Herman Melville completed his sixth and greatest novel, *Moby-Dick,* in the summer of 1851. The book must have cost him an enormous amount in terms of imaginative energy, moral effort, and sheer physical strain: and yet, within a few weeks of completing it, he was already at work again preparing his seventh novel, which was eventually to be called *Pierre: Or, The Ambiguities.* In many ways, *Pierre* represented something of a new departure for Melville. For, in the first place, it was set on land rather than at sea; and, in the second, with its aristocratic hero, its dark and fair ladies, its concern with the issues of love and money, and its use of secret letters and hidden portraits to propel or complicate the plot, it seemed to belong in a tradition of domestic romance that was immensely popular at the time. Melville, whose five books prior to *Moby-Dick* had produced an annual income of less than $1,600, clearly felt himself under some pressure to pro-

duce something that would, as he put it, pay 'the bill of the baker',[1] and in the early stages at least he appears to have been convinced that his new novel would do exactly that. At the beginning of 1852, for example, he wrote to Sophia Hawthorne to assure her that his next book would be, not 'a bowl of salt water' like his whaling story but 'a rural bowl of milk'—more suited, the implication was, not only to the delicate sensibilities of Sophia herself but to a larger, novel-reading public that was predominantly female. While only a few weeks later, in a letter to his English publisher, he was even more openly confident. *Pierre,* he insisted, was 'very much more calculated for popularity . . . being a regular romance, with a mysterious plot to it, stirring passions at work, and withall, representing a new and elevated aspect of American life'.[2]

Such declarations of confidence can hardly be read without a sense of irony now. For, far from improving Melville's standing as a professional writer, *Pierre* served to worsen it radically. Reviewers received his new, domestic romance with greater and more concerted hostility than any of his previous efforts: 'a gigantic blunder', declared one, 'an objectionable tale, clumsily told', insisted another, while a third simply dismissed it as 'the craziest fiction extant'.[3] And any hopes Melville might have had concerning its appeal with a wider reading public were soon to be disappointed: only 283 copies were sold within the first eight months of publication and over the next few years it proved considerably less popular than even *Moby-Dick* or *Mardi.* The sense of irony does not spring entirely from this, however. It stems also from the fact that any reader of the book is likely to be struck by the discrepancy, the sheer size of the gap, between what Melville apparently intended to do and what in fact he did. *Pierre* is most emphatically not 'a rural bowl of milk': on the contrary, it is one of the darkest, bleakest, and bitterest of Melville's narratives, a story that follows 'the endless, winding way' of its hero's life and its narrator's thoughts to a conclusion that is little short of nihilistic. Melville may have set out to write something that would appeal to the contemporary taste for domestic melodrama and genteel sentiment. What he ended up with, however, was something quite different: a book so thoroughgoing in its scepticism that it examines its own *raison d'être,* its own claims and assumptions and, in this respect as well as in the subversive nature of its techniques, the self-reflexive character of its idiom, seems to anticipate the post-modernist novel.

The self-reflexive, self-referential nature of *Pierre* is perhaps less surprising when one remembers the autobiographical basis of much of the book. One critic has suggested that *Pierre* represents an act of psychic withdrawal after the great, creative venture of *Moby-Dick,* another has described it as 'a Freudian exercise in psychic recovery'[4]; and, however much one may quarrel with the further implications of these remarks—the way they tend to confuse the psychological origins of the story with the story itself—they do point to certain things that are worth emphasizing and examining. First, and most obviously, they point to the fact that just as Pierre we are told, 'dropped his angle into the well of childhood, to find what fish might be there',[5] so Melville, his creator, has done exactly the same: as Henry Murray has shown, there are 'highly probable originals'[6] in Melville's life for most of the incidents, places, and people that appear in Pierre's story. The biographical detail is transposed in some cases and embellished in others; nevertheless, while writing about Pierre, Melville must have had the sense of looking at himself as if through a glass darkly—or rather, to use an image that recurs throughout the book, as though in a slightly distorting mirror. Beyond that, they also point to, or to be more accurate hint at, the centripetal structure, the inwardness of the story. Melville makes his hero a writer, writing a book that sounds very much like—and sometimes even echoes—the one in which he appears; a writer, moreover, who sets out to write something popular, using as his vehicle a thinly fictionalized version of his life, and then discovers that he cannot or will not do so. 'Who shall tell all the thoughts and feelings of Pierre', Melville asks,

> when at last the idea obtruded, that the wiser and profounder he should grow, the more and the more he lessened his chances for bread. . . .[7]

The question occurs towards the end of the narrative, by which time Melville must have recognized that his own chances for bread had radically diminished. And in reading it the reader is likely to feel, not for the first time, that he has been caught in a Chinese box of fictions, a book in which everything comments on its own origins, making, and development.

This Chinese box aspect, this sense of an artifice that calls attention to its own artificiality is perhaps most obvious at the beginning of **Pierre.** It can hardly escape the notice of even the most inattentive reader that, when we first encounter the protagonist, he is living in a world of fiction. The opening paragraph, for example, offers us what is effectively a parody of the language of conventional, pastoral romance.

> There are some strange summer mornings in the country, when he who is but a sojourner from the city shall early walk forth into the fields, and be wonder-smitten with the trance-like aspect of the green and golden world. Not a flower stirs; the trees forget to wave; and all Nature, as if suddenly become conscious of her own profound mystery, and feeling no refuge from it but silence, sinks into this wonderful and indescribable repose.[8]

That 'indescribable' might just be a touch of Melvillean irony, and the reference to silence may perhaps anticipate the narrator's later claim that Silence is the only Voice of our God: but, on the whole, this passage, with its references to the 'sojourner from the city', its clichés of thought and expression ('wonder-smitten', 'green and golden world'), its histrionic rhythms ('Not a flower stirs; the trees forget to wave . . .'), and its utter self-consciousness (a self-consciousness which is then, interestingly enough, projected on to the subject)—in all this, the passage seems

to be insisting on its status as a conventional pattern, an invented object. This, we infer, is a world of appearances, masks and mirrors: an inference justified not only by the frequent references to masquerades and reflections in subsequent pages but, more simply, by the narrator's preference for the word 'seems'.

The sense that we are being introduced to a sort of pseudoreality, a counterfeit realm, is nurtured in a variety of ways, and not least by the characters' taste for theatricality. It is not just that Pierre and his mother, and Pierre and his beloved Lucy Tartan, address each other in heightened terms, although they certainly do this—terms borrowed from *Romeo and Juliet,* say, or some other familiar text. Nor is it just that Pierre tends to see 'the illuminated scroll of his life' through the spectacles of the books he has read. It is that both the protagonist and those around him actually call attention to the artificial nature of their conversations (Pierre, for instance, concludes one flight of wit with his beloved by declaring, 'Very prettily conceited, Lucy') and seem intent on turning most of their actions and relationships into a kind of sport, a game: 'playful', for instance, is another word that recurs throughout those opening pages, most notably in the sections dealing with Pierre and his mother—who in *their* 'playfulness', we are told, introduced 'a certain fictitiousness' into 'one of the closest domestic relations of life' by referring to each other as 'brother' and 'sister'. Nor is the narrator himself immune from this tendency. For not only does he, like the characters, use an elaborately foregrounded, 'high profile' language, full of awkward neologisms ('amaranthiness', 'tinglingness', and 'preambilically' are just three random examples) and elaborate conceits ('the striped tigers of his chestnut eyes leaped in their lashed cages'); he is also inclined to remind us, in case we have forgotten, that he *is* the narrator, bound to go backward and forward in time 'as occasion calls' and compelled 'by immemorial usage' to do such things as provide a scrupulously conventional 'inventory' of Lucy's charms when she first appears. 'Is human life in its most human dimension a work of fiction?' asks Ortega y Gasset in *History as a System;* 'Is man a sort of novelist of himself who conceives the fanciful figure of a personage with its unreal occupations and then, for the sake of converting it into a reality, does all the things he does . . . ?'[9] A similar question seems to be asked by Melville at the beginning of the novel, via both the characters and the narrator; and the answer, for the moment at least, appears to be 'yes'.

Then into this dream kingdom comes another apparition: the 'mysterious, haunting face' of Isabel. To some extent, Isabel is like a figure out of Poe: associated with another realm of ghosts and the sea, endowed with 'a death-like beauty' principally focussed in her large eyes, her musical voice, and the 'flowing glossiness of her long and unimprisoned hair', she is a mixture of the Madonna and La Belle Dame Sans Merci. More relevant to the present context, however, is the opportunity she clearly offers Pierre of moral and imaginative liberation: for she is, as one critic has put it, 'the eternally baffling object of human speculation, and . . . also speculation itself'[10]—or, to put it another way, she suggests at once Otherness, the world beyond the mask and the mirror, and the Muse, that creative force that might just make a glimpse of Otherness possible. Certainly, it is in these large terms that Pierre sees her. After receiving her letter, for example, he believes that now at last he will be able to 'tear all veils', 'strike through' masks, 'see . . . hidden things', and leave his father's house (which is, surely, at once a fictive house and the house of fiction) for 'boundless expansion' and the 'infinite air'. And shortly after this—in a passage which curiously anticipates Camus's description of the moment when 'the stage sets collapse' and the feeling of the absurd rushes in on an individual—Pierre, we are told, felt 'on all sides, the physical world of solid objects now slidingly displaced . . . from around him, and . . . floated into an ether of visions'.[11]

But, and it is a large but, there are things that Pierre does not see or, if he does see, chooses not to acknowledge. Isabel, in so far as she appears to open the door to another realm of experience and indeed to suggest that realm, does not belong to the world of words, articulate speech and intelligible action. The first thing we hear from her is a primal scream, a shriek to 'split its way clear through [Pierre's] heart, and leave a yawning gap there'; and most of her life, we discover later, has apparently been spent in mysterious, anonymous places that she either cannot or will not name, places where she felt 'all visible sights and audible sounds growing stranger and stranger' to her. Of course, she has been drawn into contact of a kind with people—compelled, she reveals, by the desire to understand what words like 'father' and 'dead' signify; of course, too, she learns to read and communicate—specifically, so as to decipher 'the talismanic word' inscribed on a handkerchief that once belonged to her (and Pierre's) father; and, of course, finally she tells her story, her 'vague tale of terribleness'—or, as she puts it, enables her brother to read 'in the one poor book of Isabel'. To say all this, however, is to leave certain quite crucial things out of account. Isabel tells her story, admittedly, but sensing that it is full of 'wonders that are unimaginable and unspeakable', she relies for much of the telling on 'the utter unintelligibleness, but the infinite significancies of the sounds of the guitar' that is her constant companion. She lives in the world now, certainly, but she longs for nothing so much as to leave it, to withdraw into non-being: 'I pray for peace', she declares,

> for motionlessness—for the feeling of myself as of some plant, absorbing life without seeking it, and existing without individual sensation. I feel that there can be no perfect peace in individualness . . . I feel I am in exile here.[12]

And Pierre responds to her, it may be, but what he responds to is her *image*: at first, 'the vague impression that somewhere he had seen traits of the likeness of [her] face before' and then, later, the conviction that in her he can discern a reflection of his father as depicted in the chair portrait. The cruel paradox is that Isabel's value lies precisely in her qualities of motionlessness and worldlessness, those aspects of her that lie beyond conceptualization and verbalization, and that she cannot explain herself, or indeed be explained by others, in anything other than a fiction—or, to use the stronger terms favoured by Melville, without jugglery or imposture. At one point in the novel, when he is trying to decide what to do about Lucy now that he has committed himself to Isabel, Pierre is compared by the narrator to 'an algebraist': 'for the real Lucy', we are told.

> he, in his scheming thoughts, had substituted but a sign—some empty x—and in the ultimate solution of the problem, that empty x still figures; not the real Lucy.[13]

In a bitterly ironic way this, as it turns out, sums up what happens to Isabel as she tries to describe herself, to Pierre as he charts the rest of his course, and to Melville himself as—becoming more and more convinced that 'this world is a lie' and that even 'the truest book in the world is a lie'—he attempts to tell their tale.

'I am a nothing. It is all a dream—we dream that we dreamed we dream.'[14] Pierre makes this declaration of unbelief, couched in what are for him characteristically Romantic terms, towards the end of the novel. Long before this, however, it is clear that in committing himself to Isabel Pierre is not, as he purports to believe, committing himself to Truth but to a further if different level of illusion. Quite apart from his tendency to respond to Isabel's image, the shadowy reflections that he catches from her, there is the fact that he continues to judge people and make decisions in the most obviously fictive terms. It was not, after all, a critic or even the narrator of the book who first directed attention to the parallel between Pierre and Hamlet; Pierre himself invites this comparison and then, spurred on by what he sees as the negative example of Hamlet's indecision, decides to act at once. The sense of artifice continues, fed by references not only to Shakespeare but to Dante, and perhaps most effectively underlined by Pierre's unwillingness to acknowledge the true nature or at least the full scope of his motives, and by his continued reliance on false—which is to say, at once deceiving and self-deceiving—names. Isabel is his sister; and yet the fact that they have only known each other as adults makes her seem something other than a sister. She is also mysterious and powerfully attractive, prompting feelings that are rather more than simply fraternal. 'Now Pierre', we are told,

> began to see mysteries interpierced with mysteries and mysteries eluding mysteries; and began to seem to see the mere imaginariness of the so supposed solidest principle of human association.[15]

The brother-sister relationship has been rendered purely fictive, a matter of names and shadows; and Pierre responds to this, not by asserting a truth, but by elaborating an alternative fiction, the pretence that he and Isabel have been secretly married. Perhaps, the narrative suggests,

Pierre is prompted to adopt this course, 'the nominal conversion of a sister into a wife', by his 'previous conversational conversion of a mother into a sister'. The point is well taken: here as before, the implication is, Pierre is playing with words, constructing an artifice that enables him both to conceal and to express incestuous feelings. He has devised a new set of signs, another opaque vocabulary, with which to misinterpret things.

It is worth stressing the fact that at the very moment when Pierre, inspired by his devotion to Isabel, commits himself openly and wholeheartedly to what he calls 'the inflexible rule of holy right', the narrator does the same. 'I shall follow the endless, winding way', the narrator tells us, 'the flowing river in the cave of man'[16]: this, only two paragraphs after Pierre has declared that he will pursue the 'path' of Truth. The parallel is useful, I believe, in the sense that it highlights at least two things. In the first place, it helps to emphasize the fact that Pierre—unlike, say, Ishmael in **Moby-Dick**—is not the narrator of his own story. He writes a book eventually, but the book he writes is not the one we read: on the contrary, it is the book we read *about—within* the book that an anonymous, third-person narrator writes. The distinction is significant; for it means that whereas Ishmael (along with all Melville's other, earlier, first-person narrators) can be said in the end to stand outside his experience, discover some at least of its objective truth, and be liberated by that discovery, Pierre remains trapped like a fly in amber within the fiction that bears his name. And, in the second place, it anticipates the discovery, made eventually by author, narrator, and reader alike that the quest for Truth that **Pierre** the book embodies is just as abortive as the one upon which Pierre the character embarks. In this respect, something that Mary McCarthy said once about Vladimir Nabokov's *Pale Fire* seems relevant: when we read *Pale Fire,* she explained,

> a novel on several levels is revealed, and those 'levels' are not the customary 'levels of meaning' of modernist criticism but planes in fictive space.. . . . Each plane or level in its shadow box proves to be a false bottom; there is an infinite regression, for the book is a book of mirrors.[17]

Part of this sense that **Pierre** is, to use McCarthy's phrase, 'a book of mirrors' is due to something I have mentioned in passing already: which is the sheer obtrusiveness of the narrator, the feeling that he is always there mediating, shaping, and in the process distorting experience. Sometimes, as in the example quoted earlier, he insists on reminding us of the rules he feels compelled to obey, the conventional forms through which he and other storytellers have habitually filtered experience. At others, he emphasizes the opposite: the sheer arbitrariness of the structures he has adopted, the random nature of his fictional devices. Book XVII, for example, begins in this fashion:

> Among the various conflicting modes of writing history, there would seem to be two grand practical distinctions, under which all the rest must subordinately range. By the one mode, all contemporaneous circumstances, facts, and events must be set down contemporaneously; by the other, they are only to be set down as the general stream of the narrative shall dictate; for matters which are kindred in time, may be very irrelative in themselves. I elect neither of these; I am careless of either; both are well enough in their way; I write precisely as I please.[18]

Elsewhere, in the same vein, the reader is advised that he can 'skip' certain chapters if he prefers to, and that he must not expect a consistent portrait of Pierre but catch 'his phases as he revolves'. Whether the emphasis is on the conventional or the arbitrary, however, the effect remains the same: to focus attention on the making of the text and, by extension, on the conversion of objective experience into (to adopt Borges's useful phrase) 'a mere labyrinth of letters'.[19]

But it is not just that the narrator is conspicuously there, reminding us of his presence; he is reminding us too, and continually, of the sheer hopelessness of his task. It is idle, he admits to us, to attempt to penetrate into the heart and 'inmost life' of Pierre or indeed anyone since 'in their precise tracings-out and subtle causations, the strongest and fiercest emotions of life defy all analytical insight.' Equally, it is pointless to try to tell anyone anything,

> for—absurd as it may seem—men are only made to comprehend things which they comprehended before (though but in embryo, as it were). Things new it is impossible to make them comprehend, by merely talking to them about it.[20]

In effect, the lines of communication between author and subject and those between author and reader are all irremediably blocked: things remain resistant to explanation and there is a 'universal lurking insincerity' in 'even the greatest and purest written thoughts'. And because of this one measure of a book's authenticity, or rather its relative lack of inauthenticity, becomes the extent to which it does not even attempt to explain, does not try to contain, does not pretend that it has rendered a coherent and conclusive vision of life. As the narrator puts it:

> while the countless tribes of common novels laboriously spin veils of mystery, only to complacently clear them up at last . . . yet the profounder emanations of the human mind . . . never unravel their own intricacies, and have no proper endings: but in imperfect, unanticipated, and disappointing sequels (as mutilated stumps), hurry to abrupt intermergings with the eternal tides of time and fate.[21]

The implication of what Melville was getting his narrator to say, in passages like the one I have just quoted, were (as Melville was well aware) at once dispiriting and slightly terrifying. There is, it gradually emerges from the story of Pierre, a vacuum at the heart of things, a central emptiness, a hollowness, a silence—and 'how can a man get a Voice out of Silence?' Self-evidently, he cannot. There are, in fact, only two responsible courses of action open to him. Either he can pursue a state of non-being:

that condition of quietness, apartness, and passivity that Isabel sometimes desires—and that, as Pierre observes him, the inscrutable 'mystic-mild' Plotinus Plinlimmon seems to have achieved.[22] Or, alternatively, he can *choose* to join the 'guild of self-imposters', comforting himself with the knowledge that, while his forgeries and impostures do little real good, they will, if performed in the right spirit—which is to say, a self-reflexive, self-conscious one—do little significant harm either. 'There is infinite nonsense in the world on all . . . matters', proclaims the narrator,

> hence blame me not if I contribute my mite. It is impossible to talk or to write without throwing oneself hopelessly open; the Invulnerable Knight wears his visor down. Still, it is pleasant to chat ere we go to our beds; and speech is further incited, when like strolling improvisatores of Italy, we are paid for our breath.[23]

The casual, jokily resigned attitude that the narrator adopts here is by no means sustained throughout the book: as any reader of **Pierre** will verify, the tone fluctuates violently between irony and anger ('Oh what a vile cheat and juggler man is!'), exhausted acceptance and pure, blind rage (God is referred to at one point as 'the eminent Juggularius'), absurd humour and apocalyptic nihilism. Throughout the changes of tone, however, the essential thrust remains the same: what we are reading, the narrator reminds us, is a 'knavish pack of cards',[24] a game, a fabrication. Nor does he depend simply on telling us this; the form of the narrative, which is parodic and discontinuous, serves to remind us of it on almost every page. The literary allusions and references, for example, are quite startling in their number, breadth, and complexity, including in the opening pages not only the Shakespeare mentioned earlier but Sir Thomas Browne, De Quincey, Disraeli, Milton, and the English Romantic poets. There are deeper, more sustained parallels not only with the novel of romantic sensibility but also with Gothic romance and Jacobean drama; the style offers pastiches of a number of writers—Carlyleian twists of syntax, for instance, mingle with Biblical rhythms, while passages that recall Emerson collide with others reminiscent of Shelley; and the characters issue as much out of literature as life—with, at one end of the spectrum, Pierre reminding us of the traditional Byronic hero and, at the other, numerous minor characters recalling the porters, tinkers, and constables of Shakespeare. Given the sheer abundance and consistency of such allusiveness, and setting aside the obvious point that Melville was hardly a crowd-follower, it is difficult to see how all this can be dismissed (as it has been by some critics[25]) as an example of an author being lamely derivative. Melville knew what he was doing. Pastiche, as he was neither the first nor the last to realize, can be a useful tool in the hands of someone bent on creating a realm of surfaces, an insistently figurative, self-evidently artificial world in which books, whether by choice (as in earlier examples of this genre) or by necessity (as in **Pierre** and later examples) refer to nothing except themselves.

So, even after swearing themselves to the cause of Truth, both Pierre and his narrator remain trapped in a spider's web of words. As the narrative edges forward—one, brief section rapidly replacing another, reaching nervously in various directions and towards different points in time—the sense of inwardness, of being imprisoned in a labyrinth, grows stronger and ever more inescapable. Pierre begins writing a book in which, the narrator tells us, 'he seems to have directly plagiarized from his own experiences, to fill out the mood of his apparent author-hero'.[26] The parallel with Melville, borrowing from his own experiences to fill out the mood of *his* author-hero, is so obvious as to be hardly worth mentioning; and perhaps more interesting here is the fact that the use of the word 'plagiarized' alerts us to the fictional nature of Pierre's raw material. Pierre's life is fictive, not just because Melville has invented it, but also to the extent that (as we have seen) there is 'a certain fictitiousness' in all Pierre's relationships—and, in addition, in the sense that his entire story, from its sentimental beginnings to its Gothic conclusion, offers us a series of parodic masks; the book that he writes could consequently be described as a fiction of a fiction compounded of fictions. Not content with such dizzying involutions, our storyteller at this point takes *us* within the story he tells too. 'Let us peep over the shoulder of Pierre, he suggests, and see what he is writing there . . . Here . . . is the last sheet from his hand, the frenzied ink not yet entirely dry.'[27] At such moments, narrator and reader exist within the interior of the narrative as minor, choric characters; as a corollary of this, they, or rather we, share in the prevalent mood of narcissism—as we watch ourselves watching Melville/Pierre watching himself.

In this connection, it is worth mentioning the shadowy references to incest and incestuous feelings that run through the book and that reach their climax in the story of Pierre's 'marriage' to Isabel. It is not enough, I think, to explain these in terms of the book's parodic framework. Certainly, the tradition of the sentimental novel permitted veiled hints at such deliciously shocking matters, and the motif of incest fits in well with Melville's tendency, towards the end of the book, to present Pierre as a reflection of the Promethean Christ figure of Romantic myth. The fact that this is so, however, does not exclude the further possibility that, in playing upon the idea of incest, Melville was hoping to remind the reader of his young author-hero's narcissism and the solipsistic thrust of the narrative. Like many a young American hero, Pierre discovers that his father has failed him, that the 'niched pillar . . . which supported the entire . . . temple of his moral life'[28] has been broken; he therefore sets out to rebuild the temple by accepting the moral responsibilities which, he feels, his father has abrogated—to assume the place vacated by Mr. Glendinning and so, in effect, become his own father. All he ends by doing, however, is embracing his own image, a projection of infantile obsessions. As far as the later course of his life goes, in fact, the young American hero he most resembles—or, to be more accurate, anticipates—is Quentin Compson in William Faulkner's The Sound and the Fury. For both Pierre and Quentin end by retreating from the sound and the fury of things into a preoccupation with a 'lost sister' that at once encapsulates and exacerbates their narcissism. In both cases, it hardly matters whether or not the physical act of incest occurs since the main point is the simple fact of the attraction and its sources[29]; and in both cases, of course, a further retreat is made into suicide—self-absorption and self-enclosure leading inevitably, it seems, to self-destruction. Even this particular parallel should not be pushed too far, however. For whatever the darkness of the first three sections of *The Sound and the Fury,* Faulkner does try to locate an alternative vision in the fourth; Quentin's way is not, apparently, the only one. By contrast, as I have tried to suggest, Pierre's psychological and sexual inversion is a mocking reflection of Melville's own sense (by turns bitter, ironic, and desperate) that he has been caught in a hall of mirrors: in this respect, the book is as much of a prison for the author as it is for the hero.

By the end of the book, of course, Pierre is (if one can use the phrase in this context) quite literally in prison, in 'a low dungeon' where 'the long tiers of massive cell-galleries above [seem] partly piled on him'. The sense of being trapped in a fiction continues: 'Here then, is the untimely, timely end', Pierre declares to himself,

> —Life's last chapter well stitched into the middle; Nor book, nor author of the book, hath any sequel, though each hath its last lettering![30]

More important for our present purposes, however, Pierre feels oppressed at this juncture, not so much by laws or by people, as by 'the stone cheeks of the walls' in his 'granite hell'. As several critics have observed, references to rocks, stones, and stony structures run throughout *Pierre.*[31] The book is, after all, dedicated to 'Greylock's Most Excellent Majesty', the highest mountain in Massachusetts, which Melville could see from his writing desk; the Mount of Titans (based on Mount Greylock) and the Memnon Stone (modelled on Balance Rock, near Pittsfield) perform important functions within the narrative; and both the rural and the urban environments the characters inhabit are described principally in terms of their stoniness. It is not difficult, I think, to see the purpose of all this: rock, in this novel, becomes the central image of the material, it replaces the whale as an emblem of being—all that Wallace Stevens would later term 'things as they are'. Nor is it difficult to see what the crucial property of rock in *Pierre* (the pun on 'pierre', the French word for 'stone', may or may not be intentional) is; rock, Melville insists, is utterly impenetrable and uninterpretable, offering nothing more than a series of blank surfaces. Admittedly, attempts may be made from time to time to name an especially noticeable configuration of rocks; we are told, for instance, that 'a singular height' not far from Pierre's ancestral home has been variously (and somewhat confusingly) termed The Delectable Mountain and the Mount of the Titans— and that the Memnon Stone was thus 'fancifully christened' by Pierre himself (although very few people, the narrator adds, would either know it by this name or indeed consider it worth naming). Admittedly, too, something, some hieroglyphic or message may be inscribed on a particular rock: like the 'half-obliterate initials—"S. ye W"' that

Pierre finds 'rudely hammered' on the Memnon Stone and never satisfactorily deciphers. Such things, however, remain no more than surface scratchings, doomed efforts to name the unnameable and know the unknowable. For,

> Say what some poets will, Nature is not so much her own ever-sweet interpreter, as the mere supplier of that cunning alphabet, whereby selecting and combining as he pleases, each man reads his own peculiar lesson according to his own peculiar mind and mood.[32]

Which brings us back to Pierre, in his 'granite hell'. By the end of the novel, Pierre's attempts to name and to know the world have ceased—just as, indeed, those of Melville are about to—and he finds himself at once overpowered and mocked by the brute materiality of the world. The rocks and mountains which he christened and on which he tried to scratch some messages have now narrowed to a set of prison walls; and while he may feel like Ahab, that he would like to thrust through those walls he clearly believes that he cannot. The final paragraph, describing the tableau of Pierre and Isabel dead in one another's arms, is worth quoting here:

> 'All's o'er, and ye know him not!' came gasping from the wall; and from the fingers of Isabel dropped an empty vial—as it had been a run-out sand-glass—and shivered upon the floor; and her whole form sloped sideways, and she fell upon Pierre's heart, and her long hair ran over him, and arbored him in ebon vines.[33]

The ambiguity of those first words is surely intentional. For while most readers will assume, quite reasonably, that it is Isabel who speaks here, addressing her words to Frederic Tartan and Charlie Millthorpe, the very strangeness of the phrase 'came gasping from the wall' (combined, perhaps, with the feeling that it was never incumbent on Tartan or even Millthorpe really to know Pierre) suggests other, admittedly tentative possibilities. It could be Pierre himself, talking to the other characters, or indeed to the narrator and the reader; it would not, after all, be the first time he had referred to himself in the third person. Or, for that matter, bearing in mind the references to rocks, stones, and walls that run through the novel, it could be the visible objects of the world, addressing themselves mockingly to Melville, reminding him that for all his attempts at naming them they remain unidentified and anonymous.

"'All's o'er, and ye know him not!'": by the time Melville finished *Pierre,* there was really only one major distinction to be made between him and his young author-hero. Locked in a fictional jailhouse just as Pierre was, mocked in just the same way by the blankness of its walls, Melville at least knew, to his own profound dissatisfaction, what the alternatives were: either silence or artifice, stillness or imposture. One could either sit staring at those walls and, in a gesture of total passivity, try to assume something of their blankness and impenetrability. Or one could attempt to break through them, in the certain knowledge that all one would find beneath their immediate surface would be another surface—and then, after that, another.[34] 'Far as any geologist has yet gone down in the world', declares Melville in Book XXI of *Pierre,*

> it is found to consist of nothing but surface stratified on surface. To its axis, the world being nothing but super-induced superficies. By vast pains we mine into the pyramid; by horrible gropings we come to the central room; with joy we espy the sarcophagus; but we lift the lid—and no body is there!—appallingly vacant as vast is the soul of a man![35]

To anyone familiar with postmodernist literature, this description of superinduced superficies will probably recall not only the writers I mentioned earlier—that is, Vladimir Nabokov and Jorge Luis Borges—but also such things as, say, Roland Barthes's claim that texts can be seen

> as constructions of layers (or levels, or systems) whose body contains finally no heart, no kernel, no secret, no irreducible principle, nothing except the infinity of their own envelopes—which envelop nothing other than the unity of their own surfaces.[36]

The parallel is there, certainly: but there *is* a difference, and it is a crucial one. For there is no escaping the intense bitterness, the sheer rage and sense of betrayal, that runs through the passage from *Pierre* that I have just quoted (and, indeed, through the entire book): feelings which, it need hardly be said, are conspicuous only by their absence from Barthes's remarks and from most of the fiction of Nabokov and Borges. Part of Melville, it is clear (and a significant part of him at that), wanted to utter a thunderous 'no' to the idea of 'surface stratified on surface'; to that extent, at least, he was rather more than just a progenitor of postmodernist writing, and *Pierre* itself is something other than just a distant anticipation of books like *Ficciones* and *Pale Fire.* In his seventh novel, as in so much of his work, Melville's heart tried desperately to reject what his head told him. Which accounts not only for the book's anger, occasional awkwardness, and acidity, but also for its power as an expression of that impulse most of us feel at one time or another: the impulse to believe, that is, even if only in the possibility of belief, however perversely and despite all the evidence.

Notes

1. *Pierre; Or, The Ambiguities* (1852), p. 294. All references are to the New American Library, New York, 1964 edition.

2. *The Letters of Herman Melville* edited by Merrell R. Davis and William H. Gilman (New Haven, 1960), pp. 146, 150.

3. *Melville: The Critical Heritage* edited by Watson G. Branch (London, 1974), pp. 294, 298, 303.

4. Edward H. Rosenberry, *Melville* (London, 1979), p. 90. See also, Richard Chase, *Herman Melville: A Critical Study* (New York, 1949), p. 103.

5. P. 322.

6. 'Introduction' to *Pierre,* New York, 1949 edition, p. xxi. See also, Ronald Mason, *The Spirit Above the Dust: A Study of Herman Melville* (London, 1951), pp. 169-71.

7. P. 344.

8. P. 23. The other quotation in this paragraph is from p. 237.

9. New York, 1962. Quotations from *Pierre* in this paragraph are from pp. 25, 27, 44, 47, 58, 59, 79, 208, 297.

10. William Ellery Sedgwick, *Herman Melville: The Tragedy of the Mind* (New York, 1962), p. 153. See also, Murray, 'Introduction', pp. l-lxv.

11. P. 111. Cf. Albert Camus, *The Myth of Sisyphus* translated by Justin O'Brien (New York, 1959), p. 10. Other quotations from *Pierre* in this paragraph are from pp. 60, 91, 139.

12. P. 146. Other quotations from pp. 69, 144, 149, 152, 154, 176, 186.

13. Pp. 212-13. Other quotations from pp. 74, 241, 298.

14. P. 311.

15. P. 121. Other quotations from p. 208.

16. P. 135. Other quotations from p. 134.

17. Cited in Tony Tanner, *City of Words: American Fiction 1950-1970* (London, 1971), p. 34.

18. P. 280. Other quotations from pp. 243, 378.

19. Cited in Tanner, *City of Words,* p. 41.

20. Pp. 242-43. Other quotations from p. 92.

21. P. 170. Other quotations from p. 380.

22. There is 'something passive' about Plinlimmon, we are told; his face has 'a repose separate and apart—a repose of a face by itself'; and his features appear to express the belief that 'to respond is a suspension of isolation'. Pp. 328, 330.

23. P. 295. Other quotations from pp. 241, 242.

24. P. 380. Other quotations from pp. 298, 309.

25. See, e.g., Newton Arvin, *Herman Melville* (London, 1950), p. 227.

26. P. 342.

27. Pp. 341-42.

28. P. 94.

29. In *Pierre* the implication is that an act of incest has occurred; in *The Sound and the Fury* the implication is that it has not. A further ambiguity is introduced into *Pierre* by the fact that we never knew for certain whether or not Pierre and Isabel do have the same father.

30. P. 402. Other quotations from pp. 402, 404.

31. See, e.g., H. Bruce Franklin, *The Wake of the Gods: Melville's Mythology* (Stanford, 1963), pp. 101ff. Edgar A. Dryden, *Melville's Thematics of Form: The Great Art of Telling the Truth* (Baltimore, 1968), pp. 118ff.

32. Pp. 383-84. Other quotations from pp. 160, 161, 383.

33. P. 405.

34. See 'Bartleby' and *The Confidence-Man: His Masquerade* for later explorations of these two alternatives.

35. P. 323.

36. 'Style and its Image', in *Literary Style: A Symposium* (London, 1971). I am indebted to Harold Beaver for drawing attention to the parallel noted here.

Nicholas Canaday (essay date 1986)

SOURCE: "Pierre in the Domestic Circle," in *Studies in the Novel,* Vol. XVIII, No. 4, Winter, 1986, pp. 395-402.

[*In the following essay, Canaday explores the connection between Pierre's psychological problems and his becoming a male member of a female world as he moves from Saddle Meadows to New York City.*]

When Melville wrote to Sophia Hawthorne and promised that his new novel would be a "rural bowl of milk,"[1] he may have been referring to a central theme, which, in our predilection for irony, we have overlooked. Melville was assuring Mrs. Hawthorne, of course, that at last there would be no sailor-narrator here, that there would be a sensibility different from the rover in Polynesia, the bitter White Jacket and Redburn, or the ruminating Ishmael. As it turned out, however, the narrative voice in *Pierre* is not so different, and the phrase presenting his new hero Pierre in the clabber of domesticity is not ironic. What I am labeling the "domestic circle" is not only a setting but is also a symbolic construct in Melville's thought that, it seems to me, has a great deal of power in shaping attitudes and behavior patterns. Since there are two main domestic circles in the novel, one in Saddle Meadows and the other in New York City, we may here be observing a structural principle that will afford us some new insights.

I

Melville's *Pierre* opens with the idyllic story of Pierre and Lucy Tartan told in the extravagant, sentimental terms of the domestic romance, which Melville is parodying.[2] The substance and especially the style of the opening deservedly capture critical attention, not least because the leisure activity of courting Lucy has a central place in the life of a young man whose life is virtually all leisure. The romance, however, is spun out of the domestic circle of which Pierre is a member, and leisure entertainment—usually reading, but in this instance a kind of stagy performance featuring a series of *tableaux vivant*—is not its sole function. The romance, however, serves not merely to entertain but, more importantly, to praise the behavior and confirm the values of those in the circle. At Saddle Meadows the circle starts with two, Pierre and his mother, but Lucy and Mrs. Tartan are included, as well as other women on the social periphery. Mrs. Glendinning is the chief instrument of social authority, "conventionalness" as

Melville terms it, which shapes the domestic circle and vests its highest ranking arbiter with her power.[3]

The reader is soon given a glimpse of Pierre on a typical morning. It begins as Pierre helps his mother, whom he calls sister at her insistence, finish her toilet in front of her glass at her dressing table, passing a ribbon around her neck and fastening it with a cameo. As they talk pretty talk, he adjusts a stray ringlet of her hair and then kneels to secure the tie of her slipper. At breakfast Pierre attentively supplies his mother with all of her needs, several times admonishing the butler Dates to adjust the window sashes is order to block from his mother's neck any "unkind current of air,"[4] and to swing around a hinged painting on the wall into a favorable light. All the while the hovering Pierre takes great interest in "Sister Mary's" food. The talk between Pierre and Mrs. Glendinning here and in the other opening scenes of the novel is largely about domestic detail.

It is apparent that normal aspects of a young man's education are denied Pierre. There are books at Saddle Meadows, of course, "his father's fastidiously picked and decorous library," but because they cultivate only "delicate warmths" and "soft, imaginative flames in his heart" (p. 6), we may infer that they were chosen for a young wife. Occasionally Pierre sojourns to the city for the purpose of "mingling in a large and polished society," but that society seems to be essentially feminine, for there Pierre "had insensibly formed himself in the airier graces of life" (p. 6). Finally, Pierre is "companioned by no surnamed male Glendinning" (p. 8). Without a male model in this domestic circle, Pierre has no idea how to act in the traditional male role, and thus the folly of his longing is presented ironically in Melville's imagery: in the "vain-gloriousness of his youthful soul, he fondly hoped to have a monopoly of glory in capping the fame-column, whose tall shaft had been erected by his noble sires" (p. 8).

Pierre is unlike most other nineteen-year-old males. He keeps no secret from his mother, but, after the chance encounter with Isabel, seeing her and haunted by her face, he conceals from his mother for the first time ever a circumstance in his life and evades her questions. Mrs. Glendinning stresses Pierre's docility whenever she thinks of his character. She recalls her late husband's attitude toward women and applies it to Pierre as well: Pierre's father had said that "the noblest colts, in three points—abundant hair, swelling chest, and sweet docility—should resemble a fine woman." She adds "so should a noble youth" (p. 20). Yet in her musing she is at the same time fondling old General Glendinning's baton, part of the Saddle Meadows collection of mementos, which she recognizes as a "symbol of command" and incompatible with "sweet docility" (p. 20). But Pierre has thoroughly accepted the values of the domestic circle, as exemplified by his attitude toward the beautiful, girlish Lucy:

> Methinks one husbandly embrace would break her airy
> zone, and she exhale upward to that heaven whence

she hath hither come, condensed to a mortal sight. It can not be; I am of heavy earth, and she of airy light. By heaven, but marriage is an impious thing! (p. 58)

Frail heavenly femininity, that is, crushed by brutal earthly masculinity makes marriage itself a sacrilege, a rather unusual view about himself and sex from a nineteen-year-old male.

Pierre was unaware, as Melville writes, of the foreboding and prophetic lessons taught by Palmyra's ruins. Melville's version of the lesson of Palmyra is particularly appropriate in this context. That ancient city is said to have had an avenue lined by 750 limestone columns, each over fifty feet high topped by a statue. Melville writes only about one column: "Among those ruins is a crumbling, uncompleted shaft . . . crushed in the egg; and the proud stone that should have stood among the clouds, Time left abased beneath the soil" (p. 8). That ruin is an image of Pierre's masculinity, crushed in the egg and left abased in the domestic circle.

The baton that is incompatible with docility, the folly of aspiring to cap the fame-column, the abasement of the proud shaft—all this phallic imagery is summarized when Melville begins Book IV, which is entitled "Retrospective" and, looking back on the romantic section of the novel, brings it to an end. He begins by writing that he is dealing with the unconscious:

> In their precise tracings-out and subtle causations, the strongest and fieriest emotions of life defy all analytical insight. . . . The metaphysical writers confess, that the most impressive, sudden, and overwhelming event, as well as the minutest, is but the product of an infinite series of infinitely involved and untraceable foregoing occurrences. . . . things not wholly imputable to the immediate apparent cause, which is only one link in the chain; but to a long line of dependencies whose further part is lost in the mid-regions of the impalpable air. (p. 67)

He then suggests that the shrine in Pierre's heart, the vestibule of his religious feeling, is his late father's reputation, now laid low by the revelation of the existence of Isabel. The image of the shrine is that of a "niched pillar, deemed solid and eternal, and from whose top radiated all those innumerable sculptured scrolls and branches, which supported the entire one-pillared temple of his moral life." In the niche of the pillar "stood the perfect marble form of his departed father; without blemish, unclouded, snow-white, and serene; Pierre's fond personification of human goodness and virtue" (p. 68). The retrospective summary of the first part of the novel sees the shrine as devastated before a "withering blast" that had "stripped his holiest shrine of all overlaid bloom and buried the mild statue of the saint beneath the prostrated ruins of the soul's temple itself" (p. 69).

Melville writes specifically in this retrospective passage that Pierre's entire early life had been a product of rural influences because Pierre "had never yet become so thoroughly initiated into that darker, though truer aspect of things, which an entire residence in the city from the earliest period of his life almost invariably engraves upon the mind of any keenly observant and reflecting youth of Pierre's present years" (p. 69). This situation precisely reflects the "familial interpretation of power relations" described by Jane Gallop in her book *The Daughter's Seduction: Feminism and Psychoanalysis*. Gallop says feminism sometimes mistakenly accepts the familial interpretation as true of the world outside of what I have termed the domestic circle. Feminism, that is, complaining about men in power, "endows them with a sort of unified phallic sovereignty that characterizes an absolute monarch, and which little resembles actual power in our social, economic structures."[5] Pierre's vision of the one-pillared temple is well described by the phrase "unified phallic sovereignty," and that temple is removed by more than a country mile from the darker, truer aspects of power in citified social and economic structures.

Without a masculine role in the early part of the novel, his maleness crushed in the egg and abased in the domestic circle, Pierre is effectively a daughter, a sister. Isabel emerges from the darker, truer life of their father (the dark lady's contrast to the snow-maiden Lucy has often been noted), and thus Pierre's seduction by the father through Isabel is similar to the model outlined by Jane Gallop. The main result of this encounter is "the introduction of heterogeneity (sexuality, violence, economic class conflict) into the closed circle of the family."[6] In terms of Melville's novel, into the domestic and asexual circle of Saddle Meadows Isabel brings sexuality (Pierre's mysterious depths of attraction for Isabel never felt for Lucy), violence (his confrontation with his mother on a stairway after which he trips and falls down on the stone portico of the house), and economic class conflict (his befriending of Delly Ulver). Pierre chooses to flee, leaving the ruins of Saddle Meadows laid low by the "withering blast."

II

With crushing irony Melville shows us Pierre not escaping but transferring the domestic circle to New York City. The company of Isabel, Delly, and later Lucy in the Apostles', the three-room tenement in the abandoned church building, evidences a sensibility and a set of values exactly like that left behind at Saddle Meadows. Aside from the fact that their number makes it manifestly absurd that Pierre could ever hope to support them by his writing, this circle is completely unprepared for citified life and even for the rough, masculine democracy of the other tenants of the Apostles'. There is ready sympathy available for Pierre and his poverty-stricken household, and on one occasion willing male helpers offer protection by forcibly ejecting Lucy's brother Frederic Tartan and Pierre's cousin Glen Stanly as they attempt Lucy's rescue. Yet Pierre cannot relate to the others in any way, partly because of a lingering class consciousness, but mostly because he has no idea how to act with other men.

Pierre's domestic circle in New York is held together by certain fictions. Isabel's rhetoric maintains their brother-sister relationship except in certain moments as they sit to-gether in the dark. Yet Isabel's seductive beauty is always present, and her jealousy of Lucy surfaces with little provocation. Delly, on the other hand, because of her sense of propriety, must make an effort—and she seems success-ful in doing so—to convince herself that Pierre and Isabel are married. She knows nothing of their family relation-ship. When Lucy joins them, fleeing from her new suitor Glen Stanly and her mother and brother, and determined to sacrifice her life to Pierre's well-being, she too believes that they are married and knows nothing of their kinship. It is, ultimately, the revelation of the filial relationship, while she still believes that they have lived together as man and wife, that causes her to drop dead from shock at the climax of the novel. Incest is certainly one type of sexuality that can destroy the domestic circle and those in it as well.

Melville's way of depicting Pierre as out of place in New York City is through imagery typically applied to a young woman: "Like a flower he feels the change; his bloom is gone from his cheek; his cheek is wilted and pale" (p. 271). The verdant youth had not yet come to maturity in the summer of Saddle Meadows: "Oh, woe to that belated winter-overtaken plant which the summer could not bring to maturity! The drifting snows shall whelm it" (p. 296). To further emphasize the non-masculine nature of his ar-rested sexuality, Lucy says to Pierre that he has "no love as other men love," but "thou lovest as angels do" (p. 309). The remark is true but ironically somewhat different from the intended high compliment.

Pierre's sexual stirrings toward Isabel continue, and she encourages them by words, movement, and touch—hers is the volition, not his—but if further evidence were needed in the sometime critical disagreement as to whether their love is in fact consummated the picture of Pierre as sexu-ally immature angel should settle the disagreement.[7] Phal-lic insistence, the love that other men have, is inappropri-ate in this circle.

Since Charlie Millthorpe never appears in the Saddle Meadows section of the novel, his presence in New York City as a boyhood friend of Pierre's continues Melville's irony. In helping Pierre to find a place to live in the city, Charlie's earnest and practical kindness stands in contrast to the diffident and haughty dismissal Pierre suffers at the hands of his cousin Glen Stanly. Charlie, the son of a farmer on the Glendinning lands in Saddle Meadows, now after his father's death removed to the city with his mother and sister, attempts quite unsuccessfully in his blustery, masculine way to relate to Pierre. Eventually Charlie pays the rent for Pierre and even offers to help him move furni-ture about when Lucy arrives to join the household. Pierre smiles condescendingly at Charlie's lack of sophistication and mutters that he is "plus heart, minus head" (p. 320), but Pierre addresses Charlie only once directly in the sev-eral times they meet. That one time is after the porter bringing Lucy's belongings is dismissed: "The porter is gone then? . . . Well, Mr. Millthorpe, you will have the goodness to follow him" (p. 319).

Some expository details are given about how Pierre and Charlie played together as children in Saddle Meadows, but that happened long before Pierre's adolescence. Char-lie went on to school and to assume responsibility for his family. In contrast to Pierre, Charlie had a male presence in his life, although his father was rough, inarticulate, and given to drink. Charlie is Pierre's friend to the end, and when he holds the dead Pierre in his arms in the jail cell at the end of the novel Charlie's speech inadvertently hints at Pierre's arrested sexuality:

> Ah, Pierre! my old companion, Pierre;—school-mate—play-mate—friend!—Our sweet boy's walks within the woods! . . . What scornful innocence rests on thy lips, my friend!—Hand scorched with murderer's powder, yet how woman-soft! (p. 362)

This speech prompts Isabel's dying sentence in the same scene, essentially Pierre's epitaph: "All's o'er, and ye know him not!" (p. 362). Read as a response to Charlie, it is a remark probably not meaning that the author withheld the one secret of his character's life, his incestuous rela-tionship with Isabel,[8] but that Charlie and the world were ignorant finally of Pierre's psychosexual immaturity and his real relation with Isabel and the other women in his household.

It is, unfortunately, this same arrested sexuality that keeps Pierre from succeeding as a writer. He had promised his publisher a "popular novel," and that could have been spun out of the rural Saddle Meadows just like his life's activities there, but in the city what he writes becomes "blasphemous rhapsody" (p. 356). The controlling meta-phor of writing in the nineteenth century is "literary pater-nity" according to Sandra Gilbert and Susan Gubar in *The Madwoman in the Attic: The Woman Writer and the Nineteenth-Century Imagination.* They make the observa-tion that "male sexuality . . . is not analogically but actu-ally the essence of literary power. The poet's pen is in some sense (even more than figuratively) a penis."[9] We have seen that Pierre lacked unified phallic sovereignty, and Melville is writing in the tradition in which the liter-ary text is a manifestation of power. Again, according to Gilbert and Gubar:

> In patriarchal Western culture . . . the text's author is a father, a progenitor, a procreator, an aesthetic patriarch whose pen is an instrument of generative power like his penis. More, his pen's power, like his penis's power, is not just the ability to generate life but the power to create a posterity to which he lays claim. . . . In this respect the pen is truly mightier than its phallic coun-terpart the sword. . . .[10]

Thus unlike the idyllic harmony of Saddle Meadows, Pierre's desperation in New York City results from a grow-ing awareness of his incongruous place within the group of women who encircle him. His murderous assault on Glen Stanly with a brace of pistols stolen from the cham-bers of another inhabitant of the Apostles' is an unfocused and suicidal attempt to escape into maturity. As he leaves the Apostles' for the last time, Pierre passes through the room of Isabel, who sits in her chair as if petrified; and then through the room of Lucy, unstirring in her chair as though entranced. In the corridor between the two outer doors of each room, he pauses with outstretched arms and then breaks the domestic circle forever with this wish: "For ye two, my most undiluted prayer is now, that from your here unseen and frozen chairs ye may never stir alive" (p. 358). It is a harsh leave-taking from the women who have been close to him, but Pierre's bitter awareness of the stultifying, exclusively female, "rural bowl of milk" is a measure of Melville's response to all that was unnatural in the early life of his youthful hero and to his belated disastrous entry into a masculine world.

Notes

1. Merrell R. Davis and William H. Gilman, eds., *The Letters of Herman Melville* (New Haven: Yale Univ. Press, 1960), p. 146.

2. Melville's satirical purpose is argued convincingly by William Braswell, "The Early Love Scenes in Melville's *Pierre*," *AL* [*American Literature: A Journal of Literary History, Criticism, and Bibliography*], 22 (1950), 283-89, which essay also provides a good summary of earlier critics who had accused Melville of a lapse of taste in the opening scenes.

3. In an earlier essay, Nicholas Canaday, "Melville's Pierre: At War with Social Convention," *PLL* [*Papers on Language and Literature: A Journal for Scholars and Critics of Language and Literature*], 5 (1969), 51-62, I have characterized Pierre as a rebel against social authority.

4. Herman Melville, *Pierre; or the Ambiguities*, ed., Harrison Hayford, Hershel Parker, and G. Thomas Tanselle, Northwestern-Newberry Edition (Chicago: Northwestern Univ. Press, 1971), p. 17. All subsequent citations, which appear parenthetically in the text, are to this edition.

5. Jane Gallop, *The Daughter's Seduction: Feminism and Psychoanalysis* (Ithaca: Cornell Univ. Press, 1982), p. xv.

6. Gallop, p. xv.

7. For a summary of critical comments on this point, see Canaday, pp. 58-59. More recent support for the argument that their love is not consummated is found in Paula Miner-Quinn, "Pierre's Sexuality: A Psychoanalytic Interpretation of Herman Melville's *Pierre, or, The Ambiguities, HSL* [*University of Hartford Studies in Literature: A Journal of Interdisciplinary Criticism*], 13 (1981), 111-21.

8. Henry A. Murray, ed., *Pierre: or, The Ambiguities* by Herman Melville, Hendricks House Edition (New York: Farrar Straus, 1949), p. xcii.

9. Sandra M. Gilbert and Susan Gubar, *The Madwoman in the Attic: The Woman Writer and the Nineteenth-Century Literary Imagination* (New Haven: Yale Univ. Press, 1979), p. 4.

10. Gilbert and Gubar, p. 6.

Phillip J. Egan (essay date 1987)

SOURCE: "Isabel's Story: The Voice of the Dark Woman in Melville's *Pierre*," in *American Transcendental Quarterly: A Journal of New England Writers,* Vol. 1, No. 2, June, 1987, pp. 99-110.

[*In the following essay, Egan examines Isabel's story as a bildungsroman, or coming-of-age narrative, and interprets it in the light of several key concepts of Romanticism.*]

Isabel, the "dark" woman in Melville's *Pierre,* fascinates critics in part because she appears suddenly to tell a story that becomes the mainspring of the novel's plot. It is surprising, therefore, that her story itself has received relatively little detailed attention. It has, of course, been mined for symbols and themes in general studies of the novel. And in the past it has also been attacked by some prominent commentators. Henry Murray, for example, in his famous introduction to the Hendricks House edition of *Pierre,* dismisses Isabel's story, saying, "the incoherent flow of her shadowy memories will not be so engrossing to the reader as they are to Pierre" (xlviii). Milton Stern, writing about a decade later, appreciates the story's content but believes it to be misconceived because in it "the person who is supposed to be inarticulate becomes one of the most articulate characters in the novel" (188). Stern, moreover, objects to the form of the tale, charging that Isabel's many pauses—her most obvious trademark as a storyteller—become "peremptory and ludicrously unconvincing" (188). More positive commentators tend to reiterate certain commonplaces and to make general statements without much detail. E. L. Grant Watson noticed long ago, for example, that the story records the "birth of the conscious soul" (206), but neither he nor any successor explains much about how Melville creates this impression. More recently, Eric Sundquist tells us that the prose of the story approximates "the lithe and haunting music Isabel and her guitar make," but he does not elaborate (164). Thus the form of Isabel's story has never been fully and sympathetically treated.

Obviously, the tale is a short *bildungsroman,* an explanation not only of the events of Isabel's life but also of her coming-to-be. Less apparent are the patterns that support and constitute this *bildungsroman* and the philosophy that informs it. Properly considered, Isabel's story is nothing less than a manifesto of the Romantic artist-philosopher, complete with an implied philosophy of language. Of course, the *bildungsroman* itself, with its emphasis on stages of development and hard-won transitions to new plateaus of understanding, was a favorite form of the Romantic writers. In Isabel's story Melville manipulates this form both to display the seductive attractions of Romantic philosophy and to hint at its disastrous consequences for Pierre.

A close examination reveals first that Melville emphasizes the different stages of Isabel's development by evoking different literary genres or patterns (the fairy tale, the descent into hell, and the pastoral idyll) as backdrop for these stages. Second, the story is developmental also in its portrayal of both Isabel's psychology and her linguistic abilities. Third, the story uses motifs and ideas of Romantic origin to express a specifically Romantic vision of art and epistemology—and to express as well Melville's ambivalence about this vision. Within this context, both Isabel's rhetorical practices and her pauses are purposive, not arbitrary. If there is a problem with Isabel's characterization, it is the fact that she must fulfill a dual role: on the one hand she is a static symbol of nature, but on the other hand, the *bildungsroman* form commits her to the dynamic process of growth and change.

Of course, Isabel's story in some sense "seduces" Pierre, but the seduction, whatever its incestuous content, is primarily philosophical. Isabel revolutionizes Pierre's life not so much because she gets him to do unconventional things but because she gets him to think unconventionally and thus pulls him loose from the fixities of his early life. The trouble with Romantic philosophy is that its flexibility, imagination, and rejection of conventional order, while at first liberating, lead to a paralyzing lack of certitude and a crippling inability to deal with the world as it is. Isabel's story hints at this; Pierre's life illustrates it.

Pierre visits Isabel after sundown in a little red farm house located near a gloomy wood from which issues a "moaning, muttering, roaring, intermitted, changeful sound" including the "devilish gibberish of the forest-ghosts." Brian Higgins and Hershel Parker point out that the landscape Pierre must traverse to the cottage suggests the possible terrors that Isabel has in store for him (171-172). Isabel's cottage itself is of a piece with this setting. Overgrown with moss and adjoined at one end by a dairy-shed, it is strongly associated with nature and good food, and vaguely threatening as well. In this setting we also see the first of several manipulations of genre Melville performs in Isabel's story: by approaching the cottage, Pierre steps out of the pastoral idyll of Saddle Meadows into a fairy tale.

"'I never knew a mortal mother,'" Isabel begins (114). Her first memory is that of a crumbling mansion, perhaps a small chateau, located in a dark and threatening forest somewhere in Europe. Her original language, she believes, was French. Her foster parents, an old man and woman, treat her with frequent disdain, rarely speaking to her but often looking at her as they converse in whispers near the fire. Isabel vividly recalls an incident in which she asked to have some bread they were eating and actually touched the loaf. The man threatened to strike her, and the woman threw the loaf into the fire. Isabel sought consolation from a cat but was only hissed at. When she retreated outside to sit on a rock, the very earth seemed hostile, and its coldness caused her to faint for sheer loneliness. After this time, she says, everything she saw and heard began to be stranger and stranger to her. This early rejection and others like it powerfully shape her life, and later events (as well as her feelings even as she tells the story) consistently evoke the "starings" from her foster parents and her own "bewilderings" of this early period.

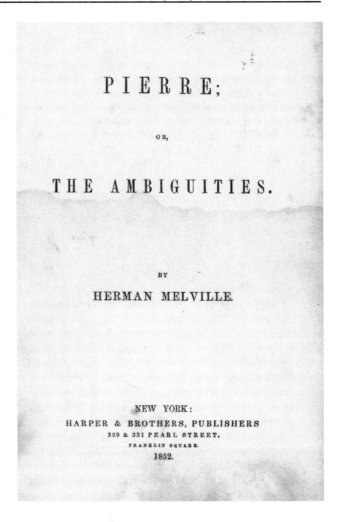

In this first part of the story, Melville evokes the world of the fairy tale. The indefinite time and place, the setting of the dark forest, the wicked foster parents, and the theme of the abandonment of a child all commonly occur in the German *märchen*. Such tales, often seen as children's stories because they express the visions and fears of childhood, are an appropriate literary reference for Isabel's early life. But Melville's use of fairy-tale conventions is subtle, not heavy-handed. None of the frankly supernatural elements common to fairy tales—gnomes, witches, and talking animals—occur here. Melville evokes the fairy tale, therefore, by selecting only those elements of it that can be reconciled with Isabel's generally realistic narrative.

Isabel does not clearly remember leaving her forest home, and she only vaguely remembers crossing the ocean to America. It is at this time, she says, that English gradually came to replace her native French. At this point, acknowledging the vagueness of her story, she gives an apology worth quoting in full:

> "Scarce know I at any time whether I tell you real things, or the unrealest dreams. Always in me, the solidest things melt into dreams, and dreams into solidities. Never have I wholly recovered from the effects of my

strange early life. This it is, that even now—this moment—surrounds thy visible form, my brother, with a mysterious mistiness; so that a second face, and a third face, and a fourth face peep at me from within thy own. Now dim, and more dim, grows in me all the memory of how thou and I did come to meet. I go groping again amid all sorts of shapes, which part to me; so that I seem to advance through the shapes; and yet the shapes have eyes that look at me. I turn round, and they look at me; I step forward, and they look at me.—Let me be silent now; do not speak to me." (117-118)

The first of five pauses that punctuate the story follows. Isabel's procedure here sets a pattern that she maintains throughout her narrative. The passage that precedes the pause consists of a repetition of certain key words and phrases—*things, dreams, face, shape,* and *look at me.* Of course, there is nothing unusual about repetition in Isabel's rhetoric even when she is not approaching a pause. Here, however, the rhetoric gives the passage cadence, a sense of ending. As she approaches the pause, her sentences and rhythms become shorter, so that the rhetoric seems to turn in upon itself and spiral down to a dead point. Such rhetorical patterns precede nearly all of her pauses. Moreover, the same general feeling brings on all her pauses, a feeling of unreality and bewilderment (or, to use Isabel's term, "bewilderingness"). Thus Isabel cannot stick to the story line; it constantly evokes feelings of loss and confusion which she emphasizes with a pause. These pauses, with their stylized introductions, impose their own rhythm on the narrative as a whole and divide it into a series of prose "stanzas" punctuated by a refrain of despair.[1] Stern condemns the device as "peremptory," but, seen as an expression of Isabel's character, these pauses become ritualistic; they both express her despair and help her to control it.

The above passage also implies Melville's critique of Romanticism. Isabel employs Coleridge's "esemplastic power" with a vengeance: she can dissolve conventional order and reconstruct things in her own imagination; however, for her even simple matters of fact are surrounded by "mistiness." As Pierre hears this, he is attracted by the very vagueness of her narrative and its implied rejection of all forms of conventional order, great and small. As one critic points out, however, anyone who can "dissolve solidities" holds much peril for Pierre ("rock") (Franklin 121). Moreover, Isabel's statement, viewed from the unsentimental perspective of modern psychology, admits that she suffers from both hallucination and paranoia.

When Isabel resumes speaking after her first pause, she describes her second habitation, a large house situated by a river. Although she never uses the term, her words clearly describe an insane asylum. The loneliness she recalls during this period brings on her second and third pauses. Here Isabel again talks to almost no one, and the sights and (more especially) the sounds, evoke both the classical and Dantean versions of hell: people are whipped, chained, and born by mutes to an invisible basement from which is-

sues a cacophony of moans and cries; and even the inmates not directly tortured are, like the inmates of hell, in a fixed state from which they will never escape. The hero of the *bildungsroman* typically passes through some personal descent into hell. Isabel's stay at this house, located in a treeless "lowland" near a "green and lagging river," is surely hers.

In the midst of this section, Isabel gives what amounts to a credo, which is all the more interesting because it contradicts what follows in the story. Rejecting happiness, she says:

> "my spirit seeks different food from happiness; for I think I have a suspicion of what it is. I have suffered wretchedness, but not because of the absence of happiness, and without praying for happiness. I pray for peace—for motionless—for the feeling of myself, as of some plant, absorbing life without seeking it, and existing without individual sensation. I feel that there can be no perfect peace in individualness. Therefore I hope one day to feel myself drank up into the pervading spirit animating all things. I feel I am an exile here." (119)

This is Isabel's clearest statement of her ideal; and, in such phrases as "the pervading spirit animating all things," we can recognize not only the transcendentalist over-soul but also the more general Romantic attitude toward nature, expressed in such poems as Wordsworth's "Tintern Abbey."[2]

Isabel's ideal, however, contradicts the movement of her character. This contradiction becomes evident in the fourth section where, as a foster daughter of a farm family, Isabel first sees natural human affection between the farm wife and her infant. This infant, says Isabel,

> "first brought me to my own mind, as it were; first made me sensible that I was something different from stones, trees, cats; first undid in me the fancy that all people were as stones, trees, cats; first filled me with the sweet idea of humanness; first made me aware of the infinite mercifulness, and tenderness, and beautifulness of humanness; and this beautiful infant first filled me with the dim thought of Beauty; and equally, and at the same time, with the feeling of the Sadness; of the immortalness and the universalness of the Sadness." (122)

This passage (which in a few sentences leads to the fourth pause) rhetorically dramatizes Isabel's change in its very diction.

Contrasted with her identity with "stones, trees, cats"—all stark objects from her early home in the forest—are the newly discovered abstractions. The passage, moreover, is poetic: it is held together by the repetition of "first" combined with parallel structures; the strategic use of "and" in the second half of the passage spaces apart the accents and creates gentle rhythms which contrast with the harsh rhythms of the first portion; even the sibilance of the repeated-*ness* is used to good effect. Here perhaps is the "music" Sundquist speaks of. And, in passages like this, it is not hard to imagine that Isabel largely accomplishes her philosophical seduction of Pierre. Rarely do abstractions sound so euphonious.

Linked with Isabel's ability to abstract comes a feeling of her separation both from nature and from the other members of the farm family. Isabel tells us that her household chores ("being busy") made her sensible of being human. As a child between the ages of nine and eleven years old, she begins to distinguish between the "human" and the "not human" in nature and concludes that "'all good, harmless men and women were human things . . . in a world of horrible and inscrutable inhumanities'" (122).

She tells us further that, "'as I grew older, I expanded in my mind. I began to learn things out of me; to see still stranger, and minuter differences'" (123). As a foster child, she does not have the same status in the family as the real children. The farmer seldom speaks to her; the wife shows more affection to her real daughters than to Isabel. And while Isabel suffers from the "starings" and "bewilderingness" she remembers from her forest home, she is thankful that the farm wife loves her even as much as she does:

> "I thanked—not God, for I had been taught no God—I thanked the bright human summer, and the joyful human sun in the sky; I thanked the human summer and the sun, that they had given me the woman; and I would sometimes steal away into the beautiful grass, and worship the kind summer and the sun; and often say over to myself the soft words, summer and the sun." (123)

Melville is trying to have it both ways in his characterization of Isabel. The very growth of her perceptions takes her toward the "individualness" she condemns in her earlier-stated credo. In other words, Isabel's development, her history of individual growth and change, conflicts with her symbolic and static identity with nature. The result is an uneasy compromise. Growing up requires the very separation from nature Isabel deplores; and, perhaps for this reason, Melville does not make the separation complete. An orphan herself, she becomes the woman who sees all of humanity as an orphan of the cosmos. Her vision, however, is not of humanity totally isolated because some parts of nature (e.g., the summer and the sun) and some objects (e.g., her guitar) are "human." Isabel grows up, then, but only part way. She has the adult's capacity to see man's condition as tragic while retaining the child's capacity to see elements of the cosmos as mystically linked with herself.

The above passage also reveals that Melville interprets this portion of Isabel's life not as a fairy tale or a descent into hell, but as a pastoral idyll. She works on the farm, but, all in all, farm life is idealized. Isabel mentions no exhausting duties, boring routines, or harsh winters. The focus is on the summer and the sun. Her idyll is based upon a measure of domestic love and completed by the visits from her father. Perhaps Melville interprets this portion of her life as an idyll for the purpose of shattering it with her father's death.

Isabel eventually learns that her father had arranged to keep her with the farmer's family by sending them money. After he dies, Isabel must leave and find work in another house. While she is there, she buys a guitar from a peddler. She seems to develop a "personal" rapport with it; when she sings to it, it answers her with its music. She says, "'the guitar was human . . . I made a loving friend of it.'" It translates "'all wonders that are unimaginable'"; it sings of "'mystic visions'" of those in the insane asylum and of "'legendary delights'" unknown to her. She ends her story abruptly with the request, "'bring me the guitar'" (125). Here Melville may, as one critic suggests, be working in the tradition of Gothic heroines who have magical musical instruments.[3] But the guitar's creative and artistic significance makes it similar as well to the eolian harp and other stringed instruments, which Romantic poets consistently used as images of both artistic inspiration and the divine presence of nature.

Melville both reinforces and critiques this association with the guitar later when he explains Pierre's domestic routine in Book XXI after the move to the city. At this time Pierre is struggling to write a "mature work" of literature and looks to Isabel's music for inspiration:

> When his day's work was done, [Isabel] sat by him in the twilight, and played her mystic guitar till Pierre felt chapter after chapter born of its wonderous suggestiveness; but alas! eternally incapable of being translated into words; for where the deepest words end, the music begins with its supersensuous and all-confounding intimations. (282)

The guitar is both inspiring but somehow inadequate. The failure of inspiration was a common crisis among the Romantic poets, particularly Coleridge, who presents "Kubla Khan" as an unrealized dream-vision, a beautiful might-have-been. In that poem Coleridge attributes his inspiration to a "damsel with a dulcimer" (I.298, l. 37) whom he can no longer hear. Pierre has his own version of this figure under his very roof, but she still does not lead to artistic production. Melville may not be alluding to "Kubla Khan" here, although he probably knew the poem. In any case he does satirize the notion, rather popular during the Romantic era, that inspiration is all. Melville makes it clear when describing Pierre's work routine in Book XXII, that, in order to get work done, Pierre must exclude Isabel from his room.

The scene that follows the introduction of Isabel's guitar is a bizarre and fitting conclusion to what has gone before. Isabel strums her guitar with a wild and wanton virtuosity, intertwining her lyrics of the "'Mystery of Isabel'" with the melodies she plays. Pierre is so enchanted that he is nearly speechless at the end. Claiming to be her "'loving, revering, most marvelling brother,'" he kisses her and departs (127).

Clearly Melville juggles different goals in Isabel's story, for upon this rather elusive narrative he tries to impose a certain realistic psychology and attempts to show the development of a philosophy. For example, the early scenes with the cruel foster parents and the insane asylum inmates powerfully affect Isabel and condition her interpretation of later events with the farm family. Here recurring image patterns are important. Isabel frequently feels alone, out in the open, barren of protection, and watched by hostile glances. The earliest habitation that she remembers is in a clearing surrounded by a forest full of threatening pines and "'unconjecturable voices'" (115). On the ship Isabel again stresses the open space surrounding her, as she does the treeless lowland that surrounds the insane asylum where she stays later. Isabel also feels, to the point of paranoia, that she is the object of hostile glances. The worst part of the rejection from her original foster parents and from the uncompanionable cat is the "starings" which she often mentions in later situations. And we have seen that, even as she speaks to Pierre, she complains of "shapes" that look at her.

At the same time Melville makes an issue of Isabel's developing linguistic consciousness. Isabel stresses, for example, that she has really no one to talk to in either her early home or the insane asylum. Furthermore, she suffers a linguistic dislocation as English gradually replaces her native French. Possibly for these reasons, Isabel is rather tentative both in her use of words and in her acceptance of their meanings. Sometimes she rejects the convenient shorthand that words offer. When she describes her voyage to America (117), she does not say immediately that she was on a ship but instead treats her listener (and the reader) to some rather puzzling description which reveals her situation gradually, somewhat as Isabel must have discovered it at the time. When she describes the insane asylum, she uses a similar tactic, except that this time she refuses to name the reality even after she describes it. She warns Pierre: "'Do not speak the word to me. That word has never passed my lips; even now, when I hear the word, I run from it; when I see it printed in a book, I run from the book. The word is wholly unendurable to me'" (121).

As her narrative progresses, she compiles an entire list of words to which she struggles to attach meanings: summer, sun, happiness, humanness, sadness, beauty, father, death. To a great extent, living has meant learning the meanings of words that name life's great realities. Even when she does not consciously fix upon a word, however, her very style demonstrates her preoccupation with the mysteries of language. Indeed her procedures imply a rejection of the rationalist attitude that language is a self-evident system of reference neatly categorizing reality. In almost all of the passages quoted above, Isabel's thoughts circle around repeated words and phrases which give even her most ordinary narrative the character of poetry or music. Her story is her work of art, and her language is part of her creation.

If her narrative is her "verse," then her pauses, as noted above, mark her stanza divisions. The plot of her story naturally invites division between the different settings Isabel lives in: the crumbling mansion, the ship, the insane asylum, the farmer's house, and her current setting. However, Isabel does not regularly pause at the changes in setting; rather—true to the Romantic faith in intuition in art—she divides the story at the dictates of her shifting feelings as she narrates.

The sudden introduction of the guitar toward the end of the story reinforces the impression that the story is about art and allows us to see Isabel's life as a portrait of a developing Romantic artist-philosopher. The Romantic artist, in this portrayal, comes to her art by a recognition of man's tragic situation—his presence among the inhumanities. This view of life happens partially as a consequence of the separations involved in growing up, both individually and as a race. Art is not primarily the result of conscious craft, but of imagination and intuition. (Isabel needs no teacher for her to play the guitar.) Art, finally, attunes the artist to nature, to childhood experience, and to the inspired visions of the mad.

Isabel's narrative, then, is artistically and philosophically sophisticated. On the one hand, it conveys a fairy-tale atmosphere in its setting and some of its elements, and it projects Isabel as a kind of enchantress. On the other hand, it employs realistic psychology both in the recurrent memories of early rejection and in the psychological and linguistic development it portrays. The story also becomes a portrait of a developing artist who displays her art not only with the guitar performance at the end but with the very lyrical order she imposes upon her story throughout. Given the fact that Pierre and even Lucy have artistic aspirations in their writing and painting, it would be wrong to read Isabel's story as Melville's last word about the artist in this novel. In Isabel, Melville portrays the subconscious sources of artistic inspiration, for Isabel is very much a creature of the subconscious. She seems to step out of Pierre's subconscious into his life with her mysterious power and vaguely incestuous appeal; her story, with its fairy-tale setting and its use of fairy-tale elements, seems to proceed from the very unconscious of humanity.

Isabel's ultimate significance, of course, lies in her effect on Pierre. In a number of ways, Isabel's story subtly forecasts the various stages of Pierre's decline. Like Isabel, Pierre comes to feel cosmically orphaned. Melville makes the point that Pierre felt he was a "soul-toddler" deserted by human parents when he first received Isabel's letter. Later, as he is working on his book and feels the indifference not only of man but also God to his aspirations, Melville reports, "the toddler was toddling entirely alone, and not without shrieks" (296). Like Isabel, who can turn dreams into solidities and solidities into dreams, Pierre increasingly loses his hold on reality. He begins having trouble with his vision and at one point suffers a fit from which he awakes in the gutter of a side street. Melville notes ominously, "if that vertigo had been also intended for another and deeper warning, he regarded such added warning not at all" (341). Finally, Pierre himself sees dreams as realities in his vision in Book XXV of Enceladus. All of these conditions are presented with attractive pathos in Isabel's narrative, but are lived out in their real sordidness by Pierre.

Finally, a point needs to be made about incest in this book. James Wilson, in *The Romantic Heroic Ideal,* points out a division among Romantic authors in their attitude toward sibling incest. British and French authors such as Lewis, Byron, Shelley, and Chateaubriand wrote of incestuous attachments with a compassion amounting to apology. Thus such incestuous pairs as Agnes and Lorenzo (*The Monk*), René and Amélie, Laon and Cynthna, Manfred and Astarte, and the poet and the "sister soul" (Shelley's "Epipsychidion") all receive gentle treatment, if not outright justification, from their respective authors. These authors, says Wilson, see incest as a "regenerating alternative to conventional, sterile morality" (135). Wilson notes that the German attitude is quite different; Schiller, Tieck, and Grillparzer all treat incest as a blasphemous crime.[4]

Isabel's story is interesting for the way it invites the British and French interpretation of her relationship with Pierre. For Isabel, the developmental heaven toward which her *bildungsroman* tends is a passionate brother-sister attachment. Sanctified by their private love, and insulated by a grand indifference to social convention, this attachment appears to offer artistic inspiration. When Pierre joins Isabel, Melville takes up the incest theme where the British and French authors leave it off, and shows the spiritual bankruptcy of their views. The promised regeneration proves elusive, and the world of their private love turns out to be a solipsistic prison isolating them from others and weakening their hold on reality.

Isabel's story has been attacked by some critics, but if there is a problem here, it is chiefly that Isabel does not live up to the expectations she creates in Book VI. She never again quite achieves the quiet power she has when she first appears. In Book VIII Melville engages in facile supernaturalism when he portrays her eliciting a melody from her guitar without actually playing it. After the move to the city, Isabel is more of a vague presence than an active character. She is occasionally jealous or seductive, but in comparison with her appearance in Book VI, she is bland. However, it would be wrong to fault Melville harshly for the difficulty that Isabel presents. Once she is on the scene, it is certainly not easy to know what to do with her. Isabel is mysterious and intuitive, and she thrives better in the misty past, where many more things seem possible, than in the clearer atmosphere of the fictional present. Nevertheless, Melville achieves a great deal by putting this "dark" woman on display in the many ways that he does, and by giving her a narrative resonant with the motifs and ideas of Romanticism.

Notes

1. Larry Edward Wegener makes a similar point though he bases it upon the repetition of Delly Ulver's footsteps heard during Isabel's pauses (xii).

2. Compare, for example, lines 95-102 of Wordsworth's poem in which he speaks of

    a sense sublime
    Of something far more deeply interfused,

    Whose dwelling is the light of setting suns,
    And the round ocean and living air,
    And the blue sky and in the mind of man:
    A motion and a spirit that impells
    All thinking things, all objects of all thought
    And rolls through all things. (II.262)

3. Newton Arvin argues that Isabel's preternatural relationship with her guitar makes her a descendant of several heroines who are associated with music in Mrs. Radcliffe's novels (41).

4. See Wilson 133-139. It seems likely that Melville knew many of the British works named here, although this is difficult to prove. Of the German works, it is quite likely that he had read Ludwig von Tieck's *Der blonde Eckbert,* which was in Carlyle's translation, *German Romance,* a two-volume set Melville borrowed from Evert Duyckink in 1850 (Sealts 47).

Works Cited

Arvin, Newton. "Melville and the Gothic Novel." *New England Quarterly* 22 (March 1949): 33-47.

Coleridge, Samuel Taylor. *The Complete Poetical Works of Samuel Taylor Coleridge.* Ed. Ernest Hartley Coleridge. 2 vols. Oxford: Clarendon Press, 1912.

Franklin, Howard Bruce. *The Wake of the Gods: Melville's Mythology.* Stanford, California: Stanford University Press, 1963.

Higgins, Brian and Hershel Parker. "The Flawed Grandeur of Melville's *Pierre.*" In *New Perspectives on Melville.* Ed. Faith Pullin. Edinburgh: Edinburgh University Press, 1978.

Melville, Herman. *Pierre; or, The Ambiguities.* Evanston: Northwestern University Press, 1971.

Murray, Henry. Introduction. In *Pierre; or, The Ambiguities.* By Herman Melville. New York: Hendricks House, 1949. xiii-ciii.

Sealts, Merton M. *Melville's Reading: A Checklist of Books Owned and Borrowed.* Madison: University of Wisconsin Press, 1966.

Stern, Milton R. *The Fine Hammered Steel of Herman Melville.* Urbana, Illinois: University of Illinois Press, 1957.

Sundquist, Eric J. *Home as Found: Authority and Genealogy In Nineteenth-Century American Literature.* Baltimore: Johns Hopkins University Press, 1979.

Watson, E. L. Grant, "Melville's *Pierre.*" *New England Quarterly* 3 (April 1930): 195-234.

Wegener, Larry Edward. Preface. In *A Concordance to Herman Melville's "Pierre, Or The Ambiguities."* Ed. Larry Edward Wegener. New York: Garland, 1985. I: xi-xx.

Wilson, James D. *The Romantic Heroic Ideal.* Baton Rouge: Louisiana State University Press, 1982.

Wordsworth, William. *The Poetical Works of William Wordsworth.* Ed. Ernest de Selincourt. 5 vols. Oxford: Clarendon Press, 1940-1949.

James C. Wilson (essay date 1987)

SOURCE: "The Sentimental Education of Pierre Glendinning: An Exploration of the Causes and Implications of Violence in Melville's *Pierre*," in *American Transcendental Quarterly: A Journal of New England Writers,* Vol. 1, No. 3, September, 1987, pp. 167-77.

[*In the following essay, Wilson notes that Melville attributes Pierre's psychological problems, especially his belief in his own capacity for heroic action, to his sentimental education.*]

Pierre; or, The Ambiguities (1852), Melville's seventh and most problematic novel, is still so little understood that critics have tended to focus on questions of authorial intent and/or composition: whether Melville intended to write a popular romance, a satire of a popular romance, or even a psychological novel;[1] and whether (and if so, why) Melville deviated from his original plot when he added the autobiographical material in the second half of the novel.[2] Little agreement has been reached on any of these questions, and meanwhile important thematic and textual matters in *Pierre* have remained unexplored.

One of the most important elements in *Pierre,* one which is central to both the Saddle Meadows and the New York sections of the novel, is the multi-layered theme of violence and its connection to the sentimental education of Pierre Glendinning, Melville's nineteen-year-old protagonist. From the very beginning of the novel, Melville repeatedly calls the reader's attention to the social influences that have shaped Pierre's life. Living at Saddle Meadows, his ancestral mansion, Pierre has been "nurtured amid the romance-engendering comforts and elegancies of life" (216). The young Glendinning has been raised as a country gentleman—steeped in tradition, social convention, and a bogus sentimentality that becomes ever more obvious as the novel progresses. In Book I we see Pierre, the grandson of a Revolutionary War hero, play at being the knight-errant and romantic lover of his betrothed, Lucy Tartan. His protestations of love are both effusive and artificial in these early mock *Romeo and Juliet* scenes. He will say, for example, "'I must away now, Lucy; see! under these colors [a flower] I march,'" to which Lucy responds in kind, "'Bravissimo! oh, my only recruit!'" (4). Their dialogue here and throughout the novel—with its use of archaic expressions like "thee," "thou," and "fie, now," and the excessive use of exclamation points—reads as though it had been copied from the kind of cheap sentimental romance that was so popular in Melville's day. In fact, Pierre attempts to measure up to what he sees as his heroic and aristocratic heritage by living according to the conventions of the sentimental romance, and he does it with a zeal that rings as false as the conventions themselves. It is significant that Pierre is repeatedly castigated, at least in the Saddle Meadows section, by the narrator of the novel, who frequently calls attention to his young protagonist's bravado, his naivete, and his romantic excesses.

Pierre maintains an equally immoderate relationship with his mother. Mrs. Glendinning, described as "an affluent, and haughty widow" (4), has rejected all suitors since the death of her husband so that she might better lavish attention on her only son. Their wealth and their insulated country life in Saddle Meadows have allowed them a "strange license" (5), a bizarre inbred familiarity that is explicitly Oedipal. With his "lover-like adoration" (16), Pierre has replaced his father, has become "lover enough" (5) for his widowed mother. Pierre and Mrs. Glendinning call each other "brother" and "sister," they engage in a kind of incestuous conversational foreplay, and they live out a pretend or mock marriage in scenes that parody the typical drawing-room marriages of the sentimental romance. The excesses of Pierre's "romantic filial love" (5) are evident throughout the early scenes of the novel.

If Pierre's love for his mother is "romantic," his love for his dead father can only be described as quasi-religious. Perhaps out of a sense of guilt for having created their own mock marriage at Saddle Meadows, both Pierre and his mother have transformed the memory of Mr. Glendinning into an icon, an image of God, the heavenly father. Mrs. Glendinning refers to him as "your dear perfect father" (19), and Pierre regards him as the "personification of perfect human goodness and virtue" (68). The dead father has become a "shrine" (68), where the son can worship the father and all that the father represents. What the father represents, as the novel makes clear, is the moral foundation (or ideological superstructure) on which Pierre's life of privilege has been constructed. Pierre's obsession with the symbolic purity of his father is yet another example of his general tendency toward absolutism, a characteristic that will prove to be self-destructive.

By the time Pierre receives the fateful letter from Isabel Banford in Book III, Melville has established most of Pierre's essential traits: his absolutism, his romantic illusions, and his emotional immaturity and volatility. These characteristics predispose Pierre to act rashly, as we see by his reaction to Isabel's letter, in which Isabel declares that she is his illegitimate sister and requests his help. Here in this first of many such instances, we see Pierre turn away from all he has held sacred and accept, without a shred of hard evidence, that Isabel is indeed his sister. Suddenly, Pierre decides, the "before undistrusted moral beauty of the world is forever fled; for thee, thy sacred father is no more a saint; all brightness hath gone from thy hills, and all peace from thy plains; and now, now, for the first time, Pierre, Truth rolls a black billow through thy soul!" (65). And just as suddenly, before he even meets Isabel, Pierre commits himself to a course of action that will have tragic consequences: "'Oh! Isabel, thou art my sister; and I will love thee, and protect thee, ay, and own thee through all'" (66).

Though Isabel's story as told in Books VI and VIII is extremely vague, and though her reasons for believing herself to be Pierre's sister are inconclusive at best, the point is that Pierre has already decided (on impulse, certainly not on any rational basis) to believe her. Thus the problem that Pierre faces is how to "protect" Isabel without publicly humiliating his mother and dishonoring the memory of his father. His solution, as dishonest as it is ultimately disastrous for everyone involved, is to announce to his mother and the world at large that he and Isabel are married. Thus Pierre goes from one pretended marriage with his mother to another pretended marriage with his (fictitious?) sister. Predictably, Mrs. Glendinning reacts with outrage and promptly disinherits her son, who leaves the mansion feeling "hurled from beneath his own ancestral roof" (185). At this crucial juncture, Pierre makes yet another rash decision—he decides to flee to New York with Isabel and Delly, a local servant woman who has recently born a child to an already married man and who is, like Isabel (and soon Pierre), a social outcast. Acting out of a "new hatefulness" (196), Pierre severs all ties with his family and his past; he symbolically burns all the family letters and miscellaneous memorials in his possession and declares: "'Henceforth, cast-out Pierre hath no paternity, and no past . . .'" (199). Here we see established a pattern that will become clearer in the second half of the novel as the action moves to New York—Pierre will decide on a particular cause to champion, will feel constrained and/or attacked by hostile forces, and will strike out impulsively and with increasing anger at all that supposedly restrains him.

Melville reminds the reader in repeated passages that Pierre suffers from an illusion that is central to his sentimental education—the illusion that he is capable of heroic action. Throughout the novel Pierre sees himself and is described as a "recruit," a "warrior," a "knight." Conventions of the literature of courtly love and the sentimental romance intermingle in one important early description of Pierre:

> In the country then Nature planted our Pierre; because Nature intended a rare and original development in Pierre. . . . She blew her wind-clarion from the blue hills, and Pierre neighed out lyrical thoughts, as at the trumpet-blast, a war-horse paws himself into a lyric of foam. . . . She lifted her spangled crest of a thickly-starred night, and . . . ten thousand mailed thoughts of heroicness started up in Pierre's soul, and glared round for some insulted good cause to defend. (13-14)

Pierre, of course, finds two of these insulted good causes in Isabel and Delly. He eagerly—and recklessly—takes it upon himself to protect and provide for both of them without understanding the consequences of his action or how the world will view it.

However, Pierre's motives in deciding to "defend" Isabel are not altogether altruistic and/or mock-heroic. Early in the novel it is apparent that Pierre's attraction to Isabel is partially, if not primarily, sexual. After he sees her for the first time at a neighbor's house, Isabel's "mystic face" (48) haunts Pierre and causes "wild reveries" (50) and a "pervading mood of semi-madness" (52). He cannot control his infatuation: "The emotions he experienced seemed to have taken hold of the deepest roots and subtlest fibers of his being. And so much the more that it was so subterranean in him, so much the more did he feel its weird inscrutableness" (48-49). Later, when Pierre agrees to meet Isabel in the little red farmhouse where she is staying, he goes to satisfy his "wild, bewildering, and incomprehensible curiosity" (47)—in other words, to possess her. To Pierre, trapped in an Oedipal relationship with his mother and an asexual courtship of Lucy, Isabel initially promises sexual release. He sees her (and in a sense creates her) as a dark, mysterious, olive-cheeked girl—in stark contrast to his cold, haughty mother, and his cold, virginal bride-to-be.

Though initially attracted, Pierre soon recoils from Isabel because his sentimental education has not prepared him for, and in fact does not allow for, open sexuality. As a victim of the idealized world of Saddle Meadows, Pierre has learned to substitute incestuous desire for genuine *Eros* or sexual love. Just as formerly he had diverted his youthful sexual desire into a mock-marriage with his mother, now he defuses his sexual response to Isabel by creating yet another fictitious, incestuous marriage. The result, of course, is that by forcing his relationship with Isabel to become hidden and illicit, Pierre ultimately destroys the relationship.

It has been a common critical assumption, at least since Henry A. Murray's seminal introduction to the Hendricks House edition of **Pierre,** that Isabel is, in Murray's words, "the personification of Pierre's unconscious" (lii). As a reflection of Pierre's unformulated and heretofore repressed desires, Isabel appears in images of sexuality and death. Indeed, the two sets of images are everywhere linked, as in this passage: "He felt a faint struggling within his clasp; her head drooped against him; his whole form was bathed in the flowing glossiness of her long and unimprisoned hair. Brushing the locks aside, he now gazed upon the death-like beauty of the face, and caught immortal sadness from it. She seemed as dead . . ." (112). In this and other passages we witness the classic struggle between *Eros* and *Thanatos* (that is, between sexual love and the death-wish) that Freud described nearly a half century after Melville. The struggle occurs both in Pierre's psyche and in the character of Isabel, and the result is that, as Pierre continues to withdraw from Isabel, *Eros,* diverted, gives way to *Thanatos.* Isabel becomes more and more associated with death. Her beauty is "death-like" and her manner "funereal"; she speaks repeatedly of a "world of horrible and inscrutable inhumanities" (122) and of the "infinite forlornness of [her] life" (123). Isabel longs for dissolution; she says at one point, "'I pray for peace—for motionlessness—for the feeling of myself, as of some plant, absorbing life without seeking it, and existing without individual sensation'" (119). Late in the novel Isabel actually attempts to commit suicide by jumping from a ship, while Pierre and Lucy restrain her.

It is significant that, as Pierre moves toward *Thanatos,* he begins to identify with literary, mythological, and historical characters who share a tragic fate. For example, in Book VII Pierre identifies with Memnon, "that dewey, royal boy, son of Aurora, and born king of Egypt, who, with enthusiastic rashness flinging himself on another's account into a rightful quarrel, fought hand to hand with his overmatch, and met his boyish and most dolorous death beneath the walls of Troy" (135); in Book IX (and elsewhere) with Hamlet, Prince of Denmark, who extinguished his royal family in an attempt to avenge the murder of his father; in Book XVI with the gladiator Spartacus, who led an unsuccessful slave revolt against Rome from 73-71 B.C.; and in Book XXV with Enceladus the Titan, the "most potent of all the giants" (345), who according to Greek mythology was killed by the thunderbolts of Zeus during a futile war on the gods. These characters share the "reckless sky-assaulting mood" (347) that Pierre is driven to emulate—by challenging infinitely greater powers, they destroy themselves.

Thus Pierre has become increasingly prone to reckless and violent behavior by the time he and Isabel leave Saddle Meadows in Book XIII. Book XIV contains the theoretical center of the novel—Plotinus Plinlimmon's pamphlet. Pierre discovers the torn, discarded pamphlet, entitled "EI" (or "IF"), in the coach that takes him to New York. To be more specific, Pierre finds a fragment of the first of the 333 lectures supposedly contained in the pamphlet. This first lecture, "Chronometricals and Horologicals," is billed as "not so much the Portal, as part of the temporary Scaffold to the Portal of this new Philosophy" (210). The point here is that the first lecture, like the pamphlet itself, is incomplete; as the narrator points out, it lacks a "conclusion," a definitive resolution to the problems that it presents.

Critics have disagreed over the meaning of "Chronometricals and Horologicals" and why Melville chose to include the pamphlet here.[3] However, it is apparent that, when considered in the context of the entire novel, the pamphlet further illuminates Pierre's essential problems—problems that are, once again, derived from his sentimental education. Plinlimmon, using the distinction between chronometric and horological time as his extended metaphor, distinguishes heavenly or "chronometric" wisdom from earthly or "horological" wisdom. He argues that, just as in China where one would not keep Greenwich time, "in things terrestial (horological) a man must not be governed by ideas celestial (chronometrical)" (214). His conclusion, though one of the most debated passages in all of *Pierre,* is really quite simple: "A virtuous expediency, then, seems the highest desirable or attainable earthly excellence for the mass of men, and is the only earthly excellence that their Creator intended for them" (214).

However, to recognize the importance of the pamphlet to Pierre, it is important to understand fully Plinlimmon's ar-

gument. To his distinction between chronometrical and horological, he adds that it "follows not" that God's truth is one thing and man's truth another. Instead, he argues that "by their very contradictions they are made to correspond" (212), and elsewhere that "this world's seeming incompatibility with God, absolutely results from its meridianal correspondence with him" (213). Finally, he promises that this correspondence, in which all contradictions are resolved, will be forthcoming in subsequent lectures, lectures that are missing from Pierre's copy of the pamphlet. The fact that these lectures are missing in Pierre's copy is significant because, unlike Plinlimmon, Pierre cannot resolve the contradictions of the world. Later in the novel he will come to refer to them as the "ambiguities."

Furthermore, embedded in the pamphlet are several passages that warn against the kind of excess and absolutism towards which Pierre is inclined. For example, at one point Plinlimmon writes that though "minor self-renunciations" are inevitable, a man "must by no means make a complete and unconditional sacrifice of himself in behalf of any other being, or any cause, or any conceit" (214). Elsewhere he writes that a man who makes an "absolute effort" to live in this world according to chronometricals will likely be led into "strange, *unique* follies and sins" (213; Melville's emphasis) and eventually "work himself woe and death" (212). These statements describe, rather obviously I think, the life of Pierre Glendinning. In fact, Plinlimmon's pamphlet can be read as an indictment of Pierre and his imprudent behavior; Pierre certainly sees it as such, which is the primary reason why he does not consciously comprehend the pamphlet, as the narrator makes clear. Because it "condemns" him, Pierre does not want to understand the pamphlet, for any treatise or sermon that "illustrates to [man] the intrinsic incorrectness and non-excellence of both the theory and the practice of his life; then that man will—more or less unconsciously—try hard to hold himself back from the self-admitted comprehension of a matter which thus condemns him" (209).

Pierre's inflexibility becomes even more apparent when he arrives in New York with Isabel and Delly. Accustomed to his life of privilege in the country, Pierre cannot adjust to the nightmarish world of greed, poverty, and sin that he discovers on his first night in the city. As a result, Pierre reacts with increasing violence in a series of brief but bitter altercations with a coach-driver, his cousin Glen Stanley, and a crowd of rowdies at a watch-house (or shelter) for the poor. When their coach-driver is insolent, Pierre flies into a "sudden wrath" (233); he "burst" open the door, "sprang ahead of the horses, and violently reined back the leaders" (233). Only the timely appearance of a policeman prevents Pierre and the driver from coming to blows. When Glen Stanley snubs Pierre because of his various affronts to conventional morality, Pierre leaps toward his cousin "like Spartacus" and only manages to restrain the "savage impulse in him" because of the presence of guests in Stanley's apartment. Even so, Pierre says, "'By Heaven, had I a knife, Glen, I could prick thee on the spot; let out all thy Glendinning blood, and then sew up the vile remainder'" (239)—a threat that looks forward to the end of the novel. Later, when he returns to the watchhouse where he has left Isabel and Delly, Pierre resorts to "an immense blow of his mailed fist" to free Isabel from one particularly aggressive "whiskerando" (241).

Pierre manages to control his violent impulses only temporarily and only by retreating with Isabel and Delly to the cloisters of the old Church of the Apostles, where they take a set of rooms in one lofty tower. The Apostles had long since outlived its "primitive purpose" (266) and had been divided, by the merchants and accountants who succeeded the priests, into offices and apartments for rent. At first the tenants had been primarily lawyers, but by the time Pierre arrives only a few lawyers remain on the ground floor, while the towers are "populous with all sorts of poets, painters, paupers and philosophers" (269). Symbolically, Pierre locates himself up above with the dreamers, sequestered in a "beggarly room" in the tower (270).

Though socially isolated in New York, Pierre is as imprisoned by his sentimental education as he was in Saddle Meadows, and he remains at heart a warrior desperate for another cause to champion. He finds his cause when he and Isabel reach the self-justifying conclusion that "'Virtue and Vice are trash!'" (273), which Pierre decides to incorporate in a book and publish to the world. The reader discovers at this point, rather belatedly, that Pierre had been a juvenile author who had enjoyed some success with silly, sentimental poetry. Characteristically, when Pierre resumes his writing career, he does it with the same excess that he displayed in courting Lucy or rushing to the aid of Isabel: he announces that he will "'gospelize the world anew, and show them deeper secrets than the Apocalypse!'" (273). However, what happens is that, as Pierre becomes more and more obsessed with his book, he loses himself in what the narrator refers to as the "devouring profundities" (305). His attempts to overturn convention and replace it with Truth (for Pierre, always capitalized) result in such passages as the following, where Vivia, the protagonist of his book, soliloquizes:

> "A deep-down, unutterable mournfulness is in me. Now I drop all humorous or indifferent disguises, and all philosophical pretensions. I own myself a brother of the clod, a child of the Primeval Gloom. Hopelessness and despair are over me, as pall on pall. Away, ye chattering apes of a sophomorean Spinoza and Plato, who once didst all but delude me that the night was day, and pain only a tickle. Explain this darkness, exorcise this devil, ye can not. Tell me not, thou inconceivable coxcomb of a Goethe, that the universe can not spare thee and thy immortality, so long as—like a hired waiter—thou makest thyself 'generally useful.' . . . Thou wert but the pretensious, heartless part of a man. Lo! I hold thee in this hand, and thou art crushed in it like an egg from which the meat hath been sucked." (302)

Here, once again, we see Pierre's anger and his instability, and we see him striking out blindly at imaginary adversaries. Above all, we see the same dangerous fanaticism that

has characterized him throughout the novel, except that here his early sentimentalism has been replaced by an equally immature nihilism. Indeed, Vivia's self-indulgent despair is just the reverse image of the sentimental rubbish that Pierre wrote and published as a youth—such poems as "The Tropical Summer: a Sonnet," "The Weather: a Thought," and "Honor: a Stanza."

Pierre never finishes his book, because finally he can only attack conventional wisdom and morality, not replace it. He cannot write the new Gospel for, as he discovers, "the more and the more that he wrote, and the deeper and the deeper that he dived, Pierre saw the everlasting elusiveness of Truth" (339). In all aspects of his life, Pierre finds himself surrounded by contradiction and uncertainty. He comes to doubt whether Isabel is truly his sister, realizing too late that the evidence supporting her claim was always tenuous and that his willingness to believe her had resulted not from fact or probability, but from an "intense procreative enthusiasm" (353)—a desire to believe. Isabel, like everything else in Pierre's life, becomes to him "an enigma, a mystery, an imaginative delirium" (354). Thus Pierre falls into the ultimate intellectual trap: he cannot live with uncertainty, and yet he cannot achieve certainty; he cannot live with the contradictions that plague him, and yet he cannot resolve those contradictions.

The final sequence of events begins when Pierre receives two letters, one from his publishers accusing him of being a swindler for sending them the early pages of his "blasphemous rapsody" instead of the "popular novel" (356) he had promised, and one from Glen Stanley and Lucy's brother accusing him of being a "villainous and perjured liar" (356) for his many crimes (which, by this time, include not only jilting Lucy and running away with Isabel, but allowing—or seducing, as they see it—Lucy to come live with them in a menage of four). To this last accusation, Pierre responds with violence; he searches out a brace of pistols and rushes into the street to meet his accusers. Earlier in the novel, after he learned that his mother had died and left the Saddle Meadows estate to Glen Stanley, Pierre had pondered the subject of murder as an intellectual possibility: "when he thought of all the ambiguities which hemmed him in; the stony walls all round that he could not overleap; the million aggravations of his most malicious lot . . .—then the utmost hate of Glen and Frederic were jubilantly welcome to him; and murder, done in the act of warding off their ignominious public blow, seemed the one only congenial sequel to such a desperate career" (337). Now idea becomes reality as Pierre, in an attempt to break out of the stasis in which he finds himself and play the hero once again, shoots and kills Glen Stanley. "'Tis speechless sweet to murder thee!'" (359), Pierre says as he slays his cousin, who has become the focus of Pierre's wrath, not only because he represents the values of the conventional society that Pierre has rejected, but because he has replaced Pierre as heir to the Glendinning estate and would-be suitor to Lucy.

Pierre is immediately "seized by a hundred contending hands" (360) and taken to the city prison. There he finds himself, like Enceladus in his dream, confined by massive stone walls "partly piled on him" (360). Likewise, he is still trapped in his belief that life is "ambiguous still" (360). Here Pierre has played out all his possibilities save one, and it is at this point that, as Isabel reasserts her power as a symbol of Pierre's unconscious death-wish, Pierre embraces the idea of suicide. Before he went out to murder Glen Stanley, Pierre had told the two women that his "'most undiluted prayer is now, that from your here unseen and frozen chairs ye may never stir alive'" (358). Now he expresses for himself this same wish for death: "'I long and long to die, to be rid of this dishonored cheek'" (360).

It is significant that, before he takes the poison that Isabel has concealed in her bosom, Pierre cries out that he is "'neuter now'" (360). Pierre is neuter both sexually and psychologically, and also in the sense that he is powerless to act the warrior now, powerless to find other "insulted good causes" to defend. Also, as we have already seen, Pierre is intellectually barren in that he has failed in his attempt to "gospelize the world anew." Neutered in all of these ways, Pierre turns to Isabel and the poison that she has hidden in her breast:

> "Girl! wife or sister, saint or fiend!"—seizing Isabel in his grasp—"in thy breasts, life for infants lodgeth not, but death-milk for thee and me!—The drug!" and tearing her bosom loose, he seized the secret vial nesting there. (360)

Isabel follows Pierre's lead and, as her "long hair ran over him and arbored him in ebon vines" (362), their final embrace is an embrace of death in a scene that mocks, at the same time it borrows, the conventions of the tragic denouement.

Henry A. Murray concluded that Melville actually "defends" Pierre's rash behavior in spite of the tragic consequences that it produces. Murray argues that Melville "defends this form of behavior [furious aggression] as stoutly as he justifies impulsiveness" (c). However, I do not think that Melville defends or justifies Pierre's extremism at all. (That Melville is more sympathetic to his protagonist toward the end of the novel does *not* constitute an endorsement of "aggression" or "impulsiveness.") Rather, what Melville has done here is to show how violence is the end result of Pierre's sentimental education, for the very qualities—his absolutism, his romantic illusions, and his emotional immaturity and volatility—that Pierre acquired in the idealized world of Saddle Meadows cause him to self-destruct once he moves out of the closed, incestuous world of his forefathers.

Melville's young protagonist is naive and self-deluded, as many critics have remarked, but he is also a victim of his society and its socially-transmitted illusions of romance and heroism. Thus, **Pierre** can be read as an indictment of the sentimental education of Pierre Glendinning and, by extension, the social world of privilege represented by Saddle Meadows. The theme of violence, and its relation to Pierre's sentimental education, is important because it helps unify an otherwise discordant novel and suggests that Melville, from the very beginning of **Pierre,** intended to subvert the genre of the popular or sentimental romance while working (more or less) within the confines of its artificial and essentially trivial form.

Notes

1. Leon Howard assumed in the Historical Note to the Northwestern-Newberry Edition of *Pierre* that Melville initially conceived of the novel in terms of a popular romance. However, other critics have viewed *Pierre* as a satire of a popular novel. For example, Robert Milder in "Melville's 'Intentions' in *Pierre*," characterizes the novel as a "diabolical parody of the romance." See also William Braswell's "The Early Love Scenes in Melville's *Pierre*," and Richard H. Brodhead's discussion of *Pierre* in *Hawthorne, Melville, and the Novel.*

   Still other critics have argued that Melville intended *Pierre* to be a psychological novel. See especially Henry A. Murray's 1949 introduction to the Hendricks House edition of *Pierre* and, more recently, the work of Hershel Parker and Brian Higgins.

2. The most thorough work on the composition of *Pierre* has been done by Hershel Parker in "Why *Pierre* Went Wrong," and in his work with Brian Higgins, including "The Flawed Grandeur of Melville's *Pierre*" and their introduction to *Critical Essays on Melville's* Pierre. For an opposite view, see Robert Milder's "Melville's 'Intentions' in *Pierre*"; Michael S. Kearns' "Interpreting Intentional Incoherence: Towards a Disambiguation of Melville's *Pierre; or, The Ambiguities*"; and William B. Dillingham's discussion of *Pierre* in *Melville's Later Novels.*

3. For a summary of the scholarship on whether Plinlimmon's pamphlet represents Melville's own views, see Brian Higgins' "Plinlimmon and the Pamphlet Again," and William B. Dillingham's discussion of the controversy in *Melville's Later Novels.*

Works Cited

Braswell, William. "The Early Love Scenes in Melville's *Pierre*." *American Literature* 22 (1950): 283-289.

Brodhead, Richard H. *Hawthorne, Melville, and the Novel.* Chicago: University of Chicago Press, 1976.

Dillingham, William B. *Melville's Later Novels.* Athens: University of Georgia Press, 1986.

Higgins, Brian. "Plinlimmon and the Pamphlet Again." *Studies in the Novel* 4 (1972): 27-38.

Higgins, Brian, and Parker, Hershel. "The Flawed Grandeur of Melville's *Pierre*," in *New Perspectives on Melville,* ed. Faith Pullin. Kent, Ohio: Kent State University Press, 1978.

———. "Introduction" to *Critical Essays on Melville's* Pierre. Boston: G. K. Hall & Company, 1983.

Kearns, Michael S. "Interpreting Intentional Incoherence: Towards a Disambiguation of Melville's *Pierre; or, The Ambiguities.*" *The Bulletin of the Midwest Modern Language Association* 16 (1983): 34-52.

Melville, Herman. *Pierre; or, The Ambiguities.* Evanston and Chicago: Northwestern University Press and The Newberry Library, 1971.

Milder, Robert. "Melville's Intentions in *Pierre.*" *Studies in the Novel* 6 (1974): 186-199.

Murray, Henry A. "Introduction" to *Pierre or The Ambiguities.* New York: Hendricks House, 1949.

Parker, Hershel. "Why *Pierre* Went Wrong." *Studies in the Novel* 8 (1976): 7-23.

Nancy Craig Simmons (essay date 1987)

SOURCE: "Why an Enthusiast?: Melville's *Pierre* and the Problem of the Imagination," in *ESQ: A Journal of the American Renaissance,* Vol. 33, No. 3, 3rd quarter, 1987, pp. 146-67.

[*In the following essay, Simmons suggests that* Pierre *presents the problem of uncontrolled imagination, and provides evidence from Melville's reading, which includes the works of Isaac Taylor.*]

Few studies of Herman Melville's *Pierre* (1852) fail to mention the hero's "enthusiasm" or to refer to Pierre as an "enthusiast," but seldom does the critic consider exactly what the word implies for our reading of the novel. Lawrance Thompson's statement is typical: "Pierre becomes the allegorical type of the 'Enthusiast'—literally, God-possessed and God-inspired. And Melville further manipulates the actions of his young enthusiast in such a way as to illuminate his own anti-Christian theological beliefs."[1] Thompson assumes we know how the "allegorical type" will act. He follows Henry Murray's explanation of Melville's "conception of his hero" as seen in the epithet "Enthusiast to Duty": the term derives from the "Socratic or Platonic notion of Eros"; it means "a man possessed by Eros, passionate love."[2] Without defining the term, Bruce Franklin discusses at length the "case against Pierre's enthusiasm," which is "more lustful than divine" and provides "the crux of *Pierre*"; and Murray Krieger devotes fourteen pages to "The Perils of 'Enthusiast' virtue" in Melville's "Enthusiast"—likewise undefined.[3] James Duban links Pierre's "quasi-religious enthusiasm" with the ideas of Jonathan Edwards, adding that Melville uses the term to "describe Pierre's excitement."[4] More recently, William B. Dillingham recognizes Melville's emphasis on the term but quickly connects it with Gnosticism; and Brian Higgins and Hershel Parker, in the *Pierre* chapter of *A Companion to Melville Studies,* state that Melville "now confronted the possibility that absolute Christlike behavior . . . might always be . . . destructive to the enthusiastic follower of Jesus."[5] The last statement indicates that our

common understanding of this undefined term has moved a great distance from Murray's assumption of a Platonic definition.

It is not surprising that scholars cannot agree on the meaning of the term; what does surprise is that no one has attempted to determine how Melville is using it, for it is basic to the character, plot, and meaning of the novel. Some form of the word occurs thirty-five times in *Pierre*—as opposed to a single use in *Moby-Dick*.[6] And the terms "idealist" and "idealism," repeatedly used to categorize the hero or the subject of Melville's attack, do not appear at all.[7] Instead, Pierre is called "our young Enthusiast," "the Enthusiast to Duty," and "the enthusiastic youth"; and his "unprecedented" decision (to atone for his father's sin by pretending that his illegitimate half-sister Isabel is his wife) is twice labelled an "enthusiast resolution."[8]

Although the "Enthusiast" is but one layer in a complex character, and although any attempt to define a single "intention" in *Pierre* would be reductive, to focus on "enthusiasm" opens the text in new ways, indicating a greater distance between Pierre and his creator than most critics have been willing to grant. *Pierre* reveals a sound knowledge of the literature of enthusiasm, which discusses the term's inherent ambiguity, often equates enthusiasm with madness, and focuses on the problem of determining the source of supposed inspiration and the difficulty of discovering truth in enigmatic situations without some extrinsic authority to provide validation of that "truth." To look at *Pierre* in this context suggests that however "prescient"[9] Melville's psychology may have been, or however aberrant Pierre's behavior may seem, Melville drew on typology and vocabulary provided by philosophers and religious thinkers of the period, which he could have expected some of his audience to recognize. Once again we see that Melville's genius lay not in his conception of original characters and plots but in his ability to transform and complicate borrowed materials in ways that simultaneously explore the recesses of his own mind, his problems as a writer, and the culture in which he lived.

In *Pierre,* Melville is refitting an old term to a new use—finding a language, as Philip Gura suggests the writers of the American Renaissance had to do, rooted in human nature rather than divine, that would speak to a post-Scriptural world, and, in the process, discovering the "ambiguity inherent in the gesture of human speech."[10] Gura's project is to show "how the terms of theological debate, particularly with regard to the accuracy and implication of scriptural revelation, when coupled with the influence of continental romanticism, were transformed into premises with deep reverberations in epistemology, theology, education, and literary form" (p. 6). My discussion will focus on a single, sometimes theological term, "enthusiasm," which helps explain not only Pierre's seemingly illogical behavior and tragic end but also Melville's use of his story to explore the problem of the imagination, especially for the writer of fiction, as a guide to action and a means to truth in a modern, secular world.

I

Melville could not have chosen a better vehicle than "enthusiasm" to convey the ambiguities of the imagination. Derived from the Greek *entheos,* which may mean either "God possessing Man or Man caught up into God," the word entered English in the Renaissance, when it "referred to religious experience, whether of possession or ecstasy,"[11] or to some form of divine inspiration, religious or poetic. Enthusiasm was the "major preoccupation of religious minds" for a hundred and fifty years (roughly 1650 to 1800), "obscuring from contemporary view the rise of atheism," according to Ronald Knox, whose study of this "chapter in the history of religion" chronicles successive eruptions of what he would prefer to call "suprasupernaturalism."[12] Spreading at this time into Lockean epistemology and evangelical religion, sentimentalism and skepticism, piety and naturalism, the term most frequently connoted delusion; beginning in the nineteenth century, "enthusiasm" more often meant "ardent zeal" (*OED*) or the mental state in which a noble selflessness replaces selfishness.[13]

The term is problematic because historically "enthusiasm" has both positive and negative connotations, as innumerable attempts to distinguish between "true" and "false" enthusiasm make clear. How, asks John Locke in his discussion of enthusiasm in Book 4 of *The Essay Concerning Human Understanding* (1690), can one "distinguish between the delusions of Satan and the inspirations of the Holy Ghost?"[14] *Pierre* is built on this ambiguity. Melville could have found a full Platonic (and positive) understanding of the word in the anonymous "editor's" "Introduction" to Edward Bulwer-Lytton's *Zanoni* (mentioned in a letter to neighbor Sarah Morewood in the fall of 1851[15]) where the Sage explains, "'Plato . . . expresses four kinds of Mania, by which I desire to understand enthusiasm, and the inspiration of the gods. Firstly, the musical; secondly, the telestic or mystic; thirdly, the prophetic; and fourthly, that which belongs to Love.'"[16] Likewise, Shaftesbury asserts in *Characteristics* (1711) (mentioned in a June 1851 letter to Hawthorne[17]) that "inspiration may justly be called divine enthusiasm; for the word itself signifies divine presence, and was made use of by the philosopher whom the earliest Christian Fathers called divine [Plato], to express whatever was sublime in human passions."[18]

Melville is clearly also aware of the word's negative sense. The enthusiast's strange behavior might not be god-inspired. Instead, "enthusiasm" was often derogatory, connoting something excessive or some form of delusion. Typical judgments called enthusiasm "mistaken . . . divine inspiration," a "misconceit of being *inspired,*" a "counterfeit of true religion," "an *imaginary,* not a *real,* inspiration." New England divine Charles Chauncy expands this last definition in his "Caveat Against Enthusiasm" (1742): "the *Enthusiast . . .* has a conceit of himself as a person favored with the extraordinary presence of the *Deity.* He mistakes the workings of his own passions for divine communications, and fancies himself inspired by

the SPIRIT of GOD, when . . . he is under no other influence than that of the over-heated imagination." Enthusiasm properly understood is a "disease, a sort of madness."[19]

John Wesley, preaching on "The Nature of Enthusiasm" (1750), goes beyond his fellow thinkers in acknowledging the ambiguity of language: the term, he insists, "is undefinable." Exploring etymology, he cautions (and Melville's critics would do well to listen) that the term is "exceeding rarely understood, even by those who use it most."[20] It is a "dark, ambiguous word";[21] its pre-Socratic Greek origins are impossible to trace; the word may mean "'in God'" or "'in sacrifice.'" In fact, Wesley states in a surprising conclusion, the word itself may be "fictitious." Fictitious or not, "enthusiasm" persists in many languages, he continues, "because men were no better agreed concerning the meaning than . . . the derivation of it. They therefore adopted the Greek word because they did not understand it: they did not translate it into their own tongues because they knew not how to translate it, it having been always a word of loose, uncertain sense, to which no determinate meaning was affixed" (*Sermons,* II, 48). Wesley soon returns to safer ground, stressing that enthusiasts mistake "imaginary" influences for the "real influence of the Spirit of God" (*Sermons,* II, 53) and that reason and Scripture provide true and clear guides to God's will.

Melville's general understanding of the term may very well derive from Locke's attack in the *Essay*: enthusiasm takes away "both reason and revelation, and substitutes the ungrounded fancies of a man's own brain."[22] Locke's discussion is extracted (without quotation marks) into the lengthy entry on "enthusiasm" in Chambers' *Cyclopedia,* which Melville owned in the 1728 edition.[23] In this passage Locke asserts that "in all ages, men, in whom melancholy has mix'd with devotion, or whose conceit of themselves, has raised them into an opinion of a greater familiarity with God, than is allowed others; have often flattered themselves with the persuasion of an immediate intercourse with the deity, and frequent communications from the divine spirit. Their minds being thus prepared," they tend to view "whatever groundless opinion comes to settle itself strongly upon their fancies [as] an illumination from the spirit of God; and whatsoever odd action they find in themselves an inclination to do, that impulse is concluded to be a call, or direction, from heaven, and must be obeyed." Locke goes on to discuss the problem of "immediate revelation, of illumination without search, and certainty without proof," and concludes that God works through natural reason or provides some "marks which reason cannot be mistaken in."[24] Melville may also have read David Hume's popular *Essays;* in "Of Superstition and Enthusiasm" (1741) Hume discusses the swollen imagination that produces "raptures, transports, and surprising flights of fancy [which] are attributed to the immediate inspiration of that Divine Being, who is the object of devotion."[25] Samuel Johnson's *Dictionary* (1755) codified the pejorative sense of "enthusiasm" in its first definition: "A vain belief of private revelation; a vain coincidence of divine favour or communication." Other meanings in the

Dictionary are more secular and neutral: "2. Heat of imagi-nation: violence of passion, confidence of opinion" and "3. Elevation of fancy; exaltation of ideas."[26]

II

Dozens of discussions of enthusiasm could be cited,[27] only a few of which we can be certain that Melville knew. And one might argue that he needed no more than the *Cyclo-paedia*'s version of Locke, with its interesting statement of the central problem of enthusiasm: "But of this seeing and feeling [of the hand of God moving within], is it a percep-tion of an inclination to do something, or of the spirit of God moving that inclination?"[28] The source of the "incli-nation to do something" is central to Pierre's "grand en-thusiast resolution": Melville examines relentlessly all the factors that can enter into a single decisive action—the nexus of fate, free will, and chance that determines human events—but his treatment is far more naturalistic, skepti-cal, and secularized than earlier discussions of enthusiasm. Pierre's bizarre behavior is most true to a type provided by one of the last significant explorations of enthusiasm, first published in 1829, which defines enthusiasm as a dis-eased imagination, a mental illness with specific causes, symptoms, and consequences: Isaac Taylor's *Natural His-tory of Enthusiasm.*

As Taylor's best-known work, the *Natural History of En-thusiasm* went through ten editions, British and American, between 1829 and 1845. A copy could have been in the "'cartload'" of books Melville's widow sold to A. F. Far-nell of Brooklyn after Melville's death, which included many "'theological' works . . . regarded as a dead loss and . . . scrapped for waste paper"[29]—a terrible loss for scholars. A wonderful compendium for the popular mind of the basic elements of "enthusiasm" as it had evolved over the two hundred years preceding its use by Melville as the subject for his rural romance, the *Natural History of Enthusiasm* would have delighted Melville's ever-questioning, alternately skeptical and believing mind: it is "a sort of historico-philosophical disquisition on the per-versions of religious imagination, . . . written with a fresh-ness and vigour which gave it an instant vogue."[30] Despite its somewhat religious orientation, however, the *Natural History* (as the title suggests) attempts to be scientific and objective in its approach to the traditional problem of dis-tinguishing true from false inspiration. Taylor's proofs are from nature, not Scripture, and he stresses worldly causes and consequences rather than heavenly ones. For Taylor, enthusiasm is the product of a diseased or disordered imagination, a natural human faculty.

This literalization of the long-metaphorical relationship between enthusiasm and madness[31] makes *Natural History of Enthusiasm* particularly useful for an understanding of *Pierre.* In much the same way that autobiographical or nautical facts structured his earlier works, the typical char-acteristics and progress of the early nineteenth-century version of the enthusiast became the framework for Melville's case study of a disease that he seemed to have

contracted. He seeks not to judge Pierre but to understand his behavior by entering his mind, thus transforming Tay-lor's type into a richer, more ambiguous figure.

The text for Wesley's sermon links enthusiasm with Melville's own personal concerns at this time: from Acts 26, 24, "And Festus said with a loud voice, Paul, thou art beside thyself," the text focuses on the problem of insanity and societal opinion of individual behavior out of confor-mity with its codes. Wesley's restatement of the problem anticipates the ideas of Melville's Plotinus Plinlimmon in the pamphlet Pierre reads on his way to the city: "It is easy to observe that the determinate thing which the world accounts madness is that utter contempt of all temporal things [Plinlimmon's 'horologicals'], and steady pursuit of things eternal [Plinlimmon's 'chronometricals']." Since Wesley wants to absolve Methodism of the derogatory charge of enthusiasm, he, like Plinlimmon, counsels "ra-tional" behavior rather than enthusiasm, which he calls a "disorder of the mind [that] greatly hinders the exercise of reason . . . , a religious madness arising from some falsely imagined influence or inspiration of God."[32] To Melville in 1850 and 1851, first struggling to complete **Moby-Dick** and then reading the early reviews of his masterpiece while writing his seventh book in as many years, recognizing that dollars damned him and yet refusing to write what would sell, and exhibiting symptoms that were causing family and reviewers to question his sanity, this subject would have great personal significance.[33] He even quoted Paul's reply to Festus, "'I am not mad, most noble Festus'" (Acts, 26, 25), in a letter to Hawthorne (November 17? 1851), when he was beginning **Pierre.** Partly because of his own worries about insanity, it seems, Melville cast Pierre in the role of the enthusiast as a way of exploring the apparently aberrant workings of the human mind a half-century before Freud.[34]

Unlike Wesley, Taylor in the *Natural History* does not want to recognize the inherently ambiguous nature of en-thusiasm. To prevent the spread of this dangerous disease, he adopts a one-sided stance. In his "Advertisement" he is dogmatic: he will describe distinctly the "perilous illusion" (enthusiasm) to "fix the sense of the term."[35] Thus he calls enthusiasm a "religion of the imagination" (p. 16), "ficti-tious piety" (p. [iii]), an "intellectual disease" (p. 98), a "common vice of the mind" (p. 16); the product of a "pam-pered imagination" (p. 17), and the "perversion of the reli-gious affections" (p. 31); it always involves an "error of imagination . . . misjudging of realities . . . [and] calcu-lations which reason condemns" (pp. 14-15); and it always connotes "folly," "weakness," "extravagance" (p. 14). But Taylor's awareness of the difficulty of "fixing" a definition creeps in at several points, as at the end of the sweeping statement that anyone who "cuts himself off from the com-mon sympathies of our nature, and makes idiot sport of the energies of moral action, and has recourse either to a jargon of sophistries, or to trivial evasions when other men act upon the intuitions of good sense . . . must be called an enthusiast, even though he were at the same time—if that were possible—a saint" (p. 92). (Compare Wesley's admission that any man "excellent in his profession . . . has . . . in his temper a strong tincture of enthusiasm"; *Sermons,* II, 48-49.) The term refuses to contain a single meaning; uprooted in empirical epistemology from any grounding in the transcendent, "enthusiasm" has become inherently ambiguous.

It is the ground between the various possibilities—the enthusiast as madman, as deluded, as suffering from an over-active imagination, as heroic or even saintly—that Melville exploits in *Pierre.* Whereas the religious writers try to contain the problem of the aberrant imagination by referring all questions to the known source of truth (Holy Scripture), Melville makes it the stuff of moral tragedy, openly playing with the ambiguity of enthusiasm as a means of raising questions about the validity of the imagination as a guide to action. On the one hand, he suggests that Pierre's is a case of "true" enthusiasm: the crisis prompted by Isabel's mysterious note leads Pierre to an "almost superhuman" resolution, and, the narrator concludes, "Thus, in the Enthusiast to Duty, the heaven-begotten Christ is born" (p. 106). "Nothing great was ever done without enthusiasm," Emerson says at the end of "Circles"; but *Pierre* comments ironically on such naivete, suggesting Pierre's may be "false" enthusiasm. For, only a few days (and a hundred pages) after the birth of the enthusiast in Pierre, as "our young Enthusiast" rides in the silent coach, away from Saddle Meadows, his past, and his patrimony, he suffers extreme doubts: "to him the Evil One propounded the possibility of the mere moonshine of all his self-renouncing Enthusiasm" (p. 205). Is his decision heroic, the only just action possible under the circumstances, a true enacting of the injunctions of Scripture? Or is Pierre a dupe of his own overactive imagination? Or is he (as he later wonders, recalling the apparent insanity of both his parents at their deaths) insane? Like "sin," "vice," and "virtue," "enthusiasm," we realize from exploring its etymology and uses, may be "another name for the other name" (p. 274)—madness, insanity, ego, sexual desire, delusion.

III

A major obstacle to critical and popular appreciation of *Pierre* has been the "revolting" nature of its title character and plot. One contemporary reviewer knew exactly why *Pierre* was "trash": "the plot . . . is monstrous, the characters unnatural, and the style a kind of prose run mad."[36] For many readers Newton Arvin's objection still holds: "Pierre is presented to us as an Enthusiast to Duty: well and good. . . . We are not prepared to believe in his acting like a madman." Arvin concludes that "Melville is chargeable in the end with an abysmal lapse of moral seriousness and coherence. . . . Pierre has behaved, not in fact like a Don Quixote, but like an Orlando Furioso.. . . he has conducted himself generally like a psychopath" (pp. 228-229). However, considering the language available to Melville in 1851, we see that Pierre behaves exactly as Taylor's scientific model predicts he will.

Taylor's genre—natural history—affords him a middle ground between theology and fiction that he peoples using narrative techniques, and the character that emerges from his analysis resembles Pierre in striking ways. From the *Natural History* we learn that the incipient enthusiast lives in a dream world, in "a sort of happy somnambulency—smiling and dreaming as he goes, unconscious of whatever is real, and busy with whatever is fantastic"; he seems both reckless and serene (p. 12). Perpetual illusion leads him to misjudge reality (pp. 14, 15); his "disordered imagination" creates a "region of fictitious happiness" in "the fields of intellectual enjoyment . . . especially of poetry and the fine arts." A "refugee" from the "vexations of common life," he lacks the "vigor necessary for continued and productive toil"; nevertheless, he wastes time on some ambitious "gaudy or preposterous extravagance of verse or picture: or perhaps [spends his] days in loading folios, shelves, and glass-cases with curious lumber of whatever kind most completely unites the qualities of rarity and worthlessness" (Taylor, pp. 13-14). To many, he seems insane.

Melville's extremely unrealistic treatment of the "dewily refreshed" Pierre in the "green and golden world" of his fathers (p. 3) and Pierre's relationships with his mother and Lucy creates in the opening chapters a subject and tone that mirror the enthusiast's unreal world, the illusory soil that engenders enthusiasm. And, although the transformation of the athletic and aristocratic Pierre of the novel's opening to dabbler in precious verse of Book XVIII is unprepared for, such dilettantism is a natural attribute of the enthusiast described by Taylor.

Taylor identifies the common element in all enthusiasts as presumption of self-importance, revealed in their demand for "sensible evidence" of God's special attentions: visions, voices, bodily commotions, natural signs. This is impiety, Taylor asserts, and the enthusiast's "experience" of such "evidence" results from uncontrolled imagination, not God's special activity on his behalf.[37] Peculiar behaviors are not evidence of God's influence. In fact, God's operations, he asserts in true Enlightenment fashion, are inscrutable because they are perfectly harmonized (Taylor, p. 66): in the human world as in nature, God works in natural ways, unseen and unperceived (p. 70), not by "extra-natural impulses, or sensible shocks upon the intellectual system" (p. 67). The "heavenly emanation which heals, cleanses, and blesses the spirit is still, and constant, and transparent" (p. 68). Taylor would agree with Melville's narrator's statement that "Silence is the only Voice of our God" (*Pierre,* pp. 204, 208). The enthusiast, however, "eager for transitory excitements" (Taylor, p. 70), demands more. Not content with the "silent rise of the well spring of purity and peace" (p. 71), his desire for palpable evidence results in "frothy agitations" and a sour "uncharitable temper," physical melancholy, and "relaxation of the moral sentiments" (p. 71). The result is a sort of bipolar manic swing from ecstasy to despondency.

Examples of Pierre's presumptuous enthusiasm abound: his belief in "divine commands upon him to befriend and champion Isabel" (p. 106), his sense that Isabel's letter is the "unmistakable cry of the godhead through her soul" (p. 174), his calling on the Terror Stone to fall on him if his vow is unjustified, and his assertion that he has "'consulted heaven itself upon [the deceitful solution to his problem], and heaven itself did not say Nay'" (p. 192). To enthusiasm, also, can be attributed Pierre's unrealistic view of the world, alternately agitated and despondent emotional state, rejection or twisting of authority and reason, and a tendency to act impulsively or leap to conclusions with insufficient evidence.

According to Taylor, the enthusiast, in his role as a "heaven-commissioned minister of religion" (p. 160), is often complacent, hypocritical, and vain (p. 175); or he may indulge in "self-renunciation" and other types of "metaphysical suicide" (p. 40—compare Pierre's "self-renouncing Enthusiasm," p. 205). The Christian should endure unnecessary suffering only when unavoidable through the use of reason (see Taylor, pp. 211, 214; compare Plinlimmon's statement that "certain minor self-renunciations" are necessary, but one must "by no means make a complete unconditional sacrifice of himself in behalf of any other human being" [*Pierre,* p. 214]). The Tayloresque enthusiast tends to blame Chance for events which actually arise from the "intricate connections of the social system" (p. 128) and to label God's actions "mysteries" (compare Pierre's increasing sense of the utter mysteriousness of life as a result of his encounter with the "mystery" of Isabel).

The variety that most closely anticipates Pierre is Taylor's intellectual enthusiast—the "heresiarch" or *"heretic by temperament"* (p. 87)—a type much like the Melville who wrote *Moby-Dick* and *Pierre.* This sort of mind enjoys the "intellectual gratifications [of] abstruse speculation": "discovery—invention—exaggeration, and paradox" (Taylor, p. 85). Yet, uncontrolled, these qualities spell danger. Heresy occurs when the imagination trespasses on forbidden territory—Scripture—"improving" and "embellishing" the source of Christian authority. Pierre's announcement, "Virtue and Vice are trash! Isabel, I will write such things—I will gospelize the world anew" (p. 273), suggests that he is such a heretic.

Taylor's mini-biography of the typical heresiarch closely parallels Melville's hero's development. The young heresiarch has "spent the earliest season of life, while yet the ingenuousness of youth remained unimpaired, in the pursuits of literature or science, and [is] ignorant of Christianity otherwise than as a system of forms and offices" (Taylor, p. 88). Likewise, Pierre "did . . . glide toward maturity thoughtless" of reality, spending many hours in his father's "fastidiously picked and decorous library; where the Spenserian nymphs had early led him into many a maze of all-bewildering beauty" that produced "soft, imaginative flames in his heart."[38] Eventually reality punctures the enthusiast's dream, producing a crisis very like that caused by Isabel's information about Pierre's father: "But the moment of awakening arrives; some appalling accident or piercing sorrow sets the interest of time in abeyance, and opens upon the soul the vast objects of immor-

tality" (Taylor, p. 88). Taylor then explores the psychology of the woe-awakened conscience. Although submission or humility may result, the enthusiast hovers over a void: "the first accidental contact with doctrinal paradox kindles the constitutional passion, and rouses the slumbering faculties to the full activity of adult vigor; contention ensues—malign sentiments, though perhaps foreign to the temper, are engendered, and these impart gloom to mysticism, and add ferocity to extravagance." The ingenuous youth becomes a "delirious bigot" (Taylor, p. 88).

Pierre's enthusiastic, imagination-based religion is the worship of his imaginary father ("without blemish, unclouded, snow-white, and serene" [p. 68]) described in Book IV. The "doctrinal paradox" is the discovery of his father's sin and the "fact" of Isabel's sisterhood; and the contention between the two occupies over a hundred pages of *Pierre,* from the moment when Pierre fearfully reads Isabel's mysterious note on pages 63 and 64 until he "crosses the Rubicon" and informs Lucy of his "unprecedented final resolution" on page 182. In this section, the narrator minutely anatomizes the mind and heart of his enthusiast ("I am more frank with Pierre than the best men are with themselves" [p. 108]), seeking the clue to his motive for choosing the perilous path and Isabel over the simple world of Saddle Meadows and Lucy. In the last of these books, Book X ("The Unprecedented Final Resolution of Pierre"), "enthusiasm" or some variant appears six times in ten pages. Pierre's crucial decision, Taylor would assert, is the natural consequence of the fundamental unreality of his life.

Taylor's and Melville's enthusiasts both ingeniously support their heresies—in Pierre's case, his simultaneous devotion to his "sister" and to his father's reputation. Spurning authority, Taylor's heresiarch hastily convinces himself of the "certainty of the new truth" (p. 87) and argues cleverly but fallaciously to buttress his false beliefs. With more "intellectual mobility" than "strength," his "ready perception of analogies gives him both facility and felicity in collecting proofs, or rather illustrations, in support of whatever opinion he adopts."[39] Certainly the most elaborate analogy in *Pierre* is that constructed by Plinlimmon to support his (heretical) argument for a "virtuous expediency" (p. 214), but Pierre recognizes and chastizes his own tendency to analogize: "'Quit thy analogies; sweet in the orator's mouth, bitter in the thinker's belly'" (p. 42). Still, when presented with what appears to be a compelling coincidence, he ignores his better reason: even before hearing the first part of Isabel's story he confirms his "presentiments" of his mother's attitude by her response to Ned and Delly's analogous situation; from this he concludes "he now perfectly knew his mother's mind, and had received forewarnings, as if from heaven" (p. 110), not to mention Isabel to her. A second coincidence—Isabel's residence in the house of Delly's father—seems one more argument for divine intent. At such times, the narrator says, one tends to ask, "chance, or God?" (p. 111). Taylor's heretic is soon duped by his self-created "false doctrine" (p. 89): "In this state of mind, of what value are the opinions of teachers and of elders? Of what weight the be-lief of the catholic church in all ages? They are nothing to be accounted of;—there seems even a glory and a hero-ism, as well as a duty, in spurning the fallible authority of man:—modesty, caution, hesitation, are treasons against conscience and heaven!" (p. 87). Pierre's examination of the "evidence" in his case—the two portraits, his aunt's story, Isabel's fragmentary memories—and his use of these products of the imagination to determine a truth, along with his failure to be honest with Lucy and his attempt to gain Falsgrave's support—in fact all of his mental machi-nations in Books IV through X—serve to justify his con-viction of the "new truth," that Isabel is indeed his sister and that he indeed must somehow help her.

The prognosis for the young heretic is dire, for the natural result of his enthusiasm is "a lamentable catastrophe." Taylor's description anticipates what happens to Pierre in New York: "when the heart is sick and faint from the ex-haustion of over activity, when the whispers of conscience have long ceased to be heard, when the emotions of genu-ine piety have become painfully strange to the soul, noth-ing is so probable as an almost sudden plunge from the pinnacle of high belief; into the bottomless gulf of univer-sal scepticism" (p. 89).

Taylor is the only writer on enthusiasm to explore in any detail the consequences of enthusiasm for the individual, and the two major dangers of the excessive imagination enumerated in Section I closely anticipate Pierre's fate and Melville's treatment of it. First, it can overcome "all other affections and motives belonging to human nature" (p. 11), sever the enthusiast from "all sympathy with the common interests of life, and . . . render a man a mere phantom" (p. 12). Taylor explains, "whoever [creates] a paradise of abstract contemplation, or of poetic imagery, where he may take refuge from the annoyances and the importunate claims of common life—whoever thus delights himself with dreams, and is insensible to realities, lives in peril of awakening from his illusions when truth comes too late" (p. 18). Imaginative indulgence tends to "indurate" (p. 17) the heart. "Artificial excitement" induced by the "religion of the imagination" (pp. 17, 16) is unhealthy and trans-forms the tender heart into "a freezing centre of solitary and unsocial indulgence. . . . No cloak of selfishness is in fact more impenetrable than that which usually envelopes a pampered imagination. The reality of woe is the very circumstance that paralyses sympathy: . . . more often than not, this kind of luxurious sensitiveness to fiction is conjoined with a callousness that enables the subject of it to pass through the affecting occasions of domestic life in immovable apathy:—the heart has become, like that of Le-viathan, 'firm as a stone—yea, hard as a piece of the nether millstone,'" (Taylor, pp. 18-19).

Whereas most discussions of enthusiasm are filled with images of heat (enthusiasm, according to Chambers, is "Prophetic rage, or fury, which . . . enflames and raises the imagination"),[40] Taylor insists it leads to coldness and stoniness: "a fictitious piety corrupts or petrifies the heart

not less certainly than does a romantic sensibility" (p. 18). When enthusiasm infects philanthropy, the "emotions of the heart are transmuted into mere pleasures of the imagi-nation" (p. 177). In monkish enthusiasm, "imaginative in-dulgences . . . petrify the heart," making "void the law of love to our neighbor, by a pretended intensity of love to God" (p. 220). (Compare Pierre's question, "Lucy or God?" p. 181.) Monastic life represents an "absolute sepa-ration from the society of man. The anchoret was a dis-joined particle, frozen deep into the mass of his own self-ishness," and Taylor concludes that "this sort of meditative insulation is the ultimate and natural issue of all enthusias-tic piety" (p. 220).

Taylor's discussion of enthusiasm's effect on the indi-vidual brings together several themes significant to Melville's exploration of the subject: selfishness, the incit-ing effect of woe, cold, the problem of fictionalizing, and, especially, stoniness—the dominant metaphor for Pierre's transformation.[41] "Enthusiastic Truth, and Earnestness, and Independence" "invariably lead" the well qualified mind to "Hyperborean Regions," according to Melville at the be-ginning of Book IX, as he explores the moral crux Pierre has involved himself in. His cutting himself off from his mother, his fiancee, his past, his patrimony, and his future; his long cold days at his desk in New York; his becoming in his dream a monolith, the armless Enceladus; his death in the low-ceilinged stone dungeon of the prison: these are all consequences of his "grand enthusiast resolution" which, the narrator points out, will require Pierre to "make a sacrifice of all objects dearest to him" (p. 106).

But, for Taylor, this is not the worst danger facing the en-thusiast: even though it severs one from the sympathy of mankind, worse can happen if enthusiasm is, by chance, aligned with "the malign passions":

> Opportunity . . . and habit may be wanting, but intrin-sic qualification for the perpetration of the worst crimes is not wanting to the man whose bosom heaves with enthusiasm, inflamed by malignancy. If checks are re-moved, if incitements are presented, if the momentum of action and custom is acquired, he will soon learn to extirpate every emotion of kindness or of pity, as if it were a treason against heaven; and will make it his am-bition to rival the achievements, not of heroes, but of fiends. (p. 18)

Similarly, Melville's narrator generalizes about those "Hy-perborean regions" to which Pierre's enthusiasm has led him: there the common maxims of social man can become inverted and confounded until one "entirely loses the di-recting compass of his mind" (p. 165). From the moment he receives Isabel's letter, Pierre behaves irrationally, si-multaneously holding conflicting goals, failing to seek evi-dence before acting, leaping over the obvious question, "*What* must I do?" to the problem of "*How* must I do it?" (pp. 87-88), and rationalizing that his quest for truth can somehow be accomplished by living a lie. It is this loss of reason that causes critics like Arvin to label Pierre an "Or-lando Furioso." The fall that Taylor predicts suggests the plot of *Pierre* from the moment when young Glendinning receives Isabel's note and swears he "will be impious" (p. 66)—a fall from innocence that climaxes when he arrives in the city. Glen's cold rejection of his woe-maddened relative issues in Pierre's "savage impulse" to murder his cousin; and Glen's dismissal of Pierre as a "'remarkable case of combined imposture and insanity'" (p. 239) is fit prelude to the descent to hell (the police station at night). From here it is a small step to Pierre's declaration that virtue and vice are "nothing" and his question, "How can one sin in a dream?" (p. 274).

The infamous actions so revolting to nineteenth-century reviewers of *Pierre* are a natural consequence of enthusiasm. Although the enthusiast may, under ordinary circumstances, suffer no ill effects from his "fictitious piety" or enthusiasm, Taylor asserts, his artificial support will "necessarily" fail him "in the hour of unusual trial." Lacking "the common principles of honor and integrity which carry worldly men with credit through difficult occasions, [the] enthusiast is . . . of all men the one who is the worst prepared to withstand peculiar seductions.—He possesses neither the heavenly armor of virtue, nor the earthly" (p. 20). In fact, the enthusiast "has only a choice of immoralities, to be determined by his temperament and circumstances" (p. 20): he may become a zealot, visionary, railer, or recluse. Hemmed in by apparently irreconcilable options—to tell the truth he must grievously wound his mother and impugn his father's reputation; to help Isabel he must reveal his father's secret or reject Lucy—Pierre convinces himself that his chosen "immorality" is the least painful for all concerned, but in return he is considered a monster, a swindler, a villainous liar, and a fiend. The "seduction" Pierre faces upon meeting his strange but beautiful "sister" is "peculiar," to say the least, and in the question of whether or not Pierre withstands this seduction in a physical sense lies the taboo subject of incest in the novel. One is reminded, too, of Plinlimmon's statement that "almost invariably, with inferior beings, the absolute effort to live in this world according to the strict letter of the chronometricals is, somehow, apt to involve those inferior beings eventually in strange, *unique* follies and sins, unimagined before" (p. 213). From the birth of his enthusiasm to his disastrous end, Pierre closely follows the naturalistic type provided by Taylor's study.

IV

Melville uses Pierre's enthusiasm to explore the question of the validity of art—the product of the imagination as interpreted by the imagination—as a guide to action and a means to truth in an artificial world where habitual fictionalizing renders all "Truth" suspect. Theological concern about enthusiasm had centered on the source of inspiration, whether it was divine or demonic; with the advent of romanticism, however, inspiration gives way to imagination, moving the locus of reality from outside to inside the individual mind. Though the terms have changed, the problem remains, as Taylor's treatment of the imagination makes clear. Thoroughly Baconian and empirical, con-

vinced of the superiority of the inductive method, Taylor distrusts abstraction in areas where (scientific) reason should prevail, and he believes the diseased imagination—enthusiasm—leads to a dangerous loss of reality. Repeatedly he emphasizes the need for authoritative reason to control the errant imagination. But his entire argument is predicated upon the very real existence of the imagination, twin to reason: both are necessary human faculties. The opening of the *Natural History,* in fact, is a paean to the imagination that introduces an immediate ambiguity into his discussion:

> Some form of beauty, engendered by the imagination . . . invests almost every object that excites desire. These illusions—if indeed they ought to be called illusions, . . . by mediating between body and spirit, reconcile the animal and intellectual propensities and give dignity and harmony to the character of man. It is these unsubstantial impressions that enrich and enliven the social affections; and these, not less than the superiority of the reasoning faculties, elevate mankind above the brute. (p. 9)

But, not only is imaginative speculation attractive; enthusiasm is necessary to human progress. Without it, "the sciences would never have moved a step in advance of the mechanic arts, much less would the high theorems of pure mathematics, or the abstruse principles of metaphysics, have been known to mankind" (p. 93). Because the imagination deals with what is not there, what is not already realized—the abstract, the metaphysical—it can theorize, invent, dream. But, misused or uncontrolled, it can create heretical doctrine, abstruse speculation, or "fictitious happiness" (p. 12), rendering the dreamer unable to deal with reality. Only a thin line separates the imagination from its perversion, enthusiasm.

Melville drops numerous "hints" that Pierre's predicament is the result of the imagination's usurping the role of reason. At the beginning of Book IV, the narrator discusses the difficulty—if not impossibility—of accounting for human emotions which can lead an individual like Pierre to behave in a way that most people consider insane. The whys and hows of human experience are lost in the chain of circumstances that leads to any event. "Idle then would it be," he concludes, to attempt to explain why Isabel's information led Pierre immediately and unquestioningly to do battle with Fate for his "sister." Nevertheless, "some random hints" may help to understand Pierre's "tumultuous mood" (p. 68). The "hints" all concern Pierre's father, but more specifically the imaginary father Pierre has confected from his own memories, his mother's attitudes, his Aunt Dorothea's stories, and the "chair-portrait" that was "stolen" by cousin Ralph. Again, in Book X, attempting to explain Pierre's "extraordinary" decision to pretend that his sister Isabel is his wife, the narrator states that in tracing "the rarest and profoundest things," their "probable origin" is often "something extremely trite or trivial" (p. 176); the very strong "hint" he offers here is the "fictitiousness" of Pierre and his mother's "brother-sister" relationship. And, in Book XII, attempting to explain Pierre's sudden hatred and destruction of the chair-portrait, the narrator "hints" that the ambiguously smiling face of his father symbolizes for Pierre the "tyranny of Time and Fate": only in the portrait does he find a link between his deceased father and the strange woman, so that the painted image, not the real man, seems to be the father of Isabel (p. 197).

All of these "hints" point to the imagination as the motivating force. Whether the medium be paint or language, the human capacity to envision and represent what is not there is the immediate cause of Pierre's acts. For the real flesh-and-blood father, Pierre has substituted an idealized version whom he worships. Another imaginative version of his father, captured in the chair-portrait, seems to speak, urging him to believe in an alternate reality; this portrait supplies him with the only bit of "evidence" to support Isabel's claim—the physical similarity Pierre noticed between the two "faces." "For the real Lucy"—the person most cruelly used in Pierre's scheme—he substitutes an abstraction, a "sign," an algebraic "*x*" (p. 181). And, for the real Isabel, he substitutes an enigma (a literary problem), the "mystery of Isabel," "wholly . . . out of the realms of mortalness, and . . . transfigured in the highest heaven of uncorrupted love" (p. 142). The products of the imagination work on each other: the "conjectured past of Isabel took mysterious hold of his father; therefore, the idea of his father tyrannized over his imagination" (p. 104). In fact, after his first "interview" with Isabel, Pierre sees all human relationships as imaginary: faced with "mysteries interpierced with mysteries, and mysteries eluding mysteries," he begins to "seem to see the mere imaginariness of the so supposed solidest principle of human association" (p. 142). However, Pierre irrationally uses this "evidence" to arrive at the "burning fact, that Isabel was his sister" (p. 170).

Only at the end of the novel does Pierre come to realize that his "grand enthusiast resolution" was predicated upon a tissue of abstractions and fictions rather than a foundation of facts. The words in Isabel's note become the key that unlocks the mystery of the father's ambiguous smile, whereas the chair-portrait becomes Pierre's only "proof," "the entire sum and substance of all possible, rakable, downright presumptive evidence" (p. 353) that Isabel is his sister. Pierre draws on the world of the imagination to fill the spaces in his knowledge; his "proofs" are insubstantial because each is the product of the imagination, and each depends on the other for validation.

Pierre begins to realize his folly soon after his arrival in New York: "Call me brother no more! How knowest thou I am thy brother? Did thy mother tell thee? Did my father say so to me?—I am Pierre, and thou Isabel, wide brother in the common humanity,—no more" (p. 273). The doubts return more forcefully after Pierre, Isabel, and Lucy visit the art gallery with its strangely evocative portraits: "How did he *know* that Isabel was his sister?" (p. 353), Pierre seems to ask as he responds to the pictures. He reviews his aunt's "nebulous legend," the "shadowy points" in

"Isabel's still more nebulous story," uncertain and blurred as it is; he recalls his "own dim reminiscences of his wandering father's death-bed"; and then he sets aside "all his own manifold and inter-enfolding mystic and transcendental persuasions,—originally born, as he now seemed to feel, purely of an intense procreative enthusiasm:—an enthusiasm no longer so all-potential with him as of yore"; and, in the light of "real naked reason," looking at the "plain, palpable facts," the central question remains, "how did he know that Isabel was his sister?" (p. 353). The crux of enthusiasm is the source of the "truth."

V

Pierre's enthusiasm is an important element in Melville's exploration of the role of the imagination in the quest for truth. In a very interesting way, Isabel's story and the chair-portrait illuminate each other at the same time that they call into question the possibility that the imagination—as both the creator and the interpreter of art—can lead to truth.[42] Both the story and the portrait are enigmas, artistic puzzles demanding solutions of their hidden meanings. Pierre is bewildered by the "enigmas" (p. 138) that invest Isabel, an "enigmatic girl" (p. 176), after she tells her "enigmatical story" (p. 128) which ends in "enigmatical obscurity" (p. 136) to the point where he begins to wonder whether "I and all mankind, beneath our garbs of common-placeness, conceal enigmas that the stars themselves, and perhaps the highest seraphim can not resolve?"[43] Pierre's handling of these enigmas, especially when compared to Taylor's discussion of this subject, is further evidence that his imagination has usurped his reason.

Taylor's concern is the problem of interpreting scriptural prophecy, since erroneous interpretation is a symptom of enthusiasm. Recognizing the difficulty of explaining God's method of speaking to men about things that have no real existence, he uses an analogy: a Biblical prophecy is like an enigma, a literary form used traditionally to manifest—and conceal—the "most important and serious truths" (p. 108). He develops at length a hint from Locke, that God provides some "extrinsical" "mark" whereby truth can be distinguished from delusion.[44] An enigma is "artfully constructed" (p. 111) so that the real subject is hidden or disguised "by some ingenuity of definition, and by some ambiguity of description" (p. 108); the enigma is *designedly* so framed as to tempt and to allow a diversity of hypothetical explanations" (p. 109); and the key to the correct interpretation of the enigma is a "special mark which shall prevent the possibility of doubt once the substance signified is seen" (p. 108).[45]

Among its ambiguities, *Pierre* contains numerous enigmas demanding solution, including Isabel's handkerchief and guitar and the carved "S. ye W." on the Memnon stone. One minor enigma satisfies all of Taylor's "laws": the apparent cooling of Pierre's once-fervid friendship with his cousin Glen. The disguise that conceals while revealing lies in the subtle change in Glen's correspondence with

Pierre; of several possible interpretations for this perceived coolness, the narrator claims, "one possible ambiguity [becomes] the only possible explanation for all the ambiguous details": the fact that Glen too has romantic feelings for Lucy, a truth Pierre arrives at, significantly, through his imagination. Here is the "master solution" that explains "all the singular enigmas in Glen": "thus read, all these riddles apparently found their cunning solution" (p. 224). Later events support this solution. As this example makes clear, Pierre's imagination may lead to truth. What is significant in "solving" an enigma is arriving at the one solution that explains all the ambiguities—Taylor's "special mark that prevents the possibility of doubt." Melville hints that Pierre may have arrived at such a solution in relation to Plinlimmon's enigmatic pamphlet; the narrator's avowed befuddlement about this enigma-within-an-enigma suggests (as the multiple critical interpretations of the piece indicate) that the pamphlet, if understood, might be the "chemic key of the cipher" (p. 70) of **Pierre.**

According to Taylor, the enigma's disguise serves three purposes: it is "a blind to the incurious—a trap to the dogmatical, and an exercise of modesty, of patience, and of sagacity, to the wise" (p. 109). The story of Isabel lures Pierre into the dogmatic trap: convinced even before she tells her story of the "fact" of Isabel's sisterhood, Pierre considers only a single interpretation. Her incoherencies add up to a terrible indictment of his father as the source of the damsel's distress. Taylor emphasizes that if the "expositor" of an enigma settles on "*any one* of the several interpretations of which an enigmatical prophecy is suceptible, and . . . claims for it a positive and exclusive preference," he "sins most flagrantly, and outrageously, against the unalterable laws of the language" (p. 111); the subsequent reading of contemporary events as fulfillments of the misinterpreted prophecy can lead the expositor to the "verge of insanity—or worse, of infidelity." "In this feverish state of the feelings, mundane interests, under the guise of faith and hope, occupy the soul to the exclusion of 'things unseen and eternal:' meanwhile the heart-affecting matters of piety and virtue become vapid to the taste, and gradually fall into forgetfulness" (p. 113).

On the other hand, Pierre's response to the chair-portrait is far more fluid and open-minded, suggesting this may be a truly imaginative interpretation, an "exercise of modesty, of patience, and of sagacity" (Taylor, p. 109). The one bit of evidence—the catalyst in Pierre's decision—is this ambiguously created, ambiguously smiling portrait. It is appropriate that this illustration of the possible deceits of the imagination be a work of art, even more important that it be the product of a series of deceits, cousin Ralph's lies about the painting he was making as he "stole" the image from the young man who became Pierre's father while that young man was wearing a smile that perhaps hid—or revealed?—his deception of the social world and of a young Frenchwoman, and that it be interpreted by a romantically sentimental sister. In trying to capture that face of deceit, the artist indeed created an enigma, "artfully constructed" to reveal and conceal the truth.

As Pierre sought to penetrate the mystery of the chair-portrait during his adolescence, the portrait had seemed to speak, to encourage him to probe deeper into the mystery behind its ambiguous smile. In the heat of Pierre's enthusiasm, Isabel's story becomes the key to the mystery—the special mark—to unlock all of its previous ambiguities, a moment of enlightenment suggestive of a religious conversion:

> But now, *now*—Isabel's letter read: swift as the first light that slides from the sun, Pierre saw all preceding ambiguities, all mysteries ripped open as if with a keen sword.. . . Now his remotest infantile reminiscences—the wandering mind of his father—the empty hand, and the ashen—the strange story of Aunt Dorothea—the mystical midnight suggestions of the portrait itself; and, above all, his mother's intuitive aversion, all overwhelmed him with reciprocal testimonies. (p. 85)

The portrait, Melville goes on to say, is "no longer wholly enigmatical, but still ambiguously smiling" (p. 87).

Later, however, at the art gallery, Pierre recognizes that the now-destroyed chair-portrait, like the similar portrait he sees, may have been "a pure fancy piece" (p. 353), a product of the imagination, and he now dismisses any similarity to the real father as "one of the wonderful coincidences" (p. 352)—whereas earlier, he had read coincidences as signs to be followed. The portrait, the coincidences—these constituted the evidence for the decision that is inexorably leading to his end. By framing Pierre's enthusiastic gesture with two apparently similar portraits whose significance can be determined only by some knowledge that resides outside of the artifacts themselves—Locke's "something extrinsical to the persuasions themselves" (*Works,* III, 157)—Melville deftly indicates the perils that attend the imagination when unrestrained by reason.

VI

The question framed by the portraits has to do with the nature and truth of art and the imagination and their relationship to human action. Is the product of the imagination "merely" a "fiction"—a lie? Is the truth that one thinks one discovers through the imagination merely an enthusiastic fantasy, the product of disordered reason? Or is that shadow land that Pierre enters when the chair portrait seems to speak to him in his adolescence—is that world more *real* than the supposedly real world of facts and surfaces, Mary Glendinning's world as represented by the drawing-room portrait? The space that Pierre's youthful mind enters in the fifth chapter of Book IV, as Melville seeks an answer to the question of the motive and cause of Pierre's immediate entrance into the lists opened by Isabel's note, resembles the moonlight world in the second story of Hawthorne's Custom-House: here are the "ever-elastic regions of evanescent invention" (*Pierre,* p. 82; compare Taylor's use of "elasticity" in reference to the "inventive power [p. 84]); in "reveries and trances" Pierre opens himself to all those ineffable hints and ambiguities, and undefined half-suggestions, which now and then people the soul's atmosphere" (p. 84); here he falls into a "midnight revery" (p. 85). It is this elastic world that engenders Pierre's enthusiasm, here that art speaks to his fluid mind and seems to convey a truth deeper than that which his social world is teaching him to know.

For the Christian addressed by most of the writers on enthusiasm, the bulwark against dangerous enthusiastic speculation is a rational approach to Scripture, the authoritative word of God which resolves all possible questions. Melville's plot indicates that this authority is unavailable to Pierre: his father (whose "pure, exalted idea" [p. 82] had once controlled his imagination) is dead and discredited; his mother failed to act her part and is now revealed to be coldly proud; and twice Pierre has discovered Falsgrave's position on the very real problem of illegitimacy, both times receiving an answer quite opposite from that taught in the Sermon on the Mount. He has come to see the social world as selfishly hypocritical, an institution whose smooth functioning depends on compromises (compare Plinlimmon's dismissal of chronometrical truth as a guide for horological life) and forms and lies, and thus he becomes his own authority, trapped in the hermetic circle of his imaginative logic.

Melville underscores this problem of the absence of an authoritative center to guide the enthusiast's actions by comparing Pierre's mood of "rebellion and horrid anarchy and infidelity" (p. 205) to that of the priest tempted to renounce his belief: whereas the priest retained his faith through the "indestructible anchors" of Christianity, Pierre has destroyed the only hard evidence he had—a work of the imagination. Moreover, Melville insists, Pierre's problem is of a different order: whereas the priest's problem concerned belief, for Pierre "it was a question whether certain vital acts of his were right or wrong." And he stresses this distinction between beliefs and acts by adding, "In this little nut lie germ-like the possible solution of some puzzling problems" (p. 205). Throughout *Pierre,* Melville is concerned with this vital question of the relationship between imagination and action—with how the "fancy pictures" created by the mind may determine human events. Despite the book's many ambiguities, Pierre's uncontrolled imagination (his "enthusiasm") is the cause of his actions.

Although Pierre's interpretations of the enigmas of Isabel and his father are clearly enthusiastic, Melville further complicates the question of the validity of the imagination by suggesting—at exactly the moment that Pierre is berating himself for his enthusiastic act, near the end of the work—that Pierre's intuitive solution may indeed have been correct. When Pierre and Isabel, side by side, view "*A stranger's head, by an unknown hand,*" they seem to respond identically, but the omniscient narrator reveals that they are seeing different things. For Pierre, the similarity between this portrait and the one he destroyed raises questions about the necessary relationship of art to life and calls into question the whole edifice upon which he built

his grand enthusiast resolution: "the original of this second portrait was as much the father of Isabel as the original of the chair-portrait. But perhaps there was no original at all to this second portrait" (p. 353). The father of Isabel produced by his imagination may not exist at all. On the other hand, Isabel apparently sees in the portrait the face of the gentleman she associates with the word "Glendinning" and remembers from her childhood; if so, the portrait provides exactly the corroborative evidence Pierre sought.

But, as Taylor warns it will, skepticism has finally replaced enthusiastic faith: recently to Pierre, the "whole story of Isabel had seemed an enigma, a mystery, an imaginative delirium" (p. 354), especially now that he, through his own art, understands the fiction-making process. Only now, when it is too late, does he come to ask himself the questions that Taylor insists one must ask when confronted with an enigma. Pierre's recognition that Isabel's story may have been an "enigma, a mystery, an imaginative delirium," as well as his rejection of coincidences as conclusive proof, represents a return to a more rational approach to the problem. Coming fast upon his severe case of enthusiasm, however, it can only plunge Pierre into "the bottomless gulf of universal scepticism" that Taylor predicts for the "young heresiarch" (p. 89).

Melville's connection of Pierre's new-found skepticism with his role as a professional "bejuggler"—a "profound" writer (p. 354)—suggests how he was using his creation of a Tayloresque enthusiast to explore the problem of the dangers and deceits, the lure and the ambiguity of the imagination he was encountering as a writer of fiction. The problem is especially acute in a selfish and scientific age when unusual behavior like Pierre's, or even Melville's, is no longer considered inspiration, but instead insanity. As opposed to his earlier belief (expressed in the review of Hawthorne's *Mosses,* 1850) in "fine authors . . . standing, as they do, for the mystical, ever-eluding Spirit of all Beauty, which ubiquitously possesses men of genius," the Melville of *Pierre* wonders whether such a writer is merely trapped in his own fictions, deluding himself and his readers. In that same review, Melville had compared Truth "in this world of lies" to a "scared white doe [fleeing] in the woodlands," revealed "only by cunning glimpses . . . covertly, and by snatches," and he had acknowledged that the writer of fiction (like Taylor's creator of enigmas) may usefully create titles "directly calculated to deceive—egregiously deceive, the superficial skimmer of pages."[46] Pierre's questions at the end of the novel suggest not only that the professional creator of serious fictions must resort to the conscious deceit of the enigma in order to conceal while revealing the most important truths, but also that those "truths" as well may be deceits. One is tempted to ridicule Pierre for his "unprecedented" method of "knowing" truth by enthusiastically creating and living a lie; but such subterfuge is endemic to professional fiction-making. Habituated to his created fictions, Melville suggests, the writer may lose the ability to distinguish between the actual and the imaginary and end by either deceiving himself and his readers or doubting the possibility of any truth. His treatment of these questions in *Pierre* shows him well on his way to the questions concerning truth and art explored in *The Confidence-Man.*

But, unlike Taylor, Melville is not dogmatic on this point: whether or not Isabel is his sister remains for Pierre an unanswered question. The imagination may have led Pierre closer to the real truth of Isabel and the social world than factual evidence ever could have. Instead, *Pierre* dramatizes the difficulty of arriving at final truth, a difficulty suggested by the progression of metaphors Melville chose to image Truth—from a "scared white doe" in 1850 to a fathomless white whale in 1851, to the "appallingly vacant" "central room" (p. 285) of the pyramid in 1852.[47] The problem is not so much that Truth is elusive (as in *Mardi* and *Moby-Dick*), but that the human instrument for seeking Truth may be unreliable. The only true fiction, then, as Melville both states and practices in *Pierre,* will be that which resists the attempt to systematize the unsystematizable as do most novels and thus remains true to the "one sensational truth" about the "complex web of life" (a learning that Pierre derives from his encounter with Isabel): "the unravelable inscrutableness of God"—or, rather, that which "all men are agreed to call by the name of *God*" (p. 141), a statement that implies another act of the imagination, possibly a way of talking about something that has no real existence.

More important, however, is Pierre's awareness of the implication of being trapped by a possible fiction: a fiction, like an enigma, is made by someone for some "cause." His new "knowledge" brings new questions, new ambiguities: who, and for what purpose, could have implanted in Isabel information that would later derail Master Pierre Glendinning as he glided on to his "choice fate" as heir to the family seat, to a life of aristocratic luxury, surrounded by adoring females? In Book I of *Pierre,* the narrator clumsily shoves the question of "Fate" and its possible role in Pierre's life at the reader through repeated foreshadowings and indirect questions ("we shall see if Fate hath not just a . . . small word or two to say" [p. 12; compare p. 14]). Taylor, however, indicates that the hows and whys of human events lie in neither the "unravelable inscrutableness of God," nor Fate, nor chance, nor some perverse human agent; instead he loads the dice in favor of "temperament and circumstances" (p. 20).

VII

Melville's type-casting of Pierre according to this naturalistic model suggests that we consider—before Darwinian ideas had emphasized heredity and environment—how large a role natural rather than supernatural causes play in the plot of human life. The "fixed threads of the warp" (*Moby-Dick,* p. 185) of Pierre's life (Taylor's "temperament and circumstances") are his "susceptible, reflective, and poetic" (p. 111) nature, his high-strung spirit, his "double revolutionary descent" (p. 20), his background, childhood, culture and education; the stimulation of his imagination and habitual fictitiousness of his life result in

predictable behavior. The element of "chance" that brings Isabel into Pierre's physical sphere would be interpreted by Taylor as the result, instead, of the "intricate connections of the social system." He goes on to explain that "The thread of every life is entangled with other threads, beyond all reach of calculation" (p. 128). Melville echoes this thought: Pierre justifies his "strange," "deceitful . . . but harmless way" out of his difficulty, explaining to Isabel, "thy true heart foreknoweth not the myriad alliances and criss-crossings among mankind, the infinite entanglements of all social things, which forbid that one thread should fly the general fabric . . . without tearing itself and tearing others" (p. 191).

The threads that led to Pierre's first "fatal" view of Isabel's face (all that has happened, he believes, "inevitably proceeded from the first hour I saw thee" [p. 192]) may include Isabel's father's (if indeed he was her father) desire to provide somewhat for his unacknowledged daughter by locating her in his vicinity; Delly's pregnancy, which deprives her family of her labor; the existence of some "necessitous emigrants" (p. 44) in the neighborhood; the Miss Pennies' deafness and resultant charitable effort in establishing a sewing circle in their home; and Mary Glendinning's role as local philanthropist. This intricate web leads to a severe psychic shock which, as Taylor predicts, results in the onset of the disease (enthusiasm) in one constitutionally susceptible as is Pierre.

Among all of these threads, the opportunity for Pierre's weaving into his destiny any measure of free will is limited.[48] As Melville says, "Fixed Fate and Free Will were arguing him, and Fixed Fate got the better in the debate" (p. 182)—"Fate" interpreted, as Taylor's work suggests, as the natural elements that produce his enthusiasm. If free will exists, Melville suggests it is located in the link between thought and action, exactly the point where Taylor fears the trespassing of the imagination. In his lengthy probing of the motives leading to Pierre's "unprecedented final resolution" in Book X, the narrator hovers over Pierre like a Greek chorus, commenting on the significance of his action "if he now acted out his most rare resolve" (p. 176). Enumerating the terrible consequences that even "impulsive Pierre" recognizes, he concludes, "Such, oh thou son of man! are the perils and the miseries thou callest down on thee, when, even in a virtuous cause, thou steppest aside from those arbitrary lines of conduct, by which the common world, however base and dastardly, surrounds thee for thy worldly good" (p. 176).

The forms, codes, lies, and hypocrisies of modern social life—justified as necessary for survival—encourage a divorce between idea and action: it is prudent to believe one thing and do another, as Falsgrave and Mary Glendinning demonstrate. Pierre has an inkling of the need for the "social lie" when he curses "the hour I acted on the thought, that Love hath no reserves. Never should I have told thee the story of that face, Lucy" (p. 37). But, even in this vital area of action, *Pierre* suggests that free will may be extremely limited: "not always in our actions are we our own factors" (p. 51), we are reminded, as Pierre ponders the "motive" that led him, for the first time, to lie to his mother. For at this point in the novel, the narrator "hints" that the clue to Pierre's fatal action may lie in the habitual fictitiousness of their relationship. Thus, Pierre finds the solution to his problem in the "baleful thought" that enters his mind as he ponders his irreconcilable motives, "that the truth should not always be paraded; . . . that sometimes a lie is heavenly, and truth infernal" (p. 92). Only one habituated to fictions would consider such a solution as the means to knowing "Truth."

The plot of Melville's *Pierre,* like Taylor's treatise and Plinlimmon's pamphlet, is a critique of enthusiasm—of acting under the delusion that one is in direct communication with God, mistaking imagination for reality, acting (in Plinlimmon's terms) chronometrically while living in a horological world. But, both Taylor and Plinlimmon recognize the possibility of a few great souls who are truly inspired, although this is not the lot of the many. Rare indeed are those who can live enthusiastically or chronometrically "without folly or sin" (p. 213). Melville's novel transcends both of these little treatises in also recognizing and dramatizing the complexities and ambiguities that surround any decisive human action, and in the process creating a frightening image of the modern world as Melville saw it—an "artificial world," as Plinlimmon calls it, where the "soul of man" is necessarily "removed from its God and . . . heavenly truth" (p. 211). In representing this world, through the artificiality, the bombast, the excess, the baroque style of *Pierre,* Melville creates an image of the artificial, imaginary world that the mass of men have come to believe is real. In the end, *Pierre,* like Plinlimmon's pamphlet, is "more the excellently illustrated restatement of a problem, than the solution of the problem itself." But, as Melville adds parenthetically to his judgment of the pamphlet, "Perhaps [such illustrations] are the only possible human solutions" (p. 210).

Pierre indeed illustrates the problem of the uncontrolled imagination in its most developed form, the diseased form of what Taylor calls the "constitutional fictions" (p. 11) all humans are subject to. It dramatizes the difficulty of right action in a situation where the voice of God is a paradoxical silence, an artificial world of lies and hypocrisies, of surfaces and masks, where the Isabels are abandoned, the Dellys are banished, and the Pierres set off shock waves; where for the lack of an authoritative center, Plinlimmon's pamphlet remains an enigma. Melville's fiction too remains enigmatic because its truth turns back upon and questions its own instruments at the same time that it indicts the artificiality of human life in a self-created imaginary world; the mind rebels when confronted with this illustration of how impossible it is for one brought up in western society to distinguish truth from falsehood, imagination from reality. Habitual fictionalizing—the creation of an artificial, antiseptic world, divorced from nature and real feeling (the insights Melville had begun to formulate in writing *Typee* six years earlier) and from any real possibility of the transcendent—makes it extremely difficult,

Melville suggests through his character Pierre, for the individual to distinguish fact from fiction, truth from lie, and thus to discover any authoritative guide to action. On this level, *Pierre* becomes a hideous allegory, demonstrating through Pierre's "enthusiasm," his diseased imagination, the problem of western man in a culture that has lost its connection with a reality beyond its own man-created world of fictions.

Notes

1. Thompson, *Melville's Quarrel With God* (Princeton: Princeton Univ. Press, 1952), pp. 267-268.

2. Murray, "Introduction," *Pierre* (New York: Hendricks House, 1949), p. lx; "Explanatory Notes," p. 460, n. 125.17; cf. p. 473, n. 244.20.

3. Franklin, *The Wake of the Gods: Melville's Mythology* (Stanford, Calif.: Stanford Univ. Press, 1963), p. 105; Krieger, *The Tragic Vision: Variations on a Theme in Literary Interpretation* (Chicago and London: Univ. of Chicago Press, 1960; Phoenix edition, 1966), pp. 195-209.

4. Duban, *Melville's Major Fiction* (Dekalb: Northern Illinois Univ. Press, 1983), p. 179.

5. Dillingham, *Melville's Later Novels* (Athens and London: Univ. of Georgia Press, 1986), p. 195 ff.; Higgins and Parker, "Reading *Pierre,*" *A Companion to Melville Studies,* ed. John Bryant (New York: Greenwood Press, 1986), p. 228.

6. Larry Edward Wegener, *A Concordance to Herman Melville's Pierre: or the Ambiguities,* 2 vols. (New York and London: Garland, 1985); Eugene F. Irey, ed., *A Concordance to Herman Melville's Moby-Dick,* 2 vols. (New York and London: Garland, 1982). Father Mapple cries out "with a heavenly enthusiasm" on p. 50 of *Moby-Dick,* ed. Harrison Hayford and Hershel Parker (New York: Norton, 1967).

7. Wegener; for Robert S. Forsythe, "Introduction," Americana Deserta ed. (New York: Knopf, 1930), *Pierre* records "the tragic downfall of a brilliant young idealist" (p. xxxi); for William Ellery Sedgwick, *Herman Melville: The Tragedy of Mind* (Cambridge, Mass.: Harvard Univ. Press, 1944), it is a "tragedy of youthful idealism" (p. 167); Murray's Pierre is "an idealistic, benevolent youth crushed by the practical, non-benevolent world" (p. xcviii); Merton M. Sealts, Jr., "Melville and the Platonic Tradition," in *Pursuing Melville, 1940-1980* (Madison: Univ. of Wisconsin Press, 1982), classes *Pierre* with Melville's "other objections to philosophical idealism" (p. 323); Milton R. Stern, *The Fine Hammered Steel of Herman Melville* (Urbana, Chicago, and London: Univ. of Illinois Press, 1968), discusses the "problem of idealism" (p. 151); Duban's Pierre is motivated by "idealistic absolutism" (p. 153). The list could be multiplied many times.

8. Herman Melville, *Pierre; or, The Ambiguities,* ed. Harrison Hayford, Hershel Parker, and G. Thomas

Tanselle (Evanston and Chicago: Northwestern Univ. and Newberry Library, 1971), pp. 204, 106, 208, 106, 111; hereafter cited parenthetically.

9. Higgins and Parker, "Reading *Pierre,*" p. 213.

10. Gura, *The Wisdom of Words* (Middletown, Conn.: Wesleyan Univ. Press, 1980), p. 4.

11. Susie I. Tucker, *Enthusiasm: A Study in Semantic Change* (Cambridge: Cambridge Univ. Press, 1972), p. 3.

12. Knox, *Enthusiasm: A Chapter in the History of Religion, with Special Reference to the XVII and XVIII Centuries* (Oxford: Clarendon Press, 1950, 1962), pp. 4, 2.

13. Walter E. Houghton, *The Victorian Frame of Mind, 1830-1870* (New Haven and London: Yale Univ. Press for Wellesley College, 1957), p. 264.

14. Locke, "Enthusiasm," *Essay Concerning Human Understanding, Works,* 10 vols. (London: 1823; rpt. Germany: Scientia Verlag Aalen, 1963), III, 155-156.

15. Melville to Sarah Morewood, September 12? 1851, *The Letters of Herman Melville,* ed. Merrell R. Davis and William H. Gilman (New Haven: Yale Univ. Press, 1960).

16. Bulwer-Lytton, *Zanoni* (New York: A. L. Burt, 1845), p. viii. Leon Howard and Parker discuss possible influences of the novel on *Pierre* in the "Historical Introduction" to the Northwestern-Newberry edition, pp. 370-372.

17. Melville to Nathaniel Hawthorne, June 1? 1851, *Letters.*

18. Anthony, Earl of Shaftesbury, *Characteristics of Men, Manners, Opinions, Times,* ed. John M. Robertson, 2 vols. in one (1711; rpt. Indianapolis: Bobbs-Merrill, 1964), I, 38.

19. "mistaken": Meric Casaubon, *A Treatise Concerning Enthusiasm, As it is an Effect of Nature: but is Mistaken by Many for Either Divine Inspiration, or Diabolical Possession* (London: by R. D. . . . , 1655); "misconceit": Henry More, *A Collection of Several Philosophical Writings of Dr. Henry More . . .* 4th ed. . . . (London: Joseph Downing, 1712), p. 2; "counterfeit": James Foster, *Sermons,* 4 vols. (London: J. Noon & A. Millar, 1755), III, 276; "imaginary": Charles Chauncy, "A Caveat Against Enthusiasm" (Boston: J. Draper . . . , 1742), p. 3.

20. Wesley, *Sermons II, Works,* ed. Albert C. Outler, (Nashville, Tenn.: Abingdon Press, 1985), II, 47. "The Nature of Enthusiasm," first printed in volume 3 of *Sermons* (1750), was separately printed in 1755 and included in the popular *Sermons on Several Occasions,* printed in seven editions in the eighteenth century and about 35 editions, English and American, in the nineteenth century prior to 1851. It is a work Melville could easily have seen.

21. Wesley, *Sermons,* II, 58.

22. Locke, *Works,* III, 149.

23. Sealts, *Melville's Reading: Revised and Enlarged Edition* (Columbia: Univ. of South Carolina, 1988), p. 164.

24. Ephraim Chambers, *Chambers' Cyclopaedia: or, An Universal Dictionary of Arts and Sciences* (London: D. Midwinter, &c., 1741), s. v. "Enthusiasm." Because the edition Melville owned (J. & J. Knapton, &c., 1728) capitalizes all substantives in the entry, a practice I find distracting, I quote the 1741 edition, which differs from the 1728 (in quoted portions) only in this respect.

25. Hume, *Essays Moral, Political, and Religious, Philosophical Works,* ed. T. H. Green & T. H. Grose, 4 vols. (London: 1882; rpt. Germany: Scientia Verlag Aalen, 1964), III, 145.

26. Johnson, *A Dictionary of the English Language . . . , 2* vols. (London: W. Strahan, 1755; rpt. New York: AMS, 1967), s. v. "Enthusiasm."

27. For extensive treatments see Knox and Tucker, cited in notes 11 and 12.

28. Locke, *Works,* III, 152, from Chambers' *Cyclopaedia,* s. v. "Enthusiasm." Locke reads, "is it a perception of an inclination or fancy to do. . . ."

29. Sealts, "Records of Melville's Reading," *Melville's Reading,* p. 10.

30. Thomas Seccombe, "Taylor, Isaac (1787-1865)," *DNB* (1898-1899).

31. Tucker is interested in "how figurative language reflects attitudes of mind" (p. 5); see her discussion in ch. 11, "Metaphors," pp. 144-161.

32. Wesley, *Sermons,* II, 47; compare *Pierre,* p. 214; *Sermons,* II, 49-50.

33. See Paul Smith, "Flux and Fixity in *Pierre,*" *ESQ* [*A Journal of the American Renaissance*], 32 (1986), 119-120, n. 1. Murray, "Introduction," discusses Melville's "exhaustion," "moral conflict," and "underlying will to wreck his self" (pp. xiv-xv), and Newton Arvin, *Herman Melville,* American Men of Letters Series (New York: William Sloane. 1950), Melville's "psychoneurotic fatigue" (p. 218). See also Sealts, "Herman Melville's 'I and My Chimney,'" *Pursuing Melville,* esp. pp. 16-22 *passim.* Higgins and Parker ("Reading *Pierre*") mention a letter revealing that in December Melville was angered by gossip about *Moby-Dick* as "'more than Blasphemous'" (p. 226). Sarah Morewood to George Duyckinck, December 28, 1851, in Eleanor Melville Metcalf, *Herman Melville, Cycle and Epicycle* (Cambridge, Mass.: Harvard Univ. Press, 1953), worried about Melville's "morbid excitement," teased him by suggesting that his reclusive life was making "city friends think he was slightly insane—he replied that long ago he came to the same conclusion himself" (p. 133). See also Melville's letters to Hawthorne of November 17? 1851 ("I am not mad, most

noble Festus") and July 17 1852, and Melville's description of the probable success of *Pierre* to English publisher Richard Bentley (April 16, 1852).

34. See Dillingham, pp. 238-243, on the therapeutic value of *Pierre* for Melville.

35. Isaac Taylor, *Natural History of Enthusiasm* (London: Holdsworth & Ball, New York: J. Leavitt, 1830). Only Murray has connected *Pierre* with Taylor's treatise: for him Pierre contradicts Taylor's model. Commenting on Melville's leniency "in allowing [his hero] to be the sole carrier of the spirit in a world of universal 'Imbecility, Ignorance, Blockheadedness and Besottedness,'" Murray writes, "As a challenger, Isaac Taylor, for one, would have proved a tough customer. In an excellent little book, *Natural History of Enthusiasm,* widely read in Melville's day, the Rev. [in fact, Taylor was not a clergyman] Mr. Taylor succeeded in accomplishing his announced intention [warning against enthusiasm]. In defending his hero against Taylor's piercing criticisms, Melville might have succeeded in forging the one positive conception that is lacking in this novel" (p. lxxvi). Knox devotes two sentences to Taylor's *History* (which he dates as 1823): "Isaac Taylor scored an instantaneous success with *The Natural History of Enthusiasm;* probably the most uniformly dull book ever written. You may read through 275 pages, in the inflated style of the period, without coming across one arresting sentiment, or one important consideration" (pp. 6-7). I do not concur.

36. *New York Commerical Advertiser,* August 11, 1852; rpt. in *Critical Essays on Herman Melville's Pierre; or, The Ambiguities,* ed. Brian Higgins and Hershel Parker (Boston: G. K. Hall, 1983), p. 35.

37. Compare Locke: Enthusiasts' "minds being thus prepared, whatever groundless opinion comes to settle itself strongly upon their fancies, is an illumination from the spirit of God, and presently of divine authority; and whatsoever odd action they find in themselves a strong inclination to do, that impulse is concluded to be a call or direction from heaven" (*Works,* III, 150).

38. *Pierre,* p. 6. Pierre's religious training has been merely formal: "At the age of sixteen, Pierre partook with his mother of the Holy Sacraments" (p. 7); his father believed "no man could be a complete gentleman . . . unless he partook of the church's sacraments" (p. 98).

39. Taylor, p. 87. Locke, *Works,* III, 151 and 153, contains an interesting discussion of the enthusiast's circular logic.

40. See Tucker, pp. 145-148; Chambers, s. v. "Enthusiasm."

41. See especially Saburo Yamaya, "The Stone Image of Melville's 'Pierre,'" *Selection,* 34 (1957), 31-58; Franklin, pp. 101-103; and Edgar Dryden, *Melville's Thematics of Form* (Baltimore and London: Johns Hopkins Univ. Press, 1968), pp. 118-127, *passim.*

42. The relationship between fictions, the fictionalizing imagination, and Melville's plot, style, and characterization in *Pierre* is explored by Dryden in *Melville's Thematics of Form,* pp. 132-138, and "The Entangled Text: Melville's *Pierre* and the Problem of Reading," *Boundary 2,* 7 (1979), 145-173; and by Brook Thomas in "The Writer's Procreative Urge in *Pierre*: Fictional Freedom or Convoluted Incest?" *Studies in the Novel,* 11 (1979), 416-430. Richard Gray explores the work's anticipation of postmodernism in its skeptical examination of "its own claims and assumptions," subversive techniques, and self-reflexive idiom in "'All's o'er, and ye know him not': A Reading of *Pierre,*" in *Herman Melville: Reassessments,* ed. A. Robert Lee (London and Totawa, N. J.: Vision and Barnes & Noble, 1984), p. 117. Richard Brodhead, *Hawthorne, Melville, and the Novel* (Chicago and London: Univ. of Chicago Press, 1976), explains Melville's use of the form of the sentimental romance to call attention to itself as fiction and the artist's recognition that he is trapped in a fiction (pp. 163-193).

43. *Pierre,* p. 139. The word "enigma" or one of its variants occurs ten times in *Pierre* (Wegener) as compared to only two uses in *Moby-Dick* (Irey), both of the adjectival form "enigmatical": Ishmael's recollection of the "enigmatical hintings" of Elijah (p. 190) and his pointing out a "strange, enigmatical object" ("the whale's penis," Hayford and Parker's note explains) on the deck (p. 350).

44. Locke, as excerpted in Chambers' *Cyclopaedia,* states, "to enable [the prophet] to judge of his inspirations, whether they be of divine original or no . . . [God] either evidences that truth by the usual methods of natural reason, or else makes it known to be a truth which he would have us assent to by his authority; and convinces us, that it is from him, by some marks, which reason cannot be mistaken in." Chambers omits Locke's emphasis on the need for "something extrinsical to the persuasions themselves" if we are to distinguish among "inspirations and delusions, truth and falsehood" (*Works,* III, 156-157).

45. Howard and Parker, in the "Historical Note" to the Northwestern-Newberry *Pierre,* quote from Bulwer-Lytton's explanation (in a later edition of *Zanoni*) that his novel is a "book of 'mysteries,'" a "story in which 'typical meanings' were concealed, and . . . each 'mystery' or 'enigma' might lend itself to a variety of interpretations by different individuals" (p. 371). This language closely parallels Taylor's definition of the enigma.

46. "Hawthorne and His Mosses," *The Piazza Tales and Other Prose Pieces, 1839-1860,* ed. Harrison Hayford *et al.* (Evanston and Chicago: Northwestern Univ. and Newberry Library, 1987), pp. 239, 244, 251.

47. Dillingham's positive reading of this passage—his insistence that it does not signify Melville's recogni-

tion of emptiness in the soul of man—is interesting but not, to my mind, convincing (pp. 168-169).

48. Although I find Brodhead's discussion perhaps the most illuminating of recent work of *Pierre,* my exploration of Pierre's enthusiasm leads to a very different conclusion from his statement that "The discovery of this discrepancy [between heavenly precepts and human behavior] allows an enthusiastic youth three choices" (p. 180). Taylor's naturalistic model suggests he has very little choice.

Priscilla Wald (essay date 1990)

SOURCE: "Hearing Narrative Voices in Melville's *Pierre,*" in *boundary 2,* Vol. 17, No. 1, Spring, 1990, pp. 100-32.

[*In the following essay, Wald characterizes* Pierre *as an endless succession of narrative voices and perspectives that requires the readers' participation in making conclusions about the events of the novel.*]

Melville's *Pierre* inaugurates the tradition of author protagonists in American literature.[1] Pierre Glendinning's declaration of independence from an authorizing cultural discourse immediately precedes his resolve to write a novel that will "gospelize the world anew." But his narrative consciousness underwrites his apparently resistless damnation, as Pierre submits precisely to those self-evident truths that he has ostensibly rejected. Pierre, we learn, is actually writing two books, and the unconsciously authored narrative that dooms him deconstructs the narrative about Vivia, himself an "author-hero," to expose Pierre's "plagiari[sm] of his own experiences." The result, *Pierre,* is a compilation of unravelings that frustrates narrative expectations as it explores the impulse to narrativize.[2]

Pierre's "plagiarism" highlights his "characterization." His resistance to autonomy is apparent both in his life and in his earliest writings. Pierre is a scribbler whose "occasional contributions to magazines and other polite periodicals" bespeak his disinclination towards the rigors of authorship. He is lauded by critics for having "Perfect Taste" and being "unquestionably a highly respectable youth . . . blameless in morals, and harmless throughout" (287). In a chapter entitled "Young America in Literature," Melville parodically assigns Pierre archetypal status in an Emersonian vision; Pierre, like the nation, is reluctant to ruffle a surface beneath which "the world seems to lie saturated and soaking with lies" (244). He is unwilling, that is, to probe the contradictions that make his legacy intolerable.

Pierre turns to authorship when his discovery of an allegedly illegitimate sister shakes his faith not only in his family myth but in American society as well. Pierre's family is indeed rooted in American history; he is the grandson of two Revolutionary War heroes and heir to a "docile homage to a venerable Faith, which the first Glendinning had brought over sea, from beneath the shadow of an English

minister" (11). He is, furthermore, the only living male surnamed Glendinning, from which he incurs sole responsibility for preserving the family line. At the commencement of *Pierre* there seems to be no problem, since Pierre is a remarkably dutiful nineteen-year-old with an appropriately tractable fiancée. But it is precisely his docility that makes him vulnerable to Isabel, a mysterious woman who claims to be his father's illegitimate daughter. Accustomed to submission, Pierre easily transfers his allegiance from his intractable mother to the equally potent Isabel.

Pierre discovers Isabel when she thrusts herself upon him, and the discovery leads him to question not only "the dear perfect father" that Mrs. Glendinning counsels him always to remember, but also the notion of legitimacy that he was raised to revere. The sullied "name of the father" calls the law itself into question, but Pierre's incapacity for ambiguity leads to his immediate reinstitution of the law; he vows to "legitimize" Isabel with a fictitious marriage that largely resembles his earlier relationship to his mother, and he leaves the idyllic Saddle Meadows for New York City where he intends to support himself by writing a novel that exposes the hypocrisy of social convention.

Melville is not subtle about Pierre's textuality:

> So perfect to Pierre had long seemed the illuminated scroll of his life thus far, that only one hiatus was discoverable by him in that sweetly-writ manuscript. A sister had been omitted from the text. He had mourned that so delicious a feeling as fraternal love had been denied him. Nor could the fictitious title, which he so often lavished upon his mother, at all supply the absent reality. . . .
>
> "Oh, had my father but had a daughter!" cried Pierre; "someone whom I might love, and protect, and fight for, if need be. It must be a glorious thing to engage in a mortal quarrel on a sweet sister's behalf! Now, of all things, would to heaven I had a sister!" (11-12)

The passive voice of the passage emphasizes Pierre's "characterization"; the script is written that he need only enact. But the script is confusing, even paradoxical. In the mid-nineteenth-century United States, the national script of identity called at once for obedience and heroism. Pierre belongs to what George B. Forgie calls "the post-heroic generation," which came of age in the period preceding the Civil War, at a time when "[a]lmost all important political, moral, and personal matters . . . were referred to, and most policy choices measured against, the heroic standards of the founding period and the lives of the founders themselves."[3] Mrs. Glendinning's consistent reminder of Pierre's ancestry is in keeping with the national reverence of the founding fathers. The age invoked heroic models in a generation to which heroism was forbidden. As Forgie notes, the founders necessarily frustrated the heroic ambitions of their successors, who could inherit the content of the rebellion, Union, only at the expense of its form, revolution. Melville himself articulates (to Evert Duyckinck) the malaise of the age in a letter written shortly before publication of *Pierre*: "We are all sons, grandsons, or nephews, or great-nephews of those who go before us. No one is his own sire."[4]

Mrs. Glendinning remarks on the paradox when she notices that Pierre's docility, so admirable in its absence of challenge, is at odds with the heroism that is also supposed to comprise his patrimony. Delighting in Pierre's manageability, she "thank[s] heaven [she] sent him not to college," that is, to a place where he might learn to think independently, but she goes on to muse that she would "almost wish him otherwise than sweet and docile . . . seeing that it must be hard for man to be an uncompromising hero and a commander among his race, and yet never ruffle any domestic brow" (27). Ultimately, however, Mrs. Glendinning favors her son's adaptation, as she "pray[s] heaven he show his heroicness in some smooth way of favoring fortune, not be called out to be a hero of some dark hope forlorn" (27).

It is characteristic both of the tragi-romantic dimensions of *Pierre* and of Pierre's reluctant authorship that both he and his mother are destroyed precisely by what "heaven" grants them in response to their invocations: Mrs. Glendinning, by Pierre's "heroism"; and Pierre, by his sister, Isabel.[5] In fact, in their fictional epithets of "brother" and "sister," both mother and son express their desire for Pierre's autonomy (by implication, from his father as well as his mother); yet, when Pierre declares his independence, both resort to madness and death. As a "fictional title" suggests, Pierre does not want to alter the text, but merely to modify it, and he is unprepared to re-write.

Endemic to Pierre's vision of his home is the inviolability of the family, particularly his dead father's perfection, and it is precisely the possibility of his imperfection that Isabel embodies and that Pierre's childlike fantasy cannot withstand. The deification of the father has an analogue in American nationalism, which Melville emblematizes in his use of "Young America," an epithet of national self-representation in the 1840s.[6] And Emerson's 1844 lecture, "The Young American," neatly fills out Pierre's Emersonian contours in the portrait of a nation so

> newborn, free, healthful, strong, the land of the laborer, of the democrat, of the philanthropist, of the believer, of the saint, she should speak for the human race. America is the country of the Future. . . . it is a country of beginnings, of projects, of vast designs, and expectations. It has no past: all has an outward and prospective look. And herein is it fitted to receive more readily every generous feature which the wisdom or the fortune of man has yet to impress.[7]

An analogous denial of history is precisely what underwrites Pierre's authorial failure; the past rushes back, unperceived, to inform one's perception of the present. Emerson returns, in this passage, to a Jeffersonian ideal, an agrarian utopianism that in fact defines progress as a return to the past; he celebrates the "happy tendency" of the young men "to withdraw from the cities, and cultivate the soil," both because of the moral benefits they will reap and because "this promised the conquering of the soil, plenty, and beyond this, the adorning of the whole continent with every advantage and ornament which labor, ingenuity, and affection for a man's home could suggest."[8] As Emerson frames conservation in progressive rhetoric, he blurs the distinction between his utopianism and the industrialization that was also hailed as utopian. "The conquering of the soil," similarly, could send attentive youths not home to cultivate their gardens but westward under the banner of "manifest destiny." Emerson and his "progressive" opponents, like the North and the South, blur their distinctions in their use of a rhetoric that summons in the same paradoxical past justification for the opposing ideals of the present.

So, against Emerson's explicitly avowed ahistoricism runs a preoccupation with history that, as Ann Douglas has documented in *The Feminization of American Culture,* characterized mid-nineteenth-century America.[9] Emerson's denial of America's past in fact obscures the present as it invigorates the narrative of history, a progressive, resistless force that impels young Americans into the future while it justifies the growing nationalism that obscured difference and made invisible the atrocities committed in the name of "manifest destiny" (the heir of the Puritans' "divine mission") at home and of the Christian salvation (missionary movement) abroad. Isabel offers Pierre the chance to introspect, the potential to examine the resistlessness of the narrative of history in America.

Illegitimate Isabel, whose childhood memories are fragments of an ocean voyage, a madhouse, a house in the woods, and a gentleman whom she presumes to be her father, is a creature of boundaries, almost, in fact, supernatural. Brian Higgins and Hershel Parker call her "an embodiment of the Unconscious," and there is something undefined and primal about her.[10] Devoid of primary relationships, she is unformed humanity, the exact opposite of her pampered brother. Isabel is the alternate discourse, the outsider who transcends cultural norms and speaks, as her mystical music makes clear, from beyond language. She is civilized, brought into the cultural symbolic, after she has already begun, vaguely, to perceive; she is, that is, brought in relatively late and as an outsider, which privileges her perspective on the values and conventions of Saddle Meadows, a perspective to which the socially indoctrinated Pierre has no access. Isabel invites Pierre to the margins of his own discourse. And since "adultery," both word and deed, has consigned Isabel to the margins, Pierre can begin his heroic inspection of social convention with an exploration of this particular prohibition, specifically of the inviolability of the home and "the name of the father" (the law, in Lacan's formulation).

But, as the narrator alerts us from the onset, Pierre resists marginality, and Isabel promotes not inspection but submission. Pierre first encounters Isabel at a sewing circle that his mother patronizes; when they see each other, she faints. Pierre responds passionately but nevertheless passively: "A wild, bewildering, and incomprehensible curiosity had seized him, to know something definite of that face. To this curiosity . . . he entirely surrendered himself" (58). The narrator continues to insist on Pierre's passivity, suggesting that "the face . . . had . . . fully possessed him for its own" (66) with a "mystic tyranny" (63) that Pierre cannot question. The "tyranny" of Isabel's face derives in fact from the internalized source into which, as we have seen, Pierre eagerly incorporates her; it is that script, rather than its human embodiment, that dominates Pierre.

The narrator offers an alternate narrative, a "history [which] goes forward and goes backward, as occasion calls" (67), that disrupts the progressive narrative of Pierre's discovery to propose an alternate narrative of his self-damnation. "Nimble center, circumference elastic you must have" (67), suggests the elusively unreliable narrator, presumably in order to understand the unperceived narratives that manifest themselves as resistless forces, like the resistless force of Emerson's disavowed historicism in the passage cited above. And it is precisely Pierre's failure to acknowledge this apparently ineluctable narrative of identity that leads him to "directly plagiarize[] from his own experiences" (352) in a text that was to mark his declaration of independence.

Isabel does not inaugurate Pierre's break with the past, with the arbitrary symbolism of Saddle Meadows, because he refamiliarizes her and draws her into the prewritten manuscript of his identity. She is, of course, the "sister [who] had been omitted from the text," the inscribed call to heroism that Pierre's legacy required him eventually to enact. But she also inherits the legacy of Pierre's interaction with his mother, who rhetorically prefigures Isabel with her fictional epithet of "sister." And, as the narrator stresses, Pierre rehearses even the pattern of his interaction with Isabel in his relationship with his mother.

What Isabel wills, though subtly articulated, replaces what Mrs. Glendinning demands; Pierre simply transfers his allegiance:

> Far as we blind moles can see, man's life seems but an acting upon mysterious hints; it is somehow hinted to us to do thus or thus. For surely no mere mortal who has at all gone down into himself will ever pretend that his slightest thought or act solely originates in his own defined identity. . . . [So Pierre's] nominal conversion of a sister into a wife . . . might have been found in the previous conversational conversion of a mother into a sister; for hereby he had habituated his voice and manner to a certain fictitiousness in one of the closest domestic relations of life. (209)

Pierre's relations with women appear to follow the pattern established by his mother, one that leaves no room for the autonomy that authorship requires. And Pierre is "no mere mortal who has gone down at all into himself"; he is neither perceptive nor analytical about his motivations. Mrs. Glendinning, we learn, returns Pierre's "romantic filial love . . . [with] triumphant maternal pride" precisely be-

cause "in the clearcut lineaments and noble air of the son, [she] saw her own graces strangely translated into the opposite sex" (9), because, it seems, he is the reflecting pool to her Narcissus. And that is how Pierre learns to love, as we see in the opening scene with Lucy, in which "the two stood silently but ardently eying each other, beholding mutual reflections of a boundless admiration and love" (7). The only reflection of which Pierre seems capable is mirroring, and he never thinks to question the fictional self that he sees thus reflected.

Insofar as Isabel resembles their father, and presumably the resemblance is strong enough to convince an albeit receptive Pierre, she must resemble—or mirror—Pierre himself. Pierre, then, does not see difference so much as similarity when he looks at Isabel. His vision constitutes the dialectical identification with the other that, in a Lacanian formulation, is preformed in the mirror-stage. The narrator uses a literal mirror to suggest that Isabel's mirroring could still jar Pierre into a contemplation of the alienation implicit in the mirror-stage of identity-formation, an alienation, that is, that can potentially elucidate the contours of Pierre's cultural subjectivity. Pierre "started at a figure in the opposite mirror. It bore the outline of Pierre, but now strangely filled with features transformed, and unfamiliar to him" (76). But such heroism is not for Pierre, as he "vainly struggle[s] with the incomprehensible power that possessed him" (76). Pierre struggles in vain, a futile effort against the vanity and the narcissism through which he repossesses Isabel as a reflection of himself; he is, it seems, incapable of any more profound self-reflection. The narrator reduces Pierre to the "umpire" between "two antagonistic agencies within him" (77) and undercuts even this degree of psychological agency with the observation that "Pierre was not arguing Fixed Fate and Free Will, now; Fixed Fate and Free Will were arguing him, and Fixed Fate got the better in the debate" (216).

Pierre's decision to turn to authorship is intrinsic to the nature of his struggle. The impulse to write, to, as he conceives of it, "gospelize the world anew," has its psychological analogue in the impulse to define oneself, to be both original and authoritative. This notion of authorship charts a departure from the theological universe in which imitation enables one to approach the divinity; imitation becomes, in this secularized world, "plagiarism," a failure to resist the authorizing discourse. And yet, as we have seen, Pierre's rhetoric belies his intention to resist; his very conception of his struggle to possess his own narrative, to authorize himself, is paradoxical and self-defeating:

> Henceforth I will know nothing but Truth; glad Truth, or sad Truth; I will know what *is*, and do what my deepest angel dictates . . . . Oh! falsely guided in the days of my Joy, am I now truly led in this night of my grief?—I will be a raver, and none shall stay me! I will lift my hand in fury, for am I not struck? I will be bitter in my breath, for is not this cup of gall? Thou Black Knight, that with visor down, thus confrontest me, and mockest at me;—I will be impious, for piety hath juggled me, and taught me to revere, where I should

spurn. From all idols, I tear all veils; henceforth I will see the hidden things; and live right out in my own hidden life!—Now I feel that nothing but Truth can move me so. (80-81)

Even at this moment, the height of his potential for self-authorization, Pierre imagines himself following "dictates," and no longer guided, he is nevertheless passively "led." Similarly, when he resolves henceforth to be impious, he juxtaposes impiety and piety in a dualistic opposition that affirms rather than negates the symbolic order from which he seeks his independence, as impiety assumes the very categories by which the culture defines "piety." In his transcendentalism, Pierre deifies "Truth," an absolute that he seeks as if it were a grail, and he resorts to images of madness, gall, and Black Knights that bespeak a marked tendency towards romanticism and that are perhaps even plagiarized from boyhood readings. His authorship has less than auspicious beginnings.

Pierre is, after all, fundamentally a believer, and he adheres fundamentally to the letter of the law. He believes the letter in which Isabel proclaims herself his sister, and he subscribes to what Donald Pease calls "the revolutionary mythos," the ahistoricism of the nation's perpetual breaking with the past.[11] Pierre removes his father's picture from the wall and, with an impressive faith in the power of the symbolic, declares, "I will no longer have a father" (Emerson's country with "no past"). But, from the first, Pierre's country was far more motherland than fatherland. The narrator again underscores Pierre's lack of preparation for the author's task:

> Nor now, though profoundly sensible that his whole previous moral being was overturned, and that for him the fair structure of the world must, in some then unknown way, be entirely rebuilded again, from the lowermost corner stone up; nor now did Pierre torment himself with the thought of that last desolation; and how the desolate place was to be made flourishing again. He seemed to feel that in his deepest soul, lurked an indefinite but potential faith, which could rule in the interregnum of all hereditary beliefs, and circumstantial persuasions; not wholly, he felt, was his soul in anarchy. The indefinite regent had assumed the scepter as its right; and Pierre was not entirely given up to his grief's utter pillage and sack. (113)

As the abundance of passive constructions and the imagery of monarchy make clear, Pierre chooses to substitute one absolute code for another rather than remain in doubt. He thus avoids the torment that he should inevitably feel under the circumstances. Pierre cannot tolerate the lack of structure implicit in his rebellion, and his metaphors belie his intention to create truly new forms in the place of the old, invalidating his declaration. Pierre, as a believer, must replace one faith with at least the "potential" of another. Insofar as Pierre is representative, Melville undermines the paradox evident in American rhetoric. The narrator makes apparent that the form of faith in the values of his inheritance belies the content of the legacy, as he rejects his Republican heritage in his preference of monarchy to self-

government and his Puritan heritage in his failure to make the desert flourish.[12] In a time of profound need of cultural affirmation, the impending Civil War's threat to the Union, the cornerstone of national identity, Pierre stands only as a reflection of the nation's failure.

Discrepancies between beliefs and discoveries that contradict them, such as Glendinning Senior's adultery, precipitate psychological crises, which, in turn, potentially facilitate insight. But as Victor Turner has pointed out in his discussion of liminality, a cultural analogue of such individual crises, the moment gives rise as well to the temptation to retreat more deeply into the sanctity of prescribed values.[13] As Nina Baym suggests, Pierre's crisis extends to grave "doubts about language" (910).[14] "Oh, hitherto," he laments, "I have but piled up words; bought books, and bought some small experiences, and builded me in libraries." Yet, just as his recognition of language and literature as the transmitters of his internalized script of cultural identity seems inevitable, Pierre again retreats into text, concluding his thought with "now I sit down and read" (110). And he similarly continues, "Oh, men are jailers all; jailers of themselves, and in Opinion's world ignorantly hold their noblest part a captive to their vilest; as disguised royal Charles when caught by peasants" (110). The metaphoric addendum, in which Pierre unconsciously preserves the equation of class distinction and nobility, distinctly undercuts the apparent sense of the initial observation, which, if followed logically, would have called the term of the metaphor into question.

Pierre's susceptibility to Isabel is, as we have seen, not so much to Isabel as to the script into which he incorporates her. Consequently, he ignores the authorial challenge that she embodies. The social isolation of her formative years brings her acquisition of language into particular focus; she is conscious of the meaning of words and of her exclusion from meaningful discourse, especially from the narrative principles that provide coherence to the stories of more socialized selves. "I can not but talk wildly upon so wild a theme" (138), she explains, as she recounts the disjointed and impressionistic details of her strange autobiography. And her meditation on the word "father" illuminates the social contours of both the term and the role:

> . . . though at the time I sometimes called him my father, and the people of the house also called him so, sometimes when speaking of him to me; yet—partly, I suppose, because of the extraordinary secludedness of my previous life—I did not then join in my mind with the word father, all those peculiar associations which the term ordinarily inspires in children. The word father only seemed a word of general love and endearment to me—little or nothing more; it did not seem to involve any claims of any sort, one way or the other. (173)

Isabel potentially affords Pierre the opportunity to examine social constructions that he had internalized unconsciously as truths. "[G]iven Melville's Emerson-derived notion of language as proceeding from a divine Author or Namer," argues Baym, "the loss of belief in an Absolute entailed the loss not only of truth in the universe but also of coherence and meaning in language."[15] Isabel actually goes further, as she points to a realm beyond language, a chaotic world that lacks coherence and meaning in general, a liminal space that temporarily illuminates the role of language in such social constructions.

At first, Isabel resists names. As she tells Pierre, "I did not ask the name of my father; for I could have had no motive to hear him named, except to individualize the person who was so peculiarly kind to me" (173-74). *"The gentleman"* and *"my father"* suffice as such particularizations for Isabel, who, furthermore, feels "there can be no perfect peace in individualness" (142). For Isabel, "individualness" means exclusion. She longs instead "to feel [her]self drank up into the pervading spirit animating all things" (142). Isabel speaks here for an alternate meaning of "union" in the "union of individuals" that United States ideology paradoxically espouses. Isabel's republic of spirit annihilates distinction; "union" means self-dissolution and is, clearly, incompatible with individualism. But "individualism," on the other hand, means exclusion and, for Isabel, has never translated even potentially into "opportunity." The will to belong, to be a part of society, supersedes even the desire to exist.

Significantly, "the gentleman's" absence prompts Isabel to forego her resolution and discover his name. Naming, and language in general, become presences that both signify and are initiated by absence.[16] On discovering writing on the handkerchief that "the gentleman" drops on his last visit to her, Isabel resolves to learn to read "in order," she tells Pierre, "that of [her]self she might learn the meaning of those faded characters" (175). Isabel's obvious social motivation again makes explicit the socializing qualities of language as it bears witness to her susceptibility to socialization. Even her (suicidal) longing to dissolve into "the pervading spirit animating all things," as we have seen, attests to a desire to be included.

Thus socialized, Isabel surrenders her agency to become a conduit for "thoughts [that] well up in [her]." She protests:

> I can not alter them, for I had nothing to do with putting them in my mind, and I never affect any thoughts, and I never adulterate any thoughts; but when I speak, think forth from the tongue, speech being sometimes before the thought; so, often, my own tongue teaches me new things. (147)

What Pierre mistakes for mysticism is in fact Isabel's submission to the "pervading spirit," the social force. Her tongue teaches her new thoughts precisely because of her submission to the process of socialization. Language dictates thought. Isabel is not a teacher who can consciously lead Pierre to the margins of discourse; rather, she is an example who dwells on, and so illuminates, those margins. She apologizes for, rather than celebrates, the incoherence of her narrative. Initially, this incoherence disturbs Pierre, who

[strives] to condense her mysterious haze into some definite and comprehensible shape. He could not but infer that the feeling of bewilderment, which she had so often hinted of during their interview, had caused her continually to go astray from the straight line of her narration; and finally to end it in an abrupt and enigmatical obscurity. But he also felt assured, that as this was entirely unintended and now, doubtless, regretted by herself, so their coming interview would help clear up much of this mysteriousness.. . . . (162)

Pierre resists the discomfort of Isabel's "bewilderment" and seeks the familiar "straight line of . . . narration" just as he clings to his faith in the fundamental values that have been instilled in him. Such narration, as Hayden White suggests, privileges causality, a principle that is particularly suited to an ideology of individualism.[17]

Gradually, however, the possibility of heroism tempts Pierre into an attraction precisely to the "bewilderment" that disturbs him. Pierre "saw, or seemed to see, that it was not so much Isabel who had by her wild idiosyncrasies mystified the narration of her history, as it was the essential and unavoidable mystery of her history itself, which had invested Isabel with such wonderful enigmas to him" (165). Unwittingly, Pierre is drawn to the paradox that Isabel embodies. The incoherence of her "narration" stems from her social exclusion; Isabel attempts to describe her experience, but there is no language that can convey the experience of illegitimacy in terms that are not social. Isabel makes every effort to use words to describe an experience that is beyond words. She attempts, in other words, to describe the outside (social exclusion) from within it, as Michel Foucault tries, with equal lack of success, to describe madness in its own terms rather than from within the language of reason.[18] Pierre has now reached the brink of another, perhaps the fundamental, social paradox; however, as we have seen, Pierre retreats from paradox. Isabel, or the experience of Isabel, "fill[s . . . Pierre] with nameless wonderings" (141), impels him beyond language. But instead of pursuing such wonderings to the margins of discourse, Pierre removes Isabel from the sphere of human experience. "[T]o him, Isabel wholly soared out of the realms of mortalness, and for him became transfigured in the highest heaven of uncorrupted Love" (170).

Pierre's idealization of Isabel also prevents his having to acknowledge his sexual attraction to her—and the incestuous implications of that attraction. Incest, which Freud and Lévi-Strauss both locate in the boundary between nature and culture, presents the possibility of ultimate defiance.[19] An incestuous relationship would allow Pierre to call into question the rudiments of civilization, the taboo from which all convention stems. But again Pierre retreats from the margins of discourse, this time into a veneration that enables him to deny his desire. Isabel, again, exists only as a character in a pre-written script. And Pierre rebels in accordance with his two favorite texts, Dante's *Inferno* and Shakespeare's *Hamlet*. Significantly, the heroes of both these works end their political rebellion and their metaphysical quests in the self-surrender of either veneration or, literally, self-destruction.

The narrator makes apparent that Pierre's reluctance to venture to the margins of discourse has at its root his inability to recognize paradox. He[20] admonishes Pierre:

> Tear thyself open, and read there the confounding story of thy blind doltishness! Thy two grand resolutions—the public acknowledgement of Isabel, and the charitable withholding of her existence from thy own mother,—these are impossible adjuncts.—Likewise, thy so magnanimous purpose to screen thy father's honorable memory from reproach, and thy other intention, the open vindication of thy fraternalness to Isabel,—these also are impossible adjuncts. And the having individually entertained four such resolves, without perceiving that once brought together, they all mutually expire; this, this ineffable folly, Pierre, brands thee in the forehead for an unaccountable infatuate. (202-3)

The narrator counsels Pierre, first of all, to recognize his own textuality—and social identity—and hence to perceive the paralysis to which his denial of agency has consigned him. In other words, the narrator advocates a course that would lead to Pierre's self-authorization. Pierre, however, prefers to retreat not only from the margins of discourse, but also from Saddle Meadows, as though a physical rather than a mental space has entrapped him. "Henceforth," he declares, "cast-out Pierre hath no paternity, and no past; and since the Future is one blank to all; therefore, twice-disinherited Pierre stands untrammeledly his ever-present self!—free to do his own self-will and present fancy to whatever end!" (235). Pierre would rather be the victim, the cast-out, than accept responsibility for his leaving, and his third person self-reference further stresses his preference to be someone else's character.

His flight to the city begins almost as an epic journey to the underworld, which, as in Dante (and his predecessors), frames the (ritualized) quest for identity in the inspection of the old order that leads to the institution of a new one. The journey begins in silence:

> All profound things, and emotions of things are preceded and attended by Silence. What a silence is that with which the pale bride precedes the responsive *I will,* to the priest's solemn question, *Wilt thou have this man for thy husband?* In silence, too, the wedded hands are clasped. . . . Silence is the only Voice of our God.
> . . .
> Now word was spoken by its inmates, as the coach bearing our young Enthusiast, Pierre, and his mournful party, sped forth through the dim dawn into the deep midnight, which still occupied, unrepulsed, the hearts of the old woods through which the road wound, very shortly after quitting the village. (240)

The marriage imagery heightens the suggestions of incest and adultery that Pierre's companions, Isabel and Delly, an adulteress, embody. And Silence, perhaps actively resisting language at the margins of cultural discourse, suggests the possibility for speaking against the arbitrary terms of that discourse. Silence precedes marriage, the ritual that marks the assumption of a new role in the social order, as though

possibility holds its breath before committing itself to the choice that marks participation in the social order, as though there were still some potential for resistance. But "Silence" becomes "no words," an alternate presence represented as absence, and the coach a prison whose "inmates" find no alternative to their captivity. "Silence is the only Voice of our God" suggestively intimates an absence that Pierre, and presumably his companions, cannot tolerate.

In fact, Pierre leaves precisely to maintain the symbolic order of Saddle Meadows. His fictitious marriage is not specifically intended as an act of defiance, but rather as an attempt to "legitimize" Isabel, to bring her into the realm of social conventions from which she has felt excluded. Pierre fails to recognize the potentially defiant implications of his departure; he leaves Saddle Meadows because to remain would be to leave Isabel outside society or to expose his father's adultery (itself a defiance of social conventions) or to commit the defiance of an incestuous marriage. His taking the adulteress, Delly, with him, in effect removes her from the eyes of Saddle Meadows. "Our young Enthusiast," ever the believer, is indeed an "inmate," imprisoned by his inability to transcend what he can no longer wholly accept, an inability that finds expression in an impotence extending as well to his inability to write.

Chaos and dream logic dominate the underworlds of epic. Apparently at the brink of the underworld, Pierre's "thoughts were very dark and wild; for a space there was rebellion and horrid anarchy and infidelity in his soul" (240). But, as the preceding paragraphs have made clear, Pierre cannot sustain such rebellion. Even here his thoughts appear to be at a distance from himself, almost as if the anarchy had invaded his soul, and he is not its source. Significantly, the narrator compares him to a priest of whom it is told that a "temporary mood . . . [once] invaded [his] heart. . . . The Evil One suddenly propounded to him the possibility of the mere moonshine of the Christian Religion. Just such now was the mood of Pierre; to him the Evil One propounded the possibility of the mere moonshine of all his self-renouncing Enthusiasm" (240-41). Like Pierre, the priest is the passive victim of a mood that he personifies as the devil. But the comparison further illustrates that Pierre has turned his self-renunciation into a kind of faith, that his actions are motivated by self-renunciation rather than self-assertion, and that he has therefore rejected psychological authorship.

The priest, who had been in the middle of administering the sacrament, "by instant and earnest prayer—closing his two eyes, with his two hands still holding the sacramental bread—. . . . had vanquished the impious Devil" (241). In other words, the priest holds on to the symbol and so dispels his doubts, which he has already successfully projected onto a personified other. He applies a preexisting system to his situation and submits himself to it—"these [tenets] were the indestructible anchors which still held the priest to his firm Faith's rock, when the sudden storm raised by the Evil One assailed him" (241). The narrator frames Pierre's dilemma in the context of the priest's:

> But Pierre—where could *he* find the Church, the monument, the Bible, which unequivocally said to him— "Go on; thou art in the Right; I endorse thee all over; go on."—So the difference between the Priest and Pierre was herein:—with the priest it was a matter, whether certain bodiless thoughts of his were true or not true; but with Pierre it was a question whether certain vital acts of his were right or wrong. (241)

And "right or wrong" again images his dilemma as a dualistic opposition that depends on a given social order. Pierre is far more eager to read than to write.

As an act of reading (Isabel's letter) begins his challenge, so an act of reading accompanies his doubt. "When, first entering the coach, Pierre had pressed his hand upon the cushioned seat to steady his way, some crumpled leaves of paper had met his fingers. He had instinctively clutched them; and the same strange clutching mood of his soul which had prompted that instinctive act, did also prevail in causing him now to retain the crumpled paper in his hand for an hour or more of that wonderful intense silence . . ." (240). Again, Pierre longs to anchor his drifting mind; he receives the paper passively and then clutches it instinctively. Pierre prefers to surrender his subjectivity to whatever is available, and the paper suits his purposes. His lack of consciousness makes it seem as though the paper had arrived magically in his grasp; "[h]e knew not how it had got there, or whence it had come, though himself had closed his own grip upon it" (242). The use of the objective "himself" further signals Pierre's characterization in a narrative he is unaware of authoring and so cannot resist. Pierre reads as an alternative to authorship: "more to force his mind away from the dark realities of things than from any other motive, Pierre finally tried his best to plunge himself into the pamphlet" (243).

Plunging, too, bespeaks a suicidal urge, an act of self-annihilation, an alternative to the self-reflection of which we have already seen Pierre consistently incapable. Here his plunge is clearly an attempt to escape from the questioning process that his emotional anarchy has begun to inspire rather than to continue to probe for truth. And plunging throughout the novel follows on turmoil, as after his first encounter with Isabel, "Pierre, gladly plunging into this welcome current of talk[,] was enabled to attend his mother home without furnishing further cause for her concern or wonderment" (60). Subsequently, plunging becomes an image of damnation in *Pierre*. Mrs. Glendinning, alarmed at the change that has come over Pierre consequent to his meeting Isabel, declares, "Let him tell me of himself, or let him slide adown!" (157). As if in fulfillment of her curse, the next section of the book begins, "Pierre plunged deep into the woods . . ." (157). And Pierre's efforts to convince Isabel to join him as his supposed wife in the city again instill plunging with forebodings of doom, "Already have I plunged! now thou canst not stay upon the bank" (227). Pierre opts continually for

self-abandonment. His "plunge" into Plinlimmon's pamphlet becomes his Narcissus's dive, his unwitting attempt to possess himself which ironically results in his self-destruction.

And like Narcissus's pond, Plinlimmon's pamphlet casts back an image that Pierre fails to recognize as his own. Plinlimmon claims to have found "the talismanic Secret [that] . . . reconcile[s] this world with [man's] own soul" (244). The "talismanic Secret," as the narrator explains, is the solution to the paradox of idealism that underlies Christian society:

> Sooner or later in this life, the earnest, or enthusiastic youth comes to know, and more or less appreciate this startling solecism:—That while, as the grand condition of acceptance to God, Christianity calls upon all men to renounce this world; yet by all odds the most Mammonish parts of this world—Europe and America—are owned by none but professed Christian nations, who glory in the owning, and seem to have some reason therefore. (243)

"Solecism" subtly emphasizes the role rhetoric plays in this grand deception, in the resolution, that is, of a paradox. And this discovery, analogous to Pierre's discovery about his father's morality, provokes a quest that could well lead to authorship. The young enthusiast's uncertainty, according to the narrator, leads to an

> earnest reperusal of the Gospels: the intense self-absorption into that greatest real miracle of all religions, the Sermon on the Mount. From that divine mount, to all earnest-loving youths, flows an inexhaustible soul-melting stream of tenderness . . . sentences which embody all the love of the Past, and all the love which can be imagined in any conceivable Future. Such emotions as that Sermon raises in the enthusiastic heart; such emotions all youthful hearts refuse to ascribe to humanity as their origin. This is of God! cries the heart, and in that cry ceases all inquisition. (244)

Here the young enthusiast, like Pierre, refuses to probe and instead plunges into the text to find answers that will end the inquisition and, thus, any possibility of doubt and autonomy. Specifically, he turns to the Sermon on the Mount in which Christ speaks with authority, not as the scriber. And indeed it is as an author, through his sentences, that Christ seduces the Christian soul into submission. His sentences emblematize completion and contain the language of the potential author (rebel), who is condemned to repeat, or plagiarize, an authorizing discourse. One who repeats is, of course, reading and not writing a text.

The pamphlet portrays a provisional world and the arbitrariness of signification. Plinlimmon suggests that while attention to the ideals keeps man from "run[ning] into utter selfishness and human demonism" (251), absolute adherence to them requires that one "commit[] a sort of suicide as to the practical things of this world . . . and, finding by experience that this is utterly impossible; in his despair, he is too apt to run clean away into all manner of moral abandonment, self-deceit, and hypocrisy. . . ." (250-51). Plinlimmon elucidates the oppositional duality through which Pierre consistently affirms rather than questions, plunges into rather than probes, the symbolic order.

But Pierre, who even rebels "in obedience," albeit "in obedience to the loftiest behest of his soul" (245), reads the pamphlet "merely to drown himself" (245). Reading, "he felt a great interest awakened in him . . . but the central conceit refused to become clear to him" (245). Pierre waits for an illumination that would undermine the narrative principle that underlies his unwitting self-definition. Pierre's pamphlet, which is literally a fragment, offers fragmentation as an alternative to the inevitable plagiarism of a narrative identity. The uncertainty that Plinlimmon regards as a condition of earthly existence could easily translate into a rejection of the "truths" of social convention, prompting a rejection of the principle of coherence that governs Western identity and masks the experience of the fragmentation that promotes introspection.

The narrative, at this juncture, blurs the distinction between itself and Plinlimmon's pamphlet, as the narrator enters into a treatise in the first person:

> That profound Silence, that only Voice of our God, which I before spoke of; from that divine thing without a name, those impostor philosophers pretend somehow to have got an answer; which is as absurd, as though they should say they had got water out of a stone; for how can a man get a Voice out of Silence? (245)

The narrator's obvious subjectivity, which disrupts the text's narrative coherence, leaves the reader with an uneasy feeling, hinted at, but less dramatically presented elsewhere in the text. If the narrator has become so resolutely a character, then who is left to guide us through the profoundly disturbing collapse of Pierre? And what principle will ensure that the events of the text will eventually make sense to us? As Ahab's vision threatens to dissolve Ishmael, and as, in fact, Ishmael's ultimate internalization of Ahab does mark a sort of Pyrrhic victory for the captain's "madness," so Pierre's confused resolve seems to provoke the narrator into a narrative surrender. He exposes the relativity of the narrative consciousness by which he has both understood and undermined Pierre.

Insofar as we come to see the narrator's perspective as an alternate narrative (as, that is, *an* other, not *the* other narrative), then perhaps Silence can indeed speak to the attuned reader. The narrative unravelling that follows undermines narrative authority and alerts the reader to the possibility of an alternate discourse. Silence (and its counterpart, meaningless noise) emerges in resistance to narrative and meaningful language, not as an absence but as an alternate presence, the *embodiment,* perhaps, of possibility. "[E]verything written," writes Maurice Blanchot, "has, for the one who writes it, the greatest meaning possible, but has also this meaning, that it is a meaning bound to chance, that it is nonmeaning."[21] Silence presents the continuous

possibility of an alternate meaning and so becomes itself an alternate meaning; it means that there are always other possible meanings. Insofar as the narrator's recovery of Pierre's unperceived narrative is itself a narrative act, *Pierre* opens itself to the possibility of a Derridean deconstruction, a reduction to noise. But as the narrator's narrative does succeed in recovering Pierre's self-annihilation in his narrative, and as Silence emerges as *a* and not *the* Voice in the text, and, finally, as Melville never fully undermines Pierre's representational status in "Young America," *Pierre* emerges as a multivocal critique of the resistless narratives that society and individuals unwittingly create and then live by.

Emblematic of such narrative reflexivity, Plinlimmon's pamphlet, which offers horological fragmentation as the earthly counterpart to chronometric silence, calls the implicitly progressive and causal form of narrative into question. Pierre is seduced by the apparent profundity of the reductive pamphlet and, especially, by the promise of consolation that the torn pamphlet never finally offers, but, as we have seen, Pierre is unable to break through the mirror image to the process of symbolization. The mirror is, for him, a Narcissus's pool in which he does not even recognize the image as himself. "For," as the narrator explains, "in this case, to comprehend, is himself to condemn himself" (246). The narrator's grammatical clumsiness itself mirrors the "highly inconvenient and uncomfortable" (246) task of such self-condemnation.

Pierre's "comprehension" (understanding) of the pamphlet would expose the futility of his quest for coherence and consistency, but "comprehension" also suggests engulfment. To "comprehend" anything is to enclose it, to impose coherence on fragmentation, and hence to "condemn" oneself to reject the possibility of self-authorization, which depends upon the perception of contradictions that disrupt coherence. The narrator continues his rhetorical performance as he retreats into the more "convenient" and "comfortable" narrative consciousness and reduces "comprehension" to the single sense of "understanding" with his assurance that "men are only made to comprehend things which they comprehended before" (246). To complicate this reading, to pause at the awkwardness that attests to textual mischief, to read, that is, in a way that is not governed by the rules of traditional narrative is to make visible the process of exclusion that is endemic to meaning and thus instigate self-authorization. Melville suggestively sends Pierre into New York wearing the pamphlet unwittingly in the lining of his coat.

Pierre's sojourn in New York is, appropriately, characterized by mirrors in which all difference is obscured beneath the unrecognized reflections of himself. The text itself mirrors earlier texts in an act of reflection that, the converse of Pierre's, elucidates rather than obscures. Pierre arrives in the city intending to find his cousin, Glendinning Stanly, whose name is the inverse of Pierre's ("pierre," French for stone; "stan," Anglo-Saxon). Lucy's predecessor in Pierre's affections, Glen even served as Pierre's earlier romantic mirror. As in Poe's "William Wilson," the double becomes increasingly the "conscience," or cultural voice (and Glendinning is even the name of one of Wilson's dupes). Whereas Glen Stanly is both real and villainous in *Pierre,* the allusion to Poe's story forces us to consider Pierre's role both in his own self-destruction and in, to some degree, his vilifying Glen. Nevertheless, Glen does assume Pierre's legacy, as he inherits Saddle Meadows and almost even Lucy. Both "stones" are, finally, equally unyielding, and the monuments of early friendship become, ironically, each other's tombstone. Pierre ultimately murders his cousin, ambiguously in self-defense, when the latter comes to retrieve Lucy, who has come to the city to join Pierre despite his "marriage" to Isabel. Like William Wilson's, Pierre's "murder" is equally a suicide. In murdering his counterpart, the cultural self he has rejected, he murders his whole self (literally, his ultimate suicide in prison).

It is tempting here to see in Pierre and Glen and analogue for the Confederacy and the Union, which, unable to compromise, face destruction and which, furthermore, fail to recognize their mirroring. What neither Pierre nor Glen can tolerate, it seems, is any violation of what Michael Kammen calls "the cult of consensus."[22] When Pierre, in quest of his kinsman, meets a "scarlet woman," Melville evokes Hawthorne's "My Kinsman, Major Molineux," in which a youth in pre-Revolutionary America comes to the city in search of his uncle, who he hopes will help him make his fortune. The only person who accosts him is a prostitute in scarlet, who tempts him into consensus, which he doesn't understand until his uncle passes, tarred and feathered, and Robin finds himself laughing uncontrollably, caught up in the contagion of "revolutionary" fervor. He also learns that "one man [may] have several voices . . . as well as two complexions," a lesson that exposes the ambiguity of the American Revolution to a listener who, like Pierre, does not seem fully able to comprehend it but is in fact comprehended by it.

The narrator pauses, after Pierre's arrival in New York, to begin "Young America in Literature" with a discussion of historiography:

> Among the various conflicting modes of writing history, there would seem to be two grand practical distinctions, under which all the rest must subordinately range. By the one mode, all contemporaneous circumstances, facts, and events must be set down contemporaneously; by the other, they are only to be set down as the general stream of the narrative shall dictate; for matters which are kindred in time, may be very irrelative in themselves. I elect neither of these; I am careless of either; both are well enough in their way; I write precisely as I please. (286)

When the narrator classifies historiography, which he assigns to either of two genres (what Hayden White would call the annals or narrative forms of historical discourse), he both explains and illustrates how exclusion underlies meaning.[23] Cultural convention is transmitted through the process of categorization which organizes data into a co-

herent and "meaningful" reality. Categories operate according to a principle of exclusion insofar as "meaning" restricts the possibility of endless interpretation.[24] Even the form of historical discourse, according to White, determines the extent to which "reality wears the mask of a meaning, the completeness and fullness of which we can only *imagine,* never experience. Insofar as historical stories can be completed, can be given narrative closure, can be shown to have had a *plot* all along, they give to reality the odor of the *ideal.*"[25]

Classification, while not itself a narrative act, is a restriction, a form of closure, and, as such, it anticipates Pierre's attempt to impose meaning on his life by narrativizing events. His effort thus to "gospelize the world anew" bespeaks the idealization that underwrites (and undercuts) his authorship. For Pierre, authorship is an absolute identity, a commitment or achievement which, therefore, entails a choice among rather than an inspection of the categories that are imposed on him through the internalized script of cultural identity. The narrator's transcendental ahistoricism, according to which his subjectivity organizes his data, recalls Pierre's declaration of independence in an act of mirroring that illustrates the failure to resist categorization, which is the goal of self-authorization.

This passage is a narrative "act" in another sense as well. It is a performance that enables the inspection that it apparently forestalls. Nina Baym views Pierre's authorship as a textual rupture in which "the uneasy union of narrator with tale dissolves." The fissure represents, in Baym's analysis, Melville's attempt to restore Pierre "to the center of the narrative."[26] Perhaps, however, as the reader is supposed to trip over such awkwardnesses as have previously been discussed, so the reader is meant to pause at the disruption marked by this juncture. The narrator willfully contradicts himself in his claim to transcendental ahistoricism in order to underscore the principle of exclusion by which Pierre converts the process of self-authorization into the ideal of authorship. Pierre's "authorship" is neither sudden nor precipitous; the consequences of Pierre's obvious textuality have been, from the onset, the dominant subject of the narrative. The narrator's intrusion indeed disrupts the narrative flow, but the reader's discomfort should instigate a questioning process. The passage illustrates how Pierre symbolizes both the *process* and the consequences of his symbolization.

In addition, Baym attributes Melville's "generic drift" to his conviction that genre, as a manifestation of literary convention, restricted rather than expanded possibilities.[27] She reads the passage that introduces Pierre's authorship as evidence of one of the central problems of the text: Melville's "fiction got in the way of the direct statement that [he] was seeking to make" (919). Yet Melville's "generic drift" calls into question the principles of classification by which, as in the passage in question, we organize the data of our world. Melville's intentional disturbance of such boundaries forces a consideration—and a reconsideration—of the effect of those principles. Perhaps the chaos of Pierre, because of which a majority of the text's critics cite the failure of Melville's project, clarifies rather than obscures the central tenets of the work.

Pierre is not, as Richard Brodhead suggests, "a draught of a draught, in a . . . desperate sense"; it does not "trace its author's discovery of the impossibility of his own creative project . . . [nor] rule out even the minimal faith in his own work that the task of revision would require of him."[28] In fact, *Pierre* is an endless series of re-visions, that, as I have suggested, compel the reader's participation, and its open-endedness completes the task that Melville had begun in *Moby Dick. Pierre* is neither historical nor ahistorical, but in some sense the history of ahistoricism. What makes the text so difficult is Melville's struggle to expose, and so to check, the compulsion to repeat the unconscious narrative of one's identity that follows on a declaration of independence. For such repetition is, as we have seen, the "comprehension" (death) of the author. To turn comprehension/engulfing into comprehension/ understanding (mastery), requires repetition to bring the narrative of identity into consciousness. Undermining narrative authority, Melville does not, as Ann Douglas suggests, "allow[] his readers no real way into the novel," but in fact allows them no real way out.[29]

The narrator, in one of the more sardonic moments in the text, startles the reader with the impossibility of the whole project:

> The world is forever babbling of originality; but there never yet was an original man, in the sense intended by the world; the first man himself—who according to the Rabbins was also the first author—not being an original; the only original author being God. (302)

As the narrator's theological stance should be, by this time, at least suspect, the sense of this declaration is unclear. But, psychologically, it re-visions authorship as a quest, an analytic process (rather than an end), to which the narrator opposes Pierre's pride, for "Pierre was proud; and a proud man . . . likes to feel himself in himself, and not by reflection in others" (304). As we have seen, a reflection in others, "mirroring," provides both the source of identity and the potential for its inspection. But as we have also seen, Pierre fails to recognize his mirroring and so succumbs to it.

Pierre declares, "I will gospelize the world anew, and show them deeper secrets than the Apocalypse!—I will write it, I will write it!" (319). His use of "gospelize" suggests that he cannot reject the basic tenets he thinks he has overthrown. Pierre wants to be the instrument through which an absolute eternal truth is filtered; he wants to transcribe rather than write. He is not only Ahab's heir, as critics have suggested, but Ishmael's as well.[30] When Ishmael ends *Moby Dick* with Rachel's searching for her children, he paraphrases a gospel that itself repeats Jeremiah in fulfillment of the prophecy. Repetition, in Matthew, is authorizing and authenticating. But in *Moby Dick,* it is a reflection of Ishmael's internalization of Ahab, his

need, that is, to find meaning in chance events, such as his survival. Ishmael, traditionally considered a foil for Ahab's megalomaniacal acts of interpretation, is in fact finally, although subtly, seduced by Ahab's point of view; his mirroring ultimately submits, to a large extent, to a reflection of rather than on Ahab.

We can perhaps understand Pierre's plagiarism specifically in conjunction with his own desire for originality. The narrator opposes "plagiarism" not to originality but to conscious repetition. Edgar Dryden underscores "plagiarize" "because Pierre's experience is composed of a series of literary fictions,"[31] but it is more particularly a reference to the narrative of identity into which those fictions, along with all other cultural transmitters, have been incorporated. In his declaration of originality, Pierre denies the narrative that, as we have seen, consequently becomes a resistless force.

Pierre's text, which also features an author-hero, mirrors both Pierre and *Pierre*; the former is, again, not conscious of the full implications of reflection, whereas the latter exploits it. Melville ridicules Pierre, whose manuscript betrays not the darkness of his vision that horrifies his publishers, but the ludicrousness that undermines his tragedy. Goethe is an "inconceivable coxcomb . . . like a hired waiter" (352). The world could "spare a million more of the same kidney . . . crushed . . . like an egg from which the meat hath been sucked" (352-53). What Pierre's text tells us about *Pierre,* however, is to look to the most apparently ridiculous moments, the disruptions, in the text for access.

What seems most ludicrous and irrelevant, as Freud told his patients, is often what is most revealing. Pierre's unconscious desires, the narrative of which he is unaware, dominate his writing. Cold, hungry, and celibate, Pierre is preoccupied by questions of employment and images of food and of the body. Similarly, when the narrative dissolves into syllabic associations, Pierre's longings are more readily revealed: "—Nor jingling sleigh-bells, nor glad Thanksgiving, nor Merry Christmas, nor jubilating New Year's:—Nor Bell, Thank, Christ, Year;—none of these are for Pierre" (354). Striking in this catalogue is "Bell," Pierre's nickname for Isabel, the forbidden object; "Christ," too, alleges the importance of Pierre's cultural ties. "Thank" and "Year" denote cultural customs and categories of organization. But what is most important here is the reading lesson; association disrupts narration, imposing personal preoccupation on the events of the narrative.

Free association foregrounds the unperceived narrative that challenges the ostensible narrative. The two narratives promote a heteroglossia that can call narrative authority in general into question.[32] Language, too, unravels into its components during the free play of association. Language breaks down as Pierre is increasingly excluded from the world, as he comes, that is, to share Isabel's alienation. As we have seen, Pierre cannot utilize his position to gain access to the margins of cultural discourse. Instead, it is a task left to the reader and the narrator, who, locating Glen's succession to Pierre's inheritance in "the hereditary syllables, Glendinning" (335), calls attention to the role of language in convention as well as to convention as a language, especially in reference to the name of the father and the authority of the law.

Without inspection, Pierre cannot change or resist the resistless force that he tragically (or pathetically) authors. His writing brings him to the precipitous discovery: "For the more and the more that he wrote, and the deeper and the deeper that he dived, Pierre saw the everlasting elusiveness of Truth; the universal lurking insincerity of even the greatest and purest written thoughts" (393). But Pierre has too much faith to make the necessary leap. If the elusiveness of Truth had led him to regard experience as relative and self-created, to perceive the terms of his unconscious narrative (the internalized script), Pierre would not have become the "most unwilling states-prisoner of letters." But his attachment to convention overpowers his authorship, as "he blindly [writes] with his eyes turned away from the paper;—thus unconsciously symbolizing the hostile necessity and distaste" (394). Necessity's "hostility" attests to the oppositional thinking to which Pierre surrenders his humanity, turning himself instead into a symbol and allowing himself to be written by a fate he authors and so potentially could alter.

Such alteration is, of course, no easy process; in fact it is, in Nick Carraway's words, "a matter of infinite hope." Typically coy, the narrator expresses a principle of interpretation that apparently chooses "the White Whale" and "the Ambiguities," over "Moby Dick" and "Pierre":

> Say what some poets will, Nature is not so much her own ever-sweet interpreter, as the mere supplier of that cunning alphabet, whereby selecting and combining as he pleases, each man reads his own peculiar lesson according to his own peculiar mind and mood. (397)

The narrator's claim, "I write precisely as I please," echoes through this passage. But "cunning" is disruptive; a "cunning alphabet" necessarily undermines linguistic free play. "Cunning" works against the narrator's claim as words signify against the intentions of their users. Language, a type of classification and cultural transmitter, organizes meaning, as "the Delectable Mountain," a mountain near Saddle Meadows rechristened by an old Baptist farmer, cast a "spell . . . [that], gazing upon [the mountain] by the light of those suggestive syllables, no poetical observer could resist" (397). The mood and the word, in intricate conjunction, conspire to mean.

Social terms invariably comprehend Pierre, organizing even—in fact, especially—his fantasies of rebellion, to which he is passive:

> one night . . . a sudden, unwonted, and all-pervading sensation seized him. He knew not where he was; he did not have any ordinary life-feeling at all. He could not see; though instinctively putting his hand to his

eyes, he seemed to feel that the lids were open. . . . During this state of semi-unconsciousness, or rather trance, a remarkable dream or vision came to him. The actual artificial objects around him slid from him, and were replaced by . . . a baseless vision. (395-97)

Under the influence of and in conformity with "his Titanic soul" (396), his particular concerns, Pierre refashions Delectable Mountain into "the Mount of the Titans" (397):

> Stark desolation; ruin, merciless and ceaseless; chills and gloom,—all here lived a hidden life, curtained by that cunning purpleness, which, from the piazza of the manor house, so beautifully invested the mountain once called Delectable, but now styled Titanic. (399)

"Cunning," which recalls the "cunning alphabet," signals the projection onto the landscape with which Pierre denies his act of authorship. The narrator shifts rhetorically at this point from a description of what "the tourist" was and did to the direct second person address, "you still ascended . . ." (399), thus forcing the reader into a specific narrative perspective. This movement parallels Pierre's surrender to a narrative that he disowns as he abandons himself to the myth of Enceladus, which finally ends his attempt at authorship. Pierre returns home in his fantasy, and he overturns his mother's genteel Christianity, but only to replace it with a pagan and emphatically social ideal. Pierre imagines himself as Enceladus, the Titan child of incest, who led an assault on the heavens and was condemned by the gods to drag the earth on a chain around his ankle. The myth fits not only Pierre's unconscious concerns but, more potently, his unconscious desires:

> . . . Enceladus was both the son and grandson of an incest; and even thus, there had been born from the organic blended heavenliness and earthliness of Pierre, another mixed, uncertain, heaven-aspiring, but still not wholly earth-emancipated mood . . .—that reckless sky-assaulting mood of his, was nevertheless on one side the grandson of the sky. For it is according to eternal fitness, that the precipitated Titan should still seek to regain his paternal birthright even by fierce escalade. Wherefore whoso storms the sky gives best proof he came from thither! (402-3)

The mytho-literary precedents for Pierre's rebellion again make clear that his "sky-assaulting mood," although directed against a paternal figure, is very much in accordance with a paternal tradition.

Most prominent, however, is the theme of incest. The monster, Enceladus, that springs from the seed of incest re-enforces the cultural prohibition. And yet, Enceladus enormously attracts Pierre in this vision. Incest has created a powerful hero, a replica of his heroic ancestors. Pierre's identification with Enceladus could foreground his attachment to his paternal ancestors, but, more important, his attraction to the myth borders on his acknowledgement of his desire for Isabel—inflamed, perhaps, by his celibacy—and, by implication, for his mother, and for himself. In other words, Pierre could potentially confront the desire through which he could shatter convention and the desire that prevents him from doing so. But his vision recovers that desire as it recovers it, and Pierre retreats for the last time from the cultural margins and the chance to resist the narrative of his identity.

Pierre seeks refuge from the intensity of his vision and from his struggle in an excursion to an art exhibit with Isabel and Lucy. Circumstances culminate his crisis as it began, in a wish that comes true—that Isabel is not in fact the sister for whom he had wished. A portrait of a nameless head in an art gallery casts doubt on Isabel and Pierre's familial ties. As Isabel's resemblance to Pierre's father's portrait convinces him that she is his sister, her resemblance to the stranger's portrait exposes the hastiness of his original conclusion. This time, however, "[t]he most tremendous displacing and revolutionizing thoughts [that] were upheaving in him, with reference to Isabel" (409), no longer pertained to heroism, but to his twin desires for Isabel and conformity. In the context of these desires, Pierre re-evaluates Isabel's story. The gallery portrait calls into question the symbol on which Pierre's chief evidence rested—the portrait of his father—and leads Pierre to wonder whether Isabel may have been consciously scripted: "By some strange arts Isabel's wonderful story might have been, someway, and for some cause, forged for her, in her childhood, and craftily impressed upon her youthful mind" (411). With no sister, Pierre has no excuse for heroism nor defiance (particularly the "danger" of incest); with no evidence of his father's adultery, he has nothing to define himself in terms of or against. Bewildered, Pierre must cast away his script and is temporarily reduced to wordless desire: "With such bewildering meditations as these in him . . . and with both Isabel and Lucy bodily touching his sides as he walked; the feelings of Pierre were entirely untranslatable into any words that can be used" (410).

Pierre, of course, is incapable of extending the limitations of language into an understanding of its inherent incapacities. And he is equally unwilling to act on his desire. But since he cannot relinquish the narrative of heroism, he channels his passion—composed of his frustrated rebellion and his desire for Isabel—into rage against the social institutions represented by the signatories of two letters he discovers on his return home. One terminates his contract with his publishing house, "Steel, Flint & Asbestos," a name that signifies impotence in its juxtaposition of fire-starters and fire-resistants. The other, from Glen Stanly and Lucy's brother, brands him "a villainous and perjured liar." Impotent against the social terms that he himself empowers, Pierre destroys himself, as we have seen, through Glen Stanly.

The final act opens on Pierre, whose metaphysical imprisonment has now taken literal form. In jail, Pierre finishes the second of his books, the one writ in blood, although his metaphors again consign him more to characterization than authorship:

> Here, then, is the untimely, timely end;—Life's last chapter well stitched into the middle! Nor book, nor

author of the book, hath any sequel, though each hath its last lettering!—It is ambiguous still. Had I been heartless now, disowned, and spurningly portioned off the girl at Saddle Meadows, then had I been happy through a long life on earth, and perchance through a long eternity in heaven! Now, 'tis merely hell in both worlds. Well, be it hell. I will mold a trumpet of the flames, and, with my breath of flame, breathe back my defiance! But give me first another body! I long and long to die, to be rid of this dishonored cheek. *Hung by the neck till thou be dead.*—Not if I forestall you, though!—Oh now to live is death, and now to die is life; now, to my soul, were a sword my midwife! (418)

Pierre appears to want to act here, in fact, to believe that he is acting, "mold[ing] a trumpet of the flames . . . and breath[ing] back [his] defiance" (418). But he is only, again, enacting a script. Deluded, he believes that "now to die is life," and he refuses to accept the nothingness of reality in death even as he recoiled from the absence of certainty in life. Enter Isabel and Lucy to play out the full tragic scene: "Lucy shrunk up like a scroll, and noiselessly fell at the feet of Pierre." Enfolded in Pierre's destiny, Lucy has herself become a text in which Pierre reads his final line, "seizing Isabel in his grasp—in thy breasts, life for infants lodgeth not, but death-milk for thee and me!—The drug!" But Pierre's finale is pathetic rather than tragic. Even his death is plagiarized, this time from Socrates, with the notable difference that Pierre's makes no point and no sense. "Midwife" suggests that Pierre believes he is being somehow reborn; he rejects the reality of his death even as he has denied the reality of his life. Pierre dies not a tragic failure, but a failed tragedy.

The end of the novel reads as a parody of a Shakespearian tragedy, and, indeed, *Hamlet* runs throughout as a pre-text for Pierre's heroism and his paralysis.[33] The three main characters lie dead or dying and the only survivors are incidental characters, but no one pronounces the lesson to be learned or the principles on which the community may be rebuilt. The apocalyptic scene is relieved only by the archaic language that undercuts any vestige of the tragedy that may have remained, beginning with Lucy's brother's exclamation:

> "Yes! Yes!—Dead! Dead! Dead!—without one visible wound—her sweet plumage hides it.—Thou hellish carrion, this is thy hellish work! Thy juggler's rifle brought down this heavenly bird! Oh, my God, my God! Thou scalpest me with this sight!"

> "The dark vein's burst, and here's the deluge-wreck—all stranded here! Ah, Pierre! my old companion, Pierre;—school-mate—playmate—friend!—Our sweet boys' walks within the woods!—Oh, I would have rallied thee, and banteringly warned thee from thy too moody ways, but thou wouldst never heed! What scornful innocence rests on thy lips, my friend!—Hand scorched with murderer's powder, yet how woman-soft!—By heaven, these fingers move!—one speechless clasp!—all's o'er!"

> "All's o'er, and ye know him not!" came gasping from the wall; and from the fingers of Isabel dropped an

empty vial—as it had been a run-out sand-glass—and shivered upon the floor; and her whole form sloped sideways, and she fell upon Pierre's heart, and her long hair ran over him, and arbored him in ebon vines. (420-21)

Pierre here conforms to the pre-written script, and his apparent bent for playing out romantic scenes brings on his senseless and melodramatic demise. The ending is apocalyptic, but no Fortinbras or Edgar, Malcolm or Lodovico, survives to profit from his tragic errors and so institute a more just rule. The stakes are simply not that high. And we assume that Pierre's text suffers the same fate.

More than one of Melville's text's initial reviewers suggested that its author be institutionalized (rather than canonized). But the intensity of its critical reception, then and now, attests to the efficacy of its formal experimentation. A book about a writer's writing a book about a writer lends itself to the prismatic introspection that Brodhead sees as a failed novel, "a draught of a draught, in a . . . desperate sense."[34] *Pierre*'s reflexivity inspects Pierre's internalization of a narrative identity that consistently foils his self-authorization, his inspection of the terms of cultural discourse, precisely because that internalization formalizes his declaration of independence. Melville's deconstruction of the national script of identity, which reads like the erratic disruptions of an unconscious, a cultural unconscious, insists on the reader's inspection of his/her own such internalization. *Pierre* confounds its readers' expectations by narrative disruptions that challenge fundamental (and internalized) assumptions about narrativity.

Notes

1. *Pierre,* in *Israel Potter, The Piazza Tales, The Confidence-Man, Uncollected Prose, Billy Budd,* with notes by Hamson Hayford (New York: The Library of America, 1984), pp. 2-421.

2. This claim runs counter to Richard Brodhead's assertion that a novel represents an author's "tacit commitment to the premise that the kind of world he wants to create can be articulated through a temporal narration, through an account of the progressive unfolding of sequential experience" (*Hawthorne, Melville, and the Novel* [Chicago: The University of Chicago Press, 1976], p. 10). However, if the difficulty of *Pierre* stems from Melville's efforts to call the concept of narrative into question within a narrative form, then what Brodhead evaluates as a failed novel may in fact be a largely successful formal experiment.

3. *Patricide in the House Divided* (New York: W. W. Norton and Co., 1979), p. 8.

4. *The Letters of Herman Melville,* ed. Merrell R. Davis and William H. Gilman (New Haven: Yale University Press, 1960), p. 78.

5. Eric Sundquist similarly notes that "[i]ronically enough, the 'sweetly-writ manuscript of his life,' whose only flaw is the omission of a sister 'from the text,' is terribly disfigured by the correction of this detail" (*Home as Found: Authority and Genealogy in Nineteenth-Century American Literature* [Baltimore: The Johns Hopkins University Press, 1979], p. 171). Sundquist precedes the observation of this irony with the more general notation that "[i]rony invokes an object of reference only to call it into question; in extremity it mutilates its own discourse and hollows out its own authority, leaving a lacuna in the stead of signification" (171). Somewhat less violently, I am calling attention here to Melville's underscoring of Pierre's unwitting authorship; he is in fact destroyed less by his wish than by his interpretation of that wish. Perhaps, as Freud might suggest, his deepest wish is for self-destruction.

6. According to Michael Paul Rogin, "Young American" and "Manifest Destiny" were the two dominant political slogans of the 1840s. Significantly, both were coined by John L. O'Sullivan, an editor and journalist with whom Melville shared a number of acquaintances. (See *Subversive Genealogy: The Politics and Art of Herman Melville* [New York: Alfred A. Knopf, 1983]). Forgie discusses the psychological implications of this metaphor in the context of earlier and later "dominant metaphors" in *Patricide in the House Divided.*

7. In *Essays and Lectures, Nature; Address, etc.,* with notes by Joel Porte (New York: The Library of America, 1983), pp. 211-30.

8. Emerson, "The Young American," p. 227.

9. Again, Forgie's discussion of the preoccupation with the founding fathers during this period is particularly illuminating in this context (see *Patricide in the House Divided*). In effect, as Michael Kammen also observes, this age witnessed a kind of historical collapse or conflation in which an ideal of the past was imposed on the present. The preoccupation with history stems, in this formulation, from a "quest for republican legitimacy" and from the desire for validation to be found in a "nostalgic vision of the Golden Age" that masks the instability that actually characterized the goals and institutions of the past (*People of Paradox: An Inquiry Concerning the Origins of American Civilization* [New York: Alfred A. Knopf, 1972], p. 51).

10. "The Flawed Grandeur of Melville's *Pierre*," in *New Perspectives on Melville,* ed. Faith Pullin (Edinburgh: Edinburgh University Press, 1978), p. 163.

11. Kammen similarly observes that "the United States may very well be the first large-scale society to have built innovation and change into its culture as a constant variable, so that a kind of 'creative destruction' continually alters the face of American life." He counterposes such "constant breaking with the past" to the American tendency to "conform to transitory norms and fashions" (*People of Paradox,* pp. 115, 110), in order to outline a central dualism that underlies American ideology.

12. In underscoring distinctions here among Melville, the narrator, and Pierre, I want to stress my departure from a reading such as Pease's. It is not Melville but Pierre who returns to a past that, as Kammen suggests, exists more in rhetoric than in actuality. In my reading, Melville does not, as Pease suggests, return to an affirmative past; instead, he demonstrates that such a return is inevitable and the attempt to deny the past merely reinforces its authority. For Melville, we are rooted in a past with an authority that we cannot escape and must, therefore, strive to understand. With his political metaphor, Melville suggestively links the authority of the past to a political system that was consciously disparaged by that (American) past (Pease, *Visionary Compacts* [Madison: University of Wisconsin Press, 1987]).

Rogin similarly underscores the political significance of Pierre's failure when he observes that Pierre's "revolution is truncated, like the 1848ers', because he steps back from its consequences. Like them he is discredited and succumbs to royal power" (*Subversive Genealogy,* p. 169).

13. *The Forest of Symbols: Aspects of Ndembu Ritual* (Ithaca: Cornell University Press, 1967).

14. See Nina Baym, "Melville's Quarrel with Fiction," *PMLA* [*Publications of the Modern Language Association of America*] 94, no. 5 (Oct. 1979): 909-23.

15. "Melville's Quarrel with Fiction," 910.

16. The Lacanian concept of "desire" is related to this idea in interesting ways. According to Lacan (and to a Lacanian reading of Freud), an object's absence precedes its earliest constitution as an object. (See Juliet Mitchell's incisive discussion in her introduction to *Feminine Sexuality,* ed. Juliet Mitchell and Jacqueline Rose, trans. Jacqueline Rose [New York and London: W. W. Norton & Co., 1982].) Isabel's exclusion from language makes the object status of language particularly apparent. Pierre's flaw stems partly from his tendency to regard language as a natural outgrowth rather than a cultural object (or artifact) that can be recontextualized and questioned.

17. See especially "The Value of Narrativity in the Representation of Reality," *On Narrative,* ed. W. J. T. Mitchell (Chicago: The University of Chicago Press, 1981), pp. 1-23. It is Pierre rather than Melville who demonstrates the "tacit commitment to the premise [of] . . . temporal narration" of which Brodhead writes (*Hawthorne,* p. 10). Melville—and the narrator—consciously seek to separate themselves from that commitment.

18. See *Madness and Civilization: A History of Insanity in the Age of Reason* (New York: Random House, 1965). Also see Jacques Derrida's critique of Foucault in "Cogito and the History of Madness," *Writing and Difference,* trans. Alan Bass (Chicago: The University of Chicago Press, 1978), pp. 31-63.

19. Fred G. See, "The Kinship of Metaphor: Incest and Language in Melville's *Pierre*," *Structuralist Review*

1, no. 2 (Winter 1978): 59. See has expanded these ideas in a fascinating study that historicizes certain aspects of contemporary critical theory (*Desire and the Sign: Nineteenth-Century American Fiction* [Baton Rouge and London: Louisiana State University Press, 1987]).

20. My pronoun is admittedly somewhat arbitrary here. However, I justify my claim of a narrative "he" on the basis of two observations. First, the intensity of identification among Melville, the narrator, and Pierre suggests a male point of view, since Melville distinguishes sharply in this text—as in most, if not all, of his works—between a male and female perspective. Secondly, Melville's women in this text—again, as in most—are more dramatically self-revealing than the calculating narrator; they tend either towards passivity (Lucy) or mystical (or shrewish) attempts to control (Isabel and Mrs. Glendinning).

21. In *The Gaze of Orpheus and Other Literary Essays,* trans. Lydia Davis (Barrytown, NY: Station Hill Press, 1981), p. 19.

22. Kammen sees the "cult of consensus . . . the desire for togetherness if not uniformity" as an outgrowth of "the quest for legitimacy and . . . the desire to reconcile our restless pluralities." He views the cult as a significant contribution to "the matrix of paradoxy in American life—unstable pluralism" (*People of Paradox,* p. 92). As it is often difficult to distinguish between—or among—political parties in the United States, it is similarly difficult to separate Pierre's goals from what he claims to be fighting.

23. See Hayden White's classification, "The Value of Narrativity."

24. This observation is perhaps a commonplace of semiotic theory. I am particularly interested in Lacan's treatment of this subject. His theories of communication, meaning, and interpretation are most pointedly articulated in this context in "The Function and Field of Speech and Language," *Ecrits,* trans. Alan Sheridan (New York and London: W. W. Norton & Co., 1977), pp. 30-113.

25. "The Value of Narrativity," p. 20.

26. "Melville's Quarrel with Fiction," p. 919.

27. This phrase was coined by Joseph Donahue of Columbia University in an American literature dissertation seminar, spring semester 1988. I have used the phrase because I think it aptly captures the almost paradoxical balance between intentionality and lack of control that Melville demonstrates here. See Baym, "Melville's Quarrel with Fiction," p. 918.

28. *Hawthorne,* pp. 189-90.

29. *The Feminization of American Culture* (New York: Alfred A. Knopf, 1977), p. 373.

30. See Brodhead, *Hawthorne,* pp. 170ff.

31. *Melville's Thematics of Form: The Great Art of Telling the Truth* (Baltimore: Johns Hopkins University Press, 1968), p. 138.

32. I am invoking Bakhtin here because of the exciting conjunction that I think remains to be developed between Bakhtin and psychoanalytic theory. These connections are rich enough to require a study of their own. Yet, I wish briefly to suggest that psychoanalysis operates by many of the principles of Bakhtin's dialogics; for example, the competing narrative voices, the heteroglossia that challenges narrative authority, are very much operative in Freud's concept of multi-determined symptoms. Schafer's competing narratives work even more directly in accordance with the concept of heteroglossia. A study of this sort could add a new voice to the growing dialogue between psychoanalytic and narrative theory.

In this context, it is interesting to note that Bakhtin, who did not have access to some of Freud's major works (including the more culturally oriented studies), attempted to restore a cultural/materialist perspective to psychoanalysis, which, he felt, was biologically reductive. See V. N. Volosinov (Bakhtin), *Freudianism: A Critical Sketch,* trans. I. R. Titunik (Bloomington and Indianapolis: Indiana University Press, 1976).

33. See also Sundquist's discussion of Melville's use of *Hamlet* in *Pierre* (Sundquist, p. 146).

34. Brodhead is hardly alone in this response (*Hawthorne,* pp. 189-90). Critics, like the initial reviewers, tend towards vehemence, albeit often qualified by their acknowledgement of Melville's stature. Newton Arvin calls *Pierre* "one of the most painfully ill-conditioned books ever to be produced by a first-rate mind" (*Herman Melville* [New York: Viking Press, 1964]). Richard Chase calls it "a book that tries to be a novel of manners and turns into a ranting melodrama" ("Introduction," *Melville: A Collection of Critical Essays* [Englewood Cliffs, N.J.: Prentice-Hall, Inc., 1962], p. 9). F. O. Matthiessen offers the somewhat more qualified view that "if *Pierre* is a failure, it must be accounted a great one, a failure in an effort to express as honestly as possible what it meant to undergo the test 'of a real impassioned onset of Life and Passion'" (*American Renaissance: Art and Expression in the Age of Emerson and Whitman* [New York and London: Oxford University Press, 1941/1966], p. 487). Interestingly, I find myself most in accord with one of the earliest responses to *Pierre*—E. L. Grant Watson's view that it "is the story of a conscious soul attempting to draw itself free from the psychic world—material in which most of mankind is unconsciously always wrapped and enfolded, as a foetus in the womb" ("Melville's *Pierre*," *New England Quarterly* 3 (April 1930): 195-234). Among contemporary readings that I find most convincing, Richard Gray's "'All's o'er, and ye know him not': A Reading of *Pierre*" (*Herman Melville: Reassessments,* ed. Robert A. Lee [London: Vision Press, 1984], pp. 116-34) most persuasively argues for a revisionist reading of *Pierre,* which, he contends, anticipates the post-modern novel in "the

subversive nature of its techniques, the self-reflexive character of its idiom" (117). It is primarily for its psychological depth and its fascinating narrative experimentation that I regard *Pierre* as a complete, successful, and brilliant work.

Gillian Brown (essay date 1990)

SOURCE: "Anti-Sentimentalism and Authorship in *Pierre,*" in *Domestic Individualism: Imagining Self in Nineteenth-Century America,* University of California Press, 1990, pp. 135-69.

[*In the following essay, Brown interprets* Pierre *as Melville's parody and critique of the typical sentimental domestic novel of his day, focusing on the author's handling of the role of the individual in American society.*]

Seventeen books into the narrative of **Pierre; or, The Ambiguities,** Melville abandons the chronology of Pierre's family history—the stuff of the sentimental novel—to announce: "I write precisely as I please."[1] This declaration of literary individualism heralds a satirical discussion of "Young America in Literature," as typified by "the juvenile author" of "that delightful love-sonnet, entitled 'The Tropical Summer'" (245). We now learn that Pierre has enjoyed some success as the author of this sentimental sonnet and other "gemmed little sketches of thought and fancy" (245).

The switch from the parodic Glendinning family plot to a lampoon of nineteenth-century American literary production sets the individual who writes precisely as he pleases against prevailing literary as well as domestic relations. For the remainder of the book Melville chronicles not only Pierre's progression from idyllic domesticity to incest and murder but his progress from celebrated "juvenile author" of popular sentimental pieces to obscure author of a "mature work." Under an individualistic imperative of authorship, Pierre flees both home and conventional literary celebrity. In what is perhaps the nineteenth century's most negative portrayal of domestic values, Melville posits authorship as an annulment of the curriculum vitae supervised by sentimental motherhood and popularized by sentimental literature. Literary subjectivity as Melville imagines it demands and offers an alternative method of self-fashioning.[2]

The disengagement of individualism from domesticity related in **Pierre** removes it from the feminine sphere, establishing a standard of masculine individualism. Melville's proposal of an authorship independent of domesticity delineates what has become the androcentric bias of American literary tradition: the alignment of the individualistic self and its representations with anti-sentimentalism.[3] Unlike Stowe, who locates in sentimentalism the individual's independence of the market, Melville regards sentimentalism as identical with the market. To read **Pierre** is to follow the ways that literary individualism appropriates the anti-market rhetoric of domestic individualism in order to distinguish male individuality from femininity, "mature" from "juvenile" authors, and, ultimately, classic American literature from mass-market publications.

It is against the marketing methods promoting such literary works as "The Tropical Summer" that Melville asserts the prerogative of writing precisely as he pleases. *Pierre* explicitly identifies sentimentalism with the procedures of the nineteenth-century literary marketplace, procedures which threaten to eclipse the writer's individuality. The accessories and paraphernalia of publication proposed to Pierre—title pages, leather-bound editions, portraits and photographs of the author—all mass-produce the writer and his work. In Melville's sarcastic ruminations upon the literary economy, marketing concerns preempt the particularity of writer and work. Contemporary publishing and advertising techniques, particularly the puffing practice of prearranged favorable reviews, thus appear in the "Young America in Literature" chapter as the silly attempts of some tailors turned publishers to make Pierre "public property" (254) by "arraying" his "productions in the library form" (247).[4] The mutual admiration society of puffing reviewers is caricatured here as the publishing industry's notion of "the broadcloth of genius" (247) available for reproduction. Against this wholesale notion of literary value, Pierre removes himself from domesticity and commerce and, moreover, institutes a domestic and commercial relation among writer, work, and reader that preserves the writer's uniqueness. We might then recognize *Pierre* as a keynote address to the program of literary individualism and as a key text in the development of the domestic hostility that has so long characterized American formulations of the literary.[5]

AUTHORSHIP AND ANONYMITY

Melville's attack on sentimentalism in *Pierre* is thus not simply a revelation of his own difficulties with finding success in the mid-nineteenth-century literary marketplace where domesticity was the primary commodity but a disquisition on the commercial and familial relations inhibiting individuality.[6] Developing the mythology of literary individualism, *Pierre* features a cult of literary obscurity in contradistinction to the cult of popular sentimental literature. This alternative literary economy begins with Pierre's disengagement from all sentimental agents, from both his family and the literary marketplace. By imagining the elimination of literary relations—the public modes and publishing methods that threaten to erode the individualistic aims of the author—*Pierre* constructs the literary estate Melville cannot find in the nineteenth-century literary marketplace.

In leaving Saddle Meadows, the Glendinning family estate, Pierre renounces, not only his mother and the sentimental ethos she represents, but his successful career as a sentimental writer. The literary motives underlying Pierre's resolve to leave home and set up housekeeping with his illegitimate half-sister Isabel become manifest as "Pierre attempts a mature work" (282). This work entails divesting himself of all the appurtenances of literary career and sentimental taste that Melville lampoons.[7] Even before his departure with Isabel to New York, Pierre removes himself from the progression of that career by refusing a series of procedures to publicize and further his literary reputation. He demurs from an offer to publish a collected edition of his "fugitive pieces," from invitations to lecture at learned societies, from magazine requests for biographies and copies of his portrait and daguerreotypes, and even from ladies' pleas for autographs. All these attentions strike Pierre as vulgar, causing him to consider "anonymousness in authorship" and to regret "that he had not started his literary career under that mask" (249). The advantage of "the inviolably anonymous method" is the "essential dignity and propriety" (249) it preserves.[8]

The system of anonymity contemplated in *Pierre* elaborates the ideas about exemplary authorship Melville conceived in his 1850 laudatory review of **"Hawthorne and His Mosses."** "Would that all excellent books were foundlings, without father or mother," Melville wishes, "that so it might be, we could glorify them, without including their ostensible authors." The anonymity of authors would enable and assure originality and genius, the marks of uniqueness. According to Melville, the author's anonymity preserves our fantasies about authors; "on a personal interview, no great author has ever come up to the idea of his reader. But that dust of which our bodies are composed, how can it ever fitly express the nobler intelligences among us?" In contrast to the reader's "ideal image of the man and his mind," the writer's own form betrays him as vulgar and commonplace.[9]

Because of this incommensurability, Pierre resists autographing as well as advertising his name. His autograph cannot match "the sublime poet Glendinning"; "owing to the very youthful and unformed character of his handwriting, his signature did not possess that inflexible uniformity, which . . . should always mark the hand of illustrious men" (253). From the opposite perspective, Pierre worries that his limited oeuvre does not merit the significance conferred by a leather-bound collected works edition. Either way, the presentation does not fit the writer.

"Anonymousness in authorship," of course, also may help the commercial success of the author, which proceeds independently of the writer's own form (249). This is the strategy adopted by nineteenth-century women writing under pen names: they assumed that under the name of an unknown man or woman, their work would not be defined by any aspect of their forms, whether sex or class or race. Anonymity also could operate as an effective publicity stunt, creating curiosity and gossip about the unknown author.[10] These commercial advantages in unknown authorship become especially clear in *Ruth Hall*, the best-selling 1855 autobiographical novel by Fanny Fern, pseudonym of Sara Payson Willis. In this satiric story of the rise of a sentimental writer, the titular heroine also writes under a pen name, the sexually indeterminate single name "Floy." Just as the question of Fern's own identity excited interest in the 1850s reading public, "there are many rumors afloat" as to who Floy can be.[11] Anonymity here publicizes the author; it epitomizes the literary commerce that Melville's ideal anonymity would jettison.

Whereas Pierre seeks the inviolability of privacy, Ruth realizes herself through public attention and approbation. For Ruth, the literary marketplace holds the possibility of personal vindication, the means for her to redress the failures of her family and associates. Another trenchant commentary on domestic myths and publishing practices, *Ruth Hall* portrays literary celebrity as the best revenge against both family cruelty and an exploitative publishing industry. Like *Pierre,* this novel aligns commercial with familial relations. All these relations appear untrustworthy and, even worse, malevolent in *Ruth Hall,* where grandparents abuse (in one case fatally) their grandchildren, parents deride and neglect their children, and publishers cheat their writers. But unlike Melville, Fern takes pains to individuate these base actions, to tabulate how the individuals in familial and commercial institutions may hinder or help the struggling heroine.

Left penniless after her husband's death and refused support from her in-laws and her own family, Ruth Hall must earn a living for herself and her two daughters. When she turns to writing for newspapers, her brother, a prominent editor, denies her aid, advising her "to seek some *unobtrusive* employment" (116). The editors and publishers Ruth meets as she tries to sell her writings recognize her talent but are similarly stingy in the "mere pittance" (140) they pay for her work. Quickly learning her "market-value" as her writing sells and gains recognition, Ruth eventually finds a properly "brotherly" publisher in John Walter, who gives her a "just compensation" (142, 143, 142), granting her "talent the moral right to a deserved remuneration" (141). In addition to securing Ruth's "welfare" in a favorable "written contract" (143), Walter makes it his business to admonish and embarrass those who had denied Ruth support. For Ruth Hall, successful publishing means getting wealth and fame, and getting back. Revenge is doubly sweet, for in this gratifying story of hard-won prosperity Fern/Willis exposed the uncharitableness of her brother Nathaniel P. Willis, the well-known editor and writer.[12]

The revenge motive in *Ruth Hall* disturbed contemporary reviewers of the book, because it seemed behavior unbefitting a woman writer. As a *New York Times* review stated:

> If Fanny Fern were a man,—a man who believed that the gratification of revenge were a proper occupation for one who has been abused, and those who have injured us are fair game, *Ruth Hall* would be a natural and excusable book. But we confess that we cannot understand how a delicate, suffering woman can hunt down even her persecutors so remorselessly. We cannot think so highly of [such] an author's womanly gentleness.[13]

Though the author acknowledges in her preface that her book "is entirely at variance with all set rules for novel-

writing" (3), she is not referring to rules of etiquette in this self-possessed statement about her writing style. Gentleness obviously is not a desirable quality to Fern/ Willis, who was also departing from domestic womanhood in telling the story of how "our heroine had become a regular business woman" (173). The crucial gender boundary the book transgresses is the line between domesticity and the market. As Ruth finds a "*real, warm-hearted, brotherly brother,* such as she had never known" (144) in her publisher, familial relations are reformed and relocated in the market. More than this, *Ruth Hall* discloses the economic and social insecurity of domestic individualism for women and advocates that women pursue individualistic interests outside the domestic sphere.[14] In this endeavor, getting even is getting one's own. The real scandal of *Ruth Hall* lies in its unabashed commitment to market individualism.

Ruth Hall locates individuality in the celebrity mass publishing creates, in the market where Ruth's literary value is realized. All the fan mail Ruth receives—"letters of friendship, love, and business" (153)—confirms her sense of self-worth, so much so that she can invest in herself. On the basis of these "proofs that I have won the public ear" (153), she decides to keep the copyright to her work for greater gain when "my book will be a success" (163). Her readers provide commensurability between the writer and her worth. If Ruth's fans ask too much—some letter writers propose marriage; some request autographs or endorsements; others seek financial assistance; one dying woman begs Ruth to adopt her baby daughter—they do so because, as one correspondent writes her, they can "read your heart in your many writings" (165).

The sociability that Ruth's writing generates and through which she gains her "true valuation" (193) undermines individuality in *Pierre*'s vision of literary relations. Whereas *Ruth Hall* equates literary talent with commercial success—"'Floy' is a genius," Walter asserts, "hence her fame and success" (151-52)—*Pierre* repudiates such a connection between literary genius and market achievement. This withdrawal of literature from the market first takes the form of an assertion of masculinity.

It is "peculiarly distasteful for Pierre to comply" with "entreaties from the young ladies that he would be pleased to grace their Albums with some nice little song" (250). In this custom of "parlor society" where "you lose your own sharp individuality and become delightfully merged in that soft social Pantheism, as it were, that rosy melting of all into one" (250), Pierre discerns an emasculation of the author—"there no one draws the sword of his own individuality" (250)—analogous to literary publicists' violation of the author's privacy and uniqueness. In order to preserve his individuality amidst "that rosy melting" (250), Pierre selects a signature more personalized than his autograph: "I will give them the actual feeling of my hand, as much as they want. And lips are still better than hands. Let them send their sweet faces to me, and I will kiss *lipographs* upon them forever and a day" (251). Pierre enacts the spirit of this plan, blowing a kiss over all the albums and returning them "accompanied with a confectioner's kiss for each album, rolled up in the most ethereal tissue" (251).

In substituting lipographs for autographs Pierre both mocks and exploits the cult of celebrity. The other side of this masculine bluff of aggressive eroticism is, predictably, the fear of his own inadequacy being exposed. The form of publicity to which he most strenuously objects, the publication of his picture, in either portrait or photograph form, is particularly threatening and troubling to Pierre's desire for proper self-representation. If he allowed his editors to make copies of his portrait, the world would see the writer Pierre Glendinning as a beardless youth without the "most noble corporeal badge of . . . the illustrious author" (253), an image unequal to Pierre's fantasy of himself as bearded genius. If he permitted publication of his daguerreotype an even worse misrepresentation would occur, for Pierre believes daguerreotypes to be a vulgar mass production of the individual "dayalizing a dunce" rather than "immortalizing a genius" (254). In an age "when every body has his portrait published, true distinction lies in not having yours published at all" (254).[15] All these forms violate Pierre's sense of propriety, a self-proprietorship so extreme that nothing other than himself can represent him. Hence the kiss serves as his truest signature, his body's imprint, impossible to forge or copy.

The crucial point here is that Pierre's kiss cannot be published and marketed. Unlike Hawthorne's Coverdale, another young bachelor sentimental writer concerned with his individuality, Pierre sees no individualistic possibilities in consumer relations. So the relation between author and market that *Ruth Hall* forges exemplifies the literary commerce from which Melville would extricate the (male) author. Blowing kisses to female autograph seekers, Pierre dismisses a feminized reading public as well as the advertising practices directed toward it. His literary individualism opposes what Ann Douglas calls the feminization of American culture.[16] But the case of *Ruth Hall* makes clear that the distrust of the feminine and the commercial— more precisely, the distrust of the feminine in the commercial—rationalizes a masculinist monopoly of literary value. The business of literature which Pierre disdains is in fact run by men, Ruth Hall discovers, and the individuals most manipulated by this economic organization are women. This is why Fanny Fern celebrates Ruth's development of business sense: her story culminates in the pictorial image of a stock certificate, printed in the penultimate chapter, which Ruth purchases from her publishing profits. Ruth's accomplishment, like Pierre's early success as a sentimental writer, proves that any individual, even a woman writer, may succeed in the literary marketplace. The market and the publishers and writers who embody it therefore strike the masculinist literary individualist as unreliable, because too elastic, indices of value.[17]

Genius and Cannibalism

The anonymity of authors recommended in the *Mosses* review and followed in ***Pierre*** thus operates to distinguish

literary value from market value. In celebrating Hawthorne's work Melville seeks to maintain the selectivity of the transcendent standard by which he measures him. The discrepancy between the bodily form of the author and the greatness of his literary work, the difference between his corporeality and his corpus (a punning association and dissociation Melville fondly elaborates throughout his own work), inaugurates a liberalized yet still selective critical standard of genius.[18] Melville speculates that the genius we attribute to great writers such as Shakespeare might in fact reside not in the man but in his membership in a brotherhood of genius: "May it not be, that this commanding mind has not been, and never will be, individually developed in any one man? And would it, indeed, appear so unreasonable to suppose that this greatness and overflowing may be, or may be destined to be, shared by a plurality of men of genius?"[19]

Melville simultaneously preserves the uniqueness of genius and extends it to new talents such as Hawthorne in his fancy of disembodied, collective genius. In this democratization of authorial achievement Melville elaborates the ideal of anonymous authorship as the submergence of the individual in the author. But the author does not disappear in this collectivity; rather, as a vehicle of brotherhood, he shines among men.[20]

This men's-club account of genius limits its membership, as *Ruth Hall* expressly demonstrates. Not all Ruth's readers recognize her "genius." Her brother brusquely tells her: "[Y]ou have no talent" (116). One of her correspondents, who signs himself "William Stearns, Professor of Greek, Hebrew, and Mathematics, in Hopetown College, and author of 'History of the Dark Ages,'" makes it his business to inform her: "You are not a genius. . . . Shakespeare was a genius. Milton was a genius," Stearns proclaims, and "the author of 'History of the Dark Ages,' which has reached its fifteenth edition, was a genius." Stearns grants himself the rank of genius because his work has warranted a "fifteenth edition"; in short, because of its marketability. Realizing that Ruth could make the same claim, Stearns adds that "the *female* mind is incapable of producing anything which may be strictly termed *literature*" (166). With this letter *Ruth Hall* exposes the misogyny of the enterprise to define and assign literary genius.

In this book's feminist critique of literary criticism, even the "brotherly" John Walter manifests masculinist assumptions about a woman's writing. Though Walter declares and defends Ruth's genius, he needs to isolate it as a phrenological phenomenon. He would explain her talent as specific to her physiognomy. Convincing Ruth to "have your head examined to please me," Walter takes her to the phrenologist Professor Finman for an analysis of the "bumps" on her head (167). Walter thinks the phrenological reading confirms his own assessment of Ruth: "The Professor has hit you off to the life" (171). Ruth, however, who has "not the slightest faith in the science" (167), disagrees. The specific point she challenges is the professor's contention that she cannot tolerate criticism. Ruth quarrels "with no one who denies my writings literary merit," but insists on "fair criticism" (172). Her disagreement with the phrenologist becomes an indictment of prejudiced literary criticism. Like the phrenological arbitrary categorization of personality according to the accidents of physical composition, criticism may misrepresent writings. Ruth allows reviewers "the right to express" their views, but denounces their irresponsible procedures:

> But to have one's book reviewed on hearsay, by persons who never looked between the covers, or to have paragraphs circulated, with words italicized, so that gross constructions might be forced upon the reader, which the author never could dream of; then to have paragraphs taken up in that state, credited to you, and commented upon by horrified moralists,—that is what I call unfair play. (172)

This rejoinder strikes at the presumptions of both phrenologists and critics, self-serving presumptions about "womanly nature" (172). Overall, Ruth gets fair play in the market, where she finds "another tribunal" (161) than her brother or Professor Stearns. For the critical program of defining genius according to Melville's masculinist prerogatives of literary individualism, it is then necessary, as the mission of Professor Stearns exhibits, to make the market a more selective index of value. Despite its anti-commercial rhetoric, Melville's literary individualism ultimately represents, not a rejection of the market, but the desire to limit it to the arbiters and adherents of a particular type of genius.[21]

In the validation of American literary genius advanced in the *Mosses* review, Melville accordingly imagines a different, masculinized, literary commerce in which the reader cannibalizes the author and his work. He speaks of having banqueted upon Hawthorne and his *Mosses,* of having "incorporated their whole stuff into my being."[22] In the process of advancing the author—of celebrating both Hawthorne and the advent of original American authorship, of a distinct American literature—Melville transforms the writer into object of consumption. The cannibalistic transfiguration of humans into food and useful resources rather curiously, and perversely, imitates and perfects the dynamics of the literary marketplace where books function as commodities. In the attempt to define a province of authorship not subject to the market delimitations Melville discerned in publishers' preferences for sentimental stories and other successful formulaic literary productions (in his own case, for the early sea tales that had sold well), Melville reenvisions literary commerce by transforming the author into his book.[23] That is, he forestalls the dissociation of the writer from his literary work when it goes to market by imagining the author as the commodity itself, the book to be banqueted upon.[24] Anonymity finally preserves the author for the right kind of commerce, in which he and his work may circulate.

Melville's feeding metaphor of literary relations reclaims and refines the metamorphoses from subjects to objects in the literary marketplace, situating subjectivity in the most extreme subjection of the self to its objective possibilities. Put more simply, the uniqueness of literary labor is secured in its consumption; the mark of authorship is most prominent when a literary production is consumed. That authorship emerges and endures in its proper commodification is the premise upon which Melville erects an American literary tradition. Far from dispensing with the consumerist relations of nineteenth-century literature so infamously associated with sentimentalism, Melville might be said to purify consumption to support literary individualism.

There could hardly be any more radical or terrifying anonymity than that of being eaten; yet this frightening reversal of anthropomorphism also images a perverse intimacy, a connection between bodies closer than kinship or sexual relations. As Melville's brotherhood of genius subsumes the individual author in order to elevate him, his incorporation of Hawthorne signifies a disappearing process that assures the perpetuation of the author: a presence so powerful as to penetrate and reside in other bodies. Anonymity appeals to the paradoxical desire of the writer to inhabit the crowd so as to be simultaneously both of and above it. In anonymity, as in orphanhood and the unknown familial status of the foundling, the self is most thinglike, least protected by the personifications of family and fame, and thus most original. The cannibalistic logic of Melville's aesthetics of anonymity works to highlight an autonomy of self. As this naturalized and masculinized literary economy is developed by *Pierre,* writing becomes a model of autogenesis.

Pierre implements the mythology of authorship Melville divulges in the *Mosses* review: in the course of the novel Pierre transforms himself into a self-generative and, ultimately, self-consuming author. This countdown to one, and then none, follows the procedure of Pierre's "lipographs," which replace standard literary relations with his own literary economy. More than a parody of the language of sentiment, the metamorphosis of autograph into kiss bespeaks the disappearance of the author's name, a system of anonymity wherein the author retains his individuality. The author's kiss translates into the candy kisses, delectable objects whose consumption recalls Melville's banqueting upon Hawthorne. Pierre also finds and protects his authorship in a model of cannibalism, a literary commerce so personal that, as we shall see, it resembles the mythology of the sentimental family it supersedes.

BODIES, BOOKS, AND FOOD

The consanguinity among author, book, and reader attained in Melville's vision of cannibalism and anonymity recapitulates the ideal of unity through food celebrated by nineteenth-century domesticians in popular cookery guides. Domestic advice writers imagined the achievement of democratic goals through food. According to William Alcott in *The Young Housekeeper, or Thoughts on Food and Cookery,* proper dietary habits would ensure "the happy day when all the family, however numerous and how little soever tied by ties of consanguinity, will be equal and free, dwelling together, eating and drinking together, and whether of one nation or another, always uniting around the same domestic altar."[25]

Preparation for this millennial moment of democracy and domesticity begins with "temperance in all things," Sarah Josepha Hale advised in her cookbook *The Good Housekeeper, or the Way to Live Well.*[26] The health and balance achieved by sensible family meals and the proper organization of the family unit prefigure the dissolution of the family into a larger family of nations. This millennial family, united through sacraments of food, implies both the expansion of domesticity (analogous to America's expanding market economy and geographical boundaries) and the disappearance of the sentimental nuclear family.

This double movement—the family magnified into great populations, the dissolution of family ties in the enlarged borders of the family—recurs in the strange mechanics of cannibalism in Melville's elaborations upon anonymity, but is there directed toward a different form of harmony. In the moment of literary brotherhood or "rosy melting," individuality is not subsumed by the community of individuals but consumed, incorporated by the masses. Melville's exemplary moment in literary relations retains the ambition of the writer, in a culture of consumption, to be consumed. This desire commits the author to the object-function at the communal feast, to becoming the meal. Furthermore, the aim of the strategy of anonymity is congruity with public taste: naturalization of the literary commodity so that the author's labor, understood as an extension of himself represented in his literary work, is preserved in the transmogrification of book to food. Melville envisions a radical intimacy like the universal endogamy of millennial domesticity but establishes his unity of relations on a perverse version of physical bonds and nurture arrangements. Whereas the apotheosis of domesticity signifies an implicitly socialistic political economy, a family transcending economic competition and fluctuation, *Pierre*'s culinary aesthetics exploit the individualistic possibilities of the literary marketplace. In this outlandishly egotistic version of commodification, the author endures in the consumption of himself.

Pierre thus advances a gastronomic organization of literary labor and consumption both to supplement and to supplant the dominant sentimental familial paradigm of literary relations. Melville's model of cannibalistic literary relations rewrites the millennial domestic meal as a literary feast, an individualistic perfection of consumerist practices in the literary marketplace. In the domestic apotheosis imagined in the great common meal, as in the ideal breakfast enacted in Rachel Halliday's kitchen in *Uncle Tom's Cabin,* all conflict and disunity are extinguished in the intimacy of eating together as one family. This ideal elaborates upon the nineteenth-century iconography of intimate transmission from mother to child during breast-feeding. The mother's role in preparing for the perfection

of domesticity, in guarding against "intemperance in eating" and forming "the habits of her children," followed from her proper regulation of breast-feeding.[27] Bad habits began in infancy, health reformer Orson Fowler warned, where "most mothers err in giving their children the breast . . . whenever they cry."[28] For Melville, such preoccupation with the effects of feeding, the implementation of education and disciplining through eating, marks precisely the sentimental family's intervention in the private life and intimacy it promises to protect.[29] If the individual becomes food, he circumvents the mediations feeding entails.

In *Pierre,* Melville satirizes these domestic investments in food and proper child-rearing in the breakfast scene between Pierre and his mother. Pierre, who "had an excellent appetite" (16), orders three bowls of milk, causing his mother to caution him playfully: "Don't be a milk-sop" (19). Yet Mary Glendinning wishes Pierre to "remain all docility" (20) to her and her "sweet programme" (19) for him. In contrast to the abundant meal of toast, tongue, pigeons, rolls, coffee, and milk in the Glendinning home, Pierre's first meal with Isabel, which he perceives as disloyalty to his mother, consists of only water and bread of Isabel's "own making" (162). Pierre calls their common meal of this bread a "real sacrament" (162), marking his flight from the maternal breast with a ritual of eating which introduces the new anti-sentimental organization of his life.

In this account of maternal nurture Melville reverses the popular sentimental metaphor of the prodigal son as a viper nursing at his mother's breast to identify the mother as the source of "such venom." Eschewing his mother's table, Pierre eschews "the too-seducing bosoms of clay" that alternately inspire flight and make men "glad to be uxorious" (180). Once Pierre has supped with his sister Isabel, prior meals seem to him like "rummaging in a pantry, like a bake-house burglar" (160); he is now resolved to leave his mother and "henceforth live together" and "eat in company" (160) with Isabel. Pierre thus rejects the table and the taste of the sentimental family, the nurture of the maternal breast, for Isabel's fare: poverty, anonymity, and finally her "death-milk," the vial of poison secreted between her breasts "where life for infants lodgeth not."

In *Pierre*'s parody of contemporary literary taste Melville literalizes taste, naturalizing the literary economy. This literalization revamps the spiritualization of nurture arrangements in domestic ideology so as to display the economy of consumption that sentimentalism simultaneously denies and propels. Melville's transubstantiation of author into book into the most natural and necessary of commodities projects a literary economy that will circumvent the marketplace variables affecting an author's success. In imagining himself as food the author anticipates and exploits the objectification of people and literature through which culture and commerce operate.

Pierre's success as a sentimental author follows from the way his literary productions are taken to be in "Perfect

Taste" (245), appealing to the consensus of literary value. To control and personalize his literary production, that is, to individuate it from other publications, Pierre eliminates the role of marketing agents—editors, publishers, biographers, and publicists—in his literary career. His literary practices compose not only a commentary on the vulgarities of the literary marketplace but an alternative literary economy. For "Pierre himself was a sort of publisher" at home (263), producing literary pieces on whatever scraps of paper he finds, strewing the house with his productions, and allowing anyone to take them gratis. So committed is Pierre to an organic relation between himself and his literary work that he needs no copyrights, no public record of himself or of his authorship other than the work itself. Indeed, he and his productions constitute an ecological system: he smokes cigars bought from his magazine publication earnings, lit by pages of his work—"His cigars were lighted in two ways: lighted by the sales of his sonnets, and lighted by the printed sonnets themselves." In this purification of the puffery system, Melville puns, "the puffs which indirectly brought his dollars were again returned, but as perfumed puffs" (262). Just as he would transform autographs into kisses and confections, literary signs into bodily gestures and pleasures, Pierre would translate literary production, both the work's materiality and its monetary value, into another oral pleasure, realizing the sentimental model of literary production as affective and nurturing.[30]

This closed cycle of literary and personal production is like the orbit of maternal influence, which is ideally a perfect congruity between the characters of mother and child. Pierre's distrust of marketplace methods of popularization, Melville's diatribe against publishers, editors, and literary hacks, expresses an absolute commitment to the model of literary production that sentimentalism seems to promote: an almost biological link between author and work analogous to the kinship between mother and son. So Pierre wants what the sentimental family and sentimental literature strive to achieve: a perfect domestic circle (like that of Rachel Halliday's kitchen) in which industry and individuality are independent from the marketplace; an intimacy between self and labor, writer and book, which assures the integrity of the individual. The representative form of this alternative formation of individuality is autobiography or, more precisely, a reconception of literature as fundamentally autobiographical—primarily self-expressive and self-determined.

In the spirit of this merger of writer with writing, Pierre imagines an autonomous, extrafamilial literary production, "too true and good to be published" (283). This perfection of sentimental ecology exacts a labor from Pierre which takes away his youth, his sight, his ambulation, his reason. His book, the book that (like its author) will not be published and placed in circulation, "whose unfathomable cravings drink his blood" and "consume all his vigor" (304-5), usurps his senses and his life; rather than extending or replicating the author's life according to the custom of the literary marketplace, Pierre's unfinished book cuts

short the author by consuming him, thereby uniting the author and literary production in the anonymity of incorporation. By divesting himself of all sentimental investments, Pierre gets his wish—"in him you behold the baby toddler, . . . forced now to stand and toddle alone"—and the punishment for his Promethean desire to be original: "he lies still—not asleep as children and day-laborers sleep," but holding "the beak of the vulture" away from his heart (305). In the images of abandoned child and punished hero inhere the possibility of an achievement untouched by, uncontaminated by, and therefore uncommon to the public and its standards. The purest autobiography undoes its author, is unwritten or, rather, is inscribed upon the author's body, slated to appear only in the decomposition of that body.

The obvious problem with Pierre's literary economy is that the project of self-objectification finally destroys the self; yet it is objectification that empowers the circulation of self, author, and books in culture. Pierre deviates from his literary culture not so much in recognizing how subjectivity inheres in its "thingness"—in the fact that selves can be appropriated, even consumed and incorporated—but in imagining his objectification as self-generation.[31] The domestic iconography of mother and child preserves subjectivity in the image of pleasurable objectivity, in the figure of the nurtured child. That is, maternal nurture cultivates the emergence of the self and its circulation, reconciling subjectivity to the inevitability of its objectivity. Pierre would claim this maternal office for himself. And this is why *Pierre* initiates its reformation of the literary economy with the displacement of the mother.[32]

THE AESTHETICS OF INCEST

The plot against the mother which complements the literary plot generates still other movements that redouble the force of *Pierre*'s anti-sentimentalism. From these symmetrical developments emerges the creative principle of Melville's ambiguities: the generation of singularity from doubleness. Pierre replaces his filial relation with a sibling relation, only finally to replace that relation with solitude and solipsism. By the end of the book, father (already removed when the story begins), mother, sister, fiancée, cousin, and Pierre himself will have disappeared. But before Pierre and his family disappear, Pierre seems engaged in extending his family, by accepting Isabel as his sister and revivifying his father.

The subversion of motherhood and the sentimental family in *Pierre* begins with the recognition of something missing from Pierre's sentimental ethos. "So perfect to Pierre had long seemed the illumined scroll of his life thus far, that only one hiatus was discoverable by him in the sweetly-writ manuscript. A sister had been omitted from the text" (7). Prior to the appearance of Isabel, Pierre had used "the fictitious title" of sister for "his pedestaled mother" (7); but even his "romantic filial love" (5) cannot "supply the absent reality" (7). Melville soon supplies the text with the missing sister, granting Pierre's wish: "[H]ad my father but had a daughter!" (7).

Upon receiving Isabel's letter in which she confides her relation to him, Pierre "could not stay in his chamber: the house contracted to a nut-shell around him; the walls smote his forehead; bare-headed he rushed from the place, and only in the infinite air, found scope for that boundless expansion of his life" (66). Pierre's home cannot contain the expansion of self Pierre experiences in the news of his sister's existence; Isabel has fortified and augmented Pierre's selfhood by presenting him with a family history anterior and antithetical to domestic life with his mother. Once having seen Isabel's "henceforth immemorial face," Pierre feels "that what he had always before considered the solid land of veritable reality, was now being audaciously encroached upon by bannered armies of hooded phantoms, disembarking in his soul, as from a flotilla of specter-boats" (49). In this haunted state, Pierre finds "the face somehow mystically appealing to his own private and individual affections" (49); "most miraculous of all," he thinks "that somewhere he had seen traces of the likeness of that face before" (49). This invasion into his soul, into his most private and individual feelings, causes him to separate himself and his thoughts from his mother, making him "a falsifyer" to her (51).

As he withdraws from his mother, Pierre tries to account for the familiarity of Isabel's face and recalls "many an old legendary family scene, which he had heard related by elderly relations" (50). The text from which a sister had been omitted contained clues to her existence. Pierre remembers his dying father wailing "My daughter, my daughter!" (70). When Isabel appears, she confirms Pierre's childhood memory of his father as well as his wish for a sister. More important, she proves that Pierre's desire for a sister *is* his memory of his dying father.

Isabel's claim to sorority with Pierre, her claim to be the daughter of his father, thus raises issues of paternity less as questions of her parentage than as questions about the biography of the father. The "family legend" (73) that Isabel prompts Pierre to reconsider is his aunt Dorothea's story about the portrait of his father she had given him. This portrait depicted "a brisk, unentangled young bachelor" who was "airily and but grazingly seated, or rather flittingly tenanting an old-fashioned chair of Malacca" (73, 72). "The mother of Pierre could never abide this picture which she had always asserted did signally belie her husband" (72). "It is not he," Mary Glendinning maintained, and "the portrait which she held to do justice to her husband" was instead "a much larger one" that showed "a middle-aged married man," which she hung in the drawing room on "the most conspicuous and honorable place on the wall" (72). Yet Pierre's aunt Dorothea, his father's elder sister, had assured Pierre that the smaller "chair-portrait" was "an excellent likeness" (79). According to Dorothea, the portrait chronicles the senior Pierre Glendinning's love affair with a young French woman. A family cousin, Ralph Winwood, having decided to paint his relative as the wooer of the French woman, "slyly picked his portrait," secretly painting him just after his visits to the woman, hoping to "catch some sort of corresponding expression" on canvas (77). Suspecting that his cousin was painting him, Glendinning instructed Ralph to either hide or destroy the picture. Dorothea explains to Pierre "that the reason your father did not want his portrait taken was because he was secretly in love with the French young lady, and did not want his secret published in the portrait" (79).

Pierre's mother's "intuitive aversion" to this portrait and Isabel's letter informing Pierre of their relation seem to Pierre "reciprocal testimonies" to Dorothea's story (85). In Isabel, in the issue of a premarital affair, and in the premarital portrait Pierre discovers another truth about his father. The picture now seems to tell Pierre: "I am thy father as he more truly was . . . I am thy real father" (83). In this more true, more real father, Pierre finds the ideal of his literary economy: an author whose true likeness is reproduced. When the chair-portrait speaks to Pierre in the voice of his father, Pierre is replacing "the latter tales and legends of his devoted wedded love" (83) with the image of the father before his marriage. The portrait enables Pierre to imagine his father unconnected with his mother. Pierre now rejects the venerated paternal character to whom his mother has testified, finding a more accurate representation in the earlier chair-portrait. Though in taking Isabel's cause Pierre resigns his patrimony, he does so not as a renunciation of paternal inheritance but as an insistence on a more truthful account of his father. The preferred, antecedent portrait that "proves" to Pierre the fact of his father fathering Isabel provides him with a model of authorship independent of the sentimental family configuration he has known. His adherence to this model representation displaces his mother, who in her allegiance to the domesticated vision of Pierre's father signifies impediments to originality. The biography of the father, the truer representation of him, antedates the sentimental mother. Pierre identifies with what escaped or predated his mother's control, and it is with this sign of his father's character that Pierre identifies his own hopes for self-determination.

Isabel provides the occasion for Pierre to summon his father, not as proof of their relation, but as the model of authorship without maternal mediations, a type of his own self-generative potential. He invokes his father, or uses Isabel's claim as an invocation of the father, to inaugurate his own genealogy and commence his own nonsentimental narrative. In the ideal sentimentalist scenario of maternal influence, a good son carries into his career the good character of his mother.[33] But then it is finally the mother's portrait, a portrait of and by the mother, that the world sees. Pierre perfects the sentimental model of authorship by erasing the mother from the paradigm of literary relations and production. Choosing to link his destiny with his sister, Pierre divorces his literary endeavor from maternal supervision.

The domestic cult, however, ascribed to sisters a maternal role; they were to assist their mothers in "forming the moral, intellectual, and physical habits of their younger brothers and sisters." In his *Advice to Young Men* William Alcott stressed that sisters "may be made the instruments of a brother's moral regeneration."[34] Getting a sister, then, is like getting another mother. Satirizing and sexualizing the sentimental idealization of mothers and sisters, Melville remarks of Pierre's desire for a sister: "He who is sisterless, is as a bachelor before his time. For much that goes to make up the deliciousness of a wife, already lies in a sister" (7). Pierre conflates sister and wife as he conflated mother and sister. But he exploits the self-defining possibilities of having a sister, her signification not of maternity or wifehood but of her brother's individuality. A sister evinces both the progenitive power of the parent(s) and the difference between male and female identity. She thus assures her brother of his particular identity, of his individuality. Her difference underlines his originality. The female sexuality of the mother is not sufficient to offer this assurance, for the mother is not also an issue of the father, not a filial representation of the father. The conception of a daughter allows the son his self by both resemblance and dissimilarity, reinforcing the bond between father and son and preserving a genetic model of representation in which the son reproduces the father.

Given that Mary Glendinning is a widow and given the actual nineteenth-century patterns of remarriage and continuous childbearing, a more likely family plot would grant Pierre a sister through his mother.[35] But it is necessary to Pierre's reformation of the sentimental family to obviate the role of the mother in reproduction and nurture. The repudiation of the mother makes way for access to the father, a union removed from the mediations of mothers and markets in patriarchal perpetuation. At the outset of *Pierre*, Melville intimates that "this strange yearning of Pierre for a sister" derived from his solitary position as "the only surnamed male Glendinning extant" (7). Since Pierre's American Revolution heroic grandfathers, the family has "run off into the female branches" (8). Now Mary Glendinning, the sentimental mother, holds and wields "the old General's baton" (20); from this phallic mother Pierre seeks to wrest his authority and "have a monopoly of glory in capping the fame-column, . . . the tall shaft erected by his noble sires" (8). A sister by the same father reasserts the homosocial structure sentimentalism obscures, thus certifying male identity.[36]

In countering the hitherto accepted portraiture of Pierre's father, Isabel thus reinstates and affirms patrilinear authority, purifying it from the claims of nurture to the development of individual identity. As such she figures as the desirable dark woman of patriarchy—antidote to sentimental womanhood and society, affirmation of masculinity, the femme fatale whose appropriation reinforces masculine power. This reinforcement explains why Pierre's alliance with her alienates and kills his mother. More than an asocial projection of the masculine imagination and Melville's fantasy of an aboriginal woman, Isabel figures the removal of maternal nurturance, the proof of a nonsymbiotic identity.

The autobiography Isabel relates to Pierre begins with the declaration that she "never knew a mortal mother." Her lips "never touched a woman's breast"; she seems "not of woman born" (114). This Athenalike origin matches Pierre's fantasy of a life without a mother. Isabel projects the possibility of an alternative life and authorship in keeping with Pierre's desire for an autonomous mode of authorship and individuality, the fantasy of nature without nurture so celebrated in Melville's travel literature.[37]

Pierre accepts Isabel as his sister because she makes the claim most appealing to his ideal of selfhood: she invokes an anti-sentimental family history. This sister embodies for Pierre the fantasy of removing himself from the sentimental family. Despite Isabel's mysteriousness, the suddenness of her appearance in Pierre's neighborhood, her lack of proofs, her lapses into incoherent murmuring when she tells Pierre of her past, Pierre immediately believes her to be his father's daughter and his own sister. He requires neither legitimation of law nor corroboration of witnesses to prove Isabel's identity. Pierre becomes even more convinced of Isabel's story through her music, in which her claims merge with the sound of her guitar. "The guitar was human," Isabel tells Pierre. "It sings to me as I to it. . . . All wonders that are unimaginable and unspeakable; all these wonders are translated in the mysterious melodiousness of the guitar" (125). The wonder translated and offered to Pierre is the possibility of such a relation, the replacement of a literary economy based on the family with one assuring absolute identity between author and book. It is this unity of body and articulation, this composition of continuity between self and expressive gestures, that seduces and enthralls Pierre.

Isabel thus provides the occasion for a reconstruction of Pierre's history, a reconstruction beginning with the destruction not just of his sentimental filial relation with his mother but also of his paternity. He then dismisses as he protects his father in his bizarre moral imperative to take Isabel's cause; having replaced sentimental family authority with patriarchal authority, having discounted, that is, his mother's "over-fond" and "over-reverential . . . imaginary image" in favor of the chair-portrait of the "real father," Pierre then "strove to banish the least trace of his altered father" (87). In order "to hold his public memory inviolate" (198), Pierre determines to destroy his father's portrait, "the one great condemning and unsuborned proof" of his profligacy (197). But the protection of his father's memory is not Pierre's only motive. Now that Isabel has "become a thing of intense and fearful love for him" (197), the portrait reminds Pierre of her illegitimacy. Because "the portrait's painted *self* seemed the real father of Isabel," the portrait remains proof of Isabel's "sinisterly becrooked, bemixed, and mutilated" status (197). To save and purify Isabel's "sweet, mournful image," to free her of this undermining parentage, Pierre must "destroy this thing" (198), must eradicate the father-portrait. Just before leaving Saddle Meadows with Isabel he burns the portrait, performing funeral rites for his father "a second time" (198): "'Henceforth, cast-out Pierre hath no paternity, and no past; and since the future is a blank to all; therefore, twice-disinherited Pierre stands untrammeledly his ever-present self!—free to do his own self-will and present fancy to whatever end!'" (199). Pierre presents his fancy to the end of making Isabel (and himself) fatherless as well as motherless, so that in fashioning his life, in imagining an autobiography modeled after Isabel's, he might make himself an orphan. The orphan, like the foundling books Melville imagined in the *Mosses* review, might be untrammeled by origins, might map his own life.

Just as in Melville's mechanics of anonymity, in which originality is achieved by a simultaneous brotherhood and orphanhood, by an increase and an extinction of relations, Pierre undoes his family through his relation to Isabel. As soon as Pierre embraces Isabel as his sister, he in effect denies their sibling relation by making her his wife. They present themselves to the world as a married couple and their relation is presented by Melville as an erotic one.[38] From a conventional sentimental point of view, the scandalous motive of Pierre's perverse enlargement of his family lies in his incestuous desire for Isabel.[39] But from this same perspective, incest involves an even more scandalous aim: Pierre's goal of dissolving the family. He "marries" his sister to divest himself of his family, including his sister. A sister *qua* sister reminds her brother of parental origins, thereby checking the autobiographical fantasy of self-generation that subtends the myth of the author. Incest with the sister, violating sibling relation and family law, enables Pierre's renovation of family for the establishment of his literary economy, a mode of authorship embedded in a self-contained family, in the notion of the self as its own family.

Incest, in Pierre's reformed sentimental family, epitomizes and literalizes the sacred tenet in sentimentalism: the bond between mother and son. But more than exposing the domestic cult's deployment of the primary familial taboo in the service of education and socialization, Melville's story of Pierre's "doubly incestuous" situation, his eroticized relations with mother and sister, discloses the familial underpinnings of aesthetic projects: how family models inform and empower myths of the writer. In a dream just before the end of his life, Pierre identifies his literary project with the exploits of the Titan Enceladus. He imagines himself as a "heaven-aspiring" being "held down to its terrestial mother," caught between "man's earthly household peace, and the ever encroaching appetite for God" (347, 345). Pierre associates Enceladus with "the wild scenery" (344) of an unapproachable mountain. But it is not only the landscape of the sublime that attracts Pierre to Enceladus; it is the Titan's incestuous genealogy that makes him sublime to Pierre. Pierre sees Enceladus as a model of selfhood because the Titan is "son and grandson of an incest," "one issue" of an endogamous family (347).[40]

Taking his sister as wife, and later, when he admits Lucy to his lodgings in New York, taking his would-be wife as sister, Pierre simultaneously denies his family ties and revises those ties to create a more endogamous family, closer

to his closed-circuit model of literary production. The endogamous, inbred family approaches the point of the family's disappearance; Pierre discovers in incest a foundation, a familial support in the form of no family at all, for his literary economy. Once established in his new familial arrangement, Pierre recedes into his work. His "author-hero Vivia" seems "directly plagiarized from his own experiences" (302). By writing this book Pierre is "thinning his blood and collapsing his heart. He is learning how to live, by rehearsing the part of death" (305). In this "accession to the personal divine" Pierre "can not eat but by force"; now become the sole source of his book, its subject and object of consumption, "his is the famishing which loathes all food" (305).[41] He famishes to be his book; in this corollary to Melville's literary cannibalism, the author is consumed by his production. The isolating movements of endogamy and incest culminate in the transformation of author into book.

A further consequence of *Pierre*'s exploitation of incest follows in an analogous change: the replacement of sentimental nurture networks by a system of self-generation. In this alternative dynamics of individualism, the unconsummated, nonprogenitive incest Melville describes between Pierre and Isabel approximates the condition of being one's own child. Pierre's "marriage" to Isabel accordingly makes him "foetal," infantilizing him as his writing debilitates him, leaving him blind and infirm, a "toddler" on his own. Subsumed by his book, his "Vivia," "Pierre was solitary as at the Pole" (338). The solitude of the autogenous self is such that nothing can intervene between the famishing author and the book that is his life. The singular literary economy projected from *Pierre*'s conversion of authors into (consumable) books, and domestic nurture into autogenesis, makes production and consumption identical: Melville's ideal (male) author *is* both the labor and the consumption of his production.

CRIME AND PUNISHMENT

The collation of *Pierre*'s perverse ecologies and genetics of family and authorship—the operations of anonymity, cannibalism, commodification, nurture, and incest I have been tracing through Melville's revision of literary economy—brings us, finally, to consider the function of death in literary individualism. If a certain misogyny inaugurated Pierre's quest for literary autonomy, a full-blown murderous misanthropy concludes it. All persons, even the person of Pierre, must disappear in this anti-sentimental narrative.

Once "isolated from the world, and intent upon his literary enterprise" (285), Pierre learns that his mother has died, leaving Saddle Meadows to his cousin Glen Stanly, who has become Lucy's suitor. Replaced by Glen Stanly and reduced to a toddler, the disinherited Pierre is at last the orphan of his dreams. In the concluding events of the narrative, Pierre literalizes the violent solipsism of his literary project, killing his cousin and Lucy's brother, thereby "slaughtering the only unoutlawed human being by the name of Glendinning" (360).

In these crimes Isabel is the woman in the case, the cause of Pierre's murderous acts. Isabel affirms the sublimity of Pierre's solitary expedition by asserting that "God called thee, Pierre, not poor Bell" (159). In the prospect of allying his fate with his sister, Pierre conflates Isabel with God, his term for the polar opposite to the mother and household; "to him, Isabel wholly soared out of the realms of mortalness" (142), replacing Lucy and his mother, emblems of the sentimental impediments to his autobiographical quest. Yet when alone at his literary task, living in alternative domesticity with Isabel, Lucy, and the servant Delly, Pierre finds himself under the surveillance of a jealous wife. Isabel sees Lucy as an obstruction to their intimacy; once Lucy decides to live with them as "a nun-like cousin" (310), Pierre's relation to Isabel seems to her mediated "through another and an intercepting zone" (334). For Isabel, intercepting zones reinforce solitariness rather than interfere with it as Pierre fears. She seeks her brother in order to overcome individualness, for, as she tells him, "there is no perfect peace in individualness" (181).[42]

Both Isabel's possessiveness and Lucy's presence disturb the peace of Pierre's individualness; this populous polar region Pierre inhabits—it is also a New York tenement—exposes the inevitable problem of other people to the imagination of self-generation, the persistence of society in the fantasy of self-containment. Yet if Isabel as well as Lucy signifies the inescapability of relations, it is less as figures of sentimental culture than as instances of the problems of intersubjectivity which the sentimental family domesticates. The sentimental family reconciles the self with others, secures the notion of selfhood in relations with others that involve the objectification, nurture, discipline, and appropriation of the self by others. The problem of other persons remains when Pierre has left the sentimental family, because selfhood requires defining the self against otherness, because identity always entails relation. As the measure of Pierre's individualness, Isabel recapitulates the sentimental mother's function, the domestic standard in the process of individuation.[43]

At this convergence of the poles *Pierre* encompasses, two portraits again figure in Pierre's aesthetics of autobiography. Visiting a portrait gallery, Pierre searches for an intriguingly labeled picture, "No. 99. A stranger's head, by an unknown hand" (349). This doubly anonymous portrait, "a real Italian gem of art" amid a "most hybrid collection of impostures" (350), shows a "comely, youthful man's head, portentously looking out of a dark, shaded ground, and ambiguously smiling" (351). To Isabel, this face holds "certain shadowy traces to her own unmistakeable likeness"; "while to Pierre, this face was in part as the resurrection of the one he had burnt" (351). In their recognition of this portrait, "Pierre was thinking of the chair-portrait: Isabel, of the living face" she remembers of her father (351). This coincidence of two referents causes Pierre to wonder about whether the congruity between "Aunt Dorothea's nebulous legend" of his father's portrait and "Isabel's still more nebulous story of her father" (353) is not merely coincidence. "How did he know that Isabel was his

sister? . . . the grand point now with Pierre was, not the general question whether his father had had a daughter, but whether, assuming he had had, *Isabel,* rather than any other living being, *was that daughter*" (353).

It is as if the recognition of Isabel's conventional relation to himself, her all too domestic claims, prompts Pierre to disown his brotherhood. But he retains the possibility of having a sister—his father still may have had a daughter. Melville sustains Pierre's literary fantasy by pairing the ambiguous picture with a copy of *The Cenci* of Guido, the portrait of the object and agent "of the two most horrible crimes . . . possible to civilized humanity—incest and parricide" (351). These portraits "exactly faced each other; so that in secret they seemed pantomimically talking over and across the living spectators below" (351). This association links Isabel with incest and parricide, so that even if she is not the orphaned sister of Pierre she is still identified with his project. Incest and parricide are crimes against relation, violations of the social (and legal) boundaries defining the family. Pierre would destroy these boundaries to rid himself of relations, of the very idea of relationship. The horror he discovers in the pictures is not the possibility that Isabel might not be his sister but the fact that she or some other remains necessary to his autobiographical project. His purified domestic economy cannot fully dispel the principle of relation. Isabel articulates this necessity of contrast to individuality when she tells Pierre: "I am called woman, and thou, man, Pierre, but there is neither man nor woman about it" (149). Sexual difference works to define not men and women but the possibility of self.[44]

Difference and resemblance, the conditions Pierre manipulates to form a self-generated, self-sustained life, bring Pierre back home to the inescapability of family. *Pierre* enacts a confusion between portraits and subjects, between representations and persons, writing and the body. The danger inherent to Pierre's fantasy of self-distinction through submersion in otherness is that of losing himself, becoming truly anonymous in anonymity. At play in the juxtaposition of the two pictures is the problem with a system of anonymous representation: the problem of determining and preserving originality when two or more representations coincide.

The quest for originality and the effort to defy the conventions of sentimental culture therefore eventually require methods of enforcement. Isabel's ultimate resemblance to Pierre's controlling sentimental mother, underscored by her resemblance to the Stranger's Head, alerts Pierre to the necessity of a law to uphold his model of the singular family. This is why the end of Pierre's mission is a chronicle of crime and punishment. His drama of individualness ends in prison, under the aegis of a legal administration of individuality. Pierre finally locates his literary economy not in heaven or at the North Pole or in any other sublime region but in sentimental culture, on the wrong side of the law. In transgressing the social order Pierre asserts his particularity and is singled out for his singularity.

Another domestic angel in Pierre's life, Isabel first enables and finally circumscribes Pierre's autobiography. The doubts the portrait raises about her identity translate into threats to Pierre's literary enterprise and his character. Two letters precipitate Pierre's resolve to shoot Glen Stanly and Lucy's brother, Frederic Tartan. The first missive, from his ironically named publishers Steel, Flint & Asbestos, accuses him of being "a swindler," of taking cash advances "under the pretenses of writing a popular novel." The publishers refuse to print any more of Pierre's "blasphemous rhapsody" and charge him for the "printing thus far" and the advances (356). The second letter, from Stanly and Tartan, also charges Pierre with a crime, denouncing him as "a villainous and perjured liar" (356). This "scornfullest and loathesomest title for a man" (357) echoes the doubt implanted in Pierre by the portrait resembling Isabel: the possibility that Isabel is not his sister but merely the object of his lust, that his literary endeavor is "a detected cheat" (357). Both his publishers and his kin strike at more than Pierre's incestuous desires; they undermine his "intense procreative enthusiasm," the myth of authorship elaborated by "his own manifold and inter-enfolding mystic and transcendental persuasions" (353) about Isabel.

To acquit himself and "get a start of the wise world's abuse" of his literary labor, Pierre spits upon his book and defies "all the world's bread and breath" (357). Unable to realize in life his Promethean quest for self-nurture, Pierre decides to meet his accusers and risk death, taking two pistols, "more wondrous" than the "wondrous tools Prometheus used" (358). Still defending the intent of his quest, the creation of a self-contained literary economy, Pierre plans the murder of his detractors as his response to their letter, literally returning their words: "[F]or the top-wadding [in the pistols], I'll send 'em back their lie, and plant it scorching in their brains! he tore off that part of Glen and Fred's letter, which more particularly gave the lie; and halving it, rammed it home among the bullets" (359). In a last-ditch implementation of his ecology of representation, he thus also literally returns his publishers' same accusation by translating steel, flint, and asbestos into instruments designed to put an end to all commerce and communication.

Murder and what is effectively matricide bring Pierre to prison and a death sentence; now that "his own hand [has] extinguished his house" (360), he can achieve his fantasy of self-nurture in the only act of self-control remaining to him: suicide. In a last and fatal act of self-nurture, he feeds himself to death with the poison Isabel keeps between her breasts. The end of Pierre's story, though, is not his but Isabel's. Joining him in death, gasping the last words "'ye know him not!' . . . she fell upon Pierre's heart, and her long hair ran over him, and arbored him in ebon vines" (362). Her words seeming to testify to Pierre's impenetrability, to his independence from his sentimental past, Isabel's dying gesture and "death-milk" actually return Pierre to the iconography of sentimental motherhood, ensconcing him in feminine bonds.

The Triumph of Sentimentalism

The return of the sentimental—the transfomation of Pierre's anti-domesticity into the final image of maternity—signifies that Pierre's anti-sentimental literary quest is precisely the cautionary tale by which domestic ideology defines and teaches individualism. Read this way, the fate of Pierre's literary individualism illustrates how bad boys get punished for blaspheming the family. To erase the family from the writer's vista turns out to be only to displace the family temporarily onto the geography of literary quest. Returning Pierre to the sovereignty of domesticity, *Pierre* exhibits a virtually paranoid sense of domestic governance. In this narrative of maternal containment of the individual, sentimental nurture blocks the writer from start to finish.

Nineteenth-century spellers, grammars, and readers represented the skills of reading and writing as extensions, if not defenses, of family values. So, for example, in the didactic practice characteristic of primer lessons which linked language usage with familial goals, the child who correctly uses the articles *a* and *the* successfully communicates the information that identifies a criminal as "the" man who had robbed and lamed her father.[45] The prominent recurrence of images of obedience and punishment in the pedagogies of reading and writing anchors literature in the family governance of individual behavior. The active and passive voices are imaged in one grammar book as an active adult figure with a whip standing over the passive child figure, reinforcing both the authority of the family and the individuality of the body the family alternately nurtures, shapes, disciplines, and punishes.[46] In the tradition of this sentimental education, Mary Glendining tutors Pierre to make him "a fine, proud, loving, docile, vigorous boy," both "sweetly docile" to herself and "a haughty hero to the world" (20). For this she dies—and for that Pierre dies. If this seems an extreme view of domestic power and responsibility, it is by no means Melville's alone.

Pierre's history bears out the predictions of sentimental child-rearing literature, testifying not only to the dangers of domestic disobedience but also to the potential delinquencies in maternal nurturance. "It is because children have been prisoners in the domestic circle—in body, mind, and soul, that they afterwards become state prisoners," William Alcott warned in his advice to mothers.[47] This imprisonment involves not the oppressive "maternal tuitions" to which Pierre was "strangely docile" but, rather, their absence. According to the contemporary popular literature of child-rearing, the mother had to realize that "the quality and quantity of food and drink, drawn in by the child at the breast, tends . . . to propagate danger and error."[48] Because mothers "sow the seeds of nearly all the good and evil in our world," only their "watchfulness" can save their children from "the verge of destruction."[49] The memory of a mother's teachings might deter a son from "the temptations which come crowding upon him" in "the busy world. . . . Even though far away, in abodes of infamy, degraded and abandoned, he must occasionally think of a broken-hearted mother."[50] This means that filial criminality is the mother's responsibility and, moreover, evidence of maternal culpability. Thus, as one mothering manual admonishes, "[I]f you are unfaithful to your child when he is young, he will be unfaithful to you when he is old."[51] In the nineteenth century's negative teleology of maternal nurture, the sins of the mother are visited upon the son. Pierre's crimes and incarceration accordingly manifest both the crime and the punishment of his mother.

When in capital punishment the birth cord is replaced with the hanging noose, the mother is relieved of her governance and responsibility; she is negated as origin and agency in the son's career. If criminality testifies to maternal neglect, and if punishment finally severs the criminal from the mother, then Pierre's crimes enable him to attain the condition of the abandoned child which sentimental criminology describes. He doubly detaches himself from his mother by causing her death and, in his own death, denying her maternity. It is the mother who is finally criminalized and punished in *Pierre*'s exposition of the outlaw writer. In what seems overkill—the excessive domestic violence of *Pierre*—Melville espouses not merely his own misogyny but what might be called the domestic tradition of misogyny.[52] For Pierre's repudiation of motherhood and home ultimately intensifies his domestic relations. His anti-sentimental literary quest is precisely the plot and psychology by which the sentimental home forwards individualism. In this light, literary individualism appears less as an oppositional mode to domestic individualism than as a certain masculine expression of it.

When Pierre resolves to leave home, the narrator remarks on the "dark, mad mystery in some human hearts, which, sometimes during the tyranny of a usurper mood, leads them to be all eagerness to cast off the most beloved bond, as a hindrance to the attainment of whatever transcendental object the usurper mood so tyrannically suggests" (180). But once the individual, in order "to embrace the boundless and unbodied air" (180), "breaks from every enfolding arm, and puts to sea in the height of a tempest," he experiences not the freedom of his own pursuit but the memory of the "household sun" he forsook (181). "For whoso once has known this sweet knowledge and then fled it; in absence, to him the avenging dream will come" (181). When Pierre renounces home, he becomes "this self-upbraiding sailor; this dreamer of the avenging dream" (181). Instead of adventure and the authority of authorship, flight entails a reconstructed home and destructive sickness; to Pierre, "who would become as immortal bachelors and gods" (180), comes a bizarre domesticity and crippling disease. Homesickness, in Melville's exposition, is not simply the effect of flight but is embodied in the conditions motivating departure. The sickness of home is that it produces a sickness for home.

This reproduction of domesticity through its internalization, an internalization Pierre tries to radicalize into a separate society of one, attests to the productive function of misogyny and anti-sentimentalism in the domestic

imagination. The desire to repudiate the mother, along with the market, is built into domestic individualism. In the genealogy of crime and punishment *Pierre* elaborates, domesticity perpetuates the demise of maternal power— the wide margins of maternal error repeatedly envisioned in nineteenth-century childcare literature—in order to preserve and replenish the sentimental legacy of individualism. *Pierre*'s testimony to domestic power suggests that the wish for self-valorization through matricide is part of what the ideology of sentimental motherhood dispenses and regulates. In this view, domesticity generates and reflects the myth of the author as the self's estrangement from the mother, a self-abandonment firmly anchored in the network called home.

Pierre's final and fatal bondage indicates that Isabel's function as the heroine through whom Pierre mirrors his ideal of individuality is ultimately in service to a sentimental literary economy. Isabel's pronouncement over Pierre's dead body to his friends that "ye know him not" (362) promotes the tale of misunderstood genius that has long circulated as the alibi of the American writer. As this tale issues from Pierre's death, he becomes the subject of a popular and frequently reissued narrative: the struggle of the male author in sentimental culture. Though Pierre fails in his authorial quest and *Pierre* failed with nineteenth-century readers, the mythology of authorship Melville expounded eventually found a select literary market— through the changing tastes and standards of the market.

The difficulty of *Pierre* and the failure of Pierre lie in the impossibility of imagining individualism outside either commerce or domesticity, of living outside the domain of self nineteenth-century America imagined—all of which is to say the impossibility of experiencing oneself as not oneself.[53] Perhaps the desire to be otherwise—to be outside the defining limits of self—is so constraining in *Pierre* because of the oppressive familiarity of alterity in individualism: the banality of utopianism in American visions of self.

Notes

1. Herman Melville, *Pierre; or, The Ambiguities;* ed. Harrison Hayford, Hershel Parker, and G. Thomas Tanselle (Evanston: Northwestern University Press and the Newberry Library, 1971), 244. All subsequent references to this text will appear in parentheses in the text.

   This chapter (without its treatment of *Ruth Hall*) first appeared as part of my 1985 dissertation, "Domesticity and the Nineteenth-Century American Imagination." Portions of it have been presented in talks at Princeton University (1985), the MLA (1985), and the University of Massachusetts at Amherst (1988).

2. My treatment of *Pierre* and domestic individualism is much influenced by Michael Rogin's insightful and intriguing discussion of the connections between nineteenth-century politics, the sentimental family, and Melville family history: *Subversive Genealogy:*

The Politics and Art of Herman Melville (New York: Knopf, 1983), 155-86.

3. The figure of the writer struggling against society dominates conceptions about American literature. Richard Poirier identifies the prominence of this archetype when he writes that "[t]he classic American writers try through style to temporarily free the hero (and the reader) from systems, to free them from the pressures of time, biology, economics, and from the social forces which are ultimately the undoing of American heroes and quite often of their creators" (*A World Elsewhere,* 5). For an exposition of the gender distinctions operating in this American mythology, see Baym, "Melodramas of Beset Manhood."

4. On the development of nineteenth-century American literary sales techniques and the puffery system, see Kelley, *Private Woman, Public Stage,* 3-27. In writing about the literary careers of nineteenth-century women writers, Kelley has coined the term *literary domesticity* to signify the "integration of private individual with published writing" that she believes these sentimental writers achieved. It is this integration of individual with literary commerce against which *Pierre* sets literary individualism.

5. The most forcefully articulated account of *Pierre* and the masculine literary career as a critique of sentimentalism and suffocating "feminine sensibility" is Ann Douglas's "Herman Melville and the Revolt against the Reader," in *The Feminization of American Culture* (New York: Avon, 1977), 349-95. In this chapter I shift from her focus to investigate what is at stake in anti-sentimentalism: the issue here is not how sentimentalism constrains but how it creates and sustains literary individualism.

6. On Melville's career difficulties see Leon Howard, "Historical Note, I," in Melville's *Pierre; or, The Ambiguities,* 365-79. The popularity of domestic literature is documented in James D. Hart, *The Popular Book: A History of America's Literary Taste* (New York: Oxford University Press, 1950); Mary Ryan, *The Empire of the Mother: American Writing about Domesticity, 1830-1860* (New York: Haworth Press, 1982), 1-43.

7. William Braswell describes Melville's satire of sentimentalism in *Pierre* in "The Early Love Scenes in *Pierre,*" *American Literature* 22 (November 1950): 283-89.

8. Melville himself, in a letter to his English publisher, considered anonymous publication for *Pierre*: letter to Richard Bentley, April 16, 1852, in *The Letters of Herman Melville,* Merrell R. Davis and William H. Gilman (New Haven: Yale University Press, 1960), 150-51.

9. Herman Melville, "Hawthorne and His Mosses," *The Literary World,* August 17 and 24, 1850, reprinted in Herman Melville, *Moby-Dick,* ed. Harrison Hayford and Hershel Parker (New York: Norton, 1967), 536.

10. Ann Douglas provides an illuminating discussion of the professional and economic aims (and necessities) of women sentimental writers in "'The Scribbling Women' and Fanny Fern: Why Women Wrote," *American Quarterly* 23 (1974): 3-24. The benefits of the strategy of anonymity for seventeeth-century French woman writers are delineated in Joan de Jean, "Lafayette's Ellipses: The Privileges of Anonymity," *PMLA* [*Publications of the Modern Language Association of America*] 99 (1984): 884-902.

In a much-debated essay ("What Is an Author?" in Josue V. Harari, ed., *Textual Strategies: Perspectives in Post-Structuralist Criticism* [Ithaca: Cornell University Press, 1979], 141-60) Michel Foucault links the rise of the "author-function" with bourgeois society, with individualism and private property. In this society the author regulates "the fictive" by limiting "the proliferation of meaning." With change, Foucault writes, this "constraint" on fiction "would then develop in the anonymity of a murmur." In other words, the agency of regulation would be less recognizable. In his effort to imagine a discourse about literature that would be attentive to political questions, Foucault advocates an "indifference" about questions of authorship and the author. Underlying this scenario of "fiction and its polysemic texts" more freely circulating and proliferating meaning is the myth of an autonomous text: the author-function does not disappear but is displaced onto the text, to which motives are now ascribed. Foucault's desire for unimpeded circulation of meaning bespeaks a new individualism—that of the text. The same vision of literary freedom that underpins Melville's myth of the anonymous author emerges in Foucault's poststructuralist myth of authorship fading into anonymity.

In a careful study of the institution of copyright, Mark Rose offers some astute qualifications to Foucault's account of authorship and individualization: "The Author as Proprietor," *Representations* 23 (Summer 1988): 51-85.

11. Fanny Fern, *Ruth Hall and Other Writings,* ed. Joyce W. Warren (New Brunswick: Rutgers University Press, 1986), 206. Subsequent references to this novel will be given in parentheses in the text.

12. Joyce Warren details Willis's treatment of his sister in her informative Introduction to *Ruth Hall and Other Writings.* This volume includes another satiric sketch Sara Willis wrote about her brother, "Apollo Hyacinth," 259-60. A much more favorable portrait of Willis emerges in Harriet Jacobs's autobiography, where, under the name of Mr. Bruce, he appears as one of Jacobs's supporters in gaining her freedom: *Incidents in the Life of a Slave Girl.*

13. Quoted in Joyce Warren, Introduction to *Ruth Hall,* ix.

14. Even though Ruth tells her daughter that "God forbid" she grow up to become a writer because "no

happy woman ever writes" (175), the book emphasizes that the domestic situation that allows women not to earn money is never a certain fate.

In an unpublished essay on *Ruth Hall* (delivered as a talk at the American Studies Association in 1986), Richard Brodhead proposes that the novel represents shifting accounts of domesticity—specifically, the shift from an agrarian domestic economy to domestic consumerism. Brodhead treats the novel's representation of literary celebrity in "Veiled Ladies: Toward a History of Antebellum Entertainment," *American Literary History* 1 (Summer 1989): 273-94. This essay, which was published after this book was written, contains interesting parallels also to my discussion of domestic values and *The Blithedale Romance.*

15. Susan Sontag traces the emergence of photography and its relation to the aesthetics of individuality and the logic of consumption in *On Photography* (New York: Farrar, Straus and Giroux, 1977), 153-80.

16. For Douglas, Melville exemplifies the serious writer's plight in a commercial culture. My reading does not presume that literature could ever be independent of socioeconomic trends. *Ruth Hall* demonstrates that the crucial issue is who controls or succeeds in commerce.

17. Jane Tompkins also analyzes the critical bias against popularity for a literary work: *Sensational Designs,* xi-xix.

18. Ahab's leg is the most memorable example of Melville's play on the relation between labor and the body; another instance is the ghostly disappearance of female physicality in the production of paper depicted in Melville's story "The Paradise of Bachelors and the Tartarus of Maids," in *Harper's Magazine* 10, no. 59 (April 1855): 670-78, reprinted in *Great Short Works of Herman Melville,* ed. Warner Berthoff (New York: Harper and Row, 1969), 202-22. Sharon Cameron has powerfully explicated the issues of body definition enacted in *Moby-Dick* in *The Corporeal Self,* 15-75.

19. "Hawthorne and His Mosses," 550.

20. In Melville's imagination, the goal of shared genius is the emergence of the individual talent. In this respect his cannibalistic brotherhood of genius distinctly differs from the myth of impersonal authorship familiar to us from T. S. Eliot's formulation of literary tradition as transcendence of history and personality: "The progress of the artist is a continual self-sacrifice, a continual extinction of personality" ("Tradition and the Individual Talent," in his *Selected Essays* [New York: Harcourt Brace Jovanovich, 1964], 7).

21. The image of a male society of privileged consumers of culture is much more fully detailed in "The Paradise of Bachelors and the Tartarus of Maids," where he considers the class and gender hierarchies of production and consumption.

22. "Hawthorne and His Mosses," 548.

23. Melville's horror of publishing practices stemmed from his own experience. Perry Miller describes Melville's literary education after the success of *Typee* as the process of learning that the publishing world was "a literary butcher shop": *The Raven and the Whale: The War of Words and Wits in the Era of Poe and Melville* (New York: Harcourt, Brace, 1956), 6-7.

24. For Melville, cannibalism also figures as the threat to subjectivity, as a sign that "individuality is a mirage." See Mitchell Breitweiser, "False Sympathy in *Typee,*" *American Quarterly* 34 (Fall 1982): 411-13.

25. William Alcott, *The Young Housekeeper, or Thoughts on Food and Cookery* (Boston: G. W. Light, 1839), 43.

26. Sarah Josepha Hale, *The Good Housekeeper, or the Way to Live Well* (Philadelphia: B. Otis, 1844), 144.

27. Hale, *The Good Housekeeper,* 144.

28. Orson S. Fowler, *Maternity* (New York: Fowler and Wells, 1855), 206.

29. The way breast-feeding can operate as a governance technique is even more explicit in the case of nineteenth-century France. Jacques Donzelot, in *The Policing of Families,* explicates how the state deployed its authority through normalization of child-nursing practices. Limiting wet-nursing to a family practice, Donzelot argues, the state invested the family with childcare responsibilities and thus internalized in the family the control of individuals.

30. Melville describes the opposite of this benign literary ecology in his portrayal of the nineteenth-century literary economy in "The Paradise of Bachelors and the Tartarus of Maids." There, the mechanical workings of the publishing industry are exposed as violations of nature. The health and beauty of the female paper-mill workers are subsumed into the paper they produce. Industry, replacing nature, does not merely alienate the worker's labor but incorporates the worker.

31. My thinking on the connections between selfhood and "thingness" has benefited from William James's discussion of subject-object relations in "The Self" in his *Psychology: Briefer Course* (1892; rpt. Cambridge: Harvard University Press, 1984), 159-91.

32. Barbara Johnson has explored the relation between mothering and autobiography with reference to the woman writer, describing the particular complications that arise in a female subject's relation to authority: the sense of monstrosity associated with female projects to mother the self in literature: "My Monster, Myself," *Diacritics* (Summer 1982): 2-10. In *Pierre,* motherhood itself is the monster preventing self-expression. The troubled relation to the mother Johnson identifies with female autobiography is in my view an effect of any autobiographical project.

33. I am following here Mary Ryan's account of the rhetoric of motherhood: *The Empire of the Mother,* 45-95.

34. William Alcott, *Advice to Young Men* (Boston: Perkins and Marvin, 1838), 135.

35. Michael Rogin suggests a Melville family model for the figure of the father's illegitimate daughter, arguing that in *Pierre* Melville is exploring the possibilities of a premarital affair his father may have had or contemplated: *Subversive Genealogy,* 192-201.

36. For a provocative discussion of other deployments of daughters by a patriarchal order, see Sandra Gilbert, "Life's Empty Pack: Notes toward a Literary Daughteronomy," *Critical Inquiry* (March 1985): 355-84.

37. This association of foreign lands and cultures with freedom from nurture is perhaps most poignant in *Typee,* where the words the traveling hero teaches the native, the characteristics by which the man of society identifies himself to the native, are *home* and *mother.*

38. Note, for example, Melville's description of Pierre's proposal to Isabel that they pretend to be married: "Over the face of Pierre there shot a terrible self-revelation; he imprinted repeated burning kisses upon her; pressed her hand; and would not let go her sweet and awful passiveness" (192).

39. The incest intimations shocked many readers of the novel. An anonymous reviewer called *Pierre* "an unhealthy mystic romance"; Julian Hawthorne characterized the story as "a repulsive, insane, and impossible romance." Both reviews are reprinted with other contemporary and subsequent assessments of *Pierre* in Brian Higgins and Hershel Parker, *Selected Essays on Melville's "Pierre"* (Boston: G. K. Hall, 1983), 73, 82.

40. Frances Ferguson elucidates the ways that individuation emerges in experiences and environments of self-vitiation: "Edmund Burke's Sublime, or the Bathos of Experience," *Glyph* 8 (1981): 62-78.

On incest and sublimity, see Thomas Weiskel, *The Romantic Sublime: Studies in the Structure and Psychology of Transcendence* (Baltimore: Johns Hopkins University Press, 1976). Michael Fried traces some relations between the sublime and family romance in his fascinating study "Realism, Writing, and Disfiguration in Thomas Eakins's *Gross Clinic,"* *Representations* 9 (Winter 1985): 73-76, reprinted in his *Realism, Writing, Disfiguration: On Thomas Eakins and Stephen Crane* (Chicago: University of Chicago Press, 1987).

Myra Jehlen also treats the relation of incest to the logic of individualism and *Pierre*'s autotelism in *American Incarnation: The Individual, the Nation, and the Continent* (Cambridge: Harvard University Press, 1986), 185-226. For yet another recent reading of *Pierre* and individualism, see Wai-chee Dimock, *Empire for Liberty: Melville and the Poetics of Individualism* (Princeton: Princeton University Press, 1989), 140-75.

41. I elaborate on eating disorders as responses to commercial culture in my discussion in the next chapter of another Melville work, "Bartleby the Scrivener."

42. Sharon Cameron points out that the distinction between self and others, individualness and relation, is itself a confusion, since if "the self cannot adequately or stably be defined, neither can distinctions between selves." Cameron reads *Moby-Dick* as a quest for self-definition through extensions of the body. I am reading *Pierre* as a different though related movement, the search for self-definition in the elimination of others, an infinite regress from connections. See *The Corporeal Self,* 56.

43. Michael Rogin also sees Isabel as figuring the return of the mother. See *Subversive Genealogy,* 192-201.

44. Many of the feminist critics published in the collection *Writing and Sexual Difference,* first published as a special issue of *Critical Inquiry,* would disagree, arguing that sexual difference determines different subjectivities and different relations to writing. But this attempt to define and even legislate a specific female subjectivity reenacts the myth of self as prior to symbolic systems, the very myth *Pierre* epitomizes and problematizes. In her astute commentary on the volume (included therein) Jane Gallop observes that this myth takes the form of a confusion about the body's relation to language, an effort to differentiate between body and language as if language did not constitute bodies, male or female: Elizabeth Abel, ed., *Writing and Sexual Difference* (Chicago: University of Chicago Press, 1982).

45. William Fletcher, "The Robber and Little Ann," *The Little Grammarian* (New York: W. B. Gilley, 1829), quoted in Clifton Johnson, *Old-time Schools and School-books* (New York: Dover, 1963), 268-270. Karl F. Kaestle and Maris A. Vinovskis explore the connections between family and education in "From Apron Strings to ABCs: Parents, Children, and Schooling in Nineteenth-Century Massachusetts," in Demos and Boocock, eds., *Turning Points,* 39-80.

46. In *The Little Grammarian,* reprinted in Johnson, *Old-Time Schools,* 370. The now standard statement on the constitution of individuality through discipline is Michel Foucault, "Docile Bodies," in his *Discipline and Punish: The Birth of the Prison,* trans. Alan Sheridan (New York: Vintage, 1977). The role of the family as an organ of authority for the socialization of individuals is delineated in Donzelot, *The Policing of Families;* David J. Rothman, *The Discovery of the Asylum: Social Order and Disorder in the New Republic* (Boston: Little, Brown, 1971), 206-36.

47. Alcott, *The Young Housekeeper,* 43.

48. Alcott, *The Young Housekeeper,* 40.

49. Alcott, *The Young Housekeeper,* 25.

50. Reverend John C. Abbott, *The Mother at Home; or, Principles of Maternal Duty* (Boston: Crocker and Brewster, 1833), 15-16.

51. Abbott, *The Mother at Home,* 20.

52. The hostility toward mothers and mothering operating in the tradition of domestic womanhood has been explicated by feminist investigations of socialization. See Nancy Chodorow, *The Reproduction of Mothering: Psychoanalysis and the Sociology of Gender* (Berkeley and Los Angeles: University of California Press, 1978); Dorothy Dinnerstein, *The Mermaid and the Minotaur: Sexual Arrangements and Human Malaise* (New York: Harper and Row, 1977).

53. In a different reading of *Pierre,* Emory Elliott attributes Pierre's failure to the fact that "he takes himself and his American heritage too seriously": "Art, Religion, and the Problem of Authority in *Pierre,*" in Sacvan Bercovitch and Myra Jehlen, eds., *Ideology and Classic American Literature* (Cambridge: Cambridge University Press, 1986), 346.

Steven C. Scheer (essay date 1990)

SOURCE: "Herman Melville: The Subversive Lie of Expedient Truth in *Pierre: Or, the Ambiguities,*" in *Pious Impostures and Unproven Words: The Romance of Deconstruction in Nineteenth-Century America,* University Press of America, 1990, pp. 67-94.

[*In the following excerpt, Scheer examines the relationship between Pierre and the narrator of* Pierre *and explores the nature of self-knowledge and virtue.*]

1. The Epistemological Ground: Or, The Expedient Lie

". . . a most singular act of pious imposture"

Because it traces the causes and effects of the inscription of this chapter, Melville's *Pierre* (1852) is perhaps the most openly deconstructive work under consideration in this book. Its "thematics" of reading and writing anticipate a number of Freudian, Nietzschean, and Derridean insights: the sublimation of repressed sexuality, the illusory nature of human "truths," and the fiction of a stable center or origin. Its basic structure is also reminiscent of biblical genetics, the loss of an always already lost innocence and the failed achievement of an always already inadequately reassuring knowledge of good and evil. Just as its "intentional incoherence" is finally interpretable as "totally coherent both internally and in its effect on the reader" (Kearns 1983: 50), so, too, its wildly divergent tonality is in the end a sign of its total narrative unity. Such paradoxical assertions about *Pierre* come in the wake of recognizing that many of its sentences "can only be understood if the reader abandons logic and accepts a principle of associational cohesion" (Kearns 1983: 40). In other words, certain "relations" the critic finds in the work are

there by the virtue of juxtaposition rather than by the virtue of inescapable logicality. This conclusion is an inevitable corollary of the way in which the story is told as well of the story which is told.

Both the act of narration and that which is narrated serve to undermine the reader's trust in the sense the human world makes of its origins and of its consequences. An almost imperceptible fissure in the fabric of the conventional world of received ideas is the opening into a text the language of which never permits unambiguous readings. Reading in *Pierre* is clearly a metaphor for the act of knowing, and the act of knowing compulsively finds itself having to recognize that the fictive is inevitably bound up with the real. According to Edgar A. Dryden, for example, "for the narrator of *Pierre* words are shadows of substance which do not help to free man from his enslavement to the world but instead bind him more tightly to its artificiality" (1968: 126). This artificiality is, in a way, the product of writing both in the literal and in the metaphorical sense, which means that it is caught up in that reading/writing dichotomy we have already seen in Hawthorne's texts and the implications of which I shall address in some detail below.

Richard H. Brodhead's reading of *Pierre* comes close to the proto-deconstructive dynamics of the work:

> The sentimental romance of *Pierre* allows Melville to recreate in the texture of his own fiction the processes of seeing and feeling that are its subjects at the dramatic level. This mode repeatedly calls attention to itself as a kind of fiction in *Pierre,* but it does this, finally, not to discredit its own worth, but rather to engage us in a consideration of the psychological dynamics out of which this kind of fiction is created—in novels and in life. (1976: 175)

The reason for this "thematic" balance between narrator and hero is further implicated by the (proto-)deconstructive texture of Melville's romance. Again, Brodhead sums up the essence of this when he states that

> [r]econciling the soul and the world, the divine and the earthly, is a problem that preoccupies the narrator as much as the hero. But he knows in addition that this problem admits of no solution. And because he knows that to obtain a voice from the silent heavens is to dupe oneself, there is only one use to which he can put his own voice. That is to tell the story of the search for final truths, the story of how this problematic state of being is entered into and endured. He cannot, he knows, announce any answer, but he can tell of the insights and impostures that cause and attend a search for one. (1976: 181)

The narrator's final attitude, in Brodhead's phrase, is to see that to "[m]ake any kind of fiction is to pretend to make sense of what defies comprehension, and to do this is to engage in conscious falsehood" (1976: 186).

Extrapolating the (proto-)deconstructive elements at work in Melville's *Pierre* entails an arbitrary separation of the otherwise inseparable epistemological and ethical "thematics" (the fact that these two dimensions are inseparable is itself of some significance). This "critical" separation, however, is unavoidable. The arbitrary nature of the "violence," therefore, with which I shall undertake this "reading" should be kept in mind. In exploring the epistemological foundations of Pierre's moral dilemma, I shall also concentrate on Melville's unique narrative technique, the narrative technique that is intricately bound up with theoretical statements about the nature of language, with the relationship between the narrator as writer (/reader) and Pierre as reader(/writer), and with the whole question of (epistemological-ethical) self-consciousness which finally leads to self-doubt rather than self-assurance.

For the narrator of **Pierre** the prototype of all words, as imaged in the "Peerage Book," is the name. If the prototype of all words is the name, it follows that the prototype of our understanding the world around us is reading. Having made the world intelligible by imparting names to all the things which constitute it, we then proceed to misread the names which we have inherited and/or invented. Because the act of reading is structurally indistinguishable from the act of misreading, the reading/writing of "names" makes for irresolvable ambiguities. In Melville's text this reading of "names" is also connected with speaking, that is, with "breath" ("spirit," the image of creation by divine fiat).

In speaking of the "Peerage Book," for example, the narrator notes that "mere names, which are also but air, do likewise revel in . . . endless descendedness" (9). The immediate context here is "empty air," that is, the air that we breathe, which is—in a sense—also our heritage in that it is the air our ancestors had already breathed. Our names, likewise, are "but air." But they not only identify us, they survive us and, at times, even survive our extinction: "grafted families successively live and die on the eternal soil of a name. In England this day, twenty-five hundred peerages are extinct; but their names survive. So that the empty air of a name is more endurable than the man, or than dynasties of men; the air fills man's lungs and puts life into a man, but man fills not the air, nor puts life into that" (10). As a theoretical statement about language, the conclusion above is ironically self-contradictory. By bestowing names on ourselves and on the things around us, we not only endow ourselves and things with life, we also perpetuate the lives of the "names" which (though not unchangeable) can haunt us with their "meanings" in unforeseeable and unexpected ways. The name as at once a convenient tag and a kind of "reading-into" is clearly delineated in the following passage:

> Say what some poets will, Nature is not so much her own ever-sweet interpreter, as the mere supplier of that cunning alphabet, whereby selecting and combining as he pleases, each man reads his own peculiar lesson according to his own peculiar mind and mood. Thus a high-aspiring, but most moody, disappointed bard, chancing once to visit the Meadows and beholding that fine eminence, christened it by the name [Mount of the

Titans] it ever after bore; completely extinguishing its former title—The Delectable Mountain—one long ago bestowed by an old Baptist farmer, an hereditary admirer of Bunyan and his most marvelous book. From the spell of that name the mountain never afterward escaped; for now, gazing upon it by the light of those suggestive syllables, no poetical observer could resist the apparent felicity of the title. For as if indeed the immemorial mount would fain adapt itself to its recent name, some people said that it had insensibly changed its pervading aspect with a score or two of winters. Nor was this strange conceit entirely without foundation, seeing that the annual displacements of huge rocks and gigantic trees were continually modifying its front and general contour. (342)

If nature does not interpret for us, that is, if nature does not provide us with her own interpretations which we simply read off, then instead of reading-off we are constantly reading-into (that is, reading-off what we have already read into). The concept of naming in this passage is intricately bound up with this issue but it is also implicitly ambiguated by it. By naming the mountain "delectable," the "old Baptist farmer" had apparently read into it a characteristic which could only be annihilated by another name, "The Mount of Titans." This second name is said to have an "apparent felicity" since it seems to be a more apt description of the rough cliffs the mountain presents to view. The name, though, has not really been "completely extinguished" which is apparent from the fact that the narrator, for example, has still heard of it. If the prior and in some sense misleading name still persists, the pleasurable facade it implies must also in a sense still be there.

This ambiguates the matter. From a distance, for example, the mountain may still look delectable, while a closer look may reveal a "stark desolation." But is this true, after all? What about the "disappointed bard" who "reads his own peculiar lesson according to his own peculiar mind and mood"? And why should the narrator say that Pierre's "remarkable dream or vision" of this mountain is a "baseless vision"? Can the vision be really baseless? Is it not based on Pierre's own "mind and mood" in his "semi-unconsciousness"? (342) And what about the ambiguity of the reading-into metaphor? A version of this metaphor is one of the first used by the narrator: "[s]o perfect to Pierre had long seemed the illuminated scroll of his life thus far, that only one hiatus was discoverable by him in that sweetly-writ manuscript. A sister had been omitted from the text. . . . Nor could the fictitious title, which he so often lavished upon his mother, at all supply the absent reality" (7). The apparently ambiguous self-contradiction may not seem hopeless here. Fictitious titles playfully bestowed seem, at any rate, unsatisfactory.

A closer examination, though, uncovers another meaning in the passage, one that will make the playful appellation of "sister" bestowed on Pierre's "mother" replete with the ambiguity of, among other things, sexual repression. But the relationship between the narrator and his hero entails even more here than the pretense of courting one's mother or the pretense of espousing one's sister. In speaking of the "richly aristocratic condition of Master Pierre Glendinning" the narrator says that his hero "stands on [a] noble pedestal; we shall see if he keeps that fine footing; we shall see if Fate hath not just a little bit of a small word or two to say in this world" (12). Read as a straightforward metaphor, the passage poses no difficulties. But if we juxtapose it to a number of other such passages, the situation soon reveals an aspect of writing reminiscent of the trial Hawthorne bestowed upon Coverdale for apparently flirting with the role of a providential interference. When discussing the benevolent effects of country life on Pierre, the narrator once more repeats the idea: "we shall see if that blessing pass from him as did the divine blessing from the Hebrews; we shall yet see again, I say, whether Fate hath not just a little bit of a word or two to say in this world" (14). But by inviting this analogy between himself and an all-powerful and fate-controlling God, the narrator also traps himself in an unexpected reversal. When later he claims that "Pierre was not arguing Fixed Fate and Free Will . . . Fixed Fate and Free Will were arguing him, and Fixed Fate got the better of the debate" (182), the narrator apparently inadvertently implies that the novelistic end in sight—Pierre's prearranged plight and inevitable catastrophe—is just as much in control of the narrator as it is in control of his hero: "I shall follow the endless, winding way . . . careless wither I be led, reckless where I land" (107).

The occasional pseudo-dialogue between the narrator and Pierre is also implicated here. When perplexed by the vision of a face (the face that will turn out to be Isabel's), Pierre seems impatient to get at the bottom of the mystery. The narrator, for the first time, addresses him directly: "[p]atience, Pierre. Ever are such mysteries best and soonest unravelled by the eventual unravelling of themselves" (53). This "unravelling" begins with Pierre's discovery that he may have a sister after all. But with this discovery comes the simultaneous collapse of his world, the loss, as it were, of his father's "innocence." Once more, the narrator addresses his hero: "for thee, the before unmistrusted moral beauty of the world is forever fled; for thee, thy sacred father is no more a saint . . . Truth rolls a black bellow through thy soul! Ah, miserable thou, to whom Truth, in his first tides, bears nothing but wrecks" (65). The next time the narrator engages his hero in pseudo-dialogue, the imposture of the novelist's providential design also manifests itself: "Pierre, thou are foolish; rebuild—no, not that, for thy shrine still stands; it stands, Pierre, firmly stands . . . Such a note as thine can easily enough be written, Pierre; impostors are not unknown in this curious world; or the brisk novelist, Pierre, will write thee fifty such notes . . . Pierre—foolish Pierre" (69-70).

This self-revelation of the "brisk novelist" as Pierre's "Fate" entails a whole maze of relationships leading into the ethical/epistemological dilemma, its causes as well as effects. The fact that Pierre can look upon his life as if it were a written text issues from the narrator's knowing that this is exactly what it is. The providential language-weaver,

then, is up to something more than his compassionate and sympathetic tone implies. By a process of "naming," he is "creating" a world, and by creating it he weaves himself into its texture, constituting himself as a part of it. But at the same time that the narrator constitutes himself he also delimits and exposes himself: "it is impossible to talk or write without apparently throwing oneself hopelessly open" (259). Through the drama of Pierre's moral dilemma and through the subsequent drama of Pierre's own novelistic enterprise, the narrator enacts the universal drama of fiction-making as a process of naming, a process of reading-into, and a process of dubious self-understanding and inadvertent self-indictment. And this final process is dubious and inadvertent precisely because the language-weaver weaves a texture of words that contains both the self that understands and the self which is indicted.

As a preliminary definition of the epistemological thrust of *Pierre,* we might say that Melville's romance both depicts and enacts a universal human dilemma which, on the level of the abstract, is represented by acts of reading which are at once also acts of writing and which, on a concrete level, exemplify the ramifications of the dilemma in question by first reversing the writing/reading hierarchy and then by reinscribing reading as the non-originary origin of writing both in the literal and in the metaphorical senses of the term. This reversal repeats the reversal of the literal/metaphorical hierarchy as well. Pierre's mental processes leading to his acceptance of Isabel as his sister are shown as a series of prior acts of metaphorical reading/writing which are going to be indirectly duplicated by his efforts as a novelist in his own right. Pierre's literal reading/writing, then, will be a consequence, an effect of his prior metaphorical reading/writing. Even though Pierre's literal reading/writing of his novel, then, will have been preceded by his experiences, it is clear in the narrator's treatment of the experiences in question that the experiences themselves represent a prior metaphorical textuality mysteriously enciphered in a series of pre/scripts.

When Pierre discovers that a "sister" may not, after all, have been "omitted from the text" of the "sweetly-writ manuscript" of his life, he plunges himself into a series of re-readings that the narrator describes in highly (proto-)deconstructive terms. The following three citations may, in fact, be taken as anticipating some crucial Derridean ideas:

> In their precise tracings-out and subtle causations, the strongest and fieriest emotions of life defy all analytical insight. . . . The metaphysical writers confess, that the most impressive, sudden, and overwhelming event, as well as the minutest, is but the product of an infinite series of infinitely involved and untraceable foregoing occurrences. [. . .]

> But is life, indeed, a thing for all infidel levities, and we, its misdeemed beneficiaries, so utterly fools and infatuate, that what we take to be our strongest tower of delight, only stands at the caprice of the minutest event—the falling of a leaf, the hearing of a voice, or the receipt of one little bit of paper scratched over with a few small characters by a sharpened feather? [. . .]

And here again, not unreasonably, might invocations go up to those Three Weird Ones, that tend Life's loom. Again we might ask them, What threads were those, oh, ye Weird Ones, that ye wove in the years foregone; that now to Pierre, they so unerringly conduct electric presentiments, that his woe is woe, his father no more a saint, and Isabel a sister indeed? . . . [I]f, in after life, Fate puts the chemic key of the cipher into his hands; then how swiftly and how wonderfully, he reads all the obscurest and most obliterate inscriptions he finds in his memory; yea, and rummages himself all over, for still hidden writings to read. (67, 69, 70)

Although his subsequent actions imply that Pierre is convinced that Isabel is his sister, his thought processes remain as constant indications that he is never absolutely certain. Even the narrator's distinction between what would convince in a court of justice as opposed to what is sufficient to convince a feverish heart is, though well taken, misleading. Upon finishing Isabel's letter, Pierre's first feeling is that the "moral beauty of the world is forever fled," that his "sacred father is no more a saint," and so he exclaims: "Henceforth I will know nothing but Truth; glad Truth, or sad Truth; I will know what *is*, and do what my deepest angel dictates." Yet, almost in the next second, "nay, but this paper thing is forged,—a base and malicious forgery, I swear." Then again, just moments later, Pierre exclaims once more: "From all idols, I tear all veils, henceforth I will see the hidden things. . . . Now I feel that nothing but truth can move me so. This letter is not forgery. Oh! Isabel, thou art my sister" (65-66, italics Melville's).

Raging between emotional and intellectual needs for certitude, for "truth," Pierre is never satisfied with his ability to uncover "hidden things," for he seems to know, even if only instinctively at this point, that every uncovering but deepens the need for further uncoverings. The best case in point is the strange but extraordinarily important "history" of the "chair-portrait," a portrait of Pierre's father painted in his youth by a cousin. An aunt, who makes a present of this chair-portrait to Pierre upon his fifteenth birthday, had told Pierre, when he was yet a child, the story of the painting. A long time ago, his aunt told Pierre, when Pierre's father may have secretly wooed a beautiful French emigrant girl, his cousin Ralph wanted to paint his portrait in that "supposed wooing way" (77). Pierre's father, however, because (according to cousin Ralph) he was "secretly in love with the French young lady, and did not want his secret published in a portrait" (79) refused to sit for the picture. Ralph, therefore, had no alternative but to "steal" the portrait (77).

Upon contemplating the resemblance between Isabel and the chair-portrait, Pierre recalls his aunt's story along with the memory of his father's dying hour in which, apparently in delirium, his father had repeatedly called out for a "daughter" (70). It is by means of these re-readings of the text of his past in the new context provided for him by Isabel's letter that Pierre decides to accept Isabel as his sister. In the final analysis Pierre's conviction rests on the perceived resemblance between the chair-portrait and the girl. But there are many moments in the romance when the status of the resemblance is itself put in question. While listening to Isabel's strange story, for example, Pierre looks at her face and sees, for an instant, "not only the nameless touchingness of that of the sewing-girl, but also the subtler expression of the portrait of his then youthful father, strangely translated, and intermarryingly blended with some before unknown, foreign feminineness" (112). What this passage implies is that there has always been a "foreign feminineness" in the chair-portrait but that it has heretofore been unread. What the passage also implies, though, is that Pierre may merely be reading this "foreign feminineness" into the chair-portrait. The "either/or" of the resemblance between the chair-portrait and the girl is constantly running the risk of being eclipsed by a "neither/nor." The narrator's most telling pinpointing of this uncertainty concerning the relationship between picture and girl comes when he states that for Pierre the "portrait's painted *self* seemed the real father of Isabel" (197, italics Melville's).

Compounding the evidential force of the resemblance for Pierre is another series of readings which may be equally right or wrong. "What subtle element could so steep this whole portrait," asks the narrator, "that, to the wife of the original, it was namelessly unpleasant and repelling? The mother of Pierre could never abide this picture, which she had always asserted did signally belie her husband." If Isabel is indeed Pierre's sister then the portrait in question does not belie Mrs. Glendinning's husband; on the contrary, it implies a truth she would rather not see. Be that as it may, the picture that Mrs. Glendinning prefers is a larger one that she commissioned herself and which even Pierre admits is a "more truthful and life-like presentation of his father" as he remembers him (72). Since the two pictures were painted in different periods of Mr. Glendinning's life, it is not at all surprising that they should be dissimilar in certain ways. The narrator's attempt to provide the reader with lucid and logical explanations does become suspect, though, especially since by doing this he appears to deviate from his standard procedure: ("[b]ut the thoughts we here indite as Pierre's are to be very carefully discriminated from those we indite concerning him" [167]) and blurs the distinction between what he says and what Pierre thinks. Of course, Pierre's mother dislikes the chair-portrait because she perceives "that the glance of the face in the portrait, is not, in some nameless way, dedicated to herself . . . whereas, the larger . . . portrait in the drawing-room, taken in the prime of life . . . indeed [resembles Mrs. Glendinning's] husband as he had really appeared to her" (82-83).

However reassuring these commonsensical explanations seem, the narrator never allows them to dissolve all suspicions. Thus, there is an ongoing fissure between what can be explained and what seems to remain inexplicable. There is, for example, the curious way in which the narrator asserts—inside Pierre's mind, as it were—that "cousin Ralph, after all, may have been not so very far from the truth, when he surmised that at one time my father did indeed cherish some passing emotion for the beautiful young French-woman. And this portrait being painted at that precise time, and indeed with the precise purpose of perpetuating some shadowy testification of the fact in the countenance of the original," the picture will naturally look as the representation of a young man in love. What makes such explanatory passages suspect is a statement made by the narrator just before he comments on them: "when the mind roams up and down in the ever-elastic regions of evanescent inventions, any definite form or feature can be assigned to the multitudinous shapes it creates out of the incessant dissolvings of its own prior creations" (82).

The tone and manner of these apparently commonsensical explanations seem to reveal a curious ambiguity. On the one hand, they are reassuring, on the other, however, they clearly indicate a process which is at once inductive and deductive. Cousin Ralph, for example, may have captured a look of love on Mr. Glendinning's face or, thinking that it was there, he may have read it into the portrait himself. And Pierre, when thinking that cousin Ralph may not have been far from the "truth," may see what the painter has read into the face or he may merely be reading something into it himself because he has been told that it is supposed to be there. Neither "nature," nor the human face, nor artistic representations of either can thus provide us with clear distinctions between reading-off and reading-into. This is borne in upon both Pierre and the reader when towards the end of the romance a third painting is introduced the function of which is to cancel all trust in representation and fill the gap between that which is represented and the representation itself with doubt. The scene is a picture gallery in New York where two pictures have a profound effect on Pierre. The first is "The Cenci of Guido" which depicts the "two most horrible crimes . . . possible to civilized humanity—incest and parricide," and the second is *A stranger's head, by an unknown hand*" (349). What is remarkable about the latter is that it is a representation of a "dark, comely, youthful man's head, portentously looking out of a shaded ground" and is, like the chair-portrait, "ambiguously smiling" (351).

The few minutes during which Pierre and Isabel contemplate this picture are full of significance. While Isabel is amazed at the resemblance between the painting and herself and of the painting's resemblance to the dim memory or dream of her father, Pierre is struck with the resemblance between the picture in question and the chair-portrait, of the existence of which Isabel knows nothing. The unreported conversation that ensues between the "siblings" after Isabel exclaims "Is it? Is it? Can it be?" is pregnant with the kind of ambiguity which grounds the entire romance and which the narrator, as non-committal and as self-indicting as ever, does not fail to point out:

> . . . here came to pass a not unremarkable thing: for though both were intensely excited by one object, yet their two minds and memories were thereby directed to entirely different contemplations; while still each, for the time—however unreasonably—might have vaguely

supposed the other occupied by one and the same contemplation. Pierre was thinking of the chair-portrait; Isabel of the living face. Yet Isabel's fervid exclamations having reference to the living face, were now, as it were, mechanically responded to by Pierre, in syllables having reference to the chair-portrait. Nevertheless, so subtile and spontaneous was it all, that neither perhaps ever afterwards discovered this contradiction. (352)

In the world of *Pierre,* then, each character lives in a realm of his or her "readings" and each character thinks that these readings are readings of "realities" shared by one and all. That the realm of "readings" he entexts for himself blurs the distinction between the fictive and the real is never explicitly borne in on Pierre. Implicitly, though, he realizes that the source of the problem is not only in the thing "read" but in the act of reading itself. When he tells Isabel that the haunting resemblance between the chair-portrait and the picture of the unknown man is but a "wonderful coincidence, nothing more," and when Isabel replies (thinking that Pierre has just referred to the resemblance between the picture and her memory of her father), "by that word . . . we but vainly seek to explain the inexplicable" (352), Pierre is already close to the never explicitly formulated basis of the entire romance itself, namely that all things are inexplicable or that all explanations are fictive. Pierre's greatest moment of clarity is also his greatest moment of doubt:

> . . . how did he *know* that Isabel was his sister? Nothing that he saw in her face could he remember as having seen in his father's. The chair-portrait, *that* was the entire sum and substance of all possible, rakable, downright presumptive evidence, which peculiarly appealed to his own separate self. Yet here was another portrait of a complete stranger . . . which was just as strong an evidence as the other. Then, the original of this second portrait was as much the father of Isabel as the original of the chair-portrait. But perhaps there was no original at all to this second portrait; it might have been a pure fancy piece. (353, italics Melville's)

Whether that which is represented is real or fictive makes no difference. The representation is in each case a lie because it is always already ambiguous enough to allow the forging of private lies which parade as public truths. The maker of the representation, the representation itself, as well as the reader/viewer of the representation are all, each in his or her own way, liars.

The novelistic enterprise is itself implicated in the problematics of representation. This applies to Melville's romance as much as to the novel Pierre is represented as writing within it. The fact that representation per se is rendered suspicious in *Pierre,* though, does not mean that the distinction between truths and lies is collapsed without a reinscription of the lie as capable of being either true or false. What is lost is the sense of certitude. Those who become cognizant of this loss (Pierre, for example, by the time he doubts the rightness of his own actions or the truthfulness of his own incipient novel) are in possession of an elusive truth, whereas those who maintain an unshakable sense of certitude remain the victims of lies mistaken for truths. Pierre's publishers, for example, accuse Pierre of being a "swindler," while cousin Glenn calls him a "villainous and perjured liar" (356). These assessments of Pierre are, of course, false precisely in proportion to their certitude, whereas Pierre's doubts concerning the rightness of his actions as well as of the truthfulness of his incipient novel remain in some sense incapable of totally annihilating a residual sense of the "truth."

Feidelson's assertion in *Symbolism and American Literature* that "when everything is fiction, fiction is nothing" (1953: 197) is belied by Melville's romance even if the comparison between **Pierre** and Gide's *Counterfeiters* is taken into consideration. It may be true, as Feidelson maintains, that in **Pierre** "Melville was not able to maintain Gide's stand" (1953: 207) of resolving rather than feeding contradictions but that may be precisely because of Melville's recognition that contradictions are themselves not immune to being contradicted. To be sure, the central issue in *The Counterfeiters,* like in **Pierre,** is "the rivalry between the real world and the representation of it which we make to ourselves. The manner in which the world of appearances imposes itself upon us, and the manner in which we try to impose upon the outside world our own interpretation—this is the drama of our lives" (Gide 1925: 205). In Melville's work, though, this question (aspects of which we have already explored above) of representation takes on the struggle of a more acutely appreciated epistemological problematic.

"All great books in the world," remarks the narrator when reflecting upon Pierre's own novelistic enterprise, "are but the mutilated shadowings-forth of invisible and eternally unembodied images in the soul; so that they are but mirrors, distortedly reflecting to us our own things; and never mind what the mirror may be, if we would see the object, we must look at the object itself, and not at its reflection" (284). The final part of this statement is highly deceptive for it is precisely the "object itself" that fails to resolve the interaction between either viewer and viewed or knower and known. There is a moment, early in the romance, when an object and its reflection represent a similar source of an inexplicable ambiguity. Pierre is going into Lucy's bedroom to fetch a "blue portfolio" in which his "affianced" keeps her pencil sketches: "crossing the magic silence of the empty chamber, he caught the snow-white bed reflected in the toilet-glass. This rooted him. For one swift instant, he seemed to see in that one glance the two separate beds—the real one and the reflected one—and an unbidden, most miserable presentiment thereupon stole into him. But in one breath it came and went" (39).

Though the precise nature of the "miserable presentiment" in question cannot be determined, it is clear that in some sense Pierre has a premonition here that he is destined not to uncover the bridal mystery of Lucy's "snow-white" bed. He cannot at this point foretell the whole maze of incest and parricide into which his rejection of Lucy's "bed"

will cast him, but he can already see that the real is somehow not the object itself nor, of course, its mere reflection but somehow the indeterminable relation between the two. By the time he undertakes the writing of his novel in New York, Pierre's previous "act of pious imposture" (173) is in full swing. Isabel, his alleged blood relative, is living with him in a pretended marital alliance, and Lucy, his erstwhile fiancée, is living with him in the pretence of a blood relationship. Meanwhile, cousin Glenn has not only usurped Pierre's place as Mrs. Glendinning's favorite but has also usurped his inheritance. Pierre's "pious imposture" has thus proliferated by means of evasions and subterfuges. On the basis of a resemblance between a picture and a young girl, which prompted a reading/misreading producing an ambivalently true/false text, Pierre has acted. His action, nobly motivated and enthusiastically undertaken, has forged a set of experiences which involve the suggestion of incest and which will eventually lead to parricide and suicide. Pierre's novel is Pierre's last attempt to untangle the entangled threads of the texture of his life. The text of his novel is both the text of his life and its "mirror image."

The implications issuing from the early passage about an object (Lucy's bed) and its reflection throw further light on Pierre's struggle to come to terms with the ambiguities of his life by the act of writing his novel. Why does Pierre, when stepping into Lucy's room, "see in . . . one glance" both the real bed and its reflection? Perhaps because only when we see the reflection simultaneously with that of which it is a reflection can it really occur to us that the "object" as such is not available for reflection by the human mind except as such, that is, except as always already a reflection in its own right. For the narrator the words of Pierre's novel (as well as perhaps of his own) represent but its reflection. The real novel, of which this verbal configuration is but an image, can never be written down except figuratively: "two books are being writ; of which the world shall only see one, and that the bungled one. The larger book, and the infinitely better, is for Pierre's own private self. That it is, whose unfathomable cravings drink his blood; the other only demands his ink. But circumstances have so decreed, that the one cannot be composed on paper, but only as the other is writ down in his soul" (304).

But if Pierre's novel is a reflection, that of which it is a reflection is not the specific experiences upon which it is based but the figurative "larger book" of the soul. The change from the youthful Pierre full of "joyous, jubilant, overflowing, upbubbling, universal life" to the still young but now worn Pierre in a "most miserable room, and at the most miserable of all pursuits of man," that of the writing of a profound novel, is precisely what is "reflected" in his work (302). "Let us peep over the shoulder of Pierre, and see what he is writing there," says the narrator. "He seems to have directly plagiarized from his own experiences, to fill out the mood of his apparent author-hero, Vivia" (302). What the fragments quoted from Pierre's novel reveal is that his book is not a verbal replica of his experiences but a series of reflections upon his emotional and intellectual struggles and of their apparent indeterminacy. "'Now I drop all humorous and indifferent disguises, and all philosophical pretentions,'" says Pierre's author-hero, because he realizes that "'the Truth and the Lie'" are unthinkable without each other, that wherever truth is lies are not far behind. To this the narrator adds that "[f]rom these random slips, it would seem, that Pierre is quite conscious of much that is so anomalously hard and bitter in his lot." Yet "knowing his condition does not one whit enable him to change or better" it (303). Pierre's book, then, is the reflection of that "larger book" in the soul which, like Isabel's music (another metaphor used for Pierre's work by the narrator), is "eternally incapable of being translated into words" (282).

Shortly after having seen Isabel's face but while still ignorant of the girl's alleged blood-relationship to him, the narrator claims that Pierre "felt that what he had always before considered the solid land of veritable reality, was now being audaciously encroached upon by bannered armies of hooded phantoms, disembarking in his soul, as from flotillas of specter-boats" (49). This is already a premonition of that eventually fatal condition which Pierre will be powerless to change. The irony is not, however, in his inability to change it, but in his mistaken belief that he has understood it. "Oh, hitherto I have but piled up words," says the narrator as though speaking for Pierre, "bought books, and bought some small experiences, and built me in libraries; now I sit down and read" (91). But reading is precisely the problem, both on the literal and on the metaphorical levels. And the problem is partially founded upon the impossibility of separating literal from metaphorical reading. The first is but a record of the second and both are forms of writing as well. This is also true of novels, those reflections or mirror images of objects where, once again, the image and the object are indeterminably connected. The narrator, Melville's most conning amanuensis as novelist, knows that conventional novels belie "reality" to the extent to which they imply that the relationship between image and object is non-problematic. Yet this relationship is nevertheless the starting point of the narrator's reflection on Pierre's literal reading:

> No slightest hope or dream had he, that what was dark and mournful in [Isabel] would ever be cleared up into some coming atmosphere of light and mirth. Like all youths, Pierre had conned his novel-lessons; had read more novels than most persons of his years; but their false, inverted attempts at systematizing eternally unsystematizable elements; their audacious, intermeddling impotency, in trying to unravel, and spread out, and classify, the more thin than gossamer threads which make up the complex web of life; these things over Pierre had no power now. Straight through their helpless miserableness he pierced; the one sensational truth in him, transfixed like beetles all the speculative lies in them. He saw that human life had truly come from that, which all men are agreed to call by the name of *God*; and that it partakes of the unravelable inscrutableness of God. By infallible presentiment he saw, that not always doth life's beginning gloom conclude in gladness; that wedding-bells peal not ever in the last scene of life's fifth act; that while the countless tribes of common novels laboriously spin veils of mystery, only to complacently clear them up at last; and while the countless tribes of common dramas do but repeat the same; yet the profounder emanations of the human mind, intended to illustrate all that can be humanly known of human life; these never unravel their own intricacies, and have no proper endings; but in imperfect, unanticipated, and disappointing sequels (as mutilated stumps), hurry with the abrupt intermergings with the eternal tides of time and fate. (141, italics Melville's)

The image/object problematic cannot be solved by mere human reflection except by what Brodhead has termed "conscious falsehood," which entails, among other things, an assumption that one has in fact unraveled God's "inscrutableness." This is also what Pierre learns by the time he attempts to write his own novel: "the more and the more that he wrote, and the deeper and the deeper that he dived, Pierre saw the everlasting elusiveness of Truth, the universal lurking insincerity of even the greatest and purest written thoughts" (339).

What the narrator's bulky verbiage amounts to (and what it attributes to Pierre's own writing at last) is a series of reflections which, like Lucy's bed, are reflections of inscrutable readings-into rather than of purely visible objects. The objects which the narrator describes or which the characters within the romance encounter are never merely apprehended except as things which are there to activate their metaphor-bound inferences. If every object is in some sense inexplicable then it follows that all explanations are but contrivances, lies. *Pierre* reverses the conventional novel's God-centered certitude not by denying God but by denying the validity of human usurpations of divine omniscience. Yet this denial is itself an invocation of the biblical account of creation by divine fiat. *Pierre* itself (as well as its hero's novelistic enterprise in the end) is a reinscription of the novel as an ambiguous reflection which, like *Hamlet,* "though a thing of life" is "but a thing of breath, evoked by the wanton magic of a creative hand, and as wantonly dismissed at last into endless halls of hell and night" (169). Thus, once the temptation of the "conscious falsehood" of apparently commonsensical explanations is put aside, what *Pierre* reflects upon is the curious phenomenon according to which in the final analysis only in the novel can we see what life is really like even as only in the mirror does Pierre really apprehend what Lucy's bed is really like. This seeing of something not by looking at it directly but by looking at its reflection in another medium, the medium of language or the equally elusive medium of the mirror's superficial depth, is paralleled by Pierre's insight into his own personal dilemma when he unwittingly uses the structure of that dilemma as the basis of his own novel, even as Melville's own insight into the act of writing/reading(-into) becomes possible in the act of writing/reading(-into) *Pierre* itself, for only in the act of writing can that which is written about be fully encountered as an always already elusive reflection.

2. The Ethical Foundation: Or, The
Subversive Truth

Pierre's moral dilemma, the thematic vicissitudes of which
are clearly underwritten by the epistemological thrust of
the romance, is a young man's improbable project in the
wake of a young man's encounter with the conventional
"wisdom" of his society. The scenario is simple enough: if
Isabel is indeed Pierre's half-sister then Pierre's father
must have committed a transgression (whether before or
after his marriage is beside the point) that not only endan-
gers the reputation of his blessed memory but would destroy the peace and tranquility of his widow. Pierre's
choice is not a choice between accepting or rejecting Isabel's claim to the Glendinning name but a way of preserving both his newly found blood relation and the reputation
of his ancestral heritage. As we have seen, he accomplishes this feat by means of a "pious imposture." By pretending to marry Isabel he bestows upon her the Glendinning name. The trouble is that in the act of achieving
justice, Pierre is forced into a number of unavoidable acts
of apparent injustice. Furthermore, as we shall shortly see,
because of the very highest ideals of the society whose
conventional "wisdom" Pierre feels compelled to reject, he
is (at the same time) impelled to keep his noble act a secret even from Lucy, lest a revelation tarnish the very nobility which is, in a sense, the goal of his "most singular
act of pious imposture."

That Pierre's noble enterprise is prompted by the young
man's enthusiasm for the highest Christian ideals (as opposed to the mere nominally "Christian" posturings Pierre
encounters in his mother and the Reverend Mr. Falsgrave)
has frequently been noted in the critical canon. No one as
yet has noted the structural similarity between Melville's
Pierre and Plato's *Republic*. Though ostensibly about the
just state, Plato's work is really an examination of the just
man. It begins with a consideration of justice and injustice. Socrates is confronted with the popular (pragmatic or
expedient) view that injustice is more profitable than justice and is, therefore, preferable to it. Socrates, who wishes
to maintain that justice is an intrinsic good, that it is its
own reward, seems momentarily to be winning the argument when two young idealists, Glaucon and Adeimantus
(who are actually on Socrates's side but who feel that the
argument for justice should be made as forcefully as
possible), challenge him to prove that justice is intrinsically better than its opposite.

At the center of the question is the typically Platonic formulation of appearance vs. reality but with a difference.
Here the recourse is not to the Forms as opposed to what
we ordinarily regard as real, but to a hypothetical reversal
of reputations (and this, as will be clear in a moment, is
the structure that Melville "takes" from Plato). Because, as
Glaucon puts it, "the highest pitch of injustice is to seem
just when you are not," Socrates has to show that the unjust man who has a reputation for justice is not better off
than the just man who has a reputation for injustice
(Pierre's case, precisely). For the just man, Glaucon main-

tains, "there must be no . . . seeming [of justice]; for if
his character were apparent, his reputation would bring
him honours and rewards, and then we should not know
whether it was for their sake that he was just or for justice's sake alone." Moreover (almost as if to make the
similarity between Pierre and the Platonic just man
stronger), Glaucon adds that the just man "must be stripped
of everything but justice, and denied every advantage the
other [the unjust man] enjoyed. Doing no wrong, he must
have the worst reputation for wrong-doing . . . and under
this life-long imputation of wickedness, let him hold on
his course of justice unwavering to the point of death. And
so, when the two men have carried their justice and injustice to the last extreme, we may judge which is the happier" (Plato i.380-70 B.C.: II.361).

Pierre wants to acknowledge Isabel as his sister without
jeopardizing his father's memory, without destroying his
mother's illusions about her late husband, and without
scandalizing his own good name. He has, of course, a
golden opportunity to replicate the situation of the Platonic just man (thereby living up to the very highest ideals
of Christianity). In other words, by doing the right thing,
Pierre will place himself, from the point of view of the
public, in the worst possible light. At first Pierre seeks
possible allies in the "public" in whose eyes his reputation
is bound to be blackened, but when his various tests bring
in failing marks, he opts for the appearance of total injustice while basking in the self-rewarding glory of its opposite. His first test case is the "wretched affair of Delly," the
servant girl who has given out-of-wedlock birth to a child
fathered by a married serving man, Ned (96). When Mrs.
Glendinning pronounces Ned to be "worse than a mur-
derer," and says that if Ned's "own legitimate boy should
now hate him, [she] could hardly blame him," even the
Reverend Mr. Falsgrave, the clergyman in whom both
Pierre and his mother seem to want to find an ally, thinks
Mrs. Glendinning is too severe. When Pierre attempts to
switch the subject to "Delly and her infant," because "their
case is miserable indeed," Mrs. Glendinning seems to become even more relentless and exclaims that the "mother
deserves" her fate. The infant, the last possible recipient of
Mrs. Glendinning's mercy, fares no better. Mrs. Glendinning insists that the "sins of the father shall be visited
upon the children to the third generation." The Reverend
Mr. Falsgrave is less adamant. His rather sententious claim
is that "because it is declared that the infamous consequences of sin shall be heredity, it does not follow that our
personal and active loathing of sin, should descend from
the sinful sinner to the sinless child." Pierre's mother's response is a rhetorical question: "if we entirely forget the
parentage of the child . . . how then is the Bible dispensation to be fulfilled?" (100)

Seeing his mother's inflexibility on the subject of a father's sins, Pierre makes one more attempt at eliciting
some semblance of mercy from her. But his inquiries concerning the attitude the legitimate child should assume toward its illegitimate counterpart only prompt Mrs. Glendinning's formulation of a foregone conclusion on the matter:

"Ask your own heart, Pierre . . . and ask the world" (101). Since Pierre knows what his own heart has to say about his predicament, he is most anxious to seek for signs that the "world" may after all underwrite his enterprise. He turns to the Reverend Mr. Falsgrave who, being a clergyman, should embody not only the wisdom of the world but that of God as well. To Pierre's pointblank question concerning the applicability of Christ's teachings to the matter at hand, the Reverend Mr. Falsgrave responds with a little speech worthy of a deconstructionist:

> "Madame and sir . . . [i]t is one of the social disadvantages which we of the pulpit labor under, that we are supposed to know more of the moral obligations of humanity than other people. And it is a still more serious disadvantage to the world, that our unconsidered, conversational opinions on the most complex problems of ethics, are too apt to be considered authoritative, as indirectly proceeding from the church itself. . . . It is not every question, however direct, Mr. Glendinning, which can be conscientiously answered with a yes or no. Millions of circumstances modify all moral questions; so that though conscience may possibly dictate freely in any known special case; yet, by one universal maxim, to embrace all moral contingencies,—this is not only impossible, but the attempt, to me, seems foolish." (102)

Though so evasive and noncommittal as to be satiric, this response is nevertheless deceptively germane to the whole question of (proto-)deconstruction in Melville's *Pierre*. As a target of satire, the Reverend Mr. Falsgrave (just as his very name implies) is hiding behind conventional words of wisdom because taking sides either with the son or the mother might win him the friendship of the one at the expense of the enmity of the other. This aside, though, his point is obviously well taken, especially the point that what comes from the clergyman will be perceived as coming from the clergy itself, thus from the "church" and, ultimately, from God Almighty. The Reverend Mr. Falsgrave's unwillingness to assume such responsibility is admirable even if his most obviously apparent intention is simply self-serving. In this way, the clergyman's position is an example of the oft-maligned "virtuous expediency" (214) we encounter in Plotinus Plinlimmon's pamphlet on "Chronometricals and Horologicals." What forces virtue to flirt with expediency at times is precisely the lack of a universal (stable) absolute standard that can be applied (centered on) any particular case.

This is precisely why Pierre divines that his "noble design" (91) must seek to fulfill itself in subterfuge. Once he has ascertained his mother's inflexibility and the clergyman's face-saving stance (after his midnight visit to the Reverend Mr. Falsgrave's house), Pierre concludes "that the truth should not always be paraded," that "sometimes a lie is heavenly, and truth infernal" (92). What makes Pierre's case ironic is not his fervent adherence to what he takes to be the "inflexible rule of holy right," but his failure to realize that this "rule" is actually the sum-total of "all conventional regardings" which he takes to be "thinner and more impalpable than airiest threads of gauze."

Pierre's trouble is not that he rejects the conventional ideals of his society but that he takes them so seriously as to actually attempt to live according to their most logically severe conclusion. "Thus," the narrator tells us, "in the Enthusiast to Duty, the heaven-begotten Christ is born" (106). It is for this reason that Pierre begs the gods to "deface in me the detested and distorted images of all the convenient lies and duty—subterfuges of the diving and ducking moralities of this earth" (107). What Pierre rejects is precisely the kind of self-serving face-saving that the Reverend Mr. Falsgrave demonstrates when he fails to abide by the "inflexible rule of holy right." Unlike the clergyman, Pierre is willing to sacrifice himself because his "sublime intuitiveness . . . points to him the sunlike glories of god-like truth and virtue; which though ever obscured by the dense fogs of the earth, still shall shine eventually in unclouded radiance, casting illustrative light upon the sapphire throne of God" (111).

Pierre's belief in the ultimately inevitable triumph of virtue is never denied by the nominally Christian society against which he rebels. His rebellion is nevertheless well taken in that the society in question will indeed honor appearances rather than realities. At the same time, the members of this society will also agree with Plato, namely, that justice is its own reward and that the truly just man will be loyal to his cause even if appearances force upon him the ill-deserved reputation of injustice. Pierre's moral dilemma, therefore, represents not so much a conflict between the ideal and the real as a conflict *within* both the ideal and the real. It is in this sense that Plotinus Plinlimmon's pamphlet is the most important subtext of Melville's *Pierre.*

It is interesting to note that even Lawrance Thompson who rejects it as a "hoax" and regards it as the "high-water mark of Melville's stylistic rascalities" (1952: 272) and who insists that it should not be taken "seriously" (1952: 275) takes it seriously enough to conclude that "Melville creates and manipulates Plinlimmon's pamphlet in such a way as to let it reflect exactly that shallow Christian doctrine against which Pierre is hopelessly fighting" (1952: 279). I think that a more careful consideration of the relationship between Plinlimmon's thesis and Pierre's moral dilemma will yield a different view of "Chronometricals and Horologicals." The first irony in the essay is that while it appears to differentiate critically between chronometers and horologes (the first being metaphorically representative of the heavenly and absolute, the second of the earthly and relative), both instruments are simply timepieces and the words themselves are etymological cousins (the first refers to the "measuring" of "time," the second to the "telling" of "hours"). Plinlimmon is, in fact, quite explicit about his attempt to reverse the chronometrical/horological hierarchy. He acknowledges that the "earthly wisdom of man may be heavenly folly to God" and that, "conversely," the "heavenly wisdom of God" may be "an earthly folly to man," but he hastens to add that it does not follow from this "that God's truth is one thing and man's truth another," for, quite to the contrary, "by their very contradictions they are made to correspond" (212).

In what sense can this paradoxical contention be maintained? The first contradictory correspondence one may note is that between "time" (chronos) and "hour" (hora). In this sense the strict difference between chronometers and horologes is not that they are set according to different standards (for don't we "tell" the "hours" in China according to their relation to Greenwich "time"?), but that the same standard cannot be applied to both at one and the same time and be *called* the same hour. The second contradictory correspondence is the reversal of the time/hour hierarchy according to which "hour" becomes the non-originary origin of all "time" which is now seen as the endless serialization of what is "measured" and "told." Since "time" (chronometer) is divine and "hour" (horologe) is human, it also follows that the non-originary origin of the divine is the human.

Melville's romance and, within it, Plinlimmon's pamphlet both depict the same fissure in the apparent failure of Pierre's "noble design." Again, the distinction is not between the ideal and the real, but the problematic nature within both the ideal and the real. Reading this highly deconstructive text, in fact, requires the awareness of a paradox. Edgar A. Dryden, for example, notes it when he says that the text of the pamphlet "seems to offer a model for human action directly contradicting that of the Sermon on the Mount since it emphasizes the incompatibility of Christian ideals and the practical demands of life in this world." At the same time, though (and this is the paradoxical awareness mentioned above) the "apparent differences between the two texts ["Chronometricals and Horologicals" and the Sermon on the Mount] are equivocated by a set of ironic similarities that exist between them" (Dryden 1979: 167-68). The problem, at any rate, seems to be that the true substance of the real does not carry the appearance of the ideal. This is why at his best, Pierre appears to be at his worst. Having saved Isabel, he sacrificed not only himself but Lucy and his mother as well. Though Lucy seems to intuit the sacrificial nature of Pierre's commitment to Isabel, Mrs. Glendinning does not. In fact, Pierre's attempt to save his mother's piece of mind also backfires. The narrator makes it quite clear that Pierre's "marriage" to Isabel may be responsible for his mother's untimely death. Plinlimmon's advice that a person "must by no means make a complete unconditional sacrifice of himself in behalf of any other being, or any cause, or any conceit" (214) is thus well taken. The pamphlet's recommendation of a "virtuous expediency" is, therefore, not a sarcastic dismissal but a recognition of the necessarily and hopelessly conflicted condition of the merely human. In the end Pierre learns enough to doubt everything he thought he knew, but what he rejects is not so much the chronometrical tendencies in his horological nature as the finally indeterminable distinction between the chronometrical and the horological.

The breakdown of this distinction between the human and the divine occurs early on in the text. The narrator is given Melville's most deconstructive statements just after Pierre has decided to save Isabel but before he has hit upon his "most singular act of pious imposture." The passage in question is a preliminary exploration of Plinlimmon's thesis but perhaps even more devastatingly anti-idealistic in appearance:

> In those hyperborean regions, to which enthusiastic Truth, and Earnestness, and Independence, will invariably lead a mind fitted by nature for profound and fearless thought, all objects are seen in a dubious, uncertain, and refracting light. Viewed through that rarified atmosphere the most immemorially admitted maxims of men begin to slide and fluctuate, and finally become wholly inverted; the very heavens themselves being not innocent of producing this confounding effect, since it is mostly in the heavens themselves that these wonderful mirages are exhibited. . . . [I]t is not for man to follow the trail of truth too far, since by so doing he entirely loses the directing compass of his mind; for arrived at the Pole, to whose barrenness only it points, there, the needle indifferently respects all points of the horizon alike. (165)

The metaphor of the compass combined with that of the chronometer/horologe offers to collapse the distinction between space and time precisely because in the human world the latter is always already "measured" or "told" ("said" as well as, in the archaic sense, "counted") in terms of the former. This collapsing of the distinction between time and space in the human world also gnaws at the "higher" distinction between the human and the divine. The metaphor of the "mirage" in the passage just quoted is a crucial "key" to the reversal of the divine/human hierarchy in Melville's text. In the context in which it is here used it represents the illusion of a "heavenly" absolute toward which deep and bold minds tend, but according to its etymological import (it comes from the Latin *mirari,* to see, to wonder at) it implies that the "absolute" is but in the eye/mind of the beholder.

If the divine/human hierarchy is *the* hierarchy to which all deconstructible hierarchies may be traced back, the question of theism vs. atheism may be raised. How may one reverse and reinscribe this fundamental or grounding hierarchy without abandoning theism and lapsing into atheism? The answer to this question is by no means easy, though there is adequate support for it in Melville's *Pierre.* The theistically human always already sees itself as secondary to the divine, but this vision is never (or cannot ever be) substantiated by something outside its own parameters. That is, the vision itself is the sole guarantee of the vision in question. To take the vision at face value, to take it "literally," in other words, is precisely what it means to have blind faith, to "see" without seeing. If we take one of Plinlimmon's traditional-sounding statements seriously, we will soon see a rather forceful anti-traditional streak running through it, undermining or subverting its apparently pro-traditional "truth": "Few of us doubt . . . that human life on this earth is but a state of probation; which among other things implies, that here below, we mortals have only to do with things provisional. Accordingly, I hold that all our so-called wisdom is likewise but provisional" (211).

If we replace the traditional Christian word "probation" with the "realistic" word "temporary," we find ourselves having to accept the provisional nature of all earthly wisdom, including the earthly wisdom that claims to coincide with heavenly wisdom. This switch from self-guaranteeing vision to self-doubting pro/vision represents a concurrent switch from "literal" to "metaphorical" faith. The metaphoric faith in question not only coincides with Plinlimmon's much-maligned "virtuous expediency," it is also grounded or founded upon that charming uncertainty which (at least theoretically) may constantly guard itself against becoming the totalizing or absolutizing authority of "literal" or blind faith. It seems to me that this argument (quite clearly implicit in Melville's romance) for the metaphoric as opposed to the literal is paralleled by the structurally identical opposition between the spirit and the letter of the law. Reinscribing the divine/human hierarchy, then, means the acceptance of the human origin of the divine and the acknowledgement of this acceptance by positing a human-divine/human hierarchy which, translated into commonsensical terms, would hold that theistic humanity guides itself on the basis of a faith in a divinely inspired human authority that (because it probably cannot ever be proved truly divinely inspired without the shadow of a doubt) must remain provisionally subject to an open and ongoing revisionism of its tenets in the light of an equally open and ongoing *humane* reading or interpretation (that is, "writing") of the results and consequences of the basically unchanged even though constantly changing tenets in question.

History clearly indicates that when this metaphoric faith is expunged by its beguiling literal counterpart the spirit is always already sacrificed on the altar of the letter of the law. This is what happened to Jesus Christ who dared to oppose the literal-mindedness of the Scribes and the Pharisees, this is what happened (in the name of Christ) to the victims of the various inquisitions, and this is also what happens in the Puritan New England depicted by Hawthorne in *The Scarlet Letter.* This is also, of course, what happens in Melville's **Pierre.** The non-originary origin of the slip from the relative (earthly) to the fiction of the (heavenly) absolute may be seen to be clearly delineated in the passage where the narrator comments on Pierre's thought processes as the latter is about to undertake the subterfuge of "marrying" his "sister":

> Ofttimes it is very wonderful to trace the rarest and profoundest things, and find their probable origin in something extremely trite and trivial. Yet so strange and complicate is the human soul; so much is confusedly involved from out itself, and such vast and varied accessions come to it from abroad, and so impossible it is always to distinguish between these two, that the wisest man were rash, positively to assign the precise and incipient origination of his final thoughts and acts. Far as we blind moles can see, man's life seems but an acting upon mysterious hints. . . . This preamble seems not entirely unnecessary as usher of the strange conceit, that possibly the latent germ of Pierre's proposed extraordinary mode of executing his proposed extraordinary resolve—namely, the nominal conversion

of a sister into a wife—might have been found in the previous conversational conversion of a mother into a sister; for hereby he had habituated his voice and manner to a certain fictitiousness in one of the closest relations of life; and since man's moral texture is very porous, and things assumed upon the surface, at last strike in—hence, this outward habituation of the above-named fictitiousness has insensibly disposed his mind to it[,] as it were; but only innocently and pleasantly as yet. If, by any possibility this general conceit be so, then to Pierre the times of sportfulness were as pregnant with the hours of earnestness; and in sport he learned the terms of woe. (176-77)

The effect of Melville's own highly provisional, tentative, probing, and cautious language clearly underwrites the oxymoronic "truth" according to which "[s]ilence is the only Voice of our God" (204). That is why Pierre's (and our own) epistemological grounds or ethical foundations cannot be clearly rested upon either subversive lies or expedient truths. Truths may become subversive, lies expedient at any moment. And that is why the slip out of the fiction of the absolute back into the reality of the provisional requires that fissure within the absolute which opens up for the person who, having followed the "Truth" too far, has lost the "directing compass of his mind," and has been bewildered by the "needle indifferently" respecting "all points of the horizon alike."

Works Cited

Feidelson, Charles. 1953. *Symbolism and American Literature,* (Chicago: Univerisity of Chicago Press).

Kearns, Michael S. 1983. "Interpreting Intentional Incoherence: Towards a Disambiguation of Melville's *Pierre: Or, The Ambiguities,*" *The Bulletin of the Midwest Modern Language Association* 16: 34–54.

Melville, Herman. *Pierre: Or, The Ambiguities.* Page references are to Vol. VII of the Northwestern—Newberry Edition of *The Writings of Herman Melville,* ed. by Harrison Hayford *et al.* (Evanston and Chicago: Northwestern UP and Newberry Library, 1971).

Pierre: Or, The Ambiguities. Page references are to Vol. VII of the Northwestern—Newberry Edition of *The Writings of Herman Melville,* ed. by Harrison Hayford *et al.* (Evanston and Chicago: Northwestern UP and Newberry Library, 1971).

Plato. i.380–370 B.C. Citation is from *The Republic of Plato,* English trans. by Francis MacDonald Cornford (New York and London: Oxford UP, 1964).

John Carlos Rowe (essay date 1991)

SOURCE: "Romancing the Stone: Melville's Critique of Ideology in *Pierre,*" in *Theorizing American Literature: Hegel, the Sign, and History,* edited by Bainard Cowan and Joseph G. Kronick, Louisiana State University Press, 1991, pp. 195-232.

[*In the following essay, Rowe discusses* Pierre *as Melville's critique of nineteenth-century literary production, suggesting that the novel is his farewell to writing as he conceived it before* Pierre, *and that it serves as a bridge to* The Confidence-Man.]

> The founders of Rome . . .—Romulus and Remus— are, according to the tradition, themselves freebooters—represented as from their earliest days thrust out from the Family, and as having grown up in a state of isolation from family affection. . . .
>
> The immoral active severity of the Romans in this private side of character necessarily finds its counterpart in the passive severity of their political union. For the severity which the Roman experienced from the State he was compensated by a severity, identical in nature, which he was allowed to indulge towards his family—a servant on the one side, a despot on the other.
>
> —Hegel, *The Philosophy of History*

In his Introduction to the 1949 Hendricks House edition of *Pierre,* Henry A. Murray criticizes Melville for not providing a clearer cultural motivation for Pierre's alienation: "Melville does not present us with a pertinent spectacle or analysis of American society, nor does he state explicitly what forces of the culture are so inimical to his spirit that he and his hero are driven to condemn it *in toto.* . . . This hiatus in emotional logic is one of the outstanding structural defects of the novel."[1] Murray very clearly identifies a central problem that has caused both contemporary reviewers and twentieth-century scholars to judge *Pierre* as Melville's most incoherent work. What little explicit commentary Melville gives the reader about social issues appears in those chapters set in New York, after Pierre has crossed his Rubicon and rebelled against his family. Indeed, what Murray terms "this hiatus in emotional logic" applies equally well to the customary division critics make between the pastoralism of the domestic romance at Saddle-Meadows and the surrealism of the episodes in the city. Instead of offering us the naturalist's microscopic examination of urban corruption, Melville focuses on Pierre's efforts to write his "infernal book." Instead of the pastoral romance of Saddle-Meadows giving way to the gritty realism of New York, we find pastoralism transformed into a metafictional romance in which virtually every urban experience relates to Pierre's problem of artistic creation. The social issues in *Pierre* thus appear to be forgotten as Melville shifts his attention from the domestic conflicts at Saddle-Meadows to Pierre's artistic problems in the city.

Yet this problem may well be a consequence of our critical methods rather than an inherent defect in the work's composition and structure. This is not to say that *Pierre* is an unacknowledged masterpiece. Quite the contrary, the novel is full of difficulties that I shall not try to resolve, intending as I do instead to use them to clarify Melville's contempt for "the man of letters" and thus for himself. Melville's wicked critique of authorship is not, however, simply a symptom of madness or uncontrolled ranting. His indictment of idealist philosophy and literary practice, especially focused on the Transcendentalists, is coherent and profound, because it recognizes how powerfully such abstractions would serve the political purposes of the new American ruling classes. At the same time, he could find no acceptable alternative to this complicity of the author with those more powerful authorities whom Melville judged to have ruined the republican dream from the beginning. Intricately worked out in the very novelistic form Melville had come to detest, his critique of ideology in *Pierre* remains a testament to the limits of literature as a force for political reform. In *Pierre,* Melville bids farewell to the literary forms of romance and the novel neither because he had lost control of them nor because he had lost control of his own life, unless we understand that life to be inseparable from his conception of his vocation as an author. What he recognizes instead is how powerfully these forms contribute to the social forces of domination they so often claim to contest. The argument of *Pierre* is thus *too* coherent and *too* convincing to result in any other conclusion than that Literature is the enemy.

Above all, it is literature's inclination to make its fantasy credible that troubles Melville, because he recognizes this tendency toward "fictional realization" as comparable to the work of ideology in naturalizing otherwise arbitrary social fictions. Among the many literary forms, romance and novel tend particularly to accomplish this work of naturalization by way of characters and dramatic situations that substitute interpersonal psychologies for more complex social and economic forces. In *Pierre,* Melville focuses on family relations both at Saddle-Meadows and in New York because he recognizes that the family is the institution through which the dramatic social changes of Jacksonian America would be rendered acceptable and normal. And it is the family as the focus of the fiction of manners—whether it be the sentimental romance or the "novel of social manners"—that had such a powerful influence on Melville's readers. As a primarily bourgeois form, the nineteenth-century novel of social manners quite obviously helped legitimate its middle-class readers and their values, often by ruthlessly criticizing aristocratic pretensions. Insofar as bourgeois values are identified with democratic sentiments, the novel became the primary literary form of urban and industrial America. It is, of course, quite conventional to notice how the novel of social manners from Jane Austen to Henry James concentrates on the specific social functions of a fictional family. More often than not, the family's class identification governs other mimetic criteria, even in writers, like Trollope and James, for whom bourgeois values are considered necessary to the well-ordered state. Even so, it is surprising how often literary critics treat such family relations in phenomenological and psychological terms. By personalizing characters and dramatizing interpersonal conflicts, novelists tempt readers to identify with characters in ways that encourage the use of psychological and phenomenological terms to understand the narrative functions of characters. One consequence of this critical inclination is the relative neglect of the social and political significance of family relations in fiction. In short, the form of the novel and the reader-competence it constructs often work contrary to the larger class significance that "character" and "the family" are supposed to convey.

Social historians traditionally have had as much difficulty studying the social functions of the family as literary scholars have had. Whereas literary critics tend to treat fictional families in psychological terms, social historians have relied on demographic statistics and other empirical data that do not adequately reflect the family as a form of social behavior. As Mark Poster has written, "While quantitative demographic studies are needed, they cannot provide historians with a concept of the family that can pose the important questions and render the family intelligible in premodern and modern Europe."[2] Only recently have works like Philippe Ariès' *Centuries of Childhood: A Social History of Family Life* and Jacques Donzelot's *The Policing of Families* begun to combine psychological and traditional sociological approaches to the family in order to understand the particular mediatory function played by families in the relation of individual behavior to communal practices.[3]

The rediscovery of the family by the social historian has interesting consequences for the literary critic. Literary critics interested in the political functions of artistic forms should find theoretical suggestions in the work of those social historians who have begun to write the "social psychology" of the family as a historical institution. The analogy between the family and art is not merely coincidental; both employ discursive practices that explicitly combine public and private terms and values. Both the family and the artistic work are representational forms that must address the bases for their actual and nominal authorities (parent and author), the origins and ends of such authority (biology and genius; history and tradition), and the status of those subject to such authorities (children and readers).

I have suggested that Melville's concentration on family relations and artistic creation in the two major movements of *Pierre* has encouraged critics like Murray to consider Melville's often strident social criticism to be unjustified or inexplicable. I want to argue that Melville's social criticism in *Pierre* is focused primarily on the social psychologies of the nineteenth-century family and Romantic theories of art. I want to demonstrate not merely how the family and art serve different social purposes, which are often disguised by the naturalness and privacy of the family and the idealism of art, but also how the family and art participate with each other in maintaining a nineteenth-century American politics of self-reliance.

The social history of the nineteenth-century American family is one of the principal concerns of Michael Paul Rogin's *Subversive Genealogy: The Politics and Art of Herman Melville*. In its attention to the socio-economic impact of Jacksonian America on the family, Rogin's study gives historical specificity to Eric Sundquist's psychoanalytical approach to the question of nineteenth-century literary authority, so often figured in metaphors of paternity, in

Home as Found. Both critics pay special attention to *Pierre* as Melville's defensive autobiography. *Pierre* is both Melville's willful rebellion against the aristocratic pretensions of his mother's family, the Gansevoorts, and the fictional confession of his failure to live up to his aristocratic ancestry. Characterizing himself in Pierre as a dilettante and literary dabbler, Melville also associates himself with Pierre's unsuccessful efforts to champion those characters exploited by the Glendinnings: the illegitimate Isabel, the vanishing Indian, the black slaves kept by Pierre's ancestors. Rogin calls *Pierre* a "bourgeois family nightmare" that employs Pierre's initiation into urban life to explore the crisis of the family occasioned by the rapid industrialization of Jacksonian America: "The adolescent male, coming of sexual age, symbolized the disruptive forces at work in Jacksonian America. Poised to break free from his family of origin, sexually and in his working life, he was the locus for Jacksonian anxieties about the disruption of the preindustrial family. The chaste woman . . . was society's agent to discipline him."[4]

The great transformation of America from an agrarian to an industrial economy in the first half of the nineteenth century brought with it the customary problems associated with industrial production: the alienation of the laborer from both the finished product and the control of his own labor, the growing division between the workplace and the home, and the migration of workers from rural towns to unfamiliar cities. It is commonplace to speak of the social consequences of the capitalist economy that began to govern American production in this period, but American capitalism did much more than merely establish the economic determinants for social changes. Ideology may be defined as the collective effect of different discursive practices designed to naturalize or normalize new social practices and working relations. In the simplest Marxist terms, this naturalization is accomplished by means of an apparently "free" exchange of labor-power for wages, whereby the disruptive and alienating owners and workers would appear to be part of a larger democratic process. Much of Marx's attention in *Capital* concerns just how this apparently "free" exchange between laborers and capitalists is, in fact, a fated, determined means of subordinating laborer to owner, thus reproducing the master/servant hierarchy at the heart of capitalism. In fact, it is the way in which capitalist ideology mystifies these master/servant relations as much as the different historical and economic conditions that distinguishes capitalist class relations from feudal hierarchies.

Another, more complicated and more subversive method of normalization, however, occurs in the diverse forms and institutions of everyday life that have little apparent connection with the means of material production. What Louis Althusser has described as the process of *interpellation* and Antonio Gramsci as hegemonic discourse approximates the complex means by which ideological values are internalized and psychically lived by apparently "free" individuals under capitalism.[5] The family is, of course, one of those social forms, even though it is directly involved in social production and reproduction. In an elementary sense, the labor force depends upon the production of the family. Yet because its means of production seems so self-evidently *natural* and *biological,* the family is an especially attractive medium for disguising ideological messages and thus contributing to the naturalization of new social relations. Engels' *The Origins of the Family, Private Property, and the State* is the classic Marxian work on the relation between private, psychological relations and ideology, but both Marx and Engels treat the family as secondary to the mode of production. As Poster observes, for Marx and Engels, "the family is epiphenomenal compared to the mode of production. In general their writings relegated the family to the backwaters of superstructure."[6]

Engels' note to the third German edition of *Capital* makes clear that the origin of the family was a troublesome issue for Marx: "Subsequent and very thorough investigations into the primitive condition of man led the author to the conclusion that it was not the family that originally developed into the tribe, but that, on the contrary, the tribe was the primitive and spontaneously developed form of human association, based on consanguinity, and that out of the first incipient loosening of the tribal bonds, the many and various forms of the family were afterwards developed."[7] As sketchy and sometimes contradictory as Marx's critical remarks on the family are, they focus with some consistency on the *bourgeois* family. Yet even the vulgar Marxian distinction between economic base and ideological superstructure permits Marx and Engels to comprehend the mystification of economic motives as *natural* attachments and the legitimation of a deceptive "individualism" achieved in the bourgeois family. For in its reflection of capitalist alienation, the bourgeois family is where the "private individual" is at home, rather than in the more public groups Marx associates with the historical origins of social organization. As Raymond Williams observes, "the dominance of the sense [of the family as a] small kingroup was probably not established before the early nineteenth century."[8] In effect, the *biological* legitimacy of the "family" belongs to nineteenth-century capitalism, and such modern kin relations are integrally related to historically contemporary conceptions of the individual.

Hegel has a great deal to say about the family, in part because his own philosophical project so explicitly attempts to legitimate bourgeois individualism. Hegel understands the family as the active and historical mediation between individual and social forms of self-consciousness. The very centrality of the family in Hegel's philosophy reflects his emphasis on individual self-consciousness, which would serve nineteenth-century American capitalism as a convenient philosophical justification for entrepreneurial practices. Nevertheless, the main thrust of Hegel's idealism was toward a concept of "self-consciousness" that would find its dialectical realization in a larger social self-consciousness rather than in the mere exchange of the father's authority for that of the capitalist or ruler. In Hegel, the family is the virtual unconscious of man's social impulse and the historical process by which such an uncon-

scious achieves conscious form involves the transformation of the family's privacy into public forms of social existence. For Hegel, the state does not merely imitate the structure of familial authority, it dialectically transforms that authority with the aim of achieving the ultimate self-governance citizens would achieve in Hegel's ideal community. In the course of such transformation, the limited authority of the family is negated.

In *Pierre,* Melville seems to criticize urban America for having forgotten or neglected the significant social role played by the family. In the pastoral world of Saddle-Meadows, social life is organized around such ruling families as the Glendinnings. In New York, Pierre encounters unruly mobs, decadent aristocrats, eccentric artists and philosophers. The carnivalesque world of the city is distinguished by the alienation of different groups and individuals, as well as by the absence of those family ties that offered Pierre some stability in the country. Even in his rebellion against his family, Pierre attempts to create a surrogate family, composed of Lucy, Isabel, and Delly, as if to compensate for the isolation they all experience in the city. In this view, Melville's social criticism appears to be quite conventional; Pierre's "fall," like that of industrial America, is his loss of those stable family associations that ought to have been the basis for his initiation into social life.

Pierre's rebellion against his family and his rejection of the stability of Saddle-Meadows, however, cannot be so easily allegorized as urban America's repudiation of the stable, preindustrial family. Like Hegel, Melville understands family and social relations to function dialectically. Melville devotes a great deal of attention to the Glendinnings' structured and closed world in order to prepare the reader for Pierre's discovery of Isabel's illegitimacy and his subsequent rejection of his heritage. The father's sin is not just his adultery with Isabel's mother but his even more pernicious refusal to accept publicly his responsibility for Isabel: that is, to establish visible signs of kinship with her. The customs and practices that encourage such secrecy are those of the preindustrial family and the class relations governed by a landed gentry. Thus it is understandable that Murray finds Melville's social criticism in *Pierre* unmotivated. Rather than exploring the significance of the Glendinnings' fatal flaw in the particular social world they govern, Melville seems to change the subject from rural to urban social issues, from aristocratic to bourgeois discursive registers. By the same token, the landed aristocracy represented by the Glendinnings seems hardly a worthwhile object for Melville's criticism. Given the rapid change from rural to urban economies in Jacksonian America, Melville's attack on an outmoded form of aristocratic rule seems unnecessary. In fact, the Glendinning family and its "secret" refer more tangibly to the plot of some European romance than to concrete social problems in nineteenth-century America.

Viewed from the perspective of Hegel's conception of the family as the "unconscious" of the state, however,

Melville's concentration on the preindustrial, aristocratic family may be an indirect approach to his criticism of American capitalism. Melville stresses the European character of the Glendinning family, as if reminding democratic Americans that they might be working to produce a society that will merely repeat the hierarchical class systems of Europe. Nineteenth-century Americans were familiar with the ways southern planters imitated the pretensions of the European aristocracy. Northern industrialists frequently justified urbanization as a way of encouraging democratization and overcoming the inherent hierarchies of landed estates. By the same token, the common nineteenth-century American assumption that agrarianism and industrialism constituted two distinct spheres is by no means historically accurate. As Carolyn Porter has shown, "farming was no more impervious to the forces of specialization, rationalization, and commodification than was household manufacture or urban life, once we recognize that America was not merely a predominantly agrarian society, but a *capitalist* agrarian society."[9] American capitalism had a vested interest in promoting the different mythologies of the country and the city, preindustrial feudalism and the "free exchange" of labor under capitalism, Old World aristocracy and American democracy. By developing the narrative contiguity of country and city, aristocratic family and democratic mob, Melville may be suggesting in *Pierre* that the origins of urban corruption are to be found in the well-ordered estates of the landed gentry.

Hegel's idealist treatment of the family's relation to the state may help us formulate this problem in terms pertinent to the romantic ethos of *Pierre*. According to Hegel, the ultimate function of the family is to serve the state, virtually by acknowledging the insufficiency or limitation of the family structure as an enduring historical principle. Hegel's version of Oedipal triangulation is supposed to effect the rite of passage from family to state, from biological repetition to historical time and change. Within the narrow family, Hegel's unrealized self is metaphorized as "brother and sister," both of whom remain in bondage to an external, abstract notion of authority that is at once the father and the divine. In the family, the dialectic of self and other is worked out in terms of brother and sister, precisely because "the brother . . . is in the eyes of the sister a being whose nature is unperturbed by desire and is ethically like her own; her recognition in him is pure and unmixed with any sexual relation."[10]

In one sense, Hegel here repeats the nineteenth century's ideology of the ideal, chaste, unsexed "family," which served the purpose of repressing and controlling those sexual energies threatening a rational social order. In this regard, Hegel's metaphor of "brother and sister" for the familial dialectic of self and other merely reinforces the ideology's spiritualization of family relations in the manner Rogin has analyzed so well: "Family ideologists sought not only to intensify the bonds between mother and son, but also to spiritualize the relations of husband to wife. Pierre's game of brother and sister is supposed to establish

the closeness of this son to his mother. But it also calls attention to those family reformers who, purifying the marriage bond of power and appetite, modeled the relations of husband and wife on those of brother and sister."[11] Pierre's habit of calling his mother "sister" certainly follows this ideology of the family. The spiritualization of family relations helps maintain a sharp distinction between the "proper family" and the impropriety or illegitimacy associated with sexuality. Melville's use of the conventions of the fair lady and dark woman to represent, respectively, Lucy and Isabel suggests how feminine propriety depended upon the repression of the sexual. In keeping with Melville's general critique of American transcendentalism, *Pierre* identifies idealization and spiritualization with psychic and cultural repression of basic drives and appetites. This idealization of family relations is the object of Melville's critique of ideology in *Pierre,* because it is one of the principal means of disguising the ruling class's legitimation of its right to rule. By doubling Pierre's treatment of his mother as "sister" and his incestuous relation with Isabel, Melville renders extremely ambiguous the customary distinctions between the proper family and illegitimate sexual relations.[12]

Hegel's interpretation of the unsexual relation of brother and sister as a model for familial self-consciousness thus appears to work in accord with those nineteenth-century family ideologists criticized by Melville. In terms of his larger social argument, however, Hegel stresses this relation of brother and sister in order to identify the limitation of the family and its necessary transcendence in the social order. Dividing unrealized self-consciousness into brother and sister, Hegel establishes an unsexual relation of self and other that is the abstract model for proper citizenship in the state. Within the narrow circle of the family, the metaphors "brother and sister" are reminders of the self's dependence on external authorities—God, father, Nature. Hegel wants to demonstrate that the apparently self-moving history of the family does not produce genuine historical growth and change but merely reproduces the same structure. Given the ways the European aristocracy based its power on complex family genealogies, Hegel's argument has immediate relevance for the changing class structures of early nineteenth-century Europe. The *desire* of the family remains purely sexual or reproductive—natural and thus not yet spiritual (or self-conscious) in the proper sense of historical *Weltgeist*. Within the family, the individual remains in bondage to natural authority, which rules that the "individual" has no particularity beyond his/her identification with the species reproduced. The *unsexual* relation of brother and sister signifies for Hegel that neither brother nor sister possesses an independent and reproductive power equivalent to the natural sexuality that continues to govern the family.

By the same token, the apparent authority of the father and mother is equally dependent upon the law of biological reproduction, which they merely follow. No matter what venerable origins or trappings of power the family employs to claim its independent identity, it continues to perform the same subservient function: the reproduction of the species. Within the family form, the child's rebellion is thus always doomed merely to repeat what it attempts to escape: the hierarchical relation of the individual to an external law. *Working* at that relation, *laboring* to overcome such externality—father, God, Nature—the son or daughter merely reproduces it in the subsequent role of husband or wife. Insofar as the son's Oedipal aggression fails to negate the family and transform it into the larger forms of social law and citizenship, the son must experience his transformation into a father as incestuous. Metaphorically, *spiritually,* such philosophical incest does weaken successive generations, since it reminds the individual that his "freedom" is already fated, that his "rebellion" is merely natural, that his "self-consciousness" is simply a biological mirage rather than a genuine product of human reason. The consequence of recognizing such a limitation to individuation in the reproduction of an unchanging and external natural law can result only in what Hegel terms "unhappy consciousness," which is his own version of philosophical madness, of absolute "ambiguity."

The "illegitimacy" of the family depends upon its failure to bring its own natural legitimation to self-consciousness: the transformation of natural law into social practice. The son realizes this potential in the family by rebelling against the father and discovering his destiny as a citizen: "The individual who seeks the 'pleasure' of enjoying his particular individuality finds it in the family life, and the 'necessity' in which that pleasure passes away is his own self-consciousness as a citizen of his nation." In short, rebellion against the family works ideally to transform the natural and biological family into the more populous social "family," insofar as Hegelian dialectics may be read in organic, evolutionary terms. Within the natural family, there are only sons and daughters, fathers and mothers; the son doubles the father, the daughter the mother. Within its own reproductive cycle, then, the natural family always grows more abstract and general, working against the destiny of the human spirit to individuate itself, to realize and complete natural law as human history. What remains purely external to the "son" within the confines of the family ought to become the internal and self-regulating principle of ethical authority within the well-ordered state: "It is knowing the 'law of his own heart' as the law of all hearts, knowing the consciousness of self to be the recognized and universal ordinance of society: it is 'virtue,' which enjoys the fruits of its own sacrifice, which brings about what it sets out to do, viz. to bring the essential nature into the light of the actual present,—and its enjoyment is this universal life."[13]

For Melville as well, the nineteenth-century family is an inadequate substitute for a truly democratic society. Melville understands, however, how the family deceives the individual with the illusion of its own self-sufficient "community" and how it is also the primal site of transformation—from self to other, nature to culture. In the former case, the "family" remains a formalist work; in the latter case, the "family" is an active social and historical force.

These different functions of the "family" may be understood primarily in the ways they organize the labor of those identified with the elementary "society" of the family. Indeed, it is the labor *of* the family—in the double sense of what the family produces and what is the social consequence of a certain family structure—that Melville recognizes as an indirect means of understanding the power and function of nineteenth-century ideology.

By her own account, Isabel achieves her initial awareness of herself as a consequence of her labor:

> "I must have been nine, or ten, or eleven years old, when the pleasant-looking woman carried me away from the large house. She was a farmer's wife; and now that was my residence, the farm-house. They taught me to sew, and work with wool, and spin the wool; I was nearly always busy now. This being busy, too, this it must have been, which partly brought to me the power of being sensible of myself as something human. Now I began to feel strange differences. When I saw a snake trailing through the grass, I said to myself, That thing is not human, but I am human."[14]

Indeed, Isabel's sense of the "old bewilderings" that haunted her adolescence are certainly associated with her sense of alienation from a stable human community. When she has grown and become a burden on the farmer's family, she asks the farmer's wife to "'hire me out to some one, let me work for some one'" (124-25). Knowing little of the ways of the world, Isabel still senses that her departure from even this adoptive family requires some change in the conditions of her labor. Whereas her labor for her adoptive family had seemed to her equivalent to the physical and psychological maintenance the family gave her, her adult labor involves her in an exchange economy, in which wages mark the difference between the labor that produces the self (labor *for* the self) and the work that produces *society*. Melville uses "The Story of Isabel" to present a critical reading of the conventional paradigm for romantic self-consciousness. In her spiritual and physical growth, Isabel—unlike Wordsworth in *The Prelude*—learns how integral concrete labor is to the development of a psychological personality. And she experiences as well the first consequences of the alienation of the worker from her proper labor, her only true product: that sensuous human activity realizable only within a social community.

Isabel's mystical guitar is a metaphor for the sort of social product that ought to issue from such human labor. Isabel tells Pierre that she bought the guitar from a peddler who "had got it slyly in part exchange from the servants of a grand house." It is especially important, I think, that Isabel specifies that "with part of my earnings, I bought the guitar. Straightway I took it to my little chamber in the gable, and softly laid it on my bed" (125). A few sentences earlier, Isabel also indicates just what sort of labor had earned her the means of buying the guitar: "My work was milking cows, and making butter, and spinning wool, and weaving carpets of strips of cloth." These bucolic labors are conventional enough, except that in series they offer a little genealogy of human labor from agrarian activities to cottage industry. Measured against Isabel, Pierre is especially inexperienced in the ways of ordinary labor, particularly those involving even the most elementary manufacturing. His "labor" in the course of the novel includes his work as a writer, occasional hunting, and the "work" of honor, which is to say the labor of melodrama.

Nevertheless, Isabel's labor does not signify some growth in the direction of social integration, even though the development of the series clearly suggests such socialization. Milk produces butter, just as wool produces cloth for carpets. Like Hester Prynne, Isabel is often shown sewing, and her labor as a seamstress seems nearly to objectify in the work of her hands the weaving and vining of her black hair. All such labor, however, fails to produce her "own" image, as labor in Hegel's ideal society promises. Exchanging money for the guitar, Isabel is prompted by some intuition or identification with the instrument, even though she confesses she "had never seen a guitar before." "There was a strange humming in my heart," she says, and it is this claim (and many others like it) that convince us that she is some version of Hawthorne's mystical women. As it turns out, the guitar is a crucial figure in the melodramatic plot, because it contains the mysterious, gilt signature, *Isabel,* which Isabel takes as her *own* name. And in Melville's romance of coincidences, the guitar is revealed to have been acquired by the peddler from the mansion at Saddle-Meadows, fueling Isabel's intuition that it was her *mother's* guitar. This would account for the guitar being in the possession of the servants, to whom it must have been given by Mary Glendinning in some equally intuitive understanding of its illegitimate associations. The peddler acquires it from the servants "slyly," suggesting some cheat in the exchange, as if the guitar must perpetuate its illegitimacy in its repeated circulation: the economy of illegitimacy. The peddler, of course, lives upon an exchange economy, insofar as he makes nothing in his own right. His "slyness" is precisely his "craft," because perfectly honest, market-value exchanges would leave him penniless. To the value of the goods he offers, he must add the "cost" of his labor, which more than anything else amounts to his "slyness."

Ironically, Isabel's wages are part of an exchange economy in which the *need* to purchase some means of self-expression (the guitar) reflects the fact that Isabel's actual labor is alien, not an integral part of her spiritual and psychological development. Indeed, Isabel's sense of her alienation from *any* society may well be her intuition of the conditions governing the laborer in such an exchange economy. And it is this sense of alienation that provokes her not just to "uncover" her family origins but also to imagine that family to be the means of *protecting* her from a hostile, alienating world. It should not surprise us, then, that guitar and family origins are so intimately related in the plot: art as a "leisure-time" expression of the inner self and the family as a "private" validation of the self are related defenses against alienating labor. Isabel's regression from socialization to the narrow circle of her lost family

heritage may also be understood as her rebellion against the romantic ideal of *Bildung* that her own story tries to sketch out. And this regression, like Pierre's own failure to grow "beyond" the love or conflict of the Glendinning family, expresses the failure of the larger social order to overcome (or at least *use productively*) the alienation of its workers.

What the guitar does for Isabel is effectively swerve her labors from her own socialization (from cows to carpets, Nature to Culture) in the direction of a self-expression that is at once sexual and illegitimate. In the context of the explicit sexual themes of **Pierre,** Isabel's first act of placing the guitar on her bed reminds us of the feminine form of the instrument. Insofar as it hides Isabel's own *assumed* name beneath a removable panel (I assume this is a decorative cover of the opening in the sound-box: a sort of hymen), the guitar serves as a sexually suggestive metonymy for Isabel herself. In this regard, we might conclude that her labor has provided her the concrete means (wages) of achieving self-expression that may communicate with the world.

Unlike the Memnon Stone, which is a mere ancient "gimmick" that simulates the voice of the divine, and unlike Westervelt's "trick" of the "Veiled Lady" in *The Blithedale Romance,* Isabel's guitar represents a genuine artistic desire to give objective, and thus communicable, form to her self-consciousness. By transforming work into wages, then into the music of the guitar, Isabel's labor initiates the transformation of individual activity into a social function, of mere existence into socially significant being. This constant metamorphosis is Emersonian, and it would place metaphor at the *heart* of the human project of bringing the world to self-consciousness. As a genuine "product" of Isabel's own labor, the guitar assumes a "real body," much in the manner of Whitman's poetic body, insofar as it "embodies" those universals by which human beings recognize each other as fundamentally social. Yet we must remember that the guitar is initially *not* the product of Isabel's own labor. The guitar *becomes* her own only as she *labors* upon it, learning how to make the music by which her story is told to others.

The guitar "plays," however, as if independent of Isabel herself, the dreamy story of her life, and Isabel understands the music to have only one purpose: to establish contact with her "brother," Pierre. In this sense, then, the music of the guitar merely plays the *family tune,* thus guaranteeing that Isabel will "legitimate" the name within the guitar as her "origin," her "mother." As such, the guitar does not serve the higher function of art in Hegel of mediating between citizen and divine, between social history and universal order, but merely "mystifies" and "enchants" Isabel and Pierre in the magic circle of the family. In effect, the guitar negates Isabel's more earthly labors, and it does so precisely by serving as a fetish for her *absent* family. This lost family is Isabel's imaginary compensation for her lack of social integration. The nineteenth-century sentimental romance used plots like Isabel's story to suggest the uniqueness of the illegitimate child's social exclusion; Melville's more encompassing plot eventually transforms Isabel's eccentric fate into the repressed story of respectable sons and daughters. By the end of the narrative, virtually every important character will have been revealed as inherently *illegitimate*. A substitute for her social labor, the guitar offers two compensations in place of a true democracy. In the plot, the guitar divulges the secret of Isabel's family lineage and origins. As a musical instrument, it provides the spiritual and ideal pleasures of art in compensation for labor that within this social context fails to produce any psychic or social growth.

Without claiming much knowledge of nineteenth-century guitar production in America, I want to suggest that the name in the guitar may well be simply a trade or model name. Even in cottage industry, the name inside a guitar would normally be taken as that of its producer rather than its owner, except in the case of some expensive, custom guitar designed for a titled aristocrat. The cottage industry serving a feudal aristocracy like that at Saddle-Meadows could *only* sign the *same name* for producer and owner, since the lord or lady of the tenant lands "owns" both the means of production and the identity of the producers. The landed gentry gives titles to all the products of its lands, legitimating those products only with its signature. One of the functions of art in such feudal societies is to provide the tokens of that name, ranging from the architecture of the manor house to the trophies and objets d'art in the great hall.

Yet the secret signature in the guitar is an *illegitimate* name, even if we assume that it is *not* the real name of the elder Pierre Glendinning's Frenchwoman. The unconscious of the aristocratic Glendinning line is its very illegitimacy, which is not to say simply that the veneer of respectability is maintained to hide the unauthorized affair of the father. Critics as various as Murray, Milton Stern, Sundquist, and Rogin have called attention to the genealogy of the Glendinnings out of Pierre's paternal great-grandfather, who, "mortally wounded, had sat unhorsed on his saddle in the grass, with his dying voice, still cheering his men" in battle against the Indians in the French and Indian War (5-6). This event, of course, gives its *name* to Saddle-Meadows, which continues to be haunted by the usurpation that initiated this American aristocratic line. As Carolyn Karcher observes, "Melville in fact comments on the double irony that America may have sold her democratic birthright for an aristocratic mess of pottage, and that the ingredients constituting that pottage—lineage, title, landed property—are all tainted."[15]

The history of aristocratic pretensions is described by Melville in terms of those "incessant restorations and creations" designed to mask their artificial origins, which on close examination generally betray the theft, piracy, and military conquest that Marx considered the means of the precapitalist accumulation of capital (10). Critics have often connected the Glendinnings' aristocratic pretensions with Pierre's fantastic conception of himself and the melo-drama that such a self-image seems to require. More interesting is Melville's contention that the rise of the bourgeoisie, which he generally traces to the execution of Charles I and the exile of Charles II, leads, not to an authentic democracy, but merely to the manufacture of new and explicitly arbitrary titles in the place of those social institutions that would transcend the family and thereby *realize* a larger human community. The history of the English peerage is a chronicle of such artificial titles: "For not Thames is so sinuous in his natural course, not the Bridgewater Canal more artificially conducted, than blood in the veins of that winding or manufactured nobility" (10).

Anticipating subsequent critics who would complain that his aristocratic romance has little to do with American democracy, Melville calls attentions to the Dutch patroons, like the Gansevoorts, whose lineages dwarf the more limited spans of their English equivalents, "those grafted families" who "successively live and die on the eternal soil of a name" (10). The difference between these American aristocrats and the English is that the former stake their claims to nobility on the property that they possess, whereas the English gentry make vain appeals to the past, often to fictionalized lineages: "But our lords, the Patroons, appeal not to the past, but they point to the present. One will show you that the public census of a county, is but part of the roll of his tenants. Ranges of mountains, high as Ben Nevis or Snowdon, are their walls; and regular armies, with staffs of officers, crossing rivers with artillery, and marching through primeval woods, and threading vast rocky defiles, have been sent out to distrain upon three thousand farmer-tenants of one landlord, at a blow" (11).

Murray points out that Melville is recalling in this passage the militiamen who set out from Albany on December 9, 1839, to subdue "a strong force of anti-rent farmers assembled on the Helderbergs" (435). The Anti-Rent protests in New York between 1839 and 1846 give strong historical credibility to Melville's argument that America does indeed have a powerful feudal aristocracy. The conventional reading of this passage as Melville's effort to defend America against English jibes at its "newness" and its "lack of history" does not address Melville's curious insistence on the appeal by American aristocrats to the present rather than to the past. Melville foresees in this passage the peculiarly American aristocrat who by the end of the Civil War would be known in caricature as "the Tycoon." This aristocrat makes no appeal to the past but relies instead on the accumulated wealth that quite literally expands his present, giving him authority over the historical moment. Indeed, this aristocrat's power is essentially anti-historical, bent as it is upon turning the "resources" of the past into the enduring image of this master. In this regard, the urban capitalist and the landed patroon have much in common.

Melville stresses the size of these feudal Dutch estates in New York by observing that they often exceed county boundaries and may include greater populations on their "rent rolls." The very mountains of the region serve as the "walls" of these estates, suggesting that the patroons' rule is not simply extensive but presumed to be *natural*. In Melville's landscape, the New York State Militia enters the picture in response to the provocation of the Anti-Rent agitators. It would not have been lost on the mid-nineteenth-century reader that such rebellion parallels quite explicitly the motives for the American Revolution.

Melville specifically associates this American aristocracy with Eastern and pre-Christian cultures: "These far-descended Dutch meadows lie steeped in a Hindooish haze; an eastern patriarchalness sways its mild crook over pastures, whose tenant flocks shall there feed, long as their own grass grows, long as their own water shall run. Such estates seem to defy Time's tooth, and by conditions which take hold of the indestructible earth seem to cotemporize their fee-simples with eternity. Unimaginable audacity of a worm that but crawls through the soil he so imperially claims!" (11). On the one hand, Melville merely seems to make these associations to stress the unexpectedly venerable character of these American princes. On the other hand, he understands how these Dutch patroons imitate the chaotic and irrational despotism that nineteenth-century westerners popularly associated with the "mysterious" Orient. Hegel is a familiar figure of this "orientalizing" by which nineteenth-century Europeans rationalized their ethnocentrism and imperialism, and he repeatedly uses India to represent the moral anarchy of the East: "If China may be regarded as nothing else but a State, Hindoo political existence presents us with a people but *no State*. Secondly, while we found a moral despotism in *China,* whatever may be called a relic of political life in *India,* is a despotism *without a principle,* without any rule of morality and religion: for morality and religion (as far as the latter has a reference to human action) have as their indispensable condition and basis the freedom of the Will. In India, therefore, the most arbitrary, wicked, degrading despotism has its full swing."[16] Melville stresses the military claims to rule both of the Glendinnings and the Dutch patroons he considers typical of an American landed aristocracy. Like Hegel's Indian monarchs, Melville's American princes are products of a social situation lacking any rational political principle that might coordinate the various and conflicting claims to power and authority. This seems confirmed by the New York State Militia, on order of Governor Seward, acting as if it were the private army of these threatened landowners.

Hegel considers the "history" of India to be no history at all, merely the record of the acts and possessions of different princes and their numerous wars. In particular, Hegel stresses how family genealogies take the place of the public events we normally associate with history: "It is the struggle of an energetic will on the part of this or that prince against a feebler one; the history of ruling dynasties, but not of peoples; a series of perpetually varying intrigues and revolts—not indeed of subjects against their rulers, but of a prince's son, for instance, against his fa-ther; of brothers, uncles and nephews in contest with each other; and of functionaries against their master."[17] For Hegel, the Hindu prince merely serves as a fetish for the still-struggling spirit of social self-governance—a spirit that Melville understands as America's democratic dream. Hegel's Hindu genealogies of princely families find their equivalence in Melville's conception in *Pierre* of the *image* or *portrait* of the father as the ultimate product or fetish of a patriarchal aristocracy. The patroon or patriarch is possible only as a consequence of a fragmented, essentially unpolitical society, like the anarchic New York that Pierre discovers on his first evening in the city with Delly and Isabel. Just this chaos of the urban realm gives special credibility to the apparently pastoral order represented by the Patroon's country estate.

In *Capital,* Marx develops Hegel's arbitrary Hindu despot as a historical and rhetorical figure for the development of capitalism. Sketching the history of cooperative labor, Marx notes, "The colossal effects of simple cooperation are to be seen in the gigantic structures erected by the ancient Asiatics, Egyptians, Etruscans, etc." For Marx, cooperation in the labor process of precapitalist societies generally depends upon "the common ownership of the conditions of production." In Marx's own myth of social origins, cooperative labor reminds us of the essentially collective motives for socialization. On the other hand, Marx recognizes that the "sporadic application of cooperation on a large scale in ancient times, in the Middle Ages, and in modern colonies, rests on direct relations of domination and servitude, in most cases on slavery." Marx is careful to distinguish this cooperation of slave-labor from capitalist cooperation, which seems to begin with the "free wage-labourer" selling "his labour-power to capital." This mystified "free-exchange" enables the capitalist to make "coordinated labor" appear to be a consequence of his ownership and management of the labor-power that he has purchased.[18] Less explicit because more subtly contrived as a "free exchange" in the rhetoric of capitalism, the capitalist's exploitation of labor nonetheless finds a precedent in the forced labor of slaves in ancient times rather than in the tribal cooperation of primitive hunting tribes or agrarian societies.

In particular, Marx calls attention to the "colossal works" of this coordinated slave labor in terms designed clearly to gloss his theory of surplus value. The monumental projects undertaken by such coordinated labor forces are generally made possible by large state surpluses often generated by military conquests. These monuments are thus testaments to the surplus value on which the ancient despot based his political power—the "capital" of domination. Indeed, the labor force is itself often composed of just such a "surplus," insofar as the slaves committed to such great works were often the spoils of war. In addition, the monuments built by such despots often serve no other purpose than to represent that arbitrary power in the form of such purely ceremonial structures as tombs, pyramids, and obelisks. Failing to recognize that it is their coordinated labor alone that produces such objects of wonder, these workers take such productions as symbols for the despot's power and authority. As such, these ancient monuments—so often appropriately dedicated to death and/or a religious or military ideal—are testaments to social waste as well as dramatic illustrations of the kind of reification that will be the ultimate product of capitalism. Having quoted a long section of Richard Jones's *Textbook of Lectures* on the economics of such colossal projects among the ancients, Marx concludes by making explicit the implications of such despotism for the rise of capitalism: "This power of Asiatic and Egyptian kings, of Etruscan theocrats, etc. has in modern society been transferred to the capitalist, whether he appears as an isolated individual or, as in the case of joint-stock companies, in combination with others."[19]

The colossal works of Hegel's and Marx's ancient despots have a curious association with Terror Rock, or the Memnon Stone, in *Pierre* and with the *name* of the Glendinning estate, Saddle-Meadows, which memorializes Pierre's great-grandfather's subjugation of the Indian. In subtler ways than the oriental despot, however, Melville's American aristocrat legitimizes his usurpation of Nature, "savage," and tenant-farmer by means of those signs and symbols (representational forms) that constitute his "estate" or "property." It is thus little wonder that on the eve of his break with his family Pierre burns the "'mementoes and monuments of the past'" that he had so fondly collected over the years. With special deliberation, he burns the chair-portrait of his father, whose image now seems to speak to him only of the father's adultery and illegitimate child, Isabel: "'It speaks merely of decay and death, and nothing more; decay and death of innumerable generations, it makes of earth one mold. How can lifelessness be fit memorial for life?'" (197). What the coordinated labor of soldiers, tenant-farmers, artisans, and painters produces is merely the *personality* of the ruler. And that personality is already a fetish for the labor of others that has actually produced such an image: the portrait of a father or the military saddle of a great-grandfather. This transformation of the living labor of the community into "heir-looms" is precisely a labor that "speaks merely of decay and death," a subtler version of Marx's "commodity fetishism" and an anticipation of Lukács' more developed conception of reification in *History and Class Consciousness*. It is a lineage without a proper history, insofar as it merely repeats the illegitimate authority of the ruler. Viewed in this manner, Pierre's grandfather's patriotism in defending "a rude but all-important stockaded fort, against the repeated combined assaults of Indians, Tories, and Regulars" during the Revolutionary War can no longer be understood as an unqualified valor in the name of democratic ideals (6). Reread according to the aristocratic lineage that such "patriotism" has produced, the grandfather's sacrifice serves to maintain only his family's power rather than the ideals of a social democracy. The grandfather merely repeats the conquering will—and its antihistorical bias—that the great-grandfather initiated in his combat with the Indian during the French and Indian War. In the course of making these close associations between the acts of "founding" the American Glendinnings by the great-grandfather and the

"founding" of America in the Revolutionary War, Melville renders ambiguous the presumed "origin" of America's break with its European heritage. And by suggesting an ironic repetition of such "origins" in the New York State Militia's suppression of the Anti-Rent protesters in 1839, Melville transforms the democratic revolution into the secret consolidation of a new, American aristocratic power.

Pierre's own gesture of rebellion, including the burning of these fetishes, ought to involve some self-conscious rejection of the limitations of the family in favor of a larger social relation. But like most "young Americans," Pierre bids instead for radical individualism: "'Henceforth, cast-out Pierre hath no paternity, and no past; and since the Future is one blank to all; therefore twice-disinherited Pierre stands untrammeledly his ever-present self!—free to do his own self-will and present fancy to whatever end!'" (199). In his own will-to-power, Pierre hardly restores America to the social revolution in which it ought to have found its origin; Pierre merely repeats that illusory "revolution" by which his ancestors supplanted the authority of others with that of their own family name.

The truth of "descendedness," Melville argues, involves an infinite regression: "For as the breath in all our lungs is hereditary, and my present breath at this moment, is further descended than the body of the present High Priest of the Jews, so far as he can assuredly trace it; so mere names, which are also but air, do likewise revel in this endless descendedness" (9). As radical breaks with the past, his ancestors' militarism and Pierre's rebellion against his family repudiate the *history* that is carried in every "name." Even as Pierre destroys the fetishes of the past, he begins to reproduce the rhetoric of such fetishism—of the oriental despot, the English aristocrat, the Dutch patroon—in his vainglorious self-reliance. For Melville, the only genuine nobility derives from our involvement in the process of constructing a human community, not from those apparently ahistorical "images" that monumentalize the family or the self. Our shared air, which circulates in the very breath of our speech, is the guarantee of a shared humanity, of a "family of man," whose only proper labor is the construction of a social habitation—that is, a *history*—for such being. For the American, such historical labor (labor *as history*) ought to involve the production of a *new* relation to Europe rather than a simple break with that inescapable past. This, I take it, is the function of the "recognition scene" near the end of *Pierre*, when Isabel and Pierre encounter "another portrait of a complete stranger—a European," which "was as much the father of Isabel as the original of the chair-portrait" (353). This scene is actually a crucial scene of *méconnaissance*, insofar as it seems to plunge Pierre into despair regarding his folly in assuming a portrait to be evidence of actual bloodliness. On the other hand, the portrait of the stranger is used by Melville not merely to absolutely mystify family origins for the sake of plot reversal or some philosophical quandary; the portrait of the European stranger reminds us how every "origin," every tradition, every *history* is the product of our social labor—whether such labor be "imaginative" or "material": "But perhaps there was no original at all to this second portrait; it might have been a pure fancy piece; to which conceit, indeed, the uncharacterizing style of the filling-up seemed to furnish no small testimony" (353). As "a pure fancy piece," the portrait serves to expose the unconscious of Pierre's determination to legitimate Isabel through his own artistic labor. Yet, as the coordinated work of the historical and social imagination, the portrait may serve as a figure for the relation to Europe that American democracy ought to be working to produce.

What inhibits this historical labor is thus not just the family, oppressive as it is represented in the lineage and fortunes of the Glendinnings, but also individualism and its contemporary cant for Melville: Emersonian self-reliance.[20] Hegel's philosophical labor and Marx's more material labor both insist that the individual can realize himself only in and through an otherness that he works to produce, transform, and ultimately internalize as his own social bond. Social history is just this perpetual process of self-transcendence as the means of self-realization. In capitalism, however, the dialectic of self and other is transformed into a dualism between worker and owner, wages and capital, change and repetition, materiality and idealism, other and self: horologicals and chronometricals. Marx's theory of surplus value describes the ways that the capitalist steals the labor-power of the worker by manipulating the working day or mystifying the amount of capital actually consumed in production. The aim of surplus value in capitalism is for Marx, however, considerably more significant than the simple accumulation and expansion of capital. The first aim is to establish the most elementary class distinction: the laborer stakes his being on his physical body, which is successively "used up" in the production process; the owner finds his being in capital, whose very accumulation is a psychic defense against his fear of illegitimacy, a constant reminder that he has a material identity that "grows" in time rather than shrinks (as does the laborer's labor-power). And because it "grows" without the capitalist's labor, surplus value assumes the appearance of a natural organicism, a simulation of the Nature that industrial capitalism displaces. This chimerical organicism finds its pre-capitalist precedent in the peculiar pastoralism of Saddle-Meadows and the special brand of American aristocracy enshrined there.

In *Pierre,* physical labor is always at odds with individual identity, with an ideal of "self-reliance." Isabel's romantic imagination equates self-consciousness with productive labor, but Isabel experiences only the alienating effects of her own labor. Indeed, the nearly mystical art of her guitar seems to be a compensation for the failure of her daily labor to produce the identity (spirit) she desires. Charlie Millthorpe's father, "a very respectable farmer," illustrates this discrepancy between what Henry James, Sr., called "doing" and "being": "Pierre well remembered old farmer Millthorpe:—the handsome, melancholy, calm-tempered, mute, old man; in whose countenance—refinedly ennobled by nature, and yet coarsely tanned and attenuated by many

a prolonged day's work in the harvest—rusticity and classicalness were strangely united. The delicate profile of his face, bespoke the loftiest aristocracy; his knobbed and bony hands resembled a beggar's" (275). Melville uses farmer Millthorpe to illustrate the general observation that "the political and social levelings and confoundings of all manner of human elements in America, produce many striking individual anomalies unknown in other lands" (275). These "anomalies," of course, ought to be the signs of an authentic American revolution, which would transform the illegitimate family of the aristocrat into a genuine democracy. But in this context, the signifier of poverty is labor; the signifier of wealth is idleness. The wear and tear of honest farming is considered *unnatural,* already hints of incipient death: "knobbed and bony hands." The "undiluted" transmission, the sheer repetition, of genetic traits is assumed to be the result of a mere inheritance that is more properly the *work of nature*: a "countenance . . . refinedly ennobled by nature."

The Millthorpes, themselves dependent on the aristocratic and feudal authority of Saddle-Meadows, "loosely and unostentatiously traced their origin to an emigrating English Knight, who had crossed the sea in the time of the elder Charles" (275). Thus, farmer Millthorpe's labor is considered a degradation of such ancestry, and it is little wonder that his poverty and death are rumored to be consequences of drunken dissipation. Insofar as the wear and tear of human labor results in nothing but the apparently enduring identity of the aristocrat, labor is quite literally dissipation and effectively "unnatural"—*other* than itself. Given these circumstances, then, it is hardly surprising that Charlie Millthorpe aspires "to be either an orator, or a poet; at any rate, a great genius of one sort or other. He recalled the ancestral Knight, and indignantly spurned the plow" (279).

Oratory, poetry, "great genius of one sort or other," we know involve Pierre's own project to "gospelize anew," to write the infernal book that would declare his rebellion against the Glendinnings' hypocrisy and assure his fortune and reputation. Indeed, the "labor" of writing is given considerable attention by Melville, both in his representation of Pierre's anguished struggle at the Church of the Apostles and in his general observations on the differences between physical and intellectual labor. Even before he rebels against his family and departs Saddle-Meadows for New York, Pierre himself has worked and earned, after a fashion, by virtue of his trivial lyrics: "The Tropical Summer: a Sonnet," "The Weather: a Thought," "Life: an Impromptu," "The late Reverend Mark Graceman: an Obituary," and so on. Like the "heirlooms" he burns, Pierre's poems are mere fetishes for his poetic self. Both literary formalism (a sonnet) and philosophical idealism (a thought) reify nature and thus speak only of the death of spiritual grace that they have helped to produce ("The late Reverend Mark Graceman: an Obituary"). The name "Reverend Mark Graceman" seems to anticipate "Mark Winsome" in *The Confidence-Man,* who quite clearly is a caricature of Emerson. The actual products of Pierre's juvenile imagination parody the idealizations of Nature and death that characterize literary transcendentalism. More specifically, Pierre's poetizing may indicate that the labor of idealism often produces the *death* of the spirit that the poet and scholar hope to *realize* in their works.

Emerson repeatedly affirms the dignity of labor that unites intellectual and manual work: "I hear therefore with joy whatever is beginning to be said of the dignity and necessity of labor to every citizen. There is virtue yet in the hoe and the spade, for the learned as well as for unlearned hands." Yet what unites different kinds of labor for Emerson is their mutual concern with the production of a spiritual self. Emerson is quick to warn us that work performed without regard for the soul it serves may well be enslaved by other temporal masters—convention and fashion: "And labor is everywhere welcome; always we are invited to work; only be this limitation observed, that a man shall not for the sake of wider activity sacrifice any opinion to the popular judgments and modes of action."[21] Emerson characteristically gives heavier weight to the work of *man* than to the work of the world. Because the "dignity of labor" requires a spiritual understanding of man's role in a natural economy, the labors of idealists—"of the poet, the priest, the lawgiver, and men of study generally"—have special authority in Emerson's division of labor. In "Man the Reformer," his address to the Mechanics' Apprentices' Library Association of Boston in 1841, Emerson seems to take perverse pleasure before such an audience in distinguishing between "intellectual exertion" and "the downright drudgery of the farmer and the smith": "I would not quite forget the venerable counsel of the Egyptian mysteries, which declared that 'there were two pairs of eyes in man, and it is requisite that the pair which are beneath should be closed, when the pair that are above them perceive, and that when the pair above are closed, those which are beneath should be opened.'" The manual laborer is all too quickly deceived by the apparent reality of the products of his labor and thus lured to accumulate and possess objects that ought to be mere symbols of the soul. The genius of the poet and scholar finds its wealth in its own activity; when genius confuses earthly and transcendental rewards, then it falls as Bellerophon did:

> He may leave to others the costly conveniences of housekeeping and large hospitality and the possession of works of art. Let him feel that genius is a hospitality, and that he who can create works of art needs not collect them. He must live in a chamber, and postpone his self-indulgence, forewarned and forearmed against that frequent misfortune of men of genius,—the taste for luxury. This is the tragedy of genius,—attempting to drive along the ecliptic with one horse of the heavens and one horse of the earth, there is only discord and ruin and downfall to chariot and charioteer.[22]

Emerson's description of the discipline and worldly privation of the man of genius is parodied in Melville's description of Pierre at work in his bare, cold room in the Church of the Apostles. And Emerson's warning that genius must not confuse the "horse of the heavens" with the "horse of the earth" or the eyes that "are above" with the eyes that "are beneath" is caricatured in Plotinus Plinlimmon's pamphlet, "Chronometricals and Horologicals."[23]

Melville criticizes Emerson's idealist foundations for human labor by suggesting that the special work of the intellect may serve merely to preserve us from the more difficult and concrete labor of producing a workable society. Emerson's labor of and for the self might require privation and "unworldliness" precisely because such alienation is its secret product. Transcendental idealism thus may be viewed as an elaborate system of psychological defense against the alienating consequences of more material labor in capitalist America. Until he faces the exigencies of earning a living for his own "family" in the city, Pierre has spent all of his literary earnings on cigars, "so that the puffs which indirectly brought him his dollars were again returned, but as perfumed puffs; perfumed with the sweet leaf of Havanna" (262). Melville parodies romantic idealism by transforming the spiritual activity of Emerson's genius or the human desire for transcendence in Wordsworth's image of "wreaths of smoke / Sent up, in silence, from among the trees" into the ephemeral vapors of self-reliant man—what T. E. Hulme terms the "circumambient gas" of romanticism.[24]

"This towering celebrity," Melville writes, "—there he would sit smoking, and smoking, mild and self-festooned as a vapory mountain" (263). This ironic identification of Pierre-as-juvenile-author with the Memnon Stone suggests that *this* formalist conception of poetic spiritualization is designed principally to obscure the self, to give it a protective outer wrapping (literally, a "white jacket" of smoke) that would protect it from the mob. Unlike the music of Isabel's guitar, the smoke from Pierre's poems and cigars protects and isolates the self, rather than serving as its virtual embodiment and medium for communication: its externalization, in Hegelian terms, in and for sociohistorical circulations.

In its own way, this figuration of Pierre as poet is the equivalent of the chair-portrait of his father. Both conceal a secret of illegitimacy that is related to their equally false claims to authority. The father's adultery is discovered in his mysterious smile in the portrait in the same way Pierre's plagiarism from other authors is revealed in his own ambitious work. Melville's description of Pierre as a "vapory mountain" also helps explain his paradoxical act of burning the chair-portrait. What Pierre intends as an act of rebellion serves as the means of protecting his father from exposure, insofar as Pierre finds in the portrait some family resemblance to Isabel:

> Painted before the daughter was conceived or born, like a dumb seer, the portrait still seemed leveling its prophetic finger at that empty air, from which Isabel did finally emerge. There seemed to lurk some mystical intelligence and vitality in the picture; because, since in his own memory of his father, Pierre could not recall any distinct lineament transmitted to Isabel, but vaguely saw such in the portrait; therefore, not Pierre's parent, as any way remembrable by him, but the portrait's

painted *self* seemed the real father of Isabel; for, so far as all sense went, Isabel had inherited one peculiar trait nowhither traceable but to it. (197)

The curiously prophetic quality of the chair-portrait, whether it be an effect of the painter's genius or merely Pierre's excited imagination, suggests an artistic function different from the defenses of Emersonian idealism or Pierre's protective veil of poetic smoke. The portrait of the father brings together the aristocrat's conscious desire for authority and the unconscious illegitimacy that fuels such desire.

Like his ancestors, Pierre wants to turn himself into an enduring figure in the landscape, precisely by protecting himself from the "mob" (such as the one that assaults Delly, Isabel, and Pierre in that infernal first night they spend in the city) and at the same time rebelling against his predecessors by willfully "authoring" his own unnatural family of Isabel, Delly, and, ultimately, Lucy. It is a family composed of nothing but "sisters" and a "brother," we are quick to notice, recalling our earlier remarks about the relation of brothers and sisters in the metaphorics of the Hegelian family. Contemptuous of the various efforts of vanity presses and journals to exploit his minor celebrity, Pierre himself merely reproduces, even in his haughty denial of their overtures, the cult of authorial "personality" these publishers *labor* to produce. Like the aristocrat and capitalist, he vainly tries to father himself and a family to render honorable such imaginative incest.

Melville's representation of Pierre as some "vapory mountain" also associates him with the natural landmark at Saddle-Meadows, Terror Rock or the Memnon Stone, which later in the narrative will come to mythic life in Pierre's dream of Enceladus, the earthbound Titan. Earlier, I interpreted the Memnon Stone as a version of those colossal monuments Hegel and Marx associated with the despotism of Asiatic and Egyptian rulers. Although a natural formation, the Memnon Stone is discovered by Pierre, "the first known publishing discoverer of this stone, which he had thereupon fancifully christened the Memnon Stone" (132). The stone becomes Pierre's colossus, his monument to the *natural* surplus the genius ought to have in reserve. The cavity at the base of the rock and its general phallic suggestiveness make the Memnon Stone a figure for a hermaphroditism that is particularly appropriate either to the false self-sufficiency of the Glendinnings or to Emerson's self-reliant genius: American aristocrat or radical individual. It is interesting to note that the Church of the Apostles' architecture is the urban equivalent of the rock, insofar as the new tower where Pierre has his rooms rises out of the courtyard of the old church. The hermaphroditism of the rural and urban forms—the former associated with the aristocracy of the Glendinnings and the latter with either Pierre's writing or the law and commerce in the buildings below—suggests the self-generative powers of the "original character" in *The Confidence-Man*: "The original character, essentially such, is like a revolving Drummond light, raying away from itself all round it—

everything is lit by it, everything starts up to it (mark how it is with Hamlet), so that, in certain minds, there follows upon the adequate conception of such a character, an effect, in its way, akin to that which in Genesis attends upon the beginning of things."[25]

Yet, such an "original" in both *Pierre* and *The Confidence-Man,* whether literary character turned author or citizen turned despot, remains Melville's grandest illusion—the secret passion of the idealist not merely to *participate* in nature's economy but to *originate* and thus *dominate* that economy. Such self-procreative and ahistorical formalism belongs only to the impossible realm of the "chronometrical," and as such it is as "self-consuming" as it is "self-producing." It is, in a word, an *incestuous* form of artistic production that merely produces its own obscurity, weakness, and ultimate death. By the same token, it obscures its actual origins, which in the case of Pierre's writing must be termed the historical conditions—necessities and exigencies—under which he must work. The unified religious authority of the old Church of the Apostles has been replaced by the apparent dualism of material *vs.* ideal, utilitarian *vs.* transcendental. The lawyers and shopkeepers in the renovated church exercise their very real powers over the workers in the city by maintaining the *illusion* of freedom represented by the dreamers and freethinkers occupying the tower. The "freedom" of such idealism (of Emerson's self-reliant genius) is, in Melville's scrutiny, merely a double of the servitude it hopes to escape; it is a *reflection* of the poverty and alienation of those who work to preserve such masters.

Such an interpretation of Pierre's art as the idealist version of the oriental despot's colossal monuments—testaments to his arbitrary power, accumulated economic surpluses, and exploitation of labor—revises considerably the conventional reading of Melville's oft-quoted glimpse into the pyramid of the human soul:

> The old mummy lies buried in cloth on cloth; it takes time to unwrap this Egyptian king. Yet now, forsooth, because Pierre began to see through the first superficiality of the world, he fondly weens he has come to the unlayered substance. But, far as any geologist has yet gone down into the world, it is found to consist of nothing but surface stratified on surface. To its axis, the world being nothing but superinduced superficies. By vast pains we mine into the pyramid; by horrible gropings we come to the central room; with joy we espy the sarcophagus; but we lift the lid—and no body is there!—appallingly vacant as vast is the soul of man! (285)

Generally interpreted in the context of Melville's nihilism or as his existential affirmation of the groundlessness of being, this passage deals less with man's essential nature (his "geology," as it were) than with the "nothingness" he produces by way of his labor to idealize the world in the service of material interests. In this passage, Melville not only indicts transcendental idealism for offering us an absolutely elusive notion of "spirit" or "soul," he also connects such idealism with those idealizing arts of political rulers who would mask their illegitimate power and their exploitation of workers in the form of majestic symbols of their supernatural authority. This political mystification initiates a historical process of labor through which we quite literally *unmake* ourselves and transform the natural energies of our bodies into alien, unnatural objects. "Nothingness" is not for Melville the essential condition for being that it would become for the twentieth-century existentialist; the vacancy in Melville's pyramid is the consequence of specific historical acts of social labor made to serve perverse gods.

Melville distinguishes Pierre's labor from that of farmer Millthorpe and even that of Isabel:

> The mechanic, the day-laborer, has but one way to live; his body must provide for his body. But not only could Pierre in some sort, do that; he could do the other; and letting his body stay lazily at home, send off his soul to labor, and his soul would come faithfully back and pay his body her wages. So, some unprofessional gentlemen of the aristocratic South, who happen to own slaves, give those slaves liberty to go and seek work, and every night return with their wages, which constitute those idle gentlemen's income. Both ambidexter and quadruple-armed is that man, who in a day-laborer's body, possesses a day-laboring soul. (261)

The spiritual slavery that Melville describes here connects Pierre's life-denying artistic idealism with the institutions of southern slavery, just as the feudalism of the Dutch patroons is associated with oriental despotism. The passage suggests that the "division of labor" in modern bourgeois culture more subtly replicates the explicit exploitation of labor in slave-holding societies. Porter considers the mythic oppositions of country and city, pastoralism and industrialism, to be characteristically American means of forgetting capitalism's deep roots in the feudalism of aristocratic class structures: "Perhaps it is partly due to a long-standing confusion in the minds of Americans over the difference between capitalist and aristocrat that they have never really been able to resist altogether the plantation myth's attractions."[26] In particular, the Transcendentalist's rejection of economic materialism often results in the substitution of an ideal economy of the self that comes dangerously close to the values and customs of the landed gentry. By explicitly feminizing Pierre's "soul" ("pay his body her wages"), Melville also returns this reflection on art and everyday labor to the psychosexual themes centering on Pierre's incestuous relation with Isabel, whose guitar plays as he writes. The "mystical" communion of Isabel and Pierre, like the spiritual "friendship" so prized by Emerson and Thoreau, is for Melville an inadequate substitute for the social product that ought to result from the coordinated labor of politically committed citizens.

Melville's association of Pierre's labor as a writer with the master-slave relation of southern slavery begins with the Emersonian cliché that writing transcends ordinary labor by coordinating physical and spiritual functions. But Melville then suggests that the function of writing may be precisely to protect its "author" from the physical depletion of ordinary labor. In this regard, authorship is explicitly related to the ownership of slaves and the idleness of the aristocrat, but with the interesting qualification that this relation between master and slave gives the slave the *illusion* of "liberty to go and seek work." That this exploitation of the slave's desire for freedom also involves the slave's desire to do his/her "own" labor is important for Melville's parable of writing. The illusion that the soul can work independently ("freely") from the body, which stays "lazily at home," is fundamental to Emersonian idealism: "Nature is the incarnation of a thought, and turns to a thought again, as ice becomes water and gas. The world is mind precipitated, and the volatile essence is forever escaping again into the state of free thought. . . . Man imprisoned, man crystallized, man vegetative, speaks to man impersonated."[27] Melville effectively reverses the terms of Emerson's triumphant transcendentalist vision, transforming the essentially free mind into a slave to the physical master, who after all *still speaks to,* or governs, this presumptively "free" spirit.

The separation of the "self" from its "labor," and the separation of physical from spiritual production, is the fundamental alienation operating in aristocratic families and in the romantic "arts" designed to "naturalize" such aristocracy. Insofar as the family does nothing but project the concept of a remote, external "law" of authority, which cannot be internalized but merely reproduced as alien and external, the family produces nothing other than alienation itself, that pure negation (*Verneinung*) that Hegel himself equated with the death of the Spirit. The move from family to society, from the Law of the Father to the internal law of self-governance, is the negation of negation, the transformation of stony externality into the self-moving principle of *Geist* as its historical movement: the *Bildungsweg* of Hegel's social theory that Marx could appropriate from an otherwise bourgeois apologist.

Pierre's "labor" in writing his "infernal book," his new gospel, is designed to reproduce this portrait of the stony self, of the Self as distinct from man's social dependency and the labor required to maintain the historical relation of self and society. We read little directly of Pierre's grand work, except those quotes from "the last sheet from his hand" and the slips he has cast to the floor. Still, we learn enough of "his apparent author-hero, Vivia," to recognize that Pierre has "directly plagiarized from his own experiences" (302). These fragments do not speak of self-consciousness as self-knowledge, as we would expect from this romantic author. Instead, Vivia speaks only of his contradiction and despair, of his hatred of life and his impotence—what Nietzsche would term his *ressentiment*: "Yet that knowing his fatal condition does not one whit enable him to change or better his condition. Conclusive proof that he has no power over his condition" (303). What Pierre/Vivia cannot know is that he has merely given objective form to a "soul," a suffering "self," produced by those contradictions in his family history that are also the disabling contradictions of a promised social democracy based upon radical individualism, whether such individualism assumes the form of the father, the military leader, the mythic hero, the Dutch patroon, the capitalist, or the visionary author.

In this regard, then, Pierre/*Pierre* reproduces the aristocratic law of the Father by means of one of those "arts" that capitalism employs for similar purposes of naturalizing and legitimating its own founding contradictions: between "self" and "society," "owner" and "laborer," "ideal" and "historical," chronometrical and horological. The art of the novel gives us a "labor" that we as readers perform only to *use up* our bodies (and our time) in the service of reproducing the "genius" of the author: Herman Melville or Pierre Glendinning. That always-absent "author" governs and controls our labors in order to take the place of the social and communal relations our work of reading ought to yield.

In *Capital*, Marx argues that it is the *identity* of the capitalist that is the true fetish, an alienated metonymy for the "labor-power" stolen from his workers in the form of "surplus value." Indeed, the growth of surplus value, the incessant drive for accumulation, seems some desperate desire on the part of the capitalist to disguise what he recognizes to be the inauthenticity of his identity: that which represents "him" is never "he himself." In a similar sense, Pierre's book is "filched" from those "vile atheists," Lucan and Voltaire, among others, who ought to remind Pierre of the impossibility of "authoring" anything outside the complex genealogy of literary and social forces. The infinite regress of *literature* and the infinite regress of *descendedness* that Melville uses to subvert aristocratic pretensions are both the preconditions for negating myths of self-reliant man and aristocratic authority in favor of that more enduring and integrated product: a social collective sustained by the labors of men and women.

Neither the aristocratic ruler nor the American capitalist wants *that* dispersed, displaced, collective authority. In *Pierre*, Melville attempted to kill romance, to take it to its ultimate extreme as a formalist prop for the ideology of America's secret aristocracy of the Spirit: economic capitalism and philosophical transcendentalism. Rogin concludes that the "self-referentiality that takes over *Pierre* brings the book's narrative to a halt" and "explains its own failure, for it is the appropriate literary form for the claustrophobic family. *Pierre* is the victim of the domestic relationship which brings both storytelling and therefore life itself to an end."[28] In this regard, we can judge Pierre's swerve back into the chivalric action of the duel and the melodrama it stages to be merely the "proper" ending for the "novel" he has written, the "infernal" new gospel of capitalist individuation as sustained by the rhetoric of literary authority. It is altogether fitting that melodrama should be Pierre's choice in the face of his literary "failure." Pierre's final "actions," however, by no means compromise his own conception of literature; such action is perfectly consistent with Pierre's literary project: the realiza-

tion of romance in experience, the substitution of the author's self for the worker's active labor. Such realization—life imitating art at last—merely enables Pierre to succumb to the "romance of the real" that is told by the authors of capitalism and enacted by their "characters," whether intellectual or manual laborers.

Yet just as the chair-portrait of Pierre's father *reveals* his kinship with Isabel and thus the very secret the portrait artist attempted to conceal with the conventional "nobility" of his subject (and the conventions of the portrait genre), so *Pierre* represents its own unconscious and thus *escapes* fleetingly its identification with Pierre and his fragmentary monument, his unfinished colossus. By so ruthlessly connecting his own craft of fiction and his own will to literary authority with the political wills of despots, aristocrats, and capitalists, Melville completes his book by undoing his own claim to legitimacy and by *characterizing* himself in his parody of an author, Pierre. Insofar as Melville accepts the social anarchy he finds at the heart of the Glendinnings' and the Gansevoorts' conceptions of "democracy," he must be "humiliated" by a literary vocation that merely serves that ideology's effort to rationalize its contradictions. Melville does not accept these conditions for labor; his rebellion is exemplified by his refusal of the customary alternatives of philosophical idealism or the "world elsewhere" of art. The "unconscious" of *Pierre* is, like the unconscious of the chair-portrait, no mystical effect of artistic intuition; it is the ideological analysis that results from deconstructing those apparently self-evident distinctions we assume govern our everyday reality: ideal and material, self and other, author and reader, owner and worker, master and servant, state and family. That Melville understands these distinctions to have special roles to play in reconciling social democracy with radical individualism makes his labor in *Pierre* especially pertinent to Jacksonian America.

Rogin and others have judged *Pierre* to be work symptomatic of Melville's ultimate self-referentiality as an author, his resignation to the delusions that later would define twentieth-century modernism. Melville deconstructs in *Pierre* the "democratic" pretensions of American capitalism by exposing the relation of radical individualism to the incestuous and claustrophobic closure of the aristocratic family. And Melville further deconstructs the new "authority" of Emerson's expressive self, both subject and object of its own labor, by revealing how literary authority participates in the naturalization of capitalist contradictions. Given his own complicity with the principal subjects of his critique, Melville can hardly be said to have mastered the problems his narrative uncovers. *Parody, irony, and satire*—mere literary terms, after all—hardly begin to address the force of Melville's critique in *Pierre*. In one sense, *Pierre* is Melville's farewell to the romance and the novel—to "literature" as he had attempted to practice it in his previous works. Yet *Pierre* is by no means the expression of incipient madness, despair, or nihilism. Quite the contrary, the book raises those questions about the ideological consequences of literary production that motivate the more socially and politically focused work of **The Confidence-Man.** Melville's critique of literary production may have devastating consequences for his own sense of vocation, but it also makes possible the active study of the genealogy of social values that Melville's Ishmael futilely attempts to "understand" from his detached vantage and by means of his romantic "negative capability" in **Moby-Dick.** By means of the deconstructive "failure" of **Pierre** as literature, Melville could make the leap from Ishmael to the confidence men, whose agitations and subversions enter the social drama, provoking the "labor" of their interlocutors, of their *readers,* either to *reproduce* the Wall Street World—America as the "tomb" of its past—or *produce* the carnival of an authentically democratic society. In **Pierre** and **The Confidence-Man,** Melville developed a mode of writing that left "literature" behind and anticipated the cultural criticism of our own present moment.

Notes

1. Henry A. Murray, Introduction to *Pierre, or The Ambiguities,* by Herman Melville (New York, 1949), xcvi.

2. Mark Poster, *Critical Theory of the Family* (London, 1978), 144.

3. Philippe Ariès, *Centuries of Childhood: A Social History of Family Life,* trans. R. Baldick (New York, 1965); Jacques Donzelot, *The Policing of Families,* trans. Robert Hurley (New York, 1979).

4. Michael Paul Rogin, *Subversive Genealogy: The Politics and Art of Herman Melville* (New York, 1983), 165; Eric Sundquist, *Home as Found: Authority and Genealogy in Nineteenth-Century American Literature* (Baltimore, 1979).

5. Louis Althusser's "Ideology and Ideological State Apparatuses (Notes toward an Investigation)," in Althusser, *Lenin and Philosophy and Other Essays,* trans. Ben Brewster (New York, 1971), provides the most extended discussion of interpellation. Antonio Gramsci develops the notion of hegemonic discourse in *The Prison Notebooks.* See Gramsci, *Selections from the Prison Notebooks,* trans. and ed. Quintin Hoare and Geoffrey Nowell Smith (New York, 1971).

6. Friedrich Engels, *The Origin of the Family, Private Property, and the State* (New York, 1942); Poster, *Critical Theory of the Family,* 43.

7. Karl Marx, *Capital,* trans. Ben Fowkes (3 vols.; New York, 1977), I, 471*n*26.

8. *Ibid.,* 472; Raymond Williams, *Keywords: A Vocabulary of Culture and Society* (Rev. ed.; New York, 1983), 133.

9. Carolyn Porter, *Seeing and Being: The Plight of the Participant Observer in Emerson, James, Adams, and Faulkner* (Middletown, Conn., 1981), 65.

10. G. W. F. Hegel, *The Phenomenology of Mind,* trans. J. B. Baillie (New York, 1967), 477.

11. Rogin, *Subversive Genealogy,* 164.

12. Williams, *Keywords,* 132, explains that the precapitalist family was often understood as "the household," rather than in terms of specific kinship relations. There is much disagreement among scholars concerning Williams' assumption that the nuclear family and the rise of the bourgeoisie are historically contemporary developments. I am not qualified to resolve these disputes, but I am struck with the central concern in the modern novel with adultery, illegitimacy, and thus the definition of "proper" family relations. Capitalism's judgment of ethical questions often involves the settlement of property rights. Kinship relations in the novel are almost always a function of property rights and the orderly transmission of those rights, rather than the other way around.

13. Hegel, *Phenomenology,* 479.

14. Herman Melville, *Pierre, or The Ambiguities* (Evanston, Ill., 1971), 122, hereinafter cited parenthetically in the text by page number.

15. Carolyn L. Karcher, *Shadow over the Promised Land: Slavery, Race, and Violence in Melville's America* (Baton Rouge, 1980), 94.

16. Hegel, *The Philosophy of History,* trans. J. Sibree (1899; rpr. New York, 1956), 161.

17. *Ibid.,* 165.

18. Marx, *Capital,* I, 451, 452.

19. *Ibid.,* 452.

20. In *Pierre,* Melville makes a number of puns on Kant's surname as part of his more general critique of transcendental idealism. Speaking of the idealists of various sorts—painters, sculptors, students, German philosophers—inhabiting the upper floors of the tower in the Church of the Apostles, Melville jibes: "While the abundance of leisure in their attics (physical and figurative), unites with the leisure of their stomachs, to fit them in an eminent degree for that undivided attention indispensable to the proper digesting of the sublimated Categories of Kant; especially as Kant (can't) is the one great palpable fact in their pervadingly impalpable lives" (267). Yet the purely *negative* palpability of Kantian idealism—its cant is its can't—finds its habitation in the "Titanic" tower that rises out of the stores and law offices into which the old church has been divided. Elsewhere, Melville judges these "theoretic and inactive" transcendentalists to be "therefore harmless," but as neighbors with the commercial and legal powers of the modern city these transcendentals must be said to serve some more active and dangerous ideological purpose, even if such a purpose depends on their apparent ineffectualness (262).

21. Ralph Waldo Emerson, "The American Scholar," in Emerson, *Nature, Addresses, and Lectures,* ed. Robert E. Spiller and Alfred R. Ferguson (Cambridge, Mass., 1971), 62, Vol. I of Joseph Slater and Douglas Emory Wilson, eds., *The Collected Works of Ralph Waldo Emerson,* 4 vols. to date.

22. Emerson, "Man the Reformer," *ibid.,* 152, 153.

23. Many critics agree that Plotinus Plinlimmon and his lecture on "chronometricals and horologicals" is Melville's intended "satire on all shallow and amiable transcendental 'reconcilers' of the 'Optimist' or 'Compensation' school," as Willard Thorp put the matter in his Introduction to *Herman Melville: Representative Selections* (New York, 1938), lxxxii. Extracted as Plinlimmon's lecture is from a series of "Three Hundred and Thirty-three Lectures" and qualified as *"not so much the Portal, as part of the temporary Scaffold to the Portal of this new Philosophy,"* Plinlimmon's very form parodies the Emersonian lecture. The title itself, *"'EI,'"* is paronomastic of Emerson's identification of the "eye" and the "I," as well as the spiritually generative qualities Emerson attributes to the crossing of the "eye" and the "I," which involves the third paronomasia: "das Ei" or "egg," as in *ab ovo.* Connecting all of these puns is, of course, their mutual philological source, the Greek philosophical term *eídos,* which variously links appearance, constitutive nature, form, type, species, and idea. I cannot recount here the complicated history of *eide* in even the restricted classical tradition from Plato to Aristotle and Plotinus, but I will simply remind the reader that classical philosophical debates concerning the relation of immanence to transcendence often focused on the particular status of *eide.* F. E. Peters in *Greek Philosophical Terms* (New York, 1967), 50, notes that by Aristotle's postulation of "the *eide* as the thoughts of God, a position that continues down through Plotinus . . . into Christianity, and at the same time . . . as immanent formal causes with an orientation toward matter, . . . an at least partial solution to the dilemma of immanence vs. transcendence was reached. But the problem continued as a serious one in Platonism, discussed at length by both Plotinus . . . and Proclus."

24. Wordsworth's lines are from "Tintern Abbey," ll. 17-18. T. E. Hulme, "Romanticism and Classicism," in *Critical Theory since Plato,* ed. Hazard Adams (New York, 1971), 769.

25. Herman Melville, *The Confidence-Man: His Masquerade,* ed. Elizabeth S. Foster (New York, 1954), 271.

26. Porter, *Seeing and Being,* 228-29.

27. Ralph Waldo Emerson, "Nature," in Emerson, *Essays: Second Series,* ed. Alfred R. Ferguson and Jean Ferguson Carr (Cambridge, Mass., 1983), 113, Vol. III of Slater and Wilson, eds., *Works.*

28. Rogin, *Subversive Genealogy,* 179-80.

James Creech (essay date 1993)

SOURCE: *"Pierre, or, The Ambiguities*: A Camp Reading," in *Closet Writing/Gay Reading: The Case of Melville's* Pierre, The University of Chicago Press, 1993, pp. 93-155.

[*In the following excerpt, Creech interprets* Pierre *as a covertly homoerotic novel, with Pierre's attraction to his father manifested through his feelings for Isabel.*]

PIERRE'S TWO FATHERS

"A WORD TO THE WISE"

Pierre has few of the . . . obviously homoerotic themes which have now been so frequently acknowledged in Melville's other novels. Even beyond these difficult questions of homoerotic content, the wink, or its audience, it is in general difficult to know at all just what Melville himself consciously thought he was doing in *Pierre.* To complicate an already complicated question, there is reason to think, for example, that the tone, if not the entire nature, of the project may actually have changed, perhaps after the first thirteen or sixteen chapters, perhaps as a result of difficulties he encountered at that time.

Brian Higgins and Hershel Parker have suggested that the bad reviews of *Moby-Dick,* which began coming in during the composition of *Pierre,* may in part explain why the novel turns so dark, destructive, and just plain weird after a certain point.[1] Melville scholars have puzzled over his promises to Richard Bentley, his English publisher, that *Pierre* would be a romance in the popular style, and his apparently sincere belief that it was the sort of book likely to generate a high volume of sales—notions that seemed as wildly improbable then as they do to anyone reading the novel today. What did Melville mean when he promised Sophia Hawthorne that his new novel would be as a "rural bowl of milk"?[2] Concerning this traditional, speculative debate about Melville's intentions in writing *Pierre,* one can, at a minimum, conclude that the novel was a site of conflicts between conscious and unconscious forces of which Melville was not fully in control. The skepticism displayed by Higgins and Parker is a necessary tonic for anyone approaching this work. "No one is ever going to demonstrate the perfect unity of *Pierre* from the opening words to the last words." Or, as they state in an earlier passage, "Our concern should be with understanding the complexity of Melville's compulsion to protect himself from others and from acknowledgement of what he had done. As Harrison Hayford said in 1946, Melville probably 'deceived himself into thinking he had submerged the profounder elements of his book far enough below the surface to allow the ordinary reader clear sailing through the romance.'"[3]

A refinement would thus seem to be in order here. We must remain open to the possibility that a literary text can wink at us about its homoerotic content without, as it were, knowing what it is doing. In such circumstances, the wink may hover ambiguously over the boundary line delineating the unavowable and the unconscious.

Melville clearly goes to considerable pains to put us on notice that there is a mystery in *Pierre.* Pierre is given "a word to the wise" which Melville no doubt meant as a wink to his readers, too: "Probe, probe a little—see—there seems one little crack there, Pierre—a wedge, a wedge. Something ever comes of all persistent inquiry; we are not so continually curious for nothing, Pierre; not for nothing, do we so intrigue and become wiley diplomatists, and glozers with our own minds, Pierre" (102, Library of America; all citations are to this ed.). His oath beneath the Terror Stone mentions "the miseries of the undisclosable things in me" (160). And perhaps most telling of all, in the last paragraph, after all speakable secrets have been revealed, Isabel in effect provides the novel with its final summation: "All's o'er, and ye know him not!" (420).

If, indeed, beyond these generic insinuations, Melville was unable to count on nineteenth-century equivalents to the code of Angora cats and house plants, it becomes crucial to look very closely at the equivalences which he himself actually constructs. Surely an important example is in the opening pages of book 1.

. . . . .

Melville repeatedly perfumes the early chapters of the novel with strong whiffs of heterosexual incest, underscoring the surprising youth and beauty of Mary Glendinning, Pierre's mother, for whom "a reverential and devoted son seemed lover enough" (8-9). Pierre's "romantic filial love," his jealousy of any potential suitor, Mary's similarity to "a conquering virgin," who etherealizes the "nameless and infinitely delicate aroma of inexpressible tenderness" which she feels in the "lover-like adoration of Pierre" (22)—all of this makes mother-son incest pervasive in the first books. Given this relationship at the outset, their subsequent rupture will have about it something of the lover's quarrel. And indeed, the incestuous link comes to seem like a relationship constructed in order to be deconstructed by subsequent events in the novel.

In the meantime, however, the mother-son incest theme will be both sustained and displaced by the habit which mother and son share of addressing each other familiarly as brother and sister: sustained, because calling each other brother and sister is a form of coeval intimacy which transgresses the rigid hierarchical taboo shaping mother-son relations in the bourgeois family; displaced, because it demonstrates at the outset that the primacy of mother-son incest is not so much the thing itself as it is one term in a potential series of analogical slippages. The putatively original (and heterosexual) desire of the son for the mother, in other words, loses some of its prestige when it can be so easily displaced and transmogrified into desire for a sister. And as the plot develops, the "brother-sister" bond between Pierre and his mother does indeed turn out to be Melville's foreshadowing of a counterbond between Pierre and Isabel, also incestuous, but a bond which will totally supplant the mother-son connection with which the novel begins. It seems that this displaceability is part of the general hostility toward the mother that surfaces steadily in the novel's first half.

. . . . .

In *Pierre,* then, Melville has not used the gothic and soon-to-be psychoanalytic trope of heterosexual incest in the

usual sense as a grounding desire from which all other forms of desire are directly or dialectically derived. If anything, heterosexually incestuous desire is itself derived from another source, and here is where the complexities and ambiguities of *Pierre* really begin. For, also beginning with book 1, Melville complicates this familiar taboo against mother-son incest with less familiar, homosexual logic:

> So perfect to Pierre had long seemed the illuminated scroll of his life thus far, that only one hiatus was discoverable by him in that sweetly-writ manuscript. A sister had been omitted from the text. He mourned that so delicious a feeling as fraternal love had been denied him. Nor could the fictitious title ["sister"], which he so often lavished upon his mother, at all supply the absent reality. This emotion was most natural; and the full cause and reason of it even Pierre did not at that time entirely appreciate. . . . For much that goes to make up the deliciousness of a wife, already lies in the sister. "Oh, had my father but had a daughter!" cried Pierre; "some one whom I might love, and protect, and fight for, if need be. . . . Now, of all things, would to heaven, I had a sister!" (11-12)

Already it seems odd that Pierre should be, in effect, mourning here for a sister he never had, when in fact the "absent reality" in his life, what had been really lost, was his father who had died seven years earlier, when Pierre was twelve.[4] Other indications of a hidden tension beneath these lines quickly follow. The proleptic "mourning" which Melville just called a "most natural emotion," is immediately, without transition, reclassified as a "strange yearning."

> *This emotion was most natural;* and the full cause and reason of it even Pierre did not at that time entirely appreciate. . . . It may have been that *this strange yearning* of Pierre for a sister, had part of its origin in that still stranger feeling of loneliness he sometimes experienced, as not only the solitary head of his family, but the only surnamed male Glendinning extant. A powerful and populous family had by degrees run off into the female branches; so that Pierre found himself . . . companioned by no surnamed male Glendinning, but the duplicate one reflected to him in the mirror. (12; my emphasis)

The logic of this passage is by normative standards incomprehensible. In schematic form it goes like this: Because Pierre is lonely as head of his family and longs to be "companioned by [a] surnamed male Glendinning," he yearns—not for a brother or a cousin, nor for the father which he in fact has lost—but for a sister. That is, Pierre's yearning for a male companion in the patriarchal position is what Melville terms the "origin" of his yearning for a sister (with which the novel's plot will provide him in short order).

Pierre's yearning for a patriarchal male Glendinning recurs elsewhere in the novel. He has exactly similar feelings when he gazes upon the "fine military portrait" of his grandfather who, like Melville's own grandfather, had been a hero of the Revolutionary War in "that patriarchal time." "Never could Pierre look upon his fine military portrait without an infinite and *mournful longing to meet his living aspect in actual life.* The majestic sweetness of this portrait was truly wonderful in its effects upon any sensitive and generous-minded young observer. For such, that portrait possessed the heavenly persuasiveness of angelic speech . . . declaring to all people, as from the Mount, that man is a *noble, god-like being, full of choicest juices; made up of strength and beauty*" (38; my emphasis). With homoerotic intensity that is today obvious, then, this "infinite and mournful longing" in Pierre is beyond any doubt desire for a male companion in the family. His mirror image of himself will not do. He longs for the fleshly reality. That this mournful longing should be infinite will come as no surprise to anyone who has considered Judith Butler's reflections on the impossibility of mourning the loss of such primary homosexual love objects.[5]

The shift to desiring a sister is, then, an unmotivated gender leap in the object of Pierre's yearning. Melville does not attempt to smooth over the displacement, but that does not prevent him from simply asserting it without commentary. For Melville to have violated the logic of narrative causality in this way, in which one, ostensibly unrelated thing is said nevertheless to cause another, he must have been responding to some conscious or unconscious desire of his own for there to be this linkage between the novel's elaborate theme of heterosexual incest (the "strange yearning") and its "origin" in a more mediated and attenuated theme of homosexual incest (the "still stranger feeling"). Homosexual incest is thus acknowledged as unavowable, with all the paradoxes implied in such a formulation: acknowledged and thus recognized; but acknowledged as being unacknowledgeable.

Here, then, is a first moment when Melville is constructing an equivalence, an embryonic code, which he cannot presume to be available at large. Because of prevailing standards of literary "competence," he can invoke Dante or Shakespeare at other junctures of the novel, fully expecting readers to "get it." Here he has to take it upon himself to rearrange normal, connotative links. And here, too, is a first wink. The path of displacement that starts with homosexual incest and travels from there to heterosexual incest begins here in book 1, and we shall find that it becomes ever more elaborately marked as the novel progresses. As a first wink, then, it begins to establish the grounds of mutual understanding that will be required for the other winks which Melville, with equal deniability, will direct at us in later pages.

. . . . .

But where does this leave us? Can we, thus, just open the closet door and peer inside? Should we just cut to the chase and state flatly that in this odd, logically disjoined passage, Melville is cruising for those longed-for readers who might understand him, trying to hook in those who might be able to discern that Isabel is a feminine cover for what logically and psychologically in this novel is a male

character? Does a camp reading require us to state crudely that *Pierre* explores the price a brave man in Melville's situation would have had to pay for owning his homosexuality frankly? Is it the story of a man who forswears his fiancé and runs away to the city with his homosexual lover, who accepts being disowned from family and rejected by society in order to heed a higher virtue of self-determination and integrity? And finally, shall we see *Pierre* as an early prototype of gay novels which, for over a century to come, would have to end in the annihilation of their gay protagonists, often in a confrontation with a straight object of their (former) affection? Yes, we shall. A great deal in the novel points precisely to such a direct transgender encoding, not unlike that performed in *A la Recherche du temps perdu* (where Albertine "is really" Albert). To the extent that one approaches it from that perspective, one would want to perform the kind of transgender decoding which George Painter and others have performed in scholarship on Proust.[6] (The tactic of changing a character's gender to disguise homosexual sensibilities is still commonly called "the Albertine strategy").

Melville's may well be a "Nathaniel/Isabel" strategy. For we must also read the novel as a necessarily transvested story of a man whose life is abruptly changed when he falls in love with another man, the way Melville did with Hawthorne, the erotic model for Isabel and for whose intelligence much of this may have been imagined. In his daring article, John D. Seelye hedgingly, but correctly, states an important part of the case. He inventories the multiple ways that autobiographical references to Hawthorne are insinuated into *Pierre,* the placement of the Ulver cottage homologously to the placement of Hawthorne's cottage at Tanglewood, for example. Add to that the detail that the cottage was red, as was Hawthorne's. He then concludes somewhat cautiously, "This is not to say that the love affair between Isabel and Pierre is a thinly-veiled allegory of Melville's friendship with Hawthorne. It is to suggest, however, that Melville seems to have been consciously drawing on his feelings toward Hawthorne as he wrote the story. The incestuous basis of the love between Pierre and Isabel hints at the unnaturalness of the attraction Melville seems to have felt for Hawthorne, later reflected in the attraction felt by Clarel towards Vine."[7] Even though we are far from wrong to read *Pierre* in this way, we must not sacrifice the crucial ambiguities which provide its subtitle, and which were an integral part of Melville's homoerotic fiction once he decided to bring it home.

A gay and lesbian studies project today must indeed undertake the simple translations and revelations where they are appropriate. It is never insignificant to discern closeted homosexual content and, where plausible, to name names. At the same time, *Pierre* must also be read as a dense reflection on the nature, function, and allure of the closet which, in a different way from *La Recherche,* forms an important aspect of its substance. The closet is itself as much the subject of *Pierre* as are any expressions of the homoerotic desire it secretes. In a different way from

Proust, and in a different way from other novels by Melville himself, the transgender fiction here is as much about the resistance to what it is seeking to express as it is about the positivity of a hidden truth. While there is hidden homosexuality in *Pierre,* as indeed there is throughout so much of Melville, in *Pierre* it is much more than a fact or an aspect of a character or a behavior observed or a temptation felt. In *Pierre,* homosexuality is explored from the perverse perspective of its impossible place, and thus its closeted space, within the still-sacred configurations of the family.

And finally, a simple transcoding of Pierre would implicitly attribute to Melville an acceptance of his desire, not only to find a male companion and soul mate (a desire he was able to own),[8] but a whole array of corollary consequences—principal among them being flight from the bonds of family and paternity—which it was simply impossible for him to imagine unequivocally. Although as a camp reading, this analysis is fundamentally enabled by the recognition that Melville, in some imprecise sense, was gay too, it does not proceed from any simple conviction about what that actually could mean in the particular life of Herman Melville, or about how it can come to legibility in his writing.

"HIS OWN LITTLE CLOSET"

The loneliness Melville ascribes to Pierre in the absence of other males at the family's patriarchal pinnacle is not autobiographically inspired since he himself was the third child in a numerous family. The singularity which he shows to be the bane of Pierre's life at this juncture is, in fact, a figuration of the closet which is all bourgeois male subjectivity conceived traditionally.

If a man competes against men for his right to occupy the privileged space of patriarchal masculinity, he loses any unmediated intimacy with other men, which explains Pierre's sense that by winning, by being alone at the top of the fame column, he will, in fact, remain lonely. Winning by default will actually mean losing male intimacy and living wholly entrapped within another closed, privatized, space—the heterosexual closet—of that (en)gendered isolation in which we can recognize "ce sexe qui est bien *un,*" to parody Luce Irigaray.

Nor does such an assumption deny the profound confusion and pain Melville surely felt because of the sexuality I am attributing to him so matter-of-factly. Indeed, *Pierre* is in part the expression of a very perplexed passion. As gay confessionals have made clear, such confusion in nineteenth-century homosexuals is in part the result of a strange kind of ignorance.[9] As we saw earlier, late in his life Melville seems to acknowledge and to lament his own ignorance in "**After the Pleasure Party**," from *Timoleon* (1891):

> Could I remake me! or set free
> This sexless bound in sex, then plunge
> Deeper than Sappho, in a lunge

> Piercing Pan's paramount mystery!
> For, Nature, in no shallow surge
> Against thee either sex may urge.[10]

This lament seems finally to embrace the closed mystery of sex with a sense of regret—"Could I remake me!"—that it took until the end of his life to accept that "Nature" can make us desire "either sex" deeply, "in no shallow surge." Though the voice here is that of a woman, her name is Urania, probably a giveaway that she is, in effect, a transvested man. *Uranian* was the word coined by Karl Ulrichs to designate homosexuals in 1864, and one can easily imagine that Melville knew the term through his association with the sex specialist, Dr. Augustus Kinsley Gardner.[11]

Although William Schurr has suggested that "**After the Pleasure Party**" might have been begun as early as 1847, the narrative voice in *Pierre* clearly does not manifest anything like this rueful acceptance and open acknowledgment. Rather, as Higgins and Parker have it, "In the early chapters Melville exploited the device of presenting situations so ambiguous that even the most brilliant reader might not be quite sure what was going on."[12] Writing this novel was, I believe, part of a lifelong process by which Melville finally did achieve at least enough calm self-acceptance to publish these remarkable lines in *Timoleon,* and other passages just as extraordinary in *Clarel.* But forty years earlier he chose a distinctly different approach when he converted his hero's primary desire for a male companion into desire for a sister.

In this perspective, then—the perspective of parallel narratives linking the evolution of overt, first-person homosexual desire in Melville's writing and the evolution of his sexual awareness—we can suggest that at the *Pierre* stage, converting homosexual desire into incestuous desire allowed him, at a minimum, to preserve homoerotic feeling, feeling which still remains palpable beneath the disguise. Recourse to a kind of transvestism was, in other words, a compromise formation and it allowed Melville to achieve more than one goal. It allowed the expression of transgressive feelings, and at the same time the novel's tragic ending punished those feelings. By picturing intense sexual longings as inadmissible because of their incestuous rather than their homosexual nature, Melville was representing sexual guilt of a kind from which he was (probably) exempt in reality. By transferring his guilt for homosexual desire to a sexual transgression of which he was innocent, he simultaneously achieves both exculpation and punishment, confession and innocence. In *Pierre,* then, Melville spins a cautionary, masochistic fantasy in which Pierre's ambiguous innocence—in this sense homologous with his own—nevertheless provokes the cataclysmic consequences of moral outrage, social ostracism, loss of family, economic destitution, failure as a writer, and death.

This exorbitant cost is, in short, the price the sea novelist feels he must pay for bringing his sexuality back home. At the same time that he exacts the price from Pierre, however, he voices rage, resentment, and criticism of the patriarchal order which inflicts such pain upon homosexuals who, nevertheless, must continue to live out their assigned roles within its ineluctable institutions. There is, then, a balanced equation in this novel. The force of the punishment which negates Pierre is matched by the iconoclastic zeal of the (disguised) homosexual evangelism which, in the midst of a marked erotic surge, he expresses rather bluntly: "I will gospelise the world anew, and show them deeper secrets than the Apocalypse!—I will write it, I will write it!" (319).

. . . . .

We must not disregard the punishment and negation that triumphs over Pierre in the end. This is not a gay-liberation tract. At the same time, it is crucial accurately to discern the other side of the equation in which is figured this potent, revolutionary force. On this second, positive, side, we begin by recognizing that by "gospelising the world anew," Pierre is certainly not trying to make the world safe for incest. The new gospel is that of his ardor for men, perhaps indeed for Hawthorne, and Melville displays a keen and subtle understanding of the nature and configuration of the forces arrayed against that possibility. One of the most important goals of a camp reading of *Pierre,* then, must be to acknowledge the novel's critique of patriarchal notions concerning access to manhood.[13] Melville uses the adjective *patriarchal* in *Pierre* (e.g., 38), but more significantly, the novel is steeped in awareness of the institution, its traditional imaginary, and its regulatory norms.

In important feminist, lesbian, and gay theory of recent date, the access route to manhood as it is regulated by patriarchy has been aptly characterized as homosocial. In the conceptual field defined by patriarchal homosociality, homosexual men are thought to seek manhood directly (e.g., sexually) through the manhood of another man. This is their mistake, however, because in the process they miss the apparently moving target of their own manhood. To achieve one's own masculine identity homosocially, and thus to achieve one's rightful place in the patriarchy, one is supposed, rather, to seek manhood not directly by reaching for that of another man but through the indirect mediation of women. As Gayle Rubin has pointed out, one's desire for manhood in such a system is to be converted into a desire for the sign of manhood which comes only in the possession and exchange of women among men.[14] Thus, one accedes to manhood only by entering into competition and conflict with other men, and only via a system founded on the exchange of women among men. According to Eve Sedgwick (who harks back to Lévi-Strauss and René Girard), it is the schematic opposition between these two systems for attaining manhood that is itself the master production of homosocial patriarchy, upon which it depends in order to constitute itself conceptually, and in order to blackmail men into accepting the strictures of patriarchal homosociality.[15] (It underlies the oedipal configuration of the bourgeois family, Freudian and Lacanian psychoanalysis, etc.) Deleuze and Guattari get off one of their funniest

lines in parodying the grim alternatives with which the law of Oedipus seems to threaten those among us who do not obey:

> *Je prends une femme autre que ma soeur pour constituer la base différenciée d'un nouveau triangle dont le sommet, tête en bas, sera mon enfant—ce qui s'appelle sortir d'OEdipe, mais aussi bien le reproduire, le transmettre plutôt que de crever tout seul, inceste, homosexuel et zombi.*[16]

> I take a woman other than my sister in order to constitute the differentiated basis for a new triangle the summit of which, turned upside down, will be my child— which is called leaving Oedipus, but which is also to reproduce it, to transmit it, rather than dying all alone, guilty of incest, a homosexual, and a zombi.

Returning to the novel, then, we can see that Pierre's originary desire for a "surnamed male Glendinning" is ambiguously situated between these two opposing schemes.

Homosexually speaking, Pierre's yearning for another male in the family is just that. Its object could be achieved in the primary homosexual incest which underlies all subsequent displacements, such as the one the text clearly performs when it transforms the desired male into a sister. Viewed homosocially, by contrast, Pierre's lack should be fulfilled by exogamous exchange of women between men and by competition among men for those objects of exchange. At least in the beginning, Pierre as scion of the Glendinning family is keenly aware of this norm and ambiguously tempted by it. That is the logic underlying his relationship with Lucy. Significantly, it is immediately after the passage on his "still stranger feeling" of need for a male that Melville first introduces the homosocial alternative with the here-significant conjunction *but*:

> It may have been that this strange yearning of Pierre for a sister, had part of its origin in that still stranger feeling of loneliness he sometimes experienced, as not only the solitary head of his family, but the only surnamed male Glendinning extant. . . . *But* in his more wonted natural mood, this thought [of being the lone male] was not wholly sad to him. Nay, sometimes it mounted into an exultant swell. For in the ruddiness, and flushfulness, and vaingloriousness of his youthful soul, he fondly hoped to have a monopoly of glory in capping the fame-column, whose tall shaft had been erected by his noble sires. (12; my emphasis)

Again—this is crucial—this caveat rebounds immediately off Melville's explanation of the "origin" of Pierre's yearning for a sister "in that still stranger feeling" of longing for another male in the family, "but in his more wonted natural mood," being the sole male at the patriarchal summit was "not wholly sad to him." The first thought was presented in its strangeness; this second one is presented as more usual for Pierre, and more natural. Indeed, the known, natural pleasure of the second scene is encoded as lusty adolescent masturbation. Melville was as clear as he dared be that the erect family shaft, in the phallocentric logic of this particular circuit, found its direct referent in the shaft immediately in hand, once again (as in the sexual semiotics of Redburn) "in the ruddiness, and flushfulness, and vaingloriousness of his youthful soul"—so to speak—as "it mounted into an exultant swell." In this version, the boy is clearly growing up to be a healthy, procreative sire of the line because, like his grandfather, he is also "full of choicest juices" (38). Melville depicts this naturalness, grounded in the empiricism of ejaculating penises, as relief from another, competing "mood" in Pierre which ranges from the "strange" to the "stranger still."

. . . . .

In summary, then, these two circuits of desire are presented explicitly in their difference from each other, within semantic fields constructed by Melville as oppositions: one is an unknown source of sadness, it is unconscious, it is strange, uncommon, and less natural; the other is more familiar, more "usual," and a kind of pleasure ("not wholly sad"). The first is a circuit of incestuously based homosexual desire for a male companion in the family (converted into desire for a sister) which progressively will take over Pierre's life; the second is a circuit of heterosexualized desire bound up in homosocial rivalry (the basis of phallocentric patriarchy) which will be acted out in Pierre's competition with Glen Stanley for Lucy Tartan. (Lucy is indeed the "tartan," of family and lineage.) In the first circuit Pierre homosexually desires the patriarchal phallus as if he lacked it. In the second circuit Pierre desires to take his "natural" place within patriarchal, phallic genealogy by virtue of the simple fact that he has a functioning penis with which he will competitively top "the fame column, whose tall shaft had been erected by his noble sires" (an imperative Melville knew all too well from within his own family's desperate situation).

In this straightforward sense of a choice between binaries, the question is whether Pierre possesses the phallus genealogically and naturally, by reference to the erect phallic glory that is already in hand, or whether his peculiar yearning is homosexual desire for his father's phallus. In more concrete terms, the question is whether he will become a man through phallic competition with Glen for Lucy—and thus mediated through her—or whether will he become a man by following a desire for an incestuous object in Isabel. The entire novel is organized around this phantasmic option which in our day has been more explicitly—but perhaps no less ideologically—theorized as an option between exogamy and endogamy, difference and sameness, otherness and narcissism, heterosexuality and homosexuality. Dramatically, and within this precise scheme, Pierre chooses the latter and leaves home to find it in the city. That choice and the (tenuous) world that emerges from it for Pierre will define the novel until the homosocial/heterosexual matrix makes its dramatic return at the novel's violent end. For although Pierre will make a clear-cut choice for an erotics grounded in homosexual incest, Melville will annihilate that choice.

At a perhaps deeper level, we might also suspect that Melville is not just reflecting his culture by refusing to let

Pierre's revolutionary choice stand. In a sense, the more profound significance of this novel might be that Pierre's coming to manhood could, however subtly, be shown to be subjected to the regulation of hypostatized gender choices at all. In that sense, the most important depiction here would be the unacceptability of sexual ambiguity, with its concomitant imposition of the obligation to choose. It is this choice which both gives Pierre a sexuality, and then wrenches his chosen sexuality out of the sphere loosely hinted at by the variety of affects attributed to him in the novel's opening development: "yearning" for "a sister," "feeling of loneliness he sometimes experienced," his "more wonted natural mood," his "exultant swell" as a result of which "he fondly hoped." In other words, this multiplicity of Pierre's boyhood feelings is presented schematically as if their original complexity and fluidity had already become unacceptable. By Melville's time, this broader range of affects is well under way toward being reduced to the rigid, binary choice Pierre has to make between the two opposing sexualities whose form we very much recognize today.

In any case, it is certain that Pierre lives in a world which acts as if there were no choice to be made. The force of the novel is in its extraordinary revelation that there is, in fact, this choice, and that society has tactics for pressuring him to make the right choice. By choosing wrongly, Pierre then forces patriarchal society to show its hand by acknowledging his choice to the extent required to confront it and to annihilate it through violence. Perversely, then, the annihilation of Pierre's choice by the forces of patriarchy (embodied in Glen and Fred) is indeed a kind of recognition. And as I have already suggested, it is a cataclysm which will remain typical of most American novels dealing with male homosexuality for a long time to come because it is one of the few forms of recognition (from straight society and, as in Melville's case, from themselves) that homosexual authors can imagine. It is a form of recognition through negation which is relayed, for example, by D. H. Lawrence's acknowledgment of Melville's deep yearnings, an acknowledgment which Lawrence, in a mode of homosexual panic all his own, cannot allow to stand. Notice his progression from description to the italicized proscription of something which he knows and fears will emerge despite its illegitimacy.

> Friendship never even made a real start in [Melville]—save perhaps his half-sentimental love for Jack Chase, in **White-Jacket.**
>
> Yet to the end he pined for this: a perfect relationship. . . . Right to the end he could never accept the fact that *perfect* relationships cannot be. Each soul is alone, and the aloneness of each soul is a double barrier to perfect relationship between two beings.
>
> Each soul *should* be alone. And in the end the desire for a "perfect relationship" is just a vicious, unmanly craving.[17]

A less panicked Lawrence might have seen that Melville has placed two competing circuits of access to manliness into play, at least in *Pierre*. A less motivated critic might have seen that Melville—precisely *unlike* Lawrence himself—did not shy away from playing out the temptation and allowing the confrontation between the emergent obligation for men to be alone, and his intense yearning that they might merge.[18] There is plenty of evidence, moreover, that the nervous disapproval displayed in Lawrence's judgment continues unabated in some Melville criticism. "Without a male model in his domestic circle," writes one recent critic, "Pierre has no idea how to act in the traditional male role, and thus the folly of his longing is presented ironically in Melville's imagery."[19]

Most radically of all, however, Melville stages this confrontation within the family. And already, it is the same family whose foundational principle will be theorized as the prohibition of incest. It is also the same family, one must quickly add, which was already showing signs of being wracked by this law of its founding, and which, in American literature, seemed even to require the invention of transgressive family romances. (One thinks, for example, of J. F. Cooper for whom symbolic incest was paradoxically a kind of solution in *The Red Rover* and *Home as Found*.[20] It is precisely this family, undermined by that which constitutes it, which is Melville's focus, the same family which would soon find its consummate exegete in Freud and its tortured representations in novels such as Lawrence's own *Sons and Lovers*.

Pierre does not question the centrality of incest as a formative desire; the novel is, however, savage in its rejection of the assumption that natural, incestuous desire begins between mother and son, and that it is what fuels the homosocial system as a positivity which results from its prohibition. The mother-son theme which is a given from the outset is precisely what Pierre rejects in order to claim a more fundamental desire for the father. The difference in the access each provides to manhood in *Pierre* is the source of the basic antagonism in the novel and the two incompatible "families" it depicts as it moves from Saddle Meadows to the Apostles'.

. . . . .

These two incompatible circuits implied fleetingly in book 1 are quickly amplified when they surface in two incompatible images of the father, correlated to two incompatible objects of desire, which quite explicitly preoccupy Pierre. The bourgeois, heterosexual paterfamilias, flower of homosocial culture, is represented by a large oil painting which hangs prominently over the mantelpiece in the drawing room. Pierre's mother admires it unambiguously. Pierre's feelings about it are, not surprisingly, confused. This official father image has its other in the small oil of Pierre senior as a young bachelor, which Pierre's mother finds "namelessly unpleasant and repellent" (88). Pierre, however, adores it and keeps it in a small chamber next to his bedroom. Melville consistently terms this space a "closet." A closet in this nineteenth-century usage was not the same wardrobe that it is today, but rather a more intimate chamber than the adjoining bedroom, a smaller space in which "privacies" could be assured (87).

Not the least of the autobiographical links between Melville and Pierre is that the descriptions of these two paintings correspond point for point with extant portraits of Melville's father Allan who died when Herman was twelve years old, portraits to which we will return below . . .

"Even to Pierre these two paintings had always seemed strangely dissimilar" (88). The larger and more formal one in the drawing room seemed to him more "truthful and life-like" because it represented the image of his father that Pierre had directly known in his boyhood. It portrays "a middle-aged, married man, and seemed to possess all the nameless and slightly portly tranquillities, incident to that condition when a felicitous one; the smaller portrait painted a brisk, unentangled, young bachelor, gayly ranging up and down in the world; light-hearted, and a very little bladish perhaps; and charged to the lips with the first uncloying morning fullness and freshness of life" (88). If this "chair portrait," as it comes to be called, portrays a "blade," he is also "gay" after a fashion that is not totally exempt from the connotations that that word has come to have in our own time. Melville describes it further by telling us that an art critic required to comment upon it might correctly have written: "An impromptu portrait of a fine-looking, *gay*-hearted, youthful gentleman. He is *lightly* and, as it were, *airily* and but *grazingly* seated in, or rather *flittingly* tenanting an old-fashioned chair of Malacca. One arm confining his hat and cane is *loungingly thrown* over the back of the chair, while the fingers of the other hand play with his gold watch-seal and key" (87; my emphasis). Reading such a description, one has to wonder if Dorian Gray can be far behind. Such a portrayal also recalls Melville's earlier descriptions of masculine beauty and grace of other characters—"matchless Jack" Chase or Billy Budd—whom Melville presents as male objects of male admiration and desire.[21] It sends us back with a new awareness to Pierre's recollection of his father's "bodily form of rare manly beauty" (83). Because Pierre's speculations about it will be crucial for the plot, Melville delves into the provenance of the chair portrait in great detail. In a flashback we are shown young Pierre learning from Pierre senior's maiden sister that the portrait was painted on the sly at a time when he had just come from visiting noble refugees of the French Revolution. It was thought that he was in love with a beautiful French woman, which explained the particular look on his face captured when his cousin Ralph first sketched the portrait without his subject realizing it. Suspicious that his likeness has been "picked" (94) like a pocket, Pierre senior seeks to gauge the danger such a portrait might represent by buying a book on "Physiognomy . . . in which the strangest and shadowiest rules were laid down for detecting people's innermost secrets by studying their faces" (96).[22] He tells cousin Ralph to destroy the painting or "at any rate, don't show it to any one, keep it out of sight" (95). Ralph perpetuates this imperative when he gives the portrait to Dorothea, "making [her] promise never to expose it anywhere" (95) that Pierre senior might see it.

This strange imperative seems to attach itself to the portrait which thereby becomes, among other things, an instrument which transfers a closeting requirement to all those who possess it. Mother Mary hates it. Pierre receives it secretly and a tacit pact requires that it never be mentioned between mother and son. "And when the portrait arrived at Saddle Meadows . . . Pierre silently hung it up in his closet; and when after a day or two his mother returned, he said nothing to her about its arrival, being still strangely alive to that certain mild mystery which invested it, and whose sacredness now he was fearful of violating, by provoking any discussion with his mother about Aunt Dorothea's gift" (98). Mary's allegiance goes, rather, to the drawingroom portrait which she herself commissioned and which addresses its patriarchal desire to her as wife and mother. The erotics of the chair portrait, on the contrary, are directed to another object, outside the family. The complex of relations and positionings which it establishes with its addressees cannot be accommodated in a bourgeois drawing room. Like any woman, surmises Pierre misogynistically, his mother has the ability "to perceive that the glance of the face in the portrait, is not, in some nameless way, dedicated to herself, but to some other and unknown object" (100).

In addition to the imperative of secrecy, another effect that seems to accompany the portrait is the strange desexualization of those who are entrusted with its secret, or more accurately in Pierre's case, a deheterosexualization. The maiden sister Dorothea is the first to figure as a vestal virgin who piously secretes the mysterious portrait away in her own chamber where she worships it privately. But then Aunt Dorothea conceives an "extravagant attachment" to her handsome nephew Pierre who is the natural addresses of the portrait and its mystery because she saw, "transformed into youth once again, the likeness and the very soul of her brother, in the fair, inheriting brow of Pierre" (89). When he turns fifteen, she therefore sends him the sacred portrait. Even in its absence, however, the virgin Dorothea remains strangely bound to the chair portrait, just as will Pierre for years to come. "Henceforth, before a gold-framed and gold-lidded ivory miniature,—a fraternal gift—aunt Dorothea now offered up her morning and her evening rites to the memory of the noblest and handsomest of brothers. Yet an annual visit to the far closet of Pierre . . . attested the earnestness of that strong sense of duty, that painful renunciation of self, which had induced her voluntarily to part with the previous memorial" (89).

The sister, now a sister in the monastic sense, assures transmission of the portrait as a virginal mission. "She sent it to him trebly boxed . . . and it was delivered . . . by an express, confidential messenger, an old gentleman of leisure, once her forlorn, because rejected gallant, but now her contented, and chatty neighbor" (89). A virgin sister sends a desexualized intermediary (reduced from "gallant" to "chatty neighbor") to deliver this image of a gay blade in heat which is so threatening that it must be "trebly boxed," and so "boxed" that it is actually treated by Pierre as a threat when he receives it. A threat to what? We are not told outright, but, without telling his mother he puts it in "his own little closet" (102).

The chair portrait is then a "closet portrait" from the beginning and acts as the vehicle for disseminating closetedness into the text: The father did not want his desire to be known, but it showed on his face; in painting his portrait, cousin Ralph "picked" the image of that secret desire. It was then the father's wish that the stolen image remain hidden. That wish to conceal became part of the representation and made those who possessed it afterward complicitious in respecting it, and thereby, partners in the secret of the desire itself. At each step, then, closeting activity itself perpetuated and acknowledged the publication of the father's pleasure as illicit. To own the portrait was vicariously to share that pleasure and to be jealously possessed by its secret—to acknowledge its wink.

The circuit followed by the chair portrait thereby reveals the paradoxical logic of the closet according to which, what it hides, in the hiding becomes knowable as a hidden secret.[23] Like the homosexual wink, closeting the portrait paradoxically acknowledges a taboo pleasure, and the pleasure of taboo, without acknowledging what about it is illicit.[24] "The face in the picture still looked at them *frankly,* and cheerfully, *as if* there was nothing kept concealed; *and yet* again, a little ambiguously and mockingly, as if slyly *winking* to some other picture" (97; my emphasis). The portrait is, then, both frank in revealing its own illicit desire and yet ironic in its campy wink, a wink acknowledging and sharing with Pierre its own truth as that which is repressed in the other portrait. The "frankness" itself with which the chair portrait expresses its own desire reveals the falsehood of the official paterfamalias represented in the drawing-room portrait. The lie perpetrated by the other picture of Pierre senior thus becomes part of the truth which is being protected by hiding the chair portrait but which, paradoxically, the chair portrait shares in a wink to its acolytes. Melville even makes the chair portrait seem to speak the message of its wink prosopopoeially to Pierre.

> Pierre, believe not the drawing-room painting; that is not thy father; or, at least is not *all* of thy father. . . . I am thy father as he more truly was. In mature life, the world overlays and varnishes us, Pierre; the thousand proprieties and polished finesses and grimaces intervene, Pierre; then, we, as it were, abdicate ourselves, and take unto us another self, Pierre; in youth we *are,* Pierre, but in age we *seem.* Look again. I am thy real father. . . . Consider this strange and ambiguous smile, Pierre; more narrowly regard this mouth. Behold, what is this too ardent and, as it were, unchastened light in these eyes, Pierre? I am thy father, boy. There was once a certain, oh, but too lovely young Frenchwoman, Pierre. Youth is hot, and temptation strong, Pierre. . . . Doth thy mother dislike me for naught? (101)

In this way did it enthrall and possess Pierre, submitting him to its example and to its secretive desire. Here we should recall Melville's description of it in terms that are remarkably like those which, historically speaking, were then becoming homosexual stereotypes: "light-hearted" and "bladish," "a brisk, unentangled, young bachelor, gaily ranging," "seated airily," "grazingly," and "flittingly" on his chair.[25] Again, his pose is worthy of Dorian Gray, "one arm confining his hat and cane is loungingly thrown over the back of the chair, while the fingers of the other hand play with his gold watch-seal and key" (87).

The transgressions of the chair portrait are then multiple. Not the least is the very representation of male desire in a male figure, rather than, as is traditional in the West, as projected dialectically outward into a female object desirable *to* men. Further, in the prosopopoeia, a father presents the images of sexual desire to his son by presenting the seductive spectacle of his own body in an erotic *blason*: "Consider *this* strange and ambiguous smile, Pierre; more narrowly regard *this* mouth. Behold, what is *this* too ardent and, as it were, unchastened light in *these* eyes, Pierre? *I* am thy father, boy," in which we cannot help hearing, mutatis mutandis, something in the semantic field of, "I am thy lover, boy." For, with the arrival of Isabel this last link will be, in effect, realized.[26]

In addressing this erotic spectacle of male desire to Pierre, the portrait of the father responds directly to the son's loneliness for another male in the family. Perhaps by analogy to Althusser's well-known term, the chair portrait erotically hails Pierre, and Pierre is brought to a dim recognition of something fundamental about himself and his longings in his spontaneous response to that hailing.[27] "This mouth" and "these eyes" address themselves to Pierre both as models of desiring and, more threateningly, as the incestuous, homosexual objects of Pierre's own desire.

Ever so coyly, Melville hints at another scene of masturbation in Pierre's long sessions before his father's portrait in this "closet sacred to the Tadmor privacies" (87).[28] The "exultant swell" of homo*social* masturbation mentioned earlier is here answered by homo*sexual* masturbation as, for hours on end Pierre remains alone and erect, "*standing guard, as it were,* before the mystical tent of the picture . . . unconsciously throwing himself open to all those ineffable hints and ambiguities" (102; my emphasis). In transcoding this closeted scene, one must recall the signifying economy that often made revery a euphemism for masturbation in Melville's time, especially when linked as here to images of liquidity.[29] The ciphered meaning then becomes obvious: "Nor did *the streams of these reveries* seem to leave any conscious sediment in his mind; they were so light and so rapid, that they rolled their own alluvial along; and seemed to leave all Pierre's thought-channels as clean and dry as though never any alluvial stream had rolled there at all" (103; my emphasis.)[30] These "trances" were such that, once over, "upbraiding himself for his self-indulgent infatuation, [Pierre] would promise never again to fall into a midnight *revery* before the chair portrait of his father." After masturbation, then, once "the stream of those reveries" have flowed, Pierre's mind is clear again for a time, the picture's power over him has been reduced, and he "upbraids" himself and vows never

to give in to such self-indulgence again. But of course, in the compulsive and circular logic of guilty masturbation, he always did.

Such conclusions about Melville's suspiciously murky prose concerning Pierre's obsessive activities in his closet seem relatively plausible. But there is a good deal more to be retrieved here, if we can compromise with the epistemological problem of referring to an extratextual source for this chair portrait. Grounds for proposing this reading are to be found in the referential link which connects Melville's description of both the chair portrait and the drawing-room portrait in *Pierre* to the real portraits of Allan Melville which were in the possession of Herman's family. The descriptions of these portraits in *Pierre* correspond point for point with those of Allan which are still extant, with the one exception that Melville calls the chair portrait of Pierre's father an oil painting, whereas the portrait of Allan is a water color. The real chair portrait, in any event, was painted in 1810 by John Rubens Smith. It is now in the Metropolitan Museum of Art, although it is not currently on display. There can be no doubt that Melville used it as the direct model for the image Pierre kept in his closet. It is still today a very queer figure.[31]

Once one actually begins to take Melville's references to the extant portrait into account, it begins to seem that the focus of Pierre's masturbatory revery is rather explicitly on his father's crotch. For in the real chair portrait of Allan Melville, lying across the figure's lap from his left to his right, is a bulging fold in the breeches which produces a clear, ithyphallic form. As an extraordinarily exaggerated fold in the breeches of a seated man, created by the downward pressure of the forearm posed laterally just above the site, this blousing bulge would ordinarily be perceived as an empty fold which the artist must have intended as innocent sartorial realism.

In this context, however, innocence is not the appropriate term to describe Melville's extended eroticization in *Pierre* of a portrait of his own father which his family actually possessed. For what are we to make of his depiction of Pierre in compulsive "reveries and trances" (103) "before the *mystical tent* of the picture; and ever watching the *strangely concealed* lights of the meanings that so mysteriously moved *to and fro within*" (102)? Read alongside the portrait of Allan, the whole passage is full of double entendres: the tent metaphor suggests that Pierre was like a soldier standing erect before the tent of the painting, in the military tradition of his family, "sentineling his own little closet" (102). The word *tent* itself is polyvalent, moreover, suggesting a canvas housing or perhaps in light of the "sacredness" (98) Pierre attaches to it, a religious tabernacle which the *Oxford English Dictionary* defines as a tent containing sacred objects. In this clearly homoerotic context, however, the tent more insinuatingly suggests a reference to the tent of cloth both hiding and hinting the paternal phallus whose exaggerated shape is so visible in the figure's lap. Just what is inside the tent formed by the cloth fold in the breeches is indeed a mystery that Lacanian psychoanalysis will see as the mystery of the phallus, hovering between full flesh and empty air, presence and absence, everything and nothing. In any case, its meanings are indeed "strangely concealed" by such a salient bulge. And as we shall see later, the text returns directly to this precise question, to just this erotic and epistemological dilemma, at the moment when Pierre's relation to his father's image undergoes a revolutionary change.

As a sexual secret betraying homosexual, incestuous desire and masturbatory indulgence before the quasi-pornographic image of his father, it is not surprising that Melville would have protected this content by carefully ciphering his private references. He seems to be reflecting on just this practice and betraying his desire to be understood despite such disguises when he wonders, "That casket, wherein we have placed our holiest and most final joy, and which we have secured by a lock of infinite deftness; can that casket be picked and desecrated at the merest stranger's touch, when we think that we alone hold the only and chosen key?" (84). And indeed, if the key was the real chair portrait, it was Melville's alone in that the portrait was a private possession.[32] If the key to the remarkable homoerotic content of these passages depends on reading ***Pierre*** with the real chair portrait before the reader's eyes, then the closet was safe enough to receive his "most final joy."

But the key figures literally in the chair portrait. We could even say that the portrait comes with key, like batteries, included, for "the fingers of the other hand play with his gold watch-seal and key." This play of fingers and hand, as we shall see shortly, are laden with distinct erotic content for Melville. Already here, however, the key that the hand is playing with may well operate as a metonymy for the organ that is the key to Pierre's reveries before the painting, and the metaphoric model of Pierre's own masturbation.

In any case, though "we think that we alone hold the only and chosen key" to our most private closet, the key to the portrait is, in fact, the object of contention between mother Mary and lover Isabel. Earlier Pierre had recognized the key in the chair portrait as the same one his mother, who hated the portrait, kept locked away "in a drawer in her wardrobe" after his father's death (96). Beyond the multiple psychoanalytic possibilities for understanding this passage, we can with certainty acknowledge that by locking away the portrait's key, Mary wants to close Pierre out of the sphere of the portrait's desire, precisely insofar as that desire is not addressed oedipally, heterosexually, and normatively to herself. On the other side of this struggle there is Isabel who, hostile to Mary and her classically patriarchal designs for her son, sends Pierre the letter—the instrument—which actually opens his secret desire and prompts this lament about his "casket" being "desecrated at the merest stranger's touch." In the contest between the opposing sociosexual spheres represented by Mary and Isabel, Mary has the literal key (which she keeps locked away), but Isabel has the more potent key of resemblance

to the chair portrait of Pierre's illicit, homosexual desire. When finally Pierre abandons Lucy/Mary for Isabel, that is, when he definitively chooses the chair portrait over the drawing-room portrait, Mary's hysterical exclamation tells all: "Thus ruthlessly to cut off, at one gross sensual dash, the fair succession of an honorable race!" (230). Sensuality (gross) and family successions (honorable) are thus irretrievably dissociated in Mary's mind and in the emergent culture which she represents. It is Pierre's transgression however, like Whitman's, to refuse that separation. Choosing Isabel, he chooses a radically different model of sensuality and succession.

But we are not yet finished with the potent allure of the chair portrait around which the whole novel indeed turns. For there are further, particularly crucial winks to decipher. As far as the senses could detect, "Isabel had inherited *one peculiar trait* nowhither traceable but to it" (233; my emphasis). And yet Melville never identifies the trait upon whose singularity and peculiarity he has so hintingly insisted. He comes back to this trait several more times, however, saying, for example, that the original body of Pierre's father was now rotted in the churchyard, and "God knows! but for *one part* . . . it may have been fit auditing" (234; my emphasis). Again, what is this singular part which Pierre knew, not from memory of his father but from the portrait itself? Here is the passage in full: "There seemed to lurk some mystical intelligence and vitality in the picture; because, since in his own memory of his father, Pierre could not recall any distinct lineament transmitted to Isabel, but vaguely saw such in the portrait; therefore, not Pierre's parent, as any way rememberable by him, but the portrait's painted *self* seemed the real father of Isabel; for, so far as all sense went, Isabel had inherited one peculiar trait nowhither traceable but to it (233)." Opaque as this text may at first seem, it nevertheless is explicit in its insistence that the only real link between the portrait and Isabel was not rational, historic, or empirical. (All Pierre's surmisings concerning the complex of circumstantial evidence for Isabel's relation to his father have already been characterized as "an endless chain of wondering" [165].) Nor could Pierre himself actually recall "any distinct lineament" in his living father that now reemerged in Isabel. He could, however, locate this distinct lineament in the chair portrait, painted before Pierre's birth. "So far as all sense went"—that is, the evidence of sense experience (sight, touch)—she "had inherited one peculiar trait" and it came not from Pierre senior but from the portrait itself.

The link between the portrait and Isabel has thus been narrowed down to a visual particular far more precise and singular than any vague family resemblance. Indeed, it is while raising precisely this question that Pierre recalls his mother's opinion: "it is my father's portrait; and yet my mother swears it is not he" (166). Thus everything about this nexus of questions is contested and mysterious.

The resemblance between the portrait and Isabel, however, is the nodal point of the entire text. How odd, then, that

Melville's writing around this crucial question is at its most tantalizingly evasive and suggestive. It is just here that he seems to signal that he is winking. "Omitting more subtle inquisition into this deftly-winding theme [of the portrait], it will be enough to hint" (233). Earlier he had the portrait tease Pierre with an erotic and epistemological taunt which is equally addressed to the reader, and which Melville's very visible hinting prompts us to recall here. "Probe, probe a little—see—there seems one little crack there, Pierre—a wedge, a wedge. Something ever comes of all persistent inquiry."

If one responds, and if one probes the text for any further clue to this mystery Melville has so visibly spun for us, one finally has to wonder if he has not indicated it in the following image of, precisely, pointing. "The portrait still seemed levelling its prophetic *finger* at *that empty air,* from which Isabel did finally emerge" (233; my emphasis). This is a passage to which virtually all commentators on *Pierre* refer, and it is surely where Melville has himself pointed out the key to the enigma of the "one peculiar trait." The problem which has prevented its understanding, however, is that his reference is not in or of the published text. Rather, he may well be invoking once again a private and personal reference to Allan Melville's portrait which was the model for the fictional portrait of Pierre's father.

There, in the chair portrait, the index finger of the right hand of the figure does indeed point, discreetly, at what is earlier described as "the mystical tent of the picture" (102), that is, at the phallomorphic bulge in the breeches which so obsessed Pierre's masturbatory moments at Saddle Meadows. . . . With all his efforts to justify his belief in his kinship to Isabel reduced to "an endless chain of wondering" (165), there remains only this "one single trait" she visibly shares with the portrait. It is this icon, "not Pierre's parent . . . but the portrait's painted self [which] seemed the real father of Isabel." In effect, then, Pierre is confessing that Isabel is a masturbatory fantasy come true.[33] This ambiguous, painted image of the paternal penis— both appropriately (as the very sign of paternity), and utterly ironically (as an empty pornographic image)—had indeed sired the companion for which Pierre had always "mourned" (11). After all the enraptured, erotic longing Pierre had addressed to this paternal representation, "Isabel did finally emerge" from it. That is, because she shared the phallic trait with the portrait, the portrait referentially sires her erotic meaning for Pierre, making her the incarnation of the homoerotic object which had heretofore been the focus of all his "reveries and trances" in the closet. In this transitional moment, the portrait itself seems to reveal the real justification for Pierre's choice of this new sister by "levelling its prophetic finger at that empty air, from which Isabel did finally emerge" (233). Though she sprang from a fantasy, Isabel's incarnate emergence has nevertheless changed all the cardinal points of Pierre's life. And foremost among those changes, instantiation in the flesh has utterly desacralized the image. The pornographic spell is broken. Because the "particular trait" in the image has now become flesh in the oneirically transvested person of

Isabel, Pierre can at last break out of the guilty thralldom which kept him night after night in his closet.

A new order has dawned as Pierre abandons Saddle Meadows. Once the portrait's "painted self" has been incarnated in Isabel, a whole regime of the dead father present in his absence—underwritten by the imaginary phallus that is both everything and nothing—has been altered. No longer will Pierre need to stand excluded and yearning before the chair portrait, stuck in an impossible mourning and desire. That version of his father is now doubly demoted to a painted image, of "empty air." No longer will he need to protect and perpetuate his father's legacy of erotic shame. By embracing Isabel, Pierre is seeking to leave his closet behind. When he comes upon the image now he is filled with "repugnance . . . augmented by an emotion altogether new. That certain lurking lineament in the portrait, whose strange transfer, blended with far other, and sweeter, and nobler characteristics, was visible in the countenance of Isabel; that lineament in the portrait was somehow now detestable; nay, altogether loathsome, ineffably so, to Pierre" (232). Pierre burns the portrait and leaves for the city with the very real Isabel.

. . . . .

There is one earlier wink which it is now possible to go back and decipher briefly. From the start Melville attributed any feelings of certainty about Isabel to Pierre's strong emotions concerning the chair portrait. Pierre's ruminations concerning an empirical, blood tie to Isabel had always "recoiled back upon him with added tribute of both certainty and insolubleness" (166). And still, despite his awareness of the "argumentative" nature of the factual evidence, the chair portrait continues to persuade him that "Isabel was indeed his sister" (166). We can now discern Melville's coyness in suggesting that, beyond rational evidence, Pierre saw "the Finger of God" (166) in this subjective certainty. "But the portrait, the chair-portrait, Pierre? Think of that. But that was painted before Isabel was born; what can that portrait have to do with Isabel?" (166). The narrator provides the answer.

> Now alive as he was to all these searching argumentative itemisings of the minutest known facts any way bearing upon the subject; and yet, at the same time, persuaded, strong as death, that in spite of them, Isabel was indeed his sister; how could Pierre, naturally poetic, and therefore piercing as he was; how could he fail to acknowledge the existence of that all-controlling and all-permeating wonderfulness, which, when imperfectly and isolatedly recognized by the generality, is *so significantly denominated* The Finger of God? But it is not merely the Finger, it is the whole outspread Hand of God; for doth not Scripture intimate, that He holdeth all of us in the hollow of His hand?—a Hollow, truly! (166; my emphasis)

In closeted language, Pierre could not fail to perceive that divine intervention, the "all-permeating wonderfulness" associated with what people call the Finger, or the hand of God, was the true guarantor of the connection between chair portrait and Isabel. But in deciphered language, how indeed could Pierre fail to see that the hand-induced pleasures of masturbation formed the only true link between the chair portrait, with its "mystical tent," and the "all-permeating wonderfulness" promised him in the flesh by Isabel. Melville smiles to think that the penis that he has been hinting as the object of Pierre's imaginary longings could be "recognized by the generality"—that is, by a sexually blind public—only as God's "so significantly denominated . . . Finger." Here Melville actually tells us that he is winking, explicitly pointing out that there is a surplus of significance in the denomination of God's "Finger" as the source of "all-permeating wonderfulness." But he cannot tell us what that significance is. Nor can he tell us why God's "so significantly denominated"—and so wittily capitalized—"Finger" is something which the "penetrating" Pierre could not miss as the link between him and Isabel. And he goes on amusingly to suggest that the divine Finger has been accompanied by the divine hand, at first "outspread," but then holding us so wonderfully in its "hollow"—wink—"A Hollow truly!"[34]

We now can see the later passage discussed above as but another gloss on this bundle of signifiers. For there, "the portrait still seemed to be levelling its prophetic finger at that empty air, from which Isabel did finally emerge." Obsessively focusing all that time on what he now realizes was only "empty air" and only a painted image of the phallus; lost in the "reveries and trances" of masturbatory ecstasy and desire for it; now, finally, that empty air has fathered sexual flesh beyond the semiotic absence of its painted self. Isabel is indeed that progeny as prophesied by Pierre's masturbatory yearning for a male companion in the family transmogrified into a sister. As Pierre's masturbatory revery-come-true, Isabel is indeed the issue of a divine hand and a pointing "Finger."[35]

. . . . .

In summary, then, the two portraits condense the terms of a conflict which we are beginning to see as profound in midcentury American culture. Recent historical and gender studies suggest that authors such as Whitman—and I would emphatically add Melville—felt compelled to resist the onslaught of impoverishment being visited upon many social relationships. Michael Moon catalogs these effects as the "privatizing, standardizing, domesticizing, misogynist, and homophobic social arrangements of industrial, commercial, and (in the post-Civil War era) corporate capitalism that eventually replaced earlier arrangements."[36] In the decades preceding the composition of *Pierre,* there is good evidence to suggest that a wide variety of social relations among men were being seized by what Sedgwick characterizes as homosexual panic, which would cast its chilling shadow on social relations of all types.

The drawing-room portrait condenses these forces which emerge everywhere in the patriarchal, heterosexual aspects of the novel. As their very image, it addresses Mary Glendinning only as wife and mother. It projects the Glendinning "fame column" which, in keeping with fam-

ily tradition, had been "erected" around this exclusive version of Pierre's father and all his previous sires, an edifice which—in his "more normal" moments—Pierre desired to extend. In opposition to this image, the chair portrait in the closet condenses and expresses the desires in Pierre which these repressive arrangements render unspeakable. That is why it must be locked away and banished from view. Something about it is intolerable to the family's class position and all its accompanying norms.[37] It represents not Pierre's desire for the glory of capping the family's fame column but his desire for a male companion to complete the deep hiatus in his life. In that sense, the chair portrait is the image of Pierre's own desire writ large on the face of his father, a desire figured homosexually as his father's phallus and the fascination it exerts on a son made lonely by his onshore alienation from other men.

Culturally, of course, there is far-reaching significance in the shifting allegiances between the portraits in which Pierre rebelliously embraces, first, the chair portrait, and then its sexual incarnation in Isabel, while Mary Glendinning defensively allies herself with the familial propriety of the drawing room portrait. The drawing room was, after all, what the middle-class American family had set for itself as a cultural ideal: a closed and regulated space characterized by the increasing loss of homosocial possibilities and same-sex intercourse which caused men such pain. Michael Moon has argued well for locating Whitman's appeal in his counterhegemonic hymn to the fluid, masturbatory realm, the same realm characterized so distinctly and so diacritically in Allan Melville's chair portrait.[38] The relief and healing, the response to a longing, which is kindled in Whitman's poems is absolutely consonant with the sensibilities which Melville displays in abundance in these passages.

. . . . .

Pierre is, of course, notable for the way it also prefigures the rigidifying oedipal structure of the bourgeois family which psychoanalysis would begin to codify in the next fifty years. Mary Glendinning is figured as a castrating, (explicitly) phallic mother who must be resisted (27, 213, etc.). Homosexual attraction among boys—"boy love," as Melville calls it—is figured as part of a latent adolescent phase which is supposed naturally to develop into heterosexual fixation on girls (253-55). In a proto-Freudian mode of female narcissism and penis envy, Mary finds her only satisfaction in her son, whom she desires narcissistically, his beauty mirroring her own (110). Pierre's internalization of the queerer paternal image is what precipitates his breaking away from his manipulating and possessive mother, as he tries (unsuccessfully) to become a separate adult in his own right. From Henry Murray to Edwin Miller, we have not lacked for psychologists to explain the pathologies of Pierre and his family in post-Freudian terms which, paradoxically, are not particularly alien to the novel. On and on, Melville anticipates all of these configurations within the bourgeois family, insights which would soon become clichés of its analysis by the psychological sciences rising up to theorize it. In 1938, Willard Thorp exclaimed, "So startling is Melville's prescience about such subjects as adolescent psychology and the unconscious and so modern in his literary use of dreams and myths that one has constantly to remind oneself of the date of the novel."[39] And indeed, exegesis of *Pierre*'s protopsychoanalytic insights, in which these and other leitmotivs figure prominently, began early in this century. Already in 1929, S. Foster Damon called it "the first novel based on morbid sex," in which Pierre was "a victim of a profound psychosis of which today we are learning a little under the misnomer, 'Oedipus complex.'"[40] More to the point, however, *Pierre* leaves no doubt that the oedipal family coming to flower in the nineteenth century was, literally, an affair among men, founded on what Luce Irigaray targets in her famous pun, as "hommo-sexuality."[41]

And yet at the same time, it is difficult to imagine a more radical rescripting of normative sexual outcomes within the oedipal family than the one which is performed when Pierre finds—not only the mediated model—but the object of his yearning in the eroticized spectacle of his father's illicit desire. Pierre keeps it in the closet not only to avoid displeasing his mother, but to isolate and protect his incestuous and homosexual "reveries and trances" from her normative incursions. We must finally acknowledge, then, that it is a yearning which links Melville powerfully with Walt Whitman in a shared awareness of what the latter described as "this terrible, irrepressible yearning, (surely more or less down underneath in most human souls)—this never-satisfied appetite for sympathy" to which Whitman, in *Leaves of Grass,* would seek to give "undisguisedly, declaredly, the openest expression."[42]

"On land," then, Pierre's closet is a device which also serves to produce the gender segregation that comes naturally in the all-male world of the sailing ship. In *Moby-Dick,* Queequeg and Ishmael can marry, bed down, kiss their phallic idol Yojo together without having to negotiate gender differences and the familial laws which order them. In Leslie Fiedler's well-put description, "[Ishmael] embraces no woman, no obvious surrogate for the banned mother, only another male, a figure patriarchal enough, in fact, to remind him of George Washington!"[43] At Saddle Meadows, however, the hovering figure of Mary and the other cognates for homosocial patriarchy (Glen Stanley, Reverend Falsgrave), though defeated in the end, are only so many obstacles to be dealt with and fended off so that Pierre's phallic idol can finally be openly and homoerotically kissed. Recent criticism of postmodern inspiration which finds in *Pierre* another confirmation of that insistent psychoanalytic nexus of father murder, guilt, displacement, and writing—whatever its merits in broader terms—must nevertheless be taxed with ignoring this fundamental figuration of homosexual eros in this particular novel.[44]

Two Objects

Two desires, represented by portraits, also organize Pierre's relation to two objects: Lucy and Isabel.

Although Lucy is Pierre's straight love interest, her character, like her physical description, is entirely formulaic:

"The world will never see another Lucy Tartan" (31).[45] She is from a good family and receives Mary's approbation as an appropriate match which will preserve family tradition. Thinking back on other Glendinning patriarchs who were lions in public and lambs at home (38), Mary sees Lucy as a daughter-in-law she can control, one who will not be an obstacle to her continuing control of Pierre. In this sense, Lucy is figured as one of the emblems of the flourishing bourgeois family order, a structure which, stereotypically, entails this continued tension and competition between mother and wife for the son's allegiance—the stuff of "family romance."

In this version of the patriarchal scenario, Lucy is the object onto which Pierre's desire for his mother should be exogamously displaced, as required when a son resolves oedipal conflicts. It is also with Lucy that Pierre could aspire to become an alpha male in the phallocentric order who has a swell of triumph at circumventing any competition from other males for the monopoly of the tall shaft. In the novel's terms, Lucy will contribute an essential element to Pierre's natural role as paterfamilias, making him worthy to be displayed in a drawing-room portrait. In psychoanalytic terms, Pierre will have the phallus thanks to mediation via Lucy who is consistently marked as pliant and without threat. In a word, Lucy is phallocentric culture's paragon object, a star in the Lacanian cinema where, in order to have the phallus, sons must give up trying to be the phallus themselves so they can receive it dialectically from women.[46] And Melville already prepared us to understand that this is a role into which Pierre can "in his more wonted natural mood" partake with "an exultant swell." Newton Arvin was undoubtedly right in writing that "Pierre's actual behavior, however, is that of a man whose unconscious is lying in wait for the first plausible opportunity to desert."[47]

And indeed, all this is only a foil, a normative frame set up to be shattered when Pierre encounters Isabel Banford who, as the incarnation of the chair portrait, fulfills his earlier yearnings for a male Glendinning, displaced onto a sister. In *Billy Budd,* Claggart would have loved Billy but for "fate and ban"; here, although "fate had done this" (*Pierre,* 170), in Isabel Melville gives Pierre a Ban-*ford.*[48]

She is a maidservant in a dairy whom Pierre first sees while she is participating in the Miss Pennies' sewing circle. She does not look up at him as he approaches her, but when finally she does, Melville resorts to a vocabulary which is both highly erotic, and quotes and mirrors Pierre's earlier loneliness for a male companion: "Anon, as yielding to the *irresistible climax* of her concealed emotion, whatever that may be, she lifts her whole marvelous countenance into the radiant candlelight. . . . Now, wonderful loveliness, and a still more wonderful *loneliness,* have with inexplicable implorings, looked up to him from that henceforth immemorial face" (58; my emphasis). During their second encounter, Melville performs a master knotting of all these threads when he writes of Isabel's face that it contained "the subtler expression of the [chair] portrait of his then youthful father, strangely translated, and intermarryingly blended with some before unknown foreign feminineness. In one breath, Memory and Prophecy and Intuition tell him—'Pierre, have no reserves; no minutest possible doubt; this being is thy sister; thou gazest on thy father's flesh'" (134). The closet portrait's homosexual, incestuous prosopopoeia of father to son—the sexual spectacle of "this mouth"—has now become his father's much desired "flesh" displaced onto and incarnated in the person of Isabel. Pierre's incestuous desire for a male, therefore, has followed a precisely prescribed trajectory by transforming itself abruptly into desire for a sister, but a sister of "before unknown foreign feminineness." Her beauty of the known feminine kind by itself cannot account for the revolution in his life. Rather, her status as transvested incarnation of the father is all-determining, a fact which will be made clear yet again when Pierre will have occasion to doubt whether or not Isabel is really his sister. To the extent that Isabel is for Pierre only a beautiful woman and the object of heterosexual desire, his later anxiety that she might not be his sister could have come as a relief. That is, if she were not his sister, a putatively painful taboo against their heterosexual passion would have thus been lifted. The reverse is true, however, and in his moments of doubt about Isabel's lineage, Pierre will feel only that he has been duped and has lost the object of his passion. All of this indicates another logic behind this passion: she is desirable only insofar as she *is* the image of his father at last made flesh. All other rationalizations and moral dilemmas are meaningless without this primary insight which the text discerns in multiple ways.

Notes

1. Higgins and Parker "The Flawed Grandeur of Melville's *Pierre*," in Higgins and Parker, eds., *Critical Essays,* 257 ff.; Higgins and Parker, "Reading *Pierre*," in Bryant, ed. Another useful survey of this argument can be found in Dillingham, *Melville's Later Novels,* 187-88 n. 7.

2. Melville, *Letters,* 146.

3. Higgins and Parker, "Reading *Pierre*," 234, 233.

4. See Tolchin. The motivation for this sister fixation also struck at least one contemporary reviewer as bizarre. In the *American Whig Review* (November 1852), he wrote, "Notwithstanding Mr. P. Glendinning's being already supplied with a mother and a mistress, he is pursued by indefinite longings for a sister" (quoted in Higgins and Parker, eds., 59).

5. Judith Butler, *Gender Trouble* (New York: Routledge, 1990), esp. 57-72. This is surely the major dynamic of grief in Melville that still needs a thorough accounting.

6. George D. Painter, *Marcel Proust: A Biography* (New York: Random House, 1959). More recently, Mark D. Guenette has performed a far more interesting and productive decoding of Proust's homosexual characters in "Le Loup et le narrateur: The Masking and Unmasking of Homosexuality in Proust's *A la re-*

cherche du temps perdu," *Romanic Review* 80, no. 2 (March 1989): 229-46. Guenette concludes that Albertine was, in fact, a displaced version of Robert de Saint-Loup.

7. Seelye, "'Ungraspable Phantom,'" 439. Higgins and Parker have summarized Seelye's conclusions approvingly, adding, "Ever since *Typee* . . . Melville had regarded his manuscripts as places to put private messages.. . . Overwhelmed by his affinity with Hawthorne as he began the book, to the point of wanting to write only for him, on an 'endless riband of foolscap' (*Letters,* p. 144) stretching from Arrowhead to the little red cottage or wherever else Hawthorne might be, Melville might well have put a private message to him or about him into *Pierre*" ("Reading *Pierre*," 221).

8. We read of Redburn's soul, "yearning to throw itself into the unbounded bosom of some immaculate friend," of Clarel's affection for Celio (who dies), or for Vine (who turns away).

9. Moving evidence of this fact can be gleaned from the responses from men born in the 1890s, in Porter and Weeks, eds. Sedgwick writes of homosexual Englishmen of Melville's class that they "operated sexually in what seems to have been startlingly close to a cognitive vacuum" (*Between Men,* 173).

10. Melville, *Selected Poems,* 134.

11. Hugh Kennedy, *Ulrichs: The Life and Works of Karl Heinrich Ulrichs* (Boston: Alyson Publications, 1988). Concerning Dr. Augustus Kinsley Gardner, see Barker-Benfield.

12. Higgins and Parker, "Reading *Pierre*," 229.

13. See David Leverenz, *Manhood and the American Renaissance* (Ithaca, NY: Cornell University Press, 1989), for many important and useful insights on this topic, esp. 291-306.

14. Gayle Rubin, "The Traffic in Women: Notes on the 'Political Economy' of Sex," in *Toward an Anthropology of Women,* ed. Rayna R. Reiter (New York: Monthly Review Press, 1975), 157-210.

15. Sedgwick, *Between Men,* 86-89; Butler, *Gender Trouble,* 38-43; Claude Lévi-Strauss, *Elementary Kinship Structures* (Boston: Beacon, 1969); René Girard, *Mensonge romantique et vérité romanesque* (Paris: Grasset, 1961).

16. Gilles Deleuze and Félix Guattari, *L'Anti-OEdipe* (Paris: Editions de Minuit, 1972), 84.

17. D. H. Lawrence, *Studies in Classic American Literature* (New York: Viking, 1964), 142.

18. In his essay on Whitman, from which I am quoting here, Lawrence attributes the same negativity to the verb *merge.* "There [in Whitman's 'Drum-Taps'] you have the progression of merging. For the great mergers, woman at last becomes inadequate. For those who love to extremes. Woman is inadequate for the

last merging. So the next step is the merging of man-for-man love. And this is on the brink of death. It slides over into death. David and Jonathan. And the death of Jonathan" (ibid., 169). This homophobic misreading of Whitman's association of love and death—as somehow different from the lengthy tradition of their linkage in heterosexual love poetry—indicates the extent of the programmatic assumption that homosexuality kills or should kill or should be killed. It is probably the same assumption which comes to full expression in the tradition of gay novels ending with the murder of one of the lovers.

19. Nicholas Canaday, "Pierre in the Domestic Circle," *Studies in the Novel* 18 (Winter 1986): 396.

20. Rogin, 8-11; Eric Sundquist, *Home as Found: Authority and Genealogy in Nineteenth-Century American Literature* (Baltimore: Johns Hopkins University Press, 1979), 15. Sundquist asserts that *Pierre* is "a fantasy of self-fathering" (170).

21. Melville describes Jack Chase in *Redburn*, 360-64, 446-47.

22. Dillingham has identified this book from Allan Melville's library as John Caspar Lavatar's *Essays on Physiognomy* (*Melville's Later Novels,* 150 ff.).

23. See Sedgwick's remarks throughout *Epistemology* on this aspect of closeted homosexuality, "the outer secret, the secret of having a secret" (205); and also D. A. Miller's influential analysis of the "open secret" in *The Novel and the Police,* esp. "Secret Subjects, Open Secrets," 207 passim.

24. *The Portrait of Dorian Gray* is another novel which links the gothic tradition of hidden portraits with the completely unspoken homosexuality behind their mystery. Dorian's friend, Basil Hallward, says, "I have grown to love secrecy. It seems to be the one thing that can make modern life mysterious or marvelous to us. The commonest thing is delightful if one only hides it" (Oscar Wilde, *Complete Works* [New York: Harper & Row, 1989], 20).

25. In *Redburn,* Melville consistently used the term *blade* in referring to the "womanly" homosexual, Harry Bolton.

26. This link, most often scotomized by critics, is so strong that already in 1950 Arvin could write that "Pierre's unconscious wish is to preserve the incestuous bond with his father by uniting himself to this mysterious girl who, as he all too readily believes, is his father's illegitimate daughter, and who at any rate strongly resembles that parent" (224). Arvin either declined to see, or was too cautious to pursue, the difficult ramifications of this insight.

27. Louis Althusser, "Idéologie, et appareils idéologiques d'Etat," in *Positions* (Paris: Editions Sociales, 1976). Throughout these passages on Pierre's enraptured sessions before his father's portrait, then, Melville's erotic imagination is clearly not working according to the (Lacanian) psychoanalytic problematic of "the gaze" which feminist theory has explored so fruitfully, e.g., in the work of Linda Williams or Kaja Silverman. I think that, from a queer studies perspective, Sue-Ellen Case got it exactly right in her recent critique when she protested that, because of the "hegemonic spread of the psychoanalytic [which] does not allow for an imaginary of the queer," feminist theory of the gaze has displaced "queer desire by retaining, in the gaze/look compound, sexual difference and its phallus/lack polarity," a perspective which "remains caught in a heterosexist reading of queer discourse." For Case, the important point lost in this discourse is that "the revels of transgression enjoyed by the queer remain outside the boundaries of heterosexist proscription" (Sue-Ellen Case, "Tracking the Vampire," *differences* 3 [Summer 1991]: 13, 11). My thanks to Valery Ross for bringing this article to my attention.

28. "Tadmor is the pre-Semitic name for the ancient city of modern Syria, Palmyra . . . ," noted for its remarkably modern comforts (Kier, *Melville Encyclopedia,* 2:992). The "privacies" in question are thus suggestive of "privies," of course, but more pertinent are sexual resonances with "privates." In his dedication to *Israel Potter,* Melville plays on the word *privacy* in a way which, according to Dillingham, designates "the external genitals" (*Melville's Later Novels,* 253 n. 16).

29. To cite another example of its currency in Melville, he writes in *White-Jacket* that as a "way of beguiling the tedious hours" sailors would "get a cosy seat somewhere, and fall into as snug a little *revery* as you can" in their grief for home and hearth, . . . "for every one knows what a luxury is grief, when you can get a *private closet* to enjoy it in, and no Paul Prys intrude" (528-29; my emphasis).

30. In *Disseminating Whitman* (59-61 passim.), Moon has discussed the place of "fluidity" in Whitman's literary-sexual universe in ways which reinforce this sense of Melville's contemporary usage here; in *The Horrors of the Half-Known Life,* Barker-Benfield elaborates on this usage in such contemporary books as Ik Marvel's *Reveries of a Bachelor,* a best seller of 1850, with thirty-nine printings before 1859 and others beyond that; and *The Student's Manual* (1835), which had run through twenty-four editions by 1854 (10, 136, 175 passim). Barker-Benfield's analysis of the nineteenth-century's "spermatic economy" (179-88) provides a further pertinent context for this passage, and he mentions, moreover, that in *Reveries of a Bachelor,* "the bachelor's fantasy also drew sustenance from other men's fantasies. One of his favorites was Melville's *Typee* (1846), [and] *Omoo* (1847)" (11).

31. My thanks to Associate Curator Carrie Ribora of the American Wing of the Metropolitan Museum of Art in New York for her kind assistance in allowing me to examine this portrait, currently held in a storage vault at the museum.

32. The records of the Metropolitan Museum do not contain information as to the portrait's provenance which would have allowed me to know whether or not the painting was actually in Melville's possession when he was writing *Pierre*. Clearly, however, even if he did not have it before his eyes while writing, he had a vivid memory of it in all its detail.

33. In this sense, I would concur with Dillingham's conclusion (*Melville's Later Novels,* 229) that "Pierre made Isabel."

34. The coy indirectness (close to incomprehensibility) of this passage reminds us of the oblique tactics Melville felt he had to use to describe the much less threatening scene involving a whale penis in *Moby-Dick*. Howard P. Vincent (*Trying-out of Moby-Dick* [Boston: Houghton Mifflin, 1949], 328) pointed out the significant unlikelihood that the great majority of readers understood that "the cossock" refers to the whale's penis. In the present context, we also recall Melville's famous pun, when a sailor literally cloaks himself in the giant penis sheath, thus becoming "a candidate for an archbishoprick," and a "lad for a Pope." Further pertinent commentary on the significance of the cossock can be found in Dillingham, *Melville's Later Novels,* 48-50. Of course, the masturbatory significance of hands and fingers finds its most universally recognized expression in *Moby-Dick,* chap. 94, on squeezing sperm: "I found myself unwittingly squeezing my co-laborers' hands in it, mistaking their hands for the gentle globules. Such an abounding, affectionate, friendly, loving feeling did this avocation beget; that at last I was continually squeezing their hands, and looking up into their eyes sentimentally; as much as to say,—Oh! my dear fellow beings. . . . Come; let us squeeze hands all round; may, let us all squeeze ourselves into each other; let us squeeze ourselves universally into the very milk and sperm of kindness" (*Redburn: White-Jacket; Moby-Dick,* 1239).

35. Such coded reference was not rare in the 1850s. G. M. Goshgarian quotes a mid-nineteenth-century anti-masturbation lecture by William Eliot whose "exceeding delicacy" was nevertheless plain to those "who had ears to hear." Eliot implored, "If not for God's sake, nor for Christ's sake, yet for your mother's sake, hold back your hand from sin!" (*To Kiss the Chastening Rod* [Ithaca, NY: Cornell University Press], 50). Martin (*Hero, Captain, and Stranger*) cites examples of encoded masturbation which are too numerous to recite. Dillingham concludes that Melville's dedication of *Pierre* to Mount Greylock "seems flippant, or even silly, unless one gets the joke—which is that he is dedicating his work of art to his male organ" (224).

36. Moon, 10.

37. See Rogin, 160 ff.

38. Moon, 9.

39. Willard Thorp, "Melville's Quest for the Ultimate," in Higgins and Parker, eds., 191-92. The same volume contains an excerpt from *American Renaissance* in which Matthiessen reviews a good number of these insights ("The Troubled Mind," 201-10).

40. Higgins and Parker, eds., 150, 151.

41. Luce Irigaray, *Speculum of the Other Woman* (Ithaca, NY: Cornell University Press, 1985), 101-3.

42. Quoted by Moon, 9.

43. Fiedler, 536.

44. A good example of this approach and this conclusion would be Joseph Riddel, "Decentering the Image: The 'Project' of 'American' Poetics?" in *Textual Strategies: Perspectives in Post-Structuralist Criticism,* ed. Josué Harari (Ithaca, NY: Cornell University Press, 1979), 323.

45. The cliché quality of her presentation can be compared with Melville's flat descriptions of Fayaway in *Typee*. His heart was clearly not in these characters. Even a contemporary reviewer noted that "Fayaway is as unreal as the scenery with which she is surrounded" (Higgins and Parker, eds., 58). Fiedler characterizes Melville's treatment of Lucy as yet "another sexless White Lady." In a rather arch but no doubt apt formulation, Fiedler goes on to claim that Melville "quite apparently . . . neither likes her nor believes in her [but] is only doing his duty" (275, 276). See also Martin, *Hero, Captain and Stranger,* 36.

46. Jacques Lacan, "The Signification of the Phallus," in *Ecrits,* trans. Alan Sheridan (New York: Norton, 1977), 281-91. See Butler's critique of Lacan in *Gender Trouble,* extended in her remarks on "wanting to have someone or wanting to be that someone," in "Imitation and Gender Insubordination," in Fuss, ed., 13-31, esp. 26 ff. Much of this analysis could be inflected usefully and differently through Butler's analysis of links between mourning and gender.

47. Arvin, 223.

48. *Pierre . . . Billy Budd,* 1394. My analysis does not support Tolchin's sense that "Pierre's relationship with his mother dominates the novel" (*Mourning, Gender, and Creativity,* 139). However overwhelming Melville's own mother may have been, Mary Glendinning is not a direct reflection of that relationship in fiction. Mary's overpowering influence on Pierre is, on the contrary, a foil for Pierre's break with her and destruction of her in the name of something else represented by Isabel. Tolchin is also at odds with this analysis, then, when he passes on the notion that "Isabel becomes Mrs. Glendinning's sexual double" or, in his own inflection, a displacement of Mary's own grief as it affects Pierre (139).

Nicola Nixon (essay date 1997)

SOURCE: "Compromising Politics and Herman Melville's *Pierre*," in *American Literature,* Vol. 69, No. 4, December, 1997, pp. 719-41.

[*In the following essay, Nixon examines* Pierre *in its historical context, maintaining that Melville preferred ambiguity to political allusion.*]

In a now rather famous chapter at the midpoint of *Pierre; or, the Ambiguities,* "Young America in Literature," Herman Melville announces a thoroughly uncompromising narrative agenda:

> Among the various conflicting modes of writing history, there would seem to be two grand practical distinctions, under which all the rest must subordinately range. By the one mode, all contemporaneous circumstances, facts, and events must be set down contemporaneously; by the other, they are only to be set down as the general stream of the narrative shall dictate; for matters which are kindred in time, may be very irrelative in themselves. I elect neither of these; I am careless of either; both are well enough in their way; I write precisely as I please.[1]

With a characteristically paraliptic flourish, in which he simultaneously posits and rejects the "conflicting modes of writing history," Melville emphasizes his refusal to abide by prescribed novelistic rules and unapologetically celebrates what appears to be narrative whimsy—the whimsy in which he has seemingly indulged in the three preceding chapters.[2] Not surprisingly, "Young America in Literature" has generated conflicting critical responses. Critics like Brian Higgins and Hershel Parker focus on "why *Pierre* went wrong," and consequently on Melville's problematic breaking of the narrative compact between readers and authors.[3] More recent critics like Gillian Brown, Myra Jehlen, and Wai-chee Dimock view the disruption of that compact as symptomatic of Melville's preoccupation with individualism and the vicissitudes of authorship in antebellum America, arguing that the protagonist is essentially a cipher for the "Young American" Melville, who was struggling to achieve authorial autonomy against the tyranny of mediocrity.[4]

I want to suggest that Melville was quite deliberate in placing "America" at the point in the novel at which he emphasizes his refusal to produce narrative continuity. *Pierre* is heterogenous by design precisely because any smoothly homogenous representation of "contemporary circumstances, facts, and events" and "matters which [were] kindred in time" would have involved a textual and ideological compromise that Melville was unwilling to make. Instead, he offers only "ambiguity." But then again, the entire idea of "compromise"—literary or otherwise—was extremely fraught, particularly in the context of an increasingly discordant sectional politics whose stridency had been exacerbated—not mitigated—by the Compromise of 1850. Published in 1852, *Pierre* reflects the ideo-logical fissures in the Union that were concretized by the incendiary rhetoric surrounding that political Compromise ostensibly between North and South, urban industrialism and rural agrarianism, democratic egalitarianism and aristocratic feudalism. The novel registers, in effect, the fissures in "Young America in [a] Literature" that forcefully and self-consciously eschews any mode of narrative union. And if Melville's contemporary critics, with their legendary attacks on his sanity and morality in reviews of *Pierre,* failed to acknowledge the degree to which Melville was representing a Union whose coherence lay increasingly in language alone, they also expressed obliquely the same romantic desire for cohesion that had characterized the placatory, concession politics of Zachary Taylor's Whig administration, which had ushered in the Compromise, and the statesmen who had argued for its acceptance.

From January to July of 1850, the Union witnessed an oratorical war of words among its most famous and venerable orator-statesmen: Henry Clay, John Calhoun, and Daniel Webster. Clay had proposed the Compromise as an omnibus bill designed to replace the contentious Wilmot Proviso and deal with the political fallout of the Mexican War, and Webster had eloquently endorsed it—much to the horror of his abolitionist supporters.[5] While the Compromise was generally achieved, neither side was satisfied. Arising from it was, of course, the newly strengthened and highly contentious Fugitive Slave Law, another unworkable compromise that not only produced far more problems than it purported to solve but galvanized abolitionists into militant civil disobedience. The enactment of the statute, when mythologized sympathetically as the plight of the runaway slave, plucked at the heart strings and consciences of all proclaiming themselves champions of freedom. Stowe's *Uncle Tom's Cabin,* for example, appeared in serialized form in 1851, only a year after Clay's bill was passed. And the enforcement of the Fugitive Slave Law pitted Melville's colleague and friend, Richard Henry Dana—author of *Two Years Before the Mast* (1841), founder of the Free Soil party, and abolitionist lawyer—against Melville's father-in-law, Lemuel Shaw, Chief Justice of Massachusetts, in the infamous Thomas Sims case of 1851.

If ultimately only a convenient metaphor, the "Union" nevertheless served a crucial iconic function for the statesmen-rhetoricians, especially when its celebration was ostensibly the touchstone for their polemic during the seven-month debate on the Compromise. South Carolina's Calhoun could thus work from the same syllogistic premises as Kentucky's Clay: both could profess to endorse the ideal of Union, testify to their good faith on the basis of that endorsement, yet arrive at mutually exclusive interpretations of it. Calhoun could conclude with a barely veiled incitement to secession, and Clay, with a reassuring resolution to conflict, both making, in the process, grand pronouncements about the essential characteristics of "North" and "South" (the "sides"). Although this hyperbolically polarized discourse proved rhetorically masterful, it reduced the North and South to a set of wholly antithetical linguistic constructs, a series of opposed attributes or qualities that were just as iconically powerful and obfuscatory as the "Union," thus ensuring that the emblematic identity of each was virtually manufactured out of the polemic. This was not, of course, the only occasion on which the Union's statesmen had had the opportunity to capitalize on factional politics; but the debates on the Compromise—the last of that scale before the Civil War—were highly publicized and exposed wide rifts that both fashioned and solidified seemingly disparate geographical and ideological constructs.

About a month into those debates Melville began writing **Moby-Dick**—a text that, not surprisingly, articulated the radical contradictions around which the Union was organized. Melville figured Ahab as embodying the opposing forces inherent in what he diagnosed as American demagoguery: how the democratic could give birth to the tyrannical, or how, as Michael Rogin suggests, one figure could combine "democratic equality . . . [and] familial hierarchy."[6] And, as various critics have pointed out, Ahab could easily represent any one of the key statesmen, the masterful rhetoricians and demagogues who hammered out or opposed the Compromise.[7] When Melville wrote **Pierre** the following year, however, he did not fuse contradictory elements into a single figure in order to map an internal trajectory from democrat to demagogue. Instead, he presented those antagonistic forces as relentless ambiguities formally and generically yoked together in two seemingly discrete narrative sides, arranged around "Young America in Literature."

Melville was not exactly misrepresenting **Pierre** when he assured Sophia Hawthorne and Richard Bentley that it was a "rural bowl of milk" and "a regular romance"; he was merely telling half the story—the first half.[8] While the initial pages of **Pierre** might indeed qualify as "romance," they are more jarringly provocative and strange than "regular," offering what Henry A. Murray describes as "an overcompensatory Eden, a poetical feudal paradise," and what Eric Sundquist judges an "insanely pastoralized opening."[9] There is no question that Melville begins the text by deploying the chivalric romance to stress the intense feudalism of the Glendinning rural seat of Saddle Meadows. Its current young lord, Pierre Glendinning, the only heir to "the historic line of Glendinning" (5) and grandson of an illustrious Revolutionary War hero and slave owner, is clearly an aristocrat. And the old Major General's captured British banners now function, ironically, as testimonies to an aristocratic heritage: they adorn the arched windows of an ancestral manor that would not shame an English peer.[10] These Glendinning aristocrats have far less kinship with the anonymous and "unobtrusive families in New England" than with the "old and oriental-like English planter families of Virginia and the South" (10) and the Dutch Patroons in the North, the "mighty lordships in the heart of a republic" (11).

Melville's allusion to the Patroons—the landed gentry "whose haughty rent-deeds are held by their thousand farmer tenants . . . [and whose] own river, Hudson, flows somewhat farther and straighter than the Serpentine brooklet in Hyde Park" (11)—is not merely ornamental. With his country seat situated somewhere in New York State, Pierre's "great genealogical and real-estate dignity" (12) is distinctly analogous to that of the Patroons, the same aristocrats whose "genealogical dignity" Melville's mother (née Maria Gansevoort) could claim. But the shared geography of Saddle Meadows and the Patroon land claims along the Hudson is not the only point of convergence between the Glendinnings and the Northern feudal lords figured by Melville. Pierre's name is the hereditary Christian name of the prominent Van Cortlandt Patroons of New York, who had, like the Glendinnings, at least three generations of Pierres. With their extensive property in the Hudson Valley, their distinguished military careers, and their involvement in Congressional politics, Pierre Van Cortlandt Sr. (1721-1814) and Pierre Jr. (1762-1848) cut fine and obtrusive figures in New York State. Pierre Sr. was, for example, George Clinton's lieutenant governor; Pierre Jr. married Clinton's eldest daughter Catherine. Born late in his father's life, Pierre III inherited the Hudson Valley properties as a young man.[11] If Pierre Van Cortlandt III thus seems to offer a Patroon prototype for Pierre Glendinning—at least in terms of his "genealogical and real-estate dignity," the location of his hereditary property, his illustrious forebears, and his name—this fictional/historical coincidence nonetheless raises some critical questions as to where to situate Pierre Glendinning geographically and historically.

When Melville assures us, in 1852, that Pierre Glendinning and Saddle Meadows represent a current landed aristocracy in New York, he seems at first not to register some rather spectacular assaults made on that hereditary stature only a few years before. New York had, after all, just experienced the violent and protracted anti-rent wars (1839-1846), wars between feudal land owners and their tenants that had heralded the waning of a coherent Northern landed gentry. When the Patroon General Van Rensselaer died in 1839, having stipulated in his will that back rents on his lands should be used to pay off his considerable debts (some $400,000), he proved the posthumous powder keg for a bitter struggle between generations of farmer-tenants, who had been treated as freeholders for years, and the Patroon families. When Van Rensselaer's son Stephen IV attempted to extract the unpaid rent from the tenants—who, of course, could no more pay large lump sums than they could claim aristocratic roots—they simply refused to pay. As justification they pointed to Northern claims to democratic freedom, relative classlessness, equal economic opportunity, and so on, claims that the North was making tirelessly in its effort to assume the moral high ground against the South. The tenants' struggle snowballed, in part because a large number of other New York tenants wanted to ensure that no precedent was set with Van Rensselaer, and in part because the Anti-Renters recognized their struggle as an acid test of the continued aristocratic status of the Northern landed gentry. After years of escalating violence, militia intervention, and political fighting, and after the Anti-Renters' successful election of the sympathetic Whig candidate John Young as governor of New York, the feudal land claims were more or less dissolved in 1846; in 1850, two years before *Pierre* was published, the Supreme Court invalidated the Van Rensselaer title and "held that the hated quarter sales, whereby a tenant who sold his farm paid one-fourth or one-third of the price to the landlord, were unconstitutional."[12]

In the midst of his panegyric upon Pierre's richly aristocratic and very American heritage, which adroitly avoids direct mention of the Van Rensselaers—or, for that matter, the similarly affected Van Cortlandts—Melville slips in a strangely provocative reference to New York's recent history:

> In midland counties of England they boast of old oaken dining-halls where three hundred men-at-arms could exercise of a rainy afternoon, in the reign of the Plantagenets. But our lords, the Patroons, appeal not to the past, but they point to the present. One will show you that the public census of a county, is but part of the roll of his tenants. Ranges of mountains, high as Ben Nevis or Snowdon, are their walls; and regular armies, with staffs of officers, crossing rivers with artillery, and marching through primeval woods, and threading vast rocky defiles, have been sent out to distrain upon three thousand farmer-tenants of one landlord, at a blow. A fact most suggestive two ways; both whereof shall be nameless here. (11)

If the English feudal lords had private men-at-arms, the Patroons had the support of "regular armies." In other words, the Northern aristocrats had their right to retain feudal lordships sanctioned and defended by a state-funded militia which, according to Melville, went to tremendous lengths to defend that right.

While not taking an overt political position on the rent-wars—Whig supporters were at first militantly opposed to any assault on the sanctity of private property, while Democrats organized support rallies for the embattled farmers—Melville nevertheless alludes to the controversy. With a rather neat paraliptic gesture, in which he at once raises and pointedly passes over the larger implications of the Patroons and the rent-wars, Melville emphasizes the controversial and recent past while nonetheless insisting that the Patroon's feudal system still exists: the "*present* patroons or lords"; "our lords, the Patroons, appeal not to the past, but they point to the *present*"; the "mighty lordships in the heart of a republic . . . survive and exist . . . and are now owned by their *present* proprietors" (11, emphases mine).

Now this seemingly anachronistic disjunction between a recent, historical interrogation of the constitutionality of feudalism and the blithely unproblematic representation of its continued existence might be explained as Melville's deliberate refusal to reconcile a fictional/historical contradiction. And such an unwillingness is certainly aided and occluded by Melville's highly burlesqued, artificial, and self-consciously antiquated version of the genre and language of romance—what Higgins and Parker dub "pseudo-Elizabethan bombast"—and his insistence on Pierre's "aristocratic condition" as established "poetically" in the first part of the novel.[13] But this disjunction does offer a historical analogue to "Young America" generally, with its problematic embracing of Manifest Destiny as its birthright.[14] Young America had, after all, not only proven itself in the Mexican War just as capable of aggressive expansionism as the Old World imperialists, but it had also found itself, as Eric Sundquist points out, "more and more an anomaly [in light of the abolition of slavery in the British West Indies in 1833 and the Dutch and French Islands in 1848], its own revolutionary drama absurdly immobilized."[15] The banners of Pierre's Revolutionary War-hero grandfather adorn the present, aristocratic Saddle Meadows, offering a mute commentary on the supposed triumph of democracy, just as the rent-wars highlighted the presence of aristocratic "mighty lordships," and just as the Compromise accentuated the coexistence of liberty and slavery within the Union. Melville can, in other words, gesture toward Old World feudalism and New World democracy as coexisting in both North and South, suggesting a political geography that was not—as the rhetoricians of the Compromise insisted—neatly delimited by the Mason-Dixon line.

What Melville challenges, then, is the absolutist, Manichean, and self-serving rhetoric that infused the Compromise—in particular, the rhetoric of Northerners who conveniently forgot their own recent history. For example, in Webster's famous speech supporting Clay's bill on 7 March—a speech bitterly denounced by the likes of Dana, Emerson, Summer, and the other Northern abolitionists who had hitherto supported Webster—the orator attacked Louisiana Senator Solomon Downs for his misconceptions of the North. Responding to Downs's unflattering comparison of the Northern laborer and the Southern slave, in which the latter allegedly enjoyed superior conditions, comforts, and happiness, Webster objected strenuously to Downs's claims, characterizing the North as unshakably and unequivocally democratic: "Why, who are the laboring people of the North? They are the whole North. They are the people who till their own farms with their own hands; freeholders, educated men, independent men. Let me say, Sir, that five sixths of the whole property of the North is in the hands of the laborers of the North."[16] Only, of course, *after* the rent-wars, only *after* the Anti-Renters had forced the sale of hundreds of thousands of acres owned by the landed gentry, could Webster deliver this statistic so confidently. But his speech also characterizes the "whole North" as either Northern laborers working with "their own hands" on their own farms or urban wage earners whose accumulated capital will eventually allow them to become freeholders.

Saddle Meadows is clearly not part of that "whole North." But Melville's bare whisper of its jeopardy or instability because of the rent-wars serves not only to remind Northern readers of their complicity in a conveniently reviled "Southern" feudalism but also to pave the way for a heralded change in the situation of the Northern landed gentry. Melville seems to acknowledge the anachronism of Saddle Meadows by gesturing to Pierre as its product: "[I]f you tell me that . . . [Pierre's inordinate pride in his ancestry] showed him no sterling Democrat, and that a truly noble man should never brag of any arm but his own; then I beg you to consider again that this Pierre was but a youngster as yet" (13); and he promises Pierre's eventual maturation: "[B]elieve me you will pronounce Pierre a thorough-going Democrat in time; perhaps a little too Radical altogether to your fancy" (13).[17] Melville thus places the chivalric romance, with its championing of aristocratic codes, beneficent feudal condescension, and patrilineal privilege, in an overtly political register, anticipating his forthcoming dissolution of romance as synonymous with Pierre's ideological emergence into the democratic field mapped out and enunciated for itself by the North. And the trigger for Pierre's emergence from an idyllic youth and a future as a young lord happily married to the angelic Lucy Tartan is the disruptive appearance of Isabel Banford, his alleged illegitimate half-sister. On a certain level, Isabel functions as the conventional mysterious dark heroine of romance, who, through her plight and sexuality, lures Pierre away from his fiancée. But her presence also galvanizes Pierre's maturation by forcing him not only to reassess his private memory of his dead father when (like Stephen Van Rensselaer) he inherits his father's problems, but also to rethink his conflicting social responsibilities to his mother, his tenants, his betrothed, and the woman his father abandoned.

Pierre's decision to preserve—for his proud mother's (and, to a degree, his own) sake—the public memory of his father as a noble and dignified family man, and also to rescue Isabel from her loneliness and obscurity, satisfies his desire to be a romance hero, to exhibit a "loftier heroism" (178). His sense of self-sacrifice encourages him to figure himself as both Christ-like and chivalric, as a true Spenserian knight. But at the same time that he embraces such a heroism, Pierre is cutting away the structures that guarantee his aristocratic position. If, as Melville suggests, the romance and its heroes are contingent on patriarchal distinction, Pierre's ostensible rejection of his heritage in order to embrace a "glorious equality" with Isabel effectively destabilizes his heroic stature. For to achieve that equality—which he articulates for Isabel as "I do not stoop to thee, nor thou to me; but we both reach up alike to a glorious ideal!" (192)—he is forced to disengage himself from his family's illustrious history: "Henceforth, cast-out Pierre hath no paternity, and no past; and since the Future is one blank to all; therefore, twice-disinherited Pierre stands untrammeledly his ever-present self!—free to do his own self-will and present fancy to whatever end!" (199). When Pierre "Crosses the Rubicon," he moves from pastoral feudalism to urban democracy, abandoning his paternal birthright; he departs from Saddle Meadows to become the embodiment of the much-celebrated Emersonian self-reliant man. As Rogin points out, in accepting the beliefs implicit in "self-reliance," the "democratic, imperial,

national self reject[s] inherited aristocratic distinctions for equal economic opportunity."[18]

But Pierre's decision to reject one social order and embrace another is not a complete rejection or even really a subversion; instead, it ultimately proves an uneasy compromise, a false marriage of irreconcilable ideals that cannot succeed because he opts to leave both intact. By pretending to be married to Isabel he can preserve untainted the (fictive) historical order, his father's public stature, and his family's distinction, even while he is apparently leaving it all behind. But the pretense of marriage equally prompts him to embrace equal social status with Isabel, which is precisely what that historic, feudal order does not admit. Pierre's inner conflict, the geographical/political crossing from Saddle Meadows to New York, thus highlights the problematic coexistence of the feudal and democratic, especially when there is no apparent intersection between them. In exchanging feudal aristocracy for democratic equality, exchanging one American social order for another, Pierre actually interrogates neither—even though his "life revolution," like the revolution of his forefathers, is ideological. Pierre's conversion or maturation from aristocrat to democrat does, however, have profound formal reverberations in the text.

More than simply a personal revolution, Pierre's break with his mother and Lucy and his escape to New York City with Delly and Isabel create a substantial narrative rupture. Parker and Higgins argue that this break marks the point at which the text begins to go seriously wrong, since it produces not the smooth progression typical of the maturation tale but a glaring inconsistency, a blatant generic substitution. At the point of rupture in Book 14 ("The Journey and the Pamphlet"), the inflated language of romance suddenly collapses, displaced first by Melville's contemplations on the virtues of textual silence, then by his seemingly wholesale incorporation of Plotinus Plinlimmon's "Chronometricals and Horologicals." The paean to silence precedes the verbose sophistry of Plinlimmon, who waxes less than eloquent on the necessity for men to compromise: to sustain a "virtuous expediency" (214), to cease trying, and failing, to unite a horological (earthly) practice with a chronometrical (celestial) ideal. Given that Melville has announced, just prior to the pamphlet, that all "profound things, and emotions of things are preceded and attended by Silence" (204), the cheap veneer of profundity in Plinlimmon's text is doubly suspect. Indeed, the pamphlet seems to present a stinging indictment of the limp logic of expedient or laissez-faire compromise—the sort of compromise, perhaps, that the Union had witnessed just two years earlier, couched in a similarly austere and earnest rhetoric, though delivered as orations rather than pamphlets.

But if Plinlimmon's pamphlet offers a tempting historical analogue for the Compromise, Melville does not drive home its larger implications. Instead, he allows it to stand as a figuration of fictional/textual compromise at precisely the point in *Pierre* when he is rejecting textual continuity.

In another apparent about-face, Book 15 begins without the slightest comment on the pamphlet and concerns itself instead with a supplemental history of Pierre's former relationship with his cousin, Glendinning Stanly. By insisting that Pierre is now on the other side of the Rubicon and can therefore recognize the essential instability of his past status, Melville shifts perspective; he focuses on the unnaturalness of Saddle Meadows, not by deploying artificial language but by offering the symptomatically aberrant fact of Pierre's youthful sexuality.

With Glen Stanly, Pierre had "cherished a much more than cousinly attachment" (216); as boys "nurtured amid the romance-engendering comforts and elegancies of life" they had shared the "empyrean of a love which only comes short, by one degree, of the sweetest sentiment entertained between the sexes" (216). Their love has "fillips and spicinesses," occasional bouts of Othello-like jealousies, sentimental sonnets, and a protracted record in two thick bundles of love letters. In fact, Pierre's rather silly and tepid feelings for Lucy appear retrospectively as pallid substitutes for the more "ardent sentiment" (218) he cherished for Glen Stanly.[19] Pierre's earlier passions are, naturally, "nurtured" at Saddle Meadows, "amid the romance-engendering comforts and elegancies of life"; and Glen Stanly's passions are "the finest feelings of the home-born nature" (218). However, through exposure to foreign travel Glen Stanly's feelings are replaced "with a fastidious superciliousness, which like the alleged bigoted Federalism of old times would not—according to a political legend—grind its daily coffee in any mill save of European manufacture, and was satirically said to have thought of importing European air for domestic consumption" (218).[20] Given that Saddle Meadows is every bit as aristocratic as an English country seat, it comes to represent just such residual (if perhaps less bigoted) "Federalism of old times," one that gives rise to homosexual passions that—despite Melville's ironic insistence that they are somehow common in boys born to "elegancies" and comforts—stand out as inbred, as perhaps symptomatic of a precious, European, aristocratic decline.

But such inbreeding was not wholly European either. The practice of intermarriage, particularly the marriage between first cousins, was very much a feature of an American aristocracy as represented in, say, Poe's "The Fall of the House of Usher" (1839) or Hawthorne's *The House of the Seven Gables* (1851). As Bertram Wyatt-Brown points out, while the practice of intermarriage had declined significantly in the North by the mid-nineteenth century, it was distinctly on the rise in the South.[21] If Poe and Hawthorne offer lurid, gothic configurations of an atrophied, diseased, or inbred American aristocracy, Melville presents something else: a male first cousin as the ironic and definitely unfruitful object-choice for the aristocratic Pierre. Indeed, with Glen Stanly established as the demonic parody of a marriageable cousin, Melville stresses not only Pierre's sexual inversion but his affiliation with both the inbred Northern Pyncheons and the equally inbred Southern Ushers.

Unlike Poe and Hawthorne, however, Melville inscribes not merely an atrophied aristocracy trembling on its last legs but a hyperbolically inflated inbreeding. All of Pierre's familial relations appear incestuous: his peculiar "romantic filial love" (5) for his mother, his brotherly romantic love for Isabel, and his romantic and cousinly love for Lucy and Glen Stanly. Rather than expanding outward generationally, Pierre's family contracts inward, co-opting anyone associated with it and determining almost all relations in familial terms only. And each family member plays numerous roles, whether or not he or she is actually a blood relation. In fact, the entire incest theme—the constantly intersecting bloodlines or confusions over them, the persistent overlapping of sexual passion and familial roles and duties, the homoeroticism—serves to represent the aristocratic Glendinnings in opposition to the plebeian, hybrid robustness and good health of Delly and the Glendinning tenants. Interestingly enough, Melville does not trace the aristocratic decline of the Glendinnings within the inflated and flowery discourse of romance, as we might expect given some of the writings of Poe and Hawthorne. Instead, he reveals Pierre's symptomatically decadent homoerotic relation with Glen Stanly at the beginning of the second part of *Pierre,* after romance has been ostentatiously rejected.

If Melville backtracks over Pierre's history with Glen Stanly to set the stage for Pierre's cruel introduction to New York City after Glen rejects him, he similarly returns to Pierre's youth to establish the means by which he can support himself in the City. Having rehearsed Pierre's past sexual proclivities, Melville introduces Pierre's talents as a young author. This oddly parallel history of Pierre as an author of sentimental sonnets is laid over the earlier narrative—in which Pierre appeared to be merely a young, leisured, feudal lord-in-training—as if it is somehow supplemental. But instead of adding to his initial inscription of Pierre's development, Melville's paraliptic rewriting of that history—or, better, his pretense of retrospectively enhancing his earlier representation of Pierre's youth—creates virtual lacunae after the fact. In other words, Melville seems to punch holes in the fabric of the earlier text only so that he can fill them with almost egregiously unlikely swatches from Pierre's apparent history. And this supplemental history is designed to call into question the smooth and untroubled romance-development of Pierre's youth by forging tenuous and dubious links between Pierre's life of idleness in Saddle Meadows and his new working life in New York.

With this reconstruction of Pierre's past, Melville at once casts a cold democratic light on the rosy elegance of the aristocratic Saddle Meadows and destabilizes Pierre's self-congratulatory heroism when it emerges in New York, the apparent locus of democratic individualism. In embracing a truly democratic selfhood, Pierre is forced to become the social equal not only of Isabel but also of the coachman who drives him from Saddle Meadows, the policeman who has to point out to him that the coachman has "rights," and Charlie Millthorpe, the son of one of his tenants. The romantically pastoral Saddle Meadows is replaced by the naturalistic New York, with its slums, red-light districts, rabble-filled police stations, and gutted and burnt-out buildings. Melville thus inverts the Emersonian idealization of the rural/pastoral as the topos of man's equality in nature and his freedom from the hierarchies and organizations that characterize the collective constructs of cities.[22] The rural in *Pierre* is no Walden-like retreat from urban strife and the mechanistic dissociation of man and nature where man can find his true connection with the world; nor is it a mythologized frontier. It is "the most aristocratic part of this earth" (13). The rural Saddle Meadows is the site of the most pronounced social hierarchies, the grossest disparities in class and privilege.

When Melville commences his tacit celebration of Pierre's decision to provide for himself and be finally self-sufficient, he contrasts Pierre not only with his former idle self but also with other such idle gentlemen: Pierre is unlike "unprofessional gentlemen of the aristocratic South, who happen to own slaves, give those slaves liberty to go and seek work, and every night return with their wages, which constitute those idle gentlemen's income" (261). Urban New York, in which Pierre can become a self-sufficient, democratic laborer, is the arena for "political and social levelings" (275). Melville plots Pierre's trajectory from hierarchical country to egalitarian city, for only in the city can Pierre reject the aristocratic idleness associated with both Saddle Meadows and Southern gentlemen, participate in an economic equality with his fellow man by laboring with his pen, and thus celebrate his "practical capacity" to live by the "wages of labor" (261).

This trajectory is, however, ironically double-edged. While Pierre may reject his aristocratic heritage, transplant himself in the truly democratic city, and thus become "his own Alpha and Omega" (261), his real Northern aristocratic counterparts are busy moving to the city precisely to maintain and perpetuate their superior social stature. The Astors, the Macys, the Van Rensselaers, and the Clintons had all relinquished their positions as landed gentry, sold off most of their land—the Van Rensselaers' was relatively late going on the auction block in 1845—and established themselves as urban plutocrats, captains of industry.[23] As Melville points out, "the more prominent among us, proudly cite the city as their seat. Too often the American that himself makes his fortune, builds him a great metropolitan house, in the most metropolitan street of the most metropolitan town" (13). Instead of emulating that move from country to city, from aristocrat to plutocrat, instead of working an expedient compromise, Pierre seems to embrace the much propagandized Northern ideal of democratic egalitarianism, with its attendant configuration of labor as constituting self-worth. Celebrating Protestant (or Emersonian) conceptions of labor as a "calling," Pierre does, in fact, begin to labor in earnest on a mature work; but he fails to recognize the basic incompatibility of his two motives for writing: to deliver to the world what he perceives as a "new, or at least miserably neglected Truth," and to "realize money" (283) by means of fictional self-glorification.

While the second half of the text contains Melville's slashing condemnation of the "dynasty of taste" in America, which decreed that decorous mediocrity would reign at the expense of writing considered "ungentlemanly" or lacking in "Taste" (245-46), Melville does not figure Pierre's attempts to write a "mature work" as representative of a good author's failure to be recognized or published.[24] Instead, the narrative constantly undercuts Pierre's efforts to deliver the "Truth" by questioning whether Pierre actually has any such truth to deliver. And thus, even though he attacks the publishing industry and its supposed slavish catering to public taste, Melville does not finally represent Pierre as one of its victims.[25] The literary elite and the public may be deeply flawed, but Pierre's gloomy "plagiariz[ing] from his own experiences" (302), his articulation of what is "hard and bitter in his lot" (303), is equally so. Ultimately Pierre's failure to transform his writing into a "practical capacity" derives from his belief that his personal experiences, his truncated autobiographical writings, have universal appeal or applicability—a belief perfectly consistent with his former position of idle privilege—and from his inability to divest himself of his romantic self-perception. His apparent ideological conversion becomes, at last, merely a form of bad faith. Regularly postulating a position for himself as superior to other men, he both celebrates and violates the North's perception of itself as wholly democratic. In other words, he cannot actually become the promised "thorough-going Democrat" because he conceives himself as substantially above yet sorely "surrounded by the base and mercenary crew" (311).

Pierre's authorial aspirations, his yearnings towards democratic selfhood, and his rejection of youthful homosexuality—all of which are opposed to his lordly idleness, his contentment with aristocratic privilege, and his embracing of Lucy as a replacement for Glen Stanly—are sutured into the text around "Young America in Literature." But, as I have suggested, Pierre's new predispositions only *seem* to offer ambiguous counterpoints to those in the first half of the text: each is compromised by Pierre's inability to divest himself completely of Saddle Meadows. What Melville posits as radical ambiguities or contradictions are, in fact, peculiar consistencies arrayed along an only apparent trajectory of psychological maturation. If, for example, the feudalism of Saddle Meadows represents a historical anomaly in the wake of the rent-wars, its aristocratic structures are simply recapitulated in urban New York through both Glen Stanly, the classic Europeanized Northern dandy, and Pierre, the would-be author with an elitist sensibility.

Pierre inscribes, in other words, a logic of substitution, in which Melville suggests that he is substituting one entire structure for its opposite—in the name of ambiguity—but the novel contains ample evidence that what is really being substituted is merely one mode for another. New York substitutes for Saddle Meadows, proffering the appearance of democratic egalitarianism for feudal aristocracy, yet only the mode of the aristocracy's representation changes. The urban aristocracy typified by Glen Stanly is just as much a "mighty lordship" in the heart of the North as its Patroon precursor—or, for that matter, as the aristocratic planter families of the South. Melville thus draws broad lines of analogy that not only challenge the representation of an iconic "whole North" but transcend as well any rigid geographical codifications of North and South. This marking of economic and political analogues that connect Saddle Meadows and the aristocratic South, New York dandies and Virginia planters, is wholly consistent with Melville's capitalizing on the spatial metaphors inherent in the etymology of "ambiguity"; *ambiguus* is Latin for "moving from side to side." Melville revels in the implications of this spatial dynamism, first by having Pierre decamp to New York City, then by having Saddle Meadows reinstate itself there.

In the midst of Pierre's failing (and flailing) efforts to discover real self-worth through the labors of his own hand, he receives a letter from his past. Lucy Tartan writes to reclaim Pierre as a romantic hero who is "too noble," has "superhuman angelical strength," and sits in the "calm, sublime heaven of heroism" (309-10). The return of Lucy signals the rearticulation of seemingly discarded, earlier textual paradigms, the return, as it were, of the repressed. In New York City, however, the position of the chivalrous, pastoral romance hero is highly problematic. When Pierre dons his gloves, seizes his dueling pistols, and sets out to avenge the blemish to his honor made by Glen Stanly, the pretender to the Glendinning inheritance, he is made almost ridiculous by the inappropriateness of his actions in the teeming metropolis. Striding purposefully down the middle of sidewalks thronged with people, Pierre is a distinct peculiarity: seeing "his wild and fatal aspect," witnesses either "took the curb" or "took the wall" (359). Simply to shoot Glen Stanly, who has struck him with his "cowhide," he has to shake off the multitudes—"the sudden white grasp of two rushing girls" (359). And after Pierre wins his duel by killing Glen Stanly, he is seized "by a hundred contending hands" (360): a duel in New York is, after all, just murder.

Melville lampoons the ludicrously anomalous and seemingly anachronistic modes of chivalry Pierre reenacts in New York, insisting that they are out of place or, rather, displaced from another context: Saddle Meadows. And the entire constellation of signifiers—Pierre's overinflated sense of his manly honor, his quest to avenge its bruising, his ostensible (although not actual) adherence to the cult of chivalry, his demand for the satisfaction of a duel—all resonate as either anachronistically Northern or currently Southern. The duel and the aristocratic cult of manly honor and chivalry had long been associated, in both the North and South, almost exclusively with the Southern planter elite.[26] By 1838, for example, when Maine Congressman Jonathan Cilley participated in a famous duel with Kentucky's William Graves, Northerners were apparently horrified. In fact, as Steven Stowe points out, the "duel was so identified with the South that commentators looked for something 'southern' in Cilley's background and temperament."[27] Clearly, the "Northerner" Pierre cannot be di-

vorced from Southerners by his "background and temperament"; the only difference between them lies in Pierre's ignorance of all the conventions of dueling: he fails to secure a second and shoots Glen Stanly before the latter has even drawn his weapon.

In invoking feudal aristocratic codes (albeit badly) in New York City, Pierre ultimately succeeds in dissolving them permanently. Pierre is the "only surnamed Glendinning," and "his own hand had extinguished his house" (360). The shooting of Glen Stanly and the final, body-piling scene in the prison, where he and Isabel take poison after Lucy has died from a stopped heart, become travesties of chivalric codes, travesties of real tragedy. Pierre's failure, as a knight and as an author, stems from his inability to adopt one role wholeheartedly, to actually cross the Rubicon in earnest by choosing between two contradictory conceptions of the individual and modes of behavior. Unchanged, he cannot be transplanted in New York amidst the democratic individualism established as a polarity to the aristocratic feudalism of Saddle Meadows; but changed, he cannot return to the unassailable sense of entitlement that is the legacy of his paternal ancestors. Some sort of transformation is, however, inevitable. As the beginning of the text suggests, "the democratic element operates as a subtile acid among us; forever producing new things by corroding the old" (9).

While Melville initially represents Saddle Meadows and the Glendinning family as eternally present, as defying Time—unlike, say, the "families [that] rise and burst like bubbles" in the cities or the "vast mass of families [that are like] blades of grass" (9)—the promised corrosion proves inevitable. The "democratic element" does finally surface at the expense of the aristocratic Glendinnings, but not necessarily because the two have clashed. The feudal House of Glendinning, at first linked with something able to resist natural progression and law, finally withers away unassisted, destroying itself, like the House of Usher, with its decadence and inability to accommodate a nonlocalized social order. Melville's initial figuration of the Glendinnings as the enduring oak trunk is eventually supplanted by the naked, impotent, and imprisoned Enceladus, whose "whole striving trunk" is inescapably rooted in the earth.[28]

When the Glendinnings become like any other American family—the metaphoric equivalent of rising and subsiding bubbles or annually replaced blades of grass—they cease to be an elite body, separated from the land-working tenants and the natural cycles, and become, like Enceladus, mere fodder for the whimsical reveries of bad artists like Pierre. In effect, the second part of *Pierre,* while deliberately disconnected from the first, offers the terms upon which the ephemeral and saccharinely artificial first half can be critiqued. Beginning with the highly problematic paraliptic rewriting of Pierre's history, a rewriting that seriously undermines the text's continuity, the second half of *Pierre* offers itself as a fictional democratic acid that corrodes the "old" romance form that preceded it. And the two halves of the text remain separated by a rocky, self-consciously failed transition because the prospect of narra-tological compromise is airily rejected out of hand in the interest of articulating Young America.

In presenting *Pierre* as a set of structural counterpoints—the chivalric romance versus the American individualist myth of ascendance through self-reliance—Melville thwarts expectations that the novel is a generically unified form. This is clearly consistent with what he does in *Mardi* (1849), in *Moby-Dick,* and later in *The Confidence-Man* (1857). But *Pierre*'s interrogation of the novelistic form and consequent glaring display of heterodoxy amounts to substantially more than Melville thumbing his nose at fic-tional conventions. When the highly self-referential narra-tor proclaims in "Young America in Literature" that, while aware of the "conflicting modes of writing history," he is "careless of either"—when he insists airily, "I write pre-cisely as I please" (244)—Melville signals that his "plea-sure" involves the inscription of coexistent opposites. Be-cause Pierre, like Young America, does not quite relinquish anything to gain its apparent opposite, his promised politi-cal conversion is suspect: his move from rural to urban, from aristocrat to democrat, from lord to wage-slave, might represent a move from side to side, but the sides are not marked geographically within an identifiable rhetoric of the Union's sides. He may cross the Rubicon, but he goes back; he may live in New York, but he imports Saddle Meadows; he may become a wage slave, but he tries to earn money by aggrandizing himself; he may be a demo-crat, but he believes himself to be a chivalric hero. In other words, Pierre bounces back and forth—geographi-cally, ideologically, historically, and politically—between oppositions supposedly determined by geography alone. And thus Melville interrogates and demystifies the firmly antithetical codifications of rural South/urban North, aris-tocratic South/democratic North, agrarian South/industrial North, Old World South/New World North.

If Melville suggests that democracy is a process, a poten-tial evolution and maturation, he never actually represents that process; instead, at the point when the transformation should take place, he renounces any concession to textual unity and proffers Plinlimmon's pamphlet as a dismissible parody of morally expedient compromise. The pamphlet stands as a metonymic figuration of both the logic of com-promise and the Plinlimmon-like compromisers them-selves. While Pierre takes his crumpled copy of Plinlim-mon's pamphlet to New York, he is never able to recover it; nor is he able to retrieve any of the other copies appar-ently disseminated there. Hidden from sight in New York City, in the deep pocket-lining of Pierre's Saddle Mead-ows coat, the pamphlet offers a potential point of conver-gence between Saddle Meadows and New York City; but it is a convergence that Melville rejects, first implicitly through parody, and later explicitly through Pierre's failure to reaffirm its limp message.

In *The Civil War World of Herman Melville* Stanton Gar-ner maintains that Melville was essentially like Abraham Lincoln: seduced by the ideal of Union and placing it be-fore the cause of abolition, Melville questioned the "merit of remedying one flaw in the national character [slavery] at the cost of the nation itself. . . . Was not gradual manu-mission preferable to irreversible rupture?"[29] Yet Clay and Webster were the authors of Compromise, and *they* were, as Sundquist remarks, quite plainly "blinded by the ideol-ogy of Union."[30] *Pierre* suggests that Melville was neither seduced nor blinded; and while he does not in *Pierre* elaborate on the upshot of that blinding to the degree he later would in *Benito Cereno,* he most certainly dismantles the premises of the Compromise in the earlier work. In fact, Melville proffers a glaringly heterogenous, ruptured narrative in *Pierre* that seems almost to anticipate a far more substantial rupture to come.

Notes

1. Herman Melville, *Pierre; or, the Ambiguities,* ed. Harrison Hayford, Hershel Parker, and G. Thomas Tanselle (Evanston and Chicago: Northwestern Univ. Press and The Newberry Library, 1971), 244. All fur-ther references to *Pierre* will be to this edition and will be cited parenthetically in the text.

2. Richard Lanham describes paralipsis (from the Greek for "disregard" or "omission") as a rhetorical figure that emphasizes through the statement of what will not be discussed; I use it that way to describe, for example, Melville's raising of the rent-wars, immedi-ately followed by his refusal to discuss their implica-tions; see Lanham, *A Handlist of Rhetorical Terms* (Chicago: Univ. of Chicago Press, 1971). Gerard Genette amplifies the sense of the term to include what he refers to as the "retrospective filling in" of a narrative, the offering of a curious supplementation where none was apparently needed or even sug-gested; see Genette, *Narrative Discourse: An Essay in Method,* trans. Jane E. Lewin (Ithaca, N.Y.: Cor-nell Univ. Press, 1980), 52. I use Genette's modifica-tion of the term to denote Melville's narration of as-pects of Pierre's youth in the second half of the novel.

3. See, for example, Brian Higgins and Hershel Parker, "The Flawed Grandeur of Melville's *Pierre,*" in *New Perspectives on Melville,* ed. Faith Pullin (Kent, Ohio: Kent State Univ. Press, 1978), 162-96; and "Why *Pierre* Went Wrong," *Studies in the Novel* 8 (Spring 1976): 7-23; Hershel Parker, *Flawed Texts and Verbal Icons* (Evanston, Ill.: Northwestern Univ. Press, 1984), 28-30.

4. Gillian Brown, *Domestic Individualism: Imagining Self in Nineteenth-Century America* (Berkeley and Los Angeles: Univ. of California Press, 1990); Myra Jehlen, *American Incarnation: The Individual, the Nation, and the Continent* (Cambridge: Harvard Univ. Press, 1986); Wai-chee Dimock, *Empire for Liberty: Melville and the Poetics of Individualism* (Princeton: Princeton Univ. Press, 1989).

5. Clay's Compromise actually failed as an omnibus bill, but passed when it was broken down into five

component bills: to admit California into the Union as a free state, to provide territorial government to newly acquired Mexican territory, to draw the border lines of Texas to exclude New Mexico and assume Texas's debts, to prohibit the slave trade but not slavery in the District of Columbia, and to strengthen the Fugitive Slave Law; see *Empire for Liberty: The Genesis and Growth of the United States of America,* vol. 1, ed. Dumas Malone and Basil Rauch (New York: Appleton Century Crofts, 1960), 569.

6. Michael Paul Rogin, *Subversive Genealogy: The Politics and Art of Herman Melville* (New York: Alfred A. Knopf, 1983), 129.

7. Melville had been accused, by William Gilmore Sims in the *Southern Quarterly Review,* of painting a "loathsome picture" of Calhoun in *Mardi* (1849), but Ahab seems an unlikely analogue for Calhoun; see *Melville: The Critical Heritage,* ed. Watson G. Branch (London: Routledge and Kegan Paul, 1974), 187. Charles Foster argues that Ahab represents Daniel Webster, the "senior senator from Massachusetts [who] had sold his soul to the devil" ("Something in Emblems: A Reinterpretation of *Moby-Dick,*" *New England Quarterly* 34 [March 1961]: 28).

8. *The Letters of Herman Melville,* ed. Merrell R. Davis and William H. Gilman (New Haven: Yale Univ. Press, 1960), 146, 150.

9. Henry A. Murray, introduction to *Pierre; or, the Ambiguities,* by Herman Melville (New York: Hendrick's House, 1949), xxxvi; Eric Sundquist, *Home as Found: Authority and Genealogy in Nineteenth-Century American Literature* (Baltimore: Johns Hopkins Univ. Press, 1979), 150.

10. Carolyn Karcher argues that "Melville in fact comments on the double irony that America might have sold her democratic birthright for an aristocratic mess of pottage, and that the ingredients constituting that pottage—lineage, title, landed property—are all tainted" (*Shadow Over the Promised Land: Slavery, Race, and Violence in Melville's America* [Baton Rouge: Louisiana State Univ. Press, 1980], 94).

11. See the *Correspondence of the Van Cortlandt Family of Cortlandt Manor: 1815-1848,* vol. 4, ed. Jacob Judd (Tarrytown, N.Y.: Sleepy Hollow Press, 1981).

12. Douglas T. Miller, *Jacksonian Aristocracy: Class and Democracy in New York, 1830-1860* (New York: Oxford Univ. Press, 1967), 69. See also David Maldwyn Ellis, *Landlords and Farmers in the Hudson-Mohawk Region: 1780-1850* (New York: Octagon, 1967); and Henry Christman, *Tin Horns and Calico: A Decisive Episode in the Emergence of Democracy* (Cornwallville, N.Y.: Hope Farm Press, 1975).

13. Higgins and Parker, "The Flawed Grandeur of Melville's *Pierre,*" 167.

14. Rogin has an acute analysis of Melville's association with the Young America crowd of John O'Sullivan

and Evert Duyckinck's literary circle in the 1840s; see *Subversive Genealogy,* 70-79.

15. Eric Sundquist, *To Wake the Nations: Race in the Making of American Literature* (Cambridge: Harvard Univ. Press, 1993), 142.

16. *The Papers of Daniel Webster,* vol. 2, *Speeches and Formal Writings, 1834-1852,* ed. Charles M. Wiltse (Hanover, N.H.: Univ. Press of New England for Dartmouth College, 1988), 545.

17. The Van Cortlandt Pierres' politics were notoriously mercurial. According to Jacob Judd, the "family members underwent rapid political transformations from Jeffersonianism, to becoming Democrats, shifting to Whiggism for a brief period, and finally, upon reexamining their true beliefs, a return to an earlier Democratic allegiance" (introduction to the *Correspondence of the Van Cortlandt Family,* xxxii). Melville suggests that Pierre's shifting politics, like those of the Van Cortlandts, are of a piece with an aristocratic immaturity.

18. Rogin, *Subversive Genealogy,* 21.

19. James Creech does not focus on Pierre's relationship with Glen Stanley as representative of Melville's interest in figuring homosexuality; instead, he argues that Isabel, as an extension of Pierre's father and the patrilineal phallus, offers the occluded masculine sexualized object: incest had an "ample degree of speakableness [which] emphatically did not apply to the other nameless awfulness of homosexuality" (*Closet Writing/Gay Reading: The Case of Melville's "Pierre"* [Chicago: Univ. of Chicago Press, 1993], 162).

20. Glen Stanly and his preferences are not necessarily of "old times" at all; rather, they could well represent New York "Knickerbocker" society. Miller describes New York socialites as typically "scorn[ing] anything American": "These aristocrats aped European fashions in everything from the cut of their clothes to language and manners. A work of art or a style of dress was not favored with fashionable approval unless it was known to be in vogue in London or Paris" (*Jacksonian Aristocracy,* 78).

21. Bertram Wyatt-Brown observes that the decrease in the number of marriages between first cousins in the North occurred at the same time as an increase in the South: "No doubt the strategy [of intermarriage in the South] reflected the concentration of wealth in an ever-narrowing circle at the top" (*Southern Honor: Ethics and Behavior in the Old South* [New York: Oxford Univ. Press, 1982], 217).

22. For a detailed examination of the rural in America, see Leo Marx, "Pastoralism in America," in *Ideology and Classic American Literature,* ed. Sacvan Bercovitch and Myra Jehlen (Cambridge: Cambridge Univ. Press, 1986), 36-69.

23. Miller, *Jacksonian Aristocracy,* 68-69.

24. Gillian Brown would not agree, arguing instead that Melville is not simply attacking the sentimental pre-

disposition of the nineteenth-century literary marketplace and its attendant cult of celebrity in the "puffery system," but also positing Pierre as the preferred individualist author/hero who can reject that marketplace wholesale because he is writing a mature work. Brown maintains that Pierre is a mouthpiece for Melville; see *Domestic Individualism,* 135-52.

25. Paul Royster argues that, unlike *Moby-Dick, Pierre* offers Melville's "negative version of the symbolic language of correspondence between man, nature, and the invisible world," and he maintains that Pierre's attempt at professional writing is a classic case of Marxist alienation: his production of a literary commodity isolates him from the "product of his labor, from his activity of producing, and from his common humanity" ("Melville's Economy of Language," in *Ideology and Classic American Literature,* 324, 327).

26. Steven Stowe observes that "[a]fter 1800 dueling rather swiftly came to be perceived as a southern phenomenon by southerners and northerners alike. . . . [T]his form of violence and self-control became distinctive of the planter-class South" (*Intimacy and Power in the Old South: Ritual in the Lives of the Planters* [Baltimore: Johns Hopkins Univ. Press, 1987], 39, 6). And Wyatt-Brown points out that the "duel set the boundaries of the upper circle of honor" in the Old South (*Southern Honor,* 352).

27. According to Stowe, the duel led to an investigation by a specially appointed "committee on House privileges," who referred, in their investigation, to the "code of honor as a 'relic of unenlightened and barbarous ages'" (*Intimacy and Power,* 39, 45).

28. For an extensive examination of the connection between the genealogical family tree of the Glendinnings and the Enceladus as its demonic counterpart, see Mark Z. Slouka, "Demonic History: Geography and Genealogy in Melville's *Pierre,*" *ESQ* [*A Journal of the American Renaissance*] 35 (Spring 1989): 147-60. Royster interprets Enceladus as a mythic figure of the bourgeois social climber, whose "upward struggle represents a middle-class image of the social process." As a "naturalized" form of bourgeois ideology, Enceladus masks Pierre's real alienation; see "Melville's Economy of Language," 332, 334.

29. Stanton Garner, *The Civil War World of Herman Melville* (Lawrence: Univ. Press of Kansas, 1993), 27.

30. Sundquist, *To Wake the Nations,* 176.

Stephen Rachman (essay date 1997)

SOURCE: "Melville's *Pierre* and Nervous Exhaustion; or, 'The Vacant Whirlingness of the Bewilderingness,'" in *Literature and Medicine,* Vol. 16, No. 2, Fall, 1997, pp. 226-49.

[*In the following essay, Rachman explores* Pierre *in the context of male hysteria, asserting that Pierre's nervous exhaustion both shapes and makes problematic the idea that the novel was written as a romance.*]

> The author . . . has succeeded in producing nothing but a powerfully unpleasant caricature of morbid thought and passion . . . [T]he details of such a mental malady as that which afflicts Pierre are almost as disgusting as those of physical disease itself.
>
> —Review of *Pierre, Graham's Magazine* 1852[1]

> So, if thou wouldst go to the gods, leave thy dog of a body behind thee.
>
> —*Pierre*[2]

FRETTED WIRES

Near the end of his most vexed novel, *Pierre, or The Ambiguities* (1852), Herman Melville describes his author/ protagonist in the thrall of nervous exhaustion, brought on by literary activity:

> Much oftener than before, Pierre laid back in his chair with the deadly feeling of faintness. Much oftener than before, came staggering home from his evening walk, and from sheer bodily exhaustion economized the breath that answered the anxious inquiries as to what might be done for him. And as if all the leagued spiritual inveteracies and malices, combined with his general bodily exhaustion, were not enough, a special corporeal affliction now descended like a sky-hawk upon him. His incessant application told upon his eyes. They became so affected, that some days he wrote with the lids nearly closed, fearful of opening them wide to the light. Through the lashes he peered upon the paper, which so seemed fretted with wires. Sometimes he blindly wrote with his eyes turned away from the paper;—thus unconsciously symbolizing the hostile necessity and distaste, the former whereof made of him this most unwilling states-prisoner of letters. (*P,* 340)

Pierre was written directly in the wake of *Moby-Dick* in the summer and winter of 1851 and early 1852, nearly a generation before a New York neurologist, George Miller Beard, popularized the amorphous diagnostic category of neurasthenia as a disease of civilization and thirty years before Jean-Martin Charcot published his studies of male hysteria. Yet Pierre's exhaustion and the extreme language Melville works up to convey it are very much in keeping with these later medical developments.[3]

In Melville's fictional world, Pierre's exhaustion becomes more than the result of being overworked and overwrought; it obstructs his vision. Because Pierre cannot fully open his eyes, he squints through his own eyelashes, as through a grating, and his writing paper appears "fretted with wires." Melville suggests that exhaustion distorts not only the author's body but also the perception of his own writing. To Pierre, the page he scribbles on becomes a projection of a "fretful" nervous condition and a cultural grid that holds him captive, a "most unwilling states-prisoner" in a panopticon of letters. The image suggests that exhaustion points simultaneously toward the body of the author and toward the network of social meaning that frames the very medium of literary activity.

It is an image in which disease and literary understanding converge, providing an opportunity for students of literature and disease to gain a purchase on the elusive issue of nervousness and, simultaneously, to approach a text as rich and strange as Melville's *Pierre.* This essay addresses this image and the key it holds for *Pierre,* for this particular moment in U.S. literary history, and for literary activity in general. How can *Pierre* inform our understanding of nineteenth-century nervous disease (or more broadly still, diseases of culture) and its connection to literature? How was it that Melville came to articulate this nervous vision?

The literary value of *Pierre* has always seemed—to the general public at least—slight at best. Though Melville assured his publisher that this book would be "very much more calculated for popularity," it never attracted a sizable audience (it sold a whopping 283 copies in its first year), and the few who read it generally loathed it or wondered what to make of it.[4] In practical terms, *Pierre* destroyed Melville's career as a novelist. The heading of the 1852 review of *Pierre* in the *New York Day Book* ran, "HERMAN MELVILLE CRAZY"; the opinion of the *Southern Quarterly Review,* "The sooner this author is put in ward the better" (*P,* 380, 383). Even after the canonization of Melville in this century, critics, sensing its flawed power, have received the book with something like muddled awe. Dr. Henry A. Murray, psychologist and one of the leading figures in recovering Melville from obscurity, remarked that *Pierre* was a "literary monster, a prodigious by-blow of genius whose appearance is marred by a variety of freakish features and whose organic worth is invalidated by the sickness of despair," summing up the oddly powerful mixture of attraction and repulsion many readers have felt.[5]

This reaction derives in part from the bizarre, racy, swerving plot of the book. In *Pierre,* Melville attempted to write a "regular romance," as he told his publishers, that is, a domestic romance of lovers, unlike the romances he had been writing previously—of Polynesian idylls and obsessed whaling captains.[6] What he produced was anything but regular. Pierre Glendinning, sole heir to a prominent Berkshire family (descended from Revolutionary War heroes), proud and reverential of his long deceased father, deeply attached to his overweening mother, prepares to make a suitable marriage to the radiant blonde Lucy Tartan when he encounters a strange dark girl named Isabel. In a series of mesmeric interviews, Isabel convinces Pierre that she is his illegitimate half-sister, daughter of his father by a Frenchwoman. His esteem for his father shattered, Pierre tries to rectify his father's sin by bringing Isabel home and introducing her as his wife. In a self-righteous pitch of moral quandary, the couple flees to New York. Expecting help from his wealthy cousin Glendinning Stanly, Pierre is instead rebuffed by him and decides to try his hand at writing. Lucy, recovered from shock, recognizes the noble nature of Pierre's sacrifice and joins the couple in their low-life apartment.

As Pierre's story of decline moves from the country to the city, from pastoral love intrigue to an urban tale of failed authorship and suicide, the reader of *Pierre* is continually made to understand how social forces become literary and nervous ones. In making Pierre an author who deflects his obsessions away from Isabel and toward his "[m]ature [w]ork," Melville shifts into an explicitly literary sphere. In their new home in "The Church of the Apostles"—a kind of transcendentalist Grub Street presided over by the elusive author Plotinus Plinlimmon—Pierre, Isabel, and Lucy are visited by squalor, bad dreams, disillusionment, and nervous debility. Eventually, Pierre murders his vengeful cousin and is thrown in prison where he, Lucy, and Isabel meet their end in a triple suicide. Pierre's story (F. O. Matthiessen calls him a Hamlet *à rebours*) records the transformation of social, filial, sexual, and revolutionary energies ("strongest and fieriest emotions" [*P,* 67]) into literary ones.[7] Pierre's family finger-pointing, social bridge-burning, and his outsized will to heroism are left to decode themselves in an arena of, among other things, frustrated writing.

Because of the plot alone, *Pierre* has encouraged and still encourages readers to find it "*symptomatic*" of the author's diseased imagination, offering many avenues of speculative diagnosis.[8] Even critics who have attempted to demonstrate that Pierre actually succeeds in aesthetic terms ("I regard *Pierre* as a complete, successful, and brilliant work," writes Patricia Wald), do so by stabilizing its eccentricities, by regarding them as the radically experimental tropes and techniques of a postmodern, subversive deconstruction of narrative.[9] The recent HarperCollins reissue of *Pierre* (1995) attempts to streamline the novel by excising the digressions into literary matters (which Melville wrote in the eleventh hour before the manuscript went to press), but this gesture once again confirms how *Pierre* continues to require a stabilization that no amount of surgical editing or elegant argumentation can finally supply. Other critics negotiate the dilemma of *Pierre* by reading it as a parody of the sentimental or melodramatic novel.[10]

And yet, despite a general validity in these assertions, there remains a sincerity, however incongruous, in Melville's novel, an investment in unconventional language, and an element of self-criticism that resists the parodic. While parody, satire, and melodrama are three of its many modes, *Pierre* is odder and perhaps more grotesque than these terms would indicate. Many funny passages in *Pierre* never wholly divest themselves of earnestness. For example, when Pierre is magnetically drawn to Isabel, the image is distortedly literal: she "seemed to swim in an electric fluid; the vivid buckler of her brow seemed as a magnetic plate" (*P,* 151). When the narrator describes the armless Titan "without one serviceable ball-and-socket above the thigh," our amusement at the perverse literalism of the amputated body is tempered by an awareness that Melville wishes us to understand this image as part of Pierre's ideal horror and the key to his actual grief (*P,* 346). If *Pierre* partakes of the burlesque, it does not ultimately ridicule its subject; it contains too many sermons.

Pierre acts out Melville's chief insight that the failure of the body is mysteriously linked to literary and cultural failure, inviting the reader, as it were, to share in Pierre's latticed vision, to see through the distorted template of nervous exhaustion. Many of *Pierre*'s terms become, in little flights of whimsy, oddly translatable into bodily ailment; colics become "*melloncolics*" (*P*, 203), "*Chronometrics*" become "the *chronic-rheumatics*" (*P*, 292), and, as Pierre says to his mother, "It is not well, well, well; but ill, ill, ill" (*P*, 56). Because Melville continually links the humor, parody, and satire in *Pierre* with disease (or at least the aura of disease) much of the book's satire appears evocatively morbid and his parody alloyed with utter gravity. I suggest that Pierre's unruly properties, while not necessarily symptomatic of anything, are more accurately captured in the review of *Pierre* from *Graham's Magazine* of 1852 (quoted as an epigraph to this essay) than one might ordinarily assume. The remark forcefully conveys the idea that Melville created the literary effect of disease, in particular a combination of physical and psychological ailments that came in time to be regularly associated with neurasthenic disease.

NERVOUS EXHAUSTION, LITERATURE, AND STIMULATION

The "morbidity" of *Pierre* situates the novel in its broad cultural context, an antebellum United States in which significant affinities between nerves and literature were readily recognized by all writers and readers. *Nervous exhaustion, breakdown, debility,* and, after 1870, *neurasthenia* were terms that doctors often applied to conditions as wide-ranging as depression, anxiety, stress, alcoholism, and what was known as the solitary vice of masturbation. These terms were also used to indicate a host of vague physical ailments that were related—as either cause or effect—to an individual's failure to cope with life's pressures. Culturally, exhaustion was the negative counterpart to the varieties of individualism that gained currency in the U.S. during the nineteenth century, from Emersonian self-reliance of the 1840s to Rooseveltian rugged individualism of the 1890s. Exhaustion appeared as a failure of self-reliance, a pathology of the strenuous life. If the Yankee was "individualism incarnate" in the eyes of one French observer of life in the U.S. in the 1830s, he was, for Oliver Wendell Holmes, Sr., in the 1850s the "Americanized European" of New England who suffered from sallow nervousness.[11] Nervous debility appeared to many contemporary observers as a cost of living in, as Henry David Thoreau described it, the "restless, nervous, bustling, trivial Nineteenth Century."[12]

By coining the term *neurasthenia* after the Civil War, Dr. Beard and his associates consolidated this wide array of physical and psychic complaints under the rubric of a new diagnostic category.[13] The cultural power of neurasthenia lay, as Charles Rosenberg has argued, in the ability to divorce nervous exhaustion from the moral and social stigma associated with older terms such as or including madness, hypochondria, melancholia, mania, and debility.[14] According-

ing to Beard, the causes of neurasthenia lay not so much in the weakness of the flesh but in the stress and pressure peculiar to modern nineteenth-century culture: the "railway, telegraph, telephone, and periodical press intensifying in ten thousand ways cerebral activity and worry."[15] Beard successfully linked the disorder to the technology of the managerial classes, giving neurasthenia the cultural cachet of modern complaint.

While artisans and factory operatives in Sylvester Graham's boardinghouses frequently suffered from excessive nervousness in the 1830s, by the 1880s neurasthenia had become a quintessentially bourgeois diagnosis, helping to mark the growing class divisions after the Civil War.[16] In trifling cases, it could be little more than a fashionable illness for melancholic, bon-bon-eating matrons, bookish lads, and dateless society debutantes ("[w]e become sad in the first place by having nothing stirring to do," Melville writes in *Pierre,* "we continue in it, because we have found a snug sofa at last" [*P*, 258-59]). In serious cases, it could be as baffling, obstinate, and tragic as anorexia nervosa is today. But in all cases, it was a disorder of culture and metaphor, inflected as much with class and gender (both masculine and feminine) as it was with neurological weakness.

Throughout the nineteenth century, nervousness and nervous stimulation were tokens of genteel literary culture. W. S. Gilbert's "greenery-yallery, Grosvenor Gallery, foot-in-the-grave young man" fixed fragile nervousness in the popular imagination as the badge of the aspiring literary aesthete.[17] The meteoric but jittery careers of the Romantic authors prominent in the early decades of the century had become regularly associated with literary aspiration well before its last decades. The neuro-literary connection was pervasive enough in 1807 that Thomas Trotter, a retired naval physician, in *A View of the Nervous Temperment* (sic), could observe, in a more positive light, of men of letters, "that all men who possess genius . . . are endued by nature with more than usual sensibility of nervous system."[18] In the *Preface* to *Lyrical Ballads,* William Wordsworth explains how the "Poet" differs from other men by invoking the terms of nervous sensibility: "Among the qualities. . . . enumerated as principally conducing to form a Poet, is implied nothing differing in kind from other men, but only in degree. . . . The Poet is chiefly distinguished from other men by a greater promptness to think and feel without immediate external excitement."[19] The same sensibility is repeated in the art-for-art's-sake prescriptions of the Pre-Raphaelites and new aesthetics of Walter Pater, Oscar Wilde, and James McNeill Whistler.[20]

One explanation for this linkage, as Raymond Williams has suggested, is that nervous sensibility helped to distinguish literary figures from society at large at a time when literary culture was engaged in a more general dissociation of itself from society.[21] Of the many ways that cultures prescribe the artistic temperament, nervousness was either a prerequisite or hazard of literary genius. It was seen as both an indicator of a literary disposition (as in

Wordsworth) and a consequence of imaginative work (as in *Pierre*). Indeed, while one can point to many celebrated literary figures who were also nervous sufferers (members of the James family and Charlotte Perkins Gilman, for example), it is hard to distinguish cause from effect, to distinguish between suffering for one's art and suffering from one's nerves.

Given that susceptibility to nervous stimulation was routinely assigned to authors, it is not surprising to find literature being assigned similar nervous (and enervating) characteristics. The commonsense orthodoxy that inveighed against romancers and their readers assailed novels as harmful stimulants to the imagination.[22] "When this poison [novel-reading] infects the mind," wrote Thomas Jefferson, "it destroys its tone and revolts it against wholesome reading. . . . Nothing can engage attention unless dressed in all the figments of fancy, and nothing so bedecked comes amiss. The result is a bloated imagination, sickly judgment, and disgust towards all the real business of life."[23]

In a pivotal moment in his career as a Romantic author and an advocate of Romantic authorship, Melville embraced this cultural prescription obliquely but powerfully when he declared in **"Hawthorne and His Mosses"** (1850) that "genius, all over the world, stands hand in hand, and one shock of recognition runs the whole circle round."[24] In this literary manifesto, Melville makes an argument for Hawthorne's genius and the U.S.'s national literature by suggesting that genius completes a global circuit of electrical recognition. "Brac[ing] the whole brotherhood," the current that passes through literary genius is joltingly powerful (**HHM,** 249). Hand in hand, genius mutually confers recognition on its brethren. The image suggests not only telegraphic but bodily communion while implying that genius itself relies on a network of confirmation. At a time when the discoveries of Luigi Galvani ("On the Force of Electricity in Muscular Movement"), Count Allessandro Volta, Michael Faraday, and Samuel Morse made the general public aware of electrical phenomena, writers did not hesitate to apply electrical metaphors to nineteenth-century culture, as Melville championed Hawthorne in terms of electro-nervous literary power. Just as Beard likened electrical transmission with neurological activity ("railway, telegraph, telephone, and periodical press intensifying in ten thousand ways cerebral activity and worry"), Melville's "shock of recognition" metaphorically connects nerves and literature as forms of electrical communication, as powerful networks of transmission, as senders and receivers of signals, as media through which authors make contact with the world around them. Hawthorne's genius resided, for Melville, in a kind of corporeal authenticity registered in his prose, the way each of the "few thoughts" that Hawthorne puts "into circulation" are "arterialized at his large warm lungs, and expanded in his honest heart" (**HHM,** 245).

By the time of *Pierre*'s composition, however, Melville raised the specter of the writers of genius who become "victims to headache, and pain in the back," whose literary productions are "born of unwillingness and the bill of the baker[;] the rickety offspring of a parent, careless of life herself, and reckless of the germ-life she contains," or works "privately published in their own brains, and suppressed there as quickly" (*P,* 258-59). Hawthorne's arterialization becomes Pierre's liability. "Builds **Pierre** the noble world of a new book? or does the Pale Haggardness unbuild the lungs and life in him?" (*P,* 304). In *Pierre,* Melville voices his skepticism about the cultural claims of authorship based on Wordsworthian excitability and stereotypical assumptions regarding bodies and literature. "Know this," the narrator explains in one of his authorial asides, "while many a consumptive dietarian has but produced the merest literary flatulencies to the world; convivial authors have alike given utterance to the sublimest wisdom, and created the least gross and most ethereal forms" (*P,* 299).

Pierre allows Melville to reorient the issue of nerves and literature: a nervous disposition reflects not the creative mark of an author but the deleterious mark of civilization on the author. While Pierre ends up depleted and deranged, he is not constitutionally frail or delicate and spends much of the novel reveling in his excesses. Similarly, Melville strains his language to equal that excess. Not only is nervous exhaustion a hazard for delicate authors, it is endemic to the modern conditions of authorship and the labor of writing. Illness does not automatically predispose one to literary activity, but literary activity may dispose one to illness. Civilization and the material realities of authorship are the sources of Pierre's nervous symptoms. "Pierre is young," the narrator argues,

> [H]eaven gave him the divinest, freshest form of a man; put light into his eye, and fire into his blood, and brawn into his arm, and a joyous, jubilant, overflowing, upbubbling, universal life in him everywhere. Now look around in that most miserable room, and at that most miserable of all the pursuits of a man, and say if here be the place, and this be the trade, that God intended him for. A rickety chair, two hollow barrels, a plank, paper, pens, and infernally black ink, four leprously dingy white walls, no carpet, a cup of water, and a dry biscuit or two. Oh, I hear the leap of the Texan Camanche, as at this moment he goes crashing like a wild deer through the green underbrush; I hear his glorious whoop of savage untameable health; and then I look in at Pierre. If physical, practical unreason make the savage, which is he? Civilization, Philosophy, Ideal Virtue! behold your victim! (*P,* 302)

Civilization both fosters and constrains authorship. Nervousness and exhaustion are not simply symptoms of a creative illness in a positive sense but a pathology of culture. An alleged physical token of an artistic sensibility that actively sought a privileged autonomy from society, nervous exhaustion in fact embodied internalized societal pressures. As Pierre struggles vainly "against all the dismal lassitude, and deathful faintness and sleeplessness, and whirlingness, and craziness" (*P,* 339), his will loses out to cultural forces, and an heroic model of authorship yields to social and historical determinism. "Sucked within the maelstrom, man must go round," the narrator explains. "Pierre was not arguing Fixed Fate and Free Will, now; Fixed Fate and Free Will were arguing him, and Fixed Fate got the better in the debate" (*P,* 182). Pierre is the most determined and *determined* of characters, and exhaustion reveals the points at which his actions are both autonomous and constrained by cultural limitations.

While Melville contests the essentialist notion of a neuro-literary disposition (intemperate authors write temperate books and vice-versa), his novel ultimately turns on the medical principle very much current in Jacksonian reform thought (through the works of Sylvester Graham borrowing from Benjamin Rush), that stimulation and excess lead to debility.[25] Dipsomania and onanism, routinely considered diseases of the nervous system through the 1870s, were seen to cause debility through stimulation, hence the concept of morbid excitement; similarly, Melville considered professional writing disease-like, subjecting the practitioner to morbid stimulation.[26] Only an internal, renunciative discipline can save the author from himself. "Elect!" Melville warns his reader (equating writing for money with the joint labor of body and soul). "Yoke the body to the soul, and put both to the plow, and the one or the other must in the end assuredly drop in the furrow. Keep, then, thy body effeminate for labor, and thy soul laboriously robust; or else thy soul effeminate for labor and thy body laboriously robust" (*P,* 261). Without restraint, without resolute effeminacy, there is only so much health a writer can have: "over the most vigorous and soaring conceits," Melville writes, "doth the cloud of Truth come stealing" (*P,* 261). The metaphors themselves experience a kind of exhaustion. Modern authorship, Melville suggests, necessitates what doctors later in the century referred to as an impelling volition, a will to preserve the self from the writing self through a kind of rest cure (with a striking association of labor with masculine and leisure with feminine) for either the literary body or soul. Pierre's downfall results from his weakness of will, his inability to "elect," to keep his body or soul effeminate for labor.

AN ILLNESS OF METAPHOR

Considered in the context of nineteenth-century theories of nervous debility and neurasthenia, *Pierre*'s engagement with exhaustion becomes not merely a problem of culture but a problem of the work that metaphors perform within culture. When Beard asserted that "there can be no doubt whatever, namely, that nervous disease scarcely exists among savages or barbarians, or semi-barbarians, or partially civilized people," he echoes the narrator's sentiments about the nature of Pierre's disease ("If physical, practical unreason make the savage, which is he? Civilization, Philosophy, Ideal Virtue! behold your victim!"), but reduces those generalized causes to specific agents.[27] Nervous exhaustion was used in a dual sense as both a distinct symptom and a name for the disorder at large, as both a part and the whole. The confusing symptomatology of exhaustion performed the cultural work of connecting the civilized body to the technological and material forces of production. In order to distinguish fatigue (a necessary condition in which, after a normal period of recuperation, one can resume activity) from exhaustion (a disorder from which recuperation does not directly or even inevitably follow), doctors attempted to account for an irrecuperable drain of energy through ambiguous medical terms that transformed diagnosis into cultural analogy.

Nervous exhaustion manifests itself as an illness of metaphor in which the terms *civilization* and *the body* may be either the tenor or vehicle. In *Pierre,* nervous debility and its hold on Melville's imagination rely on the analogical impulses that hold together such a miscellaneous congeries of symptoms. As the language of nineteenth-century medical authority veers toward the metaphoric for its explanations of exhaustion, Melville's deeply metaphoric language veers toward the symptomatic. Neurasthenia took its diagnostic imprimatur from metaphor: it disclosed the body's analogical power and engaged the body's symbolic life. Melville exploited the startling diversity of ways in which the body was capable of metaphorizing the world. *Pierre* presents the body as an alembic for culture, as self-consumption, perverse in that the forces of vitality and power appear as the culpable agents of decay. "Death's second self," William Shakespeare calls it, "Consum'd with that which it was nourish'd by."[28] In *Pierre,* Melville renders the disease as "a general and nameless torpor—some horrible foretaste of death itself" (*P,* 342). "Pierre went forth all redolent," he writes, "but alas! his body only the embalming cerements of his buried dead within" (*P,* 94).

In order to convey the analogical potential of exhausted states, Melville exhibits one of *Pierre*'s more unruly contrivances, a highly idiosyncratic atmospheric vocabulary. Melville uses extraordinary coinages that venture to communicate extreme conditions of abstraction and sensory quiddity. For example, Pierre's excitement at Lucy Tartan's touch is rendered as "feeling, softly feeling of its soft tinglingness"; the evening is described as "'an infinite starry nebulousness . . . some spangled vail of mystery'" (*P,* 36); and the after-effects of his encounter with Isabel as "'the stupor, and the torpor . . . the vacant whirlingness of the bewilderingness'" (*P,* 122). In their review of *Pierre* in *The Literary World,* the Duyckinck brothers complained of

> such infelicities of expression, such unknown words as . . . "human*ness,*" "heroic*ness,*" "patriarchal*ness,*" "descended*ness,*" "flushful*ness,*" "amaranthi*ness,*" "instantaneous*ness,*" "leapingly acknowledging," "fateful frame of mind," "protecting*ness,*" "young*ness,*" "infantile*ness,*" "visible*ness.*"[29]

Mimicking this language, *Godey's* reviewer called the work "an infinite, unbounded, inexpressible mysteriousness of nothingness."[30] Critics responded tetchily to Melville's implicit reproach of the power of English and classic English prosody to describe modern civilization. Melville's quasi-Germanic constructions, such as "the vacant whirlingness of the bewilderingness," raised hackles.

One reviewer suggested that any writer operating in the "plain, honest, Saxon style" ought to eschew the German style with its spurious mysticism and baroque prose and suggested Melville re-read Joseph Addison.[31]

Why does Melville resort to such a lexicon of supercharged neologisms, to making fey nouns out of household adjectives? Why, for example, *heroicness* rather than *heroism*? The use of the substantive *-ness* attempts to convey a categorical quality like those of nervous symptoms. Melville applies the suffix to conditions associated with exhaustion (flushfulness, whirlingness, bewilderingness), implying a more-than-local property to these states, suggesting a condition or a field rather than an instance of meaning. "'Say, Pierre,'" Isabel asks at one point, "'doth not a funerealness invest me?'" (*P*, 314). Literally Isabel refers to her dark features (especially her flowing, jet-black hair), but her language refers to her features as if they were outward symptoms of a morbid condition.

In *Pierre*, *-ness* puts into words not only the sensation of exhaustion but the structure of exhausted experience. As a suffix it implies that *any* word can become a condition, and thus part of a complex of stimulation (tinglingness) and depletion (deathful faintness, whirlingness). Through this linguistic maneuver, Pierre's fatigue and the combination of overstimulation and debility that pervades the novel are depicted not merely as part of an individual experience (something that only he feels). Instead, symptoms of fatigue are caught up in a transpersonal cultural dynamic in which feelings are connected to categories of feeling, in part culturally constructed and in part culturally determined. In *Pierre*, *-ness* imparts to ordinary language what Raymond Williams described as "structure of feeling," or a "structured formation which, because it is at the very edge of semantic availability, has many of the characteristics of a pre-formation, until specific articulations—new semantic figures—are discovered in material practice."[32] Williams argues that certain social experiences take place "*in solution,* as distinct from other social semantic formations which have been *precipitated* and are more evidently and immediately available." Paradigmatic shifts caused by great upheavals, generational shifts, landmark cultural or literary performances in some measure bring what was at the edge of articulation, the edge of "*semantic availability,*" into full-throated voice.[33]

Williams's metaphor is particularly clarifying, for if culture functions like a chemical solution in which, at any given moment, some ideas are semantically precipitated and other ideas remain in solution, writing, performing, painting—any artistic or expressive activity—would then contribute to the equilibrium or disequilibrium of that solution. For example, the terms *whirlingness* and *bewilderingness* suggest that there is also a component of a character's experience that is latent or in solution; that is to say, it is either not wholly the property of a character or is recognized by Melville's terminology as an internalization of a cultural construct. By describing nervous and literary exhaustion in this way, by turning adjectives and adverbs into force fields, Melville suggests the internalizing process by which stimulation becomes debility.

This effect is most prominent in the bizarre scene where Pierre interviews Isabel, with its weird guitar music intoning "Mystery! Mystery! Mystery of Isabel!" for it seems to have taken place in Faraday's laboratory:

> To Pierre's dilated senses Isabel seemed to swim in an electric fluid; the vivid buckler of her brow seemed as a magnetic plate. . . . For over all these things, and inter-fusing itself with the sparkling electricity in which she seemed to swim, was an ever-creeping and condensing haze of ambiguities. Often, in after-times with her, did he recall this first magnetic night, and would seem to see that she then had bound him to her by an extraordinary atmospheric spell—both physical and spiritual. . . . This spell . . . which eternally locks in mystery and in muteness the universal subject world, and the physical electricalness of Isabel seemed reciprocal with the heat-lightnings and the ground-lightnings nigh to which it had first become revealed to Pierre. She seemed molded from fire and air, and vivified at some Voltaic pile of August thunder-clouds heaped against the sunset. (*P*, 151-52)

At this moment in *Pierre,* nervous stimulation becomes incipient nervous exhaustion, the oddity of the scene reinforced by its extremely literal character. *Pierre*'s culture is figured quite literally as a solution in which sensations are equated with structures of exhausted experience. In his study of melancholia and depression, Stanley W. Jackson observed that the "late nineteenth century and the early twentieth century saw the active introduction of metaphors from the dynamics and energetics of physical science, often with a rapid loss of the sense of using a metaphor."[34] This loss of metaphoric sense seems to be endemic to nervous complaint (depression, we need to remind ourselves, is a very ancient metaphor) as well as to Melville's style and unusual diction. To look through the distorted template of nervous exhaustion and share Pierre's (and *Pierre*'s) exhausted vision, is to lose one's metaphoric senses. It is to see metaphoric states as physical conditions and to see in physical conditions metaphoric states. If Pierre believes his own droopy eyelashes to be the fretted wires of culture, this is what it means to be exhausted and to see exhaustedly.

TRANCE STATES AND THE BODY OF THE AUTHOR

Melville's opinion that civilization is a debilitating stimulus was informed by the experience of trying to support himself and his family by his pen. Biographers and critics agree that the inspiration for many elements of *Pierre* derive from the author's life, family history, and struggling career as a novelist. Biography offers us the astonishing figure of Melville, at the time of *Pierre*'s composition, suffering to some extent along with Pierre. During this period, his wife noted that he would "sit at his desk all day not eating any thing till four or five oclock—then ride to the village after dark."[35] In March 1852 Dr. Amos Nourse expressed the fear that Melville was "'devoting himself to writing with an assiduity that will cost him dear by & by.'" A neighbor and friend Sarah Morewood remarked that Melville was working "'under a state of morbid excitement which will soon injure his health,'" and "'told him that the recluse life he was leading made his city friends think that he was slightly insane.'"[36] Melville also suffered from sciatica, rheumatism, and eye trouble ("I steal abroad by twilight, owing to the twilight of my eyes," explained Melville to Evert Duyckinck, friend and editor of *The Literary World,* in the spring of 1851), and his health remained poor for three or four years after the writing of *Pierre.*[37]

The sections of the novel dealing with "Young America in Literature," "Pierre as Juvenile Author," and "The Church of the Apostles" were part of Melville's reaction to negative or indifferent reviews of *Moby-Dick,* rebuffs from his publishers, and a disenchantment with the New York literary establishment.[38] In a literary market that discouraged experimentation, Melville reacted by producing radically experimental and challenging works that frequently puzzled a readership that assumed he would repeat the charming formulae of *Typee* and *Omoo.*[39] In the late 1840s he envisioned for himself an authorship of defied expectation that might actively destabilize his public persona. "Not long ago, having published two narratives of voyages in the Pacific," the preface to *Mardi* (1849) begins, "which, in many quarters, were received with incredulity, the thought occurred to me, of indeed writing a romance of Polynesian adventure, and publishing it as such; to see whether, the fiction might not, possibly, be received for a verity: in some degree the reverse of my previous experience."[40] Encouraged by the example of Hawthorne's indirection "directly calculated to deceive—egregiously deceive" (**HHM,** 251), Melville raised the cagey antagonism of *Mardi* to the fever pitch of *Pierre.* Pierre rebels against the literary market of "*Biographico-Solicito Circulars*" that desired "a neat draft of his life," and "he had not failed to clutch with peculiar nervous detestation and contempt that ample parcel, containing the letters of his Biographico" before he destroys them (*P,* 255). This attitude, Hershel Parker has demonstrated, corresponds more or less directly to Melville's own, and is another of the many ways Melville sets the psychodrama of *Pierre* against the backdrop of his own situation.[41]

If at the time of *Mardi*'s composition Melville felt misunderstood, by the time of *Pierre* he had come to understand how his writing career had been radically altering his own identity. "From my twenty-fifth year I date my life," he explained to Hawthorne. "Three weeks have scarcely passed, at any time between then and now, that I have not unfolded within myself. But I feel that I am now come to the inmost leaf of the bulb, and that shortly the flower must fall to the mould."[42] Just entering his thirties, Melville sensed—with some justice—that he had exhausted a fundamental source of creativity. While he would go on to write many extraordinary works of intellect, imagination, and beauty, he would not do so with the extravagance of *Moby-Dick* and *Pierre.* In a very real way, the exhaustion of this phase revealed to Melville the caducous sequence of his literary career up to that moment: a series of unfoldings of a reality present all along. He also told Hawthorne, "Possibly, if you . . . direct [a letter] to Herman Melville, you will missend it—for the very fingers that now guide this pen are not precisely the same that just took it up and put it on this paper. Lord, when shall we be done changing?"[43] He reads his own development as a spectacle of Ovidian transformation as radical as that of any character he might invent, and *Pierre,* if nothing else, insists upon a similar flux of its authorial persona.

At this point in his career, Melville was particularly concerned with writing as a bodily process, as the creation of an embodied creature. His insights into nervous exhaustion and his sense of the inadequacy of nineteenth-century stereotypes about nerves and literature proceed from an awareness of how the multiple cares of writing and running his farm and household were affecting his body. Not a constitutionally frail or delicate man, Melville was certainly disturbed by his setbacks. This preoccupation percolates through *Pierre* and offers a suggestive motive for the author's strategy of having the reader share in Pierre's exhausted vision. Perhaps miserable authors love too well their readerly company. In the novel, exhaustion finds its culmination in Pierre's terrifying vision of himself as Enceladus, the Titan. Before murder and suicide bring *Pierre* to its frenzied conclusion, Pierre falls into a hallucinatory trance-state in which he envisions himself as the mythological giant who was confined in his fury by the Olympian gods beneath Mount Etna (*P,* 342). Pierre becomes the "doubly incestuous" Titan "writhing from out the imprisoning earth . . . though armless, resisting with his whole striving trunk," the mountains that the gods heaped upon him in retribution for his attack (*P,* 345). In his austere writer's garret he convulses, turning his "vast trunk into a battering-ram," hurling his "arched-out ribs again and yet again against the invulnerable steep" (*P,* 346):

> Recovered somewhat from the after-spell of this wild vision folded in his trance, Pierre composed his front as best he might, and straightway left his fatal closet. Concentrating all the remaining stuff in him, he resolved by entire and violent change, and by a willful act against his own most habitual inclinations, to wrestle with the strange malady of his eyes, this new death-fiend of the trance, and this Inferno of his Titanic vision. (*P,* 347)

As the Titan wrestles in the earth, Pierre wrestles with his breakdown. In the aftermath of the episode Pierre "writhingly strove" (*P,* 347) to gain control over his facial expression, and in Pierre's symptoms—the contortions, the chronic fatigue and the "strange malady" of the eyes—Melville finds a general criticism of culture and an epiphany of literary destiny. "'Enceladus! it is Enceladus!'—Pierre cried out in his sleep. . . . on the Titan's armless trunk, his own duplicate face and features magnifiedly gleamed upon him with prophetic discomfiture and woe" (*P,* 346).

With all its writhing neurotic content, the trance of Enceladus brings into clear relief the futility and the ineluctability of the author's embodiment. The squirming trunk of the author finds itself, like Enceladus, imprisoned by the mountain it sought to move. In the myth, Enceladus and the other giants rebelled against the new world order of the Olympian gods and were imprisoned under Mount Etna. The trance gives the physical struggle a mythic context in which physiological determinism coincides with cultural determinism.[44] "So, if thou wouldst go to the gods, leave thy dog of a body behind thee," Melville writes in *Pierre* but Enceladus and Pierre cannot go to the gods precisely because they cannot leave their bodies behind. The fragmentation of the author's identity occurs at a point where that identity and the cultural forces that police it collapse into one another. The division between the consciousness of the author and the constraints of his culture is eroded by an ambiguous set of altered states. The prison-house of letters becomes the prison-house of the body.

The "confusions and confoundings" of Pierre's "combining consciousness" are so extreme that "[h]e would fain have disowned the very memory and the mind which produced to him such an immense scandal upon his common sanity. . . . The cheeks of his soul collapsed in him: he dashed himself in blind fury . . . and fell dabbling in the vomit of his loathed identity" (*P,* 171). Through the struggle for "muscular sanity" and the verbal contortions of *Pierre,* the narrator describes exhausted writing as an attempt to counter physical and emotional torment. Out of a "profound willfulness" Pierre composes his book

> against all the dismal lassitude, and deathful faintness and sleeplessness, and whirlingness and craziness.. . . . he gave jeer for jeer, and taunted the apes that jibed him. . . . [W]ith the feeling of misery and death in him, he created forms of gladness and life. For the pangs in his heart, he put down hoots on the paper. And every thing else he disguised under the so conveniently adjustable drapery of all-stretchable Philosophy. (*P,* 339)

Melville offers a fantasy of forging literary virtue out of a lack of composure. Corporeal craziness and whirlingness become textual gladness and life; bodily pangs become paper hoots. Expressing a need to free himself from the constraints of historical narration, of cause and effect, of relevant detail, Melville abandons, in one critic's words, a "commitment to the premise that the kind of world he wants to create can be articulated through a temporal narration, through an account of the progressive unfolding of sequential experience."[45]

In other words, the trance dramatizes a crisis of agency implicit in Melville's literary exhaustion. Pierre's "state of semi-unconsciousness" (*P,* 342) returns him with smothering déjà vu to the Berkshires and Saddle Meadows, connecting the end of the novel to the beginning of the novel, allowing Pierre's scene of writing (his New York garret) to communicate with his past in Saddle Meadows, and linking Pierre's crisis of authorship with Melville's scene of writing:

The actual artificial objects around him slid from him, and were replaced by a baseless yet most imposing spectacle of natural scenery. But though a baseless vision in itself, this airy spectacle assumed very familiar features to Pierre. It was the phantasmagoria of the Mount of the Titans, a singular height standing quite detached in a wide solitude not far from the grand range of dark blue hills encircling his ancestral manor. (*P,* 342)

Here the novel most explicitly interposes into *Pierre*'s world a universe parallel to Melville's own writing environment in Pittsfield of 1851-1852. Pierre's abandonment removes him from his own scene of composition only to cast him perilously close to Melville's scene of composition (he wrote portions of *Moby-Dick* and *Pierre* at his farm in Pittsfield and a garret in New York). Pierre's piazza at Saddle Meadows corresponds to Melville's piazza "on the north side" of Arrowhead looking on Mount Greylock (also known as Saddleback Mountain) "some fifteen miles distant" (*P,* 342). In Pierre's trance, the mountain "presented a long and beautiful, but not entirely inaccessible-looking purple precipice, some two-thousand feet in air" (*P,* 342) replicating Melville's "little embrasure of a window, [near his writing desk]" as he wrote to Evert Duyckinck in 1850, "which commands so noble a view of Saddleback."[46] While the plot of *Pierre* is diverted for many pages with "the act of attempting that book" (*P,* 304), the trance brings disparate scenes of writing into momentary focus.

Pierre's "seizure" not only transports him back to the world of Saddle Meadows; it points to another portal—the origin of *Pierre* itself, the threshold between its invocation and its opening phrases:

To Greylock's Most Excellent Majesty

In old times authors were proud of the privilege of dedicating their works to Majesty. A right noble custom, which we of Berkshire must revive. For whether we will or no, Majesty is all around us here in Berkshire. . . .

But since the majestic mountain, Greylock—my own more immediate sovereign lord and king—hath now . . . been the one grand dedicatee of the earliest rays of all the Berkshire mornings, I know not how his Imperial Purple Majesty (royal-born: Porphyrogenitus) will receive the dedication of my own poor solitary ray.

Nevertheless, forasmuch as I, dwelling with my loyal neighbors . . . in the amphitheater over which his central majesty presides, have received his most bounteous and unstinted fertilizations, it is but meet, that I here devoutly kneel, and render up my gratitude, whether, thereto, The Most Excellent Purple Majesty of Greylock benignantly incline his hoary crown or no.

Pierre Just Emerging From His Teens

There are some strange summer mornings in the country, when he who is but a sojourner from the city shall early walk forth into fields, and be wonder-smitten with the trance-like aspect of the green and golden world. Not a flower stirs; the trees forget to wave; the grass itself seems to have ceased to grow; and all Nature, as if suddenly become conscious of her own profound mystery, and feeling no refuge from it but silence, sinks into this wonderful and indescribable repose. . . . The verdant trance lay far and wide; and through it nothing came but the brindled kine, dreamily wandering to their pastures followed, not driven, by ruddy-cheeked, white-footed boys. As touched and bewitched by the loveliness of this silence Pierre neared the cottage, and lifted his eyes. (*P,* 3)

Melville's world of novelistic inspiration is set beside the trance-world of the novel proper. *Pierre*'s opening, as odd as it is by itself, grows even stranger beside the not-quite-mock-heroic dedication. Together they reveal how Melville has, at the very outset, separated—like yolk and albumen—the main components of Pierre's Enceladus-trance into a quixotic pledge of fealty to Mount Greylock on one hand and an eerie scene of bucolic quiescence on the other. The Enceladus sequence, coming near *Pierre*'s conclusion, belatedly conflates the opening passage's dreamy "verdant trance" with the dedication's indifferent mountainous muse in order to give the opening retrospective meaning. A key to *Pierre*'s enigmatic, latent meanings, Enceladus invites the reader to see the whole novel through the lens of Pierre's exhausted vision. In effect, it asks the reader to reconsider the sly relation between Pierre and his book and Melville and his book heralded by the opening passages.[47]

In Enceladus's shadow, the opening can be reread as an attempt to put the reader in Pierre's position and also within the book's exhausting discourse. The retroflex movement of Pierre's trance from the urban to the rural appears at the outset as the reader's general point of view. "The trance-like aspect of the green and golden world" is displayed from the general point of view of "he who is but a sojourner from the city." The entrance to *Pierre* is literally calculated to en*trance*. We are meant to feel as if we are walking in a bucolic scene inside a paperweight, a paperweight, no doubt, resting on the author's desk. "[A] fine book is a sort of revery to us," Melville wrote at the time of *Pierre*'s composition.[48] Enceladus reorients the opening passage as a site where the reader is invited to enter the author's trance.

Pierre's vision clarifies what it might really mean to dedicate a book to a mountain. Michael Rogin has suggested that Melville's "aim was . . . to underline [the mountain's] inaccessibility."[49] Melville was also interested in how authors, readers, and texts gain access to the seemingly inaccessible. Melville allegorizes the idea that readers, authors, and texts (*Pierre,* finally, is all three) "have carried about with [them] in [their] mind[s] the thorough understanding of the book, and yet not be aware that [they] so understood it" (*P,* 294). The Enceladus-inspired trance represents a privileged moment of access to a knowledge that has been hitherto latent. Thus, the dedication connects the "unstinted fertilizations" of the mountain muse with repressed understanding. The inaccessible mountain is made accessible through nervous *access,* for, as he says, "Whether we will or no, Majesty is all around us."

The mountain represents the forces that constrain (and—ironically—sponsor) authorship, and the neurasthenic trance reveals this relation. By looking towards Mount Greylock, Melville is literally and figuratively looking away from his home and family and, at a further remove, away from New York where his literary fortunes reside. By making the mountain his patron, Melville obliquely names the real sources of patronage that rule his world, the powerful constraints of the literary marketplace. *Pierre* is a novel girded by mountains. From Greylock in the dedication to the Mount of the Titans at the end, the mountain is the site and symbol of profound literary activity and the catalyst of the most extreme literary crisis.

At the beginning of the Enceladus section Melville slips into the second person. "You stood transfixed," he writes as narrative personality dissolves into dread:

> [A] terrific towering palisade of dark mossy massiness confronted you; and trickling with unevaporable moisture, distilled upon you from its beetling brow slow thunder-showers of water-drops, chill as the last dews of death. Now you stood and shivered in that twilight, though it were high noon and burning August down the meads. All round and round, the grim scarred rocks rallied and re-rallied themselves; shot up, protruded, stretched, swelled, and eagerly reached forth; on every side bristlingly radiating with a hideous repellingness. (*P,* 344)

"Dark mossy massiness confronted you," as if Melville were addressing his protagonist, himself, and the reader at once. The second-person refuses to be either the autobiographical *I* or the objective *he.* It embraces an overwhelming sense of the traumatic present—an aura of sheer *presentness,* a disproportionate ontological sense of the here and now. Thus Melville's neologisms of -*ness*—"repellingness" and "massiness"—through their "primitive elementizing of the strange stuff" (*P,* 304) achieve the immediacy of trauma by conflating attributes with categorical forces. First-person and third-person exist in unresolved relation. *Pierre* becomes what Melville has been flirting with from the opening, you (himself) and you (the reader). In this light, Pierre's trance calls into question the autonomy of the novel's world from the world of its author.

The idea that exhaustion disrupts the autonomy of the author gives another indication of how unstable *Pierre* is, but it gives by no means a complete one. Nevertheless, in this essay I have tried to suggest some central ways that *Pierre* makes a kind of "nervous" sense. If critics have read the novel as a parody of the conventional romantic novel, the crisis of agency and autonomy built into the novel suggests a more direct challenge to the autonomy of the romantic author, and the nervous health of the author is a key element in that challenge. *Pierre* is perhaps better considered as a romance written against the idea of romantic authorship. If it is valuable for readers to see through Pierre's fretted wires and share in his "morbid" excitement and exhaustion, then Melville's unruly text may continue to prove a useful and instructive means to further our inquiries into the body of the author as well as his mind. *Pierre*'s challenge to the notion of creative malady certainly deepens our awareness of nineteenth-century assumptions about nerves and literature, challenging literary stereotypes while reinforcing connections between stimulation and debility. Melville's underlying suspicion of romantic nervousness as a mark of artistic autonomy positions **Pierre** to look forward to the neurasthenic world of the Gilded Age and back to the era of Jacksonian health reform. It is worthwhile to consider the challenge to that autonomy that **Pierre** presents. **Pierre** reminds us of the Freudian truism that novelists and imaginative literature are made against terrible resistance, but it also reminds us that novelists and literature are made in the failure of resistance. Finally, **Pierre** reminds us that exhaustion contains the potential for the loss of metaphoric sense, but in sharing in that loss we may come, once more, to our metaphoric senses.

Notes

1. Quoted in Jay Leyda, *The Melville Log: A Documentary Life of Herman Melville 1819-1891,* 2 vols. (New York: Gordian Press, 1969), I:462.

2. Herman Melville, *Pierre, or The Ambiguities* (Evanston, Ill.: Northwestern Univ. Press and The Newberry Library, 1971), 299. All subsequent quotations are from this edition and are cited parenthetically in the text with the abbreviation *P.*

3. George Miller Beard wrote several pamphlets outlining his theories, such as "Neurasthenia, or Nervous Exhaustion," *Boston Medical and Surgical Journal* 80 (1869): 245-59; and *American Nervousness, Its Causes and Consequences* (New York: G. P. Putnam's Sons, 1881). On the history of neurasthenia see Charles Rosenberg, *No Other Gods: On Science and American Social Thought* (Baltimore, Md.: The Johns Hopkins Univ. Press, 1976), 98-108; and F. G. Gosling, *Before Freud: Neurasthenia and the American Medical Community, 1870-1910* (Urbana: Univ. of Illinois Press, 1987). On male hysteria and Charcot see Mark S. Micale, "Diagnostic Discriminations: Jean-Martin Charcot and the Nineteenth-Century Idea of Masculine Hysterical Neurosis" (Ph.D. diss., Yale University, 1987); and Jan Goldstein, "The Uses of Male Hysteria: Medical and Literary Discourse in Nineteenth-Century France," *Representations* 34 (spring 1991): 134-65.

4. Merrell R. Davis and William H. Gilman, *The Letters of Herman Melville* (New Haven, Conn.: Yale Univ. Press, 1960), 150.

5. Henry A. Murray, introduction to Herman Melville, *Pierre, or The Ambiguities,* (New York: Hendricks House, Inc., 1949), xciii.

6. Davis and Gilman, 150.

7. F. O. Matthiessen, *American Renaissance: Art and Expression in the Age of Emerson and Whitman* (New York: Oxford Univ. Press, 1941), 468.

8. For a discussion of symptomatic reading in Melville see Wai-chee Dimock, *Empire for Liberty* (Princeton, N.J.: Princeton Univ. Press, 1989), 174.

9. Patricia Wald, "Hearing Narrative Voices in Melville's *Pierre,*" *boundary 2* 17, no. 1 (Spring 1990): 132 n. 34; and Sacvan Bercovitch, "How to Read Melville's Pierre," *Amerikastudien* 31 (1986): 31-49.

10. Leslie Fiedler, *Love and Death in the American Novel,* rev. (New York: Stein and Day, 1966), 93; Michael Paul Rogin, *Subversive Genealogy: The Politics and Art of Herman Melville* (New York: Alfred A. Knopf, 1983), 160; and Eric J. Sundquist, *Home as Found: Authority and Genealogy in Nineteenth-Century American Literature* (Baltimore, Md.: The Johns Hopkins Univ. Press, 1977), 175.

11. J. R. Pole, "Individualism and Conformity," in Jack P. Greene, ed., *Encyclopedia of American Political History* (New York: Charles Scribner's Sons, 1984), II:623; and Oliver Wendell Holmes, Sr., "The Americanized European," in *Lectures, Memoirs, Prefaces, and Miscellaneous Manuscripts,* Holmes Collection, Houghton Library, Harvard University, 13-75.

12. Henry David Thoreau, *Walden and Resistance to Civil Government* (New York: W. W. Norton, 1992), 220.

13. S. Weir Mitchell, *Doctor and Patient* (Philadelphia, Pa.: J. B. Lippincott, 1887). On Weir Mitchell see Richard Walker, *S. Weir Mitchell, M.D.—Neurologist: A Medical Biography* (Springfield, Ill.: Charles C. Thomas, 1970).

14. Rosenberg, 98.

15. Gosling, 13.

16. On Grahamite reform see Stephen Nissenbaum, *Sex, Diet, and Debility in Jacksonian America: Sylvester Graham and Health Reform* (Westport, Conn.: Greenwood Press, 1980), 143-57. On class and neurasthenia in the closing decades of the nineteenth century see F. G. Gosling and Tom Lutz, *American Nervousness, 1903: An Anecdotal History* (Ithaca, N.Y.: Cornell Univ. Press, 1991).

17. W. S. Gilbert and Arthur Sullivan, "Patience, or Bunthorne's Bride," Act II, in W. S. Gilbert, *The Savoy Operas: The Complete Gilbert and Sullivan Operas Originally Produced in the Years 1875-1896* (1926; rpt. London: Macmillan, 1983), 196.

18. Thomas Trotter, *A View of the Nervous Temperment* (Newcastle: Edward Walker, 1807), 39.

19. Quoted in Raymond Williams, *Culture and Society 1780-1950* (New York: Harper and Row, 1958), 46.

20. Ibid., 166-67.

21. Ibid., 30-48.

22. "Without the poison instilled [by novels] into the blood, females in ordinary life would never have been so much the slaves of vice" (from "Novel Read-

ing, a Cause of Female Depravity," *New England Quarterly* 1 [1802]: 172-74, quoted in Cathy Davidson, *Revolution and the Word: The Rise of the Novel in America* [New York: Oxford Univ. Press, 1986], 38-79, quotation p. 45.)

23. Quoted in Michael Davitt Bell, *The Development of American Romance: The Sacrifice of Relation* (Chicago: Univ. of Chicago Press, 1980), 11.

24. Herman Melville, "Hawthorne and His Mosses," in *The Piazza Tales and Other Prose Pieces 1839-1860* (Evanston, Ill.: Northwestern Univ. Press and Newberry Library, 1987), 249. Subsequent quotations are from this edition and are cited parenthetically in the text with the abbreviation *HHM*.

25. Nissenbaum, 20, 54-56, 67. See also Benjamin Rush, *Medical Inquiries and Observations,* 5 vols. (Philadelphia, Pa.: 1794-1798).

26. See, for example, the nomenclature of diseases used by J. H. Baxter in *Statistics, Medical and Anthropological of the Provost-Marshal-General's Bureau, Derived from the Records of Examination for Military Service in the Armies of the United States During the Late War of Rebellion,* 2 vols. (Washington, D.C.: Government Printing Office, 1875), I:6.

27. George Miller Beard, *American Nervousness: Its Philosophy and Treatment* (Richmond, Va.: J. W. Fergusson and Son, 1879), 6.

28. William Shakespeare, *Sonnet LXXIII.*

29. See "Historical Note" to *Pierre,* 388. See also Hershel Parker, *The Recognition of Herman Melville* (Ann Arbor: Univ. of Michigan Press, 1967), 51-56.

30. "Historical Note" to *Pierre,* 388.

31. Ibid., 384. See also Jonathan Arac, *Commissioned Spirits: The Shaping of Social Motion in Dickens, Carlyle, Melville, and Hawthorne* (New Brunswick, N.J.: Rutgers Univ. Press, 1979), 140-41.

32. Raymond Williams, *Marxism and Literature* (New York: Oxford Univ. Press, 1977), 134.

33. Ibid.

34. Stanley W. Jackson, *Melancholia and Depression: From Hippocratic Times to Modern Times* (New Haven, Conn.: Yale Univ. Press, 1986), 399.

35. Leyda, I:412. Upon Melville's working habits during the writing of *Mardi* his wife commented, "Sat in a room without fire—wrapped up" (I:283).

36. Ibid., I:441. See also Hershel Parker, "Why *Pierre* Went Wrong," *Studies in the Novel* 8 (spring 1976): 9 n. 21.

37. Melville to Evert A. Duyckinck, 26 March 1851, in Davis and Gilman, 123. Melville's eye problems of the early 1850s are well-known to his biographers, but what has been less emphasized is their relative disappearance in later years. Intrigued by this recovery, I consulted a glaucoma specialist, an expert in diseases that lead to the contraction of the visual field, who assured me of the extreme rarity of the reversal of this process in patients whose affliction has an organic basis.

38. Brian Higgins and Hershel Parker, "The Flawed Grandeur of Melville's *Pierre,*" in Myra Jehlen, ed., *Herman Melville: A Collection of Critical Essays* (Englewood Cliffs, N.J.: Prentice-Hall, 1994), 126-38.

39. William Charvat, *Literary Publishing in America, 1790-1850* (Philadelphia: Univ. of Pennsylvania Press, 1959), 36; and Michael T. Gilmore, *American Romaticism and the Marketplace* (Chicago: Univ. of Chicago Press, 1985), 113-45.

40. Melville, *Mardi, and a Voyage Thither* (1849; rpt. New York: Library of America, 1982), 661.

41. Parker, 7-23; and Richard H. Brodhead, *Hawthorne, Melville, and the Novel* (Chicago: Univ. of Chicago Press, 1976), 40.

42. Davis and Gilman, 130.

43. Ibid., 143.

44. Part of this mythic context is, of course, the taboo of incest. Enceladus and Pierre suffer their fates in part because of their incestuous lineage and their inability to remove the tainted alloy of incest from their most noble impulses. While the issue of incest is much broader than the scope of this essay, it is important to bear in mind that Melville's point about incest parallels his sense of the inevitability of the body.

45. Brodhead, 10.

46. Davis and Gilman, 111.

47. Not only does *Pierre* contain a chapter titled "Retrospective" as well as many scenes of retrospection, of intense looking backward, it can be fairly said that Melville was operating in a retrospective mode of writing after *Pierre,* especially in "Benito Cereno," "Bartleby," and *The Confidence-Man.* They are stories that practically compel the reader back to their beginnings, or, as R. W. B. Lewis said of *The Confidence-Man,* it is "more rereadable than readable" ("Afterward to *The Confidence-Man*" [New York: Signet Edition, 1964], 262).

48. Davis and Gilman, 138.

49. Rogin, 156.

Wyn Kelley (essay date 1998)

SOURCE: "*Pierre*'s Domestic Ambiguities," in *The Cambridge Companion to Herman Melville,* edited by Robert S. Levine, Cambridge University Press, 1998, pp. 91-113.

[In the following essay, Kelley suggests that Melville's notion of domesticity based on the brother/sister rather than

husband/wife relationship was too extreme for his middle-class readers, and so contributed to the novel's failure.]

In the spring of 1851, Melville wrote to his Pittsfield neighbor Nathaniel Hawthorne, pretending to review his new novel:

> "The House of the Seven Gables: A Romance. By Nathaniel Hawthorne. One vol. 16mo, pp. 344." . . . This book is like a fine old chamber, abundantly, but still judiciously, furnished. . . . There is old china with rare devices, set out on the carved buffet; there are long and indolent lounges to throw yourself upon; there is an admirable sideboard, plentifully stored with good viands; there is a smell as of old wine in the pantry; and finally, in one corner, there is a dark little black-letter volume in golden clasps, entitled "Hawthorne: A Problem."[1]

This witty letter develops into Melville's famous characterization of Hawthorne as the tragic hero who "says NO! in thunder, but the Devil himself cannot make him say *yes*" (186). Melville's opening, however, lingering as it does over the household images the novel inspired, suggests his acute awareness of Hawthorne's private side. Melville clearly knew and admired the domestic Hawthorne, inhabiting *The House of the Seven Gables* with sensual pleasure, and the letter shows that even as he was writing the ocean-going *Moby-Dick,* he contemplated house and home. In *Pierre: or the Ambiguities* Melville responds to Hawthorne's novel by making his own foray into domestic literature. But rather than uphold middle-class domestic values, as Hawthorne does, Melville offers a different kind of domesticity: one founded not on marriage and family but on the riskier relations of fraternity. In this choice, Melville may well have been influenced by contemporary women's domestic novels, which often envisioned a domestic life based on brother-sister relationships. Unfortunately, his vision of the home as a community inspired by fraternal ideals was too radical for many middle-class readers, and his book failed with that audience.[2]

Melville's letter to Hawthorne suggests that he had given considerable thought to domestic subjects and that he had, indeed, a complex response to Hawthorne's literary house. On the one hand, he seems to revel in its luxurious appointments: the lounges, viands, and wine that make this "fine old chamber" look rather more like a men's club than the little red cottage where Hawthorne lived with his wife Sophia and children Una and Julian. At the same time, with its self-conscious language and exaggerated tone, his letter mocks that luxury, revealing its shadow side. Hawthorne appears not as the gracious host, but as a dark little book entitled "Hawthorne: A Problem." Biographers and critics have long speculated on the "problem" of Hawthorne, or indeed, Melville's problematic relation with him.[3] Melville doesn't elaborate on it here, but his letter goes on to hint at a deeper consideration of Hawthorne's *House.*

He could not take up the domestic subject, though, until he had finished with his whale, saying to Hawthorne, "The tail is not yet cooked" (*Correspondence,* 196). Cooking *Pierre* would send him into new literary terrain—the family, house, and home of a young American aristocrat rather than the working-class decks of American ships—and his choice has puzzled many readers. Why, one might ask, did Melville abandon the subject he knew best and which had garnered him considerable recognition for one that seemed completely unsuited to his sensibility: domestic life, family secrets, and romantic love? "HERMAN MELVILLE CRAZY" might summarize this argument.[4]

Yet Melville knew the contemporary domestic literature well. Much of it contained issues and themes that preoccupied him deeply in the 1850s, and the success of Hawthorne's *House* stimulated him to think of a new audience. More than that, the domestic novel offered an opportunity to probe a theme that runs through much of his nautical fiction, namely, brotherhood. In *Pierre* Melville moves brotherhood from the ship to the home, from a model of comradeship between men to an equally intimate "brotherhood" between man and woman.[5] *Pierre* acts as a brother to the three women in his life: his mother Mary Glendinning, his supposed sister Isabel Banford, and later his fiancée Lucy Tartan. But whereas social convention allows a man to share almost unlimited intimacy with his brothers, closeness with sisters imposes certain constraints. If he is to achieve an ideal relationship with a sister, the brother must either adopt monastic celibacy or live in incest. *Pierre* experiments with both, with ambiguous intentions and results. Either to escape from or to protest against the patriarchal institution of marriage, *Pierre* tries to renovate the middle-class household, to achieve a fraternal communion like the one that nurtured Ishmael in *Moby-Dick.* In this sense, Melville's novel shares the antipatriarchal spirit of much domestic fiction by women writers of the 1850s. Unfortunately, the pressure of gender conventions makes *Pierre*'s quest for radical domesticity doomed. And unlike Hawthorne's *House,* which, after challenging the rules of the patriarchal family, ends by reinscribing them, Melville's *Pierre* rejects marriage, offering a warped utopian alternative. These tensions in his novel create some of the ambiguities so aptly named in its title, ambiguities that continue to perplex its readers.

Melville's choice of domestic settings and themes for *Pierre,* which takes place almost exclusively in the main characters' private homes, is not as strange as it may at first appear. Melville had considerable knowledge of the world of domesticity and of women's novels. Furthermore, he recognized and used many of the themes of domestic fiction in *Pierre,* some, it must be acknowledged, in a parodic way, but others with thought and care.[6]

Melville's knowledge of domestic life and novels began in and was sustained by his own household, which, during the early 1850s, consisted largely of women. His father Allan Melvill had died in 1832, and his older brother Gansevoort died abroad in 1846. He and his brother Allan took a New York house together when both married in 1847, but that arrangement eventually broke down, and

Melville moved his family from New York to the farm Arrowhead near Pittsfield, Massachusetts. By 1850 Melville, then, was the only male in the house besides his infant son. Meanwhile, his wife Elizabeth and his mother Maria, as well as his sisters Helen, Augusta, Catherine, and Fanny, generally kept house with him. Nor does this female-centered household appear to have irked the man who wrote in **Moby-Dick** that "man must eventually lower, or at least shift, his conceit of attainable felicity; not placing it anywhere in the intellect or the fancy; but in the wife, the heart, the bed, the table, the saddle, the fire-side, the country." Melville's letters from Arrowhead show that, on the whole, he took considerable pleasure in rural domestic life, at least in the early years. "My peace and my supper are my reward, my dear Hawthorne," he wrote, and Hawthorne praised Melville's hospitality: "If you were to see how snug and comfortable Melville makes himself and friends, I think you would not fail [to visit]." Letters from Melville's sisters confirm that he participated readily in the family's amusements and picnics, readings in the parlor, sleigh rides, and visits.[7]

Although it is not hard to reconstruct Melville's domestic life at Arrowhead, finding evidence of his reading or knowledge of what have been called the "literary domestics"—women who wrote family romances or domestic or sentimental novels—is more difficult. We do know, from a reference in **Redburn,** that Melville was familiar with Susanna Rowson's *Charlotte Temple,* one of the period's most sensational and popular stories of a woman's seduction and betrayal, Catharine Maria Sedgwick, a prolific writer of such novels as *Hope Leslie* and *The Linwoods* (which Helen Melville urged her sister Augusta to read), was a close neighbor of the Arrowhead Melvilles and a family friend. Augusta and Helen both read widely, mentioning Dickens and Thackeray in their letters, reading *Jane Eyre* as soon as it appeared in an American edition, but also reading the popular female authors published in the magazines they avidly consumed. Melville exchanged books and ideas with several women who loved to read, most notably Anne Lynch, who held lively literary soirees in New York, Sophia Hawthorne, who read **Moby-Dick** with singular appreciation, and Sarah Morewood, who sent him Harriet Martineau's *The Hour and the Man.* Nearly every day, Melville drove to Pittsfield for the mail, newspapers, and magazines, which he would bring home for family reading in the evenings. There is no direct evidence of the family reading Harriet Beecher Stowe's *Uncle Tom's Cabin,* Susan Warner's *The Wide, Wide World* and *Queechy,* Caroline Chesebro's *Isa,* or Alice Cary's *Hagar,* to name just a few of the popular women's novels published within two years of **Pierre.** But it is hard to believe that Melville and his family did not participate in the "parlor culture" of the day—the family circle reading aloud from current books and magazines.[8]

Whatever Melville may have thought of the popular women novelists, in some ways he had more in common with them socially than he did with respected male writers like Washington Irving, Hawthorne, Nathaniel Parker Wil-lis, or Longfellow. Many of the literary domestics, like their male counterparts, came from elite American families. But unlike college-educated male writers, female authors were often self-taught or did not advance beyond the typical schooling for women. Melville too, because of his family's reverses and his father's death, missed having a college education. Furthermore, the female writers tended to write out of financial necessity, often to supplement a failing husband's income, rather than because they had trained themselves for an authorial career. Melville too turned to writing out of necessity, preferring not to follow the men of his family into law, business, or politics. Many women writers, laboring under the disadvantages of economic hardship and lacking professional credentials, began their careers as "Anonymous." For **Pierre,** Melville also considered publishing the book anonymously or under the pseudonym Guy Winthrop, as if aware that this new subject matter required of him a new identity. When Melville promised Sophia Hawthorne that his new book would be a "rural bowl of milk" (**Correspondence,** 219) and informed his publisher Richard Bentley that it would have "unquestionable novelty . . . treating of utterly new scenes & characters . . . very much more calculated for popularity than anything you have yet published of mine" (**Correspondence,** 226), he may have meant only that **Pierre** concerns "home-born" characters from the countryside.[9] Clearly, however, the book has more in common with popular women's fiction than either of these two disingenuous comments would imply.

Pierre includes many of the themes that feminist scholars have identified with women's novels at midcentury. First, and most obviously, house and home are significant domains in the book. Scenes in **Pierre** take place in the Glendinning mansion's bedroom, dining room, and private closet; Lucy's aunt's cottage; Mrs. Tartan's drawing room; the Miss Pennies' sewing circle; Walter Ulver's farmhouse; Glen Stanly's bachelor apartment; and Pierre's meager dwelling at the Apostles Church in New York. Significantly too, the few outdoor scenes are often domesticated. For example, Pierre and Lucy's journey up the mountainside takes place inside the coach, and Lucy doesn't like heights. Furthermore, these domestic settings do not appear accidental or as mere backdrops but have considerable meaning in the way they encode class and character. The Glendinning house embodies the family's pride of place; Isabel's bleak home her poor, friendless condition; Lucy's cottage her middle-class domestic purity; and the Apostles' tenement Pierre's revolt against the expectations of marriage.

In its portrayal of women, **Pierre** also draws on popular stereotypes from women's fiction, such as the domestic angel, the dark temptress, the busybody, the proud matriarch, the abandoned woman, and even, briefly, the prostitute. Both Lucy and Isabel exhibit the independence and self-sufficiency of many spirited heroines, even as they subordinate themselves eventually to Pierre, in a pattern characteristic of nineteenth-century women's novels.[10] Furthermore, Pierre shares many of the traits of female protagonists. His mother worries about his "sweet docility": "Now I almost wish him otherwise than sweet and docile to me, seeing that it must be hard for man to be an un-compromising hero and a commander among his race, and yet never ruffle any domestic brow" (20). His heroism consists in his not assuming or displacing his father's po-sition in the household but rather in sacrificing his own identity and wishes to his mother's social status and Isa-bel's needs. For this sacrifice, Lucy later in the novel calls him an angel, the name usually reserved for self-negating women.[11]

Although reviewers of **Pierre** seemed appalled at the book's treatment of incest, women's fiction frequently ex-plored subliminal incestuous relationships.[12] Implied in-cest, in fact, might be seen as a primary form of socializa-tion for women, as in many women's novels heroines learn from fathers and brothers how to submit to male au-thority through love. In Susan Warner's *The Wide, Wide World* and *Queechy,* for example, Ellen and Fleda marry their "brothers," the men who have brought them up when their own parents failed them. Ellen lives for a long time in her "brother's" household, learning to tame her rebel-lious spirit, educate her mind, and adapt to a religious do-mestic ideology. Pierre's later household arrangement dif-fers from Ellen's most notably by combining marriage and brotherhood at once, whereas for Ellen, John is first a brother and then a husband.

Clearly, **Pierre** in many ways differs markedly from wom-en's novels of the period. **Pierre**'s women do not have the autonomy or credibility of many popular domestic hero-ines. The book parodies the culture's idealization of do-mesticity. Yet at the same time, it engages and takes in quite startling directions some of the women's novels' challenges to patriarchal notions of marriage, family, and the home. The question for many of **Pierre**'s readers is, why? What was Melville trying to do in his rewriting of the romantic and domestic plots?[13]

Many of **Pierre**'s readers have assumed that the novel, like women's domestic novels, has a "cover story," that it works out sensitive personal issues or presses an urgent social agenda under a socially acceptable guise.[14] A num-ber of critics have approached **Pierre** looking for an auto-biographical subtext—about Melville's family, his sexual-ity, or his relation to the literary market—for which **Pierre**'s story provides the cover. According to this argu-ment, the biographical tensions in the novel, the secrets Melville is trying to keep, help explain the book's many ambiguities.

The theory of a family plot is now well known. On the ba-sis of a letter from Melville's uncle Thomas Melvill to Herman's future father-in-law Lemuel Shaw, scholars have speculated on the possibility of there being a real Isabel in the Melville family. The letter is frustratingly elusive, de-scribing a visit by a woman and her daughter who came to claim money after the death of Herman's father, Allan Melvill. Whether the young woman was Allan's illegiti-

mate daughter or not, whether the women blackmailed Thomas Melvill or simply came with a milliner's bill, is impossible to ascertain. **Pierre** remains, however, for many readers Melville's most autobiographical novel. The bio-graphical parallels are certainly numerous, and if accurate, they suggest that **Pierre** is only a very thin cover for Melville's rage at his own family.[15]

A thicker cover might be required for another private plot, the sexual one. Edwin Haviland Miller and Newton Arvin have explored the emotional and sexual dimensions of Melville's friendship with Hawthorne as it may have col-ored the ambiguous sexuality of **Pierre.** But James Creech has been most straightforward in arguing that **Pierre** is a gay novel in which a heterosexual love story covers the hero's love for a man. In an incestuous twist, however, the real object of fascination is not a lover but the father, al-though Isabel, as the "father's flesh," provides a female cover for homoerotic passion. Melville, according to Creech, uses the portrait of his father to "wink" at the reader, showing that a hidden, subversive truth always lurks beneath the sanctioned surface. The incest in **Pierre** may be a way for Melville to deflect attention from his true concerns in the novel.[16]

Finally, the story has appeared to many readers a thin cover for Melville's attack on his publishers, editors, and audience. The book may have *begun* as a love story with a twist, but somewhere along the way—probably at about the time Melville began getting the first negative reviews of **Moby-Dick**—Melville turned Pierre into a heroic frus-trated writer, slaving away at a book that was bound to fail. Family, incest, love, women, dropped out of sight as Melville mounted his assault on meretricious editors, crit-ics, and reviewers.[17] Again the domestic plot conceals and at the same time helps to reveal a biographical imperative.

Another possibility, however, is that in **Pierre** Melville was rewriting Hawthorne's *House*; his story, then, is a cover for his reading of and relationship with Hawthorne, which was not only emotional but also literary.[18] Locating the story in the domestic sphere, as Hawthorne did in *House,* allowed Melville to focus on themes of intimacy that may have covertly alluded to his feelings for Haw-thorne. At the same time, he departed from Hawthorne's domestic politics, especially on the subject of marriage. In **Pierre,** then, Melville announced his own position, and his dissatisfaction with Hawthorne's, on the domestic novel and its readers.

Melville's **"Hawthorne and His Mosses"** and his letters to Hawthorne exhibit worshipful devotion, which many scholars have read as explicitly sexual and personal. When Melville says that "Hawthorne has dropped germinous seeds into my soul . . . and further, and further, shoots his strong New-England roots into the hot soil of my Southern soul," it is hard to miss the erotic overtones.[19] And how else are we to read a letter like this one?

> . . . I can't write what I felt. But I felt pantheistic then
> . . . your heart beat in my ribs and mine in yours, and

both in God's. A sense of unspeakable security is in me this moment, on account of your having understood the book. . . .

Whence come you, Hawthorne? By what right do you drink from my flagon of life? And when I put it to my lips—lo, they are yours and not mine. . . .

(*Correspondence,* 212-13)

Although many of the surviving letters to Hawthorne are not this sexual in their imagery, they almost all contain some personal appeal for intimacy.

But we must also remember that Hawthorne was a literary celebrity, and that nearly all the erotic language surrounds the subjects of reading and writing. Hawthorne's germinous seeds are his stories in *Mosses from an Old Manse.* Melville feels their hearts beating together when Hawthorne has read and admired **Moby-Dick.** When he touches his lips to the flagon of life and finds Hawthorne's lips there, he's trying to describe the wonder he feels at being understood. He thanks Hawthorne for having "hugged the ugly Socrates" (**Correspondence,** 213), an embrace of Melville's ideas as much as of his body. As in somewhat similar pantheistic passages in Whitman's *Song of Myself,* sexual ecstasy serves as the gateway to the spirit, sexual union as a metaphor for the merging of body and soul.[20]

I am not trying to deny that Melville had erotic feelings about Hawthorne. But whatever feelings he had existed in the context of, or alongside, an intense meeting of the minds that Melville experienced as the ecstasy of reading and being read. What better way to show his gratitude to Hawthorne than, in his next book, to show that he had read *The House of the Seven Gables* as Hawthorne had read **Moby-Dick**?

As Melville began to write his own domestic romance, he would have found Hawthorne's novel inspiring and provocative on many fronts. Rereading Hawthorne's book, he would have realized that *House* consciously attempted to work with materials that the "scribbling women" had made their own: the "true woman" or domestic angel, the separation of gender spheres, and the redemption of the male sphere by domesticity. But in several instances, Hawthorne remodeled conventions of the domestic novel for his own use. The most striking of these, in terms of Melville's handling of domesticity in **Pierre,** is the way Hawthorne locates both masculine and feminine spheres on the same site.

Many midcentury female novelists portray the home as the separate domain of women, a place where men are domesticated and the forces of capitalism and patriarchy held at bay. In Stowe's *Uncle Tom's Cabin,* Mr. Bird cannot rule his household the way he can the Congress; in Rachel Halliday's kitchen, men have a place but only under her benevolent sway. The House of the Seven Gables, however, is not a protected, sanctified home. Though presided over by a woman, Hepzibah Pyncheon, it lacks domestic warmth and cheer. Because Hepzibah is a "lady," she does

not perform the domestic labor that would make her house a home. But more problematically, the house cannot be a home because it lives under the curse of male Pyncheons who have stifled female and domestic influence.

Only when Phoebe, the country cousin, arrives can the house be redeemed, for she is a "true woman," whereas Hepzibah is a "lady."[21] Phoebe brings the old house back to life, restoring its kitchen, garden, and chambers with her busy, "cheerful" presence, her "homely witchcraft" (72). Although she succeeds partially with Hepzibah, Phoebe makes her greatest impact on the household's men. Clifford, whose soul is described as a "dark and ruinous mansion," learns to "kindle the heart's household-fire" (105) under her care. For "Phoebe's presence made a home about her—that very sphere which the outcast, the prisoner, the potentate, the wretch beneath mankind, the wretch aside from it, or the wretch above it, instinctively pines after—a home!" (141).

Phoebe also has a powerful effect on Holgrave, the mysterious daguerreotypist dwelling in the house. "Homeless . . . he had been—continually changing his whereabout, and therefore responsible neither to public opinion nor to individuals" (177). Phoebe gradually makes a home for this homeless man, who, as Pierre will be, is an enthusiast, a radical, and a philosopher. Holgrave would seem to be the antithesis of domesticity. Yet when he declares his love to Phoebe, he promises "to set out trees, to make fences—perhaps, even, in due time, to build a house for another generation" (307). At the end of the novel, she professes amazement at his zeal for making improvements in their new home.

Phoebe's homely influence, then, domesticates the House of the Seven Gables, overturning the patriarchal power of those who built the house, and especially of the murderous Jaffrey Pyncheon, who wants to keep it a great dynastic house and not a family home. In the end, Hawthorne asserts the power of home and of female domestic influence.

Men, however, remain at the center and ultimately in control of this home. As T. Walter Herbert has pointed out, Holgrave gets Phoebe's house with her hand and quietly, without fanfare, restores his own family's claim to the land.[22] Instead of providing a female-centered sphere opposed to or in retreat from the world, the Pyncheon house remains open to outside influence. Rather than separating the gender spheres, Hawthorne shows them meeting and competing within the same structure. The house is a site where masculine, dynastic house and feminine, domestic home work out their ideological struggle on the same ground. Melville uses a similar structure in **Pierre,** but with strikingly different results. Pierre resolves the conflict between patriarchal house and maternal home by leaving both behind.

In his first appearance, Pierre emerges from "the embowered and high-gabled old home of his fathers" (3), a house as ancient, patriarchal, and burdened with family secrets as

Hawthorne's. Pierre lives in domestic bliss with a much-cherished mother, their life a "softened spell which still wheeled the mother and son in one orbit of joy" (16). But as in Hawthorne's House of Pyncheon, a curse hangs over the House of Glendinning. The intervention of Isabel reveals that in house and home, Pierre has "habituated his voice and manner to a certain fictitiousness in one of the closest domestic relations of life" (177), and he sets out for New York to correct that error. Melville's treatment of domestic life eventually works to shatter middle-class norms of marriage and home.

Pierre is presented first as the heir of an honorable house. From his father, he has inherited the name that he is the last family member to bear. Should he marry as his mother wishes, he would also receive a fine estate surrounded by a landscape that with "all its hills and swales seemed as sanctified through their [the Glendinnings'] very long uninterrupted possession" (8).[23] As in Hawthorne's House of Pyncheon, with its ancestral portrait, desk, and chair, signs of patriarchal sway appear everywhere in Melville's House of Glendinning: the General's military paraphernalia, the oversized coach and pampered horses, and finally, the dignified portraits of Pierre's parents. Pierre's house, however, is managed by a more vital female presence than Hawthorne's. Whereas Hepzibah seems undone by the task of preparing breakfast for her brother, Mary Glendinning presides over an abundant table loaded with delicacies; and she never does so "in any dishabille that was not eminently becoming" (15). Although Mary, like Hepzibah, proudly upholds her family's patriarchal legacy, she also sheds a potent feminine influence over her house and son.

But does she make the House of Glendinning a home? Pierre thinks so: "it [his life with his mother] seemed almost to realize here below the sweet dreams of those religious enthusiasts, who paint to us a Paradise to come, when etherealized from all drosses and stains, the holiest passion of man shall unite all kindreds and climes in one circle of pure and unimpairable delight" (16). Mary Glendinning works as hard as any domestic angel to create that delight. Her greatest efforts go into raising Pierre as a gentleman, a Christian, and a conscientious lord of his tenants. To that end, she showers him with "maternal tuitions" (16) about how to behave: "Never rave, Pierre; and never rant. Your father never did either . . ." (19). She measures her success in Pierre's filial devotion: "For thus sweetly and religiously was the familiarity of his affections bottomed on the profoundest filial respect" (14). As in the domestic novels, Pierre and his mother sustain a private cult, founded on worship of the absent father, love for the "lovely, immaculate" (88) mother, and obedience in the "fine, proud, loving, docile, vigorous boy" (20).

Pierre's mother's domesticity supports his father's ancestral legacy by helping to nurture the next Glendinning hero. This domesticity is her feminine legacy to Pierre and, by extension, Lucy Tartan, for Lucy participates wholly in the Glendinning vision of an elegant home. Melville shows both the Glendinning mansion and Lucy's cottage as shrines to religious domesticity, the women as saints and angels, and Pierre as the Christian knight sworn in fealty to domestic goddesses. "Truly, thought the youth, [looking at Lucy] with a still gaze of inexpressible fondness; truly the skies do ope, and this invoking angel looks down" (4). Melville draws the link between mother and beloved by showing Pierre in their bedchambers; in these zones of intimacy, Pierre behaves with total reverence. Greeting his mother in her boudoir, he helps her dress for breakfast, calling himself "First Lady in waiting to the Dowager Duchess Glendinning" (14). Placing a ribbon around her neck, he kisses it, fastens a cameo, attends to her hair, and bends to tie her slipper before escorting her down to breakfast.

Lucy's domestic influence over Pierre promises to be every bit as potent as his mother's. He seems especially overcome by her bedchamber, pausing outside the door to entertain "feelings of a wonderful reverentialness. The carpet seemed as holy ground. Every chair seemed sanctified by some departed saint" (39). The room appears to him a "secret inner shrine" to Lucy and to love. And her bed seems the altar in that shrine:

> So he advanced, and with a fond and gentle joyfulness, his eye now fell upon the spotless bed itself, and fastened on a snow-white roll that lay beside the pillow. Now he started; Lucy seemed coming in upon him; but no—'tis only the foot of one of her little slippers, just peeping into view from under the narrow nether curtains of the bed. Then again his glance fixed itself upon the slender, snow-white ruffled roll; and he stood as one enchanted. (39)

Lucy's bedding elicits the same kind of fervent response as Mary Glendinning's deshabille, a response at once erotic and devotional.[24] But the eroticism is fetishized, located in ribbons, slippers, and ruffles. Toward the real women, Pierre acts with the childlike respect that the domestic cult requires.

Pierre has inherited a powerful legacy from both parents: from his male progenitors a great house and from his mother a sanctified home. To these legacies, Melville adds another: the dark stain of incest. This incest, it appears, is a necessary element of the family's house and home and has been established as a family pattern even before the advent of Isabel.

The family pattern of incest seems most obvious, of course, in the domestic fiction binding Pierre and his mother: "In the playfulness of their unclouded love, and with that strange license which a perfect confidence and mutual understanding at all points, had long bred between them, they were wont to call each other brother and sister" (5). The "strange license" of this relationship invades his later bond with his supposed sister; he admits that the "fictitiousness" (177) of his connection with his mother makes possible the incestuous union with Isabel. But other, more subtle forms of incest appear in the novel, more like what Hawthorne hints at in *House*. Pierre's Aunt Dorothea's worship of her departed brother, Pierre's father, resembles the unrequited devotion that Hepzibah feels for Clifford. Dorothea and the elder Pierre are singularly close. Like Hepzibah, she lavishes ritual attention on his miniature portrait: "before a gold-framed and gold-lidded ivory miniature,—a fraternal gift—aunt Dorothea now offered up her morning and her evening rites, to the memory of the noblest and handsomest of brothers" (73). Unlike Mary Glendinning, Dorothea cherishes the chair portrait, the picture of her brother in his "bladish" (73), erotic, wooing mood. "How much comfort that portrait has been to me" (77), she tells Pierre, claiming that she sees her brother "looking at me, and smiling at me, and nodding at me, and saying—Dorothea! Dorothea!" (79). Like the love of Hepzibah for Clifford, or of Clifford for Phoebe, this one is outwardly chaste, but it takes the form of religious devotion which supersedes all other affections.

The elder Pierre also inspires devotion and love in his cousin Ralph Winwood, the painter of the chair portrait. Ralph seduces his cousin with questions about the beautiful French emigrée in order to make him sit for a painting; the men's shared confidence and intimacy produce the only truthful portrait of Pierre's father. Melville does not make as much of this cousinly attachment as he does of the one between Pierre and his cousin Glen Stanly, which "transcends the bounds of mere boyishness, and revels for a while in the empyrean of a love which only comes short, by one degree, of the sweetest sentiment entertained between the sexes" (216). But the elder Pierre shares greater intimacy with Winwood and his sister Dorothea than he ever does with his wife, a pattern that may influence Pierre's decision to look for his closest bonds within the family rather than outside it.

House and home are not at odds in the early chapters of **Pierre** because the spheres of masculine dominance and feminine influence support the same class interests. A family religion sets the terms for domestic life, which is experienced as a tacit worship of the feminine and the home. But reverence for the family produces "a certain fictitiousness in . . . the closest domestic relations" (177), a fictitiousness that conceals fetishism and incest. It also obliterates any natural sexuality, for Mary Glendinning worships her official husband, not the wooing, erotic husband. And Pierre, contemplating his future wife, wonders, "*I* to wed this heavenly fleece? Methinks one husbandly embrace would break her airy zone" (58). Suddenly aware of the dangers of the cult of domestic purity, Pierre thinks, "I am Pluto stealing Proserpine; and every accepted lover is" (59). Pierre has only just seen Isabel's face, but it has exposed to him the hypocrisy of the family domestic fiction.

Isabel's domesticity differs radically from that of the Glendinnings and Tartans. Pierre lives in a mansion and Lucy in a cottage covered with honeysuckle and roses. Isabel dwells in a "small and low red farm-house" (110) with gables at either end, covered with moss and vines.[25] Mrs. Glendinning presides over her table or boudoir and manages her servants and tenants. Lucy works at her paint-

ing and drawing. But Isabel makes butter and cheese, sews, bakes bread, and draws water. Like Phoebe, Isabel is well versed in the domestic arts, and like her as well, she presents a social challenge to the great family in the old house. In going to her, Pierre leaves "the brilliant chandeliers of the mansion of Saddle Meadows, to join company with the wretched rushlights of poverty and woe" (111). Not only does she come from a different social class, but also she seems a real bodily presence. Whereas to enter Lucy's bedroom or to embrace her airy zone seems to him an act of Plutonic rape ("I am Pluto stealing Proserpine" [59]), Pierre unhesitatingly enters Isabel's dark room, takes her labor-hardened hand, and kisses her. Though in no way as cheerful and lightsome as Phoebe, Isabel has a similar effect in getting the aristocratic Pierre, like Clifford, to emerge from his ancestral house and escape the confinements of his class.

Although psychically and socially homeless, Isabel also teaches Pierre what a real home ought to be. Speaking for her in their final meeting before leaving for New York, he tells her, "thou wantest not the openness [of acknowledgment]; for thou dost not pine for empty nominalness, but for vital realness; what thou wantest, is not the occasional openness of my brotherly love; but its continual domestic confidence" (192). Without necessarily foreseeing how he will make a home for Isabel, Pierre nevertheless knows that his previous domesticity, his fetishistic relations with his mother and Lucy, were false. Now houseless and homeless, Pierre staggers over the threshold of the mansion: "He seemed as jeeringly hurled from beneath his own ancestral roof" (185). Pierre flees the domestic religion of his ancestors, choosing Isabel's radical, vital domesticness instead.

Up to this point in the novel, Melville adheres to an anti-patriarchal plot that shows some similarities to Hawthorne's. When Pierre leaves for New York, however, moving his family from country to city, Melville leaves Hawthorne and the world of middle-class house and home far behind. Instead Pierre commits himself to radical utopian brotherhood.

In his letter on *House,* Melville described his sense of kinship with Hawthorne: "I feel that the Godhead is broken up like the bread at the Supper, and that we are the pieces. Hence this infinite fraternity of feeling" (**Correspondence,** 212). Melville expresses the "fraternity" that he felt for Hawthorne as a spiritual union, a sacred and ideal brotherhood that resembles in some ways Ishmael's sense of divine fraternity with his shipmates: "Oh! my dear fellow beings, why should we longer cherish any social acerbities, or know the slightest ill-humor or envy! Come, let us squeeze hands all round" (416). Robert K. Martin has shown how the ethic of fraternity works to create solidarity among the *Pequod*'s crew and to resist the ship's oppressive hierarchy. Pierre similarly tries to oppose the family hierarchy by creating a spiritual fraternity that will obliterate the traditional power relations of marriage. Ironically, and perhaps not accidentally, Hawthorne was to explore the same possibilities in *The Blithedale Romance,* written at the same time as *Pierre.* Hawthorne's utopian community at Blithedale tries to base relations between the sexes on brotherhood and sisterhood. Both Hawthorne and Melville had observed a similar enterprise when they visited the Shaker community at Hancock Village in the summer of 1851.[26] After Melville's first visit to the Shakers, he bought one of their books and marked this passage: "Now let any candid person examine the causes by which associations [i.e., marriages] . . . so often fail, and he will find that it arises from the partial and selfish relations of husbands, wives and children, and other kindred relations, together with the jealousies and evil surmises naturally arising therefrom" (*Log,* 381). Melville welcomed the cultural currents challenging traditional domesticity. Brotherhood seemed preferable to the "partial and selfish" relations of marriage.

As Hawthorne shows in *The Blithedale Romance,* he may have shared some of Melville's views on marriage, but ultimately he rejected them. Erotic tensions between the Blithedale brethren and sisters destroy their community. And although marriage in this novel is nowhere near as successful or traditional as it appears in *House*—Zenobia dies seemingly out of frustrated love, Coverdale chooses a single life, and Priscilla and Hollingsworth are locked in a regressive and guilt-ridden interdependency—the fraternal experiment nevertheless fails, leaving marriage as the only alternative. Pierre, however, commits himself passionately to the fraternal ideal, joining Isabel and later Lucy in a tiny utopian community at the Apostles. As in *Blithedale,* the community fails, but in Melville's novel marriage does not take its place. Instead Pierre creates a monastic domestic sphere, a cell that replaces the house and home he had earlier revered.

Melville's choice of the city for this experiment is not accidental. Much contemporary urban fiction questioned whether a family culture nurtured in the country could survive in the city. Novelists George Lippard (*New York: Its Upper Ten and Lower Million,* 1850), E. Z. C. Judson (*The Mysteries and Miseries of New York,* 1848), Fanny Fern (*Ruth Hall,* 1855), and Walt Whitman (*Franklin Evans,* 1842) and journalists like Lydia Maria Child (*Letters from New York,* 1844) and George Foster (*New York by Gas-Light,* 1850) showed the struggles of middle- or working-class protagonists to maintain their virtue and protect their homes in the face of urban pressures.[27] Like many of these protagonists, Pierre and Isabel flee the country hoping to find new lives in the city. But New York, as Pierre bitterly says, is a place where "[m]ilk dropt from the milkman's can in December, freezes not more quickly on those stones, than does snow-white innocence, if in poverty, it chance to fall in these streets" (230). The realities of life in a city rapidly expanding in size and population, diversifying both socially and economically, and boldly displaying the widening gulf between the classes give Pierre's gloomy statement some basis in historical fact. But Melville also draws on urban literature describing the evils of the city—poverty, prostitution, drunken-

ness, and ruin—to highlight the dangers of Pierre's first foray into independent homemaking. Clearly, the conventional middle-class notions of domesticity with which Pierre was raised will prove insufficient to the economic and social challenges of New York.

Nowhere does that problem appear more obvious than in Pierre's attempts to house himself and Isabel in the city. When Pierre first announces his engagement to Lucy, his cousin Glen offers him the use of his "very charming, little old house . . . which . . . possessed great attractions for the retired billings and cooings of a honeymoon" (220). Dubbing his house the "Cooery," Glen goes on to describe how he will have it prepared for the young couple:

> . . . the venerable, grotesque, old mahoganies, and marbles, and mirror-frames, and moldings could be very soon dusted and burnished; the kitchen was amply provided with the necessary utensils for cooking; the strong box of old silver immemorially pertaining to the mansion, could be readily carted round from the vaults of the neighboring Bank; while the hampers of old china, still retained in the house, needed but little trouble to unpack; so that silver and china would soon stand assorted in their appropriate closets. . . .
>
> (121)

Glen's letter emphasizes the hard labor involved in starting up the lumbering engines of Victorian domesticity. The house filled with ancestral silver, furniture, and china weighs as heavily on its descendants as the Glendinning family history and name. In Pierre's first response, he merely thanks Glen for his trouble and reminds him to stock up on wine and coffee. After his decision to "marry" Isabel, however, Pierre writes in a different tone, thanking Glen for the offer of the house but adding that "the pre-engaged servants, and the old china, and the old silver, and the old wines, and the Mochas, were now become altogether unnecessary" (228). Pierre can no longer afford such expensive domesticity, but more than that, he now recognizes that his projected home with Lucy, the Cooery, like Saddle Meadows, is another domestic fiction that Isabel's presence has exploded. Knowing that his marriage to her is an ingenious sham, Pierre boldly refuses to adopt the trappings of middle-class domesticity.

Instead, Pierre, Isabel, and Delly settle in a tenement, the renovated church known as the Apostles. Melville details their domesticity there as fully as he does in the Saddle Meadows section, and with a similar intent: to expose the middle-class worship of house and home, this time through a dramatic contrast. At Saddle Meadows, Pierre's being Master Pierre Glendinning of the great house made him a young lord of the manor and a hero. At the Apostles, the houseless Pierre is suddenly free of that "loathed identity" (171) and can enter into a new kind of home. Tenement housing signifies the change in his social status, as he no longer owns his domestic space but rents it and shares it with "scores of those miscellaneous, bread-and-cheese adventurers, and ambiguously professional nondescripts" (267). Instead of a time-honored family mansion, he occupies a former church carved up into flats by speculators. Instead of the privacy of his bedroom and closet, he shares three small rooms with Isabel and Delly, and from his window he can see other tenants gazing back at him. Rather than separating his living space from the space of labor, he writes his novel in his bedroom, and Isabel and Delly perform their sewing and other chores on the other side of the wall. Stripped of comforts, furniture, even heat, Pierre's flat represents the polar opposite of his former luxurious home.

At the same time, it offers a freedom he previously lacked. The creative use of space at the Apostles, the motley assortment of "artists of various sorts; painters, or sculptors, or indigent students, or teachers of languages, or poets, or fugitive French politicians, or German philosophers" (267), the transitional flow of life make for a lively culture that has created its own identity. The old church retains its "romantic and lofty" (268) ambiance, which exerts a unifying influence over the tenants: "the occupants of the venerable church began to come together out of their various dens, in more social communion. . . . By-and-by . . . they . . . became organized in a peculiar society" (269). Although only nebulously defined, this community provides a loose brotherhood of like-minded souls, many like Holgrave and his friends, radicals of one kind or another. Melville's narrator mocks their transcendentalism that feasts on Graham crackers and water, presided over by the faintly ghoulish guru, Plotinus Plinlimmon. But at least Pierre has found a community congenial to his newly conceived revolt against house and home.

In this environment of spiritual fraternity and philosophical radicalism, Pierre turns to his newfound metier, writing. Whereas in the Cooery, as Lucy's husband, Pierre would have performed no labor more arduous than that of grinding coffee, the grim domesticity of the Apostles nurtures Pierre's higher calling as a writer of metaphysical fiction. As at Hawthorne's Blithedale, Pierre and his small community must live simply in order to produce finer thoughts—or, in the case of Isabel and Lucy, finer music and art. His revolt against marriage finds a congenial home at the Apostles, and at the same time this revisionist domesticity proves necessary to his art.

Furthermore, in a domesticity based on fraternity rather than marriage, Pierre hopes to formulate a response to the philosophical challenge he encountered in Plotinus Plinlimmon's tract, "Chronometricals and Horologicals." This puzzling essay addresses Pierre's metaphysical condition by proposing two mutually opposed yet coexisting standards of behavior: the chronometrical, or God-given, truth and the horological, or worldly, necessity. Plinlimmon advises mortals not to fret if they can't achieve chronometrical perfection. In fact, to do so would be to upset the whole human order: "in things terrestrial (horological) a man must not be governed by ideas celestial (chronometrical). . . . A virtuous expediency, then, seems the highest earthly excellence for the mass of men" (214). By surrendering the chronometrical ideal, humans will

thrive, according to Plinlimmon: "there would be an end to that fatal despair of becoming all good" (215).

Plinlimmon's ethic of "virtuous expediency" subverts Pierre on two fronts. The first is moral and philosophical, as Pierre begins to doubt his actions and to feel he may have chosen unwisely to defend Isabel's honor and to write a metaphysical novel. Feeling Plinlimmon's face gazing on him through the tenement window, he imagines it mocking his idealistic endeavors: "Vain! Fool! Quit!" (293). But on the domestic front as well, Plinlimmon challenges Pierre's enterprise, which, under his cynical scrutiny, comes to seem more horological than chronometrical in its aims: for "[w]hat was most terrible was the idea that by some magical means or other the face had got hold of his secret. 'Ay,' shuddered Pierre, 'the face knows that Isabel is not my wife!'" (293). Plinlimmon the voyeur sees into Pierre's unorthodox household, and although Pierre puts muslin over the window, he can't banish the all-seeing face from his mind. Pierre's distress over the pamphlet suggests, then, that just as his writing is intimately connected to his domestic life, his metaphysical doubts grow out of and return to his household secrets.

The sections of *Pierre* devoted to his writing likewise show a continuity between his literary and his domestic experiments. At Saddle Meadows, as a "highly respectable youth" (245), Pierre produced genteel poetry that was, in one critic's words, "'blameless in morals, and harmless throughout.' Another [critic], had unhesitatingly recommended his effusions to the family-circle" (246). Melville ironically condemns the parlor culture that produces such amiable young men and sustains itself by nurturing their literary effusions. When reflecting on his female admirers, all urgently requesting his autograph, Pierre thinks of the danger of this domestic culture, where "the true charm of agreeable parlor society is, that there you lose your own sharp individuality and become delightfully merged in that soft social Pantheism, as it were, that rosy melting of all into one, ever prevailing in those drawing rooms" (250). In the rosy drawing room, what can one expect to write but "that delightful love-sonnet, entitled 'The Tropical Summer'" (245)?

In the brotherhood of the Apostles, however, and in his new domestic sphere, Pierre is inspired to write a very different kind of work, an attempt to "show them deeper secrets than the Apocalypse!" (273). In this endeavor, Pierre aims not only to bring a "miserably neglected Truth to the world" (283), but also to sustain his new household. Rather than the decorative domesticity of Saddle Meadows, he expects to support "the hundred and one domestic details of how their internal arrangements were finally put into steady working order" (282). This domestic life includes Delly's therapeutic labor and companionship with Isabel, Isabel's partnership as muse and copyist in Pierre's writing, and the women's democratic sisterhood with Charlie Millthorpe's hard-working mother and sisters. In this setting of shared labor and high ideals, Pierre hopes to reform the patriarchal household and to nurture literature, philosophy, music, and art. Pierre as writer sees himself as traveling in the "orbit of his book" like an "old housewife [who] goes her daily domestic round" (298). Pierre imagines that his new domesticity will support his writing and his writing a reformed housewifery.

Melville uses the imagery of religious worship, however, to show that in a corrupt materialist culture, Pierre's new domestic arrangements are just as much a fiction as the old. In Saddle Meadows, the Christian gentleman-knight worships the saint-mother and angel-wife with elaborate adoration. The Apostles, named after Christ's brotherhood of followers, also has religious resonances, suggestive of the irony of George Lippard's name for his palace of dissolution, Monk Hall (*The Quaker City: or The Monks of Monk Hall,* 1845). Melville may certainly have been aware of the common cultural associations between Catholic orders of monks or nuns and stories of Gothic licentiousness.[28] The picture of Pierre, bundled up in blankets with hot bricks tucked around him as he writes, presents an ironic inversion of the sacred ideal, and even the narrator mocks his excessive self-discipline: "Is Pierre a shepherd, or a bishop, or a cripple?" (301).

This monastic domesticity becomes ever harder to sustain once Lucy reenters the picture. Calling her "[a] very strange cousin . . . almost a nun in her notions" (313), Pierre tries to convince Isabel and himself that Lucy can take her place in their celibate household without strain. The more experienced Delly has some inkling of the truth and begins to see the domestic façade as a lie: "'If they are not married; if I, penitentially seeking to be pure, am now but the servant to a greater sin, than I myself committed: then, pity! pity!'" (321). Lucy's presence in the house tips the delicate balance Isabel and Pierre have maintained, so that he is forced to display himself as husband rather than as brother. Meanwhile, he and Lucy have reignited their old passion and with it Isabel's resentment. The ideal of fraternity breaks down as Lucy seems to divine and by implication to expose the truth. Pierre can no longer maintain this domestic fiction, and in his despair he feels himself "a doorless and shutterless house for the four loosened winds of heaven to howl through" (339). The gothic family melodrama that has been gathering tension in the book's later sections—Lucy's dramatic break from her mother, brother, and suitor, Isabel's jealousy of Lucy, Pierre's staunch protection of the two beleaguered women—bursts into a murderous climax when Pierre kills his enemies Glen Stanly and Frederic Tartan and ends in the last of his cells, the prison.

As if to signal the end of his domestic experiment, Melville shows Pierre having a "strange vision, [that] displaced the four blank walls, the desk, and camp-bed" (346). His dream of himself as the dismembered Titan Enceladus, struggling with the gods and elements in a sublime wilderness, seems the clearest evidence that Pierre's metaphysical book has devoured his domestic life. Yet in other ways, the dream engages his domestic conflicts anew. Enceladus's story is a Titanic version of Pierre's own family ro-

mance and of many women's novels of the period. The "son and grandson of incest," Enceladus is the product and victim of monstrously bad parenting. Heroically resisting his progenitors' destructive family patterns in a spirit no less defiant than that of such female rebels as Fanny Fern's Ruth Hall or E. D. E. N. Southworth's Capitola, Pierre adopts a "reckless sky-assaulting mood" (347). Like these female protagonists, he has sought to escape the sins of his demonic fathers and grandfathers by resisting male authority and by locating his revolt in the home, creating an explicitly nonpatriarchal household.

Eventually, however, Pierre runs the ideal of domestic fraternity its full course and abandons it in despair. Exhausted by his writing labors, frustrated that he must sacrifice Lucy all over again, he finally asks the question he might have asked when he first received Isabel's letter: "How did he know that Isabel was his sister?" (353) But it is too late for him to repair the damage and for Melville to produce the conventional happy ending: "not always doth life's beginning gloom conclude in gladness; . . . wedding-bells peal not ever in the last scene of life's fifth act" (141). Rather than wedding bells, Pierre finds the dark dungeon presided over by a "squat-framed, asthmatic turnkey" (361) who jingles his bunch of keys suggestively and says, "easy, easy, till I get the picks—I'm housewife here" (361). Pierre's heroic efforts to remake middle-class domesticity run up against the law, ending in a grim joke. Midwife to an aborted experiment and housewife to his ruined family, Pierre unites himself in death with his sisters.

Although the blood-soaked ending might explain the failure of *Pierre* among "cultivated" readers in terms of literary taste, one may still ask why it produced such violent contemporary responses. And if Melville knew the market well enough to anticipate such responses, if he consciously drew from the antipatriarchal domestic novel to expose a rigid middle-class ideology, why did he destroy his own vehicle at the same time? Why does not Melville make Pierre's utopian community a triumph of ideal love and sacrifice? It is impossible to define with any certainty the intense emotional and ideological tensions in Melville that produced this self-destructive text, but clearly the novel failed with its buyers because, among other things, it could not produce wedding bells in the fifth act. Hawthorne contrives a marriage in the last few pages of *House,* reasserting the patriarchal household that the book has worked so assiduously to undermine. Fanny Fern's *Ruth Hall* goes much further than *House* in satirizing middle-class family and domestic structures, even, as in *Pierre,* replacing Ruth's marriage with a fraternal attachment to her editor John Walter. Yet in the end, Fern does not rule out the possibility of Ruth's marrying again. *Pierre,* however, boldly attacks the perversions of domesticity from within. The failure of brotherhood, Christ's own alternative to marriage, indicts the false gods and goddesses of Melville's readers. The book's revelation of corruption at the heart of the home guaranteed its commercial failure.

To readers in the twentieth century, however, **Pierre** offers a radical reading of the gender roles and domestic structures that have produced profound distress in middle-class culture. The book reveals the fault lines in the American family, not simply in extremis—in patterns of incest, abuse, betrayal, and the hypocrisy and silence that surround them—but also in the enormous and seemingly artificial labor required to maintain the illusion of ordinary, day-to-day respectability. The religion of the American family, Melville implies, demands the worship of false idols. Melville's alternative is not, as it might appear, radical individualism, for Pierre's iconoclastic writing is rooted in an egalitarian, communal domesticity. But the ideal of fraternity and sorority creates problems that neither Melville nor his fellow toiler Hawthorne could resolve. **Pierre** remains an unsettling book less because of its open defiance of conventional sexual morality than on account of its violent and ultimately inconclusive wrestling with the notion of intimacy itself and the home wherein it dwells.

Notes

1. *Correspondence*, ed. Lynn Horth (Evanston and Chicago: Northwestern University Press and the Newberry Library, 1993), 185. Further references appear in the text in parentheses.

2. Sheila Post-Lauria, however, has argued that in *Pierre* Melville was trying to reach beyond a middle-class "cultivated" audience to target more "general" readers. See her *Correspondent Colorings: Melville in the Marketplace* (Amherst: University of Massachusetts Press, 1996), 127-47.

3. Leon Howard, *Herman Melville* (Berkeley: University of California Press, 1961); Edwin Haviland Miller, *Melville* (New York: George Braziller, Inc., 1975); Laurie Robertson-Lorant, *Melville: A Biography* (New York: Clarkson N. Potter, 1996); Hershel Parker, *Herman Melville: A Biography (Volume 1, 1819-1851)* (Baltimore: Johns Hopkins University Press, 1996), 834-6.

4. Quoted in Brian Higgins and Hershel Parker, *Critical Essays on Herman Melville's Pierre, or, the Ambiguities* (Boston: G. K. Hall, 1983), 50.

5. For the theme of brotherhood, I am indebted to Robert K. Martin, *Hero, Captain, and Stranger: Male Friendship, Social Critique, and Literary Form in the Sea Novels of Herman Melville* (Chapel Hill: University of North Carolina Press, 1986).

6. See Gillian Brown, *Domestic Individualism: Imagining Self in Nineteenth-Century America* (Berkeley: University of California Press, 1990); also Post-Lauria, *Correspondent Colorings*, 82, 140; Lora Romero, "Domesticity and Fiction," in *The Columbia History of the American Novel*, ed. Emory Elliott (New York: Columbia University Press, 1991), 110-29; and William C. Spengemann, "Introduction" to Herman Melville, *Pierre, or the Ambiguities* (New York: Penguin Books, 1996).

7. *Moby-Dick*, ed. Harrison Hayford, Hershel Parker, and G. Thomas Tanselle (Evanston and Chicago:

Northwestern University Press and the Newberry Library, 1988), 416. Further references appear in the text in parentheses. *Correspondence*, 212. Jay Leyda, *The Melville Log: A Documentary Life of Herman Melville, 1819-1891* (New York: Gordian Press, 1969), 408. On Melville's life at Arrowhead, see Robertson-Lorant, *Melville: A Biography*, 239-77, and Parker, *Herman Melville*, 782-811. For Melville's domestic circle, see Hershel Parker, "*Moby-Dick* and Domesticity," in *Critical Essays on Herman Melville's Moby-Dick* (New York: G. K. Hall, 1992), 545-62. For a view of Melville's domestic tensions, see Elizabeth Renker, *Strike through the Mask: Herman Melville and the Scene of Writing* (Baltimore: Johns Hopkins University Press, 1996).

8. On domestic novels, see Nina Baym, *Woman's Fiction: A Guide to Novels by and about Women in America, 1820-1870* (Urbana and Chicago: University of Illinois Press, 1993); Baym, *Feminism and American Literary History: Essays* (New Brunswick: Rutgers University Press, 1992); Susan Harris, *19th-Century American Women's Novels: Interpretive Strategies* (New York: Cambridge University Press, 1990); Mary Kelley, *Private Woman, Public Stage: Literary Domesticity in Nineteenth-Century America* (New York: Oxford University Press, 1984). On the Melvilles and Catharine Maria Sedgwick, see Helen Melville to Augusta Melville, Oct. 8, 1835, in Additions to the Gansevoort-Lansing Collection, New York Public Library. On *Jane Eyre*, see Parker, *Herman Melville*, 583. On Melville's connections with Sophia Hawthorne and Sarah Morewood, see *Correspondence*, 218-20, 205-6. For parlor culture, see Joan Hedrick, *Harriet Beecher Stowe: A Life* (New York: Oxford University Press, 1994).

9. *Pierre, or the Ambiguities*, ed. Harrison Hayford, Hershel Parker, and G. Thomas Tanselle (Evanston and Chicago: Northwestern University Press and the Newberry Library, 1971), 218. Further references appear in the text in parentheses.

10. Nina Baym, *Woman's Fiction*, defines an overplot in woman's fiction that emphasizes female independence; Susan Harris, *19th-Century American Women's Novels*, argues that many novels showed women who did not completely challenge the marriage conventions (9).

11. See also Post-Lauria, *Correspondent Colorings*, 137.

12. See G. M. Goshgarian, *To Kiss the Chastening Rod: Domestic Fiction and Sexual Ideology in the American Renaissance* (Ithaca: Cornell University Press, 1992).

13. Higgins and Parker argue that trying to find out the "intentions" of *Pierre* imposes a New Critical unity on the novel and ignores its biographical and compositional history. See Brian Higgins and Hershel Parker, "Reading *Pierre*," in John Bryant, ed., *A Companion to Melville Studies* (New York: Greenwood Press, 1986), 211-39. Nevertheless, as my succeeding discussion shows, this question has vexed numerous readers of the book.

14. Susan Harris has shrewdly observed that *Moby-Dick* in fact has a domestic cover story: "The subversive plot of course belongs to Ahab, who represents the antithesis of domesticity" (20). But in the overplot, Ishmael rejoins the maternal *Rachel* and learns to accept "the wife, the heart, the bed" (416).

15. Herman's brother Gansevoort changed the family name from "Melvill" to "Melville." On Thomas Melvill's letter, see Henry A. Murray et al., "Allan Melvill's By-Blow," *Melville Society Extracts* 61 (February 1985): 1-6; Amy Puett Emmers, "Melville's Closet Skeleton: A New Letter About the Illegitimacy Incident in *Pierre*," in *Studies in the American Renaissance,* 1977 (Boston: Twayne, 1978), 339-42; Philip Young, *The Private Melville* (University Park: Pennsylvania State University Press, 1993). Both Robertson-Lorant and Higgins and Parker in "Reading *Pierre*" are cautious about the conclusions of Murray et. al.

16. Newton Arvin, *Herman Melville* (New York: William Sloane, 1950); James Creech, *Closet Writing, Gay Reading: The Case of Melville's Pierre* (Chicago: University of Chicago Press, 1993).

17. See Higgins and Parker, "Reading *Pierre*." On the basis of this theory, Hershel Parker has published an edition of *Pierre, or the Ambiguities* that recovers the text he feels Melville originally wrote. Called the "Kraken" edition, this book is handsomely illustrated by Maurice Sendak (New York: HarperCollins, 1995).

18. Miller, *Melville,* argues that Melville wrote *Pierre* in order to rival Hawthorne's *House* but that "in this new contest he was no match. Melville was not a domesticated person; his artistic skills did not include the intimacies of domestication or the realistic detail of this genre" (225).

19. *Piazza Tales and Other Prose Pieces, 1839-1860,* ed. Harrison Hayford, Alma MacDougall, G. Thomas Tanselle, and Merton M. Sealts, Jr. (Evanston and Chicago: Northwestern University Press and the Newberry Library, 1987), 250.

20. See David Reynolds, *Walt Whitman's America: A Cultural Biography* (New York: Random House, 1995).

21. *The House of the Seven Gables,* in *The Centenary Edition of Nathaniel Hawthorne* (Columbus: Ohio State University Press, 1965), 2:45. Further references appear in the text in parentheses.

22. T. Walter Herbert, *Dearest Beloved: The Hawthornes and the Making of the Middle-Class Family* (Berkeley: University of California Press, 1993), 102-6.

23. Samuel Otter, "The Eden of Saddle Meadows: Landscape and Ideology in *Pierre*," *American Literature* 66 (March 1994): 55-81.

24. On the connection between the religious and the erotic, see Jenny Franchot, *Roads to Rome: The Antebellum Protestant Encounter with Catholicism* (Berkeley: University of California Press, 1994).

25. See Miller, *Melville,* on the symbolism—house, moss, and vine—surrounding Hawthorne.

26. Leyda, *Log,* 422.

27. See Wyn Kelley, *Melville's City: Literary and Urban Form in Nineteenth-Century New York* (New York: Cambridge University Press, 1996); David S. Reynolds, *Beneath the American Renaissance: The Subversive Imagination in the Age of Emerson and Melville* (Cambridge: Harvard University Press, 1989).

28. See Franchot, *Roads to Rome,* 112-61.

FURTHER READING

Criticism

Barber, Patricia. "Melville's Self-Image as a Writer and the Image of the Writer in *Pierre*. In *Massachusetts Studies in English* III, No. 3 (Spring 1972): 65-71.

　　Traces parallels between Pierre as a writer and Melville himself, contending that in the novel Melville deromanticizes writing and writers.

Bell, Michael Davitt. "The Glendinning Heritage: Melville's Literary Borrowings in *Pierre*." In *Studies in Romanticism* 12, No. 4 (Fall 1973): 741-62.

　　Maintains that in *Pierre* Melville deals with the relationship between life and art and notes that all Pierre's efforts to make his life imitate art degenerate into parody.

Berthold, Michael C. "The Prison World of Melville's *Pierre* and 'Bartleby.'" In *ESQ: A Journal of the American Renaissance* 33, No. 4 (4th quarter 1987): 237-52.

　　Discusses prison imagery in *Pierre* and "Bartleby the Scrivener," suggesting that both works exhibit Melville's general contemplation of the institutional power of prisons.

Chai, Leon. "Melville and Shelley: Speculations on Metaphysics, Morals, and Poetics in *Pierre* and 'Shelley's Vision.'" In *ESQ: A Journal of the American Renaissance* 29, No. 1 (1st quarter 1983): 31-45.

　　Explores thematic connections between *Pierre* and Shelley's verse drama *The Cenci.*

Dalke, Anne French. "The Sensational Fiction of Hawthorne and Melville." In *Studies in American Fiction* 16, No. 2 (Autumn 1988): 195-207.

　　Discusses *Pierre* and *The Scarlet Letter* as sentimental fiction, focusing on their deviations from the genre.

Davis, Clark. "Asceticism and the Fictive in *Pierre*." In *ESQ: A Journal of the American Renaissance* 38, No. 2 (2nd quarter 1992): 143-59.

　　Compares the main characters' awareness of the body in *Pierre* with that of the characters in *Moby-Dick.*

Fleck, Richard F. "Stone Imagery in Melville's *Pierre*." In *Research Studies* 42 (1974): 127-30.

Discusses Melville's mastery in weaving together plot and symbol through his handling of the Memnon Stone.

Flory, Wendy Stallard. "A New Century—A New Symbol Criticism: *Pierre* and an A-Freudian Approach to Melville's Symbolizing." In *Melville Society Extracts,* No. 104 (March 1996): 25-27.

Distinguishes between a realistic and a symbolic level of reading in the novel.

Higgins, Brian and Hershel Parker. "Reading *Pierre*." In *A Companion to Melville Studies,* edited by John Bryant, pp. 211-39. New York: Greenwood Press, 1986.

Provide background on the novel, including sections on biography, criticism, intention, and composition.

Hoeveler, Diane Long. "La Cenci: The Incest Motif in Hawthorne and Melville." In *American Transcendental Quarterly: A Journal of New England Writers* No. 44 (Fall 1979): 247-59.

Explores Hawthorne's *The Marble Faun* and Melville's *Pierre* in terms of their treatment of the theme of the attempt to overthrow European roots and create a better society in America.

Hume, Beverly A. "Of Krakens and Other Monsters: Melville's *Pierre*." In *American Transcendental Quarterly: A Journal of New England Writers* 6, No. 2 (June 1992): 92-108.

Explores Melville's rendering of "feminine monstrosities" in *Pierre*.

Lackey, Kris. "The Despotic Victim: Gender and Imagination in *Pierre*." In *American Transcendental Quarterly: A Journal of New England Writers* 4, No. 1 (March 1990): 67-76.

Discusses the conflicts inherent in Melville's writing of gothic romance, both as a male author and as a revisionist of the genre.

Miner-Quinn, Paula. "Pierre's Sexuality: A Psychoanalytic Interpretation of Herman Melville's *Pierre, or, The Ambiguities*." In *University of Hartford Studies in Literature* 13, No. 2 (1981): 111-21.

Suggests that the implied themes of incest and fornication in *Pierre* deflect the reader's attention from the themes of possible impotency and homosexuality that underlie the novel's other sexual problems.

Otter, Samuel. "The Eden of Saddle Meadows: Landscape and Ideology in *Pierre*." In *American Literature* 66, No. 1 (March 1994): 55-81.

Discusses the character Pierre as both heir and victim to a deformed antebellum ideology manifested through the American landscape.

Post-Lauria, Sheila. "Genre and Ideology: The French Sensational Romance and Melville's *Pierre*." In *Journal of American Culture* 15, No. 3 (Fall 1992): 1-8.

Asserts that Melville consciously fashioned *Pierre* after the French conventions of sensation fiction.

Shepherd, Gerard W. "Pierre's Psyche and Melville's Art." In *ESQ: A Journal of the American Renaissance* 30, No. 2 (2nd quarter 1984): 83-98.

Contends that in *Pierre* Melville demonstrates a need to search for understanding despite apparent hopelessness for success.

Slouka, Mark Z. "Demonic History: Geography and Genealogy in Melville's *Pierre*." In *ESQ: A Journal of the American Renaissance* 35, No. 2 (2nd quarter 1989): 147-60.

Proposes that "Pierre's self-conscious response to the hermeneutics of landscape and selfhood that distinguish American natural theology" gives rise to Melville's nationalism.

Thomas, Brook. "The Writer's Procreative Urge in *Pierre*: Fictional Freedom or Convoluted Incest?" In *Studies in the Novel* XI, No. 4 (Winter 1979): 416-30.

Discusses Isabel's role in the novel in terms of the patriarchal order of traditional family life.

Toner, Jennifer DiLalla. "The Accustomed Signs of the Family: Rereading Genealogy in Melville's *Pierre*." In *American Literature* 70, No. 2 (June 1998): 237-63.

Explores Pierre's self-construction and self-representation in light of Melville's own image of himself as a writer.

Travis, Mildred K. "Melville's 'Furies' Continued in *Pierre*." In *ESQ: A Journal of the American Renaissance* No. 62 (Winter 1971): 33-35.

Characterizes Isabel, Lucy, and Stanly as "the personification of the pursuit of conscience" in *Pierre*.

———. "Relevant Digressions in *Pierre*." In *American Transcendental Quarterly* No. 24 (Fall 1974): 7-8.

Interprets Melville's digressions in *Pierre* as contributing to the development of Pierre as tragic hero.

Additional coverage of Melville's life and career is contained in the following sources published by the Gale Group: *Authors & Artists for Young Adults,* **Vol. 25;** *Concise Dictionary of American Literary Biography 1640-1865; Dictionary of Literary Biography,* **Vols. 3 and 74;** *DISCovering Authors; DISCovering Authors: British; DISCovering Authors: Canadian; DISCovering Authors Modules: Most-Studied Authors* **and** *Novelists; Short Story Criticism,* **Vols. 1 and 17;** *Something About the Author,* **Vol. 59; and** *World Literature Criticism.*

Richard Brinsley Sheridan
1751-1816

(Born Thomas Brinsley Sheridan.) Irish playwright, librettist, and poet. The following entry presents recent criticism of Sheridan's works. For additional discussion of Sheridan's life and career, see *NCLC,* Volume 5.

INTRODUCTION

During his brief career as a playwright, Sheridan helped revive the English Restoration comedy of manners, which depicts the amorous intrigues of wealthy society. His best-known comedies, *The Rivals* (1775) and *The School for Scandal* (1777), display Sheridan's talent for sparkling dialogue and farce. Like his Restoration predecessors William Congreve and William Wycherley, Sheridan satirized society, but, unlike them, he softened his humor with gentle morality and sentimentality. While his plays are frequently noted for a lack of incisiveness and psychological depth, they are considered by most commentators to be the work of an outstanding theatrical craftsman. Drawing from earlier dramatic conventions, Sheridan created entertaining and well-wrought comedies that have endured in their popular and critical acclaim.

BIOGRAPHICAL INFORMATION

Sheridan was born in Dublin in 1751. His father was a prominent actor and his mother a writer. The family moved to London when Sheridan was still a boy. There, Sheridan disliked his schooling, but proved to be an excellent student and began writing poetry at an early age. After composing dramatic sketches with friends, he considered becoming a playwright. His father, however, intended him to study law. When the Sheridans moved to Bath in 1770, Richard met Elizabeth Linley, a singer and famed beauty. Though she had many suitors, Linley eloped with Sheridan in 1773. Shortly after their marriage, Sheridan abandoned his legal studies in order to devote himself to writing. The initial performance of his first play, *The Rivals,* failed because of miscasting and the play's excessive length. Undaunted by the poor reception, Sheridan recast several roles, abbreviated sections of the play, and reopened it ten days later to a unanimously positive response. With the success of his opera *The Duenna; or, the Double Elopement* and the comedy *St. Patrick's Day; or, The Scheming Lieutenant* in 1775, Sheridan established himself as a prominent dramatist. Meanwhile, Sheridan purchased the Drury Lane Theatre and became its manager. In the next two years, he revived a number of Restoration comedies and wrote and staged his most well-known play, *The*

School for Scandal. By the end of the decade, Sheridan had produced his last successful stage work, *The Critic; or, Tragedy Rehearsed* (1779). In 1780 Sheridan was elected to the House of Commons. His excellence as an orator was duly noted by his contemporaries; however, Sheridan's interest in politics kept him from his theatrical endeavors and his management of the theater became haphazard. He wrote only one more play, *Pizarro*—an adaptation of August von Kotzebue's drama *Die Spanier in Peru oder Rollas Tod*—which appeared in 1799. Somewhat later, in an attempt to beautify the aging theater at Drury Lane, Sheridan had the interior completely rebuilt. The structure burned to the ground shortly thereafter, and left without resources, Sheridan was unable to finance another Parliamentary campaign. Most of Sheridan's last years were spent in poverty and disgrace; however, shortly before his death, Sheridan managed to regain his reputation as a distinguished statesman and dramatist. When he died in 1816, he was mourned widely and was buried in the Poet's Corner of Westminster Abbey.

MAJOR WORKS

In his comic drama *The Rivals* Sheridan satirizes manners using humor that is pointed but never cruel. Essentially an ironic play about character, *The Rivals* presents a number of absurd individuals and then proceeds to ridicule their flaws and idiosyncrasies. Among its range of characters, the play introduces the infamous figure of Mrs. Malaprop, from whose humorously inappropriate word usage the term "malapropism" is derived. Sheridan's libretto for the light opera *The Duenna* features characters and incidents drawn from Roman New Comedy and ends with a double marriage happily realized despite the opposition of Don Jerome—the play's stodgy father figure. Another of Sheridan's minor works, the farcical *St. Patrick's Day; or, The Scheming Lieutenant* exists very much in the mode of *The Rivals* and endeavors to amuse audiences with its affable, if preposterous, characters. *The School for Scandal* is both the most popular of Sheridan's comedies and the most strongly reminiscent of the Restoration period. This attack on a gossip-loving society demonstrates Sheridan's brilliant display of wit in its sharp indictment of manners that departs considerably from the gentle tone and approach of *The Rivals*. The story follows a double plot as it portrays the manipulative Lady Sneerwell, the hypocritical Joseph Surface, the naïve socialite Lady Teazle, the irascible Sir Peter Teazle, and the reformed libertine Charles Surface, among many other comic figures. Heavily influenced by the Duke of Buckingham's *The Rehearsal*, Sheridan's *The Critic; or, Tragedy Rehearsed* provides a satirical look at the theatrical world and is a burlesque of the vanity of artists and critics.

CRITICAL RECEPTION

Although *The Rivals* and *The School for Scandal* have been popular since their inception—the former principally for its fine characterization and the latter for its superb use of language and technical refinement—some recent critics have claimed that Sheridan was neither responsible for an English revival of comedy nor particularly innovative. Others have faulted his refusal to develop emotional subtleties in his characters, and have found his dialogue superficially witty, but lacking depth. Some have contended that the deliberate staginess of Sheridan's works detracts from their artistic value. Others have acknowledged that Sheridan chose to exaggerate and vary the traditional comedy of manners in order to heighten the theatricality of his plays and thereby intensify the audience's enjoyment. Contemporary criticism has continued to focus on Sheridan's skilled use of dialogue and manipulation of character in his major dramas, while a number of scholars have also begun to analyze Sheridan's lesser works of drama and poetry, and to study his political career.

PRINCIPAL WORKS

The Duenna; or, The Double Elopement (libretto) 1775
The Rivals (play) 1775
St. Patrick's Day; or, The Scheming Lieutenant (play) 1775
The School for Scandal (play) 1777
A Trip to Scarborough [adapter; from the drama *The Relapse* by John Vanbrugh] (play) 1777
The Critic; or, Tragedy Rehearsed (play) 1779
Pizarro [adapter; from the drama *Die Spanier in Peru oder Rollas Tod* by August von Kotzebue] (play) 1799
The Works of the Late Right Honourable Richard Brinsley Sheridan (plays) 1821
The Plays and Poems of Richard Brinsley Sheridan (plays and poetry) 1928
The Letters of Richard Brinsley Sheridan (letters) 1966
The Dramatic Works of Richard Brinsley Sheridan (plays) 1973

CRITICISM

Jack D. Durant (essay date 1975)

SOURCE: "Poet," in *Richard Brinsley Sheridan,* Twayne Publishers, 1975, pp. 47-64.

[*In the following excerpt, Durant surveys Sheridan's work as a poet.*]

Whether penning a sweet love lyric to Eliza, or dashing off a song for performance at the theater, or acknowledging some special occasion, great or small, Sheridan always displayed a bright flair for versifying. Excluding the songs in his major plays, his poetic canon includes at least sixty titles; and these poems embrace an immense variety of forms and subjects and obviously constitute a substantial segment of Sheridan's literary achievement.

I POETIC SATIRE: "THE RIDOTTO OF BATH"

Quite possibly he broke into print as a poet on May 9, 1771, with the publication in *The Bath Chronicle* of **"Hymen and Hirco: A Vision,"** a rather bland "Juvenalian" satire attacking Walter Long, the aging Wiltshire squire who for a time was contracted to marry Elizabeth Linley, Sheridan's own future bride. But a poem quite definitely Sheridan's appeared in *The Bath Chronicle* on October 10, 1771: **"The Ridotto of Bath, a Panegyrick, Being an Epistle from Timothy Screw, Under Server to Messrs. Kuhf and Fitzwater, to his brother Henry, Waiter at Almack's."** The little poem satirizes the opening ball at the New Assembly Rooms of Bath—an occasion gloriously celebrated just ten days earlier on September 30—and, in doing so, it cleverly imitates the eleventh and thirteenth letters of Christopher Anstey's roistering verse novel, the *New Bath Guide* (1766). Executed in the anapestic couplets popularized for satire by Anstey, it also features, as one critic notes, "the same chit-chat, the same mild, laughing satire upon modish follies, the same snobbishness about social risers, and even the same 'character' naming" typical of the *Guide*—e.g., Tom Handleflask, Miss Churchface, Madame Crib'em, Peg Runt.[1] Young Sheridan obviously hoped to use the credit of Anstey's popularity, but his imitation reflects an appropriate artistic tact; for by 1771 the *Guide* widely symbolized the reckless mood of Bath gaiety.

The chief merit of the **"Ridotto of Bath"** appears in its structure. After two brief preliminary sections, events proceed chronologically from seven in the evening, when the gala begins, to one in the morning, when everyone goes home; but, within the framework of this simple structure, the poet generates a system of delightful dramatic tensions and leads through them to a final, rowdy climax. Tensions take hold even at the outset where the narrator, a veteran waiter, declares this ridotto to be the grandest of his long experience. A mock ominousness compounds these tensions when in his second brief prefatory comment the narrator tells how the Mayor of Bath, on hearing that the new entertainment parlors will house a "Red Otter," threatens to cancel the grand opening. And the sense of foreboding generated by this threat takes emphasis, in turn, from the earliest description of the guests attending the ridotto, many of whom have ignored the regulations for dress specified by the master of ceremonies. Thus tensions inherent in the grandness of the affair are immediately heightened by the threat of cancellation and by signs of social anarchy within the company.

The climax toward which these tensions build is the assault upon the sideboard, which takes place in the long penultimate section of the poem. It is a climax prepared by a descriptive passage confirming in close detail the reader's worst fears about the company assembled: an undisciplined mob, highlighted by the glitter of cheap paste jewelry, mixing low and polite society, dancing grotesquely to the lilting jigs of oboe and fiddle. To elevate his climax even above this chaos of merriment, Sheridan introduces a dramatic pause into the narrative: the din subsides; the music stops; order presides. But out of this disconcerting silence soon rumbles a crushing stampede. Dinner is served:

> Our outworks they storm'd with prowess most
>   manful,
> And jellies and cakes carried off by the handful;
> While some our lines enter'd, with courage undaunted,
> Nor quitted the trench till they'd got what they
>   wanted. (122)[2]

Although the closing section of the poem covers a sizable segment of time—from the dinner hour to one o'clock in the morning—it is itself quite brief, a foreshortened denouement to the little narrative. In it, the narrator mentions the continuing "*folly, confusion,* and *pathos*" of the ridotto;

but he describes no action and generates no tension. He does nothing to dissipate the impact of the chaotic dining room scene. From beginning to end, Sheridan sustains the structural integrity of his poem, always supplying detail and controlling tensions in careful support of a single, riotous climax.

Unfortunately, very little within the poem supports its effective structure. The narrative *persona,* Timothy Screw, assumes no clear identity, though he postures after a studied comic diffidence. The young poet's ventures into dialect humor ("*Red Otter*" for "ridotto," "*Hogstyegon*" for "octagon," "*purdigiously*" for "prodigiously," "*suffocking*" for "suffocating") fare feebly at best; and his anapests stumble badly at times, e.g., "In sympathy beat the balcony above" (121). The mere thought of a grand Bath ball, says Anstey's Simkin Bernard, "Gives life to my numbers, and strength to my verse." Sheridan's Timothy Screw professes a comparable enthusiasm, but his numbers and verse fail to reflect it.

Despite its failings, however, **"The Ridotto of Bath"** earned popularity sufficient to enshrine it in the *New Foundling Hospital for Wit* (1771), a widely circulated anthology of current verse; and, by virtue of Sheridan's fine sense of drama and form, the little poem clearly elevates itself above mere "trifle" and "commonplace."[3] In being satire, of course, it ranks low on Sheridan's own scale of theoretical values—the values he suggests in his later poems **"Clio's Protest"** (1771) and **"A Familiar Epistle"** (1774). But, even while warning in these poems against the dangers of satire, he demonstrates in them as lively a satiric turn of mind as he demonstrates in **"The Ridotto of Bath."** Certainly **"Clio's Protest"** shows a mastery of Hudibrastic techniques—the driving pace, the extravagant rhymes, the casual tone, the sporadic asides, the studied digressions—and **"A Familiar Epistle"** sees these same techniques sharpened and intensified after the manner of Charles Churchill: the feminine endings dramatically reduced, the tone perceptibly darkened, the sense of order more systematically asserted. In these two poems, as in **"The Ridotto,"** the young poet has major problems with the syntax, which is loose and sometimes contrived, and in the phrasal excesses which drain many lines of their rhetorical energy and graphic interest. At the same time, however, all three poems reflect his metrical and dictional versatility and his keen ear for parody and imitation. Despite his theoretical distaste for satire, Sheridan was an effective verse satirist from the start.

II FUGITIVE VERSE

Long ago Ernest Rhys concluded that "no song or lyric can hope to reach the ear of the common people which cannot draw, as the old folksongs did, on the congenial living rhythms of its own day."[4] Sheridan's essential poetic embraces this concept, and his sharp ear for the congenial living rhythms of his day gave rise to many an easy occasional poem. Shaping his taste for lyric verse, according to Sichel, was Sheridan's schoolboy experience with Horace,

Theocritus, and Anacreon; but chiefly he immersed himself in the seventeenth-century love songs of Jonson and his school. "He stood on a lower plane than most of the Cavalier lyrists," writes Sichel, "but none the less on a plane distinguished of its kind. And he moved there with rambling footsteps."[5]

These footsteps ranged widely among lyric metrical reaches, traversing puckish anacreontics, lambent dactyls, lilting anapests, close-cropped iambs, a splendid variety of song-book measures, often used in intricate combinations, always fashioned to "read themselves into harmony," after Sheridan's characteristic manner. Taken all-in-all (Rhodes collects thirty-seven in his edition), they meet virtually every specification prescribed for good occasional poetry by Frederick Locker-Lampson, the acknowledged master of *vers de société*. For the most part, they are "graceful, refined, and fanciful, not seldom distinguished by chastened sentiment, and often playful." Their rhyme is "frequent and never forced." They are marked by "tasteful moderation, high finish and completeness"; and they project a wide spectrum of attitudes and tones: "whimsically sad," "gay and gallant," "playfully malicious," "tenderly ironical," "satirically facetious." They are rarely "flat, or ponderous, or commonplace"; and they are often graced with important "qualities of brevity and buoyancy."[6]

Sheridan's love lyrics, most of them products of his courtship with Elizabeth Linley, not only represent the largest corpus of his occasional verse but also exemplify his best lyric craftsmanship. Although many of them spring from autobiographical roots, they carefully employ the conventional generic idiom, masking personal identities behind such pastoral names as Delia, Sylvio, Eliza, and Damon. And, while Sheridan certainly lived his personal love intensely, he remains artist enough to perceive the nicest dramatic potential of a love experience and to exercise over his poems a controlled emotional detachment. The psychological ironies of love obviously fascinate him: that in the blush of youth lovers should contemplate death, that the most intense affection is liable to transiency, that the most innocent and well-intentioned love-counsel can provoke rebuff, and that a "dear delight" companions love-depair. Sheridan seeks no logical resolution to such ironies; instead, he contrives a miniature play, a sensitive little melodrama, in which the speaker tells someone (or something) about the curious awareness love has sparked in him. The distance separating the speaker from his audience varies from poem to poem, for sometimes, as in **"We Two, Each Other's Only Pride"** (240), the auditor seems close at hand, ready to reply. At other times, as in **"To the Recording Angel"** (231), he seems far removed but spiritually accessible. At yet other times, as in **"On the Death of Elizabeth Linley"** (251), the tiny drama unfolds in solemn soliloquy, not self-indulgent but affecting, the pastoral names tactfully put aside.

Just as the love poems are more often experiential than argumentative, they are often more declarative than pictorial. In **"The Grotto,"** for example, where the despairing speaker addresses first the "grotto of moss cover'd stone" then the "willow with leaves dripping dew" (232), the physical details function less as images than as agents of dialogue. Much the same concept governs the physical detail in **"To Elizabeth Linley"** in which the earnest Sylvio threatens to "hate flowers, elms, sweet bird, and grove" unless Eliza now sings to him the songs she has sung earlier to the woods and trees. The charming lyric **"To Laura"**—which vacillates irregularly between four- and five-line ballad stanzas, concluding in a stanzaic couplet—again finds a pensive speaker addressing the Nature he sees and feels; yet here the dramatic setting assumes a clarity unusual for Sheridan, picturing "a willow of no vulgar size," with shady boughs and roots providing a "moss-grown seat," the tree's bark "shatter'd" (as the poet puts it) by the inscription of Laura's name. Fretted further with emphatic images of an "azure" sky, "rosy-ting'd" sunbeams, and the "roseate wings" of May, the poem offers the most highly particularized imagery in Sheridan's love verse (possibly excepting **"On the Death of Elizabeth Linley"**); and it suggests at the same time how small a role pictorial details play in the total effect of his lyricism. With comparable generality he celebrates in other love lyrics his lady's "eye of heav'nly blue" and her "cheek of roseate hue." Obviously embarrassed by such formulaic descriptions, he succeeds best at lampooning them, as he does in an anacreontic beginning "I ne'er could any lustre see / In eyes that would not look on me" (225), a poem rivaling convention in the spirit of Shakespeare's Sonnet 130.

Most of the best qualities of Sheridan's love-lyricism appear in a sensitive three-stanza lyric **"Dry Be That Tear,"** probably dating to the courtship period 1770-72. According to Moore, this poem smacks of a French madrigal by Gibert de Montreuil, who probably had it from an Italian song by Gilles de Ménage; but Sheridan likely took the sentiment from David Hume's essay "The Epicurean," Hume having got it from Continental sources.[7] The first stanza runs as follows:

> Dry be that tear, my gentlest love,
>   Be hush'd that struggling sigh,
> Nor seasons, day, nor fate shall prove
>   More fix'd, more true than I.
> Hush'd be that sigh, be dry that tear,
> Cease boding doubt, cease anxious fear.—
>   Dry be that tear.

These lines suggest again that Sheridan's lyric imagination is aural, not visual; that it is declarative, not argumentative. As Sichel suggests, the poem "sets itself to music by the rise and fall of its melody."[8] Through patterns of repetition, it seems to savor its own sounds; its medial pauses and parallel phrases govern the tempo and sustain soft overtones even to the final muted echo: "Dry be that tear." The remaining two stanzas evince the same closely disciplined rhetoric, the same balanced phrasal patterns (modulated as here by varying accentual meters), the same six-line ballad scheme *(ababcc)* with the bobbed tail-rhyme redolent of Sir Thomas Wyatt's "My Lute Awake!" Perhaps it bears saying here that the opening lines of this lyric were borrowed from a "Dwarf Elegy on a Lady of Middle Age" by Nathaniel Brassey Halhed.[9] They so struck Sheridan's fancy that he repeated them in 1795 at the outset of an **"Elegy on the Death of a British Officer,"** a poem printed with **"Clio's Protest"** in 1819 under the title **"Verses Addressed to Laura"** and beginning "Scarce hush'd the sigh, scarce dried the [lingering] tear."

Fugitive poems not treating of love turn like the love lyrics upon subtly ironic situations, but they do so quite whimsically and often quite satirically. Again the concepts are largely declarative, not closely analyzed, not logically resolved nor imaged forth. And again many a light irony tickles the poet's fancy: an urbane lady complains that the birds in Hyde Park trouble her with country sounds (241); the founder of Brooks's Club, a great moneylender, pays at last his own moral mortgage in heaven (248); Lady Anne Hamilton, indulged in every luxury, laments her "sad" human lot (253); two eminent speakers of the House of Commons lie together dead as they had "lied" living. By technical devices Sheridan touches such ironies as these with just the right twinkling of an eye, just the right hint of a smile. Thus he lets the super-urbanized Hyde Park lady speak for herself, ingenuously, in sweeping anapests (his second use of Anstey's measure), gaily effusing the innocent vacuity of *bon ton* taste. In the **"Epitaph on Brooks,"** he mixes lugubrious tones with irreverent jingle measures. He uses separated anapestic couplets to catalogue the bright good fortunes of Lady Anne Hamilton, ending each second line with the playful phrase "——poor Anne." And, in mock incantation, as though a hymn were parodied, he eulogizes the two dead speakers of the House of Commons: "Mourn, mourn, St. Stephen's Choirs with ceaseless grieving / Two kindred spirits from the senate fled" (249).

The nice perception enabling Sheridan to define subtle social ironies also sharpens his delight in trivia—a delight inspiring, for example, a gentle mock elegy on the death of his wife's avadavat. "Each bird that is born of an egg has its date," the little poem soulfully admits. But so special a bird as this one, schooled to its song by Elizabeth's own sweet voice, will surely outsing every Muse in heaven (249). Other poems celebrating great conflicts born of trivial things include **"Lines By a Lady on the Loss of Her Trunk,"** an Anstey's measure in which each terminal word rhymes with "trunk" until the poem exhausts itself for want of available rhymes (254), and **"The Walse,"** which coolly attributes the waltz step, introduced into England in 1812, to the craftiness of the devil who had contrived that a gentleman's hand should rest upon a lady's hip, even in public (257).

In other fugitive poems, Sheridan displays a fine flair for patriotic verse and a gift for lively political caricature. As a patriotic versifier, for example, he composed on a moment's notice two rousing songs for an interlude to *Harlequin Fortunatus,* a pantomime produced at Drury Lane on January 3, 1780. Both these songs develop the *dulce et de-*

corum theme: one heartens the lonely midnight watch to thoughts of glory; the other braces the soldiers at the ramparts and rings the resolute chorus "Britons, strike home revenge your country's wrong" (239). This instinct for patriotic bravura also gives rise to a much-celebrated stanza written impromptu and appended to the National Anthem to be sung at Drury Lane in special tribute to the King, who that very evening (in 1800) had narrowly escaped assassination at the theater.

As political caricaturist, Sheridan dabbled "at various dates" in a few pasquinades, impaling on the point of a rusty doggerel those political figures whose names fell naturally into swinging anapests or amphibracs: "Johnny W---lks, Johnny W---lks;" "Jack Ch---ch---ll, Jack Ch---ch---ll;" "Captain K---th, Captain K---th," etc. (259-60). According to Crompton Rhodes, the rough-hewn, eight-line stanzas, a discrete scattering of them found among Sheridan's papers, fit the melody of a popular air beginning "Mistress Arne, Mistress Arne / It gives me concarn."[10] And while, as Moore long ago remarked, time has "removed their venom, and with it, in a great degree, their wit,"[11] the faded caricatures still suggest the writer's true eye for his subjects' foibles and his true aim in striking them down. Sheridan's real merit as a character poet, however, endures in **"A Portrait for Amoret,"** a splendid panegyric upon Mrs. Frances Crewe.

III Verse Portraiture: "A Portrait for Amoret"

"A Portrait for Amoret" was written as a prefatory compliment to be bound with a handsome manuscript copy of *The School for Scandal* presented by Sheridan to Mrs. Crewe soon after the play was introduced on May 8, 1777. Correspondence between Lord Camden and David Garrick indicates that the poem was in circulation within four months after the first performance of the play,[12] but it did not appear in print until much later, and then surreptitiously, causing Sheridan, when he saw it, to remark in a letter to his second wife that Nature had made him in his youth "an ardent romantic Blockhead."[13]

By all contemporary accounts, the incomparable Frances Crewe, only daughter of Fulke Greville, readily fired the ardor of many a fawning macaroni; but Sheridan's poem is really quite restrained and is perhaps the more ardent for its restraint. It develops in four parts: (1) an invocation to the Daughters of Calumny, promising to portray for them a lady unassailable by slander; (2) invocations to Mrs. Crewe herself ("Amoret") and to the Muse who must portray her; (3) the portrait of Amoret, which treats in turn of her splendid bearing, her captivating manner, her arresting modesty, her intriguing lips, her tactfully "irresolute" eyes, her killing smile, her ready wit, her diffident manner ("female doubt"), her spritely heart, her taste for mirth, her refined raillery, her "scorn of folly," and her high respect for talent; and (4) a grudging concession by the Daughters of Calumny that the lady portrayed, finally identified as Mrs. Crewe, does indeed defy all slander and envy.

Certainly Crompton Rhodes is right in complaining that the practice of printing Mrs. Crewe's name immediately beneath the title of the poem, a practice apparently customary in editions earlier than his own,[14] destroys the rhetorical conceit intended by Sheridan. Rhodes is right, too, in maintaining that the poem does not, as Sichel and others have held,[15] credit Mrs. Crewe with inspiring *The School for Scandal,* although the "adepts at Scandal's School" in the poem suggest the Scandal College of the play, especially as to types and varieties of scandalmongering. Quite irrespective of the play, it is Mrs. Crewe alone who has "cast a fatal gloom o'er Scandal's reign" (205). Sheridan specifies this emphasis not only by omitting from the poem all direct reference to *The School for Scandal* but also, and most importantly, by building the poem around an extended suspense conceit. Throughout all four structural segments, he withholds the true identity of his celebrated subject, heightening interest through the cumulative details of the picture. Only with the last word of the poem, spoken after an emphatic pause, does he cast aside her fictive name: "Thee my inspirer; and my model—CREWE!" And thus emphatically does he complete the portrait.

It is important to bear in mind, of course, that his device is for suspense, not for surprise. The terminal word satisfies expectation; it does not shock or outrage it. Once **"A Portrait for Amoret"** is completed, the reader delights that he has played the game of rhetorical suspense, and he then returns to the poem—as to any completed portrait—to delight further in its textures and lineaments. In view of Sheridan's liberal theories of prosody, **"A Portrait"** is the more interesting for its closely disciplined meter. It is written in heroic couplets of a highly restrictive sort. Caesuras fall customarily after the fourth, fifth, or sixth syllables. Most of the rhyming terms are "action words," either verbs or verbals, long in pronunciation. Although many shades of verbal coloring suggest themselves, Sheridan does not allow music to smother sense. Each narrow cell of sense takes interest from its own distinctive rhetoric, contributing to a rich variety of balanced constructions—sometimes with antithesis, sometimes by echo, sometimes between equal parts, showing two stressed accents on each side a medial pause, sometimes between unequal parts, showing two stressed accents on one side the pause and three on the other. Variety derives, too, from phrasal sequences, from intricate systems of repetition, from the echo of initial terms. But, amidst all this variety, the formal identity of the heroic couplet remains strong: there is virtually no enjambment between couplets.

If Sheridan still felt in 1777, as he had felt in 1771, that versification should closely complement the subject versified, it perhaps seems curious that so formal a meter should serve the subject of this poem. But since, as Wallace Cable Brown remarks, the heroic couplet is the most rigid poetic form, it is also the form in which "the greatest variations are possible without destroying the basic pattern."[16] As Sheridan pictures Mrs. Crewe, then, the strict heroic couplet is an ideal metrical form. Within the tight framework

of its basic pattern—both stanzaically and structurally—the exciting variety of Mrs. Crewe's character scintillates in the rhetorical variety of the verse.

The closing couplets of the poem mention color and outline: "And lo! each pallid hag, with blister'd tongue . . . Owns all the colours just; the outline true" (11. 121, 123), but apart from rhetorical and verbal effects, few colors or outlines really appear. What does appear is a careful modulation of tones, starting with the brusque and irritable apostrophe to the Daughters of Calumny (with the sharp imperative "Attend!" repeated at the outset of four couplets). Following, then, is tonal modulation to the quiet invocation of Amoret "Come, gentle Amoret . . . Come" (11. 25, 27). Afterward the portrait itself takes form, not in sensory detail, but in verbal tones and rhetorical schemes, helping to delineate the personal qualities of the lady portrayed. Here is a representative passage:

> Adorning Fashion, unadorn'd by dress,
> Simple from taste, and not from carelessness;
>
> Discreet in gesture, in deportment mild
> Not stiff with prudence, nor uncouthly wild;
>
> No state has Amoret! no studied mien;
> She frowns *no goddess,* and she moves *no queen.* (202)

It is the *simplex munditiis* convention again, managed here much more successfully than in the translations. In the first two of the couplets, the balanced four-stress lines, joined in each case by an unaccented syllable or by a monosyllabic "low" word (as Tillotson labels the device),[17] point in their rhetoric a simple elegance complimenting Amoret's bearing. The third couplet, which shifts to a negative emphasis, properly accents the negative terms in its scansion, most strongly stressing in each line the single iterative term "no," and thus really accenting only two syllables a line.

The shift in rhetoric, then, accompanies the shift in descriptive emphasis. In other words, rhetorical and verbal coloring help to delineate personal quality. And it is worth reiterating that Sheridan favors throughout the poem qualities of character over physical detail. The blush in Amoret's cheek betokens her modesty; her lips and eyelids move at the bidding of love; her taste for mirth bespeaks a contemplative mind. These and other high qualities receive form and vitality through apt tonal and rhetorical variations; and, in this tonal and rhetorical sense, the reader, like the Daughters of Calumny, must "Own the colours just; the outline true."

IV Theatrical Monody: "Verses to the Memory of Garrick"

A second of Sheridan's major poems—his **"Verses to the Memory of Garrick"** (1779)—also features tight heroic couplets; and again the poem achieves remarkable variety within the limitations of its medium. This time, however,

Sheridan calls more deliberately upon a subtle principle of metrical tensions—one serving to heighten the dramatic effects of oral presentation. In his study of English prosody in the eighteenth century, Paul Fussell sees this principle as originating in 1745 with Samuel Say's *Poems on Several Occasions*. It recognizes two levels of scansion in the poetic line—one based on actual sense stress, the other on theoretical or artificial stress—and holds that prosodic pleasures derive from a continuing conflict between the two levels. Where they coincide, no prosodic tensions develop; but, where they pull apart, tensions, and the consequent prosodic pleasures, result.[18] Sheridan seems to suggest this concept in his unfinished treatise on prosody, in which he insists that "A verse should read itself into harmony," asserting its own "actual rithm," but adds that "we may vary the accent as we please and the propriety is in doing so melodiously."[19] Writing in 1775, Thomas Sheridan states the concept in yet another way by declaring that "to render numbers for any time pleasing to the ear, variety is as essential as uniformity"; and he adds that "the highest ornament of versification arises from disparity in the members, equality in the whole."[20] Both the Sheridans echo Say's call for "a proper Mixture of Uniformity and Variety" to effect prosodic tension.[21]

Although written in eleven stanzas of varying lengths, the monody on Garrick falls into four distinct organizational segments; and their content suggests the discrete portions of a Classical oration. In the first, an *exordium* (11.1-20), the speaker points the aptness of this tribute to Garrick, a tribute properly paid here in the great actor's own theater. The second, a kind of *narratio* (11. 21-62), considers acting in relation to painting, sculpture, and poetry; and it concludes that of all these arts only acting stands vulnerable to time. The third, a *confirmatio* (11. 63-78), defines in sequence the qualities of the actor's art and proves the ephemerality of these qualities. The fourth, a *peroratio* (11. 79-112), urges Garrick's admirers to immortalize his artistry in their memories, since of itself it lacks enduring substance. Contemporary periodical sources indicate that "airs of a solemn nature" twice interrupt the theatrical reading of the poem.[22] The first, a setting of lines nine and ten, embellishes the *exordium;* the second, following line seventy-eight, introduces the *peroratio* (perhaps covering lines 79 through 83 as set off stanzaically in the text). The elder Thomas Linley scored these interludes, introducing into them a variety of choruses, airs, and vocal ensembles. He also composed special instrumental pieces to precede and follow the recitation. Printed in four quarto pages, the music was probably sold at the theater; but it had not the distribution, certainly, that the text of the monody had.

As published by T. Evans and others late in March, 1779, the text of the monody provides several clear signals to metrical emphasis—reduced capitals, contractions, marked caesuras, exclamation points, expletives—devices showing where the poem's theoretical scansion must be observed and where it must not. The *exordium,* for example, features a close marriage of spoken and theoretical scansions, contractions often cementing the marriage, as in line four:

"For fabled Suffe'rers, and delusive Woe."[23] Those portions of the *narratio* treating of painting and sculpture also cling to prosodic wedlock, though a capitalized "HIS WORKS" in line twenty-eight offers to shatter the bond: "With undiminish'd Awe HIS WORKS are view'd." In the third part of the *narratio* (the discourse on poetry), however, a prosodic tension takes hold, signaled by pronounced caesuras and trochaic substitutions as well as by reduced capitals: "The Pride of Glory—Pity's Sigh sincere—" (1. 53); "Such is THEIR Meed, THEIR Honors thus secure" (1.55). And this tension heralds the emotive climax of the piece: the *confirmatio* and the early portions of the *peroratio* (11. 63-78; 83-92).

Since the poem seeks throughout to be logically persuasive, it is nowhere passionate or irrational. In the *confirmatio,* however, it engages a pathos commensurate with the irony of the actor's lot. It defines in turn the qualities of his art—grace of action, adopted mien, expressive glance, gesture, harmonious speech—at last bringing the catalogue to this effective conclusion (11. 73-78).

> PASSION'S wild break,—and FROWN that awes the
>   Sense,
> And every CHARM of gentler ELOQUENCE—
> All perishable!—like the 'Electric Fire
> But strike the Frame—and as they strike expire;
> Incense too pure a bodied Flame to bear,
> It's Fragrance charms the Sense, and blends with Air.

Moore writes that certain of Sheridan's friends urged him to alter line seventy-five, causing the emphatic phrase "All perishable!" to read "All doomed to perish."[24] And, in refusing to make the change, Sheridan suggests the deliberate care with which he blends uniformity and variety not only here but at apt places throughout the poem. A wealth of metrical variety suggests itself even in these few lines quoted.

The trochaic patterns enforced by the initial terms "PASSION'S" and "Incense," for example, precisely recall the fundamental technique of "variety in uniformity" as urged in Thomas Sheridan's lectures on reading. So do the hovering medial pauses, marked typographically by the dash, and the "demicaesuras" synchronized with them to introduce "a diversity of proportion in the measurement of the pauses" (cf. 11. 73. and 76).[25] The celebrated seventy-fifth line, moreover, demonstrates in the opening phrase ("All perishable!") the intermixture of spondees and pyrrhics, a device for variety much admired by the elder Sheridan; and, in its closing phrase ("—like the 'Electric Fire"), the line engages a medial trochee calculated, as Thomas Sheridan would interpret it, to shatter melody while heightening expression.[26]

In short, appropriate variety characterizes the entire poem. The more coolly rational passages show least prosodic tension; the more emotionally excited ones place proper oral scansion at odds with regular iambic cadence. Verbal coloring everywhere supports prosodic effects—cf, "the Meed of mournful Verse" (1. 11); "Pity's sigh sincere" (1. 53) "with Force and Feeling fraught" (1. 67)—but here, as in the "Portrait for Amoret," the figurism remains much more rhetorical than sensuous. The poem always asserts its own integrity, its "actual rithm." At appropriate times, however, it signals the reader to "vary the accent," to violate the prosodic surface, to cooperate with the poetry—but not to overwhelm it—in evoking apt dramatic response.

In staging the monody as introduced at Drury Lane on March 11, 1779, Sheridan probably imitated the production ten years earlier of Garrick's own *Ode Upon Dedicating a Building and Erecting a Statue to Shakespeare at Stratford-upon-Avon,* for just as the ode featured choristers banked behind a statue of Shakespeare, with the reader (Garrick) and several soloists stationed in the foreground, so the monody featured a choir arranged "as at oratorios,"[27] with the tragic actress Mary Ann Yates standing center-forward to read the poem beside a portrait of Garrick. Except for these superficial details of production, however, the two poems are vastly unlike; for while Garrick constantly shifted the metrical pace of his poem, following the tradition of the cantata ode, Sheridan patiently plied his heroic couplets, finding metrical variety and dramatic tension in the prosodic resources of the verse.

The monody held the boards for ten performances[28]—certainly a creditable record for a funeral oration, especially in that Garrick's jubilee ode could manage only eight. And when in 1816 Lord Byron's monody on Sheridan was read at Drury Lane, its close metrical imitation of Sheridan's poem clearly attested to Byron's view that the monody on Garrick was the best "address" in the language.[29]

V THE PROLOGUES AND EPILOGUES AS POETRY

Considering Sheridan's prologues and epilogues among thousands of others, Mary Etta Knapp leaves no question that he closely embraced presiding convention in them. According with convention, he generally thought of prologues and epilogues as being dramatic presentations separate and distinct from the plays they preceded or followed. In composing them, he shamelessly pilfered weary conventional conceits. He warmed over many a stale and moldy theme, apparently always ready (despite the merit of the case he pleaded) to curry favor from an audience usually innocent of clear judgment and often jaded of taste. In short, Sheridan nowhere belies Miss Knapp's comfortable generalization that "the prologues and epilogues of the eighteenth century are characteristic of their own time, reflecting the minutiae of daily life, presenting the difficulties and triumphs of the theatre, obeying changes in taste, recording in a lively manner social and dramatic history."[30]

At the same time, however, Sheridan's pieces engage the Classic paradox of prologue writing. As Miss Knapp herself notes, and as she quotes Henry Fielding as noting in his day, the work of individual prologue-epilogue writers often asserts a striking distinctiveness, even though the general conceptual detail of their work may be largely conventional.[31] Such, certainly, is Sheridan's case. His prologues and epilogues—only twelve in sum—add little leaven to the lump; but they clearly outline his assessment of the genre itself, suggesting his views (1) that prologues and epilogues must acknowledge the privileged position of the audience; (2) that their rhetoric is usually persuasive; (3) that their office is usually instructive; and (4) that they thrive upon formal and thematic convention.

In acknowledging the privileged position of the audience, Sheridan's prologues and epilogues see the playgoers as critics in spite of themselves. They have come to the theater to be entertained; but they seem, from the poet's point of view, to have no clear idea what constitutes good entertainment. The amorphous, corporate judgment they assert needs definition; so the prologues and epilogues define the judgment. In effect, they tell the audience what it likes and why it likes what it likes, thus to contrive a union of interests (more or less specific) between the playgoers and the play they are about to see or have just seen. Actually, then, the poet maintains authority over his audience, even as he acknowledges the audience's privileged position as critic *malgré lui.* Sheridan naturally delights in this sort of psychological situation; and (at least after the success of his first play) he exploits it delightfully by quite coolly manipulating the distance between his audience and the speaker of his piece.

His earliest fully extant prologue, for example (that for the second night of ***The Rivals,*** January 28, 1775), is an acting piece spoken between a sergeant-at-law and an attorney.[32] Its scenic point of view and its rather formal concluding set speech, in which the sergeant pleads the young poet's brief, hold the audience at a respectful distance and seek favor through cautious and tentative flattery, as befits the precarious position of a beginner whose first play owes its second performance wholly to the extraordinary indulgence of a sympathetic first-night jury. Even in this tentativeness, however, the poet (through his solicitor) declares the audience (jury) his friend, promises that he seeks only to please, insists that he values good criticism, and utterly disarms hostility by placing the playgoers in a constructive critical position. In effect, he invites the playgoers to coauthorship with him in the play, thus subtly sharing with them responsibility for its success and its failure. They are therefore much inclined to admire its merits and to minimize its weaknesses, especially since this second performance (given eleven days after the first and revised in response to first-night criticism) reflects the young poet's sincerity in seeking their friendly aid.

His case at last favorably decided, he greets his tenth-night audience with a new and warmly intimate prologue[33] spoken by Mrs. Bulkley, who plays Julia Melville in the production; and in it she directly solicits the playgoer's indulgences not for the playwright but for the Muse. Again, however, he acknowledges the privileged position of the audience by having his speaker encourage between playgoers and playwrights a cooperative effort against the usurping bastard, sentimental comedy. He does not dictate taste; he rather defines among friends a cogent detail of good judgment. Such a covert but persistent tact characterizes even the most insolent of his prologues and epilogues.

Thus if the epilogue to *Edward and Eleanora* (1775) assails at the outset the marital indifference of every wife in the audience, it finally rights matters by identifying them all with the martyred heroine of the play and thereby cleverly translates insult into compliment. If the epilogue to *Semiramis* (1776) attacks the demands of taste by offering a serious epilogue after tragedy, rather than the conventional comic one,[34] it disarms criticism by applauding at last the expansive "feeling heart" of the audience. If the epilogue to *The Fatal Falsehood* (1779) fiercely offers to damn the mediocrity of bluestocking scribblers, it finally yields to a proper chivalry and ends with compliments "vastly civil to Female Talent," as Sheridan puts it in a letter to Garrick.[35] Although psychic distance may vary from piece to piece, the controlling decorum is always the same: while honoring the audience's privilege as critic and customer, the poet asserts his own professional authority, subtly shaping the playgoer's judgment after his own.

The rhetoric of such a decorum is perforce persuasive, and the thematic aim is an instructive one. Topics for instruction in Sheridan's prologues and epilogues include not only esthetic matters but also moral and theatrical ones. For example, his prologue to *The Miniature Picture* (1780) points out the difficulties of meeting anticipated production schedules and then deplores the persisting popular taste for imported entertainments.[36] His managerial disgust for foreign art (especially the ballet and the opera) again erupts in the epilogue to *The Fair Circassian* (1781), where he openly laments the high salaries paid foreign performers. Quite conventional in theme, both these pieces instruct the audience to an awareness that imported art poisons the lifeblood of the English theater. On grounds both patriotic and artistic, they champion allegiance to the native stage.

Another theatrical topic, this one treated in an epilogue for a benefit play (undated), teaches the audience that an actor's lot is not a happy one—that for him the verdant springtime, which keeps playgoers out-of-doors and away from benefit performances, is often a bitter winter of the soul. Since each item of instruction implies a consequent obligation, all the prologues and epilogues treating of theatrical matters assert a moral emphasis, a clearly defined implication of oughtness. In effect, they say that playgoers ought to support the native stage, that they ought to sympathize with the manager's scheduling problems, that they ought to attend benefit performances, despite the inviting freshness of the spring. Similarly, the esthetic pieces tell the playgoers what they ought to admire and how they ought to let art—at least some forms of it—enrich their lives.

Sheridan's understanding of the prologue-epilogue genre, his sense of its integrity, apparently presupposes extensive use of formal conventions—the acting piece,[37] the plaintiff-jury metaphor,[38] the practice of having the speaker address each level of the house in turn[39]—but, if convention dominates his work, he personalizes it, as Garrick had done, by topical involvement in it. His own political interests, for example, add substance and vitality to his several uses of the parliamentary metaphor, a structural figure used much like the plaintiff-jury convention in pointing out the judicial and legislative privilege of the audience. Similarly, his career as theater manager enlivens each topical reference to actor and stage; and his career as playwright adds natural vigor to his acting prologues and epilogues.

The persistent liveliness of his work suggests, furthermore, that he embraced convention not for want of imagination but for support of the genre itself. Since he apparently saw thematic and formal convention as nourishing the prologue and epilogue as a poetic type, he sometimes emphasized convention by deliberately departing from it. On the tenth night of **The Rivals,** therefore, he deliberately violates the settled practice of awarding the prologue to a man, underscoring his deliberateness by causing Mrs. Bulkley to declare herself "A female counsel in a female's cause."[40] Consequently, he appeals to convention—the very convention he violates—to emphasize the significance of his theme. He achieves thematic emphasis through a similarly inverse process in the epilogue to *Semiramis* where his self-conscious and openly confessed departure from the conventional comic epilogue (after tragedy) strengthens the high seriousness of his discourse on tragic pathos.

Sheridan moved comfortably, then, within the framework of convention, sometimes personalizing it by involving himself topically in it, sometimes enlarging upon its effects by deliberately departing from it. In at least one detail, moreover, he increased the body of convention itself, adapting to the genre, through his epilogue to Hannah More's *The Fatal Falsehood* (1779), the tradition of the Theophrastian character.[41] This same epilogue, incidentally, offers insight into Sheridan's poetic craftsmanship. His papers yield up a draft of the poem described by Sichel as "no less than one hundred and forty-five unrhymed, unrhythmical lines," a "disjointed farrago" (I, 543). Most of these hobbled measures Sheridan discarded; others he hammered into a Theophrastian portrait cryptically typifying the domestic and artistic ambivalence of the dedicated bluestocking. It is a portrait properly said by Rhodes to be "as consummate in its finish as the neatest raillery of Pope";[42] and, while the poet's conceptual process might well be thought an "uncouth and bewildering way of shaping verse," it is for him an incontestably successful process, as a few representative lines from the poem indicate. They are lines spoken by an indignant male poetaster who is urgently intent on driving "*female* scribblers" from the stage:

> Unfinish'd here an epigram is laid,
> And there, a mantua-maker's bill unpaid;
> Here new-born plays fore-taste the town's applause,
> There, dormant patterns pine for future gauze;
> A moral essay now is all her care,
> A satire next, and then a bill of fare:

A scene she now projects, and now a dish
Here's Act the First—and here—Remove with
    Fish. (276)

Unlike other playwright-prologuists, Sheridan made no gesture to abolish the prologue-epilogue tradition. That the poems bear little relevance to the plays sandwiched between them nowhere distressed his sense of theater. If the genre took roots in the audience's desire for a brief moment of intimacy with the stage, the clearly cooperated in that interest, finding its idiom all but natural to him. Apparently, he honored the tradition as a respectable mode of entertainment, one asserting its own integrity through distinctive and settled conventions and one meriting, by testimony of his achievement in it, a creative effort by no means casual and cheap but everywhere tightly imagined and artistically honest.

Notes

1. Martin S. Day, "Anstey and Anapestic Satire in the Late Eighteenth Century," *English Literary History,* XV (1948), 128. Cecil Price attributes "Hymen and Hirco" to Sheridan in the *Times Literary Supplement* for July 11, 1958, p. 396.

2. Except where otherwise noted, page references to Sheridan's poetry cite Volume III of *Plays and Poems.*

3. These are Sichel's judgments (I, 314).

4. Ernest Rhys, *Lyric Poetry* (London, 1913), p. 370.

5. Sichel, I, 272.

6. As quoted in *A Vers de Société Anthology,* ed. Carolyn Wells (New York, 1907), p. xxiii.

7. Moore, I, 40-41.

8. Sichel, I, 273.

9. Ibid., 274; *Plays and Poems,* III, 229.

10. *Plays and Poems,* III, 259.

11. Moore, II, 90.

12. *Plays and Poems,* III, 197.

13. [15 Oct., 1814?], *Letters,* III, 202.

14. *Plays and Poems,* III, 198.

15. Sichel, I, 551.

16. Wallace Cable Brown, *The Triumph of Form* (Chapel Hill, 1948), p. 5.

17. Geoffrey Tillotson, *On the Poetry of Pope* (Oxford, 1950), p. 150.

18. Paul Fussell, *Theory of Prosody in Eighteenth-Century England,* (New London, Conn., 1954), pp. 113-15.

19. See the beginning of Chapter 2 above. For a much fuller discussion of Sheridan's prosody in relation to the theory of tensions see Jack D. Durant, "R. B. Sheridan's 'Verses to the Memory of Garrick': Poetic Reading as Formal Theatre," *Southern Speech Journal,* XXXV (1969), 120-31.

20. Thomas Sheridan, *Lectures on the Art of Reading* (London, 1775), II, 75.

21. As quoted by Fussell, p. 113.

22. MS W. b. 479 (p. 133) in the Folger Shakespeare Library, a newspaper clipping not identified as to source (but bearing the handwritten date May 12, 1779), specifies the points at which musical interludes occur.

23. Quoting the second issue of the poem (one of several copies in the Folger collection), identical to the first except for a correction in the dedicatory epistle. A definitive text is now readily available in *The Dramatic Works of Richard Brinsley Sheridan,* ed. Cecil Price (Oxford, 1973), II, 457-62.

24. Moore, I, 176.

25. Thomas Sheridan, *Art of Reading,* II, 145.

26. Ibid., 84.

27. *Town and Country Magazine,* XI (1779), 117.

28. *The London Stage,* Pt. 5, Vol. 1, records performances at Drury Lane as follows: March 11, 13, 18, 20, 25; April 10, 21, 26; May 24; June 3.

29. George Gordon, Lord Byron, *Letters and Journals,* ed. Rowland E. Prothero (London, 1898), II, 377. For an expanded version of this discussion of the monody, see Jack D. Durant, "R. B. Sheridan's 'Verses to the Memory of Garrick': Poetic Reading as Formal Theatre," *Southern Speech Journal,* xxxv (1969), 120-31.

30. Knapp, p. 8.

31. Ibid., p. 28.

32. Cecil Price, in "The First Prologue to *The Rivals,*" *Review of English Studies,* new series, XX (1969), 192-95, prints the fragmentary first-night prologue as recently found at Somerville College, Oxford.

33. Such changes were not unusual. See Knapp, p. 2.

34. See Knapp, pp. 278-79.

35. January 10 [1778], *Letters,* I, 122.

36. For comment on this persistent theme see Knapp, pp. 178; 185.

37. Second-night prologue to *The Rivals* (*Plays and Poems,* I, 25, 26); epilogue to *The Fatal Falsehood* (*Plays and Poems,* III, 275-77). See Knapp, p. 25; 96-97.

38. Second-night prologue to *The Rivals;* cf. Knapp, p. 108 for precedents.

39. Epilogue to *Edward and Eleanora;* cf. Knapp, p. 136 for precedents.

40. *Plays and Poems,* I, 27.

41. See Knapp, pp. 307-308.

42. *Plays and Poems,* III, 277.

Jack D. Durant (essay date 1983)

SOURCE: "Sheridan's Grotesques," in *The Theatre Annual,* Vol. XXXVIII, 1983, pp. 13-30.

[*In the following essay, Durant discusses Sheridan's juxtaposition of the comic and the terrifying in his dramas.*]

From the beginning of his career as a writer, Richard Brinsley Sheridan demonstrated a distinct flair for the grotesque. His first published poem, **"The Ridotto of Bath"** (1771), pictures gaudily dressed people crowding into the new Assembly Rooms at Bath and gorging themselves in a disgustingly comic way. They disfigure themselves with chewing and swallowing; they spill food all over their clothes and trample it messily into the carpeting.[1] Another poem of the same year, actually a loose translation from the Greek poetaster Aristaenetus, presents two deformed prudes, one with a hunched back and the other with a single eye, who earn the speaker's contempt by daring to make judgments against his ladylove while suppressing torrid passions of their own. They can pretend to virtue only because they find in "blest Deformity" an "antidote to Love's attack."[2] The effects here, and in **"The Ridotto of Bath,"** qualify as "grotesque" because they assert "the co-presence of the laughable and something which is incompatible with the laughable." Displaying a "strong affinity with the *physically abnormal,*" they achieve "a mixture in some way or other of *both* the comic and the terrifying (or the disgusting, repulsive, etc.) in a problematical (i.e., not readily resolvable) way."[3] Sheridan sought such effects early, and he evoked them so persistently that they deserve notice as a major feature of his comic.

To give them the notice they deserve, however, is to commit oneself to a complicated exposition, for the subject is at once dramaturgical and historical. That is, it explores one of Sheridan's favorite means of controlling audience response while also demonstrating his evolving application of this means. The latter of these concerns, the historical arm of the exposition, calls for examining the grotesque element, its forms and functions, in each of his comedies in turn. The former of them requires that an apparent assumption of his be explained at the outset and in the clearest possible terms.

It holds that beauty and ugliness in the human form generate their own auras of expectation. To look upon beauty is to know comfort, delight, and repose. Affection flows effortlessly to it. It commands freedom and prerogative and reflects order, propriety, and harmony. To look upon ugliness, however, is to experience recoil. Affection retreats from it. It aggravates distress and scatters composure. It opposes order and nature. Neither beauty nor ugliness allows passive response; each asserts its own dynamic. But to cross, mix, and confuse the expectations attaching to the two of them is to open complex comic possibilities, and from these possibilities comes the grotesque comedy of Sheridan. By requiring his characters to confront ugliness in terms of beauty, or to pretend, in ugliness, to the prerogatives of beauty, or to blind themselves to their own ugliness while deploring the ugliness of others, or to dispense affection to ugliness and decay, he generates in his audiences internal crises as troubling as they are hilarious.

In the second act of **The Rivals,** for example, Jack Absolute communicates such a crisis to us when he contemplates the match his father has made for him. His heart, he says, is engaged to "an Angel" (Lydia Languish); he cannot countenance just any "mass of ugliness" his father might name for him. But his father, Sir Anthony, confronts him with a troubling prospect:

> Z———ds! sirrah! the lady shall be as ugly as I choose: she shall have a hump on each shoulder; she shall be as crooked as the Crescent; her one eye shall roll like the Bull's in Cox's musaeum—she shall be all this, sirrah!—yet I'll make you ogle her all day, and sit up all night to write sonnets on her beauty.
>
> (II.i.361-66)[4]

The effect here derives from diverse elements. Not only must Jack see his angel supplanted by a monstrous form; he must imagine himself embracing this form. He must proffer to ugliness the rites of beauty, and from his plight arises for us a most anxious merriment, a genuinely grotesque commingling of the laughable and the terrifying.

Nor does the matter end here. When, in act three, Jack knows the angelic Lydia to be the girl intended for him, he can feign a dutiful acquiescence in his father's wishes without risking anything. He would prefer, he says, that his wife have "the usual number of limbs, and a limited quantity of back: and tho' *one* eye may be very agreeable, yet as the prejudice has always run in favour of *two,*" he would "not wish to affect a singularity in that article" (III.i.79-82). But his principal wish is to follow his father's choice, and in doing so he is prepared to disregard all the received expectations of beauty and ugliness. To identify with Sir Anthony now is to experience with him the shock of seeing human nature go into cold suspension, an unsettling prospect even in jest, shadowed as it is by a hideous physical form. The grotesque, the co-presence of the comic and the disturbing, again afflicts the laughter.

Grotesquerie in **The Rivals** also colors the Julia—Faulkland action. In practicing his bizarre psychological cruelties against Julia, Faulkland seeks to assure himself that not the slightest human taint touches her affection for him. Any show from her of the joy, exhilaration, and sheer good luck of being in love brings her motives under suspicion and subjects them to subtle, narrow, and hair-splitting analyses. "For what quality must I love you?" she finally asks desperately, and his response probes the very sources of her affection. To love him for mind or understanding, he whines, were but to esteem him. "And for person—I have often wish'd myself deformed, to be convinced that I owed no obligation *there* for any part of your affection" (III.iii.55-59). Earnestly, but imprudently, Julia informs him that he is not the handsomest man she has ever seen. But, she says, "my heart has never asked my eyes if it were so or not." Yet even so loving an assurance as this fails to comfort him. Love, he says, must do more than simply soften defects; it must somehow transform the forbidding into the beautiful. Were he monstrous in appearance, she should, if she truly loved him, "think none so fair." Again Sheridan generates a situation requiring that the expectations attaching to beauty and ugliness be defeated. Through grotesque effects he perfectly internizes in his audience poor Julia's dilemma, the dilemma of one expected to surrender to some kind of extra-human devotion all the accustomed tendencies of human nature.

Certainly the most pervasive grotesque effect in *The Rivals* is the malapropism, which qualifies as a grotesque effect through its character as an unresolved comic device. What often astonishes people about the malapropism is that it is not a device for innuendo. When Mrs. Malaprop says that she would not wish a daughter of hers to be a "progeny" of learning but that girls need only a "supercilious" knowledge of accounts and should have enough "geometry" to know something of the "contagious" countries, the comedy derives not from innuendo but from confusion. Unintended meanings do not supplant intended ones. Mrs. Malaprop does not, like Smollett's Win Jenkins in *Humphry Clinker,* unwittingly talk dirty or ensnare herself in semantic traps. If she did so, the comic device would resolve itself in a new domain of meaning, a result which Sheridan's revisions, all of which level innuendoes, seem designed to frustrate.[5] What happens instead is that the misspoken word insists upon its own meaning quite irrespective of the intended word, and the listener struggles to construct a relationship of meaning between what is said and what is meant, between "progeny" and "prodigy," for example, or "contiguous" and "contagious." Since the actual relationship is aural and not semantic, the malapropism allows no resolution of meaning. It converts meaning into nonsense, an effect the more keenly felt because the pronunciation is studied and precise (words "ingeniously *misapplied,* without being *mispronounced,*" as Julia Melville puts it in the play [I.ii.130-31]). Like a framed grotesque drawing, the malapropism confines chaos within a boundary of order and provokes puzzled and anxious laughter.

Its way of dragging together incongruous verbal elements is, in the phrase of one commentator on grotesque literature, "a major feature of the grotesque,"[6] and its commitment to nonsense relates it to neologism, a tested grotesque stratagem, which scatters composure by shattering meaning. In observing that grotesque language characteristically creates a void where moments before had been solid ground, Neil Rhodes describes the malapropism exactly.[7] It snatches solid ground from under us. If it does not challenge the conventions of beauty and ugliness in a visual way, it certainly does so in an affective one. That is, the internal crises it aggravates are closely similar to those aggravated by grotesque visual effects, and it complements perfectly the physical appearance of Mrs. Malaprop, an *"old weather-beaten she-dragon"* whose vanity *"makes her dress up her coarse features"* and disavow her failing

eyesight (III.iii.54;59-60). She is a physical grotesque who speaks grotesquely.

A final grotesque moment in *The Rivals* comes in the fourth act when Jack Absolute answers Faukland's questions about Lydia's capricious conduct. "What can you mean?" asks Faukland; "Has Lydia chang'd her mind?—I should have thought her duty and inclination would now have pointed to the same object." And Jack gives him this remarkable answer:

> Aye, just as the eyes do of a person who squints:—when her *love eye* was fix'd on *me*—t'other—her *eye* of *duty,* was finely obliqued:—but when duty bid her point *that* the same way—off t'other turn'd on a swivel, and secured its retreat with a frown!
>
> (IV.iii.64-67)

Jack's grotesque simile endows Lydia's conduct with complex emotional resonances. What was before romantic and whimsical is now mixed with formidable and disturbing associations; it is comic still but no longer free-spirited. A main dynamic of the play, Lydia's caprice, thus assumes a deeper shading, one governed by the familiar conventions of beauty and ugliness, and through this extraordinary associational device, Sheridan colors the whole comic ambience of his second comedy, *St. Patrick's Day.*

Among the grotesque moments in *St. Patrick's Day* is a colloquy between Lieutenant O'Connor, the hero, and his lugubrious friend, Dr. Rosy, about the tendency among fashionable women to render themselves into monstrous forms by abusing cosmetic and dress. In hoops, whalebone breastplates, and turreted headgear, they fashion themselves into lumbering amazons, and they rouge their cheeks so thickly that they could not display a blush of modesty even if their midnight dissipations left them blood enough to raise one (I.I.89-96). They defeat beauty in the name of beauty. Other grotesque moments in this play—the most characteristic ones—draw upon associations of disease, decay, and dismemberment: Justice Credulous, the father of the heroine, swears that "he had rather see his Daughter in a scarlet Fever, than in the arms of a Soldier" (I.i.77-78); Lauretta, the heroine, romances about serving as the crutch of a soldier whose leg has been shot off in battle (I.ii.19). And the comic distresses aroused by these sentiments hardly touch the scope and persistence of Dr. Rosy's lamentations for his dead wife Dolly. In them, Sheridan reaches for grotesque effects a great deal more intense than anything he had tried in *The Rivals,* for here he manipulates expectations not just as they relate to beauty and ugliness but also as they relate to disease and health. Dr. Rosy is a disease lover. The fever of love had come upon him while he was treating poor Dolly for daily colics, and in her prevailing unhealth had lain his greatest joy:

> Ah! poor Dolly!—I never shall see her like again!—such an arm for a Bandage—Veins that seem'd to invite the Lancet—then her Skin—smooth and white as a Gallypot—her Mouth round, and not larger than the mouth of a penny Phial!—Her lips!—Conserve of

Roses!—then her Teeth!—none of your sturdy Fixtures—ach[e], as they would—'twas but a Pull, and out they came—I beleive [*sic*] I've drawn half a score of her poor dear Pearls—[weeps]—but what avails her Beauty,—Death has no Consideration—one must die as well as another.

(I.i.109-16)

Throughout the play Dr. Rosy grieves for this inverted Petrarchan disaster, cursing fate for carrying her beyond surgery and dosage, for cutting short her privilege of rotting and wasting above ground. Her toothless, cadaverous form broods over the play like a vulture, and it hovers round even after the play has ended, for in the closing lines Dr. Rosy superimposes the image of his Dolly upon the bright young form of Lauretta. Earlier in the play he had remarked of Lauretta "Ah! I never see her, but she reminds me of my poor dear Wife" (I.i.105), and at the end, in anticipating her marriage to O'Connor, he says to her "And I wish you may make just such a Wife, as my poor Dear Dolly—" (II.ii.217-18). Like Jack Absolute's simile of the squint-eyed person in *The Rivals,* this speech carries strong associational force, and the effect here is yet more comprehensive than it is in *The Rivals,* for it embraces the entire play. Sheridan gives the last word not to Lauretta but to Dolly, not to nuptial merriment but to grotesque of disease. He therefore robs the ending of its comfortable resolution and imbues with grotesque associations the entire recollected action of the play.

A remarkable feature of the grotesque in *The Rivals* and *St. Patrick's Day* is that very little of it actually appears upon the stage. Hints dropped in the dialogue of *The Rivals* suggest that Mrs. Malaprop is grotesque in appearance; and in the disguise of Humphrey Hum, the greasy one-eyed lummox, Lieutenant O'Connor assumes a grotesque form for one portion of *St. Patrick's Day.* But the grotesque effects in these two plays derive mainly from figurative and descriptive language. In *The Duenna,* however, Sheridan came round to objectifying his grotesques. Perhaps a moment in *St. Patrick's Day,* the one in which Humphrey Hum ardently mumbles the beautiful Lauretta (II.ii.26-32), opened to Sheridan the comic possibilities of the objective grotesque. Already resident in his mind, too, was the crone with whom Sir Anthony had threatened Jack in *The Rivals,* the one with "skin like a mummy, and the beard of a Jew" (II.i.364). From this one imaginary horror might well have sprung the two shocking forms of Margaret and Isaac, the full-fledged stage grotesques of *The Duenna.*

It ought to be emphasized that a grotesque is not simply a caricature. Caricature implies superficial distortion; it "alters the outline of a given original and gains its effect by exaggerating a part with respect to the whole," but the grotesque "is rather a distortion that penetrates to the bases of our perception of reality." It interferes in a radical and aggressive way with "the stability and constancy of the human form."[8] Caricature applies, then, to Bob Acres and Sir Lucius O'Trigger of *The Rivals.* Sheridan gives comic exaggeration to their types as cowardly bumpkin and bellicose Irishman respectively. Dr. Rosy, the lugubrious quack of *St. Patrick's Day,* also emerges as caricature, for all that his maunderings give us the grotesque Dolly. But, in Margaret and Isaac, Sheridan goes much further than exaggerating a part for the whole; he assails the human form in a radical and aggressive way. In the words of Don Jerome, the tyrannical father of *The Duenna,* old Margaret, the title character, is a "scare-crow" with "impenetrable features," a "hag" with a "dragon's front" (I.iii.122;129;130-31) down whose "deal cheeks" can only flow "tears of turpentine" (I.iii.164). Her fellow grotesque, Isaac Mendoza, sees her as having skin of "nankeen"; "for her eyes," he continues, "their utmost merit is in not squinting—

for her teeth, where there is one of ivory, its neighbor is pure ebony, black and white alternately, just like the keys of an harpsicord. Then as to her singing, and heavenly voice—by this hand, she has a shrill crack'd pipe, that sounds for all the world like a child's trumpet.

(II.iii.71-76)

In addition to these graces she sports a downy beard: "the razor wou'd'nt be amiss for either of us," says Isaac (II.ii.62). But Isaac himself has nothing to boast; nor is Margaret backward in turning tables on him:

Dares such a thing as you pretend to talk of beauty—a walking rouleau—a body that seems to owe all its consequence to the dropsy—a pair of eyes like two dead beetles in a wad of brown dough. A beard like an artichoke, with dry shrivell'd jaws that wou'd disgrace the mummy of a monkey.

(II.vii.89-93)

By actually parading upon the stage the grotesque forms of Margaret and Isaac, Sheridan manipulates with new flexibility the expectations attaching to beauty and ugliness. In one instance he draws comedy from Isaac's utter blindness to his own unloveliness: "Why, what's the matter with the face? I think it is a very engaging face; and I am sure a lady must have very little taste who could dislike my beard" (I.v.84-86). Later the comedy turns upon Isaac's misdirected hopes as he waits to meet old Margaret, whom he thinks to be the beautiful young Louisa and whose picture has been drawn for him in terms of Louisa's beauty. In the next scene the comedy rises from Isaac's disappointment and confusion as he actually meets Margaret and must confront her ugliness as though it were Louisa's beauty. Out of this meeting grows a colloquy in which Margaret presumes to the prerogatives of beauty by affecting a coy reserve; and Isaac, searching desperately for a compliment to give her, compares her to a woman very dear to him, his mother. The comedy generated here then reaches into a scene in which Isaac encounters Don Jerome and must try to determine his reasons for calling "Louisa" beautiful. When Jerome insists that her beauty combines all the best features of the family (her father's eyes, her Aunt Ursula's nose, her grandmother's forehead [II.iii.45-58]), Isaac sees these features not in the abstract, as Jerome would have him do, but in the concrete, as though transplanted from the ancient countenances who first wore them. The songs, too, assist grotesque effects in the play. Before meeting Margaret, Isaac sings a song (II.i) explaining that his standards of beauty are not high; he asks only that a woman not have a beard (a condition only old Margaret, of all women, cannot honor). And after Isaac and Margaret have met, Don Carlos (a friend to everyone in the play) constructs in song a stunning incongruity (II.ii). With the two grotesques standing beside him, he sings "Ah! sure a pair was never seen, / So justly form'd to meet by nature. / The youth excelling so in mien, / The maid in every grace of feature." In the second stanza he congratulates the children of such a pair, who stand to inherit sense, beauty, grace, and spirit. The contrast between what is seen and what is heard sharply intensifies the grotesque effect.

The antics of Margaret and Isaac thus open to Sheridan a complex repertoire of comic possibilities: ugliness confronted in terms of beauty, ugliness pretending to beauty, ugliness blind to itself, beauty promised and ugliness delivered, the received expectations of beauty and ugliness twisted through an elaborate, sometimes even ironic, system of intricate permutations. Nor is grotesquerie in **The Duenna** limited to the antics of Margaret and Isaac. Through the fat friar, Father Paul, a sleek epicure bloated by self-indulgence (but pleading flatulence from starvation), Sheridan generates a moral revulsion as dark and concentrated as any in his comedies, and again his medium is the stage grotesque, the grotesque form actually seen upon the stage.

In his book about Sheridan, Mark Auburn remarks that to move, as Sheridan did in 1776, from Covent Garden to Drury Lane was to move "from the home of 'low' comedy and comic opera to the house of 'high' and 'wit' comedy."[9] Perhaps such a sense of new surroundings motivated Sheridan to expunge every hint of grotesquerie from **A Trip to Scarborough,** his adaptation of Vanbrugh's *The Relapse.* Even so merry a grotesque moment as that in which Vanbrugh's nurse remembers the infant Hoyden at her breast—"how it used to hang at this poor tett, and suck and squeeze, and kick and sprawl it would, till the belly on't was so full it would drop off like a leech" (IV.i.108-110)[10]—fell victim to Sheridan's ax, his "little wholesome pruning" as he has one of the characters in his adaptation put it (II.i.23). But with his second major creative effort at Drury Lane, **The School for Scandal,** his flair for the grotesque emerged again and in an idiom well suited to the high and witty comedy demanded of him. It is not the broad and boisterous grotesquerie of **The Duenna;** nor does it actually appear upon the stage, but it achieves subtle and far-reaching effects.

Emerging in the dialogue of the scandal cabal in Act II, it takes the form of an accretive wit sequence in which the interlocutors build upon one another's ideas or attempt to outdo one another in formulating grotesque images. In this manner Lady Sneerwell and Sir Benjamin Backbite con-

struct the image of the Widow Ocre. To Lady Sneerwell's derogations on the way the widow "caulks her wrinkles," Sir Benjamin adds "it is not that she paints so ill—but when she has finish'd her Face she joins it so badly to her Neck that she looks like a mended Statue in which the Connoisseur sees at once that the Head's modern tho' the Trunk's antique (II.ii.54-57). A similar sequence of associations leads to Lady Teazle's description of Mrs. Prim, who, in concealing her loss of teeth in front, "draws her mouth 'till it positively resembles the aperture of a Poor's-Box, and all her words appear to slide out edgeways" (II.ii.67-69). And, in the most elaborate sequence of all, Sir Benjamin and Crabtree portray Cousin Ogle, a relative of Mrs. Candour's:

> CRABTREE. O to be sure she has herself the oddest countenance that ever was seen—'tis a collection of Features from all the different Countries of the Globe.
>
> SIR BENJ. So she has indeed.—An Irish front.
>
> CRABTREE. Caledonian Locks—
>
> SIR BENJ. Dutch nose—
>
> CRABTREE. Austrian lip—
>
> SIR BENJ. Complexion of a Spaniard—
>
> CRABTREE. And Teeth a la Chinoise—
>
> SIR BENJ. In short her Face resembles a Table d'hote at Spaw where no two guests are of a nation—
>
> CRABTREE. Or a Congress at the close of a general War—wherein all the members even to her eyes appear to have a different interest and her Nose and Chin are the only parties like to join issue.
>
> MRS. CANDOUR. Ha! ha! ha! (II.ii.115-29)

The grotesquerie generated here, and in the other such wit sequences, assists Sheridan to remarkably complex effects. It excites laughter at the expense not only of the people described and of those who describe them, the malicious scandal cabal, but also of the audience itself, whose laughter is the same as that laughed by Mrs. Candour. Through their brilliant grotesque inventions the scandal cabal display an irresistible sportiveness, the kind of sportiveness said by John Ruskin to characterize much grotesque art,[11] and through this sportiveness they woo the audience and Mrs. Candour (in spite of themselves) to their party. It is a stratagem whereby Sheridan requires everyone to share in the blame, not just the cabal and its victims, not just Mrs. Candour, but everyone delighted by a game well played, however malicious, and it demonstrates that the grotesque has a secure place in high and witty comedy.

If the grotesque moments in Sheridan's last two finished comedies are brief and few, they are certainly striking. The opening lines of **The Camp** give report of a road accident in which an old woman, a brace of chickens, and a one-eyed colt have tumbled together headlong into a ditch, a picture at once comic and formidable (I.i.1-10). Among his con games in **The Critic,** Puff includes such agonizing and disfiguring physical disorders as dropsy, for which he reports himself twice tapped, consumption, and total paralysis (I.ii.20-24;128-29). And had Sheridan finished his long-expected comedy *Affectation,* it would clearly have been the most strikingly and persistently grotesque of them all.

Textual editors differ in dating the fragments of *Affectation.* On the basis of handwriting, Cecil Price dates some parts of them to as early as 1772; Crompton Rhodes places them after *The School for Scandal,* and rumor had it that Sheridan intended after 1777 to form them into a finished play.[12] Since they suggest the language and spirit of all his comedies, they offer few internal clues for dating; but their value here turns less upon when they were written than upon their character as fragments. In representing the first stirrings of Sheridan's creative mind, they show the grotesque to be an acute and spontaneous tendency of his comic imagination.

Basically they take three forms. Some of them describe characters who might actually appear upon the stage; others seem to be rough segments of dialogue. A third, which combines properties of the first two, suggests dialogue lapsing into character or character shading into dialogue.

Representing the first of these forms is a grotesque fat woman:

> A fat woman trundling into a Room on Castors—her sitting was a leaning—rises like a Bowl on the wrong Bias—rings on her Fingers—and her fat arms strangled with Bracelet—which belted them like corded Brawn—rolling and heaving when she laugh'd with the rattles in her Throat and a most apoplectic ogle—you wish to draw her out like opera-glass (p. 813).[13]

Other figures apparently visualized as appearing on the stage include "A long lean Man, with all his Limbs rambling," who "appears roll'd out or run up against a wall" and whose standing cross-legged makes him "look like a caduceus." His obese wife ("one's a mast, and the other all Hulk") forms with him an astonishing grotesque contrast.

Dialogue carrying grotesque associations reads as follows:

> I hate to see a prettying woman studying—Looks and endeavouring to recollect an ogle, like Lady—who . . . oblig(e)s her ogle in all degrees—having le(a)rned to play eyelids like a venetian Blind. Then I hate to see an old woman putting herself Back to a girl (pp. 812-13).

And:

> Shall I be ill to Day—? shall I be nervous—your Ladyship was nervous yesterday—was I? then I'll have a cold—I haven't had a cold this Fortnight—a cold is becoming—ahem—no I'll not have a cough—that's fatiguing—no—no this Bow is very clumsy—psha!—it isn't becoming—here take it away—I'll be quite well—you become sickness—your La'ship always looks vastly well—when you're ill (p. 816)

And:

> "Shall you be at Lady————'s—I'm told the Bramin is to be there, and the new French philosopher."—No—it will be pleasanter at Lady————'s conversazione—the cow with two heads will be there."[14]

Passages of indeterminate form include the following:

> her Features so unfortunately formed that she could never dissemble or put on Sweetness enough to induce anyone to give her occasion to shew her bitterness (p. 814).

And:

> The Lodestone of true Beauty draws the hardest substances—not like the warm Dowager—who prate(s) herself into heat to get the notice of a few Papier mache Fops as you rub dutch sealing wax to draw Paper (p. 815).

In these fragments emerge many of the grotesque strategies apparent in Sheridan's finished comedies—grotesque forms seen and juxtaposed on the stage, speeches carrying grotesque associations, grotesque effects based upon disease, natural and artificial forms mixed in grotesque ways. The grotesque excites even the first stirrings of Sheridan's comic thought just as it permeates his finished work. While always holding it well within the domain of comedy, never letting it shade into horror or debilitating distress (as it might legitimately do),[15] he found himself always a ready agent of its impulses and an eager student of its possibilities. It is a basic ingredient of his comic.

We have seen that it generates in his work specific effects as various and intricate as the forms it takes. Each comedy constructs new instances of it, and each instance invites analysis in local contexts. For impressions of what it achieves generally, as part of a broad and tenacious tradition, we can turn to Philip Thomson's book on the grotesque. One general effect of the grotesque, writes Thomson, is that it tends to "bewilder and disorient, to bring the reader (or viewer) up short, jolt him out of accustomed ways of perceiving the world and confront him with a radically different, disturbing perspective."[16] It therefore generates a sense of alienation, a sense of removal from the familiar and trusted. A second general effect is that it aggravates ambivalence. It both disarms anxiety and creates it. To support this point, Thomson quotes another commentator, Thomas Cramer (in a translation by Michael Steig) as observing that 'the grotesque is the feeling of anxiety aroused by means of the comic pushed to an extreme,' but conversely that it 'is the defeat, by means of the comic, of anxiety in the face of the inexplicable.'[17] It imposes a comic perspective on the troubling aspects of experience and thus renders them less formidable to consciousness than they might otherwise be, but it never wholly neutralizes the threat they offer. Consequently the laughter it excites is never "free." In laughing at the grotesque, we experience liberation and inhibition at one and the same time, irresolubly.[18] A third general effect, then, is that the grotesque asserts the irresoluble ambiguity of life. It rejects the fiction that tragedy and comedy happen by turns and insists, as Thomson puts it, "that the vale of tears and the circus are one, that tragedy is in some ways comic and all comedy in some way tragic and pathetic."[19] Ironically, this complex vision of life gives rise to a fourth general effect of the grotesque, the effect of playfulness. To assert ambiguity and aggravate ambivalence and shatter complacency and reconstruct reality is to explore and analyze and constantly invent the means of doing so. An irrepressible sense of play thus surrounds the grotesque.[20]

In generating such effects as these, the grotesque in Sheridan's comedies provides an index to what is really most evocative about his art: its way of speaking not so much to the mind as to the visceral experience. If it is thematically thin, it is experientially very dense. If its situations and ideas flirt with shallow certitudes, its complex local effects, especially its grotesque moments, disallow all facile complacency. By frustrating expectations and dispersing internal comforts and provoking unpleasant confrontations, they send to nerve endings and emotional awarenesses the alarming message that life is not as simple as one might wish, that even playfulness and high spirit project the shadow of some desolate reality. In his book *The Ludicrous Demon,* Lee Byron Jennings makes an observation possibly applicable to Sheridan. "The grotesque," writes Jennings, "thrives in an atmosphere of disorder and is inhibited in any period characterized by a pronounced sense of dignity, an emphasis on harmony and order of life, an affinity for the typical and normal, and a prosaically realistic approach to the arts." Then he adds a point pertinent to Sheridan and his times: "If a considerable degree of grotesqueness nevertheless appears in the art of such a period, we might be justified in suspecting that it is a reaction against the prevailing standards and a symptom of their decay, that—as is often the case—the stress on prosaic and plausible things and the wish to embrace an ordered reality conceal a fascination with disorder and a yearning for unfettered exercise of the imagination."[21] It might well be true of Sheridan that his disenchantments with prevailing artistic, moral, and social standards, the frustrations and nagging apprehensions leading eventually to his burlesque play **The Critic** and his long career in opposition government, found expression too in his grotesques. His grotesques testify, in any case, to a complex comic view, one sensitive to the contradictions blighting human experience and determined to present them boldly. No drama asserts more significance to the art of Sheridan than the internal one based upon conflicts of feeling, and no such conflicts achieve greater vigor and depth in his work than the ones deriving from his grotesques.

Notes

1. See *Sheridan's Plays and Poems,* ed. R. Crompton Rhodes (1928; rpt. New York: Russell & Russell, 1962), III, 122.

2. *Sheridan's Plays and Poems,* III, 156, 158.

3. Philip Thomson, *The Grotesque* (London: Methuen, 1972), pp. 3, 9, 21.

4. References to the plays of Sheridan cite *Sheridan's Plays,* ed. Cecil Price (London: Oxford University Press, 1975).

5. For example, Mrs. Malaprop's "O he will perforate my Mistery" becomes in revision "O, he will desolve my mystery" (V.iii.193). See *The Rivals . . . Edited from the Larpent MS,* ed. Richard L. Purdy (Oxford: Clarendon, 1935), p. 115.

6. Neil Rhodes, *Elizabethan Grotesque* (London: Routledge & Kegan Paul, 1980), p. 25.

7. *Elizabethan Grotesque,* p. 26.

8. Lee Byron Jennings, *The Ludicrous Demon. Aspects of the Grotesque in German Post-Romantic Prose* (Berkeley: University of California Press), p. 9.

9. Mark S. Aubum, *Sheridan's Comedies: Their Contexts and Achievements* (Lincoln: University of Nebraska Press, 1977), p. 80.

10. As printed in *English Dramatists from Dryden to Sheridan,* 2nd ed., ed. G. H. Nettleton, A. E. Case, and G. W. Stone, Jr. (Boston: Houghton Mifflin, 1969), p. 285.

11. "The Stones of Venice," in *The Works of John Ruskin,* ed. E. T. Cook and Alexander Wedderburn (London: George Allen, 1904), XI, 151: [T]he grotesque falls into two branches, sportive grotesque and terrible grotesque; but . . . we cannot legitimately consider it under these two aspects, because . . . there are few grotesques so utterly playful as to be overcast with no shade of fearfulness, and few so fearful as absolutely to exclude all ideas of jest."

12. See Cecil Price, ed. *The Dramatic Works of Richard Brinsley Sheridan* (Oxford: Clarendon, 1973), pp. 808-10; Rhodes, *Plays and Poems,* III, 295-97. Price (p. 809) notes references made to *Affectation* in *The Morning Chronicle* for 16 October 1780 and *The Morning Post* for 6 November 1781.

13. Except in one instance (see note 14 below) the fragments of *Affectation* are quoted from Cecil Price's edition of Sheridan's *Dramatic Works.*

14. Rhodes, *Plays and Poems,* III, 302. A portion of this speech is omitted from the Price edition.

15. In "The Stones of Venice," *Works,* XI, 151, Ruskin indicates that the ludicrous and fearful elements may prevail in the grotesque to varying degrees. In the "terrible grotesque" fearful elements prevail; in the "sportive grotesque" ludicrous elements prevail.

16. Thomson, p. 58.

17. Thomson, p. 60, quoting Thomas Cramer's *Das Groteske bei E. T. A. Hoffman* (1966) as translated by Michael Steig in "Defining the Grotesque: An Attempt at Synthesis," *Journal of Aesthetics and Art Criticism,* 29 (Summer 1970), 256.

18. Thomson, p. 59.

19. Thomson, p. 63.

20. Thomson, p. 64.

21. Jennings, pp. 26-27.

Anne Parker (essay date 1986)

SOURCE: "'Absolute Sense' in Sheridan's *The Rivals*," in *Ball State University Forum*, Vol. XXVII, No. 3, Summer, 1986, pp. 10-19.

[In the following essay, Parker considers Sheridan's balance of wit and sentimentality in The Rivals.*]*

Sheridan has frequently been accused of trying to revive a moribund dramatic tradition, namely Restoration comedy. In these terms, he becomes a kind of second-hand Congreve, and not a very good one at that. Other critics, pointing to the sentiment in his plays, accuse him of being the very thing he supposedly ridicules, a sentimentalist.[1] Neither of these accusations, which in effect try to put Sheridan's comedies snugly into one of two camps, takes into account what is now starting to become a critical commonplace: the Georgian period had its own view of comedy and, in its own way, developed the laughing tradition.[2] Sheridan is no exception. At his best, he adapted the conventions of the past to his own comic ends.

Unlike what the Scotchman (in Sheridan's fragment of the same name) calls **"Grave Comedy"** (804), which strives to inculcate a serious moral, Sheridan's plays reflect folly and seek to mend it. More than that, like the Restoration comedies of the past, his plays deal with artifice, though in Sheridan's case the artifice is the sentimental pose. Comedy for Sheridan has a corrective function, directed not just at folly, which takes many forms, but also at sentimental excess. Those "things that shadow and conceal" man's true nature (Etherege III, i. 24) can, in Sheridan's terms, as easily be "witty" as they can be "sentimental."[3]

What Sheridan attempts to do in his plays is to create a balance between mirth and sentiment; he is at once benevolent and critical. What to the Restoration dramatist is a tension between the private and the public self, between appearance and reality, becomes to the sentimental dramatist an identification (Krutch 254). Eighteenth-century dramatists like Sheridan once again show the discrepancy between what is shown and what is concealed, but Sheridan does so by writing what Loftis calls "benign comedies with a satirical bite" (9).

Sheridan achieves this balance by his introduction of "absolute sense," common sense tempered by mirth and softened by good nature.[4] In this, he is very much a part of the eighteenth-century tradition. Auburn, in his study of Sheridan's comedies, mentions the importance of common sense to Georgian comic writers in general (125). Shirley Strum Kenny also argues convincingly that "the Charles Surfaces and Captain Absolutes of later eighteenth-century drama" owe much to the good sense of earlier heroes (62-63).

Therefore, freed from both salaciousness and sententiousness, Sheridan's best comedies reflect "flesh and blood" (Prologue, *The Rivals*, 1. 29). In this respect, his "mix'd character," as Congreve calls such characters in his *Amendments*, is a visible mixture of faults and virtues (453). Sheridan thereby seeks to show man's undefaced side as well as his more knavish one. His doing so places him firmly within existing dramatic traditions and not within just one camp or another. His doing so also confirms his own stature as a comic dramatist.

In his earliest play, **The Rivals** (1775), Sheridan develops his comic theme of "absolute sense" and adapts the modes of the past to his own ends.[5] Restoration playwrights dramatize the corrupting influence of the "way of the world" and frequently offer ambiguous resolutions to the struggle of the individual to survive the world and its ways. Sheridan offers the "better way" of sense at the same time that he dramatizes the excesses of the sentimental way. He mocks the absurdities of sentimental distress and delicacy of feeling. To do so, he reconciles the earlier themes of artifice and "plain-dealing" with his own treatment of virtue and sense. He reveals the folly of a world where a Puff's cant can dupe others and where a sentimental pose leads to absurdity (**The Critic**, I.ii.514).

Faulkland is one such example of absurdity,[6] and Sheridan mocks the delicate lover in the scene where Faulkland hears of Julia's social activities in the country. Here, Faulkland claims to prize the "sympathetic heart" (II.i.94) and the sentimental union of "delicate and feeling souls" (90). To be absent from his beloved is to endure an agony of mind. So, in Faulkland's terms, Julia's "violent, robust, unfeeling health" argues a happiness in his absence (92). She should be "temperately healthy" and "plaintively gay" (94). Such paradoxical statements point to Faulkland's own sentimental absurdity. He wishes Julia to be a pining heroine whose only true joy comes from her soulful union with him and whose absence from him should subdue her whole being.

But Faulkland fails to see the paradox of both his language and his demands. By wishing her to be temperate and plaintive, he in effect wishes her to be unhealthy and sad. But he does not stop there. A "truly modest and delicate woman," Faulkland says, would engage in a lively country dance only with her sentimental counterpart (94). Only then, he argues, can she preserve the sanctity of her delicate soul:

> If there be but one vicious mind in the Set, 'twill spread like a contagion—the action of their pulse beats to the lascivious movement of the jigg—their quivering, warm-breath'd sighs impregnate the very air—the atmosphere becomes electrical to love, and each amorous spark darts thro' every link of the chain! (94)

Faulkland's sexually charged speech comically undermines his role as the delicate lover.

The object of his "sentimental" ardor, Julia, refuses to play a similar role. Not only is her health robust, but she also seems to enjoy the "electrical" atmosphere of the country dance. Once branded as the "unequivocal tribute to the sentimental formula" (Kaul 141), Julia does possess a lively spirit which, at times, is critical of the over-refined temper.[7] Faulkland's jealousy receives a check from Julia, who reminds him: "If I wear a countenance of content, it is to shew that my mind holds no doubt of my Faulkland's truth" (III.ii.107). Unlike Lydia, Julia will not create an artificial sentimental distress.

In contrast, Lydia enjoys scenes of distress. To her, wealth is "that burthen on the wings of love," so she must create for herself an "undeserved persecution" (III.iii.112). She delights in the "dear delicious shifts" her lover must withstand for her sake (V.i.135). Describing one such romantic encounter with him, she uses homely, inappropriate language. Her lover is reduced to "a dripping statue," sneezing and coughing "so pathetically" as he tries to win her heart (135). They must exchange vows while the "freezing blast" numbs their joints (135).[8] Such a scene, told in such language, merely accentuates the falsity and the folly of her pretensions.

In *The Rivals*, then, Sheridan does indeed mock the aspects of sentimentalism that lead to folly. To expose these absurdities, Sheridan effectively exploits both the witty and the sentimental modes. In contrast to the artifice practised by Lydia, and the distress experienced by Julia and Faulkland, traces of the witty comic mode appear in characters like Acres, the country fop, and Mrs. Malaprop and Sir Anthony Absolute, examples of "crabbed age."[9] Acres, like many a fop before him, slavishly attempts to imitate the city gentleman, but captures only the trappings of true gentility and true wit. He, too, becomes a subject for diversion (e.g., II.i.91). And like the aging matrons of earlier comedy, Mrs. Malaprop fancies herself to be attractive and desirable, so much so that she is easily duped. The character of Sir Anthony Absolute, who attempts to bully his son into obedience, resembles another conventional character of the past, the obstinate father. At one point, he threatens to disown a son who refuses to capitulate to his wishes (99).

Foolish pretensions, like Bob Acres's *"sentimental swearing"* (96), represent a comic "echo to the sense" (95), a hollow imitation of the verbal and social mastery that Captain Absolute more truly embodies. In effect, Acres foppishly distorts both sense and sound, and applies Pope's injunction with respect to sound to a comic delivery of oaths.[10] His swearing is also a parody of the sentiment. What should exhort others to a moral truth Acres uses to bolster his courage.

Similarly, Lydia's romantic notions lead to falsity and absurdity, mere "echoes" of the sensibility and sentimental distress that Julia more truly represents.[11] So, too, with Faulkland. His refusal to forgo what he calls his "exquisite nicety" (IV.iii.131) and to follow the more sensible tactics of Captain Absolute also exemplifies an "echo to the sense," for his nicety is soon found to be caprice. There-

fore, both wit and sentiment fall into excess and affectation, a "Voluntary Disguise" which cloaks genuine feeling and genuine wit.[12]

Nearly every character in the play indulges in such excess: Mrs. Malaprop[13] with her "oracular tongue" (III.iii.110), Sir Lucius O'Trigger with his distorted view of honor, Bob Acres with his gentlemanly pretensions, Julia with her excessive good nature, Lydia with her absurd romanticism, Faulkland with his captiousness, Sir Anthony Absolute with his penchant to be "hasty in every thing" (I.i.77). These excesses are nonetheless intertwined, and their interrelationship is evident in the play's title. Contrary to the views expressed by Sen and Sherbo, the play's dual lines of action are not anomalous, but thematically linked. Here, in his first play, Sheridan does, as Auburn notes in *Sheridan's Comedies*, show himself to be a "master of comic technique."[14]

Wit and sentiment are "rival" modes, and the rivalry is established as early as the prologue, where the figure of comedy stands in opposition to the sentimental muse.[15] Julia's sweet-tempered nature, often regarded as sentimental, can be viewed only in its relation both to her lover's "captious, unsatisfied temper" (III.ii.106) and to her cousin's romantic caprice. As Rose Snider suggests, Julia's sobriety cannot be treated seriously in the context of her own absurdity.[16] Julia's fundamental good nature "rivals," as it were, the more pronounced excess of the other characters.

By pairing these characters, Sheridan strikes a balance between them. Lydia's romantic indulgences lead to imagined distresses that stand in marked contrast to Julia's own trials. While Julia's "gentle nature" will "sympathize" with her cousin's fanciful torments, her prudence will offer only chastisement (I.ii.81). Lydia realizes, too, that "one lecture from [her] grave Cousin" will persuade her to recall her banished lover (V.i.134). Later, Julia says: "If I were in spirits, Lydia, I should chide you only by laughing heartily at you" (135).

Faulkland's fretfulness also taxes Julia's good nature and, for the most part, she allows her "teasing, captious, incorrigible lover" (II.i.90) to subdue her: "but I have learn'd to think myself his debtor, for those imperfections which arise from the ardour of his attachment" (I.ii.83). In this manner, Julia herself becomes the victim of excess. Her exaggerated sense of duty to her morose lover and her belabored justifications of his treatment of her are found to be immoderate.[17]

Even though she would, no doubt, crave just such an incident to befall her, Lydia points out the absurdity of Julia's own romantic obligation to the man who rescued her from drowning. She tells Julia: "Obligation!—Why a waterspaniel would have done as much.—Well, I should never think of giving my heart to a man because he could swim!" (83) Once again, Lydia's homely comparison makes the incident more comic than sentimental.

Here, Lydia's clear-sightedness puts Julia's sentimental expostulations into perspective. By indulging Faulkland's every whim and by submitting to his sentimental notions of love, Julia tolerates his fretfulness and fosters her own excess. When Julia introduces the notions of gratitude and filial duty, for example, Faulkland tells her: "Again, Julia, you raise ideas that feed and justify my doubts" (III.ii.107). He yearns to be assured that she does in fact love him for himself alone; here she raises doubts even as she tries to remove his fears.

Finally, Julia must bear the consequences. Her indulgence eventually leads Faulkland into mistaking her sincerity for coquetry and hypocrisy. Intent on using the impending duel as "the touch-stone of Julia's sincerity and disinterestedness" (IV.iii.131), Faulkland wrongly judges Julia's love. When she hears of the duel, Julia first responds in sentimental fashion. In terms of Sheridan's theme of rivalry, the contrast between this scene of tender self-abnegation (V.i) and the scene in which Captain Absolute plays the self-sacrificing lover (III.iii) is worthy of note.

As Ensign Beverley, the captain makes use of Lydia's favorite sentimental notions. He will rescue her from her "undeserved persecution," and he pretends to revel in their anticipated poverty. He comically rhapsodizes: "Love shall be our idol and support! We will worship him with a monastic strictness; abjuring all worldly toys, to center every thought and action there" (III.iii.112). His "licensed warmth," which will "plead" for his "reward" (112), echoes Julia's pledge to her fretful lover. She willingly promises to receive "a legal claim to be the partner of [his] sorrows and tenderest comforter" (V.i.132). Jack vows to Lydia that, "proud of calamity, we will enjoy the wreck of wealth; while the surrounding gloom of adversity shall make the flame of our pure love show doubly bright" (III.iii.112). Similarly, Julia promises to Faulkland: "Then on the bosom of your wedded Julia, you may lull your keen regret to slumbering; while virtuous love, with a Cherub's hand, shall smooth the brow of upbraiding thought, and pluck the thorn from compunction" (V.i.132).

Both Jack and Julia indicate their willingness to endure hardship for the sake of love. But Julia's sentiments, prompted by Faulkland's feigned distress, follow Jack's, and his scene with Lydia is highly comic. In him, artifice clearly predominates over sensibility. The captain is trying to trick Lydia into matrimony and, after his impassioned speech, he quips in an aside: "If she holds out now the devil is in it!" (III.iii.112). His sentiments are feigned—merely to utter oaths of devotion does not ensure a disinterested heart. Julia's sentiments are more sincere and yet, because they do follow Jack's comic ones, Sheridan here inverts the conventional technique of introducing a comic scene to parody a serious one. In *The Rivals,* the serious scene "imitates" the comic one, and Sheridan thereby undermines Julia's sentiments. Faulkland likewise would trick Julia into a confession of love, unqualified by either gratitude or filial duty. Structurally and thematically, Sheridan in this way suggests the kinship between sensibility and artifice.

Soon, Julia's sensibility itself changes. Once she learns of Faulkland's deception, she resembles earlier heroines who, in the proviso scene, defend their individuality. Her language retains the syntax of the sentiment, but the content does not deal with a moral truth. Rather, she renounces him and soundly condemns his artifice (V.i.133). Delicate feelings aside, she refuses to bring further distress upon herself. To make his comic point, Sheridan prolongs Julia's diatribe, which, in its anger, recalls the tirades of the cast-off mistress. Nor can Faulkland interrupt the flow of her reproach.

At last, Faulkland's excess is checked, but not by Julia's language or her finer feelings. Although in the end he pays tribute to the reforming power of her "gentleness" and "candour" (V.iii.145), here the threat of forever losing her stirs his remorse. Julia, in witnessing the extremes to which her lover will go, also comes to realize the dangers of indulgence. Like Honeywood's in *The Good Natur'd Man,* Julia's indiscriminate good nature must be checked and restrained.

The character of Captain Absolute illustrates Sheridan's comic standard of moderation, the lesson that both Julia and Faulkland must learn. Durant remarks: "[Jack] is a sensible and practical young man; and the main thrust of the comedy comes of this practical young man's efforts to achieve sensible aims in an utterly illogical world" (27). Auburn in *Sheridan's Comedies* writes that Jack is mildly clever, motivated by honest, not entirely selfish desires, and he is "warmly human" (50). Unlike the other characters, who are "absolute" in their self-indulgent excess, the captain is "absolute" only in his sense. To Faulkland's suggestion that he immediately run away with Lydia and thus fulfill her romantic desire for a sentimental elopement, Captain Absolute retorts: "What, and lose two thirds of her fortune?" (II.i.89). Like the Restoration hero, he is willing enough to woo a lady with a substantial inheritance, but he is equally unwilling to sacrifice himself to a life of poverty. As he tells Lydia: "Come, come, we must lay aside some of our romance—a little *wealth* and *comfort* may be endur'd after all" (IV.ii.125). To live in an impoverished state may be romantic, but it is also needlessly foolish.

On another level, his moderation offsets Faulkland's sensibility. At one point, the captain urges Faulkland to "love like a man" (II.i.90), and, at another, he chides his friend even more severely: "but a captious sceptic in love—a slave to fretfulness and whim—who has no difficulties but of *his own* creating—is a subject more fit for ridicule than compassion!" (IV.iii.131). Like the balance achieved through the relationship of Lydia and Julia, the Captain's good sense also balances Faulkland's excess.

Like Faulkland's, Lydia's folly must be mended, and by the captain. After Lydia discovers that Captain Absolute and Ensign Beverley are one and the same person, he initially appeals to her sensibility. Meeting with no success, he must then challenge her very pretensions to sensibility.

He points out to Lydia how her reputation will suffer in a world where sentiment thrives only in the lending libraries or in whimsical imaginations. It is a point which, although critical of the sentimental mode, also modifies the earlier theme of artifice. Now, sentiment becomes just another form of affectation. Later, of course, in Joseph Surface, Sheridan will personify this kind of sentimental sham. Here, Sheridan indicates that the stage of the world and the world of the stage do not mutually influence each other.[18] Captain Absolute brings into comic focus the illusory and ultimately absurd nature of Lydia's attempt to transfer the fictional realm of sentimentalism into her own life.[19]

Yet, he is also a lover, "aye, and a romantic one too" (II.i.90), and this aspect of his character exemplifies Sheridan's use of convention. After his breach with Lydia, the captain agrees to a duel. Indeed, this prospect proves more successful in winning him the hand of Lydia than all his tricks, a reversal of the Restoration practice and an apparent concession to pathos.[20] But it must be stressed that, unlike Steele's treatment of the duel in *The Lying Lover,* in **The Rivals** the duel becomes an effective comic device. For both Captain Absolute and Faulkland, the duel is a gesture of despair, and Sheridan has clearly indicated the absurdity of it by juxtaposing their motives with those of O'Trigger, who would fight "genteelly" and like a Christian over some imagined insult (IV.iii.128-29).[21] The captain here momentarily forsakes sense, and he almost meets a romantic end.[22] In a final comic twist, Lydia's romantic desires are almost realized, and art does indeed almost become life. It is enough to shock all the characters into sense, and pathos is thereby averted.

Therefore, the duel exemplifies the basic rivalry between the sentimental and the witty modes, and the dangers to which both are subject. Lucy capably wears a "mask of *silliness*" and yet, like the witty servants of the past, she possesses "a pair of sharp eyes for [her] own interest under it" (I.ii.87). It is her self-interest that has led to such serious misunderstandings. The fop, too, has contributed. Seeking to master the art of "*sentimental swearing*" (II.i.96), Acres hopes to prove his courage. A blustering oath, delivered with "propriety" (95), would then achieve an effect which the cowardly "fighting Bob" could not do otherwise. But the duel shows his courage to be as suspect as his "sentimental swearing."

More important is the dual character of Ensign Beverley/Captain Absolute. His disguise also leads to misunderstandings, but he plays the key role of the man of sense. The comic excesses of the rival modes have been checked, largely through him. The rivalry between the various suitors for Lydia's hand reaches its climax at King's-Mead-Field, and the concomitant rivalry between wit and sentiment, represented by the combatants, finally ends. Out of rivalry, balance finally reigns.

The balance is reflected in Julia's concluding speech. Earlier, the actress who has played the part of Julia has deliv-

ered a prologue critical of the sentimental muse.[23] Now, at the end of the play, she delivers a word of caution: "and while Hope pictures to us a flattering scene of future Bliss, let us deny its pencil those colours which are too bright to be lasting" (V.iii.146).[24] Julia's caution highlights the folly of trusting to appearances, at the same time serving to warn against risible excess. Though couched in sentimental language, this final speech hints at the true nature of things. "Flesh and blood" (Prologue, 1.29) as mankind is, he indulges himself in the extremes of hope or despair, wit or sentiment. The "squinting eye" of excess swivels either one way or the other (IV.iii.129).

Julia's speech, then, is less a testament to a sentimental reconciliation than a plea for moderation. Sheridan has at last shown that only "absolute sense," freed from excessive wit and sentiment, will ultimately triumph.

Notes

1. Some critics who criticize Sheridan for his sentimentalism, which in their view weakens the plays' Restoration characteristics, are the following: Ernest Bernbaum, *The Drama of Sensibility* (Boston and London: Ginn, 1915) 253; Allardyce Nicoll, *British Drama: An Historical Survey from the Beginnings to the Present Time,* 5th ed., rev. (1925; London: George G. Harrap, 1964) 194; Andrew Schiller, "*The School for Scandal:* The Restoration Unrestored," *PMLA* [*Publications of the Modern Language Association of America*] 71 (March, 1956): 694-704; Marvin Mudrick, "Restoration Comedy and Later," in *English Stage Comedy,* English Institute Essays, ed. W. K. Wimsatt (New York: AMS Press, 1964), 115; Kenneth Muir, *The Comedy of Manners* (London: Hutcheson University Library, 1970), 157; A. N. Kaul, "A Note on Sheridan," in *The Action of English Comedy* (New Haven: Yale U P, 1970) 131, 136; Samuel L. Macey, "Sheridan: The Last of the Great Theatrical Satirists," *Restoration and Eighteenth-Century Theatre Research* 9 (November, 1970): 37; Leonard J. Leff, "Sheridan and Sentimentalism," *Restoration and Eighteenth-Century Theatre Research* 12 (May, 1973): 36-37, 46; Madeline Bingham, *Sheridan: The Track of a Comet* (London: Allen and Unwin, 1973) 223; Mark S. Auburn, "The Pleasures of Sheridan's *The Rivals:* A Critical Study in the Light of Stage History," *MP* [*Modern Philology: A Journal Devoted to Research in Medieval and Modern Literature*] 72 (February, 1975): 256, 264.

2. For example, recent studies argue this point convincingly: Robert D. Hume, "Goldsmith and Sheridan and the Supposed Revolution of 'Laughing' Against 'Sentimental' Comedy," in *Studies in Change and Revolution: Aspects of English Intellectual History, 1640-1800,* ed. Paul J. Korshin (Berkeley, Calif.: Scolar Press, 1972) 237-76; Robert D. Hume, *The Development of English Drama in the Late Seventeenth Century* (Oxford: Clarendon, 1976); John Loftis, *Sheridan and the Drama of Georgian England* (Cambridge, Mass.: Harvard U P, 1977); Richard W.

Bevis, *The Laughing Tradition: Stage Comedy in Garrick's Day* (Athens: U of Georgia P, 1980).

3. In *The Critic,* Puff affirms that plays "ought to be the 'abstract and brief Chronicles of the times'" (II.i.519) but, if the drama is indeed "the Mirror of Nature" (I.i.499), then the "prudery" of the time may soon yield yet another affectation. As Sneer declares: "our prudery in this respect is just on a par with the artificial bashfulness of a courtezan, who encreases the blush upon her cheek in an exact proportion to the diminution of her modesty" (501). Here, Sheridan comically exposes sentimental comedy's "bungling" efforts to reform the stage as well as the cant that goes with it. All further references will be to this edition and will be documented parenthetically.

4. Richard Brinsley Sheridan, *The Rivals,* in *Dramatic Works,* 1, ed. Cecil Price, III.i.104. All further references will be to this edition and will be documented parenthetically. Ashley Thorndike, in *English Comedy* (New York: MacMillan, 1929) 435, remarks on the importance of "good sense" in *The Rivals,* and Jack D. Durant, in "Sheridan's 'Royal Sanctuary': A Key to *The Rivals,*" *Ball State University Forum* 14 (Winter, 1973): 30, concludes that only good sense, which corrects folly and whimsy, will ultimately yield a social harmony.

5. Scattered throughout the play are references to "absolute." For example, Mrs. Malaprop has "fallen absolutely in love with a tall Irish baronet" (I.ii.81), and Acres swears "absolutely" to polish like the gentleman (II.i.95). So, too, is the captain renowned for his "absolute" sense (III.i.104). Ironically, through, to be absolute is to risk immoderation. Seldom is a character, even the captain, able to sustain a fixed mode of behavior. But he alone possesses a restraining judgment that consistently checks him at times when he could fall into excess.

6. Some critics see Faulkland as undoubtedly sentimental. See Leff, "Sheridan and Sentimentalism," 37. However, Allan Rodway, in "Goldsmith and Sheridan: Satirists of Sentiment," in *Renaissance and Modern Essays,* ed. G. R. Hibbard (London: Routledge, 1966), 71, and later Durant in "Sheridan's 'Royal Sanctuary,'" find Faulkland's presence a puzzle (28). Others, like Muir in *Comedy of Manners,* regard Faulkland as a caricature of the man of sentiment (161). Auburn, in *Sheridan's Comedies,* considers Faulkland to be Lydia's male counterpart (55), but he also explores the psychological depth of the jealous character (55-57).

7. Discussions on Sheridan's treatment of Julia vary in their emphasis. Earlier, Bernbaum, in *Drama of Sensibility,* had spoken of Faulkland's "unhappy temper," reformed by Julia's correspondingly gentle temper (253). Kaul, in "Note on Sheridan," points to Julia as "the epitome of goodness, patience, sense, sensibility" (141). And Durant, in "Sheridan's 'Royal Sanctuary,'" likewise extols her as "an authentic portrait of Sheridan's ideal woman," one who is to be "open, honest, above pretense, above caprice" (28). Rose Snider, in *Satire in the Comedies of Congreve, Sheridan, Wilde, and Coward* (1973; rpt. New York; Phaeton, 1972), 48-49, echoes Paul E. Parnell's view in "The Sentimental Mask," *PMLA,* 78 (December 1963), 529-35: the sentimental figure smugly extols his own virtue and moral superiority. Sheridan, in this view, caricatures the sentimental heroine, and treats her in a "mock-serious" manner (47). For Leff, in "Sheridan and Sentimentalism," Julia is the golden mean (41) and for Auburn, in "Pleasures of Sheridan's *The Rivals,*" the scenes between Julia and Faulkland are as sentimental as they are comic (264-65). In *Sheridan's Comedies,* Auburn calls her "passive" (48), "sensible" and "sentimental" (58). Later, James S. Malek, in "Julia as a Comic Character in *The Rivals,*" *Studies in the Humanities,* 7:1 (1978): 10-13, argues that Sheridan's treatment of her is decidedly comic.

8. As Loftis writes in *Sheridan,* the language of Sheridan's characters achieves its witty effects "by common images used in unexpected ways" (90).

9. The phrase is Elisabeth Mignon's in *Crabbed Age and Youth: The Old Man and Woman in the Restoration Comedy of Manners* (Durham: Duke U P, 1947).

10. Pope's lines read: "'Tis not enough no Harshness give Offence, / The *Sound* must seem an *Eccho* to the *Sense.*" See Alexander Pope, *An Essay on Criticism,* in *Eighteenth-Century English Literature,* eds. Geoffrey Tillotson, Paul Russell, Jr., and Marshall Waingrow (New York: Harcourt, Brace and World, 1969), 559, ll. 364-65.

11. In the eighteenth century, foolishly romantic heroines are, in many ways, traditional. Biddy in Garrick's *Miss in Her Teens,* Miss Fuz in Garrick's *A Peep Behind the Curtain,* and Biddy in Steele's *The Tender Husband* are only three examples. For a discussion of other possible sources, see Coleman O. Parsons, "Smollett's Influence on Sheridan's 'The Rivals,'" *Notes and Queries,* 164 (January, 1933): 39-41; Miriam Gabriel and Paul Mueschke, "Two Contemporary Sources of Sheridan's *The Rivals,*" *PMLA,* 43 (March, 1928): 237-50. Auburn in *Sheridan's Comedies* points to Lydia's uniqueness (55). However, Lauretta in Sheridan's own *St. Patrick's Day* and Louisa in *The Duenna* also help to illuminate Lydia's romantic inclinations and Faulkland's romantic desire to be sentimentally beloved. See *St. Patrick's Day,* in *Dramatic Works,* 1, ed. Price, I.ii.170 and II.ii.180, and *The Duenna,* in *Dramatic Works,* 1, ed. Price, I.iii.236. See also Sheridan's fragment, *The Vicar of Wakefield,* in *Dramatic Works,* 2, ed. Price, where the heroine delights in "filling her head [with] novels" (803).

12. William Congreve, "Concerning Humour in Comedy," in *The Idea of Comedy: Essays in Prose and*

Verse, Ben Jonson to George Meredith, ed. W. K. Wimsatt (Englewood Cliffs, N.J.: Prentice-Hall, 1969) 79.

13. For a discussion of Mrs. Malaprop's conventional character, see Kaul, "Note on Sheridan" 141; Hume, "Supposed Revolution" 262. Other critics stress both her conventional attributes and her uniqueness. See Sailendra Kumar Sen, "Sheridan's Literary Debt: *The Rivals* and *Humphrey Clinker,*" *MLQ* [*Modern Language Quarterly*] 21 (December, 1960): 292, 293; Auburn, "Pleasures of Sheridan's *The Rivals*" 266-67; Durant, "Sheridan's 'Royal Sanctuary'" 24, 26; Auburn, *Sheridan's Comedies,* 37.

14. Sen, "Sheridan's Literary Debt" 299-300; Arthur Sherbo, *English Sentimental Drama* (Michigan State U P, 1957), 102; Auburn, *Sheridan's Comedies,* 58.

15. *In Development of English Drama,* Hume speaks of "exemplary comedy" as an emerging "rival" mode in the 1680s (377).

16. *Satire* 48-49. See also Hume, "Supposed Revolution," 268; Leff, "Sheridan and Sentimentalism," 38; Kaul, "A Note on Sheridan," 148; Durant, "Sheridan's 'Royal Sanctuary,'" 29.

17. Malek argues, in his article "Julia as a Comic Character," that Julia is comic because there is a "disparity between what she says and what she does" (10). However, he does not think either Julia or Faulkland is reformed at the end of the play (11).

18. Contrary to the Restoration view that the stage of the theatre is a mirror that reflects the stage of the world, the eighteenth-century sentimental dramatist argues, as Steele does, that manners and customs are "transfused from the Stage to the World, which reciprocally imitate each other." For one Restoration view, see Sir John Vanbrugh, "A Short Vindication of *The Relapse* and *The Provok'd Wife* from Immorality and Profaneness," in *The Complete Works of Sir John Vanbrugh,* 1, ed. Bonamy Dobrée (Bloomsbury: Nonesuch Press, 1927), 206. For Steele's view, see *Sir Richard Steele,* "The Spectator," 370, 5 May 1772, in *The Spectator,* 3, ed. Donald F. Bond (Oxford: Clarendon, 1965), 393. Later, Wilde will dramatize the transfer of art into life and life into art. For this view, see Oscar Wilde, *The Artist as Critic: Critical Writings of Oscar Wilde,* ed. Richard Ellmann (London: W. H. Allen, 1970). In particular, see *The Decay of Lying* and *The Truth of Masks.*

19. Lydia's hiding her sentimental novels in closets and under toilets comments on the essential comedy of her attempt to live the life of a sentimental heroine. As a "female Quixote," Lydia fails to distinguish "romance from real life," as Kaul puts it in "Note on Sheridan" (147). Sir Anthony Absolute also offers a glimpse into the effect he thinks fiction, exemplified by the notorious lending libraries, can have on real life: "Madam, a circulating library in a town is, as an ever-green tree, a diabolical knowledge!—It blos-

soms through the year!—And depend on it, Mrs. Malaprop, that they who are so fond of handling the leaves, will long for the fruit at last" (I.ii.85). But his understanding is shown to be suspect. See also Durant, "Sheridan's 'Royal Sanctuary,'" 26.

20. While in *Sheridan* Loftis notes that Sheridan avoids "pathetic situations" in his comedies (10), he does not account for the duel and the distress it causes.

21. In Act III, scene iv, Sir Lucius confides to Acres that a "gay captain" has affronted him and his country (117) and yet, here, Sir Lucius mentions the "affront" only after he has successfully provoked the captain to "quarrel genteelly" (VI.iii.128).

22. For a discussion of the duel and its relation to Jack's sense, see Sen, "Sheridan's Literary Debt," 297 n. 9; Durant, "Sheridan's 'Royal Sanctuary,'" 27.

23. Leff, in "Sheridan and Sentimentalism," argues that this second prologue does not change the sentimental tone of the comedy (41). Malek, in "Julia as a Comic Character," considers both the prologue and its speaker to be appropriate, given Sheridan's portrayal of Julia (12).

24. Leff, in "Sheridan and Sentimentalism," also considers this speech to be sentimental simply because Julia utters it (41). Auburn in *Sheridan's Comedies* calls it a "moral tag" (135).

Works Cited

Auburn, Mark S. *Sheridan's Comedies: Their Contexts and Achievements.* Lincoln and London: U of Nebraska P, 1977.

Congreve, William. "Amendments of Mr. Collier's False and Imperfect Citations &c," in *The Mourning Bride: Poems, and Miscellanies,* ed. Bonamy Dobrée (Oxford U P, 1928).

Durant, Jack D. "Sheridan's 'Royal Sanctuary': A Key to *The Rivals.*" *Ball State University Forum* 14 (Winter 1973): 23-30.

Etherege, George. *The Man of Mode,* ed. W. B. Carnochan. Lincoln: U of Nebraska P, 1966.

Kenny, Shirley Strum. "Farquhar, Wilks, and Wildair; or, The Metamorphosis of the 'Fine Gentleman.'" *Philological Quarterly* 57 (1978): 46-65.

Krutch, Joseph Wood. *Comedy and Conscience After the Restoration.* 1924. New York: Columbia U P, 1949.

Loftis, John. *Sheridan and the Drama of Georgian England.* Cambridge, Mass.: Harvard U P, 1977.

Sheridan, Richard Brinsley. *A Scotchman,* in *The Dramatic Works of Richard Brinsley Sheridan.* 2 vols. Cecil Price, ed. Oxford: Clarendon P, 1973.

Robert Hogan (essay date 1986)

SOURCE: "Plot, Character, and Comic Language in Sheridan," in *Comedy from Shakespeare to Sheridan: Change* and Continuity in the English and European Dramatic Tradition, edited by A. R. Braunmuller and J. C. Bulman, Associated University Presses, 1986, pp. 274-85.

[*In the following essay, Hogan views the plotting and characterization of Sheridan's dramas as in some ways lacking, but acknowledges the brilliance of his comic language in* The Rivals, The School for Scandal, *and* The Critic.]

Oliver Goldsmith and Richard Brinsley Sheridan—these two Irishmen are inevitably considered the preeminent comic talents of the English-speaking theater in the eighteenth century. Indeed, many literary historians have said that from the retirement of Congreve and the death of Farquhar early in the eighteenth century, until the appearance of Oscar Wilde, Bernard Shaw, and W. B. Yeats late in the nineteenth century, there were no dramatists who even approached the quality of Goldsmith and Sheridan.

Like all generalizations, this one is a bit too general. This long period hardly saw the profusion of masterpieces that appeared during the reign of Elizabeth I or of Charles II, and an overwhelming number of the plays produced between 1700 and 1890 now strike us as too full of high fustian and low theatrics, and too evocative of easy tears and brainless belly laughs. Still, John Gay's *The Beggar's Opera* has outlasted Sheridan's **The Duenna,** and Henry Fielding's *Tom Thumb* stands up nicely to Sheridan's **The Critic,** while some of the straight comic work of Macklin, Murphy, Garrick, Colman the Elder, and Sheridan's own mother Frances did not in the eighteenth century fall that far short of the best of Goldsmith and Sheridan themselves. And even from the more arid nineteenth century, Dion Boucicault's *Old Heads and Young Hearts* and T. W. Robertson's *Caste* might be revived with pleasure, while the airy operettas of Gilbert and Sullivan have never been out of favor.

Still, when all of the qualifications have been made, Goldsmith and Sheridan remain unlikely to be challenged in their historical preeminence, just as their best works remain unlikely to lose their popularity on the stage.

When Sheridan's first play, **The Rivals,** was initially produced at Covent Garden in 1775, it failed. It was too long, insufficiently rehearsed, and in one instance badly cast. Sheridan quickly cut the play and replaced the offending actor with a better, and in less than two weeks, **The Rivals** had become a solid success. The play has never lost its popularity. It is one of those plays that takes a perverse genius to do badly. It is almost actor-proof and director-proof, and mediocre or even distinctly bad productions can still arouse delight. It has, nonetheless, been generally considered a lesser work than **The School for Scandal.** Yet, if there is to be any revision in the critical opinion about Sheridan, it can only be in the upgrading of **The Rivals,** and a convincing case can be made that **The Rivals** in many ways equals and in some surpasses the worth of **The School for Scandal.**

Neither play is what one would call well made, and, indeed, construction was never Sheridan's strong point.[1]

However, a tidy plot construction is probably an overrated quality in comedy, and even in tragedy the English-speaking theater has preferred Elizabethan sprawl to neoclassical trimness. Sheridan's faults in plotting **The Rivals** have been no better isolated than by the perceptive Tom Moore, who noted that

> For our insight into [the] characters, we are indebted rather to their confessions than their actions. Lydia Languish, in proclaiming the extravagance of her own romantic notions, prepares us for events much more ludicrous and eccentric, than those in which the plot allows her to be concerned; and the young lady herself is scarcely more disappointed than we are, at the tameness with which her amour concludes . . . and the wayward, captious jealousy of Faulkland, though so highly coloured in his own representation of it, is productive of no incident answerable to such an announcement.[2]

This point can be applied to the relations of other characters in the play. Bob Acres and Lydia are never brought together for a confrontation; little is made of the "love affair" of Mrs. Malaprop and Sir Lucius. Despite his usefulness to the "real" plot, Acres might just as well be cut out of the play. It would have been dramaturgically tidier for the Jack-Lydia-Mrs. Malaprop-Sir Lucius imbroglio if Jack confronted Sir Lucius without the distraction of Acres. Acres's cowardice is, however, so delicious that one would no more sacrifice it than one would the windmill episode in *Don Quixote*. Such academic strictures are sometimes just theatrically beside the point. Despite, then, the omission of several "obligatory scenes," an audience does not miss or even note what Sheridan might or should have done, because what he has done is totally absorbing and increasingly delightful: he has written a series of irresistible scenes, based either on ludicrous situations or characterizations. As each droll scene is succeeded by another of equal or greater interest, the audience remains so caught by the pleasure of the moment that the static or erratic quality of the plot is simply not noticed. Nevertheless, the plot must at least seem to move, and in **The Rivals** Sheridan's plot does lurch on toward the aborted duel. A difficulty of **The School for Scandal** is that for the first two acts the plot *seems* static.

Tom Moore sets up a persuasive but wrong-headed comparison between the language and characterization of the two plays:

> With much less wit, it [**The Rivals**] exhibits perhaps more humour than **The School for Scandal,** and the dialogue, though by no means so pointed or sparkling, is, in this respect more natural, as coming nearer the current coin of ordinary conversation; whereas, the circulating medium of **The School for Scandal** is diamonds. The characters of **The Rivals,** on the contrary, are *not* such as occur very commonly in the world; and, instead of producing striking effects with natural and obvious materials, which is the great art and difficulty of a painter of human life, he has here overcharged most of his persons with whims and absurdities.[3]

This view—that the dialogue is natural but the characters are exaggerated—strikes me as only half true. Sheridan was dealing with "humours," types, exaggerations, but the characters were not extravagant exaggerations, and so, for instance, the stage-Irishness of Sir Lucius was played down when Sheridan revised the play. The excellence of Sheridan's comic characterizations is that his types are handled with such a verve, freshness, and panache that they reinvigorate their stockness. Sir Anthony is basically the tyrannical father; Mrs. Malaprop, the superannuated dame; Sir Lucius, the Stage Irishman; and Bob Acres is a combination of rustic booby, false beau, and braggart soldier. Among the comic characters (as opposed to the straight characters of Jack and Julia), Lydia and Faulkland are the most touched with originality. Both possess the dull youth and handsomeness of innumerable young heroes and ingenues, but in Sheridan's treatment they become comic rather than straight characters because their admirable qualities are exaggerated until they become faults. In Lydia, romance becomes exaggerated to absurdity; in Faulkland, love becomes exaggerated to neurosis. Even the stock servant—a figure that has a centuries-old provenance and is little different in Wodehouse, Wilde, Vanbrugh, Machiavelli, or Terence—is made original in Sheridan. What he adds to the character of the pert servant is a charming falsity of language that the audience finds both refreshing and novel, and this addition revivifies most of Sheridan's otherwise stock characterization.

The individuality of Lydia, Faulkland, and all the less original characters, then, is established largely by their language. Rather than the natural dialogue that Tom Moore saw, the play contains a dazzling degree of unnatural and absurd dialogue. Sheridan took great pains with the writing of **The Rivals,** and it has throughout a graceful fluency that gives the impression of naturalness. It is, however, the unimportant parts of the play that are the most easy, natural, and realistic. The strongest parts, with the biggest laughs, are those in which a character uses language in a finely foolish fashion.

To take the most obvious example: the great comic lines of Mrs. Malaprop spring from an inspired misuse of words that is far too outlandish to be thought realistic or natural. Set in a surrounding dialogue of fluent naturalness, her marvelous mistakes of diction appear in bold relief. Mrs. Malaprop is funny because she is doubly pretentious: she is an aging woman who regards herself as still young and beautiful enough to be the object of a romantic love affair, and she is a stupid and vain woman who regards herself as a bluestocking. Her first pretension is deflated by the plot and by how the other characters regard her; her second pretension is deflated by her own language and by how the audience regards it. A character using the wrong word has long been a source of theatrical and fictional comedy.[4] The laughter has traditionally come from the character using a wrong word that sounds like the right one. Mrs. Malaprop's best mistakes improve on this device, for the word that she chooses not only sounds like the word she meant, but it also contains a meaning that either reduces her

thought to inspired nonsense or makes her say the opposite of what she intended. In her great speech about the education of young women (act 1, scene 2), she desires Lydia to know "something of the contagious countries," and her choice of "contagious" for "contiguous" contains a brilliant bit of nonsense that, of course, indicates her own ignorance and delights the audience.

If Mrs. Malaprop's language deflates her claims to learning, Sir Anthony's deflates his own false reasoning. In his attempts to persuade Jack to be married, Sir Anthony is thwarted, and, instead of becoming more cogent and reasonable, he becomes more incoherent and emotional. So far Sheridan follows tradition: a stock father who would be the repository of wisdom, reason, and tolerance is shown to be dense, irrational, and splenetic. Sheridan again goes beyond tradition, however, for Sir Anthony's language does not merely become incoherent with anger; at its climactic and funniest it actually becomes a parody of reasoning. His brilliant exit speech of act 2, scene 1, uses the trappings of reason but winds up in the depths of infantilism.

The success of these scenes requires two characters: the faulty speaker and the clear-eyed critic. The critic is a straight character who helps the audience see what is wrong with the comic character's language and, therefore, with his character. Thus, after Sir Anthony's great outburst, Jack acts the role of critic with his ironic remark:

> Mild, gentle, considerate father—I kiss your hands—
> What a tender method of giving his opinion in these
> matters Sir Anthony has![5]

Or, in Mrs. Malaprop's great scene in act 1, it is Sir Anthony, elsewhere himself a faulty speaker, who acts the role of critic and says:

> I must confess, that you are a truly moderate and poli-
> tic arguer, for almost every third word you say is on
> my side of the question.[6]

In the Faulkland-Julia scenes, Julia acts as the critic, and so her language needs to contrast sharply with Faulkland's. In contrast to his circuitous, emotional floridness, she must be direct, simple, and reasonable. To emphasize what is wrong with his language and character, her language and character must set the rhetorical and the moral norm. Early in their first meeting (act 3, scene 2), Sheridan controls her language well, and she makes direct and terse remarks: "I had not hoped to see you again so soon," for example, or, "Nay then, I see you have taken something ill. You must not conceal from me what it is." Such sentences contrast effectively with Faulkland's purple effusions:

> For such is my temper, Julia, that I should regard every
> mirthful moment in your absence as a treason to con-
> stancy:—The mutual tear that steals down the cheek of
> parting lovers. . . .[7]

Although the young Sheridan was already a master of comic language and here effectively mocks the language of sentiment, he was far from a master of serious language used to convey emotional intensity.[8] Consequently, Julia's later, more intense speeches become as stiff, florid, and false as Faulkland's, and we find her saying in act 5, scene 1:

> Then on the bosom of your wedded Julia, you may lull your keen regret to slumbering; while virtuous love, with a Cherub's hand, shall smooth the brow of up-braiding thought and pluck the thorn from compunction.[9]

Aside from the failure of serious language, the play is the performance of a virtuoso of dialogue fit to be ranked with Wilde and Shaw. The play may have a rather untidy plot, but the plot does provide a multitude of effective comic situations. The play may use stock types, but it also works original variations on these types. Finally, the play does provide a variety of false language hardly seen in English drama since the comedies of Congreve and Ben Jonson. The language of *The Rivals* has secured the play its high position in the English theater. It is a language that civilizes by involving its audience. It is a language that makes its audience become active critics of false language and, therefore, of false behavior.

The two main kinds of comic language are the language of humor and the language of wit. The language of humor predominates in *The Rivals,* and the language of wit in *The School for Scandal.* The language of humor misuses grammar and sentence structure and rhetorical devices to produce speech that amusingly and ignorantly diverges from a norm of commonly accepted good speech and writing. The language of wit uses grammar and sentence structure and rhetorical devices with such uncommon fluency that its speech diverges from a norm of good speech and writing by its more considerable excellence. In other words, the language of humor is purposely bad writing, and the nature of its badness is a symptom of what is wrong with the speaker. The language of wit, on the other hand, is purposely superb writing, and the nature of its excellence is a symptom of what is right with the speaker. Using the language of humor, the speaker may fail to attain a civilized norm by innate stupidity such as Dogberry's, or by lack of education such as Sam Weller's, or by provincial ignorance such as the quaint dialect flaws of the stage Irishman and Scotsman or Frenchman. Using the language of wit, as Shakespeare's Benedick and Beatrice do poorly, or as Congreve's Millamant and Mirabell do well, or as Shaw's Don Juan and Devil do consummately, the speaker exceeds the civilized norm and makes us admire his urbanity, insight, and wisdom. In the language of humor, the audience perceives a misuse of words that stems from a character fault, and the resultant laughter is critical. In the language of wit, the audience perceives a consummate use of words that stems from excellences of character, and the resultant laughter is admiring. More simply, the language of humor occasions critical laughter at stupidity, and the language of wit occasions admiring smiles at brilliance.

As the appreciation of wit is of higher worth than the perception of stupidity, so the language of wit is thought of greater worth than the language of humor. Thus a play like *The School for Scandal* is more highly regarded than a play like *The Rivals.* Yet this attitude may be suspect, for both comic languages actively engage the judgment of their auditors, and both comic languages use quite complex techniques. If there is an innate difference of value between the two comic languages, it must lie in the content. The language of wit has occasionally been used, notably in some plays by Shaw, to discuss more complex themes than the drama usually handles.

The School for Scandal, largely because of its witty language, has been Sheridan's most admired play. The play was first produced at Drury Lane on 8 May 1777 and has held the boards ever since. The scandal scenes in particular have been considered a triumph of witty language, and they will only work, indeed, because they are witty. The danger of these scenes, particularly in a poor production, is that they are static. Nothing happens in them. The plot does not advance, and one of the viewers at the play's brilliant premiere was even heard to grumble that he wondered when the author was going to get on with the story.

But, of course, the stories themselves are not well structured. To take only one example, the heroine, Maria, has quite a small part. She is off the stage through most of the crucial acts and, amazingly, is not even confronted with the hero until the very denouement in act 5. As with *The Rivals,* one could pile up a dozen instances of what Sheridan had to do with his plot and did not do. But, also as with *The Rivals,* one must admit that what he did do instead is so delightful and absorbing that his audience is thoroughly satisfied.

Sheridan makes some use of more individualized characterization in this play. There are well-defined stock types such as Mrs. Candour and Sir Benjamin Backbite, but Sir Peter and Lady Teazle are rather fuller than types, and in Charles and particularly in Joseph, Sheridan cuts beneath the surface and finds contradictions and something approaching complexity. Joseph, the apparently good but actually hypocritical brother, was regarded by Sheridan's sisters as a sketch of their own older brother, Charles. In any event, Joseph is a meaty acting role, even if not quite a fully fleshed-out one. He is, however, closer to reality than the great comic monsters of a Volpone or a Tartuffe. In Charles, it may not be stretching a point to see some of Richard Sheridan's own carelessness and casual mismanagement. But, like everyone, Sheridan had a good deal of tolerance for his own foibles, and so does his audience have a good deal of tolerance for the erring but basically good-hearted Charles. From this crucial attitude, much of the sunniness of the play can be traced.

The rhetorical showpieces of the play are the great scandal-mongering scenes of acts 1 and 2, in which the chorus of gossips, with bubbling spirits and brilliant technique, rends and shreds reputations. It is curious that the strength of these scenes arises from exquisitely phrased malice. Lady Sneerwell says in explanation that "there's no possibility of being witty without a little ill nature: the malice of a good thing is the barb that makes it stick."

Certainly it is true that Maria and Sir Peter, the unmalicious characters in the scandal scenes, are able to counter the witty malice with no more than direct statement, which is ineffective, and with honest dignity, which appears stuffy. Yet, while neither Maria nor Sir Peter is a match for witty malice, that does not mean that a match could not be found. A well-equipped Shavian wit, such as Sidney Trefusis or Don Juan, could have more than upheld the side of sense and worth with equal rhetorical cleverness and by substituting gaiety for malice.

It seems generally taken for granted that Sheridan's scandalmongers are deplorable, but it has not been much noticed that their critiques are correct. An audience would not laugh at their jokes unless their victims deserved laughter. Mrs. Evergreen, discussed in act 2, is mutton trying to pass as lamb; Miss Simper and Miss Prim are foolishly vain; Mrs. Pursy, although too fat, attempts to appear slim; Lady Stucco, although too old, attempts to appear beautiful. All of these victims deserve the lash of satire, and the audience laughs at popular pretensions deservedly deflated. The scandalmongers, then, are joke makers and, like all joke makers, are necessarily moralists. Why, then, are they themselves funny?

The reason, of course, is that they live in glass houses. The delight they take in other people's failings is wedded to their perfect ignorance of their own. Once again Sheridan worked a new twist upon old material and conveyed his truths by the vehicles of folly.

In the language of humor, which Sheridan basically used in *The Rivals,* the audience laughs at language faultily used and so becomes, en masse, a literary critic. In the language of wit, which Sheridan frequently used in *The School for Scandal,* the audience laughs at language cleverly used and becomes a literary appreciator. The point might be proved by taking any of *The School for Scandal*'s well-turned jokes and rephrasing them. Almost invariably the rephrasing lessens—if not, indeed, destroys—the strength of the joke. For instance, in act 1, the poetaster Sir Benjamin Backbite unknowingly makes a joke against his own vapid verses when he describes the appearance of his forthcoming slim volume: "a beautiful quarto page, where a neat rivulet of text shall meander through a meadow of margin." The delight of the joke comes from two sources, one obvious and one rather subliminal. The obvious point is the originality of the metaphor; the subtler point is the reinforcement of sound, first in the *t's* of "neat Rivulet of text," and next in the *m's* of "meander through a meadow of margin." To rephrase the remark in unmetaphorical and unalliterative statement is to arrive at something like: "a beautiful quarto page, where a few lines are set off by a wide margin."

We catch Sheridan's neatly conceived and deftly turned statement on the wing, and our appreciative laughter is in-

stantaneous. It is, therefore, unnecessary as well as uncivilized to spend more space in reducing clearly successful jokes to baldly tedious statements. However, it might be noted that Sheridan pushes his audience to appreciate wit in another way, and he does so by smoothly inserting some literary criteria. Several times he actually ensures that his audience will laugh by telling them what and even how to appreciate.

For instance, in the play's opening dialogue, Snake and Lady Sneerwell almost immediately launch into a rhetorical consideration of Lady Clackitt's gossip:

> LADY SNEERWELL: She certainly has Talents, but her manner is gross.
>
> SNAKE: Tis very true—she generally designs well—has a free tongue and a bold invention—but her colouring is too dark and her outline often extravagant. She wants that delicacy of Hint—and mellowness of sneer which distinguish your ladyship's Scandal.[10]

In a similar manner, Sheridan sets up the rhetorical techniques of Crabtree and Mrs. Candour.

But perhaps to say more about the high quality and the manifold techniques of Sheridan's comic language would be tedious. A good joke does not need to be explained. It startlingly explodes into perfect and unexpected obviousness, and our instantaneous laughter results from our perfect but unexpected perception. Let it merely be asserted, then, that Sheridan's command of the widest variety of rhetorical techniques is consummate. When one thinks of the flabby badinage that passes for wit between Shakespeare's Beatrice and Benedick, one can only turn with relief and delight to a Congreve, a Wilde, a Shaw—or a Sheridan.

But perhaps the greatest quality of Sheridan's comic writing is one that he shares with Goldsmith—a sunny good nature deriving from a benevolent tolerance. Neither Sheridan nor Goldsmith says much in his plays, but in their one shared, pervasive quality they imply an attitude that imparts to their work something often lacking in the work of even their greatest colleagues. That attitude is charm. Charm is usually an underrated quality, assigned to minor writers such as Charles Lamb or Kenneth Grahame. Perhaps it is easier to allow them a trivial excellence than to analyze their excellence seriously. But is charm so trivial? In Sheridan, are we not charmed because we are reminded of the vital fact that it is awfully nice to be alive? This humanity as Virginia Woolf noted, "was part of his charm" and "still warms his writing."[11]

It is too arbitrary to limit comic language to two kinds only, the language of humor and the language of wit. There is at least one other, albeit minor, kind. What of the language of imitation, the language of parody that satirizes presumptive excellence by exaggerating its faults? This is a rarer use of comic language, limited mainly to the criticism of literary forms, but it certainly does appear in plays.

The three great examples of parody or burlesque in English drama are Buckingham's *The Rehearsal* (1671), Fielding's *Tom Thumb* (1731), and Sheridan's **The Critic** (1779).[12] **The Critic** pushed *The Rehearsal* off the stage, and Fielding's delightful play presents such problems of staging that it has always been more popular in the study than on the boards. Only **The Critic** is still occasionally performed today, even though the stage style it lampooned is two centuries out of date.

Sheridan's second and third acts in **The Critic** have some brilliantly bad writing, although not nearly the profusion found in Fielding. Sheridan compensates, however, by satirizing the complete theatrical experience. Thus, he has many more visual and aural gags than does Fielding. Indeed, if we are to consider the play solely as literature, it tails off disappointingly because Sheridan does not rely on words at the conclusion but, rather, on a parody of excessive stage spectacle. In the original staging at Drury Lane, the spectacular visual conclusion satisfyingly topped everything that had gone before. On paper, little of this effect can be apparent; on the modern stage, all of this effect can be a problem.

The purely literary content, however, is so fine that the play has always been admired as the third of Sheridan's masterpieces. Indeed, he himself regarded the first act as the most finished piece of dramatic writing he had done. The act is a brilliant piece of work, and a chief excellence is that it gets its laughs while actually establishing the rules for laughing. Some of the generalizations established in act 1 are also aids for judging the ineptitudes of the play-within-the-play of acts 2 and 3.

Act 1 falls into three major scenes: the dialogue between Mr. Dangle and Sneer, the baiting of Sir Fretful Plagiary, and the rhetorical exhibition of Mr. Puff. In the Dangle-Sneer dialogue, some criticisms are made about the incompatibility of comedy and overt moralizing, which had been joined in popular sentimental comedies of Richard Steele and others. There is briefly even some criticism of the bad writing of sentimental comedy. It has too much nicety: "No double entendre, no smart innuendo admitted; even Vanburgh [*sic*] and Congreve obliged to undergo a bungling reformation!"[13] The Sir Fretful scene is a humorous criticism of a poor but egotistical playwright, *à la* Buckingham's Bayes, and the character is something of a cartoon of Richard Cumberland.[14] But even in this scene a number of axioms about false and inflated language are insinuated. For example:

> In your more serious efforts . . . your bombast would
> be less intolerable, if the thoughts were ever suited to
> the expression; but the homeliness of the sentiment
> stares thro' the fantastic encumbrance of its fine lan-
> guage, like a clown in one of the new uniforms![15]

Later, in the play-within-the-play, this fault is illustrated abundantly and with delightful inanity. Then, after the broad interlude of non-English and broken English in the little scene of the Italian singers and the French inter-preter, comes the great scene in which Mr. Puff analyzes the varieties of false language that composed contemporary advertising. The passage is too long to quote in full, but in it Sheridan bombards his audience with false fluency and, in effect, forces each member to see that it is false and to become a literary critic. For instance, part of Mr. Puff's illustration of the Puff Direct reads:

> Characters strongly drawn—highly coloured—hand of
> a master—fund of genuine humour—mine of inven-
> tion—neat dialogue—attic salt! Then for the perfor-
> mance—Mr. DODD was astonishingly great in the char-
> acter of SIR HARRY! That universal and judicious actor
> Mr. PALMER, perhaps never appeared to more advantage
> than in the COLONEL;—but it is not in the power of lan-
> guage to do justice to Mr. KING!—Indeed he more than
> merited those repeated bursts of applause which he
> drew from a most brilliant and judicious audience! As
> to the scenery—The miraculous power of Mr. DE
> LOUTHERBOURG's pencil are universally acknowl-
> edged!—In short, we are at a loss which to admire
> most,—the unrivalled genius of the author, the great at-
> tention and liberality of the managers—the wonderful
> abilities of the painter, or the incredible exertions of all
> the performers![16]

Sheridan has set up Mr. Puff's lecture on Puffing so that the audience is primed to look closely at language that Puff asserts will be effective and seem sincere in any instance. Hence, all of the descriptive phrases and all of the admiring epithets stand out in bold relief as indications of insincerity and gush. This is a considerable achievement and a healthy one.

To test Sheridan's feat, I took down from my shelves the first four volumes of contemporary dramatic criticism I put my hands on; books by Kenneth Tynan, Robert Brustein, Stanley Kauffmann, and Martin Gottfried. Still seeing with a Brinsleyan clarity, I opened each volume at random and was astonished to see that certain phrases now leapt off the page. From Mr. Tynan: "admirable, transfigured, one of the noblest performances I have ever seen, marvelously characterized, I shall never forget the skill with which. . . ."[17] From Mr. Brustein: "a spirited performance, the season's triumph, and a triumph for the American theatre. Though superlatives have a habit of sticking in my throat, I must not temporize here: this was the finest production of a Shakespeare comedy I have ever seen."[18] From Mr. Kauffmann: "production is outstandingly happy, setting is almost miraculous, vitality of the born actor and the fine control of the skillful one, we will be allowed to watch an extraordinary career develop."[19] From Mr. Gottfried: "wonderfully fluid use of stage possibilities, genuinely poetic, apt and funny, hilarious, brilliant. He is part of our theater's great tomorrow."[20]

We have seemingly wandered far afield here, but the difference between the muddy fustian of the critics and the piercing clarity of the dramatist may indicate not only how pertinent Sheridan's strictures still are but also how valid his excellence still is. It may also suggest that the clearest, shortest way to truth is not through criticism but through the work of art itself.

The language of the remaining two acts of **The Critic** illustrates, by broad parody, various kinds of bad dramatic writing. Particularly droll is the flat and intentional inadequacy of the blank verse in the "butler-maid" scene of exposition between Raleigh and Hatton. Here, of course, Sneer's axiom about homely sentiment and fine language is illustrated. Such a prosaic lameness of thought couched in words of pseudo-Shakespearian grandeur is not far-fetched. Many worthless tragedies with scarcely less awful language have succeeded for the moment on the stage: see much, if not quite all, of the work of Sheridan's young kinsman, James Sheridan Knowles.

An equally fine parody is Tilburnia's lyric purple passage that begins with the superbly stale

> Now has the whispering breath of gentle morn,
> Bad Nature's voice, and Nature's beauty rise;
> While orient Phoebus, with unborrow'd hues,
> Cloaths the wak'd loveliness which all night slept
> In heav'nly drapery! Darkness is fled.[21]

The speech ends with a lengthy catalogue of birds and flowers. Ophelia has a lot to answer for.

A chief symptom of Sheridan's parodic success is that quoting it is so irresistible. Here, then, is one final, fine, brief parody, this time of the language of rant and fustian:

WHISKERANDOS: Thou liest—base Beefeater!

BEEFEATER: Ha! Hell! the lie!
By heav'n thou'st rous'd the lion in my heart!
Off, yeoman's habit!—base disguise!—off! off![22]

By precept and example, Sheridan has established what bad theatrical language is. One does not need to be a scholar to appreciate his fun, but he has joked and punned so well that he has momentarily created an audience of laughing pundits. **The Critic** is not about life or human nature. It is about good and bad literary form; it is about taste. That fact must make it a work of lesser import than **The Rivals** or **The School for Scandal,** but it is not a work of lesser pleasure.

Three conclusions and a concluding generalization sum up Sheridan's accomplishments in his three great plays.

The plotting, although academically slovenly, is so continuously absorbing in its successive incidents that it is theatrically irresistible.

The characterization contains no original elements and scarcely ever diverges from the stereotypes worked over by Congreve, Molière, Shakespeare and Jonson, Goldoni and Plautus; upon these stock figures, however, Sheridan has mixed such new combinations and insinuated such fresh fancies of detail that they have not lost the illusion of bloom for the last two hundred years.

The comic writing, similarly, contains no original elements; and indeed, I suspect that no writer in the last two thousand years—with the dubious exception of Beckett—

has discovered a new way of making a joke. What Sheridan's comic writing does is to utilize each of the comic modes—humor, wit, and parody—and to invest these traditional manners with such fresh inventiveness of detail as to make the three great plays a perennial source of linguistic delight and even of civilized apprehension.

Sheridan wrote in one of the most constricting, simplistic, and naive forms of art, the drama. Unlike Ibsen or Strindberg or Chekhov or Granville-Barker, he did not attempt to expand the form either in technique or in content. He was a traditionalist, albeit a consummate one. A greater comic artist who did attempt to expand the form but who also thoroughly understood its traditionalism, was Bernard Shaw who remarked—not with entire truth—that dramaturgically he himself merely appropriated the characterization of Dickens and the plotting of Molière. But what Shaw further said of himself is an appropriate final generalization about Brinsley Sheridan: "He touches nothing that he does not dust and polish and put back in its place much more carefully than the last man who handled it."[23]

Notes

1. In comedy, tidy construction has given us the mechanical plots of a Feydeau or a Labiche farce, as intricate and insanely logical as clockwork and just about as inhuman. And in our own day, tidy construction in comedy has given us the rigid formula of television's half-hour "sit-com." If we recollect the glories of comic writing in the English theater, however, we might well conclude that the greatest comedy is that which diverges from or even destroys the form. Shakespeare's comedies are more often than not hopelessly slapdash in construction. In *A Midsummer Night's Dream,* the plot is concluded by the end of act 4, and nothing remains to do in act 5 except get on with the funniest part of the play, the amateur dramatic company of Bully Bottom, which really has nothing whatsoever to do with the plot. Aside from *Volpone,* the great comedies of Ben Jonson are little more than illustrative incidents effectively jumbled together; yet the warmth, vigor, and vitality of *Bartholomew Fair, The Alchemist,* and *Epicoene* are inordinately more comfortable than the cold logic of *Volpone.* The plot of Congreve's *The Way of the World* is so convoluted that no one pays much attention to it; the joy is in the glittering wit. Even the consummate comic artist Molière hastily winds up *Tartuffe* by the limpest deus ex machina. And in our own time the masterpieces of Chaplin are composed of little more than a succession of unrelated comic situations. It might almost be thought that the best made comic plots have little room for the other major elements of character and language, while the best comedies have little room for plot.

2. Thomas Moore, *Memoirs of the Life of the Right Honourable Richard Brinsley Sheridan* (London: Longman, Hurst, Rees, Orme, Brown, and Green, 1825), p. 104.

3. Ibid., pp. 103-4.

4. In her character as in some of her funniest lines, Mrs. Malaprop owes much to Mrs. Tryfort in Sheridan's mother's play, *A Journey to Bath.* See *The Plays of Frances Sheridan* (Newark: University of Delaware Press, 1984). As Sheridan's sister, when she was also borrowing some of Mrs. Tryfort's language and character in her novel *Strathallan,* remarked, however, "I am of the opinion of Charles, in *The School for Scandal,* that it is very hard if one may not make free with one's relations."

5. Cecil Price, ed., *The Dramatic Works of Richard Brinsley Sheridan* (Oxford: Clarendon Press, 1973), p. 99.

6. Ibid., p. 86.

7. Ibid., p. 106.

8. This is not an unusual fault in masters of comic language. Thus, we find Dickens's handling of Sam Weller brilliant and of Little Nell mawkish. Or we find the language of Captain Boyle and Joxer Daly consummately comic in *Juno and the Paycock;* and yet in the same play we find a serious but maudlin line like, "Ah God, Mary, have you fallen as low as that?"

9. Price, ed., *Dramatic Works,* p. 132.

10. Ibid., p. 360.

11. Virginia Woolf, *Books and Portraits* (New York: Harcourt Brace Jovanovich, 1977), p. 49.

12. One modern play might possibly be added—the first (not the revised) version of Elmer Rice's forgotten but delightful *Not for Children.*

13. Price, ed., *Dramatic Works,* p. 501. In part, Sheridan is here poking fun at his own bad practice, for in 1777 he himself had made a bungling reformation of Vanbrugh's *The Relapse,* which he staged as *A Trip to Scarborough.*

14. In this edition of Sheridan's *Works* (1874; reprint, London: Chatto & Windus, 1913), p. 630, F. Stainforth relates the following story:

    Cumberland's children induced their father to take them to see *The School for Scandal.* Every time the delighted youngsters laughed at what was going on on the stage, he pinched them, and said, "What are you laughing at, my dear little folks? you should not laugh, my angels; there is nothing to laugh at"; and then, in an undertone, "Keep still, you little dunces."—Sheridan, having been told this, said, "It was very ungrateful in Cumberland to have been displeased with his poor children for laughing at *my comedy,* for I went the other night to see *his tragedy,* and laughed at it from beginning to end."

15. Price, ed., *Dramatic Works,* p. 507.

16. Ibid., pp. 514-15.

17. Kenneth Tynan, *Curtains* (New York: Atheneum, 1961), pp. 272-73.

18. Robert Brustein, *Seasons of Discontent* (New York: Simon and Schuster, 1965), p. 276.

19. Stanley Kauffmann, *Persons of the Drama* (New York: Harper and Row, 1976), p. 175.

20. Martin Gottfried, *Opening Nights* (New York: G. P. Putnam's Sons, 1969), pp. 203-4.

21. Price, ed., *Dramatic Works,* p. 529.

22. Ibid., pp. 545-46.

23. Bernard Shaw, *Sixteen Self Sketches* (New York: Dodd, Mead, 1949), p. 183.

Christine S. Wiesenthal (essay date 1992)

SOURCE: "Representation and Experimentation in the Major Comedies of Richard Brinsley Sheridan," in *Eighteenth-Century Studies,* Vol. 25, No. 3, Spring, 1992, pp. 309-30.

[*In the following essay, Wiesenthal studies Sheridan's concern with modes of artistic representation in* The Critic, The School for Scandal, *and* The Rivals.]

In his 1825 biography of Richard Brinsley Sheridan, Thomas Moore pauses briefly to consider a "ludicrous little drama" entitled ***Ixion,*** the incomplete product of a juvenile collaboration between the nineteen-year-old Sheridan and a school chum. Insignificant in itself, the fragment, as Moore suggests, is yet "highly curious as an anticipation of ***The Critic,***" for not only is it a burletta written in the form of a rehearsal, but it also features an embryonic precursor of Sheridan's famous Mr. Puff in its main character, a playwright-critic named Simile. "It is amusing," Moore reflects by way of conclusion, "to observe how long this subject was played with by the current of Sheridan's fancy."[1]

More than merely "amusing," the fragment from Sheridan's juvenilia suggests an early, conscious fascination with the very nature of the dramatic form of representation itself. Perhaps the most manifold of the sister arts, the drama, as a type of "story unfolding through a visible enactment,"[2] offered the young Sheridan a uniquely composite narrative and pictorial medium with which to work—or perhaps more precisely, to play. For indeed, as the germinal precursor of his renowned burlesque, ***The Critic, Ixion*** attests to Sheridan's innately playful disposition towards the modes of representation involved in his chosen medium. It is such an element of "playfulness" that, as Edward Galligan has argued, constitutes the central feature of "the comic vision" in literature.[3] But most critical discussions of Sheridan's use of language, gesture, and image, limiting themselves to general considerations of his "comic dialogue" or his "comedy of situation," have failed to appreciate adequately the great extent to which Sheridan's personal "comic vision" is shaped by his play with both the themes and the actual stuff of representation. Yet one need only glance at the three major comedies, ***The Rivals***

(1775), *The School for Scandal* (1777), and *The Critic* (1779),[4] to observe not only his characteristic delight in experimenting with narrative, pictorial, and dramatic forms of representation, but his pervasive focus upon a wide range of linguistic and pictorial objects: from letters, manuscripts, and newspapers, to maps, pictures, screens, and stage props, a vast plethora of signs and symbols proliferate in Sheridan's great comedies.

Sheridan's interest in mediums of artistic representation can yield a great deal of insight into both the nature and relative merits of the individual plays, as well as to the general direction of his dramatic career as a whole. Indeed, although in one sense it may be quite rightly argued that *The Critic,* as a burlesque, cannot be evaluated alongside Sheridan's two great "neo-Restoration" comedies of manners,[5] in another, his last major work may be usefully regarded as a type of coda, which traces retrospectively the stages by which he brought his "career in comedy full circle" from that first aborted burletta.[6] In particular, *The Critic* brings to logical culmination themes about language and art, that, throughout the major works, reflect a progressively more daring and experimental play with the modes and means of representation. Words, images and gestures become increasingly less reliable, less "safe" and less effective as means of representing reality or conveying artistic intent. Sheridan's increasingly searching and sophisticated exploration of the possibilities inherent in literary and dramatic representation also provides a means of understanding *The Critic* as the logical *formal* culmination of his development as a comic dramatist, even if this last major work postdates the epitome of his dramatic achievement with the superbly crafted *The School for Scandal.* Ultimately, to trace a trajectory from *The Rivals* to *The Critic,* from his first serio-comedy to his last parodic burlesque, is to trace the genesis not only of a truly three-dimensional artistic genius, but of a more quintessentially "comic" sensibility as well.

The importance of both language and gesture in Sheridan's first comedy is subtly indicated even before the play begins, in the unusual dialogue form of the first night's prologue, a form which calls attention to the arena of discourse, an arena where words and gestures meet. Indeed, one way *The Rivals* can be read is as a play which explores dimensions of discourse, and especially that of comic language. Aptly described as a "theatrical coat of many colors . . . sometimes ridiculing sentimental comedy, sometimes echoing it,"[7] *The Rivals* also illustrates what happens when, in the inexperienced hands of an exuberant, young comic playwright, two essentially antagonistic discourses begin to compete against one another. Most critics of the play agree, in particular, that Sheridan's sentimental portrayal of the tempestuous love relationship between Julia and Faulkland in the so-called "high plot," and his simultaneous satirization of the anti-heroine, Lydia Languish, in the main plot, reveal his divided allegiances to the opposed contemporary camps of "Laughing" and "Weeping Sentimental" comedy.[8] And from early reviewers of the play to modern critics, a number of writers have

noted that "the brilliant language" of *The Rivals* seems to contribute somehow to this formal ambivalence—that it has "divisive effects" or "exact[s] a price in 'significant unity.'"[9] Beyond observing the highly stylized and peculiarly obtrusive quality of the language, however, no one has looked closely at the specific techniques and larger ramifications of Sheridan's play with comic language in *The Rivals*—some, in fact, dismissing the idea of such an exercise as tedious."[10]

The general observation that the dialogue of Sheridan's comedy is highly contrived and palpably obtrusive is actually quite unhelpful in attempting to determine the difficult matter of what is "comical" about it. For as Thomas Moore long since pointed out, both Sheridan's "witty and serious styles" are equally characterized by "false finery" and marked "effort," which, "tho' ingenious, is far too labored."[11] Moreover, not only do such "non-transparent" diction and style mark both the serious interchanges of Julia and Faulkland as well as the comic sequences of *The Rivals,* but they are also qualities intrinsic to literary or poetic language as a whole, which, as Murray Krieger observes,

> rivet[s] our attention upon its playful aesthetic presence instead of allowing us to pass through it (as we are accustomed to pass through other discourse) to the more important things it is supposed to point us toward.[12]

It is, indeed, only when one begins to consider the specific ways in which language "playfully" arrests our attention upon its "aesthetic presence" that the comic essence of Sheridan's language begins to manifest itself.

Certainly the most obvious starting point for any such discussion lies with the character of Mrs. Malaprop, merely "the duenna" of *The Rivals*' foolishly romantic Lydia Languish, in terms of the play's plot, perhaps, but the absolutely un-rivalled "queen of the dictionary" in Sheridan's comedy too (2.2). Indeed, when considering language calling attention to itself as language in an especially comical, literal way, one need look no further than this "mistress of orthodoxy" (1.2), whose malapropisms sometimes consist in an ironic confusion of the actual names of grammatical "parts of speech" for the words she intends. As she at one point confides to the hero of the play, Jack Absolute, for example, she has laid her "positive conjunctions" on Lydia never to think of Jack's "rival," Ensign Beverley, again. And, furthermore, "I have since laid Sir Anthony's preposition before her;—but I'm sorry to say she seems resolved to decline every particle that I enjoin her" (3.3). "Particles" of grammar are, in fact, also apt to surface in many of Mrs. Malaprop's own "prepositions." Hence, the punctilious "Delia" coyly confesses to her clandestine correspondent, Sir Lucius O'Trigger, after a glowing review of his charms: "Female punctuation forbids me to say more" (2.2).

Despite their undisputed prominence in this respect, however, Mrs. Malaprop's "hard words" (3.3) are not the only ones to foist their sharp verbal surfaces upon the reader's notice in humorous ways. Word games such as verbal puns, for instance, abound in *The Rivals:* French dance "lingo," such as the word "*pas,*" is phonetically juxtaposed to the clumsy "antigallican" "Paws" of the rustic fop, Bob Acres (3.4), and the names of characters furnish similar *bon mots.* Mrs. Malaprop, for example, outdoes Sir Lucious O'Trigger's pun on the "dirty acres" destined to "slip through [his] fingers" (3.4) when she blithely puns on both Sir Anthony Absolute's Christian and surnames, calling him an "absolute misanthropy" (1.2). And Sir Anthony himself similarly rechristens his newly "repentant" son from "Puppy" to "Jack" again, when he pretends to "talk sense—absolute sense" about his prospective bride (3.1).

An amusing selection of tasty tidbits, a modern Dangle and Sneer might yawn, but so what? Seemingly insubstantial in themselves, puny puns, long dismissed as "the lowest form of wit," are presently garnering a new respect in literary studies. Jonathan Culler, for one, views the pun as no less than a "paradigm for the play of language" itself, a "disquieting spectacle" of inherently unstable linguistic dynamics wherein "boundaries—between sounds, between sound and letter, between meanings," between "essence and accident . . . meaningful relations and coincidence"— "count for less than one might imagine." "[R]esponding to the call of the phoneme," the pun, Culler contends, "tell[s] of wild realms beyond the code" of our conscious, rational linguistic behavior.[13] No mere insignificant particles, puns—the quarks, not the quirks of comedy—show Sheridan working to playfully reveal the structures of language, and constitute a major aspect of the comic language of his plays.

The animated comic language of *The Rivals* not only flags itself directly as improper idiom and proper names, but it is also indirectly portrayed as an amusingly tactile realm: when Lydia not very languidly jams *The Innocent Adultery* between the chaste covers of *The Whole Duty of Man,* for example, she imparts an entirely new dimension of physicality to the notion of literary subtexts (1.2). Words are consistently personified by Sheridan as animated entities in their own right. Like a little platoon of hapless military conscripts, "a great many poor words . . . that would get their *habeas corpus* from any court in Christendom" are thus mercilessly "pressed into the service" of Mrs. Malaprop's *billet-doux* (2.2). When not "pressed' into action unwillingly, words can themselves function as the agents of active, heroic valor. "Your words," as the temporarily inspired Acres puts it to Sir Lucius, "are a grenadier's march to my heart!" (3.4). Words, in other words, like the "en-signs" of a "marching regiment" (3.1) come to town on a mission to "recruit" (2.1), effectively caricature the actions of Ensign Beverley/Captain Absolute in the main plot, even as he "mimic[s]" the language of other military characters in the play (4.3). This sort of metaphorical mimicry at the level of language itself represents an extremely subtle way, indeed, of tapping a comic resource which Freud considered as amongst the most "extraordinary" "sources of comic pleasure."[14]

Signaling its "playful aesthetic presence" through puns and personification, it becomes increasingly difficult to take the language of the play "straight." The words "pressed" into the "service" of Sheridan's comedy, that is to say, clamor so loudly and forcefully as comical actors in and of themselves that they resonate throughout the play, creating a type of unintentional, parodic "echo to the sense" (2.1) of the serious dialogues between Julia and Faulkland. To some extent, a mocking, undermining residue of humor enters into this couple's passionately intense verbal exchanges through their unhappy reliance on some of the same (or very similar) words that Mrs. Malaprop mangles in memorable lines. When Julia rightfully reproaches her neurotic lover for casting "hard aspersions on [her] fame" (5.1), for example, one is apt to hear an echo of Mrs. Malaprop's equally indignant reaction to the "brute" who dared to cast a cruel "aspersion upon [her] parts of speech!" (3.3). And as one remembers Mrs. Malaprop for her "positive conjunctions," so the gloomy and asocial Faulkland is pointedly associated with *negative* conjunctions such as "but—but." As Jack says to him in exasperation at one point, "Confound your *buts.*—You never hear anything that would make another man bless himself, but you must immediately d—n it with a *but*" (4.3). Many other comic registers come to play upon the lovers' tender scenes as a similar sort of linguistic overlay: Faulkland promises to "expiate" his "past folly" (5.1), while Lydia is warned not to attempt to "extirpate" herself from hers (1.2), and Faulkland's admission to the strange wish of having been "deformed" in order to convince himself of the integrity of Julia's affection (3.2) comes dangerously close upon the heels of Jack's reversion to the hump-backed, one-eyed bride with whom his father has earlier threatened him (3.1). A substantial measure of the "divisive effect" of language which critics have noted in *The Rivals,* then, may be seen to arise from the ironic undertow created by a comic language so exuberant that it drags upon the rhetoric of sublimity, interfering with the reader's wholly sympathetic response to Julia and Faulkland.

If Sheridan's play with language in *The Rivals* illustrates some of the drawbacks as well as the strengths of his first major work, however, it also serves to establish the central comic axis upon which his play with forms of representation will continue to hinge throughout his career. In the language of Mrs. Malaprop and Bob Acres, that is, Sheridan plays with obverse extremes of linguistic distortion which satirize the antipodes of eighteenth-century semantic theory—and he does so through a principle of comic incongruity, recognized as an essential source of laughter from the time of Aristotle.[15]

As critics have noted, it is incongruity that generates the comic force of Mrs. Malaprop's "oracular tongue, and . . . nice derangement of epitaph" (3.3), for her ingenious mis-application of "mal-a-propos" words "outrage[s]" her audience's expectations, "thrusting [them] into a wildly inept frame of reference."[16] As Sir Lucius remarks, words dare not "refuse coming" at the "call" of this "great mistress of language" even "tho' one would think [they were] quite out of hearing" (2.2). Based on a radical disparity or contrariety between words and the connotative and denotative dimensions of words, the effect of Mrs. Malaprop's comic language—as her most famous simile, "as headstrong as an allegory on the banks of the Nile" (3.3), perhaps best illustrates—is to give a whole new figurative life to figures of speech. The laughable incongruity between what Mrs. Malaprop *says* and what she really *means* is in this respect very much like the ludicrous literary style of *The Critic*'s Sir Fretful Plagiary, whose "poverty" of "thought," ever unsuited to the overly ornamental style of his poetic "expression," provokes Sneer to sniff that "the homeliness of [his] sentiment states thro' the encumberance of its fine language like a clown in one of the new uniforms" (1.1).

While Mrs. Malaprop's clownish words have received a great deal of attention by virtue of their sheer, outlandish obviousness, little heed has been paid to the "referential" swearing of Bob Acres, which actually represents the parodic obverse of Mrs. Malaprop's incongruous language. In his desire to remedy the semantic poverty of "common oaths"—which, as he feels, have "no meaning"—Acres swears by swearing only "according to" the precise "sentiment" motivating the epithet. Bob thus champions a linguistic extreme which would press for a strictly representational relation or equivalency between words and their semantic content: "the oath should be an echo to the sense," as he informs Jack, "and this we call the *oath referential* or *sentimental swearing*—ha! ha! ha! 'tis genteel isn't it?" (2.1). Acres' declared aim to drain "figures of imprecation" (2.1) of all of their figurative force, to perfect the art of literal cursing, reflects a conscious ideal of language as an absolutely transparent medium—a sort of saran wrap around thought, as it were—which contrasts directly with Mrs. Malaprop's unwitting misuse of words. Thus just as Mrs. Malaprop may be regarded as a devastating satire of the figurative ideal of language, or "affective aesthetics of taste and sentiment" in vogue during the late-eighteenth century, so Bob Acres, with his "Odds jigs and tabors" (3.4) or "Odds bullets and blades" (4.1), may be seen as a similar travesty on an old-fashioned linguistic ideal of "Lockean literalism."[17]

The theme of incongruous figurative language and "plain-speaking" literalism begun in *The Rivals* is brought to its most dramatic development in *The Critic,* wherein Sheridan plays extensively with the concept of metaphoric or poetic speech as a type of ornamental embroidery on a literal sackcloth of language, "like tambour sprigs" on "a ground of linsey-wolsey" (1.1). Puff, the genial author of "The Spanish Armada"—the "tragedy" burlesqued within Sheridan's comedy—is relentlessly satirized for the flowery heights and ludicrous lows between which his verse vacillates. Although often "obliged" to be "plain and intelligible" when his drama must convey "matter of fact," Puff's real penchant is for the "better language" of "trope, figure and metaphor," which he assiduously attempts to intersperse, "as plenty as noun substantives" (2.2). And truly,

his "panegyrical superlatives" and "variegated chips of exotic metaphor" (1.2) can be every whit as exotic as Mrs. Malaprop's Egyptian "allegories" or "contagious Countries" (1.2).

More importantly, though, in *The Critic* Sheridan plays with extremes of language in a way that pushes the funny but subtly unsettling conceptual dislocations inherent in Mrs. Malaprop's linguistic aberrations to a yet more unintelligible extreme, working steadily to undermine any complaisant faith in the simple referentiality of words. For in his satire of the theatrical convention of the tragic heroine's "mad scene," Sheridan in effect knocks back the incongruities of Mrs. Malaprop's idiosyncratic language one final remove, into the realm of utter nonsense. Hence the following indisputably "mad" speech from Puff's raving heroine, Tilburina:

> The Wind whistles—the moon rises—see
> They have kill'd my squirrel in his cage!
> Is this a grasshopper?—Ha! no, it is my
> Whiskerandos—you shall not keep him—
> I know you have him in your pocket—
> An oyster may be cross'd in love!—Who says
> A Whale's a bird?—Ha! did you call, my love?
> —He's here! He's there!—He's everywhere!
> Ah me! He's no where! (3.1)

As Ellen E. Martin has observed with respect to Jane Austen's juvenilia, such "mad" language, based on a principle of rushed metonymic associations, invites the reader to make connections or see relations between highly unlikely objects, and so reflects an essentially "non-representational aesthetic."[18] The difference between Mrs. Malaprop's "deranged epitaphs" of "allegories" on the Nile or "pineapple[s] of politeness" (*The Rivals,* 3.3) and Tilburina's nonsensical "whales" and "birds" in *The Critic,* then, is purely quantitative, not qualitative: a difference only of a degree of deferred meaning. For while one can usually, after a moment or two at most, identify the cliche or conceit behind Mrs. Malaprop's bruised and abused metaphorical "conjunctions," the significance of Tilburina's more radically disjointed words—like those of a long line of "mad" tragedy queens, including Otway's Belvidera in *Venice Preserved*—remains obscure no matter how long one puzzles over them.

A similar movement toward a progressively "non-representational aesthetic" may also be traced briefly in Sheridan's play with non-verbal forms of communication, with the gestures, "attitudes," and poses that in the drama complement language and even replace it at critical moments. In both *The Rivals* and *The School for Scandal,* Sheridan's scenes, like Puff's in "The Spanish Armada," often go "entirely for what we call Situation and Stage Effect, by which the greatest applause may be obtained, without the assistance of language, sentiment, or character: pray mark!" (*The Critic,* 3.1). Sheridan's dramaturgical excellence in this capacity is generally acknowledged, with critics typically pointing to the famous "screen scene" in *The School for Scandal* as the principal example. But although the dramatic tableau which ensues the discovery of Lady Teazle in that play is undoubtedly the most perfect instance of Sheridan's ability to crystallize a climactic narrative moment in the form of a symbolic pictorial configuration, his playful use of dramatic gesture and posture is evident throughout his major comedies. In *The Rivals,* for example, "backsides" (3.3), "side-fronts" (4.2) and "attitudes" are of the utmost importance, especially, as Bob Acres learns, when dueling. For when it is crucial to make oneself as "small" as possible, an "edge-ways" stance is infinitely preferable to the "full-front" posture advocated by Sir Lucius (5.3).

The most relentless fun with the non-verbal techniques relied upon by the drama, though, comes once again in *The Critic.* Indeed, Puff's farcical "deadlock" scene, in which six characters remain suspended, daggers pointed at each others' breasts, and all afraid "to let go first" until ordered to quit their "situation" in the name of the Queen (3.1), appears to be quite clearly intended as a parody of precisely the type of dramatic tableau Sheridan himself had utilized to such grand "STAGE EFFECT" in *The School for Scandal.* Similarly, the idea of a gestural language or "pantomic" means of communication, a concept stressed by both popular contemporary linguistic theories, such as Condillac's *"langage d'action"*[19] and the "new" school of pictorial dramaturgy which emerged in the 1770s,[20] is also caricatured by Sheridan in Puff's production. Spectators of Puff's tragedy, that is, are likely to want the same sort of "poetical second sight" with which Tilburina is happily endowed (2.2) when the character of Lord Burleigh enters upon the stage, "comes forward, shakes his head, and exit[s]": a "dumbshew" the complicated purport of which Puff must spend several minutes explicating for his confused rehearsal audience (3.1). Although language, then, is fraught with its own difficulties, the dangers of lapsing into absurdity through "dumbshew" appear yet greater.

As the dialogue format of the prologue to *The Rivals* indicates the importance of words and gestures in that play, so the dedicatory preface to *The School for Scandal,* significantly entitled "A PORTRAIT," suggests the more distinctly pictorial nature of Sheridan's most accomplished theatrical work. Although in this comedy Sheridan's love of the verbal contours of comic language is still readily apparent, his attention here shifts quite literally to the "Surfaces" of the painter's canvas. Moreover, while the comedy of this play may also be seen to hinge upon a principle of incongruity similar to that of *The Rivals, The School for Scandal* evinces a far more sophisticated and impressive awareness of the spatial as well as the narrative or temporal planes of the dramatic form. Indeed, just as comic language in *The Rivals* provides insight to that play's structural tensions, so the painterly elements of *The School for Scandal* provide a key for appreciating the consummate craftsmanship of this play, helping to unlock an intricacy of aesthetic design which belies the common critical charge of the play's "unsubtlety."

Most critics accede to the *dramaturgical* excellence of *The School for Scandal*'s use of pictorial effect, especially in its climactic "screen-scene" tableau; "as penetrating and coherent literature, however, the play claims few champions."[21] The "scandal plot," as Andrew Schiller chides, "is an awkward thing" which "fails to function," for although Lady Sneerwell and Snake open the play, "the ensuing action" does not immediately "advance" the scandal plot. "On the contrary," the matter seems to be "all but forgotten" until it is "reintroduced at the end of the play":

> The scandal group—Lady Sneerwell, Snake, Mrs. Candour, Sir Benjamin Backbite, *et al.*—are perilously close to being entirely separable from the main structure of the action. The screen scene, indeed, is the only real jointure. As a matter of fact, Sheridan originally drafted two plays, "The Slanderers,' and 'The Teazles,' and the evidence of the carpentry by which he joined them is clear enough. The most obvious evidence is that the scandal group is, in effect, a 'frame.'[22]

Although it is true that Sheridan's play does embody minor structural blemishes in the problematic role of its heroine, Maria, and her precipitous fifth-act union with the hero, Charles Surface, Schiller's argument of an "awkward" jointure of two original fragments represents an inadequate approach to the play: for one thing, it fails completely to take into account the central action of the comedy, the moral testing of the Surface brothers, Charles and Joseph, by their uncle, Sir Oliver.

Conversely, if one conceives of the "frame" of the scandal plot, not negatively, as evidence of clumsy carpentry, but, rather, positively, as the intentional structural principle upon which Sheridan's play is shaped, then *The School for Scandal* can be read as both a clever, extended play upon the notion of "framing," and as a uniquely three-dimensional comic *drama* which explores its own *spatial* performance as a *literary text.* In this sense, the concept of "literary space"[23] operating in the text may be likened to a series of coaxial Chinese boxes. In essence, Sheridan seems to take the three plots of the scandal school, the Surface family, and the Teazles—all of which revolve around a similar theme of the "art" of misrepresentation, or "framing"—and develop each one according to a different dimensional medium of representation: the first unfolds in pictorial terms, as a type of "portrait" frame; the second, in narrative terms, as a plot which unfolds sequentially over time within that former frame; and the last, in dramatic terms, as a climactic gestural or dramatic moment which occurs at the very apex of the Surface plot.

The scandal school, a school of "modish art," as the prologue has it, is thus associated with painterly images and "picture language" from the very outset. In the opening scene, Snake compares Lady Sneerwell's "paragraphs" of scandal to those of another of her school as though they are artistic illustrations, like the portraits which often did, in fact, accompany the gossip in the "scandal rags" of the day:[24]

> 'Tis very true, she generally designs well . . . but her colouring is too dark and her outline often extravagant.

She wants that delicacy of Hint—and mellowness of Sneer which distinguishes your Ladyship's Scandal. (1.1)

As Lady Sneerwell "frames" her victims in blocks and columns of print, so another prominent member of the infernal scandal "crew" (2.1), Sir Benjamin Backbite, speaks of his literary productions in the language of "*ut pictura poesis*": "Yes Madam I think you will like them—when you shall see them on a beautiful Quarto page where a neat rivulet of Text shall murmur thro' a meadow of Margin" (1.1). One can only hope that the "margins" of Sir Benjamin's pastoral landscape are absorbent enough to contain the dribble and trickle of his vapid, tepid verse. Even the scandal sessions of Sneerwell's clique turn upon extended analogies drawn from the world of art. Women who "paint" themselves cosmetically, for instance, are themselves likened to paintings and art objects: Miss Vermillion's "color" is too "fresh put on"; the "ravages of time" are evident in the mature face of Mrs. Evergreen; and the Widow Ocre, who manages to restore herself quite well by "caulk[ing] her wrinkles," nevertheless "joins" her face to her neck "so badly" that "she looks like a mended statue in which the connoisseur sees at once that the Head's modern tho' the Trunk's antique" (2.2). [Now there's a good example of clumsy carpentry for you.]

As instruction in an "art" form which thrives on "run[ning] down" or "sinking" people's reputations (2.2) by confabulating fictions which take on a life of their own, the Sneerwell school of "modish art" is travestied by Sheridan as a bitterly ironic perversion of the highest aim of legitimate art, which, as in "the Works of your Modern Raphael [Sir Joshua Reynolds], . . . gives you the strongest resemblance yet contrives to make your own portrait independent of you—so that you may Sink the Original and not hurt the Picture" (4.1). The main point, however, is that as members of a school that quite literally "kill[s] time" (2.3) with an art of "framing," the characters in the scandal plot have little to do with the typical narrative requirements of (linear) plot and character development that traditional literary critics such as Schiller once looked for.

The Surface family plot, on the other hand, has everything to do with chronological narrative time; indeed, Sir Oliver's trials of Charles and Joseph are critically dependent upon the fact of his sixteen-year absence from England. And if students of scandal tend to perceive texts as images and images as aesthetic objects, then characters in the Surface plot evince an obverse propensity to apprehend images and art objects as narratives. Just as Mrs. Malaprop remarks upon the "grammatical" "physiognomy" of Jack Absolute in *The Rivals,* for example, so Sir Oliver, a man who has remained true to his own anti-matrimonial "Text" (2.1), is able to "read husband" in the "married look" of Sir Peter's face (2.3). Sir Oliver's nephew, Charles, similarly views a room full of pictures not as a gallery of individual artistic images, but primarily as a narrative sequence documenting historical and genealogical time: "Walk in Gentlemen, pray walk in!—Here they are, the

Family of Surfaces up to the Conquest" (4.1). For Charles, then, the gallery of the "Family Canvass [sic]" (5.3) is as much a record of temporal legacy like the parchment of the "Family Tree" (4.1) as it is an art collection of perhaps dubious but nevertheless distinct aesthetic value.

In the Surface plot, unlike the scandal plot, the theme of the "art of misrepresentation" also takes on a markedly narrative rather than pictorial form. Most obviously, perhaps, Joseph, the hypocritical "Man of Sentiment" (5.3), misrepresents himself verbally, through a type of internalized "script" or "catalogue" of empty aphorisms and platitudes (5.1). And Sir Peter's contention, early in the play, that "there needs no art to discover" the true "merits" of the Surface brothers (1.2), is also proven wrong, for Sir Oliver, too, deliberately uses the art of dissimulation when he assumes the false characters of, first, "Little Premium" and then "Mr. Stanley" (3.1) in order to "make a trial" of his nephews' "Hearts" (2.3). Like Joseph's misrepresentations, Sir Oliver's impersonations mainly take the form of a verbal charade, for, significantly, he never attempts to disguise himself physically.

As the link between the predominately pictorial and narrative worlds of the scandal group, on the one hand, and the Surface family, on the other, the Teazle plot provides the means of a brilliant dramatic synthesis of representational dimensions at the very nucleus of Sheridan's play. Sir Peter discovers his wife hiding in Joseph's library, that is, not just behind any old screen, but behind one plastered with maps. Since maps are pictorial symbols that are yet "read" or deciphered like texts, they are the perfect representational form to suggest a meeting of spatial and temporal realms. In the shocked stasis which ensues Charles's dramatic "unveil[ing]" of Lady Teazle behind the screen (4.3), Sheridan's play realizes the perfect moment of the "speaking picture," a moment poised in the very midst of the incessant dialectic between word and image and act. And not only does it come as a moment of complete aesthetic equilibrium or balance, but the screen scene, as Jean Dulck first noted, also represents the very epicenter of the play in another respect as well: for beginning with Lady Teazles' entrance to the library and concluding with her confession and Joseph's disgrace, the scene constitutes a miniature five-act play within itself.[25]

In both the metadramatic form implicitly embedded within the screen scene and its manifold play with "frames," then, *The School for Scandal* clearly anticipates the overt "rehearsal" framework of *The Critic,* that modest little three-act "afterpiece," which, though it comes as something of an anticlimax after its elegantly and elaborately crafted predecessor, finally brings Sheridan's play with "frames" and planes of dramatic representation to the "surface" of a self-conscious examination. For as a parody of the illusion-making processes of theatrical—and literary—art, and a satire of the notion of the stage as "the Mirror of Nature" (1.1), *The Critic* works (hilariously) to undo and expose all the clanking contrivance that *The School for Scandal* for the most part gracefully conceals within itself, thus consistently subverting the aesthetic "gratification" of theatrical artifice by revealing it as "gratifiction."[26]

Significantly, Sheridan's play with the motif of pictorial art from *The Rivals* to *The School for Scandal* charts a movement that follows in the wake of the direction taken by his experimentation with linguistic and non-discursive mediums of expression, toward an ever more slippery and unstable "non-representational aesthetic." The integrity of the heroes of both *The Rivals* and *The School for Scandal,* for example, is tested by their willingness, or non-willingness, to relinquish the image or "copy" of an "original" who has a legitimate moral claim upon their "Hearts." Happily, both Jack Absolute and Charles Surface pass their "tests." But in the earlier play, although Jack's miniature "copy" of Lydia "is not equal" to its "original" "in beauty," it has a reassuring "merit" in "being still the same," and it is upon this basis of resemblance that Jack "cannot find it in [his] heart to part with it" (4.2). In *The School for Scandal,* on the other hand, Charles Surface cannot rely upon such a faithful correspondence between image and referent to guide his actions: indeed, it is precisely because he *does* trust unquestioningly to the referential "merit" of his pictures as "Inveterate likeness[es]— all stiff and Aukward [sic] as the Originals" that he comes perilously close to committing an unforgivable "*ex post facto* Parricide" in the eyes of his uncle (4.1). For in this play, of course, the all-important portrait of "the ill-looking little fellow over the settee" (4.1) bears not the slightest resemblance (any more) to its "original," who, unbeknownst to Charles, stands before his very eyes, highly amused at the ironical truth of his nephew's observation that his "Uncle Noll" is "so much changed lately that his nearest Relations don't know him" (3.3).

Once again, it is in *The Critic* that representational veracity becomes most tenuous, albeit in this play, Sheridan focuses his parody specifically upon the status of "original" dramatic works of art and their "copies." And rather than pressing the idea of radical incongruities or gaps between art and life, *The Critic* plays raucously, instead, with the notion of an infinitely referential ripple of intertextual echoes amongst works within a common cultural body of art. From its satire of Richard Cumberland in the figure of Sir Fretful Plagiary, and its comic exploitation of Sheridan's own reputation as the occasionally plagiarizing hack of the "Drury Lane Theatre" (1.1), to its farcical exposure of the casual "coincidences" between Puff's "Spanish Armada" and some of Shakespeare's gems, *The Critic*—itself a sort of rehearsal of Villiers's *The Rehearsal*—evinces a trenchant and wry awareness of the essential derivativeness of all literary works, itself included, as forms of "plagiarisms" of earlier works of art.[27] Freely and frankly, Sheridan's last major comedy plays with those nasty "starts of recollection" or "appearances of plagiary" which the author of *The Rivals* sought so hard to avoid.[28] As Puff puts it, succinctly: "[Y]ou see I don't attempt to strike out any thing new—but I take it I improve on the established modes" (2.2).

Louis Kronenberger has rightfully contended that, unlike the pre-eminent Restoration "original" whose dramas he "copied" and adapted for his own late-eighteenth-century audience, Sheridan, the "modern Congreve," was not at liberty to "attack appearances" in his comedies, but rather, "had himself some to keep up."[29] And yet as a final barometer of Sheridan's disposition toward his medium, *The Critic* clearly illustrates the great extent to which, over the course of his career, his need to maintain "appearances"— like "gratifications" of "newness" and "originality"—had lessened. Indeed, not only does *The Critic,* in its playful poke at the subject of plagiarism, denote a far more casual and unillusioned authorial attitude toward the status of art in general, but it also indicates a corollary conception of the status of *comic* art in particular: for just as the play suggests that "art" need not pretend to be "original," so it also unequivocally endorses the idea that the art of comedy need not pretend to teach. Indeed, the early satire in *Ixion* of Simile's belief that "the stage should be a place of rational entertainment," of "grave comedy" formed "so that it is no laughing, giggling piece of work,"[30] finds its most mature and mordant expression in *The Critic,* in Sheridan's sneer at Sneer's advocacy of "The Reformed Housebreaker": a "new type" of "truly moral" comedy which proposes to "dramatize the penal laws and make the Stage a court of ease to the Old Bailey" (1.1).

Sheridan's gay parody of the comic stage as a "court of ease" to a burdened and groaning Old Bailey—a type of laxative to "ease" the cramped channels of a "constirpated" judicial system (to echo one of Mrs. Malaprop's more memorable gaffes)—provides an apt indication of just how far he has come toward eliminating, so to speak, from *The Critic* those "didactic excrescences" which critics object to in *The Rivals.*[31] For although the famous tenth-night prologue to that play clearly implies that "comedy" is not "form'd to teach" (and although Lydia Languish certainly serves the comic cause in this respect, by using the pages of *Fordyce's Sermons* to curl her hair [1.2]), the drama itself also plainly reflects the obligation Sheridan felt to "coax some Moral from his Play," as the epilogue puts it. It is such "coaxing," all too evident in Julia's somewhat strained final speech, which mars the ending of *The Rivals.* Even if one takes into account its serio-comic nature, the play's perfunctory nod at didactic convention is problematic, for it ultimately leads Sheridan to request that his audience believe the unbelievable: namely, that the "unhappy temper" of Faulkland, which has clearly disclosed itself by this time as a species of compulsive neurosis, is really a character flaw amenable to "reform[ation]" (5.3).

The School for Scandal, on the other hand, evinces Sheridan's increasing unwillingness to oblige his characters to undergo precisely such a "bungling reformation" (*The Critic,* 1.1). Interestingly, this play has often been criticized upon the very ground that it does not thrust home its moral vigorously enough, that Sheridan relies lamely upon emphasizing benevolence and virtue rewarded at the expense of properly thrashing vice. According to one such critic, the play "clicks its heels before conventional morality"; intended primarily as a "box-office success," it "no where boldly challenges fashionable opinion or assaults fashionable complacency."[32] And yet the fact that Sheridan allows Joseph Surface to exit, ways unmended, still blithering protestations that are "moral to the last drop," and the fact that he has only one "licentiate" of the "Scandalous College" opt out of the "Diploma" program for good (5.3), can also be considered in terms of Robert Heilman's theory of "comic acceptance." According to Heilman, comedy, as an essentially "unillusioned" and "jesting awareness" of the "habitual and indeed incurable ironies of life in the world," "rarely proposes amendment, alternatives, or avoidance" of the world.[33] It accepts as inevitable any defects in society which "a sensed norm" or "common sense" perceives that "it would be foolish or perverse not to accept."[34]

It is perhaps not in the generic disposition of comedy, then, to go about "boldly challenging" or "assaulting" inevitable and incurable human weaknesses such as hypocrisy and slander. As an avid gossip and hypocrite herself, Mrs. Candour, of course, has a vested interest in "accepting" such vices as "inevitable" "Ways of the World," but in a very real sense, she is the voice of this comic truth in Sheridan's play. As she replies to Maria's rather pious protestations about "impertinent" tongues: "Very true Child but what's to be done? People will talk—there's no preventing it—Why it was but yesterday, I was told . . ." (1.1). Ultimately, if in its portrayal of Charles Surface and the "good" characters *The School for Scandal* posits a roseate, sentimental faith in the essential goodness of humanity, then it is a view nicely balanced—not by satire, but by a truly comical, "jesting awareness"—that slick "surfaces" such as Joseph and sour slanderers such as Lady Sneerwell, the "Oil and Vinegar" of society (5.3), will always exist, and that to call for their sudden "reformation" at the end of the play would merely be to "bungle" another ending.

After the commendable restraint exercised in *The School for Scandal, The Critic* comes as a final, ringing affirmation of Sheridan's ultimate adherence to the Johnsonian dictum that "the great end to comedy" is neither corrective nor didactic, but simply, to entertain and divert by "making an audience merry."[35] And despite the views of centuries of critics on *The Critic* who insist that Sheridan's burlesque is primarily a bitter and vindictive work—a real "snarler," as one put it[36]—it is by far his most playful and unillusioned work. Neither straining, like *The Rivals,* to extract an elusive kernel of didactic value from within itself, nor striving, artfully, for the superbly crafted form of *The School for Scandal, The Critic* acknowledges and revels in a sense of its own exuberant chaos and slipshod imperfection. It is a play that reflects the irrepressible spirit and enthusiasm of that endearing "Practitioner of Panegyrick" (1.2), Puff, a playwright who knows he is "luxuriant" (2.1) and cares not to restrain himself: "Now then for my magnificence!" he thunders, "—my battle!—my noise!—my procession!" (3.1). As Puff

watches his grand finale, the pomp and pageantry of his "fete Brittania [sic]" (3.1), of his drums, trumpets, cannonry, and his splendid parade of rivers, he "applauds everything" even as he cheerfully accedes that there are some rough edges to be worked out: "Well, pretty well— but not quite Perfect—So ladies and gentlemen, if you please, we'll rehearse this piece again tomorrow" (3.1). It is a closure which captures especially well that affirmative spirit of comic willingness for compromise, for acceptance of the less-than-perfect, which theorists such as Heilman hail as the definitive feature of the comic genre.

Ultimately, one way to view Sheridan's abiding penchant for experimentation with the composite dimensions of dramatic representation is as a type of progressive education or induction into the comic truth or "jesting awareness" of the desires and dangers simultaneously inherent in framing things: words within margins, images within picture frames, bodies within stage sets, ideas within conceptual frameworks. In this respect, his major works chart the progress of a playwright learning how to cope creatively with the maddening fact of the irrevocable clash between the artist's compulsive need to shape and contain, frame feelings and thoughts in images and words, on the one hand, and the representational and referential liabilities of attempting to do so, on the other. If the critic may indulge in a "gratifiction" of her own for a moment, Sheridan's career in comedy might be said to begin by being touched by a thin Faulklandish note of anxious insecurity and reserve, but ends with a happy blare and bang when, with the effervescent Puff, Sheridan finally indulges the creative process for the unalloyed glee and fun of it.

In a more general sense, Sheridan's manifold experimentation with forms of comic drama, and his play with forms of representation within those forms, stand as a testimony to the essentially fluid and protean nature of his comedy, which manifests itself, finally, as a spirit or an attitude, more than a literary or dramatic "form" with definable contours shaped by rigid generic laws. Indeed, unlike "the art of puffing" in *The Critic,* the art of Sheridan's comedy cannot be "scientifically treated, nor reduced to rule" (1.2). The varying textures of his major plays, each with its own unique blend of the sentimental and the satirical, point to only a few of the thoroughly composite and ever-malleable "forms" within which his comic spirit resides.

One thing is certain. From the time he prefaced *The Rivals* by bringing forth upon the stage "the Figure of Comedy," with the injunction to his audience to "Look on this form," to the time the cannon dust settled after the final curtain drop of *The Critic,* the creator of "Puff" knew all about the beauty and the elusiveness of the "forms" of both his dramatic medium and his comic mode.

Notes

1. Thomas Moore, *Memoirs of the Life of the Rt. Hon. Richard Brinsley Sheridan,* vol. I (1858; New York: Greenwood, 1968), pp. 19, 24.

2. Martin Meisel, *Realizations: Narrative, Pictorial, and Theatrical Arts in Nineteenth-Century England* (Princeton: Princeton University Press, 1983), p. 3.

3. Edward L. Galligan, *The Comic Vision in Literature* (Athens: University of Georgia Press, 1984). Galligan uses the word in the sense of "play" as a recurring motif in comic literature, intending it as "a label that is part noun, part adjective, and part verb," to denote "both the activity, play, the manner, playful," and "the injunction, play!" (p. 36).

4. Most critics agree upon Sheridan's "major" works as these three, which have never been out of the theatrical repertoire since they were first presented. While most of Sheridan's other works are minor, "occasional" pieces, such as the two-act farce, *St. Patrick's Day,* or adaptations, such as *A Trip to Scarborough* or the much later *Pizarro, The Duenna,* a comic opera, was a huge success during its time. Now deemed an operatic "museum piece" by John Loftis (*Sheridan and the Drama of Georgian England* [Cambridge, Mass.: Harvard University Press, 1977], p. 73), *The Duenna,* although it falls beyond the scope of the present essay, merits closer study as another of Sheridan's self-consciously multidimensional productions.

5. See, for example, Mark Auburn, *Sheridan's Comedies: Their Contexts and Achievements* (Lincoln: University of Nebraska Press, 1977), pp. 165ff.

6. Jack Durant, *Richard Brinsley Sheridan* (Boston: Twayne, 1975), p. 108. In an interesting way, *The Critic* provides a broad overview of all the dramatic forms Sheridan experimented with along the way, including glances at the comic opera, the military farce, and adaptations, as well as at his comedies of manners.

7. Louis Kronenberger, "The Polished Surface," in *Sheridan: Comedies,* ed. Peter Davison (London: MacMillan Education, 1986), p. 176.

8. The most compelling arguments to suggest that Sheridan intended Julia and Faulkland as a serious, nonsatiric portrayal of sentimental love are advanced by Leonard L. Leff, "Sheridan and Sentimentalism," *Restoration and Eighteenth-Century Theatre Research* 12 (1973): 36-48, and Auburn, pp. 31-60.

9. Durant, p. 72; and Otto Reinert, as cited by Durant, p. 71. Most early reviewers objected to the "defective" language of Mrs. Malaprop on the grounds of its "shameful" departure from the speech of "common life and common manners," anon. rev. of *The Rivals, The Public Ledger* 18 January 1775, reprinted in Davison, pp. 82 and 81-95 passim.

10. Robert Hogan, "Plot, Character, and Comic Language in Sheridan," in *Comedy from Shakespeare to Sheridan: Change and Continuity in the English and European Dramatic Tradition,* ed. & intro. A. R. Braunmiller and J. C. Bulman (Newark: University of Delaware; London: Associated University Press, 1986), pp. 274-285.

11. Moore I, p. 97. On the highly artificial nature of *all* dramatic dialogue, even "naturalistic," see Robert Cohen, "Spoken Dialogue in Written Drama," *Essays in Theater* 4 (1986): 85-97.

12. Murray Krieger, *Words about Words about Words: Theory, Criticism, and the Literary Text* (Baltimore: Johns Hopkins University Press, 1988), p. 231.

13. Jonathan Culler, ed., *On Puns: The Foundation of Letters* (Oxford: Basil Blackwell, 1988), pp. 3-5.

14. Sigmund Freud, "Jokes and the Comic," in *Comedy: Meaning and Form,* ed. Robert W. Corrigan, 2nd ed. (New York: Harper, 1981), p. 169.

15. As Stuart Tave has shown, it was primarily the principle of incongruity—or the "mixture of *relation* and *contrariety* in things"—upon which the prevailing late-eighteenth-century theory of "joyful and kindly" laughter was based. See *The Amiable Humorist: A Study in the Comic Theory and Criticism of the Eighteenth and Early Nineteenth Centuries* (Chicago: University of Chicago Press, 1960).

16. Durant, p. 70.

17. See Murray Cohen, *Sensible Words: Linguistic Practise in England, 1640-1785* (Baltimore: Johns Hopkins University Press, 1977), p. 45. It is interesting to note here that Sheridan's father, Thomas Sheridan, was a leading exponent of the new "language of emotion" that signaled the eighteenth-century departure from the simple representationism it inherited from the previous century (pp. 108-109). Another incisive overview of contemporary linguistic and aesthetic theory is presented by Stephen Land, *From Signs to Propositions: The Concept of Form in Eighteenth-Century Semantic Theory* (London: Longman, 1974), esp. pp. 21-74.

18. Ellen E. Martin, "The Madness of Jane Austen: Metonymic Style and Literature's Resistance to Interpretation," *Persuasions* 9 (1987): 76-84.

19. Land, pp. 90-92.

20. Meisel, pp. 40-41.

21. Durant, p. 100.

22. Andrew Schiller, "*The School for Scandal:* The Restoration Unrestored," in *Sheridan: Comedies,* ed. Davison, op. cit., p. 162.

23. W. J. T. Mitchell, *Iconology: Image, Text, Ideology* (Chicago: University of Chicago Press, 1986), p. 96.

24. See Cecil Price, ed., *Sheridan: Plays* (London: Oxford University Press, 1975), p. 227, n. 3.

25. Jean Dulck, *Les Comedies de Sheridan* (Paris: Didier, 1962), as cited by Durant, p. 105. According to Dulck and Durant, the servants' interruptions to announce Sir Peter, Charles, and finally Lady Sneerwell break the first three "acts"; the fourth concludes with the fall of the screen, and the last, "a seriocomic resolution to the whole scene," presents the "aftermath" of the collapse (pp. 105-106).

26. Krieger, p. 256. For a good but by no means exhaustive discussion of *The Critic* as a metadrama, see Philip K. Jason, "A Twentieth-Century Response to

The Critic," *Theatre Survey: The American Journal of Theater History* (1974), rpt, in Davison, pp. 204-209.

27. On this subject, see Raymond Federman's excellent essay, "Imagination as Plagiarism: [An Unfinished Paper . . .]," *New Literary History* 7 (1976): 563-578.

28. Sheridan, *Dramatic Works,* in Price, p. 6.

29. Kronenberger, p. 176.

30. Quoted in Moore I, p. 3.

31. Auburn, p. 26.

32. Kronenberger, pp. 179-180.

33. Robert B. Heilman, *The Ways of the World: Comedy and Society* (Seattle: University of Washington Press, 1978), pp. 236, 41.

34. Ibid., p. 179.

35. James Boswell, *Life of Johnson,* ed. R. W. Chapman (Oxford: Oxford University Press, 1970), p. 525.

36. W. C. Oulton, *The History of the Theatres of London . . . 1771 to 1795* (1796), as cited in Cecil Price, ed., *The Dramatic Works of Richard Brinsley Sheridan,* vol. 2 (Oxford: Clarendon Press, 1973), p. 484.

Richard C. Taylor (essay date 1995)

SOURCE: "'Future Retrospection': Rereading Sheridan's Reviewers," in *Sheridan Studies,* edited by James Morwood and David Crane, Cambridge University Press, 1995, pp. 47-57.

[*In the following essay, Taylor examines early critical reaction to Sheridan's satirical drama* The Rivals.]

The withdrawal of **The Rivals** after a disastrous opening performance at Covent Garden on 17 January 1775 is a well-established part of theatrical lore: a combination of sloppy acting and miscasting doomed the initial staging, and eleven days and some quick rewriting and recasting later, the play was successfully remounted, and it held the stage for fifteen nights. Since then it has become a mainstay of theatrical repertories, one of a handful of works representing the sprawling and diverse field of eighteenth-century theatre.

The responses of London newspaper critics to the first production suggest another possible reason for the initial failure of **The Rivals:** Sheridan had written a self-consciously novel play, one that set tradition and contemporaneity in conflict and satirized both. This theme is delightfully expressed by Mrs Malaprop in her muddled announcement: 'our retrospection will now be all to the future' (IV. ii. 136-7). Theatrical and social convention run up against the romantic sentimentalism in vogue and the patriarchal challenges of the novel and its readers. To some extent, because of the novelty of the play in its set-

ting, characterization, language and ideology, convention-bound critics and audience members essentially missed the point. Withdrawing it from production, ostensibly for revision, served another purpose: to let the novelty of the experience sink in, to allow a second reading by an audience not so stunned by its originality.

Mark Auburn argues that the play's 'pleasure derives from individual effects and not from a sophisticated overall informing aesthetic design'.[1] Yet it is this purposefully confused double gaze, forward and backward, that unifies the play—that informs its language, its characterizations, its plot conflict—and also helps explain the difficulties it presented to its first audience and reviewers. Critics and producers who conflate **The Rivals** with *The Man of Mode,* or *The Way of the World,* or *The Beaux' Stratagem* are also missing the point: Sheridan did not write Restoration comedies. The play itself inscribes a theatrical tradition for satiric purposes, but its newness is its *raison d'être,* its structure, its language, its thematic centre. It is a rivalry of a triumphant present over a ridiculous past. John Loftis argues that Sheridan 'took promising dramatic materials' from Restoration comedy, 'reworking them in his own idiom'.[2] This new idiom—and not the well-rehearsed plot conventions that critics denounced—is the central dramatic vehicle, established in the opening dialogue between the Coachman and Fag:

> FAG . . . none of the London whips of any degree of Ton wear *wigs* now.
>
> COACH More's the pity! more's the pity, I say.—Odd's life! when I heard how the lawyers and doctors had took to their own hair, I thought how 'twould go next . . . believe me, Mr Fag: and look'ee, I'll never gi' up mine—the lawyers and doctors may do as they will. (I.i.71-8)

It is a new age to which all the characters respond: the enlightened have discarded their wigs; Bath, not London, is the centre of fashion and intrigue; young women pillage circulating libraries rather than plundering reputations at cabalistic card parties; the female protagonist conspires to lose her inheritance and marry a poor man—we are in a world turned upside down. Sheridan writes for an audience of novel readers, an audience familiar with Smollett and Mackenzie, the scandalous romances of mid-century, the idea of female quixotism. His audience must have been well aware, also, of the persistent Tory attacks against the novel as a threat to patriarchal control—attacks that are pilloried as mindless and dictatorial, just as the new 'romanticism' of the young is lampooned. The real rivalry is between those struggling awkwardly and pretentiously for novelty and those who would squelch it.

Two years later, audiences were ready to applaud, and critics to accept, Sheridan's novelty. **The School for Scandal** was 'admirably suited to the present aera' (*Gazetteer,* 10 May 1777). The reviewer for the *London Evening Post* announced: 'Under this *poetical St George,* we may expect to see the Dragon of *mere sentimental drama* entirely subdued, and the standard of *real comedy* once more unfurled' (8-10 May 1777). The propaganda war passed from Goldsmith to Sheridan had been won: while somehow becoming the new Congreve, as the *Gazetteer* proclaimed, Sheridan apparently captained the triumph of the new laughing comedy over sentimentalism. The reviewer for the *Morning Chronicle* suggests that with some revision the new play might have been titled *The Man of Sentiment* (24 May 1777). Sentiment, though, was not a dragon to be slain, but the conceptual embodiment of modernity. It was the vortex around which swirled ideological confusion, hypocrisy, and misjudgement—a rivalry of competing definitions and sensibilities. Sheridan's triumph, here, lies not in his savaging the reigning genres of sentimentalism, but in offering a clarifying corrective: dropping the screen of ambiguity that veiled contemporary treatments of the sentimental ideal and offering his own comic vision.

Is *The School for Scandal* somehow a better play than *The Rivals*? Did Sheridan's dramatic abilities mature to such an extent that in less than two years he could develop from a clumsy hack to the greatest dramatist of his generation—as his reviewers would seem to have it? Attempts to explain the difference between the two plays have, by and large, followed a critical line established by Thomas Moore in his *Memoirs of Sheridan*: 'With much less wit, it [*The Rivals*] exhibits perhaps more humour than *The School for Scandal*.'³ Such impressionistic analysis is almost completely unhelpful in revealing why one play succeeded and one failed upon their initial appearances. Perhaps the two plays are much more of a piece than critics have been willing to accept: both topical and colloquial, both structured around ideological rivalries, both offering linguistic inventiveness and new character types, rather than original 'fables', for comic effect.

The Rivals was the only new comic mainpiece mounted at Covent Garden in the 1774-5 season. Four days before its opening, the company revived *She Stoops to Conquer,* which had begun its initial run on 15 March 1773.⁴ The revival might have been an attempt to prepare audiences for the new comedy—with the implicit message: *The Rivals* is the same sort of comedy as Goldsmith's hit. The character of Acres was easily recognizable as 'a second Tony Lumpkin' (*Public Ledger,* 18 January 1775). Jane Green, who had played Mrs Hardcastle, was cast as Mrs Malaprop. As a veteran performer of 'conspiratorial chambermaids, eccentric maiden ladies, and silly hostesses', Green appeared to be the perfect choice to create Mrs Malaprop.⁵ Edward Shuter, a veteran of three decades on the stage and Goldsmith's first Hardcastle, seemed an equally apt choice for Sir Anthony Absolute.⁶ Both casting choices reinforced the idea of *The Rivals* as the new *She Stoops,* a new 'laughing comedy' antidote for the ills of sentimental comedy.

Critics of the opening performance enumerated a series of damning flaws. 'This Comedy was acted so imperfectly, either from the Timidity of the Actors on a first Night's Performance, or from an improper Distribution of Parts,

that it was generally disapproved' (*St James Chronicle,* 17-19 January 1775); 'Shuter was . . . shamefully imperfect' (*Morning Chronicle,* 18 January 1775). Reviewers barely noticed Jane Green's Mrs Malaprop until the play was returned. How is it that veteran cast members, many of whom had appeared in apparently similar roles, by all accounts botched the opening performance? In her study of experimental language in Sheridan's plays, Christine Wiesenthal provides a partial answer: 'in the inexperienced hands of an exuberant, young comic playwright, two essentially antagonistic discourses begin to compete against one another'.⁷ What critics have identified as a structural ambivalence, reflected in the play's awkward diction, further reinforces the central conflict in the play: both the romantic excesses of novelty and the eccentricities and irrationality of the old order are exposed and placed in conflict—a confusion embodied in Mrs Malaprop's infectious verbal chaos. Incredibly, critics seemed to miss the Malaprop game so central to the play's comic inventiveness: 'The diction is an odd mixture of the elegant and the absurd. Some of the scenes are written in a very masterly stile; others in a low, farcical kind of dialogue' (*St James Chronicle,* 17-19 January 1775); 'in language it is defective to an extreme' (*Public Ledger,* 18 January 1775). Such is the result of the clashing cultural assumptions that Sheridan is recording, but for reviewers characters such as Malaprop were not 'copied from nature' and her language was a 'defect' in the playwright's skill (*Morning Chronicle,* 18 January 1775). The *Public Ledger* condemned the 'shameful absurdities in language' apparently without recognizing the source and satiric intention of these 'absurdities' (18 January 1775). While it is possible that the acting difficulties were a product of laziness on the part of Shuter and others, it is equally plausible that the performers were unprepared for the complex play of language and the demands of creating new character types.

For at least one observer, the language of the play was strikingly realistic, 'more natural, as coming nearer the current coin of ordinary conversation' than *The School for Scandal.*⁸ The younger characters employ a contemporary jargon replete with allusions to the social milieu of the mid-1770s. Such a commitment to contemporaneity was another breach of decorum.

Also singled out for critical condemnation was John Lee's Sir Lucius O'Trigger. Irish stereotypes and social prejudice against the Irish generally were so commonplace that the sanctimonious objections to Lee's O'Trigger are somewhat surprising. Lee was another well-established performer who had acted in Ireland in the early 1770s and who had also managed at Bath, ideal credentials, one might assume, for the role.⁹ And yet response to his character was universally hostile: 'What the Devil Business can he have with the Part of a mere Irishman?' (*St James Chronicle,* 17-19 January 1775); 'This representation of Sir Lucius is indeed an affront to the common sense of an audience, and is so far from giving the manners of our brave and worthy neighbours, that it scarce equals the picture of a *respectable* Hotentot' (*Morning Chronicle,* 18

January 1775); 'the casting Mr Lee for the part of *Lucius O'Trigger,* is a blunder of the first brogue' (*Morning Chronicle,* 20 January 1775). This latter review pointed to inconsistencies in dialect and the fact that Lee was not 'Irish enough' to pull off the role. A correspondent to the *Morning Post* claimed never to have seen 'a portrait of an Irish Gentleman, permitted so openly to insult the country upon the boards of an English theatre' (*Morning Post,* 21 January 1775). The revised and recast O'Trigger is largely stripped of ethnic identity: he is an old fool, whose function is to articulate antiquated ideas about honour and courtship—most notably realized in his promoting the ludicrous duel between Acres and Absolute. His interference, like that of the other old fools in the play, invites the possibility of a murderous outcome to the various romantic intrigues.

The objections to the original O'Trigger anticipate a serious problem in producing Sheridan: the racist and anti-Semitic epithets mouthed by fools and heroes alike. 'I hated your poor dear uncle before marriage as if he'd been a black-a-moor,' proclaims Mrs Malaprop (I.ii.174-5); 'the lady shall be as ugly as I choose . . . she shall have a skin like a mummy, and the beard of a Jew' (II.i.361-4); 'though I were an æthiop, you'd think none so fair' (III.ii.65-6). The anti-Semitism that runs throughout *The School for Scandal* produces palpable discomfort in contemporary audiences, and no amount of directorial cutting easily eliminates it. Ironically, London audiences now seem less sensitive—or perhaps more accustomed—to Irish stereotypes than to these other forms of bigotry.

Another moral objection to the play was to its 'numberless oaths' (*Morning Chronicle,* 27 January 1775). For Sheridan, though, cursing is more than an isolated technique for character development or a means of achieving shock value; it is a means of underscoring his theme: new-fangled cursing versus ludicrously outdated cursing, both of which add to a delightful bewilderment that interferes with communication and causes further generational separation. For reviewers, though, cursing was a violation of decorum and delicacy, and 'One of the Pit', writing to the *Morning Chronicle,* threatens the author on this subject: 'the English are not sudden, but strong in their resentments, and if he persists in such scandalous negligence of his duty, he may one day experience it' (27 January 1775). Absolute remarks that Acres' 'Odds whips and wheels' and 'Odd's Blushes and Blooms' and 'Odds Crickets' represent 'an odd kind of a new method of swearing' (II.i.258-9). Acres blunders, as do his cohorts in foolishness, in trying to modernize himself. His efforts are foiled by a comic duality: he opposes the modern system of 'Sentimental swearing' (II.i.268) and is tradition-bound. Of oaths he declares that 'nothing but their antiquity makes them respectable . . . the "oath should be an echo to the sense"' (II.i.263-7). He is a perverse upholder of the 'old learning', of the Augustan aesthetic, and so his own attempts at novelty are hopelessly outmoded, another instance of 'future retrospection'.

Reviewers also complained about the excessive length of the play: 'insufferably tedious' (*Morning Chronicle,* 18 January 1775); 'lulled several of the middle gallery spectators into a profound SLEEP' (*Public Ledger,* 18 January 1775); 'a *full hour* longer in the representation than any piece on the stage' (*Morning Chronicle,* 20 January 1775). This response is most puzzling given the almost invariable sprightliness of Sheridan's plays in performance. Was his first audience asleep? Some of those attending the first revival apparently hissed when they noticed that a comic scene involving Lydia had been cut (*Morning Post,* 30 January 1775). Audiences had, indeed, been accustomed to shorter pieces designed to accommodate the double-billing that was typical at both Drury Lane and Covent Garden.

Another possible solution concerns the novelty of the plot. Novel-readers in the audience might have recognized a structural looseness and digressiveness typical in the fiction of the period. In the plot and language of *The Rivals* and in its patterns of allusion, Sheridan inscribes a rivalry between the drama and the novel. The relationship between late-eighteenth-century theatre and the novel was roughly analogous to the current one between the novel and television: one medium overtaken in popularity and influence by another; a form of entertainment struggling for currency and relevance while acutely aware of the cultural ascendancy of another form. Much like the self-reflexive concern with novel-reading and readers in the novels themselves, Sheridan's play, in another act of 'future retrospection', lampoons the theatrical tradition while pillorying the influence of the novel on custom and language.

If the opening conversation about wiglessness signifies a struggle between the old and new in fashion, the dialogue that opens Scene ii between Lucy and Lydia establishes the female protagonist as a woman of the moment, a devourer of novels and a denizen of circulating libraries. The items on her latest novelistic menu were all recent publications, two, *The Fatal Connection* (1773) and *The Tears of Sensibility* (1773), published only a year before the play was written. Like Charlotte Lennox's Arabella, Sheridan's Lydia had been nursed on the romance; but unlike Arabella, who had educated herself on bad translations of old French romances, Lydia's preferences were strictly modern. She is the embodiment of a Tory nightmare: a young woman scorning paternal authority, hell-bent on an improper alliance, devoid of common sense. Arcane and serious tomes such as *The Whole Duty of Man* (1659) are useful only for hair-pressing—a moribund ideology impressed into the service of modishness.

At the same time, Lydia functions to mock the outmoded manner of courtship preferred by her aunt, Mrs Malaprop, who assumes the hackneyed pastoral pseudonym 'Delia', and who has chosen as her object of affection a 'tall Irish baronet'—presumably an equal affront to fashion (I.ii.49). When her aunt and Sir Anthony Absolute approach, the trappings of modernity must be hidden and the furnishings of propriety displayed: James Fordyce's sermons and *Lord*

Chesterfield's Letters conceal Smollett and Mackenzie and Lydia's volumes of scandalous memoirs (I.ii.137-46). Sir Anthony then harangues against 'teaching girls to read' (I.ii.186), while his rhetorical partner Mrs Malaprop insists that Lydia 'illiterate' her lover from her memory (I.ii.154). By the time Mrs Malaprop speaks out against serious education for women, Sheridan's audience should have learned to read her ironically. Clearly, Mrs Malaprop's charm-school view is as empty a system as Lydia's education-by-novel.

Another obvious influence of the novel in **The Rivals** is its 'sentimentalism', evidenced by its characterizations, by overt textual treatment of the idea, and by the critical reaction to the play. The principals are novelistic protagonists to the extent that they conceive of romance and of themselves as lovers. Even the relatively pragmatic Julia describes her lover Faulkland as a typical romantic hero: 'being unhackney'd in the passion, his affection is ardent and sincere; and as it engrosses his whole soul, he expects every thought and emotion of his mistress to move in unison with his' (I.ii.103-6). Captain Absolute, too, is a self-described sentimentalist. Like Malaprop's diction, Lydia's romanticism is contagious, and her lover admits: 'Am not *I* a lover; aye, and a romantic one, too? Yet do I carry every where with me such a confounded farago of doubts, fears, hopes, wishes, and all the flimsy furniture of a country Miss's brain!' (II.i.74-6). Like Lydia, the Captain sees duty and obedience as a dusty veneer concealing passion and independence. The idea of arranged marriage is an anachronistic fraud—his father, after all, 'married himself for love' (II.i.397)—to be defeated by ingenuity. Yet when his scheming goes awry, he blames his lover's sentimental inclinations: 'Lydia is romantic—dev'lish romantic, and very absurd of course' (V.ii.49-50). Sentimentalism, as a code-word for modishness, is a satiric target—'sentimental swearing' or the 'sentimental elopement' Lydia had planned—and the antithesis of a 'Smithfield bargain' view of courtship that is equally ridiculous.

Reviewers of **The Rivals** did not know what to make of this theme: 'the characters of Faulkland and Julia are even beyond the pitch of *sentimental* comedy, and may be not improperly stiled *metaphysical*' (*Morning Chronicle,* 18 January 1775). Clearly, if the play had indeed been marketed as a successor to *She Stoops to Conquer,* Sheridan had been positioning his work in opposition to sentimental comedy. In 'An Essay on the Theatre' for *Westminster Magazine* (January 1773), Goldsmith advocated 'laughing comedy', in which category theatre historians have subsequently placed Sheridan's works, as a sort of antidote to sentimentalism. However, Sheridan's reviewers almost unanimously accused him of outré sentimentalism, without recognizing his satiric aim.

Among critics, however, the word *sentimental* was not entirely pejorative. Responding to the revised production, the *Morning Chronicle* extols 'some of the most affecting sentimental scenes I ever remember to have met with' (*Morning Chronicle,* 27 January 1775). On the other hand,

the tenor of the *Morning Post* reviewer's comments of 31 January 1775 more or less reflects the play's subsequent reputation: 'sentimental blockheads, so much admired by the gaping multitude of our century, were not a little disappointed at the success of Mr Sheridan'. The play, then, lives as a triumph over sentimentalism. Sheridan's comedy survives, and rival offerings such as Isaac Bickerstaff's *Love in a Village,* Ambrose Phillips' *The Distress'd Mother* and Thomas Francklin's *Matilda* are forgotten.

John Loftis casts Sheridan as a social conservative: 'His authorial judgments . . . reveal a reverence for English social institutions as marked as that of Henry Fielding.'[10] Yet **The Rivals** was in many ways a risky undertaking, an attack levelled on both the ancients and moderns. There is no Alworthy among Sheridan's aristocrats: they have hollow notions of honour, their authority is suspect, their language gibberish, their education vapid. If, as reviewers complained, the plot conflicts and resolution of **The Rivals** are wildly implausible, and its structure loose and digressive, Sheridan is responding satirically to the influence of a fashionable sentimentalism inscribed in the novel. The important rivalry, here, is not between suitors but between the foolishness of the old and the absurdities of the young. The result is miscommunication, malapropism, a purposeful clash of styles which critics, bound by absolute notions of decorum, could only describe as the flaws of an inexperienced playwright. Loftis describes the world of **The Rivals** as one 'of social and financial practicality familiar in Restoration and eighteenth-century comedy, in which a rich and repulsive suitor such as Bob Acres might be rejected in favour of a rich and attractive suitor such as Jack Absolute, but in which misalliances do not occur except as a form of punishment, outside the absurd fantasies of a girl whose head has been turned by reading novels'.[11] What separates the play from its comic predecessors and situates it in mid-1770s London is its novelty, its idiomatic contemporaneity, its confusion of language and cultural identity. Mackenzie has met Lord Chesterfield; Smollett is duelling with 'the learned and pious author of *The Whole Duty of Man*'; the 'deep play' has moved from London to Bath and—more ominously—from the theatre to the novel.

By 1777, when Drury Lane introduced **The School for Scandal,** critics were prepared to overlook the playwright's derivative plotting and linguistic 'awkwardness'. They recognized the topicality of Sheridan's moral concern and that Sheridan was targeting hypocrisy, one of the 'prevailing vices of the times' through which many 'assume the appearance of men of virtue and sentiment' (*Morning Chronicle,* 9 May 1777). Beyond its titular concern with gossip and its archaic Wycherley-like plot, the play is an arena for competing visions of modernity—specifically, for defining a moral ideal, the idea of sentiment that dominated late-eighteenth-century discourse. Hypocrites and debauchees, young and old—all appropriate and misappropriate the term in their efforts to make moral judgements. The rivalry in this play is not so much a generational one, but a semantic one between competing visions of the sentimental ideal.

Sheridan's first scene establishes the social problem or challenge that unifies the play: distinguishing the 'man of Sentiment' from the 'Sentimental Knave'. The audience must recognize that the scandal school has corrupted the virtues of 'sensibility' and 'sentiment': Surface speaks of Mr Snake's 'sensibility and discernment'; and Surface is 'moral' because he is *'a man of Sentiment'*; he mistrusts Snake because he 'hasn't Virtue enough to be faithful even to his own Villainy' (I.i.73-122). Scandal is the machinery that has circulated this ethical perversion.

In the National Theatre's 1990 production at the Olivier, Peter Wood's visual metaphor for this process was newsprint, which covered the flat surfaces of the set; even the furniture was papered over by scandal. If the 'country wife' plot has recognizable seventeenth-century roots, the implicit attack on the ascendant print culture is distinctly late Georgian, when the threat, as Sir Peter puts it, of being 'paragraph'd—in the news-Papers' is a prevailing trope for loss of reputation (I.ii.13-14).

Like *The Rivals, The School for Scandal* has its 'old fools': Mrs Candour, a variation of the Mrs Malaprop character, asks Lady Sneerwell, 'how have you been this Century' (I.i.165-6); Sir Peter is essentially a 'Pinchwife'. Their principal fault, though, is in either distorting or failing to comprehend the modern idea of sentiment. Sir Peter mistakes Joseph Surface as 'a man of Sentiment' (I.ii.51). For Lady Sneerwell, sentiment is merely an affectation to 'study' (I.i.351-2). For Joseph, 'sentimental' is little more than the characteristic of his favourite French plate (V.ii.106-7). The young lovers Maria and Charles represent true sentiment, Maria for her discernment, Charles for his generosity and honesty. The importance of this theme lies not only in Sheridan's verbal insistence upon it throughout the play but also in the climactic comic moment. When Charles throws down the screen—arguably one of the most sublimely funny moments in all of comedy—hypocrisy is unveiled, and virtue revealed. The punchline, here, is Charles's mocking echo of Sir Peter: 'there's nothing in the world so noble as a man of Sentiment!' (IV.iii.385-6). The stage directions then suggest a long silence: the point has been made; nothing further remains to be said.

If Goldsmith had established a self-serving critical rivalry between laughing comedy and sentimental comedy, Sheridan weaves this rivalry into the fabric of his two best-known plays. Sentimentalism becomes a comic theme, a pivotal issue that separates generations and divides the virtuous and the fraudulent. Further confusing the rivalry between an antiquated and paternalistic older generation and an absurdly 'romantic' younger one is the obscuring medium of gossip—private conflict made public. Newsprint becomes the metaphor for 'future retrospection': language used to distort and deceive, past values and current fashions jumbled. Clarity of vision and expression become heroic acts.

While bad acting probably contributed to sabotaging the initial performance of *The Rivals,* the evidence of critical

response suggests that audiences and reviewers were unprepared for a new play about newness. Strategically linking the production to Goldsmith's *She Stoops to Conquer* failed because, quite obviously, Sheridan is not Goldsmith. Unlike Goldsmith's comedy, Sheridan's plays attempt to inscribe a historical present: where clear communication has become nearly impossible, where equally absurd new and old systems of thought compete, where deception is fashionable. Given the thematic and linguistic complexity of his plays, it is hardly surprising that Sheridan's work needed to 'sink in'. Even the critical reception of *The School for Scandal* involved a sort of 'future retrospection': Sheridan captures the modern era because he is a new Congreve—*The Way of the World* in 1777. Needless to say, Sheridan is not Congreve either.

Notes

1. M. S. Auburn, *Sheridan's Comedies: Their Contexts and Achievements* (Lincoln, NB, 1977), p. 36.

2. J. Loftis, *Sheridan and the Drama of Georgian England* (Oxford, 1976), p. 43.

3. T. Moore, *Memoirs of the Life of the Right Honourable Richard Brinsley Sheridan* (London, 1815), i, p. 141.

4. C. B. Hogan, ed., *The London Stage, 1660-1800, Part Five, 1776-1800* (Carbondale, IL, 1968).

5. P. H. Highfill, Jr, K. A. Burnim, and E. A. Langhans, *A Biographical Dictionary of Actors, Actresses, Musicians, Dancers, Managers and Other Stage Personnel in London, 1660-1800,* vi (Carbondale, IL, 1978), pp. 328-35.

6. *A Biographical Dictionary,* xiii (1991), pp. 370-84.

7. C. S. Wiesenthal, 'Representation and Experimentation in the Major Comedies of Richard Brinsley Sheridan', *Eighteenth-Century Studies,* xxv(3) (Spring 1992), 311.

8. Moore, *Life,* i, p. 141.

9. *A Biographical Dictionary,* ix (1984), pp. 201-9.

10. Loftis, *Sheridan and the Drama of Georgian England,* p. 46.

11. Ibid., pp. 46-7.

Christopher Clayton (essay date 1995)

SOURCE: "The Political Career of Richard Brinsley Sheridan," in *Sheridan Studies,* edited by James Morwood and David Crane, Cambridge University Press, 1995, pp. 131-50.

[*In the following essay, Clayton recounts Sheridan's actions and reputation as a Whig politician and a member of Parliament.*]

When Thomas Moore was preparing his biography of Sheridan he was told by Lord Thanet that Sheridan never liked any allusion to his being a dramatic writer.[1] Outstanding success as a playwright eased, and arguably enabled, Sheridan's introduction to the society of the Westminster political world, but his theatrical work, both as writer and manager, was a potent reminder that Sheridan had to work for a living and did not spring from a background of landed wealth and aristocratic leisure. This background remained the most powerful qualification for political leadership amongst the Whig élite—far more powerful than the recommendation of talent by itself. Charles James Fox could offer both talent and aristocratic pedigree, and in that fact lies the single most important explanation of why Fox could lead the Whigs, in spite of his manifest lack of judgement on occasion, and why Sheridan could never be seen as a legitimate Whig leader. Not only did allusions to Sheridan's theatrical background carry a clear message of his status as a parvenu on the political stage, but association with the theatre carried with it a distinctly disreputable aura. As the young George Canning explained to his mother, an actress: 'there is perhaps no subject on which public opinion decides more positively than on the respectability or *dis*respectability of different pursuits and occupations . . . the world is capricious and unjust—but it is peremptory—and to explain myself fully—need I do more than ask you—to what cause is Mr Sheridan's want of success and popularity to be attributed?'[2]

Had Sheridan been prepared to sacrifice his views on matters connected with the constitution, the problems of Ireland, the removal of religious disabilities and the plight of the poor and politically unenfranchised, he too, by joining his talents to those who served Pitt, might, like Canning, have achieved high office, but at the cost of sacrificing political principles and political friendship. Refusal to sacrifice either tied Sheridan's political fortunes to a set of politicians whose prejudices were aristocratic and exclusive. Sheridan's political career can thus be seen as a demonstration of the limited opportunities available to a non-aristocratic 'man of talent' in the Whig party of the late eighteenth and early nineteenth centuries. This has wider implications concerning both the development of political parties in this period and the progress of liberal reform. In particular, the weakness of the Whig party in the first decades of the nineteenth century can be explained by the deflection of ambitious, talented non-aristocrats of liberal temperament into the Tory camp, where their liberal aspirations were frustrated, often by monarchical prejudice. Sheridan's experience in politics at the hands of the Whig leadership can help to explain why this happened. This essay seeks to show why Sheridan's political career was a failure in comparison with his brief, glittering success as a playwright in the 1770s. It is also contended that his was not a dishonourable failure; he did remain loyal to political friendships and principles.

Sheridan's political career can be divided into four, broadly distinct, chronological periods. During the first decade of his parliamentary career Sheridan rose steadily to a position of considerable prominence in the House of Commons, making his mark as a notable exponent of the Rockingham/Foxite Whig thesis that the events of these years demonstrated an alarming growth of executive power. There were occasional flashes of independence, as when he disagreed with Fox on the latter's Bill to replace the existing Marriage Act on 15 June 1781,[3] and when he objected to Pitt's Irish commercial propositions in 1785 from a perspective that was specifically defensive of Irish constitutional rights rather than of British manufacturers' rights. Speaking in the debate of 30 May 1785 he declared that 'he was the mouth of no party . . . nor was he the tool of any party'.[4] This was perhaps to protect his arguments from the odium in which the Foxites were then held as a result of Pitt's victory in 1784. But that he *was* a party man was acknowledged by his sister, Betsy Sheridan, who commented 'he acts on this occasion from his own feelings, totally independent of any wish *his party* may have to harass the Minister' (my italics).[5]

The second period dates from 1789-90, when the impact of the French Revolution began to be felt on British politics. Sheridan acquired an unjustified reputation for dangerous radicalism and acted as a catalyst in the process which led to the break-up of the Whig party in 1794. During the 1790s Sheridan steadfastly supported Fox in his stand against the war with France and in his belief that the real danger to British liberties derived from the growth of executive power and not from popular radicalism. But from 1797, the third period of his career, Sheridan appeared to follow a much more independent line, refusing to join the Foxite secession from Parliament in 1797 and calling for a united, patriotic resistance to the danger of a French invasion. During Addington's ministry he was in open disagreement with Fox's parliamentary tactics, although after 1804 he appeared to be reconciled again with his political colleagues. The fourth period encompasses the years 1806-12. The disappointment of Sheridan's political ambitions when the Ministry of All the Talents was formed in 1806 produced the final estrangement from the Whigs, led after Fox's death by Grey and Grenville. From 1807 he owed his seat in Parliament to the Prince of Wales's patronage. From 1809 he seemed to be moving closer to George Canning, who, before serving in Pitt's ministry, had been a protégé of Sheridan. Sheridan's career ended in 1812 when he failed to win back his seat in Stafford.

In thirty-two years in Parliament Sheridan enjoyed three brief spells in government: as Under-Secretary for Foreign Affairs in the short-lived Rockingham administration of 1782; as Joint Secretary to the Treasury in the Fox-North coalition in 1783 and finally, in January 1806, as Treasurer of the Navy in the Ministry of All the Talents. This was a post vacated by the much younger George Canning which Sheridan had been promised almost twenty years previously at the time of the first Regency Crisis.[6] This was the rather feeble reward for having been 'Thirty years a Whig Politician and six and twenty years in Parliament, and having expended full £20,000 of my own money to maintain my seat there and in all the course of political life struggling thro' great di[f]ficulties and risking the existence of the only Property I had'.[7] That Sheridan did not have more opportunities to serve in government is due to his party loyalty and the antagonism of George III to the Rockingham/Foxite Whigs. But that Sheridan did not rise higher within the party when the opportunity afforded is due in large measure to the conservative aristocratic ethos of the leaders of that party, including Fox. Why and how Sheridan became a Foxite Whig is, therefore, a central question.

The evidence concerning Sheridan's earliest political thinking indicates little common ground with the Rockingham Whigs. A letter published in the *Public Advertiser* on 16 October 1769, chiefly intended to criticize the style of a correspondent who signed himself 'Novus', contained an oblique defence of Lord Bute, who was regarded by the Newcastle/Rockingham Whigs as the tool of George III and the means of their downfall in 1762.[8] A draft for an essay entitled *Essay on Absentees,* probably written about 1778, criticized the behaviour of Irish landlords, such as the Marquis of Rockingham and other Whig landowners, for the problems which their absenteeism caused in Ireland.[9] Jottings made probably in 1776 for a reply to Johnson's *Taxation No Tyranny* had, however, shown sympathy for the Whig point of view on the issue of America, in that Sheridan sought to show that taxation of the American colonists could not be justified by theories of virtual representation.[10]

Sheridan was drawn first into metropolitan Whig social life, and then into Whig politics, for two principal reasons. First, his marriage to the beautiful singer, Elizabeth Linley, who was much sought after for private recitals in the homes of the nobility, obtained for Sheridan an entry to Devonshire House society, at the heart of the Whig élite. Subsequently, in 1780, Georgiana, Duchess of Devonshire, a member of the Spencer family, was to exert the Spencer interest in Stafford to help secure Sheridan's election to the House of Commons.[11]

The second factor was Sheridan's developing friendship with Charles James Fox. Thomas Moore relates that Fox was immediately impressed by Sheridan's wit on first meeting him, probably in 1776 or 1777.[12] At that time Fox himself was only just moving towards political co-operation with the Rockingham Whigs under the influence of Edmund Burke.[13] As a former member of North's government, and the son of Henry Fox, who loomed almost as large as Bute in the Whig demonology, Fox was hardly an orthodox Whig. Fox presided over Sheridan's election to the Literary Club on 11 March 1777 and after the success of *The School for Scandal* later that year was known to regard Sheridan as 'the first Genius of these times'.[14] Apart from mutual admiration there was their shared family connections with the deposed Stuart dynasty to draw them together. Fox, whose first two names were more than usually significant, could trace his ancestry back through his mother and the Dukes of Richmond to Charles II. In contrast with Sheridan, Fox could lay claim to high aristocratic pedigree, but the uncle of Sheridan's grandfather

had been secretary to James II in exile and his grandfather's cousin had been knighted during the 1745 Jacobite rebellion by the Young Pretender.[15]

From a letter written on 4 January 1773, it is clear that Sheridan had been contemplating a career in politics. Rejecting a life of private enjoyment he asked, 'Was it meant that we should shrink from the active Principles of Virtue, and consequent[ly] of true Happiness . . . ?'[16] It was not surprising that Sheridan's ambition was kindled by the admiration of members of the political élite. Sheridan now saw a political life as the means to social elevation and personal satisfaction. As he put it in another letter, written on 24 February 1773,

> The Track of a Comet is as regular to the eye of God as the orbit of a planet . . . as God very often pleases to let down great Folks from the elevated stations which they might claim as their Birthright, there can be no reason for us to suppose that He does not mean that others should ascend etc.[17]

Speaking in the House of Commons in June 1804 he uttered similar sentiments: 'there is nothing of honour, emolument or wealth which is not within the reach of a man of merit . . . I would call on the humblest peasant to defend his son's title to the great seal of England.'[18]

Such views were too advanced for the Whig party to which Sheridan became attached through his connection with Fox. But Sheridan's talents were useful assets to the forces fighting Lord North's alleged incompetence and the supposed growth of executive power which threatened to unbalance the constitution. In particular, Sheridan was able to provide a link between the Whig leaders in Parliament and the sources of extra-parliamentary discontent. He contributed to a periodical, *The Englishman,* addressed to the 'freeholders of England', urging them to turn against the alleged corruption of the North ministry. Along with other Whigs, Sheridan was present at the founding meeting of the Westminster Committee of Association, established to join the pressure for parliamentary reform being exerted by Christopher Wyvill's county association movement; two months later he was present at the inaugural meeting of the Society for Constitutional Information. Under Sheridan's chairmanship a sub-committee of the Westminster Association, established to enquire into the 'state of the Representation', produced a report which considered that the representative system was even more unfair at representing property (assessed through regional land tax contributions) than electors. It was perhaps because of the influence of Sheridan and Fox that the Westminster Committee was diverted from more radical solutions than those being advocated by Wyvill's country gentlemen, but as popular pressure for reform began to decline, so Sheridan's attendances at committee meetings became fewer.[19] When Sheridan entered the House of Commons in September 1780 he was already an established Foxite. A promising political future seemed to beckon as North's ministry tottered.

In Parliament Sheridan consolidated his position as a loyal Foxite. He was at least as vehement as Fox in his condemnation of Shelburne's behaviour during the Rockingham administration and did not hesitate to follow Fox into opposition when Shelburne succeeded Rockingham as First Lord of the Treasury. There is some doubt as to what he really thought about the wisdom of the Fox-North coalition and of introducing the East India Bill at that time,[20] but Sheridan later played a prominent part in attacking Pitt's own Bill, introduced in 1784, and in the impeachment proceedings against Warren Hastings, in each case with the intention of vindicating Fox's coalition government and its actions.[21] In 1788 Sheridan wrote *A Comparative Statement of the Two Bills for the Better Government of the British Possessions in India,* which contained a systematic attack on the principles underlying Pitt's style of government. He was central to the Foxites' attempts to create a favourable impression of themselves in the newspapers and he took over the difficult, but vital, brief of opposition spokesman on financial and taxation affairs, in which Fox had no interest at all.[22] He was a zealous proponent of the view that the manner in which Pitt and the King were able to overwhelm the Fox-North coalition in 1783-4 was proof of a constitutional crisis, in which the House of Commons was losing power and influence as a result of the contrivances of a wily, ambitious king and unscrupulous ministers. Although he supported parliamentary reform when the question was brought forward in Parliament, Sheridan did not offend the conservative aristocratic Whigs by unnecessarily pressing the issue. When he was asked to bring forward the question of reform of the notoriously corrupt Scottish burghs by a committee of delegates from the burghs in 1787, he brought forward his motion very late in the session. Even after 1789, when there was more political capital to be gained from supporting such a measure, as popular interest in reform revived under the impact of the French Revolution, Sheridan was cautious in his approach, prompting the historian John Cannon to comment that his campaign on behalf of the burghs had 'the impetuosity of a slow bicycle race'.[23] Parliamentary reform was never a fundamental principle of Foxite belief. Sheridan, more than most politicians of his generation, was aware of the value of courting extra-parliamentary opinion, but even he was reported to have said in November 1794 'in the hearing of Lord Fitzwilliam' at Brooks's that it was 'the present intention of the Friends of the People to abandon all thoughts of Parliamentary Reform unless called for by two-thirds of the People'.[24] If this is true, Sheridan was obviously trying to conciliate those aristocrats whose fear of reform in the context of the French Revolution was driving them into alliance with Pitt.

In spite of Sheridan's manifest loyalty and usefulness, tension was generated within the party by Sheridan's equally manifest ambition. He believed his talents entitled him in due course to a position of leadership. This did not fit the Whig view that for liberty to survive in the balanced constitution established at the Glorious Revolution, the leading parts in government must be undertaken by men of wealth, property and education, who could be relied upon to be independent and were thus immune to the blandish-

ments of ambitious kings.[25] Such men could only be aristocrats and they took on governmental office as an obligation and not primarily as an object of ambition.

Particularly worrying to the other Foxites was Sheridan's closeness to the Prince of Wales. In 1786 Sheridan had been involved in trying to sort out the Prince's finances—a grave embarrassment to the Foxites who had so clearly attempted to secure the Prince's favour. It was Sheridan who managed to save the situation in 1787, after Fox had denied there was any truth in the rumour of a marriage between the Prince and Mrs Fitzherbert. This exploit enhanced Sheridan's position at Carlton House and irritated Fox. Fox was further irritated by Sheridan's assumption of a leadership role in November 1788 when the Regency Crisis developed while Fox was abroad. The Duchess of Devonshire recorded two quarrels between Fox and Sheridan at this time—on 20 December and 2 January.[26] Fox was not the only one to be alarmed at Sheridan's assumption of a position of eminence. Charles Grey believed Sheridan had deliberately humiliated him in front of the Prince.[27] Later in 1789 another quarrel between Grey and Sheridan nearly produced a duel.[28] The Duke of Portland was reported to be offended by the close consultation between the Prince and Sheridan in November 1788[29] and at the end of January 1789 Portland declared his determination 'not to act with Mr Sheridan in council'.[30]

More significantly for the events to come, Sheridan's relations with Burke were deteriorating. Burke was deeply irritated by the manner in which both Sheridan and Fox began to lose interest in the impeachment of Warren Hastings once it became clear that it would not undermine Pitt. To Burke, the Hastings trial was a moral issue, not a question of party politics. Sheridan's advance presented a direct challenge to Burke's own influence over Fox; the fact that Burke's advice during the Regency Crisis was ignored seemed to demonstrate the effects of Sheridan's rise. Fox's enthusiastic support for the removal of the legal penalties on the Dissenters seemed to show that Fox was being pushed in the direction of more radical and dangerous ideas and this was ascribed to Sheridan's influence. This impression was confirmed by the enthusiastic reception that Fox and Sheridan gave to the French Revolution.

Burke's resentment exploded on 9 February 1790 in the debate on the Army Estimates, when Burke and Fox clashed openly on the subject of the French Revolution. Sheridan then vehemently disagreed with Burke.[31] Although Sheridan seems 'to have expressed some contrition for his conduct on the very evening the conversation passed',[32] there was no wish for reconciliation on Burke's part. From this point on, there was an open struggle for the nature of the Whig party's beliefs. Sheridan was depicted by Burke and his son—and others alarmed at his apparent influence over Fox—as a dangerous demagogic manipulator. In Burke's opinion 'They who cry up the French Revolution, cry down the [Whig] Party', which was 'an aristocratic Party . . . a Party, in its composition and in its principles connected with the solid permanent long possessed property of the Country'.[33] Sheridan and others in the party were said to be 'running into Democracy'.[34]

In reality, Sheridan, and others like Charles Grey, whose social origins were more elevated, sought a moderate parliamentary reform for conservative reasons. Moderate reform was the best means of restoring the constitutional balance framed in the Revolution Settlement of 1689 and of conciliating the extra-parliamentary reformers to the substance of that settlement. Nor were the aristocratic Whig leaders to whom Burke was appealing taken in by Burke's claim that Fox and Sheridan had become the leaders of the 'New French Whigs' who cared not at all for the traditional Whig approach. There was a degree of resentment at the way in which Burke seemed to polarize the situation, pushing Fox into a more determined defence of the French Revolution and benefiting Pitt's government by dividing the opposition. But Sheridan's humble origins and rapid rise to political prominence, together with his connections with the popular societies, made him ideal for fostering the aristocrats' fears. The satirical prints delighted in portraying Sheridan as a revolutionary regicide.[35] Burke's claim that Sheridan intended to put himself at the head of a spirit of innovation and to gain by the resulting confusion had plausibility. This propaganda, articulated in the context of the issues raised by the French Revolution, derived from antecedent tensions and rivalries based on resentment of Sheridan as a parvenu who did not know the proper limits to set to his own political ambition.

Sheridan's radicalism in the 1790s consisted of support for a measure of parliamentary reform to reverse the growth in executive power when there was sufficient popular support for such a measure; resistance to Pitt's innovatory, repressive legislation of the 1790s; and rejection of the war against France as unnecessary and insidious, designed to extend executive power in Britain and restore despotism in France. With all this Fox could agree. Where they differed might have been in Sheridan's stated belief that Britain's constitution helped to create 'a people among whom all that is advantageous in private acquisition, all that is honourable in public ambition [is] equally open to the efforts, the industry and the abilities of all—among whom no sullen line of demarkation (sic) separates and cuts off the several orders from each other'.[36] Fox, on the other hand, told Lord Holland, just before the Whig split in 1794, 'You know I am one who think both property and rank of great importance in this country in a party view'.[37] By 1799, regarding the political situation in Britain with despair, he wrote that he could not 'help feeling every day more and more, that in this country at least, an aristocratic party is absolutely necessary to the preservation of liberty'.[38] Although Fox carried little or no ideological baggage, he recognized that the only way to power after Pitt's resignation in 1801, and then after his death in 1806, was through broadening the party to bring in those aristocratic elements whose prejudices were not compatible with Sheridan's ambition. Sheridan was to reap little reward for continuing the parliamentary fight against Pitt during the Foxite secession.

Lord Holland told James Mackintosh that Sheridan's failure to reach the highest levels of party leadership was due to his 'peculiarities' rather than to Whig snobbery. He claimed that if distinctions based on birth mattered 'They were in fact less in the real and practical estimation of the Party called Whigs than of that of the Society in which they lived'.[39] For a party that claimed to stand for the public interest, aristocratic exclusivity was hard to admit openly. Lady Bessborough stated that she 'should approve of a great deal in his [Sheridan's] language and conduct . . . but then a great deal is quite disgusting and it is impossible to trust him for a moment'.[40] Before the French Revolution Sheridan had been portrayed as Bardolph or compared with Joseph Surface.[41] But behind-the-scenes intrigue, whether at Carlton House or in Grub Street, was one way in which Sheridan had made himself useful to the Whigs. And there was an argument, conceded even by Lady Holland, that Sheridan was driven to intrigue to overcome the prejudice he encountered.[42] In the early nineteenth century, when the Whigs maintained their unity through the long years of opposition by developing a Foxite cult,[43] there was a need to denigrate Sheridan because detailed examination of his career could expose serious shortcomings in Fox's. In 1818 Lord Byron told Thomas Moore, who was preparing his biography: 'The Whigs abuse him; however, he never left them, and such blunderers deserve neither credit nor compassion . . . Don't let yourself be led away by clamour, but compare him with the coalitioner Fox, and the pensioner Burke, as a man of principle, and with ten hundred thousand in personal views and with more in talent for he beat them all *out* and *out*.'[44] How justified was Whig exclusion of Sheridan on the basis of 'peculiarity'?

Sheridan's refusal to join the secession from Parliament in 1797, his advocacy of a united patriotic resistance to the danger of a French invasion and his willingness to support the Volunteer movement set up to counteract this threat—all this irritated his colleagues.[45] The apparently loyalist and aggressively anti-Napoleonist sentiments given voice in *Pizarro* bewildered them; Fox described it as the 'worst thing possible'.[46] More significantly, Fox was greatly exasperated by Sheridan's attempt to bolster the Addington government against the possibility of Pitt's return to office and consequently his rejection of the idea of an understanding with the Grenvilles in opposition to Addington. Sheridan was not alone in opposing an arrangement of political co-operation with the Grenvilles, however informal,[47] but in opposing such a link Sheridan exposed the Foxites and the Grenvilles to the same sort of condemnation that had been so damaging to the Fox-North coalition—that an unprincipled alliance was trying to restrict the king's choice of ministers. Sheridan and other anti-Grenville Foxites believed such an alliance would damage their reputation. But a sub-text to this argument was a battle for influence over Fox and the Prince of Wales. Grey was a keen supporter of co-operation with the Grenvilles, even if it meant co-operation with Pitt.[48] Fox was not in the best of health and such was his diffidence about politics that he could retire at any time. Sheridan was known to be keen to take over the prestigious constituency of Westminster in this event. Battle had been joined for the succession to Fox as leader and Sheridan had the audacity to regard himself as a realistic contender. But in the quarrel over parliamentary tactics between 1801 and 1804 Sheridan lost the battle for Fox's ear and confidence to Grey and consequently lost any hope of asserting his right to a leading position in any ministry the Foxites and their new allies might form.

Sheridan's behaviour during this quarrel provided some evidence to those who wished to prove that he lacked integrity and could not be trusted. In December, 1802, he was accused of inserting in the newspapers 'puffs' of himself alongside 'the most violent abuse' of Fox.[49] Fox claimed that he remained sympathetic to Sheridan in spite of the provocations afforded by his behaviour both in and out of Parliament, and indeed he expressed willingness for Sheridan to succeed him in Westminster. Referring to Sheridan's alleged interference in the newspapers, he told Denis O'Bryen 'that what I most feel in it is the advantages it gives to those who hate him . . . to justify suspicions which in my conscience I believe to be wholly unfounded'.[50] Yet Fox himself described Sheridan as 'mad with vanity and folly'[51] just two days before the latter made a speech calling upon Members of Parliament to show unanimity and 'not to waste that time and those talents in party spirit and intrigue, which might be so much more worthily employed in performing the sublime and animated duties of patriotism'.[52] On hearing this, Fox considered that Sheridan had 'outdone his usual outdoings. Folly beyond all the past'.[53]

Sheridan's relations with Fox reached their lowest point in early 1804, just before Pitt returned to power. Unwisely he allowed Thomas Creevey to overhear him 'damning Fox in the midst of his enemies'.[54] Creevey believed that Sheridan was 'basely playing an under game as Fox's friend in the event of defeat to him and his Dr'.[55] Although Sheridan admitted to his wife that he saw 'Fox every day—and Addington almost every evening',[56] he had never made any secret of his goodwill towards Addington's government, once it had become clear that Addington was no mere Pittite stooge. Sheridan's conduct did possess integrity, however galling it was to his colleagues. Opposition to Pitt provided a connecting thread of consistency through his conduct. Although he had called for a spirit of patriotic unity to resist French aggression in 1798, he had at the same time stated his 'irreconcilable' enmity to Pitt's government as well as his 'unaltered and unalterable' attachment to Fox and his political principles.[57] The rationale of his support for Addington was that he had made peace with the French and destroying him would only produce Pitt's return to power. Pitt was damnable in Sheridan's eyes. He practised a debased, cynical and unprincipled form of politics for the purposes of personal advancement. He had fatally weakened the cause of reform in British politics by allowing the king to defy the majority of the House of Commons in 1783, and the combined effect of the revolutionary war and the accompanying repressive

legislation had been to undermine British liberties and the balanced constitution itself. Sheridan's support for Addington was only the converse of hostility to Pitt. Sheridan was scrupulous in refusing any position for himself or his son in Addington's ministry unless the Foxites came in as a body—unlike George Tierney who accepted the post of Treasurer of the Navy, but nevertheless, because of his friendship with Grey, later went on to become a leader of the Whigs in the House of Commons. Once the return of Pitt to government was assured, Sheridan could with consistency resume co-operation with Fox, even in concert with the formerly Pittite Grenvilles. Sheridan might, with justification, claim that he had remained loyal to Foxite principles, even if that had involved friction with Fox himself. He did, however, continue to differ from Fox in believing that Napoleon was motivated by a desire for territorial conquest and not for peace. He also believed it was unwise to agitate the issue of Catholic emancipation for the purpose of embarrassing Pitt while George III remained on the throne, because the only result would be to raise Catholic hopes, simply to have them dashed against the king's intransigence, with possibly disastrous consequences in Ireland. In both these judgements he was arguably more astute than Fox and Grey. When the Foxites finally took office in 1806, with the Grenvilles and the followers of Sidmouth, the Whig leaders could easily claim that Sheridan was too much of a maverick to claim the senior position in the ministry which his long service to the party and his abilities deserved. Consequently Sheridan felt no qualms about opposing his own government's plans for the country's defences in July 1806.[58]

Having crushed Sheridan's aspirations for high office, the Whig leaders, Grey and Grenville, made sure that Sheridan did not inherit Fox's seat in Westminster after his death in September 1806. Although Sheridan successfully insisted on his candidature in the general election held shortly after the by-election, the Whig party leaders did not over-exert themselves in Sheridan's interest, although he was elected. He was not so fortunate in the general election of May 1807, after the collapse of the Talents Ministry. Westminster's independent electors could no longer trust the Whigs or their representatives to support the cause of reform and Sheridan was only able to return to Parliament as Member of Parliament for a pocket borough in the gift of the Prince.[59]

Thereafter, the Whigs and Sheridan drifted further apart. Significantly, when Grey moved to the House of Lords on the death of his father in November 1807, Grenville placed an absolute veto on any aspirations Sheridan, Whitbread and Windham might have had to take over Grey's role as leader of the Whigs in the House of Commons.[60] All three were non-aristocrats. In July 1808, Grey would tell Lady Holland 'As to Sheridan's conduct in a party view that is past praying for; and in truth it is of no consequence.'[61] By 1810 Sheridan had acquired an amused detachment from the squabbles over leadership among the Whigs in the Commons. He told Lady Bessborough that the struggle for pre-eminence 'threaten'd to subdivide the subdivisions of

Op[position] till they became like Atoms known to exist, but too numerous to count—and too small to be felt'.[62] After Canning's resignation from the Portland ministry in 1809, Sheridan tried to establish closer relations with him. Lady Holland described Canning as one who 'abhors titles and the aristocracy of hereditary nobility'.[63] In 1810 Sheridan claimed that he would defend Canning 'thro' thick and thin'.[64] Alliance with Canning was a means of maintaining liberal principles while at the same time challenging the exclusive, aristocratic ethos represented by Grey and Grenville.

Any remaining connection Sheridan might have had with the party led by Grey and Grenville was shattered by the events of 1810-12. With the onset of the King's terminal illness in November 1810, proceedings were set in train for the establishment of a regency. Grenville and Grey were thoroughly angered when their proposed draft for the Prince's reply to the terms of the regency offered by Perceval was altered by Sheridan. Haughtily, Grey told his wife that he had remonstrated 'on the impropriety of having the advice which Ld. Grenville and I were called upon to give subjected in this manner to the examination of an inferior council'.[65] Sheridan was accused of undermining the Prince's official advisers in the manner of Bute or Shelburne, but even Lord Holland had to admit that there was nothing official in the position of Grey and Grenville.[66] Inevitably, Sheridan was blamed for the failure of the Whigs to gain office when the limited regency came to an end and George III's incapacity seemed permanent. Holland was aware, however, that Sheridan had hoped for the non-cabinet post of Chief Secretary to Ireland in a ministry headed by Grey and Grenville. This was 'peremptorily rejected by Lord Grenville . . . Lord Grenville and Lord Grey showed upon that and every other occasion a repugnance to consult or to court him'.[67] Grey said that sending Sheridan to Ireland would have been like sending a man with a lighted torch into a magazine of gunpowder, but if it were merely a question of 'giving him a place, however high, with large emoluments, nobody would be more ready to consent to it than I should be'.[68] This was precisely the stipulation that Fitzwilliam had made in 1792 when he had said that Sheridan 'might have a lucrative place, but never could be admitted to one of trust and confidence'.[69] Finally the Whig leaders claimed that they had been deliberately misled by Sheridan into thinking that they would not be able to have control of appointments within the Prince's Household if they came into office after the assassination of Perceval in May 1812. Acting under this impression the Whig leaders refused to form a government. Sheridan was therefore given the blame for the re-establishment of a ministry unsympathetic to Catholic emancipation, under the leadership of Lord Liverpool. Thus Sheridan's reputation for double-dealing and untrustworthiness was assured.[70] But Sheridan had written to the Prince to tell him that 'a proscription of Lord Grey in the formation of a new administration would be a proceeding equally injurious to the estimation of your personal dignity and the maintenance of the Public Interests'.[71] Sheridan seems to have worked towards a coalition of groups united in their policy on the war, on the Catholic question and on Ireland; what he called 'that extended and efficient administration which the country was desirous of having'.[72] Sheridan did not want to see the continuation of an anti-Catholic administration and he refused to consider playing any part in such an administration.

In the summer of 1812 Sheridan declared his determination to work with Canning in politics from then on.[73] Anxious to prove his independence from the Prince of Wales and his ministers, he offered himself once again for his old constituency of Stafford at the general election held in October. He came bottom of the poll. The *Staffordshire Advertiser* claimed that there had been 'groundless reports' spread to injure his cause by 'vulgar and illiterate people'.[74] Sheridan claimed he had been denied money he was owed by the Drury Lane Theatre trustees under Samuel Whitbread's chairmanship.[75] Possibilities of a return to the House of Commons as representative for Wootton Bassett and subsequently Westminster came to nothing. Sheridan's political career, including his influence with the Prince, was at an end.

Writing to William Eden on 16 January 1789, the Archbishop of Canterbury, noticing the rivalries among the Foxite Whigs, drily observed that 'it is thought that things are not yet ripe enough for the manager of Drury Lane to be manager of the House of Commons'.[76] The anonymous writer of a political pamphlet published in 1794 perceptively pointed out that Sheridan had 'quit a path [in the theatre] which must have led to honest fame and competence, to prostitute his talents to a faction, who, though they pretend to reject the pretensions of illustrious extraction, still are secretly so much swayed by ancient prejudice, that they will never acknowledge the son of an actor as their leader, however superior may be his capacity'.[77] Making sure that his message was quite clear, the author added that it was Sheridan's fate 'to live for ever the drudge of a party who distrust him while they employ him; who despise his obscure birth, while they avail themselves of his talents'.[78]

The party into which Sheridan was drawn by his friendship with Charles Fox was an aristocratic party. For those who constituted the Rockingham Whig party, known after 1782 as the Foxite Whig party, the preservation of political liberty was essentially a matter of balancing out powers within the state and particularly of preventing the development of an over-mighty executive, especially monarchical, power. The Rockinghams, descendants of the 'Old Corps' Whigs who had monopolized governmental office in the previous two reigns, had adopted and adapted the arguments of the opposition to their predecessors. In the Rockingham view, however, aristocrats were cast as the guardians of constitutional liberty because not only did they possess a physical stake in the country, through the ownership of land, but they possessed the independent means to guarantee their capacity to act independently, and thus to withstand the tendency inherent in a monarchy to degenerate into despotism. Fox's objection to Pitt and Addington was that they lacked the personal fortune to be anything other than royal puppets, whereas Grenville, by contrast, had the wealth and intelligence which gave him the freedom to challenge the Crown, if the need arose. Unlike Pitt, the Grenvilles were seen as capable of becoming good party men.

Sheridan could happily agree, especially after the events of 1783-4, that the overwhelmingly important question in British politics was the danger of a growth in executive power at the expense of Parliament and the country's liberties. He could support the Whigs out of conviction, not just because of personal connections. In Shelburne's machinations in 1782 Sheridan could sense the motions of an ambitious king; the installation of Pitt in power in 1783 evinced a contempt for Parliament; Pitt's reforms of the government in India and of the trading relationship with Ireland betrayed a system hostile to constitutional rights. The repressive legislation of the 1790s convinced Sheridan that there was a deep-laid plot to introduce despotism into the country.[79] Even as late as February 1810 Sheridan could state his belief that the source of the downfall of the nations of Europe, under the Napoleonic flail, was 'the want of that salutary controul (*sic*) upon their governments, that animating source of public spirit and national exertion', provided by a free press.[80] All this could be accepted by the most aristocratic of Whigs. What could not be accepted was Sheridan's blithe assertion that 'it was the most amiable and valuable fruit of our happy constitution, that every path of honourable ambition was open to talents and industry, without distinction of ranks'.[81] Sheridan's views on liberty went beyond the traditional Whig view to something more akin to the nineteenth-century Liberal belief in equality of opportunity. Equally unsettling to his more traditional colleagues was his recognition that politics could not be confined to the Palace of Westminster. Sheridan was assiduous and adept at cultivating a wide range of political contacts outside Parliament, particularly among the popular societies and within the journalistic field.

Professor John Cannon has shown that between 1782 and 1820 sixty-five individuals held Cabinet office of whom forty-three were peers and of the remaining twenty-two fourteen were sons of peers. By his reckoning only six were genuinely non-aristocratic.[82] Of these, only William Windham could put forward any claim to having been a Rockinghamite/Foxite Whig. Significantly, two of the others on the list, Addington and George Canning, were linked politically with Sheridan. It is true that in 1806-7 the Whigs were prepared to admit Addington—a man whose origins and abilities they had previously scorned—to the Cabinet table, but on this occasion it suited their own political ambition to do so; Addington had already been raised to the peerage as Lord Sidmouth and he was from outside the party, which somehow made it more acceptable. Sheridan and Whitbread, both non-aristocratic Foxites, were excluded. Sheridan was forced to accept that cultivating the Prince of Wales and acquiring influence in

the extra-parliamentary world would not be enough to overcome Whig social prejudices. By 1812 Sheridan was of the opinion that only a new party could cater for the man of talent with liberal convictions. Pittite 'Tories' were unwilling to force reform on unwilling, reactionary monarchs, although men of humble extraction could prosper well enough in their ranks if they possessed enough talent and were prepared to sacrifice any reforming proclivities. Whigs had the right ideas about civil, religious and political liberties, but remained wedded to traditional ideas of rank and deference.

In one of his last speeches in Parliament, Sheridan declared that he would never 'endure that this great country must be suffered to go drooping to perdition, because there are none but those two parties competent to direct its energies'.[83] But, failing to be elected in 1812, he never had the opportunity to see whether forging a political alliance with that other scion of the theatrical world, George Canning, would produce anything of substance in a party view. After his death in 1816 he was buried in Poets' Corner. Even in death the Whigs insisted on keeping him in his proper place.

Notes

1. *Memoirs, Journal and Correspondence of Thomas Moore,* ed. Lord J. Russell (London, 1853-6), iii, 233.

2. W. Hinde, *George Canning* (London, 1973), p. 21 (quoting from Leeds City Archives, Harewood MSS. 2: George Canning to his mother, 13 June 1791.)

3. *The Parliamentary History of England from the Earliest Period to the Year 1803,* ed. W. Cobbett (London, 1806-20), xxii, 415 (cited hereafter as *PH*).

4. *PH,* xxv, 766.

5. *Betsy Sheridan's Journal: Letters from Sheridan's Sister 1784-86; 1788-90,* ed. W. LeFanu (London, 1960), p. 58 (15-20 June 1785).

6. British Library Add. MSS. 41579 fo. 4; The Journal of Lady Elizabeth Foster.

7. *The Letters of Richard Brinsley Sheridan,* ed. C. Price (Oxford, 1966), ii, 260: To the Duke of Bedford, 12 February 1806.

8. Ibid. i, 6-11. Sheridan's father had been granted a pension by the Bute government and Henry Fox, the father of Charles James, led for the government in the House of Commons when Bute was First Lord of the Treasury.

9. T. Moore, *Memoirs of the Life of Richard Brinsley Sheridan* (single volume edition, London, 1825), pp. 205-10.

10. Ibid., pp. 110-12.

11. Price, *Letters,* i, 135: to the Duchess of Devonshire, 19 September 1780.

12. Moore, *Life of Sheridan,* p. 211.

13. L. G. Mitchell, *Charles James Fox* (Oxford, 1992), pp. 25-45. In view of Sheridan's later difficulties with the Whigs' aristocratic ethos, and the fact that Sheridan's primary political attachment was to Fox, not the Rockinghamite leadership, it is significant that Mitchell states (p. 25) that 'In 1782, Fox was not a Whig in the sense that he had foreclosed on all other options . . . The lack of firm principle, which had marked his early years, still gave him total flexibility.'

14. *The Dramatic Works of Richard Brinsley Sheridan,* ed. C. Price (Oxford, 1973), i, 331, quoting from Folger Shakespeare Library, Washington DC, Folger MS. Wb. 478 opp. p. 254.

15. I am grateful to Professor Ian Christie for drawing my attention to the Jacobite connections in Sheridan's family; W. Sichel, *Sheridan* (London, 1909), i, 209-18.

16. Price, *Letters,* i, 72: to Thomas Grenville, 4 January 1773. Thomas Grenville was the elder brother of William Wyndham Grenville, 1st Baron Grenville, who led the Whig party jointly with Grey after Fox's death. Thomas Grenville had been a pupil in Sheridan's father's school of oratory at Bath.

17. Price, *Letters,* i, 77: to Thomas Grenville.

18. *The Parliamentary Debates from the year 1803 to the present time,* ed. T. C. Hansard (London, 1812-20), ii, 728-38. (Hereafter *PD*).

19. BL Add. MSS. 38593-5: Minutes of the Westminster Committee of Association.

20. *Memorials and Correspondence of Charles James Fox,* ed. Lord J. Russell (London, 1853-7), ii, 21-5: Lord John Townshend to Lord Holland, 15 June and 23 June 1830; *PH*, XXIV, 490; J. Watkins, *Memoirs of the Public and Private Life of the Rt Hon. Richard Brinsley Sheridan, with a particular account of his family and connections* (London, 1817), i, 240-50; Moore, *Journal,* ii, 316; *PH*, xxvi, 187.

21. *PH,* xxiv, 1199; xxvi, 274-302.

22. L. T. Werkmeister, *The London Daily Press 1772-92* (Nebraska, 1963), pp. 10-12, 69-70. A. Aspinall, *Politics and the Press c. 1780-1850* (London, 1949), pp. 271-2; Scottish Record Office, Blair Adam MSS: W. Woodfall to W. Adam, 24 February 1784.

23. J. A. Cannon, *Parliamentary Reform 1640-1832* (Cambridge, 1972), p. 113.

24. *Political Memoranda of the 5th Duke of Leeds,* ed. O. Browning (Camden Society, 1884), pp. 209-10.

25. See E. A. Smith, *Lord Grey 1764-1845* (Oxford, 1990), p. 11.

26. Sichel, *Sheridan,* ii, 418, 422-3.

27. Chatsworth House, Derbyshire, MSS. Journal of Lady Elizabeth Foster, 2 December 1788.

28. *Ibid.,* 5 June 1789.

29. Duke of Buckingham and Chandos, *Memoirs of the Courts and Cabinets of George III, from original family documents* (London, 1853), i, 451.

30. *The Journal and Correspondence of William, Lord Auckland,* ed. Bishop of Bath and Wells (London, 1861-2), ii, 279.

31. *PH,* xviii, 344-72.

32. *The Life and Letters of Sir Gilbert Elliot, 1st Earl of Minto, 1750-1806,* ed. Countess of Minto (London, 1874), i, 351.

33. *The Correspondence of Edmund Burke,* general ed. T. Copeland (Cambridge, 1958-70), vii, 52-63: Burke to W. Weddell, 31 January 1792.

34. Ibid., 409: R. Burke to Fitzwilliam, 16 August 1793.

35. M. D. George, *English Political Caricature: A Study of Opinion and Propaganda, 1793-1832* (Oxford, 1959), pp. 213-21.

36. *PH,* xxxi, 1072.

37. Russell, *Memorials and Correspondence,* iii, 67.

38. Ibid., 149.

39. L. G. Mitchell, *Holland House* (London, 1980), p. 67.

40. *The Private Correspondence of Lord Granville Leveson Gower, 1781-1821,* ed. Castalia Countess Grenville (London, 1916), i, 427: Lady B to GLG, 17 August 1803.

41. M. D. George, *Catalogue of Political and Personal Satires preserved . . . in the British Museum* (London, 1978), vi, nos. 6974; 7380; 7528; *Morning Post,* 14 August 1788.

42. *The Journal of Elizabeth, Lady Holland (1791-1811),* ed. Earl of Ilchester (London, 1908), i, 221-2.

43. Mitchell, *Fox,* p. 262; Mitchell, *Holland House,* chapters 2 and 3.

44. *Byron: A Self-Portrait. Letters and Diaries 1798 to 1824,* ed. P. Quennell (Oxford, 1990), p. 432.

45. *PH,* xxxvi 1698; *Morning Chronicle,* 9 February 1804.

46. *Recollections of the Table-Talk of Samuel Rogers,* ed. A. Dyce (3rd edition, London, 1856), p. 97.

47. Moore, *Sheridan,* pp. 607-8. Beinecke Library, Yale University, Im. Sh. 53+w825a.

48. Smith, *Grey,* pp. 89-91.

49. BL Add. MSS. 47566 fos. 134-5: Fox to D. O'Bryen, 24 December 1802.

50. Ibid.

51. Russell, *Memorials and Correspondence,* iii, 412.

52. *PH,* xxxvi, 1698.

53. Russell, *Memorials and Correspondence,* iv, 11.

54. *The Creevey Papers: A Selection from the Correspondence and Diaries of the late Thomas Creevey*

M.P. 1768-1838, ed. Sir H. Maxwell (London, 1903), i, 21: Creevey to Currie, 21 January 1804.

55. Ibid., i, 25: Creevey to Currie, 2 April 1804. Addington was disparagingly referred to as 'the Doctor' because his father had been a mere physician.

56. Price, *Letters,* ii, 215-6: to his wife 27 February 1804.

57. *PH,* xxxiii, 1427.

58. *PD,* vii, 1115.

59. See C. A. Clayton, *The Political Career of Richard Brinsley Sheridan* (unpublished D. Phil. thesis, Oxford University, 1992), chapter VI.

60. J. J. Sack, *The Grenvillites, 1801-1829. Party Politics and Factionalism in the Age of Pitt and Liverpool* (London, 1979), p. 135.

61. Durham University Library, Grey MSS: Grey to Lady Holland, 2 July 1808.

62. Granville, *Private Correspondence,* ii, 353: Lady B to GLG, 1810.

63. *Lady Holland's Journal,* i, 217.

64. Granville, *Private Correspondence,* ii, 353.

65. Grey MSS: Grey to Lady Grey, 12 January 1811.

66. Lord Holland, *Further Memoirs of the Whig Party,* ed. Lord Stavordale (London, 1905), p. 84.

67. Ibid., p. 73.

68. Grey MSS: Grey to Lady Grey, 29 January 1811.

69. *The Diaries and Correspondence of James Harris, 1st Earl of Malmesbury,* ed. by his grandson (London, 1844), ii, 465.

70. See Sir J. Barrington, *Personal Sketches of his Own Times* (London, 1827), i, 298-9.

71. Price, *Letters,* iii, 158: To the Prince of Wales, 1 June 1812.

72. *PD,* xxiii, 623.

73. Granville, *Private Correspondence,* ii, 444: G. Canning to GLG, 18 August 1812.

74. *Staffordshire Advertiser,* 17 October 1812.

75. Price, *Letters,* iii, 163: to Samuel Whitbread, 1 November 1812.

76. *Auckland Correspondence,* ii, 267.

77. *The Whig Club or a Sketch of the Manners of the Age* (London, 1794), p. 19.

78. Ibid., p. 24.

79. *PH,* xxxii, 665.

80. *PD,* xv, 341.

81. *PD,* xvi, 33. Speech of 23 March 1810.

82. J. Cannon, *Aristocratic Century, The Peerage of Eighteenth-Century England* (Cambridge, 1984), p. 117.

83. *PD,* xxiii, 612.

Julie A. Carlson (essay date 1996)

SOURCE: "Trying Sheridan's *Pizarro,*" in *Texas Studies in Literature and Language,* Vol. 38, Nos. 3-4, Fall-Winter, 1996, pp. 359-78.

[*In the following essay, Carlson analyzes the dynamics of language, colonial oppression, and filial responsibility in Sheridan's adapted play* Pizarro.]

The most popular play of the 1790s in London and the second most popular play of the entire eighteenth century is Richard Brinsley Sheridan's *Pizarro,* adapted from the German of August von Kotzebue. Featuring an all-star cast of John Kemble, Sarah Siddons, and Dorothy Jordan, Sheridan's *Pizarro* dramatizes Peruvian struggles for independence against Spain as announced by Kotzebue's title, *Die Spanier in Peru oder Rollas Tod.* Virtually forgotten now, the play was so popular then that to be "*pizarroed* out of my memory and recollection, in every company I enter" was apparently a comprehensible phrase and experience in London society during the early summer of 1799 (Simpson 90). The play ran continuously from May to July of 1799, in the process restoring the dwindling coffers of Drury Lane and "swallow[ing] up every other Competitor" for public attention on stage and off. Already by 1800 the English version of the play had seen fifteen editions and numerous extended critical commentaries.[1]

Today those few scholars who know the play view it as a literary embarrassment for Sheridan. The bombast of its speeches and the improbability of its actions, scenes, and outcome undermine Sheridan's reputation as playwright and his own plays' attack on sentimentalism.[2] If *Pizarro* has any merit for these scholars, it lies in its historical interest, both in its depictions of history and the implications of this history for Sheridan's reputation as a politician. In this case, present-day critics focus not on the play's explicit setting in Peru but its allusions to England's relations with India, made perceptible by the speech that both they and commentators at the time identify as the play's most powerful passage: the speech of the Peruvian commander Rolla, in which he rallies his compatriots to resist the Spanish invaders. This speech casts into an otherwise faithful translation of Kotzebue images from Sheridan's most popular political speech ever—his famous Begums speech delivered during the impeachment trial of Warren Hastings for "high crimes and misdemeanors" conducted during his tenure as Governor General of Bengal.[3] Responsible at its first hearing for bringing Hastings to trial, Sheridan's Begums speech is partially responsible for bringing the "oppressions of millions of unfortunate persons in India" to the attention of the English public.

The most "original" contribution of Sheridan's to *Pizarro,* Rolla's speech repeats the Begums speech which is itself a repeat performance. Sheridan first delivered it in the House of Commons on February 7, 1787, as the fourth of twenty-two charges brought by Edmund Burke against Hastings in 1786. This charge, known as the Begums Charge, accused

Hastings of violating a prior agreement between the East India Company and the ruling family of Oudh that guaranteed the protection of lands and treasures to the mother and grandmother (the Begums) of the Nawab Wazir of Oudh. It claimed that in 1781, on a contrived pretext of the women's hostility to the British, Hastings compelled the Wazir to resume his mother and grandmother's lands, to seize most of their treasure, and to pay the proceeds to the company. In presenting this charge, Sheridan accentuates the criminality of Hastings's violation not of contract but of "filial piety," a tactic which, according to one prominent historian of the trial, "recovered at a stroke" the "momentum of the prosecution, so laboriously built up during 1786" (Marshall 52). After hearing only six of the twenty-two charges, the House voted to impeach Hastings on May 10, 1787. The ensuing trial for impeachment opened in Westminster Hall on February 13, 1788 and ended with Hastings's acquittal on April 23, 1795. This time Sheridan presented the Begums Charge over a period of four days, June 3, 6, 10, and 13, 1788, in a speech still viewed as the high point of the trial and of oratorical performances throughout the eighteenth century. In Fox's reckoning, compared to this speech, all other speeches "dwindled into nothing, and vanished like vapour before the sun."[4]

Gaining access to the Begums speech through Rolla's speech, contemporary scholars prize *Pizarro* for preserving this triumph of Sheridan's parliamentary career even as they censure *Pizarro* for damaging Sheridan's claims to literary achievement, originality, and sound judgment. Yet agreement on the power of Rolla's speech begins to identify the relevance of *Pizarro* for performance studies of (pre)romanticism and for theorists of performativity working in the area of colonial culture studies. As a member of Parliament and manager of Drury Lane, Sheridan himself embodies the lack of distinction not in but between aesthetic and political arenas that performance studies endorse. More specifically, contemporary accounts of the Begums speech stress the highly theatrical nature of the Hastings trial and foreground long-standing performative alliances among oratory, theater, and law. Descriptions of Sheridan's performance in Westminster Hall anticipate descriptions of the conditions for Rolla's debut: a four-hour wait for admission, tickets going for as much as fifty pounds, a rush for seating which "nearly proved fatal to many," and attendance by "persons of the first distinction" (*Speeches* 2: 55).[5] They describe him as highly theatric, especially in his concluding tableau in which he collapses into Burke's arms uttering as final words, "My Lords, I have done."[6] Public perceptions of Sheridan's theatrics identify a second cultural service performed by the trial. If its rendering India familiar to a sizable portion of the English public is important for colonial culture studies, its making social concerns good entertainment is an operating principle of performativity—and of "Old Sherry."

The most compelling recent account of the trial of *Pizarro* connects the dramaturgical implications of staging the play to its negotiation of colonial relations. Sara Suleri's analysis of the "recollection" out of which English audiences were "pizarroed" stresses a crucial linkage between repression and viewing that is often overlooked by theorists of performance who promote a politics of visibility. In her account, audiences at the time were hearing at least two things in Rolla's speech: a "literal return" of the repressed, *Pizarro* being the only cultural artifact to "disseminate the colonial guilt surrounding a trial whose implications were too soon repressed"; and nothing at all, owing to the overwhelming nature of spectacle (68). The scenic splendor of the staging, especially the Incan Temple of the Sun and Pizarro's pavilion, is claimed to rival the strength of acting (Price 630). By representing the ascendancy of spectacle over speech, *Pizarro* alters dramaturgical conditions in intensifying scenic illusion throughout the century. By collapsing "colonial space into melodramatic space," it depicts the "inefficacy of discourse to halt colonial logic" (Suleri 68). In this respect, *Pizarro* forecasts what even the Managers of the trial were not in a position to see: the anachronism of impeachment in the late eighteenth century and the inadequacy of dramaturgical categories like hero and victim, innocence and guilt, to comprehend the "impersonality" of colonial relations. As *Pizarro* makes clear, this impersonality is particularly intimate in colonial settings where "dividing lines between 'they' and 'we' bec[o]me increasingly impossible to maintain" (73).

By recognizing that Rolla's speech appeals to a nation's repressed memories, Suleri alters the sense of timing often associated with performance and reminds us that there is no time like "the present" in theater. But by posing as an opposition spectacle and speech, Suleri oversimplifies the mechanism of theater's double time and conflicting modes of identification—between the sympathetic version developing in the eighteenth century and unconscious processes articulated by psychoanalysis. Rolla's speech is a moving speech in part because it is seen and (not) heard—or heard to eschew the need for words to say what "we" all feel. Its means of gaining sympathy appeal to unconscious processes that perceive the stranger as ourselves through modes of identification that precede the solidification of our "self." Both the trial and the tragedy depict this conflict in anchoring identity in "primal bonds" of family. In this regard, Suleri underplays the uncanny nature of theater in deeming dramaturgical categories like "hero" anachronistic. We are formed on such ideal images, even if they are fiction.

Rolla's speech is also moving because its historical referents change with the times. While present-day and contemporary commentators agree on the power of Rolla's speech, they hear in it different lessons for different times. In 1799 commentators praise the speech for its "happy allusions" to current events between England and France and hear Rolla rallying the English to resist the threatened French invasion (Britton 141). Rolla's speech is printed in every newspaper account of the play, and Sheridan is credited with performing a patriotic service to the nation. At a minimum, Rolla's speech answers to five alarms of invasion. Besides those sounding between Peru and Spain, India and England, and England and France, Rolla's speech also raises alarms over the literary invasion of England by Germany in the 1790s and the perpetually immanent invasion of Ireland by England in the same years. It answers by enlisting an us/them rhetoric that arouses patriotic sentiment in any state and by using words to deny the necessity of words to say what "we" all feel:

> *Rol.* Yet never was the hour of peril near, when to inspire [soldiers] words were so little needed. My brave associates—partners of my toil, my feelings and my fame!—can Rolla's words add vigour to the virtuous energies which inspire your hearts?—No—You have judged as I have, . . . the motives, which, in a war like this, can animate *their* minds, and Ours.—They, by a strange frenzy driven, fight for power, for plunder, and extended rule—We, for our country, our altars, and our homes.—They follow an Adventurer whom they fear—and obey a power which they hate—We serve a Monarch whom we love—A God whom we adore. . . . They boast, they come but to improve our state, enlarge our thoughts, and free us from the yoke of error! . . . They offer us their protection—Yes, such protection as vultures give to lambs—covering and devouring them! (*P* 2. 2. 11-14, 17-21, 24-25, 27-28).

To such offers, the last of which repeats Sheridan's depiction of Hastings's offers of "protection" as "fraught with a similar security; like that of a Vulture to a Lamb," Rolla asserts:

> Be our plain answer this: The throne We honour is the People's Choice—the laws we reverence are our brave Fathers' legacy—the faith we follow teaches us to live in bonds of charity with all mankind, and die with hope of bliss beyond the grave. Tell your invaders this, and tell them too, we seek no change; and, least of all, such change as they would bring us (*P* 2. 2. 30-35).

This speech speaks volumes about the lack of identity between affect and reason that constitutes powers of persuasion in oratory, theater, and law. Analyzing its content in the context of its mobility raises important challenges to the performative mode. What were audiences hearing in a speech that rallied them to two contradictory judgments regarding England? What can it tell us about the ease with which national characters make the shift from victimizer to victim? Does cognitive dissonance produce emotional intensity? What is the relevant difference between a "subject position" and a subject who constantly changes position? In the case of Rolla's speech, its capacity to address multiple, even contradictory, situations depends on its saying nothing new. Rolla's disavowal of words is (not) rhetorical: there is no rational need to repeat what we feel, but the repetition is key to achieving conviction. Rolla specifies one psychic function of theater by allying patriotism to nonrational faculties. Both theater and national sentiment depend on a suspension of disbelief that requires audiences to remain unenlightened.

In saying nothing new, Rolla's speech is an allegory of the broader rhetorical practices that enable it: the British elocutionary movement of the eighteenth century and theories and practices of translation in Germany. Both projects pursue the same cultural challenges as the trial of Warren Hastings: to envision "humanity" as and for a particularity; to render the foreign familiar; to find a language that expresses commonalities among peoples; to intensify meaning by eschewing information. Both practices in this period also occasion alarms of invasion within England, the elocutionary movement from its location in Ireland, the "rage" for German translations culminating in an English protectionism directed against Kotzebue. To recover *Pizarro,* then, is to confront alarms of invasion on multiple borders—between nations, between people, within persons—and to encounter conflicting times of identification through theater's combination of text and vision. As we will see, Sheridan answers these alarms by appealing to primal bonds of family as the paradigm for rendering the foreign familiar. The conflicts that ensue are to a certain extent negotiable through taking seriously the generic point of departure for *Pizarro:* adaptation. Skill in adaptation as literary mode and technique of survival is what makes Sheridan of value for performance studies today.

I. Trial Runs

Considering Rolla's speech in the context of the elocutionary movement in Britain establishes important preconditions for understanding Sheridan's adaptation, *Pizarro.* It foregrounds the visual dimensions of speech by advocating the centrality of tone, look, and gesture in oratorical training. It highlights the patriotic service of the orator by considering public speaking as the most effective means for preserving a people's liberty. Undergirding the commitment to strengthen the arts of delivery are three related assumptions that apply to performative domains generally: persuasion is best achieved by addressing the passions rather than the understanding of an audience; passion employs the language of tone, look, and gesture; this language speaks to the widest possible audience and evokes similar emotions in its receivers. All three assumptions are crucial to a broader shift in political authority from coercion to consent, the goal of which is to make sociality natural by appealing to what people share (Fliegelman 28-34).

The emphasis on delivery makes oratorical training indispensable to both houses of representation in which Sheridan performs. But for Sheridan oratorical training is also an in-house operation owing to contingencies of birth. The father—or, to accept Wilbur Howell's assessment, "second" father—of the British elocutionary movement is Thomas Sheridan, the father of the adoptive father of *Pizarro* (169). In his chosen occupations, Thomas Sheridan embodies the close alliance between oratory and theater, as does his lifelong plan to open a school for oratory as an annex to the theater and his occasional use of his home for the former purpose. The father's lessons condition Rolla's speech in form and content: to speak universally is to accentuate the visual dimensions of speech and to take as one's subject "filial piety."

Thomas Sheridan initiates *A Course of Lectures on Elocution* with a critique of Locke's *Essay Concerning Human*

Understanding for the ways that its views on language have led to the deterioration of Britain's moral and political health. By restricting the mind to understanding and thus words to the representation of ideas, Locke's *Essay* neglects to account for the seats of passion and of fancy and the languages appropriate to them. This restriction reinforces the "extravagant idea entertained of the power of writing" in Britain, to which Sheridan attributes the "propagation of selfishness" currently eroding the nation and statemen's ability to achieve political reform (xii, 181). Cultivation of speech generally, especially the arts of delivery, is the remedy for Britain's "dissocial" condition. Acquiring skill in the language of looks and gestures, what Sheridan calls the "hand-writing of nature," guarantees a wider and more receptive audience than that convoked by print. Artificial, divisive, ambiguous, and arbitrary: written language opposes sociality and the means of consent.

We are right to reject this opposition between speaking and writing, the mystifications of which have been deconstructed by grammatologists and critics of liberalism. But the quest for common ground need not be abandoned just because we have abandoned notions like "ground" and the binarisms that support it. The elder Sheridan provides reasons to pursue his pursuit of a more universal language, despite his antagonism toward writing. For one thing, his view of speech does not contain the terms opposed to writing as Derrida has named them. To give only two, neither self-presence nor truth are operative categories for an orator whose power stems from theater and theater's cultivation of the *appearance* of sincerity, the reality of which remains immaterial.[7] For another, Sheridan's goal in standardizing pronunciation is mobility, both economic and geographic. Standardizing pronunciation removes the social distinctions perpetuated by designations of dialect. The site to which Sheridan imagines students from all the British colonies coming to acquire proficiency in English is Ireland, not the "court-end" of London.[8]

The importance Sheridan ascribes to body language also keeps the quest for a common language from supporting conformist agendas, though in a less conscious manner. As a man of theater, Sheridan has some experience with the problems of predicting how bodies are received. This awareness at times leads him to invert the logic that equates gesture with universality by arguing that body language is less capable of standardization than the language of words. However, this diversity of language becomes a virtue—even a hallmark of national character—because the "bad consequences" that follow from the "confusion of tongues at Babel" do not attend it (126). Recognizing that there is a wish behind this belief should not blind us to what Sheridan's project makes visible: the deftness with which diversity affirms the "singularity" of British character and the reasons viewing audiences do not always perceive similarity in diversity (118). The trial of Hastings and the tragedy of **Pizarro** dramatize what this father and son "know" only too well. Limits to sympathy begin at home. That site of natural social relations has estrangement at the heart of it.

THE BEGUMS SPEECH: "PRIMAL BONDS" OF FAMILY

Agreement exists on the heights represented by Sheridan's Begums speech and on the reason for its success: strength of material. Apparently there is something irresistible about charges that a man in high places plundered defenseless women, invaded their strongholds, accused them of inciting a rebellion, and employed his own son as the agent of ill against his mother. Agreement also exists on the strongest part of this strong material. The "celebrated delineation" of "filial piety" occurring on the final day of the charge is highlighted more frequently than any other part of the speech (Moore 2: 24). Part of the enduring fascination of this charge is how its irresistibility is positioned within two potentially contradictory sites of conviction: evidence and feeling. The case against Hastings appears strongest in this charge, and the persuasiveness of the case has little to do with the accuracy with which the evidence is presented.[9] Conviction results from something "beyond argument" and before the law, about which it "would be superfluous to speak" were it not the Manager's "duty" to do so. It results from "filial piety," that

> gratitude founded upon a conviction of obligations, not remembered, but the more binding because not remembered,—because conferred before the tender reason could acknowledge, or the infant memory record them—a gratitude and affection, which no circumstances should subdue, and which few can strengthen[10]

and against which Hastings has transgressed in instigating a son to plunder his mother. The superfluity of words, besides occasioning an outpouring of words that present nothing remotely resembling evidence, articulates a lasting message regarding the interconnection between reason and feeling in achieving convictions. What links affect to evidence is self-evidence, which it is the role of the family to supply.

To accuse Hastings of crimes against the family simplifies a number of problems of evidence that have already complicated and eventually undermine the prosecution's ability to make the case against Hastings. First, the Managers experience difficulties in amassing evidence for a crime whose scene is halfway around the globe and most of whose witnesses are accomplices to the crime. A related difficulty is determining the status of the evidence emerging from this distant scene—whether legal codes are universal or particular and on what points "Hindoo custom" and English law agree. Early on in the trial Burke does what he can to circumvent both of these problems by presenting both a "Historical Detail of Local Occurrences and Observations" relative to governing in India and a "map, as it were, of the moral world" that depicts the absurdity of "geographical morality"—"as if conscience and moral feeling were the creatures of points and parallels—existences, which like certain animals, drooped beneath the *line*" (*Trial* 1: 11). A third procedural difficulty concerns the determination of under which branch of law in England, common law or the custom of parliament, evidence is to be evaluated in the case of impeachment.[11] Sheridan's

depiction of Hastings's crime as against the family simplifies, by suspending, all three complications. "To condemn
crimes like these, we need not talk of laws or of human
rules—their foulness, their deformity does not depend
upon local constitutions, upon human institutes or religious creeds." The "persons who perpetrate" these deeds
are "monsters who violate the primitive condition, upon
which the earth was given to man—they are guilty by the
general verdict of human kind" (Moore 25).

The evidence against Hastings provided by the universal
sanctity of the family extends to the family's particular
function in making evident a "self." This function resolves
two opposing problems that the Managers experience in
interpreting character. The first betrays a prosecutorial
schizophrenia in characterizing the identity of this criminal—and determining whether he has an identity at all. Is
Hastings a criminal "of the blackest dye" whose evil is unprecedented in all the records of crime (*Speeches* 1: 277,
287; 2: 113)? Or is he "but a petty Nucleus, involved in its
Lamina, scarcely seen or thought of" because dependent
on others for his crimes and successes (*Speeches* 2: 56;
see also 2: 93)? More to the (defense's) point, to what extent is a company man accountable as an individual at
all?[12] To stress the enormity of his crimes keeps the lordships's "eyes" on Hastings and the validity of impeachment. It also renders self-evident the Managers' efface-
ment of self in their function as delegates of nature
speaking in the voice of "the commons of Great Britain."
So speaking mutes public outcry over the "private spleen"
evident in their "harsh language" and bullying demeanor
toward Hastings (*Trial* 2: 56).

So much evidence for and against these selves won the
day on the strength of the self-evidence of the value of
family. On its first hearing, Pitt specified as one of the
"two great points" that "fully proved" the "criminality of
Mr. Hastings" his making "the son the instrument of rob-
bing the mother" (*Speeches* 1: 297). The success of its
second airing proved that partisanship is suspendable when
the cause is humanity while also delivering positive evidence for the speaker's self: Sheridan's strength *is* his
feeling which makes the allegedly uncharacteristic sentimentalism of *Pizarro* his own.[13] But both the trial and the
tragedy present this evidence against the self: what is self-
evident is often manifestly untrue. This point about evidence never emerges as an articulated lesson of the trial,
though several perceptions hint in this direction: especially
that Sheridan's heart was not in the trial and that his repetition of his father's lessons did not lessen the distance
between them.[14] Nor is *Pizarro* perceived to uncover this
truth, even though the play demystifies filial piety and undermines any claims for the consistency of Sheridan's political feelings. If Pitt complains that he has heard Rolla's
speech before at Hastings's trial, William Cobbett, as we
will see, is outraged over the number of times and varying
circumstances under which this speech is heard.[15]

In the case of the trial, the problem is not that the charge
brings its own evidence against filial piety. We can accept

Sheridan's arguments that this son could not resist the
master's instructions to plunder his mother. Power differ-
entials between countries place serious limitations on the
autonomy of family relations in them. But this fact does
not explain away the record provided by Sheridan of this
family's history of resistance to each other, which he gives
while ostensibly countering the defense's charge that the
Begums were hostile to the British. Sentimental scenarios
of a loving wife and self-sacrificing mother have a way of
turning nasty. In one, the mother interposes her body between the "scymeter" of her husband and the son he is intent on "cutting down" (*Speeches* 2: 66).[16] In another, enmity against the son is now transferred from father to
mother. Testimony against the charge that the Begums in-
cited the rebellion produces this set piece of evidence.
"The elder Begum did express great dislike to [the Nabob,
her son], but I cannot pretend to say it was on account of
his connexion with the English." "What were the marks of
dissatisfaction?" "It was her practice to throw away the
musnod on which he sat, as a mark of her dislike or contempt, but what her motives were for it, I cannot say."[17]
Others did say. According to P. J. Marshall, hers was an
"unnatural" son, whose "homosexuality, extravagance, and
incompetence were notorious" (110n).

The revelation of these family secrets in the context of the
Hastings trial, however, indicates how such secrets remain
hidden: they get displaced. The attempt to render India familiar by focusing on what we all feel about familial attachment backfires. To English eyes, this family is less es-
tranged than foreign, exotic.[18] Records of audience
response to the trial set the limits to sympathy where processes of identification frequently encounter difficulties:
the site of the mother.[19] Special difficulties accrue around
the effort to gain sympathy for the Begums, either as elderly women or persons whose private quarters have been
invaded. As a way of linking Hastings's invasion of the
zenanas with rape, Sheridan emphasizes testimony regarding the sanctity with which the "sequestration" of Indian
women is viewed, especially by the women themselves
who elect to retire from the public eye because they view
being viewed as "profanation" (*Speeches* 2: 64; *Trial* 1:
70). This was a gross miscalculation according to the court
recorder who observes that "the female part of the audience did not seem to feel his distress" (*Trial* 1: 55). They
may also have experienced the testimony as fighting words
aimed at their interest in seeing and being seen at the
trial.[20]

*Trial to Tragedy: "What Could Subdue Attachment So
Begun?"*

The audience's negative reaction to this comparison,
coupled with the difficulties of ascertaining what Sheridan
means by drawing it, should render more interesting the
question of why the *zenana* is the other feature from the
trial that Sheridan imports into *Pizarro.* The reappearance
of "Rolla's" speech is less surprising, at least on the score
of one great performance deserving another. What made
these two moments from the trial feel of a piece when

Sheridan was adapting Kotzebue's piece for the English stage—beyond the opportunism of self-borrowing, the dismissability of which is not so self-evident either? After all, self-borrowing constitutes a time-honored strategy of composition but not a principle of selection, and there were many more auspicious candidates for inclusion in the play. An initial answer comes from considering the logic that makes Rolla's speech consistent with the spectacle of women's private quarters. On the level of content, the two passages connect the inviolability of home to the borders of the motherland and the gendered division of labor necessary to protect these spheres: conquest and confinement. On the level of representation, the two affirm a sexual difference between speech and spectacle at the same time that both make their appeal by disavowing their proper spheres of representation. Rolla asserts that never were words so little needed before launching into the longest speech of the play. Elvira and Cora both affirm that visibility is woman's primary mode of influence. The exemplary Peruvian wife and mother Cora repeatedly disobeys Alonzo's and Rolla's entreaties to "hasten then to the concealment" (*P* 2. 1. 42). The Spanish mistress Elvira asserts that the "mould" of her mind is not "formed for tame sequestered love" (*P* 3. 3. 155).

These passages from the trial seem at home in *Pizarro,* then, because Kotzebue's play similarly foregrounds familial relations in order to place the "foreign" on familiar territory. The play's Peruvian heroes, Rolla and Alonzo, fight for their country out of the strength of their natural attachments. Indeed, thematizing the nature of attachment is what justifies otherwise extraneous characters and scenes.[21] But it also generates the conflict between countries and men. Initiating the tragedy is Alonzo's transfers of allegiance from Spain and Pizarro to Peru and Father Las-Casas, transfers that validate the shift from primal to willed affiliations. To Valverde's query regarding the prior filial relation between Pizarro and Alonzo, "What could subdue attachment so begun?" the dejected Pizarro responds: Las-Casas's "canting precepts of humanity" which "raised in Alonzo's mind a new enthusiasm . . . to forego his country's claims for those of human nature" (*P* 1.1. 89-92). Similarly, what solidifies the friendship between Rolla and Alonzo is Rolla's decision to "resign his claim" to Cora upon finding that she "preferred" Alonzo (*P* 1. 1. 281-83).

These ringing endorsements of choice in attachment conflict with the play's depiction of the formation and effect of early attachments. Indeed, *Pizarro* goes out of its way to denaturalize primal bonds wherever they are depicted, so far as to characterize the child's first words as the "grateful sound of, Father, Mother!" (*P* 2. 1. 16-22).[22] Everyone has difficulty relating to Cora's baby. Not only does the baby boy "rob" Alonzo of Cora's "caresses," but whether he "resembles" Alonzo is a question from the start (*P* 2. 1. 1-6). What allows Rolla to resolve the question in his favor depends on Cora's prior performance as an "unnatural" mother (*P* 5. 1. 96). Her son is taken by Spanish soldiers when Cora abandons the "veiled" infant

to rush into Alonzo's arms. He is placed back into her arms by a mortally wounded Rolla whose dying words proclaim, "'Tis my blood, Cora." Nor are European attachments less perverse. Pizarro enlists his mistress Elvira in both methods of subduing the foreigner on the grounds that she is more man than his men (*P* 3. 3. 18). His expectation that she will participate not in battle but in Pizarro's marriage to the Peruvian king's daughter effects her change of heart. What differentiates Elvira from other women is less that she is attached to a man who has murdered her brother and occasioned her mother's death; for, in the case of women, conjugal relations naturally destroy prior ties. Her problem is that sexual relations do not change her identifications. When Pizarro stops acting the part of the hero on which her love was formed, Elvira is drawn to the other side. This couple's attachment, moreover, is determined along gender lines demarcating spectacle from speech. Like Desdemona, Elvira first "waked to love" by tales depicting Pizarro's grandeur. Pizarro dies still captivated by his first sight of Elvira.[23]

In specifying the trouble that Drury Lane audiences experienced in accepting these scenes, contemporary reviews provide further evidence for the self-evidence of primal sympathy. They invert the verdict leveled against Sheridan's prior attempts to make India familiar to English audiences by objecting that depictions of the natural goodness of the Peruvians make them look too much like Europeans and that these particular Europeans do not look like "us" at all.[24] Consequently, perversions of family go unremarked in both cases. With "them," the exemplarity of their natures as heroes and mothers hides their familial derangement (Bardsley 44). With "us," the obvious violations of marital conventions obscure the realism with which the fixation and mobility of desire are portrayed. The popularity of this tragedy, and domestic tragedy more generally, suggests that there is more to gaining visibility than becoming visible. As stage history displays, perversions of family have been in our faces a long time without making a noticeable difference in our perceptions of family. This, too, suggests a logic by which Rolla's speech and the spectacle of the *zenanas* are at home in *Pizarro.* Both depict borders in relation to which alarms of invasion prove particularly alarming. Attending to the dynamic by which alarms galvanize resistance may provide a less mystified view of familial and national attachments. On the one hand, destabilizing borders does not automatically weaken defenses but tends to intensify them. In addition, perversions in the family are always capable of being externalized, whether in objects down the block or around the globe. On the other hand, through proximity over time individuals learn to adapt. *Pizarro* makes this modification to Kristeva's precondition for nations without nationalism: it acknowledges the stranger that is the family who makes the individual like it (*Strangers* 182-88).

II. ADAPTING

"Taken from the German of Kotzebue," the title page of *Pizarro* already announces the "ordeal of the foreign" that all acts of translation imply (Berman vii). As a German translation in the 1790s, *Pizarro* enters a particularly charged field of interlingual exchange in terms of both the intensity of literary commerce between England and Germany and tensions within practices of translation coming from Germany.[25] As Walter Benjamin contends, translations in Germany at this period prepare for the revelation that "languages are not strangers to one another" (72). Facilitating this recognition is the way that translation differs from other linguistic activities in exaggerating the gap between content and word. "Enveloping its content like a royal robe with ample folds," the language of translation makes apprehensible the "pure" language toward which individual languages are heading that is occluded by the tighter fit between intent and mode in the original language (75). Translation also realigns the times of meaning, concentrating on the virtuality of composition and the afterlife of reception. These tasks of translation, even as they effect a universal language, accomplish the ends that Kristeva seeks in universalizing strangeness. Translation redefines kinship such that it has little to do with resemblance or likeness, not least because it reforms the origin in the process of becoming "foreign." It also redefines meaning such that it has nothing to do with saying something new.

The transmission and reception of *Pizarro,* however, bears all the marks of what Benjamin and Antoine Berman call a "bad translation." To the extent translation aims at transmitting information, it effects a "systematic negation of the strangeness of the foreign work" (Berman 5). Refusal to be affected by the foreign characterizes English literary reactions against Kotzebue to an extraordinary degree. The rage for Kotzebue in the 1790s unleashes rage against German language, sentiment, and feeling, occasioning a full-scale endorsement of protectionism in English letters. With *Pizarro* rage against German takes the form of critical enthusiasm for Sheridan's English that leaves no trace of "foreign idiom" in the language of the play.

The supremacy of English and of Sheridan's accomplishments in and as English find expression in the popular verdict regarding *Pizarro* that "the *body* may be *Kotzebue's,* but the Soul is Sheridan's."[26] Yet at least one commentator discerns the inadequacy of the body-soul analogy to depict the relation between Sheridan's and Kotzebue's achievements. For one thing, the analogy misconstrues the nature of Sheridan's performance, which is not a translation but an adaptation of two English translations for the stage. For another, it misrepresents a process that, in his depiction, is all body:

> It has been said, by some remarkers on this play, that *Kotzebue is the body, but Sheridan is the soul. . . .* I would rather say, that *Kotzebue was the naked body,* and Sheridan had clothed and dressed him from his own wardrobe, with suitable paraphernalia for the present season and *prevailing fashions of the times* (Britton 142-43).

Not explicitly motivated by a desire to distance himself from English protectionism, Britton's formulation of the differing tasks of translation and adaptation foregrounds the efficacy of performance to resolve, by diffusing, national, interpersonal, and intrapsychic border disputes. Substituting one surface for another, adaptation makes impossible the demarcation of what separates mine from yours, native from foreign, interior from exterior, old from new.

By taking up the body language that is lost in translation, moreover, adaptation brings translation theory into contact with performance studies in ways that modify both. To considerations of the language that is exchanged in translation is added a change in the media of performance—from drama to theater, novel to film—discussions of which foreground sociological concerns regarding assumed alliances between specific artistic forms and particular groups. On the other hand, transferring translation's conception of the evolutionary unfolding of language to visual media makes the "now" of performance less a thing of the "present." The different wardrobes ascribed to translation and adaptation measure further gains in the sociology of adaptation. The royal robe of translation does not suit the prevailing fashions of adaptation. The former addresses a future encoded in the virtuality of words, the latter adapts surfaces to the appearance of their times. This nearer miss of the present effects a corresponding change in the mode and time of reaction to invasions associated with the foreign. Unlike translation, adaptation does not seek to preempt invasion either by resisting contact or dissolving it in a "pure" language. It views invasion as having already occurred; foreign bodies are within a body without defined interiors. This perception does not make adaptation less defensive about its properties, but, in defending them, it begins from someplace other than origin.

On these grounds, *Pizarro* appears to be "about" what it "is" only in its English form of adaptation, though Sheridan clearly gets the message from the German title and the character who embodies the Spaniard in the Peruvian. On national, interpersonal, and intrapsychic levels, invasion has already occurred before the curtains rise. What remains is adapting to it. *Pizarro* extends the project of adaptation to a new ending which both eliminates Pizarro—the only character who is self-made and visibly resistant to change—and leaves the (good) Spaniards in Peru.[27] The latter event would seem to contradict Rolla's speech advocating resistance to invasion, except that the concluding lines of his speech have already done so. The saying "no/yes" to words is repeated in the speech's changing reaction to change, "Tell your invaders this, and tell them too, we seek no change; and, least of all, such change as they would bring us" (*P* 2. 2. 34-35).

Rolla's speech also introduces the chief challenge of adaptation that must be addressed before theorists of performance adopt it for political ends. From where, let alone which side, is a speaker speaking when he moves easily from "be *our* plain answer this" to "tell *your* invaders this"? On which battlefield do your invaders differ from mine? Such questions regarding sides are leveled repeatedly at Sheridan, though never so aggressively as by Cobbett who, in 1803, devotes a series of open letters to analyzing Sheridan's "consistency" as exemplified in Rolla's speech. In September of 1803, answering to another alarm of invasion from France, Sheridan recirculates Rolla's speech as "Sheridan's Address to the People" in support of "Our King, our Country, and our God."[28] In Cobbett's view, resurrecting Rolla's speech at this moment and in this manner makes opportunity indistinguishable from opportunism. Its new objects—king, war, volunteers—overturn Sheridan's history of opposition in championing France, Napoleon, and the Prince of Wales. Worse, the shift to loyalty is itself provisional. Sheridan times Rolla's appearance to suit the "taste and fashion" of support for Napoleon.[29] He retains the placeholder of revolution in specifying as the "Throne we honour" the "People's Choice." The only consistent thing about this speech is the way that it suits Sheridan's private interests. Sheridan's sponsorship of the Vote of Thanks to the volunteers, his various visits to the corps, his "industrious circulation" of Rolla's speech: all prepare for Drury Lane's revival of *Pizarro,* at which *"the members of all the Volunteer Corps were expected to attend!"* (389).

Despite its large share of private spleen and its eventual perfect fit for him, Cobbett's attack on Sheridan's consistency raises relevant questions. In the absence of "soul" or incontrovertible principles, on what grounds are limits to adaptability set? This question cannot be settled in advance of the circumstances that occasion it, but we can prepare for it by determining the conditions under which speech-acts move. Sheridan-Rolla-Sheridan's speech provides an occasion to evaluate the mobility achieved by proper speech and the orator's preeminence in rousing a people to protect their freedom. Its enabling conditions in oratory, legal trials, and translation suggest one facet of a moving speech in the feature they share: transmission of information is not the point. *Pizarro* dramatizes this insight by elevating the act over the content of speaking when it speaks to the regulation of international affairs. "Tell your invaders this;" or "Tell them [the rulers of Spain], that the pursuits of avarice, conquest, and ambition, never yet made a people happy, or a nation great" (*P* 5. 4. 29-30). In this respect, speeches in *Pizarro* point up a certain wishfulness to J. L. Austin's desire to cordon off the performative from theater. On the other hand, the various occasions for Sheridan-Rolla's speech indicate that determining proper occasions for speech is not an all-or-nothing affair. Originality is not paramount, but even the most moving speech does not move all the time or every person.

Moving Through Time

The speech's initial airing in the trial of Warren Hastings underscores one limit to even the most powerful speeches: time. The "unprecedented" length of the trial is adduced as a chief reason for Hastings's acquittal in ways that specify the interconnections between identity and time. Passage of time heightened sympathy for the "victim" and weakened

the appearance of evidence against him (Marshall 76-87). Moreover, it strengthened the evidence by showing how force of personality proves no match for force of events. Applied to Sheridan, this nonmatch acknowledges the minor role that not only he but speechmaking in general played in a trial, the tedium of whose procedural disputes, oral reports, and cross examinations dragged on for years. Applied to Hastings, the force of world events, particularly the French Revolution, changed his identity from chief villain to hero of Britain. Four years after Sheridan charges Hastings with destroying the British name in India, events credit Hastings with preserving "the British empire *entire* in India, when it had been convulsed and torn to pieces in other parts of the globe" (*Trial* 2: 309).

Yet this nonmatch is not a matter of alternatives, as if events negate the effects of personality, however anachronistic its conceptualization. Events make Hastings appear as a hero in his own eyes and those of others. What the nonmatch stresses is the interdependence of events and personality on differing levels of identification. Ego ideals govern in ways that complicate the identification of good government. Their power disrupts the predictability of sympathy. Stressing the "unprecedented hardship" of the trial on Hastings finally outweighs the oppression of "millions of unfortunate persons in India" (*Speeches* 1: 275). This has to do with Hastings's familiarity as English but also with his singularity. Sympathy needs individuals. Understanding as he does the blockage that attends the mathematical sublime, Burke fights fire with fire: "Mr. Burke replied with much heat and violence . . . that if Mr. Hastings had been abused, so had he too" (*Trial* 2: 272). Sheridan is less inclined to this line of defense, but he adapts it to Elvira: "but didst thou know my story, Rolla, thou would'st pity me" (*P* 4. 2. 75). In neither instance does the personalizing of pain go very far in redressing collective oppression. More often, it allows subjects to dwell on their pain and leaves collective suffering to reform itself on more transferential models.

Yet the particularizing of pain does bring us closer to what moves in speeches like Rolla's. Literally, what moves the Begums speech into *Pizarro* is a figure: the image of a vulture protecting a lamb. As image, it suggests adaptation's proximity to symbol but not its identity in the eternal, the universal, the one. This proximity underscores the capaciousness of images: England can resemble India on the level of generality depicted by "lamb." The adaptability of this image points up adaptation's position in the spaces between "particular" and "universal." It stations itself in two in-betweens: general but not abstract; generalizable but not universalizable. The latter is visible in what does not follow from Elvira's bid for sympathy. She is never given the words to tell her story and occasions no one's pity. "Lamb" is a large but not a universal category. It does not suit women who have a history of preying upon men. Nor does it apply to ruling men who prefer the sexual favors of men or to mothers who meddle in their son's affairs.

Viewed over the long run, **Pizarro** can adapt our thinking about histories of oppression. Its "topicality" is ongoing. Rolla's speech speaks against what Louise Fradenburg identifies as contemporary criticism's penchant to overemphasize the alterity of the past in advocating the cause of difference ("Pleasures" 375-78). Oppressive practices have a way of resembling each other across space and time. Moving speeches move because of the countless times that we have heard them before. Recognizing how a nation is moved by "veteran similes" suggests a way to modify them without denying the hold of figures on people: not by overreacting with a reaffirmation of reason, consciousness, and control but by adapting dimensions of the objects on which our earliest attachments are formed.[30] Here is a value of family—at least as translation and transference conceive it. The task of the translator and the analyst is to "invite us to come back constantly to our origins in order better to transcend them"—that is, to transcend through adapting them (Kristeva, *Nations* 4).[31] Changing what counts as "lamb," "black sheep," or even "wolf's clothing" moves us closer to strangers as ourselves.

Recalling the very short run of the first appearance of **Pizarro** on stage brings up a final promising feature of adaptation. No audience saw that performance again—not because every performance is unique but because people complained that this performance was "much, very much too long."[32] Within days, Sheridan cut the performance time by almost two hours, and this very last-minute adaptation, more than any other of his adaptations, is credited with ensuring the lengthy run of the play. Such an ability to modify mistakes and to restage events marks a clear difference between world and stage but also a point of congruence, not simply for Sheridan. Performance meets sociality at adaptation, a space-time in which moving speeches can remake social relations while allowing persons to make a living.

Notes

1. For accounts of the success of *Pizarro,* see Donohue 125-28 and excerpts from newspaper accounts given in the critical remarks to the play, Price 2: 631-41.

2. See Loftis, 125. Marshall Brown, whose chapter on Sheridan is one of the best recent treatments of him, dismisses *Pizarro* as a "mediocre tragedy" (232).

3. For accounts of the differences between Kotzebue's and Sheridan's plays, see Donohue, 129-35 and Sinko, 11-20.

4. Headnote to the speech of 7 February 1787 in *Speeches of the Late Right Honourable Richard Brinsley Sheridan.*

5. Suleri echoes the newspaper and court-recorded accounts of the trial by drawing attention to their highly theatrical nature (57-60).

6. Rae cites letters substantiating the outpouring of tears ("I never remember to have cried so heartily and so copiously on any public occasion") 2: 71.

7. See T. Sheridan, 121, 5; also Fliegelman, 2.

8. See T. Sheridan, 28-30; also Howell, 220.

9. See Marshall, 109, 110-29. Sheridan introduces the Presents Charge (2 April 1787) by admitting that "the present charge . . . was not, perhaps, of that nature which came home most effectually to the feelings of men; it could not excite those sensations of commiseration or abhorrence which a ruined prince, a royal family reduced to want and wretchedness, the desolation of kingdoms, or the sacrilegious invasion of palaces, would certainly inspire" (*Trial* 1: 344).

10. Moore 2: 24; see *Speeches* 2: 117.

11. See *Trial* 1: 23-25; Marshall, 64-70; Suleri, 49-50.

12. Sheridan's parody of this tactic suggests his sense of its power. "Major Scott, says [Hastings], take care of my consistency;—Mr. Middleton, you have my *memory* in commission!—Prove me a financier, Mr. Shore.—Answer for me, Mr. Holt (all journeymen, good enough for the house of commons, though not for your lordships)" (*Trial* 2: 62-63).

13. See *The Daily Universal Register:* "an oration, that an heart, flowing with the softest feelings of God-like humanity, could alone pour forth—and which no head, be it ever so good, would be able to supply, unless aided by a heart feelingly alive to the distresses of his fellow-creatures" (8 February 1787).

14. Moore reprints letters from Burke to Mrs. Sheridan, encouraging her to ensure Sheridan's presence at the trial (2: 10-12). Early on the report circulated of Sheridan's wish that "Hastings would run away and Burke after him" (cited in Suleri 68). According to Rae, Sheridan "waited in vain" for a "letter of congratulation from his father," though his sister Alicia reported that "[Thomas Sheridan] seems truly pleased that men should say, 'There goes the father of Gaul'" (2: 64-66).

15. See his series of open letters to Sheridan in *The Political Register* of 1803, modified and reissued as *The Political Proteus* (London: Cox, Son, and Baylis, 1804).

16. These scenes also feature deathbed pledges of protection by Hastings to the husband of the Behu Begum (2: 65-66).

17. *London Chronicle* 5-7 June; *Trial* 1: 125.

18. Records report considerable amusement over the "singularity of Indian names and appellations" (*Trial* 1: 37, 46).

19. See the "Turkish tale" Burke introduces as evidence of the "sanctity with which women were held" in India: starring the "*mama of Demetrius Cantemar* who supplied him with some hundreds" of "young virgins" whom "he received and treated kindly—*just once* before consigning them to the *Zenana,* never more to be treated thus kindly again!" (*Trial* 1: 70-72).

20. Courtroom and newspaper accounts delight in dwelling on the status, wardrobe, and beauty of the women in attendance (*Trial* 1: 5, 16, 36, 43, 58, 73).

21. See *P* 1. 1. 240-305; 2. 4. 10-13, 22-30; and Rolla's exchange with the soldier guarding the dungeon of Alonzo, from whom he gains access by awakening thoughts of the soldier's wife and children (4. 1. 55-80).

22. Kotzebue names "Father, Mother," but the "grateful sound" is Sheridan's.

23. The stage directions are telling: "At this moment [as Pizarro is poised to kill Alonzo], Elvira enters, habited as when Pizarro first beheld her [in the convent].—Pizarro appalled, staggers back. Alonzo renews the Fight, and slays him." See Bardsley, 22.

24. See Bardsley: "Instead of a half-civilized Slave (such as the best of the Peruvians must have been) we find Rolla's character represented as a compound of the European gallantry of a former age, mixed with modern German Sentiment, and a tolerable sprinkling of English Manners." Elvira is "an outrage against probability" (44, 28, 29).

25. See Rault, 83-89; Simpson, 84-94.

26. Britton ascribes this sentiment to "the elegant and learned Dr. Bisset" 131.

27. See especially 1. 1. 45; 1. 1. 100-01; 3. 3. 142; 4. 2. 129.

28. See Letter 4 (10 September 1803) in Cobbett's *Political Register* (385-97).

29. "When [Napoleon] was 'in a scrape,' in 1799, he was Pizarro; when he was crowned with laurels, in 1800, he was Hannibal; when he was, as you thought, at least, in another 'scrape' in 1803, then he became Pizarro again. I wish, Sir, he may continue Pizarro" (397).

30. See Tietjen-Meyer's expansion of Kristeva's concept of dissident speech (56-62, 106-15).

31. See Fradenburg "'Be not far from me'" for a fuller account of this process.

32. Quoted in *The Sun*. See Donohue on the decreasing times of each performance (128-29).

Works Cited

Bardsley, Samuel. *Critical Remarks on Pizarro, a tragedy, taken from the German drama of Kotzebue, and adapted to the English stage by Richard Brinsley Sheridan.* London: T. Cadell, Junior and W. Davies, 1800.

Benjamin, Walter. "The Task of the Translator." *Illuminations.* Trans. Harry Zorn. New York: Schocken Books, 1978.

Berman, Antoine. *The Experience of the Foreign: Culture and Translation in Romantic Germany.* Trans. S. Heyvaert. Albany: State U of New York P, 1992.

Britton, John. *Sheridan and Kotzebue. The Enterprising Adventures of Pizarro, preceded by a Brief Sketch of the Voyages and Discoveries of Columbus and Cortez: to which are subjoined the Histories of Alonzo and Cora, on which Kotzebue founded his two celebrated Plays of the Virgin of the Sun and The Death of Rolla. Also Varieties and Oppositions of The Whole Forming a Comprehensive Account of those Plays and the grand ballads of Cora, and Rolla and Cora, at the Royal Circus, and Royal Amphitheatre.* London: J. Fairburn, 1799.

Brown, Marshall. *Preromanticism.* Stanford: Stanford UP, 1991.

Cobbett, William. *The Political Proteus.* London: Cox, Son, and Baylis, 1804.

———. *The Political Register.* 1803.

Donohue, Joseph. *Dramatic Character in the English Romantic Age.* Princeton: Princeton UP, 1970.

Fliegelman, Jay. *Declaring Independence: Jefferson, Natural Language, and the Culture of Performance.* Stanford: Stanford UP, 1993.

Fradenburg, Louise. "'Be Not Far From Me': Psychoanalysis, Medieval Studies and the Subject of Religion." *Exemplaria* 7 (1995): 41-54.

Fradenburg, Louise, and Carla Freccero. "The Pleasures of History." *GLQ* 1, 4 (1995): 371-84.

Great Britain, Parliament, House of Commons. *The Trial of Warren Hastings, Esq.* 2 vols. London: J. Owen, 1794.

Howell, Wilbur Samuel. *Eighteenth-Century British Logic and Rhetoric.* Princeton: Princeton UP, 1971.

Kristeva, Julia. *Nations without Nationalism.* Trans. Leon Roudiez. New York: Columbia UP, 1993.

———. *Strangers to Ourselves.* Trans. Leon Roudiez. New York: Columbia UP, 1993.

Liu, Alan. "Local Transcendence: Cultural Criticism, Postmodernism, and the Romanticism of Detail." *Representations* 32 (1990): 75-113.

Loftis, John. *Sheridan and the Drama of Georgian England.* Oxford: Basil Blackwell, 1976.

Marshall, P. J. *The Impeachment of Warren Hastings.* Oxford: Oxford UP, 1965.

Meyers, Diana Tietjens. *Subjection and Subjectivity: Psychoanalytic Feminism and Moral Philosophy.* New York and London: Routledge, 1994.

Moore, Thomas. *Memoirs of the Life of the Right Honourable Richard Brinsley Sheridan.* 2 vols. New York: W. J. Widdleton, 1826.

Rae, W. Fraser. *Sheridan: A Biography.* 2 vols. London: Bentley and Son, 1896.

Rault, André. "Die Spanier in Peru oder die Deutschen in England: Englisches und deutsches Theater, 1790-1810." *Wissenschaftliche Zeitschrift der Ernst-Moritz-Arndt Universität.* 32.3-4 (1983): 83-89.

Sheridan, Richard Brinsley. *Sheridan's Plays.* Ed. Cecil Price. Oxford: Oxford UP, 1975.

Sheridan, Thomas. *A Course of Lectures on Elocution: Together with Two Dissertations on Language; and some other Tracts relative to those Subjects.* London: W. Strahan, 1762; rpt. New York: Benjamin Blom, 1968.

Simpson, David. *Romanticism, Nationalism, and the Revolt against Theory.* Chicago: U of Chicago P, 1993.

Sinko, Grzegorz. *Sheridan and Kotzebue: A Comparative Essay.* Wroclaw: Nakladem Wroclawskiego Towarzystwa Naukowego, 1949.

Speeches of the Late Right Honourable Richard Brinsley Sheridan. Ed. by a Constitutional Friend. 2 vols. London: Patrick Martin, 1816.

Suleri, Sara. *The Rhetoric of English India.* Chicago: U of Chicago P, 1992.

FURTHER READING

Biography

Durant, Jack D. "*Truth* for Sheridan: The Biographical Dilemma." In *A Fair Day in the Affections: Literary Essays in Honor of Robert B. White, Jr.,* edited by Jack D. Durant and M. Thomas Hester, pp. 119-30. Raleigh, N. C.: The Winston Press, 1980.

Surveys numerous injustices done to Sheridan by biographers since his death.

Criticism

Choudhury, Mita. "Sheridan, Garrick, and a Colonial Gesture: *The School for Scandal* on the Calcutta Stage." In *Theatrical Journal* 46, No. 3 (October 1994): 303-21.

Studies the use of Sheridan's *The School for Scandal,* produced in Calcutta in 1782, as a means of putting an innocent face on British colonial expansion.

Durant, Jack D. "Sheridan, Burke, and Revolution." In *Eighteenth Century Life* 6, Nos. 2-3 (January-May 1981): 103-13.

Summarizes Sheridan's political differences with the conservative thinker Edmund Burke.

———. "Sheridan's Picture-Auction Scene: A Study in Contexts." In *Eighteenth Century Life* 11, No. 3 (November 1987): 34-47.

Probes the comic potential of the picture-auction scene (Act IV, scene i) in *The School for Scandal,* calling it a "theatrical *tour de force.*"

Ellis, Frank H. "Folklore Motifs and the Plot of Comedy." In *Restoration* 11, No. 2 (Fall 1987): 94-106.

Schematizes *The School for Scandal* and William Congreve's *The Way of the World* as these dramas present numerous characters and themes from folklore.

Hess-Lüttich, Ernest W. B. "Maxims of Maliciousness: Sheridan's School for Conversation." In *Poetics* 11, Nos. 4-6 (December 1982): 419-37.

Presents an interpretation of rhetorical and conversational techniques in *The School for Scandal* that particularly notes the intersection between satire and sentiment in eighteenth-century drama.

McVeagh, John. "*Robinson Crusoe*'s Stage Début: The Sheridan Pantomime of 1781." In *Journal of Popular Culture* 24, No. 2 (Fall 1990): 137-52.

Reconstructs the stage pantomime for the 1781 production of Sheridan's *Robinson Crusoe.*

Picker, John M. "Disturbing Surfaces: Representations of the Fragment in *The School for Scandal.*" In *ELH* 65, No. 3 (Fall 1998): 637-52.

Suggests the fragmentary nature of *The School for Scandal* which, while pleasing, is rife with disjunction and incongruity.

Troost, Linda V. "The Characterizing Power of Song in Sheridan's *The Duenna.*" In *Eighteenth-Century Studies* 20, No. 2 (Winter 1986-87): 153-72.

Analyzes Sheridan's popular comic opera *The Duenna,* a work that critics have frequently dismissed as superficial, frivolous entertainment.

Wills, Jack C. "Lord Byron and 'Poor Dear Sherry,' Richard Brinsley Sheridan." In *Lord Byron and His Contemporaries,* edited by Charles E. Robinson, pp. 85-104. East Brunswick, N. J.: Associated University Presses, 1982.

Details Sheridan and Lord Byron's friendship and mutual influence upon each other.

Wood, Peter. "On Producing Sheridan." In *Sheridan Studies,* edited by James Morwood and David Crane, pp. 178-88. Cambridge: Cambridge University Press, 1995.

Interview with director Peter Wood, who discusses his impressions while staging *The Rivals* and *The School for Scandal.*

Anne Louise Germaine Necker, Baronne de Staël-Holstein
1766-1817

French critic, novelist, historian, and playwright. The following entry presents recent criticism of de Staël. For further discussion of de Staël's life and career, see *NCLC*, Volume 3.

INTRODUCTION

Madame de Staël is credited with infusing the theories of Romanticism into French literary and political thought. Her belief that critical judgment is relative and based on a sense of history sharply altered French literary attitudes of her time. In her *De la littérature considérée dans ses rapports avec les institutions sociales* (1800; *The Influence of Literature upon Society*), de Staël delineated the distinction between the classical literature of southern Europe, and northern Europe's Romantic literature. Though her fiction, including the novels *Delphine* (1802) and *Corinne; ou, L'Italie* (1807; *Corinne; or, Italy*), has attracted the attention of modern scholars, it is generally considered to be secondary to her historical and critical works, which influenced a generation of writers.

BIOGRAPHICAL INFORMATION

The daughter of Louis XVI's minister of finance, de Staël was raised in Paris. Her intellectual interests were encouraged by her parents, whose literary salon included such notables as Edward Gibbon, Denis Diderot, and Friedrich Grimm. She was married in 1786 to the Swedish ambassador in Paris, Eric de Staël-Holstein. Though de Staël had begun to write at fifteen, it was not until she published *Lettres sur les ouvrages et le caractère de J. J. Rousseau* (1788; *Letters on the Works and Character of J. J. Rousseau*) that she became known as a theorist. Published just before the outbreak of the French Revolution, the book advocated liberal thinking and the ideas of the Enlightenment as antidotes to the growing political crisis. During the revolution, her husband's political immunity enabled de Staël to remain in France and arrange for the escape of numerous refugees. Ultimately, however, she was forced to flee to Switzerland. Upon her return to Paris in 1797, de Staël began what many critics consider to be the most brilliant segment of her career. She published several important political and literary essays, notably *De l'influence des passions sur le bonheur des individus et des nations* (1796; *A Treatise on the Influence of the Passions upon the Happiness of Individuals and Nations*).

During this time she met the French painter and author Benjamin Constant, who became one of her lovers and exposed de Staël to the German philosophy that influenced this and other works. Outspoken in politics, de Staël provoked the ire of Napoleon, who viewed her as a personal enemy; when she formed a liberal opposition to his political aims, he banished her to Switzerland in 1803. During this time she established a well-known coterie of writers and intellectuals at Coppet, wrote two novels, and produced *De l'Allemagne* (1810; *Germany*). Napoleon found *De l'Allemagne* subversive, and ordered its proof sheets to be destroyed. By 1812, finding that she was no longer safe in Switzerland, de Staël fled across Europe, eventually retreating to England. Napoleon's abdication in March of 1813 allowed her to return home; she spent the remainder of her life in Paris and Coppet.

MAJOR WORKS

Among De Staël's earliest mature works are several dramas, notably *Jane Grey, tragédie en cinq actes et en vers* (1790) concerning the Englishwoman who chose death rather than recant her beliefs. The essays of *Lettres sur les ouvrages et le caractère de J. J. Rousseau* attest to the profound influence of Rousseau's writing and thought on de Staël, and contain analyses of his novels and political works, as well as an assessment of his life. *De l'influence des passions sur le bonheur des individus et des nations* considers such topics as passionate love, ambition, vanity, friendship, and religion. In *Essai sur les fictions* (1795), de Staël champions the novel as a legitimate literary genre. This work also suggests some of the ideas de Staël was to explore more fully in *The Influence of Literature upon Society,* which states that a literary work must reflect the moral and historical reality, the *Zeitgeist,* of the country in which it is created. The epistolary novel *Delphine* follows an intricate plot as it confronts the multitude of social problems faced by women in the early nineteenth century. Part travelogue and part romantic novel *Corinne* features the ill-fated affair of its heroine Corinne, a poet of genius, and Oswald, a young Englishman traveling through Italy. *De l'Allemagne* offers a study of the *Sturm und Drang* movement and a discussion of German Idealism, particularly the philosophy of Immanuel Kant. *Dix années d'exil* (1818; Ten Years' Exile) is de Staël's memoir of the years 1803 to 1813.

CRITICAL RECEPTION

An influential literary and political figure in the late eighteenth and early nineteenth centuries, de Staël has been associated with the hegemony of Romantic thought during this period. Critics have noted that the clarity and objectivity of de Staël's literary theories greatly influenced writers to follow, notably Charles Augustin Sainte-Beuve and Victor Hugo. Commentators have also acknowledged that she awakened an interest in foreign literature in France and sought to transform the aging spirit of classicism into the new currents of Romanticism. Additionally, she has been viewed as an early and outstanding proponent of feminism. Thus, while scholars have tended to privilege de Staël's criticism over her fictional works, contemporary interest in the novels *Delphine* and *Corinne* as significant feminist texts has remained strong.

PRINCIPAL WORKS

Lettres sur les ouvrages et le caractère de J. J. Rousseau [*Letters on the Works and Character of J. J. Rousseau*] (essays) 1788

Jane Grey, tragédie en cinq actes et en vers (verse drama) 1790

*Recueil de morceaux détachés (essays and novels) 1795

De l'influence des passions sur le bonheur des individus et des nations [*A Treatise on the Influence of the Passions upon the Happiness of Individuals and Nations*] (essays) 1796

De la littérature considérée dans ses rapports avec les institutions sociales [*A Treatise on Ancient and Modern Literature,* also published as *The Influence of Literature upon Society*] (criticism) 1800

Delphine [*Delphine*] (novel) 1802

Corinne; ou, L'Italie [*Corinne; or, Italy*] (novel) 1807

De l'Allemagne. 3 vols. [*Germany*] (history and criticism) 1810

Réflexions sur le suicide (essay) 1813

Considérations sur les principaux événements française. 3 vols. (criticism) 1818

Dix années d'exil [*Ten Years' Exile; or, Memoirs of That Interesting Period of the Life of the Baroness the Staël Holstein, Written by Herself*] (memoirs) 1818

Oeuvres complètes de Mme la Baronne de Staël. 17 vols. (novels, essays, criticism, and memoirs) 1820-21

Des circonstances actuelles qui peuvent terminer la Révolution et des principes qui doivent fonder la république en France (essay) 1906

Madame de Staël on Politics, National Character (essays) 1964

*Contains *Epître au malheur; Essai sur les fictions; Trois nouvelles: Mirza, ou Lettre d'un voyageur, Adelaïde et Théodore, Histoire de Pauline.*

CRITICISM

Noreen J. Swallow (essay date 1981)

SOURCE: "Portraits: A Feminist Appraisal of Mme de Staël's *Delphine*," in *Atlantis,* Vol. 7, No. 1, Fall, 1981, pp. 65-76.

[*In the following essay, Swallow assesses* Delphine *as it depicts "the oppressive effects of patriarchal hegemony."*]

Madame de Staël has suffered from superficial and fallacious criticism disposed to dismiss her novels as clumsy, dated romans à clef. Certainly there are weaknesses in Staël's writing—she is, for example, annoyingly prone to prolixity and repetition—but her contribution as a writer of fiction has been unduly minimized, especially by critics prepared to see no more in Staëlien theme and characterization than hysterical retaliation and posturing self-pity. Approached thus, her two major works of fiction, ***Delphine*** and ***Corinne,*** become mere outbursts of self-dramatization, their many characters reduced to vindictive portrayals of resented relatives and out-of-favour lovers.[1] And such criticism assumes that, the novels' sensational value having inevitably declined, ***Delphine*** and ***Corinne*** lack both merit and interest and may, with justification, be relegated to fictional limbo.

In spite of such dismissal, Mme de Staël's heroines have maintained a curiosity value as contemporaries of melancholy loners like Oberman and René.[2] And in recent years there has been renewed interest in *Corinne* for its presentation of the female artist in society.[3] But these approaches, too, have been misguided and inadequate, failing to do the novelist justice. For to identify Delphine and Corinne with neurotic romantic heroes is to diminish their appeal as women and overlook the sexist nature of their conflict. And to concentrate attention on *Corinne* as the portrait of an exceptional female is to disregard Mme de Staël's concerned interest in problems common to all women.[4]

More recently, given careful and sympathetic reading, analyzed intrinsically, and approached in the light of current feminist writing, Staël's fiction has begun to take on significant new life.[5] Indeed, liberated from prejudgement as autobiographical ranting, inferior Chateaubriand or gifted heroinism, the novels emerge as perceptive studies of the destructive effects of entrenched sexist discrimination. This is particularly true of *Delphine,* describing as it does the struggles of a young woman and her friends desperately trying to sort out their lives as female persons in late eighteenth-century Paris society. Though written in 1802, *Delphine* strikes today's reader as uncannily topical in theme and characterization.

Society in the novel is a patriarchal power structure in which state and church work together to foster and protect "traditional values"; that is, as the author emphasizes throughout, to maintain a system of attitudes, laws and customs created and perpetuated by the world of men principally for the pleasure, security and advancement of men. Anticipating modern feminist literature by over one hundred and fifty years, Mme de Staël sets to work to expose these deeply ingrained, chauvinistic values, showing how they operate, often below the level of consciousness, to obstruct the development and fulfillment of women, to undermine relations between the sexes, and to poison the moral outlook of society. Since the era of *Delphine,* woman's subjection to the forces of male superiority has, of course, outwardly diminished. However, because the novel focuses on underlying tendencies which perennially subvert female self-realization, and because sexist attitudes are still at work in society today, Mme de Staël's representation is fascinatingly relevant.

As one would expect, the author makes her most sustained and powerful assault on the destructiveness of male-dominated society through her presentation of the character and fortunes of the heroine, Delphine d'Albémar. Staël adds support to this central attack with descriptions of the characters and careers of a number of women who make up the circle of Delphine's acquaintances—women of varying tastes and capabilities who, far from being unique or superior, are ordinary individuals facing the social pressures of everyday life under a patriarchal regime. Permit-

ted no reality beyond their male-related roles, they live in a world where females are routinely channelled towards lives of service and subservience to men. Should marriage, the approved route to woman's "fulfilment," prove impossible or untenable, retreat to the non-life of a waiting convent is the only condoned alternative. In *Delphine*'s gallery of female portraits we see women trapped in these realities, victimized whether they resist or comply. Nonconformity brings alienation from society and conformity brings alienation from self.

Elise de Lebensei, for example, finds herself ostracized for defying the barbaric custom of arranged marriages enthusiastically promoted under a system of patriarchal tyranny. As Mme de Lebensei succinctly puts it when referring to her early marriage: "Il . . . me demanda, m'obtint . . ."[6] (p. 405) Contrary to custom, however, Elise fought to gain freedom from the misery and frustration of an incompatible union; persevering against masculine threats of violence and financial reprisal, she finally gained deliverance through a Dutch divorce.[7]

Inexorably, as Mme de Staël demonstrates, Elise's entrapment is re-established by French society. Woman's fealty in marriage lasts forever in a system that subordinates female worth to wifely duty, and society in the novel cannot tolerate a woman who throws off the ties of matrimony to seek personal fulfillment. Furthermore, divorced Elise is guilty of the ultimate defiance as "une femme qui s'est remariée pendant que son premier mari vivait encore." (p. 401) Mme de Lebensei must be punished. Ostracism is her lot. Although her second husband is relatively untouched by harassment and continues to function forcefully in the business community, lonely, sequestered Elise pays the price for challenging convention, rejected by friends, family and Church.

Another female who rebels against the limits set for women and incurs the wrath of society, is Mme de R. Separated, childless and in her thirties, Mme de R. attempts to pursue her personal and social life as a kind of swinging single, propelled dizzily "de distractions en distractions" (p. 550) through several indiscreet affairs. Similar conduct in a male might be condoned, even applauded, but Mme de R.'s reputation is soon irreparably damaged. Like Elise she must pay woman's penalty for flouting the rules. In public Mme de R. is snubbed, not only by the ladies, but also by the gentlemen—the very men who may well have pursued her in private. As Delphine observes, ". . . ils veulent, en séduisant les femmes, conserver le droit de les en punir." (p. 383)

In contrast to Mme de R.'s free-wheeling defiance of feminine limits, Mme de Cerlebe's separation is cautiously restrained. Disenchanted with love and marriage (". . . je ne crois point au bonheur de l'amour . . . ," [p. 582]) she quietly moves out, accompanied by the children. Because such action, though discreet, leaves Mme de Cerlebe liable to public attack as a derelict wife, it is followed by her immediate withdrawal into rural seclusion.

Mme de Cerlebe is not able to pursue her new-found independence, however, even in isolation, for society rearranges and re-establishes its hold upon her through the children. Socially conditioned to feel guilty and apprehensive about the uncertainties of single parenthood, separated Mme de Cerlebe over-compensates for marital break-up by compressing her own existence into the narrow confines of meticulous maternity. As she admits to Delphine, "Dans la route du devoir, l'incertitude n'existe plus. . . ." (p. 582) By sacrificing her briefly-revived individuality to the duties of motherhood, Mme de Cerlebe has followed alienation from society with alienation from self.

Obviously ostracism is a common punishment imposed by the conforming establishment upon the rebel who breaks the rules. But it may also be used as self-castigation by a conformist conditioned to see herself as inadequate or remiss. Such is the case of pathetic Thérèse d'Ervins, a young wife processed by society for unquestioning conformity. Wed as a sensitive girl of fourteen to a hard-nosed opportunist twenty-five years her senior, Thérèse is so accustomed to non-existence, to a life shaped by chauvinistic forces in the world of men, that she has in fact lost all sense of her own identity. When, at twenty-four, she falls in love with charming M. de Serbellane, she cannot conceive of her own right to happiness, even after her husband's timely death. On the contrary, overcome by guilt feelings, utterly confused and unable to cope, society's child sentences herself to society's punishment: Thérèse d'Ervins retreats from a self she cannot recognize and a world she scarcely knows to pass the rest of her days in a convent, "immolant sa jeunesse, ensevelissant elle-même sa destinée." (p. 421)

It is the essence of female entrapment as observed by Mme de Staël that those who conform are those most victimized. While outwardly respecting male-oriented convention, women undergo, knowingly or not, an inward form of alienation more crippling than social ostracism—an insidious warping of the soul, often so complete as to eclipse or destroy the victim's natural self. Sophie de Vernon, for example, leads a life of conventional, outward propriety and reaps the rewards of acceptance and acclaim. In fact, hers is an existence that bears testimony to the power of the establishment to pervert and destroy.

Sophie began life with all the attributes of vulnerability: she was orphaned; she was poor; she was female—a gentle, trusting child delivered into the charge of a boorish male relative for whom female children were amusing toys and female adults witless mistresses. When her guardian decides to marry her off to an unprepossessing stranger, Sophie recoils in panic and disgust. But she is powerless to resist. Penniless, haphazardly educated, threatened with the alternative of banishment to a convent, she enters into marriage with a frightened hatred for the forces of power that festers for the rest of her days, albeit hidden beneath a controlled and congenial exterior. For Sophie's defense against the injustice of female oppression is neither outward revolt nor physical retreat; it is cynical conformity. Suppressing all natural feeling, operating with calculated dissimulation, Mme de Vernon cultivates for her own and her daughter's protection a façade of domestic devotion and respectful restraint.

Not until death is imminent does Sophie risk articulating her grievances against a social structure that destroyed her as a person long before the approach of physical death. Bitterly but rationally she explains her views to Delphine:

> Je crus fermement que le sort des femmes les condamnait à la fausseté; je me confirmai dans l'idée conçue dès mon enfance, que j'étais, par mon sexe et par le peu de fortune que je possédais, une malheureuse esclave à qui toutes les ruses étaient permises avec son tyran. (p. 445)

> . . . les femmes étant victimes de toutes les institutions de la société, elles sont dévouées au malheur, si elles s'abandonnent le moins du monde à leurs sentiments, si elles perdent de quelque manière l'empire d'elles-mêmes. (p. 446)

Cynical, deceitful and manipulative, Sophie de Vernon's warped existence is an example of the corruptive power of a society that thrives on the vulnerability of its female victims, insidiously processing them through self-betrayal for the perpetuation of their own oppression.

Mlle d'Albémar, Delphine's unmarried sister-in-law, conforms so completely to society's standards that she both accepts and inflicts her own alienation. Louise's problem stems initially from her lack of physical attractiveness. As a girl, she never knew the capricious attention awarded by men to pretty young faces; as a lonely adult, she refers frequently to her "désavantages naturels." (p. 528) Not able to attract and not expected to want to, Louise accepts the fact that as an ugly "old-maid" she is an unwholesome oddity in the world of men: ". . . j'ai l'extérieur du monde le moins agréable; . . . je ne suis point faite pour inspirer de l'amour . . . Il était ridicule pour moi d'aimer. . . ." (p. 346) Well aware, as she reminds Delphine, that ". . . la société . . . n'a permis qu'un seul bonheur aux femmes, l'amour dans le mariage . . ." (p. 470), Mlle d'Albémar anticipates unhappiness from her out-of-step role as spinster. Indeed, with her singleness a disturbingly unfinished state in the eyes of society, Louise finds that she is increasingly unwanted, her presence an embarrassment to others, as well as to herself. Rather than exist in the world without social dignity, she retires to a distant convent, preferring to live vicariously through beautiful Delphine. In complying with society's value system for women, Mlle d'Albémar has had to betray her innate intelligence and her sense of self-worth, condone her own social rejection and inflict upon herself society's penalty for those who are different—isolation.

Like Louise, Léontine de Ternan accepts society's high evaluation of youthful female beauty. Unlike Louise, Léontine was born pretty. Her looks have brought her marriage, glory as a social decoration, and wide popularity as a flattered booster of male vanity.

But in a society where female youth and beauty are loudly fêted, female middle and old age are equated with loss of worth. Through flashbacks of Léontine de Ternan's life, Mme de Staël touchingly recreates the tragedy of society's beautiful woman who panics and despairs at the fatal touch of decline and death. Staël's character reacts with all the horror that growing old and "unfeminine" holds for a woman who has, with masculine encouragement, staked her existence on sexual attractiveness. Once courted and pursued, now rejected and replaced, Mme de Ternan sums up her life and her dilemma: "J'ai été fort belle, et j'ai cinquante ans. . . ." (p. 575)

Léontine's commitment to masculine praise as the ultimate reality, though superficially and temporarily gratifying, has in the long run brought personal, domestic and social alienation. It has blinded her to her own self-worth, warped her growth as a person, sabotaged her relationship with her family and, finally, provoked her humiliating withdrawal from the system to which she has so completely accommodated. On the verge of breakdown, Léontine de Ternan enters a convent and subsequently takes her vows.

Two of Delphine's acquaintances, Matilde de Vernon and Mme de Mondoville, have been so "successfully" absorbed into the male value system that they are themselves active promoters of the status quo, proud to defend as woman's reality the warping sexist abstractions imposed on society by the world of men. Both women conceive of no raison d'être for female existence beyond the servicing, male-related roles of domesticity, in marriages initiated primarily as business contracts. Protectively cloaked in the social prestige denied rebels like Mme de R. and outsiders like Louise d'Albémar, they seem oblivious to their own want of soul and are prepared to stake their lives and those of their children on the reliable rewards of conformity.

Mme de Staël depicts such women as the bedrock of society, guaranteeing by their actions and their attitudes the continued prosperity of the patriarchal structure. Predictably, these women are appalled and repelled by Delphine's displays of "unfeminine" assertiveness. Matilde speaks for both of them when she cautions the heroine: ". . . vous prenez une mauvaise route, soit pour votre bonheur intérieur, soit pour votre considération dans le monde." (p. 339)

Like other non-conformists in the novel, Delphine d'Albémar finds herself attacked and alienated when her attempts at self-expression offend the conventions of female behaviour established and sanctified by the collective forces of society. Delphine is assaulted on two fronts: through Léonce de Mondoville, her intimate and peer, and through her moral inferiors in the social set—people like small-minded Mme du Marset and gossipy M. de Fierville. The heroine's inferiors arm themselves for the attack with society's weapons—slander, cruelty, sexism, fraud—all wielded in the guise of moral and religious authority against the woman whose assertive self defies the dictates of convention and threatens society's existence. Wounded externally by the onslaught of her inferiors and weakened internally through her love for rigidly conformist Léonce, the heroine is doomed to destruction.

Delphine has, from early childhood, been propelled toward the role of misfit in a man's world. An orphan, she was raised in the country by elderly, eccentric M. d'Albémar—first her indulgent guardian and then, in name only, her solicitous husband. The recipient, according to acerbic Sophie de Vernon, of "une éducation à la fois toute philosophique et toute romanesque" (p. 351), Delphine has grown up with the aura of a creature from a better world. She is "notre angélique Delphine" (p. 527) to her friends, and newly-smitten Léonce de Mondoville feels that ". . . elle respire ce qui est bien, comme un air pur, comme le seul dans lequel son âme généreuse puisse vivre." (p. 370) Celestial analogy is reinforced by the heroine's lack of human "roots." No mention is made of her antecedents; nothing is recalled of her infancy. Consequently, no intervention of family background or patriarchal heritage colours the purity of the character's presentation; nor does it dull the freshness of her emergence into reality when, newly widowed, she moves from the quiet security of rural seclusion into the conflict and hustle of Paris life. In fact, at twenty years of age, Delphine is Rousseau's newborn babe entering the world with loving, generous and trusting heart, her full-blown sensibility vulnerable to the onslaught of self-serving society. That Delphine's innocence is not accompanied by unsureness or fear is attributable, paradoxically, to the insulated cocoon of her pastoral upbringing, an idyllic existence that has served as a liberating force, permitting and encouraging her to follow proudly the promptings of her own heart: ". . . c'est de mon Dieu et de mon propre coeur que je fais dépendre ma conduite." (p. 362) Furthermore, because M. d'Albémar married her only to ensure her inheritance, Delphine emerges into life not only young, self-confident and beautiful, but financially independent ("indépendante par ma situation et ma fortune" [p. 519]).

Therein lie the seeds of conflict, and therein lies the force of Mme de Staël's presentation. Orphaned, widowed, without male relatives or friends, lacking a male-related female model on which to pattern herself, personally free, therefore, from the dictates of patriarchal authority, Delphine moves naïvely into a patriarchal system with its established values and conventions. How will the heroine, confidently expecting to put her moral and financial freedom into practice, cope with the restraints of male prejudice? How will she react upon encountering the divergence between ideal and real? If she follows her personal credo: "Je ne suis rien, si je ne puis être moi" (p. 585), conflict is certain. And because she is female, defeat at the hands of society is highly likely.

The chauvinistic establishment into which the heroine moves is represented by male relatives and friends of the women who appear in Staël's gallery of portraits, men who, however weak or insignificant as individuals, possess and project an acknowledged social identity as citizens, workers and heads of households. By virtue of power and prestige based on recognized legal, educational and economic foundations, such men are, in their relations with women, lords and masters, entitled by their superiority to be exactors of service and receivers of sacrifice. Accordingly, Staël's men purchase child-brides, own wives and pursue mistresses. But while relatively free to seek their pleasures within the framework of male-oriented convention (". . . ayant fait les lois, les hommes sont les maîtres de les interpréter ou de les braver" [p. 430]), men are also touchy defenders of name and honour, neurotically preoccupied with externals. Of great importance to male characters in **Delphine,** therefore, is the public image of their women—fiancées and wives whose finest function in the eyes of society is to appear beautiful, dutiful and virtuous, a credit to their owners and an enhancement to the family name.

Léonce de Mondoville, Delphine's love and the principal male character in the novel, is the product and the advocate of the patriarchal system. In the ultra-conventional Mondoville family, a man's name is of the highest importance, public opinion is a supreme force, and visible identification with that which is unconventional or scandalous is to be avoided at all costs. On the public stage (but within the broad context of masculine privilege) a Mondoville performs not only for general acceptance, but preferably for admiring approbation. These are the principles that have molded young Léonce, inducing him to suppress his natural sensibility (an unpredictable, "feminine" quality) and encouraging him, through constant surveillance, to cultivate for himself and to demand in a prospective spouse an image of admirable and irreproachable correctness. These are the standards that, as a superior male, he confidently expects to bring to bear on spontaneous Delphine: ". . . elle soumettra, j'en suis sûr, ses actions à mes désirs . . ." (p. 376) Tragically, in the process of asserting his masculine values, Léonce belittles Delphine as a person, fractures an inherently harmonious union and precipitates the heroine's untimely demise.

Delphine d'Albémar is not the first woman destined for Léonce. Before the novel begins, the hero has committed himself to the imminent reality of an acceptable, arranged marriage, common practice when female suitability is a prime requisite for matrimony, and engagements are more often decided by money, appearance and reputation than by love. Designated as bride-to-be is Delphine's pious cousin, Matilde de Vernon, a brittle beauty whom Léonce has never seen, but whose qualifications are vouched for by his family. Before the wedding plans are finalized, however, Léonce and widowed Delphine meet for the first time and are overwhelmed by mutual attraction and the delicate sensibility they have in common: "Ah! nos âmes avaient été créées l'une pour l'autre . . ." (p. 567) Although Léonce aims almost immediately at halting his proposed union with Matilde so that he may marry Del-

phine, he does not abandon his instilled priorities. On the contrary, fascinated by the charm, goodness and sensitivity of Delphine (". . . elle n'attache du prix qu'à plaire et à être aimée" [p. 386]), Léonce envisages her as the perfect wife for him to possess: a woman whose many qualities may be directed toward delightful enhancement of the Mondoville image and, as a marvellous "plus," a loving spouse promising the private bliss of physical compatibility and a touching union of souls. It is, regardless of the excitement of mutual attraction, a conventional vision, with emphasis on Delphine's role as an enlargement of her husband's self-image and an extension of the Mondoville identity. Writing to his mother of Delphine's appropriateness, Léonce assures her, ". . . que n'obtiendrai-je donc pas d'elle, et pour vous, et pour moi." (p. 386)

As their romance continues and Léonce's "idea" of Delphine meshes more and more with his cherished "idea" of self and family, Delphine the person is pushed increasingly aside, her beautiful soul superseded by her beautiful image. Naturally, as a Mondoville acquisition she is expected to parade her dream-come-true perfection in the public arena for general viewing, thereby flattering Léonce's social vanity and augmenting his pride in himself and his name. Certainly Léonce places high value on the heroine as a precious, fascinating object, a possession a man may be proud of, may display with a heady mixture of jealousy and exhilaration. Describing Delphine dancing at a party before the assembled guests, Mondoville reports excitedly, "Les hommes et les femmes montèrent sur les bancs pour voir danser Delphine; je sentis mon coeur battre avec une grande violence quand tous les yeux se tournèrent sur elle . . ." (p. 377) But while social accomplishments like beautiful dancing and sparkling conversation may be encouraged by man for his woman, acting on her own decisions is not. Increasingly concerned that Delphine's assertive sensibility, admittedly a positive force and quite charming in private, may nevertheless prove publicly embarrassing, Léonce craves a Delphine without the risks of independent action. When, inevitably, his "intended" acts on her own in a non-conforming way, asserting herself as a free person, as subject rather than object, Léonce is confused and angry.

Such is the case early in their relationship when the heroine conspicuously crosses the floor at a court function to sit with tearful, ostracized Mme de R.—a defiant act that antagonizes society and embarrasses Léonce. When vindictive gossips hint that Delphine shares Mme de R.'s promiscuous lifestyle, thin-skinned Léonce sinks into credulous despair, racked by fears for the Mondoville name. Delphine's explanation that she acted "par un mouvement de pitié tout à fait irréfléchi" (p. 384) gives shaky comfort to the man whose self-centered scale of values is clearly revealed in a subsequent admonition: ". . . soyez plus fière que sensible, quand il s'agit de la réputation de votre ami." (p. 523)

Léonce's egotistic apprehensions are justified, for Delphine continues sympathetically helping those in need, regardless of risk to her own reputation. She is dismayed to find, however, that she now hesitates before acting, increasingly aware of Léonce's reputation and disturbed by fears of the young man's disapproval ("la crainte de déplaire à Léonce, cette crainte toujours présente" [p. 383]).

Delphine's fears are shortly realized. Prompted by pity, she allows unhappily married Thérèse d'Ervins and the latter's admirer, M. de Serbellane, to meet in her home—a move that brings scandal, death and charges of immorality against Delphine. Léonce is traumatized; in a rage of anger, jealousy and self-pity he abandons Delphine, and rushes vengefully into marriage with arid but untarnished Matilde.

Léonce's hasty marriage, with its bitter aftermath, points up the nefarious potential of a social structure built on male privilege. Favoured by virtue of his sex with a superior role as arbiter of female destinies, and protected by a system that encourages him to capitalize on his own weaknesses, vain and vacillating Léonce is able to move selfishly from Matilde to Delphine, to Matilde, to exonerated Delphine, adversely affecting the lives of both women. Through the arrogant imposition of Léonce's will both Matilde and Delphine are devalued as individuals, a fulfilling relationship between Léonce and either woman is rendered impossible, and Delphine begins her tragic decline into disillusionment and death. At the same time, the hero initiates his own descent from the proud heights of private impeccability, shamelessly preying now on the virtues of his female inferiors.

Nowhere is Léonce's egocentricity more apparent than in his post-marriage pursuit of the recently absolved heroine. As Matilde's husband doggedly pushes for re-establishment of a relationship with Delphine, he manoeuvres the lives of both women in a display of male egotism appalling for its frank denigration of female worth. Smugly Matilde is dismissed with distaste and Delphine tempted with flattery: "Songez quel est mon supplice . . . renfermé dans ma maison, avec une femme qui a pris ta place" (p. 460); presumptuously the heroine is pressed for discreet tête-à-tête, to be arranged "sans jamais causer la moindre peine à Matilde." (p. 468) Resorting to specious logic, reproach, self-pity and plain threat, Léonce in fact urges Delphine to become his mistress—the man who had required of Delphine-as-fiancée that she live up to his and society's most demanding expectations now using every ploy to prevent her from doing so. Dismissing as irrelevant the gods of tradition, conformity and opinion (". . . oublie tout ce qui n'est pas nous; . . . anéantissons l'univers dans notre pensée, et soyons heureux" (p. 461), Léonce calculatingly assures Delphine that ". . . rien de pareil à notre situation ne s'est encore rencontré; . . . devant ton Dieu, nous sommes libres." (p. 460) Cunningly Delphine's own sensibility is used against her: "Je ne te reconnais pas, mon amie; tu permets à tes idées sur la vertu d'altérer ton caractère: prends garde, tu vas l'endurcir . . ." (p. 461) Ruthlessly the reluctant heroine has thrust upon her full responsibility for Léonce's own life and for Matilde's

well-being: ". . . me croyez-vous si loin de la mort . . ." (p. 460); ". . . savez-vous qui souffrira de ma douleur? Matilde, oui, Matilde, à qui vous me sacrifiez." (p. 463) With the ultimate in male arrogance, Delphine—spurned as wife, pursued as mistress—is reminded: ". . . il faut que tu renonces pour moi à l'existence que je ne puis te promettre dans le monde. . . . Mais, j'en suis sûr, tu me feras volontiers ce sacrifice . . ." (p. 457)

Finally coerced into seeing Léonce on a regular basis after he has stationed himself in front of her galloping horses threatening suicide, Delphine makes every effort to remain "virtuous." But she must constantly check the increasing demands of her aspiring lover, his pregnant young wife forgotten and all but deserted.

Through Delphine's renewed involvement with Léonce, Staël shows how society accepts (and expects) from a man behaviour that it savagely condemns in a female, even when the woman is a victim of circumstance—or of circumstantial evidence. Predictably, Delphine's liaison with Léonce swells the undercurrents of gossip long directed against her independent behaviour, until they burst forth. When Léonce attacks M. de Valorbe outside Delphine's home at one in the morning, it is Delphine who is publicly condemned. Accused of brazenly juggling late-night assignations with two lovers—one a married man with a saintly young wife—the innocent heroine is confronted by Matilde, sneered at by the gossips and publicly snubbed. Notwithstanding, she visits unhappy Valorbe in his room, not reappearing for several hours. Her reputation now in shreds, Delphine knows she is the victim of society's accepted double standard: as a man, Léonce may with impunity dabble in adultery; as a man, Valorbe may without reproach detain a woman in his room; but as a woman accused of having loose morals, Delphine d'Albémar is ruined. In fact, Delphine is destroyed for not sufficiently controlling appearances, even when she has nothing to hide. Fearing Léonce's wrath, and totally disillusioned with the injustices of patriarchal reality, Delphine commits herself to the seclusion of a Swiss convent, agreeing to take her vows: "Qu'est-ce donc que je sacrifie? une liberté dont je ne puis faire aucun usage . . ." (p. 594)

In being shunned by society, accepting exile and betraying her conscience by taking the veil, Delphine becomes yet another victim of a social structure that preys on and is nourished by vulnerability, a structure openly committed to the exploitation of its traditionally most vulnerable element—the female. Although Delphine's flight to the non-life of a convent removes her from exposure to overt daily exploitation, it represents, as she despairingly realizes, her acceptance of the ultimate in suppression—total passivity, a prelude to physical death as annihilation of the heroine's assertive self.

Mme de Staël has documented Delphine's pathetic descent from the pre-Léonce, halcyon days of liberated vitality, through the Léonce-dominated era of anguished ambivalence, to the painful resignation of passivity and approaching death. That Delphine in her vigour should have been susceptible to such mutation is attributable to a particular aspect of her refined sensibility, to the "flaw" that did indeed bring tragedy—her urge for an intimate human relationship, for a soul-mate. Sophie de Vernon answered the need to some extent as friend, but when critically wounded Léonce appeared on the scene—handsome, sensitive and in need of tender care—Delphine fell into romantic love, fantasizing him as the perfect mate, a superior being to serve and cherish, her key to domestic bliss. The enraptured heroine began viewing herself in relation to Léonce, and felt thrillingly humbled by his socially bestowed superiority: ". . . je jouis de me sentir inférieure à lui." (p. 489) In a flight of fancy she enthused to Louise d'Albémar, "Il me semble que je suis née pour lui obéir autant que pour l'adorer . . ." (p. 490); and in her imagination Léonce became the symbol of life itself: "Je ne suis rien que par Léonce . . ." (p. 628)

Crushed by Léonce's betrayal and the perverseness of his union with a woman he did not love, Delphine declined rapidly. Her agony was aggravated by the realization that however passionately the young man was attracted to her, his real "love" was not for a woman, but for a concept—the Mondoville image. So that, even if he were again free to do so, Léonce could not bring himself to marry discredited Delphine. Eventually Delphine acknowledges Léonce's frailties, but having once committed her love to him, having once confirmed their communion of souls on which, as a woman of sensibility, she places the highest value, the heroine is pathetically ensnared. Desperately she has tried to compensate in her imagination for the revealed Léonce, actually willing herself to inferiority and dependence: "Léonce, que ferais-je seule? . . . je ne puis rien pour moi-même. . . ." (p. 625) Such self-abasement is fatal, even when interpreted ideally as an act of will.

Tragically, commitment to Léonce has brought Delphine not wholeness, but fragmentation: "J'étais d'accord avec moi-même autrefois . . ." (p. 488); not confirmation of self but its diminution: ". . . je n'ai point de confiance en mes propres forces . . ." (p. 625) Instead of continuing to look within herself for her identity, she has looked for it in Léonce's distorted gaze ("Léonce, Léonce! est-il donc devenu ma conscience . . ." [p. 380]) and her agonized awareness of such alienation of self is articulated in a terse but moving reproach to Mondoville: ". . . je souffre pour mériter votre estime . . ." (p. 464) By the time she enters the convent, sliding into inertia, Delphine d'Albémar is not far from death.

But retreat brings only temporary respite from outside intervention, for Léonce—his wife and infant son both dead—appears suddenly at the convent, threatening suicide now that Delphine is no longer available. He is dissuaded from death only when Delphine agrees to renounce her vows and run away with him. However, in the midst of flight and increasingly vague talk about marriage, Léonce deserts the heroine, tormented by thoughts of public condemnation of his intent to marry a *religieuse*. Mon-

doville is located in Verdun where, though not actually a member of the émigré forces, he has been made prisoner and condemned to death. Just before Léonce is shot, Delphine takes poison and dies.[8]

From a moral point of view death is the only solution for Delphine d'Albémar in a society where virtue goes unrewarded and love does not triumph. In feminist terms, Delphine's death is complete suppression, the total eradication of a woman of intelligence and sensitivity whose qualities have been constantly devalued and whose potential has been destroyed. It is the establishment's final triumph. Significantly, Léonce perishes too, suggesting that Staël's heroine is victim of a system that, in its self-satisfied commitment to male prerogative, in effect betrays both sexes. By systematically undermining the strengths of the female and openly serving the weaknesses of the male, the patriarchal system in ***Delphine*** sabotages women, men, marriage and society.

With Delphine's shattered portrait rounding out Staël's gallery of oppressed women, one might well ask if there are no undiminished females in the novel. Hidden among the persecuted wives, lonely outsiders and warped conformists is there no portrait of a female fulfilled? Is there no woman enjoying even the socially approved paradise of "l'amour dans le mariage?" (p. 471) Mme de Staël does indeed include such a portrait—that of Mme de Belmont.

The de Belmonts appear to be the perfect family unit: mother, father and two children living together in love and admiration, rejoicing in one another's company, leading an idyllic existence in a country cottage where all is harmony and joy. The key to their domestic bliss is, along with the competent involvement of Mme de Belmont, the complete devotion of M. de Belmont to his wife and family. There is, however, an ironic twist: M. de Belmont is blind. Dependent on the eyes, arm and voice of his wife, unable to function without her, he has no duties or distractions in the outside world, traditional purlieu of male endeavour; on the contrary, as he explains to Delphine, home is life and ". . . tout mon être est concentré dans le sentiment . . ." (p. 483)

Indeed, the de Belmont household challenges the cultural definition of "husband" and "wife"; cut off from the socially imposed, masculine image of self-seeking lord and master, handicapped, impecunious M. de Belmont blends effortlessly into the traditionally female scene, into the *sensible* atmosphere of domesticity. At the same time, his wife, though largely disinherited for her undesirable marriage, begins to emerge as an individual, secure in the knowledge that her presence and her small annuity are vital to the welfare of husband and family. In society's eyes, of course, a man without economic status and the woman who is his equal or superior are both inferior to the masculine ideal promoted in and by that society. Because in the "real" world the de Belmonts would be made to suffer the rejection of pity or derision, it is indeed fortunate that they enjoy country life.

As the result of an asocial reshuffling of male and female roles and the creation of a self-contained utopia in physical and psychological isolation from the status quo, Mme de Belmont's happiness is hardly a tribute to convention. Indeed, the obvious irony of Mme de Staël's "de Belmont solution" to sexism—fulfillment through mutilation and segregation—underscores the hopelessness of woman's lot within the patriarchal system. Self-realization with an un-crippled mate in a social setting seems a reasonable expectation. Yet to function "normally" in the system a woman must betray herself and her sex by accepting values that belittle, restrict and victimize the female. To demur is to condemn oneself to excommunication. Delphine d'Albémar resisted and perished. Her creator was exiled.

While the action of **Delphine** is necessarily played out in the context of a patriarchal structure with masculine values permeating the scene, and while there are constant references in letters and conversations to husbands, guardians and male relatives, comparatively few men perform up front. Léonce, M. de Serbellane, Henri de Lebensei and M. de Valorbe are the principal male characters, while standard male social types such as doctors, tutors, soldiers, priests and valets form a backdrop. In **Delphine** it is, fittingly, the female characters who appear in the foreground. It is the women in the novel who come across as three-dimensional and who, although socially defined in terms of their male-related roles, are portrayed as individuals in relation one to another, and in their own right.

Infancy, childhood, youth, mid-life, old-age; daughter, fiancée, wife, mother; spinster, mistress, widow, nun—the novel is a striking collection of female portraits, testifying to the author's interest in and concern for woman's oppressed state in a sexist society. Anticipating modern feminism by almost two hundred years, Mme de Staël clearly recognized that the key to female oppression lay in the self-perpetuating nature of the tradition, as she observed women like Delphine and her friends caught up in the double bind of powerlessness victimized by power, and power sustained and nurtured by the powerless. The novel **Delphine** is a dramatization of that fact, a fact that Staël had noted two years earlier when writing on women in **De la littérature:**

> . . . si elles veulent acquérir de l'ascendant, on leur fait un crime d'un pouvoir que les lois ne leur ont pas donné; si elles restent esclaves, on opprime leur destinée. (Seconde partie, chapitre IV)[9]

Notes

1. The following statement is typical: ". . . in *Delphine,* Madame de Staël took her revenge on Talleyrand and portrayed him in the character of Madame de Vernon. . . ." J. Christopher Herold, *Mistress to an Age* (New York: Bobbs-Merril, 1958), p. 93.

   Corinne's British hero, Oswald, Lord Nelvil, has been variously identified as Benjamin Constant, Prosper de Barante, Vincenzo Monti, Dom Pedro de Souza e Holstein, Lord John Campbell, le chevalier de Pange and Edward Gibbon.

2. Chateaubriand's *René* first appeared in April, 1802; *Delphine* in December, 1802; Senancour's *Oberman* in 1804; *Corinne* in 1807.

3. See "Performing Heroinism: The Myth of *Corinne,*" Ellen Moers, *Literary Women* (New York: Anchor Press, 1977), pp. 263-319.

4. Exclusive emphasis on Corinne-as-genius or Delphine-as-paragon leads to faulty generalisations like the following: "Madame de Staël believed in the rights of the exceptional individual but was quite uninterested in the condition of the majority." Claire Tomalin, *The Life and Death of Mary Wollstonecraft* (New York: Mentor, 1976), p. 153.

5. See Madelyn Gutwirth, *Madame de Staël, Novelist: The Emergence of the Artist as Woman* (Urbana: University of Illinois Press, 1978).

6. All references to *Delphine* are to Volume I of the *Oeuvres complètes de Madame la baronne de Staël-Holstein* (3 Vols.; Paris, 1861; rpt. Genève: Slatkine, 1967).

7. Elise obtained her divorce in Holland in the mid 1780's. Henri de Lebensei, eloquently promoting divorce for France in a letter to Delphine dated September 2, 1791, states that ". . . le divorce doit être décrété dans un mois par l'assemblée constituante . . ." (p. 531) By 1792 a law establishing divorce had been passed.

8. Sensitive to criticism that she advocated suicide, Mme de Staël wrote a revised ending which appeared in the 1820 edition of her complete works: emotionally exhausted and physically frail after her sojourn in the convent, Delphine declines further at evidence of Léonce's mounting reluctance to wed a *religieuse.* Decline leads to death. A month after Delphine's demise, Léonce is killed in action in the Vendée.

9. Mme de Staël, Vol. I, p. 301.

Madelyn Gutwirth (essay date 1985)

SOURCE: "Forging a Vocation: Germaine de Staël on Fiction, Power, and Passion," in *Bulletin of Research in the Humanities,* Vol. 86, No. 3, 1983-1985, pp. 242-54.

[In the following essay, Gutwirth analyzes de Staël's views on love, passion, and ambition as expressed in De l'influence des passions.*]*

> *Quelle époque ai-je choisie pour faire un traité sur le bonheur des individus et des nations!* (What an age I have chosen to write a treatise on the happiness of individuals and nations!)
>
> —STAËL *De l'influence des passions* . . . Introduction

"Marat," wrote Germaine de Staël in her account of the French Revolution, "was using his newspaper day after day [in the summer of 1792] to threaten the royal family and its defenders with the most atrocious of tortures. Never had one witnessed a human tongue so denatured; the roaring of wild beasts could have been translated into the language he used."[1]

Daughter of Jacques Necker, the ill-starred last pre-revolutionary prime minister of Louis XVI, Germaine Necker had made her entry into society both at Versailles—under the sway of courtly manners and traditions—and at home in the salon of her mother Suzanne Necker—under the aegis of the Enlightenment's radical if sometimes archly ornamented interrogation of those traditions. Her eager and precocious intelligence had first fed principally upon literature, but her father's earlier spell as Finance Minister and her subsequent marriage to the Swedish ambassador to Louis' court had awakened her increasingly to questions of government. Already a deeply engaged observer of the Revolution from its earliest stages, by 1792, at twenty-six years of age, she was also the author of several fictions and of an ambitious volume of essays on Rousseau. Now she maintained a distinguished and political salon where people of diverse tendencies gathered for conversation, and most of the guests professed to admire their hostess's sagacity, wit—and advocacy of rational political policies. In her emotional life, however, reason had not prevailed: she had suffered great affective upheaval as she pursued an ostentatious liaison with her lover the Comte de Narbonne, an affair which made her an object both of public ridicule and of maternal censure.

The omens, like Marat's summonses to slaughter, that preceded the Reign of Terror were therefore deeply disquieting to Germaine de Staël. If the lives of the monarchs, whose right to exist she still defended, were so clearly menaced, so was the possibility for rational discourse or for any pacific constitutional resolution. So, too, was the very world where she had loved and struggled threatened with extinction by the unleashing of a typhoon of human passion.

If she had already conceived the idea of writing her essays *Concerning the Influence of the Passions upon the Happiness of Individuals and of Nations,* in the Paris of 1792 the daily threats of exile, imprisonment, summary trial, and execution—to her friends and acquaintances as well as to herself—would have prevented her from concentrating on such meditative labors. After narrowly escaping assassination in the Place de Grève, she fled to her father's home in Coppet, Switzerland, in September of that year, and in November she gave birth to her second son. By December she would be restlessly off again, eventually stopping in England where she joined Narbonne. It was there, at Juniper Hall in Surrey early in 1793, that she began to concentrate in earnest upon her interrupted treatise; after her return to Coppet in May her work was again pre-empted by sentimental and political events, as the full force of the Reign of Terror battered and tore at France and a new lover presented her with a conflict between loyalty and desire. She understandably turned her back on both politics and passion to write her *Essay on Fiction*

(*Essai sur les fictions*), published in 1795, a work which exhibits some striking contrasts in tone with the *Passions,* even as it skirts some of the same themes. Only after she had finished this essay did she return to the *Passions,* completing that labored and tortured work in 1795. It in turn would be published in 1796, her thirtieth year.[2]

Written in exile, these two texts bear the marks of her personal disarray as well as that of her nation: the political rejection of the father she idolized; her abandonment by Narbonne, the lover whose career she had so shamelessly fostered and who had fathered her two sons; her brief but intense love affair, in the wake of Narbonne's defection, with the Swedish political exile Adolph Ribbing von Leuven; the collapse of the ideal of constitutional monarchy to which she had been so passionately committed; the disintegration not merely of civic order but of all the civilized forms of discourse and manners that had given structure to the values sustaining that order.

These are works that intuit rather than fully grasp the measure of this collapse, and that seek, picking among the cinders, those few glowing brands out of which to light the new fires needed to sustain life. They illustrate, page by page, a nostalgic hearkening back to past certainties and a candid sense of being unmoored, rudderless before the tide of human unreason. Emerging throughout, not unexpectedly, are the themes of power and its uses, of the just allocation of energies to public and private spheres, of the avoidance of pain, and, always, of the problematics of woman's love and ambition. The fascination of these texts lies in their daringly open, exhibitionistic probing of the female self and its responses to the range of the passions. Amidst the flow of apparent endorsement of conventional positions, it is in the places where Staël unmoors herself that she displays her courageous mobility and shows us shafts of keen brightness. To paraphrase the words of Luce Irigaray, she dares here to let us see what she is becoming, even as she clings to "what she could have been, might be."[3] For like her contemporary Rahel Varnhagen, whose complex attitudes concerning her identity have been so probingly explored by Hannah Arendt, Germaine de Staël in these works exhibits the stages of triumph over her "eternal dissembling," her "being reasonable," her "yielding . . . and swallowing her own insights."[4] Staël adopts the first person, speaking, as a woman, with candid openness of the love which overwhelms her and of the power for which she longs but to which she is denied access. An autobiographical, perhaps even a self-therapeutic project is in progress here.

In its very structure, the *Passions* is an exceedingly ambitious work, one in which Staël sought to establish the voice of a serious thinker, a *moraliste* in the tradition of Montaigne, La Rochefoucauld, La Bruyère, or Chamfort. Yet she opens on a confessional note closer to Rousseau's than to any of theirs: "condemned to celebrity but without being truly known, I find the need to allow the public to judge me through my writings. Ceaselessly slandered, I have given in to the hope that in publishing this fruit of my mediations I should be giving some genuine notion . . . of my character" (Introduction).[5] The work is, then, a *réplique* to a fantasized jury, an act of defense, and a counterattack. Here is displayed that quality of *apologia* which distinguishes Staël's writing posture. Her concomitant pose of victim, warranted though it was, since slander against her descended to depths and rose to paroxysms of intensity normally reserved for statesmen and crowned heads,[6] gives her prose a bitter flavor. So undone is she by her plight that she cannot forbear making this explicit plea for understanding which, by virtue of its importunate insistency, has the ironic effect of raising the very barrier between herself and the reader that she is trying to eliminate.

Riddled with intimations of the betrayal of her personal ambition and of her loves as well as deep moral dismay at the parlous times, the **Passions** was originally designed to be presented in two parts, the first an abstract treatment of the effects of passionate impulses on the individual, the second a practical application of her observations to political theory and actual government; but the second part was never published, if indeed it was ever written.[7] Part one, our actual text, is far more extensive than may be suggested by my isolation of the few issues which center on love and ambition.[8] There are three sections: the first consisting of reflections upon glory, ambition, vanity, love, gambling, avarice, drunkenness, envy and vengeance, partisanship, and criminality; the second devoted to those feelings intermediate between passion and self-containment which involve another as well as the self—friendship, filial and conjugal tenderness, and religiosity; the third moving on to the true inner resources that Staël believed could provide a bulwark against the ravages of the passions: philosophy, study, and generosity. It is clear that the trajectory was intended to move one *away* from the horror and confusion of passionate obsession, toward calm, rational joys. Thus the structure of the work is rationalistic, though its execution continually betrays this rational scheme and falls into passionate defense or postures of advocacy for the passions that can only be termed Romantic.

The **Passions** might best be termed the Staëlian "psychology." In her analyses, however, indifferent to consistency she will come full circle: after proclaiming that the passions are a force for sorrow alone, she will end up nonetheless by restoring them (in sorrow) to preeminence. In the process she has managed to set forth her notions concerning human failings and to elaborate her conception of motivation.

Her inner struggle can be glimpsed at once in the fine early Romantic dualism she proposes near the opening of her essay, between the passionate and the unimpassioned. The latter enjoy a tranquility, she writes, whose base is "the certainty of never being agitated or dominated by any feeling stronger than self-love" (Introduction). She cannot really find much to admire in such people; for her rising Rousseauist generation these were the cold and soulless *non-engagés*. Yet revolted as she is by such anomie as theirs, she balks at the notion that passion is essential. Although compelled to concede that there *is* something sublime in passion, the motor in us, she admits, of much that is generous and inspired, she nonetheless insists that it is unfavorable to the commonweal, hence basically to be feared. Defining it as an "impulsive force that draws man on independent of his will," she sees passion as a natural impediment both to individual and to social happiness. If a rationalist were to ask her, "Why not direct the passions rather than destroy them?" she would reply, "I am unable to understand how one can direct that which thrives only on domination; there are but two states in man: either he is certain of being master of himself, and in that case he has no passion; or he feels he is ruled by a force within him stronger than himself, in which case he is entirely dependent upon it. . . ." She concludes, "all these treaties one makes with passion are purely imaginary: like all true tyrants, it is either enthroned or in chains" (Introduction).

This all-or-nothing formulation reflects the nascent Romantic ethos as well as Germaine de Staël's personal truth. Although she will often encourage sanity and moderation in her arguments, she can be no true apostle of any cult of sobriety. As she wrote this essay she was well aware to what extent those passions that had dominated her could be destructive to herself and to others. The passions, however alluring, had themselves to be destroyed—by writing them out of existence. Such is the overt design. The passions, however, are not so easily read out of court.

A detailed discussion of the passions follows this curiously disorienting prelude. Dominating the first section is Staël's treatment of the quest for *gloire*.[9] So high is it on her own pyramid of value that she will revert to it several times. The search for glory, she tells us, can never be appeased by ephemeral celebrity: it is rather to "the world and to posterity" that we look "to ratify the gift of so august a crown; it must therefore be bestowed only for genius or for virtue" (I i). Of the literary genius for which she later professes so much admiration, in the **Fictions,** she speaks here but disparagingly: for it will never, like the *gloire* of the active life, yield that unique sense of physical and moral strength combined that "insures the exercise of all the faculties" and "inebriates with the certainty of one's powers of being." Literature being the mode of her enterprise, we read this as a deliberate devaluation of the writer's own ambition, to exalt another kind beyond her grasp. In this passage she identifies completely with the splendor of fully realized potential and affirms the realm of action as supreme.

By way of contrast with the purity of the love of *gloire,* ambition is decried as "the passion that has no object save power, that is, the possession of status, of wealth and those honors that accompany these." In its perfection the love of *gloire* "comes out of true talent and aspires to nothing but the aura of fame" (I ii). Yet even the pursuit of such perfection, she is troubled to acknowledge, is often achieved at society's expense. She is struck, too, by the degree to which reverses of fame bring in their wake "a sense of defeat and of mortality; no one," she points out, "has ever descended painlessly from a rank which placed him higher than other men" (II ii). This empathy of hers for the plight of the high fallen low is a preoccupation that stays with her, an echo of her father's fall from power, she tumbling after him.[10]

To follow the vicissitudes of Staël's idea of *gloire,* I digress here to consider her *Fictions.* A defense and illustration of the importance of imaginative literature, this essay appears to be a precise attempt to explore the capacity of this terrain as a fulfilling alternative to the glory of the active life of politics or war. Unlike the *Passions,* which backs and fills meanderingly, offering digressive personal judgments on her own formulations, the *Fictions* is brief, brisk, and tightly organized. In it she reviews three types of fiction: the allegorical, the historical, and that which imitates life. She demonstrates little appreciation of the first two categories.[11] The meat of her argument appears in the last section, where she presents an unexpectedly elevated image of fiction in answer to its detractors:[12] it is "one of the fairest of all the products of the human spirit, one of the most influential upon the mores of individuals and that which, in the end, gives shape to social customs" (III). Novels, then, must be useful, but in order to be so they must expand our understanding of the emotions. The art in the novel she sees as essential to its power to act upon us, to improve us, making us better able to contend with our complex of passions, better armed to combat them. Notice the vigor of her language (my emphasis added): "We must *animate* virtue, so that it may *win the battle* with the passions; we must bring into being a kind of exaltation that will lend an attraction to sacrifice." We rediscover here with a shock of recognition some of that enthusiasm we perceived earlier in her description of *gloire.*

A great reforming zeal remains visible here, inadequately covering her underlying political goal: literature simply replaces politics as the theatre of action. She writes of the Revolution that is still in process, "Dante's Hell was less extreme than the crimes to which we have been witness." In our own times, following the Hitlerian and other terrors, we have been driven to ask, as was Germaine de Staël, whence they could arise and how they might be prevented. The answer she proffered to her own time was that such a deficiency in the human soul (somewhat akin to the "banality" that Hannah Arendt saw in Adolph Eichmann) could only be cured by the soul's intensive development. It is her hope to preserve from crime those in whom all sense of obligation is simply absent—by "developing in them the capacity to be moved." This it is that makes her newly reverent of the role of the artist, the mission of the novelist. Approving this mission, she consents too to what she regards as a soothing power, that of fiction, and concludes: "In this life through which we pass rather than truly live, anyone who distracts man from himself and from his fellows, who suspends the action of the passions and substitutes for them independent pleasures is the dispenser of the only true happiness human nature can enjoy . . ." (III). Here we have the link with the interrupted

work on the *Passions*: fiction can be their antidote, or at least their sedative.

The intriguing, frequently quoted passage from the *Fictions* in which she suggests a future course for the novel is concerned precisely with its treatment of the passions.

> The destiny of those women, the happiness of those men who are not called upon to govern empires often depends for the rest of their lives on the share they have given in youth to the importunity of love; but they forget completely at a certain age the impression it originally made upon them; they take on another nature; they are entirely given over to other objects, other passions; and it is to these new interests that novels should be devoted. A new career would then open up . . . for those authors with the talent to portray all the phases of the human heart and to convince us by their intimate knowledge of it. Ambition, pride, avarice, vanity might be the principal object of novels whose incidents would then be fresher and whose situations might prove more varied than those that have love as their subject. (III)

This view was not altogether new. The theatre had already undergone a similar critique of its subject matter, and d'Alembert, for example, had proposed the exploration of an expanded panorama of fictional and dramatic passions.[13] Yet an anomaly it was indeed for a woman to call, as did Germaine de Staël, for the other passions of humankind, so long subordinated to the tyrant love in fiction though not necessarily in life, to be given their full share in the novelist's art. She herself was never wholly freed from the chase after love, and all of her fictions are suffused with its aura. It is not merely a concern that equal time be allotted to the other passions that motivates her wish to dethrone love from its pedestal. I would hold that she arrived at this position because she subliminally perceived that the fictional dominance of love, through those very moral effects of the novel of which she had shown herself so conscious, was an instrument in maintaining women in a state of subservience and in that permanent latency that had baffled her own development.

Her stand here is an implicit rejection of such subservience by a subtle undermining of the love mystique. She would appear to be trying to pry the novel loose from the sentimental trap into which it had so completely fallen.[14] Her challenge does not lack a spark of rebellion: here is a woman writer resolutely rising above the cliché of her time that love, as Voltaire had put it, was all a woman ever took any interest in. Expressing her hope of one day seeing "the Lovelace of the ambitious," Staël illustrated the truth of what d'Alembert had affirmed: that it was not "natural" that all women should dwell eternally and exclusively on sexual conquest.

To be worthy of Germaine de Staël's attention, then, as a substitute for the worldly powers to which she felt herself equal, fiction could be no mere pastime but a serious, even elevated, enterprise. We see her theory pointing in the direction she believed Rousseau's *Nouvelle Héloise* had indicated: fiction must become a vehicle of exploration of the individual mind and soul in the torment of self discovery, a search undertaken for the sake of a higher morality. There is an underground layer of rationalization in this very work on fiction, as well as in the **Passions,** for the turn of her own aspirations away from politics and toward letters. As we sense her personal struggle to validate and lend authority to her evolving decision, we return with interest to those parts of the work she will now complete that deal with women and power.

In one such passage, significantly the chapter devoted not to ambition but to vanity, her inner struggle becomes apparent in literally every line of the text. She begins as she so often felt impelled to do in speaking of her sex, by making a ritual concession to the conventional view of woman's nature.[15] "The origin of all women," she intones, "is heavenly, for it is to nature's gifts that they owe their powers; in preoccupying themselves with pride and ambition, they cause all that is magical in their charms to be dissipated." She states this proposition, so puzzlingly relevant to her own case, first in its most negatively monitory form, as if attempting to bring its implications to full consciousness. Her consciousness, however, is in fact quite lucid. She remarks that no respect or esteem can follow a woman who makes a display of ambition, for women thereby "animate against themselves the passions of those who wish to think of them in no other way than to love them." Seeing so clearly the weight of male mentality against her project, she seems to abandon it, for her very next statement is despairing, full of disparagement of women's (that is, her own) aspirations. "The only real absurdity, that which arises from a discord with the essence of things, attaches to their efforts: when they set themselves against the plans and ambitions of men, they excite the lively resentment that all unexpected obstacles produce" (I iii). Necker's own strictures on his daughter's ambitions had been magnified a thousandfold by the nature of the public censure of her: consequently, she has learned to censure herself. Yet, since she cannot help chafing under these strictures, she goes on to try out a softened version of the traditional line: "These reflections are not at all intended to deflect women from all serious occupation, but from the misfortune of ever taking themselves to be the end of their own efforts." We now perceive that while giving the impression of criticizing female ambition, she has given the subject the twist needed for her to find some egress. In casting about to uncover something more basic about the taboo on ambition in women, she has hit on a fresh way of characterizing it. It is the absurd fate of precisely the woman who, like herself, desires to be an end in herself, subject rather than object, that perplexes her. Even as she declares her revulsion against herself, pacifying her public, making a show of agreement with the traditions that condemn her, she cannot help turning the matter round and about. Women, she writes, can participate in ambition by guiding the destinies of those they love, but only if their lovers should happen to be leaders of affairs would it be acceptable for them to act through them, for in that case, "they love, they are women; but," she cautions pre-

scriptively, "when they give themselves over to being *active personalities,* when they try to have all events center around them . . . then they are scarcely worthy of that ephemeral applause that rewards dignified victories" (I iii, emphasis added).

Given Germaine de Staël's restive, ambitious, egocentric, yet generous nature, these passages are a patent form of propitiatory self-flagellation, calculated to challenge the very laws she claims to accept. Men, she continues, pursuing her picture of the ravages of ambition to women's lives, whether iniquitously or justly, find no utility in encouraging success in women, and "any praise not founded in utility is neither deep, durable, nor universal." Unreasonably, however, she adds this quite unexpected note: "Chance sometimes makes for exceptions: if there are a few souls driven either by their talent or character, they may perhaps depart from the common rule, and some palms of glory may one day crown their efforts; but they will not escape the inevitable misfortune that is linked with their destiny" (I iii). Thus she provides a personal escape hatch for persisting, as she cannot help doing, in her own ambitious project. She will try, despite all the disclaimers, to be one of that handful of female exceptions to the rule who may be granted the right to succeed, provided only that they expressly renounce happiness and resolve to suffer for their transgression.

As we might have predicted from the previous evidences of conflict in the text, when Staël comes to the point of juxtaposing woman with that most powerful of passions, the desire for *gloire,* she can imagine no means whatever of reconciling the two. This time, however, in her rethinking of the problem she adds the social critique that could only be inferred in her earlier statement. She writes: "A woman cannot exist through herself alone; *gloire* itself would not sufficiently sustain her; and the insurmountable weakness of her nature *and her position in the social order* have placed her in an eternal dependency such that even immortal genius could not make her immune to it" (emphasis added). In the context of the need for love, then, it is no longer a question of merely lamenting that a woman whose ambition makes her take herself as an end will be resented. That aspiration to *gloire,* for her so much greater than ambition, would place a woman so thoroughly beyond the pale, would divorce her so thoroughly from all connection with others that it suggests to Germaine de Staël a total disintegration of being as punishment. Cowering emotionally before this terrifying conclusion, she turns all the way back and, at the end of this passage, affirms that it is the status of object—*femme aimée*—that is the highest good for woman. Acceding to her fear that no woman can be an end in herself, she thus casts self aside and, vindictively embracing her own negation, affirms what she has been taught: few of those who seek fame or glory for themselves, she concludes, have lives "that can rival in worth the most obscure life of one who is a loved woman and happy mother" (I iii).

That this view is not firmly anchored but expresses her guilt and anxiety rather than any fixed conviction appears to be borne out by other passages in which Staël assumes an altogether contrary feminist stance and vigorously, in smooth, strong prose that lacks the tormented parentheses and meanderings of her propitiatory statements, goes on the attack and deplores women's powerlessness. "Nature and society have disinherited half of humankind: strength, courage, genius, and independence all belong to men, and if they cover our youth with flattery, it is so as to give themselves the pleasure of overturning our throne; it is much as it is with children, who are allowed to command, so long as it is understood that they possess no real power of making others obey" (I iv). She does, in fact, perceive how the double standard makes a mockery of women's power, in love and outside it. In this rare direct apostrophe she speaks to women, exhorting them, "O women, you victims in the temple where you are told you are adored, listen to me! . . . Stay within the bounds of virtue . . . but if you do let yourselves give way to the need to be loved, men are the masters of public opinion, men have the power over their lives; men will overthrow your existence for the sake of a few moments in their own" (I iv).

Although Germaine de Staël derides the passions on virtually every page of her work, on each page we nevertheless discern how much they still enthrall her, even though she may deplore their hold. In these two texts, the ***Passions*** and the ***Fictions,*** we find enacted that drama in which her sense of self has begun to assume proportions rivalling those of her awe of love. As her statement concerning the future content of the novel already suggests, she had become conscious that passion, though precious, must not prevail unchallenged; that independent pursuits can yield their own fulfillments, that silence and loneliness often provide a surer sense of self and of the world than can be gained by being perpetually involved with others in the struggle to dominate or to avoid domination. She concludes her tortured meditation with this devastating praise of her subject: "The passions are the striving of man toward some other destiny; they make us feel the disquiet in our faculties, the emptiness in life; they perhaps presage a future existence, but meanwhile they rip this one to shreds." Her early Rousseauesque ideal of ecstasy in experience having faltered, she strives in this text to reject it, at least intellectually. Passion's violent relentlessness, itself an anti-ideal, somehow suggests to her an ideal life of passion purified that can never be realized on earth. This dual sense of loss and longing will find its fullest expression in her greatest imaginative work, the Romantic novel of the woman as genius, ***Corinne.***[16]

Mystified by the collapse of values during the Terror and in her own personal experience, Germaine de Staël was impelled to probe human frailty in a search to uncover what path might remain to her, a woman both passionate and aspiring. Building, in these texts, upon the masochistic energy generated out of her reiterated, reified repression of self in the passages where she overtly rejects the idea of woman's ambition, she yet manages to piece together for herself a new writer's persona: that of accursed exception to the rule of female subservience. In this newly fabricated

posture she assumes her oracular role as servant to the newly espoused creative imagination by presaging the Romantic vision. Heaven alone holds promise of redemption, earthly passions having vilified humankind. And in that heaven where passion might at last fulfill rather than destroy us, the powers of women, we divine, would be sacrificed no longer.

Notes

1. *Considérations sur les principaux événements de la Révolution française* (1818 [posthumous]) III vii (the translation is my own; references are to part and chapter).

2. Staël also wrote two important political tracts during this period: *Réflexions sur le procès de la reine* (1793) and the *Réflexions sur la paix addressées à M. Pitt* (1795). See Simone Balayé *Madame de Staël, lumières et liberté* (Paris: Klincksieck 1979), 51-60 for an overview of the biographical chronology and general content of these works.

3. Luce Irigaray "When Our Lips Speak Together" *Signs* 6:i (1980) 76.

4. Hannah Arendt *Rahel Varnhagen, The Life of a Jewish Woman* (NY: Harcourt Brace Jovanovich 1956) 13. Arendt never poses Varnhagen's identity problem as a problematic of femaleness, but rather of female Jewishness. Yet some of the parallels in the psychic postures of the two women are striking. The basic point of Arendt's study is that in espousing Christianity as she had striven to do Rahel had also to assimilate the anti-semitism inherent in it, which she finally balked at accepting. An analogous struggle took place for Germaine de Staël with the misogyny inherent in the culture's limitations on women's aspirations.

5. References to the *Passions* in the text refer to part and chapter only; those to the *Fictions* to the section, since a standard edition does not exist. All translations from the French are my own.

6. See ch. 3 of my *Madame de Staël, Novelist: The Emergence of the Artist as Woman* (Urbana: Univ. of Illinois Press 1978) for a more extensive discussion of the effects of the slander against Staël during the 90s upon her writing.

7. It is quite probable that the recently re-edited text of *Des Circonstances actuelles qui peuvent terminer la Révolution en France* Lucia Omacini, ed (Geneva: Droz 1980) represents that attempt to formulate a praxis. Half political pamphlet, half notes toward a political theory, this piece was never worked through to completion and remained unpublished until 1902.

8. Mme de Staël also wrote a short and intense work of fiction, *Zulma,* published in 1794, which she had originally intended to append to this text. I deal with it in my *Madame de Staël, Novelist* 72-75. In her preface she speaks of her wish to depict the effects of love by a portrayal of "the most dreadful of all

misfortunes and the most passionate of all characters." Such feeling could find its full expression only in a person with the soul of a savage, but whose mind was fully cultivated, since "the power of judgment so greatly augments the experience of pain."

9. The French conception of *gloire* inherited from the seventeenth century is, as the career of General De Gaulle reminds us, not easily transposed into English. The scholar Robert Mauzi sees it as the public dimension of the search for personal recognition.

10. Necker's recall from exile on July 15, like his original dismissal from power, was one of the key events of the French Revolution. His triumphant return on July 30 was a day of such *gloire* that it became virtually the high point of Staël's life. Her father's subsequent loss of popularity was swift: it was never to be recovered.

11. Although I am unable to deal with them in this context, these sections are worthy of scrutiny, for she makes interesting, if debatable, statements in them; for example as she rejects the epic, or the role of the gods in Homer, or demands that fiction "make us hang suspended on every word" as it elaborates the feelings of its characters.

12. See Georges May *Le Dilemme du roman au XVIIIe siècle* (Paris: Presses Universitaires Françaises 1963) for its excellent account of the eighteenth century's polemics over the worth of the novel.

13. See Jean d'Alembert "Lettre à Jean-Jacques Rousseau, citoyen de Genève," *Oeuvres complètes* (Paris: Belin 1821-22), IV 450.

14. Pierre Fauchery *La Destinée féminine dans le roman européen du dix-neuvième siècle* (Paris: Armand Colin 1972) gives ample documentation of this phenomenon, more probingly discussed too from the woman's standpoint by Nancy Miller in *The Heroine's Text* (NY: Columbia Univ. Press 1981).

15. For another example of this concessive, ambivalent behavior, see my article "Madame de Staël, Rousseau and the Woman Question," *Publications of the Modern Language Association* 86:i (1971) 100-09.

16. In the aftermath of these treatises she will write all her important works: *De la littérature* (1800); *Delphine* (1802); *Corinne* (1807); *De l'Allemagne* (1810); and the *Considérations sur les principaux événements de la Révolution française* (1818 [posthumous]).

Charlotte Hogsett (essay date 1987)

SOURCE: "History and Story," in *The Literary Existence of Germaine de Staël,* Southern Illinois University Press, 1987, pp. 71-93.

[*In the following excerpt, Hogsett examines de Staël's attempts to insert feminine ways of narration into a masculine-oriented history and literature in* De la littérature considérée dans ses rapports avec les institutions sociales *and* Delphine.]

Staël published nothing between *Passions* in 1796 and *On Literature* in 1800. Simone Balayé speculates that between 1796 and late 1798, when she began the writing of *On Literature,* she was perhaps working on the second part of the *Passions.*[1] That does indeed seem likely, especially in the light of her failure to complete "On Current Circumstances . . ." whose subject matter was closely related to the *Passions* project. Realizing the impossibility of doing that piece of work, she began to cast about for a potentially more successful project. Her search seems to have taken two forms. In the first place, she apparently decided that part of her problem was the subject matter she had proposed for herself in the *Passions,* namely, the science of government. Our examination of reasons why government did not energize her writing, a fact all the more odd given her intense interest in it, suggested that Staël felt, in spite of herself, that it was not a topic a woman writer could adequately or appropriately treat. If that is so, it is logical to conclude that she would be looking for a viable topic. She found it in literature, a subject with which women had been traditionally associated. At the same time, Staël thought of a way of treating literature that would enable her to incorporate some of the research she had already done on forms of government through the ages and which would at least partly satisfy her desire to talk about politics. The full title of her work reveals this approach: *De la littérature considérée dans ses rapports avec les institutions sociales* (*On Literature Considered in Its Relationship with Social Institutions*).[2] One of the "social institutions" that she will treat insofar as it impinged on literary production is, of course, political organization. In little over a year she had written and published her work, so that it seems that she had indeed rethought her topic in a way that allowed her writing to move ahead rather than to remain stymied.

The second reason why the work on the *Passions* presented obstacles to the flow of writing was her plan to include both masculine and feminine ways of thinking and writing in the same book and to present them as "analogous." In her work of the turn of the century, Staël has found a new way of approaching that problem. During this time she writes not only *On Literature* but also *Delphine,* an epistolary novel, her next literary project after the work on literature.[3] These two works are a pair, the first belonging to the "male" series laid out in the *Essay on Fiction* and the second to the "female" series. The first is a work of history that recounts public events and arranges them according to a theory of history. The second is a fictional work that reveals the happenings and feelings of private life, inspired by events actually observed or lived by the author. Rather than trying to write the masculine and the feminine together, as she had attempted in the *Passions,* Staël is now separating them into two distinct works, not claiming any particular relationship between them, making no attempt to show their "analogies." She must have felt that this was a successful approach. Between 1803 and 1810 she wrote another pair of works, one expository, the other one fictional. Toward the end of her career she can be shown to have been projecting still another such pair.

In composing books by pairs, Germaine de Staël has found a most interesting solution to the problem of sexual writing identity. Members of a pair are both associated and dissociated. The latter effect—dissociation—is, I claim, the one actually sought by Staël herself. The androgyny of a male/female work, like the **Passions,** of which she dreamed but which she did not complete, made her uncomfortable. Perceiving maleness and femaleness to be a dichotomy, she could more easily deal with creating works that she could think of as adhering to its parts rather than questioning them by the act of establishing analogies. Writing works in pairs thus satisfied this need to keep the dichotomy intact. Meanwhile, however, it is the associative quality of pairs that is the more interesting and critically useful phenomenon here. If it can be shown that the male and female members of a pair are in fact "analogous" after all, we may conclude that, like it or not, Staël had a single identity that insistently manifested itself whenever she wrote, no matter how different the types of works she created may seem. These assessments differ from that of Simone Balayé who, in comparing the fictional and nonfictional works of Staël has written, "The critical and political work of Madame de Staël proposes, constructs, comforts, while the novelistic work destroys, expressing the anguish of the author."[4] While evidence to support this claim can certainly be gathered in the overt themes of the works in question, their deep structure constantly asserts unity rather than duality.

That **Delphine** and **On Literature** are a pair can be demonstrated by reference to both their tonal and their structural affinities. A major tone struck by both works is that of nostalgia. As **On Literature** ends Staël thinks back to the period ten years earlier, depicting herself as "entrant dans le monde" (entering the world). This is the same phrase by which the Staël of the 1814 preface to the Rousseau letters was to use to characterize her status in the late 1780s and early 1790s. She contrasts the hopeful and confident young woman she was then with the guarded person she has become. The action of the novel **Delphine** takes place in the same time period. Her central character describes herself at that time with this same phrase: "I am entering the world . . ." This nostalgic note is emphasized by the presence of parental figures in both books, **Delphine** being the book of the mother, **On Literature,** the book of the father.[5]

The epigraph of **Delphine** is "A man must be able to defy opinion, a woman, to submit to it."[6] This aphorism was written by Staël's mother. The novel comments on it by featuring a man who submits to public opinion and a woman who defies it. Thus, the qualities that should be associated, according to Suzanne Necker, with a man are exhibited by a woman who permits herself masculine behavior. The appropriate quality has been transferred to the

inappropriate sex, so that a crossing, or a chiasmus, has resulted. Staël has crossed or gone against the values of her mother, but in the same ambivalent way that we have already observed, for example, in her attitude toward moral philosophy in the **Essay.** She has indeed created a plot in which the female character fails to act in the way prescribed by the maternal aphorism. However, Delphine is severely punished for each failure. At the same time she is without any doubt the heroine of the novel. Her character is exalted, her actions are blameless, her way of being is valorized. Suzanne Necker had been dead since 1794, and yet even now when her daughter crosses her, she must do so in a shifting way, her aggressive moves tempered by attempted appeasements. **Delphine** is in part a response to Suzanne Necker. The memory of her moral lessons, of her interpretation to her daughter of woman's proper place, is present even before the actual beginning of the novel, and, as Madelyn Gutwirth demonstrates, the "complicity in woman's fate" of both good and evil mothers is depicted and analyzed in the book.[7]

The attitude toward the father, however, is quite different. **On Literature** traces the history of literature and thought in their relation to various other social phenomena from the time of the Greeks through the French Revolution in a first part. Its second part is an attempt to project the nature of the literature of the future, a literature she hopes will develop somewhere in the world, perhaps in France, perhaps in America, when an enlightened and free nation comes into being. In her penultimate chapter, entitled "Du Style des Ecrivains et de celui des Magistrats," (On the Style of Writers and of Magistrates), she discusses her father in terms that recall the Rousseau letters. Her father is the best example of a magistrate/writer and stands as one to be emulated in this essential endeavor. If the first part of the book leads up to the French Revolution, the second part leads up to Necker. He has then a significant place in the overall plan of his daughter's book. The father is not crossed; he is apotheosized.

That **Delphine** is conceived as a response to the mother and **On Literature** to the father, suggests the dissociation between the male and the female Staël seems to have wished to bring about in these two works. Yet structurally, the two works are similar in that they share a central preoccupation and organizing principle: both are stories and thus both are arranged diachronically. Narrations are grounded in some fundamental informing conception of temporality and causality. The writer must arrange chosen or invented events in temporal succession and show how they derive from prior events and lead to those that follow. The events will be related in a way that forms a pattern of development in time and of causation. **On Literature,** the book of the father, is man's history, the story of development in the public realm. **Delphine,** the book of the mother, is a novel which depicts the world of a woman in her relation to the man she loves and of that part of the man's life that is carried out in the private arena. The distinctions Staël set up in the **Essay** lead us to expect that we will be dealing with different stories in the two cases.

The public story will be abstract, exclusive of certain elements. In telling it, one will be working under some theory of history according to which one will order events and interpretations. The private story will have to conform to the contours of experience. Some of Staël's critics have adopted this dichotomized picture of her performance. Simone Balayé says, "There are for her novels tragic endings, for her philosophical and political works endings which are never closures" and discerns "a fundamental difference of orientation between these two manners of expressing her genius."[8] James Hamilton, however, senses a "structural polarity" in *On Literature,* two levels of reasoning, the one dialectical and the other "unconscious and skeptical."[9] There is indeed a tension in that work, rather than openings into hope. In fact, the stories of the two books bear striking similarities that provide evidence for a certain Staëlian conception of temporal sequence and of causality, which imposed itself on her rendering of both man's and woman's story. That conception comes from her unmistakable female identity.

In the book on literature, Staël's theory of history is a particularly insistent version of perfectibility, an idealized interpretation that she found in a number of sources. Rousseau, one of the first to use the word perfectibility (in his *Second Discourse,* 1755), actually meant by it "capacity for change," a change that can move toward amelioration or degeneration. Condorcet, probably the most immediate influence on her theory, claimed progress in the development of the human mind but saw little advancement for human kind itself in his "Essay on the history of the progress of the human mind," 1793-1794. Staël wishes to adopt a stronger attitude still, to claim progress for humankind as well as progress in thought. She words her initial presentation of the theory in such a way as to underplay the distinction between progress of the mind and improvement in the human lot. "In looking at the revolutions of the world and at the succession of centuries, there is one prime idea which I keep constantly in mind: the perfectibility of *human kind.* I do not think that this great work of moral nature has ever been abandoned, in periods of enlightenment as in centuries of darkness, the *gradual march of the human mind* has not been interrupted" (emphasis added).[10] The shift in terminology (from "human kind" to "human mind") is not brought out and explained but rather slipped in so as to blur the distinction. The implication is that Staël wishes to claim progress for human kind, but because she cannot do so with an entirely clear intellectual conscience, she expresses herself ambiguously on the point. The strong claim she wishes to make is one that finally she cannot entirely bring herself to make even at this initial, introductory stage. Lucia Omacini discovers this same pattern in Staël's very syntax: "The syntactical structure transmits and reflects at once optimism, faith in perfectibility, hope in a better future, but, if one can read between the lines, it hides traps which lie in wait for the irreparable calamities of humanity."[11]

In this same passage Staël posits an agent (moral nature) which has set out on and continually pursues its activity, that of creating a work. The work is a readable, understandable, sensible story. Human kind and the human mind or both gradually march forward under its influence. There is a force at work that somehow moves events along in such a way as to form a pattern of progress. The causal principle behind the movement posited here is a hidden but active intelligence. "Time reveals to us a design, in the sequence of events that seemed to be only the pure result of chance; and one sees a thought emerge, always the same thought, from the abyss of facts and centuries."[12]

The importance to Staël of this theory of history is emphasized when, in her second preface to the book, she reiterates her claims, now citing a number of other writers who have professed the same theory in answer to her critics. It is a system, she says, that "promises to men on this earth some of the benefits of immortality, a limitless future, continuity without interruption!"[13] This passage specifies that the movement of history which Staël wishes to recount will be characterized not only by an upward linear progression but also by a particular articulation of events—they must be continuous, uninterrupted, their lines unbroken, smoothly linking from one to the next. But the passage also betrays the scarcely spoken skepticism Staël felt about her cherished theory. She says it "promises" various benefits.

In the Preliminary Discourse of her book (p. 208) Staël calls her theory a "une croyance philosophique" (a philosophical belief). At the same time she claims that it is not a "vain theory" but rather that it is based on the "observation of facts." She does not, however, state what those observations are, so that the word *belief* seems to fit well. What she says about this belief does not amount to a proof of its truth but rather to an appeal to its advantages. It serves to combat discouragement, the feeling that one's efforts are pointless. Thus Staël's attitude toward her theory of history is characterized both by an adamant insistence on the importance of its moral and emotional role and by an inherent implicit skepticism about its foundation in demonstrable fact. The story of perfectibility must be told and believed, but it is not necessarily a true story. Staël made a valiant effort to tell that story, but she does not manage to make it work smoothly and convincingly. The structure of the story being told works at cross purposes with that of the story Staël wanted to tell. Decadence taints perfectibility. Senselessness threatens sense. Circularity bends linearity.

Every story must have a beginning. Staël does not show as much interest in beginnings, though, as such eighteenth-century thinkers as Rousseau and Condillac, who discussed at length the origins of language, knowledge, and society. Rather she sets history in motion abruptly. Facts about our origins are missing; lacking anything upon which to base our ideas, we speculate in vain. Yet it is necessary to posit some sort of a beginning and some force that explains why there was a beginning at all. Staël brings in a quite general principle. She claims simply that "moral nature" acquires quickly what is needed. "For example, . . . language is the instrument that is necessary for the acquisition of all other developments; and, by a sort of miracle, this instrument exists."[14] The initial step of human kind is inexplicable; one can only appeal to some unknown force, a divine hand, a quasi-magic thrust into existence from nothingness. Once the elements of humanity and society are in motion, further developments come slowly, in steps, which lend themselves to study and to understanding. But the beginning leaps into being surprisingly, irrationally.

Staël's attitude toward the originators of Western civilization, for her, the Greeks, is decidedly ambivalent. This is a second factor that gets her story off to an uncertain start. She does not admire them as much as she does the Romans, saying that they, in disappearing from history, leave "few regrets" (part I, chapter 4). Yet emotions and thought, as well as the literature which expressed them, existed in a pristine state, uncomplicated by precedents, which can never be recaptured. Staël does show some nostalgia for this state. Regret for a lost past is not compatible with the theory of perfectibility that theoretically should involve looking ahead with anticipation and behind with the assurance that the past existed mainly to serve the present and the future. From the outset nostalgia coexists uneasily with perfectibility.

The main characters of the next episode are the Romans. If the theory of perfectibility is valid, then they must be both different from the Greeks (that is, the Romans must be superior to them), and different from modern France (that is, inferior to it). On the first point, Staël has little difficulty. Rome borrowed from Greece and integrated its borrowings into its own distinctive culture. On the second point, however, there are some obstacles. Modern France may be superior to ancient Rome, but not in all ways. Roman historical writing, for instance, is better than French. Or again, in many ways, France is neither better nor worse than Rome, but similar. To point out a few resemblances between ancient and modern times does not at first glance seem to threaten necessarily the theory of perfectibility. But if the examples of similarity become too numerous, then history will start seeming to repeat itself and thus be more like a circle than a straight line. That is why Staël, whenever she makes a comparison, is potentially endangering her entire hypothetical structure.

In fact, Staël does much more than point out resemblances. She sees a structural similarity between the history of the Romans and that of the French. Everyone knows and Staël repeats the story of the Romans, whose civilization flourished and then declined and fell. One cannot talk about Rome without talking about decadence, that major enemy of perfectibility. Naturally, then, when Staël treats the fall of the Roman Empire she is working in an area mined with danger to her system. It presents a strong case for the countertheory to that of Staël: inevitable periodic decadence. "Some have claimed that the decadence of the arts and letters of empires must necessarily occur after a certain degree of splendor."[15] Staël combats this hypothesis by recourse to a distinction she was careful to make at the beginning of the account and which she reiterates throughout: that the arts are not indefinitely perfectible (the classical ideal of a "point of perfection"), whereas thought can progress indeterminably. This distinction can certainly guard perfectibility from the threat of decadence in the realm of the arts, but it provides no defense if decadence can be demonstrated in the realm of thought. Faced with this threat Staël makes a very dangerous move. "Moral nature tends to be perfected. Previous improvement is a cause for future improvement; this chain can be interrupted by accidental events that impede future progress but that are not the consequences of previous progress."[16] She introduces the element of chance, of accident, disconnecting the chain of events that, she had claimed, leads continually from one to the next. She has given up a great deal here, abandoned, in fact, the cornerstone of her entire claim, the uninterrupted continuity of progress. Yet she proceeds as if this capitulation had not taken place. She goes on to claim that whereas the Romans did indeed decline, decadence is not an inevitable thrust within history and that there is every reason to believe that it will not happen again. The argument is that decadence is not destined to occur; it comes as the result of certain causes, so that when the causes are eliminated or diminished the effect will cease or be attenuated. But the case is not very strongly argued. Reference is made to Montesquieu for factual proof of the thesis. Yet, as in her discussion of perfectibility, the appeal is not to demonstrable evidence but to emotional necessity; it would be too depressing to contemplate an inevitable succession of falls. Furthermore, in the case of at least one cause, that of the atrocities committed as the Roman Empire declined, it can only be demonstrated that that cause does not exist any more by eliminating the fact of the Terror. If one took this Terror into consideration, rather than refusing to consider it, as Staël suggests, one's conclusion would be quite different. The price of the proof is abstraction. And even so, Staël cannot bring herself to claim triumphantly that decadence no longer threatens, only that the threat has diminished in intensity.

Next, Staël has to deal with the "Dark Ages," with what appear to have been ten centuries of decadence, a period that would indeed seem to question the idea of perfectibility. But even in those times events were not left to chance development; a mysterious force was at work. The narrative language of the chapter on the Middle Ages (part I, chapter 8), depends on the functioning of some hidden but active intelligence. The force is strongly reminiscent of the one Staël used to set history in motion. The process of creation is described in terms similar to those used in the discussion of this process of re-creation after the neochaos which followed the fall of the Roman Empire. Staël must deny chance as an explanatory factor in the unfolding of history (and this in spite of her own occasional slips). But at the essential moments of articulation, as at the moment of creation, she cannot manage to assert and demonstrate a chain of cause and effect. She relies instead on a behind-the-scenes, mysterious power that energizes what might otherwise have remained in nothingness or reverted to it. Neither the thrust nor the processes of history seem to be marching along.

Halting and questionable as the progress has been up to this point, however, Staël moves on to the Renaissance. Here modern history begins. It is to be, she asserts, different from the past. Resolutely taking the side of the Moderns rather than the Ancients, Staël points to a new era that has already begun and which will now progress without further interruption. She calls upon the reader to look ahead. Looking back is associated with depression or discouragement, looking forward with renewed life, fecundity, hope, the excitement of voyage. Theoretically, whatever threats decadence may have posed before the Renaissance are now past, overcome. One may proceed into a continuously progressive future.

But that is not by any means how the story really goes on, for Staël soon arrives at the Revolution. "Thus time was marching toward the conquest of freedom . . . Ah! . . . Every time the course of ideas leads us to reflect upon the destiny of man, the revolution appears!"[17] The only answer to this despair is a renewed rhetorical exhortation: "Nevertheless, let us not succumb to this discouragement. Let us return to general observations."[18] Moreover, when Staël turns from the past to the future, in the second part of her work, projecting what further progress is foreshadowed in the events and developments of her own time, her projections do not seem to promise continuity and progress any more than her retrospections. It begins in this way: "I have followed the history of the human mind from Homer until 1789. In my national pride, I viewed the time of the French Revolution as a new era for the intellectual world."[19] The Renaissance was supposed to be a new era that was to proceed without interruption. But now there has been another interruption, the Revolution, and there is to be a second new era. Is history not repeating itself?

It certainly seems to be doing so. The similarities between the state of things at the fall of the Roman Empire and now, in the aftermath of the French Revolution, are overwhelming. The structure of the two situations is the same, and Staël brings it out very clearly herself. In the first case, the friendly force of history had to bring about a reconciliation between two opposing sides, the barbarian invaders from the north and the decadent invaded from the south. The linking factor was the Christian religion. In the second, contemporary, case, the opposing sides are the decadent aristocracy invaded by the lower classes. How, Staël asks, can they be reconciled? The problem is the same: opposing forces to be united. The very natures of the two sides in the two cases are parallel. And the solutions, Christianity in the first case and now, as Staël shows in the latter chapters of her book, enthusiasm, are strikingly similar.

As Staël says, in her projections of the future she has depended upon her observations about the past. Indeed, people say that one studies history in order to learn from it; no doubt that is in general a good thing to do. But

within the system of Staël, when the past is so inescapably like the present, the backlash from learning the lessons of history is that history begins to look circular. There is a double bind here: one cannot profit from the contemplation of the past unless history does repeat itself; but in that event we must face the fact that past events may recur and with the same results as before, and recur again and again. That, for Staël, is a very depressing thought. "It is impossible to condemn thought to retrace its steps, without hope and with regret; the human mind, deprived of a future, would fall into the most miserable degradation. Let us then look for this future, in literary productions and in philosophical ideas."[20] Again, in the face of threatened decadence, the rhetorical exhortation. History does not have tense, not the past, nor the present, nor the future. It has only mode, and that mode is the imperative. It is the "let us affirm, let us look, let us not give up." In this book Staël wanted to make the past make sense by the power of the word, but she could not finally tell the story she wanted to tell. The chain of perfectibility is constantly buffeted by the fear of decadence. The projected future is a wish; the only hope for its realization is to write rhetorically in such a way that the reader will want to share the "philosophical belief."

Thus Staël's theory of history and her development of events and their causes are troubled, proceed by fits and starts, demonstrate the opposite of what she claims, and veer finally away from history into rhetoric. In her epistolary novel *Delphine*[21] projections just as optimistic meet with equally disappointing results. In the preface to her novel, Staël does not immediately announce a definite shape that it supposedly will have, but she does make her explanatory factor quite clear. Destiny is formed by morality. The moral life of the characters will determine the elaboration of their stories. "Fictions should explain to us, by our virtues and our feelings, the mysteries of our fate."[22] Whatever happens to us, mysterious as it may temporarily seem, is finally explainable, can ultimately be shown to spin out of what we are and do. In the novel, the reader can expect to find a linking of events which makes sense of their succession and direction. The implication is that if the characters are virtuous, their stories should be, like history, a continuous improvement. That, in any event, is the prediction the main character Delphine naïvely makes about herself as the novel opens. "I am entering the world with a good and true character, wit, youth and fortune; why would these gifts of Providence not make me happy?"[23]

But here is briefly what happens: When the hero, Léonce, and Delphine meet, the former is engaged to be married to a cousin of Delphine, Mathilde de Vernon, who is also the daughter of the woman whom Delphine considers to be her closest friend, Sophie de Vernon. Since the announcement of the engagement has not yet been made nor all of the arrangements completed, Léonce would be able, at the beginning, to change his mind and marry Delphine instead of Mathilde. Certainly the two of them recognize very soon their irresistible attraction to each other. But a villain intervenes. Sophie de Vernon, it turns out, is a treacherous woman who has taken advantage of Delphine's friendship and generosity. Now she intends that her daughter will marry the wealthy and charming Léonce and uses Delphine's innocence, credulity, and spontaneity against her, once she has perceived that Léonce's preferences do not go toward her daughter. She tricks Léonce into believing that Delphine is involved with another man. Disappointed, Léonce quickly marries Mathilde (part I).

Delphine does not understand why Léonce has acted as he has, so that following the marriage there is a period of misunderstanding. At length, however, Léonce and Delphine both discover the truth about Madame de Vernon's perfidy, but too late: Léonce is already bound to Mathilde (part II). Delphine realizes that under the circumstances she should leave Paris, refuse to see Léonce, and thereby eliminate the risk of allowing their relationship to continue and deepen. But Léonce prevails upon her not to leave, and continually finding new excuses to blind herself to her duty, Delphine stays. The position of the would-be lovers becomes more and more untenable, so that finally Delphine manages to leave Paris without telling Léonce where she is going or indeed without even announcing her departure to him (parts III and IV).

Now, two more villains: one Monsieur de Valorbe, who wishes the reluctant Delphine to marry him, and Madame de Ternan, sister and eventually agent of Léonce's mother, whose aim it is to separate her son from the threat that Delphine presents to his marriage. Hounded by the first and perfidiously encouraged by the other, Delphine takes religious vows, (part V), ironically at the same time that Léonce is being freed from his marriage by the death of his wife. At this point it is Delphine who is bound and Léonce who is at liberty to marry. If only Delphine could be persuaded to abjure her vows . . . But she knows that Léonce would never be able to accept that solution: What would people say of his marrying a defrocked nun? The only real solution is the one that is worked out in each of two endings: the death of the lovers (part VI).

In **Delphine,** the claim is made that character leads to destiny. To some extent, that is true. To be sure, Delphine's character produces the spontaneous actions that turn out to be so compromising in the eyes of Léonce. This exchange of properties which results in chiasmus causes the lovers to be not so much star-crossed as character-crossed. The actions of the villains as well as those of characters who innocently, or at times with good intention but blunderingly, end by placing obstacles to the progress of the lovers are explainable and explained by the characters. But something else is at work in the formation of destiny that makes it depend not only on the tightly-conceived interaction of people but also, to an important degree, on chance and fate.

One can best see the design of **Delphine** by outlining the major actions of the plot.

a. Part I: Léonce marries Mathilde instead of Delphine.
b. Part II: Léonce and Delphine find out the truth about what has separated them.
c. Parts III and IV: Delphine leaves Paris.
d. Part V: Delphine takes religious vows, thus making marriage impossible.
e. Part VI: The lovers die.

The working out of these actions does not proceed always in the same way. In fact, there are two series of actions, viewed from this standpoint. Actions (a), (b), and (d) differ from actions (c) and (e). Novelistically, the first series is superior to the second. In the former case, Staël skillfully and gradually presents a number of characters whose complex interaction moves the story along. Essential here are the machinations of villains, Sophie de Vernon, first, and then Monsieur de Valorbe and Madame de Ternan. They take advantage of Delphine's well intentioned help for her friends, of her naïve trustfulness, and of her tendency to act spontaneously, without sufficiently foreseeing the repercussions for herself. In the case of the second series, however, there is little real story. At the beginning of part III and at the beginning of part VI, the climactic action is so predictable that the letters consist of a sequence of avoidance maneuvers that merely postpone the inevitable. The first series is more dynamic than the second.

The factors at work in the second series are malevolent chance and, on the part of the characters, an indecision that would put the most hardened procrastinator to shame. In part III, Delphine announces her departure three times, but in each case Léonce uses emotional blackmail, the threat that he will die if she leaves, and in each case she submits to his threats. In part IV, still knowing she should leave, she insists that her much-admired sister-in-law, Mademoiselle d'Albémar, decide for her. The latter, herself much influenced by Léonce's threats, decides that she should stay. But her staying becomes more and more problematic. Chance events make the situation as unendurable as possible, but still her decision is not forthcoming. Finally, Delphine reveals the truth about the feelings between herself and Léonce to Mathilde, whose ability not to see them make her a model wife for a faithless husband. But this action on Delphine's part is not an action at all. She describes her state of mind during the confession as irrational; she did not know what she was doing. Her "decision" was not based on a reasoning process but on an irresistible inner movement. Then in the aftermath of the encounter, Delphine depicts herself as a helpless victim, waiting for someone else, in this case, Mathilde, to make the final determination. Mathilde, not surprisingly, requires that she leave, but even now fifteen more letters intervene before the departure.

In these two parts (III and IV) the plot is not one of suspense, but of suspension. Whatever happens, happens despite the characters, not only the interventions of chance but even their own so-called actions. The inevitable outcome is postponed at great length, so that the characters exist always in a state of waiting, of living-until, of uncertainty and loudly proclaimed helplessness, the victims not of themselves but of circumstance.

In fact, suspension is present also in the parts in which more really motivated action takes place. The moment of truth that concludes part II is postponed, for example, when by chance Delphine does not find the person to whom she needed to deliver an essential letter, and she trustingly, foolishly, gives it to Madame de Vernon to send. The latter takes advantage of the contretemps in order to keep the lovers separated and in darkness longer than would have otherwise been possible. In part V, Delphine takes the vows that will separate her from Léonce at the very time when he is becoming free; had she waited just a little while, the situation that seemed to be forcing her into that drastic solution could have been dispelled.

Not even the actions of villains have the expected force. Their actions represent negative and destructive forces, but they are at least dynamic, emanating from character, evil though it be. It is useful to compare Madame de Vernon to a character Staël probably had in mind when she created her, Pierre de Laclos' Marquise de Merteuil. The marquise, in working her evil designs on her innocent victims, intended and maintained her actions and her character to the very end. Madame de Vernon intended what she did, but she ends by repenting, explaining her motivations in such a way as to expiate her crimes, at least in the eyes of Delphine. The same is true of Monsieur de Valorbe. Even Madame de Ternan, who does not repent, gives a lengthy explanation of her actions, designed to attenuate the evil of her character. Staël, unlike Laclos, will not allow evil to persist in her book; she must purge it, explain it away, make it acceptable. But in this refusal of evil she is undercutting an essential active force, softening her plot, turning away from what she had used as a principle of story-advancing action.

Decision is postponed and finally thrust upon the characters; the plot depends on chance; the villains are defused. Where the characters and their actions should be present, if we are to believe that out of our essence spins our story, there are voids. The analysis of the plot gives negative view of human action that people are not involved in a series of events that either make sense or are related in a pattern of consequence.

The atmosphere of the novel confirms it. In fact, the book is a romance that bathes in the atmosphere of medieval chivalry. Conventional motifs from that system abound. On two major occasions, when she falls in love and when she travels into Switzerland upon leaving Paris, Delphine has the impression of a passage from the ordinary world into a new one, dangerous but perhaps promising transformation and salvation. In several scenes, she is depicted in a carriage, being led away from the old world by dizzyingly swift horses. There are what the characters take to be supernatural premonitions of the future: when Delphine has taken her vows, she accidentally breaks the portrait of Léonce, signaling, she believes, the coming of some ominous event. A wise older woman, latter-day crone, tries to help the heroine. A blind man represents a happiness into which the lovers are denied access and a warning of that denial. There are festivals, a masked ball, scenes in dark churches. The love of Léonce and Delphine is that of Tristan and Isolde, a love-passion which leads to death through a series of separations and reunions. Realistic scenes, that is, scenes in which the characters are shown in their social settings, do not lack. Yet actually society is not so much the background against which the story is played out as a stock character of medieval romance, the villain, "this modern fate,"[24] "an uncontrollable, irrational, destructive, counter-natural force."[25] Such conventional motifs set up certain expectations about destiny. A dark fate hangs over the characters, and it will not be carried out in linear, logical fashion. The arbitrary is in the service of the inevitable.

Are we, then, responsible for our actions? Apparently not, if the actions based on our characters are as fated as those visited upon us by others or by circumstance. But what does, finally, explain destiny? The book comments on the question but by no means addresses itself to it effectively. The plot explains nothing, gives no coherent vision of destiny, because the way events are articulated within it does not make sense of them. Naturally, the only appeal possible is to an obscure external force sometimes called chance and sometimes, fate. In **Delphine** the force is more openly acknowledged than in **On Literature,** where it is imbedded, implicit in the language but not overtly discussed. But it is, nonetheless, recognizable as the kind of agent *ex machina* that Staël brought in at crucial junctures of that story as well. Both books deal uneasily with consequence.

Whereas sequence of events caused Staël a great deal of difficulty in **On Literature,** the shape of destiny is clear in **Delphine.** That shape bears an interesting and revealing relationship to history as Staël tells it. The story in **Delphine** follows the archetypal pattern of Tristan and Isolde. The protagonists meet and fall in love despite the fact that one of them is already engaged to marry someone else. They share a moment of happiness and intimacy (in Staël the intimacy is spiritual only) but are separated by the marriage of one. However, they do come together later, (in the case of Delphine and Léonce, twice) but are again separated after each reunion. Their final encounter brings death. Thus the pattern is one of alternating presence and absence. In the description of the shared moments (six in all), several qualities are gradually developed and linked: bliss, timelessness,[26] music, and death.

The recurrence of the same motifs in each of the encounters creates a circularly shaped plot, consisting of a sequence of returns to and banishments from ideal moments. In shape, therefore, the story of Delphine strongly resembles the history of **On Literature,** not, to be sure, the latter's asserted movement of perfectibility, but its tendency to fall away from linear progression into a cycle of rise and fall.

Thus the story Staël wanted to tell—a story of temporal progress and comprehensible causality—becomes constantly distorted into another quite different one, characterized instead by circularity and senselessness. Despite the assertions she made about her conception of history on the one hand and the novel, as a genre, on the other, they both actually tell the same story. Some unwilled but inexorable pattern seems to impose itself, weakening the links of the desired narrations and molding them into a common shape. It is, then, in the very "weakness" of the plot that Staël expresses herself most strongly. Nancy K. Miller's work on novels by eighteenth-century women, often accused of implausibility and lack of verisimilitude, directs attention to this kind of strength: "The peculiar shape of a heroine's destiny in novels by women, the implausible twists of plot so common in these novels, is a form of insistence about the relationship of women to writing . . . The attack on female plots and plausibilities assumes that women writers cannot or will not obey the rules of fiction . . . but . . . the fictions of desire behind the desiderata of fiction are masculine and not universal constructs."[27] The case of Germaine de Staël illustrates and is illuminated by these perceptions.

The associations Staël spells out in her *Essay* are crucial: speculative philosophy, history, abstract, invented, and public are linked with the male; the opposites, imaginative fiction, concrete, imitative, private, are related to the female. In these two books she separates the two domains into two supposedly different works, thereby theoretically dividing herself into two people, the one functioning in man's terms with the mind of a man and the other in woman's terms with the sensitivity of a woman. Staël could not, of course, successfully execute such a polarized plan. One cannot function alternately in two preconceived modes. Rather, one functions always in the same mode, one's own, informed by the place in the world one occupies as male or female and by one's interpretation of that place. Thus, Staël could not finally set history aside as an idealized and abstract form that she could use to tell a story of progress and continuity. It is difficult to believe in a story one has not participated in and even more so to lend credence to a story that does not ring true when judged according to one's own experience.

It is to Staël's credit that she devoted considerable thought to the nature and relationship of the stories of man and of woman. In the *Passions* she states that love for woman is a story but for man it is an episode.[28] Man's story is public and recounted by history. In his story, woman, who belongs to private life, figures only incidentally, in those "vast empty spaces" that are not included in the narration of public events of the past. In man's story woman is present only in the absent parts—in other words, she figures not at all. If she tries to tell that story herself she will inevitably find herself not included in it. Can one tell a story from which one has been erased in advance? In *On Germany,* some ten years after the publication of the two books under consideration here, Staël put the matter somewhat differently: "Women try to arrange themselves like a novel; men, like a history"[29] This reflection implies that a woman will design her story along the lines of the private life she leads rather than in the manner of the story in which she has no part. This is in fact what Staël did in composing her two histories. She aspired to the telling of man's story in what she perceives as man's way, but she could not carry it off. She ends instead by telling twice the story whose structure she had personally experienced.

There is, however, one element in the book on history that indicates that Staël was making an effort to go beyond the impasse she had reached in trying to tell two separate stories. This effort takes two forms in *On Literature:* the first is to find a place for women in male history; the second is to write a new story with parts for both men and women.

The search for a place within male history was most fundamentally for Staël a search for a place for herself, that is, a place for a special woman, different from others, more talented, more energetic, more ambitious, unwilling to be relegated to the domestic life that other women accept. At the beginning of her chapter on women, the reader may be led to expect a general treatment of the place of women in society and a call, like that of Mary Wollstonecraft, for improvement in the status of woman through education. But after this general introduction, Staël passes immediately to the subject of her real interest, revealed in the very title of the essay, **"On Women Who Cultivate Letters"** (part II, chapter 4). She particularly examines the place of woman writers in a monarchy and in a republic. As the essay draws to a close she depicts the vicissitudes of the female literary figure in a way all too obviously calculated to attract pity to herself. Politically, this chapter amounts simply to an appeal that some few, elite, superior women be allowed a role in man's history. The chapter does not foresee any impact on that history that would exceed its limits.

The second effort is more imaginative and may reach further. Staël promises in the introduction to show what impact the status ("mode d'existence") of women before and after the establishment of Christianity had on the development of literature. Such an initiative would potentially involve a new history that would integrate both man's story and woman's story into one story. Thus two inadequacies of history, as Staël saw it, would be overcome. No longer would there be vast empty spaces that remain when one tells public history only, thereby leaving out the private. No longer would woman's story be an often-omitted episode in a story in which she did not participate. Both man's and woman's story would thereby be completed, complemented, supplemented by each other.

That Staël even envisaged such a history is quite impressive. To this day it has not been written, although feminist historians are at work to increase the knowledge about women in the past to a point that would make it possible to attempt such an integration. That Staël did not succeed is not surprising. Even in her introduction one realizes that her insight has not gone far enough, for she writes of woman's influence in a list of many other factors that includes forms of government, religion, and climate that have had an impact on the history of literature. Obviously woman is not the focal point of her concern. Moreover, in this introduction, the influence of woman is subsumed under another apparently more influential category, the establishment of Christianity.

In the remainder of the book, Staël does not actually limit herself to woman's place before and after Christianity. Possibly she introduced her topic in such a timid and limited way in order to avoid criticism that she, as a woman, was giving inordinate attention to the place of women. Identifying herself with women, making common cause with "them," was not part of her approach. Her desire to write a book which would be admired by men and accepted as a piece of writing as fine as any man had done would have turned her away from any bolder move. Each mention of women in the work, in fact, has the same double movement which we are noting here: a claim rich in suggestions followed by an undercutting of those suggestions or of the claim. I will give a few examples of this phenomenon.

Staël states that in Homer there is little "true sensitivity." It seems, she says, that the ability to love has increased with other progress the human mind has made, especially in modern times when women are called upon to share man's destiny (part I, chapter 1, FD I, p. 212). The fact that the Greeks had only limited relationships with women, who were kept rigidly in certain roles, in turn limited the sensitivity and thereby the profundity of their works. Here she seems to be pointing toward a new society. A society that includes both men and women functions best. Any other society will be constrained and restricted, its works of art concomitantly vitiated. Yet only a few sentences later Staël specifies the role that she envisages for woman: she will be mentally equal, submissive because of love, "a companion who will be happy to dedicate her faculties, her time, her feelings, to complete another existence."[30] Here the particular kind of "sharing man's destiny" is specified. Woman is depicted in her traditional secondary and private role. Destiny still belongs to man, this second passage states clearly. Woman may share it but only by remaining in a derivative place.

Before Christianity, women were virtual slaves, Staël states. Christianity made them morally and spiritually equal (FD I, p. 239). This equality, limited as Staël indicates by her qualifiers, admitted women to the role they now have: they have not composed, she says, truly superior works but they have served the cause of literary progress because of what men have learned from them in their relationships. Or again, as Staël begins her discussion of contemporary literature, she stresses woman's influence. "All the feelings which they are permitted to have, the fear of death,

regret for life, endless devotion, measureless indignation, enrich literature with new expressions."[31] The beginning of the chapter attaches great importance to women in the transformation of ancient into modern literature. Here again an attempt at integration of the private and the public is at least sketched. But the influence of women is limited (I, 151) to works of imagination and, within that category, to certain aspects—delicate sensibility, variety of situations, knowledge of the human heart. Furthermore, Staël's references to women are always in the third person, indicating a distancing and dissociation from the group to which she in fact belonged. In short, many times suggestions are made but their implications are immediately restricted to relatively small and delimited areas that are not outside the traditional realm of women.

Timid and consistently undercut claims bear witness to troubled and unresolved feelings, which are really at the heart of the narrative difficulties of *Delphine* and *On Literature*. In her chapter on women of letters Staël says "The existence of woman in society is still uncertain in many ways . . . Everything is arbitrary in their success as well as in their failures . . . In present society, they are, for the most part, neither in the order of nature nor in that of society."[32] Observing that her actions have unpredictable results, a woman may well find it difficult to believe in continuity and causality, to depict an order to which she does not belong, to speak with certainty from a position of uncertainty. Staël's desire to function within the world of men conflicted with society's dictates concerning woman's proper place. Her desire to believe that there was a forward-looking, progressive, continuous male story in which she might herself take some part, albeit indirect, conflicted with her observation of the story she seemed to be living out herself. In these two books she works in a troubled half-light with these conflicts. Her tremendous energy and ambition are still at work, but they become enmeshed in circularity and senselessness because she has found no resolution, no certain ground on which to stand and from which she can function. She refuses solidarity with other women, cannot find a satisfactory place for herself in man's world, and finds no way to reconcile the two.[33]

Staël was both bold and timid. Her audacity made her writing possible; her timidity undermined its effectiveness. The uncertain position of their author generates the peculiar status of these strong and yet insecure works. She had not enough courage to object to that status openly, not enough fear to accept it, and not enough blindness to ignore it. Here she has seen through to the true nature of woman's, of her own, story. She has told it once and again, always with the same structure, no matter what the difference in terms. Therein lies her deeply female vision and her implicit "j'accuse."

Notes

1. Balayé, Simone. *Madame de Staël: Lumiéres et Liberté,* 1979, p. 248.

2. The critical edition of this work is Madame de Staël, *De la littérature considérée dans ses rapports avec*

les institutions sociales, edited by Paul van Tieghem (Geneva: Droz, 1959).

3. Des femmes has recently published an "édition féministe" of *Delphine,* edited by Claudine Herrmann (Paris: Des femmes, 1981).

4. "A propos du 'préromantisme': continuité ou rupture chez Madame de Staël," p. 168. (L'Oeuvre critique et politique de Madame de Staël propose; construit, réconforte, pendant que l'oeuvre romanesque détruit en exprimant l'angoisse de l'écrivain.)

5. Gutwirth, Madelyn. *Madame de Staël, Novelist: The Emergence of the Artist as Woman,* 1979, pp. 77-80 and 157.

6. Un homme doit savoir braver l'opinion, une femme s'y soumettre. (FD I, p. 334)

7. Gutwirth, pp. 108-10 and 113-21.

8. Balayé, pp. 136, and 243. (Il y a pour ses romans des fins tragiques, pour ses oeuvres philosophiques et politiques des fins qui ne sont jamais des fermetures . . . une différence fondamentale d'orientation entre ces deux manières d'exprimer son propre génie.)

9. James Hamilton, "Structural Polarity in Madame de Staël's *De la litterature, French Review* 50, no. 5 (April 1977):706-12.

10. En parcourant les révolutions du monde et la succession des siècles, il est une idée première dont je ne détourne jamais mon attention: c'est la perfectibilité de *l'espèce humaine.* Je ne pense pas que ce grand oeuvre de la nature morale ait jamais été abandonné; dans les périodes lumineuses, comme dans les siècles de ténèbres, *la marche graduelle de l'esprit humain* n'a point été interrompue. (Discours Préliminaire, FD I, p. 207)

11. Lucia Omacini, "Pour une typologie du discours staëlien," p. 379.

12. Le temps nous découvre un dessein dans la suite des événements qui semblaient n'être que le pur effet du hasard; et l'on voit surgir une pensée, toujours la même, de l'abîme des faits et des siècles. (Part I, chapter 8; FD I, p. 236)

13. Promet aux hommes sur cette terre quelques-uns des bienfaits d'une vie immortelle, un avenir sans bornes, une continuité sans interruption! (P. 198)

14. Par exemple, . . . le langage est l'instrument nécessaire pour acquérir tous les autres développements; et, par une sorte de prodige, cet instrument existe. (Part I, chapter 1. FD I, p. 210)

15. On a prétendu que la décadence des arts, des lettres et des empires, devait arriver nécessairement après un certain degré de splendeur. (Part I, chapter 7. FD I, p. 234)

16. La nature morale tend à se perfectionner. L'amélioration précédente est une cause de l'amélioration future; cette chaîne peut être interrompue par des événements accidentels qui contrarient

les progrès à venir, mais qui ne sont point la conséquence des progres antérieurs. (Part I, chapter 7. FD I, p. 234)

17. Ainsi marchait le siècle vers la conquête de la liberté . . . Ah! . . . Toutes les fois que le cours des idées ramène à réfléchir sur la destinée de l'homme, la révolution nous apparaît. (Part I, chapter 9. FD I, p. 245)

18. Ne succombons pas néanmoins à cet abattement. Revenons aux observations générales.

19. J'ai suivi l'histoire de l'esprit humain depuis Homère jusqu'en 1789. Dans mon orgueil national je regardais l'époque de la révolution de France comme une ère nouvelle pour le monde intellectuel. (Part I, chapter 1. FD I, p. 288)

20. Il est impossible de condamner la pensée à revenir sur ses pas, avec l'espérance de moins et les regrets de plus; l'esprit humain, privé d'avenir, tomberait dans la dégradation la plus misérable. Cherchons-le donc cet avenir dans les productions littéraires et les idées philosophiques. (Part II, chapter 1. FD I, p. 289)

21. For a discussion of the novel's epistolarity as well as of its revelation of Staël's depiction of the Revolution, see Madelyn Gutwirth, "La *Delphine* de Madame de Staël: Femme, Révolution, et Mode Epistolaire," in *Cahiers Staëliens,* nos. 26-27 (1979):151-65.

22. Les fictions doivent nous expliquer, par nos vertus et nos sentiments, les mystères de notre sort. (FD I, p. 335)

23. J'entre dans le monde avec un caractère bon et vrai, de l'esprit, de la jeunesse et de la fortune; pourquoi ces dons de la Providence ne me rendraient-ils pas heureuse? (Part I, letter 3. FD I, p. 341)

24. Balayé, p. 136.

25. Gutwirth, p. 106.

26. I take the desire to stop time altogether to be a more fundamental mode of temporal sensibility than the "hâte de vivre," the desire to make time move more quickly, isolated and analyzed by Georges Poulet, *Etudes sur le temps humain,* 1946. Reprint (Paris: Plon, 1956), 194.

27. Nancy K. Miller, "Emphasis Added: Plots and Plausibilities in Women's Fiction," *Publications of the Modern Language Association,* 96 no. 1 (January 1981):44, 46. This article has been reprinted in *Feminist Criticism: Essays on Women, Literature, and Theory,* 339-60 edited by Elaine Showalter, (New York: Pantheon, 1985), 339-60.

28. Section I, chapter 4. FD I, p. 137.

29. Les femmes cherchent à s'arranger commen un roman, et les hommes comme une histoire. (Part III, chapter 18. FD II, p. 217.)

30. Une compagne de la vie, heureuse de consacrer ses facultés, ses jours, ses sentiments, à compléter une autre existence. (Part I, chapter 8. FD I, p. 212)

31. Tous les sentiments auxquels il leur est permis de se livrer, la crainte de la mort, le regret de la vie, le dévouement sans bornes, l'indignation sans mesure, enrichissent la littérature d'expressions nouvelles. (Part I, chapter 9. FD I, p. 243)

32. L'existence des femmes en société est encore incertaine sous beaucoup de rapports. . . . Tout est arbitraire dans leurs succès comme dans leurs revers. . . . Dans l'état actual, elles ne sont pour la plupart ni dans l'ordre de la nature, ni dans l'ordre de la société. (Part II, chapter 4. FD I, p. 301)

33. Two articles which treat Staël's attitude toward women in society are Madelyn Gutwirth, "Madame de Staël, Rousseau, and the Woman Question," and Joanne Kitchen, "La littérature et les femmes selon Madame de Staël." The latter, in the main, juxtaposes passages in which Staël treated the subject, whereas the former is marked by reflection and analysis.

Deborah Heller (essay date 1990)

SOURCE: "Tragedy, Sisterhood, and Revenge in *Corinne*," in *Papers on Language & Literature,* Vol. 26, No. 2, Spring, 1990, pp. 212-32.

[*In the following essay, Heller evaluates the impact of de Staël's feminist narrative in* Corinne *on twentieth century readers.*]

1

The publication of Avriel H. Goldberger's new translation of Germaine de Staël's *Corinne ou l'Italie* makes accessible to an American readership the novel that Ellen Moers, in her early pioneering study of women's literature, called "*the* book of the woman of genius" and whose "enormous influence on literary women" she traced throughout the nineteenth century (173, 174). Coinciding with a burgeoning interest in women's studies, Goldberger's translation comes at an opportune time. Thirty years ago, Staël's American biographer was content to write off her novels as period pieces; comparing Staël unfavorably to her contemporary, Jane Austen, J. Christopher Herold observed that while the problems of Austen's characters "are of the commonplace or eternally human variety . . . the problems of Germaine's characters are those of her age and place." However questionable this distinction, it led him to an undeniable truth, which he presented as right and just: "Jane is still read, and Germaine is not" (232). The contemporary American Staël scholar, Madelyn Gutwirth, takes a different view of *Corinne* in her back cover quote for Goldberger's new translation: "It will set this building block of women's literature firmly back into the foundation of the edifice, where it belongs."

Which is it, then, to be—a book for scholars only, or a book that speaks to our contemporary concerns? In any case, the time is ripe for our considering *Corinne ou l'Italie* anew, for in her fundamental concern with the status of women, Madame de Staël addresses issues that touch us deeply today. She challenges female stereotypes that still afflict us and poses problems that remain relevant to our experience. Yet it will hardly surprise if *Corinne* cannot be read by us in quite the same defiant and self-affirmative spirit in which it was written, or if in challenging many attitudes and social conventions that were detrimental to female development, the novel nonetheless upholds others equally damaging. Our most valiant efforts to achieve critical distance from the intellectual and social climate in which we have developed must, necessarily, remain in some way part of that context. The tension between what is challenged and what is accepted constitutes the hidden drama of *Corinne.*

That Staël was "not only unmilitant but often quite reactionary in her own statements about women" has been aptly demonstrated by Madelyn Gutwirth with regard to the gradual and cautious evolution of Staël's theoretical position ("Madame de Staël" 101). This essay is concerned with the complementary issue of the unarticulated logic behind Staël's dramatic treatment of women in *Corinne.* The novel makes extraordinary claims for an exceptional heroine, and appears to defy an ideology that opposes the flowering of her talent; but it also endorses a system of values destructive to the heroine and ultimately calls into question the genius it claims for her.[1]

Explicitly, *Corinne* is presented as a tragedy of a woman of genius defeated by the restrictive forces of narrow social conventions and expectations. By now, the story of how female potential is thwarted by the limitations of social possibility is easily recognizable as a familiar "woman's plot,"[2] a variant of a more general pattern in the nineteenth-century novel—the thwarting of individual potential by social constraint; but for the "woman's plot" the social constraints are much greater, the obstacles much more pronounced. Viewed in this context, Staël's 1807 novel prefigures subsequent versions of the same general conflict that embody in a manner particular to women a perpetual human dilemma. *Corinne,* however, is immediately distinguishable from later, more typical nineteenth-century treatments of this theme by its unremitting insistence on the *fulfilled* genius of its heroine: when we first see Corinne she is being crowned for her artistic achievement at the Capitol in Rome.

Staël makes plain, however, that such appreciative social recognition of female genius is possible only in Italy. Late in the novel Corinne reveals herself as the daughter of an English lord and a Florentine mother, who from the ages of fifteen to twenty-one had lived in a small town in England, where she was made to feel the crushing weight of social disapproval for any activity or interest that departed from the narrowest interpretation of female domestic duty. The best advice from her father was to exercise her talents in secret, so as not to excite envy. With less conviction he extended the feeble hope that with luck she might be fortunate enough to find a husband who would take pleasure in her talents. But when Corinne spent time alone to cultivate her talents, her stepmother became angry and resentful. "What is the good of all that," she would ask with chilling Utilitarian logic, broaching what emerges as an important underlying question throughout the novel: "Will you be any happier for it?" (365). Corinne's naive belief that happiness consists in the development of our faculties was met with her stepmother's correction that a woman's role was to care for her husband and children, and that all other ambitions could only cause trouble. In Staël's account, English provincial life appears more wholly suffocating and stultifying than it does in the novels of Jane Austen or George Eliot, lacking even a shred of hollow approval for such female "accomplishments" as piano playing or sketching, which their works satirize. Hence, when Corinne comes into an independent income after her father's death, recognizing that her energies and enthusiasm need encouragement if she is to develop her talents, she flees the death-in-life of English provincial society and returns to her native Italy. Corinne's past history, then, circumscribed within a single retrospective, autobiographical "book" of the novel, presents the reader only with a tragedy-that-might-have-been, one averted by the wise choice of a nurturing environment.

Still, Simone Balayé surely reads Staël's intention correctly when she describes the "essential theme" of the novel as "the conflict of the woman of genius with society" (137), although our reading will suggest ways in which the text that emerges is less simple than the apparent intention behind it. In its broadest outlines the opposition between social requirements and female genius is clear enough, for though Corinne appears to have escaped the asphyxiating influence of English social attitudes, her triumph is short-lived. To summarize a complex plot: at the moment of greatest glory in her career—her coronation at the Capitol—she meets and falls in love with Oswald Lord Nelvil, peer of Scotland, in whom are deeply rooted the very prejudices of British society that Corinne has fled. While in Italy and under the direct influence of Corinne, with whom he falls in love, Oswald subjects these attitudes to scrutiny, concluding that the exceptional qualities of her genius and personality are more desirable than the self-effacing domestic virtues that his society has taught him to value most in women. Nevertheless, he feels bound by filial devotion to do nothing that might contradict the wishes of his dead father. Only late in the novel does Corinne reveal that Oswald's father had met her in England and thought her unsuitable to be his son's wife, preferring Corinne's younger half sister Lucile instead. Corinne's revelation does not initially alter Oswald's intention to remain faithful; but when his regiment summons him back to England, he learns more about his father's disapproval of Corinne as a marriage choice, hears her disparaged by her stepmother, and meets the angelic, socially conventional Lucile. Influenced as well by a series of improbable coincidences and the mistaken belief that Corinne has lost interest in him, Oswald betrays Corinne by marrying her sister, as his father had wished, and Corinne retires

from the world to die. As social forces hostile to Corinne's genius converge to assist her defeat, the novel follows the broad pattern of classical tragedy, dramatizing the fall of a protagonist from her initial position of grandeur, and sidesteps the tragedy *manquée* (which will become more typical of the nineteenth-century novel) of a protagonist whose exceptional sensibilities are inhibited by circumstance from developing fully.

Other embryonic tragedies in ***Corinne*** are also adumbrated but not pursued. The most important of these is the conflict between the demands of love and genius in a woman. Corinne openly pursues and delights in glory, an attitude commonly regarded as praiseworthy in men but unseemly in women. Yet, while it is abundantly clear that her happiness depends on the full and free exercise of her talents, once she falls in love with Oswald his love becomes equally necessary to her. Italy—as much a construct of Staël's myth-making imagination as a product of her powers of observation—is presented as the required sustaining soil for the full flowering of her genius.[3] This fact, implicit in her life history, is made explicit late in the book in a letter by Oswald's father to Corinne's father, antedating the action proper of the novel and underscoring the importance of contextuality in determining identity and possibility: "such rare talents must necessarily excite the desire to develop them . . . [Corinne] would necessarily lead my son outside of England; for such a woman can not be happy here; and only Italy is suited to her." But, the letter continues, whereas English provincial domestic life is entirely unsuitable to Corinne, "a man born in our happy fatherland must be English above all." In short, the politically responsible male citizen and the woman artist must necessarily prove incompatible, because "in countries where political institutions provide men with honorable opportunities to act and to prove themselves, women must remain in the shadows" (466-67; bk. 16, ch. 8). The late Lord Nelvil's letter only confirms the potential conflict that has cast its menacing shadow over the love story all along. A good Englishman, Oswald needs England; an artist and a woman, Corinne needs Italy. What Lord Nelvil could not predict, however, is that, as a passionate, loving nature, Corinne would need Oswald as well.

The potential conflicts between Oswald's love for Corinne and his role as a Scottish peer, military man, and devoted son, and between Corinne's needs as an artist and a woman in love, are carefully constructed. But they are not sustained, and the focus of the tragedy shifts elsewhere. Back in England, Oswald does wonder how to reconcile loyalty to his father with his oft-sworn fidelity to Corinne. A compromise they had earlier discussed—his returning to her in Italy as a devoted, loving friend—hovers unsatisfactorily in his mind as a hazy, ill-defined alternative. But Oswald does not clearly confront the problem of how frustrating such an existence might prove to him in the long run. This is partly because the novel offers no convincing proof that he has any real *work* from which an idle residence in Italy, passed in single-minded devotion to Corinne, would keep him. (His exploits of military bravery after his marriage are presented more as desperate attempts at self-destruction than anything else.) More fundamentally, he never faces directly the potential conflict between love and vocation because his newly awakened love for Lucile, the insufficiency of his prior love for Corinne, his moral scruples regarding his father's wishes, and his faulty interpretation of Corinne's silence all combine with his deep-rooted prejudices to lead him, confusedly and almost passively, into his precipitous marriage with her half sister.

In the presentation of Corinne, the potential conflict between love and career—in her case, between love and genius—is more abundantly prepared for and more completely abandoned. Throughout the novel Staël scatters indications of an inherent conflict between Corinne's increasing dependency on Oswald, which characterizes her love, and the necessary independence of spirit required for her artistic creativity. Yet as long as Oswald remains with her, this embryonic conflict results in no appreciable ill effects. Indeed, as long as she is sure of Oswald's love and he remains with her, she is perfectly happy. The very idea of marriage appears distasteful to her, especially when she contemplates that it would force her to leave Italy to live in England. Ultimately, however, she does come to hope that Oswald will want to marry her as she recognizes that "he conceived of happiness only in domestic life and that he could never renounce the plan of marrying her except by loving her less" (397; bk. 15, ch. 2). In fact, she assures him, "if you wished to spend your days in the remotest part of Scotland, I would be happy to live and die there by your side; but far from giving up my imagination, it would serve me the better to enjoy Nature" (366; bk. 14, ch. 1). But how can the reader believe this sudden turn after all we have read? There has been abundant preparation that might have led to the tragic ramifications of an unreconcilable conflict between Corinne's need for Oswald's love *and* for an environment and state of mind conducive to her uninhibited development as an artist, as well as between the demands of marriage and those of a woman's creative self-fulfillment; but such preparation is not followed up. Instead of pursuing the internal dynamics of Corinne's contrasting needs and desires, the focus of the tragedy shifts to Oswald's betrayal and his failure to appreciate adequately Corinne's extraordinary worth and love for him.

The tragedy growing out of a woman's contradictory needs and desires would have conferred a more contemporary, even a more feminist, flavor to the novel. The tragedy of a woman's misplaced affections and her betrayal by an unworthy man is, sadly, a more conventional as well as a conceptually less interesting plot. A particularly dated aspect of the structure Staël develops is that, in the contrast between the intensity of Corinne's love and the insufficiency of Oswald's, Oswald is portrayed not only as psychologically weak and indecisive, but also as morally culpable. Although Corinne repeatedly affirms she wants Oswald's love freely given and never seeks marriage as a means of holding him against his will, his failure to reciprocate the intensity of her love is presented, in the context of the novel's moral structure, as objectively blameworthy. This judgment, implicit throughout, is made explicit in several authorial statements on greater female vulnerability—both emotional and social—in love, and is reiterated near the end by Prince Castel-Forte, who pronounces definitively on Oswald's guilt by pointing above all to women's greater vulnerability "in the world's opinion" (563; bk. 20, ch. 2). Interestingly, Staël might have bolstered her view of Oswald's culpability by developing the implications of a situation which, again, she introduces and then declines to pursue dramatically. She repeatedly shows Corinne's concealing from Oswald the extent to which she is "compromising" herself when she sets off from Rome to travel alone with him to other parts of Italy; but when Corinne returns from these travels unmarried, though her friends are surprised, her social position has in no way suffered. Even after she is abandoned, her friends esteem her as highly and remain as eager for her company as before. The issue of Corinne's social vulnerability is raised only to be dropped. On the other hand, Corinne's angry reproach near the end, "what have you done with so much love?" (572; bk. 20, ch. 3), echoes the novel's sustained viewpoint, implicit throughout, that a love as exceptional as Corinne's somehow "deserves" to be returned. It is her emotional, rather than her social, vulnerability that proves her undoing. It may be, of course, that the author does not really believe in the idyllic social context she has constructed for her heroine. But as the novel is written, Corinne becomes a victim of her love for Oswald because of forces within herself, not within society.

2

A modern reading of the novel might want to overlook the emphasis attributed to Oswald's "fault," and to locate the deeper tragedy in the way in which all of Corinne's extraordinary talents, her intellectual and artistic energies, ultimately fail to help her when she is wounded in love. Such a reading would lead us to re-view, in a sadly ironic light, Corinne's earlier conversations with her stepmother, in which Lady Edgermond questioned the worth of female genius and Corinne expressed unhesitating confidence in the intrinsic value of cultivating her faculties. With a logic that recalls Rousseau as it anticipates Stendhal, Staël reiterates that the very power of Corinne's faculties—the richness of her sensibilities, intellect, and imagination—only serves to increase her unhappiness.

However, if we attempt to "update" the novel by ignoring the clearly expressed view of Oswald's responsibility for Corinne's death and by viewing the profounder tragedy as the heroine's own emotional vulnerability, we encounter an unavoidable difficulty: it is not at all plain that we are being invited to regard Corinne's monomaniacal fixation on Oswald's betrayal and her determined drift toward death as tragic. Rather, her withdrawal from the world and her death from a broken heart are presented, finally, as more triumphant than tragic. How this happens may best be seen by considering the roles of the two other women in the novel whose relation to Oswald can be compared to

Corinne's. One is her half sister with whom at the end she develops a strange bond, which has been sensitively commented on by feminist critics and which we shall examine shortly. The other is Mme. d'Arbigny, Oswald's first love, the other "other woman" in *Corinne,* who typically receives only the briefest possible mention from critics, if they do not ignore her entirely. Mme. d'Arbigny deserves considerably more attention if we are to understand the values implicit in *Corinne*—its ideology—and the problems the novel poses for contemporary readers.

Mme. d'Arbigny belongs to the prehistory of the narrative proper, existing only in Oswald's account of his earlier life. A foil to Corinne, whose honesty and naturalness are everywhere insisted upon, d'Arbigny appears from the beginning as calculating and deceitful. The aristocratic widow of a rich, older husband whom she had married without love to escape financial hardship, she inveigles herself into Oswald's affections by flattering and always agreeing with him. After her brother's execution, following Oswald's return to Scotland, she lures Oswald back to revolutionary France by appealing to his sense of chivalry, untruthfully expressing anxiety about her financial plight and pretending to be more friendless than she is. However, her interest in him is not venal, any more than Corinne's. She loves as much as one can when "one conducts the affairs of the heart like a political intrigue" (318; bk. 12, ch. 2). In Oswald's account, she is also somehow at fault for failing to resist his overtures of physical passion: "as it was part of her plan to captivate me at any cost, I thought I perceived that she was not invariably set on rejecting my desires; and now that I think back over what happened between us, it seems to me that she hesitated from motives that were foreign to love"—this implies that true love would have fortified her resistance—"and that her apparent struggles were secret deliberations." Afterwards, "She showed more unhappiness and remorse than perhaps she actually felt, and bound me tightly to her destiny by her very repentance" (319; bk. 12, ch. 2). She refuses Oswald's entreaties to return with him to England to obtain his father's consent to their marriage, urging him instead to marry her first and threatening to give herself up to assassins if he leaves. Finally, in response to his sick father's repeated urgent summonses, he is on the point of departing alone when she pretends to be pregnant and claims his departure will cause the death of her unborn child as well as herself.

Ultimately, Oswald is released from his agonizing moral dilemma by the disclosures of M. de Maltigues, a close relative and confidant of Mme. d'Arbigny, whom, Oswald learns belatedly, she has been planning to marry should Oswald leave her, "for under no circumstances did she want to appear as an abandoned woman" 'car elle ne voulait à aucun prix passer pour une femme abandonnée' (321; bk. 12, ch. 2). An engaging cynic, M. de Maltigues reveals Mme. d'Arbigny as "a person of great wisdom . . . who, even when she is in love herself, always takes wise precautions for the eventuality that she will no longer be loved." Exposing Mme. d'Arbigny's pregnancy as a

hoax, M. de Maltigues advises Oswald against marrying her ("she is too crafty [rusée] for you"), while relieving him of possible moral scruples: "She will weep, because she loves you; but she will recover, because she is a woman too reasonable to want to be unhappy, and above all, to appear to be so. Within three months she will be Madame de Maltigues" (329-31; bk. 12, ch. 3). M. de Maltigues's prophesy seems to provide a satisfying closure to this episode in Oswald's history. Oswald returns to Scotland, but too late to see his father alive; blaming himself for his father's death, he is left with an unassuageable sense of guilt.

Mme. d'Arbigny's absence from the rest of the novel, however, is deceptive, for her unacknowledged, invisible presence hovers over much of what follows. While her most obvious dramatic function is to intensify Oswald's deference toward his father's wishes regarding his choice of a wife, structurally and thematically she also serves other functions. Her many differences from Corinne throw into relief aspects of the heroine's character—Corinne's simplicity and naturalness, and her refusal to try to hold Oswald against his will or scruples by marriage or, indeed, by any stratagem or ruse. Moreover, the love affair between Oswald and Mme. d'Arbigny also emphasizes the different nature of his romance with Corinne; although Oswald is forever clasping Corinne to his heart in outbursts of passionate intensity, the novel makes clear that their love is chaste:

> Several times he pressed Corinne to his heart, several times he moved away, then returned, then moved away again, in order to respect the woman who was to be the companion of his life. Corinne gave no thought to the dangers which might have alarmed her, for such was her esteem for Oswald, that, if he had asked for the full gift of her being, she would not have doubted that this prayer was his solemn oath to marry her; but she was quite glad that he would triumph over himself and honour her by this sacrifice. . . . (288; bk. 11, ch.1)

She assures him, "I am confident you will respect the woman who loves you; you know a simple prayer from you would be all-powerful; therefore it is you who are answerable for me; it is you who would refuse me forever as your wife if you rendered me unworthy of so being" (289; bk. 11, ch. 1). In short, they both subscribe to the familiar double standard, whereby female chastity is an unquestioned virtue, and men are thought to have stronger sexual feelings than women and are permitted greater sexual liberties—but not with women they truly respect. Tellingly, the story of Oswald's romance with Mme. d'Arbigny arouses no feelings of jealousy in Corinne—indeed, having listened to his lengthy tale, Corinne wastes not a word or even a thought on her predecessor in Oswald's affections. By contrast, Corinne's account of her chaste relationships with two prior suitors arouses considerable jealousy in Oswald.[4] The novel thus implicitly admonishes the reader not to confuse the unabashed public display of female talent, intelligence, and eloquence with emotional lightness or sexual unchastity. Whatever other literary and social conventions Corinne may violate, female chastity is not one of them. Sadly, it is in part by insisting on a code of sexual propriety more stringent than any Staël herself followed, that the novel seeks to validate Corinne's right to lead the free life of an artist.

That the sexually freer "other woman" is in reality less passionate than the virtuous virgin heroine is not in itself implausible. We may want to recognize, however, that this polarity has appeared particularly congenial to women novelists in a world unreceptive to the unconventional, "unfeminine" public display of talent, eloquence, and emotional intensity which writing necessarily entails. It can be understood as a kind of back-handed defense of passion, a way of demonstrating its compatibility with virtue. The same pattern appears later in the century in *Jane Eyre,* whose sexually chaste heroine is more truly passionate than any of the four "looser" "other women" in Rochester's past (his Creole wife or his three continental mistresses). Charlotte Brontë, herself a passionate writer, lived under severely circumscribed social conditions; moreover, the value she placed on Jane's "virtue" corresponded to her own ethical beliefs. Staël's beliefs, as well as her personal conduct, were different. But despite this—and the vastly greater social rank and economic independence enjoyed by her and her fictional heroine—the pattern of polarities that separates Corinne and Mme. d'Arbigny are essentially the same as in Brontë's novel.

Mme. d'Arbigny's shallowness is revealed not only in her sexual "looseness," but also, and perhaps chiefly, in her ability to recover from her disappointment in love and to transfer her affections to another man, "car elle ne voulait à aucun prix passer pour une femme abandonnée". The predefined role of "la femme abandonnée" was to be contemptible, ridiculous, or pathetic. By outliving a lover's rejection and redirecting her affections a woman might escape the stigma of being "une femme abandonnée," but only at the cost of confirming her fundamental "lightness," compromising the dignity and integrity of her prior feelings of love, and, in turn, her own dignity and integrity as a human being.

In the broadest outlines, Mme. d'Arbigny is a kind of prototype of Corinne, despite all the differences already noted. In relation to Oswald, both are enticing foreign women, both in some ways too clever for him, but also too clever for their own good. Oswald's father disapproves of each as a wife for his son. The most significant similarity, however, is that both are abandoned by him. Oswald's story of Mme. d'Arbigny, with its stern assessment of her, might well serve Corinne as a cautionary tale, though no evidence is given that it does. However, it conveys to the reader the author's view of the appropriate attitude toward Corinne's death. Reminding us of the unflattering associations attached to *la femme abandonnée,* while demonstrating the indignity that, alternately, attaches to a woman who accepts rejection and carries on with her life, the episode helps us to recognize the predicament that Corinne goes on to demonstrate—only through death can the aban-

doned woman escape the stigma of being thought light, ridiculous, pitiable, or contemptible. A woman who loves unwisely can reaffirm her dignity and worth only by proving the absolute and uncompromising purity of her love, and this affirmation can be achieved only through her complete and demonstrated inability to sustain its loss.[5] Corinne may come to recognize at the end that Oswald "is not the man I thought he was" (565; bk. 20, ch. 2), but this discovery only makes it more imperative for her to prove that her love is "unique au monde." Corinne's death distinguishes her from the other "other woman" of the novel, and thus becomes a means of heroic self-vindication, rather than tragic defeat.

The Mme. d'Arbigny episode leads to other reflections. If Corinne feels no bonds of "sisterhood" between herself and Mme. d'Arbigny, it would be strange if the same were true of the author who created them both. On the simplest level, among the cosmopolitan cast which populates *Corinne,* Mme. d'Arbigny is the only Frenchwoman. And who could be more French than her Paris-born author, who yearned throughout years of exile to return to her native city? Both character and author were the widows of much older husbands, whom they married without love; yet both pursued love and were sexually accessible. And while Mme. d'Arbigny's approach to her love affair with Oswald, as well as her reaction to his loss, may have been totally alien to Corinne, her conduct cannot have been entirely so to Staël. Although Staël was not particularly looking for another husband, Oswald's accounts of Mme. d'Arbigny's scenes—her tears, hysterics, operatic demonstrations of suffering, her threats of suicide, her swooning at his feet in attempts to renew a cooling lover's ardour—all have a familiar ring to readers acquainted with Staël's biography. Equally familiar is Oswald's account of Mme. d'Arbigny's calculated strategies, her attempts to hold a current lover by stressing her dependence, while yet encouraging a future one—above all, her desire not to pass for an abandoned woman. Moreover, as has been widely noted only in relation to the author's difference from Corinne, Staël herself survived and recovered from rejection by lovers—indeed, more repeatedly than Mme. d'Arbigny.

If aspects of Staël's experience found their way into the creation of this resilient, unchaste Frenchwoman, however, such an identification—even if a "negative identification"[6]—is unlikely to have been conscious. Her portrayal is so generally negative as to have not only prevented critics from appreciating her complex function in the novel, but also to have rendered her all but invisible to them.[7] Perhaps we require a Jean Rhys to rediscover this overlooked woman.[8] In a novel deliberately designed to challenge so many conventional ideas about women, the harsh, dismissive judgment passed on Mme. d'Arbigny reminds us how difficult it is for even a writer as boldly unconventional as Staël to break free from entrenched ways of thinking about her own sex.

3

While critics have failed to recognize any kinship between Mme. d'Arbigny and her creator, and Corinne herself experiences not the slightest bond of sympathy with Oswald's first love, the same neglect has not attached itself to the figure of the more obvious "other woman" in the novel whom Oswald finally does marry.[9] Half sisters in fact, Corinne and Lucile, near the end of the novel, establish a bond of spiritual "sisterhood" as well, which benefits them both. Through her bond with Lucile, Corinne assures the triumphant nature of her death. Five years after his marriage, Oswald returns to Italy with his wife and daughter. Corinne, in the final stages of her gradual and deliberate drift toward death, asks to see her niece, Juliette. In what become daily visits to her aunt, "the child made inconceivable progress in all fields" as Corinne "took the greatest pains to instruct her and communicate all her talents, as a legacy she took pleasure in bequeathing her while she was still alive" (575; bk. 20, ch. 4). Thus, the child of her half sister and her perfidious lover will become the vehicle of Corinne's immortality. Moreover, Lucile also takes to visiting her sister, at first out of pique, but then to benefit from the talents that Corinne is so generously ready to share. In passing on the legacy of her talents to niece and sister, Corinne insures her continued spiritual presence in Oswald's daily life. Corinne teaches Juliette to imitate her on the harp by playing a Scots tune with which, formerly, she had deeply touched Oswald's emotions, and she teaches Lucile to complement her own virtues with those of her dying sister: "You must be you and me at the same time" (578; bk. 20, ch. 4). While Corinne's pedagogical undertakings ostensibly reflect her generosity of spirit and desire to sweeten Oswald's life with the pleasures she was once able to give him, they also, transparently, constitute a means of triumphant self-affirmation, a victorious superimposition of her presence on the future lives of niece, sister, and lost lover. Despite the patina of Christian resignation which colours Corinne's last weeks, her generosity, as critics have noted, far from being selfless, can be seen as a form of triumphant revenge (Goldberger xli-xlii; Gutwirth, *Madame de Staël* 251-57; Moers 175).

However, Corinne's relationships with Lucile and Juliette create a serious difficulty for the reader in reconciling what the novel claims with what it actually shows. It is clear enough how Corinne is able to perpetuate her memory, but just how she might be able to perpetuate her talents and genius (terms used interchangeably) poses an embarrassing question. Corinne has been presented as a universal genius—poet, writer, above all *improvisatrice* in the first definition; as the novel proceeds, her talents multiply. She acts, dances, paints, sculpts, sings, plays the harp, translates, and writes plays. The common thread is that she is "an inspired priestess who devoted herself . . . to the cult of genius" (68; bk. 2, ch. 4) and "a priestess of Apollo," while at the same time a perfectly natural and unaffected woman (52; bk. 2, ch. 1). The superlative nature of the multifaceted talents claimed for Corinne may

lead us to wonder how the "legacy" of such genius can be transmitted in a few weeks, or months, to a five-year-old girl, or a young British-educated wife and mother. Of all her many talents, what can—and does—Corinne actually teach?

The text provides some startling answers. Regarding Juliette, we may quote the whole of a passage cited earlier in part: "in a few days the child made inconceivable progress in all fields. Her Italian teacher was enraptured with her pronunciation. Her music teachers already admired her first efforts." Enrapturing Italian pronunciation and admirable "premiers essais" in music, in addition to learning how to imitate Corinne on the harp, are the only concrete evidence of Corinne's legacy to her niece which the novel provides—along with the more general statement that "the lessons . . . added to her attractions [agréments] in a most remarkable manner" (575; bk. 20, ch. 4). The key summarizing word appears to be "agréments"—those attractions, or adornments, that render us pleasing 'agréable' to others.

Corinne's legacy to Lucile is similar. After his wife's first visit to Corinne, Oswald is struck by the increased interest she shows in conversation, and after several days he observes that his wife "appeared [se montrait] constantly more likeable [aimable] and more lively than usual" (576-77; bk. 20, ch. 4). It is no accident that Lucile's gains are seen through Oswald's eyes, since what we actually see Corinne teaching her sister is the art of pleasing her man:

> Knowing his character perfectly, she made Lucile understand why he needed to find in the woman he loved *a manner* that was in some respects different from his own . . . Corinne depicted herself in her days of splendour . . . and warmly showed Lucile how *agreeable* [*agréable*] a person would be who, with the most proper conduct and the most rigid morality, nevertheless would have all the *charm,* all the abandon, all *the desire to please* [*le désir de plaire*] which is sometimes inspired by the need to redress errors. (578; bk. 20, ch.4; emphasis added)

The lesson continues in this vein, with Corinne helping Lucile to understand how she should seek "to appear more likeable" '*à se montrer plus aimable*' and should recognize "that your virtues never justify you in neglecting in the least bit your attractions" 'vos agréments' (578; bk. 20, ch. 4). Lucile's studies to "resemble the person whom Oswald loved the most" are rewarded, as her husband daily observes in her "new grace(s)" (579; bk. 20, ch. 4). The former crowned priestess of Apollo and the cult of genius, repeatedly likened to the Sibyl of Domenichino, here, through her essential legacy, all but transforms herself into a geisha girl.

Staël thus trivializes her heroine's genius and undermines the claims she has made for her. Even considering that the art of conversation and the social skills of pleasing a cultivated audience were more highly valued in the eighteenth-century Paris salon society in which Staël grew up than they are in our own culture, the conclusion of the novel may still come as a shock. While Corinne's own need for a receptive audience is integral to her conception, and has received abundant critical attention (Moers; Starobinski; Gutwirth; Poulet), at least Corinne seeks an audience for her genius. But her decision to privilege her skill in pleasing an audience of one as the essence of the legacy she bequeaths may find the reader so unprepared as scarcely to absorb the sudden turn in the narrative. If readers have overlooked the strange dénouement and ignored its implications, it is a tribute to the imaginative power of Staël's original conception, which succeeded in inspiring generations of female readers (cf. Blanchard). But the full daring of that conception may be better appreciated if we face the extent to which Corinne's "legacy"—and hence her chosen immortality—represent a radical retreat from the novel's previous bold claims. This finale also adds to the difficulty of any attempt to regard the tragedy as the failure of all Corinne's talents to sustain her in the loss of Oswald. For if this were the crux of her tragedy, then how could her ability to pass on to his wife and daughter the art of knowing how to please and the secret of acquiring "*agréments*" be seen as adequate, no less triumphant, "revenge"?

Still, there is a disturbing coherence between the dénouement and what the narrative has revealed. Corinne can scarcely transmit her artistic and intellectual attainments as their own reward, since they have manifestly not proven so to her. At the same time, the fact that her profoundest legacy should be the art of pleasing enables Corinne to effect a specific revenge. In her autobiographical letter, Corinne described the visit of Oswald's father seven years earlier, when he came to look her over as a potential wife for his son, and she speculated on the causes for his disapproval: "When Lord Nelvil arrived, I wanted to please him, perhaps I wanted it too much, and I gave myself infinitely more pains to succeed than were necessary; I showed him all my talents, I danced, I sang, I improvised for him, and my spirit, contained for too long, was perhaps too lively in breaking its chains." Her account of her performance as a kind of trained pet is sad to read, as it must be for her to reflect on—especially as it was, she fears, her very eagerness to please which made her seem to his father unsuitable as a wife for Oswald. She goes on to suggest, however, that with her greater age and experience she would actually better please Lord Nelvil today, were he alive to see her: "After seven years, experience has calmed me; I am not so eager to show myself off. . . . I have, I know it, improved after seven years" (373-74; bk. 14, ch. 2).

A pitiable plea, and with cause. For Corinne is caught in a classic female double bind. Women are supposed to seek to please, but to please only a very restricted few, or a select "one," and they are not supposed to reveal their intentions too obviously. Corinne's failure lies in the transparency of her youthful efforts to please, and what this suggests about her need for a wide audience, not in the efforts themselves. Her speculations about Lord Nelvil's reaction, in fact, prove correct, as he writes to her father,

"No doubt your daughter has received from you, has found in her heart, only the purest principles and feelings; *but* she has the need to please, to captivate, to make an impression" '*mais* elle a besoin de plaire, de captiver, de faire effet' (466; bk. 16, ch. 8; emphasis added). Once deemed unsuitable for Oswald because of her excessive zeal in wanting to please, Corinne, through the legacy she bequeaths during her last days, has the satisfaction of passing on to his wife and daughter precisely that talent for which she was too hastily condemned and whose lack in Lucile Oswald has felt painfully for the last five years. The demure, retiring Lucile is encouraged to become a synthesis of herself and Corinne, not by assimilating her sister's genius, but by learning how "de plaire, de captiver," without falling into Corinne's youthful error of visibly striving to "faire effet."[10]

Our discomfort with what is presented as Corinne's final triumph is only one more instance of the difficulty a modern reader experiences in responding to **Corinne** in the spirit in which it was written, or even first read. The discrepancies between our contemporary response and the author's intentions, however, may prove instructive, as they clarify important aspects of her world and our own, and dramatize the insidious power of the constraints Staël had to overcome in her bid for a woman's right to lead a full, unfettered existence. Certainly, we can still respond to her concern with the obstacles that society places in the way of woman's quest for self-fulfillment. But since Oswald appears so clearly undeserving of Corinne, and since her world apart from him—her Italy—has proved so attractive to female readers precisely because it seems to offer women all but unlimited possibility for self-development, it is easier for us to appreciate **Corinne** for what it suggests about a woman's own inner conflicts and what it demonstrates about the dynamics of her incomplete liberation from the social codes she has internalized, than for what it shows about her struggles with external obstacles. Although we recognize ways in which women are disadvantaged by society, we feel more comfortable in our literature with tragedy that grows out of internal conflicts and contrasting needs and desires, or that reveals the insufficiency of even great strengths in the face of great needs. On the other hand, the opposition between Corinne's need for independence and her counterbalancing need for love, as the opposition between healthy female identity and marriage, though only adumbrated, finds as ready a response in modern readers as the portrayal of Corinne's all-too-human pain and suffering in the face of loss, despite her acclaimed genius and achievement.

We are less comfortable with the notion of blame in a failed romance, and prefer, at least in theory, to see people take responsibility for their own choices, even for their own mistakes. Implicit in the novel's focus on Oswald's fault and betrayal is a dangerous diminution of Corinne's stature, her uncongenial transformation into a passive victim of someone else's inadequacy. Similarly, her uncompromising rejection of life as a means of remaining "uncompromised" by her unfortunate bestowal of love on an unworthy object is apt to diminish rather than elevate her in our eyes; our instinctive sympathy is with survivors, not with those who seek in what Dickens was to call the "vanity of suffering" a source of triumphant revenge. Nor do we believe—any more than did Staël in her own life—that a woman must deny her sexuality to preserve her dignity and deserve our sympathy. And we regret, even as we try to understand, Staël's need to uphold in fiction those standards—so demeaning and divisive to women—by which she did not want to live. In Corinne's heroic death and in her failure to acknowledge any spiritual kinship with her resilient, sexually freer predecessor in Oswald's affections, we recognize the tenacious hold, on both author and heroine, of values that are deeply destructive to women. Corinne's closing bond of sisterhood with her actual sister, on the other hand, would strike us as satisfyingly "modern," were it not for the questionable object of their alliance. The final element of Corinne's apparent revenge, in which she and her author choose to trivialize her talent and genius in favor of her "agréments" and ability to please an undeserving lover, can best be appreciated as an eloquent demonstration of the unconscious imperatives and double binds at work in both author and heroine. Read in this way, as the valiant and sadly flawed attempt of two extraordinary women (one real, one fictional) to free themselves from a pattern of internalized sexist demands and inhibitions which ultimately prove too strong for them, the novel may still engage us, move us, and even make us weep.

Notes

1. Corinne's defeat itself, of course, has never been in question, but explanations for it vary—from the view of Corinne's death as expressing simple pessimism regarding the fate of the exceptional woman in a world unreceptive to her claims, to Madelyn Gutwirth's recent suggestion that it reflects Mme. de Staël's guilt over her own transgression of the limits placed on female achievement by a patriarchal society and by her own father in particular. This view informs Gutwirth's 1978 full-length study (154-310, 157, 207-08, 224-27). While I am in broad sympathy with Gutwirth's argument, I believe, and shall argue here, that in Staël's presentation of Corinne's death—its logic as well as Corinne's own active role—and in her attempt to transmute tragedy into a victory so powerful as virtually to annihilate its tragic aspects, the novelist has internalized more values destructive to women, and with less self-awareness, than has generally been acknowledged. On Corinne's willed death, see also Starobinski.

2. While the pattern is too familiar to require examples, the "Prelude" to George Eliot's *Middlemarch* succinctly states the conflict as "a certain spiritual grandeur ill-matched with the meanness of opportunity."

3. The status of Staël's "Italy," which had an enormous impact on subsequent nineteenth-century representations of that country, has been the subject of extensive commentary. Moers and Gutwirth in particular have discussed Staël's construction of Italy as a land uniquely favorable to female possibility. For further reading on parallels between that Italy and women, see Hogsett 117-22.

4. Because Gutwirth refers to Corinne's "[living] freely, taking and leaving lovers" (162), I have dwelt on the extreme care Staël takes to clarify the unconsummated nature of the love between Oswald and Corinne and the latter's unimpugned "virtue." The corollary of this is that the term "lovers" can be applied to the men in Corinne's life only if we understand it in its nineteenth-century sense—roughly equivalent to "suitors."

5. One may be reminded here of Racine's Phèdre or Richardson's Clarissa, who also bring about their own deaths as a means of regaining or achieving heroic stature after the consequences of their feelings and judgment threaten to leave them irrevocably compromised. The pattern is a familiar one, though the circumstances and complex of meanings surrounding each heroine's death vary from text to text.

6. I am using this term in its popular psychoanalytic sense, introduced by Erik Erikson, in which a "negative identity" embodies all those qualities one fears most to recognize in oneself, but by which, for that very reason, one feels particularly threatened.

7. For example, Balayé, in the Introduction to her recent edition of the novel, while reminding us, "Mme. de Staël n'est jamais tout entière chez l'un ou l'autre des protagonistes," goes only so far as to add, "on la trouve un peu partout même chez d'Erfeuil. Lui, Corinne et Oswald, dans leurs dissemblances, representent des moments de Mme. de Staël" (18-22)—ignoring Mme. d'Arbigny entirely. Goldberger's Introduction to the American edition does mention Mme, d'Arbigny, but only in passing, as "one of the three characters who represent France in the novel [she ignores M. de Maltigues] . . . a product of the Parisian society that has corrupted her ability to be honest" (xxxii). Similarly, Gutwirth's extensive discussion of *Corinne* in *Madame de Staël* makes only the briefest passing reference to Mme. d'Arbigny, wholly accepting Oswald's view of his first beloved and all but dismissing her as a kind of villainess preying on innocence (162, 224, 235, 196). In her discussion of *Corinne* in *Lumières et Liberté,* Balayé also makes only the briefest passing reference to Mme. d'Arbigny ("une femme . . . intriguante et fausse"), relating this episode in Oswald's past to the situation of Constant's Adolphe in Germany (149). Hogsett's book discusses various autobiographical elements in *Corinne,* but never mentions Mme. d'Arbigny. This dismissive assessment of Mme. d'Arbigny possibly owes something to Sainte-Beuve's early identification of her as a "portrait" based on a real-life model (Mme. de Flahaut) (155), a reminder that is picked up by Gennari when she dismisses Mme. d'Arbigny as a "peinture assez conventionelle de l'hypocrisie mondaine" (123).

8. Rhys's *Wide Sargasso Sea* offers, of course, the classic revisionist view of *Jane Eyre*'s mad Mrs. Rochester. The literary critical equivalent of this is in Gilbert and Gubar, which has called our attention to suppressed bonds of kinship among unlikely literary and fictional women.

9. See Gutwirth, *Madame de Staël* 237-45; Goldberger xl-xlii. Sensitively arguing that "the sisters represent . . . the divided part of what ought to be a unity" (241), Gutwirth nonetheless simply ignores Mme. d'Arbigny completely when she asserts, "Mme. de Staël always ends by embracing another woman's plight imaginatively" (245). Goldberger, who also praises the vision of sisterhood conveyed in the bond between "the dark woman and the fair lady," refers to Lucile without qualification as "the 'other woman' in the novel" (xl).

10. In keeping with the quite separate roles envisioned for men and women, Oswald is loved by three women in the novel without *his* taking the least pains to please any of them; nor would any reader accuse him of being excessively "agréable." Indeed, Corinne loves him precisely for his tortured, melancholy reserve, in which he distinguishes himself from her more agreeable continental admirers, whose deficiency, articulated by the British M. Edgermond, is tacitly confirmed by Corinne's love for Oswald: "Men in Italy have nothing to do but to please women" (204; bk. 8, ch. 1). This correspondence can also be seen as part of a more general correlation suggested by the novel between the position of women and Italy (or Italians) with regard to their shared lack of political power.

Works Cited

Balayé, Simone. *Madame de Staël: Lumières et Liberté.* Paris: Klincksieck, 1979.

Blanchard, Paula. "*Corinne* and the 'Yankee Corinna': Madame de Staël and Margaret Fuller." In Goldberger 39-47.

Gennari, Geneviève. *Le Premier Voyage de Madame de Staël en Italie et la Genèse de Corinne.* Paris: Boivin, 1947.

Gilbert, Sandra M., and Susan Gubar. *The Madwoman in the Attic.* New Haven: Yale UP, 1979.

Goldberger, Avriel H., ed. *Woman as Mediatrix: Essays on Nineteenth-Century European Women Writers.* Westport, CT: Greenwood, 1987.

Gutwirth, Madelyn. *Madame de Staël, Novelist: The Emergence of the Artist as Woman.* Urbana: U of Illinois P, 1978.

———. "Madame de Staël, Rousseau, and the Woman Question." *PMLA* [*Publications of the Modern Language Association of America*] 86 (1971): 100-09.

Herold, J. Christopher. *Mistress to an Age: A Life of Mme de Staël.* London: Hamilton, 1959.

Hogsett, Charlotte. *The Literary Existence of Germaine de Staël.* Carbondale: Southern Illinois UP, 1987.

Moers, Ellen. *Literary Women.* New York: Doubleday, 1976.

Poulet, Georges. "'Corinne' et 'Adolphe': deux romans conjugués." *Revue d'histoire littéraire de la France* (1978): 580-97.

Sainte-Beuve, Charles Augustin. *Portraits de Femmes.* Paris: Garnier, 1847.

Staël, Germaine de. *Corinne, or Italy.* Trans and ed. Avriel H. Goldberger. New Brunswick: Rutgers UP, 1987.

———. *Corinne ou l'Italie.* Ed. Simone Balayé. France: Gallimard, 1985. [This is the edition cited in the text; translations are mine.]

Starobinski, Jean. "Suicide et mélancolie chez Mme de Staël." *Madame de Staël et l'Europe: Colloque de Coppet.* Paris: Klincksieck, 1970. 242-53.

Frank Paul Bowman (essay date 1991)

SOURCE: "Communication and Power in Germaine de Staël: Transparency and Obstacle," in *Germaine de Staël: Crossing the Borders,* edited by Madelyn Gutwirth, Avriel Goldberger, and Karyna Szmurlo, Rutgers University Press, 1991, pp. 55-68.

[*In the following essay, Bowman considers the problem of communication in de Staël's writing.*]

> One of the results of absolute power which most contributed to Napoleon's downfall was that, bit by bit, no one dared any longer tell him the truth about anything. He ended up unaware that winter arrived in Moscow in November because none of his courtiers was Roman enough to tell him something even that simple.[1]

Because of this remark, and many others like it, I shall try to present here an overall view of a major problem in Staël's writing, which she never analyzes in a systematic way, but where her thought is very rich: how communication is impeded or interrupted by silence, lying, hypocrisy, the debasement of language.[2] We tend, incorrectly, to associate the problematics of language and communication solely with the crisis of modernity; they were also of great concern for the Groupe de Coppet. The problem is linguistic, but also moral and political, and Staël discusses it in all her various sorts of writing. My goal is in part to demonstrate the homogeneity of her thought as novelist, critic, philosopher, and political theoretician. For lack of space, I shall have to be schematic; the subject merits a book.

Adelaide and Theodore, an early work, (1786), prefigures in many ways the obstacles to communication typical of Staël's later writings. Adelaide is secretly married to Theodore. His mother's opposition makes declaring that marriage impossible. Because a friend of hers is in love with

Count d'Elmont, Adelaide often entertains d'Elmont; Theodore is understandably jealous, but she cannot betray her friend's secret. She becomes pregnant, but does not dare tell Theodore, whence the crisis scene:

> Adelaide, who was on the point of telling him about the new tie between them, was deeply wounded by his coldness, and so kept silent. They moved toward each other, their secrets were about to be revealed, but some strange eagerness for unhappiness imposed silence, and Theodore rushed off with the painful cry, "Adelaide, adieu."[3]

She runs after him, shouting, but "her voice could not be heard." He falls fatally ill with pulmonary trouble (other heroes get wounded in the chest, all interfering with speech). She goes to see him, but in hiding, does not even dare ask where he is. When they do get together, his mother arrives, and she can say nothing. Theodore dies, and Adelaide stays alive long enough to bear their child and then commits suicide. She does leave her son an autobiographical text which tells all, but when communication is finally established, the protagonists are all dead. Otherwise, communication fails throughout the text, and each failure produces a new disaster.

The plot is quite similar to that of *Delphine* but, as Simone Balayé has shown, *Delphine* is also a political novel in which communication is impeded not only because of the amorous plot but also because of political and social factors and because of woman's status.[4] Staël was the first woman to obtain fame in France not only as a novelist but as an essayist, in philosophy, esthetics, history, and politics. In all these areas she is concerned with the problem of communication.

Despotism as an Obstacle to Communication

The clearest case is that represented by my opening quotation about Napoleon and the Moscow winters. Political theoreticians, from Machiavelli to Max Weber and Erving Goffmann, have lengthily analyzed how the possession of power prevents effective communication. It is one of Staël's major criticisms of Napoleon: "The fear he created was such that no one dared tell him the truth about anything."[5] She also faults the ancien régime for the same reason, as she does the first Restoration; even a simple Swiss peasant knew that Napoleon was apt to return, but court etiquette and ministerial pretensions were such that no one could state the obvious.[6] There are historical exceptions: Louis XII, Henri IV with his attacks on flattery, the English—who are "as truthful about their failures as about their successes,"[7] but generally despotism produces flattery, and he who is flattered cannot know the truth.[8] The Duke of Mendoce in *Delphine* is a nice satirical portrait of such a flatterer, and the play *Jane Grey* offers several others, but one could say that in *Delphine* salon life is similarly vitiated by the despotism of opinion. Staël's thinking here is hardly original, except in two respects. One is her thesis that the obstacles despotism poses to communication can be remedied by the use of allegory or the fantas-

tic, stating the truth in a veiled manner.[9] The other is that, despite flattery, the truth will out, history will destroy the lie, it will snow in Moscow in November.[10] I leave aside the related but well-known matter of her opposition to censorship to discuss how political abuse of language can create obstacles to communication.

The Debasement of Language

Staël is primarily concerned here with two phenomena: the abuse of revolutionary language during the Terror and the problem of calumny—of which women, including Marie Antoinette and Staël herself, are particularly victims. But she reflects the same concern with the debasement of language in her discussion of what we have referred to since Heidegger as "inauthentic discourse," in salon life as well as elsewhere. Here she is a precursor of Flaubert: the abuse of language deprives words of their proper meaning and results in a reversal of moral values, where virtue becomes associated with the weak and duped, vice with the strong.[11] Calumny and revolutionary eloquence "deprive words of their natural power and reason, exhausted by error and sophistry, can no longer perceive the truth" (*On Literature* 405). *On Literature* contains a long and violent attack against revolutionary eloquence, which abuses the names of all the virtues to justify every crime (407-409). In a close analysis of a sentence by Couthon, she shows how it is well organized and logically constructed, but only to the end that reason can become the arm of crime. And here, in contrast to what happens with flattery, history tends to espouse and realize the abuse of language. These false ideas, dressed up in exaggerated images, lead to the most sanguinary furies; all proper judgment is destroyed.[12] Words that are so abused become arid and powerless to move, and the language of liberty particularly loses that power.[13] A special study should be made of Staël's proposals for controlling calumny, where she and Constant had some trouble reconciling their hatred of libel with their love of the freedom of the press. But the main problem for her was that words and eloquence, which should be instruments of freedom, had become the instruments of terror and oppression. As an example of her deep concern, I cite one of the few really cruel passages she ever wrote, about Robespierre's death. "His jaw was smashed by a pistol shot; he could not even talk to defend himself, he who had talked so much in order to destroy others! One might say that divine justice does not refuse, when it wishes, to strike the imagination by powerfully moving circumstances" (*Considerations* 315).

Under Napoleon, matters became worse in the sense that he not only censored the press and speech but also created a controlled press that spewed forth lies and falsehoods, creating "a despotism which took its delights in language" (*Circumstances* 294). Napoleon manipulated language, indulged in the "active lie."[14] He practiced political dissimulation not by silence but by floods of words; it is easier to mislead by speaking, by lying actively, than by silence.[15] To the tyranny of gossip he added the gossip of tyranny.[16] And this abuse of language, created by the Revolution and intensified by Napoleonic despotism, she felt, was now invading all forms of discourse; one can only learn what it is safe to say, and not what is.[17]

THE TREATISE ON GOOD ELOQUENCE

A contemporary reader is astonished by the importance Staël attributes to eloquence in *On Literature,* but for her, eloquence is a necessary and indispensable political instrument badly in need of rehabilitation. And Staël, a firm believer in perfectibility, does not despair; indeed, with progress in literacy and democracy good eloquence will become more and more necessary, for "reason and eloquence are the natural links of any republican association."[18] Her recipe for rehabilitating the eloquence that the Revolution and Napoleon had perverted is a simple one; one must have recourse to reason, imagination, and sentiment, and the three must be harmoniously combined.[19] The spread of printing, as opposed to oral communication, has made right reason even more essential: geometric precision and logical ordering are required when the text can be read closely and reexamined.[20] But truth and the ornaments of truth must be effectively combined, expression and sentiment derived from the same source.[21] Also, one must be brave and dare to speak the truth. Notably, truth is for Staël necessary not only in political discourse but also in the novel, a theory she has already developed in *Essay on Fiction;* fiction must also harmoniously combine reason, sentiment, and imagination.[22]

But the task is not a simple one, and we must make a detour here to discuss another problem.

THE POWERS AND DANGERS OF THE IRONIC WIT OF THE ENLIGHTENMENT

Eighteenth-century authors, particularly Voltaire, says Staël, employed "an allegorical manner of expressing the truth effectively in an age when error reigned."[23] *On Literature* offers an interesting historical explanation for this phenomenon in France. The power of the French monarchy was limitless in fact but uncertain and limited in principle (*droit*). Power could be arbitrary, but at the same time liberty of thought and expression was both possible and necessary when it took the form of wit and even ridicule, and could contribute to the progressive struggle against error and oppression. This wit is peculiarly French: in Russia, the nobility is too uneducated, the government too despotic; in Italy, again for political reasons, wit can only deal with matters of love, esthetics, and so forth; in Germany, people are too concerned with the truth to practice wit; in England, there are no intermediate conversational bodies between the family and Parliament where wit could find political play.[24]

Elsewhere, however, Staël can be quite negative about this ironic wit, which is too often used to attack behavior that does not conform to social norms. The "noble simplicity" that should characterize speech in a republic has been replaced by this clattering of syllables, the product of despotism. It is a discourse of vanity and not of energy. In the novels it is often the weapon of slander.[25] More interestingly, she associates language of this sort with that "metaphysic which links all our ideas to our sensations." Staël is convinced to the contrary, that the superficial comes from outside impressions, serious discourse reflects the depths of the soul.[26] Her rejection of eighteenth-century wit is connected with her option for transcendental rather than sensualist or ideological philosophy. But that choice raises another question.

IS A PURELY TRANSPARENT LANGUAGE POSSIBLE?

Staël associated Transcendentalism first and foremost with Kant, including the categorical imperative and the Kantian injunction to refuse lying in all its forms. Kant, as she notes, respected truth to the point where one should not even lie when a scoundrel asks you if your friend whom he is pursuing is hidden in your house.[27] Staël concluded, in the context of the Terror suggested by the above example, that there are occasions when one must lie in order to protect others, whence her preference for Jacobi over Kant, for a somewhat flexible ethics inspired by religious sentiment over logical rigorism.[28] *Delphine* echoes this debate in her preference for religion as opposed to honor as the ethical principle. In ethics, Staël, a novelist, thinks about concrete, not abstract situations, as she does in politics, and concludes that good must often compromise with evil.[29] It is noteworthy in this respect that, in her essay on Rousseau, she does not praise his claim of absolute sincerity in his *Confessions.* Her minor literary texts are full of "white lies"; indeed Jane Grey's excellence stems from her lying about her political attitudes, from the lie she tells in order to save her husband's life, and *M. de Kernadec* is all about the invention of a rather preposterous white lie so that crossed lovers can be married. Elsewhere, she is more ambiguous. Her comments on Rousseau's *Nouvelle Héloïse* on the one hand admire Julie's refusal to tell all to M. de Wolmar, but then she adds, "How I should appreciate a movement which would lead her to reveal everything."[30] Her *Story of Pauline* offers an exemplary illustration of this ambiguity. Mme de Verneuil, who is good, encourages Pauline to lie in order to get out of the clutches of her seducer and start a new life, then to lie about her past in order to marry her true love, Edouard; but when Edouard does discover the past, the result is a duel where he is fatally wounded. The text concludes that what most caused his despair was Pauline's silence about her past failings.[31] In the same way, in *Delphine* the "white lie" is usually the lie of silence—Léonce about his would-be assassins, Delphine about her political opinions, about the love of Thérèse d'Ervins for M. de Serbellane, about her gifts to Matilde, and her refusal, at Barton's suggestion, to tell Léonce what she has discovered about Mme de Vernon. But many of these lies of silence, while morally justified, eventually produce disaster; Delphine's silence about Thérèse, for instance, leads Léonce to marry Matilde. The absolute refusal to lie demanded by Kant is then not only impossible, but can even be immoral. When one must lie, it is best to lie by silence, and even then the "virtuous" lie exacts a price of suffering. Nor was Staël unaware that almost everyone thinks that his or her lie is virtuous; Mme de Vernon gives a rather good speech to that effect on her deathbed.

English Eloquence and Lucile's Silence

The Anglophilia which dominates much of Staël's thought is less strong when it comes to the problem of communication. On the one hand she admires the seriousness of English political discourse, the fairness of legal eloquence, the absence of a declamatory style and of sophistry.[32] On the other, she not only criticizes, as noted above, the absence of political discussions outside Parliament, but above all she deplores the silence that women in England are reduced to. They do not participate in discussions, creating a lack of general conversation, of familiarity.[33] *Corinne* offers an ample case study of this English failing, not only with Lady Edgermond but with Edgermond himself and above all with Lucile. Lucile's refusal to tell Oswald about the dangers of crossing the Alps is all too reminiscent of the courtiers' refusal to tell Napoleon about the November weather in Moscow. Staël interestingly (if incorrectly) complains that in England there are no memoirs, confessions, autobiographical literature; a too severe refusal to talk about the self vitiates English literature.[34] According to Staël, silence, particularly the silence imposed on women in England, is not golden.

The Forms of Impeded Communication

I should now like to propose a categorization of the forms of impeded communication in Staël's texts, though I must admit that my categories are heteroclite and not watertight. The "degré zéro" would of course be what I have already discussed, Silence. In addition to the white lie of silence, it should be noted that in many cases silence is either anodine or clearly virtuous—Oswald's silencing of praises about his heroic conduct at the fire of Ancona, for example. It should also be noted, however, that silence is often imposed by an excess of emotion, or more importantly by someone who is more powerful (Mme de Vernon on Delphine, Lady Edgermond on Corinne, or the way in which Corinne cannot improvise in front of Edgermond, the incarnation of English power).

Nonverbal Communication

In many cases, communication is effected by nonverbal means, particularly when an excess of emotion imposes silence. Staël was familiar with de Gérando's theory that language was not the only or even the most important system of communication—one recalls the rather comic Kalmouk prince of *Ten Years of Exile* who, unable to converse with the ladies who delight him, gives them diamonds instead—but the innumerable instances where gesture or glance replace language in Staël's novels should be studied, particularly because they are associated with

Communication by Displaced Discourse

Direct discourse is often replaced by singing a song, often accompanied on a harp (usually in order to declare one's

passion), or by citing a poem, or by evoking a work of literature, or, most importantly and frequently, by discussing a painting or a sculpture. Delphine is as much a master of this art as Corinne. Sophie and Pauline also use displaced discourse, and in her esthetic writings Staël discusses at length the communicability of music. But all these are instances where straightforward verbal communication breaks down, usually because of varying degrees of emotional intensity or incompatibility.

To Speak or to Write?

The same problematics of communication appear in the numerous discussions in Staël's writing about the written versus the spoken word. Here again, her thought is complex. Serious subjects should be treated in writing, she feels, not in conversation.[35] Yet, the spoken word is often more sincere than the written word, and she admires the English obligation to improvise rather than read a speech. (She does not seem to have known the considerable discussions of contemporary theoreticians of eloquence about the relative merits of improvising, learning by heart, reading, or speaking from a detailed outline.) Both Léonce and Geneviève de Brabant insist on speaking rather than writing because it is more sincere, but Corinne, Mme de Lebensei, and Mlle d'Albémar know moments when they must substitute writing for speaking, out of timidity, *pudeur,* or intense emotion. Mme de Vernon prefers writing to speaking because it is easier to manipulate and control what one writes. And, of course, there is the problem of the extent to which the form of the epistolary novel requires that one substitute writing for speaking.

Opinion as an Obstacle to Transparent Communication

In the salon, opinion reigns, and, even if the salon exists for conversation, opinion imposes silence and lying. *Delphine*'s epigram is a quotation from Mme Necker, "A man should know how to defy opinion, a woman how to submit to it," a theory repeated in the novel not by Delphine but by Matilde.[36] In politics, it is necessary but also difficult to go counter to opinion; one must know how to flatter, how to please.[37] But generally Staël attacks the way opinion imposes dishonesty and lying, to the extent that this reader at least likes the jesuitical proposal of Mme d'Artenas that Delphine should become publicly reconciled with Mme de Vernon and at the same time be as nasty as possible about her behind her back. To do so would be to enter into the world of submission to opinion, of hypocrisy and lying. The Staël heroine refuses even if Staël's mother recommended it.

Inauthentic Discourse

Staël refuses this, much as she does ironic wit. She considers it "bavardage qui use l'esprit," chit chat which destroys the mind, gossiping sprinkled with name-dropping, a waste of time where the soul is sacrificed to the taste of the day.[38] The exigencies of inauthentic conversation destroy sincerity of character and treat thought as a sickness that requires a strict diet of pap.[39] In *On Germany* she gives some nice examples, including the man who begins by fulsomely praising an actress he has just seen; the sardonic smiles of his audience make him temper his praise bit by bit until he ends up saying, "The poor devil did what she could" (1:103); inauthenticity leads to lies. The problem is fully represented in the novels, epitomized in *Corinne* by M. d'Erfeuil who, though *sympathique,* claims that proper form can justify any kind of content. It is more nefarious, more widespread and vitiating in *Delphine,* where it is associated with slander and suffering. But my favorite example is in the play *The Mannequin.* Sophie practices a white lie in order to avoid marriage with the egotistical and loquacious Count Erville (Erfeuil, Ervins—*air vain?*). Erville, who chatters and never listens, is put before a mannequin who pleases him endlessly; she is beautiful, never interrupts him, and admires everything he says. He asks her hand, freeing Sophie. Inauthentic discourse is here not the chirping of birds, but a means of reducing the other to a mute object.

IMPEDED COMMUNICATION AS A PRINCIPLE OF PLOT STRUCTURE

Often in Staël's novels, it is lies, silence, and hypocrisy which create misunderstandings but also determine the action and create suspense for the reader—all the more so because of dramatic irony: the reader knows what the characters cannot say or be told. Almost all of *Delphine* is constructed on this principle: the heroine's unspoken love for Léonce, the unsaid reasons why she receives M. de Serbellane, the occultation of Mme de Vernon's perfidy, the silence toward Matilde demanded by Mme de Vernon on her deathbed. It is noteworthy that it is a child, Thérèse's daughter, hence an innocent outside the social system, who reveals the truth. The purest case is probably the play *Sappho*; but there, as in *Delphine* and elsewhere, the anagnorisis, far from solving matters, produces tragedy. When the obstacle disappears and communication becomes transparent, tragedy and death result.

IMPEDED COMMUNICATION AND THE CRISIS SCENE

Significantly, the crisis scenes in Staël's writings occur when communication is impossible: Corinne, hidden spectator of Lucile and Oswald's marriage, where at the most she can communicate by sending a ring; Delphine, at Léonce's marriage to Matilde (with its tense build-up), hidden behind a pillar, veiled. One could add many others—the scene in the garden at night, the scene at the theater when *Tancrède* is being played, and so on. As Simone Balayé notes, a symbolic system of hidden gestures, veils, masks, and separating screens, governs the whole novel, showing that Delphine and Léonce can never get together.[40] It is this symbolic system which comes into play in the crisis scenes that articulate the plot.

THE MOTHER AS IMPEDER OF COMMUNICATION

The classic case is surely Lady Edgermond. Silence reigns in her house, and what conversation there is is completely inauthentic and concerns the weather. Corinne cannot talk to her; moreover, here again, Staël weaves a symbolic system to underline Lady Edgermond's role—her silencing the Italian musicians, the fact that she becomes mute a month before her death. Mme de Vernon is a more complex case. She will not let Delphine reveal her love to Léonce, or to Mme de Vernon herself, and she manipulates what can and especially what cannot be said, practicing both hypocrisy and censorship. "I'll hear," she says, "Delphine's confession of her love when I want to, but I don't intend to for a while, so I have freedom of action."[41] She has an intense dislike for moments when one says what one thinks or tells all.[42] She does tell all on her deathbed, but only in order to impose a new kind of silence on Delphine and Léonce. One could do a similar analysis of the mother in *Sophie* or *Sappho* or elsewhere. It is often, of course, the mother not of the heroine but of the heroine's enemy. This is a comforting kind of transference, but still the epigram of *Delphine* about how women must bend to opinion is from Mme Necker. Grist for the mill of psychoanalytical critics . . .

HYPOCRISY DONE AND UNDONE: FROM OBSTACLE TO TRAGIC TRANSPARENCE

Mme de Vernon could take as her motto Talleyrand's supposed quip, "language was given to man to hide his thoughts"; indeed, she has often been read as a caricature of the famed diplomat. Among the vices, hypocrisy in particular provokes Staël's wrath. In a noted attack in *On Literature* hypocrites are described as charlatans of vice, mockers of the sensitive soul, of all moral principles, who should themselves be ridiculed, handed over to the mockery of children.[43] Elsewhere she emphasizes how hypocrisy perverts its practitioners.[44] The exemplary hypocrite in her political writings is less Talleyrand than Napoleon, particularly in his dealings with the Poles and Czar Alexander. Once more, however, I underline that when Mme de Vernon does at her deathbed drop her mask of hypocrisy, she does so only to ask Léonce and Delphine to practice hypocrisy, thus heightening the tragedy. The same thing happens elsewhere, notably in *Jane Grey,* where Surrey and Northumberland are both consummate hypocrites; the latter, like Mme de Vernon, unveils all the horrors of his crime but in so doing only precipitates the tragedy. If hypocrisy is the worst of vices, is it perhaps also a necessary vice?

THAT LOVE WHICH CANNOT BE EXPRESSED

Love should create total transparency between two beings, but more than any other relationship in Staël's writings, it is vitiated by the obstacles to communication. Oswald does not dare declare his love for Corinne to Edgermond, to Erfeuil, or to Corinne, creating endless misunderstandings; she cannot declare her love, nor the details of her past, not even her name, to him; Lucile finds herself in a similar impossibility. From her first meeting with Léonce, Delphine cannot talk with him, and if Léonce can declare his love for her to Barton, he cannot to Delphine. The preface evokes "those sentiments of affection which cannot be stated" and the plot is created by the obstacles to the communication of love. The play *Sophie* probably offers the quintessential treatment of the theme. The Count cannot declare his love for Sophie, or Sophie hers for the Count, and the Countess refuses to state anything concerning these loves. When the love is revealed, it is without saying for whom, or the revelation is created by breaking taboos. The obviously incestuous overtones of the play may explain why love cannot be declared here in so intense a fashion, but as Sophie herself observes, "When passions achieve a certain degree of violence, they are almost always veiled in silence."[45] The main obstacles to communication are located on the *Carte du Tendre*.

CONCLUSION

I have probably exhausted my reader's patience, but I have not exhausted the subject. One could analyze those occasions where people refuse to speak because to do so would be to wound, to create suffering; the cases of blackmail, where saying does destroy; the refusal to state what the hero must discover on his own (see *La Sunamite*); the way in which transparent communication can deteriorate into the trite and the inauthentic, and then into silence. I have not discussed Staël's correspondence here, which would offer rich material for the subject. The problem in Staël should be compared to incommunicability in Constant (well studied) and in Mme de Charrière. Much of what I have been describing is a commonplace of political discourse and indeed of the tradition of the novel and the theater, but I do think that Staël's texts reveal an exceptionally high incidence of preoccupation with the failures of communication. For her, the problem is a central one. "Nature created me for conversation," she says in her proposed panegyric.[46] She loved to converse and to communicate, and her fear of exile and hatred of despotism were deeply motivated by the fact that both provided obstacles to communication. She lived in an age that was very aware of the problematics of language and of communication, of the uses and abuses of eloquence. In many texts, she suggests an almost frenetic confidence in the potential and power of language. Language offers an inexhaustible resource and no sincere word is every wholly lost.[47] In her political writings, however, as in her fiction and plays, she shows an intense and acute awareness that there are obstacles to communication and also that transparency can be dangerous. My title is derived from Starobinski's remarkable study of Rousseau, but the world of Staël's fiction is not the utopia of the *Nouvelle Héloïse*, and she never chose to strive for transparency the way Rousseau did in his *Confessions*. Between the two occurred the Terror (where many, like Corinne, did not dare give their names) and Napoleonic despotism, under which **On Germany** was given more drastic treatment than that given the *Encyclopédie* under the ancien régime. Rousseau was a man, Staël a woman, and, as Marie-Claire Vallois says, her novels exemplify "the aphasic character of feminine discourse."[48] She is reported to have said of her second husband, John Rocca, that "words were not his language"; perhaps Rocca is to be envied. But in **Corinne,** as Madelyn Gutwirth notes, and often elsewhere, silence conquers language.[49] The result, if inevitable, is nonetheless tragic.

Notes

1. *Considérations sur la Révolution française,* ed. Jacques Godechot (Paris: Tallandier, 1983) 427. Hereafter *Considérations*.

2. The problem has of course been discussed, regarding particular texts, by Staël scholars, but never in an overall analysis. Most notable are Madelyn Gutwirth, "Du silence de Corinne et de la parole," in *Benjamin Constant, Mme de Staël et le Groupe de Coppet* (Oxford: Voltaire Foundation; Lausanne: Institut Benjamin Constant, 1982) 427-434; Simone Balayé, "Les gestes de la dissimulation dans *Delphine,*" *Cahiers de l'Association internationale des études françaises* 26 (1974): 189-202; and Marie-Claire Vallois, *Fictions féminines: Mme de Staël et la voix de la Sibylle* (Stanford: Stanford French Studies, Anma Libri, 1987).

3. Germaine de Staël, *Oeuvres complètes,* vol. 1 (Paris: Treuttel and Würtz, 1844) 83. Hereafter *OC*.

4. Simone Balayé, "*Delphine,* roman des lumières; pour une lecture politique," in *Le Siècle de Voltaire, Hommage à René Pomeau* (ed. Christiane Mervaud and Sylvain Menant) (Oxford: Voltaire Foundation, 1987) 37-45.

5. *Considérations* 427; see 482, 590; *Dix années d'exil,* ed. Simone Balayé (Paris: Bibliothèque 10/18, 1966) 136. Hereafter *Dix années*.

6. *Considérations* 162; *Dix années* 225, 228-229.

7. *Considérations* 72, 74; *Dix années* 201.

8. *Considérations* 76.

9. *Essai sur les fictions,* in *OC* 1: 66; *De la littérature considérée dans ses rapports avec les institutions sociales,* ed. Paul Van Tieghem (Geneva: Droz, 1959) 164. Hereafter *Littérature*.

10. See her criticism of Alfieri's *Octavie* in *Corinne, ou l'Italie,* ed. Simone Balayé (Paris: Gallimard, 1985) 185.

11. *Littérature* 349; see *Des circonstances actuelles qui peuvent terminer la Révolution,* ed. Lucia Omacini (Geneva: Droz, 1979) 288. Hereafter *Circonstances*.

12. *Circonstances* 295.

13. *Littérature* 170; *Circonstances* 294.

14. *Considérations* 340-343, 410.

15. *Considérations* 362.

16. *Considérations* 368.

17. *Considérations* 590.

18. *Littérature* 31; see also 293, 416; *De l'Allemagne,* ed. Simone Balayé (Paris: Garnier Flammarion, 1968) 1:81.

19. *Littérature* 23.

20. *Circonstances* 281.

21. *Littérature* 306.

22. *Essai sur les fictions,* in *OC* 1:63, 65.

23. *Littérature* 28; *Considérations* 79.

24. *Dix années* 213; *Littérature* 161, 213; *De l'Allemagne* 1: 55-56, 174; see 1: 111 concerning interruptions of discourse in French and German.

25. *Littérature* 297, 300; *Dix années* 89.

26. *De l'Allemagne* 2:116; see *Littérature* 382.

27. *De l'Allemagne* 2:197. This debate among the Coppet group has been much studied. See B. Munteano, "Episodes kantiens en Suisse et en France," *Revue de littérature comparée* 15 (1935): 387-459; A. Monchoux, "Mme de Staël interprète de Kant," *Revue d'histoire littéraire de la France* 66 (1966): 71-84; Ernst Behler, "Kant vu par le Groupe de Coppet," in *Le Groupe de Coppet, Deuxième colloque* (Paris: Champion, 1977) 135-167.

28. *De l'Allemagne* 2:205.

29. *Réflexions sur la paix intérieure* (1798), in *OC* 1:58; *De l'Allemagne* 2:202.

30. *Essai sur les fictions,* in *OC* 1:68.

31. *Histoire de Pauline,* in *OC* 1:100.

32. *Littérature* 232; *De l'Allemagne* 2:18; *Considérations* 531, 556; *Littérature* 242.

33. *Considérations* 556-557.

34. *Littérature* 238.

35. *De l'Allemagne* 1:47.

36. *Delphine,* 5th ed. (1809) 1:11.

37. *Circonstances* 192; *Littérature,* chap. 18.

38. *De l'Allemagne* 1:94, 91, 101.

39. *De l'Allemagne* 1:103, 90.

40. Balayé, "Les gestes de la dissimulation," 193.

41. *Delphine* 1:203; 2:257.

42. *Delphine* 2:257.

43. *Littérature,* 350.

44. *De l'Allemagne* 2:246.

45. *Sophie,* in *OC* 2:152.

46. *Circonstances* 120.

47. *De l'Allemagne* 1:142; 2:308.

48. *Fictions féminines* 15.

49. "Du silence de Corinne" 433.

Naomi Schor (essay date 1994)

SOURCE: "*Corinne*: The Third Woman," in *L'Esprit Créateur,* Vol. XXXIV, No. 3, Fall, 1994, pp. 99-106.

[*In the following essay, Schor examines the relationship between death and femininity in* Corinne.]

> On eût dit que dans ces lieux, comme dans la tragédie de Hamlet, les ombres erraient autour du palais où se donnaient les festins.
>
>   Madame de Staël, *Corinne ou l'Italie*

In March, 1992, while on leave in Paris, I prepared a synopsis of a paper on death in Staël's *Corinne* that I proposed to give at the annual fall meeting of Nineteenth-Century French Studies. A month later I was being operated on at the Hôpital Saint-Antoine for a life-threatening liver failure.

Little did I realize at the time that I was entering a new stage in my life, a stage of serial illnesses from which I have yet to emerge. Consequently, what I viewed with apt modesty as a "small" paper has come to seem to me despite its restricted dimensions a strangely prophetic project insistently calling into question the very relationship of the mind and body I had spent a lifetime repressing. Did I feel the need to write about death because I was in fact and unbeknownst to me silently dying? And when did that dying begin, when I sat at my word processor before my illness declared itself in full-blown visible, visualizable, and quantifiable symptoms but heralded its crisis in so called "non-specific" symptoms: extreme fatigue, depression, loss of inspiration? Shortly before his unexpected and untimely death my father produced two atypically morbid works: a large self portrait in livid hues of muddy greens and ghoulish blues—the face of a drowned man—and an oversize brass mask where in one empty socket one could see a doll-like male figure dangling from a spring—the effigy of a man who has hung himself. Did life imitate art when my father's heart failed him or did some Lethe-like fluid guide his hand as he created those works?

Like so many other projects I was engaged in at the time, the paper on *Corinne* was a casualty of my illness and recovery. The celebration of the life work of Mme Tison-Braun, the beloved teacher who first awakened and recognized in me an interest in French literature, is the happy occasion of my at last but with no lesser sense of urgency writing the paper I had outlined when I still counted myself among the healthy.

          . . . . .

I want in what follows to make and, hopefully, substantiate an outlandish claim: because of the disparity between the chronology of events and the narrative organization of the material, when Corinne first appears in the novel that bears her name, she is already dead, a victim of patriarchy, a gendered ghost, the ghost of gender. In other words, *Corinne* is neither, as the narrator suggests, a mere retelling of the archetypal story of Sheherazade, who enlists narrative in the deferral of death,[1] nor, by the same token, a reworking of what Peter Brooks has called Freud's masterplot, the dawdlings and detours of the death-driven *Beyond the Pleasure Principle.* Death in *Corinne* is not the telos to be avoided, but the disaster which has already occurred, which sets the narrative in motion and brings it finally to its foreordained conclusion, the physical enactment of a symbolic death.

Much has been written about women and death in art and fiction, and a consensus has emerged regarding the proliferation of dead or dying female figures in the European art produced during a time period extending from the mid-eighteenth to the late nineteenth century. Following Michel Foucault's periodization, which dovetails with that of Philippe Ariès, Elizabeth Bronfen in her ambitious Lacanian exercise in "thanatopoetics," *Over Her Dead Body,* sees the end of the eighteenth century as marked by an epistemic shift in the function and representation of death. What characterizes this new understanding of death is its ambivalence: viewed as a means of attaining scientific truth, the corpse is simultaneously seen as a source of pollution which must be distanced from the city; viewed as a means of individuation, death constantly threatens the living with the return of the repressed Other:

> By the nineteenth century, "love" and "death" were culturally constructed as the two realms where savage nature could break into "man"'s city, at the same historical moment that society believed that its achievements in technology and rationalism had served to colonise nature completely. Since it combines these two disruptive elements, the dead body of a woman served as a particularly effective figure for this triumph over "violent nature" and its failure to expulse the Other completely; a superlative figure for the inevitable return of the repressed.[2]

There are in fact (at least) two epistemic shifts which coincide at the turn of the eighteenth century: on the one hand death is reconfigured, secularized, individualized, on the other, femininity is invented through the convergence of a set of emerging disciplinary discourses and in response to increasingly urgent political pressures (*OHDB* 78). Hence the feminization of the corpse, the killing of women form a nexus which becomes by mid-century a stereotype: "her dead body." It is this coming together that distinguishes post-revolutionary literary and pictorial representations of dead women from those that immediately precede that historical break in France, for of course representations of women as dead or death itself goes back as far as classical mythology; as Madelyn Gutwirth observes:

> A fascination with female frailty certainly recurs in Western art with some reliability over the centuries, remaining one of the stock of topoi available to it. But no glut of such foredoomed figures exists in modern times before the waning of the Age of Enlightenment and in the century that copes with this heritage.[3]

The crucial factor is that what is at stake in both Bronfen's and Gutwirth's studies is the triangle constituted by death, femininity, and a male author or artist. Or, to paraphrase Bronfen: Her body/His text. Gutwirth mentions only one woman in her article, Mme Riccoboni, and not in her capacity as a writer, rather her role as a critic of Laclos's *Liaisons Dangereuses.* Bronfen does include two novels by women in her book, Charlotte Brontë's *Jane Eyre* and Mary Shelley's *Frankenstein,* but she reserves her discussion of women writers and artists and death for a final chapter entitled, "From muse to creatrix—Snow White unbound." This transmutation is emphatically a twentieth-century phenomenon. What tends then to get lost in these accounts is the specificity of representations of dead women in pre-twentieth-century works by women artists and authors. Even when they are cited, gender difference is elided.

It may well be that in the historical context in which *Corinne* appeared it was impossible for a woman writer, however rebellious, to break with the dominant models of representation. And yet *Corinne* is in so many other respects an iconoclastic novel that it strains credulity that Corinne's dead body is indistinguishable from that of Ellénore, Benjamin Constant's counter example in *Adolphe,* and that what distinguishes them is unrelated to the sexual divide that separates their authors. It is the same difference as that between suicide and matricide.

From the very first page the prominence of death in this deeply melancholic early romantic novel is made clear, but it is not, as one might expect, the heroine's, or any other woman's for that matter, but the hero's father's. When we first encounter Oswald Lord Nelvil he is on a journey to Italy for medical reasons: "La plus intime de toutes les douleurs, la perte d'un père, était la cause de sa maladie" ("The most personal of all griefs, the loss of a father, had provoked his illness" (*C* 28/3). Implicit in this phrase is a maxim which goes something like: his father's death is man's greatest sorrow. When, as is the case for Oswald, that irreparable loss is overlayed with guilt, then the disease is as we in time discover incurable. Afflicted with a bad case of what Margaret Waller has wittily called "the male malady"[4] (a.k.a. the *mâle de siècle*), Oswald is a severely depressed Oedipus. It is in this state that he encounters Corinne, who is at the very pinnacle of her success. I am referring, of course, to the celebrated scene of her crowning at the Capitol. From that moment on Corinne takes it upon herself to cure the unhappy Oswald. This is tourism as therapy: she will cure him by making him see Italy and its beauties, for like Oedipus at Colonnus Oswald in Italy is blind, sightless: "Oswald parcourut la Marche d'Ancone et l'Etat ecclésiastique jusqu'à Rome sans rien observer" ("Oswald crossed the Marches and the Papal States as far as Rome without noticing anything" [*C* 46/17]); "il ne remarqua point les lieux antiques et célèbres à travers lesquels passait le char de Corinne" ("he took no notice whatever of the ancient places traversed by Corinne's chariot" [*C* 53/22]). The cure is homeopathic, in that it fights grief with grief; the burden of Oswald's mourning of his dead father is offset by a visit to the cemetery outside the city gates where Corinne guides Oswald to the funerary monument dedicated by a Roman citizen to the memory of his dead daughter, Cecilia Métalla.[5]

But above all to see Italy is to see Corinne; the cure for Oswald's undone grief work is gazing at Corinne. Gazing at Corinne is a moral imperative for Oswald, for as the prince Castel-Forte enjoins him: "regardez Corinne" ("Behold Corinne" [*C* 58/25]).

What does it mean to "behold" Corinne? Corinne, when Oswald first sees her, is the picture of health; at the height of her powers she is the most animated of heroines. It is this animation that I want to hold up to scrutiny, for it is illusory; the solar Corinne conceals a cold lunar landscape. She radiates a life force that is the after-glow of a star long dead. In this strange temporality, the reading of the novel that would have Corinne waste away as a result of Oswald's craven abandonment is a partial reading that too readily accepts conventional causality as its organizing principle, that is too quick to charge the male protagonist—absent a male author—with murder. It forgets one of the crucial lessons of Lacan's mirror stage, the impossibility of representing the body in pieces except from the perspective of the body as whole. The disjointed body of the infant can only be reconstructed from the vantage point of an imaginary identity. In the words of Jane Gallop: "The image of the body in bits and pieces is fabricated retroactively from the mirror stage. It is only the anticipated 'orthopedic' form of totality that can define—retroactively—the body as insufficient."[6] Corinne must reach the pinnacle of success for her underlying inexistence to become visible. Stardom—and Corinne, the performance artist, is nothing if not a star—is ghostly, a state of haunting.

Let us recall that when Corinne at last provides the key to the enigma of her identity, her missing patronym, she makes the following crucial avowal: after her father Lord Edgermond's death in England, she is driven into exile by her step-mother, who makes a diabolical bargain with her:

> . . . si vous prenez un parti qui vous déshonore dans l'opinion, vous devez à votre famille de changer de nom et de vous faire passer pour morte.

> [". . . should you decide on a course of action that will dishonor you in public opinion, you owe it to your family to change your name and pass for dead." (*C* 382/267)]

> Oui, sans doute, m'écriais-je, passons pour morte dans ces lieux où mon existence n'est qu'un sommeil agité. Je revivrai avec la nature, avec le soleil, avec les beaux-arts, et les froides lettres que composent mon nom, inscrites sur un vain tombeau, tiendront, aussi bien que moi, ma place dans ce séjour sans vie.

> ["Yes! Why not?" I exclaimed. "In this place where my life is no more than a troubled sleep, let them think me dead. With nature, with the sun, with the arts, I shall come alive again; and in this lifeless world, the cold letters of my name engraved on an empty tomb will surely take my place as well as ever I could." (*C* 383-84/268)]

Though by virtue of its history Italy is the land of ruins and crumbling tombstones, England by virtue of its rigid ideology of separate spheres is at least for women the "land of the living dead" (*MM* 76-79).[7] English society is

a cemetery where a brilliant public woman like Corinne can only be buried alive, racked by nightmares—"perchance to dream." To leave England is to rise Lazarus-like from the dead, yet at the same time to leave England is to leave behind more than the lifeless letters that make up one's patronym, rather one's mortal envelope; to return to Italy is to (re)enter the land of the living but to do so in spectral form.

> Si la vie est offerte aux morts dans les tombeaux, ils ne soulèveraient pas la pierre qui les couvre avec plus d'impatience que je n'en éprouvais pour écarter de moi tous mes linceuls, et reprendre possession de mon imagination, de mon génie, de la nature.

> [Were life offered to the dead in their graves, they would not lift off their tombstones with greater impatience than I felt to cast off my shrouds, and repossess nature, my imagination, and my genius. (*C* 385/268)]

Paradoxically, however, Corinne can only arise from the dead by faking her real death, staging her disappearance. Well before Oswald journeys to Italy to restore his health, Corinne is rumored to have done the same, so that Oswald on page one repeats Corinne's earlier gesture, for in what Derrida calls the "logic of spectrality"[8] there is no separating the first time from its repetition.

> Ma belle-mère me manda qu'elle avait répandu le bruit que les médecins m'avaient ordonné le voyage du midi pour rétablir ma santé, et que j'étais morte dans la traversée.

> [My stepmother gave me to understand that she had spread word of my death on a trip to the south prescribed by the doctors for my health. (*C* 386/269)]

Every crossing in *Corinne* evokes the fatal passage of the Styx: thus, when at the end of the novel Oswald returns to Italy with his wife and child, the river Taro is transformed into a dangerous torrent:

> le brouillard était tel que le fleuve se confondait avec l'horizon, et ce spectacle rappelait bien plutôt les descriptions poétiques des rives du Styx, que ces eaux bienfaisantes qui doivent charmer les regards des habitants brûlés par les rayons du soleil.

> [The fog was so thick that the river merged with the horizon, and the spectacle recalled the poetic descriptions of the banks of the river Styx, rather than the benevolent waters meant to charm the eyes of a population burnt by the rays of the sun. (*C* 558/397)]

The extraordinary Corinne that Oswald sees is then posthumous, not literally a dead female body, but a dead female soul: "on dirait que je suis une ombre qui veut encore rester sur la terre, quand les rayons du jour, quand l'approche des vivants, la forcent à disparaître" ("It is as if I were a shade still wanting to remain on earth when the light of day, the approach of the living, compel it to disappear" [*C* 522/371]), she writes when she is wasting away. She does not become a ghost because she was abandoned, rather, she is abandoned precisely because of her ghostliness.

From the moment of *Corinne*'s publication readers were stumped by the pairing of Oswald and Corinne: what do these two characters have in common? what does Corinne, the exceptional woman, see in Oswald, the conventional albeit new "sensitive" man? What prevents Oswald from choosing the profound Corinne over her superficial half sister Lucille? There is, of course, no single answer to this question, and over the years the answers have ranged from the humorous (Eliot's in *The Mill on the Floss*) to the scathing: the readings of contemporary feminists who view Corinne as a paradigm of the exceptional woman and the post-revolutionary killing into allegory of woman. Curiously, the psychoanalytic dimension has been neglected, yet it sheds light on this conundrum: Oswald abandons Corinne not only because of his father's law, not only because he is culturally unsuited to love a woman who does not adhere to the ideal of domesticity, but because Corinne represents death in the manner of Freud's third woman in his neat little essay of 1913, "The Theme of the Three Caskets." Unlike Freud's archetypal male, however, who fools destiny by selecting the inevitable, Oswald, who otherwise is always placing himself in harm's way, flees death in the shape of a comely woman, "the fairest, best, most desirable and the most lovable of women."[9] Because Oswald is a narcissist he rejects the Other and the Death-Goddess is the ultimate Other. The third woman is the woman who subverts the function assigned Woman in the male imaginary, that of guarantor of man's exclusive subjectivity and sense of phallic invulnerability. Is it any wonder then that narcissistic men, whose very self is threatened by female alterity and the death it signifies for their majestic Ego, chose unthreatening love objects that enhance their sense of omnipotence and immortality?

And what of the third woman? Can the third woman die? Yes: there is a double dying in *Corinne*. But in *Corinne* the Goddess of Death is dumb no more, Atropos speaks, writes, and what is more leaves a legacy. Not only does she stage her death, but she stages her swan song. More important, by the means of feminist pedagogy, the transmission of her wisdom to Lucille and Lucille and Oswald's daughter Juliette, she lives on. The specter of the exceptional woman haunts the nineteenth century.

Notes

1. Madame de Staël, *Corinne ou l'Italie* (Paris: Folio, 1985), 133; *Corinne, or Italy,* trans. Avriel H. Goldberger (New Brunswick: Rutgers UP, 1987), 81. Subsequent page references to these editions will be given within the text under the abbreviation *C,* with the English page numbers in italics.

2. Elizabeth Bronfen, *Over Her Dead Body: Death, Femininity, and the Aesthetic* (New York: Routledge, 1992), 86; hereafter abbreviated as (*OHDB*).

3. Madelyn Gutwirth, "The Engulfed Beloved: Representations of Dead and Dying Women in the Art and Literature of the Revolutionary Era," in Sara E. Melzer and Leslie W. Rabine, eds., *Rebel Daughters: Women and the French Revolution* (New York: Oxford UP, 1992), 198.

4. Margaret Waller, *The Male Malady: Fictions of Impotence in the French Romantic Novel* (New Brunswick: Rutgers UP, 1994). Hereafter (*MM*).

5. This detail is glossed by Nancy K. Miller, *Subject to Change: Reading Feminist Writing* (New York: Columbia UP, 1988), 172-73.

6. Jane Gallop, *Reading Lacan* (Ithaca: Cornell University Press, 1985), 86.

7. Cf. Jean Starobinski's congruent description of Corinne as "une morte-vivante" ("a living-dead woman") in his article, "Suicide et mélancolie chez Mme de Staël," in *Madame de Staël et l'Europe, Colloque de Coppet* (Paris: Klincksieck, 1970), 246. Starobinski's concern is the psychology of Staël and her heroines. The (virtual) abandoned woman is kept alive through the artificial means of a love whose withdrawal determines an "ontological catastrophe" (247).

8. Jacques Derrida, *Spectres de Marx* (Paris: Galilée, 1993), 24.

9. Sigmund Freud, "The Theme of the Three Caskets," *Character and Culture* (New York: Collier, 1963), 76.

Gretchen Rous Besser (essay date 1994)

SOURCE: "Forays into Fiction: *Delphine,*" in *Germaine de Staël Revisited,* Twayne Publishers, 1994, pp. 64-76.

[In the following excerpt, Besser surveys the story, theme, and critical reception of Delphine.*]*

Staël's two principal novels were to earn her spectacular success. Her first full-length work of fiction, and her only experiment with the epistolary form,[1] was the hugely popular *Delphine.* Recapitulating themes touched on in her short stories, *Delphine* has a well-developed if convoluted plot, presents a number of sharply defined characters, exemplifies social criticism at its most daring, and marks Staël's emergence as a best-selling writer. The book's conception dates from April 1800. Staël began writing that summer, as she apprised Adélaïde de Pastoret on 9 June 1800: "I am writing a novel . . . and preparing for a literary career. Contrary to the usual sequence, I started with generalities and have now embarked on a work of the imagination. We shall see what happens." (Solovieff, 176). By September, she informed Pastoret that she was focusing on women's condition: "I am continuing my *novel,* which has become the story of women's destiny presented under various guises" (181).

Delphine appeared in December 1802. By the following May, it was in its fourth edition; two translations had come out in London and three in Germany. Although Staël specified that political polemics would have no part in her novel, she situated the action during the last years of the Revolution. This time gap facilitated treating such tinderbox questions as divorce and monastic vows, which are germane to the plot.[2] The book's dedication—a quotation from Mme Necker's posthumous *Mélanges*—sums up the fictional dilemma: "A man must be able to challenge public opinion, a woman to submit." The tragedy of *Delphine* arises from the reversal of these sex-related roles; the hero is incapable of defying society, while the heroine is incapable of yielding.

The preface to the first edition, summarizing the history of fiction in a single paragraph, is like a précis of the *Essai sur les fictions.* Although writing fiction may appear easy (witness the slew of mediocre novels), in effect it requires uncommon imagination and sensitivity. Like Henry Fielding's *Tom Jones* (1749), *Clarissa, La Nouvelle Héloïse,* and *Werther* (titles already mentioned in *Fictions*), the novel must probe hidden feelings and inculcate moral lessons. While explaining the tenor of knightly romance and granting nodding recognition to Marie-Madeleine de La Fayette, Staël places fictional mastery firmly in eighteenth-century England. Overlooking Chateaubriand's devastating critique of *Littérature,* she lauds his "original, extraordinary, overwhelming imagination" ([*Oeuvres complètes,* henceforth *OC*], 5:xlv) in the *Génie du christianisme* (*The Genius of Christianity*, 1802) while at the same time specifying that creative inspiration is antithetical to religious dictates.

The first part of *Delphine,* which begins in April 1790, initiates a confrontation between two rivals for the same man and highlights their personality clashes. With the generosity that will be her downfall, Delphine d'Albémar offers a gift of land to facilitate marriage between her cousin-in-law Matilde de Vernon and Léonce de Mondoville. (This is the first of many ironical twists of plot, for it is Matilde's eventual marriage to Léonce, accomplished by duplicity when he and Delphine are already in love, that will doom the heroine to suffering and death.) The contrast between the two women is a product of character and upbringing. Raised in the Catholic church, Matilde is a cold, self-righteous religious bigot, whose conformity to convention provides a counterpoint to Delphine's candor and spontaneity. The latter's moral character has been formed, not by church dogma, but by her late husband. (Like Adélaïde and Pauline, she was married young to a much older man[3] but was genuinely fond of her husband, who was more like a father than a spouse.)[4] Delphine echoes her husband's (and Staël's) humanistic creed: "He believed in God and trusted in the soul's immortality; virtue based on goodness constituted his cult toward the supreme Being" (*OC,* 5:17). Staël's valuation of natural goodness over ritual (and of Protestantism over Catholicism)[5] is concretized by Delphine's later serving as lay confessor to Matilde's dying mother and as moral mentor to Léonce. Functioning as Delphine's confidante and surrogate mother, her sister-in-law Louise d'Albémar warns against the unscrupulous ambition of Sophie de Vernon, Matilde's mother and Delphine's close friend. Ugly and deformed,[6] Louise has buried herself in the country because her physical defects have eradicated any hope of love or marriage.

Léonce de Mondoville's composite background—half Spanish, half French[7]—supposedly accounts for his hypersensitivity and prickly code of honor. He explains (prophetically) to his preceptor Barton why he has not yet fallen in love: "I was afraid to love a woman who might not agree with me about the importance I attach to people's opinion, and whose charm would ensnare me while her way of thinking made me suffer" (*OC,* 5:104). The stage is set for an impasse between the impulsive, unconventional heroine and the tradition-bound hero. While recognizing the disparity between Léonce's character and her own, Delphine is smitten by pity when she sees him pale and in pain. Among Staël's heroines, sympathy for a suffering hero is an invariable prelude to love.

Staël inserts vignettes of the duc de Mendoce, a "flatterer," Mme du Marset, a busybody, and M. d'Ervins, a man consumed by self-interest. These social "types," like those traced in *Passions,* create the background of conventional attitudes against which Delphine's story will be played out. Societal pressures are exemplified in the famous incident when Delphine, accompanying Sophie de Vernon and Léonce to the Tuileries to see the queen, defies the assembled society by befriending Mme de R., who has been collectively snubbed.[8]

Delphine's guileless generosity precipitates her disgrace and Léonce's desertion. In a weak moment, she agrees to lend her home for a tryst between her friend Thérèse d'Ervins and M. de Serbellane, Thérèse's lover. When the irate husband discovers the couple, he challenges Serbellane to a duel and is killed. Delphine confesses her part in this event to her presumed friend Sophie who, while promising to exonerate her to Léonce, in actuality persuades him that Serbellane is Delphine's lover and hastens his marriage to Matilde. Delphine attends the church ceremony, hidden behind a pillar, where Léonce imagines he sees her reaching out to him.

In the second part, Matilde's absorption in religious duties prompts Léonce to describe the void of his marriage, in terms that reflect Staël's own marital deception: "Side by side we will proceed along the path that leads to the grave—a road we ought to travel together; the journey will be as silent and somber as its destination" (*OC,* 5:256). Matilde's bigotry extends to a cousin who has divorced and remarried, whom the more open-minded Delphine visits and whose story she learns. After a miserable first marriage, Elise fell in love with Henri de Lebensei. Although his strength of character and complete indifference to other people's opinion have provided a bulwark against the world's disfavor, she has been obliged to withdraw from the society she defied for the sake of love.

At a performance of *Tancrède* (a play Staël repeatedly favored), Delphine spies Léonce hidden in a cloak, shaking with sobs as the hero expresses his love for Aménaïde and despair at her infidelity. Realizing that she has been maligned, Delphine determines to regain Léonce's esteem. Thérèse decides meanwhile to become a nun and entrust her daughter Isore to Delphine's care. When Léonce learns from the child that Serbellane was courting her mother and not Delphine, he implores the latter to tell him the truth, but she refuses to exculpate herself for fear of angering him against his mother-in-law.

Summoned suddenly to Sophie's deathbed, Delphine is handed a confessional letter tracing the steps that led the older woman from a tormented childhood to a perverted, amoral, self-centered adulthood.[9] Orphaned at age three, she was brought up by an unprincipled tutor and then forced to marry a man she detested lest she be confined to a convent forever; her only recourse was hypocrisy and deception. Although she led a life of pleasure, she gave her daughter a strict Catholic education. Afraid of losing an inheritance when d'Albémar married Delphine, she studied the young woman's character carefully: "I soon realized that you were governed by your good qualities—kindness, generosity, confidence—as others are controlled by passion, and that it was almost as difficult for you to resist your virtues, however unpremeditated, as for others to withstand their vices" (*OC,* 5:459). Because she resented Delphine for endangering Matilde's marriage, she did not intercede with Léonce after d'Ervins's death, as she had promised. Ironically, a child (Isore) uncovered her duplicity. Now that she is dying, she can speak the truth. Delphine is the only person she ever loved, who sometimes made her doubt her heartless calculations. Countermanding Matilde's order to send for a priest, Sophie asks Delphine to hear her prayers. In replacing the traditional clergyman, the heroine plays the role of confessor whose saintly ministrations rehabilitate the sinner and whose religious morality, untainted by dogma or prejudice, supersedes the arid rigidity of Matilde's creed. After the emotional turmoil of Léonce's unexpected arrival, his furious denunciation of his mother-in-law's treachery and deceit, and Sophie's death, Delphine falls dangerously ill.

In the third part, Léonce—disregarding his customary subservience to social pressure, and with no qualms about the risk to Delphine's reputation—begs her to live with him as man and wife. When she refuses to see him again, Léonce first threatens to inform Matilde of their love, then contrives to change Delphine's mind with the prospect of reforming him spiritually as she had Sophie. In confirmation of Staël's assertion in *Passions* that true love means merging one's self with the beloved, Delphine tells Léonce: "At present I am merely a creature who lives for the man she loves and exists only for the interest and glory of the object she has chosen" (*OC,* 6:50-51). Léonce announces his presentiment that he will die young, happy to perish in the full ardor of love, before age makes the heart grow cold (another Staëlian notion).

Like Théodore before him, Léonce grows jealous of Delphine's social success as the center of attention in every salon, where men and women stand three deep to hear her. Wanting her all to himself, he asks to spend the winter together at her country house of Bellerive—again inducing Delphine to flaunt convention. While there, he admires her

DE

L'INFLUENCE DES PASSIONS

SUR

LE BONHEUR DES INDIVIDUS

ET

DES NATIONS.

PAR

MAD. LA BARONNE STAEL DE HOLSTEIN.

Quæsivit cœlo lucem ingemuitque repertâ.

A LAUSANNE *en Suisse,*

Chez { JEAN MOURER, Libraire.
     { HIGNOU ET COMPᵉ. Imp. Lib.

1796.

unsuspected housewifely skills,[10] and they visit the Belmont ménage, which exemplifies marital happiness. Mme de Belmont gave up a fortune to marry a blind man, whom she loves and nurtures. With their two children, they form a picture of self-contained domestic bliss, as Belmont describes it: "Life offers no greater joy than the union of marriage and the affection of children, which is only perfect when one cherishes their mother. . . . No relationship outside marriage is permanent. External events or natural disinclinations shatter once-solid bonds. Opinion pursues you . . . and poisons your happiness" (*OC,* 6:116). For Staël, love in marriage is still the ultimate utopia.

Uneasy about the imminent arrival in Paris of a man named Valorbe (who will play the villain's role assigned to Meltin in *Pauline*), Delphine asks Louise to dissuade him from visiting her. A royalist, Léonce is pained by Delphine's prorevolutionary sentiments. Like her creator, she claims to detest factionalism and to cherish liberty. Before entering the cloister, Thérèse begs Léonce not to damn her by making Delphine "guilty." In the furious belief that Delphine is conspiring to leave him, he insists she prove her love by swearing, at the very altar where he took his marriage vow, that she will be his; if not, he will kill himself on the spot. Praying heaven to protect her, Delphine falls in a faint.[11]

In the fourth part, Delphine's rash generosity once again incurs society's stigma. Having unwisely granted Valorbe political asylum for the night, thereby provoking an altercation between him and Léonce, she is maligned for giving an assignation to two men in one night. Léonce cannot avenge the affront to Delphine's honor because, as Lebensei explains, "we can only protect the bonds that society sanctions—a wife, a sister, a daughter—but never the one who is linked to us by love alone" (*OC,* 6:312-13). Lebensei also furnishes philosophical and moral arguments in favor of divorce (which the Constituent Assembly is about to ratify): society encourages marriages of convenience without permitting a means of escape (including adultery); a bad, irreversible marriage makes for a hopeless old age; youthful inexperience can entail a lifetime of misery; children are adversely affected by "the eternal circle of suffering formed by an ill-assorted and indissoluble union" (327). This liberal position—a courageous stand for women's rights and a refutation of Mme Necker's posthumous work opposing divorce—was to cost the author dearly in social and critical disapproval. Although at one point she considered divorcing her husband and marrying Narbonne,[12] Staël eventually gave up the idea, as she has Delphine reject it. The latter returns to society in a futile attempt to silence wagging tongues. Ostracized at a social gathering, she flees in humiliation (a reversal of the incident when she alone befriended Mme de R.). Having learned that Matilde is carrying Léonce's child, she departs incognito for Switzerland with Isore.

The fifth part begins on 7 December 1791, as Delphine crosses the border. The bleak weather and bare trees remind her of death. In a rare allusion to the harmony between nature and mood, a storm on the lake mirrors her agitation.[13] She flees to Zurich on learning that Valorbe, who has vowed to stop at nothing either to win or to punish her, is in Lausanne. When she takes up residence in a convent run by Mme de Ternan, Léonce's aunt, Delphine is warned by a new friend, Henriette de Cerlebe, against the abbess's authoritarian and self-centered character. Afraid that the new divorce law will encourage Léonce to abandon Matilde for Delphine, Mme de Mondoville asks her sister, the abbess, to do everything in her power to separate the two. Mme de Ternan resolves to make Delphine a nun. At the latter's behest, Lebensei tries to dissuade Léonce from joining the émigré forces to fight against France. His arguments against civil war and party prejudices repeat ideas contained in *Passions.* Like Staël, Lebensei voices the patriotic duty not to tolerate foreign armies in the land and declaims that "liberty . . . is the prime happiness and sole glory of the social order; history is adorned by the virtues of free peoples" (*OC,* 7:84). This type of liberal dissertation, upholding freedom and revolutionary ideals, particularly irked Bonaparte.

Henriette de Cerlebe tries to persuade Delphine to accept Valorbe; not believing in romantic love, she lauds filial and maternal affections instead. She recounts her life story: at her father's urging, she retired to the country to raise her children herself; she has learned to enjoy domestic duties and the calm contemplation of nature in company with a sensitive, intelligent, and indulgent father (with whom she enjoys the creator's fantasized relationship with the widowed Necker). Delphine spurns Henriette's suggestion; death is preferable to a mismatched marriage. Indignant at her rejection, Valorbe vows to pursue and possess her.

Yielding unwisely to pity when he is arrested for debt, Delphine travels to nearby Zell to bail him out. The ingrate locks her up in his house; if she will not marry him, he will dishonor her by publicizing the fact that they spent the night together. Upon Delphine's return to the convent next morning, Mme de Ternan threatens to expel her unless she takes the veil. After learning that Valorbe has threatened to carry her off by force and Matilde has borne a child, Delphine tearfully accedes. When he finds out what she has done, Valorbe clears her name, then kills himself. Henriette points up the ironic twist: "A week after pronouncing her vows, she learned that the terrible sacrifice she had made was for nought" (*OC,* 7:179).

When the sixth part opens, Matilde and her newborn son have died; her last wish was that Léonce marry Delphine. Lebensei is dispatched to find the hero, who has left for Switzerland. Having heard of a nameless woman resembling Delphine in Paradise Abbey, Léonce is ecstatic at the prospect of seeing her. But when she appears, veiled in black, he shakes the grill in anguish. "Matilde is dead," he cries. "Delphine, can you be mine?" "No," she replies, "but I can die!" (*OC,* 7:223). To save the two, Lebensei proposes that Delphine return to France, where monastic vows can be broken by law, and there live with Léonce in defiance of "absurd prejudices" (229). Always the voice of rational judgment, Lebensei urges Léonce to disregard social convention, citing reasons why Delphine's impetuous act should not bind her eternally. Although Léonce ostensibly agrees, Delphine worries about his underlying conviction. For health reasons, she receives permission to spend two months at Baden with him.

In the original ending, Delphine realizes that Léonce is still troubled by other people's opinion when a crowd murmurs against her in public and he complains that life without honor is unbearable. Aware that they cannot be happy together, she swears that she will never be his wife; Léonce swears in turn that he will not survive without her. He writes to announce his intention of joining the émigré army: the only way he can reconcile the conflict between his character and his love is to sacrifice his life.

With Serbellane's help, Delphine finds Léonce in a Verdun prison, where he is about to be judged and shot. He tells Delphine that the proximity of death has made him understand life's priorities; if she obtains his pardon, they can be happy together. At her insistence, Léonce prays to God for the first time in his life. By dint of eloquent supplication, Delphine prevails on the judge to release him,[14] but a commissioner from Paris rescinds the order. Serbellane arrives with a reprieve, provided Léonce declares he did not intend to bear arms against France, but he refuses lest people think he signed falsely; at the point of death, he still bows to public opinion. (This last-minute pardon, with an untenable alternative to execution, echoes *Jane Gray*).

After swallowing poison in "a moment of convulsion and despair" (*OC*, 7:346), Delphine accompanies Léonce to his execution so that she may serve him (as she did Sophie) in lieu of a priest. In the tumbrel, she prays for and with him; their love will endure forever: "Those who succumb slowly beneath the weight of time can believe in destruction, for they have experienced it in advance; but we who approach the grave full of life attest to immortality!" (350-51). Just as Léonce tells the firing squad to dispense with a blindfold and aim at his heart, Delphine collapses and dies. The deeply affected soldiers are ready to spare the prisoner, but he hurls insults until one of them fires and kills him. After burying the lovers in the same grave, Serbellane muses: "Léonce should have defied opinion . . . when happiness and love made it his duty to do so; Delphine, to the contrary, over-confident of her heart's purity, was never able to respect the power of opinion to which women must submit; but do nature and conscience teach the same moral lesson as society, which imposes contrary rules on men and women? and did my unfortunate friends have to suffer so much for such pardonable errors?" (357).

This ending, consonant with the tenor of the story and the character of the protagonists, makes Delphine a suicide-for-love and Léonce a misguided hero to the last. It reenacts with greater pathos the execution scenes sketched in *Jane Gray* and **"L'Epître au malheur."** The conclusion echoes Staël's youthful credo that it is better to die at the height of love than to witness its decline. Serbellane's final reflection emphasizes the antithetical roles of hero and heroine: if Léonce had disregarded convention (as a man may) and Delphine had observed it (as a woman must), their tragedy would have been averted.

Because Staël herself was caught between Scylla and Charybdis—between braving and submitting to public opinion—her personal dilemma reflects that of her heroine. Long after *Delphine* appeared, its author took certain criticism to heart and, unlike her heroine, ceded to public outcry. Not only did she write a preface defending her moral intentions, but she even penned an alternative, non-suicidal ending in order to appease her detractors. It was her son Auguste, rummaging among his mother's papers after her death, who discovered this alternative denouement as well as the apologetic "Quelques réflexions sur le but moral de *Delphine*" (Thoughts on the moral goal of *Delphine*), which he published with her collected works.

In the new ending, Léonce solemnly confirms his promise to marry Delphine by placing a ring on her finger in the presence of the rising sun. Back in Mondoville, near the royalist enclave of the Vendée region, it is soon rumored that the young lord is about to dishonor himself by wedding a nun. An old soldier of his father's accuses Léonce of disgracing the family name; when Delphine overhears

him explain that he cannot abandon a woman who has sacrificed everything for him, these words take a mortal toll. Dying, she writes Léonce to explain the basic discord between her sensitivity and society. Weary of suffering, she is content to die before love palls. Sophie de Vernon was right: the differences in their characters would have prevented their being happy, even if there had been no obstacle to their union. She asks to have music played during her last night (like Mme Necker) and dies at dawn. At her request, Léonce entrusts Isore to Louise d'Albémar, then departs for the Vendée, where he is killed in his first encounter.

In this second ending, Léonce's liaison with Delphine is legitimized in a ring ceremony under the aegis of nature, if not of the church; Delphine manages to die for love without committing suicide; there is no religious conversion by Léonce and no priestly ministrations by Delphine. If the situation is artificial and lackluster, the underlying message is twisted to hold Delphine, not society, responsible for her tragedy. We may dismiss this alternative as an inauthentic compromise with the very conventions that Staël's novel seeks to undermine.

Despite the mediocrity of this new denouement, "Le but moral de *Delphine*" is a significant critical and feminist text. Insisting that her novel stands on its own merits, without apology, Staël states that a literary work is vindicated by "the imposing impartiality of time" (*OC*, 5:v). Because society as a collective personality tries to maintain the status quo and ensure that outward conventions are observed, it feels threatened by extraordinary individuals—especially women—and judges them harshly. Delphine's difficulties arise out of her character; Staël never intended to present her as a model to emulate—the epigraph blames both Léonce and Delphine. She considers her novel useful because it stresses goodness in a postrevolutionary period when sympathy toward misfortune is imperative. It teaches women not to trust their good qualities but to respect opinion, else it will crush them. The author also feels that *Delphine* admonishes society to deal kindly with those of exceptional mind and spirit; otherwise it commits a disproportionate injustice that may ruin a promising career.

In balancing a graceless Matilde against a superior Delphine, Staël claims to have demonstrated the overriding force of morality, for, in spite of her cold religiosity, Matilde's honesty outweighs all Delphine's qualities and charm. Although men may sometimes escape punishment, "the social order makes it impossible for women to avoid the unhappiness that results from wrongdoing" (*OC*, 5:xix). Once a man has obtained a woman's affection—unless their bond is sanctified by marriage—his ardor cools first: "[Men's] lot is too independent, their lives too dynamic, their future too certain, for them to experience the secret terror of loneliness that ceaselessly pursues even those women whose destiny is most brilliant" (xxiv). *Delphine* can help those who are victimized by their feelings (as another way of instilling the lesson of *Passions*). "We do not sufficiently realize the dire combination, for our happiness, of being endowed with a mind that judges and with a heart that suffers from the truths the mind reveals" (xxvii). Mirza was also meant to illustrate the dichotomy of reason and emotion.

Staël professes that she changed the ending for various reasons, but not because some readers objected to Delphine's suicide.[15] A writer does not express a personal opinion when characters act in a certain way. Nor can an argument be found for or against suicide in the example of a woman who lacks the strength to endure life after the man she loves has gone to the scaffold. Moral severity must be tempered with sympathy and understanding (attributes Staël claimed for herself in *Passions*): "One must have suffered in order to be heard by those who suffer and . . . to have tried a dagger on one's own heart before asserting it does not hurt" (*OC,* 5:xxxvi).

According to her stated intention, Staël populated *Delphine* with an assortment of women whose lives represent the various possibilities open to their sex, none of which is satisfactory. In spite of a loving heart and sensitive nature, Louise d'Albémar is condemned to spinsterhood for no reason other than her physical unattractiveness. Thérèse d'Ervins, like Elise de Lebensei and countless others, is married against her will to a despicable husband. Her attempt to find happiness in adulterous love is doomed; not only is she ostracized by society, but she is forced to bury herself in a convent, that is, to embrace a living death. Elise de Lebensei depicts the woman shamed by divorce who, in embracing love, must retreat from society. Furthermore, her decision requires collaboration by a man strong enough and willing to support her in her isolation. Mme de Belmont epitomizes the fulfillment of perfect love in marriage; however, it must be noted that her husband, being blind, depends on her like a child.[16] Henriette de Cerlebe celebrates the joys of maternity and domestic tranquillity in a rural setting, where she rears her children herself—but with the help and emotional support of a loving father. Mme de Ternan's story exemplifies women's destiny: while young and beautiful, she turned men's heads; when her beauty faded, life lost its meaning. In her latter years, she had no option but the cloister. Sophie de Vernon illustrates the depravity to which an inadequate or uncaring upbringing can lead. However selfish and deceitful she has been, however deeply she has wronged Delphine, her "confession" explains her character defects according to woman's obligatory status. As a youngster, Sophie's feelings and intellect were repressed. She was forced to marry a man she loathed because the alternative was life imprisonment in a convent (a centuries-old way of coercing women into wedlock). While deploring her stunted character, Staël is careful to show that circumstance forced her to become what she was. She also has Sophie properly repent before she dies.

Although fictional characters are often composites of people the author may have known, critics over the centuries have enjoyed the game of designating Staël's probable models. In this respect, *Delphine* has been a fertile field for treasure seekers. The title character shares a number of her creator's traits. Clever, kind, and impetuous, she is an impassioned lover, faithful friend, and champion of freedom. Ambivalent about social conventions, she flaunts them while acknowledging their abusive power. Delphine is also pictured as beautiful—an attribute her creator sadly believed she lacked.[17] Some contemporaries and present-day critics take Sophie de Vernon to be the portrait of Talleyrand in skirts.[18] Because she is married to an older man and is one of the most seductive beauties of her time, Thérèse d'Ervins has been likened to Juliette Récamier (Levaillant, 37). Louise d'Albémar resembles Suzanne Necker to some extent, although she is more sympathetic than Staël ever believed her mother to be. Gutwirth calls Matilde "Mme Necker's grossly caricatured surrogate" (112) because, while pious and prudish, she is also critical of and a rival to Delphine. Léonce is supposedly a combination of Narbonne and Ribbing, with greater emphasis on the first.

Contrary to Staël's naive assumption, *Delphine* did not win the approbation of the first consul. Quite the opposite. A number of elements in the book were almost guaranteed to arouse Bonaparte's ire. To begin with, Staël's bold dedication "to silent and enlightened France" was a backhanded slap in the face. Her defense of divorce and denigration of Catholic ritual in favor of a humanistic Protestantism appeared soon after Napoleon signed a concordat with the pope. Her running indictment of society and arranged marriages was regarded as a criticism of the status quo, as were the liberal views she expressed via Lebensei. Her profeminist attitudes were also anathema to a man who felt that women were good for only one thing—childrearing.

Bonaparte was all the more incensed when *Delphine*'s appearance in December 1802 became an epochal event. To counteract its popularity, he instigated a virulent press campaign. The *Journal des Débats* of December 1802 attacked Staël's immortality in denying divine revelation and advocating divorce. Bonaparte criticized both book and author: "I do not like women who try to be men any more than I like men who are effeminate. . . . I cannot abide that woman." In May 1803 one Emmanuel Dupaty staged a parody entitled *Delphine, ou l'Opinion* (Delphine, or, Opinion), satirizing both Staël and one of her detractors, Félicité de Genlis, but a coalition of Staël's friends ensured the play's swift demise. Charles de Villers was ecstatic about Staël's novel; he wrote her on 4 May 1803: "Your work sparkles with beauties of detail, observations, perspicacious and profound views, and passages of eloquence, purity, grace, and breath of feeling. . . . You have feminized Rousseau's pen."

Delphine may retain the prolix and sentimentalized excesses of its period, the epistolary form (also symptomatic of its age) may be artificial and confining, and the proliferation of plot and subplot may tax the patience of today's reader; nevertheless, the novel has much to recommend it.

The characters, especially the gallery of female portraits, are lifelike and appealing. When not enraging, the love story is engaging. The heroine is not a two-dimensional stereotype but a woman of multiple facets and accomplishments. Her early, isolated education, like Emile's, fostered the very spontaneity and impulsive generosity that bring her into conflict with the severe social arbiters among whom she is thrust. Her suicide at the end is as much a gesture of defiance as despair.

From a feminist point of view, as Noreen Swallow aptly points out in her excellent analysis of **Delphine** (65-76), Staël's heroine is the victim of a patriarchal society whose dictates are reinforced by the very women it represses. Church and society collaborate in maintaining women within a circumscribed role wherein their primary function is to marry and bear children. The laws, customs, and attitudes sanctioned by society contribute to the subjugation of women while perpetuating the pleasure and security of men: "Anticipating modern feminist literature by over one hundred and fifty years, Mme de Staël sets to work to expose these deeply ingrained, chauvinistic values, showing how they operate, often below the level of consciousness, to obstruct the development and fulfillment of women, to undermine relations between the sexes, and to poison the moral outlook of society" (66).

In the course of the novel, Delphine's inveterate kindness and affection are consistently disparaged by a Greek chorus of minor characters, many of them women. It is Delphine's mischance to fall in love with a man who lives by the patriarchal code she challenges. Léonce does not merely represent a contrasting attitude toward societal traditions. He embodies masculine freedom from the values that govern women's lives. He can marry as he chooses, leave his pregnant wife to woo another woman, and scuttle back and forth between the two without a hint of disapprobation. He is selfish enough to try to force Delphine into the kind of behavior he excoriates—and although her "virtue" remains intact, her reputation is tattered: "Through the arrogant imposition of Léonce's will both Matilde and Delphine are devalued as individuals." (Swallow, 72). The book reinforces Staël's contention that society accepts in a man behavior it finds contemptible in a woman.

Staël's criticism of patriarchal society repeatedly calls into question the double standard governing men's and women's lives. The same frustration in the face of convention, the same struggle between love and independence, the same destruction of woman's potential by man's selfish privilege, pervades Staël's fictional masterpiece **Corinne,** which carries woman's fight for love and self-fulfillment onto a higher and more complex plane.

Notes

1. Although Simone Balayé credits *La Nouvelle Héloïse* and *Werther* as providing Staël with forceful examples of epistolary fiction, she fails to mention Richardson's *Pamela* (1740-41) and *Clarissa* (1747-48) or Choderlos de Laclos's *Liaisons dangereuses*

(1782) as other probable models (*Delphine,* 2 vols., ed. Simone Balayé and Lucia Omacini [Geneva: Droz, 1987-90], 1:12).

2. Staël gave Charles de Villers yet another reason (3 June 1803): "For the struggle between prejudice and reason, there is no more favorable period than the French Revolution" (Jasinski, 4:628).

3. Adélaïde, Pauline, Delphine, and Corinne are all orphans; Corinne alone has been shaped by a mother's influence. All but Corinne have been married and widowed young; all are independently wealthy. Their married status (for Corinne, her exceptional prestige as a poet) and personal fortune endow these heroines with the freedom of action that would be unthinkable for an unmarried woman or an impecunious widow at the turn of the nineteenth century.

4. Not only does the concept of a paternal husband reflect Staël's subconscious wish; it mirrors the real-life example of her intimate friend Juliette Récamier.

5. Staël acknowledged to Suard on 4 November 1802 that her novel was slightly "anti-Catholic" because the plot places "the heart's religion above Catholicism" (Jasinski, 4:570).

6. Louise is supposedly modeled on Benjamin Constant's hunchbacked cousin Rosalie.

7. The antinomy of a binational upbringing will resurface in the conflicts of Corinne's character.

8. This scene is a precise rendition of Staël's rescue at a reception by Delphine de Sabran (see ch. 1).

9. Despite lack of evidence that Staël ever read Laclos's *Liaisons dangereuses,* both Hogsett and Gutwirth detect resemblances between this novel and Staël's work. Hogsett sees a similarity between Théodore's seduction of Pauline and the seductions in *Liaisons* (20 n. 12), while Gutwirth discerns a basic correspondence between Sophie de Vernon's and Mme de Merteuil's autobiographical backgrounds (119 n. 13).

10. Staël finds it important to endow even Corinne, the freest spirit she has engendered, with domestic capabilities.

11. This scene recalls Edouard's threat to kill himself unless Pauline vows to wed him; she, too, faints away.

12. Cf. letters to Narbonne of 2 and 23 October 1792 (Jasinski, 2:37, 53).

13. Elsewhere Staël emphasizes nature's indifference to human emotions. When Delphine visits the waterfall of the Rhine, she is struck by the contrast between her private sorrow and the majestic, impassive movement of the waters (*OC,* 7:151-52). She is again horrified by the brilliant sun shining on the morning of Léonce's execution.

14. According to Diesbach, this scene is a replay of Staël's impassioned defense and rescue of Jacques de Norvins before General Lemoine under the Terror (200-01).

15. Noreen Swallow maintains that the heroine's death marks the ultimate stage in the repressive process by which patriarchal society undermines her independence, fragments her identity, and nullifies her personality: "In feminist terms, Delphine's death is . . . the total eradication of a woman of intelligence and sensitivity whose qualities have been constantly devalued and whose potential has been destroyed. It is the establishment's final triumph" ("Portraits: A Feminist Appraisal of Mme de Staël's *Delphine,*" *Atlantis* 7, no. 1 [Fall-Automne 1981]: 75; hereafter cited in the text [as Swallow]).

16. The Belmont *ménage* reverses the sex roles of the principals: "In the 'perfect union' of the Belmonts, the wife plays precisely the sort of role which society had always assigned to the male partner in marriage: she provides for his needs, and his whole life, intellectual and moral, is filtered through her" (Gutwirth, 126).

17. "Delphine is Mme de Staël as she conceived herself to be morally and as she would have liked to be viewed physically" (Diesbach, 245). Staël's description of herself to Ribbing in a letter of 1 December 1793 tallies with Delphine's character: "All my thoughts and feelings slip out in spite of myself, and my only strength lies in the truth" (Jasinski 2:510).

18. Gutwirth considers Suzanne Necker a far more important source: "The sole importance Talleyrand has as a model was as an inspiration for the depiction of perfidy in a charming and dearly loved friend" (118). Jasinski detects a resemblance between Sophie de Vernon and Narbonne, especially in connection with her flippant wit and love of gambling (2:xviii).

Works Cited

Diesbach, Ghislain de. *Madame de Staël.* Paris: Perrin, 1983.

Jasinski, Béatrice W., ed. *Correspondance générale.* 6 vols. Paris: Jean-Jacques Pauvert, 1962-74; Hachette, 1985; Klincksieck, 1993.

Solovieff, Georges, ed. *Choix de lettres de Mme de Staël (1778-1817).* Paris: Klincksieck, 1970.

Françoise Massardier-Kenney (essay date 1994)

SOURCE: "Staël, Translation, and Race," in *Translating Slavery: Gender and Race in French Women's Writing, 1783-1823,* edited by Doris Y. Kadish and Françoise Massardier-Kenney, Kent State University Press, 1994, pp. 135-45.

[*In the following essay, Massardier-Kenney investigates de Staël's critique of cultural values in her work, particularly in the antislavery sentiment of* Mirza.]

Germaine de Staël (1766-1817) is the only major woman author of the nineteenth century, with the exception of George Sand, who has managed to break through the silence in literary history surrounding women's writing during that time. Still, until recently her reputation has rested mostly on having introduced German Romanticism in France in *De l'Allemagne* (1810), on her opposition to Napoleon, and on her affair with Benjamin Constant, which he fictionalized in *Adolphe.* Her works have been hard to find and her major pieces had not been available in current re-editions. The last two decades have seen a flurry of revisionist studies, of critical editions and translations,[1] which bear witness to the considerable interest that Staël's *oeuvre* holds for anyone interested in nineteenth-century intellectual movements and literature. Yet, her important connection to race and to translation has been ignored, except for Avriel Goldberger's pioneering article on the translation of *Corinne.*[2] The 1934 description of Staël's lifelong interest in the question of slavery by her descendant Comtesse Jean de Pange—"Mme de Staël et les nègres"—gives useful facts but does not analyze either her particular sensitivity as a woman author to the plight of slaves or her idea of culture based on differences and cross-influences. Staël's connection to race, gender, and translation needs to be examined.

Germaine de Staël is the quintessential figure of the translator; she embodies the ideal of translation. She is that "voice from the other side" who throughout her life and works forced her audience to become aware of their own culture through an appeal to the culture of others, be they German, English, or African. Her subtle but unrelenting questioning of the values of French culture through a discourse describing different discourses present in other cultures makes her an "exemplary intellectual," as Pierre Barbéris has called her.[3] She provides us with the point of view of one who is on the margin of mainstream culture and public life.

Staël and her family were, in a subtle way, outsiders. She was born in 1766 to Suzanne Curchod Necker, a Swiss-born, highly educated woman who had visited Rousseau and Voltaire during her years as governess to the children of the Swiss pastor Moulton. Suzanne Curchod married the Protestant Swiss banker Jacques Necker who became famous as finance minister under Louis XVI and as a financial innovator who used massive borrowings to restore French finances. Mme Necker's Parisian salon was one of the most famous of the times. Germaine Necker thus entered the world in a prominent family, and from her earliest years benefitted from the company of the most famous men; but the Neckers were Swiss and Protestant in a French Catholic society, and of course they were commoners.

The primacy of the spoken voice was to be a prominent feature of Staël's fiction. Suzanne Necker, a Rousseau disciple, devoted much time to her daughter's education and kept her with her in her salon. She was apparently unable to show her affection or approval, and her relations with her daughter were strained, both women focusing their love on Jacques Necker, the "patriarchal God of the household."[4] However, through her mother, Germaine Necker first encountered the life of the intellect in conversations, and she herself became a conversationalist well before she became a writer. The importance of the oral is obvious in the poetic improvisations of her famous heroine Corinne, but also, among the readings in this volume, in the early hymns of her Jolof character Mirza. Very early in her life and in her writing career, Staël abstains from valorizing the values of Western Europe, of "civilization." Her emphasis on the oral rather than on the written made her particularly suited to accept cultures from Africa and to appreciate their oral traditions. Her partial exclusion from written discourse because of her gender allowed her to be inclusive racially, and her early concern about the question of slavery would last throughout her life.

This privileging of the spoken voice also came as a transformation of an all too real denial of access to the written word. Germaine Necker's mother Suzanne had started a non-fictional work that she had to abandon at her husband's request. Jacques Necker disapproved of women writing. Later, when the Neckers' daughter began to write, both parents made light of her efforts, and the father reiterated that writing was to be the sole province of men. Between a father whom she adored but who disapproved of her writing, and a mother whom she disliked and who had suppressed her own writing, Staël would have little space in which to maneuver, and her literary strategies would tend to be indirect.

Staël's entry into the world of letters coincided with her gaining some distance from her father. In 1786 Germaine Necker married the Swedish ambassador to France, Eric-Magnus de Staël, and opened a Parisian salon that would soon become famous. Her first work titled *Lettres sur les ouvrages et le caractère de Jean-Jacques Rousseau* (1788) was published anonymously, but everyone knew she was the author. This first act of writing already bore the marks of Staël's strategy: seeming to obey the paternal injunction not to write (she published the work anonymously, she was no longer Mademoiselle Necker, and the work is a praise to another male role model), while nonetheless engaging in the act of writing (she did write and publish, and her authorship was known). This work was to attract a great deal of attention and be re-edited a number of times. Composed of five letters (a borderline genre between the oral and the written), it is a defense of Rousseau and approves of his views on women (i.e., that they should not play a role in public life.)[5] Thus in her first publication of nonfiction Staël took a firm position as a liberal[6] (her subject is a philosopher who questions the most basic institutions of the monarchy), but she also endorsed the paternalistic views of her male model, an endorsement which prefigured the Revolution's relegating women to the private sphere. A radical activist like Olympe de Gouges could publish a *Déclaration des droits de la femme et de la citoyenne* (1791), and women formed clubs of their own (Les Amies de la Vérité, and Citoyennes révolutionnaires),

but the Convention abolished them in October 1793 and Gouges's efforts on women's behalf were to end on the guillotine. What we can learn from comparing Staël to Gouges is that Gouges's efforts on behalf of women and of people of color were more direct and urgent, and immediately thwarted. Her play *L'esclavage des noirs* was immediately brought down by the powerful colonists' club Massiac while Staël's more timorous, but perhaps more timely efforts (more specifically her intervention on behalf of the Guadeloupean Pelasge in 1803,[7] her preface to Wilberforce's essay against slavery in 1814), would go unimpeded.

Staël's paradox was to be that having accepted the paternal male denial of women's involvement in writing and in public life, she would, perhaps indirectly but steadily, write and make for herself a place in public life by using her writing differently from more radical figures like Gouges. A major strategy of Staël's (a major one, but by no means a conscious one), was the timing of the publication of her works so that she would avoid being silenced the way women like Gouges had been. It is perhaps not by chance that a work like *Lettres* (a work not concerned with gender or race) was the first piece she published. It gave her a public voice which she would later use to disseminate her more unsettling works, those sensitive to women, slaves, and cultural differences. Throughout her career she would interspace essays and works of fiction from which a dialogue of different voices would be heard. At the time she published *Lettres,* she had already written three short stories, the publication of which was delayed until 1795 with the *Essai sur les fictions* in a book titled *Recueil de morceaux détachés.* (It is noticeable that it is her short stories that Staël chose to have "détaché" [removed, cut off] while Gouges had her head "détachée.") The short stories not published earlier include *Mirza, ou lettre d'un voyageur, Adélaïde et Théodore,* and *Histoire de Pauline.* In her preface to *Mirza,* Staël indicated that the stories were written before the Revolution and when "she was not twenty yet."[8] Although these stories have not been dated with certainty, if we take Staël's word, we are led to conclude that they were written before she married, and before she published the *Lettres.* They can be read as a counterpoint to *Lettres,* or at least as another point of view, one Staël seemingly did not choose to make public when she was still Mademoiselle Necker.

During the revolution, Staël became active politically in a perhaps limited but real way. At the beginning of the revolution, she returned to Paris with her parents, her father having been recalled to the ministry of finance by public acclaim. She stayed in Paris until 1792 when the Terror forced her to take refuge in Switzerland. She spent the rest of the revolution in exile in England and in Coppet, the family estate in Switzerland Necker had bought previously. In 1795 the Convention freed slaves in the colonies, and that same year Staël returned to Paris where she became active politically. She publicly espoused republicanism, and in 1797 founded the Club Constitutionnel with Benjamin Constant among others. She soon became disenchanted with the government of Napoleon, who banned several of her works and exiled her from Paris. It is only in 1815 after the fall of Napoleon that she would be free to come back to Paris.

During the years of the revolution, Staël experimented with a number of forms and developed a theory of literature grounded on the necessity of cross influences from foreign literatures. She first published several plays (*Sophie, Jane Gray,* both written in 1786) depicting women's sacrificial love, as well as several newspaper articles: **"Réflexions sur le procès de la reine"** (1793), **"Réflexions sur la paix"** (published in 1794 in Switzerland and in 1795 in France). At the same time she published *Zulma,* another short story probably written a few years earlier, and an essay on politics entitled *De l'influence des passions* (1796). She expressed her views of literature both in the *Essai sur les fictions* (1795) and in *De la littérature considérée dans ses rapports avec les institutions sociales* (1800), where she argues that the revolution has changed the conditions in which literature is produced. It is no longer a matter of entertaining, of writing according to the rules and taste of a privileged class, but of expressing "the situation of the individual in modern society."[9] Her ideal is one of the republican novel, "the novel, in republican France, shall depict personalities, personal feelings, teaching man about himself and his relations with his fellowmen and with society [la collectivité]."[10] This republican novel will benefit from "graftings" from other, foreign literatures. Such a program could not endear her to Napoleon whose ambition was to forge a unified France that would be inwardly turned and would shun enemy influences coming from the countries around it (or "surrounding" it, as Napoleonic ideology would have phrased it).

Staël practiced in her own works the kind of intralingual translation that she advocated in her theoretical works. In 1802 she published *Delphine,* a fictional reworking of the themes of *De la littérature,* and which rekindled the controversy created by that work, with the result that Bonaparte forbade her to stay in Paris. As Pierre Barbéris has insightfully noted, Staël constituted the "legitimization of another language."[11] Her militant cosmopolitanism is but a way to question the unexamined values of French culture, what Barbéris calls "franco-centrism" and "voltairo-centrism."[12] Thus the Germany she appeals to in *De la littérature* is used not as a historical reference, but as a utopian antidote to France, an open culture "which, because of its versatility, lends itself to antagonistic exchanges."[13] This appeal to the foreign in order to acknowledge and question the limits of one's culture and language is original: Staël is not interested in describing the picturesque or the exotic. She focuses on the essential: how sentiments are expressed and how power is exercised. In order to do so, she moves between fiction and essays, between what is French and what is foreign in a movement that makes her an exemplary practitioner of intralingual translation. She is interested in the ways in which cultural hybridization can be apprehended as a gain for the culture that lets in influences from the outside. In fact, she

seems to sense that culture is "cultural capital," to use Pierre Bourdieu's term,[14] but that it should not be immobilized by trade barriers.

During the years 1803-13, Staël traveled to Germany and Italy and would write her major works. The outcome of her travels to Italy was the publication of *Corinne* (1807), which became an immediate success. In 1810 she published *De l'Allemagne,* which was immediately banned by Napoleon (before it was even distributed) and caused her to be sent back to her Swiss retreat at Coppet. *De l'Allemagne* finally appeared in 1813 in London (still in French). During this same decade, she published two anti-slavery pieces: **"Préface pour la traduction d'un ouvrage de M. Wilberforce"** (1814), written in London and translated into English by her daughter Albertine; and **"Appel aux Souverains"** (1814), in which she went back in nonfictional form to the concerns expressed at the beginning of her career in *Mirza* and *Histoire de Pauline.* Her abolitionist pleas were already voiced in the opening of *Pauline* written some twenty years earlier: "These scorching climates where men, solely occupied with a barbaric trade and gain, seem, for the most part, to have lost the ideas and feelings which could make them recoil in horror from such a trade."[15]

She spent her last years actively fighting Napoleon's regime, and during these years of political opposition, perhaps not accidentally, she published her last work *De l'esprit des traductions* (1816) in Milan where it was to create a major debate and to influence the development of Italian Romanticism. In this essay Staël advocates translation as the necessary condition to keep national literatures alive. She conceives of translation not as an imitation of what is foreign, but as a way to move free from obsolete literary conventions. She argues that it is through the influence of translation that a national literature can learn and develop new forms.[16] Staël's conception of translation is political, or rather, ideological in that she perceives that literature is a cultural product that functions like a commodity. She herself uses the term "circulation of ideas" and links translation to "other forms of commerce." In a very modern way, she perceives that translation is the agent of change which acknowledges that culture is determined by the society and the times in which it thrives, and that translation is a sort of ideological distancing from and criticism of existing national modes of writing. Her repeated use of the metaphor of gold to represent literature emphasizes that literature is a form of capital, and like a good liberal, she wants that capital to circulate freely between countries.

Her survey of the situation of translation in different countries emphasizes that literatures, without or with little translation, are dead literatures, precisely because they are severed from the influence and the test of other literatures. For Staël, a literature can thrive only if it is part of the great chain of other signifying practices. In her conclusion she calls for the practitioners of Italian literature to turn outward and to let translation rejuvenate their writing.

When it has been mentioned at all, *Mirza* has been dismissed absent-mindedly as "an awkward work,"[17] or patronizingly as "strictly a curiosity, of merely marginal interest."[18] Yet *Mirza*'s depiction of gender and race makes it an important text in the tradition of women's writing and antislavery. It may even be that it is this very conjunction of race and gender that has placed *Mirza* in the "margins," that space in established discourse which Staël was to use and appropriate to create a theory of cultural identity based on maintaining oppositions and differences, not on erasing them. As Pierre Macherey has observed, "it became possible for her to think about cultures, not from within, but from the gaps that, separating them from themselves, projected them outside of their own constitution."[19] From this perspective, Switzer's charges that "she is incapable of reacting to any kind of beauty that is not strictly within the scope of Western European standards,"[20] that she "indulges in the same kind of stereotypes adopted by Hugo in *Bug Jargal*,"[21] are unfounded. Whereas *Bug Jargal* presents stereotypical descriptions of people of color (i.e., childlike, violent, or overly physical figures), *Mirza*'s black characters are intellectual, sensitive, and their sexuality is not emphasized. Moreover, the title character Mirza is endowed with qualities which historical accounts tell us characterize the author. This identification of the implied author with the black character is the opposite of what happens in a work like *Bug Jargal*. Last, these characters are not simply "African"; they belong to two different tribes, a distinction of importance.

Anyway, Staël does not depict "real" Africans any more than she would later depict "real" Germans. She is using the depiction of the other, of the foreigner, to bring out particularities and deficiencies in her own culture. In a perhaps extremely perceptive and honest move, she seems to know that the other point of view can be used to place in question her own culture; but that its representation is inevitably mediated by the gender, the class, the culture, in brief, the ideology of the author, that the recognition of the limits of such a representation is at the center of her refusal to endorse culturocentrism.

Mirza clearly links antislavery sentiments and women. First, the preface, written several years after Staël wrote the story but before it was published in 1895, reclaims the narrative and its authorship. The presence of the preface provides a frame for the narrative, made by a male European to an unknown woman, so that, although the narrator is male, both the author and the addressee are women. This story of women and slavery is thus doubly gendered. Secondly, the title character Mirza, the African heroine, is first presented as the eloquent voice of antislavery. The character Ximeo first hears her speak: "The love of freedom, the horror of slavery were the subjects of the noble hymns that filled me with a rapturous admiration." Moreover, it is made clear in the story that Mirza, an orphan member of the Jolof tribe,[22] opposes the male warriors' custom of selling their war prisoners as slaves. The female character is thus the only one not ideologically implicated in the slave system. Revealingly, after offering herself as a substitute slave to save Ximeo[23] and after being saved by the French Governor, Mirza chooses to die. The superficial reason is her broken heart over Ximeo's faithlessness; but another motive, more indirect but still significant, is the impossibility for the independent woman to owe her life and her freedom to a European colonialist, generous as he may be. Thus Mirza dies while Ximeo heads a European-style plantation, answering the naive and patronizing questions of the European narrator about his superior ability to speak French and to run a smooth plantation. Ximeo only escapes the power structure master/slave, superior/inferior, European/African which links him to the European visitor through the retelling of Mirza's story (her story of abandonment and death, but also of rebellion): indeed, while the author carefully avoids using direct discourse between the European male narrator and Ximeo, thus sidestepping the question of using "tu" (the usual form for an intimate or an inferior) or "vous" (the form reserved for equality or formality), Ximeo finally addresses the narrator as "tu," an astonishing "tu" that acknowledges the significance of telling Mirza's story as a way to undermine confidence in the value, let alone superiority, of the European.

Lest this significant use of "tu" be interpreted as a sign of Ximeo's lack of mastery of the French language (the enduring stereotype was that Africans spoke "petit nègre," the French version of Pidgin English), the narrator had earlier emphasized Ximeo's native command of French. One sees here that, although superficially correct, the charge of Franco-centrism waged against Staël or other women writers for making their African characters speak perfect French needs to be reexamined. If a French author depicts foreign characters (be they Jolof like Mirza or Italian as in *Corinne*), their language will inevitably be a translation. The question is whether this translation will emphasize their lack of control of language through a stereotypical distortion of standard French or whether the translation will be transparent[24] (i.e., emphasize what they say rather than how inadequately they express themselves or how peculiar they sound). Thus Staël shifts the difference of her characters away from the grammatical forms of their language (from *langue*) to voice, a more individual, less collectively determined language (to *parole*); she is engaged in the representation of different modes of thinking and speaking. And speak is precisely what Mirza does, unlike Ximeo who is left speechless when Mirza improvises on the theme of freedom. Throughout the narrative, Staël emphasizes the power of Mirza's voice. When, at the end, she speaks up to the slave traders in favor of Ximeo, he is again speechless. Staël is here suggesting that Mirza's kind of voice, the voice of passion, of antislavery, of female difference, of the spoken, can silence and counterbalance—for a moment—the discourse of the male, patriarchal, European colonialism and deceit. When asked by Ximeo to speak about love, Mirza opposes herself to the other tribe. She tells Ximeo "do not expect me to speak with the artfulness of the women of your country." Mirza opposes the "naturalness" of her speech, which is the sincere outpouring of feelings, to a language which is deceitful. Through Mirza Staël criticizes the classical, regulated language of traditional French literature as well as the oppressive language of Ximeo. Mirza's language is a utopian language which is opposed to patriarchal language. At the same time, Staël refuses to create a mythical figure of an "African" who would speak a "pure" language; she distinguishes between Ximeo from Cayor and Mirza, the Jolof.

The link between patriarchy, political division, and deceit is made clear by Ximeo who, after writing a letter to Mirza about his departure and his alleged trip, attempts to justify himself: "my father would never have called daughter a woman from the Jolof country." The inability of one culture to accept an exterior element is directly linked to the father's discourse. *Mirza* does present a series of oppositions—Mirza/Ximeo, Africa/Europe, woman/man, voice/written discourse, antislavery/patriarchy—but these oppositions are not static binary oppositions. Shifts occur, change is possible, the language from without can enter and rejuvenate the culture from within. The male Ximeo shifts from the weak listener and writer position to that of speaker: "But I have wished to speak of her." The male character redeems himself by telling the woman's story, by learning to understand and speak her language. The link between race and gender is made once again.

Ximeo the African prince is to the European colonialist as woman is to man. Ximeo's feminization is suggested early in the story. The European male narrator describes him in ways which emphasize, not so much his Europeanness, but his feminine aspect. His features are "ravissantes" (beautiful), he is "trop mince pour un homme" (too thin for a man), he has "beaux yeux" (beautiful eyes), he has more "délicatesse" (frailty) than "force" (strength). Staël's description of Ximeo's physical appearance, which runs counter to the stereotype of the black man as threatening because of his size and his physicality, is in fact one of her indirect ways of connecting race and gender. Ximeo is black and thus feminine in the eyes of the European (and it is the narrator who comments on Ximeo's lack of the "defects of the men of his race").[25] Revealingly, the female heroine Mirza is hardly described at all; rather, she is situated in a utopian elsewhere outside of the economy of static subject/object positions. The European male gaze of the narrator has not seen her and Ximeo has been subjugated by her voice.

Staël's strong liberal position and the indirect strategies she used to link gender and race, and to present the oppression of Africans and women by the French male patriarchy, seem to be the salient features which would direct the "siting" of the translation of *Mirza.* While Staël could not transcend the limits placed on her by her times and place, her opposition to Francocentrism, to slavery, and to patriarchy should not be minimized and decontextualized. In the same way as Staël used transparency yet allowed for the voice of difference, the translator translating *Mirza* for a modern American audience has to both work with a tone and a vocabulary that seem at home in English, and give an indication that the text comes from a culture which

is different from ours but which can be apprehended without "cannibalizing" the source text, without erasing its difference. Avriel Goldberger has similarly stated about her translation of *Corinne,* "[t]he translator has sought as 'timeless' a language as possible, avoiding both an imitation of nineteenth-century English which can so easily sound like a parody, and the obviously twentieth-century which would give a false modernity to the text."[26] This transparency, which nonetheless admits to the existence of a distance between the French and the English text, is a working in translation of the circulation of a specific cultural capital, a capital whose value determines how the translation is sited. This notion of transparency is quite different from the "bad" transparency described by Tejaswini Niranjana.[27] It does not aim at fixing a colonized discourse but at showing the modernity of Staël's notion of culture as something that should not be fixed by national boundaries.

In specific terms, the passionate, Romantic voice of Mirza could have been toned down to adapt to our contemporary mode of writing and to avoid skirting the ridiculous, but its dissident force would have been lost or trivialized. To keep the distance, yet to "familiarize" the text in English (to reuse the well-known Russian formalist notion of "defamiliarization"), I turned to the English romantics for texts of a similar sensibility but also remote in time. Perhaps not unsurprisingly, the most useful parallel text turned out to be Mary Shelley's *Frankenstein.*

For that same "familiarization" effect, Staël's careful feminization of Ximeo, her use of the passive voice to render his lack of agency, had to be kept without pushing her text in the direction of parody. Similarly, the terms used to describe Africans (nègre, nègresse) had to be carefully thought out since they now have a negative connotation which was not necessarily present in the original French text.[28] However, since the term Negro was endorsed by African Americans until recently, and since the translated text is obviously sited as an older text, not as a modernization, the term was kept.[29] A more ideologically loaded issue was Staël's reference to the African share of responsibilities in the slave trade (in the same way as Aphra Behn had done previously in English). The choice was either to tone down the statement so as to fit our expected audience's ideological expectations (i.e., to focus on the responsibility of the colonizer not on the complicity of the victims), or to keep it in as an integral part of the liberal antiabolitionist argument of the time. Since Staël also refers again to the African custom of slavery in her later piece on slavery, **"Appel aux souverains,"** the statement was kept as is.

Other syntactic issues such as Ximeo's sudden use of "tu" have been handled in the "margin" of the translation, i.e., the introduction, which, like Staël's preface, is a necessary part of the text since it contextualizes the translated text and brings attention to its status as translation. I have noted earlier Staël's valorization of the oral over the written, and I would argue that her whole *oeuvre* is a valorization of the process of translation over original "pure," "uncontaminated" texts, that she optimistically emphasizes that it is in the retelling of the story in another language or from another point of view that cultures can be revitalized.[30]

Notes

1. See in particular Simone Balayé, *Corinne* (Paris: Gallimard, 1985) and *Madame de Staël: lumières et liberté* (Paris: Klincksieck, 1979); Madelyn Gutwirth, *Madame de Staël, Novelist* (Urbana, Ill.: University of Illinois Press, 1978) and "Madame de Staël, Rousseau and the Woman Question," *PMLA* [*Publications of the Modern Language Association of America*] 86 (January 1971): 100-109; Charlotte Hogsett, *The Literary Existence of Germaine de Staël* (Carbondale, Ill.: Southern Illinois University Press, 1987); Avriel Goldberger, ed. and trans., *Corinne* (New Brunswick, N.J.: Rutgers University Press, 1987).

2. Avriel Goldberger, "Germaine De Staël's *Corinne*: Challenges to the Translator in the 1980s," *French Review* 63 (April 1990): 800-809. In this article, Goldberger analyzes previous translations of *Corinne* and describes the strategies she used for her own translation. Although she does not assess Staël's own connection to translation, her own self-consciousness about translating Staël provides useful insights.

3. Pierre Barbéris, "Madame de Staël: du romantisme, de la littérature et de la France nouvelle," *Europe* 693 (1987): 11.

4. For an insightful account of the relations between Germaine Necker and her mother, see Madelyn Gutwirth, *Madame de Staël, Novelist,* chapter 1.

5. For a discussion of *Lettres* in relation to Staël's position as a woman, see Gutwirth's "Madame de Staël, Rousseau and the Woman Question."

6. I am using the term liberal in its nineteenth-century context of one who follows the philosophical and political system based on individual liberties and equality. The liberalism of Staël is opposed to the despotism of Napoleon or the royalist Restoration which followed him.

7. For a description of her efforts to get Pelasge out of jail, see Comtesse Jean de Pange, "Madame de Staël et les nègres," *Revue de France* 5 (Oct. 1934): 425-34.

8. Germaine de Staël, "Mirza," in *Oeuvres complètes* (Geneva: Slatkine, 1967), 72.

9. Henri Coulet, "Révolution et roman selon Madame de Staël," *Revue d'histoire littéraire de France* 87 (1987): 646.

10. Ibid., 65.

11. Barbéris, "Madame de Staël," 15.

12. Ibid., 12.

13. Pierre Macherey, "Un imaginaire cosmopolite: la pensée littéraire de Madame de Staël," in *A quoi pense la littérature* (Paris: Presses Universitaires de France, 1990), 34.

14. For a discussion of this concept, see Pierre Bourdieu, *Distinction. A Social Critique of Taste,* trans. Richard Nice (Cambridge, Mass.: Harvard University Press, 1984).

15. Staël, *Oeuvres complètes,* 1:88.

16. For a discussion of the ways in which translation can enrich a culture, see Albrecht Neubert and Gregory M. Shreve, *Translation as Text* (Kent, Ohio: Kent State University Press, 1992), 3.

17. Coulet, "Révolution," 647.

18. Richard Switzer, "Mme de Staël, Mme de Duras and the Question of Race," *Kentucky Romance Quarterly* 20 (1973): 308.

19. Macherey, *A quoi pense la littérature,* 36.

20. Switzer, "Mme de Staël," 306.

21. Ibid., 304.

22. Jolof refers to an authentic tribe, but it was a "kingdom," of which "Cayor" was a part. Staël has reversed the importance of the two groups.

23. Actually, the Jolofs have no reason not to trade Mirza since the distinction they make is not between friends and enemies, but between kin and non-kin. Since Mirza is an orphan of unclear origin, she may very well be considered non-kin. For a comprehensive study of slavery in Africa, see Patrick Manning, *Slavery and African Life* (London: Cambridge University Press, 1983) and Paul Lovejoy, *Transformations in Slavery* (London: Cambridge University Press, 1990).

24. For a discussion of the notion of "transparency" in translation see chapter 1 of this volume.

25. This is not to say that *Mirza* is completely free of Eurocentrism. After all Mirza gets her "culture" from a French exile, and the workers on Ximeo's plantation are represented as longing for their former games of bows and arrows, a rather patronizing view of what their culture may have entailed. On the other hand, Staël does not represent the topos of "the" African and is careful to distinguish between two West African tribes.

26. Goldberger, "Challenges to the Translator," 808–9.

27. Tejaswini Niranjana, *Siting Translation: History, Post-Structuralism, and the Colonial Context* (Berkeley: University of California Press, 1992), 3.

28. For a discussion of the term "nègre," see chapter 1.

29. For an interesting discussion of the use of the term "nègre" in another context, see James A. Arnold's article on the translation of Aimé Césaire. His discussion shows that a translation may go astray if it does not distance itself from its own ideology. James A. Arnold, "Translating/Editing 'Race' and 'Culture' from Caribbean French," in *Translating Latin*

America, ed. William Luis and Julio Rodriguez-Luis (Binghamton, N.Y.: SUNY University Press, 1991), 215–22.

30. Of course, this hope was in complete opposition to the building of the European colonial empire in the sense that what Europe did in the nineteenth century was to attempt to export its values to its colonies and to impose them on other cultures.

Jennifer Birkett (essay date 1995)

SOURCE: "Speech in Action: Language, Society, and Subject in Germaine de Staël's *Corinne,*" in *Eighteenth-Century Fiction,* Vol. 7, No. 4, July, 1995, pp. 393-408.

[*In the following essay, Birkett discusses the dynamics of subjective and collective narrative voice within the feminist text of* Corinne.]

A central preoccupation in Germaine de Staël's **Corinne, ou l'Italie** (1807),[1] and one which is returning to contemporary agendas with a political urgency equal to that of its feminist theme, is the problematic of the relation between the individual subject and the social and political community. In his influential collection of lectures, *The Philosophical Discourse of Modernity* (1985),[2] Jürgen Habermas has renewed the debate with two fresh contributions: his concept of the "communication community," and his meditations on modernity's consciousness of time. In this essay, I use Habermas's insights to illuminate the modernity of **Corinne,** and in particular to explore the mechanics and the meaning of the heroine's improvisation exercises, which, I argue, are simultaneously improvisations of self and improvisations of society. At the same time, I want to maintain a feminist perspective (not one of Habermas's preoccupations) with a consideration of Staël's emphasis on the distinctive role of the ideal feminine voice in the improvisatory process. The "modernity" of **Corinne,** read in these selected perspectives, is twofold. It presents a dynamic model of the subject's founding in intersubjectivity, within a process of discursive exchange in which the individual is engaged both as an autonomous self-creating subject and as a representative of the groups of which society is constituted. It also presents a ground-breaking account of creative feminine voice as the fulcrum of the model, speaking a subject that is both open and receptive to otherness *and* resistant in its own right.

THE MODERN PERSPECTIVE

I) SUBJECT TO REASON: HABERMAS AND THE COMMUNICATION COMMUNITY

In its own context, Habermas's theory of the "communication community" addresses a different agenda from Madame de Staël's text, and it is important to avoid temptations to anachronism and opportunism in bringing the two together. A short preliminary account of Habermas's posi-

tion should bring out both the differences in their perspective and the areas of significant overlapping interest.

In his preface to *The Philosophical Discourse of Modernity,* Habermas explains that his aim is to reconstruct the philosophical discourse of modernity in the light of the challenge from the neostructuralist critique of reason. The modern definition of modernity, he argues, arose in the course of the eighteenth century with the replacement of the Christian concept of the world of the future as a world still to come, a last day yet to dawn, by a secular concept which "expresses the conviction that the future has already begun. It is the epoch that lives for the future, that opens itself up to the novelty of the future."[3] The concept of modernity implies the inauguration of a new historical-philosophical perspective, in which the present finds itself as it recognizes its status in history, but not as a carrier of the norms of the past; rather, it defines itself in terms of the radical break it has made with the past (pp. 6-7). Habermas evokes Walter Benjamin's productive characterization in his "Theses on the Philosophy of History" of the time-consciousness of modernity, a now-time (*Jetztzeit*) shot through with fragments of Messianic time: an authentic, startling awareness of the immediacy of the present, lit by openings to an unknown future which spring directly from renewed perception of the past.[4]

Other thinkers have been less successful than Benjamin in finding ways of formulating the relationship between past and present that secure the independence and innovative capacity of the immediate moment without cutting it off entirely from its formative origins. As Habermas sees it, the problem of modernity has from the start been that of finding philosophical justification for its own norms and values. In the process of wrestling with that problem, philosophers from Hegel to Nietzsche (most recently, in the generation preceding our own, Theodor Adorno and Max Horkheimer) have succeeded in discrediting notions of reason, subjectivity, and subject, which are rooted in Enlightenment thinking. And, along with these notions, they have discredited the beneficial products of Enlightenment reason on which the structures of contemporary Western society were built, what Habermas describes as "the rational content of cultural modernity that was captured in bourgeois ideals (and also instrumentalized along with them)."[5] Among such benefits, Habermas lists speculative thought ("the specific theoretical dynamic that continually pushes the sciences . . . *beyond* merely engendering technically useful knowledge"); universal principles of law and morality which, he says, have been incorporated into the formative structures of societies and subjects ("the institutions of constitutional government, into the forms of democratic will formation, and into individualist patterns of identity formation"); the new, varied, and qualitatively different kinds of aesthetic experience which become available to a subjectivity liberated from merely conventional and end-directed activity; and, not least, the enriched range of values proper to self-realization that such aesthetic experiences help engender (p. 113). (It is worth noting at this early stage that these are all values—creativity, freedom, innovation, democratic ethics—which are embodied in *Corinne*.)

Habermas develops his concept of the communication community as a way of enabling contemporary thinking to reconcile the notion of values and the notion of modernity. To re-establish the notion of values, it is necessary to re-store the concept of validity. Since Nietzsche, with his as-similation of reason and power, and his insistence that all individual evaluations and formulations of the world are subjective and interested, it has been impossible to sustain the original presumption of Enlightenment philosophy that individual subjects participate in an objective and univer-sally valid Reason. Habermas proposes that thinking should no longer start from the notion that Heidegger, Foucault, and Derrida have rightly challenged of a meta-physically isolated subject, observer, and dominator of the world, the sole validator of its self-established norms (p. 296). The subject should be conceived of as grounded within intersubjectivity, and for that there needs to be es-tablished a "paradigm of mutual understanding" founded in the way the speech community works. Habermas de-fines this community as "an interpersonal relationship structured by the system of reciprocally interlocked per-spectives among speakers, hearers and non-participants who happen to be present at the time. On the level of grammar, this corresponds to the system of personal pro-nouns. Whoever has been trained in this system has learned how, in the performative attitude, to take up and transform into one another the perspectives of the first, second and third persons."[6]

Habermas argues that subjects are effectively constituted in this paradigm, since they are accustomed to the interac-tions of the language community, to shifting subject posi-tions within discourse, experiencing being *I, you, s/he* as positions with equal power, having to recapitulate and un-derstand the positions of others before they themselves speak. He argues further that this speech situation must be considered as a segment of the "lifeworld" that forms the horizons of those who participate in the interlocutory ex-change. The lifeworld "offers a store of things taken for granted in the given culture, from which communicative participants draw consensual interpretative patterns in their efforts at interpretation" (p. 298). The values and working assumptions of the lifeworld are consolidated in groups ("The solidarities of groups integrated by values and the competences of socialized individuals belong, as do cultur-ally ingrained background assumptions, to the components of the lifeworld," p. 298) and are reproduced through the medium of communicative action. In this paradigm, par-ticipants in the communication community are not con-ceived of as masterful subjects but as individual speakers with group origins: "interaction participants . . . no longer appear as originators who master situations with the help of accountable actions, but as the *products* of the tradi-tions in which they stand, of the solidary groups to which they belong, and of the socialization processes within which they grow up" (p. 299).

The writing of *Corinne* is certainly unconscious of any need to tackle the philosophical problem of the grounding of values, which is where Habermas starts. But the text equally certainly addresses the philosophical and political questions Habermas associates with that problem (questions of competing subjectivities and groups) and looks for solutions in similar directions. In its simplest terms, the problem for Staël's novel is to find less oppres-sive and more productive modes of coexistence for indi-viduals, groups (men/women, fathers/sons), and nations, and the solution incorporates two notions: the concept of the individual as product of the group, and the idea of communicative action as the point where the "lifeworld" (to use Habermas's term) is actualized and reproduced. In Staël's novel, however, there is one significant difference. The lifeworld is not merely reproduced through Corinne's improvisations and exchanges but is also re-formed. Corinne, half-Italian and half-English, finds herself not simply reproducing the values and competences of the groups that produced her, but acting as a point where a multitude of different national, class, and gender values in-tersect and interact, opening the potential for something radically new.

II) THE FEMININE VOICE

Feminist interpretations of "the feminine voice" oscillate, sometimes disconcertingly, between two poles. On the one hand, there are Lacanian-inspired versions of speech dis-empowered by its origins in a language constructed in the Name of the Father, a symbolic in which woman is simply non-existent and the best that can be managed is a hysteri-cal or silent deployment of women's status as victim. On the other, there are celebratory visions of the feminine ca-pacity to produce a Utopian discourse, which can both found a distinctive feminine identity and embrace a plural-ity of others. Staël's *Corinne* negotiates between the two extremes. It clearly acknowledges the limits set to wom-en's speech by the discourse(s) of patriarchal society.[7] But in the last analysis it also offers a construction of the ideal feminine voice as one which aims to generate from within those limits a different model of speaking and being, di-rected towards openness, pluralism, and the negotiation of change.

There has in recent years been an explosion of innovative feminist criticism exploring the nature of the feminine voice in *Corinne*. Two books are of particular importance. *Germaine de Staël: Crossing the Borders* (1991) includes some excellent essays which offer insights into the inter-play of male and female discourses in Staël's work, ex-ploring its biographical and psychoanalytical hinterland, the tensions between repression and self-affirmation, self-realization through speech and the failure of communica-tion.[8] Marie-Claire Vallois's stimulating monograph *Fic-tions féminines: Madame de Staël et les voix de la Sibylle* (1987)[9] reads *Corinne* as a quest for the absent mother and the recovery of archaic female space, a "drama of dis-placement and substitution that deconstructs language as privileged cultural edifice," and argues that in place of language the gestures of fragmentation offered by Corinne, grounded in the ultimate ruin of the self that is suicide, convey women's struggle for authentic communication.[10]

In a considerable number of these critics, emphasis leans towards the negatives in the text, such as Corinne's death or the landscape of ruins and tombs from which she speaks. As a result, attention has been over-directed towards the disempowerment of the female by the irresistible power of the Father, to female failure and silence, and to the concept of an essentially female inheritance of things falling apart, fragments cobbled desperately together.[11] My own reading would emphasize, out of a consciously complex text, the countervailing forces which Staël herself foregrounds in, for example, her presentation of Corinne's competences as musician and poet and her particular skill in interweaving her voice with other voices to put differences and dissonances in unifying harmonies. In this process, she is shown taking fragments of traditional airs, motifs, and rhythms and bringing them to coherence through rhythms and variations of her own inspiration. Or again, Staël offers a passage set in the ruins of Ancient Rome (discussed in detail below), where Corinne speaks not as a woman scrabbling to recover sense from the ruins of a dead world but as a member of an artistic tradition that links across the ages musicians, poets, and, most of all, architects—those builders of the new, skilled in the remaking of the perspectives of ancient landscape. As artist, Corinne shares the capacity for remaking tradition of some of her male predecessors. She invents her own inheritance, remaking her language as the great artists of Renaissance Italy she invokes remade theirs. The parallel might be drawn with contemporary writers such as Hélène Cixous or Julia Kristeva, whose feminine voice acknowledges its identity with its male modernist forerunners, Mallarmé, Kafka, Joyce, and Beckett, architects of new linguistic worlds.

Every word in Staël's text recognizes the constitutive force and the dominant pull of the past, inscribed in that vast sequence of present landscapes over which Corinne travels and whose history both she and the narrative voice evoke (France, England, and all the varied regions of Italy, city-states and rural landscapes), and carried by the individuals of different cultures who make up Corinne's various audiences. Corinne herself, though, is not a hostage to the past, or to tradition, or to any of the cultures she addresses. Her mixed parentage, her formative years spent in both Italy and England, her fluency in many languages, her diverse artistic talents, are all so many passports to free movement. She lives by making her own choices, emphasizing her autonomy. She chose Italian rather than English as her language and nationality because, as she explains, she recognized the parallels between her own talents and preferences and those of Italian society (both prize culture, thought, poetic speech). She chooses her own destiny. Her decision to leave for Naples with Oswald, despite the comte d'Erfeuil's warnings, is stamped by clear assertion of her own self-knowledge and her will to determine her own purposes: "Je souffre, je jouis, je sens à ma manière,

et ce serait moi seule qu'il faudrait observer, si l'on voulait influer sur mon bonheur" (1:265). Corinne's choices are potent ones that determine the destinies of others. Crossing the sea to Naples, with Oswald, she takes the veiled moon for her symbol; in the concluding tableau of the text, on her deathbed, she makes it the orientating focus of the transformed community she leaves behind.

Failure and silencing are at least as much a masculine as a feminine fate in Staël's text, which offers a range of examples of good men destroyed by unfortunate fate, weak men destroyed by their own lack of nerve, and sons over-awed and silenced by patriarchal power. Oswald, locked to duty, obsessed by the responsibility he feels to perpetuate a patriarchal order figured not only by his own father but by the English state that summons him to war, is not merely the ungrateful lover but also the representative, in this lifeworld, of all sons. As Castel-Forte explains, men's capacity for creative speech is limited because they are rooted in social formations, by their work and duties. Women are freer. Were that not so, all men might follow Corinne's example: "nous suivrions ses traces, nous serions hommes comme elle est femme, si les hommes pouvaient, comme les femmes, se créer un monde dans leur propre cœur, et si notre génie, nécessairement dépendant des relations sociales et des circonstances extérieures, pouvait s'allumer tout entier au seul flambeau de la poésie" (1:51). Castel-Forte's own statement is a model of the conceptual prejudices which, as much as their social commitments, limit men's capacity to initiate change. Where he posits mutually exclusive alternatives (dream or engagement, feeling or action, poetry or politics, private or public spheres), *Corinne* begins with the presumption that all possibilities can be reconciled. This is the difference that makes unlocking the closed categories of the present and creating a fresh future pre-eminently, for Staël, a function of feminine voice.

IMPROVISING SELF/IMPROVISING SOCIETY

The remainder of this essay will look at some of the key improvisatory moments of the novel and try to substantiate the contentions made above with a critical analysis of the processes and nature of the "communication community" realized through Corinne's voice. Certain key characteristics recur. The predominant discursive mode is one of negotiation and reconciliation. Apparently contradictory standpoints, viewed from a larger, distancing perspective—the third-person position, taken by Corinne—are separately analysed and grasped in their difference, and then reformulated to create a dynamic invocation of something new. Construction of an improvisation is a matter of mixing learned discourse, technical skill, and rhetorical competence with spontaneous and enthusiastic inspiration.[12] The starting material consists of poetic clichés, quotations, borrowings from the common cultural stock. This material—the social given—is transformed as Corinne glimpses through it some inspiration of her own. At its best, her improvisations are a fusion of subjective and collective inspiration, bringing together personal and public preoccupations. In that form, they move into rhythms of her own invention and the building blocks of poetic cliché are replaced, we are told, by original lyrical prose. We never actually discover what fresh rhythms and syntax that prose might consist of: all the text offers are the French representations of the presumedly Italian original. What Corinne makes possible are the conditions of a different performance. The different performance itself is not capable of direct representation, being one that can only be fully grasped in the presence of its making.

Presence is the mark of Corinne's first improvisation (which is also her first appearance in the novel), which takes place on the Capitol and marks her incorporation into the pantheon of Italian poetic genius. The episode is dramatically delayed in the narrative (vol. 1, book 3) by a lengthy preliminary account of Oswald's journey to Italy, its motivation, and his guilt-ridden attachment to the past. The contrast between the two character presentations is striking. Oswald's tale is a third-person, single-dimensional narrative of his actions and thoughts, conducted predominantly in the past historic. It reads as a relentless self-accounting of son to father, establishing a monolinear continuity between past, present, and a predictably drab future. Corinne is not a tale but a presence, a speech-product, generated by a plurality of voices in a range of tenses in which the past has its role but where the present quickly dominates. Corinne appears as pre-eminently a subject in discourse, a construction in the present voice.

The narrative voice of the text, dominant in the presentation of Oswald, is muted for Corinne into a supporting function. It enables her to make an authoritative entry onto a public stage which contemporary readers would otherwise expect to be the particular province of masculine subjects. It presents (subordinated into indirect speech) a series of mediating and legitimizing voices which before she opens her own mouth establish her as a subject in her own right. Through those same voices, it identifies the range of different speaking positions in the Italian communication community (people, aristocracy, laymen, poets) and a new element—the English private and political sensibility represented by Oswald—all of which her voice will in turn address, legitimize, and transform.

Corinne moves through the various personal pronouns identified in Habermas's analysis. She first appears as "she," both in the adulatory clichés of the crowd ("c'est une divinité entourée de nuages," 1:45) and in the introductory panegyric delivered by her noble friend Castel-Forte, the father-figure who throughout the text displays a lover's devotion. Castel-Forte establishes her in threefold person: as the object of her Italian audience, as a subject in her own right, and as mediatory third (1:50). What Italy appreciates, he says, is her ability to bring unity out of diversity, uniting knowledge of many languages and cultures. He emphasizes the originality of her talent, the spark of distinctive genius she displays in all her artistic talents: "cette trace de feu, cette trace d'elle." And equally, he identifies her social place and mediatory function:

"Corinne est le lien de ses amis entre eux." Corinne mediates time, harmonizing past, present, and future. The product of Italy's climate and culture, she also figures the best of what Italy might be: "Nous nous plaisons à la contempler comme une admirable production de notre climat, de nos beaux-arts, comme un rejeton du passé, comme une prophétie de l'avenir." Corinne herself, in effect, embodies for Italy Walter Benjamin's Messianic moment: the bearer of a reformulated past, tradition recuperated and transformed in the living delight of the present, caught up in the dynamic promise of an equally delightful, unknowable, living future.

Oswald's first response to the eulogies offered by Corinne's fellow citizens is a jealous desire to compete: "Déjà lord Nelvil souffrait de cette manière de louer Corinne; il lui semblait déjà qu'en la regardant il aurait fait à l'instant même un portrait d'elle plus juste, plus vrai, plus détaillé, un portrait enfin qui ne pût convenir qu'à Corinne" (1:47). Corinne's improvisation responds to the range of competing interests in the audience—competing not only with each other but also with her, in their desire to make her the image of their own desire. She turns competition into negotiation. Her speech takes an overview of its audience, identifies its polarized elements (Italy and Oswald), and reproduces and recombines selected characteristics of each. The theme of her improvisation, and its first movement, is dictated by the crowd: "la gloire et le bonheur d'Italie." The second movement incorporates Oswald, taking its subject from the mourning he is wearing for his father. Corinne sings of death Italian style, which is not, in her version, the obliteration of the isolated subject, but entry into a glorious cultural community, life lived in the light of an unknown posterity: "Peut-être un des charmes secrets de Rome est-il de réconcilier l'imagination avec le long sommeil" (1:58). The narrative voice returns to prominence to point out to the reader that it is not the given material but what Corinne does with it—the form and style of her improvisation—that is the strength of her work. Contrast is its key, produced by her thematic yoking of death and glory, and by the distinctive tonal variation of her voice, which combines the sonority of the Italian language with her own compassionate timbre. The crowd acclaims her in acknowledgment of the understanding conveyed by her voice. The narrative voice further emphasizes that in her turn Corinne is herself transformed and empowered by her own act of speaking, redefined within the collective response: "elle venait de parler . . . l'enthousiasme le remportait sur la timidité. Ce n'était plus une femme craintive, mais une prêtresse inspirée, qui se consacrait avec joie au culte du génie" (1:59).

At her best, as she explains to Oswald, Corinne's improvisations are an enthusiastic collocation of personal and public statements. This double definition of individual subject as simultaneously engaged in public and private speech, reaching for new perspectives for the common good beyond the limits of the given,[13] is the model she urges on Oswald as she guides him round Rome in the second improvisatory moment I want to consider (1:83-133). In effect, this is a sequence of improvisations elaborating that first insight which sparked on the Capitol between her, Oswald, and the crowd: that death in Italy is a doorway to new life. Speech here engages transformatively with the Roman landscape to unlock the creative energies of past communities crystallized in its crumbling buildings and monuments. In the present, the creative potential of both Oswald and Corinne is released as, in dialogue, they reformulate their perception of the ruins as the raw material of a future: "Ils étaient des amis qui voyageaient ensemble: ils commencaient à dire *nous*" (1:99). The transformation is more obvious in Oswald, who starts in the near-silence of a language mortgaged to his dead father and ends declaring "vous avez réveillé mon imagination" (1:131). But Corinne, too, is changed in this relationship, confronting and coming to productive terms with a degree of material resistance to her enthusiasms unmatched since her disastrous childhood visit to England.[14] The past, even as represented by Oswald, can be a constitutive, not a destructive force.

Corinne, in Oswald's own words, *interprets* Rome to him (1:93). Her speech repositions him within the cultural landscape in every possible sense, physical, moral, and intellectual. It rearticulates his structures of perception, changing the relationships between himself and the things he sees, and, potentially, between the things themselves. The ruins remain ruins, but in Corinne's version they exist in a context where continuity of larger values, not supersession of individual objects and persons, is the centre of interest. Corinne urges Oswald away from an exclusive focus on isolated details (including, by implication, his father's death) towards the larger comprehension of an expanding, interrelated whole (1:96). In a planned progression through the Pantheon, commenting on its pagan symbolization of the divinity of life, by Hadrian's tomb, and towards St Peter's, she reads out of the ruins the continuity of such concepts as nobility and beauty, freedom, and disinterested socially-rooted morality.[15] Her rhetorical skills are enhanced by a sense of theatre which turns the material landscape into a well-planned stage. As her argument reaches its climax, Oswald is allowed to see Saint Peter's for the first time, in full dazzling sunlight, the living embodiment in modern Italy of Corinne's thesis. She emphasizes its status as an artefact, designed by Michelangelo to blend pagan images and Christian dogma so as to release death into life: "[L]a pensée est détournée de la contemplation d'un cercueil par les chefs-d'œuvre du génie. Ils rappellent l'immortalité sur l'autel même de la mort; et l'imagination, animée par l'admiration qu'ils inspirent, ne sent pas, comme dans le Nord, le silence et le froid, immuables gardiens des sépulcres" (1:98). This demonstration that traditional discourse is not an absolute but a construct, and that it is in the hands of succeeding generations to reconfigure it, is not lost on Oswald, who sets against the Latin tradition the cold gloom of his own Ossianic mythology and, already, acknowledges his disinclination to choose change: "Ici, vous voulez oublier et jouir; je ne sais si je désirerais que votre beau ciel me fît ce genre de bien" (1:98).

Oswald understands fully that Corinne represents for him his opportunity to negotiate a passage out of the dead-end of patriarchal philosophy and politics: "recevoir par l'imagination une vie nouvelle, renaître pour l'avenir, sans rompre avec le passé" (1:61). The competitiveness that from the beginning, on the Capitol, first attracted him to her now stands in his way. Even in the first dazzling flush of love, standing with her in the ruins of the Coliseum at the end of the second day of their tour of Rome, he cannot respond to her attempts to write a pluralist version of history that is a charter for other voices and values. Corinne is dismayed as he argues the case for the self-centred ego: "L'imagination exaltée peut produire les miracles du genie; mais ce n'est qu'en se dévouant à son opinion, ou à ses sentiments, qu'on est vraiment vertueux: c'est alors seulement qu'une puissance céleste subjugue en nous l'homme mortel" (1:107). His possessive, would-be dominant voice, speaking the language of his father, clings to its rights of denial and interdict. For him, the past is a way of avoiding, not facilitating, renewal in the present: "il répétait souvent à Corinne, que s'il n'avait pas eu dans son pays de nobles intérêts à servir, il n'aurait trouvé la vie supportable que dans les contrées ou les monuments tiennent lieu de l'existence présente" (2:24). In this spirit, he pries Corinne away from the varied interactions of her community (her friends, her public activities) and into exclusive dialogue with himself—a discourse of two isolated subjects with no present third to resolve it. As they travel away from Rome across the lonely Pontine marshes ("où l'on ne voit pas une seule habitation," 2:7), Corinne drifts into silent sleep, in the foul air, while Oswald, in a new protective role, finds fresh speech: "bien qu'il fût silencieux naturellement, il était inépuisable en sujets de conversation, toujours soutenus, toujours nouveaux, pour l'empêcher de succomber un moment à ce fatal sommeil" (2:8). The crisis comes when the two exchange the stories of their lives, at Oswald's instigation: Oswald in speech, which concludes with the manuscript of his father's last words that he gives Corinne to read out, and then Corinne, in writing. In this way, subjects-in-process become irretrievably fixed in the past, and in the past, subject to the Father, Corinne is necessarily lost. In the first conversation that follows Oswald's reading of Corinne's account (2:117-19), the balance of pronouns marks a new inequality: in Oswald's speech, "je" predominates, whereas for Corinne the leading pronoun is chiefly "vous."[16]

The conclusion of the novel, after Corinne has returned Oswald's ring, charts Corinne's construction of another communication community both like and strikingly different from the one in which her story opened. Having abandoned Rome, too marked by memories of Oswald, she settles in Tuscany, drawn by its republican spirit, the purity of Florentine Italian, and its fine instances of Renaissance art. In this last, most difficult, extended improvisation, her only interlocutor, to begin with, is the notebook in which she writes disjointed utterances of a grief almost impossible to express. But gradually another audience collects, first in the form of the faithful Castel-Forte, then the penitent Oswald, and finally (a new element) the Englishwomen who are Corinne's closest family: her niece Juliette and her sister Lucile, Oswald's daughter and wife. This extension of the communicative community creates in Italy a liberating opportunity for those English female voices whom English politics have suppressed. It also creates a way of holding open a future place in the community to an Oswald (and by extension, an England) Corinne herself can only reject.

Corinne's final discourse is not in itself an improvisation. Lacking the energy for extempore creativity, she writes out her text, which is delivered before the Academy of Florence by a young woman. The text gestures towards a community that echoes out into time and space. Through her mediator, Corinne addresses her fellow citizens, God, Italy, posterity, Rome, as well as the "tombeaux silencieux" to which she must finally turn. The parallels are emphasized between this final act of communication and that on which the narrative opened. The subject—death—is that presented by Oswald at the beginning, but, as then, made Corinne's own with a steer towards life. The voice of the young presenter, like Corinne's younger voice, modifies the message by its tone, providing a contrast which brings serenity into despair. Death in Italy, as in that first improvisation, is demonstrably a way of living in the community of creative genius. As her niece Juliette repeats Corinne's song for Oswald in the domestic sphere, the young singer pursues Corinne's public address.

What is finally to be made of the deathbed tableau, and the symbol of the veiled moon, is settled in the closing utterances in which the reader is invited to participate, drawn into the communication community of the text by the direct address of the narrative voice. In its own final improvisatory twist, the voice of the text takes the past tense of the death of Corinne and the remorse of Oswald, identifying the latter—the squandered potential of the son—as the key problem for resolution. The voice turns past into active present, free of guilt, concluding on a note that leaves future options structured, certainly, but still open for further discussion by the next speakers in the chain. ("Se pardonna-t-il sa conduite passée? Le monde qui l'approuva le consola-t-il? se contenta-t-il d'un sort commun, après ce qu'il avait perdu? Je l'ignore; je ne veux à cet égard ni le blâmer ni l'absoudre," 2:303.) The death of the heroine does not represent the failure of feminine voice; what **Corinne** establishes is the continuity of that network of voices which is the feminine text, both in itself and in its interpellation of the reader's world. Speech in **Corinne,** caught in action, consolidates and extends the community of language, society, and individual subject.

Notes

1. Germaine de Staël, *Corinne, ou l'Italie*, ed. Claudine Herrmann, 2 vols (Paris: Éditions des femmes, 1979). References are to this edition. I have modernized the spelling in all quotations.

2. Jürgen Habermas, *Der philosophische Diskurs der Moderne: Zwölf Vorlesungen* (Frankfurt-am-Main: Suhrkamp Verlag, 1985), trans. Frederick Lawrence, *The Philosophical Discourse of Modernity* (Cambridge: Polity Press, 1987). References are to this edition. I am grateful to Lois McNay's book *Foucault and Feminism* (Cambridge: Polity Press, 1992) for first drawing my attention to Habermas's notion of a discourse ethics and its interest for "feminist and other attempts to understand the intersubjective dimension of social relations" (McNay, p. 182). As I complete this essay, I note the advertised appearance of a new collection of essays for January 1995 by Johanna Meehan (*Habermas and Feminism*, London: Routledge).

3. Habermas, "Modernity's Consciousness of Time and its Need for Self-Reassurance," *Philosophical Discourse,* p. 5.

4. Walter Benjamin, "Theses on the Philosophy of History," in *Illuminations* (New York: Harcourt, Brace and World, 1968), first published as *Schriften* (Frankfurt-am-Main: Suhrkamp Verlag, 1955).

5. Habermas, "The Entwinement of Myth and Enlightenment: Horkheimer and Adorno," *Philosophical Discourse,* p. 113.

6. Habermas, "An Alternative Way out of the Philosophy of the Subject: Communicative versus Subject-Centred Reason," *Philosophical Discourse,* pp. 296-97.

7. Limits vary, according to the text, between Italy, where women have relative freedom of speech, and England, where public order has been made dependent on the subordination and silencing of women's voice.

8. *Germaine de Staël: Crossing the Borders,* ed. Madelyn Gutwirth, Avriel Goldberger, and Karyna Szmurlo (New Brunswick, N.J.: Rutgers University Press, 1991). See particularly in this collection Frank Bowman, "Communication and Power in Germaine de Staël: Transparency and Obstacle," Ellen Peel, "Corinne's Shift to Patriarchal Mediation: Rebirth or Regression?," and Margaret Higonnet, "Suicide as Self-Construction." Higonnet's essay concludes on an aside close to my present theme, picking up Staël's social theory of art, her linking of language and social power, and the relationship of creative speaker and audience in improvisation: "By linking the genius of her heroines to the public performance of inspired dialogue and fragments, Staël underscores the dynamic role of reception that is central to her social theory of art" (p. 81). For another angle on the theme of performance and audience in *Corinne,* see Nancy K. Miller, "Performances of the Gaze: Staël's *Corinne, or Italy," Subject to Change: Reading Feminist Writing* (New York: Columbia University Press, 1988). For completeness, I also note Simone Balayé's collection of essays on *Corinne, Madame de Staël—écrire, lutter, vivre* (Geneva: Droz, 1994), which I have yet been able to consult.

9. Marie-Claire Vallois, *Fictions féminines: Madame de Staël et les voix de la Sibylle* (Saratoga, Calif.: ANMA Libri, 1987).

10. I adapt here the admirable summary of Higonnet (p. 80), which it would be hard to better.

11. However, see the short but pointed pieces in Gutwirth et al, by English Showalter ("Corinne as an Autonomous Heroine") and Nancy K. Miller ("Politics, Feminism and Patriarchy: Rereading *Corinne*").

12. Corinne offers her own analysis of how her improvisations are constructed in an early informal conversation with Oswald (1:75-78).

13. "[J]e me sens poète, non pas seulement quand un heureux choix de rimes ou de syllabe harmonieuse, quand une heureuse réunion d'images éblouit les auditeurs, mais quand mon âme s'élève, quand elle dédaigne du plus haut l'égoïsme et la bassesse, enfin quand une belle action me serait plus facile: c'est alors que mes vers ont les meilleurs. Je suis poète, lorsque j'admire, lorsque je méprise, lorsque je hais, non par des sentiments personnels, non pour ma propre cause, mais pour la dignité de l'espèce humaine et la gloire du monde" (1:77-78).

14. Well known but worth recalling here is the political context of the composition of *Corinne,* which Madame de Staël began in the summer of 1805, a month after Napoleon had been crowned King of Italy, when it was still her hope that union with a strong and well-organized France might reinvigorate the creative potential of the new state. The Corinne-Oswald couple play out the interaction of complementary strengths and weaknesses out of which a new community might be forged.

15. The social rooting of values continues to be developed throughout the text, most notably in Corinne's comments on the open-air living represented in the architecture of Pompeii: "Il semble que le caractère des entretiens de la société doit être tout autre avec de telles habitudes, que dans les pays où la rigueur du froid force à se renfermer dans les maisons. On comprend mieux les dialogues de Platon, en voyant ces portiques sous lesquels les anciens se promenaient la moitié du jour. Ils étaient sans cesse animés par le spectacle d'un beau ciel: l'ordre social, tels qu'ils le concevaient, n'était point l'aride combinaison du calcul et de la force, mais un heureux ensemble d'institutions qui excitaient les facultés, développaient l'âme, et donnaient à l'homme pour but le perfectionnement de lui-même et de ses semblables" (2:23).

16. See for example the exchange towards the end of this sequence: "Cruel! s'écria Corinne avec désespoir, vous ne répondez rien, vous ne combattez pas ce que je vous dis! Ah! c'est donc vrai! Hélas! tout en le disant, je ne le croyais pas encore—J'ai retrouvé, grâce à vos soins, répondit Oswald, la vie que j'étais prêt à perdre; cette vie appartient à mon pays pendant la guerre. Si je puis m'unir à vous, nous ne nous quitterons plus, et je vous rendrai votre nom et votre existence en Angleterre" (2:118).

Patrick Coleman (essay date 1995)

SOURCE: "Exile and Narrative Voice in *Corinne,*" in *Studies in Eighteenth-Century Culture,* Vol. 24, 1995, pp. 91-105.

[*In the following essay, Coleman contends that the influential narrative voice of* Corinne *is traceable "to Staël's own experience with exile and other political expressions."*]

Exile was a decisive experience for Germaine de Staël, shaping not only the course of her life but the character of her work as well. If women's fame, in Staël's phrase, can be defined as "le deuil éclatant du bonheur,"[1] her own reluctant career, out of which emerged such works as *Corinne* and *De l'Allemagne,* provides the most striking example of this intimate yet painful connection between separation and success. For in Staël's most important books the physical distancing of exile and the psychological separation of mourning combine to produce new connections between political, moral, and literary thought. In her masterpieces about Italy and Germany, geographical breadth goes hand in hand with a concern for the inner spirit of persons and nations. I want to suggest that Staël's response to exile may also help us understand her experiments with narrative voice. *Corinne* is in fact the first modern French novel to use an external narrator in what may be called the realist manner, anticipating in many respects the method of her nineteenth-century successors. Except for brief interventions in the first person (a device that will reappear in *Le Rouge et le noir* and *Madame Bovary*), Staël's narrator occupies a position close to but outside the world of the story. I would argue that the special intimacy of tone and the adoption of an external standpoint go together, and that the emergence of this influential novelistic attitude can be traced, at least in part, to the cultural dislocations that shaped Staël's career.

Staël gave her memoirs the title *Dix années d'exil.* In that work she compared exile to a kind of moral death, claiming that "on rencontre plus de braves contre l'échafaud que contre la perte de sa patrie."[2] She added that the threat of exile was particularly painful for women, "qui sont destinées à soutenir et à récompenser l'enthousiasme," for even more than men will they stifle their "sentiments généreux, s'il doit en résulter ou qu'elles soient enlevées aux objets de leur tendresse, ou qu'ils leur sacrifient leur existence en les suivant en exil" (62). Yet, what is most significant about Staël's experience is that it does not conform to this rather conventional view of women's role. If we except the early episode of her father's banishment in 1787, Staël's forced departures resulted primarily from her own political and intellectual activity. Furthermore, while

Paris would always be Staël's emotional and intellectual home, and while she would suffer because it was difficult for her to see the friends who continued to live there, her experience of other countries and cultures inspired a philosophy in which the notion of exile is redefined. In the pluralistic Europe imagined by the Coppet circle,[3] there is no one center. Staël's heroine Corinne, for example, is at home (and in exile) in both England and Italy. The pain of separation may not be less intense, but the sorrow, whether personal or political, can no longer be traced to a single source or relieved by pursuing a single goal.

The exaggerated conventionality of Staël's rhetoric in **Dix années d'exil** betrays the author's discomfort with a mode of expression that should also be left behind. Why does Staël not do so? One reason is that these memoirs were composed in 1811-1812 to rally European opposition to Napoleon. Under the circumstances, Staël felt obliged to minimize her own involvement in the French Revolution and in political activity generally. Another is Staël's ambivalence about women's presence on any public stage, even as witness and writer. She accepts the need to exile herself from her own work. "Je me flatte," she tells us, "de me faire souvent oublier en racontant ma propre histoire" (2). Staël's difficulties in negotiating her participation in the public sphere have been ably described by a number of scholars.[4] But I would also suggest a third reason that applies to some male authors as well. The sentence I have just quoted is echoed in other works of the period, for example in Benjamin Constant's *Adolphe,* which is also a tale of wandering and dispossession. Speaking of his earlier self, the narrator notes that "tout en ne m'intéressant qu'à moi, je m'intéressais faiblement à moi-même."[5] In a number of pre-romantic authors, talk of exile, mourning, or some other form of loss, becomes a way of expressing a discursive problem. How, in a dislocated world, can one accept the centrality of individual experience in artistic creation while asserting the subordination of that experience to the symbolic forms art must produce to help repair the damage, and which, to succeed, must transcend the limits of what Charles Taylor has called the "punctual" self?[6]

One influential solution was to view the writer's vocation as a kind of secular priesthood, endowing his experience with exemplary, even sacred meaning. Rousseau played a crucial role here, and Paul Bénichou has traced the extension of this idea in the late eighteenth and early nineteenth centuries.[7] But while post-revolutionary French culture may have produced the most inflated claims for the writer's mission, culminating in Victor Hugo's cosmic will, it also fostered the most sceptical, even systematically reductive conceptions of the scope of artistic action. This is most apparent in the long tradition of academic criticism which, from the Imperial period on, saw Romanticism as a pernicious foreign import for which Staël deserved much of the blame. But it also can be seen in the sometimes paralyzing self-doubt and second thoughts of those writers who, like Constant and Staël, wonder just how possible—or socially responsible—it is to enhance the ordinary with a higher, more privileged, poetic self. Her mixture of enthusiasm and scruple on this point has not helped Staël's literary reputation. French critics of the right dismissed her work as insufficiently objective and restrained; those of the left, as lacking in practical zeal. For more sympathetic critics steeped in English or German Romanticism, Staël is too hesitant about embracing the subjective impersonality of the poetic self. In an influential essay, Georges Poulet praised Staël's search for a new artistic consciousness in which the self's immediate concerns would be subordinated to a more authentic apprehension of human consciousness in time.[8] But critics close to Poulet, such as Jean Starobinski and Paul de Man, characterized Staël's reluctance to give up the empirical self's demands and commit herself to art as a serious flaw.[9]

More recent critics, writing from a feminist point of view, have asked whether the ideal of aesthetic transcendence was not a trap for a writer struggling to overcome the handicap of a gender role in which aesthetic categories themselves became a tool for cultural marginalization. Joan de Jean, for example, includes Staël in her study of the image of Sappho, the suffering woman whose transcendent lyricism has been praised at the expense of her female identity and whose work has suffered even more by the problematic and reductive equation of the two.[10] From this point of view, artistic authenticity, far from giving the self a new anchor in the deepest structures of consciousness, only masks another kind of exile. What is needed is to set Staël's work more firmly in its cultural context by analyzing its relationship to the circumstances of its time, to the vocabularies and images available to women for creative appropriation or subversion.

These two viewpoints may appear poles apart, but I suggest we keep them both in mind, for both derive in some degree from Staël's own discussion of literature in **De la littérature** and **De l'Allemagne.** Each of these works combines a sociological approach to literature with an idealist doctrine of art and attempts to reconcile them within a broad philosophy of history.[11] In sketching an interpretation of **Corinne**'s narrative form that seeks to relate the inner dynamic of the novel's form to its cultural context, I hope to be faithful to Staël's own example and to recover some of the literary-historical significance of her work.[12]

Staël's choice of an external narrator is particularly revealing in this regard because it seems to contradict rather than conform to her ideas about the relationship between fictional form and the progress of human sensibility. For Staël, the modern spirit finds its most advanced expression in the epistolary novel. This was the form she chose for her first full-length fiction, **Delphine,** and in **De l'Allemagne** she would claim that the epistolary narration is the truly modern form:

> Les romans par lettres supposent toujours plus de sentiments que de faits; jamais les Anciens n'auraient imaginé de donner cette forme à leurs fictions; et ce n'est même que depuis deux siècles que la philosophie s'est assez introduite en nous-mêmes pour que l'analyse de

ce qu'on éprouve tienne une si grande place dans les livres. Cette manière de concevoir les romans n'est pas aussi poétique, sans doute, que celle qui consiste tout entière dans les récits; mais l'esprit humain est maintenant bien moins avide des événements même les mieux combinés, que des observations sur ce qui se passe dans le coeur.[13]

Staël's stark opposition between "récit" and "observation" may not be fair to the subtleties of a novel such as Lafayette's *La Princesse de Clèves* (1678), but it does reflect the broad history of novelistic techniques in France. In the seventeenth century, third-person narration was most often linked to a disenchanted view of life in which the chance and often blind acts of the characters were framed by a kind of transcendent, impersonal necessity. The form almost disappeared in the eighteenth century, replaced initially by the first-person, autobiographical novel that focused on the achievement of a limited but genuine self-knowledge, then by the epistolary novel, with its emphasis on what the characters thought and felt at particular moments in relation to each other. Of course, a controlling consciousness was at work in all these forms, but it is as if that consciousness could not be made explicit without spoiling the integrity of the fictional world. I speak here of France, because in England Frances Burney, to cite one writer known to Staël, had set an important example in moving from the epistolary form of *Evelina* (1778) to the external narrator of *Cecilia* (1782). Burney's novels, however, include a comic element, largely absent from Staël's work, that connects Burney's choice of narrator with a long-established use of the third person for comic commentary. The most famous eighteenth-century example was *Tom Jones,* a novel Staël admired,[14] but which was quite foreign to the French tradition in which old distinctions between comic and serious modes persisted much longer. Only in the ironic novels of Diderot and Sade (largely unappreciated, of course, in the post-revolutionary period) did this tradition start to break down.

Thus *Corinne*'s reintroduction of the distinction between the world of the characters and that of the commentary in a novel of sentiment marks a new stage in the evolution of French narrative. Staël's novel contains, it is true, a long letter in which the heroine tells her own story, as well as lengthy speeches in which the characters open their hearts, but its overall form does not foster a feeling of immediacy. The ebb and flow of correspondence is replaced by a series of twenty clearly divided "books," each with its own title. The narrator does enter the story at the very end of the novel, but this final, first-person remark only underscores the distance between narrator and character. Speaking of Oswald's regret at abandoning Corinne in favor of the more docile but vapid Lucile, the narrator asks: "se pardonna-t-il sa conduite passée? Le monde qui l'approuva le consola-t-il? Se contenta-t-il d'un sort commun, après ce qu'il avait perdu? Je l'ignore, et ne veux, à cet égard, ni le blâmer, ni l'absoudre."[15] Judged by Staël's "modern" standard, the inability to supply this information is a sign of aesthetic inadequacy, not only because we do not learn what Oswald feels, but because it is implied we do not

need to know: the story is over. Although *Corinne* is hardly stingy in its "observations sur ce qui se passe dans le coeur," it ends by asserting the precedence of a "récit" with its own distinct coherence and closure.

The narrative perspective of *Corinne* is nonetheless very different from that of *La Princesse de Clèves*. Instead of chance and necessity, Staël's book dramatizes contingency and probability. The characters' actions are determined by any number of social or psychological causes, but their relative weight can be assessed and their probable effects, in other circumstances, could be predicted. The relation between the narrator and the characters is also different. Lafayette's authoritative narrator lays bare hidden motives only to show that the human heart remains unknowable.[16] The last lines of *Corinne* express a different relationship between ignorance and knowledge. One could, in theory, find out what Oswald felt. The limits to the narrator's knowledge do not reflect a necessary incapacity. Like everyone else's, the narrator's knowledge is real, but precisely because it is like everyone else's it is only a partial perspective, not the whole truth. Even within its sphere of competence, it suggests rather than defines absolutely.

Yet, Staël's strategy should also be distinguished from that of the fictional "editor" of an epistolary novel like *Les Liaisons dangereuses*. Was Valmont a libertine right to the end? Laclos' editor inserts a footnote saying that because nothing in the correspondence entrusted to him resolves this question he has decided to suppress a last letter by Valmont expressing remorse over his betrayal of Madame de Tourvel.[17] Here the uncertainty is ostensibly attributed to a lack of external evidence in the "society" which produced the correspondence. Laclos uses that uncertainty, however, to damn Valmont all the more effectively by excluding his letter which in itself is held to possess no evidential value. Staël's tentativeness is also ironic—Oswald *is* being judged—but the tenor of that irony is different. In Laclos, the absence of external evidence means paradoxically that the editor's decision cannot be appealed. Staël's narrator does not attribute her ignorance to the same definite cause. The kind of evidence that might or might not resolve the issue is left an open question. But although its narrator is less peremptory, *Corinne* is in one sense less dependent on its social intertext than *Les Liaisons*. Within the fictional terms of the "found" correspondence, the possibility that other evidence might turn up still exists—a pretext used by other novelists of the time to publish sequels to popular books. Laclos has done his best to forestall that possibility by composing a tightly-woven plot, but the eighteenth-century French novel situates itself within a larger communicative network in which stories are exchanged and revised.[18] The indeterminate basis for Staël's "je l'ignore," a statement whose social location cannot be identified—or, if so, only in the space between French, English, and Italian societies—really means we can only support or appeal the narrator's judgment by referring to the story itself. Incomplete and unrooted as it may be, the novel in an important sense becomes its own context.

Staël's narrator, at once inside and outside the world of the story, freely asserting an independent point of view yet refusing to assume a position of final authority, may be seen as an attempt to mediate between the central and the exiled, marginal self whose duality lies at the heart of pre-romantic French writing. The goal of this mediation is neither wholly aesthetic nor wholly practical. Rather, it is to redefine these fields through the symbolic construct of the work. Detailed evidence about the formal genesis of *Corinne* is still unavailable,[19] but we can get some insight into what was at stake from a review of the novel written by August Wilhelm Schlegel, who accompanied Staël throughout her travels in Italy and played an important role in her aesthetic education.[20] This little-known essay is significant in that Schlegel, perhaps mindful of the kind of thinking that led Staël to praise the epistolary novel as the form most expressive of "modern" interiority, tries to justify Staël's choice of form. He does so in the name of a literary imagination that has managed to combine what Staël earlier called the poetry of story with the insight of analysis.

The problem with *Delphine,* according to Schlegel, was that the heroine's "imagination of the heart" (and by implication, the author's identification with that imagination, expressed in the choice of the epistolary form) had overwhelmed every other form of imagination. The narrative form chosen in *Corinne* is "unquestionably preferable." First, because it is more "concise"—the implication being that otherwise the novel would have been much longer than it is! Second, and more important, because it allows for a presentation of the characters that is both clearer and more plausible.

> The constant use of the epistolary form is subject to many inconveniences: the characters have to be constrained by their individual situation, and yet they have to be endowed with a power that is incompatible with their condition, a power to observe themselves and others so that the reader can understand them and their illusions more clearly, and so the stage can be set for what comes next. Narrative on the other hand can allow itself to look down calmly and impartially on the players with a kind of poetic omniscience.[21]

At first glance, Schlegel's defence seems rather strained. In Richardson and Rousseau there was no incompatibility between the characters' limited awareness and their capacity for analysis. Indeed, their novels turn on the complex interplay between the two. Why would *Corinne* need to be more explicit? I think we have to read the issue of plausibility and the need to accommodate the reader's understanding as two aspects of the same problem, which is that of increasing cultural diversification. The unifying sociability of Ancien Régime culture which enabled one to appeal, beyond differences and disagreements, to a common realm of general opinion, has broken down. Staël is writing for a post-revolutionary Europe defined no longer as a homogeneous audience but as groups of readers reflecting distinct national cultures. Things may have to be explained that earlier could be taken for granted. The fictional world

in which the characters move is also more radically diverse, too much so for the effects of cultural difference to be dramatized in a purely immanent way.

And yet, a unifying framework cannot simply be imposed from outside: that would be to reproduce Napoleon's oppressive parody of European unity. The relatively autonomous narrator Staël devises for *Corinne* offers a possible alternative. Schlegel speaks of poetic omniscience, but that omniscience is not simply assumed by the authorial consciousness. The latter strives to achieve it by a moral effort we can feel, and through which the narrative strives to overcome the limited "imagination of the heart" in favor of a more "serene and impartial" perspective. However detached and impersonal that perspective, it remains linked to the ordinary self, to the "moi-même" behind the "moi." To put it another way, the author is also a reader in search of clarity. It is to Schlegel's credit that he does not impute the author's difficulty to the fact that she is a woman, although the terms he uses could easily lend themselves to a gender-saturated discourse. Staël's struggle is interpreted instead, most suggestively I think, in a broad context of formal and cultural considerations. Again, according to Schlegel, a narrator is needed not only to explain the characters' situation to each other and to the reader, but also to "set the stage for what comes next." I think we can read this not only in terms of plot developments that have to be anticipated, but more broadly as a call to include within the novel a more explicit sense of the agency that shapes it.

In *Corinne,* this struggle for perspective is thematized in various ways. One is Corinne and Oswald's discussion of aesthetic principles as they examine the paintings and monuments of Rome. In spite of what Schlegel says, their clash of views, as modern critics have noted, provides an illuminating commentary on the novel's evolving articulation.[22] But Staël also resorts to a device that has not received the attention it deserves. At critical points in the book she includes excerpts from her father's writings.[23] Necker's comments on the consolations of religion, quoted extensively, are not simply illustrative. Rather, they are the interventions of a super-narrator who for a moment takes the place of the novel's own narrator, as if the latter were unable or unwilling to carry the full burden of omniscience. Staël's adoption of a presiding external perspective is clearly made possible by her identification with her father.

The gesture is thus a problematic one, involving what to us is an all-too-enthusiastic idealization of paternal authority. Yet, on the level of the book's composition, if not of its themes, Necker is not primarily a symbol of law. The novel's reverence for his memory does not lead to the paralysis we see in Oswald's relationship with his father. Rather, it increases the novel's range of sympathy by allowing for a more nuanced portrayal of Oswald's weakness, despite the latter's injustice to Corinne. This achievement builds on the insight that in an important sense the two characters share a common father. That father is no longer the real father (good or bad), for the latter is no longer present (and we recall that Staël's own father died in between the writing of *Delphine* and *Corinne*). Paternity becomes a figure for the novel's own more inclusive understanding. This understanding, it seems, needs to be grounded in something more than the attempt to reconcile moral and aesthetic categories in Corinne and Oswald's debates. The latter, after all, lead to an impasse. The two lovers agree to disagree, but the differences in their viewpoints—Oswald looking more to moral energy and Corinne to ideal sympathy, the one accused of narrow-mindedness, the other of passive indulgence—anticipate a more serious emotional estrangement that will not be overcome.

The choice of narrative form can be read as an attempt to bridge the gap at a higher level: Not so much by subsuming art and morality together under religion[24] as by postulating an ideal point where sympathetic intimacy and an energizing distance of perspective no longer contradict each other. For while the quotations from Necker help establish a narrative perspective of broad sympathy, the way that perspective takes narrative form also sets limits to the characters' scope of action. The suspense plot chosen by Staël requires that many things not be said in the early parts of the book. Oswald and Corinne must long remain in ignorance of essential facts about each other. While their long discussions about historical monuments and art works give them clues about each other's state of mind, they cannot entirely replace those other, more ordinary opportunities to test their powers of self-observation that earlier novelists provided through interaction with other characters. The mute stones may speak, but, in the decorous world of *Corinne,* they don't talk back. Nor are the secondary characters granted any real access to the protagonists' thoughts or feelings.

From the point of view of today's reader, the effect is not always a happy one. Ellen Peel, for example, has expressed some scepticism about the novel's feminist thrust on the grounds that Corinne has no female friends.[25] We should recognize, however, that this is in part a formal problem. The move from the epistolary to the third-person form eliminates the structural need for confidantes, and so we should more correctly say that in this respect, as in some others, *Corinne* exploits too simplistically the powers its narrator enjoys. But these powers also play an essential role in giving the novel its integrity as a work of art. The form of Staël's novel underscores the contrast between the logic of its plot and the heroine's talent for improvisation. Now, it is true that Corinne's transcendent genius can be rendered only imperfectly. But it is significant that, in contrast to earlier aesthetic practice, which would either simply declare the impossibility of conveying perfection or epitomize it through brief quotation, Staël offers extended approximations of Corinne's Italian poems in French prose. In doing so, and perhaps despite herself, she gives the heroine's aesthetic expression a more conditional value.

This also applies, ironically, to Corinne's one sustained written composition: the narration of her own life story.

Oswald has told her his story in person, but Corinne, out of consideration for his feelings as well as her own, refuses to do the same. She writes her story and compounds the distancing effect of her choice by postponing as long as she can its communication to Oswald. When the story finally reaches him, it is too late: the lovers' separation is inevitable. One could say that Corinne's narrative takes retrospection too far. It is prematurely posthumous, anticipating the final retrospection that belongs to a consciousness beyond the limits of the story's action. If Corinne can only improvise in the presence of admirers who look up to her, she can only narrate when the reply she seeks could only come from an ideal Oswald who didn't belong to the real, imperfect world, an Oswald who would incarnate within that world the transcendent paternal super-narrator. According to Margaret Waller, the fact that Corinne writes her confession "thematizes the link between conventional narrative imperatives and a repressive paternal line."[26] Waller's insight is suggestive, although formulated too broadly. Many women writers have, after all, used conventional narrative forms (the romance and the Gothic, for example) for their own subversive purposes. In the first instance, the figure of the father in *Corinne* is a liberating one, opening up the emotional range of the story. The problem, however, comes from identifying too much with that transcendent guarantee, to the point where the pluralism of outlook it initially made possible collapses into a self-destructive withdrawal from the ordinary world. For Corinne, as opposed to the character-narrators of earlier epistolary novels, there is no middle ground between unreflective action and a retrospective stance that renounces any further initiative on the practical level. To return to utilitarian calculation would undermine the authenticity of the reflective insight. This polarization of interest and "disinterest," it should be stressed, has to be understood in political as well as psychological terms, for it is part of Staël's response to the Terror's fusion of partisan interest and the rhetoric of disinterest in Robespierre's Republic of Virtue. As Corinne's fate shows, however, too strenuous a defence against that fusion leads to another kind of oppression.

The problems associated with Corinne as self-narrator support Schlegel's point about the suitability of the omniscient perspective for a novelist standing outside the story from the beginning. For what no longer works at the level of the character may be rearticulated at the level of the novel's overall composition. Because it is a fiction, the novel stands apart from the world of action. But not entirely. A novel that portrays realistic characters in the ordinary world involves, to the extent that it gives those characters a destiny, a series of decisions that readers (and often authors) may interpret as matters of craft but also as moral actions.[27] The key issue, on which Corinne and Oswald disagree in their discussions of various artworks mentioned in the novel, is to what extent aesthetic form relativizes and mediates moral imperatives, or is itself undercut by them. Looking again at the narrator's final words, we can read them as an attempt to establish a balance between the exercise and suspension of moral judgment, of intervention and reflection, that should character-ize the work as a whole.

The sense of equilibrium in the narrator's final words de-pends for its effect, however, on the refusal to specify what happens to Oswald in the indefinite future. A nega-tive gesture of this kind is not enough to resolve the prob-lems raised by the closure of the story itself. For to com-plete the novel means finishing off the heroine. As Carla Peterson puts it, "the narrator . . . comes to displace Corinne as the center of the novel. If unity and singleness of personality are finally achieved, if morcellation is over-come, these accomplishments occur at the expense of Corinne herself, at the level of the narrator, not of the character."[28] Toward the end of the novel, when she has re-tired to Florence to waste away and die, Corinne tries to write, that is, to compose from day to day as an artist would for whom writing is part of life, a vocation or a ca-reer. But we are told her poetic gift has left her. Although art arises from melancholy, too strong a sadness destroys the capacity to create. At this point, we are made to reflect on the crucial artistic difference between the heroine and the narrator who is about to complete the story of Corinne.

In recent years, a number of critics have asked us to con-sider the death of a fictional character from an ethical point of view. Feminist critics in particular have ques-tioned the relationship between Manon Lescaut's death, for example, and the sentimental lyricism it occasions. Is the one the price of the other? Or does such a question re-flect a blurring of the boundary between life and litera-ture?[29] Without pretending to answer this question, I would like to suggest that it is connected to the problems with which we began: about Staël's reluctance to abandon an instrumental view of art, and about the problematic dis-tinction between the kinds of self displayed in French pre-romantic writing. It has been observed that while Staël's major works of criticism end optimistically, both her nov-els end on a mournful note with the death of the heroine.[30] What readers like to think of as the "natural" consequence of a broken heart and society's hostility must, in the light of Staël's own reflections on literature as moral action, be seen as no less—or no more—the result of an artistic deci-sion than the death of, say, Constant's Éléonore.

Although in one sense *Corinne*'s conclusion is less tragic than that of *Delphine,* since something of her is transmit-ted to Oswald and Lucile's daughter Julie, through whom Corinne will live on, in another sense her death is more problematic precisely because of Staël's choice of narra-tive form. In an epistolary fiction like *Delphine,* the char-acter seems in some degree to be in control, if not of her life, at least of her story. A third-person narrative like *Corinne,* however strong its investment in the character, subordinates the heroine's agency to its own logic. Be-cause the narrator is now located outside the world of the story, the character may seem that much more the object of the writer's whim. This would be especially true in a literature that had earlier abandoned the external narrator because the transcendent authority that grounded it had

come to appear arbitrary. Staël's gamble in *Corinne* is that the apparent concession to the centrality of the writing self will allow, on the contrary, for a more nuanced perspective in which specific actions can be productively contextual-ized within a larger, more differentiated symbolic world.

The appeal to a paternal super-narrator is one way Staël tries to achieve this perspective. But by itself it would have brought the novel too close to the model of *Wilhelm Meister,* a book Staël praised,[31] but with serious reserva-tions about the disproportion between the impartial point of view and the sensibility of the Mignon story, whose pa-thos is sacrificed to Goethe's overarching scheme. A sec-ond kind of framework is therefore needed to mitigate the oppressive effect of premature closure. It is provided by the conception of Italy as a maternal world. Marie-Claire Vallois has very perceptively analyzed *Corinne*'s evoca-tion of Italy as a pre-Oedipal containing context which is opposed to the harsh—yet in many ways admirable—world of English political virtue where the separation of private and public spheres is held to be vital to self-government in every sense of that term. She sees Corinne's exploration of Italy's ruins as an attempt to recover a creative maternal power that has been devastated by the laws of history.[32]

Vallois' insightful interpretation needs to be qualified, however: first, because Corinne's maternal Italy is not truly pre-symbolic. It is very much, in the Schillerian sense, a sentimental reconstruction. When Corinne dresses up as a sybil, for example, she imitates, not an ancient im-age, but Domenichino's painting.[33] Fusion with the mater-nal is never a real possibility. It is rehearsed, instead, so that the seductiveness of such a fusion can be felt but then put in perspective. Oswald's criticism of the sentimental-ism of religion in Rome and the common people's super-stitiousness clearly reflects Staël's own point of view, as does his praise of Britain's more masculine political en-ergy. It is the containing rather than directly creative power of the maternal to which Staël appeals. Staël's survey of Italy emphasizes above all what endures beyond destruc-tion—even the destruction caused by the heroine's (or the author's) own initiative.

If in giving shape, coherence, and closure to her story through the use of the external narrator Staël identifies with an image of the father, the maternal image of Italy al-lows us to put story-telling in perspective by showing us what remains beyond the drama of rise and fall. At first glance, what remains is a collection of ruins, but the pa-thos of fragmentation is to some extent compensated by the energizing appreciation of the way different layers of time and different cultural productions coexist for the ob-serving eye. As Roland Mortier has pointed out, the ruin is "the meeting-point of nature and art, of determinism and freedom, of voluntaristic creation and fate."[34] But that meeting-point lies in the consciousness of the viewer, a consciousness that cannot rest on any one point, but must work to supply the missing pieces. Appreciation of Italy may in this sense be opposed to the prematurely posthu-mous closure of Corinne's self-narration, which was placed under the sign of the father. For better and for worse, Italy is a land of contradiction and diversity, where actions, as Corinne tries to show the stiff-mannered Oswald, may have more than one meaning. Italy's story is not a happy one, but it is unfinished. Italy provided a home for Corinne after Lady Edgermond, the wicked stepmother, demanded she accept the fiction of her death so as not to sully the family's reputation. One could say that Italy makes it possible for Staël to have Corinne die a second time for the sake of her novel without that gesture carrying the burden of authorial anxiety it might otherwise have done. As containing context, "Italy" inscribes that gesture in the *longue durée* and stumbling progress of the human spirit.

In the end, though, there is no one context. About the only thing we know about the shaping of **Corinne** is Staël's uncertainty whether her novel would be a love story contained in a travel book, or a travel book contained in a love story.[35] From the formal point of view, this can be seen as a hesitation between a unitary and a looser narrative logic. Similarly, **Corinne** depends on both a paternal and a maternal model, neither of which has any clear priority—if indeed we can clearly distinguish the contours of each. For one could say that, contrary to expectation, the inwardness of the love story belongs to the former, while the expansiveness of the travel book belongs to the latter. Staël's adoption and transformation of the external narrator is an attempt to relativize the hierarchy of these models without abandoning the ideal of an ultimate context of meaning. That context can no longer be apprehended immediately, still less inhabited as one would a home. Corinne's final wish, "tout dire et tout éprouver à la fois" (579), can only be realized in her dying song. The experience of exile cannot be erased. But if there is no single home, then exile loses its privilege as the definitive cultural metaphor. A more suitable analogy for the mobility and cross-fertilization of discursive contexts attempted in **Corinne** may be found in an activity whose broad cultural importance to the diversity of the modern world Staël was one of the first to recognize: translation.[36]

Notes

1. Germaine de Staël, *De l'Allemagne,* ed. Simone Balayé (Paris: Garnier-Flammarion, 1968), 2:218 (pt. 3, chap. 19).

2. Germaine de Staël, *Dix années d'exil,* preface by Emmanuel d'Astier, introduction and notes by Simone Balayé (Paris: Union générale d'éditions, 1966), 61. References to this edition will be included in the text. The work is available in English under the title *Ten Years of Exile,* trans. Doris Beik (New York: Saturday Review Press, 1972).

3. Coppet, Staël's home in Switzerland, attracted a circle of friends and admirers.

4. See especially Madelyn Gutwirth's pathbreaking *Madame de Staël, Novelist: The Emergence of the Artist as Woman* (Urbana: University of Illinois Press, 1978); Simone Balayé, *Madame de Staël: Lumières et liberté* (Paris: Klincksieck, 1979); and the various

perspectives included in *Germaine de Staël: Crossing the Borders,* ed. Madelyn Gutwirth, Avriel Goldberger, and Karyna Szmurlo (New Brunswick, NJ: Rutgers University Press, 1991).

5. Benjamin Constant, *Oeuvres* (Paris: Gallimard, 1957), 14. The quotation is from the first chapter of *Adolphe.*

6. I take the expression "punctual self" from Charles Taylor's illuminating discussion of modernity in *Sources of the Self: The Making of the Modern Identity* (Cambridge: Harvard University Press, 1989), 159ff.

7. Paul Bénichou, *Le Sacre de l'écrivain* (Paris: Corti, 1973).

8. Georges Poulet, "Madame de Staël," in *Mesure de l'instant* (Paris: Plon, 1968), 193-212.

9. Jean Starobinski, "Suicide et mélancolie chez Mme de Staël," *Madame de Staël et l'Europe. Colloque de Coppet (18-24 juillet 1966)* (Paris: Klincksieck, 1970), 242-52; Paul de Man, "Madame de Staël and Jean-Jacques Rousseau," in *Critical Writings 1953-1978,* ed. Lindsay Waters (Minneapolis: University of Minnesota Press, 1989), 171-78 (originally published in French in *Preuves* 190 [Dec. 1966]: 35-40).

10. Joan de Jean, *Fictions of Sappho 1546-1937* (Chicago: University of Chicago Press, 1989), especially 161-86.

11. For a suggestive recent introduction to Staël's views on literary history, see the introduction to Madame de Staël, *De la littérature,* ed. Gérard Gengembre and Jean Goldzink (Paris: Flammarion, 1991).

12. Marie-Claire Vallois' *Fictions féminines: Mme de Staël et les voix de la Sibylle* (Saratogo, CA: Anima Libri, 1987) includes some valuable remarks on the third person in *Corinne* as an "autobiographie dédoublée" (165-69). Susan Sniader Lanser, in *Fictions of Authority: Women Writers and Narrative Voice* (Ithaca: Cornell University Press, 1992), 162-64, argues on the contrary that the third-person voice of the novel means that Corinne is prevented from becoming a full Romantic subject. Carla Peterson, in *The Determined Reader: Gender and Culture in the Novel from Napoleon to Victoria* (New Brunswick, NJ: Rutgers University Press, 1986), asserts instead that "Staël attests to the indomitability of the female genius in her creation of an omniscient narrator, superior to Corinne, who strives to heal madness, reconcile conflict . . . in her own narrative" (59). My own approach is closest to Peterson's and has been influenced by the discussions of novelistic realism in Michael Bell, *The Sentiment of Reality* (London: George Allen and Unwin, 1983), and Marshall Brown, "The Logic of Realism: A Hegelian Approach," *PMLA* 96 (1981): 224-41.

13. *De l'Allemagne,* 2:43 (pt. 2, chap. 28).

14. *De la littérature,* 244.

15. Germaine de Staël, *Corinne ou l'Italie,* ed. Simone Balayé (Paris: Gallimard, 1985), 587. For the English text, see *Corinne, or Italy,* trans. Avriel Goldberger (New Brunswick, NJ: Rutgers University Press, 1987), 419.

16. As J. W. Scott points out in *Madame de Lafayette: La Princesse de Clèves* (London, 1983), the narrator uses the word "perhaps" only ironically, when the unflattering truth is obvious. But I would claim the irony is double-edged, pointing to the fundamental untrustworthiness of one's own ability to achieve a clear understanding of human affairs.

17. Choderlos de Laclos, *Oeuvres complètes,* ed. Laurent Versini (Paris: Gallimard, 1979), 352n (note to letter 154).

18. See William Ray, *Story and History* (Oxford: Blackwell, 1990). A good example of such supplementary exchange is the "préface dialoguée" Rousseau himself added to *Julie.*

19. According to Avriel Goldberger, *Corinne, or Italy,* xxxvii and n. 21, fragments of early drafts do exist, but they have yet to be published. The edition of Staël's complete correspondence, which is progressing very slowly, does not cover the period of *Corinne*'s revision and publication.

20. A. W. Schlegel, review of *Corinne,* in *Werke* (Leipzig, 1846), 12:188-206. It originally appeared in the *Jenaischen allgemeinen Literatur-Zeitung* no. 152, in 1807. The text is also available in Emil Staiger's selection of Schlegel's *Kritische Schriften* (Zürich: Artemis, 1962), 326-41. It has been translated into French as "Une étude critique de Corinne ou l'Italie," by A. Blschke and J. Arnaud, *Cahiers staëliens* n.s. 16 (June 1973): 57-71.

21. "Die in der Corinna gewälte erzählende Form ist unstreitig der Abfassung eines Roman in Briefen vorzuziehen. Erstlich ist sie weit gedrängter; ferner ist der durchgängige Gebrauch der Briefform vielen Unbequemlichkeiten unterworfen: die Personen sollen in ihrer jedesmaligen Lage Befangen sein, und doch muss ihnen eine damit unverträgliche Beobachtung ihrer selbst und anderer verliehen werden, um den Leser über sie und ihre Täuchungen ins klare zu setzen und die Zukunft vorzubereiten. Die Erzählung hingegen darf mit einer gewissen dichterischen Allwissenheit ruhig und unparteiisch auf die Mithandelnden herabschauen." Staiger edition, 339-40, my translation.

22. In addition to the books by Gutwirth and Balayé, see the articles listed in the latter's edition of *Corinne.*

23. See bk. 8, chap. 1, and bk. 12, chap. 2.

24. Staël was inclined to such a view, but her views on this point, which need to be studied alongside and against those of Chateaubriand and others of the period, cannot be discussed here.

25. Ellen Peel, "Contradictions of Form and Feminism in *Corinne, ou l'Italie,*" *Essays in Literature* 14 (1987): 281-98. I am not sure Staël meant to give this impression, but it is significant that the only woman in Rome we are told Corinne visits is referred to as the "wife of a friend" (*Corinne,* 125).

26. Margaret Waller, *The Male Malady: Fictions of Impotence in the French Romantic Novel* (New Brunswick, NJ: Rutgers University Press, 1993), 76.

27. For a discussion of the perplexed, often unproductive attempts to establish the cultural status of the novel in France, see Georges May, *Le Dilemme du roman au XVIIIe siècle* (Paris: Presses universitaires de France, 1963). A good example of the attempt in Staël's circle to modify the terms of the debate is Constant's discussion of *Corinne* in "De Madame de Staël et de ses ouvrages," *Oeuvres,* 834: "Un ouvrage d'imagination ne doit pas avoir un but moral, mais un résultat moral."

28. Peterson, *The Determined Reader,* 61.

29. See for example Naomi Segal, *The Unintended Reader: Feminism and Manon Lescaut* (Cambridge: Cambridge University Press, 1986); Nancy K. Miller, "1735: The Gender of the Memoir Novel," in *A New History of French Literature,* ed. Denis Hollier (Cambridge: Harvard University Press, 1989), 436-42; and Patrick Coleman, "From the *Mémoires* to *Manon*: Mourning and Narrative Control in Prévost," *Nottingham French Studies* 29:2 (1990): 3-11.

30. Balayé, *Madame de Staël,* 136.

31. Staël, *De l'Allemagne* 2:44-45.

32. Vallois, *Fictions féminines,* chap. 3.

33. *Corinne,* 52 (bk. 2, chap. 1).

34. Roland Mortier, *La Poétique des ruines en France* (Geneva: Droz, 1970), 10.

35. For the genesis of the novel; see Simone Balayé, *Les Carnets de voyage de Madame de Staël: contribution à la genèse de ses oeuvres* (Geneva: Droz, 1971), 93-103, and Staël's letter of 9 April 1805 to Jean-Baptiste Suard in *Madame de Staël, Correspondance générale,* ed. Beatrice W. Jasinski, vol. 5, pt. 2 (Paris: Hachette, 1985), 531-32 and notes.

36. See "De l'esprit des traductions," in Staël's *Oeuvres* (Paris, 1821), 17:387-99.

John Isbell (essay date 1996)

SOURCE: "The Painful Birth of the Romantic Heroine: Staël as Political Animal, 1786-1818," in *Romanic Review,* Vol. 87, No. 1, January, 1996, pp. 59-66.

[*In the following essay, Isbell argues that de Staël chose to produce literary art in response to her exclusion from politics as a woman.*]

1. *On a raison d'exclure les femmes des affaires politiques et civiles.* Staël, 1810.

2. Depuis la Révolution, les hommes ont pensé qu'il était politiquement et moralement utile de réduire les femmes à la plus absurde médiocrité. Staël, 1800[1].

One author, two verdicts. What is going on? This paper argues that Staël chose art only when banned by men from politics, under Napoleon in particular. The "Romantic heroine" her life and works handed to posterity was a fallback position, used by a woman exiled from the Revolutionary stage. Staël's complete works make this clear, splitting into four periods.

1. ANCIEN RÉGIME.

Born in 1766, Staël is writing short moral comedies by the age of twelve—***Les Inconvénients de la vie de Paris.*** In 1786, she marries and turns twenty, and her output now slowly pushes the envelope of discourse expected by society of a very young *salonnière*: outlines of novels; portraits and *éloges; synonymes,* a remarkable *Folle,* and *vers de circonstance* published in Grimm's *Correspondance* for the royal courts of Europe. In 1786-7, she completes two plays, ***Sophie ou les sentiments secrets*** and ***Jane Grey,*** and prepares her ***Lettres sur Rousseau.*** This output may seem pre-political, but it is already breaking the hermetic seal of Versailles and of women's private art, moving toward Paris and the citizen's public arena. ***Jane Grey*** is only the first of Staël's five Voltairean political tragedies of 1787-97, including ***Montmorency,*** soon to be published at last, and the lost ***Jean de Witt.*** Domenech also has brilliantly shown how Staël uses Rousseau in 1788 as an *homme de paille* for Necker, giving her father free publicity on the eve of the *Etats-généraux*—a diversionary strategy she will repeat throughout her career. Staël's correspondence shows this same move toward politics, linked to her growing maturity, a change of mood in France, Necker's role as *Premier Ministre* and her own marriage to the Swedish ambassador; thus, her bulletins on French politics for the King of Sweden[2].

2. REVOLUTION.

Staël's most familiar works in this decade again seem at first largely "female", or private and apolitical: ***Zulma*** and the ***Recueil de morceaux détachés,*** 1794-5, and her treatise on the influence of the passions, 1796. But three facts destroy that first impression.

First, the politics in these fine and under-studied works. ***Mirza*** and ***Zulma*** from the ***Recueil*** are tragic heroines with a *public* voice; its ***Epître au malheur*** and her book on the passions explicitly discuss the effects of the Terror, title of her lover Constant's later brochure. Staël adds that her volume's three *nouvelles* date from before 1786, but ***Mirza*** and ***Pauline*** already attack the slave trade, another constant of Staël's life up to her work with Wilberforce in 1814. Often, in Staël's case, full titles reveal our misleading shorthand: thus, ***De l'influence des passions sur le bonheur des individus et des nations.***

Second, other published material: her 1790 ***Eloge*** of the strategist Guibert; her 1791 tract on public opinion; her three series of ***Réflexions,*** 1793-5, on the queen's trial, on peace—her first signed work, in 1794—and on domestic peace; and her 1798 treatise on how to establish the Republic. Again, these texts are little-studied. Like de Gaulle, Guibert had warned of mobile armies amid a caste who favoured fortifications; Staël's lover Narbonne faces that same resistance as Minister for War in 1791-2, before their views conquer Europe. Her 1791 tract on how to identify a national majority pinpoints the way extremists in Paris could hijack a Revolution once desired by the nation as a whole: a common theme two centuries later. Her thorough series of Réflexions appeal for common sense from the French government and people, and practical solutions to civil unrest—mud in the eye for those who dismiss her as irrational. And her 400-page tract on how to ground the Republic continues these themes, including the elements of a draft constitution.

Third, unknown material. The 1995 ***Cahier staëlien*** contains 29 unknown Staël texts, including ten short political pieces, and a 163-item repertoire of her complete works, roughly twice the list in the last bibliography. Three anonymous prefaces Staël adds to her short volumes of Necker extracts show the clear continuity of her method—she uses Necker as shield and springboard in six different publications over thirty years. A new preface in 1798 stresses the politics in her ***Lettres sur Rousseau.*** Beside drafts of political memoirs for Narbonne and Ribbing, and her 1795 Republican declaration, stands her work on Narbonne's speeches to the *Législative* in 1791-2, on the eve of Europe's 23-year war: Staël and Narbonne divided their efforts, he preparing France for invasion, and she adding a populist political agenda to his frequent speeches before the wary *députés.* Here is their desperate bid to save France from disaster, at a bleak moment in its history. From all these texts, published and unpublished, the same clear political ideal emerges: a centrist government of notables and conciliation, empowered by the silent nation. Living and collaborating with Staël, Constant in his turn reworks this model in 1796-7: her latest *protégé*[3]. Finally, we publish three possible collaborations with Talleyrand: a speech on the death of Mirabeau, one on the value of French colonies, and above all, evidence that Staël wrote his famous *Rapport* on the education of women—spur to Mary Wollstonecraft, who dedicated to him her superb *Vindication of the Rights of Women* the next year.

Seen as a unit, this impressive bloc of material will radically change our grasp of Staël's place in Revolutionary France. But the story of the 1791 *Rapport* merits special attention, focussing as it does on the woman question at the heart of this paper.

Wollstonecraft in her *Vindication* attacks Staël for accepting Rousseau's demeaning view of women in 1788. Oddly, she claims that Staël's text was "*accidentally* put into my hands", though she had reviewed it in 1789: she may not want hints of intellectual debt. This also seems unfair to a text which talks in 1788 of *esclavage domestique* (***LR*** 4), rejects marriage as doomed and defends women writers amid a long and subtle discussion. Gutwirth crisply reviews Staël's evolving thought on women's fate, putting in brilliant relief a series of four brief "manifesti", from the Bastille to Waterloo. Staël's other feminist texts confirm Gutwirth's conclusions: the chapters on vanity, friendship, love and tenderness in her book on the passions; her articles on Aspasia, Cleopatra and her mother for the *Biographie Michaud;* and almost all her fictions. *Corinne* and *Delphine* are forceful arias in this symphonic development. It seems only fitting, if Staël did indeed write Talleyrand's *Rapport,* that Wollstonecraft should inadvertently dedicate her famous *Vindication* to a fellow authoress and precursor whom she misrepresents in its pages[4].

Throughout this development, Staël offers women a loser's choice between marriage and public existence. Certain from Rousseau's Julie onward that love in marriage is a dream, she gives it in 1796 one closing paragraph in her chapter on the subject; public life meanwhile is a fool's gamble, braving slander, hatred, and abandonment for an ersatz reward, the "deuil éclatant du bonheur". As Gutwirth shows, Staël is happier with both options by 1814, shrugging off not only her own lived sorrows but the dead weight of her father, blissfully married and outspoken against women authors. Yet this is largely a rich woman's dilemma; Staël's works say little of poorer women's burdens, and capitalism's new choice for them between home as a prison or life on the streets. The *Rapport* fills that gap.

Staël, Talleyrand and Narbonne shared an agenda in 1791. Besides circumstantial evidence of Staël's help with this *Rapport,* the text also speaks for itself. Its detailed review of women in society, ignored throughout Talleyrand's later career, precisely echoes Staël's own idiosyncratic views, and her bizarre mix of feminist polemic and resignation. For a man agreeing with his male colleagues that they are right to want women at home, its immediate appeal to the Pandora's Box of women's rights is a jolt to say the least: "First, we cannot here separate questions relative to women's education from the examination of their political rights." If, says the text, we grant women the same rights as men, we must give them the same means to apply them, and it continues with a tableau: "Half the human race excluded by the other from all participation in government; people native by fact and foreign by law to the land that saw their birth; proprietors with no direct influence and no representation: these are political phenomena which seem in abstract principle impossible to explain"[5].

Re-reading this government plan for women's future, a shocking absence gradually appears: despite an appeal to men and women's "bonheur commun", despite much talk about mothers and daughters, marriage receives not a word. A fate too horrible to contemplate? Senseless for Talleyrand, this void is natural for Staël, whose feelings are clear. Indeed, the whole tract is written beneath the sign of sacrifice: "que sont un petit nombre d'exceptions brillantes? Autorisent-elles à déranger le plan général de la nature?" Such women, it argues, must sacrifice their tal-

ents to the good of the Benthamite majority, show themselves "au-dessus de leur sexe en le jugeant, en lui marquant sa véritable place, et ne pas demander qu'en livrant les femmes aux mêmes études que nous, on les sacrifie toutes pour avoir peut-être dans un siècle quelques hommes de plus". Why does an appeal to exceptional women fill almost half a legislative proposal for poor women's vocational schools? Why does it ask such women to *mark* their sex's place, when it is itself doing just that? This senseless series makes sudden sense if we see Staël's sad hand behind it, resigning "de chimériques espérances" before the hard facts of sexism. Eternal pragmatist, Staël unlike Gouges or Méricourt here seeks little gains for her sex: a little public space; "des ressources pour les exceptions et des remèdes pour le malheur"; and above all, "les moyens de subsister *indépendantes,* par le produit de leur travail"[6].

3. CONSULATE AND EMPIRE.

Under Napoleon, Staël could hold on to her public voice only by using code, in artistic fictions. The break is clear: Staël after *brumaire* locks away her nearly-completed treatise on grounding the Republic, to publish *De la littérature* instead. The Revolution had early pushed women off the political stage, and we have seen Staël's own complicity with some of these tenets, but Napoleon will be far more systematic. In the 1790s, even in 1798, Staël used no excuse to talk politics: for the rest of her life, excuses are there. Even in 1817, at the age of fifty, she still pretends that her considerations on the French Revolution are but a daughter's memoirs of her father's glorious career[7].

A book "on literature" may sound innocuous, but three facts inflect that judgement. Staël's *full* title is *De la littérature considérée dans ses rapports avec les institutions sociales;* many modern critics also see it as the inventor of sociocriticism; and finally, like almost all her works, it faced a barrage of controversy in the press. Chateaubriand launched his career with a long attack on the work as too liberal, which he signed prematurely as "by the author of the *Génie du christianisme*". For the next decade, Staël signed and published just five texts: the novels *Delphine* and *Corinne ou l'Italie;* a private biography of her father; a volume of extracts from the Prince de Ligne; and her pulped masterpiece, *De l'Allemagne,* in 1810. Whatever Staël's actual agenda, all her *labels* announce woman's private sphere: novels; literature; inspiring her men friends. It is no coincidence that her best seller here was the Prince de Ligne text: the Emperor's reviewers must have sighed with relief to see this woman at last shut up about politics and publish another man's jottings, as good women should. Many men still label Staël an *Egérie* today[8].

Nor is Staël's *unpublished* work in this period explicitly political: around 1805, she even tried verse, as the next *Cahier staëlien* reveals. In 1805-11, she returned to the theatre, staging several plays at her château in Coppet, and writing at least seven more: experimental Romantic dramas like *Agar, Geneviève de Brabant, Sapho* and *La Su-*

namite; and very funny comedies which may have influenced Musset—*La Signora Fantastici, Le Mannequin, Le Capitaine Kernadec.* In *Le Mannequin,* a man who wants a pliable wife ends up married to a tailor's dummy, a curious presage of Hoffmann's *Der Sandmann*: he may have heard the story through their mutual friend Chamisso.

Has Staël then finally accepted the muzzle, like her tailor's dummy, in the face of bitter male hostility to what the language still calls a *femme publique*? Her titles certainly suggest it. And yet, once again, behind this docile mask her politics survive. Staël was born with a political voice: it resurfaces throughout her life, behind her wide range of alleged subjects. Balayé recently finished an elegant series of *lectures politiques* for *Delphine, Corinne* and *De l'Allemagne.* Staël's talk of her father, *vainqueur de la Bastille,* is another excuse for Revolution, and even her Prince de Ligne speaks for a defeated Europe. Titles here are again deceitful: Staël's *Réflexions sur le suicide,* of all things, contains her fierce indictment of Germany's political quietism before 1813, neatly sidestepped in *De l'Allemagne* itself. *De l'Allemagne*'s own pulping simply made such politics explicit[9].

Yet despite the politics that inflects all Staël's thought, her focus of interest has now subtly shifted, reflecting both her new experience, and the iron hand of patriarchy. Muzzled by the Imperial government, Staël takes her Romantic heroine, who in her pre-1800 writings appears in counterpoint to political discussion, and brings her center stage. In a sense, these are all the same heroine, Staël's eternal feminine; reaching from *Pauline, Mirza,* and the *Folle* of 1786, up to her own posthumous persona in the *Dix années d'exil.* Many have complained that this heroine is Staël herself, dressed up in different costumes; that much is obvious; but she is also any woman, before or since, who has felt her talent crushed by the dead weight of male opinion. This is a vast subject, after all, which Staël treats with rich variety.

There are some splendid studies of Staël's Romantic heroine, unhappy witness to male needs for a silent and servile companion buried within the private sphere. What deserves further study is the massive impact this heroine evidently had on her readers, especially women: Margaret Fuller named herself "the Yankee Corinna", and both Corinne and Delphine are still standard names in France today. At the height of French Romanticism, 1830-48, France alone published 17 editions of *Corinne ou l'Italie,* or one a year, in an age flooded with novels; 1850-70 saw another fifteen editions. Before George Sand, I argue that almost nowhere else in literature could romantic women, young or old, find a soul-sister with a *public* voice: heroines were domestic animals. And in fact, almost nothing before *Corinne* had put *any* exceptional creative genius, man or woman, so gloriously center stage: Ossian hints at it, Byron completes the process; but Byron wrote in 1812, after *Corinne.* Did Staël then invent the Romantic hero, and do so in the feminine[10]?

4. RESTORATION.

After 1814, after fleeing via unburnt Moscow in 1812, Staël at last escapes the muzzle; free to speak again in public, to influence the state. In 1804, she had hinted at politics by reviewing her father. Her new works—*De l'Allemagne*'s new preface, some short pieces in the next *Cahier staëlien,* and her two political testaments, *Dix années d'exil* and the *Considérations sur la Révolution française*—use that same excuse, with Staël carefully guarding her "political virginity" by telling men what they want to hear; that she had never had a political role (this while Alexander, Wellington and the Duc d'Orléans visit her salon). But a bizarre new element separates these new texts from her talk of politics in the 1790s: suddenly, Staël's Romantic heroine has stepped through fiction's mirror to enter her political discourse. Staël is reinventing herself as one of her own heroines, a Delphine-like victim longing for the private sphere. Above all, she is a victim; indeed, she is the Emperor's victim. And clearly this is more than a mere excuse to publish. In inventing the Romantic heroine, and perhaps in watching her friend Byron at work, Staël has glimpsed this suffering figure's enormous power; here is the electric, indeed *female* link with that ocean of romantic readers she has sought throughout her career. Ironically, she had used it already, as Poulet remarks, in her first great work on Rousseau, before feeling the call of discursive objectivity for two decades thereafter[11].

It is also ironic that Staël's modest lie was not enough for her male heirs, who heavily censored both posthumous texts. One incident will illustrate their methods: every edition of the *Considérations* carries a note from Staël's son Auguste, saying that her chapter on the French constitution was unfinished. That chapter has sat in manuscript for two hundred years, as fully revised as her manuscript constitution of 1798; waiting for a time when women could again speak in public. Staël's life and work, in short, from childhood to death-bed—indeed, on through her posthumous career—bear eloquent witness to her age's sexual contract, and to its pressing desire to ban all women from the public arena[12].

Notes

1. This is bitter counsel: Staël states that if *bonheur* is to be denied them, "il vaut mieux renfermer les femmes comme esclaves [. . .] que des les lancer au milieu du monde"; *De l'Allemagne* [*DA*], in Staël, *Œuvres complètes* [*OC*], 3 vols (Paris: Treuttel & Würtz 1834), II 218. Indeed, her term here for women's fame—*un deuil éclatant du bonheur*—was brewing by 1796: "les femmes doivent penser que, pour la gloire même, il faut renoncer au bonheur". She adds, "ce n'est pas en renonçant au sort fixé par la société, que les femmes peuvent échapper au malheur". *De l'influence des passions* [*IP*] in *OC* I 130, 138. Lastly, as 1793 made explicit, the Revolutionary *zoon politikon* of our title was male, and predicated upon privatised female "helots".

Staël, *DA* 218; *De la litterature considérée dans ses rapports avec les institutions sociales* [*DL*], in *OC* I 335. Other texts mentioned here are in the 1995 *Cahier staëlien,* which lists all Staël's known works—not forgetting the magnificent *Correspodance générale.*

2. Jacques Domenech, "L'éloge de Rousseau prétexte à l'hagiographie de Necker chez Madame de Staël", in *Etudes Jean-Jacques Rousseau* 3 (Reims: A l'Ecart, 1989), 69-83.

3. These parallels are discussed in John Isbell, "Le contrat social selon Benjamin Constant et Mme de Staël, ou la liberté a-t-elle un sexe?", *Cahiers de l'Association internationale des études françaises,* 1996.

4. John Cleary, "Madame de Staël, Rousseau, and Mary Wollstonecraft", in *Romance Notes* 21 (1980/81), 329-31; and Madelyn Gutwirth, "Madame de Staël, Rousseau, and the Woman Question", in *PMLA* [*Publications of the Modern Language Association of America*], 1970, 100-9. An odd footnote is Staël's debate on whether monarchies or republics can better use women leaders: in 1800, she claims that they offer ridicule and hatred respectively (*DL* 302). But elsewhere Staël is more pointed: reviewing in 1788 Rousseau's desire to "empêcher les femmes de se mêler des affaires publiques", she suggests that in a republic, "cet usage est préférable", while in a monarchy, women perhaps conserve "more feelings of independence and pride than men"; *Lettres sur* [. . .] *J.-J. Rousseau* [*LR*], in *OC* I 4. In 1811, Staël says the reverse: in monarchies, one feels "une sorte d'éloignement" for women who mess with public affairs; "il semble qu'elles deviennent les rivales des hommes [. . .]; mais dans une république, la politique étant le premier intérêt de tous les hommes, ils ne seraient point associés du fond de l'âme avec les femmes qui ne partageraient pas cet intérêt" ("Aspasie", in *OC* II 297). By amazing coincidence, Staël's change of heart echoes who was in power. On this subject, see Susan Tenenbaum, "Montesquieu and Mme de Staël: The Woman as a Factor in Political Analysis"; in *Political Theory* 1.i, February 1973, 92-103.

5. Compare Staël's near-identical phrase in 1796, "la nature et la société ont déshérité la moitié de l'espèce humaine" (*IP* 137). An appeal here to men against women "rivals" has special reason to be her work: "Ne faites pas des rivaux des compagnes de votre vie: laissez, laissez dans ce monde subsister une union qu'aucun intérêt, qu'aucune rivalité ne puisse rompre." Surely any man among men would instead have said *laissons?* Also, this repeated term, *rivalry,* while hardly a man's choice, is crucial to Staël's world view, from 1796 to 1814: "faudrait-il devenir leurs rivaux"?; "rivaux parmi les femmes"; "rivalité avec les hommes" (*IP* 138; *DL* 304; *DA* 218). In the new 1814 preface to her work on Rousseau, Staël imagines verdicts on female talent: "nous voulons

que cet esprit ne leur inspire pas le désir [. . .] d'entrer en rivalité avec les hommes" (*LR* 2). Another parallel stresses women's free choice, with some irony: the *Rapport* says of ex-nuns, "elles prendront envers la Société des engagements d'autant plus sacrés, qu'ils seront plus libres", and Staël's review of Sophie says that wives "contribueraient peut-être autant au bonheur de leur époux, si elles se bornaient à leur destinée *par choix plutôt que par incapacité*" (*LR* 13).

6. On these *hommes de plus,* note Staël's old dream, shared by Sand, of being a man—saying of her heroine in 1786, "ce n'était plus une femme, c'était un poète"; imagining a woman who "s'élèverait par sa pensée au sort des hommes les plus célèbres"; noting that "Aspasie influait sur la nation entière", or that her mother "fut élevée [. . .] comme pourrait l'être un homme" (*Mirza,* in *OC* I 74; *IP* 130; "Aspasie" 298; *Biographie Michaud* 31, "Madame Necker"). The *Rapport* itself twice mentions female *gloire.* On Staël's realism amid these dreams, compare her remark in 1796, *Corinne in nuce:* "les avantages d'un caractère élevé [. . .] détachent à la longue tout ce qui lui serait inférieur". With equal simplicity, she adds that "les hommes sont maîtres de l'opinion" (*IP* 137-8).

7. Compare Staël's reflections on domestic peace, printed but never released in 1795. Staël had always liked the scene where Emile carries Sophie. She shows us bad women, like Cleopatra in 1813 who "ne sut pas placer sa gloire dans celle de l'objet de son choix; elle ne cessa de se préférer à ce qu'elle aimait"; or Adélaïde in 1786, who "n'aurait pu vivre sans Théodore, mais [. . .] pouvait s'amuser sans lui" ("Cléopâtre", in *OC* II 301; *Adélaïde et Théodore,* in *OC* I 83). Facing them are good women like the queen, whose only early concern in affairs was to "accomplir quelques actes de bienfaisance ou de générosité"; or Zulma who remarks of her beloved, "c'est au bruit de sa gloire que j'apprenais mon bonheur"; or indeed her mother, "entourée d'un grand nombre d'hommes d'esprit [. . .] qu'elle faisait valoir par l'admiration qu'elle montrait pour leur esprit et leur talent" (*Réflexions sur le procès de la reine,* in *OC* I 25; *Zulma,* in *OC* I 105; "Madame Necker"). Mother also shares the queen's requisite penchant for *bienfaisance* and hospices; codes of female behavior were no less strict on paper. Staël thus remarks on the dangers run by "cette puissance inconnue qu'on appelle une femme"—above all, that "on l'accuserait de toutes les actions de ses amis" (*DL* 304). The simple solution was to state repeatedly and to all comers that one had had no public role whatsoever.

8. On *De la littérature,* see Burkhart Steinwachs, *Epochenbewuβtsein und Kunsterfahrung* [. . .] (München: Fink 1986), 62-86, a splendid study. Which other Staël texts are epoch-making? Poulet begins his history of modern criticism, *La Conscience*

critique, with Staël's letters on Rousseau; all quote *De l'Allemagne* at the birth of Romantic theory. Gwynne claims that with her *Considérations,* "la Révolution entre pour ainsi dire dans l'histoire", in *Madame de Staël et la Révolution française. Politique, philosophie, littérature* (Paris: Nizet, 1969), 299. I make a case for *Corinne ou l'Italie* below. Five texts? Enough, surely, for any author.

9. Simone Balayé, "Pour une lecture politique de *De l'Allemagne* de Madame de Staël", in *Stendhal: l'écrivain, la société et le pouvoir* (Grenoble: Presses universitaires de Grenoble, 1984), 129-43; "*Delphine,* roman des Lumières: pour une lecture politique", in *Le Siècle de Voltaire, hommage à René Pomeau* (Oxford: Voltaire Foundation, 1987), I 37-46; "Pour une lecture politique de *Corinne*", in *Il Gruppo di Coppet e l'Italia* (Pisa: Pascini 1988), 7-16. Also John Isbell, *The Birth of European Romanticism: Truth and propaganda in Staël's De l'Allemagne* (Cambridge: C.U.P. 1994).

10. See Madelyn Gutwirth, "Woman as Mediatrix: From Jean-Jacques Rousseau to Germaine de Staël", in A. Goldberger, ed., *Woman as Mediatrix. Essays on Nineteenth-Century European Women Writers* (Westport: Greenwood Press, 1987), 13-29. Simone Balayé points out that Corinne never writes politics—what Staël failed to do; in "Comment peut-on être Madame de Staël? Une femme dans l'institution littéraire", *Romantisme* 77 (1992), 21.

11. Georges Poulet, *La Conscience critique* (Paris: Corti 1971).

12. On the Revolution, see Candice Proctor, *Women, Equality and the French Revolution* (Westport: Greenwood Press 1990), Olwen Hufton, *Women and the Limits of Citizenship in the French Revolution* (Toronto: University of Toronto Press, 1992), and Madelyn Gutwirth, *Twilight of the Goddesses: Representations of Women in the French Revolution* (New Brunswick: Rutgers U.P. 1993). On women's raw deal in contract theory and liberal economics, see Carole Pateman, *The Sexual Contract* (Stanford: Stanford U.P., 1988); also John Isbell, "Inventing the French Revolution: Staël considers national credit, 1789-1818", in the acts of the 1994 Hofstra Colloquium on French Women Writers. Finally, a superb complement to this whole argument is Enzo Caramaschi, *Voltaire, Madame de Staël, Balzac* (Padova: Liviana, 1977), 137-98.

Renee Winegarten (essay date 1998)

SOURCE: "An Early Dissident: Madame de Staël," in *The New Criterion,* Vol. 16, No. 9, May, 1998, pp. 17-22.

[In the following essay, Winegarten probes the results of de Staël's exile from France during the Napoleonic regime.]

> There is a world elsewhere.
>
> —*Coriolanus* Act III, scene iii

Exile is a terrible fate, a source of bitterness and grief since the time of the ancient Hebrews as they sat down by the waters of Babylon and wept. In our own tormented era, a great many people have felt what it means to be forcibly cut off, perhaps forever, from their treasured familiar culture. On this theme, Anne Louise Germaine Necker, Mme. de Staël (1766-1817), the great forerunner of the modern literary and political dissidents, still has much of value to communicate. For a woman as highly strung and imaginative as she was, exile figured as grimly as death itself—and she was by no means the first to think in that way. She often remembered that, nearly a hundred years earlier, the statesman and writer Viscount Bolingbroke had associated exile and death. Her thoughts also turned to the Roman poet Ovid sent into exile by the Emperor Augustus and left to bemoan his fate among the Scythians on the shores of the Black Sea, where he died.

Tradition has it that Ovid was exiled for a poem that gave offense as well as for involvement in a sexual-cum-political scandal. Mme. de Staël's fault in the eyes of the leaders of the Committee of Public Safety in 1795, of the Directory in 1799, and, most potently, of Napoleon Bonaparte from 1800, was not sexual (though her private life and her numerous love affairs were a source of prurient gossip). It was literary and political. Napoleon condemned her to banishment from Paris and to internal exile under constant surveillance in the French provinces (so that eventually she felt driven to flee abroad). This was because she had offended him with her outspoken criticism and her writings which, he felt, undermined directly or obliquely the policies of his personal rule. Having grown accustomed to sycophancy, he was absolutely furious because she not only failed to praise his mighty exploits, but also she omitted to mention them in her books. She was used to the freedom of talk that had flourished under the ancien régime in the days immediately before the French Revolution of 1789, and so she thought she could criticize his dictatorship in private and in society with similar impunity. Whatever her virtues—and she was certainly courageous—prudence was not among them. For a long time, she did not comprehend that in Napoleon she was dealing with a new phenomenon. It was one that would prefigure many of the authoritarian tendencies familiar to the modern era.

Her indiscreet remarks and her sometimes defiant actions were perfectly well known to Napoleon through his ubiquitous spies. Even when in Germany or Russia, busily engaged in the wars, he took the trouble to be well informed about her sayings and doings. He would find time to write to Joseph Fouché, the supreme spymaster, then minister of police, urging him to tighten measures against "this real bird of ill omen," "this whore," as Napoleon graciously called her. Since she often conversed with his actual or putative enemies at home and abroad, in his eyes she was a seriously tiresome troublemaker, and he suspected her of actively plotting against him. He said that people always left her salon plainly less well disposed toward himself. She had offended him, and that was sufficient cause for punishment. There could be no redress against giving offense to an absolute ruler, she once observed.

She soon came to realize that others did not regard exile as so dreadful a fate. As early as 1803, she had written to a friend that "people will get used to my exile and will be surprised at my whim to extricate myself from it." That elevated and self-regarding writer, Chateaubriand, visited her at Coppet, her handsome family mansion near the shores of Lake Geneva. He expressed astonishment that a person of large means like herself, who resided in a beautiful house, attended by servants and with all the amenities of unspoiled nature around her, could be so unhappy at her banishment from Paris. He was drawn to conclude that, whereas he would be well content with the pleasures of solitude in such conditions, there were others of different temperament who could not be reconciled to it.

It was in a state of near collapse and terror that, on May 23, 1812, Mme. de Staël left Coppet, and carrying only her fan entered her carriage, ostensibly to go for a drive with her daughter Albertine. Riding alongside for a short distance was her son Auguste, who tried to cheer her with the thought that she was going (of necessity secretly and circuitously) to England, a land she had long idealized as the seat of freedom. Coppet had fallen under Napoleon's rule some fourteen years earlier when he invaded Switzerland. For many months, the local *préfet* had been limiting her movements to a few miles from her home, so that she was virtually under house arrest.

The few close friends who had ventured to visit her were in their turn punished with internal exile. (They were not always as apolitical as she averred.) Others warned her that she might well suffer the same fate as Mary Queen of Scots, who had been imprisoned for almost two decades by Queen Elizabeth I, and then beheaded. After all, it was only a few years since the duc d'Enghien had been kidnapped on foreign soil and hastily executed at Vincennes—a crime famously judged by a cynic to be a "mistake," and one sufficiently extraordinary at the time to linger in the collective memory. Indeed, her own arrest was a distinct possibility, and her fears were not illusory. In 1811 the zealous local *préfet* informed General René Savary (who had succeeded Fouché as minister of police) that the order for her arrest had not been issued "for the moment." Clearly, the authorities had imprisonment in view. It can readily be imagined how furious Napoleon and his bureaucratic underlings were when they discovered that she had managed to escape their long surveillance and constant harassment. After months of secret planning and diversionary tactics, she was embarking on the first stage of a momentous journey that was to take her across war-torn Europe, through Austria, Poland, Russia, Sweden, to her ultimate goal, freedom in England, Napoleon's bitterest foe.

Out of that perilous journey would come one of the most fascinating books of the nineteenth century, *Dix années d'exil.* The ten years of exile to which the title alludes, from 1803 to 1813, were in fact only one part of the story because she had known banishment earlier. This splendid work is a broken monument, for it is unfinished. It was written at different periods, separated by an interval of some five years. She did not live to correct the manuscript, although it was her custom to make many drafts. Part of it she removed and inserted into one of her major works, her reflections on the French Revolution, later published by her son Auguste in the year following his mother's untimely death in 1817. Her health had been deteriorating, not just through her intense emotional overdrive in her often stormy personal relationships, through a difficult pregnancy when in her mid forties, and her abuse of opium, but also as a result of the constant agitation and mental stress caused by persecution and banishment.

Auguste eventually decided to publish also her account of her years of exile, but he took it upon himself to modify the style, alter the text, and cut passages that might have some risky current political implication or that referred to persons who were still living. This is the version that has largely been available until now, superseded at last by a superb new edition that is unlikely to be surpassed.[1] It even includes the "disguised manuscripts" where, fearing discovery, she concealed her views beneath allusions to the history of England so that, for instance, Mary Queen of Scots stands for the duc d'Enghien. Now, for the first time we can read the work more or less as it came from Mme. de Staël's hand.

Why is this incomplete work so telling even today? Here is a gripping personal memoir of her meetings with General Bonaparte in 1797, when he returned to Paris crowned with laurel as the great republican hero and liberator, the heir of the Revolution—an image that some could never bring themselves to renounce. (She would be distressed by the enduring admiration for Napoleon, war or no war, displayed by blinkered British fellow travelers, on meeting them in London in 1813.) In those early days, however, she also was under the spell of Bonaparte the military genius, in a manner more imaginatively and romantically intense than she was later prepared to admit. He did not respond, treating her—as he did many women whom he considered unlikely to be of use to him—with soldierly coarse and brutal misogyny. Master of the apparently sightless stare, he intimidated her to such a degree that, although she was renowned for her fascinating talk and witty repartee, she was reduced to silence. It did not help if she prepared in advance what she was going to say.

The work also tells of her growing awareness of the First Consul's monarchical ambitions and his drive to absolute power. From 1800, when she encouraged Benjamin Constant to stand up for free speech in the Tribunate, and was ostracized for her pains, she kept to her principles in mingled pride and dread. Moreover, she describes vividly the persecution she endured at Bonaparte's hands, not only in France but also in the realms he conquered and wherever fears of his displeasure predominated. Her words ring down the ages: "If tyranny only had its direct advocates on its side, it would never prosper. The astounding thing, and one that above all bears witness to the depths of human abasement, is that most mediocre men are at the service of the event. . . ." This inclination she attributed not only to weakness of character but also to the fact that mankind has a sort of need to prove fate right, in order to live in peace with it. She remarked that there are always those who are able to find philosophical reasons to be content with the powers that be.

As to the constant harassment she endured, known today down to the last petty detail from the patient research of scholars into police archives, she does not reveal the half of it. All the same, what she does relate is powerful enough in its indictment of the abuse of power. The book aims to encompass Napoleon's downfall and the establishment of a new republican regime in France. And, along the way, it is a kind of travel book whose depiction of Russia in 1812 remains memorable. She crossed the Russian frontier at Brody in Galicia shortly after the invading French armies traversed the river Niemen, and she was one of the last independent foreign observers to see Moscow before the inhabitants defiantly put it to the torch.

The fact was that her exile, however painful, opened her mind to new and fruitful experiences. Because of the French invasion of Russia, she was obliged to make a large detour via Kiev before she could reach Moscow. Although the country was struggling against the French invader, she was surprised at the kindness and hospitality shown her. However, she soon became aware of the vast difference between the "Asiatic" magnificence of the princes and aristocrats who entertained her in such an extravagant manner and the miserable existence of the serfs. There is no third estate here, she remarked, noting the absence of a middle class concerned with culture and enlightenment as she had known it in France. Her Russian hosts kept silent on serious matters, she reflected, because they knew that it was dangerous to express a personal opinion.

In St. Petersburg, she conferred with British agents like Lord William Bentinck; with diplomats like Baron Heinrich von Stein, one of the leading German opponents of Napoleon's regime, whom she inspired; and John Quincy Adams, future president of the United States. Czar Alexander I and his family welcomed her as an honored guest, and he discussed public affairs with her as an equal. He was in his liberal phase, and he assured her that he intended to improve the condition of the serfs at an opportune moment. Later, in London, when a lady ill-advisedly spoke to her about the existence of a free society in Russia, Mme. de Staël swiftly countered that she had never known freedom to coexist with serfdom. Her book is more flattering to Alexander than her true opinions would suggest. In general, her comments were acute. She observed that though there was much imitation of French, German, and British modes and manners, it was only skin deep.

What lay at the root of her opposition to Napoleon's regime? He once said that he found the French crown lying on the ground and that he quite simply picked it up. Crowned emperor in 1804, he created a Bonapartist aristocracy and a court, and placed his brothers and sisters on the thrones of Europe. That was not what the daughter of Jacques Necker—Louis XVI's reformist minister of finance, whom she had seen welcomed with ecstasy by the populace in 1789—ever anticipated. What need was there now, after the regime of the Bourbons had been abolished at such a high cost in blood, for a new royalty and a new caste? Some of her friends among the old nobility had hastened to renounce their privileges at the beginning of the Revolution. She would remain faithful to the generous libertarian ideals that had inspired them and that had been betrayed by the Jacobin Terror of 1793-4. Then there were Napoleon's endless wars with their terrible casualties. When thousands of his soldiers lay dead on the battlefield, she heard how Napoleon had insouciantly remarked that one night in Paris would make up the numbers. He liked to shock with his brutal remarks and let everyone know who was master.

The Corsican-born General Bonaparte did not care for intellectuals and thinkers in general (*idéologues* as some were then known), whereas for Mme. de Staël the ability to think for oneself was preeminent. When advised to be more discreet, she replied, "It is the truth, it is what I think and I shall say so." He particularly disliked women who took an interest in political affairs, and that distaste necessarily embraced Mme. de Staël, who was fascinated by politics. As a very young girl, she had listened intently to the eminent political figures and the leading *philosophes* who frequented her mother's salon. Even then, she had contributed not a little to the conversation, much to the disapproval of Mme. de Genlis, that critic of her upbringing and stickler for social niceties.

The art of conversation, supreme refinement of eighteenth-century French civilization, as Mme. de Staël knew it in the salons of Paris, was as necessary to her as the air she breathed. It was not to be mistaken for mere idle chatter or regarded simply as a diversion, entertaining though it might prove. Without concern for distinctions of rank, gifted people met together in the salons to discuss with ease and wit every kind of topic. She knew men who were not great readers but who became knowledgeable and cultivated through their contact with the salons. Napoleon was familiar with each person's weakness, and he had no trouble in finding hers. Most people he could win by their desire for preferment, by awarding them lucrative posts and high-sounding titles. Mme. de Staël could not be corrupted in that way. Her real weakness, though, was her acute susceptibility to boredom and melancholy that made her long for the company of her friends, for discourse and discussion. These helped to cover the dark chasm of nothingness that might appear at any moment. By condemning her to live forty leagues from Paris, in some provincial town like Auxerre that she called a veritable Scythia, Napoleon found exactly how to make her suffer.

She was open to attack, too, on the ground of nationality. Born in Paris, naturally she always considered herself to be French. Many French people, though, did not regard her as one of themselves, and journalists (who were mostly on Napoleon's payroll) encouraged them in their prejudice. That kind of disinclination to accept certain categories of people born in France as genuine citizens was to persist into the Vichy regime and beyond. Her parents were both Swiss-born Protestants long resident in France. Her father had loyally served the Catholic crown without too much ado about his nationality and religion, even if these were sometimes called into question. Matters were complicated for her when, on her marriage to a Swedish diplomat, she became Swedish herself. Sometimes, of course, she found it expedient to make use of this when in a tight corner. It enabled her to help friends to escape to Switzerland during the Terror.

On her husband's death, as the French-born widow of a foreigner, she should have been able to revert to being French. In her manner and outlook, she was French to her fingertips, as writers who met her, like Goethe and Schiller and others in Weimar or Berlin, or Byron in London, were agreed. Yet this Corsican general, born "Buonaparte" in Ajaccio in 1769 (a mere three months after the French finally defeated the Corsican patriots), ruled indisputably over France. There was galling irony here in the fact that, though born in Paris, she was forced to flee by order of a man "less French than I."

Besides, she could not believe that she, Necker's daughter, the celebrated author of novels like *Delphine* and *Corinne,* of influential works on literature and on the passions, writings that had created a great stir throughout Europe, could be treated in this cruel way. She had mistakenly believed that her fame was her defense. She was a child of the Enlightenment, after all: she believed in reason and progress, in the high ideals of freedom and fairness that had inspired the eighteenth-century movement for the reform of many abuses. In benighted quarters today, the Enlightenment is under attack as the purlieu of self-interested imperialist white males, despite the fact that—however imperfect, like all human endeavors—it sought disinterestedly to promote toleration and justice for all. Often purchased at great personal cost, these were, and remain, the values of a civilized society. In their light, the authoritarian regime of Napoleon seemed to Mme. de Staël to be an aberration. Surely Bonaparte must be amenable to reasoned argument.

Such a notion has endured as the great liberal delusion. There are always those who are not amenable to reason, or who choose evil as their good. Following Ovid, who addressed poems of complaint to Rome (and has been criticized for self-pity as a result), she went on writing embarrassing letters of self-justification, presenting her case—not without a certain casuistry at times—in a manner that seemed eminently reasonable to her. True, the situation was not simple and clear-cut. There were people she knew well in Napoleon's entourage whom she engaged to intercede on her behalf, notably his elder brother Joseph, her lifelong friend (who, she says in *Dix années d'exil* in farfetched partisanship, was forced against his will to be king of Spain). All such effort proved vain: the emperor was adamant.

A woman of penetrating insight, gifted as she well knew with an analytical mind and the impressive ability to deduce general ideas from her observations, she was also the victim of blindness where Napoleon was concerned. For a long time, she thought he just wanted to frighten her into submission. Indeed, not until 1810, when Napoleon personally gave orders for the destruction of all copies of *De l'Allemagne,* her epoch-making book on German culture, did she begin to realize that his aim was to silence her, or worse. It was not so much a question of the nature and significance of his form of authoritarianism, which she understood and made evident better than most: it was rather, for a while, her failure to grasp the full extent of it.

This combination of insight and blindness would eventually lead her to an impasse. France was at war, yet she believed that she could now fight Napoleon while, as it were, separating him and his supporters from the fate of France itself. It was as if, despite all her criticism of their baseness and barbarity, she could ultimately ignore his numerous committed followers. Napoleon's wholehearted adherents must be "Corsicans" or "Africans" like him, not true Frenchmen. As she saw it, the allies would defeat the tyrant, and France would at once return to the body of civilized nations, rather as though the entire Napoleonic era and its wars had not intervened. She did not see that in victory the Allies would exact an extremely heavy price in reparations, and that France would suffer defeat as well as Napoleon.

It was at a lavish entertainment on Prince Naryshkin's country estate overlooking the gulf of Finland, when a toast was proposed to Anglo-Russian victory over the French, that she suddenly realized her view was not shared. She protested, and would drink only to the defeat of the Corsican despot. She did not foresee the consequences of her fight to topple Napoleon. Given her distaste for the Bourbons, she did not want their return. Consequently, she ardently promoted the cause of General Bernadotte, now Crown Prince of Sweden, as the republican leader of integrity to replace Napoleon. Despite her advocacy, few were converted for long to the cause of the procrastinating Bernadotte, and in 1814 the Allies restored the Bourbons to the French throne in the person of Louis XVIII. In a sense, then, her passionate practical activity was to be frustrated, and on her return to France one of the bitterest shocks of her life was to see the Cossacks encamped on the Champs-Elysées. Her more lasting contribution lay elsewhere as she battled against political fanaticism. She envisaged a body of intellectuals united across frontiers in "the cult of truth." Until recently, the values for which she strove formed an essential part of the civilized humane ideal.

Napoleon later remarked to his recalcitrant younger brother Lucien: "I was wrong. Mme. de Staël raised more enemies against me during her exile than she would have done in France." In her book, she presents herself as the victim, not as the tireless active opponent, but Napoleon himself knew better, and it was not often that he admitted having made a mistake. She provoked the lion. He pushed her beyond endurance. They are like two models of the endlessly repeated struggle between imagination and humanity on the one hand, and the abuse of power on the other. In the conflict between sword and spirit, it is the writer who ultimately emerges as the moral victor. In that light, passing fantasies about the nonexistence of the author and modish nihilistic theories about truth that undermine humanist values pale into insignificance.

Notes

1. *Dix années d'exil,* by Mme. de Staël, edited by Simone Balayé and Mariella Vianello Bonifacio; Arthème Fayard, pages 588, 180 FF.

FURTHER READING

Criticism

Borowitz, Helen O. "The Unconfessed *Précieuse*: Madame de Staël's Debt to Mademoiselle de Scudéry." In *Nineteenth-Century French Studies* 11, Nos. 1 & 2 (Fall-Winter 1982-83): 32-59.
    Explores de Staël's use of Mlle de Scudéry's literary self-portrait as a model for her fictional heroine Corinne.

Bruschini, Enrico and Alba Amoia. "Rome's Monuments and Artistic Treasures in Mme de Staël's *Corinne* (1807): Then and Now." In *Nineteenth-Century French Studies* 22, Nos. 3 & 4 (Spring-Summer 1994): 311-47.
    Considers *Corinne* as a "novel-cum-guidebook" to Italian travel.

DeJean, Joan. "Staël's *Corinne*: The Novel's Other Dilemma." In *Stanford French Review* XI (Spring 1987): 77-87.
    Examines de Staël's adoption of the patriarchal third-person perspective and rejection of the first-person, conversational form in *Corinne*.

Deneys-Tunney, Anne. "*Corinne* by Madame de Staël: The Utopia of Feminine Voice as Music within the Novel." In *Dalhousie French Studies* 28 (Fall 1994): 55-63.
    Discusses the crisis of the feminine voice portrayed in *Corinne*.

Goldberger, Avriel H. "Introduction." In *Corinne, or Italy,* by Madame de Staël, translated and edited by Avriel H. Goldberger, pp. xv-liv. New Brunswick, N. J.: Rutgers University Press, 1987.
    Surveys de Staël's life and analyzes *Corinne,* calling it "one of the three most important novels of early French Romanticism."

———. "Germaine de Staël's *Corinne*: Challenges to the Translator in the 1980s. In *The French Review* 63, No. 5 (April 1990): 800-09.
    Summarizes the problems associated with twentieth-century translation of *Corinne*.

Higonnet, Margaret R. "Madame de Staël and Schelling." In *Comparative Literature* 38, No. 2 (Spring 1986): 159-80.
    Probes de Staël's adaptation of German Idealist philosophy for a French audience in *De l'Allemagne*.

Lind, L. R. "Madame de Staël and the Battle of the Books." In *Classical and Modern Literature* 14, No. 1 (Fall 1994): 7-24.
    Comments on de Staël's view of the relative merits of classic versus modern literature, including her greater sympathies with the latter.

Mortimer, Armine Kotin. "Male and Female Plots in Staël's *Corinne*." In *Correspondances: Studies in Literature, History, and the Arts in Nineteenth-Century France,* edited by Keith Busby, pp. 149-55. Amsterdam: Rodopi, 1992.
    Concentrates on male subjugation of the fallen woman in de Staël's *Corinne*.

Nash, Suzanne. "*De l'Allemagne* and the Creation of a French Germany." In *The Shaping of the Text: Style, Imagery, and Structure in French Literature: Essays in Honor of John Porter Houston,* edited by Emanuel J. Mickel Jr., pp. 80-87. Cranbury, N. J.: Associated University Presses, 1993.
    Recounts de Staël's "myth of a liberal Germany" in *De l'Allemagne* and its effect on subsequent French intellectual history.

Pacini, Giulia. "Hidden Politics in Germaine de Staël's *Corinne ou l'Italie*." In *French Forum* 24, No. 2 (May 1999): 163-77.
    Elucidates the "strong, yet subtle" critique of French politics in *Corinne*.

Peel, Ellen. "Contradictions of Form and Feminism in *Corinne ou l'Italie*." In *Essays in Literature* XIV, No. 2 (Fall 1987): 281-98.
    Analyzes patterns and oppositions in the feminism of de Staël's novel *Corinne*.

Vallois, Marie-Claire. "Voice as Fossil, Madame de Staël's *Corinne or Italy*: An Archaeology of Feminine Discourse." In *Tulsa Studies in Women's Literature* 6, No. 1 (Spring 1987): 47-60.
    Interprets de Staël's use of passive and impersonal modes of narration in *Corinne*.

How to Use This Index

The main references

Calvino, Italo
1923-1985 .... CLC **5, 8, 11, 22, 33, 39,
73; SSC 3**

list all author entries in the following Gale Literary Criticism series:

BLC = *Black Literature Criticism*
CLC = *Contemporary Literary Criticism*
CLR = *Children's Literature Review*
CMLC = *Classical and Medieval Literature Criticism*
DA = *DISCovering Authors*
DAB = *DISCovering Authors: British*
DAC = *DISCovering Authors: Canadian*
DAM = *DISCovering Authors: Modules*
    DRAM: *Dramatists Module;* *MST:* *Most-Studied Authors Module;*
    MULT: *Multicultural Authors Module;* *NOV:* *Novelists Module;*
    POET: *Poets Module;* *POP:* *Popular Fiction and Genre Authors Module*
DC = *Drama Criticism*
HLC = *Hispanic Literature Criticism*
LC = *Literature Criticism from 1400 to 1800*
NCLC = *Nineteenth-Century Literature Criticism*
NNAL = *Native North American Literature*
PC = *Poetry Criticism*
SSC = *Short Story Criticism*
TCLC = *Twentieth-Century Literary Criticism*
WLC = *World Literature Criticism, 1500 to the Present*

The cross-references

See also CANR 23; CA 85-88;
obituary CA116

list all author entries in the following Gale biographical and literary sources:

AAYA = *Authors & Artists for Young Adults*
AITN = *Authors in the News*
BEST = *Bestsellers*
BW = *Black Writers*
CA = *Contemporary Authors*
CAAS = *Contemporary Authors Autobiography Series*
CABS = *Contemporary Authors Bibliographical Series*
CANR = *Contemporary Authors New Revision Series*
CAP = *Contemporary Authors Permanent Series*
CDALB = *Concise Dictionary of American Literary Biography*
CDBLB = *Concise Dictionary of British Literary Biography*
DLB = *Dictionary of Literary Biography*
DLBD = *Dictionary of Literary Biography Documentary Series*
DLBY = *Dictionary of Literary Biography Yearbook*
HW = *Hispanic Writers*
JRDA = *Junior DISCovering Authors*
MAICYA = *Major Authors and Illustrators for Children and Young Adults*
MTCW = *Major 20th-Century Writers*
SAAS = *Something about the Author Autobiography Series*
SATA = *Something about the Author*
YABC = *Yesterday's Authors of Books for Children*

Literary Criticism Series
Cumulative Author Index

A/C Cross
See Lawrence, T(homas) E(dward)

Abasiyanik, Sait Faik 1906-1954
See Sait Faik
See also CA 123

Abbey, Edward 1927-1989 .... **CLC 36, 59**
See also CA 45-48; 128; CANR 2, 41; DA3; MTCW 2

Abbott, Lee K(ittredge) 1947- .... **CLC 48**
See also CA 124; CANR 51; DLB 130

Abe, Kobo 1924-1993 ...... **CLC 8, 22, 53, 81; DAM NOV**
See also CA 65-68; 140; CANR 24, 60; DLB 182; MTCW 1, 2

Abelard, Peter c. 1079-c. 1142 ...... **CMLC 11**
See also DLB 115, 208

Abell, Kjeld 1901-1961 .... **CLC 15**
See also CA 111

Abish, Walter 1931- .... **CLC 22**
See also CA 101; CANR 37; DLB 130, 227

Abrahams, Peter (Henry) 1919- .... **CLC 4**
See also BW 1; CA 57-60; CANR 26; DLB 117, 225; MTCW 1, 2

Abrams, M(eyer) H(oward) 1912- ... **CLC 24**
See also CA 57-60; CANR 13, 33; DLB 67

Abse, Dannie 1923- .... **CLC 7, 29; DAB; DAM POET**
See also CA 53-56; CAAS 1; CANR 4, 46, 74; DLB 27; MTCW 1

Achebe, (Albert) Chinua(lumogu)
1930- ...... **CLC 1, 3, 5, 7, 11, 26, 51, 75, 127; BLC 1; DA; DAB; DAC; DAM MST, MULT, NOV; WLC**
See also AAYA 15; BW 2, 3; CA 1-4R; CANR 6, 26, 47; CLR 20; DA3; DLB 117; MAICYA; MTCW 1, 2; SATA 38, 40; SATA-Brief 38

Acker, Kathy 1948-1997 .... **CLC 45, 111**
See also CA 117; 122; 162; CANR 55

Ackroyd, Peter 1949- .... **CLC 34, 52**
See also CA 123; 127; CANR 51, 74; DLB 155; INT 127; MTCW 1

Acorn, Milton 1923- .... **CLC 15; DAC**
See also CA 103; DLB 53; INT 103

Adamov, Arthur 1908-1970 .... **CLC 4, 25; DAM DRAM**
See also CA 17-18; 25-28R; CAP 2; MTCW 1

Adams, Alice (Boyd) 1926-1999 .. **CLC 6, 13, 46; SSC 24**
See also CA 81-84; 179; CANR 26, 53, 75, 88; DLBY 86; INT CANR-26; MTCW 1, 2

Adams, Andy 1859-1935 .... **TCLC 56**
See also YABC 1

Adams, Brooks 1848-1927 .... **TCLC 80**
See also CA 123; DLB 47

Adams, Douglas (Noel) 1952- .... **CLC 27, 60; DAM POP**
See also AAYA 4, 33; BEST 89:3; CA 106; CANR 34, 64; DA3; DLBY 83; JRDA; MTCW 1; SATA 116

Adams, Francis 1862-1893 .... **NCLC 33**

Adams, Henry (Brooks)
1838-1918 .... **TCLC 4, 52; DA; DAB; DAC; DAM MST**
See also CA 104; 133; CANR 77; DLB 12, 47, 189; MTCW 1

Adams, Richard (George) 1920- ... **CLC 4, 5, 18; DAM NOV**
See also AAYA 16; AITN 1, 2; CA 49-52; CANR 3, 35; CLR 20; JRDA; MAICYA; MTCW 1, 2; SATA 7, 69

Adamson, Joy(-Friederike Victoria)
1910-1980 .... **CLC 17**
See also CA 69-72; 93-96; CANR 22; MTCW 1; SATA 11; SATA-Obit 22

Adcock, Fleur 1934- .... **CLC 41**
See also CA 25-28R, 182; CAAE 182; CAAS 23; CANR 11, 34, 69; DLB 40

Addams, Charles (Samuel)
1912-1988 .... **CLC 30**
See also CA 61-64; 126; CANR 12, 79

Addams, Jane 1860-1945 .... **TCLC 76**

Addison, Joseph 1672-1719 .... **LC 18**
See also CDBLB 1660-1789; DLB 101

Adler, Alfred (F.) 1870-1937 .... **TCLC 61**
See also CA 119; 159

Adler, C(arole) S(chwerdtfeger)
1932- .... **CLC 35**
See also AAYA 4; CA 89-92; CANR 19, 40; JRDA; MAICYA; SAAS 15; SATA 26, 63, 102

Adler, Renata 1938- .... **CLC 8, 31**
See also CA 49-52; CANR 5, 22, 52; MTCW 1

Ady, Endre 1877-1919 .... **TCLC 11**
See also CA 107

A.E. 1867-1935 .... **TCLC 3, 10**
See also Russell, George William

Aeschylus 525B.C.-456B.C. .. **CMLC 11; DA; DAB; DAC; DAM DRAM, MST; DC 8; WLCS**
See also DLB 176

Aesop 620(?)B.C.-(?)B.C. .... **CMLC 24**
See also CLR 14; MAICYA; SATA 64

Affable Hawk
See MacCarthy, Sir(Charles Otto) Desmond

Africa, Ben
See Bosman, Herman Charles

Afton, Effie
See Harper, Frances Ellen Watkins

Agapida, Fray Antonio
See Irving, Washington

Agee, James (Rufus) 1909-1955 ...... **TCLC 1, 19; DAM NOV**
See also AITN 1; CA 108; 148; CDALB 1941-1968; DLB 2, 26, 152; MTCW 1

Aghill, Gordon
See Silverberg, Robert

Agnon, S(hmuel) Y(osef Halevi)
1888-1970 .... **CLC 4, 8, 14; SSC 30**
See also CA 17-18; 25-28R; CANR 60; CAP 2; MTCW 1, 2

Agrippa von Nettesheim, Henry Cornelius
1486-1535 .... **LC 27**

Aguilera Malta, Demetrio 1909-1981
See also CA 111; 124; CANR 87; DAM MULT, NOV; DLB 145; HLCS 1; HW 1

Agustini, Delmira 1886-1914
See also CA 166; HLCS 1; HW 1, 2

Aherne, Owen
See Cassill, R(onald) V(erlin)

Ai 1947- .... **CLC 4, 14, 69**
See also CA 85-88; CAAS 13; CANR 70; DLB 120

Aickman, Robert (Fordyce)
1914-1981 .... **CLC 57**
See also CA 5-8R; CANR 3, 72

Aiken, Conrad (Potter) 1889-1973 .... **CLC 1, 3, 5, 10, 52; DAM NOV, POET; PC 26; SSC 9**
See also CA 5-8R; 45-48; CANR 4, 60; CDALB 1929-1941; DLB 9, 45, 102; MTCW 1, 2; SATA 3, 30

Aiken, Joan (Delano) 1924- .... **CLC 35**
See also AAYA 1, 25; CA 9-12R, 182; CAAE 182; CANR 4, 23, 34, 64; CLR 1, 19; DLB 161; JRDA; MAICYA; MTCW 1; SAAS 1; SATA 2, 30, 73; SATA-Essay 109

Ainsworth, William Harrison
1805-1882 .... **NCLC 13**
See also DLB 21; SATA 24

Aitmatov, Chingiz (Torekulovich)
1928- .... **CLC 71**
See also CA 103; CANR 38; MTCW 1; SATA 56

Akers, Floyd
See Baum, L(yman) Frank

Akhmadulina, Bella Akhatovna
1937- .... **CLC 53; DAM POET**
See also CA 65-68

Akhmatova, Anna 1888-1966 ..... **CLC 11, 25, 64, 126; DAM POET; PC 2**
See also CA 19-20; 25-28R; CANR 35; CAP 1; DA3; MTCW 1, 2

Aksakov, Sergei Timofeyvich
1791-1859 .... **NCLC 2**
See also DLB 198

Aksenov, Vassily
See Aksyonov, Vassily (Pavlovich)

Akst, Daniel 1956- .... CLC 109
See also CA 161

Aksyonov, Vassily (Pavlovich)
1932- .... CLC 22, 37, 101
See also CA 53-56; CANR 12, 48, 77

Akutagawa, Ryunosuke
1892-1927 .... TCLC 16
See also CA 117; 154

Alain 1868-1951 .... TCLC 41
See also CA 163

Alain-Fournier TCLC 6
See also Fournier, Henri Alban
See also DLB 65

Alarcon, Pedro Antonio de
1833-1891 .... NCLC 1

Alas (y Urena), Leopoldo (Enrique Garcia)
1852-1901 .... TCLC 29
See also CA 113; 131; HW 1

Albee, Edward (Franklin III) 1928- . CLC 1,
2, 3, 5, 9, 11, 13, 25, 53, 86, 113; DA;
DAB; DAC; DAM DRAM, MST; DC
11; WLC
See also AITN 1; CA 5-8R; CABS 3;
CANR 8, 54, 74; CDALB 1941-1968;
DA3; DLB 7; INT CANR-8; MTCW 1, 2

Alberti, Rafael 1902-1999 .... CLC 7
See also CA 85-88; 185; CANR 81; DLB
108; HW 2

Albert the Great 1200(?)-1280 ...... CMLC 16
See also DLB 115

Alcala-Galiano, Juan Valera y
See Valera y Alcala-Galiano, Juan

Alcott, Amos Bronson 1799-1888 .... NCLC 1
See also DLB 1, 223

Alcott, Louisa May 1832-1888 . NCLC 6, 58,
83; DA; DAB; DAC; DAM MST, NOV;
SSC 27; WLC
See also AAYA 20; CDALB 1865-1917;
CLR 1, 38; DA3; DLB 1, 42, 79, 223;
DLBD 14; JRDA; MAICYA; SATA 100;
YABC 1

Aldanov, M. A.
See Aldanov, Mark (Alexandrovich)

Aldanov, Mark (Alexandrovich)
1886(?)-1957 .... TCLC 23
See also CA 118; 181

Aldington, Richard 1892-1962 .... CLC 49
See also CA 85-88; CANR 45; DLB 20, 36,
100, 149

Aldiss, Brian W(ilson) 1925- . CLC 5, 14, 40;
DAM NOV; SSC 36
See also CA 5-8R; CAAS 2; CANR 5, 28,
64; DLB 14; MTCW 1, 2; SATA 34

Alegria, Claribel 1924- .... CLC 75; DAM
MULT; HLCS 1; PC 26
See also CA 131; CAAS 15; CANR 66;
DLB 145; HW 1; MTCW 1

Alegria, Fernando 1918- .... CLC 57
See also CA 9-12R; CANR 5, 32, 72; HW
1, 2

Aleichem, Sholom TCLC 1, 35; SSC 33
See also Rabinovitch, Sholem

Aleixandre, Vicente 1898-1984
See also CANR 81; HLCS 1; HW 2

Alepoudelis, Odysseus
See Elytis, Odysseus

Aleshkovsky, Joseph 1929-
See Aleshkovsky, Yuz
See also CA 121; 128

Aleshkovsky, Yuz CLC 44
See also Aleshkovsky, Joseph

Alexander, Lloyd (Chudley) 1924- ... CLC 35
See also AAYA 1, 27; CA 1-4R; CANR 1,
24, 38, 55; CLR 1, 5, 48; DLB 52; JRDA;
MAICYA; MTCW 1; SAAS 19; SATA 3,
49, 81

Alexander, Meena 1951- .... CLC 121
See also CA 115; CANR 38, 70

Alexander, Samuel 1859-1938 .... TCLC 77

Alexie, Sherman (Joseph, Jr.)
1966- .... CLC 96; DAM MULT
See also AAYA 28; CA 138; CANR 65;
DA3; DLB 175, 206; MTCW 1; NNAL

Alfau, Felipe 1902- .... CLC 66
See also CA 137

Alfred, Jean Gaston
See Ponge, Francis

Alger, Horatio Jr., Jr. 1832-1899 .... NCLC 8,
83
See also DLB 42; SATA 16

Algren, Nelson 1909-1981 ..... CLC 4, 10, 33;
SSC 33
See also CA 13-16R; 103; CANR 20, 61;
CDALB 1941-1968; DLB 9; DLBY 81,
82; MTCW 1, 2

Ali, Ahmed 1910- .... CLC 69
See also CA 25-28R; CANR 15, 34

Alighieri, Dante
See Dante

Allan, John B.
See Westlake, Donald E(dwin)

Allan, Sidney
See Hartmann, Sadakichi

Allan, Sydney
See Hartmann, Sadakichi

Allen, Edward 1948- .... CLC 59

Allen, Fred 1894-1956 .... TCLC 87

Allen, Paula Gunn 1939- .... CLC 84; DAM
MULT
See also CA 112; 143; CANR 63; DA3;
DLB 175; MTCW 1; NNAL

Allen, Roland
See Ayckbourn, Alan

Allen, Sarah A.
See Hopkins, Pauline Elizabeth

Allen, Sidney H.
See Hartmann, Sadakichi

Allen, Woody 1935- .... CLC 16, 52; DAM
POP
See also AAYA 10; CA 33-36R; CANR 27,
38, 63; DLB 44; MTCW 1

Allende, Isabel 1942- . CLC 39, 57, 97; DAM
MULT, NOV; HLC 1; WLCS
See also AAYA 18; CA 125; 130; CANR
51, 74; DA3; DLB 145; HW 1, 2; INT
130; MTCW 1, 2

Alleyn, Ellen
See Rossetti, Christina (Georgina)

Allingham, Margery (Louise)
1904-1966 .... CLC 19
See also CA 5-8R; 25-28R; CANR 4, 58;
DLB 77; MTCW 1, 2

Allingham, William 1824-1889 ...... NCLC 25
See also DLB 35

Allison, Dorothy E. 1949- .... CLC 78
See also CA 140; CANR 66; DA3; MTCW
1

Allston, Washington 1779-1843 .... NCLC 2
See also DLB 1

Almedingen, E. M. CLC 12
See also Almedingen, Martha Edith von
See also SATA 3

Almedingen, Martha Edith von 1898-1971
See Almedingen, E. M.
See also CA 1-4R; CANR 1

Almodovar, Pedro 1949(?)- .... CLC 114;
HLCS 1
See also CA 133; CANR 72; HW 2

Almqvist, Carl Jonas Love
1793-1866 .... NCLC 42

Alonso, Damaso 1898-1990 .... CLC 14
See also CA 110; 131; 130; CANR 72; DLB
108; HW 1, 2

Alov
See Gogol, Nikolai (Vasilyevich)

Alta 1942- .... CLC 19
See also CA 57-60

Alter, Robert B(ernard) 1935- .... CLC 34
See also CA 49-52; CANR 1, 47

Alther, Lisa 1944- .... CLC 7, 41
See also CA 65-68; CAAS 30; CANR 12,
30, 51; MTCW 1

Althusser, L.
See Althusser, Louis

Althusser, Louis 1918-1990 .... CLC 106
See also CA 131; 132

Altman, Robert 1925- .... CLC 16, 116
See also CA 73-76; CANR 43

Alurista 1949-
See Urista, Alberto H.
See also DLB 82; HLCS 1

Alvarez, A(lfred) 1929- .... CLC 5, 13
See also CA 1-4R; CANR 3, 33, 63; DLB
14, 40

Alvarez, Alejandro Rodriguez 1903-1965
See Casona, Alejandro
See also CA 131; 93-96; HW 1

Alvarez, Julia 1950- .... CLC 93; HLCS 1
See also AAYA 25; CA 147; CANR 69;
DA3; MTCW 1

Alvaro, Corrado 1896-1956 .... TCLC 60
See also CA 163

Amado, Jorge 1912- .... CLC 13, 40, 106;
DAM MULT, NOV; HLC 1
See also CA 77-80; CANR 35, 74; DLB
113; HW 2; MTCW 1, 2

Ambler, Eric 1909-1998 .... CLC 4, 6, 9
See also CA 9-12R; 171; CANR 7, 38, 74;
DLB 77; MTCW 1, 2

Amichai, Yehuda 1924- ... CLC 9, 22, 57, 116
See also CA 85-88; CANR 46, 60; MTCW
1

Amichai, Yehudah
See Amichai, Yehuda

Amiel, Henri Frederic 1821-1881 .... NCLC 4

Amis, Kingsley (William)
1922-1995 ...... CLC 1, 2, 3, 5, 8, 13, 40,
44, 129; DA; DAB; DAC; DAM MST,
NOV
See also AITN 2; CA 9-12R; 150; CANR 8,
28, 54; CDBLB 1945-1960; DA3; DLB
15, 27, 100, 139; DLBY 96; INT
CANR-8; MTCW 1, 2

Amis, Martin (Louis) 1949- .... CLC 4, 9, 38,
62, 101
See also BEST 90:3; CA 65-68; CANR 8,
27, 54, 73; DA3; DLB 14, 194; INT
CANR-27; MTCW 1

Ammons, A(rchie) R(andolph)
1926- ... CLC 2, 3, 5, 8, 9, 25, 57, 108;
DAM POET; PC 16
See also AITN 1; CA 9-12R; CANR 6, 36,
51, 73; DLB 5, 165; MTCW 1, 2

Amo, Tauraatua i
See Adams, Henry (Brooks)

Amory, Thomas 1691(?)-1788 .... LC 48

Anand, Mulk Raj 1905- .. CLC 23, 93; DAM
NOV
See also CA 65-68; CANR 32, 64; MTCW
1, 2

Anatol
See Schnitzler, Arthur

Anaximander c. 610B.C.-c.
546B.C. .... CMLC 22

Anaya, Rudolfo A(lfonso) 1937- ...... CLC 23;
DAM MULT, NOV; HLC 1
See also AAYA 20; CA 45-48; CAAS 4;
CANR 1, 32, 51; DLB 82, 206; HW 1;
MTCW 1, 2

Andersen, Hans Christian
1805-1875 .... NCLC 7, 79; DA; DAB;
DAC; DAM MST, POP; SSC 6; WLC
See also CLR 6; DA3; MAICYA; SATA
100; YABC 1

Anderson, C. Farley
   See Mencken, H(enry) L(ouis); Nathan, George Jean

Anderson, Jessica (Margaret) Queale
   1916- .... **CLC 37**
   See also CA 9-12R; CANR 4, 62

Anderson, Jon (Victor) 1940- . **CLC 9; DAM POET**
   See also CA 25-28R; CANR 20

Anderson, Lindsay (Gordon)
   1923-1994 .... **CLC 20**
   See also CA 125; 128; 146; CANR 77

Anderson, Maxwell 1888-1959 .... **TCLC 2; DAM DRAM**
   See also CA 105; 152; DLB 7, 228; MTCW 2

Anderson, Poul (William) 1926- .... **CLC 15**
   See also AAYA 5, 34; CA 1-4R; CAAE 181; CAAS 2; CANR 2, 15, 34, 64; CLR 58; DLB 8; INT CANR-15; MTCW 1, 2; SATA 90; SATA-Brief 39; SATA-Essay 106

Anderson, Robert (Woodruff)
   1917- .... **CLC 23; DAM DRAM**
   See also AITN 1; CA 21-24R; CANR 32; DLB 7

Anderson, Sherwood 1876-1941 ..... **TCLC 1, 10, 24; DA; DAB; DAC; DAM MST, NOV; SSC 1; WLC**
   See also AAYA 30; CA 104; 121; CANR 61; CDALB 1917-1929; DA3; DLB 4, 9, 86; DLBD 1; MTCW 1, 2

Andier, Pierre
   See Desnos, Robert

Andouard
   See Giraudoux, (Hippolyte) Jean

Andrade, Carlos Drummond de CLC 18
   See also Drummond de Andrade, Carlos

Andrade, Mario de 1893-1945 .... **TCLC 43**

Andreae, Johann V(alentin)
   1586-1654 .... **LC 32**
   See also DLB 164

Andreas-Salome, Lou 1861-1937 ... **TCLC 56**
   See also CA 178; DLB 66

Andress, Lesley
   See Sanders, Lawrence

Andrewes, Lancelot 1555-1626 .... **LC 5**
   See also DLB 151, 172

Andrews, Cicily Fairfield
   See West, Rebecca

Andrews, Elton V.
   See Pohl, Frederik

Andreyev, Leonid (Nikolaevich)
   1871-1919 .... **TCLC 3**
   See also CA 104; 185

Andric, Ivo 1892-1975 .... **CLC 8; SSC 36**
   See also CA 81-84; 57-60; CANR 43, 60; DLB 147; MTCW 1

Androvar
   See Prado (Calvo), Pedro

Angelique, Pierre
   See Bataille, Georges

Angell, Roger 1920- .... **CLC 26**
   See also CA 57-60; CANR 13, 44, 70; DLB 171, 185

Angelou, Maya 1928- .... **CLC 12, 35, 64, 77; BLC 1; DA; DAB; DAC; DAM MST, MULT, POET, POP; WLCS**
   See also AAYA 7, 20; BW 2, 3; CA 65-68; CANR 19, 42, 65; CDALBS; CLR 53; DA3; DLB 38; MTCW 1, 2; SATA 49

Anna Comnena 1083-1153 .... **CMLC 25**

Annensky, Innokenty (Fyodorovich)
   1856-1909 .... **TCLC 14**
   See also CA 110; 155

Annunzio, Gabriele d'
   See D'Annunzio, Gabriele

Anodos
   See Coleridge, Mary E(lizabeth)

Anon, Charles Robert
   See Pessoa, Fernando (Antonio Nogueira)

Anouilh, Jean (Marie Lucien Pierre)
   1910-1987 .... **CLC 1, 3, 8, 13, 40, 50; DAM DRAM; DC 8**
   See also CA 17-20R; 123; CANR 32; MTCW 1, 2

Anthony, Florence
   See Ai

Anthony, John
   See Ciardi, John (Anthony)

Anthony, Peter
   See Shaffer, Anthony (Joshua); Shaffer, Peter (Levin)

Anthony, Piers 1934- .... **CLC 35; DAM POP**
   See also AAYA 11; CA 21-24R; CANR 28, 56, 73; DLB 8; MTCW 1, 2; SAAS 22; SATA 84

Anthony, Susan B(rownell)
   1916-1991 .... **TCLC 84**
   See also CA 89-92; 134

Antoine, Marc
   See Proust, (Valentin-Louis-George-Eugene-) Marcel

Antoninus, Brother
   See Everson, William (Oliver)

Antonioni, Michelangelo 1912- .... **CLC 20**
   See also CA 73-76; CANR 45, 77

Antschel, Paul 1920-1970
   See Celan, Paul
   See also CA 85-88; CANR 33, 61; MTCW 1

Anwar, Chairil 1922-1949 .... **TCLC 22**
   See also CA 121

Anzaldua, Gloria 1942-
   See also CA 175; DLB 122; HLCS 1

Apess, William 1798-1839(?) .... **NCLC 73; DAM MULT**
   See also DLB 175; NNAL

Apollinaire, Guillaume 1880-1918 .. **TCLC 3, 8, 51; DAM POET; PC 7**
   See also Kostrowitzki, Wilhelm Apollinaris de
   See also CA 152; MTCW 1

Appelfeld, Aharon 1932- .... **CLC 23, 47**
   See also CA 112; 133; CANR 86

Apple, Max (Isaac) 1941- .... **CLC 9, 33**
   See also CA 81-84; CANR 19, 54; DLB 130

Appleman, Philip (Dean) 1926- .... **CLC 51**
   See also CA 13-16R; CAAS 18; CANR 6, 29, 56

Appleton, Lawrence
   See Lovecraft, H(oward) P(hillips)

Apteryx
   See Eliot, T(homas) S(tearns)

Apuleius, (Lucius Madaurensis)
   125(?)-175(?) .... **CMLC 1**
   See also DLB 211

Aquin, Hubert 1929-1977 .... **CLC 15**
   See also CA 105; DLB 53

Aquinas, Thomas 1224(?)-1274 ..... **CMLC 33**
   See also DLB 115

Aragon, Louis 1897-1982 .. **CLC 3, 22; DAM NOV, POET**
   See also CA 69-72; 108; CANR 28, 71; DLB 72; MTCW 1, 2

Arany, Janos 1817-1882 .... **NCLC 34**

Aranyos, Kakay
   See Mikszath, Kalman

Arbuthnot, John 1667-1735 .... **LC 1**
   See also DLB 101

Archer, Herbert Winslow
   See Mencken, H(enry) L(ouis)

Archer, Jeffrey (Howard) 1940- ...... **CLC 28; DAM POP**
   See also AAYA 16; BEST 89:3; CA 77-80; CANR 22, 52; DA3; INT CANR-22

Archer, Jules 1915- .... **CLC 12**
   See also CA 9-12R; CANR 6, 69; SAAS 5; SATA 4, 85

Archer, Lee
   See Ellison, Harlan (Jay)

Arden, John 1930- .... **CLC 6, 13, 15; DAM DRAM**
   See also CA 13-16R; CAAS 4; CANR 31, 65, 67; DLB 13; MTCW 1

Arenas, Reinaldo 1943-1990 . **CLC 41; DAM MULT; HLC 1**
   See also CA 124; 128; 133; CANR 73; DLB 145; HW 1; MTCW 1

Arendt, Hannah 1906-1975 .... **CLC 66, 98**
   See also CA 17-20R; 61-64; CANR 26, 60; MTCW 1, 2

Aretino, Pietro 1492-1556 .... **LC 12**

Arghezi, Tudor 1880-1967 .... **CLC 80**
   See also Theodorescu, Ion N.
   See also CA 167

Arguedas, Jose Maria 1911-1969 .... **CLC 10, 18; HLCS 1**
   See also CA 89-92; CANR 73; DLB 113; HW 1

Argueta, Manlio 1936- .... **CLC 31**
   See also CA 131; CANR 73; DLB 145; HW 1

Arias, Ron(ald Francis) 1941-
   See also CA 131; CANR 81; DAM MULT; DLB 82; HLC 1; HW 1, 2; MTCW 2

Ariosto, Ludovico 1474-1533 .... **LC 6**

Aristides
   See Epstein, Joseph

Aristophanes 450B.C.-385B.C. .... **CMLC 4; DA; DAB; DAC; DAM DRAM, MST; DC 2; WLCS**
   See also DA3; DLB 176

Aristotle 384B.C.-322B.C. .... **CMLC 31; DA; DAB; DAC; DAM MST; WLCS**
   See also DA3; DLB 176

Arlt, Roberto (Godofredo Christophersen)
   1900-1942 .... **TCLC 29; DAM MULT; HLC 1**
   See also CA 123; 131; CANR 67; HW 1, 2

Armah, Ayi Kwei 1939- . **CLC 5, 33; BLC 1; DAM MULT, POET**
   See also BW 1; CA 61-64; CANR 21, 64; DLB 117; MTCW 1

Armatrading, Joan 1950- .... **CLC 17**
   See also CA 114; 186

Arnette, Robert
   See Silverberg, Robert

Arnim, Achim von (Ludwig Joachim von Arnim) 1781-1831 ..... **NCLC 5; SSC 29**
   See also DLB 90

Arnim, Bettina von 1785-1859 .... **NCLC 38**
   See also DLB 90

Arnold, Matthew 1822-1888 ..... **NCLC 6, 29, 89; DA; DAB; DAC; DAM MST, POET; PC 5; WLC**
   See also CDBLB 1832-1890; DLB 32, 57

Arnold, Thomas 1795-1842 .... **NCLC 18**
   See also DLB 55

Arnow, Harriette (Louisa) Simpson
   1908-1986 .... **CLC 2, 7, 18**
   See also CA 9-12R; 118; CANR 14; DLB 6; MTCW 1, 2; SATA 42; SATA-Obit 47

Arouet, Francois-Marie
   See Voltaire

Arp, Hans
   See Arp, Jean

Arp, Jean 1887-1966 .... **CLC 5**
   See also CA 81-84; 25-28R; CANR 42, 77

Arrabal
   See Arrabal, Fernando

Arrabal, Fernando 1932- ... **CLC 2, 9, 18, 58**
   See also CA 9-12R; CANR 15

Arreola, Juan Jose 1918- .... **SSC 38; DAM MULT; HLC 1**
See also CA 113; 131; CANR 81; DLB 113; HW 1, 2

Arrick, Fran CLC 30
See also Gaberman, Judie Angell

Artaud, Antonin (Marie Joseph)
1896-1948 .. **TCLC 3, 36; DAM DRAM**
See also CA 104; 149; DA3; MTCW 1

Arthur, Ruth M(abel) 1905-1979 ..... **CLC 12**
See also CA 9-12R; 85-88; CANR 4; SATA 7, 26

Artsybashev, Mikhail (Petrovich)
1878-1927 .... **TCLC 31**
See also CA 170

Arundel, Honor (Morfydd)
1919-1973 .... **CLC 17**
See also CA 21-22; 41-44R; CAP 2; CLR 35; SATA 4; SATA-Obit 24

Arzner, Dorothy 1897-1979 .... **CLC 98**

Asch, Sholem 1880-1957 .... **TCLC 3**
See also CA 105

Ash, Shalom
See Asch, Sholem

Ashbery, John (Lawrence) 1927- .. **CLC 2, 3, 4, 6, 9, 13, 15, 25, 41, 77, 125; DAM POET; PC 26**
See also CA 5-8R; CANR 9, 37, 66; DA3; DLB 5, 165; DLBY 81; INT CANR-9; MTCW 1, 2

Ashdown, Clifford
See Freeman, R(ichard) Austin

Ashe, Gordon
See Creasey, John

Ashton-Warner, Sylvia (Constance)
1908-1984 .... **CLC 19**
See also CA 69-72; 112; CANR 29; MTCW 1, 2

Asimov, Isaac 1920-1992 ..... **CLC 1, 3, 9, 19, 26, 76, 92; DAM POP**
See also AAYA 13; BEST 90:2; CA 1-4R; 137; CANR 2, 19, 36, 60; CLR 12; DA3; DLB 8; DLBY 92; INT CANR-19; JRDA; MAICYA; MTCW 1, 2; SATA 1, 26, 74

Assis, Joaquim Maria Machado de
See Machado de Assis, Joaquim Maria

Astley, Thea (Beatrice May) 1925- .. **CLC 41**
See also CA 65-68; CANR 11, 43, 78

Aston, James
See White, T(erence) H(anbury)

Asturias, Miguel Angel 1899-1974 .... **CLC 3, 8, 13; DAM MULT, NOV; HLC 1**
See also CA 25-28; 49-52; CANR 32; CAP 2; DA3; DLB 113; HW 1; MTCW 1, 2

Atares, Carlos Saura
See Saura (Atares), Carlos

Atheling, William
See Pound, Ezra (Weston Loomis)

Atheling, William, Jr.
See Blish, James (Benjamin)

Atherton, Gertrude (Franklin Horn)
1857-1948 .... **TCLC 2**
See also CA 104; 155; DLB 9, 78, 186

Atherton, Lucius
See Masters, Edgar Lee

Atkins, Jack
See Harris, Mark

Atkinson, Kate CLC 99
See also CA 166

Attaway, William (Alexander)
1911-1986 .... **CLC 92; BLC 1; DAM MULT**
See also BW 2, 3; CA 143; CANR 82; DLB 76

Atticus
See Fleming, Ian (Lancaster); Wilson, (Thomas) Woodrow

Atwood, Margaret (Eleanor) 1939- ... **CLC 2, 3, 4, 8, 13, 15, 25, 44, 84; DA; DAB; DAC; DAM MST, NOV, POET; PC 8; SSC 2; WLC**
See also AAYA 12; BEST 89:2; CA 49-52; CANR 3, 24, 33, 59; DA3; DLB 53; INT CANR-24; MTCW 1, 2; SATA 50

Aubigny, Pierre d'
See Mencken, H(enry) L(ouis)

Aubin, Penelope 1685-1731(?) .... **LC 9**
See also DLB 39

Auchincloss, Louis (Stanton) 1917- .. **CLC 4, 6, 9, 18, 45; DAM NOV; SSC 22**
See also CA 1-4R; CANR 6, 29, 55, 87; DLB 2; DLBY 80; INT CANR-29; MTCW 1

Auden, W(ystan) H(ugh) 1907-1973 . **CLC 1, 2, 3, 4, 6, 9, 11, 14, 43; DA; DAB; DAC; DAM DRAM, MST, POET; PC 1; WLC**
See also AAYA 18; CA 9-12R; 45-48; CANR 5, 61; CDBLB 1914-1945; DA3; DLB 10, 20; MTCW 1, 2

Audiberti, Jacques 1900-1965 .... **CLC 38; DAM DRAM**
See also CA 25-28R

Audubon, John James 1785-1851 . **NCLC 47**

Auel, Jean M(arie) 1936- .... **CLC 31, 107; DAM POP**
See also AAYA 7; BEST 90:4; CA 103; CANR 21, 64; DA3; INT CANR-21; SATA 91

Auerbach, Erich 1892-1957 .... **TCLC 43**
See also CA 118; 155

Augier, Emile 1820-1889 .... **NCLC 31**
See also DLB 192

August, John
See De Voto, Bernard (Augustine)

Augustine 354-430 .... **CMLC 6; DA; DAB; DAC; DAM MST; WLCS**
See also DA3; DLB 115

Aurelius
See Bourne, Randolph S(illiman)

Aurobindo, Sri
See Ghose, Aurabinda

Austen, Jane 1775-1817 ...... **NCLC 1, 13, 19, 33, 51, 81; DA; DAB; DAC; DAM MST, NOV; WLC**
See also AAYA 19; CDBLB 1789-1832; DA3; DLB 116

Auster, Paul 1947- .... **CLC 47, 131**
See also CA 69-72; CANR 23, 52, 75; DA3; DLB 227; MTCW 1

Austin, Frank
See Faust, Frederick (Schiller)

Austin, Mary (Hunter) 1868-1934 . **TCLC 25**
See also CA 109; 178; DLB 9, 78, 206, 221

Averroes 1126-1198 .... **CMLC 7**
See also DLB 115

Avicenna 980-1037 .... **CMLC 16**
See also DLB 115

Avison, Margaret 1918- .... **CLC 2, 4, 97; DAC; DAM POET**
See also CA 17-20R; DLB 53; MTCW 1

Axton, David
See Koontz, Dean R(ay)

Ayckbourn, Alan 1939- ...... **CLC 5, 8, 18, 33, 74; DAB; DAM DRAM; DC 13**
See also CA 21-24R; CANR 31, 59; DLB 13; MTCW 1, 2

Aydy, Catherine
See Tennant, Emma (Christina)

Ayme, Marcel (Andre) 1902-1967 ... **CLC 11; SSC 41**
See also CA 89-92; CANR 67; CLR 25; DLB 72; SATA 91

Ayrton, Michael 1921-1975 .... **CLC 7**
See also CA 5-8R; 61-64; CANR 9, 21

Azorin CLC 11
See also Martinez Ruiz, Jose

Azuela, Mariano 1873-1952 . **TCLC 3; DAM MULT; HLC 1**
See also CA 104; 131; CANR 81; HW 1, 2; MTCW 1, 2

Baastad, Babbis Friis
See Friis-Baastad, Babbis Ellinor

Bab
See Gilbert, W(illiam) S(chwenck)

Babbis, Eleanor
See Friis-Baastad, Babbis Ellinor

Babel, Isaac
See Babel, Isaak (Emmanuilovich)

Babel, Isaak (Emmanuilovich)
1894-1941(?) .... **TCLC 2, 13; SSC 16**
See also CA 104; 155; MTCW 1

Babits, Mihaly 1883-1941 .... **TCLC 14**
See also CA 114

Babur 1483-1530 .... **LC 18**

Baca, Jimmy Santiago 1952-
See also CA 131; CANR 81, 90; DAM MULT; DLB 122; HLC 1; HW 1, 2

Bacchelli, Riccardo 1891-1985 .... **CLC 19**
See also CA 29-32R; 117

Bach, Richard (David) 1936- .... **CLC 14; DAM NOV, POP**
See also AITN 1; BEST 89:2; CA 9-12R; CANR 18; MTCW 1; SATA 13

Bachman, Richard
See King, Stephen (Edwin)

Bachmann, Ingeborg 1926-1973 .... **CLC 69**
See also CA 93-96; 45-48; CANR 69; DLB 85

Bacon, Francis 1561-1626 .... **LC 18, 32**
See also CDBLB Before 1660; DLB 151

Bacon, Roger 1214(?)-1292 .... **CMLC 14**
See also DLB 115

Bacovia, George TCLC 24
See also Vasiliu, Gheorghe
See also DLB 220

Badanes, Jerome 1937- .... **CLC 59**

Bagehot, Walter 1826-1877 .... **NCLC 10**
See also DLB 55

Bagnold, Enid 1889-1981 ...... **CLC 25; DAM DRAM**
See also CA 5-8R; 103; CANR 5, 40; DLB 13, 160, 191; MAICYA; SATA 1, 25

Bagritsky, Eduard 1895-1934 .... **TCLC 60**

Bagrjana, Elisaveta
See Belcheva, Elisaveta

Bagryana, Elisaveta 1893-1991 .... **CLC 10**
See also Belcheva, Elisaveta
See also CA 178; DLB 147

Bailey, Paul 1937- .... **CLC 45**
See also CA 21-24R; CANR 16, 62; DLB 14

Baillie, Joanna 1762-1851 .... **NCLC 71**
See also DLB 93

Bainbridge, Beryl (Margaret) 1934- . **CLC 4, 5, 8, 10, 14, 18, 22, 62, 130; DAM NOV**
See also CA 21-24R; CANR 24, 55, 75, 88; DLB 14; MTCW 1, 2

Baker, Elliott 1922- .... **CLC 8**
See also CA 45-48; CANR 2, 63

Baker, Jean H. TCLC 3, 10
See also Russell, George William

Baker, Nicholson 1957- .... **CLC 61; DAM POP**
See also CA 135; CANR 63; DA3; DLB 227

Baker, Ray Stannard 1870-1946 .... **TCLC 47**
See also CA 118

Baker, Russell (Wayne) 1925- .... **CLC 31**
See also BEST 89:4; CA 57-60; CANR 11, 41, 59; MTCW 1, 2

Bakhtin, M.
See Bakhtin, Mikhail Mikhailovich
Bakhtin, M. M.
See Bakhtin, Mikhail Mikhailovich
Bakhtin, Mikhail
See Bakhtin, Mikhail Mikhailovich
Bakhtin, Mikhail Mikhailovich
1895-1975 .... **CLC 83**
See also CA 128; 113
Bakshi, Ralph 1938(?)- .... **CLC 26**
See also CA 112; 138
Bakunin, Mikhail (Alexandrovich)
1814-1876 .... **NCLC 25, 58**
Baldwin, James (Arthur) 1924-1987 . **CLC 1,**
2, 3, 4, 5, 8, 13, 15, 17, 42, 50, 67, 90,
127; BLC 1; DA; DAB; DAC; DAM
MST, MULT, NOV, POP; DC 1; SSC
10, 33; WLC
See also AAYA 4, 34; BW 1; CA 1-4R; 124;
CABS 1; CANR 3, 24; CDALB 1941-
1968; DA3; DLB 2, 7, 33; DLBY 87;
MTCW 1, 2; SATA 9; SATA-Obit 54
Ballard, J(ames) G(raham)
1930-1964 ...... **CLC 3, 6, 14, 36; DAM**
NOV, POP; SSC 1
See also AAYA 3; CA 5-8R; CANR 15, 39,
65; DA3; DLB 14, 207; MTCW 1, 2;
SATA 93
Balmont, Konstantin (Dmitriyevich)
1867-1943 .... **TCLC 11**
See also CA 109; 155
Baltausis, Vincas
See Mikszath, Kalman
Balzac, Honore de 1799-1850 ... **NCLC 5, 35,**
53; DA; DAB; DAC; DAM MST, NOV;
SSC 5; WLC
See also DA3; DLB 119
Bambara, Toni Cade 1939-1995 ...... **CLC 19,**
88; BLC 1; DA; DAC; DAM MST,
MULT; SSC 35; WLCS
See also AAYA 5; BW 2, 3; CA 29-32R;
150; CANR 24, 49, 81; CDALBS; DA3;
DLB 38; MTCW 1, 2; SATA 112
Bamdad, A.
See Shamlu, Ahmad
Banat, D. R.
See Bradbury, Ray (Douglas)
Bancroft, Laura
See Baum, L(yman) Frank
Banim, John 1798-1842 .... **NCLC 13**
See also DLB 116, 158, 159
Banim, Michael 1796-1874 .... **NCLC 13**
See also DLB 158, 159
Banjo, The
See Paterson, A(ndrew) B(arton)
Banks, Iain
See Banks, Iain M(enzies)
Banks, Iain M(enzies) 1954- .... **CLC 34**
See also CA 123; 128; CANR 61; DLB 194;
INT 128
Banks, Lynne Reid CLC 23
See also Reid Banks, Lynne
See also AAYA 6
Banks, Russell 1940- .... **CLC 37, 72**
See also CA 65-68; CAAS 15; CANR 19,
52, 73; DLB 130
Banville, John 1945- .... **CLC 46, 118**
See also CA 117; 128; DLB 14; INT 128
Banville, Theodore (Faullain) de
1832-1891 .... **NCLC 9**
Baraka, Amiri 1934- . **CLC 1, 2, 3, 5, 10, 14,**
33, 115; BLC 1; DA; DAC; DAM MST,
MULT, POET, POP; DC 6; PC 4;
WLCS
See also Jones, LeRoi
See also BW 2, 3; CA 21-24R; CABS 3;
CANR 27, 38, 61; CDALB 1941-1968;
DA3; DLB 5, 7, 16, 38; DLBD 8; MTCW
1, 2

Barbauld, Anna Laetitia
1743-1825 .... **NCLC 50**
See also DLB 107, 109, 142, 158
Barbellion, W. N. P. TCLC 24
See also Cummings, Bruce F(rederick)
Barbera, Jack (Vincent) 1945- .... **CLC 44**
See also CA 110; CANR 45
Barbey d'Aurevilly, Jules Amedee
1808-1889 .... **NCLC 1; SSC 17**
See also DLB 119
Barbour, John c. 1316-1395 .... **CMLC 33**
See also DLB 146
Barbusse, Henri 1873-1935 .... **TCLC 5**
See also CA 105; 154; DLB 65
Barclay, Bill
See Moorcock, Michael (John)
Barclay, William Ewert
See Moorcock, Michael (John)
Barea, Arturo 1897-1957 .... **TCLC 14**
See also CA 111
Barfoot, Joan 1946- .... **CLC 18**
See also CA 105
Barham, Richard Harris
1788-1845 .... **NCLC 77**
See also DLB 159
Baring, Maurice 1874-1945 .... **TCLC 8**
See also CA 105; 168; DLB 34
Baring-Gould, Sabine 1834-1924 ... **TCLC 88**
See also DLB 156, 190
Barker, Clive 1952- ...... **CLC 52; DAM POP**
See also AAYA 10; BEST 90:3; CA 121;
129; CANR 71; DA3; INT 129; MTCW
1, 2
Barker, George Granville
1913-1991 .... **CLC 8, 48; DAM POET**
See also CA 9-12R; 135; CANR 7, 38; DLB
20; MTCW 1
Barker, Harley Granville
See Granville-Barker, Harley
See also DLB 10
Barker, Howard 1946- .... **CLC 37**
See also CA 102; DLB 13
Barker, Jane 1652-1732 .... **LC 42**
Barker, Pat(ricia) 1943- .... **CLC 32, 94**
See also CA 117; 122; CANR 50; INT 122
Barlach, Ernst (Heinrich)
1870-1938 .... **TCLC 84**
See also CA 178; DLB 56, 118
Barlow, Joel 1754-1812 .... **NCLC 23**
See also DLB 37
Barnard, Mary (Ethel) 1909- .... **CLC 48**
See also CA 21-22; CAP 2
Barnes, Djuna 1892-1982 .... **CLC 3, 4, 8, 11,**
29, 127; SSC 3
See also CA 9-12R; 107; CANR 16, 55;
DLB 4, 9, 45; MTCW 1, 2
Barnes, Julian (Patrick) 1946- .... **CLC 42;**
DAB
See also CA 102; CANR 19, 54; DLB 194;
DLBY 93; MTCW 1
Barnes, Peter 1931- .... **CLC 5, 56**
See also CA 65-68; CAAS 12; CANR 33,
34, 64; DLB 13; MTCW 1
Barnes, William 1801-1886 .... **NCLC 75**
See also DLB 32
Baroja (y Nessi), Pio 1872-1956 ..... **TCLC 8;**
HLC 1
See also CA 104
Baron, David
See Pinter, Harold
Baron Corvo
See Rolfe, Frederick (William Serafino Aus-
tin Lewis Mary)
Barondess, Sue K(aufman)
1926-1977 .... **CLC 8**
See also Kaufman, Sue
See also CA 1-4R; 69-72; CANR 1

Baron de Teive
See Pessoa, Fernando (Antonio Nogueira)
Baroness Von S.
See Zangwill, Israel
Barres, (Auguste-) Maurice
1862-1923 .... **TCLC 47**
See also CA 164; DLB 123
Barreto, Afonso Henrique de Lima
See Lima Barreto, Afonso Henrique de
Barrett, (Roger) Syd 1946- .... **CLC 35**
Barrett, William (Christopher)
1913-1992 .... **CLC 27**
See also CA 13-16R; 139; CANR 11, 67;
INT CANR-11
Barrie, J(ames) M(atthew)
1860-1937 .... **TCLC 2; DAB; DAM**
DRAM
See also CA 104; 136; CANR 77; CDBLB
1890-1914; CLR 16; DA3; DLB 10, 141,
156; MAICYA; MTCW 1; SATA 100;
YABC 1
Barrington, Michael
See Moorcock, Michael (John)
Barrol, Grady
See Bograd, Larry
Barry, Mike
See Malzberg, Barry N(athaniel)
Barry, Philip 1896-1949 .... **TCLC 11**
See also CA 109; DLB 7, 228
Bart, Andre Schwarz
See Schwarz-Bart, Andre
Barth, John (Simmons) 1930- ... **CLC 1, 2, 3,**
5, 7, 9, 10, 14, 27, 51, 89; DAM NOV;
SSC 10
See also AITN 1, 2; CA 1-4R; CABS 1;
CANR 5, 23, 49, 64; DLB 2, 227; MTCW
1
Barthelme, Donald 1931-1989 ... **CLC 1, 2, 3;**
5, 6, 8, 13, 23, 46, 59, 115; DAM NOV;
SSC 2
See also CA 21-24R; 129; CANR 20, 58;
DA3; DLB 2; DLBY 80, 89; MTCW 1, 2;
SATA 7; SATA-Obit 62
Barthelme, Frederick 1943- ...... **CLC 36, 117**
See also CA 114; 122; CANR 77; DLBY
85; INT 122
Barthes, Roland (Gerard)
1915-1980 .... **CLC 24, 83**
See also CA 130; 97-100; CANR 66;
MTCW 1, 2
Barzun, Jacques (Martin) 1907- ...... **CLC 51**
See also CA 61-64; CANR 22
Bashevis, Isaac
See Singer, Isaac Bashevis
Bashkirtseff, Marie 1859-1884 .... **NCLC 27**
Basho
See Matsuo Basho
Basil of Caesaria c. 330-379 .... **CMLC 35**
Bass, Kingsley B., Jr.
See Bullins, Ed
Bass, Rick 1958- .... **CLC 79**
See also CA 126; CANR 53; DLB 212
Bassani, Giorgio 1916- .... **CLC 9**
See also CA 65-68; CANR 33; DLB 128,
177; MTCW 1
Bastos, Augusto (Antonio) Roa
See Roa Bastos, Augusto (Antonio)
Bataille, Georges 1897-1962 .... **CLC 29**
See also CA 101; 89-92
Bates, H(erbert) E(rnest)
1905-1974 . **CLC 46; DAB; DAM POP;**
SSC 10
See also CA 93-96; 45-48; CANR 34; DA3;
DLB 162, 191; MTCW 1, 2
Bauchart
See Camus, Albert

Baudelaire, Charles 1821-1867 . NCLC 6, 29, 55; DA; DAB; DAC; DAM MST, POET; PC 1; SSC 18; WLC
See also DA3

Baudrillard, Jean 1929- .... CLC 60

Baum, L(yman) Frank 1856-1919 ... TCLC 7
See also CA 108; 133; CLR 15; DLB 22; JRDA; MAICYA; MTCW 1, 2; SATA 18, 100

Baum, Louis F.
See Baum, L(yman) Frank

Baumbach, Jonathan 1933- .... CLC 6, 23
See also CA 13-16R; CAAS 5; CANR 12, 66; DLBY 80; INT CANR-12; MTCW 1

Bausch, Richard (Carl) 1945- .... CLC 51
See also CA 101; CAAS 14; CANR 43, 61, 87; DLB 130

Baxter, Charles (Morley) 1947- ...... CLC 45, 78; DAM POP
See also CA 57-60; CANR 40, 64; DLB 130; MTCW 2

Baxter, George Owen
See Faust, Frederick (Schiller)

Baxter, James K(eir) 1926-1972 .... CLC 14
See also CA 77-80

Baxter, John
See Hunt, E(verette) Howard, (Jr.)

Bayer, Sylvia
See Glassco, John

Baynton, Barbara 1857-1929 .... TCLC 57

Beagle, Peter S(oyer) 1939- .... CLC 7, 104
See also CA 9-12R; CANR 4, 51, 73; DA3; DLBY 80; INT CANR-4; MTCW 1; SATA 60

Bean, Normal
See Burroughs, Edgar Rice

Beard, Charles A(ustin)
1874-1948 .... TCLC 15
See also CA 115; DLB 17; SATA 18

Beardsley, Aubrey 1872-1898 .... NCLC 6

Beattie, Ann 1947- ..... CLC 8, 13, 18, 40, 63; DAM NOV, POP; SSC 11
See also BEST 90:2; CA 81-84; CANR 53, 73; DA3; DLBY 82; MTCW 1, 2

Beattie, James 1735-1803 .... NCLC 25
See also DLB 109

Beauchamp, Kathleen Mansfield 1888-1923
See Mansfield, Katherine
See also CA 104; 134; DA; DAC; DAM MST; DA3; MTCW 2

Beaumarchais, Pierre-Augustin Caron de
1732-1799 .... DC 4
See also DAM DRAM

Beaumont, Francis 1584(?)-1616 .... LC 33; DC 6
See also CDBLB Before 1660; DLB 58, 121

Beauvoir, Simone (Lucie Ernestine Marie Bertrand) de 1908-1986 .... CLC 1, 2, 4, 8, 14, 31, 44, 50, 71, 124; DA; DAB; DAC; DAM MST, NOV; SSC 35; WLC
See also CA 9-12R; 118; CANR 28, 61; DA3; DLB 72; DLBY 86; MTCW 1, 2

Becker, Carl (Lotus) 1873-1945 ..... TCLC 63
See also CA 157; DLB 17

Becker, Jurek 1937-1997 .... CLC 7, 19
See also CA 85-88; 157; CANR 60; DLB 75

Becker, Walter 1950- .... CLC 26

Beckett, Samuel (Barclay)
1906-1989 .. CLC 1, 2, 3, 4, 6, 9, 10, 11, 14, 18, 29, 57, 59, 83; DA; DAB; DAC; DAM DRAM, MST, NOV; SSC 16; WLC
See also CA 5-8R; 130; CANR 33, 61; CD-BLB 1945-1960; DA3; DLB 13, 15; DLBY 90; MTCW 1, 2

Beckford, William 1760-1844 .... NCLC 16
See also DLB 39

Beckman, Gunnel 1910- .... CLC 26
See also CA 33-36R; CANR 15; CLR 25; MAICYA; SAAS 9; SATA 6

Becque, Henri 1837-1899 .... NCLC 3
See also DLB 192

Becquer, Gustavo Adolfo 1836-1870
See also DAM MULT; HLCS 1

Beddoes, Thomas Lovell
1803-1849 .... NCLC 3
See also DLB 96

Bede c. 673-735 .... CMLC 20
See also DLB 146

Bedford, Donald F.
See Fearing, Kenneth (Flexner)

Beecher, Catharine Esther
1800-1878 .... NCLC 30
See also DLB 1

Beecher, John 1904-1980 .... CLC 6
See also AITN 1; CA 5-8R; 105; CANR 8

Beer, Johann 1655-1700 .... LC 5
See also DLB 168

Beer, Patricia 1924- .... CLC 58
See also CA 61-64; 183; CANR 13, 46; DLB 40

Beerbohm, Max -1956
See Beerbohm, (Henry) Max(imilian)

Beerbohm, (Henry) Max(imilian)
1872-1956 .... TCLC 1, 24
See also CA 104; 154; CANR 79; DLB 34, 100

Beer-Hofmann, Richard
1866-1945 .... TCLC 60
See also CA 160; DLB 81

Begiebing, Robert J(ohn) 1946- .... CLC 70
See also CA 122; CANR 40, 88

Behan, Brendan 1923-1964 ...... CLC 1, 8, 11, 15, 79; DAM DRAM
See also CA 73-76; CANR 33; CDBLB 1945-1960; DLB 13; MTCW 1, 2

Behn, Aphra 1640(?)-1689 ...... LC 1, 30, 42; DA; DAB; DAC; DAM DRAM, MST, NOV, POET; DC 4; PC 13; WLC
See also DA3; DLB 39, 80, 131

Behrman, S(amuel) N(athaniel)
1893-1973 .... CLC 40
See also CA 13-16; 45-48; CAP 1; DLB 7, 44

Belasco, David 1853-1931 .... TCLC 3
See also CA 104; 168; DLB 7

Belcheva, Elisaveta 1893- .... CLC 10
See also Bagryana, Elisaveta

Beldone, Phil "Cheech"
See Ellison, Harlan (Jay)

Beleno
See Azuela, Mariano

Belinski, Vissarion Grigoryevich
1811-1848 .... NCLC 5
See also DLB 198

Belitt, Ben 1911- .... CLC 22
See also CA 13-16R; CAAS 4; CANR 7, 77; DLB 5

Bell, Gertrude (Margaret Lowthian)
1868-1926 .... TCLC 67
See also CA 167; DLB 174

Bell, J. Freeman
See Zangwill, Israel

Bell, James Madison 1826-1902 ... TCLC 43; BLC 1; DAM MULT
See also BW 1; CA 122; 124; DLB 50

Bell, Madison Smartt 1957- ...... CLC 41, 102
See also CA 111; 183; CAAE 183; CANR 28, 54, 73; MTCW 1

Bell, Marvin (Hartley) 1937- ...... CLC 8, 31; DAM POET
See also CA 21-24R; CAAS 14; CANR 59; DLB 5; MTCW 1

Bell, W. L. D.
See Mencken, H(enry) L(ouis)

Bellamy, Atwood C.
See Mencken, H(enry) L(ouis)

Bellamy, Edward 1850-1898 ...... NCLC 4, 86
See also DLB 12

Belli, Gioconda 1949-
See also CA 152; HLCS 1

Bellin, Edward J.
See Kuttner, Henry

Belloc, (Joseph) Hilaire (Pierre Sebastien Rene Swanton) 1870-1953 ...... TCLC 7, 18; DAM POET; PC 24
See also CA 106; 152; DLB 19, 100, 141, 174; MTCW 1; SATA 112; YABC 1

Belloc, Joseph Peter Rene Hilaire
See Belloc, (Joseph) Hilaire (Pierre Sebastien Rene Swanton)

Belloc, Joseph Pierre Hilaire
See Belloc, (Joseph) Hilaire (Pierre Sebastien Rene Swanton)

Belloc, M. A.
See Lowndes, Marie Adelaide (Belloc)

Bellow, Saul 1915- . CLC 1, 2, 3, 6, 8, 10, 13, 15, 25, 33, 34, 63, 79; DA; DAB; DAC; DAM MST, NOV, POP; SSC 14; WLC
See also AITN 2; BEST 89:3; CA 5-8R; CABS 1; CANR 29, 53; CDALB 1941-1968; DA3; DLB 2, 28; DLBD 3; DLBY 82; MTCW 1, 2

Belser, Reimond Karel Maria de 1929-
See Ruyslinck, Ward
See also CA 152

Bely, Andrey TCLC 7; PC 11
See also Bugayev, Boris Nikolayevich
See also MTCW 1

Belyi, Andrei
See Bugayev, Boris Nikolayevich

Benary, Margot
See Benary-Isbert, Margot

Benary-Isbert, Margot 1889-1979 .... CLC 12
See also CA 5-8R; 89-92; CANR 4, 72; CLR 12; MAICYA; SATA 2; SATA-Obit 21

Benavente (y Martinez), Jacinto
1866-1954 .... TCLC 3; DAM DRAM, MULT; HLCS 1
See also CA 106; 131; CANR 81; HW 1, 2; MTCW 1, 2

Benchley, Peter (Bradford) 1940- . CLC 4, 8; DAM NOV, POP
See also AAYA 14; AITN 2; CA 17-20R; CANR 12, 35, 66; MTCW 1, 2; SATA 3, 89

Benchley, Robert (Charles)
1889-1945 .... TCLC 1, 55
See also CA 105; 153; DLB 11

Benda, Julien 1867-1956 .... TCLC 60
See also CA 120; 154

Benedict, Ruth (Fulton)
1887-1948 .... TCLC 60
See also CA 158

Benedict, Saint c. 480-c. 547 .... CMLC 29

Benedikt, Michael 1935- .... CLC 4, 14
See also CA 13-16R; CANR 7; DLB 5

Benet, Juan 1927- .... CLC 28
See also CA 143

Benet, Stephen Vincent 1898-1943 . TCLC 7; DAM POET; SSC 10
See also CA 104; 152; DA3; DLB 4, 48, 102; DLBY 97; MTCW 1; YABC 1

Benet, William Rose 1886-1950 .... TCLC 28; DAM POET
See also CA 118; 152; DLB 45

Benford, Gregory (Albert) 1941- ..... CLC 52
See also CA 69-72; 175; CAAE 175; CAAS 27; CANR 12, 24, 49; DLBY 82

Bengtsson, Frans (Gunnar)
1894-1954 .... TCLC 48
See also CA 170

Benjamin, David
See Slavitt, David R(ytman)
Benjamin, Lois
See Gould, Lois
Benjamin, Walter 1892-1940 .... **TCLC 39**
See also CA 164
Benn, Gottfried 1886-1956 .... **TCLC 3**
See also CA 106; 153; DLB 56
Bennett, Alan 1934- .... **CLC 45, 77; DAB; DAM MST**
See also CA 103; CANR 35, 55; MTCW 1, 2
Bennett, (Enoch) Arnold
1867-1931 .... **TCLC 5, 20**
See also CA 106; 155; CDBLB 1890-1914; DLB 10, 34, 98, 135; MTCW 2
Bennett, Elizabeth
See Mitchell, Margaret (Munnerlyn)
Bennett, George Harold 1930-
See Bennett, Hal
See also BW 1; CA 97-100; CANR 87
Bennett, Hal CLC 5
See also Bennett, George Harold
See also DLB 33
Bennett, Jay 1912- .... **CLC 35**
See also AAYA 10; CA 69-72; CANR 11, 42, 79; JRDA; SAAS 4; SATA 41, 87; SATA-Brief 27
Bennett, Louise (Simone) 1919- ...... **CLC 28; BLC 1; DAM MULT**
See also BW 2, 3; CA 151; DLB 117
Benson, E(dward) F(rederic)
1867-1940 .... **TCLC 27**
See also CA 114; 157; DLB 135, 153
Benson, Jackson J. 1930- .... **CLC 34**
See also CA 25-28R; DLB 111
Benson, Sally 1900-1972 .... **CLC 17**
See also CA 19-20; 37-40R; CAP 1; SATA 1, 35; SATA-Obit 27
Benson, Stella 1892-1933 .... **TCLC 17**
See also CA 117; 155; DLB 36, 162
Bentham, Jeremy 1748-1832 .... **NCLC 38**
See also DLB 107, 158
Bentley, E(dmund) C(lerihew)
1875-1956 .... **TCLC 12**
See also CA 108; DLB 70
Bentley, Eric (Russell) 1916- .... **CLC 24**
See also CA 5-8R; CANR 6, 67; INT CANR-6
Beranger, Pierre Jean de
1780-1857 .... **NCLC 34**
Berdyaev, Nicolas
See Berdyaev, Nikolai (Aleksandrovich)
Berdyaev, Nikolai (Aleksandrovich)
1874-1948 .... **TCLC 67**
See also CA 120; 157
Berdyayev, Nikolai (Aleksandrovich)
See Berdyaev, Nikolai (Aleksandrovich)
Berendt, John (Lawrence) 1939- ...... **CLC 86**
See also CA 146; CANR 75; DA3; MTCW 1
Beresford, J(ohn) D(avys)
1873-1947 .... **TCLC 81**
See also CA 112; 155; DLB 162, 178, 197
Bergelson, David 1884-1952 .... **TCLC 81**
Berger, Colonel
See Malraux, (Georges-)Andre
Berger, John (Peter) 1926- .... **CLC 2, 19**
See also CA 81-84; CANR 51, 78; DLB 14, 207
Berger, Melvin H. 1927- .... **CLC 12**
See also CA 5-8R; CANR 4; CLR 32; SAAS 2; SATA 5, 88
Berger, Thomas (Louis) 1924- .. **CLC 3, 5, 8, 11, 18, 38; DAM NOV**
See also CA 1-4R; CANR 5, 28, 51; DLB 2; DLBY 80; INT CANR-28; MTCW 1, 2

Bergman, (Ernst) Ingmar 1918- ...... **CLC 16, 72**
See also CA 81-84; CANR 33, 70; MTCW 2
Bergson, Henri(-Louis) 1859-1941 . **TCLC 32**
See also CA 164
Bergstein, Eleanor 1938- .... **CLC 4**
See also CA 53-56; CANR 5
Berkoff, Steven 1937- .... **CLC 56**
See also CA 104; CANR 72
Bermant, Chaim (Icyk) 1929- .... **CLC 40**
See also CA 57-60; CANR 6, 31, 57
Bern, Victoria
See Fisher, M(ary) F(rances) K(ennedy)
Bernanos, (Paul Louis) Georges
1888-1948 .... **TCLC 3**
See also CA 104; 130; DLB 72
Bernard, April 1956- .... **CLC 59**
See also CA 131
Berne, Victoria
See Fisher, M(ary) F(rances) K(ennedy)
Bernhard, Thomas 1931-1989 ..... **CLC 3, 32, 61**
See also CA 85-88; 127; CANR 32, 57; DLB 85, 124; MTCW 1
Bernhardt, Sarah (Henriette Rosine)
1844-1923 .... **TCLC 75**
See also CA 157
Berriault, Gina 1926-1999 .... **CLC 54, 109; SSC 30**
See also CA 116; 129; 185; CANR 66; DLB 130
Berrigan, Daniel 1921- .... **CLC 4**
See also CA 33-36R; CAAS 1; CANR 11, 43, 78; DLB 5
Berrigan, Edmund Joseph Michael, Jr.
1934-1983
See Berrigan, Ted
See also CA 61-64; 110; CANR 14
Berrigan, Ted CLC 37
See also Berrigan, Edmund Joseph Michael, Jr.
See also DLB 5, 169
Berry, Charles Edward Anderson 1931-
See Berry, Chuck
See also CA 115
Berry, Chuck CLC 17
See also Berry, Charles Edward Anderson
Berry, Jonas
See Ashbery, John (Lawrence)
Berry, Wendell (Erdman) 1934- ... **CLC 4, 6, 8, 27, 46; DAM POET; PC 28**
See also AITN 1; CA 73-76; CANR 50, 73; DLB 5, 6; MTCW 1
Berryman, John 1914-1972 ... **CLC 1, 2, 3, 4, 6, 8, 10, 13, 25, 62; DAM POET**
See also CA 13-16; 33-36R; CABS 2; CANR 35; CAP 1; CDALB 1941-1968; DLB 48; MTCW 1, 2
Bertolucci, Bernardo 1940- .... **CLC 16**
See also CA 106
Berton, Pierre (Francis Demarigny)
1920- .... **CLC 104**
See also CA 1-4R; CANR 2, 56; DLB 68; SATA 99
Bertrand, Aloysius 1807-1841 .... **NCLC 31**
Bertran de Born c. 1140-1215 .... **CMLC 5**
Besant, Annie (Wood) 1847-1933 ..... **TCLC 9**
See also CA 105; 185
Bessie, Alvah 1904-1985 .... **CLC 23**
See also CA 5-8R; 116; CANR 2, 80; DLB 26
Bethlen, T. D.
See Silverberg, Robert
Beti, Mongo CLC 27; BLC 1; DAM MULT
See also Biyidi, Alexandre
See also CANR 79

Betjeman, John 1906-1984 ...... **CLC 2, 6, 10, 34, 43; DAB; DAM MST, POET**
See also CA 9-12R; 112; CANR 33, 56; CDBLB 1945-1960; DA3; DLB 20; DLBY 84; MTCW 1, 2
Bettelheim, Bruno 1903-1990 .... **CLC 79**
See also CA 81-84; 131; CANR 23, 61; DA3; MTCW 1, 2
Betti, Ugo 1892-1953 .... **TCLC 5**
See also CA 104; 155
Betts, Doris (Waugh) 1932- ...... **CLC 3, 6, 28**
See also CA 13-16R; CANR 9, 66, 77; DLBY 82; INT CANR-9
Bevan, Alistair
See Roberts, Keith (John Kingston)
Bey, Pilaff
See Douglas, (George) Norman
Bialik, Chaim Nachman
1873-1934 .... **TCLC 25**
See also CA 170
Bickerstaff, Isaac
See Swift, Jonathan
Bidart, Frank 1939- .... **CLC 33**
See also CA 140
Bienek, Horst 1930- .... **CLC 7, 11**
See also CA 73-76; DLB 75
Bierce, Ambrose (Gwinett)
1842-1914(?) .... **TCLC 1, 7, 44; DA; DAC; DAM MST; SSC 9; WLC**
See also CA 104; 139; CANR 78; CDALB 1865-1917; DA3; DLB 11, 12, 23, 71, 74, 186
Biggers, Earl Derr 1884-1933 .... **TCLC 65**
See also CA 108; 153
Billings, Josh
See Shaw, Henry Wheeler
Billington, (Lady) Rachel (Mary)
1942- .... **CLC 43**
See also AITN 2; CA 33-36R; CANR 44
Binyon, T(imothy) J(ohn) 1936- .... **CLC 34**
See also CA 111; CANR 28
Bion 335B.C.-245B.C. .... **CMLC 39**
Bioy Casares, Adolfo 1914-1999 ... **CLC 4, 8, 13, 88; DAM MULT; HLC 1; SSC 17**
See also CA 29-32R; 177; CANR 19, 43, 66; DLB 113; HW 1, 2; MTCW 1, 2
Bird, Cordwainer
See Ellison, Harlan (Jay)
Bird, Robert Montgomery
1806-1854 .... **NCLC 1**
See also DLB 202
Birkerts, Sven 1951- .... **CLC 116**
See also CA 128; 133; 176; CAAE 176; CAAS 29; INT 133
Birney, (Alfred) Earle 1904-1995 .. **CLC 1, 4, 6, 11; DAC; DAM MST, POET**
See also CA 1-4R; CANR 5, 20; DLB 88; MTCW 1
Biruni, al 973-1048(?) .... **CMLC 28**
Bishop, Elizabeth 1911-1979 ... **CLC 1, 4, 9, 13, 15, 32; DA; DAC; DAM MST, POET; PC 3**
See also CA 5-8R; 89-92; CABS 2; CANR 26, 61; CDALB 1968-1988; DA3; DLB 5, 169; MTCW 1, 2; SATA-Obit 24
Bishop, John 1935- .... **CLC 10**
See also CA 105
Bissett, Bill 1939- .... **CLC 18; PC 14**
See also CA 69-72; CAAS 19; CANR 15; DLB 53; MTCW 1
Bissoondath, Neil (Devindra)
1955- .... **CLC 120; DAC**
See also CA 136
Bitov, Andrei (Georgievich) 1937- ... **CLC 57**
See also CA 142
Biyidi, Alexandre 1932-
See Beti, Mongo
See also BW 1, 3; CA 114; 124; CANR 81; DA3; MTCW 1, 2

Bjarme, Brynjolf
See Ibsen, Henrik (Johan)

Bjoernson, Bjoernstjerne (Martinius)
1832-1910 .... **TCLC 7, 37**
See also CA 104

Black, Robert
See Holdstock, Robert P.

Blackburn, Paul 1926-1971 .... **CLC 9, 43**
See also CA 81-84; 33-36R; CANR 34;
DLB 16; DLBY 81

Black Elk 1863-1950 .... **TCLC 33; DAM
MULT**
See also CA 144; MTCW 1; NNAL

Black Hobart
See Sanders, (James) Ed(ward)

Blacklin, Malcolm
See Chambers, Aidan

Blackmore, R(ichard) D(oddridge)
1825-1900 .... **TCLC 27**
See also CA 120; DLB 18

Blackmur, R(ichard) P(almer)
1904-1965 .... **CLC 2, 24**
See also CA 11-12; 25-28R; CANR 71;
CAP 1; DLB 63

Black Tarantula
See Acker, Kathy

Blackwood, Algernon (Henry)
1869-1951 .... **TCLC 5**
See also CA 105; 150; DLB 153, 156, 178

Blackwood, Caroline 1931-1996 .... **CLC 6, 9,
100**
See also CA 85-88; 151; CANR 32, 61, 65;
DLB 14, 207; MTCW 1

Blade, Alexander
See Hamilton, Edmond; Silverberg, Robert

Blaga, Lucian 1895-1961 .... **CLC 75**
See also CA 157; DLB 220

Blair, Eric (Arthur) 1903-1950
See Orwell, George
See also CA 104; 132; DA; DAB; DAC;
DAM MST, NOV; DA3; MTCW 1, 2;
SATA 29

Blair, Hugh 1718-1800 .... **NCLC 75**

Blais, Marie-Claire 1939- .... **CLC 2, 4, 6, 13,
22; DAC; DAM MST**
See also CA 21-24R; CAAS 4; CANR 38,
75; DLB 53; MTCW 1, 2

Blaise, Clark 1940- .... **CLC 29**
See also AITN 2; CA 53-56; CAAS 3;
CANR 5, 66; DLB 53

Blake, Fairley
See De Voto, Bernard (Augustine)

Blake, Nicholas
See Day Lewis, C(ecil)
See also DLB 77

Blake, William 1757-1827 .... **NCLC 13, 37,
57; DA; DAB; DAC; DAM MST,
POET; PC 12; WLC**
See also CDBLB 1789-1832; CLR 52;
DA3; DLB 93, 163; MAICYA; SATA 30

Blasco Ibanez, Vicente
1867-1928 .... **TCLC 12; DAM NOV**
See also CA 110; 131; CANR 81; DA3; HW
1, 2; MTCW 1

Blatty, William Peter 1928- .... **CLC 2; DAM
POP**
See also CA 5-8R; CANR 9

Bleeck, Oliver
See Thomas, Ross (Elmore)

Blessing, Lee 1949- .... **CLC 54**

Blight, Rose
See Greer, Germaine

Blish, James (Benjamin) 1921-1975 . **CLC 14**
See also CA 1-4R; 57-60; CANR 3; DLB
8; MTCW 1; SATA 66

Bliss, Reginald
See Wells, H(erbert) G(eorge)

Blixen, Karen (Christentze Dinesen)
1885-1962
See Dinesen, Isak
See also CA 25-28; CANR 22, 50; CAP 2;
DA3; MTCW 1, 2; SATA 44

Bloch, Robert (Albert) 1917-1994 .... **CLC 33**
See also AAYA 29; CA 5-8R, 179; 146;
CAAE 179; CAAS 20; CANR 5, 78;
DA3; DLB 44; INT CANR-5; MTCW 1;
SATA 12; SATA-Obit 82

Blok, Alexander (Alexandrovich)
1880-1921 .... **TCLC 5; PC 21**
See also CA 104; 183

Blom, Jan
See Breytenbach, Breyten

Bloom, Harold 1930- .... **CLC 24, 103**
See also CA 13-16R; CANR 39, 75, 92;
DLB 67; MTCW 1

Bloomfield, Aurelius
See Bourne, Randolph S(illiman)

Blount, Roy (Alton), Jr. 1941- .... **CLC 38**
See also CA 53-56; CANR 10, 28, 61; INT
CANR-28; MTCW 1, 2

Bloy, Leon 1846-1917 .... **TCLC 22**
See also CA 121; 183; DLB 123

Blume, Judy (Sussman) 1938- .. **CLC 12, 30;
DAM NOV, POP**
See also AAYA 3, 26; CA 29-32R; CANR
13, 37, 66; CLR 2, 15; DA3; DLB 52;
JRDA; MAICYA; MTCW 1, 2; SATA 2,
31, 79

Blunden, Edmund (Charles)
1896-1974 .... **CLC 2, 56**
See also CA 17-18; 45-48; CANR 54; CAP
2; DLB 20, 100, 155; MTCW 1

Bly, Robert (Elwood) 1926- .... **CLC 1, 2, 5,
10, 15, 38, 128; DAM POET**
See also CA 5-8R; CANR 41, 73; DA3;
DLB 5; MTCW 1, 2

Boas, Franz 1858-1942 .... **TCLC 56**
See also CA 115; 181

Bobette
See Simenon, Georges (Jacques Christian)

Boccaccio, Giovanni 1313-1375 ... **CMLC 13;
SSC 10**

Bochco, Steven 1943- .... **CLC 35**
See also AAYA 11; CA 124; 138

Bodel, Jean 1167(?)-1210 .... **CMLC 28**

Bodenheim, Maxwell 1892-1954 .... **TCLC 44**
See also CA 110; DLB 9, 45

Bodker, Cecil 1927- .... **CLC 21**
See also CA 73-76; CANR 13, 44; CLR 23;
MAICYA; SATA 14

Boell, Heinrich (Theodor)
1917-1985 ..... **CLC 2, 3, 6, 9, 11, 15, 27,
32, 72; DA; DAB; DAC; DAM MST,
NOV; SSC 23; WLC**
See also CA 21-24R; 116; CANR 24; DA3;
DLB 69; DLBY 85; MTCW 1, 2

Boerne, Alfred
See Doeblin, Alfred

Boethius 480(?)-524(?) .... **CMLC 15**
See also DLB 115

Boff, Leonardo (Genezio Darci) 1938-
See also CA 150; DAM MULT; HLC 1;
HW 2

Bogan, Louise 1897-1970 .... **CLC 4, 39, 46,
93; DAM POET; PC 12**
See also CA 73-76; 25-28R; CANR 33, 82;
DLB 45, 169; MTCW 1, 2

Bogarde, Dirk 1921-1999
See Van Den Bogarde, Derek Jules Gaspard
Ulric Niven

Bogosian, Eric 1953- .... **CLC 45**
See also CA 138

Bograd, Larry 1953- .... **CLC 35**
See also CA 93-96; CANR 57; SAAS 21;
SATA 33, 89

Boiardo, Matteo Maria 1441-1494 .... **LC 6**

Boileau-Despreaux, Nicolas 1636-1711 . **LC 3**

Bojer, Johan 1872-1959 .... **TCLC 64**

Boland, Eavan (Aisling) 1944- .. **CLC 40, 67,
113; DAM POET**
See also CA 143; CANR 61; DLB 40;
MTCW 2

Boll, Heinrich
See Boell, Heinrich (Theodor)

Bolt, Lee
See Faust, Frederick (Schiller)

Bolt, Robert (Oxton) 1924-1995 ...... **CLC 14;
DAM DRAM**
See also CA 17-20R; 147; CANR 35, 67;
DLB 13; MTCW 1

Bombal, Maria Luisa 1910-1980 ...... **SSC 37;
HLCS 1**
See also CA 127; CANR 72; HW 1

Bombet, Louis-Alexandre-Cesar
See Stendhal

Bomkauf
See Kaufman, Bob (Garnell)

Bonaventura NCLC 35
See also DLB 90

Bond, Edward 1934- .... **CLC 4, 6, 13, 23;
DAM DRAM**
See also CA 25-28R; CANR 38, 67; DLB
13; MTCW 1

Bonham, Frank 1914-1989 .... **CLC 12**
See also AAYA 1; CA 9-12R; CANR 4, 36;
JRDA; MAICYA; SAAS 3; SATA 1, 49;
SATA-Obit 62

Bonnefoy, Yves 1923- .. **CLC 9, 15, 58; DAM
MST, POET**
See also CA 85-88; CANR 33, 75; MTCW
1, 2

Bontemps, Arna(ud Wendell)
1902-1973 ..... **CLC 1, 18; BLC 1; DAM
MULT, NOV, POET**
See also BW 1; CA 1-4R; 41-44R; CANR
4, 35; CLR 6; DA3; DLB 48, 51; JRDA;
MAICYA; MTCW 1, 2; SATA 2, 44;
SATA-Obit 24

Booth, Martin 1944- .... **CLC 13**
See also CA 93-96; CAAS 2; CANR 92

Booth, Philip 1925- .... **CLC 23**
See also CA 5-8R; CANR 5, 88; DLBY 82

Booth, Wayne C(layson) 1921- .... **CLC 24**
See also CA 1-4R; CAAS 5; CANR 3, 43;
DLB 67

Borchert, Wolfgang 1921-1947 .... **TCLC 5**
See also CA 104; DLB 69, 124

Borel, Petrus 1809-1859 .... **NCLC 41**

Borges, Jorge Luis 1899-1986 ... **CLC 1, 2, 3,
4, 6, 8, 9, 10, 13, 19, 44, 48, 83; DA;
DAB; DAC; DAM MST, MULT; HLC
1; PC 22; SSC 4, 41; WLC**
See also AAYA 26; CA 21-24R; CANR 19,
33, 75; DA3; DLB 113; DLBY 86; HW 1,
2; MTCW 1, 2

Borowski, Tadeusz 1922-1951 .... **TCLC 9**
See also CA 106; 154

Borrow, George (Henry)
1803-1881 .... **NCLC 9**
See also DLB 21, 55, 166

Bosch (Gavino), Juan 1909-
See also CA 151; DAM MST, MULT; DLB
145; HLCS 1; HW 1, 2

Bosman, Herman Charles
1905-1951 .... **TCLC 49**
See also Malan, Herman
See also CA 160; DLB 225

Bosschere, Jean de 1878(?)-1953 ... **TCLC 19**
See also CA 115; 186

Boswell, James 1740-1795 ...... **LC 4, 50; DA;
DAB; DAC; DAM MST; WLC**
See also CDBLB 1660-1789; DLB 104, 142

Bottoms, David 1949- .... **CLC 53**
  See also CA 105; CANR 22; DLB 120;
  DLBY 83
Boucicault, Dion 1820-1890 .... **NCLC 41**
Bourget, Paul (Charles Joseph)
  1852-1935 .... **TCLC 12**
  See also CA 107; DLB 123
Bourjaily, Vance (Nye) 1922- .... **CLC 8, 62**
  See also CA 1-4R; CAAS 1; CANR 2, 72;
  DLB 2, 143
Bourne, Randolph S(illiman)
  1886-1918 .... **TCLC 16**
  See also CA 117; 155; DLB 63
Bova, Ben(jamin William) 1932- ...... **CLC 45**
  See also AAYA 16; CA 5-8R; CAAS 18;
  CANR 11, 56; CLR 3; DLBY 81; INT
  CANR-11; MAICYA; MTCW 1; SATA 6,
  68
Bowen, Elizabeth (Dorothea Cole)
  1899-1973 . **CLC 1, 3, 6, 11, 15, 22, 118;**
  DAM NOV; SSC 3, 28
  See also CA 17-18; 41-44R; CANR 35;
  CAP 2; CDBLB 1945-1960; DA3; DLB
  15, 162; MTCW 1, 2
Bowering, George 1935- .... **CLC 15, 47**
  See also CA 21-24R; CAAS 16; CANR 10;
  DLB 53
Bowering, Marilyn R(uthe) 1949- .... **CLC 32**
  See also CA 101; CANR 49
Bowers, Edgar 1924-2000 .... **CLC 9**
  See also CA 5-8R; CANR 24; DLB 5
Bowie, David **CLC 17**
  See also Jones, David Robert
Bowles, Jane (Sydney) 1917-1973 ..... **CLC 3,**
  68
  See also CA 19-20; 41-44R; CAP 2
Bowles, Paul (Frederick) 1910-1999 . **CLC 1,**
  2, 19, 53; SSC 3
  See also CA 1-4R; 186; CAAS 1; CANR 1,
  19, 50, 75; DA3; DLB 5, 6; MTCW 1, 2
Box, Edgar
  See Vidal, Gore
Boyd, Nancy
  See Millay, Edna St. Vincent
Boyd, William 1952- .... **CLC 28, 53, 70**
  See also CA 114; 120; CANR 51, 71
Boyle, Kay 1902-1992 .... **CLC 1, 5, 19, 58,**
  121; SSC 5
  See also CA 13-16R; 140; CAAS 1; CANR
  29, 61; DLB 4, 9, 48, 86; DLBY 93;
  MTCW 1, 2
Boyle, Mark
  See Kienzle, William X(avier)
Boyle, Patrick 1905-1982 .... **CLC 19**
  See also CA 127
Boyle, T. C. 1948-
  See Boyle, T(homas) Coraghessan
Boyle, T(homas) Coraghessan
  1948- .... **CLC 36, 55, 90; DAM POP;**
  SSC 16
  See also BEST 90:4; CA 120; CANR 44,
  76, 89; DA3; DLBY 86; MTCW 2
Boz
  See Dickens, Charles (John Huffam)
Brackenridge, Hugh Henry
  1748-1816 .... **NCLC 7**
  See also DLB 11, 37
Bradbury, Edward P.
  See Moorcock, Michael (John)
  See also MTCW 2
Bradbury, Malcolm (Stanley)
  1932- .... **CLC 32, 61; DAM NOV**
  See also CA 1-4R; CANR 1, 33, 91; DA3;
  DLB 14, 207; MTCW 1, 2

Bradbury, Ray (Douglas) 1920- .... **CLC 1, 3,**
  10, 15, 42, 98; DA; DAB; DAC; DAM
  MST, NOV, POP; SSC 29; WLC
  See also AAYA 15; AITN 1, 2; CA 1-4R;
  CANR 2, 30, 75; CDALB 1968-1988;
  DA3; DLB 2, 8; MTCW 1, 2; SATA 11,
  64
Bradford, Gamaliel 1863-1932 .... **TCLC 36**
  See also CA 160; DLB 17
Bradley, David (Henry), Jr. 1950- ... **CLC 23,**
  118; BLC 1; DAM MULT
  See also BW 1, 3; CA 104; CANR 26, 81;
  DLB 33
Bradley, John Ed(mund, Jr.) 1958- . **CLC 55**
  See also CA 139
Bradley, Marion Zimmer
  1930-1999 .... **CLC 30; DAM POP**
  See also AAYA 9; CA 57-60; 185; CAAS
  10; CANR 7, 31, 51, 75; DA3; DLB 8;
  MTCW 1, 2; SATA 90; SATA-Obit 116
Bradstreet, Anne 1612(?)-1672 ...... **LC 4, 30;**
  DA; DAC; DAM MST, POET; PC 10
  See also CDALB 1640-1865; DA3; DLB
  24
Brady, Joan 1939- .... **CLC 86**
  See also CA 141
Bragg, Melvyn 1939- .... **CLC 10**
  See also BEST 89:3; CA 57-60; CANR 10,
  48, 89; DLB 14
Brahe, Tycho 1546-1601 .... **LC 45**
Braine, John (Gerard) 1922-1986 . **CLC 1, 3,**
  41
  See also CA 1-4R; 120; CANR 1, 33; CD-
  BLB 1945-1960; DLB 15; DLBY 86;
  MTCW 1
Bramah, Ernest 1868-1942 .... **TCLC 72**
  See also CA 156; DLB 70
Brammer, William 1930(?)-1978 ...... **CLC 31**
  See also CA 77-80
Brancati, Vitaliano 1907-1954 .... **TCLC 12**
  See also CA 109
Brancato, Robin F(idler) 1936- .... **CLC 35**
  See also AAYA 9; CA 69-72; CANR 11,
  45; CLR 32; JRDA; SAAS 9; SATA 97
Brand, Max
  See Faust, Frederick (Schiller)
Brand, Millen 1906-1980 .... **CLC 7**
  See also CA 21-24R; 97-100; CANR 72
Branden, Barbara **CLC 44**
  See also CA 148
Brandes, Georg (Morris Cohen)
  1842-1927 .... **TCLC 10**
  See also CA 105
Brandys, Kazimierz 1916- .... **CLC 62**
Branley, Franklyn M(ansfield)
  1915- .... **CLC 21**
  See also CA 33-36R; CANR 14, 39; CLR
  13; MAICYA; SAAS 16; SATA 4, 68
Brathwaite, Edward (Kamau)
  1930- ...... **CLC 11; BLCS; DAM POET**
  See also BW 2, 3; CA 25-28R; CANR 11,
  26, 47; DLB 125
Brautigan, Richard (Gary)
  1935-1984 .... **CLC 1, 3, 5, 9, 12, 34, 42;**
  DAM NOV
  See also CA 53-56; 113; CANR 34; DA3;
  DLB 2, 5, 206; DLBY 80, 84; MTCW 1;
  SATA 56
Brave Bird, Mary 1953-
  See Crow Dog, Mary (Ellen)
  See also NNAL
Braverman, Kate 1950- .... **CLC 67**
  See also CA 89-92
Brecht, (Eugen) Bertolt (Friedrich)
  1898-1956 .... **TCLC 1, 6, 13, 35; DA;**
  DAB; DAC; DAM DRAM, MST; DC
  3; WLC
  See also CA 104; 133; CANR 62; DA3;
  DLB 56, 124; MTCW 1, 2

Brecht, Eugen Berthold Friedrich
  See Brecht, (Eugen) Bertolt (Friedrich)
Bremer, Fredrika 1801-1865 .... **NCLC 11**
Brennan, Christopher John
  1870-1932 .... **TCLC 17**
  See also CA 117
Brennan, Maeve 1917-1993 .... **CLC 5**
  See also CA 81-84; CANR 72
Brent, Linda
  See Jacobs, Harriet A(nn)
Brentano, Clemens (Maria)
  1778-1842 .... **NCLC 1**
  See also DLB 90
Brent of Bin Bin
  See Franklin, (Stella Maria Sarah) Miles
  (Lampe)
Brenton, Howard 1942- .... **CLC 31**
  See also CA 69-72; CANR 33, 67; DLB 13;
  MTCW 1
Breslin, James 1930-1996
  See Breslin, Jimmy
  See also CA 73-76; CANR 31, 75; DAM
  NOV; MTCW 1, 2
Breslin, Jimmy **CLC 4, 43**
  See also Breslin, James
  See also AITN 1; DLB 185; MTCW 2
Bresson, Robert 1901- .... **CLC 16**
  See also CA 110; CANR 49
Breton, Andre 1896-1966 .. **CLC 2, 9, 15, 54;**
  PC 15
  See also CA 19-20; 25-28R; CANR 40, 60;
  CAP 2; DLB 65; MTCW 1, 2
Breytenbach, Breyten 1939(?)- .. **CLC 23, 37,**
  126; DAM POET
  See also CA 113; 129; CANR 61; DLB 225
Bridgers, Sue Ellen 1942- .... **CLC 26**
  See also AAYA 8; CA 65-68; CANR 11,
  36; CLR 18; DLB 52; JRDA; MAICYA;
  SAAS 1; SATA 22, 90; SATA-Essay 109
Bridges, Robert (Seymour)
  1844-1930 ... **TCLC 1; DAM POET; PC**
  28
  See also CA 104; 152; CDBLB 1890-1914;
  DLB 19, 98
Bridie, James **TCLC 3**
  See also Mavor, Osborne Henry
  See also DLB 10
Brin, David 1950- .... **CLC 34**
  See also AAYA 21; CA 102; CANR 24, 70;
  INT CANR-24; SATA 65
Brink, Andre (Philippus) 1935- . **CLC 18, 36,**
  106
  See also CA 104; CANR 39, 62; DLB 225;
  INT 103; MTCW 1, 2
Brinsmead, H(esba) F(ay) 1922- ...... **CLC 21**
  See also CA 21-24R; CANR 10; CLR 47;
  MAICYA; SAAS 5; SATA 18, 78
Brittain, Vera (Mary) 1893(?)-1970 . **CLC 23**
  See also CA 13-16; 25-28R; CANR 58;
  CAP 1; DLB 191; MTCW 1, 2
Broch, Hermann 1886-1951 .... **TCLC 20**
  See also CA 117; DLB 85, 124
Brock, Rose
  See Hansen, Joseph
Brodkey, Harold (Roy) 1930-1996 ... **CLC 56**
  See also CA 111; 151; CANR 71; DLB 130
Brodskii, Iosif
  See Brodsky, Joseph
Brodsky, Iosif Alexandrovich 1940-1996
  See Brodsky, Joseph
  See also AITN 1; CA 41-44R; 151; CANR
  37; DAM POET; DA3; MTCW 1, 2
Brodsky, Joseph 1940-1996 ..... **CLC 4, 6, 13,**
  36, 100; PC 9
  See also Brodskii, Iosif; Brodsky, Iosif Al-
  exandrovich
  See also MTCW 1
Brodsky, Michael (Mark) 1948- .... **CLC 19**
  See also CA 102; CANR 18, 41, 58

Bromell, Henry 1947- .... **CLC 5**
See also CA 53-56; CANR 9
Bromfield, Louis (Brucker)
1896-1956 .... **TCLC 11**
See also CA 107; 155; DLB 4, 9, 86
Broner, E(sther) M(asserman)
1930- .... **CLC 19**
See also CA 17-20R; CANR 8, 25, 72; DLB
28
Bronk, William (M.) 1918-1999 .... **CLC 10**
See also CA 89-92; 177; CANR 23; DLB
165
Bronstein, Lev Davidovich
See Trotsky, Leon
Bronte, Anne 1820-1849 .... **NCLC 4, 71**
See also DA3; DLB 21, 199
Bronte, Charlotte 1816-1855 ...... **NCLC 3, 8,
33, 58; DA; DAB; DAC; DAM MST,
NOV; WLC**
See also AAYA 17; CDBLB 1832-1890;
DA3; DLB 21, 159, 199
Bronte, Emily (Jane) 1818-1848 ... **NCLC 16,
35; DA; DAB; DAC; DAM MST, NOV,
POET; PC 8; WLC**
See also AAYA 17; CDBLB 1832-1890;
DA3; DLB 21, 32, 199
Brooke, Frances 1724-1789 .... **LC 6, 48**
See also DLB 39, 99
Brooke, Henry 1703(?)-1783 .... **LC 1**
See also DLB 39
Brooke, Rupert (Chawner)
1887-1915 .... **TCLC 2, 7; DA; DAB;
DAC; DAM MST, POET; PC 24; WLC**
See also CA 104; 132; CANR 61; CDBLB
1914-1945; DLB 19; MTCW 1, 2
Brooke-Haven, P.
See Wodehouse, P(elham) G(renville)
Brooke-Rose, Christine 1926(?)- ...... **CLC 40**
See also CA 13-16R; CANR 58; DLB 14
Brookner, Anita 1928- .... **CLC 32, 34, 51;
DAB; DAM POP**
See also CA 114; 120; CANR 37, 56, 87;
DA3; DLB 194; DLBY 87; MTCW 1, 2
Brooks, Cleanth 1906-1994 . **CLC 24, 86, 110**
See also CA 17-20R; 145; CANR 33, 35;
DLB 63; DLBY 94; INT CANR-35;
MTCW 1, 2
Brooks, George
See Baum, L(yman) Frank
Brooks, Gwendolyn 1917- ...... **CLC 1, 2, 4, 5,
15, 49, 125; BLC 1; DA; DAC; DAM
MST, MULT, POET; PC 7; WLC**
See also AAYA 20; AITN 1; BW 2, 3; CA
1-4R; CANR 1, 27, 52, 75; CDALB 1941-
1968; CLR 27; DA3; DLB 5, 76, 165;
MTCW 1, 2; SATA 6
Brooks, Mel CLC 12
See also Kaminsky, Melvin
See also AAYA 13; DLB 26
Brooks, Peter 1938- .... **CLC 34**
See also CA 45-48; CANR 1
Brooks, Van Wyck 1886-1963 .... **CLC 29**
See also CA 1-4R; CANR 6; DLB 45, 63,
103
Brophy, Brigid (Antonia)
1929-1995 .... **CLC 6, 11, 29, 105**
See also CA 5-8R; 149; CAAS 4; CANR
25, 53; DA3; DLB 14; MTCW 1, 2
Brosman, Catharine Savage 1934- ..... **CLC 9**
See also CA 61-64; CANR 21, 46
Brossard, Nicole 1943- .... **CLC 115**
See also CA 122; CAAS 16; DLB 53
Brother Antoninus
See Everson, William (Oliver)
The Brothers Quay
See Quay, Stephen; Quay, Timothy
Broughton, T(homas) Alan 1936- ..... **CLC 19**
See also CA 45-48; CANR 2, 23, 48

Broumas, Olga 1949- .... **CLC 10, 73**
See also CA 85-88; CANR 20, 69
Brown, Alan 1950- .... **CLC 99**
See also CA 156
Brown, Charles Brockden
1771-1810 .... **NCLC 22, 74**
See also CDALB 1640-1865; DLB 37, 59,
73
Brown, Christy 1932-1981 .... **CLC 63**
See also CA 105; 104; CANR 72; DLB 14
Brown, Claude 1937- .... **CLC 30; BLC 1;
DAM MULT**
See also AAYA 7; BW 1, 3; CA 73-76;
CANR 81
Brown, Dee (Alexander) 1908- . **CLC 18, 47;
DAM POP**
See also AAYA 30; CA 13-16R; CAAS 6;
CANR 11, 45, 60; DA3; DLBY 80;
MTCW 1, 2; SATA 5, 110
Brown, George
See Wertmueller, Lina
Brown, George Douglas
1869-1902 .... **TCLC 28**
See also CA 162
Brown, George Mackay 1921-1996 ... **CLC 5,
48, 100**
See also CA 21-24R; 151; CAAS 6; CANR
12, 37, 67; DLB 14, 27, 139; MTCW 1;
SATA 35
Brown, (William) Larry 1951- .... **CLC 73**
See also CA 130; 134; INT 133
Brown, Moses
See Barrett, William (Christopher)
Brown, Rita Mae 1944- .... **CLC 18, 43, 79;
DAM NOV, POP**
See also CA 45-48; CANR 2, 11, 35, 62;
DA3; INT CANR-11; MTCW 1, 2
Brown, Roderick (Langmere) Haig-
See Haig-Brown, Roderick (Langmere)
Brown, Rosellen 1939- .... **CLC 32**
See also CA 77-80; CAAS 10; CANR 14,
44
Brown, Sterling Allen 1901-1989 ...... **CLC 1,
23, 59; BLC 1; DAM MULT, POET**
See also BW 1, 3; CA 85-88; 127; CANR
26; DA3; DLB 48, 51, 63; MTCW 1, 2
Brown, Will
See Ainsworth, William Harrison
Brown, William Wells 1813-1884 ... **NCLC 2,
89; BLC 1; DAM MULT; DC 1**
See also DLB 3, 50
Browne, (Clyde) Jackson 1948(?)- ... **CLC 21**
See also CA 120
Browning, Elizabeth Barrett
1806-1861 ...... **NCLC 1, 16, 61, 66; DA;
DAB; DAC; DAM MST, POET; PC 6;
WLC**
See also CDBLB 1832-1890; DA3; DLB
32, 199
Browning, Robert 1812-1889 . **NCLC 19, 79;
DA; DAB; DAC; DAM MST, POET;
PC 2; WLCS**
See also CDBLB 1832-1890; DA3; DLB
32, 163; YABC 1
Browning, Tod 1882-1962 .... **CLC 16**
See also CA 141; 117
Brownson, Orestes Augustus
1803-1876 .... **NCLC 50**
See also DLB 1, 59, 73
Bruccoli, Matthew J(oseph) 1931- ... **CLC 34**
See also CA 9-12R; CANR 7, 87; DLB 103
Bruce, Lenny CLC 21
See also Schneider, Leonard Alfred
Bruin, John
See Brutus, Dennis
Brulard, Henri
See Stendhal
Brulls, Christian
See Simenon, Georges (Jacques Christian)

Brunner, John (Kilian Houston)
1934-1995 .... **CLC 8, 10; DAM POP**
See also CA 1-4R; 149; CAAS 8; CANR 2,
37; MTCW 1, 2
Bruno, Giordano 1548-1600 .... **LC 27**
Brutus, Dennis 1924- .... **CLC 43; BLC 1;
DAM MULT, POET; PC 24**
See also BW 2, 3; CA 49-52; CAAS 14;
CANR 2, 27, 42, 81; DLB 117, 225
Bryan, C(ourtlandt) D(ixon) B(arnes)
1936- .... **CLC 29**
See also CA 73-76; CANR 13, 68; DLB
185; INT CANR-13
Bryan, Michael
See Moore, Brian
Bryan, William Jennings
1860-1925 .... **TCLC 99**
Bryant, William Cullen 1794-1878 . **NCLC 6,
46; DA; DAB; DAC; DAM MST,
POET; PC 20**
See also CDALB 1640-1865; DLB 3, 43,
59, 189
Bryusov, Valery Yakovlevich
1873-1924 .... **TCLC 10**
See also CA 107; 155
Buchan, John 1875-1940 .... **TCLC 41; DAB;
DAM POP**
See also CA 108; 145; DLB 34, 70, 156;
MTCW 1; YABC 2
Buchanan, George 1506-1582 .... **LC 4**
See also DLB 152
Buchheim, Lothar-Guenther 1918- .... **CLC 6**
See also CA 85-88
Buchner, (Karl) Georg 1813-1837 . **NCLC 26**
Buchwald, Art(hur) 1925- .... **CLC 33**
See also AITN 1; CA 5-8R; CANR 21, 67;
MTCW 1, 2; SATA 10
Buck, Pearl S(ydenstricker)
1892-1973 .... **CLC 7, 11, 18, 127; DA;
DAB; DAC; DAM MST, NOV**
See also AITN 1; CA 1-4R; 41-44R; CANR
1, 34; CDALBS; DA3; DLB 9, 102;
MTCW 1, 2; SATA 1, 25
Buckler, Ernest 1908-1984 .... **CLC 13; DAC;
DAM MST**
See also CA 11-12; 114; CAP 1; DLB 68;
SATA 47
Buckley, Vincent (Thomas)
1925-1988 .... **CLC 57**
See also CA 101
Buckley, William F(rank), Jr. 1925- . **CLC 7,
18, 37; DAM POP**
See also AITN 1; CA 1-4R; CANR 1, 24,
53; DA3; DLB 137; DLBY 80; INT
CANR-24; MTCW 1, 2
Buechner, (Carl) Frederick 1926- . **CLC 2, 4,
6, 9; DAM NOV**
See also CA 13-16R; CANR 11, 39, 64;
DLBY 80; INT CANR-11; MTCW 1, 2
Buell, John (Edward) 1927- .... **CLC 10**
See also CA 1-4R; CANR 71; DLB 53
Buero Vallejo, Antonio 1916- ...... **CLC 15, 46**
See also CA 106; CANR 24, 49, 75; HW 1;
MTCW 1, 2
Bufalino, Gesualdo 1920(?)- .... **CLC 74**
See also DLB 196
Bugayev, Boris Nikolayevich
1880-1934 .... **TCLC 7; PC 11**
See also Bely, Andrey
See also CA 104; 165; MTCW 1
Bukowski, Charles 1920-1994 ... **CLC 2, 5, 9,
41, 82, 108; DAM NOV, POET; PC 18**
See also CA 17-20R; 144; CANR 40, 62;
DA3; DLB 5, 130, 169; MTCW 1, 2
Bulgakov, Mikhail (Afanas'evich)
1891-1940 . **TCLC 2, 16; DAM DRAM,
NOV; SSC 18**
See also CA 105; 152

Bulgya, Alexander Alexandrovich
1901-1956 .... TCLC 53
See also Fadeyev, Alexander
See also CA 117; 181

Bullins, Ed 1935- .... CLC 1, 5, 7; BLC 1;
DAM DRAM, MULT; DC 6
See also BW 2, 3; CA 49-52; CAAS 16;
CANR 24, 46, 73; DLB 7, 38; MTCW 1,
2

Bulwer-Lytton, Edward (George Earle
Lytton) 1803-1873 .... NCLC 1, 45
See also DLB 21

Bunin, Ivan Alexeyevich
1870-1953 .... TCLC 6; SSC 5
See also CA 104

Bunting, Basil 1900-1985 ..... CLC 10, 39, 47;
DAM POET
See also CA 53-56; 115; CANR 7; DLB 20

Bunuel, Luis 1900-1983 .. CLC 16, 80; DAM
MULT; HLC 1
See also CA 101; 110; CANR 32, 77; HW
1

Bunyan, John 1628-1688 ... LC 4; DA; DAB;
DAC; DAM MST; WLC
See also CDBLB 1660-1789; DLB 39

Burckhardt, Jacob (Christoph)
1818-1897 .... NCLC 49

Burford, Eleanor
See Hibbert, Eleanor Alice Burford

Burgess, Anthony -1993 .... CLC 1, 2, 4, 5, 8,
10, 13, 15, 22, 40, 62, 81, 94; DAB
See Wilson, John (Anthony) Burgess
See also AAYA 25; AITN 1; CDBLB 1960
to Present; DLB 14, 194; DLBY 98;
MTCW 1

Burke, Edmund 1729(?)-1797 .... LC 7, 36;
DA; DAB; DAC; DAM MST; WLC
See also DA3; DLB 104

Burke, Kenneth (Duva) 1897-1993 ... CLC 2,
24
See also CA 5-8R; 143; CANR 39, 74; DLB
45, 63; MTCW 1, 2

Burke, Leda
See Garnett, David

Burke, Ralph
See Silverberg, Robert

Burke, Thomas 1886-1945 .... TCLC 63
See also CA 113; 155; DLB 197

Burney, Fanny 1752-1840 .. NCLC 12, 54, 81
See also DLB 39

Burns, Robert 1759-1796 . LC 3, 29, 40; DA;
DAB; DAC; DAM MST, POET; PC 6;
WLC
See also CDBLB 1789-1832; DA3; DLB
109

Burns, Tex
See L'Amour, Louis (Dearborn)

Burnshaw, Stanley 1906- .... CLC 3, 13, 44
See also CA 9-12R; DLB 48; DLBY 97

Burr, Anne 1937- .... CLC 6
See also CA 25-28R

Burroughs, Edgar Rice 1875-1950 . TCLC 2,
32; DAM NOV
See also AAYA 11; CA 104; 132; DA3;
DLB 8; MTCW 1, 2; SATA 41

Burroughs, William S(eward)
1914-1997 .. CLC 1, 2, 5, 15, 22, 42, 75,
109; DA; DAB; DAC; DAM MST,
NOV, POP; WLC
See also AITN 2; CA 9-12R; 160; CANR
20, 52; DA3; DLB 2, 8, 16, 152; DLBY
81, 97; MTCW 1, 2

Burton, SirRichard F(rancis)
1821-1890 .... NCLC 42
See also DLB 55, 166, 184

Busch, Frederick 1941- .... CLC 7, 10, 18, 47
See also CA 33-36R; CAAS 1; CANR 45,
73, 92; DLB 6

Bush, Ronald 1946- .... CLC 34
See also CA 136

Bustos, F(rancisco)
See Borges, Jorge Luis

Bustos Domecq, H(onorio)
See Bioy Casares, Adolfo; Borges, Jorge
Luis

Butler, Octavia E(stelle) 1947- .... CLC 38,
121; BLCS; DAM MULT, POP
See also AAYA 18; BW 2, 3; CA 73-76;
CANR 12, 24, 38, 73; CLR 65; DA3;
DLB 33; MTCW 1, 2; SATA 84

Butler, Robert Olen (Jr.) 1945- .... CLC 81;
DAM POP
See also CA 112; CANR 66; DLB 173; INT
112; MTCW 1

Butler, Samuel 1612-1680 .... LC 16, 43
See also DLB 101, 126

Butler, Samuel 1835-1902 . TCLC 1, 33; DA;
DAB; DAC; DAM MST, NOV; WLC
See also CA 143; CDBLB 1890-1914; DA3;
DLB 18, 57, 174

Butler, Walter C.
See Faust, Frederick (Schiller)

Butor, Michel (Marie Francois)
1926- .... CLC 1, 3, 8, 11, 15
See also CA 9-12R; CANR 33, 66; DLB
83; MTCW 1, 2

Butts, Mary 1892(?)-1937 .... TCLC 77
See also CA 148

Buzo, Alexander (John) 1944- .... CLC 61
See also CA 97-100; CANR 17, 39, 69

Buzzati, Dino 1906-1972 .... CLC 36
See also CA 160; 33-36R; DLB 177

Byars, Betsy (Cromer) 1928- .... CLC 35
See also AAYA 19; CA 33-36R, 183; CAAE
183; CANR 18, 36, 57; CLR 1, 16; DLB
52; INT CANR-18; JRDA; MAICYA;
MTCW 1; SAAS 1; SATA 4, 46, 80;
SATA-Essay 108

Byatt, A(ntonia) S(usan Drabble)
1936- ..... CLC 19, 65; DAM NOV, POP
See also CA 13-16R; CANR 13, 33, 50, 75;
DA3; DLB 14, 194; MTCW 1, 2

Byrne, David 1952- .... CLC 26
See also CA 127

Byrne, John Keyes 1926-
See Leonard, Hugh
See also CA 102; CANR 78; INT 102

Byron, George Gordon (Noel)
1788-1824 .... NCLC 2, 12; DA; DAB;
DAC; DAM MST, POET; PC 16; WLC
See also CDBLB 1789-1832; DA3; DLB
96, 110

Byron, Robert 1905-1941 .... TCLC 67
See also CA 160; DLB 195

C. 3. 3.
See Wilde, Oscar (Fingal O'Flahertie Wills)

Caballero, Fernan 1796-1877 .... NCLC 10

Cabell, Branch
See Cabell, James Branch

Cabell, James Branch 1879-1958 .... TCLC 6
See also CA 105; 152; DLB 9, 78; MTCW
1

Cable, George Washington
1844-1925 .... TCLC 4; SSC 4
See also CA 104; 155; DLB 12, 74; DLBD
13

Cabral de Melo Neto, Joao 1920- ... CLC 76;
DAM MULT
See also CA 151

Cabrera Infante, G(uillermo) 1929- . CLC 5,
25, 45, 120; DAM MULT; HLC 1; SSC
39
See also CA 85-88; CANR 29, 65; DA3;
DLB 113; HW 1, 2; MTCW 1, 2

Cade, Toni
See Bambara, Toni Cade

Cadmus and Harmonia
See Buchan, John

Caedmon fl. 658-680 .... CMLC 7
See also DLB 146

Caeiro, Alberto
See Pessoa, Fernando (Antonio Nogueira)

Cage, John (Milton, Jr.) 1912-1992 . CLC 41
See also CA 13-16R; 169; CANR 9, 78;
DLB 193; INT CANR-9

Cahan, Abraham 1860-1951 .... TCLC 71
See also CA 108; 154; DLB 9, 25, 28

Cain, G.
See Cabrera Infante, G(uillermo)

Cain, Guillermo
See Cabrera Infante, G(uillermo)

Cain, James M(allahan) 1892-1977 .. CLC 3,
11, 28
See also AITN 1; CA 17-20R; 73-76;
CANR 8, 34, 61; DLB 226; MTCW 1

Caine, Hall 1853-1931 .... TCLC 97

Caine, Mark
See Raphael, Frederic (Michael)

Calasso, Roberto 1941- .... CLC 81
See also CA 143; CANR 89

Calderon de la Barca, Pedro
1600-1681 .... LC 23; DC 3; HLCS 1

Caldwell, Erskine (Preston)
1903-1987 .. CLC 1, 8, 14, 50, 60; DAM
NOV; SSC 19
See also AITN 1; CA 1-4R; 121; CAAS 1;
CANR 2, 33; DA3; DLB 9, 86; MTCW
1, 2

Caldwell, (Janet Miriam) Taylor (Holland)
1900-1985 .. CLC 2, 28, 39; DAM NOV,
POP
See also CA 5-8R; 116; CANR 5; DA3;
DLBD 17

Calhoun, John Caldwell
1782-1850 .... NCLC 15
See also DLB 3

Calisher, Hortense 1911- ..... CLC 2, 4, 8, 38,
134; DAM NOV; SSC 15
See also CA 1-4R; CANR 1, 22, 67; DA3;
DLB 2; INT CANR-22; MTCW 1, 2

Callaghan, Morley Edward
1903-1990 ...... CLC 3, 14, 41, 65; DAC;
DAM MST
See also CA 9-12R; 132; CANR 33, 73;
DLB 68; MTCW 1, 2

Callimachus c. 305B.C.-c.
240B.C. .... CMLC 18
See also DLB 176

Calvin, John 1509-1564 .... LC 37

Calvino, Italo 1923-1985 .... CLC 5, 8, 11, 22,
33, 39, 73; DAM NOV; SSC 3
See also CA 85-88; 116; CANR 23, 61;
DLB 196; MTCW 1, 2

Cameron, Carey 1952- .... CLC 59
See also CA 135

Cameron, Peter 1959- .... CLC 44
See also CA 125; CANR 50

Camoens, Luis Vaz de 1524(?)-1580
See also HLCS 1

Camoes, Luis de 1524(?)-1580 .... PC 31
See also HLCS 1

Campana, Dino 1885-1932 .... TCLC 20
See also CA 117; DLB 114

Campanella, Tommaso 1568-1639 .... LC 32

Campbell, John W(ood, Jr.)
1910-1971 .... CLC 32
See also CA 21-22; 29-32R; CANR 34;
CAP 2; DLB 8; MTCW 1

Campbell, Joseph 1904-1987 .... CLC 69
See also AAYA 3; BEST 89:2; CA 1-4R;
124; CANR 3, 28, 61; DA3; MTCW 1, 2

Campbell, Maria 1940- .... CLC 85; DAC
See also CA 102; CANR 54; NNAL

Campbell, (John) Ramsey 1946- ..... **CLC 42;
SSC 19**
See also CA 57-60; CANR 7; INT CANR-7
Campbell, (Ignatius) Roy (Dunnachie)
1901-1957 .... **TCLC 5**
See also CA 104; 155; DLB 20, 225;
MTCW 2
Campbell, Thomas 1777-1844 .... **NCLC 19**
See also DLB 93; 144
Campbell, Wilfred **TCLC 9**
See also Campbell, William
Campbell, William 1858(?)-1918
See Campbell, Wilfred
See also CA 106; DLB 92
Campion, Jane **CLC 95**
See also AAYA 33; CA 138; CANR 87
Camus, Albert 1913-1960 ...... **CLC 1, 2, 4, 9,
11, 14, 32, 63, 69, 124; DA; DAB;
DAC; DAM DRAM, MST, NOV; DC
2; SSC 9; WLC**
See also CA 89-92; DA3; DLB 72; MTCW
1, 2
Canby, Vincent 1924- .... **CLC 13**
See also CA 81-84
Cancale
See Desnos, Robert
Canetti, Elias 1905-1994 .. **CLC 3, 14, 25, 75,
86**
See also CA 21-24R; 146; CANR 23, 61,
79; DA3; DLB 85, 124; MTCW 1, 2
Canfield, Dorothea F.
See Fisher, Dorothy (Frances) Canfield
Canfield, Dorothea Frances
See Fisher, Dorothy (Frances) Canfield
Canfield, Dorothy
See Fisher, Dorothy (Frances) Canfield
Canin, Ethan 1960- .... **CLC 55**
See also CA 131; 135
Cannon, Curt
See Hunter, Evan
Cao, Lan 1961- .... **CLC 109**
See also CA 165
Cape, Judith
See Page, P(atricia) K(athleen)
Capek, Karel 1890-1938 ... **TCLC 6, 37; DA;
DAB; DAC; DAM DRAM, MST, NOV;
DC 1; SSC 36; WLC**
See also CA 104; 140; DA3; MTCW 1
Capote, Truman 1924-1984 . **CLC 1, 3, 8, 13,
19, 34, 38, 58; DA; DAB; DAC; DAM
MST, NOV, POP; SSC 2; WLC**
See also CA 5-8R; 113; CANR 18, 62;
CDALB 1941-1968; DA3; DLB 2, 185,
227; DLBY 80, 84; MTCW 1, 2; SATA
91
Capra, Frank 1897-1991 .... **CLC 16**
See also CA 61-64; 135
Caputo, Philip 1941- .... **CLC 32**
See also CA 73-76; CANR 40
Caragiale, Ion Luca 1852-1912 ...... **TCLC 76**
See also CA 157
Card, Orson Scott 1951- ..... **CLC 44, 47, 50;
DAM POP**
See also AAYA 11; CA 102; CANR 27, 47,
73; DA3; INT CANR-27; MTCW 1, 2;
SATA 83
Cardenal, Ernesto 1925- .... **CLC 31; DAM
MULT, POET; HLC 1; PC 22**
See also CA 49-52; CANR 2, 32, 66; HW
1, 2; MTCW 1, 2
Cardozo, Benjamin N(athan)
1870-1938 .... **TCLC 65**
See also CA 117; 164
Carducci, Giosue (Alessandro Giuseppe)
1835-1907 .... **TCLC 32**
See also CA 163
Carew, Thomas 1595(?)-1640 . **LC 13; PC 29**
See also DLB 126

Carey, Ernestine Gilbreth 1908- ...... **CLC 17**
See also CA 5-8R; CANR 71; SATA 2
Carey, Peter 1943- .... **CLC 40, 55, 96**
See also CA 123; 127; CANR 53, 76; INT
127; MTCW 1, 2; SATA 94
Carleton, William 1794-1869 .... **NCLC 3**
See also DLB 159
Carlisle, Henry (Coffin) 1926- .... **CLC 33**
See also CA 13-16R; CANR 15, 85
Carlsen, Chris
See Holdstock, Robert P.
Carlson, Ron(ald F.) 1947- .... **CLC 54**
See also CA 105; CANR 27
Carlyle, Thomas 1795-1881 .. **NCLC 70; DA;
DAB; DAC; DAM MST**
See also CDBLB 1789-1832; DLB 55; 144
Carman, (William) Bliss
1861-1929 .... **TCLC 7; DAC**
See also CA 104; 152; DLB 92
Carnegie, Dale 1888-1955 .... **TCLC 53**
Carossa, Hans 1878-1956 .... **TCLC 48**
See also CA 170; DLB 66
Carpenter, Don(ald Richard)
1931-1995 .... **CLC 41**
See also CA 45-48; 149; CANR 1, 71
Carpenter, Edward 1844-1929 .... **TCLC 88**
See also CA 163
Carpentier (y Valmont), Alejo
1904-1980 ..... **CLC 8, 11, 38, 110; DAM
MULT; HLC 1; SSC 35**
See also CA 65-68; 97-100; CANR 11, 70;
DLB 113; HW 1, 2
Carr, Caleb 1955(?)- .... **CLC 86**
See also CA 147; CANR 73; DA3
Carr, Emily 1871-1945 .... **TCLC 32**
See also CA 159; DLB 68
Carr, John Dickson 1906-1977 .... **CLC 3**
See also Fairbairn, Roger
See also CA 49-52; 69-72; CANR 3, 33,
60; MTCW 1, 2
Carr, Philippa
See Hibbert, Eleanor Alice Burford
Carr, Virginia Spencer 1929- .... **CLC 34**
See also CA 61-64; DLB 111
Carrere, Emmanuel 1957- .... **CLC 89**
Carrier, Roch 1937- .... **CLC 13, 78; DAC;
DAM MST**
See also CA 130; CANR 61; DLB 53;
SATA 105
Carroll, James P. 1943(?)- .... **CLC 38**
See also CA 81-84; CANR 73; MTCW 1
Carroll, Jim 1951- .... **CLC 35**
See also AAYA 17; CA 45-48; CANR 42
Carroll, Lewis -1898 .... **NCLC 2, 53; PC 18;
WLC**
See also Dodgson, Charles Lutwidge
See also CDBLB 1832-1890; CLR 2, 18;
DLB 18, 163, 178; DLBY 98; JRDA
Carroll, Paul Vincent 1900-1968 ...... **CLC 10**
See also CA 9-12R; 25-28R; DLB 10
Carruth, Hayden 1921- ..... **CLC 4, 7, 10, 18,
84; PC 10**
See also CA 9-12R; CANR 4, 38, 59; DLB
5, 165; INT CANR-4; MTCW 1, 2; SATA
47
Carson, Rachel Louise 1907-1964 ... **CLC 71;
DAM POP**
See also CA 77-80; CANR 35; DA3;
MTCW 1, 2; SATA 23
Carter, Angela (Olive) 1940-1992 ...... **CLC 5,
41, 76; SSC 13**
See also CA 53-56; 136; CANR 12, 36, 61;
DA3; DLB 14, 207; MTCW 1, 2; SATA
66; SATA-Obit 70
Carter, Nick
See Smith, Martin Cruz

Carver, Raymond 1938-1988 ..... **CLC 22, 36,
53, 55, 126; DAM NOV; SSC 8**
See also CA 33-36R; 126; CANR 17, 34,
61; DA3; DLB 130; DLBY 84, 88;
MTCW 1, 2
Cary, Elizabeth, Lady Falkland
1585-1639 .... **LC 30**
Cary, (Arthur) Joyce (Lunel)
1888-1957 .... **TCLC 1, 29**
See also CA 104; 164; CDBLB 1914-1945;
DLB 15, 100; MTCW 2
Casanova de Seingalt, Giovanni Jacopo
1725-1798 .... **LC 13**
Casares, Adolfo Bioy
See Bioy Casares, Adolfo
Casely-Hayford, J(oseph) E(phraim)
1866-1930 ...... **TCLC 24; BLC 1; DAM
MULT**
See also BW 2; CA 123; 152
Casey, John (Dudley) 1939- .... **CLC 59**
See also BEST 90:2; CA 69-72; CANR 23
Casey, Michael 1947- .... **CLC 2**
See also CA 65-68; DLB 5
Casey, Patrick
See Thurman, Wallace (Henry)
Casey, Warren (Peter) 1935-1988 .... **CLC 12**
See also CA 101; 127; INT 101
Casona, Alejandro **CLC 49**
See also Alvarez, Alejandro Rodriguez
Cassavetes, John 1929-1989 .... **CLC 20**
See also CA 85-88; 127; CANR 82
Cassian, Nina 1924- .... **PC 17**
Cassill, R(onald) V(erlin) 1919- ... **CLC 4, 23**
See also CA 9-12R; CAAS 1; CANR 7, 45;
DLB 6
Cassirer, Ernst 1874-1945 .... **TCLC 61**
See also CA 157
Cassity, (Allen) Turner 1929- .... **CLC 6, 42**
See also CA 17-20R; CAAS 8; CANR 11;
DLB 105
Castaneda, Carlos (Cesar Aranha)
1931(?)-1998 .... **CLC 12, 119**
See also CA 25-28R; CANR 32, 66; HW 1;
MTCW 1
Castedo, Elena 1937- .... **CLC 65**
See also CA 132
Castedo-Ellerman, Elena
See Castedo, Elena
Castellanos, Rosario 1925-1974 .... **CLC 66;
DAM MULT; HLC 1; SSC 39**
See also CA 131; 53-56; CANR 58; DLB
113; HW 1; MTCW 1
Castelvetro, Lodovico 1505-1571 .... **LC 12**
Castiglione, Baldassare 1478-1529 ...... **LC 12**
Castle, Robert
See Hamilton, Edmond
Castro (Ruz), Fidel 1926(?)-
See also CA 110; 129; CANR 81; DAM
MULT; HLC 1; HW 2
Castro, Guillen de 1569-1631 .... **LC 19**
Castro, Rosalia de 1837-1885 ... **NCLC 3, 78;
DAM MULT**
Cather, Willa -1947
See Cather, Willa Sibert
Cather, Willa Sibert 1873-1947 ...... **TCLC 1,
11, 31, 99; DA; DAB; DAC; DAM
MST, NOV; SSC 2; WLC**
See also Cather, Willa
See also AAYA 24; CA 104; 128; CDALB
1865-1917; DA3; DLB 9, 54, 78; DLBD
1; MTCW 1, 2; SATA 30
Catherine, Saint 1347-1380 .... **CMLC 27**
Cato, Marcus Porcius
234B.C.-149B.C. .... **CMLC 21**
See also DLB 211
Catton, (Charles) Bruce 1899-1978 . **CLC 35**
See also AITN 1; CA 5-8R; 81-84; CANR
7, 74; DLB 17; SATA 2; SATA-Obit 24

Catullus c. 84B.C.-c. 54B.C. .... **CMLC 18**
See also DLB 211

Cauldwell, Frank
See King, Francis (Henry)

Caunitz, William J. 1933-1996 .... **CLC 34**
See also BEST 89:3; CA 125; 130; 152;
CANR 73; INT 130

Causley, Charles (Stanley) 1917- .... **CLC 7**
See also CA 9-12R; CANR 5, 35; CLR 30;
DLB 27; MTCW 1; SATA 3, 66

Caute, (John) David 1936- .... **CLC 29; DAM NOV**
See also CA 1-4R; CAAS 4; CANR 1, 33,
64; DLB 14

Cavafy, C(onstantine) P(eter)
1863-1933 ...... **TCLC 2, 7; DAM POET**
See also Kavafis, Konstantinos Petrou
See also CA 148; DA3; MTCW 1

Cavallo, Evelyn
See Spark, Muriel (Sarah)

Cavanna, Betty **CLC 12**
See also Harrison, Elizabeth Cavanna
See also JRDA; MAICYA; SAAS 4; SATA
1, 30

Cavendish, Margaret Lucas
1623-1673 .... **LC 30**
See also DLB 131

Caxton, William 1421(?)-1491(?) .... **LC 17**
See also DLB 170

Cayer, D. M.
See Duffy, Maureen

Cayrol, Jean 1911- .... **CLC 11**
See also CA 89-92; DLB 83

Cela, Camilo Jose 1916- .... **CLC 4, 13, 59, 122; DAM MULT; HLC 1**
See also BEST 90:2; CA 21-24R; CAAS
10; CANR 21, 32, 76; DLBY 89; HW 1;
MTCW 1, 2

Celan, Paul **CLC 10, 19, 53, 82; PC 10**
See also Antschel, Paul
See also DLB 69

Celine, Louis-Ferdinand **CLC 1, 3, 4, 7, 9, 15, 47, 124**
See also Destouches, Louis-Ferdinand
See also DLB 72

Cellini, Benvenuto 1500-1571 .... **LC 7**

Cendrars, Blaise 1887-1961 ...... **CLC 18, 106**
See also Sauser-Hall, Frederic

Cernuda (y Bidon), Luis
1902-1963 .... **CLC 54; DAM POET**
See also CA 131; 89-92; DLB 134; HW 1

Cervantes, Lorna Dee 1954-
See also CA 131; CANR 80; DLB 82;
HLCS 1; HW 1

Cervantes (Saavedra), Miguel de
1547-1616 .. **LC 6, 23; DA; DAB; DAC; DAM MST, NOV; SSC 12; WLC**

Cesaire, Aime (Fernand) 1913- . **CLC 19, 32, 112; BLC 1; DAM MULT, POET; PC 25**
See also BW 2, 3; CA 65-68; CANR 24,
43, 81; DA3; MTCW 1, 2

Chabon, Michael 1963- .... **CLC 55**
See also CA 139; CANR 57

Chabrol, Claude 1930- .... **CLC 16**
See also CA 110

Challans, Mary 1905-1983
See Renault, Mary
See also CA 81-84; 111; CANR 74; DA3;
MTCW 2; SATA 23; SATA-Obit 36

Challis, George
See Faust, Frederick (Schiller)

Chambers, Aidan 1934- .... **CLC 35**
See also AAYA 27; CA 25-28R; CANR 12,
31, 58; JRDA; MAICYA; SAAS 12;
SATA 1, 69, 108

Chambers, James 1948-
See Cliff, Jimmy
See also CA 124

Chambers, Jessie
See Lawrence, D(avid) H(erbert Richards)

Chambers, Robert W(illiam)
1865-1933 .... **TCLC 41**
See also CA 165; DLB 202; SATA 107

Chamisso, Adelbert von
1781-1838 .... **NCLC 82**
See also DLB 90

Chandler, Raymond (Thornton)
1888-1959 .... **TCLC 1, 7; SSC 23**
See also AAYA 25; CA 104; 129; CANR
60; CDALB 1929-1941; DA3; DLB 226;
DLBD 6; MTCW 1, 2

Chang, Eileen 1920-1995 .... **SSC 28**
See also CA 166

Chang, Jung 1952- .... **CLC 71**
See also CA 142

Chang Ai-Ling
See Chang, Eileen

Channing, William Ellery
1780-1842 .... **NCLC 17**
See also DLB 1, 59

Chao, Patricia 1955- .... **CLC 119**
See also CA 163

Chaplin, Charles Spencer
1889-1977 .... **CLC 16**
See also Chaplin, Charlie
See also CA 81-84; 73-76

Chaplin, Charlie
See Chaplin, Charles Spencer
See also DLB 44

Chapman, George 1559(?)-1634 .... **LC 22; DAM DRAM**
See also DLB 62, 121

Chapman, Graham 1941-1989 .... **CLC 21**
See also Monty Python
See also CA 116; 129; CANR 35

Chapman, John Jay 1862-1933 .... **TCLC 7**
See also CA 104

Chapman, Lee
See Bradley, Marion Zimmer

Chapman, Walker
See Silverberg, Robert

Chappell, Fred (Davis) 1936- ..... **CLC 40, 78**
See also CA 5-8R; CAAS 4; CANR 8, 33,
67; DLB 6, 105

Char, Rene(-Emile) 1907-1988 .... **CLC 9, 11, 14, 55; DAM POET**
See also CA 13-16R; 124; CANR 32;
MTCW 1, 2

Charby, Jay
See Ellison, Harlan (Jay)

Chardin, Pierre Teilhard de
See Teilhard de Chardin, (Marie Joseph)
Pierre

Charlemagne 742-814 .... **CMLC 37**

Charles I 1600-1649 .... **LC 13**

Charriere, Isabelle de 1740-1805 .. **NCLC 66**

Charyn, Jerome 1937- .... **CLC 5, 8, 18**
See also CA 5-8R; CAAS 1; CANR 7, 61;
DLBY 83; MTCW 1

Chase, Mary (Coyle) 1907-1981 .... **DC 1**
See also CA 77-80; 105; DLB 228; SATA
17; SATA-Obit 29

Chase, Mary Ellen 1887-1973 .... **CLC 2**
See also CA 13-16; 41-44R; CAP 1; SATA
10

Chase, Nicholas
See Hyde, Anthony

Chateaubriand, Francois Rene de
1768-1848 .... **NCLC 3**
See also DLB 119

Chatterje, Sarat Chandra 1876-1936(?)
See Chatterji, Saratchandra
See also CA 109

Chatterji, Bankim Chandra
1838-1894 .... **NCLC 19**

Chatterji, Saratchandra -1938 .... **TCLC 13**
See also Chatterje, Sarat Chandra
See also CA 186

Chatterton, Thomas 1752-1770 ..... **LC 3, 54; DAM POET**
See also DLB 109

Chatwin, (Charles) Bruce
1940-1989 . **CLC 28, 57, 59; DAM POP**
See also AAYA 4; BEST 90:1; CA 85-88;
127; DLB 194, 204

Chaucer, Daniel -1939
See Ford, Ford Madox

Chaucer, Geoffrey 1340(?)-1400 .. **LC 17, 56; DA; DAB; DAC; DAM MST, POET; PC 19; WLCS**
See also CDBLB Before 1660; DA3; DLB
146

Chavez, Denise (Elia) 1948-
See also CA 131; CANR 56, 81; DAM
MULT; DLB 122; HLC 1; HW 1, 2;
MTCW 2

Chaviaras, Strates 1935-
See Haviaras, Stratis
See also CA 105

Chayefsky, Paddy **CLC 23**
See also Chayefsky, Sidney
See also DLB 7, 44; DLBY 81

Chayefsky, Sidney 1923-1981
See Chayefsky, Paddy
See also CA 9-12R; 104; CANR 18; DAM
DRAM

Chedid, Andree 1920- .... **CLC 47**
See also CA 145

Cheever, John 1912-1982 ..... **CLC 3, 7, 8, 11, 15, 25, 64; DA; DAB; DAC; DAM MST, NOV, POP; SSC 1, 38; WLC**
See also CA 5-8R; 106; CABS 1; CANR 5,
27, 76; CDALB 1941-1968; DA3; DLB
2, 102, 227; DLBY 80, 82; INT CANR-5;
MTCW 1, 2

Cheever, Susan 1943- .... **CLC 18, 48**
See also CA 103; CANR 27, 51, 92; DLBY
82; INT CANR-27

Chekhonte, Antosha
See Chekhov, Anton (Pavlovich)

Chekhov, Anton (Pavlovich)
1860-1904 .... **TCLC 3, 10, 31, 55, 96; DA; DAB; DAC; DAM DRAM, MST; DC 9; SSC 2, 28, 41; WLC**
See also CA 104; 124; DA3; SATA 90

Chernyshevsky, Nikolay Gavrilovich
1828-1889 .... **NCLC 1**

Cherry, Carolyn Janice 1942-
See Cherryh, C. J.
See also CA 65-68; CANR 10

Cherryh, C. J. **CLC 35**
See also Cherry, Carolyn Janice
See also AAYA 24; DLBY 80; SATA 93

Chesnutt, Charles W(addell)
1858-1932 .. **TCLC 5, 39; BLC 1; DAM MULT; SSC 7**
See also BW 1, 3; CA 106; 125; CANR 76;
DLB 12, 50, 78; MTCW 1, 2

Chester, Alfred 1929(?)-1971 .... **CLC 49**
See also CA 33-36R; DLB 130

Chesterton, G(ilbert) K(eith)
1874-1936 . **TCLC 1, 6, 64; DAM NOV, POET; PC 28; SSC 1**
See also CA 104; 132; CANR 73; CDBLB
1914-1945; DLB 10, 19, 34, 70, 98, 149,
178; MTCW 1, 2; SATA 27

Chiang, Pin-chin 1904-1986
See Ding Ling
See also CA 118

Ch'ien Chung-shu 1910- .... **CLC 22**
See also CA 130; CANR 73; MTCW 1, 2

Child, L. Maria
   See Child, Lydia Maria
Child, Lydia Maria 1802-1880 .. NCLC 6, 73
   See also DLB 1, 74; SATA 67
Child, Mrs.
   See Child, Lydia Maria
Child, Philip 1898-1978 .... CLC 19, 68
   See also CA 13-14; CAP 1; SATA 47
Childers, (Robert) Erskine
   1870-1922 .... TCLC 65
   See also CA 113; 153; DLB 70
Childress, Alice 1920-1994 .. CLC 12, 15, 86,
      96; BLC 1; DAM DRAM, MULT,
      NOV; DC 4
   See also AAYA 8; BW 2, 3; CA 45-48; 146;
      CANR 3, 27, 50, 74; CLR 14; DA3; DLB
      7, 38; JRDA; MAICYA; MTCW 1, 2;
      SATA 7, 48, 81
Chin, Frank (Chew, Jr.) 1940- .... DC 7
   See also CA 33-36R; CANR 71; DAM
      MULT; DLB 206
Chislett, (Margaret) Anne 1943- ...... CLC 34
   See also CA 151
Chitty, Thomas Willes 1926- .... CLC 11
   See also Hinde, Thomas
   See also CA 5-8R
Chivers, Thomas Holley
   1809-1858 .... NCLC 49
   See also DLB 3
Choi, Susan CLC 119
Chomette, Rene Lucien 1898-1981
   See Clair, Rene
   See also CA 103
Chomsky, (Avram) Noam 1928- ..... CLC 132
   See also CA 17-20R; CANR 28, 62; DA3;
      MTCW 1, 2
Chopin, Kate TCLC 5, 14; DA; DAB; SSC
      8; WLCS
   See also Chopin, Katherine
   See also AAYA 33; CDALB 1865-1917;
      DLB 12, 78
Chopin, Katherine 1851-1904
   See Chopin, Kate
   See also CA 104; 122; DAC; DAM MST,
      NOV; DA3
Chretien de Troyes c. 12th cent. - . CMLC 10
   See also DLB 208
Christie
   See Ichikawa, Kon
Christie, Agatha (Mary Clarissa)
   1890-1976 .... CLC 1, 6, 8, 12, 39, 48,
      110; DAB; DAC; DAM NOV
   See also AAYA 9; AITN 1, 2; CA 17-20R;
      61-64; CANR 10, 37; CDBLB 1914-1945;
      DA3; DLB 13, 77; MTCW 1, 2; SATA 36
Christie, (Ann) Philippa
   See Pearce, Philippa
   See also CA 5-8R; CANR 4
Christine de Pizan 1365(?)-1431(?) .... LC 9
   See also DLB 208
Chubb, Elmer
   See Masters, Edgar Lee
Chulkov, Mikhail Dmitrievich
   1743-1792 .... LC 2
   See also DLB 150
Churchill, Caryl 1938- .... CLC 31, 55; DC 5
   See also CA 102; CANR 22, 46; DLB 13;
      MTCW 1
Churchill, Charles 1731-1764 .... LC 3
   See also DLB 109
Chute, Carolyn 1947- .... CLC 39
   See also CA 123
Ciardi, John (Anthony) 1916-1986 . CLC 10,
      40, 44, 129; DAM POET
   See also CA 5-8R; 118; CAAS 2; CANR 5,
      33; CLR 19; DLB 5; DLBY 86; INT
      CANR-5; MAICYA; MTCW 1, 2; SAAS
      26; SATA 1, 65; SATA-Obit 46

Cicero, Marcus Tullius
   106B.C.-43B.C. .... CMLC 3
   See also DLB 211
Cimino, Michael 1943- .... CLC 16
   See also CA 105
Cioran, E(mil) M. 1911-1995 .... CLC 64
   See also CA 25-28R; 149; CANR 91; DLB
      220
Cisneros, Sandra 1954- . CLC 69, 118; DAM
      MULT; HLC 1; SSC 32
   See also AAYA 9; CA 131; CANR 64; DA3;
      DLB 122, 152; HW 1, 2; MTCW 2
Cixous, Helene 1937- .... CLC 92
   See also CA 126; CANR 55; DLB 83;
      MTCW 1, 2
Clair, Rene CLC 20
   See also Chomette, Rene Lucien
Clampitt, Amy 1920-1994 .... CLC 32; PC 19
   See also CA 110; 146; CANR 29, 79; DLB
      105
Clancy, Thomas L., Jr. 1947-
   See Clancy, Tom
   See also CA 125; 131; CANR 62; DA3;
      DLB 227; INT 131; MTCW 1, 2
Clancy, Tom CLC 45, 112; DAM NOV, POP
   See also Clancy, Thomas L., Jr.
   See also AAYA 9; BEST 89:1, 90:1; MTCW
      2
Clare, John 1793-1864 ... NCLC 9, 86; DAB;
      DAM POET; PC 23
   See also DLB 55, 96
Clarin
   See Alas (y Urena), Leopoldo (Enrique
      Garcia)
Clark, Al C.
   See Goines, Donald
Clark, (Robert) Brian 1932- .... CLC 29
   See also CA 41-44R; CANR 67
Clark, Curt
   See Westlake, Donald E(dwin)
Clark, Eleanor 1913-1996 .... CLC 5, 19
   See also CA 9-12R; 151; CANR 41; DLB 6
Clark, J. P.
   See Clark Bekedermo, J(ohnson) P(epper)
   See also DLB 117
Clark, John Pepper
   See Clark Bekedermo, J(ohnson) P(epper)
Clark, M. R.
   See Clark, Mavis Thorpe
Clark, Mavis Thorpe 1909- .... CLC 12
   See also CA 57-60; CANR 8, 37; CLR 30;
      MAICYA; SAAS 5; SATA 8, 74
Clark, Walter Van Tilburg
   1909-1971 .... CLC 28
   See also CA 9-12R; 33-36R; CANR 63;
      DLB 9, 206; SATA 8
Clark Bekedermo, J(ohnson) P(epper)
   1935- .. CLC 38; BLC 1; DAM DRAM,
      MULT; DC 5
   See also Clark, J. P.; Clark, John Pepper
   See also BW 1; CA 65-68; CANR 16, 72;
      MTCW 1
Clarke, Arthur C(harles) 1917- .... CLC 1, 4,
      13, 18, 35; DAM POP; SSC 3
   See also AAYA 4, 33; CA 1-4R; CANR 2,
      28, 55, 74; DA3; JRDA; MAICYA;
      MTCW 1, 2; SATA 13, 70, 115
Clarke, Austin 1896-1974 ... CLC 6, 9; DAM
      POET
   See also CA 29-32; 49-52; CAP 2; DLB 10,
      20
Clarke, Austin C(hesterfield) 1934- .. CLC 8,
      53; BLC 1; DAC; DAM MULT
   See also BW 1; CA 25-28R; CAAS 16;
      CANR 14, 32, 68; DLB 53, 125
Clarke, Gillian 1937- .... CLC 61
   See also CA 106; DLB 40

Clarke, Marcus (Andrew Hislop)
   1846-1881 .... NCLC 19
Clarke, Shirley 1925- .... CLC 16
Clash, The
   See Headon, (Nicky) Topper; Jones, Mick;
      Simonon, Paul; Strummer, Joe
Claudel, Paul (Louis Charles Marie)
   1868-1955 .... TCLC 2, 10
   See also CA 104; 165; DLB 192
Claudius, Matthias 1740-1815 .... NCLC 75
   See also DLB 97
Clavell, James (duMaresq)
   1925-1994 .. CLC 6, 25, 87; DAM NOV,
      POP
   See also CA 25-28R; 146; CANR 26, 48;
      DA3; MTCW 1, 2
Cleaver, (Leroy) Eldridge
   1935-1998 . CLC 30, 119; BLC 1; DAM
      MULT
   See also BW 1, 3; CA 21-24R; 167; CANR
      16, 75; DA3; MTCW 2
Cleese, John (Marwood) 1939- .... CLC 21
   See also Monty Python
   See also CA 112; 116; CANR 35; MTCW 1
Cleishbotham, Jebediah
   See Scott, Walter
Cleland, John 1710-1789 .... LC 2, 48
   See also DLB 39
Clemens, Samuel Langhorne 1835-1910
   See Twain, Mark
   See also CA 104; 135; CDALB 1865-1917;
      DA; DAB; DAC; DAM MST, NOV; DA3;
      DLB 11, 12, 23, 64, 74, 186, 189; JRDA;
      MAICYA; SATA 100; YABC 2
Clement of Alexandria
   150(?)-215(?) .... CMLC 41
Cleophil
   See Congreve, William
Clerihew, E.
   See Bentley, E(dmund) C(lerihew)
Clerk, N. W.
   See Lewis, C(live) S(taples)
Cliff, Jimmy CLC 21
   See also Chambers, James
Cliff, Michelle 1946- .... CLC 120; BLCS
   See also BW 2; CA 116; CANR 39, 72;
      DLB 157
Clifton, (Thelma) Lucille 1936- .... CLC 19,
      66; BLC 1; DAM MULT, POET; PC
      17
   See also BW 2, 3; CA 49-52; CANR 2, 24,
      42, 76; CLR 5; DA3; DLB 5, 41; MAI-
      CYA; MTCW 1, 2; SATA 20, 69
Clinton, Dirk
   See Silverberg, Robert
Clough, Arthur Hugh 1819-1861 ... NCLC 27
   See also DLB 32
Clutha, Janet Paterson Frame 1924-
   See Frame, Janet
   See also CA 1-4R; CANR 2, 36, 76; MTCW
      1, 2
Clyne, Terence
   See Blatty, William Peter
Cobalt, Martin
   See Mayne, William (James Carter)
Cobb, Irvin S(hrewsbury)
   1876-1944 .... TCLC 77
   See also CA 175; DLB 11, 25, 86
Cobbett, William 1763-1835 .... NCLC 49
   See also DLB 43, 107, 158
Coburn, D(onald) L(ee) 1938- .... CLC 10
   See also CA 89-92
Cocteau, Jean (Maurice Eugene Clement)
   1889-1963 .... CLC 1, 8, 15, 16, 43; DA;
      DAB; DAC; DAM DRAM, MST, NOV;
      WLC
   See also CA 25-28; CANR 40; CAP 2;
      DA3; DLB 65; MTCW 1, 2

Codrescu, Andrei 1946- .... **CLC 46, 121; DAM POET**
　See also CA 33-36R; CAAS 19; CANR 13, 34, 53, 76; DA3; MTCW 2

Coe, Max
　See Bourne, Randolph S(illiman)

Coe, Tucker
　See Westlake, Donald E(dwin)

Coen, Ethan 1958- .... **CLC 108**
　See also CA 126; CANR 85

Coen, Joel 1955- .... **CLC 108**
　See also CA 126

The Coen Brothers
　See Coen, Ethan; Coen, Joel

Coetzee, J(ohn) M(ichael) 1940- ...... **CLC 23, 33, 66, 117; DAM NOV**
　See also CA 77-80; CANR 41, 54, 74; DA3; DLB 225; MTCW 1, 2

Coffey, Brian
　See Koontz, Dean R(ay)

Coffin, Robert P(eter) Tristram
　　1892-1955 .... **TCLC 95**
　See also CA 123; 169; DLB 45

Cohan, George M(ichael)
　　1878-1942 .... **TCLC 60**
　See also CA 157

Cohen, Arthur A(llen) 1928-1986 ...... **CLC 7, 31**
　See also CA 1-4R; 120; CANR 1, 17, 42; DLB 28

Cohen, Leonard (Norman) 1934- ...... **CLC 3, 38; DAC; DAM MST**
　See also CA 21-24R; CANR 14, 69; DLB 53; MTCW 1

Cohen, Matt 1942-1999 .... **CLC 19; DAC**
　See also CA 61-64; CAAS 18; CANR 40; DLB 53

Cohen-Solal, Annie 19(?)- .... **CLC 50**

Colegate, Isabel 1931- .... **CLC 36**
　See also CA 17-20R; CANR 8, 22, 74; DLB 14; INT CANR-22; MTCW 1

Coleman, Emmett
　See Reed, Ishmael

Coleridge, Hartley 1796-1849 .... **NCLC 90**
　See also DLB 96

Coleridge, M. E.
　See Coleridge, Mary E(lizabeth)

Coleridge, Mary E(lizabeth)
　　1861-1907 .... **TCLC 73**
　See also CA 116; 166; DLB 19, 98

Coleridge, Samuel Taylor
　　1772-1834 .... **NCLC 9, 54; DA; DAB; DAC; DAM MST, POET; PC 11; WLC**
　See also CDBLB 1789-1832; DA3; DLB 93, 107

Coleridge, Sara 1802-1852 .... **NCLC 31**
　See also DLB 199

Coles, Don 1928- .... **CLC 46**
　See also CA 115; CANR 38

Coles, Robert (Martin) 1929- .... **CLC 108**
　See also CA 45-48; CANR 3, 32, 66, 70; INT CANR-32; SATA 23

Colette, (Sidonie-Gabrielle)
　　1873-1954 . **TCLC 1, 5, 16; DAM NOV; SSC 10**
　See also CA 104; 131; DA3; DLB 65; MTCW 1, 2

Collett, (Jacobine) Camilla (Wergeland)
　　1813-1895 .... **NCLC 22**

Collier, Christopher 1930- .... **CLC 30**
　See also AAYA 13; CA 33-36R; CANR 13, 33; JRDA; MAICYA; SATA 16, 70

Collier, James L(incoln) 1928- .... **CLC 30; DAM POP**
　See also AAYA 13; CA 9-12R; CANR 4, 33, 60; CLR 3; JRDA; MAICYA; SAAS 21; SATA 8, 70

Collier, Jeremy 1650-1726 .... **LC 6**

Collier, John 1901-1980 .... **SSC 19**
　See also CA 65-68; 97-100; CANR 10; DLB 77

Collingwood, R(obin) G(eorge)
　　1889(?)-1943 .... **TCLC 67**
　See also CA 117; 155

Collins, Hunt
　See Hunter, Evan

Collins, Linda 1931- .... **CLC 44**
　See also CA 125

Collins, (William) Wilkie
　　1824-1889 .... **NCLC 1, 18**
　See also CDBLB 1832-1890; DLB 18, 70, 159

Collins, William 1721-1759 . **LC 4, 40; DAM POET**
　See also DLB 109

Collodi, Carlo 1826-1890 .... **NCLC 54**
　See also Lorenzini, Carlo
　See also CLR 5

Colman, George 1732-1794
　See Glassco, John

Colt, Winchester Remington
　See Hubbard, L(afayette) Ron(ald)

Colter, Cyrus 1910- .... **CLC 58**
　See also BW 1; CA 65-68; CANR 10, 66; DLB 33

Colton, James
　See Hansen, Joseph

Colum, Padraic 1881-1972 .... **CLC 28**
　See also CA 73-76; 33-36R; CANR 35; CLR 36; MAICYA; MTCW 1; SATA 15

Colvin, James
　See Moorcock, Michael (John)

Colwin, Laurie (E.) 1944-1992 .... **CLC 5, 13, 23, 84**
　See also CA 89-92; 139; CANR 20, 46; DLBY 80; MTCW 1

Comfort, Alex(ander) 1920- .... **CLC 7; DAM POP**
　See also CA 1-4R; CANR 1, 45; MTCW 1

Comfort, Montgomery
　See Campbell, (John) Ramsey

Compton-Burnett, I(vy)
　　1884(?)-1969 .... **CLC 1, 3, 10, 15, 34; DAM NOV**
　See also CA 1-4R; 25-28R; CANR 4; DLB 36; MTCW 1

Comstock, Anthony 1844-1915 ...... **TCLC 13**
　See also CA 110; 169

Comte, Auguste 1798-1857 .... **NCLC 54**

Conan Doyle, Arthur
　See Doyle, Arthur Conan

Conde (Abellan), Carmen 1901-
　See also CA 177; DLB 108; HLCS 1; HW 2

Conde, Maryse 1937- .... **CLC 52, 92; BLCS; DAM MULT**
　See also BW 2, 3; CA 110; CANR 30, 53, 76; MTCW 1

Condillac, Etienne Bonnot de
　　1714-1780 .... **LC 26**

Condon, Richard (Thomas)
　　1915-1996 ...... **CLC 4, 6, 8, 10, 45, 100; DAM NOV**
　See also BEST 90:3; CA 1-4R; 151; CAAS 1; CANR 2, 23; INT CANR-23; MTCW 1, 2

Confucius 551B.C.-479B.C. .. **CMLC 19; DA; DAB; DAC; DAM MST; WLCS**
　See also DA3

Congreve, William 1670-1729 .... **LC 5, 21; DA; DAB; DAC; DAM DRAM, MST, POET; DC 2; WLC**
　See also CDBLB 1660-1789; DLB 39, 84

Connell, Evan S(helby), Jr. 1924- . **CLC 4, 6, 45; DAM NOV**
　See also AAYA 7; CA 1-4R; CAAS 2; CANR 2, 39, 76; DLB 2; DLBY 81; MTCW 1, 2

Connelly, Marc(us Cook) 1890-1980 . **CLC 7**
　See also CA 85-88; 102; CANR 30; DLB 7; DLBY 80; SATA-Obit 25

Connor, Ralph **TCLC 31**
　See also Gordon, Charles William
　See also DLB 92

Conrad, Joseph 1857-1924 .... **TCLC 1, 6, 13, 25, 43, 57; DA; DAB; DAC; DAM MST, NOV; SSC 9; WLC**
　See also AAYA 26; CA 104; 131; CANR 60; CDBLB 1890-1914; DA3; DLB 10, 34, 98, 156; MTCW 1, 2; SATA 27

Conrad, Robert Arnold
　See Hart, Moss

Conroy, Pat
　See Conroy, (Donald) Pat(rick)
　See also MTCW 2

Conroy, (Donald) Pat(rick) 1945- ... **CLC 30, 74; DAM NOV, POP**
　See also Conroy, Pat
　See also AAYA 8; AITN 1; CA 85-88; CANR 24, 53; DA3; DLB 6; MTCW 1

Constant (de Rebecque), (Henri) Benjamin
　　1767-1830 .... **NCLC 6**
　See also DLB 119

Conybeare, Charles Augustus
　See Eliot, T(homas) S(tearns)

Cook, Michael 1933- .... **CLC 58**
　See also CA 93-96; CANR 68; DLB 53

Cook, Robin 1940- .... **CLC 14; DAM POP**
　See also AAYA 32; BEST 90:2; CA 108; 111; CANR 41, 90; DA3; INT 111

Cook, Roy
　See Silverberg, Robert

Cooke, Elizabeth 1948- .... **CLC 55**
　See also CA 129

Cooke, John Esten 1830-1886 .... **NCLC 5**
　See also DLB 3

Cooke, John Estes
　See Baum, L(yman) Frank

Cooke, M. E.
　See Creasey, John

Cooke, Margaret
　See Creasey, John

Cook-Lynn, Elizabeth 1930- . **CLC 93; DAM MULT**
　See also CA 133; DLB 175; NNAL

Cooney, Ray **CLC 62**

Cooper, Douglas 1960- .... **CLC 86**

Cooper, Henry St. John
　See Creasey, John

Cooper, J(oan) California (?)- .... **CLC 56; DAM MULT**
　See also AAYA 12; BW 1; CA 125; CANR 55; DLB 212

Cooper, James Fenimore
　　1789-1851 .... **NCLC 1, 27, 54**
　See also AAYA 22; CDALB 1640-1865; DA3; DLB 3; SATA 19

Coover, Robert (Lowell) 1932- ...... **CLC 3, 7, 15, 32, 46, 87; DAM NOV; SSC 15**
　See also CA 45-48; CANR 3, 37, 58; DLB 2, 227; DLBY 81; MTCW 1, 2

Copeland, Stewart (Armstrong)
　　1952- .... **CLC 26**

Copernicus, Nicolaus 1473-1543 .... **LC 45**

Coppard, A(lfred) E(dgar)
　　1878-1957 .... **TCLC 5; SSC 21**
　See also CA 114; 167; DLB 162; YABC 1

Coppee, Francois 1842-1908 .... **TCLC 25**
　See also CA 170

Coppola, Francis Ford 1939- ... **CLC 16, 126**
　See also CA 77-80; CANR 40, 78; DLB 44

Corbiere, Tristan 1845-1875 .... **NCLC 43**

Corcoran, Barbara 1911- .... **CLC 17**
See also AAYA 14; CA 21-24R; CAAS 2; CANR 11, 28, 48; CLR 50; DLB 52; JRDA; SAAS 20; SATA 3, 77

Cordelier, Maurice
See Giraudoux, (Hippolyte) Jean

Corelli, Marie 1855-1924 .... **TCLC 51**
See also Mackey, Mary
See also DLB 34, 156

Corman, Cid 1924- .... **CLC 9**
See also Corman, Sidney
See also CAAS 2; DLB 5, 193

Corman, Sidney 1924-
See Corman, Cid
See also CA 85-88; CANR 44; DAM POET

Cormier, Robert (Edmund) 1925- ... **CLC 12, 30; DA; DAB; DAC; DAM MST, NOV**
See also AAYA 3, 19; CA 1-4R; CANR 5, 23, 76; CDALB 1968-1988; CLR 12, 55; DLB 52; INT CANR-23; JRDA; MAICYA; MTCW 1, 2; SATA 10, 45, 83

Corn, Alfred (DeWitt III) 1943- .... **CLC 33**
See also CA 179; CAAE 179; CAAS 25; CANR 44; DLB 120; DLBY 80

Corneille, Pierre 1606-1684 ..... **LC 28; DAB; DAM MST**

Cornwell, David (John Moore) 1931- .... **CLC 9, 15; DAM POP**
See also le Carre, John
See also CA 5-8R; CANR 13, 33, 59; DA3; MTCW 1, 2

Corso, (Nunzio) Gregory 1930- .... **CLC 1, 11**
See also CA 5-8R; CANR 41, 76; DA3; DLB 5, 16; MTCW 1, 2

Cortazar, Julio 1914-1984 ... **CLC 2, 3, 5, 10, 13, 15, 33, 34, 92; DAM MULT, NOV; HLC 1; SSC 7**
See also CA 21-24R; CANR 12, 32, 81; DA3; DLB 113; HW 1, 2; MTCW 1, 2

Cortes, Hernan 1484-1547 .... **LC 31**

Corvinus, Jakob
See Raabe, Wilhelm (Karl)

Corwin, Cecil
See Kornbluth, C(yril) M.

Cosic, Dobrica 1921- .... **CLC 14**
See also CA 122; 138; DLB 181

Costain, Thomas B(ertram)
1885-1965 .... **CLC 30**
See also CA 5-8R; 25-28R; DLB 9

Costantini, Humberto 1924(?)-1987 . **CLC 49**
See also CA 131; 122; HW 1

Costello, Elvis 1955- .... **CLC 21**

Costenoble, Philostene
See Ghelderode, Michel de

Cotes, Cecil V.
See Duncan, Sara Jeannette

Cotter, Joseph Seamon Sr.
1861-1949 ...... **TCLC 28; BLC 1; DAM MULT**
See also BW 1; CA 124; DLB 50

Couch, Arthur Thomas Quiller
See Quiller-Couch, SirArthur (Thomas)

Coulton, James
See Hansen, Joseph

Couperus, Louis (Marie Anne)
1863-1923 .... **TCLC 15**
See also CA 115

Coupland, Douglas 1961- .... **CLC 85, 133; DAC; DAM POP**
See also AAYA 34; CA 142; CANR 57, 90

Court, Wesli
See Turco, Lewis (Putnam)

Courtenay, Bryce 1933- .... **CLC 59**
See also CA 138

Courtney, Robert
See Ellison, Harlan (Jay)

Cousteau, Jacques-Yves 1910-1997 .. **CLC 30**
See also CA 65-68; 159; CANR 15, 67; MTCW 1; SATA 38, 98

Coventry, Francis 1725-1754 .... **LC 46**

Cowan, Peter (Walkinshaw) 1914- .... **SSC 28**
See also CA 21-24R; CANR 9, 25, 50, 83

Coward, Noel (Peirce) 1899-1973 . **CLC 1, 9, 29, 51; DAM DRAM**
See also AITN 1; CA 17-18; 41-44R; CANR 35; CAP 2; CDBLB 1914-1945; DA3; DLB 10; MTCW 1, 2

Cowley, Abraham 1618-1667 .... **LC 43**
See also DLB 131, 151

Cowley, Malcolm 1898-1989 .... **CLC 39**
See also CA 5-8R; 128; CANR 3, 55; DLB 4, 48; DLBY 81, 89; MTCW 1, 2

Cowper, William 1731-1800 . **NCLC 8; DAM POET**
See also DA3; DLB 104, 109

Cox, William Trevor 1928- ... **CLC 9, 14, 71; DAM NOV**
See also Trevor, William
See also CA 9-12R; CANR 4, 37, 55, 76; DLB 14; INT CANR-37; MTCW 1, 2

Coyne, P. J.
See Masters, Hilary

Cozzens, James Gould 1903-1978 . **CLC 1, 4, 11, 92**
See also CA 9-12R; 81-84; CANR 19; CDALB 1941-1968; DLB 9; DLBD 2; DLBY 84, 97; MTCW 1, 2

Crabbe, George 1754-1832 .... **NCLC 26**
See also DLB 93

Craddock, Charles Egbert
See Murfree, Mary Noailles

Craig, A. A.
See Anderson, Poul (William)

Craik, Dinah Maria (Mulock)
1826-1887 .... **NCLC 38**
See also DLB 35, 163; MAICYA; SATA 34

Cram, Ralph Adams 1863-1942 ..... **TCLC 45**
See also CA 160

Crane, (Harold) Hart 1899-1932 .... **TCLC 2, 5, 80; DA; DAB; DAC; DAM MST, POET; PC 3; WLC**
See also CA 104; 127; CDALB 1917-1929; DA3; DLB 4, 48; MTCW 1, 2

Crane, R(onald) S(almon)
1886-1967 .... **CLC 27**
See also CA 85-88; DLB 63

Crane, Stephen (Townley)
1871-1900 ...... **TCLC 11, 17, 32; DA; DAB; DAC; DAM MST, NOV, POET; SSC 7; WLC**
See also AAYA 21; CA 109; 140; CANR 84; CDALB 1865-1917; DA3; DLB 12, 54, 78; YABC 2

Cranshaw, Stanley
See Fisher, Dorothy (Frances) Canfield

Crase, Douglas 1944- .... **CLC 58**
See also CA 106

Crashaw, Richard 1612(?)-1649 .... **LC 24**
See also DLB 126

Craven, Margaret 1901-1980 .... **CLC 17; DAC**
See also CA 103

Crawford, F(rancis) Marion
1854-1909 .... **TCLC 10**
See also CA 107; 168; DLB 71

Crawford, Isabella Valancy
1850-1887 .... **NCLC 12**
See also DLB 92

Crayon, Geoffrey
See Irving, Washington

Creasey, John 1908-1973 .... **CLC 11**
See also CA 5-8R; 41-44R; CANR 8, 59; DLB 77; MTCW 1

Crebillon, Claude Prosper Jolyot de (fils)
1707-1777 .... **LC 1, 28**

Credo
See Creasey, John

Credo, Alvaro J. de
See Prado (Calvo), Pedro

Creeley, Robert (White) 1926- .. **CLC 1, 2, 4, 8, 11, 15, 36, 78; DAM POET**
See also CA 1-4R; CAAS 10; CANR 23, 43, 89; DA3; DLB 5, 16, 169; DLBD 17; MTCW 1, 2

Crews, Harry (Eugene) 1935- ..... **CLC 6, 23, 49**
See also AITN 1; CA 25-28R; CANR 20, 57; DA3; DLB 6, 143, 185; MTCW 1, 2

Crichton, (John) Michael 1942- .... **CLC 2, 6, 54, 90; DAM NOV, POP**
See also AAYA 10; AITN 2; CA 25-28R; CANR 13, 40, 54, 76; DA3; DLBY 81; INT CANR-13; JRDA; MTCW 1, 2; SATA 9, 88

Crispin, Edmund CLC 22
See also Montgomery, (Robert) Bruce
See also DLB 87

Cristofer, Michael 1945(?)- ... **CLC 28; DAM DRAM**
See also CA 110; 152; DLB 7

Croce, Benedetto 1866-1952 .... **TCLC 37**
See also CA 120; 155

Crockett, David 1786-1836 .... **NCLC 8**
See also DLB 3, 11

Crockett, Davy
See Crockett, David

Crofts, Freeman Wills 1879-1957 .. **TCLC 55**
See also CA 115; DLB 77

Croker, John Wilson 1780-1857 .... **NCLC 10**
See also DLB 110

Crommelynck, Fernand 1885-1970 .. **CLC 75**
See also CA 89-92

Cromwell, Oliver 1599-1658 .... **LC 43**

Cronin, A(rchibald) J(oseph)
1896-1981 .... **CLC 32**
See also CA 1-4R; 102; CANR 5; DLB 191; SATA 47; SATA-Obit 25

Cross, Amanda
See Heilbrun, Carolyn G(old)

Crothers, Rachel 1878(?)-1958 .... **TCLC 19**
See also CA 113; DLB 7

Croves, Hal
See Traven, B.

Crow Dog, Mary (Ellen) (?)- .... **CLC 93**
See also Brave Bird, Mary
See also CA 154

Crowfield, Christopher
See Stowe, Harriet (Elizabeth) Beecher

Crowley, Aleister TCLC 7
See also Crowley, Edward Alexander

Crowley, Edward Alexander 1875-1947
See Crowley, Aleister
See also CA 104

Crowley, John 1942- .... **CLC 57**
See also CA 61-64; CANR 43; DLBY 82; SATA 65

Crud
See Crumb, R(obert)

Crumarums
See Crumb, R(obert)

Crumb, R(obert) 1943- .... **CLC 17**
See also CA 106

Crumbum
See Crumb, R(obert)

Crumski
See Crumb, R(obert)

Crum the Bum
See Crumb, R(obert)

Crunk
See Crumb, R(obert)

Crustt
See Crumb, R(obert)

Cruz, Victor Hernandez 1949-
See also BW 2; CA 65-68; CAAS 17; CANR 14, 32, 74; DAM MULT, POET; DLB 41; HLC 1; HW 1, 2; MTCW 1

Cryer, Gretchen (Kiger) 1935- .... **CLC 21**
See also CA 114; 123

Csath, Geza 1887-1919 .... **TCLC 13**
See also CA 111

Cudlip, David R(ockwell) 1933- .... **CLC 34**
See also CA 177

Cullen, Countee 1903-1946 .... **TCLC 4, 37; BLC 1; DA; DAC; DAM MST, MULT, POET; PC 20; WLCS**
See also BW 1; CA 108; 124; CDALB 1917-1929; DA3; DLB 4, 48, 51; MTCW 1, 2; SATA 18

Cum, R.
See Crumb, R(obert)

Cummings, Bruce F(rederick) 1889-1919
See Barbellion, W. N. P.
See also CA 123

Cummings, E(dward) E(stlin) 1894-1962 .... **CLC 1, 3, 8, 12, 15, 68; DA; DAB; DAC; DAM MST, POET; PC 5; WLC**
See also CA 73-76; CANR 31; CDALB 1929-1941; DA3; DLB 4, 48; MTCW 1, 2

Cunha, Euclides (Rodrigues Pimenta) da 1866-1909 .... **TCLC 24**
See also CA 123

Cunningham, E. V.
See Fast, Howard (Melvin)

Cunningham, J(ames) V(incent) 1911-1985 .... **CLC 3, 31**
See also CA 1-4R; 115; CANR 1, 72; DLB 5

Cunningham, Julia (Woolfolk) 1916- .... **CLC 12**
See also CA 9-12R; CANR 4, 19, 36; JRDA; MAICYA; SAAS 2; SATA 1, 26

Cunningham, Michael 1952- .... **CLC 34**
See also CA 136

Cunninghame Graham, R. B.
See Cunninghame Graham, Robert (Gallnigad) Bontine

Cunninghame Graham, Robert (Gallnigad) Bontine 1852-1936 .... **TCLC 19**
See also Graham, R(obert) B(ontine) Cunninghame
See also CA 119; 184; DLB 98

Currie, Ellen 19(?)- .... **CLC 44**

Curtin, Philip
See Lowndes, Marie Adelaide (Belloc)

Curtis, Price
See Ellison, Harlan (Jay)

Cutrate, Joe
See Spiegelman, Art

Cynewulf c. 770-c. 840 .... **CMLC 23**

Czaczkes, Shmuel Yosef
See Agnon, S(hmuel) Y(osef Halevi)

Dabrowska, Maria (Szumska) 1889-1965 .... **CLC 15**
See also CA 106

Dabydeen, David 1955- .... **CLC 34**
See also BW 1; CA 125; CANR 56, 92

Dacey, Philip 1939- .... **CLC 51**
See also CA 37-40R; CAAS 17; CANR 14, 32, 64; DLB 105

Dagerman, Stig (Halvard) 1923-1954 .... **TCLC 17**
See also CA 117; 155

Dahl, Roald 1916-1990 ...... **CLC 1, 6, 18, 79; DAB; DAC; DAM MST, NOV, POP**
See also AAYA 15; CA 1-4R; 133; CANR 6, 32, 37, 62; CLR 1, 7, 41; DA3; DLB

139; JRDA; MAICYA; MTCW 1, 2; SATA 1, 26, 73; SATA-Obit 65

Dahlberg, Edward 1900-1977 .. **CLC 1, 7, 14**
See also CA 9-12R; 69-72; CANR 31, 62; DLB 48; MTCW 1

Daitch, Susan 1954- .... **CLC 103**
See also CA 161

Dale, Colin TCLC 18
See also Lawrence, T(homas) E(dward)

Dale, George E.
See Asimov, Isaac

Dalton, Roque 1935-1975
See also HLCS 1; HW 2

Daly, Elizabeth 1878-1967 .... **CLC 52**
See also CA 23-24; 25-28R; CANR 60; CAP 2

Daly, Maureen 1921-1983 .... **CLC 17**
See also AAYA 5; CANR 37, 83; JRDA; MAICYA; SAAS 1; SATA 2

Damas, Leon-Gontran 1912-1978 .... **CLC 84**
See also BW 1; CA 125; 73-76

Dana, Richard Henry Sr. 1787-1879 .... **NCLC 53**

Daniel, Samuel 1562(?)-1619 .... **LC 24**
See also DLB 62

Daniels, Brett
See Adler, Renata

Dannay, Frederic 1905-1982 . **CLC 11; DAM POP**
See also Queen, Ellery
See also CA 1-4R; 107; CANR 1, 39; DLB 137; MTCW 1

D'Annunzio, Gabriele 1863-1938 ... **TCLC 6, 40**
See also CA 104; 155

Danois, N. le
See Gourmont, Remy (-Marie-Charles) de

Dante 1265-1321 .... **CMLC 3, 18, 39; DA; DAB; DAC; DAM MST, POET; PC 21; WLCS**
See also Alighieri, Dante
See also DA3

d'Antibes, Germain
See Simenon, Georges (Jacques Christian)

Danticat, Edwidge 1969- .... **CLC 94**
See also AAYA 29; CA 152; CANR 73; MTCW 1

Danvers, Dennis 1947- .... **CLC 70**

Danziger, Paula 1944- .... **CLC 21**
See also AAYA 4; CA 112; 115; CANR 37; CLR 20; JRDA; MAICYA; SATA 36, 63, 102; SATA-Brief 30

Da Ponte, Lorenzo 1749-1838 .... **NCLC 50**

Dario, Ruben 1867-1916 .... **TCLC 4; DAM MULT; HLC 1; PC 15**
See also CA 131; CANR 81; HW 1, 2; MTCW 1, 2

Darley, George 1795-1846 .... **NCLC 2**
See also DLB 96

Darrow, Clarence (Seward) 1857-1938 .... **TCLC 81**
See also CA 164

Darwin, Charles 1809-1882 .... **NCLC 57**
See also DLB 57, 166

Daryush, Elizabeth 1887-1977 ...... **CLC 6, 19**
See also CA 49-52; CANR 3, 81; DLB 20

Dasgupta, Surendranath 1887-1952 .... **TCLC 81**
See also CA 157

Dashwood, Edmee Elizabeth Monica de la Pasture 1890-1943
See Delafield, E. M.
See also CA 119; 154

Daudet, (Louis Marie) Alphonse 1840-1897 .... **NCLC 1**
See also DLB 123

Daumal, Rene 1908-1944 .... **TCLC 14**
See also CA 114

Davenant, William 1606-1668 .... **LC 13**
See also DLB 58, 126

Davenport, Guy (Mattison, Jr.) 1927- .... **CLC 6, 14, 38; SSC 16**
See also CA 33-36R; CANR 23, 73; DLB 130

Davidson, Avram (James) 1923-1993
See Queen, Ellery
See also CA 101; 171; CANR 26; DLB 8

Davidson, Donald (Grady) 1893-1968 .... **CLC 2, 13, 19**
See also CA 5-8R; 25-28R; CANR 4, 84; DLB 45

Davidson, Hugh
See Hamilton, Edmond

Davidson, John 1857-1909 .... **TCLC 24**
See also CA 118; DLB 19

Davidson, Sara 1943- .... **CLC 9**
See also CA 81-84; CANR 44, 68; DLB 185

Davie, Donald (Alfred) 1922-1995 ... **CLC 5, 8, 10, 31; PC 29**
See also CA 1-4R; 149; CAAS 3; CANR 1, 44; DLB 27; MTCW 1

Davies, Ray(mond Douglas) 1944- ... **CLC 21**
See also CA 116; 146; CANR 92

Davies, Rhys 1901-1978 .... **CLC 23**
See also CA 9-12R; 81-84; CANR 4; DLB 139, 191

Davies, (William) Robertson 1913-1995 .... **CLC 2, 7, 13, 25, 42, 75, 91; DA; DAB; DAC; DAM MST, NOV, POP; WLC**
See also BEST 89:2; CA 33-36R; 150; CANR 17, 42; DA3; DLB 68; INT CANR-17; MTCW 1, 2

Davies, Walter C.
See Kornbluth, C(yril) M.

Davies, William Henry 1871-1940 ... **TCLC 5**
See also CA 104; 179; DLB 19, 174

Da Vinci, Leonardo 1452-1519 ..... **LC 12, 57, 60**

Davis, Angela (Yvonne) 1944- .... **CLC 77; DAM MULT**
See also BW 2, 3; CA 57-60; CANR 10, 81; DA3

Davis, B. Lynch
See Bioy Casares, Adolfo; Borges, Jorge Luis

Davis, B. Lynch
See Bioy Casares, Adolfo

Davis, H(arold) L(enoir) 1894-1960 . **CLC 49**
See also CA 178; 89-92; DLB 9, 206; SATA 114

Davis, Rebecca (Blaine) Harding 1831-1910 .... **TCLC 6; SSC 38**
See also CA 104; 179; DLB 74

Davis, Richard Harding 1864-1916 .... **TCLC 24**
See also CA 114; 179; DLB 12, 23, 78, 79, 189; DLBD 13

Davison, Frank Dalby 1893-1970 ..... **CLC 15**
See also CA 116

Davison, Lawrence H.
See Lawrence, D(avid) H(erbert Richards)

Davison, Peter (Hubert) 1928- .... **CLC 28**
See also CA 9-12R; CAAS 4; CANR 3, 43, 84; DLB 5

Davys, Mary 1674-1732 .... **LC 1, 46**
See also DLB 39

Dawson, Fielding 1930- .... **CLC 6**
See also CA 85-88; DLB 130

Dawson, Peter
See Faust, Frederick (Schiller)

Day, Clarence (Shepard, Jr.) 1874-1935 .... **TCLC 25**
See also CA 108; DLB 11

Day, Thomas 1748-1789 .... **LC 1**
See also DLB 39; YABC 1

Day Lewis, C(ecil) 1904-1972 . **CLC 1, 6, 10;**
DAM POET; PC 11
See also Blake, Nicholas
See also CA 13-16; 33-36R; CANR 34;
CAP 1; DLB 15, 20; MTCW 1, 2
Dazai Osamu 1909-1948 .. **TCLC 11; SSC 41**
See also Tsushima, Shuji
See also CA 164; DLB 182
de Andrade, Carlos Drummond 1892-1945
See Drummond de Andrade, Carlos
Deane, Norman
See Creasey, John
Deane, Seamus (Francis) 1940- ...... **CLC 122**
See also CA 118; CANR 42
de Beauvoir, Simone (Lucie Ernestine Marie
Bertrand)
See Beauvoir, Simone (Lucie Ernestine
Marie Bertrand) de
de Beer, P.
See Bosman, Herman Charles
de Brissac, Malcolm
See Dickinson, Peter (Malcolm)
de Campos, Alvaro
See Pessoa, Fernando (Antonio Nogueira)
de Chardin, Pierre Teilhard
See Teilhard de Chardin, (Marie Joseph)
Pierre
Dee, John 1527-1608 .... **LC 20**
Deer, Sandra 1940- .... **CLC 45**
See also CA 186
De Ferrari, Gabriella 1941- .... **CLC 65**
See also CA 146
Defoe, Daniel 1660(?)-1731 .... **LC 1, 42; DA;**
DAB; DAC; DAM MST, NOV; WLC
See also AAYA 27; CDBLB 1660-1789;
CLR 61; DA3; DLB 39, 95, 101; JRDA;
MAICYA; SATA 22
de Gourmont, Remy(-Marie-Charles)
See Gourmont, Remy (-Marie-Charles) de
de Hartog, Jan 1914- .... **CLC 19**
See also CA 1-4R; CANR 1
de Hostos, E. M.
See Hostos (y Bonilla), Eugenio Maria de
de Hostos, Eugenio M.
See Hostos (y Bonilla), Eugenio Maria de
Deighton, Len **CLC 4, 7, 22, 46**
See Deighton, Leonard Cyril
See also AAYA 6; BEST 89:2; CDBLB
1960 to Present; DLB 87
Deighton, Leonard Cyril 1929-
See Deighton, Len
See also CA 9-12R; CANR 19, 33, 68;
DAM NOV, POP; DA3; MTCW 1, 2
Dekker, Thomas 1572(?)-1632 . **LC 22; DAM**
DRAM; DC 12
See also CDBLB Before 1660; DLB 62, 172
Delafield, E. M. 1890-1943 .... **TCLC 61**
See also Dashwood, Edmee Elizabeth
Monica de la Pasture
See also DLB 34
de la Mare, Walter (John)
1873-1956 ..... **TCLC 4, 53; DAB; DAC;**
DAM MST, POET; SSC 14; WLC
See also CA 163; CDBLB 1914-1945; CLR
23; DA3; DLB 162; MTCW 1; SATA 16
Delaney, Franey
See O'Hara, John (Henry)
Delaney, Shelagh 1939- .... **CLC 29; DAM**
DRAM
See also CA 17-20R; CANR 30, 67; CD-
BLB 1960 to Present; DLB 13; MTCW 1
Delany, Mary (Granville Pendarves)
1700-1788 .... **LC 12**
Delany, Samuel R(ay, Jr.) 1942- .. **CLC 8, 14,**
38; BLC 1; DAM MULT
See also AAYA 24; BW 2, 3; CA 81-84;
CANR 27, 43; DLB 8, 33; MTCW 1, 2

De La Ramee, (Marie) Louise 1839-1908
See Ouida
See also SATA 20
de la Roche, Mazo 1879-1961 .... **CLC 14**
See also CA 85-88; CANR 30; DLB 68;
SATA 64
De La Salle, Innocent
See Hartmann, Sadakichi
Delbanco, Nicholas (Franklin)
1942- .... **CLC 6, 13**
See also CA 17-20R; CAAS 2; CANR 29,
55; DLB 6
del Castillo, Michel 1933- .... **CLC 38**
See also CA 109; CANR 77
Deledda, Grazia (Cosima)
1875(?)-1936 .... **TCLC 23**
See also CA 123
Delgado, Abelardo (Lalo) B(arrientos) 1930-
See also CA 131; CAAS 15; CANR 90;
DAM MST, MULT; DLB 82; HLC 1; HW
1, 2
Delibes, Miguel **CLC 8, 18**
See also Delibes Setien, Miguel
Delibes Setien, Miguel 1920-
See Delibes, Miguel
See also CA 45-48; CANR 1, 32; HW 1;
MTCW 1
DeLillo, Don 1936- ..... **CLC 8, 10, 13, 27, 39,**
54, 76; DAM NOV, POP
See also BEST 89:1; CA 81-84; CANR 21,
76, 92; DA3; DLB 6, 173; MTCW 1, 2
de Lisser, H. G.
See De Lisser, H(erbert) G(eorge)
See also DLB 117
De Lisser, H(erbert) G(eorge)
1878-1944 .... **TCLC 12**
See also de Lisser, H. G.
See also BW 2; CA 109; 152
Deloney, Thomas 1560(?)-1600 .... **LC 41**
See also DLB 167
Deloria, Vine (Victor), Jr. 1933- ...... **CLC 21,**
122; DAM MULT
See also CA 53-56; CANR 5, 20, 48; DLB
175; MTCW 1; NNAL; SATA 21
Del Vecchio, John M(ichael) 1947- .. **CLC 29**
See also CA 110; DLBD 9
de Man, Paul (Adolph Michel)
1919-1983 .... **CLC 55**
See also CA 128; 111; CANR 61; DLB 67;
MTCW 1, 2
DeMarinis, Rick 1934- .... **CLC 54**
See also CA 57-60, 184; CAAE 184; CAAS
24; CANR 9, 25, 50
Dembry, R. Emmet
See Murfree, Mary Noailles
Demby, William 1922- .... **CLC 53; BLC 1;**
DAM MULT
See also BW 1, 3; CA 81-84; CANR 81;
DLB 33
de Menton, Francisco
See Chin, Frank (Chew, Jr.)
Demetrius of Phalerum c.
307B.C.- .... **CMLC 34**
Demijohn, Thom
See Disch, Thomas M(ichael)
de Molina, Tirso 1584(?)-1648 .... **DC 13**
See also HLCS 2
de Montherlant, Henry (Milon)
See Montherlant, Henry (Milon) de
Demosthenes 384B.C.-322B.C. ...... **CMLC 13**
See also DLB 176
de Natale, Francine
See Malzberg, Barry N(athaniel)
Denby, Edwin (Orr) 1903-1983 .... **CLC 48**
See also CA 138; 110
Denis, Julio
See Cortazar, Julio
Denmark, Harrison
See Zelazny, Roger (Joseph)

Dennis, John 1658-1734 .... **LC 11**
See also DLB 101
Dennis, Nigel (Forbes) 1912-1989 ...... **CLC 8**
See also CA 25-28R; 129; DLB 13, 15;
MTCW 1
Dent, Lester 1904(?)-1959 .... **TCLC 72**
See also CA 112; 161
De Palma, Brian (Russell) 1940- ...... **CLC 20**
See also CA 109
De Quincey, Thomas 1785-1859 ..... **NCLC 4,**
87
See also CDBLB 1789-1832; DLB 110; 144
Deren, Eleanora 1908(?)-1961
See Deren, Maya
See also CA 111
Deren, Maya 1917-1961 .... **CLC 16, 102**
See also Deren, Eleanora
Derleth, August (William)
1909-1971 .... **CLC 31**
See also CA 1-4R; 29-32R; CANR 4; DLB
9; DLBD 17; SATA 5
Der Nister 1884-1950 .... **TCLC 56**
de Routisie, Albert
See Aragon, Louis
Derrida, Jacques 1930- .... **CLC 24, 87**
See also CA 124; 127; CANR 76; MTCW 1
Derry Down Derry
See Lear, Edward
Dersonnes, Jacques
See Simenon, Georges (Jacques Christian)
Desai, Anita 1937- ..... **CLC 19, 37, 97; DAB;**
DAM NOV
See also CA 81-84; CANR 33, 53; DA3;
MTCW 1, 2; SATA 63
Desai, Kiran 1971- .... **CLC 119**
See also CA 171
de Saint-Luc, Jean
See Glassco, John
de Saint Roman, Arnaud
See Aragon, Louis
Descartes, Rene 1596-1650 .... **LC 20, 35**
De Sica, Vittorio 1901(?)-1974 .... **CLC 20**
See also CA 117
Desnos, Robert 1900-1945 .... **TCLC 22**
See also CA 121; 151
de Staël, Germaine 1766-1817
See also de Staël-Holstein, Anne Louise
Germaine Necker Baronn
Destouches, Louis-Ferdinand
1894-1961 .... **CLC 9, 15**
See also Celine, Louis-Ferdinand
See also CA 85-88; CANR 28; MTCW 1
de Tolignac, Gaston
See Griffith, D(avid Lewelyn) W(ark)
Deutsch, Babette 1895-1982 .... **CLC 18**
See also CA 1-4R; 108; CANR 4, 79; DLB
45; SATA 1; SATA-Obit 33
Devenant, William 1606-1649 .... **LC 13**
Devkota, Laxmiprasad 1909-1959 . **TCLC 23**
See also CA 123
De Voto, Bernard (Augustine)
1897-1955 .... **TCLC 29**
See also CA 113; 160; DLB 9
De Vries, Peter 1910-1993 ..... **CLC 1, 2, 3, 7,**
10, 28, 46; DAM NOV
See also CA 17-20R; 142; CANR 41; DLB
6; DLBY 82; MTCW 1, 2
Dewey, John 1859-1952 .... **TCLC 95**
See also CA 114; 170
Dexter, John
See Bradley, Marion Zimmer
Dexter, Martin
See Faust, Frederick (Schiller)
Dexter, Pete 1943- .. **CLC 34, 55; DAM POP**
See also BEST 89:2; CA 127; 131; INT 131;
MTCW 1
Diamano, Silmang
See Senghor, Leopold Sedar

Diamond, Neil 1941- .... **CLC 30**
See also CA 108

Diaz del Castillo, Bernal 1496-1584 .. **LC 31; HLCS 1**

di Bassetto, Corno
See Shaw, George Bernard

Dick, Philip K(indred) 1928-1982 ... **CLC 10, 30, 72; DAM NOV, POP**
See also AAYA 24; CA 49-52; 106; CANR 2, 16; DA3; DLB 8; MTCW 1, 2

Dickens, Charles (John Huffam) 1812-1870 .... **NCLC 3, 8, 18, 26, 37, 50, 86; DA; DAB; DAC; DAM MST, NOV; SSC 17; WLC**
See also AAYA 23; CDBLB 1832-1890; DA3; DLB 21, 55, 70, 159, 166; JRDA; MAICYA; SATA 15

Dickey, James (Lafayette) 1923-1997 .... **CLC 1, 2, 4, 7, 10, 15, 47, 109; DAM NOV, POET, POP**
See also AITN 1, 2; CA 9-12R; 156; CABS 2; CANR 10, 48, 61; CDALB 1968-1988; DA3; DLB 5, 193; DLBD 7; DLBY 82, 93, 96, 97, 98; INT CANR-10; MTCW 1, 2

Dickey, William 1928-1994 .... **CLC 3, 28**
See also CA 9-12R; 145; CANR 24, 79; DLB 5

Dickinson, Charles 1951- .... **CLC 49**
See also CA 128

Dickinson, Emily (Elizabeth) 1830-1886 ..... **NCLC 21, 77; DA; DAB; DAC; DAM MST, POET; PC 1; WLC**
See also AAYA 22; CDALB 1865-1917; DA3; DLB 1; SATA 29

Dickinson, Peter (Malcolm) 1927- .. **CLC 12, 35**
See also AAYA 9; CA 41-44R; CANR 31, 58, 88; CLR 29; DLB 87, 161; JRDA; MAICYA; SATA 5, 62, 95

Dickson, Carr
See Carr, John Dickson

Dickson, Carter
See Carr, John Dickson

Diderot, Denis 1713-1784 .... **LC 26**

Didion, Joan 1934- .... **CLC 1, 3, 8, 14, 32, 129; DAM NOV**
See also AITN 1; CA 5-8R; CANR 14, 52, 76; CDALB 1968-1988; DA3; DLB 2, 173, 185; DLBY 81, 86; MTCW 1, 2

Dietrich, Robert
See Hunt, E(verette) Howard, (Jr.)

Difusa, Pati
See Almodovar, Pedro

Dillard, Annie 1945- .. **CLC 9, 60, 115; DAM NOV**
See also AAYA 6; CA 49-52; CANR 3, 43, 62, 90; DA3; DLBY 80; MTCW 1, 2; SATA 10

Dillard, R(ichard) H(enry) W(ilde) 1937- .... **CLC 5**
See also CA 21-24R; CAAS 7; CANR 10; DLB 5

Dillon, Eilis 1920-1994 .... **CLC 17**
See also CA 9-12R; 182; 147; CAAE 182; CAAS 3; CANR 4, 38, 78; CLR 26; MAICYA; SATA 2, 74; SATA-Essay 105; SATA-Obit 83

Dimont, Penelope
See Mortimer, Penelope (Ruth)

Dinesen, Isak -1962 .. **CLC 10, 29, 95; SSC 7**
See also Blixen, Karen (Christentze Dinesen)
See also MTCW 1

Ding Ling CLC 68
See also Chiang, Pin-chin

Diphusa, Patty
See Almodovar, Pedro

Disch, Thomas M(ichael) 1940- ... **CLC 7, 36**
See also AAYA 17; CA 21-24R; CAAS 4; CANR 17, 36, 54, 89; CLR 18; DA3; DLB 8; MAICYA; MTCW 1, 2; SAAS 15; SATA 92

Disch, Tom
See Disch, Thomas M(ichael)

d'Isly, Georges
See Simenon, Georges (Jacques Christian)

Disraeli, Benjamin 1804-1881 ... **NCLC 2, 39, 79**
See also DLB 21, 55

Ditcum, Steve
See Crumb, R(obert)

Dixon, Paige
See Corcoran, Barbara

Dixon, Stephen 1936- .... **CLC 52; SSC 16**
See also CA 89-92; CANR 17, 40, 54, 91; DLB 130

Doak, Annie
See Dillard, Annie

Dobell, Sydney Thompson 1824-1874 .... **NCLC 43**
See also DLB 32

Doblin, Alfred TCLC 13
See also Doeblin, Alfred

Dobrolyubov, Nikolai Alexandrovich 1836-1861 .... **NCLC 5**

Dobson, Austin 1840-1921 .... **TCLC 79**
See also DLB 35; 144

Dobyns, Stephen 1941- .... **CLC 37**
See also CA 45-48; CANR 2, 18

Doctorow, E(dgar) L(aurence) 1931- ...... **CLC 6, 11, 15, 18, 37, 44, 65, 113; DAM NOV, POP**
See also AAYA 22; AITN 2; BEST 89:3; CA 45-48; CANR 2, 33, 51, 76; CDALB 1968-1988; DA3; DLB 2, 28, 173; DLBY 80; MTCW 1, 2

Dodgson, Charles Lutwidge 1832-1898
See Carroll, Lewis
See also CLR 2; DA; DAB; DAC; DAM MST, NOV, POET; DA3; MAICYA; SATA 100; YABC 2

Dodson, Owen (Vincent) 1914-1983 .... **CLC 79; BLC 1; DAM MULT**
See also BW 1; CA 65-68; 110; CANR 24; DLB 76

Doeblin, Alfred 1878-1957 .... **TCLC 13**
See also Doblin, Alfred
See also CA 110; 141; DLB 66

Doerr, Harriet 1910- .... **CLC 34**
See also CA 117; 122; CANR 47; INT 122

Domecq, H(onorio Bustos)
See Bioy Casares, Adolfo

Domecq, H(onorio) Bustos
See Bioy Casares, Adolfo; Borges, Jorge Luis

Domini, Rey
See Lorde, Audre (Geraldine)

Dominique
See Proust, (Valentin-Louis-George-Eugene-) Marcel

Don, A
See Stephen, SirLeslie

Donaldson, Stephen R. 1947- .... **CLC 46; DAM POP**
See also CA 89-92; CANR 13, 55; INT CANR-13

Donleavy, J(ames) P(atrick) 1926- .... **CLC 1, 4, 6, 10, 45**
See also AITN 2; CA 9-12R; CANR 24, 49, 62, 80; DLB 6, 173; INT CANR-24; MTCW 1, 2

Donne, John 1572-1631 .... **LC 10, 24; DA; DAB; DAC; DAM MST, POET; PC 1; WLC**
See also CDBLB Before 1660; DLB 121, 151

Donnell, David 1939(?)- .... **CLC 34**

Donoghue, P. S.
See Hunt, E(verette) Howard, (Jr.)

Donoso (Yanez), Jose 1924-1996 ... **CLC 4, 8, 11, 32, 99; DAM MULT; HLC 1; SSC 34**
See also CA 81-84; 155; CANR 32, 73; DLB 113; HW 1, 2; MTCW 1, 2

Donovan, John 1928-1992 .... **CLC 35**
See also AAYA 20; CA 97-100; 137; CLR 3; MAICYA; SATA 72; SATA-Brief 29

Don Roberto
See Cunninghame Graham, Robert (Gallnigad) Bontine

Doolittle, Hilda 1886-1961 . **CLC 3, 8, 14, 31, 34, 73; DA; DAC; DAM MST, POET; PC 5; WLC**
See also H. D.
See also CA 97-100; CANR 35; DLB 4, 45; MTCW 1, 2

Dorfman, Ariel 1942- ...... **CLC 48, 77; DAM MULT; HLC 1**
See also CA 124; 130; CANR 67, 70; HW 1, 2; INT 130

Dorn, Edward (Merton) 1929-1999 .... **CLC 10, 18**
See also CA 93-96; CANR 42, 79; DLB 5; INT 93-96

Dorris, Michael (Anthony) 1945-1997 .... **CLC 109; DAM MULT, NOV**
See also AAYA 20; BEST 90:1; CA 102; 157; CANR 19, 46, 75; CLR 58; DA3; DLB 175; MTCW 2; NNAL; SATA 75; SATA-Obit 94

Dorris, Michael A.
See Dorris, Michael (Anthony)

Dorsan, Luc
See Simenon, Georges (Jacques Christian)

Dorsange, Jean
See Simenon, Georges (Jacques Christian)

Dos Passos, John (Roderigo) 1896-1970 ... **CLC 1, 4, 8, 11, 15, 25, 34, 82; DA; DAB; DAC; DAM MST, NOV; WLC**
See also CA 1-4R; 29-32R; CANR 3; CDALB 1929-1941; DA3; DLB 4, 9; DLBD 1, 15; DLBY 96; MTCW 1, 2

Dossage, Jean
See Simenon, Georges (Jacques Christian)

Dostoevsky, Fedor Mikhailovich 1821-1881 . **NCLC 2, 7, 21, 33, 43; DA; DAB; DAC; DAM MST, NOV; SSC 2, 33; WLC**
See also DA3

Doughty, Charles M(ontagu) 1843-1926 .... **TCLC 27**
See also CA 115; 178; DLB 19, 57, 174

Douglas, Ellen CLC 73
See also Haxton, Josephine Ayres; Williamson, Ellen Douglas

Douglas, Gavin 1475(?)-1522 .... **LC 20**
See also DLB 132

Douglas, George
See Brown, George Douglas

Douglas, Keith (Castellain) 1920-1944 .... **TCLC 40**
See also CA 160; DLB 27

Douglas, Leonard
See Bradbury, Ray (Douglas)

Douglas, Michael
See Crichton, (John) Michael

Douglas, (George) Norman
1868-1952 .... **TCLC 68**
See also CA 119; 157; DLB 34, 195
Douglas, William
See Brown, George Douglas
Douglass, Frederick 1817(?)-1895 .. **NCLC 7, 55; BLC 1; DA; DAC; DAM MST, MULT; WLC**
See also CDALB 1640-1865; DA3; DLB 1, 43, 50, 79; SATA 29
Dourado, (Waldomiro Freitas) Autran
1926- .... **CLC 23, 60**
See also CA 25-28R, 179; CANR 34, 81; DLB 145; HW 2
Dourado, Waldomiro Autran 1926-
See Dourado, (Waldomiro Freitas) Autran
See also CA 179
Dove, Rita (Frances) 1952- .... **CLC 50, 81; BLCS; DAM MULT, POET; PC 6**
See also BW 2; CA 109; CAAS 19; CANR 27, 42, 68, 76; CDALBS; DA3; DLB 120; MTCW 1
Doveglion
See Villa, Jose Garcia
Dowell, Coleman 1925-1985 .... **CLC 60**
See also CA 25-28R; 117; CANR 10; DLB 130
Dowson, Ernest (Christopher)
1867-1900 .... **TCLC 4**
See also CA 105; 150; DLB 19, 135
Doyle, A. Conan
See Doyle, Arthur Conan
Doyle, Arthur Conan 1859-1930 .... **TCLC 7; DA; DAB; DAC; DAM MST, NOV; SSC 12; WLC**
See also AAYA 14; CA 104; 122; CDBLB 1890-1914; DA3; DLB 18, 70, 156, 178; MTCW 1, 2; SATA 24
Doyle, Conan
See Doyle, Arthur Conan
Doyle, John
See Graves, Robert (von Ranke)
Doyle, Roddy 1958(?)- .... **CLC 81**
See also AAYA 14; CA 143; CANR 73; DA3; DLB 194
Doyle, Sir A. Conan
See Doyle, Arthur Conan
Doyle, Sir Arthur Conan
See Doyle, Arthur Conan
Dr. A
See Asimov, Isaac; Silverstein, Alvin
Drabble, Margaret 1939- ...... **CLC 2, 3, 5, 8, 10, 22, 53, 129; DAB; DAC; DAM MST, NOV, POP**
See also CA 13-16R; CANR 18, 35, 63; CDBLB 1960 to Present; DA3; DLB 14, 155; MTCW 1, 2; SATA 48
Drapier, M. B.
See Swift, Jonathan
Drayham, James
See Mencken, H(enry) L(ouis)
Drayton, Michael 1563-1631 ..... **LC 8; DAM POET**
See also DLB 121
Dreadstone, Carl
See Campbell, (John) Ramsey
Dreiser, Theodore (Herman Albert)
1871-1945 .... **TCLC 10, 18, 35, 83; DA; DAC; DAM MST, NOV; SSC 30; WLC**
See also CA 106; 132; CDALB 1865-1917; DA3; DLB 9, 12, 102, 137; DLBD 1; MTCW 1, 2
Drexler, Rosalyn 1926- .... **CLC 2, 6**
See also CA 81-84; CANR 68
Dreyer, Carl Theodor 1889-1968 ...... **CLC 16**
See also CA 116
Drieu la Rochelle, Pierre(-Eugene)
1893-1945 .... **TCLC 21**
See also CA 117; DLB 72

Drinkwater, John 1882-1937 .... **TCLC 57**
See also CA 109; 149; DLB 10, 19, 149
Drop Shot
See Cable, George Washington
Droste-Hulshoff, Annette Freiin von
1797-1848 .... **NCLC 3**
See also DLB 133
Drummond, Walter
See Silverberg, Robert
Drummond, William Henry
1854-1907 .... **TCLC 25**
See also CA 160; DLB 92
Drummond de Andrade, Carlos
1902-1987 .... **CLC 18**
See also Andrade, Carlos Drummond de
See also CA 132; 123
Drury, Allen (Stuart) 1918-1998 .... **CLC 37**
See also CA 57-60; 170; CANR 18, 52; INT CANR-18
Dryden, John 1631-1700 .... **LC 3, 21; DA; DAB; DAC; DAM DRAM, MST, POET; DC 3; PC 25; WLC**
See also CDBLB 1660-1789; DLB 80, 101, 131
Duberman, Martin (Bauml) 1930- ..... **CLC 8**
See also CA 1-4R; CANR 2, 63
Dubie, Norman (Evans) 1945- .... **CLC 36**
See also CA 69-72; CANR 12; DLB 120
Du Bois, W(illiam) E(dward) B(urghardt)
1868-1963 ... **CLC 1, 2, 13, 64, 96; BLC 1; DA; DAC; DAM MST, MULT, NOV; WLC**
See also BW 1, 3; CA 85-88; CANR 34, 82; CDALB 1865-1917; DA3; DLB 47, 50, 91; MTCW 1, 2; SATA 42
Dubus, Andre 1936-1999 ..... **CLC 13, 36, 97; SSC 15**
See also CA 21-24R; 177; CANR 17; DLB 130; INT CANR-17
Duca Minimo
See D'Annunzio, Gabriele
Ducharme, Rejean 1941- .... **CLC 74**
See also CA 165; DLB 60
Duclos, Charles Pinot 1704-1772 .... **LC 1**
Dudek, Louis 1918- .... **CLC 11, 19**
See also CA 45-48; CAAS 14; CANR 1; DLB 88
Duerrenmatt, Friedrich 1921-1990 ... **CLC 1, 4, 8, 11, 15, 43, 102; DAM DRAM**
See also CA 17-20R; CANR 33; DLB 69, 124; MTCW 1, 2
Duffy, Bruce 1953(?)- .... **CLC 50**
See also CA 172
Duffy, Maureen 1933- .... **CLC 37**
See also CA 25-28R; CANR 33, 68; DLB 14; MTCW 1
Dugan, Alan 1923- .... **CLC 2, 6**
See also CA 81-84; DLB 5
du Gard, Roger Martin
See Martin du Gard, Roger
Duhamel, Georges 1884-1966 .... **CLC 8**
See also CA 81-84; 25-28R; CANR 35; DLB 65; MTCW 1
Dujardin, Edouard (Emile Louis)
1861-1949 .... **TCLC 13**
See also CA 109; DLB 123
Dulles, John Foster 1888-1959 .... **TCLC 72**
See also CA 115; 149
Dumas, Alexandre (pere)
See Dumas, Alexandre (Davy de la Pailleterie)
Dumas, Alexandre (Davy de la Pailleterie)
1802-1870 ...... **NCLC 11, 71; DA; DAB; DAC; DAM MST, NOV; WLC**
See also DA3; DLB 119, 192; SATA 18
Dumas, Alexandre (fils)
1824-1895 .... **NCLC 71; DC 1**
See also AAYA 22; DLB 192

Dumas, Claudine
See Malzberg, Barry N(athaniel)
Dumas, Henry L. 1934-1968 .... **CLC 6, 62**
See also BW 1; CA 85-88; DLB 41
du Maurier, Daphne 1907-1989 .. **CLC 6, 11, 59; DAB; DAC; DAM MST, POP; SSC 18**
See also CA 5-8R; 128; CANR 6, 55; DA3; DLB 191; MTCW 1, 2; SATA 27; SATA-Obit 60
Du Maurier, George 1834-1896 ..... **NCLC 86**
See also DLB 153, 178
Dunbar, Paul Laurence 1872-1906 . **TCLC 2, 12; BLC 1; DA; DAC; DAM MST, MULT, POET; PC 5; SSC 8; WLC**
See also BW 1, 3; CA 104; 124; CANR 79; CDALB 1865-1917; DA3; DLB 50, 54, 78; SATA 34
Dunbar, William 1460(?)-1530(?) .... **LC 20**
See also DLB 132, 146
Duncan, Dora Angela
See Duncan, Isadora
Duncan, Isadora 1877(?)-1927 .... **TCLC 68**
See also CA 118; 149
Duncan, Lois 1934- .... **CLC 26**
See also AAYA 4, 34; CA 1-4R; CANR 2, 23, 36; CLR 29; JRDA; MAICYA; SAAS 2; SATA 1, 36, 75
Duncan, Robert (Edward)
1919-1988 .... **CLC 1, 2, 4, 7, 15, 41, 55; DAM POET; PC 2**
See also CA 9-12R; 124; CANR 28, 62; DLB 5, 16, 193; MTCW 1, 2
Duncan, Sara Jeannette
1861-1922 .... **TCLC 60**
See also CA 157; DLB 92
Dunlap, William 1766-1839 .... **NCLC 2**
See also DLB 30, 37, 59
Dunn, Douglas (Eaglesham) 1942- .... **CLC 6, 40**
See also CA 45-48; CANR 2, 33; DLB 40; MTCW 1
Dunn, Katherine (Karen) 1945- .... **CLC 71**
See also CA 33-36R; CANR 72; MTCW 1
Dunn, Stephen 1939- .... **CLC 36**
See also CA 33-36R; CANR 12, 48, 53; DLB 105
Dunne, Finley Peter 1867-1936 ...... **TCLC 28**
See also CA 108; 178; DLB 11, 23
Dunne, John Gregory 1932- .... **CLC 28**
See also CA 25-28R; CANR 14, 50; DLBY 80
Dunsany, Edward John Moreton Drax Plunkett 1878-1957
See Dunsany, Lord
See also CA 104; 148; DLB 10; MTCW 1
Dunsany, Lord -1957 .... **TCLC 2, 59**
See also Dunsany, Edward John Moreton Drax Plunkett
See also DLB 77, 153, 156
du Perry, Jean
See Simenon, Georges (Jacques Christian)
Durang, Christopher (Ferdinand)
1949- .... **CLC 27, 38**
See also CA 105; CANR 50, 76; MTCW 1
Duras, Marguerite 1914-1996 . **CLC 3, 6, 11, 20, 34, 40, 68, 100; SSC 40**
See also CA 25-28R; 151; CANR 50; DLB 83; MTCW 1, 2
Durban, (Rosa) Pam 1947- .... **CLC 39**
See also CA 123
Durcan, Paul 1944- .... **CLC 43, 70; DAM POET**
See also CA 134

Durkheim, Emile 1858-1917 .... **TCLC 55**
Durrell, Lawrence (George)
   1912-1990 .... **CLC 1, 4, 6, 8, 13, 27, 41;**
   DAM NOV
      See also CA 9-12R; 132; CANR 40, 77;
      CDBLB 1945-1960; DLB 15, 27, 204;
      DLBY 90; MTCW 1, 2
Durrenmatt, Friedrich
      See Duerrenmatt, Friedrich
Dutt, Toru 1856-1877 .... **NCLC 29**
Dwight, Timothy 1752-1817 .... **NCLC 13**
      See also DLB 37
Dworkin, Andrea 1946- .... **CLC 43**
      See also CA 77-80; CAAS 21; CANR 16,
      39, 76; INT CANR-16; MTCW 1, 2
Dwyer, Deanna
      See Koontz, Dean R(ay)
Dwyer, K. R.
      See Koontz, Dean R(ay)
Dwyer, Thomas A. 1923- .... **CLC 114**
      See also CA 115
Dye, Richard
      See De Voto, Bernard (Augustine)
Dylan, Bob 1941- .... **CLC 3, 4, 6, 12, 77**
      See also CA 41-44R; DLB 16
E. V. L.
      See Lucas, E(dward) V(errall)
Eagleton, Terence (Francis) 1943- .. **CLC 63,**
      132
      See also CA 57-60; CANR 7, 23, 68;
      MTCW 1, 2
Eagleton, Terry
      See Eagleton, Terence (Francis)
Early, Jack
      See Scoppettone, Sandra
East, Michael
      See West, Morris L(anglo)
Eastaway, Edward
      See Thomas, (Philip) Edward
Eastlake, William (Derry)
      1917-1997 .... **CLC 8**
      See also CA 5-8R; 158; CAAS 1; CANR 5,
      63; DLB 6, 206; INT CANR-5
Eastman, Charles A(lexander)
      1858-1939 .... **TCLC 55; DAM MULT**
      See also CA 179; CANR 91; DLB 175;
      NNAL; YABC 1
Eberhart, Richard (Ghormley)
      1904- .. **CLC 3, 11, 19, 56; DAM POET**
      See also CA 1-4R; CANR 2; CDALB 1941-
      1968; DLB 48; MTCW 1
Eberstadt, Fernanda 1960- .... **CLC 39**
      See also CA 136; CANR 69
Echegaray (y Eizaguirre), Jose (Maria
      Waldo) 1832-1916 .... **TCLC 4; HLCS 1**
      See also CA 104; CANR 32; HW 1; MTCW
      1
Echeverria, (Jose) Esteban (Antonino)
      1805-1851 .... **NCLC 18**
Echo
      See Proust, (Valentin-Louis-George-
      Eugene-) Marcel
Eckert, Allan W. 1931- .... **CLC 17**
      See also AAYA 18; CA 13-16R; CANR 14,
      45; INT CANR-14; SAAS 21; SATA 29,
      91; SATA-Brief 27
Eckhart, Meister 1260(?)-1328(?) ... **CMLC 9**
      See also DLB 115
Eckmar, F. R.
      See de Hartog, Jan
Eco, Umberto 1932- .... **CLC 28, 60; DAM**
      NOV, POP
      See also BEST 90:1; CA 77-80; CANR 12,
      33, 55; DA3; DLB 196; MTCW 1, 2
Eddison, E(ric) R(ucker)
      1882-1945 .... **TCLC 15**
      See also CA 109; 156

Eddy, Mary (Ann Morse) Baker
      1821-1910 .... **TCLC 71**
      See also CA 113; 174
Edel, (Joseph) Leon 1907-1997 .. **CLC 29, 34**
      See also CA 1-4R; 161; CANR 1, 22; DLB
      103; INT CANR-22
Eden, Emily 1797-1869 .... **NCLC 10**
Edgar, David 1948- .. **CLC 42; DAM DRAM**
      See also CA 57-60; CANR 12, 61; DLB 13;
      MTCW 1
Edgerton, Clyde (Carlyle) 1944- ...... **CLC 39**
      See also AAYA 17; CA 118; 134; CANR
      64; INT 134
Edgeworth, Maria 1768-1849 .... **NCLC 1, 51**
      See also DLB 116, 159, 163; SATA 21
Edmonds, Paul
      See Kuttner, Henry
Edmonds, Walter D(umaux)
      1903-1998 .... **CLC 35**
      See also CA 5-8R; CANR 2; DLB 9; MAI-
      CYA; SAAS 4; SATA 1, 27; SATA-Obit
      99
Edmondson, Wallace
      See Ellison, Harlan (Jay)
Edson, Russell CLC 13
      See also CA 33-36R
Edwards, Bronwen Elizabeth
      See Rose, Wendy
Edwards, G(erald) B(asil)
      1899-1976 .... **CLC 25**
      See also CA 110
Edwards, Gus 1939- .... **CLC 43**
      See also CA 108; INT 108
Edwards, Jonathan 1703-1758 .... **LC 7, 54;**
      DA; DAC; DAM MST
      See also DLB 24
Efron, Marina Ivanovna Tsvetaeva
      See Tsvetaeva (Efron), Marina (Ivanovna)
Ehle, John (Marsden, Jr.) 1925- ...... **CLC 27**
      See also CA 9-12R
Ehrenbourg, Ilya (Grigoryevich)
      See Ehrenburg, Ilya (Grigoryevich)
Ehrenburg, Ilya (Grigoryevich)
      1891-1967 .... **CLC 18, 34, 62**
      See also CA 102; 25-28R
Ehrenburg, Ilyo (Grigoryevich)
      See Ehrenburg, Ilya (Grigoryevich)
Ehrenreich, Barbara 1941- .... **CLC 110**
      See also BEST 90:4; CA 73-76; CANR 16,
      37, 62; MTCW 1, 2
Eich, Guenter 1907-1972 .... **CLC 15**
      See also CA 111; 93-96; DLB 69, 124
Eichendorff, Joseph Freiherr von
      1788-1857 .... **NCLC 8**
      See also DLB 90
Eigner, Larry CLC 9
      See also Eigner, Laurence (Joel)
      See also CAAS 23; DLB 5
Eigner, Laurence (Joel) 1927-1996
      See Eigner, Larry
      See also CA 9-12R; 151; CANR 6, 84; DLB
      193
Einstein, Albert 1879-1955 .... **TCLC 65**
      See also CA 121; 133; MTCW 1, 2
Eiseley, Loren Corey 1907-1977 .... **CLC 7**
      See also AAYA 5; CA 1-4R; 73-76; CANR
      6; DLBD 17
Eisenstadt, Jill 1963- .... **CLC 50**
      See also CA 140
Eisenstein, Sergei (Mikhailovich)
      1898-1948 .... **TCLC 57**
      See also CA 114; 149
Eisner, Simon
      See Kornbluth, C(yril) M.
Ekeloef, (Bengt) Gunnar
      1907-1968 ... **CLC 27; DAM POET; PC**
      23
      See also CA 123; 25-28R

Ekelof, (Bengt) Gunnar
      See Ekeloef, (Bengt) Gunnar
Ekelund, Vilhelm 1880-1949 .... **TCLC 75**
Ekwensi, C. O. D.
      See Ekwensi, Cyprian (Odiatu Duaka)
Ekwensi, Cyprian (Odiatu Duaka)
      1921- ...... **CLC 4; BLC 1; DAM MULT**
      See also BW 2, 3; CA 29-32R; CANR 18,
      42, 74; DLB 117; MTCW 1, 2; SATA 66
Elaine TCLC 18
      See also Leverson, Ada
El Crummo
      See Crumb, R(obert)
Elder, Lonne III 1931-1996 .... **DC 8**
      See also BLC 1; BW 1, 3; CA 81-84; 152;
      CANR 25; DAM MULT; DLB 7, 38, 44
Eleanor of Aquitaine 1122-1204 ... **CMLC 39**
Elia
      See Lamb, Charles
Eliade, Mircea 1907-1986 .... **CLC 19**
      See also CA 65-68; 119; CANR 30, 62;
      DLB 220; MTCW 1
Eliot, A. D.
      See Jewett, (Theodora) Sarah Orne
Eliot, Alice
      See Jewett, (Theodora) Sarah Orne
Eliot, Dan
      See Silverberg, Robert
Eliot, George 1819- . **NCLC 4, 13, 23, 41, 49,**
      89; DA; DAB; DAC; DAM MST, NOV;
      PC 20; WLC
      See also CDBLB 1832-1890; DA3; DLB
      21, 35, 55
Eliot, John 1604-1690 .... **LC 5**
      See also DLB 24
Eliot, T(homas) S(tearns)
      1888-1965 ...... **CLC 1, 2, 3, 6, 9, 10, 13,**
      15, 24, 34, 41, 55, 57, 113; DA; DAB;
      DAC; DAM DRAM, MST, POET; PC
      5, 31; WLC
      See also AAYA 28; CA 5-8R; 25-28R;
      CANR 41; CDALB 1929-1941; DA3;
      DLB 7, 10, 45, 63; DLBY 88; MTCW 1,
      2
Elizabeth 1866-1941 .... **TCLC 41**
Elkin, Stanley L(awrence)
      1930-1995 .. **CLC 4, 6, 9, 14, 27, 51, 91;**
      DAM NOV, POP; SSC 12
      See also CA 9-12R; 148; CANR 8, 46; DLB
      2, 28; DLBY 80; INT CANR-8; MTCW
      1, 2
Elledge, Scott CLC 34
Elliot, Don
      See Silverberg, Robert
Elliott, Don
      See Silverberg, Robert
Elliott, George P(aul) 1918-1980 .... **CLC 2**
      See also CA 1-4R; 97-100; CANR 2
Elliott, Janice 1931- .... **CLC 47**
      See also CA 13-16R; CANR 8, 29, 84; DLB
      14
Elliott, Sumner Locke 1917-1991 ..... **CLC 38**
      See also CA 5-8R; 134; CANR 2, 21
Elliott, William
      See Bradbury, Ray (Douglas)
Ellis, A. E. CLC 7
Ellis, Alice Thomas CLC 40
      See also Haycraft, Anna (Margaret)
      See also DLB 194; MTCW 1
Ellis, Bret Easton 1964- ..... **CLC 39, 71, 117;**
      DAM POP
      See also AAYA 2; CA 118; 123; CANR 51,
      74; DA3; INT 123; MTCW 1
Ellis, (Henry) Havelock
      1859-1939 .... **TCLC 14**
      See also CA 109; 169; DLB 190
Ellis, Landon
      See Ellison, Harlan (Jay)

Ellis, Trey 1962- .... **CLC 55**
   See also CA 146; CANR 92
Ellison, Harlan (Jay) 1934- ... **CLC 1, 13, 42;**
   DAM POP; SSC 14
   See also AAYA 29; CA 5-8R; CANR 5, 46;
   DLB 8; INT CANR-5; MTCW 1, 2
Ellison, Ralph (Waldo) 1914-1994 .... **CLC 1,**
   3, 11, 54, 86, 114; BLC 1; DA; DAB;
   DAC; DAM MST, MULT, NOV; SSC
   26; WLC
   See also AAYA 19; BW 1, 3; CA 9-12R;
   145; CANR 24, 53; CDALB 1941-1968;
   DA3; DLB 2, 76, 227; DLBY 94; MTCW
   1, 2
Ellmann, Lucy (Elizabeth) 1956- ..... **CLC 61**
   See also CA 128
Ellmann, Richard (David)
   1918-1987 .... **CLC 50**
   See also BEST 89:2; CA 1-4R; 122; CANR
   2, 28, 61; DLB 103; DLBY 87; MTCW
   1, 2
Elman, Richard (Martin)
   1934-1997 .... **CLC 19**
   See also CA 17-20R; 163; CAAS 3; CANR
   47
Elron
   See Hubbard, L(afayette) Ron(ald)
Eluard, Paul **TCLC 7, 41**
   See also Grindel, Eugene
Elyot, Sir Thomas 1490(?)-1546 .... **LC 11**
Elytis, Odysseus 1911-1996 .... **CLC 15, 49,**
   100; DAM POET; PC 21
   See also CA 102; 151; MTCW 1, 2
Emecheta, (Florence Onye) Buchi
   1944- .. **CLC 14, 48, 128; BLC 2; DAM**
   MULT
   See also BW 2, 3; CA 81-84; CANR 27,
   81; DA3; DLB 117; MTCW 1, 2; SATA
   66
Emerson, Mary Moody
   1774-1863 .... **NCLC 66**
Emerson, Ralph Waldo 1803-1882 . **NCLC 1,**
   38; DA; DAB; DAC; DAM MST,
   POET; PC 18; WLC
   See also CDALB 1640-1865; DA3; DLB 1,
   59, 73, 223
Eminescu, Mihail 1850-1889 .... **NCLC 33**
Empson, William 1906-1984 ... **CLC 3, 8, 19,**
   33, 34
   See also CA 17-20R; 112; CANR 31, 61;
   DLB 20; MTCW 1, 2
Enchi, Fumiko (Ueda) 1905-1986 ..... **CLC 31**
   See also CA 129; 121; DLB 182
Ende, Michael (Andreas Helmuth)
   1929-1995 .... **CLC 31**
   See also CA 118; 124; 149; CANR 36; CLR
   14; DLB 75; MAICYA; SATA 61; SATA-
   Brief 42; SATA-Obit 86
Endo, Shusaku 1923-1996 ..... **CLC 7, 14, 19,**
   54, 99; DAM NOV
   See also CA 29-32R; 153; CANR 21, 54;
   DA3; DLB 182; MTCW 1, 2
Engel, Marian 1933-1985 .... **CLC 36**
   See also CA 25-28R; CANR 12; DLB 53;
   INT CANR-12
Engelhardt, Frederick
   See Hubbard, L(afayette) Ron(ald)
Engels, Friedrich 1820-1895 .... **NCLC 85**
   See also DLB 129
Enright, D(ennis) J(oseph) 1920- .. **CLC 4, 8,**
   31
   See also CA 1-4R; CANR 1, 42, 83; DLB
   27; SATA 25
Enzensberger, Hans Magnus
   1929- .... **CLC 43; PC 28**
   See also CA 116; 119
Ephron, Nora 1941- .... **CLC 17, 31**
   See also AITN 2; CA 65-68; CANR 12, 39,
   83

Epicurus 341B.C.-270B.C. .... **CMLC 21**
   See also DLB 176
Epsilon
   See Betjeman, John
Epstein, Daniel Mark 1948- .... **CLC 7**
   See also CA 49-52; CANR 2, 53, 90
Epstein, Jacob 1956- .... **CLC 19**
   See also CA 114
Epstein, Jean 1897-1953 .... **TCLC 92**
Epstein, Joseph 1937- .... **CLC 39**
   See also CA 112; 119; CANR 50, 65
Epstein, Leslie 1938- .... **CLC 27**
   See also CA 73-76; CAAS 12; CANR 23,
   69
Equiano, Olaudah 1745(?)-1797 .... **LC 16;**
   BLC 2; DAM MULT
   See also DLB 37, 50
ER **TCLC 33**
   See also CA 160; DLB 85
Erasmus, Desiderius 1469(?)-1536 ...... **LC 16**
Erdman, Paul E(mil) 1932- .... **CLC 25**
   See also AITN 1; CA 61-64; CANR 13, 43,
   84
Erdrich, Louise 1954- .... **CLC 39, 54, 120;**
   DAM MULT, NOV, POP
   See also AAYA 10; BEST 89:1; CA 114;
   CANR 41, 62; CDALBS; DA3; DLB 152,
   175, 206; MTCW 1; NNAL; SATA 94
Erenburg, Ilya (Grigoryevich)
   See Ehrenburg, Ilya (Grigoryevich)
Erickson, Stephen Michael 1950-
   See Erickson, Steve
   See also CA 129
Erickson, Steve 1950- .... **CLC 64**
   See also Erickson, Stephen Michael
   See also CANR 60, 68
Ericson, Walter
   See Fast, Howard (Melvin)
Eriksson, Buntel
   See Bergman, (Ernst) Ingmar
Ernaux, Annie 1940- .... **CLC 88**
   See also CA 147
Erskine, John 1879-1951 .... **TCLC 84**
   See also CA 112; 159; DLB 9, 102
Eschenbach, Wolfram von
   See Wolfram von Eschenbach
Eseki, Bruno
   See Mphahlele, Ezekiel
Esenin, Sergei (Alexandrovich)
   1895-1925 .... **TCLC 4**
   See also CA 104
Eshleman, Clayton 1935- .... **CLC 7**
   See also CA 33-36R; CAAS 6; DLB 5
Espriella, Don Manuel Alvarez
   See Southey, Robert
Espriu, Salvador 1913-1985 .... **CLC 9**
   See also CA 154; 115; DLB 134
Espronceda, Jose de 1808-1842 ..... **NCLC 39**
Esquivel, Laura 1951(?)-
   See also AAYA 29; CA 143; CANR 68;
   DA3; HLCS 1; MTCW 1
Esse, James
   See Stephens, James
Esterbrook, Tom
   See Hubbard, L(afayette) Ron(ald)
Estleman, Loren D. 1952- ..... **CLC 48; DAM**
   NOV, POP
   See also AAYA 27; CA 85-88; CANR 27,
   74; DA3; DLB 226; INT CANR-27;
   MTCW 1, 2
Euclid 306B.C.-283B.C. .... **CMLC 25**
Eugenides, Jeffrey 1960(?)- .... **CLC 81**
   See also CA 144
Euripides c. 485B.C.-406B.C. .... **CMLC 23;**
   DA; DAB; DAC; DAM DRAM, MST;
   DC 4; WLCS
   See also DA3; DLB 176

Evan, Evin
   See Faust, Frederick (Schiller)
Evans, Caradoc 1878-1945 .... **TCLC 85**
Evans, Evan
   See Faust, Frederick (Schiller)
Evans, Marian
   See Eliot, George
Evans, Mary Ann
   See Eliot, George
Evarts, Esther
   See Benson, Sally
Everett, Percival L. 1956- .... **CLC 57**
   See also BW 2; CA 129
Everson, R(onald) G(ilmour) 1903- . **CLC 27**
   See also CA 17-20R; DLB 88
Everson, William (Oliver)
   1912-1994 .... **CLC 1, 5, 14**
   See also CA 9-12R; 145; CANR 20; DLB
   212; MTCW 1
Evtushenko, Evgenii Aleksandrovich
   See Yevtushenko, Yevgeny (Alexandrovich)
Ewart, Gavin (Buchanan)
   1916-1995 .... **CLC 13, 46**
   See also CA 89-92; 150; CANR 17, 46;
   DLB 40; MTCW 1
Ewers, Hanns Heinz 1871-1943 ..... **TCLC 12**
   See also CA 109; 149
Ewing, Frederick R.
   See Sturgeon, Theodore (Hamilton)
Exley, Frederick (Earl) 1929-1992 .... **CLC 6,**
   11
   See also AITN 2; CA 81-84; 138; DLB 143;
   DLBY 81
Eynhardt, Guillermo
   See Quiroga, Horacio (Sylvestre)
Ezekiel, Nissim 1924- .... **CLC 61**
   See also CA 61-64
Ezekiel, Tish O'Dowd 1943- .... **CLC 34**
   See also CA 129
Fadeyev, A.
   See Bulgya, Alexander Alexandrovich
Fadeyev, Alexander **TCLC 53**
   See also Bulgya, Alexander Alexandrovich
Fagen, Donald 1948- .... **CLC 26**
Fainzilberg, Ilya Arnoldovich 1897-1937
   See Ilf, Ilya
   See also CA 120; 165
Fair, Ronald L. 1932- .... **CLC 18**
   See also BW 1; CA 69-72; CANR 25; DLB
   33
Fairbairn, Roger
   See Carr, John Dickson
Fairbairns, Zoe (Ann) 1948- .... **CLC 32**
   See also CA 103; CANR 21, 85
Falco, Gian
   See Papini, Giovanni
Falconer, James
   See Kirkup, James
Falconer, Kenneth
   See Kornbluth, C(yril) M.
Falkland, Samuel
   See Heijermans, Herman
Fallaci, Oriana 1930- .... **CLC 11, 110**
   See also CA 77-80; CANR 15, 58; MTCW
   1
Faludy, George 1913- .... **CLC 42**
   See also CA 21-24R
Faludy, Gyoergy
   See Faludy, George
Fanon, Frantz 1925-1961 ... **CLC 74; BLC 2;**
   DAM MULT
   See also BW 1; CA 116; 89-92
Fanshawe, Ann 1625-1680 .... **LC 11**
Fante, John (Thomas) 1911-1983 ..... **CLC 60**
   See also CA 69-72; 109; CANR 23; DLB
   130; DLBY 83

Farah, Nuruddin 1945- ...... **CLC 53; BLC 2; DAM MULT**
See also BW 2, 3; CA 106; CANR 81; DLB 125

Fargue, Leon-Paul 1876(?)-1947 .... **TCLC 11**
See also CA 109

Farigoule, Louis
See Romains, Jules

Farina, Richard 1936(?)-1966 .... **CLC 9**
See also CA 81-84; 25-28R

Farley, Walter (Lorimer)
1915-1989 .... **CLC 17**
See also CA 17-20R; CANR 8, 29, 84; DLB 22; JRDA; MAICYA; SATA 2, 43

Farmer, Philip Jose 1918- .... **CLC 1, 19**
See also AAYA 28; CA 1-4R; CANR 4, 35; DLB 8; MTCW 1; SATA 93

Farquhar, George 1677-1707 ... **LC 21; DAM DRAM**
See also DLB 84

Farrell, J(ames) G(ordon)
1935-1979 .... **CLC 6**
See also CA 73-76; 89-92; CANR 36; DLB 14; MTCW 1

Farrell, James T(homas) 1904-1979 . **CLC 1, 4, 8, 11, 66; SSC 28**
See also CA 5-8R; 89-92; CANR 9, 61; DLB 4, 9, 86; DLBD 2; MTCW 1, 2

Farren, Richard J.
See Betjeman, John

Farren, Richard M.
See Betjeman, John

Fassbinder, Rainer Werner
1946-1982 .... **CLC 20**
See also CA 93-96; 106; CANR 31

Fast, Howard (Melvin) 1914- .. **CLC 23, 131; DAM NOV**
See also AAYA 16; CA 1-4R, 181; CAAE 181; CAAS 18; CANR 1, 33, 54, 75; DLB 9; INT CANR-33; MTCW 1; SATA 7; SATA-Essay 107

Faulcon, Robert
See Holdstock, Robert P.

Faulkner, William (Cuthbert)
1897-1962 .... **CLC 1, 3, 6, 8, 9, 11, 14, 18, 28, 52, 68; DA; DAB; DAC; DAM MST, NOV; SSC 1, 35; WLC**
See also AAYA 7; CA 81-84; CANR 33; CDALB 1929-1941; DA3; DLB 9, 11, 44, 102; DLBD 2; DLBY 86, 97; MTCW 1, 2

Fauset, Jessie Redmon
1884(?)-1961 .... **CLC 19, 54; BLC 2; DAM MULT**
See also BW 1; CA 109; CANR 83; DLB 51

Faust, Frederick (Schiller)
1892-1944(?) .... **TCLC 49; DAM POP**
See also CA 108; 152

Faust, Irvin 1924- .... **CLC 8**
See also CA 33-36R; CANR 28, 67; DLB 2, 28; DLBY 80

Fawkes, Guy
See Benchley, Robert (Charles)

Fearing, Kenneth (Flexner)
1902-1961 .... **CLC 51**
See also CA 93-96; CANR 59; DLB 9

Fecamps, Elise
See Creasey, John

Federman, Raymond 1928- .... **CLC 6, 47**
See also CA 17-20R; CAAS 8; CANR 10, 43, 83; DLBY 80

Federspiel, J(uerg) F. 1931- .... **CLC 42**
See also CA 146

Feiffer, Jules (Ralph) 1929- ..... **CLC 2, 8, 64; DAM DRAM**
See also AAYA 3; CA 17-20R; CANR 30, 59; DLB 7, 44; INT CANR-30; MTCW 1; SATA 8, 61, 111

Feige, Hermann Albert Otto Maximilian
See Traven, B.

Feinberg, David B. 1956-1994 .... **CLC 59**
See also CA 135; 147

Feinstein, Elaine 1930- .... **CLC 36**
See also CA 69-72; CAAS 1; CANR 31, 68; DLB 14, 40; MTCW 1

Feldman, Irving (Mordecai) 1928- ..... **CLC 7**
See also CA 1-4R; CANR 1; DLB 169

Felix-Tchicaya, Gerald
See Tchicaya, Gerald Felix

Fellini, Federico 1920-1993 .... **CLC 16, 85**
See also CA 65-68; 143; CANR 33

Felsen, Henry Gregor 1916-1995 ..... **CLC 17**
See also CA 1-4R; 180; CANR 1; SAAS 2; SATA 1

Fenno, Jack
See Calisher, Hortense

Fenollosa, Ernest (Francisco)
1853-1908 .... **TCLC 91**

Fenton, James Martin 1949- .... **CLC 32**
See also CA 102; DLB 40

Ferber, Edna 1887-1968 .... **CLC 18, 93**
See also AITN 1; CA 5-8R; 25-28R; CANR 68; DLB 9, 28, 86; MTCW 1, 2; SATA 7

Ferguson, Helen
See Kavan, Anna

Ferguson, Niall 1967- .... **CLC 134**

Ferguson, Samuel 1810-1886 .... **NCLC 33**
See also DLB 32

Fergusson, Robert 1750-1774 .... **LC 29**
See also DLB 109

Ferling, Lawrence
See Ferlinghetti, Lawrence (Monsanto)

Ferlinghetti, Lawrence (Monsanto)
1919(?)- .... **CLC 2, 6, 10, 27, 111; DAM POET; PC 1**
See also CA 5-8R; CANR 3, 41, 73; CDALB 1941-1968; DA3; DLB 5, 16; MTCW 1, 2

Fern, Fanny 1811-1872
See Parton, Sara Payson Willis

Fernandez, Vicente Garcia Huidobro
See Huidobro Fernandez, Vicente Garcia

Ferre, Rosario 1942- .... **SSC 36; HLCS 1**
See also CA 131; CANR 55, 81; DLB 145; HW 1, 2; MTCW 1

Ferrer, Gabriel (Francisco Victor) Miro
See Miro (Ferrer), Gabriel (Francisco Victor)

Ferrier, Susan (Edmonstone)
1782-1854 .... **NCLC 8**
See also DLB 116

Ferrigno, Robert 1948(?)- .... **CLC 65**
See also CA 140

Ferron, Jacques 1921-1985 .... **CLC 94; DAC**
See also CA 117; 129; DLB 60

Feuchtwanger, Lion 1884-1958 .... **TCLC 3**
See also CA 104; DLB 66

Feuillet, Octave 1821-1890 .... **NCLC 45**
See also DLB 192

Feydeau, Georges (Leon Jules Marie)
1862-1921 .... **TCLC 22; DAM DRAM**
See also CA 113; 152; CANR 84; DLB 192

Fichte, Johann Gottlieb
1762-1814 .... **NCLC 62**
See also DLB 90

Ficino, Marsilio 1433-1499 .... **LC 12**

Fiedeler, Hans
See Doeblin, Alfred

Fiedler, Leslie A(aron) 1917- .. **CLC 4, 13, 24**
See also CA 9-12R; CANR 7, 63; DLB 28, 67; MTCW 1, 2

Field, Andrew 1938- .... **CLC 44**
See also CA 97-100; CANR 25

Field, Eugene 1850-1895 .... **NCLC 3**
See also DLB 23, 42, 140; DLBD 13; MAICYA; SATA 16

Field, Gans T.
See Wellman, Manly Wade

Field, Michael 1915-1971 .... **TCLC 43**
See also CA 29-32R

Field, Peter
See Hobson, Laura Z(ametkin)

Fielding, Henry 1707-1754 ..... **LC 1, 46; DA; DAB; DAC; DAM DRAM, MST, NOV; WLC**
See also CDBLB 1660-1789; DA3; DLB 39, 84, 101

Fielding, Sarah 1710-1768 .... **LC 1, 44**
See also DLB 39

Fields, W. C. 1880-1946 .... **TCLC 80**
See also DLB 44

Fierstein, Harvey (Forbes) 1954- .... **CLC 33; DAM DRAM, POP**
See also CA 123; 129; DA3

Figes, Eva 1932- .... **CLC 31**
See also CA 53-56; CANR 4, 44, 83; DLB 14

Finch, Anne 1661-1720 .... **LC 3; PC 21**
See also DLB 95

Finch, Robert (Duer Claydon)
1900- .... **CLC 18**
See also CA 57-60; CANR 9, 24, 49; DLB 88

Findley, Timothy 1930- . **CLC 27, 102; DAC; DAM MST**
See also CA 25-28R; CANR 12, 42, 69; DLB 53

Fink, William
See Mencken, H(enry) L(ouis)

Firbank, Louis 1942-
See Reed, Lou
See also CA 117

Firbank, (Arthur Annesley) Ronald
1886-1926 .... **TCLC 1**
See also CA 104; 177; DLB 36

Fisher, Dorothy (Frances) Canfield
1879-1958 .... **TCLC 87**
See also CA 114; 136; CANR 80; DLB 9, 102; MAICYA; YABC 1

Fisher, M(ary) F(rances) K(ennedy)
1908-1992 .... **CLC 76, 87**
See also CA 77-80; 138; CANR 44; MTCW 1

Fisher, Roy 1930- .... **CLC 25**
See also CA 81-84; CAAS 10; CANR 16; DLB 40

Fisher, Rudolph 1897-1934 .. **TCLC 11; BLC 2; DAM MULT; SSC 25**
See also BW 1, 3; CA 107; 124; CANR 80; DLB 51, 102

Fisher, Vardis (Alvero) 1895-1968 ...... **CLC 7**
See also CA 5-8R; 25-28R; CANR 68; DLB 9, 206

Fiske, Tarleton
See Bloch, Robert (Albert)

Fitch, Clarke
See Sinclair, Upton (Beall)

Fitch, John IV
See Cormier, Robert (Edmund)

Fitzgerald, Captain Hugh
See Baum, L(yman) Frank

FitzGerald, Edward 1809-1883 .... **NCLC 9**
See also DLB 32

Fitzgerald, F(rancis) Scott (Key)
1896-1940 .. **TCLC 1, 6, 14, 28, 55; DA; DAB; DAC; DAM MST, NOV; SSC 6, 31; WLC**
See also AAYA 24; AITN 1; CA 110; 123; CDALB 1917-1929; DA3; DLB 4, 9, 86; DLBD 1, 15, 16; DLBY 81, 96; MTCW 1, 2

Fitzgerald, Penelope 1916- ... **CLC 19, 51, 61**
See also CA 85-88; CAAS 10; CANR 56, 86; DLB 14, 194; MTCW 2

Fitzgerald, Robert (Stuart)
1910-1985 .... **CLC 39**
See also CA 1-4R; 114; CANR 1; DLBY 80

FitzGerald, Robert D(avid)
1902-1987 .... **CLC 19**
See also CA 17-20R

Fitzgerald, Zelda (Sayre)
1900-1948 .... **TCLC 52**
See also CA 117; 126; DLBY 84

Flanagan, Thomas (James Bonner)
1923- .... **CLC 25, 52**
See also CA 108; CANR 55; DLBY 80; INT 108; MTCW 1

Flaubert, Gustave 1821-1880 .... **NCLC 2, 10, 19, 62, 66; DA; DAB; DAC; DAM MST, NOV; SSC 11; WLC**
See also DA3; DLB 119

Flecker, Herman Elroy
See Flecker, (Herman) James Elroy

Flecker, (Herman) James Elroy
1884-1915 .... **TCLC 43**
See also CA 109; 150; DLB 10, 19

Fleming, Ian (Lancaster) 1908-1964 . **CLC 3, 30; DAM POP**
See also AAYA 26; CA 5-8R; CANR 59; CDBLB 1945-1960; DA3; DLB 87, 201; MTCW 1, 2; SATA 9

Fleming, Thomas (James) 1927- ...... **CLC 37**
See also CA 5-8R; CANR 10; INT CANR-10; SATA 8

Fletcher, John 1579-1625 .... **LC 33; DC 6**
See also CDBLB Before 1660; DLB 58

Fletcher, John Gould 1886-1950 .... **TCLC 35**
See also CA 107; 167; DLB 4, 45

Fleur, Paul
See Pohl, Frederik

Flooglebuckle, Al
See Spiegelman, Art

Flying Officer X
See Bates, H(erbert) E(rnest)

Fo, Dario 1926- .... **CLC 32, 109; DAM DRAM; DC 10**
See also CA 116; 128; CANR 68; DA3; DLBY 97; MTCW 1, 2

Fogarty, Jonathan Titulescu Esq.
See Farrell, James T(homas)

Follett, Ken(neth Martin) 1949- ..... **CLC 18; DAM NOV, POP**
See also AAYA 6; BEST 89:4; CA 81-84; CANR 13, 33, 54; DA3; DLB 87; DLBY 81; INT CANR-33; MTCW 1

Fontane, Theodor 1819-1898 .... **NCLC 26**
See also DLB 129

Foote, Horton 1916- .... **CLC 51, 91; DAM DRAM**
See also CA 73-76; CANR 34, 51; DA3; DLB 26; INT CANR-34

Foote, Shelby 1916- ..... **CLC 75; DAM NOV, POP**
See also CA 5-8R; CANR 3, 45, 74; DA3; DLB 2, 17; MTCW 2

Forbes, Esther 1891-1967 .... **CLC 12**
See also AAYA 17; CA 13-14; 25-28R; CAP 1; CLR 27; DLB 22; JRDA; MAICYA; SATA 2, 100

Forche, Carolyn (Louise) 1950- .... **CLC 25, 83, 86; DAM POET; PC 10**
See also CA 109; 117; CANR 50, 74; DA3; DLB 5, 193; INT 117; MTCW 1

Ford, Elbur
See Hibbert, Eleanor Alice Burford

Ford, Ford Madox 1873-1939 ... **TCLC 1, 15, 39, 57; DAM NOV**
See also Chaucer, Daniel
See also CA 104; 132; CANR 74; CDBLB 1914-1945; DA3; DLB 162; MTCW 1, 2

Ford, Henry 1863-1947 .... **TCLC 73**
See also CA 115; 148

Ford, John 1586-(?) .... **DC 8**
See also CDBLB Before 1660; DAM DRAM; DA3; DLB 58

Ford, John 1895-1973 .... **CLC 16**
See also CA 45-48

Ford, Richard 1944- .... **CLC 46, 99**
See also CA 69-72; CANR 11, 47, 86; DLB 227; MTCW 1

Ford, Webster
See Masters, Edgar Lee

Foreman, Richard 1937- .... **CLC 50**
See also CA 65-68; CANR 32, 63

Forester, C(ecil) S(cott) 1899-1966 ... **CLC 35**
See also CA 73-76; 25-28R; CANR 83; DLB 191; SATA 13

Forez
See Mauriac, Francois (Charles)

Forman, James Douglas 1932- .... **CLC 21**
See also AAYA 17; CA 9-12R; CANR 4, 19, 42; JRDA; MAICYA; SATA 8, 70

Fornes, Maria Irene 1930- . **CLC 39, 61; DC 10; HLCS 1**
See also CA 25-28R; CANR 28, 81; DLB 7; HW 1, 2; INT CANR-28; MTCW 1

Forrest, Leon (Richard) 1937-1997 .. **CLC 4; BLCS**
See also BW 2; CA 89-92; 162; CAAS 7; CANR 25, 52, 87; DLB 33

Forster, E(dward) M(organ)
1879-1970 ...... **CLC 1, 2, 3, 4, 9, 10, 13, 15, 22, 45, 77; DA; DAB; DAC; DAM MST, NOV; SSC 27; WLC**
See also AAYA 2; CA 13-14; 25-28R; CANR 45; CAP 1; CDBLB 1914-1945; DA3; DLB 34, 98, 162, 178, 195; DLBD 10; MTCW 1, 2; SATA 57

Forster, John 1812-1876 .... **NCLC 11**
See also DLB 144, 184

Forsyth, Frederick 1938- .... **CLC 2, 5, 36; DAM NOV, POP**
See also BEST 89:4; CA 85-88; CANR 38, 62; DLB 87; MTCW 1, 2

Forten, Charlotte L. TCLC 16; BLC 2
See also Grimke, Charlotte L(ottie) Forten
See also DLB 50

Foscolo, Ugo 1778-1827 .... **NCLC 8**

Fosse, Bob CLC 20
See also Fosse, Robert Louis

Fosse, Robert Louis 1927-1987
See Fosse, Bob
See also CA 110; 123

Foster, Stephen Collins
1826-1864 .... **NCLC 26**

Foucault, Michel 1926-1984 . **CLC 31, 34, 69**
See also CA 105; 113; CANR 34; MTCW 1, 2

Fouque, Friedrich (Heinrich Karl) de la Motte 1777-1843 .... **NCLC 2**
See also DLB 90

Fourier, Charles 1772-1837 .... **NCLC 51**

Fournier, Pierre 1916- .... **CLC 11**
See also Gascar, Pierre
See also CA 89-92; CANR 16, 40

Fowles, John (Philip) 1926- .. **CLC 1, 2, 3, 4, 6, 9, 10, 15, 33, 87; DAB; DAC; DAM MST; SSC 33**
See also CA 5-8R; CANR 25, 71; CDBLB 1960 to Present; DA3; DLB 14, 139, 207; MTCW 1, 2; SATA 22

Fox, Paula 1923- .... **CLC 2, 8, 121**
See also AAYA 3; CA 73-76; CANR 20, 36, 62; CLR 1, 44; DLB 52; JRDA; MAICYA; MTCW 1; SATA 17, 60

Fox, William Price (Jr.) 1926- .... **CLC 22**
See also CA 17-20R; CAAS 19; CANR 11; DLB 2; DLBY 81

Foxe, John 1516(?)-1587 .... **LC 14**
See also DLB 132

Frame, Janet 1924- . **CLC 2, 3, 6, 22, 66, 96; SSC 29**
See also Clutha, Janet Paterson Frame

France, Anatole TCLC 9
See also Thibault, Jacques Anatole Francois
See also DLB 123; MTCW 1

Francis, Claude 19(?)- .... **CLC 50**

Francis, Dick 1920- .... **CLC 2, 22, 42, 102; DAM POP**
See also AAYA 5, 21; BEST 89:3; CA 5-8R; CANR 9, 42, 68; CDBLB 1960 to Present; DA3; DLB 87; INT CANR-9; MTCW 1, 2

Francis, Robert (Churchill)
1901-1987 .... **CLC 15**
See also CA 1-4R; 123; CANR 1

Frank, Anne(lies Marie)
1929-1945 . **TCLC 17; DA; DAB; DAC; DAM MST; WLC**
See also AAYA 12; CA 113; 133; CANR 68; DA3; MTCW 1, 2; SATA 87; SATA-Brief 42

Frank, Bruno 1887-1945 .... **TCLC 81**
See also DLB 118

Frank, Elizabeth 1945- .... **CLC 39**
See also CA 121; 126; CANR 78; INT 126

Frankl, Viktor E(mil) 1905-1997 ...... **CLC 93**
See also CA 65-68; 161

Franklin, Benjamin
See Hasek, Jaroslav (Matej Frantisek)

Franklin, Benjamin 1706-1790 .. **LC 25; DA; DAB; DAC; DAM MST; WLCS**
See also CDALB 1640-1865; DA3; DLB 24, 43, 73

Franklin, (Stella Maria Sarah) Miles (Lampe) 1879-1954 .... **TCLC 7**
See also CA 104; 164

Fraser, (Lady) Antonia (Pakenham)
1932- .... **CLC 32, 107**
See also CA 85-88; CANR 44, 65; MTCW 1, 2; SATA-Brief 32

Fraser, George MacDonald 1925- ...... **CLC 7**
See also CA 45-48, 180; CAAE 180; CANR 2, 48, 74; MTCW 1

Fraser, Sylvia 1935- .... **CLC 64**
See also CA 45-48; CANR 1, 16, 60

Frayn, Michael 1933- .... **CLC 3, 7, 31, 47; DAM DRAM, NOV**
See also CA 5-8R; CANR 30, 69; DLB 13, 14, 194; MTCW 1, 2

Fraze, Candida (Merrill) 1945- .... **CLC 50**
See also CA 126

Frazer, J(ames) G(eorge)
1854-1941 .... **TCLC 32**
See also CA 118

Frazer, Robert Caine
See Creasey, John

Frazer, Sir James George
See Frazer, J(ames) G(eorge)

Frazier, Charles 1950- .... **CLC 109**
See also AAYA 34; CA 161

Frazier, Ian 1951- .... **CLC 46**
See also CA 130; CANR 54

Frederic, Harold 1856-1898 .... **NCLC 10**
See also DLB 12, 23; DLBD 13

Frederick, John
See Faust, Frederick (Schiller)

Frederick the Great 1712-1786 .... **LC 14**

Fredro, Aleksander 1793-1876 .... **NCLC 8**

Freeling, Nicolas 1927- .... **CLC 38**
See also CA 49-52; CAAS 12; CANR 1, 17, 50, 84; DLB 87

Freeman, Douglas Southall
1886-1953 .... **TCLC 11**
See also CA 109; DLB 17; DLBD 17

Freeman, Judith 1946- .... **CLC 55**
See also CA 148

Freeman, Mary E(leanor) Wilkins
1852-1930 .... **TCLC 9; SSC 1**
See also CA 106; 177; DLB 12, 78, 221

Freeman, R(ichard) Austin
1862-1943 .... **TCLC 21**
See also CA 113; CANR 84; DLB 70

French, Albert 1943- .... **CLC 86**
See also BW 3; CA 167

French, Marilyn 1929- .... **CLC 10, 18, 60; DAM DRAM, NOV, POP**
See also CA 69-72; CANR 3, 31; INT CANR-31; MTCW 1, 2

French, Paul
See Asimov, Isaac

Freneau, Philip Morin 1752-1832 ... **NCLC 1**
See also DLB 37, 43

Freud, Sigmund 1856-1939 .... **TCLC 52**
See also CA 115; 133; CANR 69; MTCW 1, 2

Friedan, Betty (Naomi) 1921- .... **CLC 74**
See also CA 65-68; CANR 18, 45, 74; MTCW 1, 2

Friedlander, Saul 1932- .... **CLC 90**
See also CA 117; 130; CANR 72

Friedman, B(ernard) H(arper)
1926- .... **CLC 7**
See also CA 1-4R; CANR 3, 48

Friedman, Bruce Jay 1930- .... **CLC 3, 5, 56**
See also CA 9-12R; CANR 25, 52; DLB 2, 28; INT CANR-25

Friel, Brian 1929- .... **CLC 5, 42, 59, 115; DC 8**
See also CA 21-24R; CANR 33, 69; DLB 13; MTCW 1

Friis-Baastad, Babbis Ellinor
1921-1970 .... **CLC 12**
See also CA 17-20R; 134; SATA 7

Frisch, Max (Rudolf) 1911-1991 ... **CLC 3, 9, 14, 18, 32, 44; DAM DRAM, NOV**
See also CA 85-88; 134; CANR 32, 74; DLB 69, 124; MTCW 1, 2

Fromentin, Eugene (Samuel Auguste)
1820-1876 .... **NCLC 10**
See also DLB 123

Frost, Frederick
See Faust, Frederick (Schiller)

Frost, Robert (Lee) 1874-1963 .. **CLC 1, 3, 4, 9, 10, 13, 15, 26, 34, 44; DA; DAB; DAC; DAM MST, POET; PC 1; WLC**
See also AAYA 21; CA 89-92; CANR 33; CDALB 1917-1929; DA3; DLB 54; DLBD 7; MTCW 1, 2; SATA 14

Froude, James Anthony
1818-1894 .... **NCLC 43**
See also DLB 18, 57, 144

Froy, Herald
See Waterhouse, Keith (Spencer)

Fry, Christopher 1907- .... **CLC 2, 10, 14; DAM DRAM**
See also CA 17-20R; CAAS 23; CANR 9, 30, 74; DLB 13; MTCW 1, 2; SATA 66

Frye, (Herman) Northrop
1912-1991 .... **CLC 24, 70**
See also CA 5-8R; 133; CANR 8, 37; DLB 67, 68; MTCW 1, 2

Fuchs, Daniel 1909-1993 .... **CLC 8, 22**
See also CA 81-84; 142; CAAS 5; CANR 40; DLB 9, 26, 28; DLBY 93

Fuchs, Daniel 1934- .... **CLC 34**
See also CA 37-40R; CANR 14, 48

Fuentes, Carlos 1928- .... **CLC 3, 8, 10, 13, 22, 41, 60, 113; DA; DAB; DAC; DAM MST, MULT, NOV; HLC 1; SSC 24; WLC**
See also AAYA 4; AITN 2; CA 69-72; CANR 10, 32, 68; DA3; DLB 113; HW 1, 2; MTCW 1, 2

Fuentes, Gregorio Lopez y
See Lopez y Fuentes, Gregorio

Fuertes, Gloria 1918- .... **PC 27**
See also CA 178, 180; DLB 108; HW 2; SATA 115

Fugard, (Harold) Athol 1932- . **CLC 5, 9, 14, 25, 40, 80; DAM DRAM; DC 3**
See also AAYA 17; CA 85-88; CANR 32, 54; DLB 225; MTCW 1

Fugard, Sheila 1932- .... **CLC 48**
See also CA 125

Fukuyama, Francis 1952- .... **CLC 131**
See also CA 140; CANR 72

Fuller, Charles (H., Jr.) 1939- .... **CLC 25; BLC 2; DAM DRAM, MULT; DC 1**
See also BW 2; CA 108; 112; CANR 87; DLB 38; INT 112; MTCW 1

Fuller, John (Leopold) 1937- .... **CLC 62**
See also CA 21-24R; CANR 9, 44; DLB 40

Fuller, Margaret
See Ossoli, Sarah Margaret (Fuller marchesa d')

Fuller, Roy (Broadbent) 1912-1991 ... **CLC 4, 28**
See also CA 5-8R; 135; CAAS 10; CANR 53, 83; DLB 15, 20; SATA 87

Fuller, Sarah Margaret 1810-1850
See Ossoli, Sarah Margaret (Fuller marchesa d')

Fulton, Alice 1952- .... **CLC 52**
See also CA 116; CANR 57, 88; DLB 193

Furphy, Joseph 1843-1912 .... **TCLC 25**
See also CA 163

Fussell, Paul 1924- .... **CLC 74**
See also BEST 90:1; CA 17-20R; CANR 8, 21, 35, 69; INT CANR-21; MTCW 1, 2

Futabatei, Shimei 1864-1909 .... **TCLC 44**
See also CA 162; DLB 180

Futrelle, Jacques 1875-1912 .... **TCLC 19**
See also CA 113; 155

Gaboriau, Emile 1835-1873 .... **NCLC 14**

Gadda, Carlo Emilio 1893-1973 .... **CLC 11**
See also CA 89-92; DLB 177

Gaddis, William 1922-1998 ... **CLC 1, 3, 6, 8, 10, 19, 43, 86**
See also CA 17-20R; 172; CANR 21, 48; DLB 2; MTCW 1, 2

Gage, Walter
See Inge, William (Motter)

Gaines, Ernest J(ames) 1933- ...... **CLC 3, 11, 18, 86; BLC 2; DAM MULT**
See also AAYA 18; AITN 1; BW 2, 3; CA 9-12R; CANR 6, 24, 42, 75; CDALB 1968-1988; CLR 62; DA3; DLB 2, 33, 152; DLBY 80; MTCW 1, 2; SATA 86

Gaitskill, Mary 1954- .... **CLC 69**
See also CA 128; CANR 61

Galdos, Benito Perez
See Perez Galdos, Benito

Gale, Zona 1874-1938 .... **TCLC 7; DAM DRAM**
See also CA 105; 153; CANR 84; DLB 9, 78, 228

Galeano, Eduardo (Hughes) 1940- . **CLC 72; HLCS 1**
See also CA 29-32R; CANR 13, 32; HW 1

Galiano, Juan Valera y Alcala
See Valera y Alcala-Galiano, Juan

Galilei, Galileo 1546-1642 .... **LC 45**

Gallagher, Tess 1943- ...... **CLC 18, 63; DAM POET; PC 9**
See also CA 106; DLB 212

Gallant, Mavis 1922- .. **CLC 7, 18, 38; DAC; DAM MST; SSC 5**
See also CA 69-72; CANR 29, 69; DLB 53; MTCW 1, 2

Gallant, Roy A(rthur) 1924- .... **CLC 17**
See also CA 5-8R; CANR 4, 29, 54; CLR 30; MAICYA; SATA 4, 68, 110

Gallico, Paul (William) 1897-1976 ..... **CLC 2**
See also AITN 1; CA 5-8R; 69-72; CANR 23; DLB 9, 171; MAICYA; SATA 13

Gallo, Max Louis 1932- .... **CLC 95**
See also CA 85-88

Gallois, Lucien
See Desnos, Robert

Gallup, Ralph
See Whitemore, Hugh (John)

Galsworthy, John 1867-1933 .... **TCLC 1, 45; DA; DAB; DAC; DAM DRAM, MST, NOV; SSC 22; WLC**
See also CA 104; 141; CANR 75; CDBLB 1890-1914; DA3; DLB 10, 34, 98, 162; DLBD 16; MTCW 1

Galt, John 1779-1839 .... **NCLC 1**
See also DLB 99, 116, 159

Galvin, James 1951- .... **CLC 38**
See also CA 108; CANR 26

Gamboa, Federico 1864-1939 .... **TCLC 36**
See also CA 167; HW 2

Gandhi, M. K.
See Gandhi, Mohandas Karamchand

Gandhi, Mahatma
See Gandhi, Mohandas Karamchand

Gandhi, Mohandas Karamchand
1869-1948 .... **TCLC 59; DAM MULT**
See also CA 121; 132; DA3; MTCW 1, 2

Gann, Ernest Kellogg 1910-1991 ..... **CLC 23**
See also AITN 1; CA 1-4R; 136; CANR 1, 83

Garber, Eric 1943(?)-
See Holleran, Andrew
See also CANR 89

Garcia, Cristina 1958- .... **CLC 76**
See also CA 141; CANR 73; HW 2

Garcia Lorca, Federico 1898-1936 . **TCLC 1, 7, 49; DA; DAB; DAC; DAM DRAM, MST, MULT, POET; DC 2; HLC 2; PC 3; WLC**
See also Lorca, Federico Garcia
See also CA 104; 131; CANR 81; DA3; DLB 108; HW 1, 2; MTCW 1, 2

Garcia Marquez, Gabriel (Jose)
1928- .... **CLC 2, 3, 8, 10, 15, 27, 47, 55, 68; DA; DAB; DAC; DAM MST, MULT, NOV, POP; HLC 1; SSC 8; WLC**
See also Marquez, Gabriel (Jose) Garcia
See also AAYA 3, 33; BEST 89:1, 90:4; CA 33-36R; CANR 10, 28, 50, 75, 82; DA3; DLB 113; HW 1, 2; MTCW 1, 2

Garcilaso de la Vega, El Inca 1503-1536
See also HLCS 1

Gard, Janice
See Latham, Jean Lee

Gard, Roger Martin du
See Martin du Gard, Roger

Gardam, Jane 1928- .... **CLC 43**
See also CA 49-52; CANR 2, 18, 33, 54; CLR 12; DLB 14, 161; MAICYA; MTCW 1; SAAS 9; SATA 39, 76; SATA-Brief 28

Gardner, Herb(ert) 1934- .... **CLC 44**
See also CA 149

Gardner, John (Champlin), Jr.
1933-1982 ...... **CLC 2, 3, 5, 7, 8, 10, 18, 28, 34; DAM NOV, POP; SSC 7**
See also AITN 1; CA 65-68; 107; CANR 33, 73; CDALBS; DA3; DLB 2; DLBY 82; MTCW 1; SATA 40; SATA-Obit 31

Gardner, John (Edmund) 1926- ...... **CLC 30; DAM POP**
See also CA 103; CANR 15, 69; MTCW 1

Gardner, Miriam
See Bradley, Marion Zimmer

Gardner, Noel
See Kuttner, Henry

Gardons, S. S.
See Snodgrass, W(illiam) D(e Witt)

Garfield, Leon 1921-1996 .... CLC 12
　　See also AAYA 8; CA 17-20R; 152; CANR
　　38, 41, 78; CLR 21; DLB 161; JRDA;
　　MAICYA; SATA 1, 32, 76; SATA-Obit 90
Garland, (Hannibal) Hamlin
　　1860-1940 .... TCLC 3; SSC 18
　　See also CA 104; DLB 12, 71, 78, 186
Garneau, (Hector de) Saint-Denys
　　1912-1943 .... TCLC 13
　　See also CA 111; DLB 88
Garner, Alan 1934- ..... CLC 17; DAB; DAM
　　POP
　　See also AAYA 18; CA 73-76, 178; CAAE
　　178; CANR 15, 64; CLR 20; DLB 161;
　　MAICYA; MTCW 1, 2; SATA 18, 69;
　　SATA-Essay 108
Garner, Hugh 1913-1979 .... CLC 13
　　See also CA 69-72; CANR 31; DLB 68
Garnett, David 1892-1981 .... CLC 3
　　See also CA 5-8R; 103; CANR 17, 79; DLB
　　34; MTCW 2
Garos, Stephanie
　　See Katz, Steve
Garrett, George (Palmer) 1929- .. CLC 3, 11,
　　51; SSC 30
　　See also CA 1-4R; CAAS 5; CANR 1, 42,
　　67; DLB 2, 5, 130, 152; DLBY 83
Garrick, David 1717-1779 .... LC 15; DAM
　　DRAM
　　See also DLB 84
Garrigue, Jean 1914-1972 .... CLC 2, 8
　　See also CA 5-8R; 37-40R; CANR 20
Garrison, Frederick
　　See Sinclair, Upton (Beall)
Garro, Elena 1920(?)-1998
　　See also CA 131; 169; DLB 145; HLCS 1;
　　HW 1
Garth, Will
　　See Hamilton, Edmond; Kuttner, Henry
Garvey, Marcus (Moziah, Jr.)
　　1887-1940 ...... TCLC 41; BLC 2; DAM
　　MULT
　　See also BW 1; CA 120; 124; CANR 79
Gary, Romain CLC 25
　　See also Kacew, Romain
　　See also DLB 83
Gascar, Pierre CLC 11
　　See also Fournier, Pierre
Gascoyne, David (Emery) 1916- .... CLC 45
　　See also CA 65-68; CANR 10, 28, 54; DLB
　　20; MTCW 1
Gaskell, Elizabeth Cleghorn
　　1810-1865 .... NCLC 70; DAB; DAM
　　MST; SSC 25
　　See also CDBLB 1832-1890; DLB 21, 144,
　　159
Gass, William H(oward) 1924- . CLC 1, 2, 8,
　　11, 15, 39, 132; SSC 12
　　See also CA 17-20R; CANR 30, 71; DLB
　　2, 227; MTCW 1, 2
Gassendi, Pierre 1592-1655 .... LC 54
Gasset, Jose Ortega y
　　See Ortega y Gasset, Jose
Gates, Henry Louis, Jr. 1950- .... CLC 65;
　　BLCS; DAM MULT
　　See also BW 2, 3; CA 109; CANR 25, 53,
　　75; DA3; DLB 67; MTCW 1
Gautier, Theophile 1811-1872 .. NCLC 1, 59;
　　DAM POET; PC 18; SSC 20
　　See also DLB 119
Gawsworth, John
　　See Bates, H(erbert) E(rnest)
Gay, John 1685-1732 .. LC 49; DAM DRAM
　　See also DLB 84, 95
Gay, Oliver
　　See Gogarty, Oliver St. John
Gaye, Marvin (Penze) 1939-1984 ..... CLC 26
　　See also CA 112

Gebler, Carlo (Ernest) 1954- .... CLC 39
　　See also CA 119; 133
Gee, Maggie (Mary) 1948- .... CLC 57
　　See also CA 130; DLB 207
Gee, Maurice (Gough) 1931- .... CLC 29
　　See also CA 97-100; CANR 67; CLR 56;
　　SATA 46, 101
Gelbart, Larry (Simon) 1923- .... CLC 21, 61
　　See also CA 73-76; CANR 45
Gelber, Jack 1932- .... CLC 1, 6, 14, 79
　　See also CA 1-4R; CANR 2; DLB 7, 228
Gellhorn, Martha (Ellis)
　　1908-1998 .... CLC 14, 60
　　See also CA 77-80; 164; CANR 44; DLBY
　　82, 98
Genet, Jean 1910-1986 .. CLC 1, 2, 5, 10, 14,
　　44, 46; DAM DRAM
　　See also CA 13-16R; CANR 18; DA3; DLB
　　72; DLBY 86; MTCW 1, 2
Gent, Peter 1942- .... CLC 29
　　See also AITN 1; CA 89-92; DLBY 82
Gentile, Giovanni 1875-1944 .... TCLC 96
　　See also CA 119
Gentlewoman in New England, A
　　See Bradstreet, Anne
Gentlewoman in Those Parts, A
　　See Bradstreet, Anne
George, Jean Craighead 1919- .... CLC 35
　　See also AAYA 8; CA 5-8R; CANR 25;
　　CLR 1; DLB 52; JRDA; MAICYA; SATA
　　2, 68
George, Stefan (Anton) 1868-1933 . TCLC 2,
　　14
　　See also CA 104
Georges, Georges Martin
　　See Simenon, Georges (Jacques Christian)
Gerhardi, William Alexander
　　See Gerhardie, William Alexander
Gerhardie, William Alexander
　　1895-1977 .... CLC 5
　　See also CA 25-28R; 73-76; CANR 18;
　　DLB 36
Gerstler, Amy 1956- .... CLC 70
　　See also CA 146
Gertler, T. CLC 34
　　See also CA 116; 121; INT 121
Ghalib NCLC 39, 78
　　See also Ghalib, Hsadullah Khan
Ghalib, Hsadullah Khan 1797-1869
　　See Ghalib
　　See also DAM POET
Ghelderode, Michel de 1898-1962 ..... CLC 6,
　　11; DAM DRAM
　　See also CA 85-88; CANR 40, 77
Ghiselin, Brewster 1903- .... CLC 23
　　See also CA 13-16R; CAAS 10; CANR 13
Ghose, Aurabinda 1872-1950 .... TCLC 63
　　See also CA 163
Ghose, Zulfikar 1935- .... CLC 42
　　See also CA 65-68; CANR 67
Ghosh, Amitav 1956- .... CLC 44
　　See also CA 147; CANR 80
Giacosa, Giuseppe 1847-1906 .... TCLC 7
　　See also CA 104
Gibb, Lee
　　See Waterhouse, Keith (Spencer)
Gibbon, Lewis Grassic TCLC 4
　　See also Mitchell, James Leslie
Gibbons, Kaye 1960- .... CLC 50, 88; DAM
　　POP
　　See also AAYA 34; CA 151; CANR 75;
　　DA3; MTCW 1; SATA 117
Gibran, Kahlil 1883-1931 .... TCLC 1, 9;
　　DAM POET, POP; PC 9
　　See also CA 104; 150; DA3; MTCW 2
Gibran, Khalil
　　See Gibran, Kahlil

Gibson, William 1914- .. CLC 23; DA; DAB;
　　DAC; DAM DRAM, MST
　　See also CA 9-12R; CANR 9, 42, 75; DLB
　　7; MTCW 1; SATA 66
Gibson, William (Ford) 1948- ... CLC 39, 63;
　　DAM POP
　　See also AAYA 12; CA 126; 133; CANR
　　52, 90; DA3; MTCW 1
Gide, Andre (Paul Guillaume)
　　1869-1951 . TCLC 5, 12, 36; DA; DAB;
　　DAC; DAM MST, NOV; SSC 13; WLC
　　See also CA 104; 124; DA3; DLB 65;
　　MTCW 1, 2
Gifford, Barry (Colby) 1946- .... CLC 34
　　See also CA 65-68; CANR 9, 30, 40, 90
Gilbert, Frank
　　See De Voto, Bernard (Augustine)
Gilbert, W(illiam) S(chwenck)
　　1836-1911 .... TCLC 3; DAM DRAM,
　　POET
　　See also CA 104; 173; SATA 36
Gilbreth, Frank B., Jr. 1911- .... CLC 17
　　See also CA 9-12R; SATA 2
Gilchrist, Ellen 1935- ...... CLC 34, 48; DAM
　　POP; SSC 14
　　See also CA 113; 116; CANR 41, 61; DLB
　　130; MTCW 1, 2
Giles, Molly 1942- .... CLC 39
　　See also CA 126
Gill, Eric 1882-1940 .... TCLC 85
Gill, Patrick
　　See Creasey, John
Gilliam, Terry (Vance) 1940- .... CLC 21
　　See also Monty Python
　　See also AAYA 19; CA 108; 113; CANR
　　35; INT 113
Gillian, Jerry
　　See Gilliam, Terry (Vance)
Gilliatt, Penelope (Ann Douglass)
　　1932-1993 .... CLC 2, 10, 13, 53
　　See also AITN 2; CA 13-16R; 141; CANR
　　49; DLB 14
Gilman, Charlotte (Anna) Perkins (Stetson)
　　1860-1935 .... TCLC 9, 37; SSC 13
　　See also CA 106; 150; DLB 221; MTCW 1
Gilmour, David 1949- .... CLC 35
　　See also CA 138, 147
Gilpin, William 1724-1804 .... NCLC 30
Gilray, J. D.
　　See Mencken, H(enry) L(ouis)
Gilroy, Frank D(aniel) 1925- .... CLC 2
　　See also CA 81-84; CANR 32, 64, 86; DLB
　　7
Gilstrap, John 1957(?)- .... CLC 99
　　See also CA 160
Ginsberg, Allen 1926-1997 .... CLC 1, 2, 3, 4,
　　6, 13, 36, 69, 109; DA; DAB; DAC;
　　DAM MST, POET; PC 4; WLC
　　See also AAYA 33; AITN 1; CA 1-4R; 157;
　　CANR 2, 41, 63; CDALB 1941-1968;
　　DA3; DLB 5, 16, 169; MTCW 1, 2
Ginzburg, Natalia 1916-1991 .... CLC 5, 11,
　　54, 70
　　See also CA 85-88; 135; CANR 33; DLB
　　177; MTCW 1, 2
Giono, Jean 1895-1970 .... CLC 4, 11
　　See also CA 45-48; 29-32R; CANR 2, 35;
　　DLB 72; MTCW 1
Giovanni, Nikki 1943- .... CLC 2, 4, 19, 64,
　　117; BLC 2; DA; DAB; DAC; DAM
　　MST, MULT, POET; PC 19; WLCS
　　See also AAYA 22; AITN 1; BW 2, 3; CA
　　29-32R; CAAS 6; CANR 18, 41, 60, 91;
　　CDALBS; CLR 6; DA3; DLB 5, 41; INT
　　CANR-18; MAICYA; MTCW 1, 2; SATA
　　24, 107
Giovene, Andrea 1904- .... CLC 7
　　See also CA 85-88

Gippius, Zinaida (Nikolayevna) 1869-1945
See Hippius, Zinaida
See also CA 106
Giraudoux, (Hippolyte) Jean
1882-1944 .... **TCLC 2, 7; DAM DRAM**
See also CA 104; DLB 65
Gironella, Jose Maria 1917- .... **CLC 11**
See also CA 101
Gissing, George (Robert)
1857-1903 .... **TCLC 3, 24, 47; SSC 37**
See also CA 105; 167; DLB 18, 135, 184
Giurlani, Aldo
See Palazzeschi, Aldo
Gladkov, Fyodor (Vasilyevich)
1883-1958 .... **TCLC 27**
See also CA 170
Glanville, Brian (Lester) 1931- .... **CLC 6**
See also CA 5-8R; CAAS 9; CANR 3, 70;
DLB 15, 139; SATA 42
Glasgow, Ellen (Anderson Gholson)
1873-1945 .... **TCLC 2, 7; SSC 34**
See also CA 104; 164; DLB 9, 12; MTCW
2
Glaspell, Susan 1882(?)-1948 . **TCLC 55; DC
10; SSC 41**
See also CA 110; 154; DLB 7, 9, 78, 228;
YABC 2
Glassco, John 1909-1981 .... **CLC 9**
See also CA 13-16R; 102; CANR 15; DLB
68
Glasscock, Amnesia
See Steinbeck, John (Ernst)
Glasser, Ronald J. 1940(?)- .... **CLC 37**
Glassman, Joyce
See Johnson, Joyce
Glendinning, Victoria 1937- .... **CLC 50**
See also CA 120; 127; CANR 59, 89; DLB
155
Glissant, Edouard 1928- . **CLC 10, 68; DAM
MULT**
See also CA 153
Gloag, Julian 1930- .... **CLC 40**
See also AITN 1; CA 65-68; CANR 10, 70
Glowacki, Aleksander
See Prus, Boleslaw
Gluck, Louise (Elisabeth) 1943- .. **CLC 7, 22,
44, 81; DAM POET; PC 16**
See also CA 33-36R; CANR 40, 69; DA3;
DLB 5; MTCW 2
Glyn, Elinor 1864-1943 .... **TCLC 72**
See also DLB 153
Gobineau, Joseph Arthur (Comte) de
1816-1882 .... **NCLC 17**
See also DLB 123
Godard, Jean-Luc 1930- .... **CLC 20**
See also CA 93-96
Godden, (Margaret) Rumer
1907-1998 .... **CLC 53**
See also AAYA 6; CA 5-8R; 172; CANR 4,
27, 36, 55, 80; CLR 20; DLB 161; MAI-
CYA; SAAS 12; SATA 3, 36; SATA-Obit
109
Godoy Alcayaga, Lucila 1889-1957
See Mistral, Gabriela
See also BW 2; CA 104; 131; CANR 81;
DAM MULT; HW 1, 2; MTCW 1, 2
Godwin, Gail (Kathleen) 1937- ..... **CLC 5, 8,
22, 31, 69, 125; DAM POP**
See also CA 29-32R; CANR 15, 43, 69;
DA3; DLB 6; INT CANR-15; MTCW 1,
2
Godwin, William 1756-1836 .... **NCLC 14**
See also CDBLB 1789-1832; DLB 39, 104,
142, 158, 163
Goebbels, Josef
See Goebbels, (Paul) Joseph
Goebbels, (Paul) Joseph
1897-1945 .... **TCLC 68**
See also CA 115; 148

Goebbels, Joseph Paul
See Goebbels, (Paul) Joseph
Goethe, Johann Wolfgang von
1749-1832 ...... **NCLC 4, 22, 34, 90; DA;
DAB; DAC; DAM DRAM, MST,
POET; PC 5; SSC 38; WLC**
See also DA3; DLB 94
Gogarty, Oliver St. John
1878-1957 .... **TCLC 15**
See also CA 109; 150; DLB 15, 19
Gogol, Nikolai (Vasilyevich)
1809-1852 . **NCLC 5, 15, 31; DA; DAB;
DAC; DAM DRAM, MST; DC 1; SSC
4, 29; WLC**
See also DLB 198
Goines, Donald 1937(?)-1974 . **CLC 80; BLC
2; DAM MULT, POP**
See also AITN 1; BW 1, 3; CA 124; 114;
CANR 82; DA3; DLB 33
Gold, Herbert 1924- .... **CLC 4, 7, 14, 42**
See also CA 9-12R; CANR 17, 45; DLB 2;
DLBY 81
Goldbarth, Albert 1948- .... **CLC 5, 38**
See also CA 53-56; CANR 6, 40; DLB 120
Goldberg, Anatol 1910-1982 .... **CLC 34**
See also CA 131; 117
Goldemberg, Isaac 1945- .... **CLC 52**
See also CA 69-72; CAAS 12; CANR 11,
32; HW 1
Golding, William (Gerald)
1911-1993 ..... **CLC 1, 2, 3, 8, 10, 17, 27,
58, 81; DA; DAB; DAC; DAM MST,
NOV; WLC**
See also AAYA 5; CA 5-8R; 141; CANR
13, 33, 54; CDBLB 1945-1960; DA3;
DLB 15, 100; MTCW 1, 2
Goldman, Emma 1869-1940 .... **TCLC 13**
See also CA 110; 150; DLB 221
Goldman, Francisco 1954- .... **CLC 76**
See also CA 162
Goldman, William (W.) 1931- ...... **CLC 1, 48**
See also CA 9-12R; CANR 29, 69; DLB 44
Goldmann, Lucien 1913-1970 .... **CLC 24**
See also CA 25-28; CAP 2
Goldoni, Carlo 1707-1793 .... **LC 4; DAM
DRAM**
Goldsberry, Steven 1949- .... **CLC 34**
See also CA 131
Goldsmith, Oliver 1728-1774 . **LC 2, 48; DA;
DAB; DAC; DAM DRAM, MST, NOV,
POET; DC 8; WLC**
See also CDBLB 1660-1789; DLB 39, 89,
104, 109, 142; SATA 26
Goldsmith, Peter
See Priestley, J(ohn) B(oynton)
Gombrowicz, Witold 1904-1969 .... **CLC 4, 7,
11, 49; DAM DRAM**
See also CA 19-20; 25-28R; CAP 2
Gomez de la Serna, Ramon
1888-1963 .... **CLC 9**
See also CA 153; 116; CANR 79; HW 1, 2
Goncharov, Ivan Alexandrovich
1812-1891 .... **NCLC 1, 63**
Goncourt, Edmond (Louis Antoine Huot) de
1822-1896 .... **NCLC 7**
See also DLB 123
Goncourt, Jules (Alfred Huot) de
1830-1870 .... **NCLC 7**
See also DLB 123
Gontier, Fernande 19(?)- .... **CLC 50**
Gonzalez Martinez, Enrique
1871-1952 .... **TCLC 72**
See also CA 166; CANR 81; HW 1, 2
Goodman, Paul 1911-1972 ..... **CLC 1, 2, 4, 7**
See also CA 19-20; 37-40R; CANR 34;
CAP 2; DLB 130; MTCW 1

Gordimer, Nadine 1923- ...... **CLC 3, 5, 7, 10,
18, 33, 51, 70; DA; DAB; DAC; DAM
MST, NOV; SSC 17; WLCS**
See also CA 5-8R; CANR 3, 28, 56, 88;
DA3; DLB 225; INT CANR-28; MTCW
1, 2
Gordon, Adam Lindsay
1833-1870 .... **NCLC 21**
Gordon, Caroline 1895-1981 . **CLC 6, 13, 29,
83; SSC 15**
See also CA 11-12; 103; CANR 36; CAP 1;
DLB 4, 9, 102; DLBD 17; DLBY 81;
MTCW 1, 2
Gordon, Charles William 1860-1937
See Connor, Ralph
See also CA 109
Gordon, Mary (Catherine) 1949- .... **CLC 13,
22, 128**
See also CA 102; CANR 44, 92; DLB 6;
DLBY 81; INT 102; MTCW 1
Gordon, N. J.
See Bosman, Herman Charles
Gordon, Sol 1923- .... **CLC 26**
See also CA 53-56; CANR 4; SATA 11
Gordone, Charles 1925-1995 .... **CLC 1, 4;
DAM DRAM; DC 8**
See also BW 1, 3; CA 93-96; 180; 150;
CAAE 180; CANR 55; DLB 7; INT 93-
96; MTCW 1
Gore, Catherine 1800-1861 .... **NCLC 65**
See also DLB 116
Gorenko, Anna Andreevna
See Akhmatova, Anna
Gorky, Maxim 1868-1936 ..... **TCLC 8; DAB;
SSC 28; WLC**
See also Peshkov, Alexei Maximovich
See also MTCW 2
Goryan, Sirak
See Saroyan, William
Gosse, Edmund (William)
1849-1928 .... **TCLC 28**
See also CA 117; DLB 57, 144, 184
Gotlieb, Phyllis Fay (Bloom) 1926- .. **CLC 18**
See also CA 13-16R; CANR 7; DLB 88
Gottesman, S. D.
See Kornbluth, C(yril) M.; Pohl, Frederik
Gottfried von Strassburg fl. c.
1210- .... **CMLC 10**
See also DLB 138
Gould, Lois .... **CLC 4, 10**
See also CA 77-80; CANR 29; MTCW 1
Gourmont, Remy (-Marie-Charles) de
1858-1915 .... **TCLC 17**
See also CA 109; 150; MTCW 2
Govier, Katherine 1948- .... **CLC 51**
See also CA 101; CANR 18, 40
Goyen, (Charles) William
1915-1983 .... **CLC 5, 8, 14, 40**
See also AITN 2; CA 5-8R; 110; CANR 6,
71; DLB 2; DLBY 83; INT CANR-6
Goytisolo, Juan 1931- .... **CLC 5, 10, 23, 133;
DAM MULT; HLC 1**
See also CA 85-88; CANR 32, 61; HW 1,
2; MTCW 1, 2
Gozzano, Guido 1883-1916 .... **PC 10**
See also CA 154; DLB 114
Gozzi, (Conte) Carlo 1720-1806 .... **NCLC 23**
Grabbe, Christian Dietrich
1801-1836 .... **NCLC 2**
See also DLB 133
Grace, Patricia Frances 1937- .... **CLC 56**
See also CA 176
Gracian y Morales, Baltasar
1601-1658 .... **LC 15**
Gracq, Julien .... **CLC 11, 48**
See also Poirier, Louis
See also DLB 83
Grade, Chaim 1910-1982 .... **CLC 10**
See also CA 93-96; 107

Graduate of Oxford, A
See Ruskin, John
Grafton, Garth
See Duncan, Sara Jeannette
Graham, John
See Phillips, David Graham
Graham, Jorie 1951- .... **CLC 48, 118**
See also CA 111; CANR 63; DLB 120
Graham, R(obert) B(ontine) Cunninghame
See Cunninghame Graham, Robert
(Gallnigad) Bontine
See also DLB 98, 135, 174
Graham, Robert
See Haldeman, Joe (William)
Graham, Tom
See Lewis, (Harry) Sinclair
Graham, W(illiam) S(ydney)
1918-1986 .... **CLC 29**
See also CA 73-76; 118; DLB 20
Graham, Winston (Mawdsley)
1910- .... **CLC 23**
See also CA 49-52; CANR 2, 22, 45, 66;
DLB 77
Grahame, Kenneth 1859-1932 ...... **TCLC 64;**
DAB
See also CA 108; 136; CANR 80; CLR 5;
DA3; DLB 34, 141, 178; MAICYA;
MTCW 2; SATA 100; YABC 1
Granovsky, Timofei Nikolaevich
1813-1855 .... **NCLC 75**
See also DLB 198
Grant, Skeeter
See Spiegelman, Art
Granville-Barker, Harley
1877-1946 .... **TCLC 2; DAM DRAM**
See also Barker, Harley Granville
See also CA 104
Grass, Guenter (Wilhelm) 1927- ... **CLC 1, 2,**
4, 6, 11, 15, 22, 32, 49, 88; DA; DAB;
DAC; DAM MST, NOV; WLC
See also CA 13-16R; CANR 20, 75; DA3;
DLB 75, 124; MTCW 1, 2
Gratton, Thomas
See Hulme, T(homas) E(rnest)
Grau, Shirley Ann 1929- . **CLC 4, 9; SSC 15**
See also CA 89-92; CANR 22, 69; DLB 2;
INT CANR-22; MTCW 1
Gravel, Fern
See Hall, James Norman
Graver, Elizabeth 1964- .... **CLC 70**
See also CA 135; CANR 71
Graves, Richard Perceval 1945- .... **CLC 44**
See also CA 65-68; CANR 9, 26, 51
Graves, Robert (von Ranke)
1895-1985 .. **CLC 1, 2, 6, 11, 39, 44, 45;**
DAB; DAC; DAM MST, POET; PC 6
See also CA 5-8R; 117; CANR 5, 36; CD-
BLB 1914-1945; DA3; DLB 20, 100, 191;
DLBD 18; DLBY 85; MTCW 1, 2; SATA
45
Graves, Valerie
See Bradley, Marion Zimmer
Gray, Alasdair (James) 1934- .... **CLC 41**
See also CA 126; CANR 47, 69; DLB 194;
INT 126; MTCW 1, 2
Gray, Amlin 1946- .... **CLC 29**
See also CA 138
Gray, Francine du Plessix 1930- ..... **CLC 22;**
DAM NOV
See also BEST 90:3; CA 61-64; CAAS 2;
CANR 11, 33, 75, 81; INT CANR-11;
MTCW 1, 2
Gray, John (Henry) 1866-1934 ...... **TCLC 19**
See also CA 119; 162
Gray, Simon (James Holliday)
1936- .... **CLC 9, 14, 36**
See also AITN 1; CA 21-24R; CAAS 3;
CANR 32, 69; DLB 13; MTCW 1

Gray, Spalding 1941- ..... **CLC 49, 112; DAM**
POP; DC 7
See also CA 128; CANR 74; MTCW 2
Gray, Thomas 1716-1771 .... **LC 4, 40; DA;**
DAB; DAC; DAM MST; PC 2; WLC
See also CDBLB 1660-1789; DA3; DLB
109
Grayson, David
See Baker, Ray Stannard
Grayson, Richard (A.) 1951- .... **CLC 38**
See also CA 85-88; CANR 14, 31, 57
Greeley, Andrew M(oran) 1928- ..... **CLC 28;**
DAM POP
See also CA 5-8R; CAAS 7; CANR 7, 43,
69; DA3; MTCW 1, 2
Green, Anna Katharine
1846-1935 .... **TCLC 63**
See also CA 112; 159; DLB 202, 221
Green, Brian
See Card, Orson Scott
Green, Hannah
See Greenberg, Joanne (Goldenberg)
Green, Hannah 1927(?)-1996 .... **CLC 3**
See also CA 73-76; CANR 59
Green, Henry 1905-1973 .... **CLC 2, 13, 97**
See also Yorke, Henry Vincent
See also CA 175; DLB 15
Green, Julian (Hartridge) 1900-1998
See Green, Julien
See also CA 21-24R; 169; CANR 33, 87;
DLB 4, 72; MTCW 1
Green, Julien CLC **3, 11, 77**
See also Green, Julian (Hartridge)
See also MTCW 2
Green, Paul (Eliot) 1894-1981 .... **CLC 25;**
DAM DRAM
See also AITN 1; CA 5-8R; 103; CANR 3;
DLB 7, 9; DLBY 81
Greenberg, Ivan 1908-1973
See Rahv, Philip
See also CA 85-88
Greenberg, Joanne (Goldenberg)
1932- .... **CLC 7, 30**
See also AAYA 12; CA 5-8R; CANR 14,
32, 69; SATA 25
Greenberg, Richard 1959(?)- .... **CLC 57**
See also CA 138
Greene, Bette 1934- .... **CLC 30**
See also AAYA 7; CA 53-56; CANR 4; CLR
2; JRDA; MAICYA; SAAS 16; SATA 8,
102
Greene, Gael CLC **8**
See also CA 13-16R; CANR 10
Greene, Graham (Henry)
1904-1991 .... **CLC 1, 3, 6, 9, 14, 18, 27,**
37, 70, 72, 125; DA; DAB; DAC; DAM
MST, NOV; SSC 29; WLC
See also AITN 2; CA 13-16R; 133; CANR
35, 61; CDBLB 1945-1960; DA3; DLB
13, 15, 77, 100, 162, 201, 204; DLBY 91;
MTCW 1, 2; SATA 20
Greene, Robert 1558-1592 .... **LC 41**
See also DLB 62, 167
Greer, Germaine 1939- .... **CLC 131**
See also AITN 1; CA 81-84; CANR 33, 70;
MTCW 1, 2
Greer, Richard
See Silverberg, Robert
Gregor, Arthur 1923- .... **CLC 9**
See also CA 25-28R; CAAS 10; CANR 11;
SATA 36
Gregor, Lee
See Pohl, Frederik
Gregory, Isabella Augusta (Persse)
1852-1932 .... **TCLC 1**
See also CA 104; 184; DLB 10
Gregory, J. Dennis
See Williams, John A(lfred)

Grendon, Stephen
See Derleth, August (William)
Grenville, Kate 1950- .... **CLC 61**
See also CA 118; CANR 53
Grenville, Pelham
See Wodehouse, P(elham) G(renville)
Greve, Felix Paul (Berthold Friedrich)
1879-1948
See Grove, Frederick Philip
See also CA 104; 141, 175; CANR 79;
DAC; DAM MST
Grey, Zane 1872-1939 . **TCLC 6; DAM POP**
See also CA 104; 132; DA3; DLB 212;
MTCW 1, 2
Grieg, (Johan) Nordahl (Brun)
1902-1943 .... **TCLC 10**
See also CA 107
Grieve, C(hristopher) M(urray)
1892-1978 ..... **CLC 11, 19; DAM POET**
See also MacDiarmid, Hugh; Pteleon
See also CA 5-8R; 85-88; CANR 33;
MTCW 1
Griffin, Gerald 1803-1840 .... **NCLC 7**
See also DLB 159
Griffin, John Howard 1920-1980 ..... **CLC 68**
See also AITN 1; CA 1-4R; 101; CANR 2
Griffin, Peter 1942- .... **CLC 39**
See also CA 136
Griffith, D(avid Lewelyn) W(ark)
1875(?)-1948 .... **TCLC 68**
See also CA 119; 150; CANR 80
Griffith, Lawrence
See Griffith, D(avid Lewelyn) W(ark)
Griffiths, Trevor 1935- .... **CLC 13, 52**
See also CA 97-100; CANR 45; DLB 13
Griggs, Sutton (Elbert)
1872-1930 .... **TCLC 77**
See also CA 123; 186; DLB 50
Grigson, Geoffrey (Edward Harvey)
1905-1985 .... **CLC 7, 39**
See also CA 25-28R; 118; CANR 20, 33;
DLB 27; MTCW 1, 2
Grillparzer, Franz 1791-1872 .... **NCLC 1;**
SSC 37
See also DLB 133
Grimble, Reverend Charles James
See Eliot, T(homas) S(tearns)
Grimke, Charlotte L(ottie) Forten
1837(?)-1914
See Forten, Charlotte L.
See also BW 1; CA 117; 124; DAM MULT,
POET
Grimm, Jacob Ludwig Karl
1785-1863 .... **NCLC 3, 77; SSC 36**
See also DLB 90; MAICYA; SATA 22
Grimm, Wilhelm Karl 1786-1859 .. **NCLC 3,**
77; SSC 36
See also DLB 90; MAICYA; SATA 22
Grimmelshausen, Johann Jakob Christoffel
von 1621-1676 .... **LC 6**
See also DLB 168
Grindel, Eugene 1895-1952
See Eluard, Paul
See also CA 104
Grisham, John 1955- .... **CLC 84; DAM POP**
See also AAYA 14; CA 138; CANR 47, 69;
DA3; MTCW 2
Grossman, David 1954- .... **CLC 67**
See also CA 138
Grossman, Vasily (Semenovich)
1905-1964 .... **CLC 41**
See also CA 124; 130; MTCW 1
Grove, Frederick Philip TCLC **4**
See also Greve, Felix Paul (Berthold
Friedrich)
See also DLB 92
Grubb
See Crumb, R(obert)

Grumbach, Doris (Isaac) 1918- . **CLC 13, 22, 64**
See also CA 5-8R; CAAS 2; CANR 9, 42, 70; INT CANR-9; MTCW 2

Grundtvig, Nicolai Frederik Severin 1783-1872 .... **NCLC 1**

Grunge
See Crumb, R(obert)

Grunwald, Lisa 1959- .... **CLC 44**
See also CA 120

Guare, John 1938- .... **CLC 8, 14, 29, 67; DAM DRAM**
See also CA 73-76; CANR 21, 69; DLB 7; MTCW 1, 2

Gudjonsson, Halldor Kiljan 1902-1998
See Laxness, Halldor
See also CA 103; 164

Guenter, Erich
See Eich, Guenter

Guest, Barbara 1920- .... **CLC 34**
See also CA 25-28R; CANR 11, 44, 84; DLB 5, 193

Guest, Edgar A(lbert) 1881-1959 ... **TCLC 95**
See also CA 112; 168

Guest, Judith (Ann) 1936- .... **CLC 8, 30; DAM NOV, POP**
See also AAYA 7; CA 77-80; CANR 15, 75; DA3; INT CANR-15; MTCW 1, 2

Guevara, Che **CLC 87; HLC 1**
See also Guevara (Serna), Ernesto

Guevara (Serna), Ernesto 1928-1967 .... **CLC 87; DAM MULT; HLC 1**
See also Guevara, Che
See also CA 127; 111; CANR 56; HW 1

Guicciardini, Francesco 1483-1540 ..... **LC 49**

Guild, Nicholas M. 1944- .... **CLC 33**
See also CA 93-96

Guillemin, Jacques
See Sartre, Jean-Paul

Guillen, Jorge 1893-1984 .... **CLC 11; DAM MULT, POET; HLCS 1**
See also CA 89-92; 112; DLB 108; HW 1

Guillen, Nicolas (Cristobal) 1902-1989 ..... **CLC 48, 79; BLC 2; DAM MST, MULT, POET; HLC 1; PC 23**
See also BW 2; CA 116; 125; 129; CANR 84; HW 1

Guillevic, (Eugene) 1907- .... **CLC 33**
See also CA 93-96

Guillois
See Desnos, Robert

Guillois, Valentin
See Desnos, Robert

Guimaraes Rosa, Joao 1908-1967
See also CA 175; HLCS 2

Guiney, Louise Imogen 1861-1920 .... **TCLC 41**
See also CA 160; DLB 54

Guiraldes, Ricardo (Guillermo) 1886-1927 .... **TCLC 39**
See also CA 131; HW 1; MTCW 1

Gumilev, Nikolai (Stepanovich) 1886-1921 .... **TCLC 60**
See also CA 165

Gunesekera, Romesh 1954- .... **CLC 91**
See also CA 159

Gunn, Bill **CLC 5**
See also Gunn, William Harrison
See also DLB 38

Gunn, Thom(son William) 1929- .. **CLC 3, 6, 18, 32, 81; DAM POET; PC 26**
See also CA 17-20R; CANR 9, 33; CDBLB 1960 to Present; DLB 27; INT CANR-33; MTCW 1

Gunn, William Harrison 1934(?)-1989
See Gunn, Bill
See also AITN 1; BW 1, 3; CA 13-16R; 128; CANR 12, 25, 76

Gunnars, Kristjana 1948- .... **CLC 69**
See also CA 113; DLB 60

Gurdjieff, G(eorgei) I(vanovich) 1877(?)-1949 .... **TCLC 71**
See also CA 157

Gurganus, Allan 1947- . **CLC 70; DAM POP**
See also BEST 90:1; CA 135

Gurney, A(lbert) R(amsdell), Jr. 1930- ..... **CLC 32, 50, 54; DAM DRAM**
See also CA 77-80; CANR 32, 64

Gurney, Ivor (Bertie) 1890-1937 ... **TCLC 33**
See also CA 167

Gurney, Peter
See Gurney, A(lbert) R(amsdell), Jr.

Guro, Elena 1877-1913 .... **TCLC 56**

Gustafson, James M(oody) 1925- ... **CLC 100**
See also CA 25-28R; CANR 37

Gustafson, Ralph (Barker) 1909- ..... **CLC 36**
See also CA 21-24R; CANR 8, 45, 84; DLB 88

Gut, Gom
See Simenon, Georges (Jacques Christian)

Guterson, David 1956- .... **CLC 91**
See also CA 132; CANR 73; MTCW 2

Guthrie, A(lfred) B(ertram), Jr. 1901-1991 .... **CLC 23**
See also CA 57-60; 134; CANR 24; DLB 212; SATA 62; SATA-Obit 67

Guthrie, Isobel
See Grieve, C(hristopher) M(urray)

Guthrie, Woodrow Wilson 1912-1967
See Guthrie, Woody
See also CA 113; 93-96

Guthrie, Woody **CLC 35**
See also Guthrie, Woodrow Wilson

Gutierrez Najera, Manuel 1859-1895
See also HLCS 2

Guy, Rosa (Cuthbert) 1928- .... **CLC 26**
See also AAYA 4; BW 2; CA 17-20R; CANR 14, 34, 83; CLR 13; DLB 33; JRDA; MAICYA; SATA 14, 62

Gwendolyn
See Bennett, (Enoch) Arnold

H. D. **CLC 3, 8, 14, 31, 34, 73; PC 5**
See also Doolittle, Hilda

H. de V.
See Buchan, John

Haavikko, Paavo Juhani 1931- .. **CLC 18, 34**
See also CA 106

Habbema, Koos
See Heijermans, Herman

Habermas, Juergen 1929- .... **CLC 104**
See also CA 109; CANR 85

Habermas, Jurgen
See Habermas, Juergen

Hacker, Marilyn 1942- ...... **CLC 5, 9, 23, 72, 91; DAM POET**
See also CA 77-80; CANR 68; DLB 120

Haeckel, Ernst Heinrich (Philipp August) 1834-1919 .... **TCLC 83**
See also CA 157

Hafiz c. 1326-1389(?) .... **CMLC 34**

Hafiz c. 1326-1389 .... **CMLC 34**

Haggard, H(enry) Rider 1856-1925 .... **TCLC 11**
See also CA 108; 148; DLB 70, 156, 174, 178; MTCW 2; SATA 16

Hagiosy, L.
See Larbaud, Valery (Nicolas)

Hagiwara Sakutaro 1886-1942 ..... **TCLC 60; PC 18**

Haig, Fenil
See Ford, Ford Madox

Haig-Brown, Roderick (Langmere) 1908-1976 .... **CLC 21**
See also CA 5-8R; 69-72; CANR 4, 38, 83; CLR 31; DLB 88; MAICYA; SATA 12

Hailey, Arthur 1920- ..... **CLC 5; DAM NOV, POP**
See also AITN 2; BEST 90:3; CA 1-4R; CANR 2, 36, 75; DLB 88; DLBY 82; MTCW 1, 2

Hailey, Elizabeth Forsythe 1938- ..... **CLC 40**
See also CA 93-96; CAAS 1; CANR 15, 48; INT CANR-15

Haines, John (Meade) 1924- .... **CLC 58**
See also CA 17-20R; CANR 13, 34; DLB 212

Hakluyt, Richard 1552-1616 .... **LC 31**

Haldeman, Joe (William) 1943- .... **CLC 61**
See also Graham, Robert
See also CA 53-56, 179; CAAE 179; CAAS 25; CANR 6, 70, 72; DLB 8; INT CANR-6

Hale, Sarah Josepha (Buell) 1788-1879 .... **NCLC 75**
See also DLB 1, 42, 73

Haley, Alex(ander Murray Palmer) 1921-1992 . **CLC 8, 12, 76; BLC 2; DA; DAB; DAC; DAM MST, MULT, POP**
See also AAYA 26; BW 2, 3; CA 77-80; 136; CANR 61; CDALBS; DA3; DLB 38; MTCW 1, 2

Haliburton, Thomas Chandler 1796-1865 .... **NCLC 15**
See also DLB 11, 99

Hall, Donald (Andrew), Jr. 1928- ...... **CLC 1, 13, 37, 59; DAM POET**
See also CA 5-8R; CAAS 7; CANR 2, 44, 64; DLB 5; MTCW 1; SATA 23, 97

Hall, Frederic Sauser
See Sauser-Hall, Frederic

Hall, James
See Kuttner, Henry

Hall, James Norman 1887-1951 ..... **TCLC 23**
See also CA 123; 173; SATA 21

Hall, Radclyffe -1943
See Hall, (Marguerite) Radclyffe
See also MTCW 2

Hall, (Marguerite) Radclyffe 1886-1943 .... **TCLC 12**
See also CA 110; 150; CANR 83; DLB 191

Hall, Rodney 1935- .... **CLC 51**
See also CA 109; CANR 69

Halleck, Fitz-Greene 1790-1867 .... **NCLC 47**
See also DLB 3

Halliday, Michael
See Creasey, John

Halpern, Daniel 1945- .... **CLC 14**
See also CA 33-36R

Hamburger, Michael (Peter Leopold) 1924- .... **CLC 5, 14**
See also CA 5-8R; CAAS 4; CANR 2, 47; DLB 27

Hamill, Pete 1935- .... **CLC 10**
See also CA 25-28R; CANR 18, 71

Hamilton, Alexander 1755(?)-1804 .... **NCLC 49**
See also DLB 37

Hamilton, Clive
See Lewis, C(live) S(taples)

Hamilton, Edmond 1904-1977 .... **CLC 1**
See also CA 1-4R; CANR 3, 84; DLB 8

Hamilton, Eugene (Jacob) Lee
See Lee-Hamilton, Eugene (Jacob)

Hamilton, Franklin
See Silverberg, Robert

Hamilton, Gail
See Corcoran, Barbara

Hamilton, Mollie
See Kaye, M(ary) M(argaret)

Hamilton, (Anthony Walter) Patrick 1904-1962 .... **CLC 51**
See also CA 176; 113; DLB 191

Hamilton, Virginia 1936- ...... **CLC 26; DAM MULT**
See also AAYA 2, 21; BW 2, 3; CA 25-28R; CANR 20, 37, 73; CLR 1, 11, 40; DLB 33, 52; INT CANR-20; JRDA; MAICYA; MTCW 1, 2; SATA 4, 56, 79

Hammett, (Samuel) Dashiell 1894-1961 .... **CLC 3, 5, 10, 19, 47; SSC 17**
See also AITN 1; CA 81-84; CANR 42; CDALB 1929-1941; DA3; DLB 226; DLBD 6; DLBY 96; MTCW 1, 2

Hammon, Jupiter 1711(?)-1800(?) . **NCLC 5; BLC 2; DAM MULT, POET; PC 16**
See also DLB 31, 50

Hammond, Keith
See Kuttner, Henry

Hamner, Earl (Henry), Jr. 1923- ...... **CLC 12**
See also AITN 2; CA 73-76; DLB 6

Hampton, Christopher (James) 1946- .... **CLC 4**
See also CA 25-28R; DLB 13; MTCW 1

Hamsun, Knut **TCLC 2, 14, 49**
See also Pedersen, Knut

Handke, Peter 1942- .... **CLC 5, 8, 10, 15, 38, 134; DAM DRAM, NOV**
See also CA 77-80; CANR 33, 75; DLB 85, 124; MTCW 1, 2

Handy, W(illiam) C(hristopher) 1873-1958 .... **TCLC 97**
See also BW 3; CA 121; 167

Hanley, James 1901-1985 ..... **CLC 3, 5, 8, 13**
See also CA 73-76; 117; CANR 36; DLB 191; MTCW 1

Hannah, Barry 1942- .... **CLC 23, 38, 90**
See also CA 108; 110; CANR 43, 68; DLB 6; INT 110; MTCW 1

Hannon, Ezra
See Hunter, Evan

Hansberry, Lorraine (Vivian) 1930-1965 ..... **CLC 17, 62; BLC 2; DA; DAB; DAC; DAM DRAM, MST, MULT; DC 2**
See also AAYA 25; BW 1, 3; CA 109; 25-28R; CABS 3; CANR 58; CDALB 1941-1968; DA3; DLB 7, 38; MTCW 1, 2

Hansen, Joseph 1923- .... **CLC 38**
See also CA 29-32R; CAAS 17; CANR 16, 44, 66; DLB 226; INT CANR-16

Hansen, Martin A(lfred) 1909-1955 .... **TCLC 32**
See also CA 167

Hanson, Kenneth O(stlin) 1922- .... **CLC 13**
See also CA 53-56; CANR 7

Hardwick, Elizabeth (Bruce) 1916- .... **CLC 13; DAM NOV**
See also CA 5-8R; CANR 3, 32, 70; DA3; DLB 6; MTCW 1, 2

Hardy, Thomas 1840-1928 .. **TCLC 4, 10, 18, 32, 48, 53, 72; DA; DAB; DAC; DAM MST, NOV, POET; PC 8; SSC 2; WLC**
See also CA 104; 123; CDBLB 1890-1914; DA3; DLB 18, 19, 135; MTCW 1, 2

Hare, David 1947- .... **CLC 29, 58**
See also CA 97-100; CANR 39, 91; DLB 13; MTCW 1

Harewood, John
See Van Druten, John (William)

Harford, Henry
See Hudson, W(illiam) H(enry)

Hargrave, Leonie
See Disch, Thomas M(ichael)

Harjo, Joy 1951- ...... **CLC 83; DAM MULT; PC 27**
See also CA 114; CANR 35, 67, 91; DLB 120, 175; MTCW 2; NNAL

Harlan, Louis R(udolph) 1922- .... **CLC 34**
See also CA 21-24R; CANR 25, 55, 80

Harling, Robert 1951(?)- .... **CLC 53**
See also CA 147

Harmon, William (Ruth) 1938- .... **CLC 38**
See also CA 33-36R; CANR 14, 32, 35; SATA 65

Harper, F. E. W.
See Harper, Frances Ellen Watkins

Harper, Frances E. W.
See Harper, Frances Ellen Watkins

Harper, Frances E. Watkins
See Harper, Frances Ellen Watkins

Harper, Frances Ellen
See Harper, Frances Ellen Watkins

Harper, Frances Ellen Watkins 1825-1911 ...... **TCLC 14; BLC 2; DAM MULT, POET; PC 21**
See also BW 1, 3; CA 111; 125; CANR 79; DLB 50, 221

Harper, Michael S(teven) 1938- ... **CLC 7, 22**
See also BW 1; CA 33-36R; CANR 24; DLB 41

Harper, Mrs. F. E. W.
See Harper, Frances Ellen Watkins

Harris, Christie (Lucy) Irwin 1907- .... **CLC 12**
See also CA 5-8R; CANR 6, 83; CLR 47; DLB 88; JRDA; MAICYA; SAAS 10; SATA 6, 74; SATA-Essay 116

Harris, Frank 1856-1931 .... **TCLC 24**
See also CA 109; 150; CANR 80; DLB 156, 197

Harris, George Washington 1814-1869 .... **NCLC 23**
See also DLB 3, 11

Harris, Joel Chandler 1848-1908 ... **TCLC 2; SSC 19**
See also CA 104; 137; CANR 80; CLR 49; DLB 11, 23, 42, 78, 91; MAICYA; SATA 100; YABC 1

Harris, John (Wyndham Parkes Lucas) Beynon 1903-1969
See Wyndham, John
See also CA 102; 89-92; CANR 84

Harris, MacDonald **CLC 9**
See also Heiney, Donald (William)

Harris, Mark 1922- .... **CLC 19**
See also CA 5-8R; CAAS 3; CANR 2, 55, 83; DLB 2; DLBY 80

Harris, (Theodore) Wilson 1921- ..... **CLC 25**
See also BW 2, 3; CA 65-68; CAAS 16; CANR 11, 27, 69; DLB 117; MTCW 1

Harrison, Elizabeth Cavanna 1909-
See Cavanna, Betty
See also CA 9-12R; CANR 6, 27, 85

Harrison, Harry (Max) 1925- .... **CLC 42**
See also CA 1-4R; CANR 5, 21, 84; DLB 8; SATA 4

Harrison, James (Thomas) 1937- ...... **CLC 6, 14, 33, 66; SSC 19**
See also CA 13-16R; CANR 8, 51, 79; DLBY 82; INT CANR-8

Harrison, Jim
See Harrison, James (Thomas)

Harrison, Kathryn 1961- .... **CLC 70**
See also CA 144; CANR 68

Harrison, Tony 1937- .... **CLC 43, 129**
See also CA 65-68; CANR 44; DLB 40; MTCW 1

Harriss, Will(ard Irvin) 1922- .... **CLC 34**
See also CA 111

Harson, Sley
See Ellison, Harlan (Jay)

Hart, Ellis
See Ellison, Harlan (Jay)

Hart, Josephine 1942(?)- .... **CLC 70; DAM POP**
See also CA 138; CANR 70

Hart, Moss 1904-1961 .... **CLC 66; DAM DRAM**
See also CA 109; 89-92; CANR 84; DLB 7

Harte, (Francis) Bret(t) 1836(?)-1902 ... **TCLC 1, 25; DA; DAC; DAM MST; SSC 8; WLC**
See also CA 104; 140; CANR 80; CDALB 1865-1917; DA3; DLB 12, 64, 74, 79, 186; SATA 26

Hartley, L(eslie) P(oles) 1895-1972 ... **CLC 2, 22**
See also CA 45-48; 37-40R; CANR 33; DLB 15, 139; MTCW 1, 2

Hartman, Geoffrey H. 1929- .... **CLC 27**
See also CA 117; 125; CANR 79; DLB 67

Hartmann, Sadakichi 1867-1944 ... **TCLC 73**
See also CA 157; DLB 54

Hartmann von Aue c. 1160-c. 1205 .... **CMLC 15**
See also DLB 138

Hartmann von Aue 1170-1210 ...... **CMLC 15**

Haruf, Kent 1943- .... **CLC 34**
See also CA 149; CANR 91

Harwood, Ronald 1934- .... **CLC 32; DAM DRAM, MST**
See also CA 1-4R; CANR 4, 55; DLB 13

Hasegawa Tatsunosuke
See Futabatei, Shimei

Hasek, Jaroslav (Matej Frantisek) 1883-1923 .... **TCLC 4**
See also CA 104; 129; MTCW 1, 2

Hass, Robert 1941- ... **CLC 18, 39, 99; PC 16**
See also CA 111; CANR 30, 50, 71; DLB 105, 206; SATA 94

Hastings, Hudson
See Kuttner, Henry

Hastings, Selina **CLC 44**

Hathorne, John 1641-1717 .... **LC 38**

Hatteras, Amelia
See Mencken, H(enry) L(ouis)

Hatteras, Owen **TCLC 18**
See also Mencken, H(enry) L(ouis); Nathan, George Jean

Hauptmann, Gerhart (Johann Robert) 1862-1946 .... **TCLC 4; DAM DRAM; SSC 37**
See also CA 104; 153; DLB 66, 118

Havel, Vaclav 1936- ... **CLC 25, 58, 65; DAM DRAM; DC 6**
See also CA 104; CANR 36, 63; DA3; MTCW 1, 2

Haviaras, Stratis **CLC 33**
See also Chaviaras, Strates

Hawes, Stephen 1475(?)-1523(?) .... **LC 17**
See also DLB 132

Hawkes, John (Clendennin Burne, Jr.) 1925-1998 .. **CLC 1, 2, 3, 4, 7, 9, 14, 15, 27, 49**
See also CA 1-4R; 167; CANR 2, 47, 64; DLB 2, 7, 227; DLBY 80, 98; MTCW 1, 2

Hawking, S. W.
See Hawking, Stephen W(illiam)

Hawking, Stephen W(illiam) 1942- . **CLC 63, 105**
See also AAYA 13; BEST 89:1; CA 126; 129; CANR 48; DA3; MTCW 2

Hawkins, Anthony Hope
See Hope, Anthony

Hawthorne, Julian 1846-1934 .... **TCLC 25**
See also CA 165

Hawthorne, Nathaniel 1804-1864 . **NCLC 39; DA; DAB; DAC; DAM MST, NOV; SSC 3, 29, 39; WLC**
See also AAYA 18; CDALB 1640-1865; DA3; DLB 1, 74, 223; YABC 2

Haxton, Josephine Ayres 1921-
See Douglas, Ellen
See also CA 115; CANR 41, 83

Hayaseca y Eizaguirre, Jorge
See Echegaray (y Eizaguirre), Jose (Maria Waldo)

Hayashi, Fumiko 1904-1951 .... TCLC 27
See also CA 161; DLB 180

Haycraft, Anna (Margaret) 1932-
See Ellis, Alice Thomas
See also CA 122; CANR 85, 90; MTCW 2

Hayden, Robert E(arl) 1913-1980 . CLC 5, 9,
14, 37; BLC 2; DA; DAC; DAM MST,
MULT, POET; PC 6
See also BW 1, 3; CA 69-72; 97-100; CABS
2; CANR 24, 75, 82; CDALB 1941-1968;
DLB 5, 76; MTCW 1, 2; SATA 19; SATA-
Obit 26

Hayford, J(oseph) E(phraim) Casely
See Casely-Hayford, J(oseph) E(phraim)

Hayman, Ronald 1932- .... CLC 44
See also CA 25-28R; CANR 18, 50, 88;
DLB 155

Haywood, Eliza (Fowler)
1693(?)-1756 .... LC 1, 44
See also DLB 39

Hazlitt, William 1778-1830 ...... NCLC 29, 82
See also DLB 110, 158

Hazzard, Shirley 1931- .... CLC 18
See also CA 9-12R; CANR 4, 70; DLBY
82; MTCW 1

Head, Bessie 1937-1986 .... CLC 25, 67; BLC
2; DAM MULT
See also BW 2, 3; CA 29-32R; 119; CANR
25, 82; DA3; DLB 117, 225; MTCW 1, 2

Headon, (Nicky) Topper 1956(?)- .... CLC 30

Heaney, Seamus (Justin) 1939- ..... CLC 5, 7,
14, 25, 37, 74, 91; DAB; DAM POET;
PC 18; WLCS
See also CA 85-88; CANR 25, 48, 75, 91;
CDBLB 1960 to Present; DA3; DLB 40;
DLBY 95; MTCW 1, 2

Hearn, (Patricio) Lafcadio (Tessima Carlos)
1850-1904 .... TCLC 9
See also CA 105; 166; DLB 12, 78, 189

Hearne, Vicki 1946- .... CLC 56
See also CA 139

Hearon, Shelby 1931- .... CLC 63
See also AITN 2; CA 25-28R; CANR 18,
48

Heat-Moon, William Least CLC 29
See also Trogdon, William (Lewis)
See also AAYA 9

Hebbel, Friedrich 1813-1863 .... NCLC 43;
DAM DRAM
See also DLB 129

Hebert, Anne 1916-2000 .... CLC 4, 13, 29;
DAC; DAM MST, POET
See also CA 85-88; CANR 69; DA3; DLB
68; MTCW 1, 2

Hecht, Anthony (Evan) 1923- ...... CLC 8, 13,
19; DAM POET
See also CA 9-12R; CANR 6; DLB 5, 169

Hecht, Ben 1894-1964 .... CLC 8
See also CA 85-88; DLB 7, 9, 25, 26, 28,
86

Hedayat, Sadeq 1903-1951 .... TCLC 21
See also CA 120

Hegel, Georg Wilhelm Friedrich
1770-1831 .... NCLC 46
See also DLB 90

Heidegger, Martin 1889-1976 .... CLC 24
See also CA 81-84; 65-68; CANR 34;
MTCW 1, 2

Heidenstam, (Carl Gustaf) Verner von
1859-1940 .... TCLC 5
See also CA 104

Heifner, Jack 1946- .... CLC 11
See also CA 105; CANR 47

Heijermans, Herman 1864-1924 .... TCLC 24
See also CA 123

Heilbrun, Carolyn G(old) 1926- .... CLC 25
See also CA 45-48; CANR 1, 28, 58

Heine, Heinrich 1797-1856 .... NCLC 4, 54;
PC 25
See also DLB 90

Heinemann, Larry (Curtiss) 1944- .. CLC 50
See also CA 110; CAAS 21; CANR 31, 81;
DLBD 9; INT CANR-31

Heiney, Donald (William) 1921-1993
See Harris, MacDonald
See also CA 1-4R; 142; CANR 3, 58

Heinlein, Robert A(nson) 1907-1988 . CLC 1,
3, 8, 14, 26, 55; DAM POP
See also AAYA 17; CA 1-4R; 125; CANR
1, 20, 53; DA3; DLB 8; JRDA; MAICYA;
MTCW 1, 2; SATA 9, 69; SATA-Obit 56

Helforth, John
See Doolittle, Hilda

Hellenhofferu, Vojtech Kapristian z
See Hasek, Jaroslav (Matej Frantisek)

Heller, Joseph 1923-1999 . CLC 1, 3, 5, 8, 11,
36, 63; DA; DAB; DAC; DAM MST,
NOV, POP; WLC
See also AAYA 24; AITN 1; CA 5-8R;
CABS 1; CANR 8, 42, 66; DA3; DLB 2,
28, 227; DLBY 80; INT CANR-8; MTCW
1, 2

Hellman, Lillian (Florence)
1906-1984 .. CLC 2, 4, 8, 14, 18, 34, 44,
52; DAM DRAM; DC 1
See also AITN 1, 2; CA 13-16R; 112;
CANR 33; DA3; DLB 7, 228; DLBY 84;
MTCW 1, 2

Helprin, Mark 1947- .... CLC 7, 10, 22, 32;
DAM NOV, POP
See also CA 81-84; CANR 47, 64;
CDALBS; DA3; DLBY 85; MTCW 1, 2

Helvetius, Claude-Adrien 1715-1771 .. LC 26

Helyar, Jane Penelope Josephine 1933-
See Poole, Josephine
See also CA 21-24R; CANR 10, 26; SATA
82

Hemans, Felicia 1793-1835 .... NCLC 71
See also DLB 96

Hemingway, Ernest (Miller)
1899-1961 ..... CLC 1, 3, 6, 8, 10, 13, 19,
30, 34, 39, 41, 44, 50, 61, 80; DA;
DAB; DAC; DAM MST, NOV; SSC 1,
25, 36, 40; WLC
See also AAYA 19; CA 77-80; CANR 34;
CDALB 1917-1929; DA3; DLB 4, 9, 102,
210; DLBD 1, 15, 16; DLBY 81, 87, 96,
98; MTCW 1, 2

Hempel, Amy 1951- .... CLC 39
See also CA 118; 137; CANR 70; DA3;
MTCW 2

Henderson, F. C.
See Mencken, H(enry) L(ouis)

Henderson, Sylvia
See Ashton-Warner, Sylvia (Constance)

Henderson, Zenna (Chlarson)
1917-1983 .... SSC 29
See also CA 1-4R; 133; CANR 1, 84; DLB
8; SATA 5

Henkin, Joshua CLC 119
See also CA 161

Henley, Beth CLC 23; DC 6
See also Henley, Elizabeth Becker
See also CABS 3; DLBY 86

Henley, Elizabeth Becker 1952-
See Henley, Beth
See also CA 107; CANR 32, 73; DAM
DRAM, MST; DA3; MTCW 1, 2

Henley, William Ernest 1849-1903 .. TCLC 8
See also CA 105; DLB 19

Hennissart, Martha
See Lathen, Emma
See also CA 85-88; CANR 64

Henry, O. TCLC 1, 19; SSC 5; WLC
See also Porter, William Sydney

Henry, Patrick 1736-1799 .... LC 25

Henryson, Robert 1430(?)-1506(?) ...... LC 20
See also DLB 146

Henry VIII 1491-1547 .... LC 10
See also DLB 132

Henschke, Alfred
See Klabund

Hentoff, Nat(han Irving) 1925- .... CLC 26
See also AAYA 4; CA 1-4R; CAAS 6;
CANR 5, 25, 77; CLR 1, 52; INT CANR-
25; JRDA; MAICYA; SATA 42, 69;
SATA-Brief 27

Heppenstall, (John) Rayner
1911-1981 .... CLC 10
See also CA 1-4R; 103; CANR 29

Heraclitus c. 540B.C.-c. 450B.C. ... CMLC 22
See also DLB 176

Herbert, Frank (Patrick)
1920-1986 .... CLC 12, 23, 35, 44, 85;
DAM POP
See also AAYA 21; CA 53-56; 118; CANR
5, 43; CDALBS; DLB 8; INT CANR-5;
MTCW 1, 2; SATA 9, 37; SATA-Obit 47

Herbert, George 1593-1633 ..... LC 24; DAB;
DAM POET; PC 4
See also CDBLB Before 1660; DLB 126

Herbert, Zbigniew 1924-1998 ..... CLC 9, 43;
DAM POET
See also CA 89-92; 169; CANR 36, 74;
MTCW 1

Herbst, Josephine (Frey)
1897-1969 .... CLC 34
See also CA 5-8R; 25-28R; DLB 9

Heredia, Jose Maria 1803-1839
See also HLCS 2

Hergesheimer, Joseph 1880-1954 ... TCLC 11
See also CA 109; DLB 102, 9

Herlihy, James Leo 1927-1993 .... CLC 6
See also CA 1-4R; 143; CANR 2

Hermogenes fl. c. 175- .... CMLC 6

Hernandez, Jose 1834-1886 .... NCLC 17

Herodotus c. 484B.C.-429B.C. .... CMLC 17
See also DLB 176

Herrick, Robert 1591-1674 .... LC 13; DA;
DAB; DAC; DAM MST, POP; PC 9
See also DLB 126

Herring, Guilles
See Somerville, Edith

Herriot, James 1916-1995 ..... CLC 12; DAM
POP
See also Wight, James Alfred
See also AAYA 1; CA 148; CANR 40;
MTCW 2; SATA 86

Herris, Violet
See Hunt, Violet

Herrmann, Dorothy 1941- .... CLC 44
See also CA 107

Herrmann, Taffy
See Herrmann, Dorothy

Hersey, John (Richard) 1914-1993 .... CLC 1,
2, 7, 9, 40, 81, 97; DAM POP
See also AAYA 29; CA 17-20R; 140; CANR
33; CDALBS; DLB 6, 185; MTCW 1, 2;
SATA 25; SATA-Obit 76

Herzen, Aleksandr Ivanovich
1812-1870 .... NCLC 10, 61

Herzl, Theodor 1860-1904 .... TCLC 36
See also CA 168

Herzog, Werner 1942- .... CLC 16
See also CA 89-92

Hesiod c. 8th cent. B.C.- .... CMLC 5
See also DLB 176

Hesse, Hermann 1877-1962 ... **CLC 1, 2, 3, 6, 11, 17, 25, 69; DA; DAB; DAC; DAM MST, NOV; SSC 9; WLC**
See also CA 17-18; CAP 2; DA3; DLB 66; MTCW 1, 2; SATA 50

Hewes, Cady
See De Voto, Bernard (Augustine)

Heyen, William 1940- .... **CLC 13, 18**
See also CA 33-36R; CAAS 9; DLB 5

Heyerdahl, Thor 1914- .... **CLC 26**
See also CA 5-8R; CANR 5, 22, 66, 73; MTCW 1, 2; SATA 2, 52

Heym, Georg (Theodor Franz Arthur)
1887-1912 .... **TCLC 9**
See also CA 106; 181

Heym, Stefan 1913- .... **CLC 41**
See also CA 9-12R; CANR 4; DLB 69

Heyse, Paul (Johann Ludwig von)
1830-1914 .... **TCLC 8**
See also CA 104; DLB 129

Heyward, (Edwin) DuBose
1885-1940 .... **TCLC 59**
See also CA 108; 157; DLB 7, 9, 45; SATA 21

Hibbert, Eleanor Alice Burford
1906-1993 .... **CLC 7; DAM POP**
See also BEST 90:4; CA 17-20R; 140; CANR 9, 28, 59; MTCW 2; SATA 2; SATA-Obit 74

Hichens, Robert (Smythe)
1864-1950 .... **TCLC 64**
See also CA 162; DLB 153

Higgins, George V(incent)
1939-1999 .... **CLC 4, 7, 10, 18**
See also CA 77-80; 186; CAAS 5; CANR 17, 51, 89; DLB 2; DLBY 81, 98; INT CANR-17; MTCW 1

Higginson, Thomas Wentworth
1823-1911 .... **TCLC 36**
See also CA 162; DLB 1, 64

Highet, Helen
See MacInnes, Helen (Clark)

Highsmith, (Mary) Patricia
1921-1995 .... **CLC 2, 4, 14, 42, 102; DAM NOV, POP**
See also CA 1-4R; 147; CANR 1, 20, 48, 62; DA3; MTCW 1, 2

Highwater, Jamake (Mamake)
1942(?)- .... **CLC 12**
See also AAYA 7; CA 65-68; CAAS 7; CANR 10, 34, 84; CLR 17; DLB 52; DLBY 85; JRDA; MAICYA; SATA 32, 69; SATA-Brief 30

Highway, Tomson 1951- .... **CLC 92; DAC; DAM MULT**
See also CA 151; CANR 75; MTCW 2; NNAL

Higuchi, Ichiyo 1872-1896 .... **NCLC 49**

Hijuelos, Oscar 1951- .... **CLC 65; DAM MULT, POP; HLC 1**
See also AAYA 25; BEST 90:1; CA 123; CANR 50, 75; DA3; DLB 145; HW 1, 2; MTCW 2

Hikmet, Nazim 1902(?)-1963 .... **CLC 40**
See also CA 141; 93-96

Hildegard von Bingen 1098-1179 . **CMLC 20**
See also DLB 148

Hildesheimer, Wolfgang 1916-1991 .. **CLC 49**
See also CA 101; 135; DLB 69, 124

Hill, Geoffrey (William) 1932- ...... **CLC 5, 8, 18, 45; DAM POET**
See also CA 81-84; CANR 21, 89; CDBLB 1960 to Present; DLB 40; MTCW 1

Hill, George Roy 1921- .... **CLC 26**
See also CA 110; 122

Hill, John
See Koontz, Dean R(ay)

Hill, Susan (Elizabeth) 1942- .... **CLC 4, 113; DAB; DAM MST, NOV**
See also CA 33-36R; CANR 29, 69; DLB 14, 139; MTCW 1

Hillerman, Tony 1925- . **CLC 62; DAM POP**
See also AAYA 6; BEST 89:1; CA 29-32R; CANR 21, 42, 65; DA3; DLB 206; SATA 6

Hillesum, Etty 1914-1943 .... **TCLC 49**
See also CA 137

Hilliard, Noel (Harvey) 1929- .... **CLC 15**
See also CA 9-12R; CANR 7, 69

Hillis, Rick 1956- .... **CLC 66**
See also CA 134

Hilton, James 1900-1954 .... **TCLC 21**
See also CA 108; 169; DLB 34, 77; SATA 34

Himes, Chester (Bomar) 1909-1984 .. **CLC 2, 4, 7, 18, 58, 108; BLC 2; DAM MULT**
See also BW 2; CA 25-28R; 114; CANR 22, 89; DLB 2, 76, 143, 226; MTCW 1, 2

Hinde, Thomas .... **CLC 6, 11**
See also Chitty, Thomas Willes

Hine, (William) Daryl 1936- .... **CLC 15**
See also CA 1-4R; CAAS 15; CANR 1, 20; DLB 60

Hinkson, Katharine Tynan
See Tynan, Katharine

Hinojosa(-Smith), Rolando (R.) 1929-
See also CA 131; CAAS 16; CANR 62; DAM MULT; DLB 82; HLC 1; HW 1, 2; MTCW 2

Hinton, S(usan) E(loise) 1950- .... **CLC 30, 111; DA; DAB; DAC; DAM MST, NOV**
See also AAYA 2, 33; CA 81-84; CANR 32, 62, 92; CDALBS; CLR 3, 23; DA3; JRDA; MAICYA; MTCW 1, 2; SATA 19, 58, 115

Hippius, Zinaida .... **TCLC 9**
See also Gippius, Zinaida (Nikolayevna)

Hiraoka, Kimitake 1925-1970
See Mishima, Yukio
See also CA 97-100; 29-32R; DAM DRAM; DA3; MTCW 1, 2

Hirsch, E(ric) D(onald), Jr. 1928- .... **CLC 79**
See also CA 25-28R; CANR 27, 51; DLB 67; INT CANR-27; MTCW 1

Hirsch, Edward 1950- .... **CLC 31, 50**
See also CA 104; CANR 20, 42; DLB 120

Hitchcock, Alfred (Joseph)
1899-1980 .... **CLC 16**
See also AAYA 22; CA 159; 97-100; SATA 27; SATA-Obit 24

Hitler, Adolf 1889-1945 .... **TCLC 53**
See also CA 117; 147

Hoagland, Edward 1932- .... **CLC 28**
See also CA 1-4R; CANR 2, 31, 57; DLB 6; SATA 51

Hoban, Russell (Conwell) 1925- . **CLC 7, 25; DAM NOV**
See also CA 5-8R; CANR 23, 37, 66; CLR 3; DLB 52; MAICYA; MTCW 1, 2; SATA 1, 40, 78

Hobbes, Thomas 1588-1679 .... **LC 36**
See also DLB 151

Hobbs, Perry
See Blackmur, R(ichard) P(almer)

Hobson, Laura Z(ametkin)
1900-1986 .... **CLC 7, 25**
See also CA 17-20R; 118; CANR 55; DLB 28; SATA 52

Hochhuth, Rolf 1931- .. **CLC 4, 11, 18; DAM DRAM**
See also CA 5-8R; CANR 33, 75; DLB 124; MTCW 1, 2

Hochman, Sandra 1936- .... **CLC 3, 8**
See also CA 5-8R; DLB 5

Hochwaelder, Fritz 1911-1986 .... **CLC 36; DAM DRAM**
See also CA 29-32R; 120; CANR 42; MTCW 1

Hochwalder, Fritz
See Hochwaelder, Fritz

Hocking, Mary (Eunice) 1921- .... **CLC 13**
See also CA 101; CANR 18, 40

Hodgins, Jack 1938- .... **CLC 23**
See also CA 93-96; DLB 60

Hodgson, William Hope
1877(?)-1918 .... **TCLC 13**
See also CA 111; 164; DLB 70, 153, 156, 178; MTCW 2

Hoeg, Peter 1957- .... **CLC 95**
See also CA 151; CANR 75; DA3; MTCW 2

Hoffman, Alice 1952- ... **CLC 51; DAM NOV**
See also CA 77-80; CANR 34, 66; MTCW 1, 2

Hoffman, Daniel (Gerard) 1923- . **CLC 6, 13, 23**
See also CA 1-4R; CANR 4; DLB 5

Hoffman, Stanley 1944- .... **CLC 5**
See also CA 77-80

Hoffman, William M(oses) 1939- ..... **CLC 40**
See also CA 57-60; CANR 11, 71

Hoffmann, E(rnst) T(heodor) A(madeus)
1776-1822 .... **NCLC 2; SSC 13**
See also DLB 90; SATA 27

Hofmann, Gert 1931- .... **CLC 54**
See also CA 128

Hofmannsthal, Hugo von
1874-1929 ...... **TCLC 11; DAM DRAM; DC 4**
See also CA 106; 153; DLB 81, 118

Hogan, Linda 1947- .. **CLC 73; DAM MULT**
See also CA 120; CANR 45, 73; DLB 175; NNAL

Hogarth, Charles
See Creasey, John

Hogarth, Emmett
See Polonsky, Abraham (Lincoln)

Hogg, James 1770-1835 .... **NCLC 4**
See also DLB 93, 116, 159

Holbach, Paul Henri Thiry Baron
1723-1789 .... **LC 14**

Holberg, Ludvig 1684-1754 .... **LC 6**

Holcroft, Thomas 1745-1809 .... **NCLC 85**
See also DLB 39, 89, 158

Holden, Ursula 1921- .... **CLC 18**
See also CA 101; CAAS 8; CANR 22

Holderlin, (Johann Christian) Friedrich
1770-1843 .... **NCLC 16; PC 4**

Holdstock, Robert
See Holdstock, Robert P.

Holdstock, Robert P. 1948- .... **CLC 39**
See also CA 131; CANR 81

Holland, Isabelle 1920- .... **CLC 21**
See also AAYA 11; CA 21-24R; 181; CAAE 181; CANR 10, 25, 47; CLR 57; JRDA; MAICYA; SATA 8, 70; SATA-Essay 103

Holland, Marcus
See Caldwell, (Janet Miriam) Taylor (Holland)

Hollander, John 1929- .... **CLC 2, 5, 8, 14**
See also CA 1-4R; CANR 1, 52; DLB 5; SATA 13

Hollander, Paul
See Silverberg, Robert

Holleran, Andrew 1943(?)- .... **CLC 38**
See also Garber, Eric
See also CA 144

Holley, Marietta 1836(?)-1926 .... **TCLC 99**
See also CA 118; DLB 11

Hollinghurst, Alan 1954- .... **CLC 55, 91**
See also CA 114; DLB 207

Hollis, Jim
 See Summers, Hollis (Spurgeon, Jr.)
Holly, Buddy 1936-1959 .... **TCLC 65**
Holmes, Gordon
 See Shiel, M(atthew) P(hipps)
Holmes, John
 See Souster, (Holmes) Raymond
Holmes, John Clellon 1926-1988 ...... **CLC 56**
 See also CA 9-12R; 125; CANR 4; DLB 16
Holmes, Oliver Wendell, Jr.
 1841-1935 .... **TCLC 77**
 See also CA 114; 186
Holmes, Oliver Wendell
 1809-1894 .... **NCLC 14, 81**
 See also CDALB 1640-1865; DLB 1, 189;
 SATA 34
Holmes, Raymond
 See Souster, (Holmes) Raymond
Holt, Victoria
 See Hibbert, Eleanor Alice Burford
Holub, Miroslav 1923-1998 .... **CLC 4**
 See also CA 21-24R; 169; CANR 10
Homer c. 8th cent. B.C.- .. **CMLC 1, 16; DA;**
 DAB; DAC; DAM MST, POET; PC
 23; WLCS
 See also DA3; DLB 176
Hongo, Garrett Kaoru 1951- .... **PC 23**
 See also CA 133; CAAS 22; DLB 120
Honig, Edwin 1919- .... **CLC 33**
 See also CA 5-8R; CAAS 8; CANR 4, 45;
 DLB 5
Hood, Hugh (John Blagdon) 1928- . **CLC 15,**
 28
 See also CA 49-52; CAAS 17; CANR 1,
 33, 87; DLB 53
Hood, Thomas 1799-1845 .... **NCLC 16**
 See also DLB 96
Hooker, (Peter) Jeremy 1941- .... **CLC 43**
 See also CA 77-80; CANR 22; DLB 40
hooks, bell **CLC 94; BLCS**
 See also Watkins, Gloria Jean
 See also MTCW 2
Hope, A(lec) D(erwent) 1907- .... **CLC 3, 51**
 See also CA 21-24R; CANR 33, 74; MTCW
 1, 2
Hope, Anthony 1863-1933 .... **TCLC 83**
 See also CA 157; DLB 153, 156
Hope, Brian
 See Creasey, John
Hope, Christopher (David Tully)
 1944- .... **CLC 52**
 See also CA 106; CANR 47; DLB 225;
 SATA 62
Hopkins, Gerard Manley
 1844-1889 .... **NCLC 17; DA; DAB;**
 DAC; DAM MST, POET; PC 15; WLC
 See also CDBLB 1890-1914; DA3; DLB
 35, 57
Hopkins, John (Richard) 1931-1998 .. **CLC 4**
 See also CA 85-88; 169
Hopkins, Pauline Elizabeth
 1859-1930 ...... **TCLC 28; BLC 2; DAM**
 MULT
 See also BW 2, 3; CA 141; CANR 82; DLB
 50
Hopkinson, Francis 1737-1791 .... **LC 25**
 See also DLB 31
Hopley-Woolrich, Cornell George 1903-1968
 See Woolrich, Cornell
 See also CA 13-14; CANR 58; CAP 1; DLB
 226; MTCW 2
Horace 65B.C.-8B.C. .... **CMLC 39**
 See also DLB 211
Horatio
 See Proust, (Valentin-Louis-George-
 Eugene-) Marcel

Horgan, Paul (George Vincent
 O'Shaughnessy) 1903-1995 . **CLC 9, 53;**
 DAM NOV
 See also CA 13-16R; 147; CANR 9, 35;
 DLB 212; DLBY 85; INT CANR-9;
 MTCW 1, 2; SATA 13; SATA-Obit 84
Horn, Peter
 See Kuttner, Henry
Hornem, Horace Esq.
 See Byron, George Gordon (Noel)
Horney, Karen (Clementine Theodore
 Danielsen) 1885-1952 .... **TCLC 71**
 See also CA 114; 165
Hornung, E(rnest) W(illiam)
 1866-1921 .... **TCLC 59**
 See also CA 108; 160; DLB 70
Horovitz, Israel (Arthur) 1939- ...... **CLC 56;**
 DAM DRAM
 See also CA 33-36R; CANR 46, 59; DLB 7
Horton, George Moses
 1797(?)-1883(?) .... **NCLC 87**
 See also DLB 50
Horvath, Odon von
 See Horvath, Oedoen von
 See also DLB 85, 124
Horvath, Oedoen von 1901-1938 ... **TCLC 45**
 See also Horvath, Odon von; von Horvath,
 Oedoen
 See also CA 118
Horwitz, Julius 1920-1986 .... **CLC 14**
 See also CA 9-12R; 119; CANR 12
Hospital, Janette Turner 1942- .... **CLC 42**
 See also CA 108; CANR 48
Hostos, E. M. de
 See Hostos (y Bonilla), Eugenio Maria de
Hostos, Eugenio M. de
 See Hostos (y Bonilla), Eugenio Maria de
Hostos, Eugenio Maria
 See Hostos (y Bonilla), Eugenio Maria de
Hostos (y Bonilla), Eugenio Maria de
 1839-1903 .... **TCLC 24**
 See also CA 123; 131; HW 1
Houdini
 See Lovecraft, H(oward) P(hillips)
Hougan, Carolyn 1943- .... **CLC 34**
 See also CA 139
Household, Geoffrey (Edward West)
 1900-1988 .... **CLC 11**
 See also CA 77-80; 126; CANR 58; DLB
 87; SATA 14; SATA-Obit 59
Housman, A(lfred) E(dward)
 1859-1936 .... **TCLC 1, 10; DA; DAB;**
 DAC; DAM MST, POET; PC 2;
 WLCS
 See also CA 104; 125; DA3; DLB 19;
 MTCW 1, 2
Housman, Laurence 1865-1959 .... **TCLC 7**
 See also CA 106; 155; DLB 10; SATA 25
Howard, Elizabeth Jane 1923- ..... **CLC 7, 29**
 See also CA 5-8R; CANR 8, 62
Howard, Maureen 1930- .... **CLC 5, 14, 46**
 See also CA 53-56; CANR 31, 75; DLBY
 83; INT CANR-31; MTCW 1, 2
Howard, Richard 1929- .... **CLC 7, 10, 47**
 See also AITN 1; CA 85-88; CANR 25, 80;
 DLB 5; INT CANR-25
Howard, Robert E(rvin)
 1906-1936 .... **TCLC 8**
 See also CA 105; 157
Howard, Warren F.
 See Pohl, Frederik
Howe, Fanny (Quincy) 1940- .... **CLC 47**
 See also CA 117; CAAS 27; CANR 70;
 SATA-Brief 52
Howe, Irving 1920-1993 .... **CLC 85**
 See also CA 9-12R; 141; CANR 21, 50;
 DLB 67; MTCW 1, 2
Howe, Julia Ward 1819-1910 .... **TCLC 21**
 See also CA 117; DLB 1, 189

Howe, Susan 1937- .... **CLC 72**
 See also CA 160; DLB 120
Howe, Tina 1937- .... **CLC 48**
 See also CA 109
Howell, James 1594(?)-1666 .... **LC 13**
 See also DLB 151
Howells, W. D.
 See Howells, William Dean
Howells, William D.
 See Howells, William Dean
Howells, William Dean 1837-1920 .. **TCLC 7,**
 17, 41; SSC 36
 See also CA 104; 134; CDALB 1865-1917;
 DLB 12, 64, 74, 79, 189; MTCW 2
Howes, Barbara 1914-1996 .... **CLC 15**
 See also CA 9-12R; 151; CAAS 3; CANR
 53; SATA 5
Hrabal, Bohumil 1914-1997 .... **CLC 13, 67**
 See also CA 106; 156; CAAS 12; CANR
 57
Hroswitha of Gandersheim c. 935-c.
 1002 .... **CMLC 29**
 See also DLB 148
Hsun, Lu
 See Lu Hsun
Hubbard, L(afayette) Ron(ald)
 1911-1986 .... **CLC 43; DAM POP**
 See also CA 77-80; 118; CANR 52; DA3;
 MTCW 2
Huch, Ricarda (Octavia)
 1864-1947 .... **TCLC 13**
 See also CA 111; DLB 66
Huddle, David 1942- .... **CLC 49**
 See also CA 57-60; CAAS 20; CANR 89;
 DLB 130
Hudson, Jeffrey
 See Crichton, (John) Michael
Hudson, W(illiam) H(enry)
 1841-1922 .... **TCLC 29**
 See also CA 115; DLB 98, 153, 174; SATA
 35
Hueffer, Ford Madox
 See Ford, Ford Madox
Hughart, Barry 1934- .... **CLC 39**
 See also CA 137
Hughes, Colin
 See Creasey, John
Hughes, David (John) 1930- .... **CLC 48**
 See also CA 116; 129; DLB 14
Hughes, Edward James
 See Hughes, Ted
 See also DAM MST, POET; DA3
Hughes, (James) Langston
 1902-1967 .... **CLC 1, 5, 10, 15, 35, 44,**
 108; BLC 2; DA; DAB; DAC; DAM
 DRAM, MST, MULT, POET; DC 3;
 PC 1; SSC 6; WLC
 See also AAYA 12; BW 1, 3; CA 1-4R; 25-
 28R; CANR 1, 34, 82; CDALB 1929-
 1941; CLR 17; DA3; DLB 4, 7, 48, 51,
 86, 228; JRDA; MAICYA; MTCW 1, 2;
 SATA 4, 33
Hughes, Richard (Arthur Warren)
 1900-1976 .... **CLC 1, 11; DAM NOV**
 See also CA 5-8R; 65-68; CANR 4; DLB
 15, 161; MTCW 1; SATA 8; SATA-Obit
 25
Hughes, Ted 1930-1998 . **CLC 2, 4, 9, 14, 37,**
 119; DAB; DAC; PC 7
 See also Hughes, Edward James
 See also CA 1-4R; 171; CANR 1, 33, 66;
 CLR 3; DLB 40, 161; MAICYA; MTCW
 1, 2; SATA 49; SATA-Brief 27; SATA-
 Obit 107
Hugo, Richard F(ranklin)
 1923-1982 .... **CLC 6, 18, 32; DAM**
 POET
 See also CA 49-52; 108; CANR 3; DLB 5,
 206

Hugo, Victor (Marie) 1802-1885 .... **NCLC 3, 10, 21; DA; DAB; DAC; DAM DRAM, MST, NOV, POET; PC 17; WLC**
See also AAYA 28; DA3; DLB 119, 192; SATA 47

Huidobro, Vicente
See Huidobro Fernandez, Vicente Garcia

Huidobro Fernandez, Vicente Garcia
1893-1948 .... **TCLC 31**
See also CA 131; HW 1

Hulme, Keri 1947- .... **CLC 39, 130**
See also CA 125; CANR 69; INT 125

Hulme, T(homas) E(rnest)
1883-1917 .... **TCLC 21**
See also CA 117; DLB 19

Hume, David 1711-1776 .... **LC 7, 56**
See also DLB 104

Humphrey, William 1924-1997 .... **CLC 45**
See also CA 77-80; 160; CANR 68; DLB 212

Humphreys, Emyr Owen 1919- .... **CLC 47**
See also CA 5-8R; CANR 3, 24; DLB 15

Humphreys, Josephine 1945- ..... **CLC 34, 57**
See also CA 121; 127; INT 127

Huneker, James Gibbons
1857-1921 .... **TCLC 65**
See also DLB 71

Hungerford, Pixie
See Brinsmead, H(esba) F(ay)

Hunt, E(verette) Howard, (Jr.)
1918- .... **CLC 3**
See also AITN 1; CA 45-48; CANR 2, 47

Hunt, Francesca
See Holland, Isabelle

Hunt, Kyle
See Creasey, John

Hunt, (James Henry) Leigh
1784-1859 .... **NCLC 1, 70; DAM POET**
See also DLB 96, 110, 144

Hunt, Marsha 1946- .... **CLC 70**
See also BW 2, 3; CA 143; CANR 79

Hunt, Violet 1866(?)-1942 .... **TCLC 53**
See also CA 184; DLB 162, 197

Hunter, E. Waldo
See Sturgeon, Theodore (Hamilton)

Hunter, Evan 1926- .... **CLC 11, 31; DAM POP**
See also CA 5-8R; CANR 5, 38, 62; DLBY 82; INT CANR-5; MTCW 1; SATA 25

Hunter, Kristin (Eggleston) 1931- .... **CLC 35**
See also AITN 1; BW 1; CA 13-16R; CANR 13; CLR 3; DLB 33; INT CANR-13; MAICYA; SAAS 10; SATA 12

Hunter, Mary
See Austin, Mary (Hunter)

Hunter, Mollie 1922- .... **CLC 21**
See also McIlwraith, Maureen Mollie Hunter
See also AAYA 13; CANR 37, 78; CLR 25; DLB 161; JRDA; MAICYA; SAAS 7; SATA 54, 106

Hunter, Robert (?)-1734 .... **LC 7**

Hurston, Zora Neale 1903-1960 .. **CLC 7, 30, 61; BLC 2; DA; DAC; DAM MST, MULT, NOV; DC 12; SSC 4; WLCS**
See also AAYA 15; BW 1, 3; CA 85-88; CANR 61; CDALBS; DA3; DLB 51, 86; MTCW 1, 2

Husserl, E. G.
See Husserl, Edmund (Gustav Albrecht)

Husserl, Edmund (Gustav Albrecht)
1859-1938 .... **TCLC 100**
See also CA 116; 133

Huston, John (Marcellus)
1906-1987 .... **CLC 20**
See also CA 73-76; 123; CANR 34; DLB 26

Hustvedt, Siri 1955- .... **CLC 76**
See also CA 137

Hutten, Ulrich von 1488-1523 .... **LC 16**
See also DLB 179

Huxley, Aldous (Leonard)
1894-1963 .... **CLC 1, 3, 4, 5, 8, 11, 18, 35, 79; DA; DAB; DAC; DAM MST, NOV; SSC 39; WLC**
See also AAYA 11; CA 85-88; CANR 44; CDBLB 1914-1945; DA3; DLB 36, 100, 162, 195; MTCW 1, 2; SATA 63

Huxley, T(homas) H(enry)
1825-1895 .... **NCLC 67**
See also DLB 57

Huysmans, Joris-Karl 1848-1907 ... **TCLC 7, 69**
See also CA 104; 165; DLB 123

Hwang, David Henry 1957- .. **CLC 55; DAM DRAM; DC 4**
See also CA 127; 132; CANR 76; DA3; DLB 212; INT 132; MTCW 2

Hyde, Anthony 1946- .... **CLC 42**
See also CA 136

Hyde, Margaret O(ldroyd) 1917- ..... **CLC 21**
See also CA 1-4R; CANR 1, 36; CLR 23; JRDA; MAICYA; SAAS 8; SATA 1, 42, 76

Hynes, James 1956(?)- .... **CLC 65**
See also CA 164

Hypatia c. 370-415 .... **CMLC 35**

Ian, Janis 1951- .... **CLC 21**
See also CA 105

Ibanez, Vicente Blasco
See Blasco Ibanez, Vicente

Ibarbourou, Juana de 1895-1979
See also HLCS 2; HW 1

Ibarguengoitia, Jorge 1928-1983 ...... **CLC 37**
See also CA 124; 113; HW 1

Ibsen, Henrik (Johan) 1828-1906 ... **TCLC 2, 8, 16, 37, 52; DA; DAB; DAC; DAM DRAM, MST; DC 2; WLC**
See also CA 104; 141; DA3

Ibuse, Masuji 1898-1993 .... **CLC 22**
See also CA 127; 141; DLB 180

Ichikawa, Kon 1915- .... **CLC 20**
See also CA 121

Idle, Eric 1943- .... **CLC 21**
See also Monty Python
See also CA 116; CANR 35, 91

Ignatow, David 1914-1997 .. **CLC 4, 7, 14, 40**
See also CA 9-12R; 162; CAAS 3; CANR 31, 57; DLB 5

Ignotus
See Strachey, (Giles) Lytton

Ihimaera, Witi 1944- .... **CLC 46**
See also CA 77-80

Ilf, Ilya TCLC 21
See also Fainzilberg, Ilya Arnoldovich

Illyes, Gyula 1902-1983 .... **PC 16**
See also CA 114; 109

Immermann, Karl (Lebrecht)
1796-1840 .... **NCLC 4, 49**
See also DLB 133

Ince, Thomas H. 1882-1924 .... **TCLC 89**

Inchbald, Elizabeth 1753-1821 ...... **NCLC 62**
See also DLB 39, 89

Inclan, Ramon (Maria) del Valle
See Valle-Inclan, Ramon (Maria) del

Infante, G(uillermo) Cabrera
See Cabrera Infante, G(uillermo)

Ingalls, Rachel (Holmes) 1940- .... **CLC 42**
See also CA 123; 127

Ingamells, Reginald Charles
See Ingamells, Rex

Ingamells, Rex 1913-1955 .... **TCLC 35**
See also CA 167

Inge, William (Motter) 1913-1973 .... **CLC 1, 8, 19; DAM DRAM**
See also CA 9-12R; CDALB 1941-1968; DA3; DLB 7; MTCW 1, 2

Ingelow, Jean 1820-1897 .... **NCLC 39**
See also DLB 35, 163; SATA 33

Ingram, Willis J.
See Harris, Mark

Innaurato, Albert (F.) 1948(?)- ... **CLC 21, 60**
See also CA 115; 122; CANR 78; INT 122

Innes, Michael
See Stewart, J(ohn) I(nnes) M(ackintosh)

Innis, Harold Adams 1894-1952 .... **TCLC 77**
See also CA 181; DLB 88

Ionesco, Eugene 1909-1994 ... **CLC 1, 4, 6, 9, 11, 15, 41, 86; DA; DAB; DAC; DAM DRAM, MST; DC 12; WLC**
See also CA 9-12R; 144; CANR 55; DA3; MTCW 1, 2; SATA 7; SATA-Obit 79

Iqbal, Muhammad 1873-1938 .... **TCLC 28**

Ireland, Patrick
See O'Doherty, Brian

Iron, Ralph
See Schreiner, Olive (Emilie Albertina)

Irving, John (Winslow) 1942- ... **CLC 13, 23, 38, 112; DAM NOV**
See also AAYA 8; BEST 89:3; CA 25-28R; CANR 28, 73; DA3; DLB 6; DLBY 82; MTCW 1, 2

Irving, Washington 1783-1859 . **NCLC 2, 19; DA; DAB; DAC; DAM MST; SSC 2, 37; WLC**
See also CDALB 1640-1865; DA3; DLB 3, 11, 30, 59, 73, 74, 186; YABC 2

Irwin, P. K.
See Page, P(atricia) K(athleen)

Isaacs, Jorge Ricardo 1837-1895 ... **NCLC 70**

Isaacs, Susan 1943- .... **CLC 32; DAM POP**
See also BEST 89:1; CA 89-92; CANR 20, 41, 65; DA3; INT CANR-20; MTCW 1, 2

Isherwood, Christopher (William Bradshaw)
1904-1986 .. **CLC 1, 9, 11, 14, 44; DAM DRAM, NOV**
See also CA 13-16R; 117; CANR 35; DA3; DLB 15, 195; DLBY 86; MTCW 1, 2

Ishiguro, Kazuo 1954- . **CLC 27, 56, 59, 110; DAM NOV**
See also BEST 90:2; CA 120; CANR 49; DA3; DLB 194; MTCW 1, 2

Ishikawa, Hakuhin
See Ishikawa, Takuboku

Ishikawa, Takuboku
1886(?)-1912 ... **TCLC 15; DAM POET; PC 10**
See also CA 113; 153

Iskander, Fazil 1929- .... **CLC 47**
See also CA 102

Isler, Alan (David) 1934- .... **CLC 91**
See also CA 156

Ivan IV 1530-1584 .... **LC 17**

Ivanov, Vyacheslav Ivanovich
1866-1949 .... **TCLC 33**
See also CA 122

Ivask, Ivar Vidrik 1927-1992 .... **CLC 14**
See also CA 37-40R; 139; CANR 24

Ives, Morgan
See Bradley, Marion Zimmer

Izumi Shikibu c. 973-c. 1034 .... **CMLC 33**

J. R. S.
See Gogarty, Oliver St. John

Jabran, Kahlil
See Gibran, Kahlil

Jabran, Khalil
See Gibran, Kahlil

Jackson, Daniel
See Wingrove, David (John)

Jackson, Helen Hunt 1830-1885 .... **NCLC 90**
See also DLB 42, 47, 186, 189

Jackson, Jesse 1908-1983 .... **CLC 12**
See also BW 1; CA 25-28R; 109; CANR 27; CLR 28; MAICYA; SATA 2, 29; SATA-Obit 48

Jackson, Laura (Riding) 1901-1991
See Riding, Laura
See also CA 65-68; 135; CANR 28, 89;
DLB 48
Jackson, Sam
See Trumbo, Dalton
Jackson, Sara
See Wingrove, David (John)
Jackson, Shirley 1919-1965 . **CLC 11, 60, 87;
DA; DAC; DAM MST; SSC 9, 39;
WLC**
See also AAYA 9; CA 1-4R; 25-28R; CANR
4, 52; CDALB 1941-1968; DA3; DLB 6;
MTCW 2; SATA 2
Jacob, (Cyprien-)Max 1876-1944 .... **TCLC 6**
See also CA 104
Jacobs, Harriet A(nn)
1813(?)-1897 .... **NCLC 67**
Jacobs, Jim 1942- .... **CLC 12**
See also CA 97-100; INT 97-100
Jacobs, W(illiam) W(ymark)
1863-1943 .... **TCLC 22**
See also CA 121; 167; DLB 135
Jacobsen, Jens Peter 1847-1885 .... **NCLC 34**
Jacobsen, Josephine 1908- .... **CLC 48, 102**
See also CA 33-36R; CAAS 18; CANR 23,
48
Jacobson, Dan 1929- .... **CLC 4, 14**
See also CA 1-4R; CANR 2, 25, 66; DLB
14, 207, 225; MTCW 1
Jacqueline
See Carpentier (y Valmont), Alejo
Jagger, Mick 1944- .... **CLC 17**
Jahiz, al- c. 780-c. 869 .... **CMLC 25**
Jakes, John (William) 1932- . **CLC 29; DAM
NOV, POP**
See also AAYA 32; BEST 89:4; CA 57-60;
CANR 10, 43, 66; DA3; DLBY 83; INT
CANR-10; MTCW 1, 2; SATA 62
James, Andrew
See Kirkup, James
James, C(yril) L(ionel) R(obert)
1901-1989 .... **CLC 33; BLCS**
See also BW 2; CA 117; 125; 128; CANR
62; DLB 125; MTCW 1
James, Daniel (Lewis) 1911-1988
See Santiago, Danny
See also CA 174; 125
James, Dynely
See Mayne, William (James Carter)
James, Henry Sr. 1811-1882 .... **NCLC 53**
James, Henry 1843-1916 ..... **TCLC 2, 11, 24,
40, 47, 64; DA; DAB; DAC; DAM
MST, NOV; SSC 8, 32; WLC**
See also CA 104; 132; CDALB 1865-1917;
DA3; DLB 12, 71, 74, 189; DLBD 13;
MTCW 1, 2
James, M. R.
See James, Montague (Rhodes)
See also DLB 156
James, Montague (Rhodes)
1862-1936 .... **TCLC 6; SSC 16**
See also CA 104; DLB 201
James, P. D. 1920- .... **CLC 18, 46, 122**
See also White, Phyllis Dorothy James
See also BEST 90:2; CDBLB 1960 to
Present; DLB 87; DLBD 17
James, Philip
See Moorcock, Michael (John)
James, William 1842-1910 .... **TCLC 15, 32**
See also CA 109
James I 1394-1437 .... **LC 20**
Jameson, Anna 1794-1860 .... **NCLC 43**
See also DLB 99, 166

Jami, Nur al-Din 'Abd al-Rahman
1414-1492 .... **LC 9**
Jammes, Francis 1868-1938 .... **TCLC 75**
Jandl, Ernst 1925- .... **CLC 34**
Janowitz, Tama 1957- .. **CLC 43; DAM POP**
See also CA 106; CANR 52, 89
Japrisot, Sebastien 1931- .... **CLC 90**
Jarrell, Randall 1914-1965 .... **CLC 1, 2, 6, 9,
13, 49; DAM POET**
See also CA 5-8R; 25-28R; CABS 2; CANR
6, 34; CDALB 1941-1968; CLR 6; DLB
48, 52; MAICYA; MTCW 1, 2; SATA 7
Jarry, Alfred 1873-1907 . **TCLC 2, 14; DAM
DRAM; SSC 20**
See also CA 104; 153; DA3; DLB 192
Jawien, Andrzej
See John Paul II, Pope
Jaynes, Roderick
See Coen, Ethan
Jeake, Samuel, Jr.
See Aiken, Conrad (Potter)
Jean Paul 1763-1825 .... **NCLC 7**
Jefferies, (John) Richard
1848-1887 .... **NCLC 47**
See also DLB 98, 141; SATA 16
Jeffers, (John) Robinson 1887-1962 .. **CLC 2,
3, 11, 15, 54; DA; DAC; DAM MST,
POET; PC 17; WLC**
See also CA 85-88; CANR 35; CDALB
1917-1929; DLB 45, 212; MTCW 1, 2
Jefferson, Janet
See Mencken, H(enry) L(ouis)
Jefferson, Thomas 1743-1826 .... **NCLC 11**
See also CDALB 1640-1865; DA3; DLB
31
Jeffrey, Francis 1773-1850 .... **NCLC 33**
See also DLB 107
Jelakowitch, Ivan
See Heijermans, Herman
Jellicoe, (Patricia) Ann 1927- .... **CLC 27**
See also CA 85-88; DLB 13
Jemyma
See Holley, Marietta
Jen, Gish CLC 70
See also Jen, Lillian
Jen, Lillian 1956(?)-
See Jen, Gish
See also CA 135; CANR 89
Jenkins, (John) Robin 1912- .... **CLC 52**
See also CA 1-4R; CANR 1; DLB 14
Jennings, Elizabeth (Joan) 1926- ...... **CLC 5,
14, 131**
See also CA 61-64; CAAS 5; CANR 8, 39,
66; DLB 27; MTCW 1; SATA 66
Jennings, Waylon 1937- .... **CLC 21**
Jensen, Johannes V. 1873-1950 ...... **TCLC 41**
See also CA 170
Jensen, Laura (Linnea) 1948- .... **CLC 37**
See also CA 103
Jerome, Jerome K(lapka)
1859-1927 .... **TCLC 23**
See also CA 119; 177; DLB 10, 34, 135
Jerrold, Douglas William
1803-1857 .... **NCLC 2**
See also DLB 158, 159
Jewett, (Theodora) Sarah Orne
1849-1909 .... **TCLC 1, 22; SSC 6**
See also CA 108; 127; CANR 71; DLB 12,
74, 221; SATA 15
Jewsbury, Geraldine (Endsor)
1812-1880 .... **NCLC 22**
See also DLB 21
Jhabvala, Ruth Prawer 1927- . **CLC 4, 8, 29,
94; DAB; DAM NOV**
See also CA 1-4R; CANR 2, 29, 51, 74, 91;
DLB 139, 194; INT CANR-29; MTCW 1,
2

Jibran, Kahlil
See Gibran, Kahlil
Jibran, Khalil
See Gibran, Kahlil
Jiles, Paulette 1943- .... **CLC 13, 58**
See also CA 101; CANR 70
Jimenez (Mantecon), Juan Ramon
1881-1958 .... **TCLC 4; DAM MULT,
POET; HLC 1; PC 7**
See also CA 104; 131; CANR 74; DLB 134;
HW 1; MTCW 1, 2
Jimenez, Ramon
See Jimenez (Mantecon), Juan Ramon
Jimenez Mantecon, Juan
See Jimenez (Mantecon), Juan Ramon
Jin, Ha
See Jin, Xuefei
Jin, Xuefei 1956- .... **CLC 109**
See also CA 152; CANR 91
Joel, Billy CLC 26
See also Joel, William Martin
Joel, William Martin 1949-
See Joel, Billy
See also CA 108
John, Saint 7th cent. - .... **CMLC 27**
John of the Cross, St. 1542-1591 .... **LC 18**
John Paul II, Pope 1920- .... **CLC 128**
See also CA 106; 133
Johnson, B(ryan) S(tanley William)
1933-1973 .... **CLC 6, 9**
See also CA 9-12R; 53-56; CANR 9; DLB
14, 40
Johnson, Benj. F. of Boo
See Riley, James Whitcomb
Johnson, Benjamin F. of Boo
See Riley, James Whitcomb
Johnson, Charles (Richard) 1948- .... **CLC 7,
51, 65; BLC 2; DAM MULT**
See also BW 2, 3; CA 116; CAAS 18;
CANR 42, 66, 82; DLB 33; MTCW 2
Johnson, Denis 1949- .... **CLC 52**
See also CA 117; 121; CANR 71; DLB 120
Johnson, Diane 1934- .... **CLC 5, 13, 48**
See also CA 41-44R; CANR 17, 40, 62;
DLBY 80; INT CANR-17; MTCW 1
Johnson, Eyvind (Olof Verner)
1900-1976 .... **CLC 14**
See also CA 73-76; 69-72; CANR 34
Johnson, J. R.
See James, C(yril) L(ionel) R(obert)
Johnson, James Weldon
1871-1938 .. **TCLC 3, 19; BLC 2; DAM
MULT, POET; PC 24**
See also BW 1, 3; CA 104; 125; CANR 82;
CDALB 1917-1929; CLR 32; DA3; DLB
51; MTCW 1, 2; SATA 31
Johnson, Joyce 1935- .... **CLC 58**
See also CA 125; 129
Johnson, Judith (Emlyn) 1936- .... **CLC 7, 15**
See Sherwin, Judith Johnson
See also CA 25-28R; 153; CANR 34
Johnson, Lionel (Pigot)
1867-1902 .... **TCLC 19**
See also CA 117; DLB 19
Johnson, Marguerite (Annie)
See Angelou, Maya
Johnson, Mel
See Malzberg, Barry N(athaniel)
Johnson, Pamela Hansford
1912-1981 .... **CLC 1, 7, 27**
See also CA 1-4R; 104; CANR 2, 28; DLB
15; MTCW 1, 2
Johnson, Robert 1911(?)-1938 .... **TCLC 69**
See also BW 3; CA 174
Johnson, Samuel 1709-1784 . **LC 15, 52; DA;
DAB; DAC; DAM MST; WLC**
See also CDBLB 1660-1789; DLB 39, 95,
104, 142

Johnson, Uwe 1934-1984 .. **CLC 5, 10, 15, 40**
See also CA 1-4R; 112; CANR 1, 39; DLB 75; MTCW 1

Johnston, George (Benson) 1913- .... **CLC 51**
See also CA 1-4R; CANR 5, 20; DLB 88

Johnston, Jennifer (Prudence) 1930- . **CLC 7**
See also CA 85-88; CANR 92; DLB 14

Joinville, Jean de 1224(?)-1317 ..... **CMLC 38**

Jolley, (Monica) Elizabeth 1923- ..... **CLC 46; SSC 19**
See also CA 127; CAAS 13; CANR 59

Jones, Arthur Llewellyn 1863-1947
See Machen, Arthur
See also CA 104; 179

Jones, D(ouglas) G(ordon) 1929- ..... **CLC 10**
See also CA 29-32R; CANR 13, 90; DLB 53

Jones, David (Michael) 1895-1974 .... **CLC 2, 4, 7, 13, 42**
See also CA 9-12R; 53-56; CANR 28; CDBLB 1945-1960; DLB 20, 100; MTCW 1

Jones, David Robert 1947-
See Bowie, David
See also CA 103

Jones, Diana Wynne 1934- .... **CLC 26**
See also AAYA 12; CA 49-52; CANR 4, 26, 56; CLR 23; DLB 161; JRDA; MAICYA; SAAS 7; SATA 9, 70, 108

Jones, Edward P. 1950- .... **CLC 76**
See also BW 2, 3; CA 142; CANR 79

Jones, Gayl 1949- ..... **CLC 6, 9, 131; BLC 2; DAM MULT**
See also BW 2, 3; CA 77-80; CANR 27, 66; DA3; DLB 33; MTCW 1

Jones, James 1921-1977 ..... **CLC 1, 3, 10, 39**
See also AITN 1, 2; CA 1-4R; 69-72; CANR 6; DLB 2, 143; DLBD 17; DLBY 98; MTCW 1

Jones, John J.
See Lovecraft, H(oward) P(hillips)

Jones, LeRoi CLC 1, 2, 3, 5, 10, 14
See also Baraka, Amiri
See also MTCW 2

Jones, Louis B. 1953- .... **CLC 65**
See also CA 141; CANR 73

Jones, Madison (Percy, Jr.) 1925- ..... **CLC 4**
See also CA 13-16R; CAAS 11; CANR 7, 54, 83; DLB 152

Jones, Mervyn 1922- .... **CLC 10, 52**
See also CA 45-48; CAAS 5; CANR 1, 91; MTCW 1

Jones, Mick 1956(?)- .... **CLC 30**

Jones, Nettie (Pearl) 1941- .... **CLC 34**
See also BW 2; CA 137; CAAS 20; CANR 88

Jones, Preston 1936-1979 .... **CLC 10**
See also CA 73-76; 89-92; DLB 7

Jones, Robert F(rancis) 1934- .... **CLC 7**
See also CA 49-52; CANR 2, 61

Jones, Rod 1953- .... **CLC 50**
See also CA 128

Jones, Terence Graham Parry 1942- .... **CLC 21**
See also Jones, Terry; Monty Python
See also CA 112; 116; CANR 35; INT 116

Jones, Terry
See Jones, Terence Graham Parry
See also SATA 67; SATA-Brief 51

Jones, Thom (Douglas) 1945(?)- .... **CLC 81**
See also CA 157; CANR 88

Jong, Erica 1942- .... **CLC 4, 6, 8, 18, 83; DAM NOV, POP**
See also AITN 1; BEST 90:2; CA 73-76; CANR 26, 52, 75; DA3; DLB 2, 5, 28, 152; INT CANR-26; MTCW 1, 2

Jonson, Ben(jamin) 1572(?)-1637 .. **LC 6, 33; DA; DAB; DAC; DAM DRAM, MST, POET; DC 4; PC 17; WLC**
See also CDBLB Before 1660; DLB 62, 121

Jordan, June 1936- .... **CLC 5, 11, 23, 114; BLCS; DAM MULT, POET**
See also AAYA 2; BW 2, 3; CA 33-36R; CANR 25, 70; CLR 10; DLB 38; MAICYA; MTCW 1; SATA 4

Jordan, Neil (Patrick) 1950- .... **CLC 110**
See also CA 124; 130; CANR 54; INT 130

Jordan, Pat(rick M.) 1941- .... **CLC 37**
See also CA 33-36R

Jorgensen, Ivar
See Ellison, Harlan (Jay)

Jorgenson, Ivar
See Silverberg, Robert

Josephus, Flavius c. 37-100 .... **CMLC 13**

Josiah Allen's Wife
See Holley, Marietta

Josipovici, Gabriel (David) 1940- ...... **CLC 6, 43**
See also CA 37-40R; CAAS 8; CANR 47, 84; DLB 14

Joubert, Joseph 1754-1824 .... **NCLC 9**

Jouve, Pierre Jean 1887-1976 .... **CLC 47**
See also CA 65-68

Jovine, Francesco 1902-1950 .... **TCLC 79**

Joyce, James (Augustine Aloysius) 1882-1941 .. **TCLC 3, 8, 16, 35, 52; DA; DAB; DAC; DAM MST, NOV, POET; PC 22; SSC 3, 26; WLC**
See also CA 104; 126; CDBLB 1914-1945; DA3; DLB 10, 19, 36, 162; MTCW 1, 2

Jozsef, Attila 1905-1937 .... **TCLC 22**
See also CA 116

Juana Ines de la Cruz 1651(?)-1695 .... **LC 5; HLCS 1; PC 24**

Judd, Cyril
See Kornbluth, C(yril) M.; Pohl, Frederik

Juenger, Ernst 1895-1998 .... **CLC 125**
See also CA 101; 167; CANR 21, 47; DLB 56

Julian of Norwich 1342(?)-1416(?) . **LC 6, 52**
See also DLB 146

Junger, Ernst
See Juenger, Ernst

Junger, Sebastian 1962- .... **CLC 109**
See also AAYA 28; CA 165

Juniper, Alex
See Hospital, Janette Turner

Junius
See Luxemburg, Rosa

Just, Ward (Swift) 1935- .... **CLC 4, 27**
See also CA 25-28R; CANR 32, 87; INT CANR-32

Justice, Donald (Rodney) 1925- .. **CLC 6, 19, 102; DAM POET**
See also CA 5-8R; CANR 26, 54, 74; DLBY 83; INT CANR-26; MTCW 2

Juvenal c. 60-c. 13 .... **CMLC 8**
See also Juvenalis, Decimus Junius
See also DLB 211

Juvenalis, Decimus Junius 55(?)-c. 127(?)
See Juvenal

Juvenis
See Bourne, Randolph S(illiman)

Kacew, Romain 1914-1980
See Gary, Romain
See also CA 108; 102

Kadare, Ismail 1936- .... **CLC 52**
See also CA 161

Kadohata, Cynthia CLC 59, 122
See also CA 140

Kafka, Franz 1883-1924 . **TCLC 2, 6, 13, 29, 47, 53; DA; DAB; DAC; DAM MST, NOV; SSC 5, 29, 35; WLC**
See also AAYA 31; CA 105; 126; DA3; DLB 81; MTCW 1, 2

Kahanovitsch, Pinkhes
See Der Nister

Kahn, Roger 1927- .... **CLC 30**
See also CA 25-28R; CANR 44, 69; DLB 171; SATA 37

Kain, Saul
See Sassoon, Siegfried (Lorraine)

Kaiser, Georg 1878-1945 .... **TCLC 9**
See also CA 106; DLB 124

Kaletski, Alexander 1946- .... **CLC 39**
See also CA 118; 143

Kalidasa fl. c. 400- .... **CMLC 9; PC 22**

Kallman, Chester (Simon) 1921-1975 .... **CLC 2**
See also CA 45-48; 53-56; CANR 3

Kaminsky, Melvin 1926-
See Brooks, Mel
See also CA 65-68; CANR 16

Kaminsky, Stuart M(elvin) 1934- ..... **CLC 59**
See also CA 73-76; CANR 29, 53, 89

Kandinsky, Wassily 1866-1944 .... **TCLC 92**
See also CA 118; 155

Kane, Francis
See Robbins, Harold

Kane, Paul
See Simon, Paul (Frederick)

Kanin, Garson 1912-1999 .... **CLC 22**
See also AITN 1; CA 5-8R; 177; CANR 7, 78; DLB 7

Kaniuk, Yoram 1930- .... **CLC 19**
See also CA 134

Kant, Immanuel 1724-1804 ..... **NCLC 27, 67**
See also DLB 94

Kantor, MacKinlay 1904-1977 .... **CLC 7**
See also CA 61-64; 73-76; CANR 60, 63; DLB 9, 102; MTCW 2

Kaplan, David Michael 1946- .... **CLC 50**

Kaplan, James 1951- .... **CLC 59**
See also CA 135

Karageorge, Michael
See Anderson, Poul (William)

Karamzin, Nikolai Mikhailovich 1766-1826 .... **NCLC 3**
See also DLB 150

Karapanou, Margarita 1946- .... **CLC 13**
See also CA 101

Karinthy, Frigyes 1887-1938 .... **TCLC 47**
See also CA 170

Karl, Frederick R(obert) 1927- .... **CLC 34**
See also CA 5-8R; CANR 3, 44

Kastel, Warren
See Silverberg, Robert

Kataev, Evgeny Petrovich 1903-1942
See Petrov, Evgeny
See also CA 120

Kataphusin
See Ruskin, John

Katz, Steve 1935- .... **CLC 47**
See also CA 25-28R; CAAS 14, 64; CANR 12; DLBY 83

Kauffman, Janet 1945- .... **CLC 42**
See also CA 117; CANR 43, 84; DLBY 86

Kaufman, Bob (Garnell) 1925-1986 . **CLC 49**
See also BW 1; CA 41-44R; 118; CANR 22; DLB 16, 41

Kaufman, George S. 1889-1961 ...... **CLC 38; DAM DRAM**
See also CA 108; 93-96; DLB 7; INT 108; MTCW 2

Kaufman, Sue CLC 3, 8
See also Barondess, Sue K(aufman)

Kavafis, Konstantinos Petrou 1863-1933
See Cavafy, C(onstantine) P(eter)
See also CA 104

Kavan, Anna 1901-1968 .... **CLC 5, 13, 82**
See also CA 5-8R; CANR 6, 57; MTCW 1

Kavanagh, Dan
See Barnes, Julian (Patrick)

Kavanagh, Julie 1952- .... **CLC 119**
See also CA 163

Kavanagh, Patrick (Joseph)
1904-1967 .... **CLC 22**
See also CA 123; 25-28R; DLB 15, 20;
MTCW 1

Kawabata, Yasunari 1899-1972 ..... **CLC 2, 5, 9, 18, 107; DAM MULT; SSC 17**
See also CA 93-96; 33-36R; CANR 88;
DLB 180; MTCW 2

Kaye, M(ary) M(argaret) 1909- .... **CLC 28**
See also CA 89-92; CANR 24, 60; MTCW
1, 2; SATA 62

Kaye, Mollie
See Kaye, M(ary) M(argaret)

Kaye-Smith, Sheila 1887-1956 .... **TCLC 20**
See also CA 118; DLB 36

Kaymor, Patrice Maguilene
See Senghor, Leopold Sedar

Kazan, Elia 1909- .... **CLC 6, 16, 63**
See also CA 21-24R; CANR 32, 78

Kazantzakis, Nikos 1883(?)-1957 .... **TCLC 2, 5, 33**
See also CA 105; 132; DA3; MTCW 1, 2

Kazin, Alfred 1915-1998 ..... **CLC 34, 38, 119**
See also CA 1-4R; CAAS 7; CANR 1, 45,
79; DLB 67

Keane, Mary Nesta (Skrine) 1904-1996
See Keane, Molly
See also CA 108; 114; 151

Keane, Molly **CLC 31**
See Keane, Mary Nesta (Skrine)
See also INT 114

Keates, Jonathan 1946(?)- .... **CLC 34**
See also CA 163

Keaton, Buster 1895-1966 .... **CLC 20**

Keats, John 1795-1821 ...... **NCLC 8, 73; DA; DAB; DAC; DAM MST, POET; PC 1; WLC**
See also CDBLB 1789-1832; DA3; DLB
96, 110

Keble, John 1792-1866 .... **NCLC 87**
See also DLB 32, 55

Keene, Donald 1922- .... **CLC 34**
See also CA 1-4R; CANR 5

Keillor, Garrison **CLC 40, 115**
See also Keillor, Gary (Edward)
See also AAYA 2; BEST 89:3; DLBY 87;
SATA 58

Keillor, Gary (Edward) 1942-
See Keillor, Garrison
See also CA 111; 117; CANR 36, 59; DAM
POP; DA3; MTCW 1, 2

Keith, Michael
See Hubbard, L(afayette) Ron(ald)

Keller, Gottfried 1819-1890 .... **NCLC 2; SSC 26**
See also DLB 129

Keller, Nora Okja **CLC 109**

Kellerman, Jonathan 1949- .. **CLC 44; DAM POP**
See also BEST 90:1; CA 106; CANR 29,
51; DA3; INT CANR-29

Kelley, William Melvin 1937- .... **CLC 22**
See also BW 1; CA 77-80; CANR 27, 83;
DLB 33

Kellogg, Marjorie 1922- .... **CLC 2**
See also CA 81-84

Kellow, Kathleen
See Hibbert, Eleanor Alice Burford

Kelly, M(ilton) T(errence) 1947- ...... **CLC 55**
See also CA 97-100; CAAS 22; CANR 19,
43, 84

Kelman, James 1946- .... **CLC 58, 86**
See also CA 148; CANR 85; DLB 194

Kemal, Yashar 1923- .... **CLC 14, 29**
See also CA 89-92; CANR 44

Kemble, Fanny 1809-1893 .... **NCLC 18**
See also DLB 32

Kemelman, Harry 1908-1996 .... **CLC 2**
See also AITN 1; CA 9-12R; 155; CANR 6,
71; DLB 28

Kempe, Margery 1373(?)-1440(?) ... **LC 6, 56**
See also DLB 146

Kempis, Thomas a 1380-1471 .... **LC 11**

Kendall, Henry 1839-1882 .... **NCLC 12**

Keneally, Thomas (Michael) 1935- ... **CLC 5, 8, 10, 14, 19, 27, 43, 117; DAM NOV**
See also CA 85-88; CANR 10, 50, 74; DA3;
MTCW 1, 2

Kennedy, Adrienne (Lita) 1931- ..... **CLC 66; BLC 2; DAM MULT; DC 5**
See also BW 2, 3; CA 103; CAAS 20;
CABS 3; CANR 26, 53, 82; DLB 38

Kennedy, John Pendleton
1795-1870 .... **NCLC 2**
See also DLB 3

Kennedy, Joseph Charles 1929-
See Kennedy, X. J.
See also CA 1-4R; CANR 4, 30, 40; SATA
14, 86

Kennedy, William 1928- .. **CLC 6, 28, 34, 53; DAM NOV**
See also AAYA 1; CA 85-88; CANR 14,
31, 76; DA3; DLB 143; DLBY 85; INT
CANR-31; MTCW 1, 2; SATA 57

Kennedy, X. J. **CLC 8, 42**
See also Kennedy, Joseph Charles
See also CAAS 9; CLR 27; DLB 5; SAAS
22

Kenny, Maurice (Francis) 1929- ..... **CLC 87; DAM MULT**
See also CA 144; CAAS 22; DLB 175;
NNAL

Kent, Kelvin
See Kuttner, Henry

Kenton, Maxwell
See Southern, Terry

Kenyon, Robert O.
See Kuttner, Henry

Kepler, Johannes 1571-1630 .... **LC 45**

Kerouac, Jack **CLC 1, 2, 3, 5, 14, 29, 61**
See also Kerouac, Jean-Louis Lebris de
See also AAYA 25; CDALB 1941-1968;
DLB 2, 16; DLBD 3; DLBY 95; MTCW
2

Kerouac, Jean-Louis Lebris de 1922-1969
See Kerouac, Jack
See also AITN 1; CA 5-8R; 25-28R; CANR
26, 54; DA; DAB; DAC; DAM MST,
NOV, POET, POP; DA3; MTCW 1, 2;
WLC

Kerr, Jean 1923- .... **CLC 22**
See also CA 5-8R; CANR 7; INT CANR-7

Kerr, M. E. **CLC 12, 35**
See also Meaker, Marijane (Agnes)
See also AAYA 2, 23; CLR 29; SAAS 1

Kerr, Robert **CLC 55**

Kerrigan, (Thomas) Anthony 1918- .. **CLC 4, 6**
See also CA 49-52; CAAS 11; CANR 4

Kerry, Lois
See Duncan, Lois

Kesey, Ken (Elton) 1935- ..... **CLC 1, 3, 6, 11, 46, 64; DA; DAB; DAC; DAM MST, NOV, POP; WLC**
See also AAYA 25; CA 1-4R; CANR 22,
38, 66; CDALB 1968-1988; DA3; DLB
2, 16, 206; MTCW 1, 2; SATA 66

Kesselring, Joseph (Otto)
1902-1967 .... **CLC 45; DAM DRAM, MST**
See also CA 150

Kessler, Jascha (Frederick) 1929- ...... **CLC 4**
See also CA 17-20R; CANR 8, 48

Kettelkamp, Larry (Dale) 1933- .... **CLC 12**
See also CA 29-32R; CANR 16; SAAS 3;
SATA 2

Key, Ellen 1849-1926 .... **TCLC 65**

Keyber, Conny
See Fielding, Henry

Keyes, Daniel 1927- ...... **CLC 80; DA; DAC; DAM MST, NOV**
See also AAYA 23; CA 17-20R, 181; CAAE
181; CANR 10, 26, 54, 74; DA3; MTCW
2; SATA 37

Keynes, John Maynard
1883-1946 .... **TCLC 64**
See also CA 114; 162, 163; DLBD 10;
MTCW 2

Khanshendel, Chiron
See Rose, Wendy

Khayyam, Omar 1048-1131 .... **CMLC 11; DAM POET; PC 8**
See also DA3

Kherdian, David 1931- .... **CLC 6, 9**
See also CA 21-24R; CAAS 2; CANR 39,
78; CLR 24; JRDA; MAICYA; SATA 16,
74

Khlebnikov, Velimir **TCLC 20**
See also Khlebnikov, Viktor Vladimirovich

Khlebnikov, Viktor Vladimirovich 1885-1922
See Khlebnikov, Velimir
See also CA 117

Khodasevich, Vladislav (Felitsianovich)
1886-1939 .... **TCLC 15**
See also CA 115

Kielland, Alexander Lange
1849-1906 .... **TCLC 5**
See also CA 104

Kiely, Benedict 1919- .... **CLC 23, 43**
See also CA 1-4R; CANR 2, 84; DLB 15

Kienzle, William X(avier) 1928- ..... **CLC 25; DAM POP**
See also CA 93-96; CAAS 1; CANR 9, 31,
59; DA3; INT CANR-31; MTCW 1, 2

Kierkegaard, Soren 1813-1855 ..... **NCLC 34, 78**

Kieslowski, Krzysztof 1941-1996 .... **CLC 120**
See also CA 147; 151

Killens, John Oliver 1916-1987 .... **CLC 10**
See also BW 2; CA 77-80; 123; CAAS 2;
CANR 26; DLB 33

Killigrew, Anne 1660-1685 .... **LC 4**
See also DLB 131

Killigrew, Thomas 1612-1683 .... **LC 57**
See also DLB 58

Kim
See Simenon, Georges (Jacques Christian)

Kincaid, Jamaica 1949- .... **CLC 43, 68; BLC 2; DAM MULT, NOV**
See also AAYA 13; BW 2, 3; CA 125;
CANR 47, 59; CDALBS; CLR 63; DA3;
DLB 157, 227; MTCW 2

King, Francis (Henry) 1923- .... **CLC 8, 53; DAM NOV**
See also CA 1-4R; CANR 1, 33, 86; DLB
15, 139; MTCW 1

King, Kennedy
See Brown, George Douglas

King, Martin Luther, Jr.
1929-1968 .... **CLC 83; BLC 2; DA; DAB; DAC; DAM MST, MULT; WLCS**
See also BW 2, 3; CA 25-28; CANR 27,
44; CAP 2; DA3; MTCW 1, 2; SATA 14

King, Stephen (Edwin) 1947- .... **CLC 12, 26, 37, 61, 113; DAM NOV, POP; SSC 17**
See also AAYA 1, 17; BEST 90:1; CA 61-
64; CANR 1, 30, 52, 76; DA3; DLB 143;
DLBY 80; JRDA; MTCW 1, 2; SATA 9,
55

King, Steve
See King, Stephen (Edwin)

King, Thomas 1943- ... **CLC 89; DAC; DAM MULT**
See also CA 144; DLB 175; NNAL; SATA 96

Kingman, Lee CLC 17
See also Natti, (Mary) Lee
See also SAAS 3; SATA 1, 67

Kingsley, Charles 1819-1875 .... **NCLC 35**
See also DLB 21, 32, 163, 190; YABC 2

Kingsley, Sidney 1906-1995 .... **CLC 44**
See also CA 85-88; 147; DLB 7

Kingsolver, Barbara 1955- .... **CLC 55, 81, 130; DAM POP**
See also AAYA 15; CA 129; 134; CANR 60; CDALBS; DA3; DLB 206; INT 134; MTCW 2

Kingston, Maxine (Ting Ting) Hong 1940- .... **CLC 12, 19, 58, 121; DAM MULT, NOV; WLCS**
See also AAYA 8; CA 69-72; CANR 13, 38, 74, 87; CDALBS; DA3; DLB 173, 212; DLBY 80; INT CANR-13; MTCW 1, 2; SATA 53

Kinnell, Galway 1927- ..... **CLC 1, 2, 3, 5, 13, 29, 129; PC 26**
See also CA 9-12R; CANR 10, 34, 66; DLB 5; DLBY 87; INT CANR-34; MTCW 1, 2

Kinsella, Thomas 1928- .... **CLC 4, 19**
See also CA 17-20R; CANR 15; DLB 27; MTCW 1, 2

Kinsella, W(illiam) P(atrick) 1935- . **CLC 27, 43; DAC; DAM NOV, POP**
See also AAYA 7; CA 97-100; CAAS 7; CANR 21, 35, 66, 75; INT CANR-21; MTCW 1, 2

Kinsey, Alfred C(harles) 1894-1956 .... **TCLC 91**
See also CA 115; 170; MTCW 2

Kipling, (Joseph) Rudyard 1865-1936 .... **TCLC 8, 17; DA; DAB; DAC; DAM MST, POET; PC 3; SSC 5; WLC**
See also AAYA 32; CA 105; 120; CANR 33; CDBLB 1890-1914; CLR 39, 65; DA3; DLB 19, 34, 141, 156; MAICYA; MTCW 1, 2; SATA 100; YABC 2

Kirkland, Caroline M. 1801-1864 . **NCLC 85**
See also DLB 3, 73, 74; DLBD 13

Kirkup, James 1918- .... **CLC 1**
See also CA 1-4R; CAAS 4; CANR 2; DLB 27; SATA 12

Kirkwood, James 1930(?)-1989 .... **CLC 9**
See also AITN 2; CA 1-4R; 128; CANR 6, 40

Kirshner, Sidney
See Kingsley, Sidney

Kis, Danilo 1935-1989 .... **CLC 57**
See also CA 109; 118; 129; CANR 61; DLB 181; MTCW 1

Kivi, Aleksis 1834-1872 .... **NCLC 30**

Kizer, Carolyn (Ashley) 1925- ... **CLC 15, 39, 80; DAM POET**
See also CA 65-68; CAAS 5; CANR 24, 70; DLB 5, 169; MTCW 2

Klabund 1890-1928 .... **TCLC 44**
See also CA 162; DLB 66

Klappert, Peter 1942- .... **CLC 57**
See also CA 33-36R; DLB 5

Klein, A(braham) M(oses) 1909-1972 . **CLC 19; DAB; DAC; DAM MST**
See also CA 101; 37-40R; DLB 68

Klein, Norma 1938-1989 .... **CLC 30**
See also AAYA 2; CA 41-44R; 128; CANR 15, 37; CLR 2, 19; INT CANR-15; JRDA; MAICYA; SAAS 1; SATA 7, 57

Klein, T(heodore) E(ibon) D(onald) 1947- .... **CLC 34**
See also CA 119; CANR 44, 75

Kleist, Heinrich von 1777-1811 ...... **NCLC 2, 37; DAM DRAM; SSC 22**
See also DLB 90

Klima, Ivan 1931- .... **CLC 56; DAM NOV**
See also CA 25-28R; CANR 17, 50, 91

Klimentov, Andrei Platonovich 1899-1951 .... **TCLC 14**
See also CA 108

Klinger, Friedrich Maximilian von 1752-1831 .... **NCLC 1**
See also DLB 94

Klingsor the Magician
See Hartmann, Sadakichi

Klopstock, Friedrich Gottlieb 1724-1803 .... **NCLC 11**
See also DLB 97

Knapp, Caroline 1959- .... **CLC 99**
See also CA 154

Knebel, Fletcher 1911-1993 .... **CLC 14**
See also AITN 1; CA 1-4R; 140; CAAS 3; CANR 1, 36; SATA 36; SATA-Obit 75

Knickerbocker, Diedrich
See Irving, Washington

Knight, Etheridge 1931-1991 . **CLC 40; BLC 2; DAM POET; PC 14**
See also BW 1, 3; CA 21-24R; 133; CANR 23, 82; DLB 41; MTCW 2

Knight, Sarah Kemble 1666-1727 .... **LC 7**
See also DLB 24, 200

Knister, Raymond 1899-1932 .... **TCLC 56**
See also CA 186; DLB 68

Knowles, John 1926- . **CLC 1, 4, 10, 26; DA; DAC; DAM MST, NOV**
See also AAYA 10; CA 17-20R; CANR 40, 74, 76; CDALB 1968-1988; DLB 6; MTCW 1, 2; SATA 8, 89

Knox, Calvin M.
See Silverberg, Robert

Knox, John c. 1505-1572 .... **LC 37**
See also DLB 132

Knye, Cassandra
See Disch, Thomas M(ichael)

Koch, C(hristopher) J(ohn) 1932- .... **CLC 42**
See also CA 127; CANR 84

Koch, Christopher
See Koch, C(hristopher) J(ohn)

Koch, Kenneth 1925- .... **CLC 5, 8, 44; DAM POET**
See also CA 1-4R; CANR 6, 36, 57; DLB 5; INT CANR-36; MTCW 2; SATA 65

Kochanowski, Jan 1530-1584 .... **LC 10**

Kock, Charles Paul de 1794-1871 . **NCLC 16**

Koda Rohan 1867-
See Koda Shigeyuki

Koda Shigeyuki 1867-1947 .... **TCLC 22**
See also CA 121; 183; DLB 180

Koestler, Arthur 1905-1983 ... **CLC 1, 3, 6, 8, 15, 33**
See also CA 1-4R; 109; CANR 1, 33; CDBLB 1945-1960; DLBY 83; MTCW 1, 2

Kogawa, Joy Nozomi 1935- .... **CLC 78, 129; DAC; DAM MST, MULT**
See also CA 101; CANR 19, 62; MTCW 2; SATA 99

Kohout, Pavel 1928- .... **CLC 13**
See also CA 45-48; CANR 3

Koizumi, Yakumo
See Hearn, (Patricio) Lafcadio (Tessima Carlos)

Kolmar, Gertrud 1894-1943 .... **TCLC 40**
See also CA 167

Komunyakaa, Yusef 1947- .... **CLC 86, 94; BLCS**
See also CA 147; CANR 83; DLB 120

Konrad, George
See Konrad, Gyoergy

Konrad, Gyoergy 1933- .... **CLC 4, 10, 73**
See also CA 85-88

Konwicki, Tadeusz 1926- .... **CLC 8, 28, 54, 117**
See also CA 101; CAAS 9; CANR 39, 59; MTCW 1

Koontz, Dean R(ay) 1945- .... **CLC 78; DAM NOV, POP**
See also AAYA 9, 31; BEST 89:3, 90:2; CA 108; CANR 19, 36, 52; DA3; MTCW 1; SATA 92

Kopernik, Mikolaj
See Copernicus, Nicolaus

Kopit, Arthur (Lee) 1937- ..... **CLC 1, 18, 33; DAM DRAM**
See also AITN 1; CA 81-84; CABS 3; DLB 7; MTCW 1

Kops, Bernard 1926- .... **CLC 4**
See also CA 5-8R; CANR 84; DLB 13

Kornbluth, C(yril) M. 1923-1958 .... **TCLC 8**
See also CA 105; 160; DLB 8

Korolenko, V. G.
See Korolenko, Vladimir Galaktionovich

Korolenko, Vladimir
See Korolenko, Vladimir Galaktionovich

Korolenko, Vladimir G.
See Korolenko, Vladimir Galaktionovich

Korolenko, Vladimir Galaktionovich 1853-1921 .... **TCLC 22**
See also CA 121

Korzybski, Alfred (Habdank Skarbek) 1879-1950 .... **TCLC 61**
See also CA 123; 160

Kosinski, Jerzy (Nikodem) 1933-1991 .... **CLC 1, 2, 3, 6, 10, 15, 53, 70; DAM NOV**
See also CA 17-20R; 134; CANR 9, 46; DA3; DLB 2; DLBY 82; MTCW 1, 2

Kostelanetz, Richard (Cory) 1940- .. **CLC 28**
See also CA 13-16R; CAAS 8; CANR 38, 77

Kostrowitzki, Wilhelm Apollinaris de 1880-1918
See Apollinaire, Guillaume
See also CA 104

Kotlowitz, Robert 1924- .... **CLC 4**
See also CA 33-36R; CANR 36

Kotzebue, August (Friedrich Ferdinand) von 1761-1819 .... **NCLC 25**
See also DLB 94

Kotzwinkle, William 1938- ..... **CLC 5, 14, 35**
See also CA 45-48; CANR 3, 44, 84; CLR 6; DLB 173; MAICYA; SATA 24, 70

Kowna, Stancy
See Szymborska, Wislawa

Kozol, Jonathan 1936- .... **CLC 17**
See also CA 61-64; CANR 16, 45

Kozoll, Michael 1940(?)- .... **CLC 35**

Kramer, Kathryn 19(?)- .... **CLC 34**

Kramer, Larry 1935- .. **CLC 42; DAM POP; DC 8**
See also CA 124; 126; CANR 60

Krasicki, Ignacy 1735-1801 .... **NCLC 8**

Krasinski, Zygmunt 1812-1859 .... **NCLC 4**

Kraus, Karl 1874-1936 .... **TCLC 5**
See also CA 104; DLB 118

Kreve (Mickevicius), Vincas 1882-1954 .... **TCLC 27**
See also CA 170; DLB 220

Kristeva, Julia 1941- .... **CLC 77**
See also CA 154

Kristofferson, Kris 1936- .... **CLC 26**
See also CA 104

Krizanc, John 1956- .... **CLC 57**

Krleza, Miroslav 1893-1981 .... **CLC 8, 114**
See also CA 97-100; 105; CANR 50; DLB 147

Kroetsch, Robert 1927- . **CLC 5, 23, 57, 132; DAC; DAM POET**
See also CA 17-20R; CANR 8, 38; DLB 53; MTCW 1

Kroetz, Franz
See Kroetz, Franz Xaver

Kroetz, Franz Xaver 1946- .... **CLC 41**
See also CA 130

Kroker, Arthur (W.) 1945- .... **CLC 77**
See also CA 161

Kropotkin, Peter (Aleksieevich)
1842-1921 .... **TCLC 36**
See also CA 119

Krotkov, Yuri 1917- .... **CLC 19**
See also CA 102

Krumb
See Crumb, R(obert)

Krumgold, Joseph (Quincy)
1908-1980 .... **CLC 12**
See also CA 9-12R; 101; CANR 7; MAI-CYA; SATA 1, 48; SATA-Obit 23

Krumwitz
See Crumb, R(obert)

Krutch, Joseph Wood 1893-1970 ..... **CLC 24**
See also CA 1-4R; 25-28R; CANR 4; DLB 63, 206

Krutzch, Gus
See Eliot, T(homas) S(tearns)

Krylov, Ivan Andreevich
1768(?)-1844 .... **NCLC 1**
See also DLB 150

Kubin, Alfred (Leopold Isidor)
1877-1959 .... **TCLC 23**
See also CA 112; 149; DLB 81

Kubrick, Stanley 1928-1999 .... **CLC 16**
See also AAYA 30; CA 81-84; 177; CANR 33; DLB 26

Kueng, Hans 1928-
See Kung, Hans
See also CA 53-56; CANR 66; MTCW 1, 2

Kumin, Maxine (Winokur) 1925- ..... **CLC 5, 13, 28; DAM POET; PC 15**
See also AITN 2; CA 1-4R; CAAS 8; CANR 1, 21, 69; DA3; DLB 5; MTCW 1, 2; SATA 12

Kundera, Milan 1929- . **CLC 4, 9, 19, 32, 68, 115; DAM NOV; SSC 24**
See also AAYA 2; CA 85-88; CANR 19, 52, 74; DA3; MTCW 1, 2

Kunene, Mazisi (Raymond) 1930- ... **CLC 85**
See also BW 1, 3; CA 125; CANR 81; DLB 117

Kung, Hans 1928- .... **CLC 130**
See also Kueng, Hans

Kunikida Doppo 1869-1908 .... **TCLC 99**
See also DLB 180

Kunitz, Stanley (Jasspon) 1905- .. **CLC 6, 11, 14; PC 19**
See also CA 41-44R; CANR 26, 57; DA3; DLB 48; INT CANR-26; MTCW 1, 2

Kunze, Reiner 1933- .... **CLC 10**
See also CA 93-96; DLB 75

Kuprin, Aleksander Ivanovich
1870-1938 .... **TCLC 5**
See also CA 104; 182

Kureishi, Hanif 1954(?)- .... **CLC 64**
See also CA 139; DLB 194

Kurosawa, Akira 1910-1998 .... **CLC 16, 119; DAM MULT**
See also AAYA 11; CA 101; 170; CANR 46

Kushner, Tony 1957(?)- .... **CLC 81; DAM DRAM; DC 10**
See also CA 144; CANR 74; DA3; DLB 228; MTCW 2

Kuttner, Henry 1915-1958 .... **TCLC 10**
See also CA 107; 157; DLB 8

Kuzma, Greg 1944- .... **CLC 7**
See also CA 33-36R; CANR 70

Kuzmin, Mikhail 1872(?)-1936 ...... **TCLC 40**
See also CA 170

Kyd, Thomas 1558-1594 .... **LC 22; DAM DRAM; DC 3**
See also DLB 62

Kyprianos, Iossif
See Samarakis, Antonis

La Bruyere, Jean de 1645-1696 .... **LC 17**

Lacan, Jacques (Marie Emile)
1901-1981 .... **CLC 75**
See also CA 121; 104

Laclos, Pierre Ambroise Francois Choderlos de 1741-1803 .... **NCLC 4, 87**

Lacolere, Francois
See Aragon, Louis

La Colere, Francois
See Aragon, Louis

La Deshabilleuse
See Simenon, Georges (Jacques Christian)

Lady Gregory
See Gregory, Isabella Augusta (Persse)

Lady of Quality, A
See Bagnold, Enid

La Fayette, Marie (Madelaine Pioche de la Vergne Comtes 1634-1693 .... **LC 2**

Lafayette, Rene
See Hubbard, L(afayette) Ron(ald)

La Fontaine, Jean de 1621-1695 .... **LC 50**
See also MAICYA; SATA 18

Laforgue, Jules 1860-1887 . **NCLC 5, 53; PC 14; SSC 20**

Lagerkvist, Paer (Fabian)
1891-1974 ...... **CLC 7, 10, 13, 54; DAM DRAM, NOV**
See also Lagerkvist, Par
See also CA 85-88; 49-52; DA3; MTCW 1, 2

Lagerkvist, Par SSC 12
See also Lagerkvist, Paer (Fabian)
See also MTCW 2

Lagerloef, Selma (Ottiliana Lovisa)
1858-1940 .... **TCLC 4, 36**
See also Lagerlof, Selma (Ottiliana Lovisa)
See also CA 108; MTCW 2; SATA 15

Lagerlof, Selma (Ottiliana Lovisa)
See Lagerloef, Selma (Ottiliana Lovisa)
See also CLR 7; SATA 15

La Guma, (Justin) Alex(ander)
1925-1985 .... **CLC 19; BLCS; DAM NOV**
See also BW 1, 3; CA 49-52; 118; CANR 25, 81; DLB 117, 225; MTCW 1, 2

Laidlaw, A. K.
See Grieve, C(hristopher) M(urray)

Lainez, Manuel Mujica
See Mujica Lainez, Manuel
See also HW 1

Laing, R(onald) D(avid) 1927-1989 . **CLC 95**
See also CA 107; 129; CANR 34; MTCW 1

Lamartine, Alphonse (Marie Louis Prat) de
1790-1869 . **NCLC 11; DAM POET; PC 16**

Lamb, Charles 1775-1834 ..... **NCLC 10; DA; DAB; DAC; DAM MST; WLC**
See also CDBLB 1789-1832; DLB 93, 107, 163; SATA 17

Lamb, Lady Caroline 1785-1828 ... **NCLC 38**
See also DLB 116

Lamming, George (William) 1927- ... **CLC 2, 4, 66; BLC 2; DAM MULT**
See also BW 2, 3; CA 85-88; CANR 26, 76; DLB 125; MTCW 1, 2

L'Amour, Louis (Dearborn)
1908-1988 ...... **CLC 25, 55; DAM NOV, POP**
See also AAYA 16; AITN 2; BEST 89:2; CA 1-4R; 125; CANR 3, 25, 40; DA3; DLB 206; DLBY 80; MTCW 1, 2

Lampedusa, Giuseppe (Tomasi) di
1896-1957 .... **TCLC 13**
See also Tomasi di Lampedusa, Giuseppe
See also CA 164; DLB 177; MTCW 2

Lampman, Archibald 1861-1899 ... **NCLC 25**
See also DLB 92

Lancaster, Bruce 1896-1963 .... **CLC 36**
See also CA 9-10; CANR 70; CAP 1; SATA 9

Lanchester, John CLC 99

Landau, Mark Alexandrovich
See Aldanov, Mark (Alexandrovich)

Landau-Aldanov, Mark Alexandrovich
See Aldanov, Mark (Alexandrovich)

Landis, Jerry
See Simon, Paul (Frederick)

Landis, John 1950- .... **CLC 26**
See also CA 112; 122

Landolfi, Tommaso 1908-1979 .... **CLC 11, 49**
See also CA 127; 117; DLB 177

Landon, Letitia Elizabeth
1802-1838 .... **NCLC 15**
See also DLB 96

Landor, Walter Savage
1775-1864 .... **NCLC 14**
See also DLB 93, 107

Landwirth, Heinz 1927-
See Lind, Jakov
See also CA 9-12R; CANR 7

Lane, Patrick 1939- ... **CLC 25; DAM POET**
See also CA 97-100; CANR 54; DLB 53; INT 97-100

Lang, Andrew 1844-1912 .... **TCLC 16**
See also CA 114; 137; CANR 85; DLB 98, 141, 184; MAICYA; SATA 16

Lang, Fritz 1890-1976 .... **CLC 20, 103**
See also CA 77-80; 69-72; CANR 30

Lange, John
See Crichton, (John) Michael

Langer, Elinor 1939- .... **CLC 34**
See also CA 121

Langland, William 1330(?)-1400(?) ... **LC 19; DA; DAB; DAC; DAM MST, POET**
See also DLB 146

Langstaff, Launcelot
See Irving, Washington

Lanier, Sidney 1842-1881 ..... **NCLC 6; DAM POET**
See also DLB 64; DLBD 13; MAICYA; SATA 18

Lanyer, Aemilia 1569-1645 .... **LC 10, 30**
See also DLB 121

Lao-Tzu
See Lao Tzu

Lao Tzu fl. 6th cent. B.C.- .... **CMLC 7**

Lapine, James (Elliot) 1949- .... **CLC 39**
See also CA 123; 130; CANR 54; INT 130

Larbaud, Valery (Nicolas)
1881-1957 .... **TCLC 9**
See also CA 106; 152

Lardner, Ring
See Lardner, Ring(gold) W(ilmer)

Lardner, Ring W., Jr.
See Lardner, Ring(gold) W(ilmer)

Lardner, Ring(gold) W(ilmer)
1885-1933 .... **TCLC 2, 14; SSC 32**
See also CA 104; 131; CDALB 1917-1929; DLB 11, 25, 86; DLBD 16; MTCW 1, 2

Laredo, Betty
See Codrescu, Andrei

Larkin, Maia
See Wojciechowska, Maia (Teresa)

Larkin, Philip (Arthur) 1922-1985 ... **CLC 3, 5, 8, 9, 13, 18, 33, 39, 64; DAB; DAM MST, POET; PC 21**
See also CA 5-8R; 117; CANR 24, 62; CD-BLB 1960 to Present; DA3; DLB 27; MTCW 1, 2

Larra (y Sanchez de Castro), Mariano Jose de 1809-1837 .... **NCLC 17**

Larsen, Eric 1941- .... **CLC 55**
See also CA 132

Larsen, Nella 1891-1964 .... **CLC 37; BLC 2; DAM MULT**
See also BW 1; CA 125; CANR 83; DLB 51

Larson, Charles R(aymond) 1938- .. **CLC 31**
See also CA 53-56; CANR 4

Larson, Jonathan 1961-1996 .... **CLC 99**
See also AAYA 28; CA 156

Las Casas, Bartolome de 1474-1566 ... **LC 31**

Lasch, Christopher 1932-1994 .... **CLC 102**
See also CA 73-76; 144; CANR 25; MTCW 1, 2

Lasker-Schueler, Else 1869-1945 ... **TCLC 57**
See also CA 183; DLB 66, 124

Laski, Harold 1893-1950 .... **TCLC 79**

Latham, Jean Lee 1902-1995 .... **CLC 12**
See also AITN 1; CA 5-8R; CANR 7, 84; CLR 50; MAICYA; SATA 2, 68

Latham, Mavis
See Clark, Mavis Thorpe

Lathen, Emma CLC 2
See also Hennissart, Martha; Latsis, Mary J(ane)

Lathrop, Francis
See Leiber, Fritz (Reuter, Jr.)

Latsis, Mary J(ane) 1927(?)-1997
See Lathen, Emma
See also CA 85-88; 162

Lattimore, Richmond (Alexander)
1906-1984 .... **CLC 3**
See also CA 1-4R; 112; CANR 1

Laughlin, James 1914-1997 .... **CLC 49**
See also CA 21-24R; 162; CAAS 22; CANR 9, 47; DLB 48; DLBY 96, 97

Laurence, (Jean) Margaret (Wemyss)
1926-1987 . **CLC 3, 6, 13, 50, 62; DAC; DAM MST; SSC 7**
See also CA 5-8R; 121; CANR 33; DLB 53; MTCW 1, 2; SATA-Obit 50

Laurent, Antoine 1952- .... **CLC 50**

Lauscher, Hermann
See Hesse, Hermann

Lautreamont, Comte de
1846-1870 .... **NCLC 12; SSC 14**

Laverty, Donald
See Blish, James (Benjamin)

Lavin, Mary 1912-1996 . **CLC 4, 18, 99; SSC 4**
See also CA 9-12R; 151; CANR 33; DLB 15; MTCW 1

Lavond, Paul Dennis
See Kornbluth, C(yril) M.; Pohl, Frederik

Lawler, Raymond Evenor 1922- .... **CLC 58**
See also CA 103

Lawrence, D(avid) H(erbert Richards)
1885-1930 .... **TCLC 2, 9, 16, 33, 48, 61, 93; DA; DAB; DAC; DAM MST, NOV, POET; SSC 4, 19; WLC**
See also CA 104; 121; CDBLB 1914-1945; DA3; DLB 10, 19, 36, 98, 162, 195; MTCW 1, 2

Lawrence, T(homas) E(dward)
1888-1935 .... **TCLC 18**
See also Dale, Colin
See also CA 115; 167; DLB 195

Lawrence of Arabia
See Lawrence, T(homas) E(dward)

Lawson, Henry (Archibald Hertzberg)
1867-1922 .... **TCLC 27; SSC 18**
See also CA 120; 181

Lawton, Dennis
See Faust, Frederick (Schiller)

Laxness, Halldor CLC 25
See also Gudjonsson, Halldor Kiljan

Layamon fl. c. 1200- .... **CMLC 10**
See also DLB 146

Laye, Camara 1928-1980 ... **CLC 4, 38; BLC 2; DAM MULT**
See also BW 1; CA 85-88; 97-100; CANR 25; MTCW 1, 2

Layton, Irving (Peter) 1912- .... **CLC 2, 15; DAC; DAM MST, POET**
See also CA 1-4R; CANR 2, 33, 43, 66; DLB 88; MTCW 1, 2

Lazarus, Emma 1849-1887 .... **NCLC 8**

Lazarus, Felix
See Cable, George Washington

Lazarus, Henry
See Slavitt, David R(ytman)

Lea, Joan
See Neufeld, John (Arthur)

Leacock, Stephen (Butler)
1869-1944 .... **TCLC 2; DAC; DAM MST; SSC 39**
See also CA 104; 141; CANR 80; DLB 92; MTCW 2

Lear, Edward 1812-1888 .... **NCLC 3**
See also CLR 1; DLB 32, 163, 166; MAICYA; SATA 18, 100

Lear, Norman (Milton) 1922- .... **CLC 12**
See also CA 73-76

Leautaud, Paul 1872-1956 .... **TCLC 83**
See also DLB 65

Leavis, F(rank) R(aymond)
1895-1978 .... **CLC 24**
See also CA 21-24R; 77-80; CANR 44; MTCW 1, 2

Leavitt, David 1961- ..... **CLC 34; DAM POP**
See also CA 116; 122; CANR 50, 62; DA3; DLB 130; INT 122; MTCW 2

Leblanc, Maurice (Marie Emile)
1864-1941 .... **TCLC 49**
See also CA 110

Lebowitz, Fran(ces Ann) 1951(?)- ... **CLC 11, 36**
See also CA 81-84; CANR 14, 60, 70; INT CANR-14; MTCW 1

Lebrecht, Peter
See Tieck, (Johann) Ludwig

le Carre, John CLC 3, 5, 9, 15, 28
See also Cornwell, David (John Moore)
See also BEST 89:4; CDBLB 1960 to Present; DLB 87; MTCW 2

Le Clezio, J(ean) M(arie) G(ustave)
1940- .... **CLC 31**
See also CA 116; 128; DLB 83

Leconte de Lisle, Charles-Marie-Rene
1818-1894 .... **NCLC 29**

Le Coq, Monsieur
See Simenon, Georges (Jacques Christian)

Leduc, Violette 1907-1972 .... **CLC 22**
See also CA 13-14; 33-36R; CANR 69; CAP 1

Ledwidge, Francis 1887(?)-1917 .... **TCLC 23**
See also CA 123; DLB 20

Lee, Andrea 1953- ... **CLC 36; BLC 2; DAM MULT**
See also BW 1, 3; CA 125; CANR 82

Lee, Andrew
See Auchincloss, Louis (Stanton)

Lee, Chang-rae 1965- .... **CLC 91**
See also CA 148; CANR 89

Lee, Don L. CLC 2
See also Madhubuti, Haki R.

Lee, George W(ashington)
1894-1976 .... **CLC 52; BLC 2; DAM MULT**
See also BW 1; CA 125; CANR 83; DLB 51

Lee, (Nelle) Harper 1926- . **CLC 12, 60; DA; DAB; DAC; DAM MST; WLC**
See also AAYA 13; CA 13-16R; CANR 51; CDALB 1941-1968; DA3; DLB 6; MTCW 1, 2; SATA 11

Lee, Helen Elaine 1959(?)- .... **CLC 86**
See also CA 148

Lee, Julian
See Latham, Jean Lee

Lee, Larry
See Lee, Lawrence

Lee, Laurie 1914-1997 .... **CLC 90; DAB; DAM POP**
See also CA 77-80; 158; CANR 33, 73; DLB 27; MTCW 1

Lee, Lawrence 1941-1990 .... **CLC 34**
See also CA 131; CANR 43

Lee, Li-Young 1957- .... **PC 24**
See also CA 153; DLB 165

Lee, Manfred B(ennington)
1905-1971 .... **CLC 11**
See also Queen, Ellery
See also CA 1-4R; 29-32R; CANR 2; DLB 137

Lee, Shelton Jackson 1957(?)- .... **CLC 105; BLCS; DAM MULT**
See also Lee, Spike
See also BW 2, 3; CA 125; CANR 42

Lee, Spike
See Lee, Shelton Jackson
See also AAYA 4, 29

Lee, Stan 1922- .... **CLC 17**
See also AAYA 5; CA 108; 111; INT 111

Lee, Tanith 1947- .... **CLC 46**
See also AAYA 15; CA 37-40R; CANR 53; SATA 8, 88

Lee, Vernon TCLC 5; SSC 33
See also Paget, Violet
See also DLB 57, 153, 156, 174, 178

Lee, William
See Burroughs, William S(eward)

Lee, Willy
See Burroughs, William S(eward)

Lee-Hamilton, Eugene (Jacob)
1845-1907 .... **TCLC 22**
See also CA 117

Leet, Judith 1935- .... **CLC 11**

Le Fanu, Joseph Sheridan
1814-1873 ..... **NCLC 9, 58; DAM POP; SSC 14**
See also DA3; DLB 21, 70, 159, 178

Leffland, Ella 1931- .... **CLC 19**
See also CA 29-32R; CANR 35, 78, 82; DLBY 84; INT CANR-35; SATA 65

Leger, Alexis
See Leger, (Marie-Rene Auguste) Alexis Saint-Leger

Leger, (Marie-Rene Auguste) Alexis Saint-Leger 1887-1975 .. **CLC 4, 11, 46; DAM POET; PC 23**
See also CA 13-16R; 61-64; CANR 43; MTCW 1

Leger, Saintleger
See Leger, (Marie-Rene Auguste) Alexis Saint-Leger

Le Guin, Ursula K(roeber) 1929- ..... **CLC 8, 13, 22, 45, 71; DAB; DAC; DAM MST, POP; SSC 12**
See also AAYA 9, 27; AITN 1; CA 21-24R; CANR 9, 32, 52, 74; CDALB 1968-1988; CLR 3, 28; DA3; DLB 8, 52; INT CANR-32; JRDA; MAICYA; MTCW 1, 2; SATA 4, 52, 99

Lehmann, Rosamond (Nina)
1901-1990 .... **CLC 5**
See also CA 77-80; 131; CANR 8, 73; DLB 15; MTCW 2

Leiber, Fritz (Reuter, Jr.)
1910-1992 .... **CLC 25**
See also CA 45-48; 139; CANR 2, 40, 86;
DLB 8; MTCW 1, 2; SATA 45; SATA-
Obit 73

Leibniz, Gottfried Wilhelm von
1646-1716 .... **LC 35**
See also DLB 168

Leimbach, Martha 1963-
See Leimbach, Marti
See also CA 130

Leimbach, Marti CLC 65
See also Leimbach, Martha

Leino, Eino TCLC 24
See also Loennbohm, Armas Eino Leopold

Leiris, Michel (Julien) 1901-1990 ..... **CLC 61**
See also CA 119; 128; 132

Leithauser, Brad 1953- .... **CLC 27**
See also CA 107; CANR 27, 81; DLB 120

Lelchuk, Alan 1938- .... **CLC 5**
See also CA 45-48; CAAS 20; CANR 1, 70

Lem, Stanislaw 1921- .... **CLC 8, 15, 40**
See also CA 105; CAAS 1; CANR 32;
MTCW 1

Lemann, Nancy 1956- .... **CLC 39**
See also CA 118; 136

Lemonnier, (Antoine Louis) Camille
1844-1913 .... **TCLC 22**
See also CA 121

Lenau, Nikolaus 1802-1850 .... **NCLC 16**

L'Engle, Madeleine (Camp Franklin)
1918- .... **CLC 12; DAM POP**
See also AAYA 28; AITN 2; CA 1-4R;
CANR 3, 21, 39, 66; CLR 1, 14, 57; DA3;
DLB 52; JRDA; MAICYA; MTCW 1, 2;
SAAS 15; SATA 1, 27, 75

Lengyel, Jozsef 1896-1975 .... **CLC 7**
See also CA 85-88; 57-60; CANR 71

Lenin 1870-1924
See Lenin, V. I.
See also CA 121; 168

Lenin, V. I. TCLC 67
See also Lenin

Lennon, John (Ono) 1940-1980 .. **CLC 12, 35**
See also CA 102; SATA 114

Lennox, Charlotte Ramsay
1729(?)-1804 .... **NCLC 23**
See also DLB 39

Lentricchia, Frank (Jr.) 1940- .... **CLC 34**
See also CA 25-28R; CANR 19

Lenz, Siegfried 1926- .... **CLC 27; SSC 33**
See also CA 89-92; CANR 80; DLB 75

Leonard, Elmore (John, Jr.) 1925- . **CLC 28,
34, 71, 120; DAM POP**
See also AAYA 22; AITN 1; BEST 89:1,
90:4; CA 81-84; CANR 12, 28, 53, 76;
DA3; DLB 173, 226; INT CANR-28;
MTCW 1, 2

Leonard, Hugh CLC 19
See also Byrne, John Keyes
See also DLB 13

Leonov, Leonid (Maximovich)
1899-1994 .... **CLC 92; DAM NOV**
See also CA 129; CANR 74, 76; MTCW 1,
2

Leopardi, (Conte) Giacomo
1798-1837 .... **NCLC 22**

Le Reveler
See Artaud, Antonin (Marie Joseph)

Lerman, Eleanor 1952- .... **CLC 9**
See also CA 85-88; CANR 69

Lerman, Rhoda 1936- .... **CLC 56**
See also CA 49-52; CANR 70

Lermontov, Mikhail Yuryevich
1814-1841 .... **NCLC 47; PC 18**
See also DLB 205

Leroux, Gaston 1868-1927 .... **TCLC 25**
See also CA 108; 136; CANR 69; SATA 65

Lesage, Alain-Rene 1668-1747 .... **LC 2, 28**

Leskov, Nikolai (Semyonovich)
1831-1895 .... **NCLC 25; SSC 34**

Lessing, Doris (May) 1919- ... **CLC 1, 2, 3, 6,
10, 15, 22, 40, 94; DA; DAB; DAC;
DAM MST, NOV; SSC 6; WLCS**
See also CA 9-12R; CAAS 14; CANR 33,
54, 76; CDBLB 1960 to Present; DA3;
DLB 15, 139; DLBY 85; MTCW 1, 2

Lessing, Gotthold Ephraim 1729-1781 . **LC 8**
See also DLB 97

Lester, Richard 1932- .... **CLC 20**

Lever, Charles (James)
1806-1872 .... **NCLC 23**
See also DLB 21

Leverson, Ada 1865(?)-1936(?) .... **TCLC 18**
See also Elaine
See also CA 117; DLB 153

Levertov, Denise 1923-1997 .. **CLC 1, 2, 3, 5,
8, 15, 28, 66; DAM POET; PC 11**
See also CA 1-4R, 178; 163; CAAE 178;
CAAS 19; CANR 3, 29, 50; CDALBS;
DLB 5, 165; INT CANR-29; MTCW 1, 2

Levi, Jonathan CLC 76

Levi, Peter (Chad Tigar) 1931- .... **CLC 41**
See also CA 5-8R; CANR 34, 80; DLB 40

Levi, Primo 1919-1987 . **CLC 37, 50; SSC 12**
See also CA 13-16R; 122; CANR 12, 33,
61, 70; DLB 177; MTCW 1, 2

Levin, Ira 1929- .... **CLC 3, 6; DAM POP**
See also CA 21-24R; CANR 17, 44, 74;
DA3; MTCW 1, 2; SATA 66

Levin, Meyer 1905-1981 .... **CLC 7; DAM
POP**
See also AITN 1; CA 9-12R; 104; CANR
15; DLB 9, 28; DLBY 81; SATA 21;
SATA-Obit 27

Levine, Norman 1924- .... **CLC 54**
See also CA 73-76; CAAS 23; CANR 14,
70; DLB 88

Levine, Philip 1928- .. **CLC 2, 4, 5, 9, 14, 33,
118; DAM POET; PC 22**
See also CA 9-12R; CANR 9, 37, 52; DLB
5

Levinson, Deirdre 1931- .... **CLC 49**
See also CA 73-76; CANR 70

Levi-Strauss, Claude 1908- .... **CLC 38**
See also CA 1-4R; CANR 6, 32, 57; MTCW
1, 2

Levitin, Sonia (Wolff) 1934- .... **CLC 17**
See also AAYA 13; CA 29-32R; CANR 14,
32, 79; CLR 53; JRDA; MAICYA; SAAS
2; SATA 4, 68

Levon, O. U.
See Kesey, Ken (Elton)

Levy, Amy 1861-1889 .... **NCLC 59**
See also DLB 156

Lewes, George Henry 1817-1878 ... **NCLC 25**
See also DLB 55, 144

Lewis, Alun 1915-1944 .... **TCLC 3; SSC 40**
See also CA 104; DLB 20, 162

Lewis, C. Day
See Day Lewis, C(ecil)

Lewis, C(live) S(taples) 1898-1963 .... **CLC 1,
3, 6, 14, 27, 124; DA; DAB; DAC;
DAM MST, NOV, POP; WLC**
See also AAYA 3; CA 81-84; CANR 33,
71; CDBLB 1945-1960; CLR 3, 27; DA3;
DLB 15, 100, 160; JRDA; MAICYA;
MTCW 1, 2; SATA 13, 100

Lewis, Janet 1899-1998 .... **CLC 41**
See Winters, Janet Lewis
See also CA 9-12R; 172; CANR 29, 63;
CAP 1; DLBY 87

Lewis, Matthew Gregory
1775-1818 .... **NCLC 11, 62**
See also DLB 39, 158, 178

Lewis, (Harry) Sinclair 1885-1951 . **TCLC 4,
13, 23, 39; DA; DAB; DAC; DAM
MST, NOV; WLC**
See also CA 104; 133; CDALB 1917-1929;
DA3; DLB 9, 102; DLBD 1; MTCW 1, 2

Lewis, (Percy) Wyndham
1882(?)-1957 .... **TCLC 2, 9; SSC 34**
See also CA 104; 157; DLB 15; MTCW 2

Lewisohn, Ludwig 1883-1955 .... **TCLC 19**
See also CA 107; DLB 4, 9, 28, 102

Lewton, Val 1904-1951 .... **TCLC 76**

Leyner, Mark 1956- .... **CLC 92**
See also CA 110; CANR 28, 53; DA3;
MTCW 2

Lezama Lima, Jose 1910-1976 .... **CLC 4, 10,
101; DAM MULT; HLCS 2**
See also CA 77-80; CANR 71; DLB 113;
HW 1, 2

L'Heureux, John (Clarke) 1934- ...... **CLC 52**
See also CA 13-16R; CANR 23, 45, 88

Liddell, C. H.
See Kuttner, Henry

Lie, Jonas (Lauritz Idemil)
1833-1908(?) .... **TCLC 5**
See also CA 115

Lieber, Joel 1937-1971 .... **CLC 6**
See also CA 73-76; 29-32R

Lieber, Stanley Martin
See Lee, Stan

Lieberman, Laurence (James)
1935- .... **CLC 4, 36**
See also CA 17-20R; CANR 8, 36, 89

Lieh Tzu fl. 7th cent. B.C.-5th cent.
B.C. .... **CMLC 27**

Lieksman, Anders
See Haavikko, Paavo Juhani

Li Fei-kan 1904-
See Pa Chin
See also CA 105

Lifton, Robert Jay 1926- .... **CLC 67**
See also CA 17-20R; CANR 27, 78; INT
CANR-27; SATA 66

Lightfoot, Gordon 1938- .... **CLC 26**
See also CA 109

Lightman, Alan P(aige) 1948- .... **CLC 81**
See also CA 141; CANR 63

Ligotti, Thomas (Robert) 1953- ...... **CLC 44;
SSC 16**
See also CA 123; CANR 49

Li Ho 791-817 .... **PC 13**

Liliencron, (Friedrich Adolf Axel) Detlev
von 1844-1909 .... **TCLC 18**
See also CA 117

Lilly, William 1602-1681 .... **LC 27**

Lima, Jose Lezama
See Lezama Lima, Jose

Lima Barreto, Afonso Henrique de
1881-1922 .... **TCLC 23**
See also CA 117; 181

Limonov, Edward 1944- .... **CLC 67**
See also CA 137

Lin, Frank
See Atherton, Gertrude (Franklin Horn)

Lincoln, Abraham 1809-1865 .... **NCLC 18**

Lind, Jakov CLC 1, 2, 4, 27, 82
See also Landwirth, Heinz
See also CAAS 4

Lindbergh, Anne (Spencer) Morrow
1906- .... **CLC 82; DAM NOV**
See also CA 17-20R; CANR 16, 73; MTCW
1, 2; SATA 33

Lindsay, David 1876(?)-1945 .... **TCLC 15**
See also CA 113

Lindsay, (Nicholas) Vachel
1879-1931 . **TCLC 17; DA; DAC; DAM
MST, POET; PC 23; WLC**
See also CA 114; 135; CANR 79; CDALB
1865-1917; DA3; DLB 54; SATA 40

Linke-Poot
See Doeblin, Alfred

Linney, Romulus 1930- .... **CLC 51**
See also CA 1-4R; CANR 40, 44, 79

Linton, Eliza Lynn 1822-1898 .... **NCLC 41**
See also DLB 18

Li Po 701-763 .... **CMLC 2; PC 29**

Lipsius, Justus 1547-1606 .... **LC 16**

Lipsyte, Robert (Michael) 1938- ..... **CLC 21; DA; DAC; DAM MST, NOV**
See also AAYA 7; CA 17-20R; CANR 8, 57; CLR 23; JRDA; MAICYA; SATA 5, 68, 113

Lish, Gordon (Jay) 1934- ... **CLC 45; SSC 18**
See also CA 113; 117; CANR 79; DLB 130; INT 117

Lispector, Clarice 1925(?)-1977 .... **CLC 43; HLCS 2; SSC 34**
See also CA 139; 116; CANR 71; DLB 113; HW 2

Littell, Robert 1935(?)- .... **CLC 42**
See also CA 109; 112; CANR 64

Little, Malcolm 1925-1965
See Malcolm X
See also BW 1, 3; CA 125; 111; CANR 82; DA; DAB; DAC; DAM MST, MULT; DA3; MTCW 1, 2

Littlewit, Humphrey Gent.
See Lovecraft, H(oward) P(hillips)

Litwos
See Sienkiewicz, Henryk (Adam Alexander Pius)

Liu, E 1857-1909 .... **TCLC 15**
See also CA 115

Lively, Penelope (Margaret) 1933- .. **CLC 32, 50; DAM NOV**
See also CA 41-44R; CANR 29, 67, 79; CLR 7; DLB 14, 161, 207; JRDA; MAICYA; MTCW 1, 2; SATA 7, 60, 101

Livesay, Dorothy (Kathleen) 1909- ... **CLC 4, 15, 79; DAC; DAM MST, POET**
See also AITN 2; CA 25-28R; CAAS 8; CANR 36, 67; DLB 68; MTCW 1

Livy c. 59B.C.-c. 17 .... **CMLC 11**
See also DLB 211

Lizardi, Jose Joaquin Fernandez de 1776-1827 .... **NCLC 30**

Llewellyn, Richard
See Llewellyn Lloyd, Richard Dafydd Vivian
See also DLB 15

Llewellyn Lloyd, Richard Dafydd Vivian 1906-1983 .... **CLC 7, 80**
See also Llewellyn, Richard
See also CA 53-56; 111; CANR 7, 71; SATA 11; SATA-Obit 37

Llosa, (Jorge) Mario (Pedro) Vargas
See Vargas Llosa, (Jorge) Mario (Pedro)

Lloyd, Manda
See Mander, (Mary) Jane

Lloyd Webber, Andrew 1948-
See Webber, Andrew Lloyd
See also AAYA 1; CA 116; 149; DAM DRAM; SATA 56

Llull, Ramon c. 1235-c. 1316 .... **CMLC 12**

Lobb, Ebenezer
See Upward, Allen

Locke, Alain (Le Roy) 1886-1954 . **TCLC 43; BLCS**
See also BW 1, 3; CA 106; 124; CANR 79; DLB 51

Locke, John 1632-1704 .... **LC 7, 35**
See also DLB 101

Locke-Elliott, Sumner
See Elliott, Sumner Locke

Lockhart, John Gibson 1794-1854 .. **NCLC 6**
See also DLB 110, 116, 144

Lodge, David (John) 1935- ... **CLC 36; DAM POP**
See also BEST 90:1; CA 17-20R; CANR 19, 53, 92; DLB 14, 194; INT CANR-19; MTCW 1, 2

Lodge, Thomas 1558-1625 .... **LC 41**

Lodge, Thomas 1558-1625 .... **LC 41**
See also DLB 172

Loennbohm, Armas Eino Leopold 1878-1926
See Leino, Eino
See also CA 123

Loewinsohn, Ron(ald William) 1937- .... **CLC 52**
See also CA 25-28R; CANR 71

Logan, Jake
See Smith, Martin Cruz

Logan, John (Burton) 1923-1987 .... **CLC 5**
See also CA 77-80; 124; CANR 45; DLB 5

Lo Kuan-chung 1330(?)-1400(?) .... **LC 12**

Lombard, Nap
See Johnson, Pamela Hansford

London, Jack **TCLC 9, 15, 39; SSC 4; WLC**
See also London, John Griffith
See also AAYA 13; AITN 2; CDALB 1865-1917; DLB 8, 12, 78, 212; SATA 18

London, John Griffith 1876-1916
See London, Jack
See also CA 110; 119; CANR 73; DA; DAB; DAC; DAM MST, NOV; DA3; JRDA; MAICYA; MTCW 1, 2

Long, Emmett
See Leonard, Elmore (John, Jr.)

Longbaugh, Harry
See Goldman, William (W.)

Longfellow, Henry Wadsworth 1807-1882 .... **NCLC 2, 45; DA; DAB; DAC; DAM MST, POET; PC 30; WLCS**
See also CDALB 1640-1865; DA3; DLB 1, 59; SATA 19

Longinus c. 1st cent. - .... **CMLC 27**
See also DLB 176

Longley, Michael 1939- .... **CLC 29**
See also CA 102; DLB 40

Longus fl. c. 2nd cent. - .... **CMLC 7**

Longway, A. Hugh
See Lang, Andrew

Lonnrot, Elias 1802-1884 .... **NCLC 53**

Lopate, Phillip 1943- .... **CLC 29**
See also CA 97-100; CANR 88; DLBY 80; INT 97-100

Lopez Portillo (y Pacheco), Jose 1920- .... **CLC 46**
See also CA 129; HW 1

Lopez y Fuentes, Gregorio 1897(?)-1966 .... **CLC 32**
See also CA 131; HW 1

Lorca, Federico Garcia
See Garcia Lorca, Federico

Lord, Bette Bao 1938- .... **CLC 23**
See also BEST 90:3; CA 107; CANR 41, 79; INT 107; SATA 58

Lord Auch
See Bataille, Georges

Lord Byron
See Byron, George Gordon (Noel)

Lorde, Audre (Geraldine) 1934-1992 ... **CLC 18, 71; BLC 2; DAM MULT, POET; PC 12**
See also BW 1, 3; CA 25-28R; 142; CANR 16, 26, 46, 82; DA3; DLB 41; MTCW 1, 2

Lord Houghton
See Milnes, Richard Monckton

Lord Jeffrey
See Jeffrey, Francis

Lorenzini, Carlo 1826-1890
See Collodi, Carlo
See also MAICYA; SATA 29, 100

Lorenzo, Heberto Padilla
See Padilla (Lorenzo), Heberto

Loris
See Hofmannsthal, Hugo von

Loti, Pierre **TCLC 11**
See also Viaud, (Louis Marie) Julien
See also DLB 123

Lou, Henri
See Andreas-Salome, Lou

Louie, David Wong 1954- .... **CLC 70**
See also CA 139

Louis, Father M.
See Merton, Thomas

Lovecraft, H(oward) P(hillips) 1890-1937 ...... **TCLC 4, 22; DAM POP; SSC 3**
See also AAYA 14; CA 104; 133; DA3; MTCW 1, 2

Lovelace, Earl 1935- .... **CLC 51**
See also BW 2; CA 77-80; CANR 41, 72; DLB 125; MTCW 1

Lovelace, Richard 1618-1657 .... **LC 24**
See also DLB 131

Lowell, Amy 1874-1925 .... **TCLC 1, 8; DAM POET; PC 13**
See also CA 104; 151; DLB 54, 140; MTCW 2

Lowell, James Russell 1819-1891 ... **NCLC 2, 90**
See also CDALB 1640-1865; DLB 1, 11, 64, 79, 189

Lowell, Robert (Traill Spence, Jr.) 1917-1977 .... **CLC 1, 2, 3, 4, 5, 8, 9, 11, 15, 37, 124; DA; DAB; DAC; DAM MST, NOV; PC 3; WLC**
See also CA 9-12R; 73-76; CABS 2; CANR 26, 60; CDALBS; DA3; DLB 5, 169; MTCW 1, 2

Lowenthal, Michael (Francis) 1969- .... **CLC 119**
See also CA 150

Lowndes, Marie Adelaide (Belloc) 1868-1947 .... **TCLC 12**
See also CA 107; DLB 70

Lowry, (Clarence) Malcolm 1909-1957 .... **TCLC 6, 40; SSC 31**
See also CA 105; 131; CANR 62; CDBLB 1945-1960; DLB 15; MTCW 1, 2

Lowry, Mina Gertrude 1882-1966
See Loy, Mina
See also CA 113

Loxsmith, John
See Brunner, John (Kilian Houston)

Loy, Mina **CLC 28; DAM POET; PC 16**
See also Lowry, Mina Gertrude
See also DLB 4, 54

Loyson-Bridet
See Schwob, Marcel (Mayer Andre)

Lucan 39-65 .... **CMLC 33**
See also DLB 211

Lucas, Craig 1951- .... **CLC 64**
See also CA 137; CANR 71

Lucas, E(dward) V(errall) 1868-1938 .... **TCLC 73**
See also CA 176; DLB 98, 149, 153; SATA 20

Lucas, George 1944- .... **CLC 16**
See also AAYA 1, 23; CA 77-80; CANR 30; SATA 56

Lucas, Hans
See Godard, Jean-Luc

Lucas, Victoria
See Plath, Sylvia

Lucian c. 120-c. 180 .... **CMLC 32**
See also DLB 176

Ludlam, Charles 1943-1987 .... **CLC 46, 50**
See also CA 85-88; 122; CANR 72, 86
Ludlum, Robert 1927- .... **CLC 22, 43; DAM NOV, POP**
See also AAYA 10; BEST 89:1, 90:3; CA 33-36R; CANR 25, 41, 68; DA3; DLBY 82; MTCW 1, 2
Ludwig, Ken CLC 60
Ludwig, Otto 1813-1865 .... **NCLC 4**
See also DLB 129
Lugones, Leopoldo 1874-1938 ...... **TCLC 15; HLCS 2**
See also CA 116; 131; HW 1
Lu Hsun 1881-1936 .... **TCLC 3; SSC 20**
See also Shu-Jen, Chou
Lukacs, George CLC 24
See also Lukacs, Gyorgy (Szegeny von)
Lukacs, Gyorgy (Szegeny von) 1885-1971
See Lukacs, George
See also CA 101; 29-32R; CANR 62; MTCW 2
Luke, Peter (Ambrose Cyprian)
1919-1995 .... **CLC 38**
See also CA 81-84; 147; CANR 72; DLB 13
Lunar, Dennis
See Mungo, Raymond
Lurie, Alison 1926- .... **CLC 4, 5, 18, 39**
See also CA 1-4R; CANR 2, 17, 50, 88; DLB 2; MTCW 1; SATA 46, 112
Lustig, Arnost 1926- .... **CLC 56**
See also AAYA 3; CA 69-72; CANR 47; SATA 56
Luther, Martin 1483-1546 .... **LC 9, 37**
See also DLB 179
Luxemburg, Rosa 1870(?)-1919 ..... **TCLC 63**
See also CA 118
Luzi, Mario 1914- .... **CLC 13**
See also CA 61-64; CANR 9, 70; DLB 128
Lyly, John 1554(?)-1606 .... **LC 41; DAM DRAM; DC 7**
See also DLB 62, 167
L'Ymagier
See Gourmont, Remy (-Marie-Charles) de
Lynch, B. Suarez
See Bioy Casares, Adolfo; Borges, Jorge Luis
Lynch, B. Suarez
See Bioy Casares, Adolfo
Lynch, David (K.) 1946- .... **CLC 66**
See also CA 124; 129
Lynch, James
See Andreyev, Leonid (Nikolaevich)
Lynch Davis, B.
See Bioy Casares, Adolfo; Borges, Jorge Luis
Lyndsay, Sir David 1490-1555 .... **LC 20**
Lynn, Kenneth S(chuyler) 1923- ...... **CLC 50**
See also CA 1-4R; CANR 3, 27, 65
Lynx
See West, Rebecca
Lyons, Marcus
See Blish, James (Benjamin)
Lyre, Pinchbeck
See Sassoon, Siegfried (Lorraine)
Lytle, Andrew (Nelson) 1902-1995 ... **CLC 22**
See also CA 9-12R; 150; CANR 70; DLB 6; DLBY 95
Lyttelton, George 1709-1773 .... **LC 10**
Maas, Peter 1929- .... **CLC 29**
See also CA 93-96; INT 93-96; MTCW 2
Macaulay, Rose 1881-1958 .... **TCLC 7, 44**
See also CA 104; DLB 36
Macaulay, Thomas Babington
1800-1859 .... **NCLC 42**
See also CDBLB 1832-1890; DLB 32, 55

MacBeth, George (Mann)
1932-1992 .... **CLC 2, 5, 9**
See also CA 25-28R; 136; CANR 61, 66; DLB 40; MTCW 1; SATA 4; SATA-Obit 70
MacCaig, Norman (Alexander)
1910- .... **CLC 36; DAB; DAM POET**
See also CA 9-12R; CANR 3, 34; DLB 27
MacCarthy, Sir(Charles Otto) Desmond
1877-1952 .... **TCLC 36**
See also CA 167
MacDiarmid, Hugh CLC 2, 4, 11, 19, 63; PC 9
See also Grieve, C(hristopher) M(urray)
See also CDBLB 1945-1960; DLB 20
MacDonald, Anson
See Heinlein, Robert A(nson)
Macdonald, Cynthia 1928- .... **CLC 13, 19**
See also CA 49-52; CANR 4, 44; DLB 105
MacDonald, George 1824-1905 .... **TCLC 9**
See also CA 106; 137; CANR 80; DLB 18, 163, 178; MAICYA; SATA 33, 100
Macdonald, John
See Millar, Kenneth
MacDonald, John D(ann)
1916-1986 .. **CLC 3, 27, 44; DAM NOV, POP**
See also CA 1-4R; 121; CANR 1, 19, 60; DLB 8; DLBY 86; MTCW 1, 2
Macdonald, John Ross
See Millar, Kenneth
Macdonald, Ross CLC 1, 2, 3, 14, 34, 41
See also Millar, Kenneth
See also DLBD 6
MacDougal, John
See Blish, James (Benjamin)
MacDougal, John
See Blish, James (Benjamin)
MacEwen, Gwendolyn (Margaret)
1941-1987 .... **CLC 13, 55**
See also CA 9-12R; 124; CANR 7, 22; DLB 53; SATA 50; SATA-Obit 55
Macha, Karel Hynek 1810-1846 .... **NCLC 46**
Machado (y Ruiz), Antonio
1875-1939 .... **TCLC 3**
See also CA 104; 174; DLB 108; HW 2
Machado de Assis, Joaquim Maria
1839-1908 ..... **TCLC 10; BLC 2; HLCS 2; SSC 24**
See also CA 107; 153; CANR 91
Machen, Arthur TCLC 4; SSC 20
See also Jones, Arthur Llewellyn
See also CA 179; DLB 36, 156, 178
Machiavelli, Niccolo 1469-1527 .... **LC 8, 36; DA; DAB; DAC; DAM MST; WLCS**
MacInnes, Colin 1914-1976 .... **CLC 4, 23**
See also CA 69-72; 65-68; CANR 21; DLB 14; MTCW 1, 2
MacInnes, Helen (Clark)
1907-1985 .... **CLC 27, 39; DAM POP**
See also CA 1-4R; 117; CANR 1, 28, 58; DLB 87; MTCW 1, 2; SATA 22; SATA-Obit 44
Mackenzie, Compton (Edward Montague)
1883-1972 .... **CLC 18**
See also CA 21-22; 37-40R; CAP 2; DLB 34, 100
Mackenzie, Henry 1745-1831 .... **NCLC 41**
See also DLB 39
Mackintosh, Elizabeth 1896(?)-1952
See Tey, Josephine
See also CA 110
MacLaren, James
See Grieve, C(hristopher) M(urray)
Mac Laverty, Bernard 1942- .... **CLC 31**
See also CA 116; 118; CANR 43, 88; INT 118

MacLean, Alistair (Stuart)
1922(?)-1987 .. **CLC 3, 13, 50, 63; DAM POP**
See also CA 57-60; 121; CANR 28, 61; MTCW 1; SATA 23; SATA-Obit 50
Maclean, Norman (Fitzroy)
1902-1990 .... **CLC 78; DAM POP; SSC 13**
See also CA 102; 132; CANR 49; DLB 206
MacLeish, Archibald 1892-1982 ... **CLC 3, 8, 14, 68; DAM POET**
See also CA 9-12R; 106; CANR 33, 63; CDALBS; DLB 4, 7, 45; DLBY 82; MTCW 1, 2
MacLennan, (John) Hugh
1907-1990 . **CLC 2, 14, 92; DAC; DAM MST**
See also CA 5-8R; 142; CANR 33; DLB 68; MTCW 1, 2
MacLeod, Alistair 1936- .... **CLC 56; DAC; DAM MST**
See also CA 123; DLB 60; MTCW 2
Macleod, Fiona
See Sharp, William
MacNeice, (Frederick) Louis
1907-1963 .... **CLC 1, 4, 10, 53; DAB; DAM POET**
See also CA 85-88; CANR 61; DLB 10, 20; MTCW 1, 2
MacNeill, Dand
See Fraser, George MacDonald
Macpherson, James 1736-1796 .... **LC 29**
See also Ossian
See also DLB 109
Macpherson, (Jean) Jay 1931- .... **CLC 14**
See also CA 5-8R; CANR 90; DLB 53
MacShane, Frank 1927-1999 .... **CLC 39**
See also CA 9-12R; 186; CANR 3, 33; DLB 111
Macumber, Mari
See Sandoz, Mari(e Susette)
Madach, Imre 1823-1864 .... **NCLC 19**
Madden, (Jerry) David 1933- .... **CLC 5, 15**
See also CA 1-4R; CAAS 3; CANR 4, 45; DLB 6; MTCW 1
Maddern, Al(an)
See Ellison, Harlan (Jay)
Madhubuti, Haki R. 1942- . **CLC 6, 73; BLC 2; DAM MULT, POET; PC 5**
See also Lee, Don L.
See also BW 2, 3; CA 73-76; CANR 24, 51, 73; DLB 5, 41; DLBD 8; MTCW 2
Maepenn, Hugh
See Kuttner, Henry
Maepenn, K. H.
See Kuttner, Henry
Maeterlinck, Maurice 1862-1949 ... **TCLC 3; DAM DRAM**
See also CA 104; 136; CANR 80; DLB 192; SATA 66
Maginn, William 1794-1842 .... **NCLC 8**
See also DLB 110, 159
Mahapatra, Jayanta 1928- .... **CLC 33; DAM MULT**
See also CA 73-76; CAAS 9; CANR 15, 33, 66, 87
Mahfouz, Naguib (Abdel Aziz Al-Sabilgi)
1911(?)-
See Mahfuz, Najib
See also BEST 89:2; CA 128; CANR 55; DAM NOV; DA3; MTCW 1, 2
Mahfuz, Najib CLC 52, 55
See also Mahfouz, Naguib (Abdel Aziz Al-Sabilgi)
See also DLBY 88
Mahon, Derek 1941- .... **CLC 27**
See also CA 113; 128; CANR 88; DLB 40

Mailer, Norman 1923- ... **CLC 1, 2, 3, 4, 5, 8, 11, 14, 28, 39, 74, 111; DA; DAB; DAC; DAM MST, NOV, POP**
See also AAYA 31; AITN 2; CA 9-12R; CABS 1; CANR 28, 74, 77; CDALB 1968-1988; DA3; DLB 2, 16, 28, 185; DLBD 3; DLBY 80, 83; MTCW 1, 2

Maillet, Antonine 1929- .. **CLC 54, 118; DAC**
See also CA 115; 120; CANR 46, 74, 77; DLB 60; INT 120; MTCW 2

Mais, Roger 1905-1955 .... **TCLC 8**
See also BW 1, 3; CA 105; 124; CANR 82; DLB 125; MTCW 1

Maistre, Joseph de 1753-1821 .... **NCLC 37**

Maitland, Frederic 1850-1906 .... **TCLC 65**

Maitland, Sara (Louise) 1950- .... **CLC 49**
See also CA 69-72; CANR 13, 59

Major, Clarence 1936- . **CLC 3, 19, 48; BLC 2; DAM MULT**
See also BW 2, 3; CA 21-24R; CAAS 6; CANR 13, 25, 53, 82; DLB 33

Major, Kevin (Gerald) 1949- . **CLC 26; DAC**
See also AAYA 16; CA 97-100; CANR 21, 38; CLR 11; DLB 60; INT CANR-21; JRDA; MAICYA; SATA 32, 82

Maki, James
See Ozu, Yasujiro

Malabaila, Damiano
See Levi, Primo

Malamud, Bernard 1914-1986 .. **CLC 1, 2, 3, 5, 8, 9, 11, 18, 27, 44, 78, 85; DA; DAB; DAC; DAM MST, NOV, POP; SSC 15; WLC**
See also AAYA 16; CA 5-8R; 118; CABS 1; CANR 28, 62; CDALB 1941-1968; DA3; DLB 2, 28, 152; DLBY 80, 86; MTCW 1, 2

Malan, Herman
See Bosman, Herman Charles; Bosman, Herman Charles

Malaparte, Curzio 1898-1957 .... **TCLC 52**

Malcolm, Dan
See Silverberg, Robert

Malcolm X CLC 82, 117; BLC 2; WLCS
See also Little, Malcolm

Malherbe, Francois de 1555-1628 .... **LC 5**

Mallarme, Stephane 1842-1898 ...... **NCLC 4, 41; DAM POET; PC 4**

Mallet-Joris, Francoise 1930- .... **CLC 11**
See also CA 65-68; CANR 17; DLB 83

Malley, Ern
See McAuley, James Phillip

Mallowan, Agatha Christie
See Christie, Agatha (Mary Clarissa)

Maloff, Saul 1922- .... **CLC 5**
See also CA 33-36R

Malone, Louis
See MacNeice, (Frederick) Louis

Malone, Michael (Christopher)
1942- .... **CLC 43**
See also CA 77-80; CANR 14, 32, 57

Malory, (Sir) Thomas
1410(?)-1471(?) .... **LC 11; DA; DAB; DAC; DAM MST; WLCS**
See also CDBLB Before 1660; DLB 146; SATA 59; SATA-Brief 33

Malouf, (George Joseph) David
1934- .... **CLC 28, 86**
See also CA 124; CANR 50, 76; MTCW 2

Malraux, (Georges-)Andre
1901-1976 .... **CLC 1, 4, 9, 13, 15, 57; DAM NOV**
See also CA 21-22; 69-72; CANR 34, 58; CAP 2; DA3; DLB 72; MTCW 1, 2

Malzberg, Barry N(athaniel) 1939- ... **CLC 7**
See also CA 61-64; CAAS 4; CANR 16; DLB 8

Mamet, David (Alan) 1947- .. **CLC 9, 15, 34, 46, 91; DAM DRAM; DC 4**
See also AAYA 3; CA 81-84; CABS 3; CANR 15, 41, 67, 72; DA3; DLB 7; MTCW 1, 2

Mamoulian, Rouben (Zachary)
1897-1987 .... **CLC 16**
See also CA 25-28R; 124; CANR 85

Mandelstam, Osip (Emilievich)
1891(?)-1938(?) .... **TCLC 2, 6; PC 14**
See also CA 104; 150; MTCW 2

Mander, (Mary) Jane 1877-1949 ... **TCLC 31**
See also CA 162

Mandeville, John fl. 1350- .... **CMLC 19**
See also DLB 146

Mandiargues, Andre Pieyre de CLC 41
See also Pieyre de Mandiargues, Andre
See also DLB 83

Mandrake, Ethel Belle
See Thurman, Wallace (Henry)

Mangan, James Clarence
1803-1849 .... **NCLC 27**

Maniere, J.-E.
See Giraudoux, (Hippolyte) Jean

Mankiewicz, Herman (Jacob)
1897-1953 .... **TCLC 85**
See also CA 120; 169; DLB 26

Manley, (Mary) Delariviere
1672(?)-1724 .... **LC 1, 42**
See also DLB 39, 80

Mann, Abel
See Creasey, John

Mann, Emily 1952- .... **DC 7**
See also CA 130; CANR 55

Mann, (Luiz) Heinrich 1871-1950 ... **TCLC 9**
See also CA 106; 164; 181; DLB 66, 118

Mann, (Paul) Thomas 1875-1955 ... **TCLC 2, 8, 14, 21, 35, 44, 60; DA; DAB; DAC; DAM MST, NOV; SSC 5; WLC**
See also CA 104; 128; DA3; DLB 66; MTCW 1, 2

Mannheim, Karl 1893-1947 .... **TCLC 65**

Manning, David
See Faust, Frederick (Schiller)

Manning, Frederic 1887(?)-1935 ... **TCLC 25**
See also CA 124

Manning, Olivia 1915-1980 .... **CLC 5, 19**
See also CA 5-8R; 101; CANR 29; MTCW 1

Mano, D. Keith 1942- .... **CLC 2, 10**
See also CA 25-28R; CAAS 6; CANR 26, 57; DLB 6

Mansfield, Katherine -1923 .. **TCLC 2, 8, 39; DAB; SSC 9, 23, 38; WLC**
See also Beauchamp, Kathleen Mansfield
See also DLB 162

Manso, Peter 1940- .... **CLC 39**
See also CA 29-32R; CANR 44

Mantecon, Juan Jimenez
See Jimenez (Mantecon), Juan Ramon

Manton, Peter
See Creasey, John

Man Without a Spleen, A
See Chekhov, Anton (Pavlovich)

Manzoni, Alessandro 1785-1873 .... **NCLC 29**

Map, Walter 1140-1209 .... **CMLC 32**

Mapu, Abraham (ben Jekutiel)
1808-1867 .... **NCLC 18**

Mara, Sally
See Queneau, Raymond

Marat, Jean Paul 1743-1793 .... **LC 10**

Marcel, Gabriel Honore 1889-1973 . **CLC 15**
See also CA 102; 45-48; MTCW 1, 2

March, William 1893-1954 .... **TCLC 96**

Marchbanks, Samuel
See Davies, (William) Robertson

Marchi, Giacomo
See Bassani, Giorgio

Margulies, Donald CLC 76
See also DLB 228

Marie de France c. 12th cent. - ..... **CMLC 8; PC 22**
See also DLB 208

Marie de l'Incarnation 1599-1672 ...... **LC 10**

Marier, Captain Victor
See Griffith, D(avid Lewelyn) W(ark)

Mariner, Scott
See Pohl, Frederik

Marinetti, Filippo Tommaso
1876-1944 .... **TCLC 10**
See also CA 107; DLB 114

Marivaux, Pierre Carlet de Chamblain de
1688-1763 .... **LC 4; DC 7**

Markandaya, Kamala CLC 8, 38
See also Taylor, Kamala (Purnaiya)

Markfield, Wallace 1926- .... **CLC 8**
See also CA 69-72; CAAS 3; DLB 2, 28

Markham, Edwin 1852-1940 .... **TCLC 47**
See also CA 160; DLB 54, 186

Markham, Robert
See Amis, Kingsley (William)

Marks, J
See Highwater, Jamake (Mamake)

Marks-Highwater, J
See Highwater, Jamake (Mamake)

Markson, David M(errill) 1927- .... **CLC 67**
See also CA 49-52; CANR 1, 91

Marley, Bob CLC 17
See also Marley, Robert Nesta

Marley, Robert Nesta 1945-1981
See Marley, Bob
See also CA 107; 103

Marlowe, Christopher 1564-1593 ...... **LC 22, 47; DA; DAB; DAC; DAM DRAM, MST; DC 1; WLC**
See also CDBLB Before 1660; DA3; DLB 62

Marlowe, Stephen 1928-
See Queen, Ellery
See also CA 13-16R; CANR 6, 55

Marmontel, Jean-Francois 1723-1799 .. **LC 2**

Marquand, John P(hillips)
1893-1960 .... **CLC 2, 10**
See also CA 85-88; CANR 73; DLB 9, 102; MTCW 2

Marques, Rene 1919-1979 ..... **CLC 96; DAM MULT; HLC 2**
See also CA 97-100; 85-88; CANR 78; DLB 113; HW 1, 2

Marquez, Gabriel (Jose) Garcia
See Garcia Marquez, Gabriel (Jose)

Marquis, Don(ald Robert Perry)
1878-1937 .... **TCLC 7**
See also CA 104; 166; DLB 11, 25

Marric, J. J.
See Creasey, John

Marryat, Frederick 1792-1848 .... **NCLC 3**
See also DLB 21, 163

Marsden, James
See Creasey, John

Marsh, Edward 1872-1953 .... **TCLC 99**

Marsh, (Edith) Ngaio 1899-1982 .... **CLC 7, 53; DAM POP**
See also CA 9-12R; CANR 6, 58; DLB 77; MTCW 1, 2

Marshall, Garry 1934- .... **CLC 17**
See also AAYA 3; CA 111; SATA 60

Marshall, Paule 1929- .. **CLC 27, 72; BLC 3; DAM MULT; SSC 3**
See also BW 2, 3; CA 77-80; CANR 25, 73; DA3; DLB 33, 157, 227; MTCW 1, 2

Marshallik
See Zangwill, Israel

Marsten, Richard
  See Hunter, Evan
Marston, John 1576-1634 .... **LC 33; DAM
    DRAM**
  See also DLB 58, 172
Martha, Henry
  See Harris, Mark
Marti (y Perez), Jose (Julian)
    1853-1895 ...... **NCLC 63; DAM MULT;
    HLC 2**
  See also HW 2
Martial c. 40-c. 104 .... **CMLC 35; PC 10**
  See also DLB 211
Martin, Ken
  See Hubbard, L(afayette) Ron(ald)
Martin, Richard
  See Creasey, John
Martin, Steve 1945- .... **CLC 30**
  See also CA 97-100; CANR 30; MTCW 1
Martin, Valerie 1948- .... **CLC 89**
  See also BEST 90:2; CA 85-88; CANR 49,
    89
Martin, Violet Florence
    1862-1915 .... **TCLC 51**
Martin, Webber
  See Silverberg, Robert
Martindale, Patrick Victor
  See White, Patrick (Victor Martindale)
Martin du Gard, Roger
    1881-1958 .... **TCLC 24**
  See also CA 118; DLB 65
Martineau, Harriet 1802-1876 .... **NCLC 26**
  See also DLB 21, 55, 159, 163, 166, 190;
    YABC 2
Martines, Julia
  See O'Faolain, Julia
Martinez, Enrique Gonzalez
  See Gonzalez Martinez, Enrique
Martinez, Jacinto Benavente y
  See Benavente (y Martinez), Jacinto
Martinez Ruiz, Jose 1873-1967
  See Azorin; Ruiz, Jose Martinez
  See also CA 93-96; HW 1
Martinez Sierra, Gregorio
    1881-1947 .... **TCLC 6**
  See also CA 115
Martinez Sierra, Maria (de la O'LeJarraga)
    1874-1974 .... **TCLC 6**
  See also CA 115
Martinsen, Martin
  See Follett, Ken(neth Martin)
Martinson, Harry (Edmund)
    1904-1978 .... **CLC 14**
  See also CA 77-80; CANR 34
Marut, Ret
  See Traven, B.
Marut, Robert
  See Traven, B.
Marvell, Andrew 1621-1678 .. **LC 4, 43; DA;
    DAB; DAC; DAM MST, POET; PC
    10; WLC**
  See also CDBLB 1660-1789; DLB 131
Marx, Karl (Heinrich) 1818-1883 . **NCLC 17**
  See also DLB 129
Masaoka Shiki **TCLC 18**
  See also Masaoka Tsunenori
Masaoka Tsunenori 1867-1902
  See Masaoka Shiki
  See also CA 117
Masefield, John (Edward)
    1878-1967 ..... **CLC 11, 47; DAM POET**
  See also CA 19-20; 25-28R; CANR 33;
    CAP 2; CDBLB 1890-1914; DLB 10, 19,
    153, 160; MTCW 1, 2; SATA 19
Maso, Carole 19(?)- .... **CLC 44**
  See also CA 170

Mason, Bobbie Ann 1940- ... **CLC 28, 43, 82;
    SSC 4**
  See also AAYA 5; CA 53-56; CANR 11, 31,
    58, 83; CDALBS; DA3; DLB 173; DLBY
    87; INT CANR-31; MTCW 1, 2
Mason, Ernst
  See Pohl, Frederik
Mason, Lee W.
  See Malzberg, Barry N(athaniel)
Mason, Nick 1945- .... **CLC 35**
Mason, Tally
  See Derleth, August (William)
Mass, William
  See Gibson, William
Master Lao
  See Lao Tzu
Masters, Edgar Lee 1868-1950 .... **TCLC 2,
    25; DA; DAC; DAM MST, POET; PC
    1; WLCS**
  See also CA 104; 133; CDALB 1865-1917;
    DLB 54; MTCW 1, 2
Masters, Hilary 1928- .... **CLC 48**
  See also CA 25-28R; CANR 13, 47
Mastrosimone, William 19(?)- .... **CLC 36**
  See also CA 186
Mathe, Albert
  See Camus, Albert
Mather, Cotton 1663-1728 .... **LC 38**
  See also CDALB 1640-1865; DLB 24, 30,
    140
Mather, Increase 1639-1723 .... **LC 38**
  See also DLB 24
Matheson, Richard Burton 1926- .... **CLC 37**
  See also AAYA 31; CA 97-100; CANR 88;
    DLB 8, 44; INT 97-100
Mathews, Harry 1930- .... **CLC 6, 52**
  See also CA 21-24R; CAAS 6; CANR 18,
    40
Mathews, John Joseph 1894-1979 .. **CLC 84;
    DAM MULT**
  See also CA 19-20; 142; CANR 45; CAP 2;
    DLB 175; NNAL
Mathias, Roland (Glyn) 1915- .... **CLC 45**
  See also CA 97-100; CANR 19, 41; DLB
    27
Matsuo Basho 1644-1694 .... **PC 3**
  See also DAM POET
Mattheson, Rodney
  See Creasey, John
Matthews, (James) Brander
    1852-1929 .... **TCLC 95**
  See also DLB 71, 78; DLBD 13
Matthews, Greg 1949- .... **CLC 45**
  See also CA 135
Matthews, William (Procter, III)
    1942-1997 .... **CLC 40**
  See also CA 29-32R; 162; CAAS 18; CANR
    12, 57; DLB 5
Matthias, John (Edward) 1941- .... **CLC 9**
  See also CA 33-36R; CANR 56
Matthiessen, F(rancis) O(tto)
    1902-1950 .... **TCLC 100**
  See also CA 185; DLB 63
Matthiessen, Peter 1927- ... **CLC 5, 7, 11, 32,
    64; DAM NOV**
  See also AAYA 6; BEST 90:4; CA 9-12R;
    CANR 21, 50, 73; DA3; DLB 6, 173;
    MTCW 1, 2; SATA 27
Maturin, Charles Robert
    1780(?)-1824 .... **NCLC 6**
  See also DLB 178
Matute (Ausejo), Ana Maria 1925- .. **CLC 11**
  See also CA 89-92; MTCW 1
Maugham, W. S.
  See Maugham, W(illiam) Somerset

Maugham, W(illiam) Somerset
    1874-1965 ... **CLC 1, 11, 15, 67, 93; DA;
    DAB; DAC; DAM DRAM, MST, NOV;
    SSC 8; WLC**
  See also CA 5-8R; 25-28R; CANR 40; CD-
    BLB 1914-1945; DA3; DLB 10, 36, 77,
    100, 162, 195; MTCW 1, 2; SATA 54
Maugham, William Somerset
  See Maugham, W(illiam) Somerset
Maupassant, (Henri Rene Albert) Guy de
    1850-1893 . **NCLC 1, 42, 83; DA; DAB;
    DAC; DAM MST; SSC 1; WLC**
  See also DA3; DLB 123
Maupin, Armistead 1944- ..... **CLC 95; DAM
    POP**
  See also CA 125; 130; CANR 58; DA3;
    INT 130; MTCW 2
Maurhut, Richard
  See Traven, B.
Mauriac, Claude 1914-1996 .... **CLC 9**
  See also CA 89-92; 152; DLB 83
Mauriac, Francois (Charles)
    1885-1970 .... **CLC 4, 9, 56; SSC 24**
  See also CA 25-28; CAP 2; DLB 65;
    MTCW 1, 2
Mavor, Osborne Henry 1888-1951
  See Bridie, James
  See also CA 104
Maxwell, William (Keepers, Jr.)
    1908- .... **CLC 19**
  See also CA 93-96; CANR 54; DLBY 80;
    INT 93-96
May, Elaine 1932- .... **CLC 16**
  See also CA 124; 142; DLB 44
Mayakovski, Vladimir (Vladimirovich)
    1893-1930 .... **TCLC 4, 18**
  See also CA 104; 158; MTCW 2
Mayhew, Henry 1812-1887 .... **NCLC 31**
  See also DLB 18, 55, 190
Mayle, Peter 1939(?)- .... **CLC 89**
  See also CA 139; CANR 64
Maynard, Joyce 1953- .... **CLC 23**
  See also CA 111; 129; CANR 64
Mayne, William (James Carter)
    1928- .... **CLC 12**
  See also AAYA 20; CA 9-12R; CANR 37,
    80; CLR 25; JRDA; MAICYA; SAAS 11;
    SATA 6, 68
Mayo, Jim
  See L'Amour, Louis (Dearborn)
Maysles, Albert 1926- .... **CLC 16**
  See also CA 29-32R
Maysles, David 1932- .... **CLC 16**
Mazer, Norma Fox 1931- .... **CLC 26**
  See also AAYA 5; CA 69-72; CANR 12,
    32, 66; CLR 23; JRDA; MAICYA; SAAS
    1; SATA 24, 67, 105
Mazzini, Guiseppe 1805-1872 .... **NCLC 34**
McAlmon, Robert (Menzies)
    1895-1956 .... **TCLC 97**
  See also CA 107; 168; DLB 4, 45; DLBD
    15
McAuley, James Phillip 1917-1976 .. **CLC 45**
  See also CA 97-100
McBain, Ed
  See Hunter, Evan
McBrien, William (Augustine)
    1930- .... **CLC 44**
  See also CA 107; CANR 90
McCabe, Patrick 1955- .... **CLC 133**
  See also CA 130; CANR 50, 90; DLB 194
McCaffrey, Anne (Inez) 1926- .... **CLC 17;
    DAM NOV, POP**
  See also AAYA 6, 34; AITN 2; BEST 89:2;
    CA 25-28R; CANR 15, 35, 55; CLR 49;
    DA3; DLB 8; JRDA; MAICYA; MTCW
    1, 2; SAAS 11; SATA 8, 70, 116
McCall, Nathan 1955(?)- .... **CLC 86**
  See also BW 3; CA 146; CANR 88

McCann, Arthur
See Campbell, John W(ood, Jr.)
McCann, Edson
See Pohl, Frederik
McCarthy, Charles, Jr. 1933-
See McCarthy, Cormac
See also CANR 42, 69; DAM POP; DA3;
MTCW 2
McCarthy, Cormac 1933- ...... **CLC 4, 57, 59,
101**
See also McCarthy, Charles, Jr.
See also DLB 6, 143; MTCW 2
McCarthy, Mary (Therese)
1912-1989 .. **CLC 1, 3, 5, 14, 24, 39, 59;
SSC 24**
See also CA 5-8R; 129; CANR 16, 50, 64;
DA3; DLB 2; DLBY 81; INT CANR-16;
MTCW 1, 2
McCartney, (James) Paul 1942- . **CLC 12, 35**
See also CA 146
McCauley, Stephen (D.) 1955- .... **CLC 50**
See also CA 141
McClure, Michael (Thomas) 1932- ... **CLC 6,
10**
See also CA 21-24R; CANR 17, 46, 77;
DLB 16
McCorkle, Jill (Collins) 1958- .... **CLC 51**
See also CA 121; DLBY 87
McCourt, Frank 1930- .... **CLC 109**
See also CA 157
McCourt, James 1941- .... **CLC 5**
See also CA 57-60
McCourt, Malachy 1932- .... **CLC 119**
McCoy, Horace (Stanley)
1897-1955 .... **TCLC 28**
See also CA 108; 155; DLB 9
McCrae, John 1872-1918 .... **TCLC 12**
See also CA 109; DLB 92
McCreigh, James
See Pohl, Frederik
McCullers, (Lula) Carson (Smith)
1917-1967 .... **CLC 1, 4, 10, 12, 48, 100;
DA; DAB; DAC; DAM MST, NOV;
SSC 9, 24; WLC**
See also AAYA 21; CA 5-8R; 25-28R;
CABS 1, 3; CANR 18; CDALB 1941-
1968; DA3; DLB 2, 7, 173, 228; MTCW
1, 2; SATA 27
McCulloch, John Tyler
See Burroughs, Edgar Rice
McCullough, Colleen 1938(?)- .... **CLC 27,
107; DAM NOV, POP**
See also CA 81-84; CANR 17, 46, 67; DA3;
MTCW 1, 2
McDermott, Alice 1953- .... **CLC 90**
See also CA 109; CANR 40, 90
McElroy, Joseph 1930- .... **CLC 5, 47**
See also CA 17-20R
McEwan, Ian (Russell) 1948- .... **CLC 13, 66;
DAM NOV**
See also BEST 90:4; CA 61-64; CANR 14,
41, 69, 87; DLB 14, 194; MTCW 1, 2
McFadden, David 1940- .... **CLC 48**
See also CA 104; DLB 60; INT 104
McFarland, Dennis 1950- .... **CLC 65**
See also CA 165
McGahern, John 1934- ... **CLC 5, 9, 48; SSC
17**
See also CA 17-20R; CANR 29, 68; DLB
14; MTCW 1
McGinley, Patrick (Anthony) 1937- . **CLC 41**
See also CA 120; 127; CANR 56; INT 127
McGinley, Phyllis 1905-1978 .... **CLC 14**
See also CA 9-12R; 77-80; CANR 19; DLB
11, 48; SATA 2, 44; SATA-Obit 24
McGinniss, Joe 1942- .... **CLC 32**
See also AITN 2; BEST 89:2; CA 25-28R;
CANR 26, 70; DLB 185; INT CANR-26

McGivern, Maureen Daly
See Daly, Maureen
McGrath, Patrick 1950- .... **CLC 55**
See also CA 136; CANR 65
McGrath, Thomas (Matthew)
1916-1990 ..... **CLC 28, 59; DAM POET**
See also CA 9-12R; 132; CANR 6, 33;
MTCW 1; SATA 41; SATA-Obit 66
McGuane, Thomas (Francis III)
1939- .... **CLC 3, 7, 18, 45, 127**
See also AITN 2; CA 49-52; CANR 5, 24,
49; DLB 2, 212; DLBY 80; INT CANR-
24; MTCW 1
McGuckian, Medbh 1950- .... **CLC 48; DAM
POET; PC 27**
See also CA 143; DLB 40
McHale, Tom 1942(?)-1982 .... **CLC 3, 5**
See also AITN 1; CA 77-80; 106
McIlvanney, William 1936- .... **CLC 42**
See also CA 25-28R; CANR 61; DLB 14,
207
McIlwraith, Maureen Mollie Hunter
See Hunter, Mollie
See also SATA 2
McInerney, Jay 1955- .... **CLC 34, 112; DAM
POP**
See also AAYA 18; CA 116; 123; CANR
45, 68; DA3; INT 123; MTCW 2
McIntyre, Vonda N(eel) 1948- .... **CLC 18**
See also CA 81-84; CANR 17, 34, 69;
MTCW 1
McKay, Claude **TCLC 7, 41; BLC 3; DAB;
PC 2**
See also McKay, Festus Claudius
See also DLB 4, 45, 51, 117
McKay, Festus Claudius 1889-1948
See McKay, Claude
See also BW 1, 3; CA 104; 124; CANR 73;
DA; DAC; DAM MST, MULT, NOV,
POET; MTCW 1, 2; WLC
McKuen, Rod 1933- .... **CLC 1, 3**
See also AITN 1; CA 41-44R; CANR 40
McLoughlin, R. B.
See Mencken, H(enry) L(ouis)
McLuhan, (Herbert) Marshall
1911-1980 .... **CLC 37, 83**
See also CA 9-12R; 102; CANR 12, 34, 61;
DLB 88; INT CANR-12; MTCW 1
McMillan, Terry (L.) 1951- .... **CLC 50, 61,
112; BLCS; DAM MULT, NOV, POP**
See also AAYA 21; BW 2, 3; CA 140;
CANR 60; DA3; MTCW 1
McMurtry, Larry (Jeff) 1936- .. **CLC 2, 3, 7,
11, 27, 44, 127; DAM NOV, POP**
See also AAYA 15; AITN 2; BEST 89:2;
CA 5-8R; CANR 19, 43, 64; CDALB
1968-1988; DA3; DLB 2, 143; DLBY 80,
87; MTCW 1, 2
McNally, T. M. 1961- .... **CLC 82**
McNally, Terrence 1939- ... **CLC 4, 7, 41, 91;
DAM DRAM**
See also CA 45-48; CANR 2, 56; DA3;
DLB 7; MTCW 2
McNamer, Deirdre 1950- .... **CLC 70**
McNeal, Tom **CLC 119**
McNeile, Herman Cyril 1888-1937
See Sapper
See also CA 184; DLB 77
McNickle, (William) D'Arcy
1904-1977 .... **CLC 89; DAM MULT**
See also CA 9-12R; 85-88; CANR 5, 45;
DLB 175, 212; NNAL; SATA-Obit 22
McPhee, John (Angus) 1931- .... **CLC 36**
See also BEST 90:1; CA 65-68; CANR 20,
46, 64, 69; DLB 185; MTCW 1, 2
McPherson, James Alan 1943- .. **CLC 19, 77;
BLCS**
See also BW 1, 3; CA 25-28R; CAAS 17;
CANR 24, 74; DLB 38; MTCW 1, 2

McPherson, William (Alexander)
1933- .... **CLC 34**
See also CA 69-72; CANR 28; INT
CANR-28
Mead, George Herbert 1873-1958 . **TCLC 89**
Mead, Margaret 1901-1978 .... **CLC 37**
See also AITN 1; CA 1-4R; 81-84; CANR
4; DA3; MTCW 1, 2; SATA-Obit 20
Meaker, Marijane (Agnes) 1927-
See Kerr, M. E.
See also CA 107; CANR 37, 63; INT 107;
JRDA; MAICYA; MTCW 1; SATA 20,
61, 99; SATA-Essay 111
Medoff, Mark (Howard) 1940- ... **CLC 6, 23;
DAM DRAM**
See also AITN 1; CA 53-56; CANR 5; DLB
7; INT CANR-5
Medvedev, P. N.
See Bakhtin, Mikhail Mikhailovich
Meged, Aharon
See Megged, Aharon
Meged, Aron
See Megged, Aharon
Megged, Aharon 1920- .... **CLC 9**
See also CA 49-52; CAAS 13; CANR 1
Mehta, Ved (Parkash) 1934- .... **CLC 37**
See also CA 1-4R; CANR 2, 23, 69; MTCW
1
Melanter
See Blackmore, R(ichard) D(oddridge)
Melies, Georges 1861-1938 .... **TCLC 81**
Melikow, Loris
See Hofmannsthal, Hugo von
Melmoth, Sebastian
See Wilde, Oscar (Fingal O'Flahertie Wills)
Meltzer, Milton 1915- .... **CLC 26**
See also AAYA 8; CA 13-16R; CANR 38,
92; CLR 13; DLB 61; JRDA; MAICYA;
SAAS 1; SATA 1, 50, 80
Melville, Herman 1819-1891 ..... **NCLC 3, 12,
29, 45, 49, 91; DA; DAB; DAC; DAM
MST, NOV; SSC 1, 17; WLC**
See also AAYA 25; CDALB 1640-1865;
DA3; DLB 3, 74; SATA 59
Menander c. 342B.C.-c. 292B.C. ... **CMLC 9;
DAM DRAM; DC 3**
See also DLB 176
Menchu, Rigoberta 1959-
See also HLCS 2
Menchu, Rigoberta 1959-
See also CA 175; HLCS 2
Mencken, H(enry) L(ouis)
1880-1956 .... **TCLC 13**
See also CA 105; 125; CDALB 1917-1929;
DLB 11, 29, 63, 137; MTCW 1, 2
Mendelsohn, Jane 1965(?)- .... **CLC 99**
See also CA 154
Mercer, David 1928-1980 .... **CLC 5; DAM
DRAM**
See also CA 9-12R; 102; CANR 23; DLB
13; MTCW 1
Merchant, Paul
See Ellison, Harlan (Jay)
Meredith, George 1828-1909 .. **TCLC 17, 43;
DAM POET**
See also CA 117; 153; CANR 80; CDBLB
1832-1890; DLB 18, 35, 57, 159
Meredith, William (Morris) 1919- .... **CLC 4,
13, 22, 55; DAM POET; PC 28**
See also CA 9-12R; CAAS 14; CANR 6,
40; DLB 5
Merezhkovsky, Dmitry Sergeyevich
1865-1941 .... **TCLC 29**
See also CA 169
Merimee, Prosper 1803-1870 ... **NCLC 6, 65;
SSC 7**
See also DLB 119, 192
Merkin, Daphne 1954- .... **CLC 44**
See also CA 123

Merlin, Arthur
See Blish, James (Benjamin)

Merrill, James (Ingram) 1926-1995 .. **CLC 2, 3, 6, 8, 13, 18, 34, 91; DAM POET; PC 28**
See also CA 13-16R; 147; CANR 10, 49, 63; DA3; DLB 5, 165; DLBY 85; INT CANR-10; MTCW 1, 2

Merriman, Alex
See Silverberg, Robert

Merriman, Brian 1747-1805 .... **NCLC 70**

Merritt, E. B.
See Waddington, Miriam

Merton, Thomas 1915-1968 ..... **CLC 1, 3, 11, 34, 83; PC 10**
See also CA 5-8R; 25-28R; CANR 22, 53; DA3; DLB 48; DLBY 81; MTCW 1, 2

Merwin, W(illiam) S(tanley) 1927- ... **CLC 1, 2, 3, 5, 8, 13, 18, 45, 88; DAM POET**
See also CA 13-16R; CANR 15, 51; DA3; DLB 5, 169; INT CANR-15; MTCW 1, 2

Metcalf, John 1938- .... **CLC 37**
See also CA 113; DLB 60

Metcalf, Suzanne
See Baum, L(yman) Frank

Mew, Charlotte (Mary) 1870-1928 .. **TCLC 8**
See also CA 105; DLB 19, 135

Mewshaw, Michael 1943- .... **CLC 9**
See also CA 53-56; CANR 7, 47; DLBY 80

Meyer, Conrad Ferdinand
1825-1905 .... **NCLC 81**
See also DLB 129

Meyer, June
See Jordan, June

Meyer, Lynn
See Slavitt, David R(ytman)

Meyer-Meyrink, Gustav 1868-1932
See Meyrink, Gustav
See also CA 117

Meyers, Jeffrey 1939- .... **CLC 39**
See also CA 73-76; CAAE 186; CANR 54; DLB 111

Meynell, Alice (Christina Gertrude Thompson) 1847-1922 .... **TCLC 6**
See also CA 104; 177; DLB 19, 98

Meyrink, Gustav **TCLC 21**
See also Meyer-Meyrink, Gustav
See also DLB 81

Michaels, Leonard 1933- .... **CLC 6, 25; SSC 16**
See also CA 61-64; CANR 21, 62; DLB 130; MTCW 1

Michaux, Henri 1899-1984 .... **CLC 8, 19**
See also CA 85-88; 114

Micheaux, Oscar (Devereaux)
1884-1951 .... **TCLC 76**
See also BW 3; CA 174; DLB 50

Michelangelo 1475-1564 .... **LC 12**

Michelet, Jules 1798-1874 .... **NCLC 31**

Michels, Robert 1876-1936 .... **TCLC 88**

Michener, James A(lbert)
1907(?)-1997 .... **CLC 1, 5, 11, 29, 60, 109; DAM NOV, POP**
See also AAYA 27; AITN 1; BEST 90:1; CA 5-8R; 161; CANR 21, 45, 68; DA3; DLB 6; MTCW 1, 2

Mickiewicz, Adam 1798-1855 .... **NCLC 3**

Middleton, Christopher 1926- .... **CLC 13**
See also CA 13-16R; CANR 29, 54; DLB 40

Middleton, Richard (Barham)
1882-1911 .... **TCLC 56**
See also DLB 156

Middleton, Stanley 1919- .... **CLC 7, 38**
See also CA 25-28R; CAAS 23; CANR 21, 46, 81; DLB 14

Middleton, Thomas 1580-1627 .... **LC 33; DAM DRAM, MST; DC 5**
See also DLB 58

Migueis, Jose Rodrigues 1901- .... **CLC 10**

Mikszath, Kalman 1847-1910 .... **TCLC 31**
See also CA 170

Miles, Jack **CLC 100**

Miles, Josephine (Louise)
1911-1985 .. **CLC 1, 2, 14, 34, 39; DAM POET**
See also CA 1-4R; 116; CANR 2, 55; DLB 48

Militant
See Sandburg, Carl (August)

Mill, John Stuart 1806-1873 .... **NCLC 11, 58**
See also CDBLB 1832-1890; DLB 55, 190

Millar, Kenneth 1915-1983 ... **CLC 14; DAM POP**
See also Macdonald, Ross
See also CA 9-12R; 110; CANR 16, 63; DA3; DLB 2, 226; DLBD 6; DLBY 83; MTCW 1, 2

Millay, E. Vincent
See Millay, Edna St. Vincent

Millay, Edna St. Vincent
1892-1950 .... **TCLC 4, 49; DA; DAB; DAC; DAM MST, POET; PC 6; WLCS**
See also CA 104; 130; CDALB 1917-1929; DA3; DLB 45; MTCW 1, 2

Miller, Arthur 1915- ...... **CLC 1, 2, 6, 10, 15, 26, 47, 78; DA; DAB; DAC; DAM DRAM, MST; DC 1; WLC**
See also AAYA 15; AITN 1; CA 1-4R; CABS 3; CANR 2, 30, 54, 76; CDALB 1941-1968; DA3; DLB 7; MTCW 1, 2

Miller, Henry (Valentine)
1891-1980 .... **CLC 1, 2, 4, 9, 14, 43, 84; DA; DAB; DAC; DAM MST, NOV; WLC**
See also CA 9-12R; 97-100; CANR 33, 64; CDALB 1929-1941; DA3; DLB 4, 9; DLBY 80; MTCW 1, 2

Miller, Jason 1939(?)- .... **CLC 2**
See also AITN 1; CA 73-76; DLB 7

Miller, Sue 1943- .... **CLC 44; DAM POP**
See also BEST 90:3; CA 139; CANR 59, 91; DA3; DLB 143

Miller, Walter M(ichael, Jr.) 1923- ... **CLC 4, 30**
See also CA 85-88; DLB 8

Millett, Kate 1934- .... **CLC 67**
See also AITN 1; CA 73-76; CANR 32, 53, 76; DA3; MTCW 1, 2

Millhauser, Steven (Lewis) 1943- .... **CLC 21, 54, 109**
See also CA 110; 111; CANR 63; DA3; DLB 2; INT 111; MTCW 2

Millin, Sarah Gertrude 1889-1968 ... **CLC 49**
See also CA 102; 93-96; DLB 225

Milne, A(lan) A(lexander)
1882-1956 ..... **TCLC 6, 88; DAB; DAC; DAM MST**
See also CA 104; 133; CLR 1, 26; DA3; DLB 10, 77, 100, 160; MAICYA; MTCW 1, 2; SATA 100; YABC 1

Milner, Ron(ald) 1938- .... **CLC 56; BLC 3; DAM MULT**
See also AITN 1; BW 1; CA 73-76; CANR 24, 81; DLB 38; MTCW 1

Milnes, Richard Monckton
1809-1885 .... **NCLC 61**
See also DLB 32, 184

Milosz, Czeslaw 1911- ...... **CLC 5, 11, 22, 31, 56, 82; DAM MST, POET; PC 8; WLCS**
See also CA 81-84; CANR 23, 51, 91; DA3; MTCW 1, 2

Milton, John 1608-1674 .... **LC 9, 43; DA; DAB; DAC; DAM MST, POET; PC 19, 29; WLC**
See also CDBLB 1660-1789; DA3; DLB 131, 151

Min, Anchee 1957- .... **CLC 86**
See also CA 146

Minehaha, Cornelius
See Wedekind, (Benjamin) Frank(lin)

Miner, Valerie 1947- .... **CLC 40**
See also CA 97-100; CANR 59

Minimo, Duca
See D'Annunzio, Gabriele

Minot, Susan 1956- .... **CLC 44**
See also CA 134

Minus, Ed 1938- .... **CLC 39**
See also CA 185

Miranda, Javier
See Bioy Casares, Adolfo

Miranda, Javier
See Bioy Casares, Adolfo

Mirbeau, Octave 1848-1917 .... **TCLC 55**
See also DLB 123, 192

Miro (Ferrer), Gabriel (Francisco Victor)
1879-1930 .... **TCLC 5**
See also CA 104; 185

Mishima, Yukio 1925-1970 .... **CLC 2, 4, 6, 9, 27; DC 1; SSC 4**
See also Hiraoka, Kimitake
See also DLB 182; MTCW 2

Mistral, Frederic 1830-1914 .... **TCLC 51**
See also CA 122

Mistral, Gabriela **TCLC 2; HLC 2**
See also Godoy Alcayaga, Lucila
See also MTCW 2

Mistry, Rohinton 1952- .... **CLC 71; DAC**
See also CA 141; CANR 86

Mitchell, Clyde
See Ellison, Harlan (Jay); Silverberg, Robert

Mitchell, James Leslie 1901-1935
See Gibbon, Lewis Grassic
See also CA 104; DLB 15

Mitchell, Joni 1943- .... **CLC 12**
See also CA 112

Mitchell, Joseph (Quincy)
1908-1996 .... **CLC 98**
See also CA 77-80; 152; CANR 69; DLB 185; DLBY 96

Mitchell, Margaret (Munnerlyn)
1900-1949 . **TCLC 11; DAM NOV, POP**
See also AAYA 23; CA 109; 125; CANR 55; CDALBS; DA3; DLB 9; MTCW 1, 2

Mitchell, Peggy
See Mitchell, Margaret (Munnerlyn)

Mitchell, S(ilas) Weir 1829-1914 .... **TCLC 36**
See also CA 165; DLB 202

Mitchell, W(illiam) O(rmond)
1914-1998 .. **CLC 25; DAC; DAM MST**
See also CA 77-80; 165; CANR 15, 43; DLB 88

Mitchell, William 1879-1936 .... **TCLC 81**

Mitford, Mary Russell 1787-1855 ... **NCLC 4**
See also DLB 110, 116

Mitford, Nancy 1904-1973 .... **CLC 44**
See also CA 9-12R; DLB 191

Miyamoto, (Chujo) Yuriko
1899-1951 .... **TCLC 37**
See also CA 170, 174; DLB 180

Miyazawa, Kenji 1896-1933 .... **TCLC 76**
See also CA 157

Mizoguchi, Kenji 1898-1956 .... **TCLC 72**
See also CA 167

Mo, Timothy (Peter) 1950(?)- ... **CLC 46, 134**
See also CA 117; DLB 194; MTCW 1

Modarressi, Taghi (M.) 1931- .... **CLC 44**
See also CA 121; 134; INT 134

Modiano, Patrick (Jean) 1945- .... **CLC 18**
    See also CA 85-88; CANR 17, 40; DLB 83
Moerck, Paal
    See Roelvaag, O(le) E(dvart)
Mofolo, Thomas (Mokopu)
    1875(?)-1948 .. **TCLC 22; BLC 3; DAM MULT**
    See also CA 121; 153; CANR 83; DLB 225; MTCW 2
Mohr, Nicholasa 1938- .... **CLC 12; DAM MULT; HLC 2**
    See also AAYA 8; CA 49-52; CANR 1, 32, 64; CLR 22; DLB 145; HW 1, 2; JRDA; SAAS 8; SATA 8, 97; SATA-Essay 113
Mojtabai, A(nn) G(race) 1938- ..... **CLC 5, 9, 15, 29**
    See also CA 85-88; CANR 88
Moliere 1622-1673 ..... **LC 10, 28; DA; DAB; DAC; DAM DRAM, MST; DC 13; WLC**
    See also DA3
Molin, Charles
    See Mayne, William (James Carter)
Molnar, Ferenc 1878-1952 .. **TCLC 20; DAM DRAM**
    See also CA 109; 153; CANR 83
Momaday, N(avarre) Scott 1934- ...... **CLC 2, 19, 85, 95; DA; DAB; DAC; DAM MST, MULT, NOV, POP; PC 25; WLCS**
    See also AAYA 11; CA 25-28R; CANR 14, 34, 68; CDALBS; DA3; DLB 143, 175; INT CANR-14; MTCW 1, 2; NNAL; SATA 48; SATA-Brief 30
Monette, Paul 1945-1995 .... **CLC 82**
    See also CA 139; 147
Monroe, Harriet 1860-1936 .... **TCLC 12**
    See also CA 109; DLB 54, 91
Monroe, Lyle
    See Heinlein, Robert A(nson)
Montagu, Elizabeth 1720-1800 .... **NCLC 7**
Montagu, Elizabeth 1917- .... **NCLC 7**
    See also CA 9-12R
Montagu, Mary (Pierrepont) Wortley
    1689-1762 .... **LC 9, 57; PC 16**
    See also DLB 95, 101
Montagu, W. H.
    See Coleridge, Samuel Taylor
Montague, John (Patrick) 1929- ..... **CLC 13, 46**
    See also CA 9-12R; CANR 9, 69; DLB 40; MTCW 1
Montaigne, Michel (Eyquem) de
    1533-1592 .... **LC 8; DA; DAB; DAC; DAM MST; WLC**
Montale, Eugenio 1896-1981 ... **CLC 7, 9, 18; PC 13**
    See also CA 17-20R; 104; CANR 30; DLB 114; MTCW 1
Montesquieu, Charles-Louis de Secondat
    1689-1755 .... **LC 7**
Montgomery, (Robert) Bruce 1921(?)-1978
    See Crispin, Edmund
    See also CA 179; 104
Montgomery, L(ucy) M(aud)
    1874-1942 .... **TCLC 51; DAC; DAM MST**
    See also AAYA 12; CA 108; 137; CLR 8; DA3; DLB 92; DLBD 14; JRDA; MAICYA; MTCW 2; SATA 100; YABC 1
Montgomery, Marion H., Jr. 1925- .... **CLC 7**
    See also AITN 1; CA 1-4R; CANR 3, 48; DLB 6
Montgomery, Max
    See Davenport, Guy (Mattison, Jr.)
Montherlant, Henry (Milon) de
    1896-1972 ..... **CLC 8, 19; DAM DRAM**
    See also CA 85-88; 37-40R; DLB 72; MTCW 1

Monty Python
    See Chapman, Graham; Cleese, John (Marwood); Gilliam, Terry (Vance); Idle, Eric; Jones, Terence Graham Parry; Palin, Michael (Edward)
    See also AAYA 7
Moodie, Susanna (Strickland)
    1803-1885 .... **NCLC 14**
    See also DLB 99
Mooney, Edward 1951-
    See Mooney, Ted
    See also CA 130
Mooney, Ted CLC 25
    See also Mooney, Edward
Moorcock, Michael (John) 1939- ...... **CLC 5, 27, 58**
    See also Bradbury, Edward P.
    See also AAYA 26; CA 45-48; CAAS 5; CANR 2, 17, 38, 64; DLB 14; MTCW 1, 2; SATA 93
Moore, Brian 1921-1999 ... **CLC 1, 3, 5, 7, 8, 19, 32, 90; DAB; DAC; DAM MST**
    See also CA 1-4R; 174; CANR 1, 25, 42, 63; MTCW 1, 2
Moore, Edward
    See Muir, Edwin
Moore, G. E. 1873-1958 .... **TCLC 89**
Moore, George Augustus
    1852-1933 .... **TCLC 7; SSC 19**
    See also CA 104; 177; DLB 10, 18, 57, 135
Moore, Lorrie CLC 39, 45, 68
    See also Moore, Marie Lorena
Moore, Marianne (Craig)
    1887-1972 .... **CLC 1, 2, 4, 8, 10, 13, 19, 47; DA; DAB; DAC; DAM MST, POET; PC 4; WLCS**
    See also CA 1-4R; 33-36R; CANR 3, 61; CDALB 1929-1941; DA3; DLB 45; DLBD 7; MTCW 1, 2; SATA 20
Moore, Marie Lorena 1957-
    See Moore, Lorrie
    See also CA 116; CANR 39, 83
Moore, Thomas 1779-1852 .... **NCLC 6**
    See also DLB 96, 144
Moorhouse, Frank 1938- .... **SSC 40**
    See also CA 118; CANR 92
Mora, Pat(ricia) 1942-
    See also CA 129; CANR 57, 81; CLR 58; DAM MULT; DLB 209; HLC 2; HW 1, 2; SATA 92
Moraga, Cherrie 1952- .... **CLC 126; DAM MULT**
    See also CA 131; CANR 66; DLB 82; HW 1, 2
Morand, Paul 1888-1976 .... **CLC 41; SSC 22**
    See also CA 184; 69-72; DLB 65
Morante, Elsa 1918-1985 .... **CLC 8, 47**
    See also CA 85-88; 117; CANR 35; DLB 177; MTCW 1, 2
Moravia, Alberto 1907-1990 .... **CLC 2, 7, 11, 27, 46; SSC 26**
    See also Pincherle, Alberto
    See also DLB 177; MTCW 2
More, Hannah 1745-1833 .... **NCLC 27**
    See also DLB 107, 109, 116, 158
More, Henry 1614-1687 .... **LC 9**
    See also DLB 126
More, Sir Thomas 1478-1535 .... **LC 10, 32**
Moreas, Jean TCLC 18
    See also Papadiamantopoulos, Johannes
Morgan, Berry 1919- .... **CLC 6**
    See also CA 49-52; DLB 6
Morgan, Claire
    See Highsmith, (Mary) Patricia
Morgan, Edwin (George) 1920- .... **CLC 31**
    See also CA 5-8R; CANR 3, 43, 90; DLB 27
Morgan, (George) Frederick 1922- .. **CLC 23**
    See also CA 17-20R; CANR 21

Morgan, Harriet
    See Mencken, H(enry) L(ouis)
Morgan, Jane
    See Cooper, James Fenimore
Morgan, Janet 1945- .... **CLC 39**
    See also CA 65-68
Morgan, Lady 1776(?)-1859 .... **NCLC 29**
    See also DLB 116, 158
Morgan, Robin (Evonne) 1941- .... **CLC 2**
    See also CA 69-72; CANR 29, 68; MTCW 1; SATA 80
Morgan, Scott
    See Kuttner, Henry
Morgan, Seth 1949(?)-1990 .... **CLC 65**
    See also CA 185; 132
Morgenstern, Christian 1871-1914 .. **TCLC 8**
    See also CA 105
Morgenstern, S.
    See Goldman, William (W.)
Moricz, Zsigmond 1879-1942 .... **TCLC 33**
    See also CA 165
Morike, Eduard (Friedrich)
    1804-1875 .... **NCLC 10**
    See also DLB 133
Moritz, Karl Philipp 1756-1793 .... **LC 2**
    See also DLB 94
Morland, Peter Henry
    See Faust, Frederick (Schiller)
Morley, Christopher (Darlington)
    1890-1957 .... **TCLC 87**
    See also CA 112; DLB 9
Morren, Theophil
    See Hofmannsthal, Hugo von
Morris, Bill 1952- .... **CLC 76**
Morris, Julian
    See West, Morris L(anglo)
Morris, Steveland Judkins 1950(?)-
    See Wonder, Stevie
    See also CA 111
Morris, William 1834-1896 .... **NCLC 4**
    See also CDBLB 1832-1890; DLB 18, 35, 57, 156, 178, 184
Morris, Wright 1910-1998 .. **CLC 1, 3, 7, 18, 37**
    See also CA 9-12R; 167; CANR 21, 81; DLB 2, 206; DLBY 81; MTCW 1, 2
Morrison, Arthur 1863-1945 .... **TCLC 72; SSC 40**
    See also CA 120; 157; DLB 70, 135, 197
Morrison, Chloe Anthony Wofford
    See Morrison, Toni
Morrison, James Douglas 1943-1971
    See Morrison, Jim
    See also CA 73-76; CANR 40
Morrison, Jim CLC 17
    See also Morrison, James Douglas
Morrison, Toni 1931- . **CLC 4, 10, 22, 55, 81, 87; BLC 3; DA; DAB; DAC; DAM MST, MULT, NOV, POP**
    See also AAYA 1, 22; BW 2, 3; CA 29-32R; CANR 27, 42, 67; CDALB 1968-1988; DA3; DLB 6, 33, 143; DLBY 81; MTCW 1, 2; SATA 57
Morrison, Van 1945- .... **CLC 21**
    See also CA 116; 168
Morrissy, Mary 1958- .... **CLC 99**
Mortimer, John (Clifford) 1923- ..... **CLC 28, 43; DAM DRAM, POP**
    See also CA 13-16R; CANR 21, 69; CDBLB 1960 to Present; DA3; DLB 13; INT CANR-21; MTCW 1, 2
Mortimer, Penelope (Ruth)
    1918-1999 .... **CLC 5**
    See also CA 57-60; CANR 45, 88
Morton, Anthony
    See Creasey, John

Mosca, Gaetano 1858-1941 .... **TCLC 75**
Mosher, Howard Frank 1943- .... **CLC 62**
  See also CA 139; CANR 65
Mosley, Nicholas 1923- .... **CLC 43, 70**
  See also CA 69-72; CANR 41, 60; DLB 14,
  207
Mosley, Walter 1952- .... **CLC 97; BLCS;**
  DAM MULT, POP
  See also AAYA 17; BW 2; CA 142; CANR
  57, 92; DA3; MTCW 2
Moss, Howard 1922-1987 ...... **CLC 7, 14, 45,**
  50; DAM POET
  See also CA 1-4R; 123; CANR 1, 44; DLB
  5
Mossgiel, Rab
  See Burns, Robert
Motion, Andrew (Peter) 1952- .... **CLC 47**
  See also CA 146; CANR 90; DLB 40
Motley, Willard (Francis)
  1909-1965 .... **CLC 18**
  See also BW 1; CA 117; 106; CANR 88;
  DLB 76, 143
Motoori, Norinaga 1730-1801 .... **NCLC 45**
Mott, Michael (Charles Alston)
  1930- .... **CLC 15, 34**
  See also CA 5-8R; CAAS 7; CANR 7, 29
Mountain Wolf Woman 1884-1960 .. **CLC 92**
  See also CA 144; CANR 90; NNAL
Moure, Erin 1955- .... **CLC 88**
  See also CA 113; DLB 60
Mowat, Farley (McGill) 1921- .... **CLC 26;**
  DAC; DAM MST
  See also AAYA 1; CA 1-4R; CANR 4, 24,
  42, 68; CLR 20; DLB 68; INT CANR-24;
  JRDA; MAICYA; MTCW 1, 2; SATA 3,
  55
Mowatt, Anna Cora 1819-1870 ..... **NCLC 74**
Moyers, Bill 1934- .... **CLC 74**
  See also AITN 2; CA 61-64; CANR 31, 52
Mphahlele, Es'kia
  See Mphahlele, Ezekiel
  See also DLB 125
Mphahlele, Ezekiel 1919- .... **CLC 25, 133;**
  BLC 3; DAM MULT
  See also Mphahlele, Es'kia
  See also BW 2, 3; CA 81-84; CANR 26,
  76; DA3; DLB 225; MTCW 2
Mqhayi, S(amuel) E(dward) K(rune Loliwe)
  1875-1945 ...... **TCLC 25; BLC 3; DAM**
  MULT
  See also CA 153; CANR 87
Mrozek, Slawomir 1930- .... **CLC 3, 13**
  See also CA 13-16R; CAAS 10; CANR 29;
  MTCW 1
Mrs. Belloc-Lowndes
  See Lowndes, Marie Adelaide (Belloc)
Mtwa, Percy (?)- .... **CLC 47**
Mueller, Lisel 1924- .... **CLC 13, 51**
  See also CA 93-96; DLB 105
Muir, Edwin 1887-1959 .... **TCLC 2, 87**
  See also CA 104; DLB 20, 100, 191
Muir, John 1838-1914 .... **TCLC 28**
  See also CA 165; DLB 186
Mujica Lainez, Manuel 1910-1984 ... **CLC 31**
  See also Lainez, Manuel Mujica
  See also CA 81-84; 112; CANR 32; HW 1
Mukherjee, Bharati 1940- ...... **CLC 53, 115;**
  DAM NOV; SSC 38
  See also BEST 89:2; CA 107; CANR 45,
  72; DLB 60; MTCW 1, 2
Muldoon, Paul 1951- .... **CLC 32, 72; DAM**
  POET
  See also CA 113; 129; CANR 52, 91; DLB
  40; INT 129
Mulisch, Harry 1927- .... **CLC 42**
  See also CA 9-12R; CANR 6, 26, 56

Mull, Martin 1943- .... **CLC 17**
  See also CA 105
Muller, Wilhelm NCLC 73
Mulock, Dinah Maria
  See Craik, Dinah Maria (Mulock)
Munford, Robert 1737(?)-1783 .... **LC 5**
  See also DLB 31
Mungo, Raymond 1946- .... **CLC 72**
  See also CA 49-52; CANR 2
Munro, Alice 1931- .... **CLC 6, 10, 19, 50, 95;**
  DAC; DAM MST, NOV; SSC 3;
  WLCS
  See also AITN 2; CA 33-36R; CANR 33,
  53, 75; DA3; DLB 53; MTCW 1, 2; SATA
  29
Munro, H(ector) H(ugh) 1870-1916
  See Saki
  See also CA 104; 130; CDBLB 1890-1914;
  DA; DAB; DAC; DAM MST, NOV; DA3;
  DLB 34, 162; MTCW 1, 2; WLC
Murdoch, (Jean) Iris 1919-1999 ... **CLC 1, 2,**
  3, 4, 6, 8, 11, 15, 22, 31, 51; DAB;
  DAC; DAM MST, NOV
  See also CA 13-16R; 179; CANR 8, 43, 68;
  CDBLB 1960 to Present; DA3; DLB 14,
  194; INT CANR-8; MTCW 1, 2
Murfree, Mary Noailles 1850-1922 ... **SSC 22**
  See also CA 122; 176; DLB 12, 74
Murnau, Friedrich Wilhelm
  See Plumpe, Friedrich Wilhelm
Murphy, Richard 1927- .... **CLC 41**
  See also CA 29-32R; DLB 40
Murphy, Sylvia 1937- .... **CLC 34**
  See also CA 121
Murphy, Thomas (Bernard) 1935- ... **CLC 51**
  See also CA 101
Murray, Albert L. 1916- .... **CLC 73**
  See also BW 2; CA 49-52; CANR 26, 52,
  78; DLB 38
Murray, Judith Sargent
  1751-1820 .... **NCLC 63**
  See also DLB 37, 200
Murray, Les(lie) A(llan) 1938- .... **CLC 40;**
  DAM POET
  See also CA 21-24R; CANR 11, 27, 56
Murry, J. Middleton
  See Murry, John Middleton
Murry, John Middleton
  1889-1957 .... **TCLC 16**
  See also CA 118; DLB 149
Musgrave, Susan 1951- .... **CLC 13, 54**
  See also CA 69-72; CANR 45, 84
Musil, Robert (Edler von)
  1880-1942 .... **TCLC 12, 68; SSC 18**
  See also CA 109; CANR 55, 84; DLB 81,
  124; MTCW 2
Muske, Carol 1945- .... **CLC 90**
  See also Muske-Dukes, Carol (Anne)
Muske-Dukes, Carol (Anne) 1945-
  See Muske, Carol
  See also CA 65-68; CANR 32, 70
Musset, (Louis Charles) Alfred de
  1810-1857 .... **NCLC 7**
  See also DLB 192
Mussolini, Benito (Amilcare Andrea)
  1883-1945 .... **TCLC 96**
  See also CA 116
My Brother's Brother
  See Chekhov, Anton (Pavlovich)
Myers, L(eopold) H(amilton)
  1881-1944 .... **TCLC 59**
  See also CA 157; DLB 15
Myers, Walter Dean 1937- ..... **CLC 35; BLC**
  3; DAM MULT, NOV
  See also AAYA 4, 23; BW 2; CA 33-36R;
  CANR 20, 42, 67; CLR 4, 16, 35; DLB
  33; INT CANR-20; JRDA; MAICYA;
  MTCW 2; SAAS 2; SATA 41, 71, 109;
  SATA-Brief 27

Myers, Walter M.
  See Myers, Walter Dean
Myles, Symon
  See Follett, Ken(neth Martin)
Nabokov, Vladimir (Vladimirovich)
  1899-1977 .... **CLC 1, 2, 3, 6, 8, 11, 15,**
  23, 44, 46, 64; DA; DAB; DAC; DAM
  MST, NOV; SSC 11; WLC
  See also CA 5-8R; 69-72; CANR 20;
  CDALB 1941-1968; DA3; DLB 2; DLBD
  3; DLBY 80, 91; MTCW 1, 2
Naevius c. 265B.C.-201B.C. .... **CMLC 37**
  See also DLB 211
Nagai Kafu 1879-1959 .... **TCLC 51**
  See also Nagai Sokichi
  See also DLB 180
Nagai Sokichi 1879-1959
  See Nagai Kafu
  See also CA 117
Nagy, Laszlo 1925-1978 .... **CLC 7**
  See also CA 129; 112
Naidu, Sarojini 1879-1943 .... **TCLC 80**
Naipaul, Shiva(dhar Srinivasa)
  1945-1985 .... **CLC 32, 39; DAM NOV**
  See also CA 110; 112; 116; CANR 33;
  DA3; DLB 157; DLBY 85; MTCW 1, 2
Naipaul, V(idiadhar) S(urajprasad)
  1932- .... **CLC 4, 7, 9, 13, 18, 37, 105;**
  DAB; DAC; DAM MST, NOV; SSC 38
  See also CA 1-4R; CANR 1, 33, 51, 91;
  CDBLB 1960 to Present; DA3; DLB 125,
  204, 206; DLBY 85; MTCW 1, 2
Nakos, Lilika 1899(?)- .... **CLC 29**
Narayan, R(asipuram) K(rishnaswami)
  1906- . **CLC 7, 28, 47, 121; DAM NOV;**
  SSC 25
  See also CA 81-84; CANR 33, 61; DA3;
  MTCW 1, 2; SATA 62
Nash, (Frediric) Ogden 1902-1971 . **CLC 23;**
  DAM POET; PC 21
  See also CA 13-14; 29-32R; CANR 34, 61;
  CAP 1; DLB 11; MAICYA; MTCW 1, 2;
  SATA 2, 46
Nashe, Thomas 1567-1601(?) .... **LC 41**
  See also DLB 167
Nashe, Thomas 1567-1601 .... **LC 41**
Nathan, Daniel
  See Dannay, Frederic
Nathan, George Jean 1882-1958 .... **TCLC 18**
  See also Hatteras, Owen
  See also CA 114; 169; DLB 137
Natsume, Kinnosuke 1867-1916
  See Natsume, Soseki
  See also CA 104
Natsume, Soseki 1867-1916 .... **TCLC 2, 10**
  See also Natsume, Kinnosuke
  See also DLB 180
Natti, (Mary) Lee 1919-
  See Kingman, Lee
  See also CA 5-8R; CANR 2
Naylor, Gloria 1950- .... **CLC 28, 52; BLC 3;**
  DA; DAC; DAM MST, MULT, NOV,
  POP; WLCS
  See also AAYA 6; BW 2, 3; CA 107; CANR
  27, 51, 74; DA3; DLB 173; MTCW 1, 2
Neihardt, John Gneisenau
  1881-1973 .... **CLC 32**
  See also CA 13-14; CANR 65; CAP 1; DLB
  9, 54
Nekrasov, Nikolai Alekseevich
  1821-1878 .... **NCLC 11**
Nelligan, Emile 1879-1941 .... **TCLC 14**
  See also CA 114; DLB 92
Nelson, Willie 1933- .... **CLC 17**
  See also CA 107

Nemerov, Howard (Stanley)
1920-1991 .... CLC 2, 6, 9, 36; DAM
POET; PC 24
See also CA 1-4R; 134; CABS 2; CANR 1,
27, 53; DLB 5, 6; DLBY 83; INT CANR-
27; MTCW 1, 2

Neruda, Pablo 1904-1973 .. CLC 1, 2, 5, 7, 9,
28, 62; DA; DAB; DAC; DAM MST,
MULT, POET; HLC 2; PC 4; WLC
See also CA 19-20; 45-48; CAP 2; DA3;
HW 1; MTCW 1, 2

Nerval, Gerard de 1808-1855 ... NCLC 1, 67;
PC 13; SSC 18

Nervo, (Jose) Amado (Ruiz de)
1870-1919 .... TCLC 11; HLCS 2
See also CA 109; 131; HW 1

Nessi, Pio Baroja y
See Baroja (y Nessi), Pio

Nestroy, Johann 1801-1862 .... NCLC 42
See also DLB 133

Netterville, Luke
See O'Grady, Standish (James)

Neufeld, John (Arthur) 1938- .... CLC 17
See also AAYA 11; CA 25-28R; CANR 11,
37, 56; CLR 52; MAICYA; SAAS 3;
SATA 6, 81

Neumann, Alfred 1895-1952 .... TCLC 100
See also CA 183; DLB 56

Neville, Emily Cheney 1919- .... CLC 12
See also CA 5-8R; CANR 3, 37, 85; JRDA;
MAICYA; SAAS 2; SATA 1

Newbound, Bernard Slade 1930-
See Slade, Bernard
See also CA 81-84; CANR 49; DAM
DRAM

Newby, P(ercy) H(oward)
1918-1997 .... CLC 2, 13; DAM NOV
See also CA 5-8R; 161; CANR 32, 67; DLB
15; MTCW 1

Newlove, Donald 1928- .... CLC 6
See also CA 29-32R; CANR 25

Newlove, John (Herbert) 1938- .... CLC 14
See also CA 21-24R; CANR 9, 25

Newman, Charles 1938- .... CLC 2, 8
See also CA 21-24R; CANR 84

Newman, Edwin (Harold) 1919- ...... CLC 14
See also AITN 1; CA 69-72; CANR 5

Newman, John Henry 1801-1890 .. NCLC 38
See also DLB 18, 32, 55

Newton, (Sir)Isaac 1642-1727 .... LC 35, 52

Newton, Suzanne 1936- .... CLC 35
See also CA 41-44R; CANR 14; JRDA;
SATA 5, 77

Nexo, Martin Andersen
1869-1954 .... TCLC 43

Nezval, Vitezslav 1900-1958 .... TCLC 44
See also CA 123

Ng, Fae Myenne 1957(?)- .... CLC 81
See also CA 146

Ngema, Mbongeni 1955- .... CLC 57
See also BW 2; CA 143; CANR 84

Ngugi, James T(hiong'o) CLC 3, 7, 13
See also Ngugi wa Thiong'o

Ngugi wa Thiong'o 1938- .. CLC 36; BLC 3;
DAM MULT, NOV
See also Ngugi, James T(hiong'o)
See also BW 2; CA 81-84; CANR 27, 58;
DLB 125; MTCW 1, 2

Nichol, B(arrie) P(hillip) 1944-1988 . CLC 18
See also CA 53-56; DLB 53; SATA 66

Nichols, John (Treadwell) 1940- .... CLC 38
See also CA 9-12R; CAAS 2; CANR 6, 70;
DLBY 82

Nichols, Leigh
See Koontz, Dean R(ay)

Nichols, Peter (Richard) 1927- .... CLC 5, 36,
65
See also CA 104; CANR 33, 86; DLB 13;
MTCW 1

Nicolas, F. R. E.
See Freeling, Nicolas

Niedecker, Lorine 1903-1970 ..... CLC 10, 42;
DAM POET
See also CA 25-28; CAP 2; DLB 48

Nietzsche, Friedrich (Wilhelm)
1844-1900 .... TCLC 10, 18, 55
See also CA 107; 121; DLB 129

Nievo, Ippolito 1831-1861 .... NCLC 22

Nightingale, Anne Redmon 1943-
See Redmon, Anne
See also CA 103

Nightingale, Florence 1820-1910 ... TCLC 85
See also DLB 166

Nik. T. O.
See Annensky, Innokenty (Fyodorovich)

Nin, Anais 1903-1977 ..... CLC 1, 4, 8, 11, 14,
60, 127; DAM NOV, POP; SSC 10
See also AITN 2; CA 13-16R; 69-72;
CANR 22, 53; DLB 2, 4, 152; MTCW 1,
2

Nishida, Kitaro 1870-1945 .... TCLC 83

Nishiwaki, Junzaburo 1894-1982 .... PC 15
See also CA 107

Nissenson, Hugh 1933- .... CLC 4, 9
See also CA 17-20R; CANR 27; DLB 28

Niven, Larry CLC 8
See also Niven, Laurence Van Cott
See also AAYA 27; DLB 8

Niven, Laurence Van Cott 1938-
See Niven, Larry
See also CA 21-24R; CAAS 12; CANR 14,
44, 66; DAM POP; MTCW 1, 2; SATA
95

Nixon, Agnes Eckhardt 1927- .... CLC 21
See also CA 110

Nizan, Paul 1905-1940 .... TCLC 40
See also CA 161; DLB 72

Nkosi, Lewis 1936- ... CLC 45; BLC 3; DAM
MULT
See also BW 1, 3; CA 65-68; CANR 27,
81; DLB 157, 225

Nodier, (Jean) Charles (Emmanuel)
1780-1844 .... NCLC 19
See also DLB 119

Noguchi, Yone 1875-1947 .... TCLC 80

Nolan, Christopher 1965- .... CLC 58
See also CA 111; CANR 88

Noon, Jeff 1957- .... CLC 91
See also CA 148; CANR 83

Norden, Charles
See Durrell, Lawrence (George)

Nordhoff, Charles (Bernard)
1887-1947 .... TCLC 23
See also CA 108; DLB 9; SATA 23

Norfolk, Lawrence 1963- .... CLC 76
See also CA 144; CANR 85

Norman, Marsha 1947- .... CLC 28; DAM
DRAM; DC 8
See also CA 105; CABS 3; CANR 41;
DLBY 84

Normyx
See Douglas, (George) Norman

Norris, Frank 1870-1902 .... SSC 28
See also Norris, (Benjamin) Frank(lin, Jr.)
See also CDALB 1865-1917; DLB 12, 71,
186

Norris, (Benjamin) Frank(lin, Jr.)
1870-1902 .... TCLC 24
See also Norris, Frank
See also CA 110; 160

Norris, Leslie 1921- .... CLC 14
See also CA 11-12; CANR 14; CAP 1; DLB
27

North, Andrew
See Norton, Andre

North, Anthony
See Koontz, Dean R(ay)

North, Captain George
See Stevenson, Robert Louis (Balfour)

North, Milou
See Erdrich, Louise

Northrup, B. A.
See Hubbard, L(afayette) Ron(ald)

North Staffs
See Hulme, T(homas) E(rnest)

Norton, Alice Mary
See Norton, Andre
See also MAICYA; SATA 1, 43

Norton, Andre 1912- .... CLC 12
See also Norton, Alice Mary
See also AAYA 14; CA 1-4R; CANR 68;
CLR 50; DLB 8, 52; JRDA; MTCW 1;
SATA 91

Norton, Caroline 1808-1877 .... NCLC 47
See also DLB 21, 159, 199

Norway, Nevil Shute 1899-1960
See Shute, Nevil
See also CA 102; 93-96; CANR 85; MTCW
2

Norwid, Cyprian Kamil
1821-1883 .... NCLC 17

Nosille, Nabrah
See Ellison, Harlan (Jay)

Nossack, Hans Erich 1901-1978 .... CLC 6
See also CA 93-96; 85-88; DLB 69

Nostradamus 1503-1566 .... LC 27

Nosu, Chuji
See Ozu, Yasujiro

Notenburg, Eleanora (Genrikhovna) von
See Guro, Elena

Nova, Craig 1945- .... CLC 7, 31
See also CA 45-48; CANR 2, 53

Novak, Joseph
See Kosinski, Jerzy (Nikodem)

Novalis 1772-1801 .... NCLC 13
See also DLB 90

Novis, Emile
See Weil, Simone (Adolphine)

Nowlan, Alden (Albert) 1933-1983 . CLC 15;
DAC; DAM MST
See also CA 9-12R; CANR 5; DLB 53

Noyes, Alfred 1880-1958 ...... TCLC 7; PC 27
See also CA 104; DLB 20

Nunn, Kem CLC 34
See also CA 159

Nwapa, Flora 1931- .... CLC 133; BLCS
See also BW 2; CA 143; CANR 83; DLB
125

Nye, Robert 1939- . CLC 13, 42; DAM NOV
See also CA 33-36R; CANR 29, 67; DLB
14; MTCW 1; SATA 6

Nyro, Laura 1947- .... CLC 17

Oates, Joyce Carol 1938- .. CLC 1, 2, 3, 6, 9,
11, 15, 19, 33, 52, 108, 134; DA; DAB;
DAC; DAM MST, NOV, POP; SSC 6;
WLC
See also AAYA 15; AITN 1; BEST 89:2;
CA 5-8R; CANR 25, 45, 74; CDALB
1968-1988; DA3; DLB 2, 5, 130; DLBY
81; INT CANR-25; MTCW 1, 2

O'Brien, Darcy 1939-1998 .... CLC 11
See also CA 21-24R; 167; CANR 8, 59

O'Brien, E. G.
See Clarke, Arthur C(harles)

O'Brien, Edna 1936- ..... CLC 3, 5, 8, 13, 36,
65, 116; DAM NOV; SSC 10
See also CA 1-4R; CANR 6, 41, 65; CD-
BLB 1960 to Present; DA3; DLB 14;
MTCW 1, 2

O'Brien, Fitz-James 1828-1862 ..... NCLC 21
See also DLB 74

O'Brien, Flann CLC 1, 4, 5, 7, 10, 47
See also O Nuallain, Brian

O'Brien, Richard 1942- .... CLC 17
See also CA 124

O'Brien, (William) Tim(othy) 1946- . **CLC 7, 19, 40, 103; DAM POP**
See also AAYA 16; CA 85-88; CANR 40, 58; CDALBS; DA3; DLB 152; DLBD 9; DLBY 80; MTCW 2

Obstfelder, Sigbjoern 1866-1900 .... **TCLC 23**
See also CA 123

O'Casey, Sean 1880-1964 .... **CLC 1, 5, 9, 11, 15, 88; DAB; DAC; DAM DRAM, MST; DC 12; WLCS**
See also CA 89-92; CANR 62; CDBLB 1914-1945; DA3; DLB 10; MTCW 1, 2

O'Cathasaigh, Sean
See O'Casey, Sean

Occom, Samson 1723-1792 .... **LC 60**
See also DLB 175; NNAL

Ochs, Phil(ip David) 1940-1976 .... **CLC 17**
See also CA 185; 65-68

O'Connor, Edwin (Greene)
1918-1968 .... **CLC 14**
See also CA 93-96; 25-28R

O'Connor, (Mary) Flannery
1925-1964 .... **CLC 1, 2, 3, 6, 10, 13, 15, 21, 66, 104; DA; DAB; DAC; DAM MST, NOV; SSC 1, 23; WLC**
See also AAYA 7; CA 1-4R; CANR 3, 41; CDALB 1941-1968; DA3; DLB 2, 152; DLBD 12; DLBY 80; MTCW 1, 2

O'Connor, Frank **CLC 23; SSC 5**
See also O'Donovan, Michael John
See also DLB 162

O'Dell, Scott 1898-1989 .... **CLC 30**
See also AAYA 3; CA 61-64; 129; CANR 12, 30; CLR 1, 16; DLB 52; JRDA; MAI-CYA; SATA 12, 60

Odets, Clifford 1906-1963 ..... **CLC 2, 28, 98; DAM DRAM; DC 6**
See also CA 85-88; CANR 62; DLB 7, 26; MTCW 1, 2

O'Doherty, Brian 1934- .... **CLC 76**
See also CA 105

O'Donnell, K. M.
See Malzberg, Barry N(athaniel)

O'Donnell, Lawrence
See Kuttner, Henry

O'Donovan, Michael John
1903-1966 .... **CLC 14**
See also O'Connor, Frank
See also CA 93-96; CANR 84

Oe, Kenzaburo 1935- .... **CLC 10, 36, 86; DAM NOV; SSC 20**
See also CA 97-100; CANR 36, 50, 74; DA3; DLB 182; DLBY 94; MTCW 1, 2

O'Faolain, Julia 1932- .... **CLC 6, 19, 47, 108**
See also CA 81-84; CAAS 2; CANR 12, 61; DLB 14; MTCW 1

O'Faolain, Sean 1900-1991 ...... **CLC 1, 7, 14, 32, 70; SSC 13**
See also CA 61-64; 134; CANR 12, 66; DLB 15, 162; MTCW 1, 2

O'Flaherty, Liam 1896-1984 .... **CLC 5, 34; SSC 6**
See also CA 101; 113; CANR 35; DLB 36, 162; DLBY 84; MTCW 1, 2

Ogilvy, Gavin
See Barrie, J(ames) M(atthew)

O'Grady, Standish (James)
1846-1928 .... **TCLC 5**
See also CA 104; 157

O'Grady, Timothy 1951- .... **CLC 59**
See also CA 138

O'Hara, Frank 1926-1966 .... **CLC 2, 5, 13, 78; DAM POET**
See also CA 9-12R; 25-28R; CANR 33; DA3; DLB 5, 16, 193; MTCW 1, 2

O'Hara, John (Henry) 1905-1970 . **CLC 1, 2, 3, 6, 11, 42; DAM NOV; SSC 15**
See also CA 5-8R; 25-28R; CANR 31, 60; CDALB 1929-1941; DLB 9, 86; DLBD 2; MTCW 1, 2

O Hehir, Diana 1922- .... **CLC 41**
See also CA 93-96

Ohiyesa
See Eastman, Charles A(lexander)

Okigbo, Christopher (Ifenayichukwu)
1932-1967 ... **CLC 25, 84; BLC 3; DAM MULT, POET; PC 7**
See also BW 1, 3; CA 77-80; CANR 74; DLB 125; MTCW 1, 2

Okri, Ben 1959- .... **CLC 87**
See also BW 2, 3; CA 130; 138; CANR 65; DLB 157; INT 138; MTCW 2

Olds, Sharon 1942- ... **CLC 32, 39, 85; DAM POET; PC 22**
See also CA 101; CANR 18, 41, 66; DLB 120; MTCW 2

Oldstyle, Jonathan
See Irving, Washington

Olesha, Yuri (Karlovich) 1899-1960 .. **CLC 8**
See also CA 85-88

Oliphant, Laurence 1829(?)-1888 .. **NCLC 47**
See also DLB 18, 166

Oliphant, Margaret (Oliphant Wilson)
1828-1897 .... **NCLC 11, 61; SSC 25**
See also DLB 18, 159, 190

Oliver, Mary 1935- .... **CLC 19, 34, 98**
See also CA 21-24R; CANR 9, 43, 84, 92; DLB 5, 193

Olivier, Laurence (Kerr) 1907-1989 . **CLC 20**
See also CA 111; 150; 129

Olsen, Tillie 1912- .... **CLC 4, 13, 114; DA; DAB; DAC; DAM MST; SSC 11**
See also CA 1-4R; CANR 1, 43, 74; CDALBS; DA3; DLB 28, 206; DLBY 80; MTCW 1, 2

Olson, Charles (John) 1910-1970 .. **CLC 1, 2, 5, 6, 9, 11, 29; DAM POET; PC 19**
See also CA 13-16; 25-28R; CABS 2; CANR 35, 61; CAP 1; DLB 5, 16, 193; MTCW 1, 2

Olson, Toby 1937- .... **CLC 28**
See also CA 65-68; CANR 9, 31, 84

Olyesha, Yuri
See Olesha, Yuri (Karlovich)

Ondaatje, (Philip) Michael 1943- .... **CLC 14, 29, 51, 76; DAB; DAC; DAM MST; PC 28**
See also CA 77-80; CANR 42, 74; DA3; DLB 60; MTCW 2

Oneal, Elizabeth 1934-
See Oneal, Zibby
See also CA 106; CANR 28, 84; MAICYA; SATA 30, 82

Oneal, Zibby **CLC 30**
See also Oneal, Elizabeth
See also AAYA 5; CLR 13; JRDA

O'Neill, Eugene (Gladstone)
1888-1953 .... **TCLC 1, 6, 27, 49; DA; DAB; DAC; DAM DRAM, MST; WLC**
See also AITN 1; CA 110; 132; CDALB 1929-1941; DA3; DLB 7; MTCW 1, 2

Onetti, Juan Carlos 1909-1994 ... **CLC 7, 10; DAM MULT, NOV; HLCS 2; SSC 23**
See also CA 85-88; 145; CANR 32, 63; DLB 113; HW 1, 2; MTCW 1, 2

O Nuallain, Brian 1911-1966
See O'Brien, Flann
See also CA 21-22; 25-28R; CAP 2

Ophuls, Max 1902-1957 .... **TCLC 79**
See also CA 113

Opie, Amelia 1769-1853 .... **NCLC 65**
See also DLB 116, 159

Oppen, George 1908-1984 ...... **CLC 7, 13, 34**
See also CA 13-16R; 113; CANR 8, 82; DLB 5, 165

Oppenheim, E(dward) Phillips
1866-1946 .... **TCLC 45**
See also CA 111; DLB 70

Opuls, Max
See Ophuls, Max

Origen c. 185-c. 254 .... **CMLC 19**

Orlovitz, Gil 1918-1973 .... **CLC 22**
See also CA 77-80; 45-48; DLB 2, 5

Orris
See Ingelow, Jean

Ortega y Gasset, Jose 1883-1955 ... **TCLC 9; DAM MULT; HLC 2**
See also CA 106; 130; HW 1, 2; MTCW 1, 2

Ortese, Anna Maria 1914- .... **CLC 89**
See also DLB 177

Ortiz, Simon J(oseph) 1941- . **CLC 45; DAM MULT, POET; PC 17**
See also CA 134; CANR 69; DLB 120, 175; NNAL

Orton, Joe **CLC 4, 13, 43; DC 3**
See also Orton, John Kingsley
See also CDBLB 1960 to Present; DLB 13; MTCW 2

Orton, John Kingsley 1933-1967
See Orton, Joe
See also CA 85-88; CANR 35, 66; DAM DRAM; MTCW 1, 2

Orwell, George -1950 ...... **TCLC 2, 6, 15, 31, 51; DAB; WLC**
See also Blair, Eric (Arthur)
See also CDBLB 1945-1960; DLB 15, 98, 195

Osborne, David
See Silverberg, Robert

Osborne, George
See Silverberg, Robert

Osborne, John (James) 1929-1994 .... **CLC 1, 2, 5, 11, 45; DA; DAB; DAC; DAM DRAM, MST; WLC**
See also CA 13-16R; 147; CANR 21, 56; CDBLB 1945-1960; DLB 13; MTCW 1, 2

Osborne, Lawrence 1958- .... **CLC 50**

Osbourne, Lloyd 1868-1947 .... **TCLC 93**

Oshima, Nagisa 1932- .... **CLC 20**
See also CA 116; 121; CANR 78

Oskison, John Milton 1874-1947 .. **TCLC 35; DAM MULT**
See also CA 144; CANR 84; DLB 175; NNAL

Ossian c. 3rd cent. - .... **CMLC 28**
See also Macpherson, James

Ossoli, Sarah Margaret (Fuller marchesa d')
1810-1850 .... **NCLC 5, 50**
See also Fuller, Margaret; Fuller, Sarah Margaret
See also CDALB 1640-1865; DLB 1, 59, 73, 83, 223; SATA 25

Ostriker, Alicia (Suskin) 1937- .... **CLC 132**
See also CA 25-28R; CAAS 24; CANR 10, 30, 62; DLB 120

Ostrovsky, Alexander 1823-1886 .. **NCLC 30, 57**

Otero, Blas de 1916-1979 .... **CLC 11**
See also CA 89-92; DLB 134

Otto, Rudolf 1869-1937 .... **TCLC 85**

Otto, Whitney 1955- .... **CLC 70**
See also CA 140

Ouida **TCLC 43**
See also De La Ramee, (Marie) Louise
See also DLB 18, 156

Ousmane, Sembene 1923- ... **CLC 66; BLC 3**
See also BW 1, 3; CA 117; 125; CANR 81; MTCW 1

Ovid 43B.C.-17 . **CMLC 7; DAM POET; PC 2**
See also DA3; DLB 211
Owen, Hugh
See Faust, Frederick (Schiller)
Owen, Wilfred (Edward Salter)
1893-1918 .... **TCLC 5, 27; DA; DAB; DAC; DAM MST, POET; PC 19; WLC**
See also CA 104; 141; CDBLB 1914-1945; DLB 20; MTCW 2
Owens, Rochelle 1936- .... **CLC 8**
See also CA 17-20R; CAAS 2; CANR 39
Oz, Amos 1939- ...... **CLC 5, 8, 11, 27, 33, 54; DAM NOV**
See also CA 53-56; CANR 27, 47, 65; MTCW 1, 2
Ozick, Cynthia 1928- .... **CLC 3, 7, 28, 62; DAM NOV, POP; SSC 15**
See also BEST 90:1; CA 17-20R; CANR 23, 58; DA3; DLB 28, 152; DLBY 82; INT CANR-23; MTCW 1, 2
Ozu, Yasujiro 1903-1963 .... **CLC 16**
See also CA 112
Pacheco, C.
See Pessoa, Fernando (Antonio Nogueira)
Pacheco, Jose Emilio 1939-
See also CA 111; 131; CANR 65; DAM MULT; HLC 2; HW 1, 2
Pa Chin CLC 18
See also Li Fei-kan
Pack, Robert 1929- .... **CLC 13**
See also CA 1-4R; CANR 3, 44, 82; DLB 5
Padgett, Lewis
See Kuttner, Henry
Padilla (Lorenzo), Heberto 1932- ..... **CLC 38**
See also AITN 1; CA 123; 131; HW 1
Page, Jimmy 1944- .... **CLC 12**
Page, Louise 1955- .... **CLC 40**
See also CA 140; CANR 76
Page, P(atricia) K(athleen) 1916- ...... **CLC 7, 18; DAC; DAM MST; PC 12**
See also CA 53-56; CANR 4, 22, 65; DLB 68; MTCW 1
Page, Thomas Nelson 1853-1922 .... **SSC 23**
See also CA 118; 177; DLB 12, 78; DLBD 13
Pagels, Elaine Hiesey 1943- .... **CLC 104**
See also CA 45-48; CANR 2, 24, 51
Paget, Violet 1856-1935
See Lee, Vernon
See also CA 104; 166
Paget-Lowe, Henry
See Lovecraft, H(oward) P(hillips)
Paglia, Camille (Anna) 1947- .... **CLC 68**
See also CA 140; CANR 72; MTCW 2
Paige, Richard
See Koontz, Dean R(ay)
Paine, Thomas 1737-1809 .... **NCLC 62**
See also CDALB 1640-1865; DLB 31, 43, 73, 158
Pakenham, Antonia
See Fraser, (Lady) Antonia (Pakenham)
Palamas, Kostes 1859-1943 .... **TCLC 5**
See also CA 105
Palazzeschi, Aldo 1885-1974 .... **CLC 11**
See also CA 89-92; 53-56; DLB 114
Pales Matos, Luis 1898-1959
See also HLCS 2; HW 1
Paley, Grace 1922- .... **CLC 4, 6, 37; DAM POP; SSC 8**
See also CA 25-28R; CANR 13, 46, 74; DA3; DLB 28; INT CANR-13; MTCW 1, 2
Palin, Michael (Edward) 1943- .... **CLC 21**
See also Monty Python
See also CA 107; CANR 35; SATA 67
Palliser, Charles 1947- .... **CLC 65**
See also CA 136; CANR 76

Palma, Ricardo 1833-1919 .... **TCLC 29**
See also CA 168
Pancake, Breece Dexter 1952-1979
See Pancake, Breece D'J
See also CA 123; 109
Pancake, Breece D'J CLC 29
See also Pancake, Breece Dexter
See also DLB 130
Pankhurst, Emmeline (Goulden)
1858-1928 .... **TCLC 100**
See also CA 116
Panko, Rudy
See Gogol, Nikolai (Vasilyevich)
Papadiamantis, Alexandros
1851-1911 .... **TCLC 29**
See also CA 168
Papadiamantopoulos, Johannes 1856-1910
See Moreas, Jean
See also CA 117
Papini, Giovanni 1881-1956 .... **TCLC 22**
See also CA 121; 180
Paracelsus 1493-1541 .... **LC 14**
See also DLB 179
Parasol, Peter
See Stevens, Wallace
Pardo Bazan, Emilia 1851-1921 .... **SSC 30**
Pareto, Vilfredo 1848-1923 .... **TCLC 69**
See also CA 175
Parfenie, Maria
See Codrescu, Andrei
Parini, Jay (Lee) 1948- .... **CLC 54, 133**
See also CA 97-100; CAAS 16; CANR 32, 87
Park, Jordan
See Kornbluth, C(yril) M.; Pohl, Frederik
Park, Robert E(zra) 1864-1944 ..... **TCLC 73**
See also CA 122; 165
Parker, Bert
See Ellison, Harlan (Jay)
Parker, Dorothy (Rothschild)
1893-1967 .... **CLC 15, 68; DAM POET; PC 28; SSC 2**
See also CA 19-20; 25-28R; CAP 2; DA3; DLB 11, 45, 86; MTCW 1, 2
Parker, Robert B(rown) 1932- .... **CLC 27; DAM NOV, POP**
See also AAYA 28; BEST 89:4; CA 49-52; CANR 1, 26, 52, 89; INT CANR-26; MTCW 1
Parkin, Frank 1940- .... **CLC 43**
See also CA 147
Parkman, Francis Jr., Jr.
1823-1893 .... **NCLC 12**
See also DLB 1, 30, 186
Parks, Gordon (Alexander Buchanan)
1912- .... **CLC 1, 16; BLC 3; DAM MULT**
See also AITN 2; BW 2, 3; CA 41-44R; CANR 26, 66; DA3; DLB 33; MTCW 2; SATA 8, 108
Parmenides c. 515B.C.-c. 450B.C. .... **CMLC 22**
See also DLB 176
Parnell, Thomas 1679-1718 .... **LC 3**
See also DLB 94
Parra, Nicanor 1914- ...... **CLC 2, 102; DAM MULT; HLC 2**
See also CA 85-88; CANR 32; HW 1; MTCW 1
Parra Sanojo, Ana Teresa de la 1890-1936
See also HLCS 2
Parrish, Mary Frances
See Fisher, M(ary) F(rances) K(ennedy)
Parson
See Coleridge, Samuel Taylor
Parson Lot
See Kingsley, Charles

Parton, Sara Payson Willis
1811-1872 .... **NCLC 86**
See also DLB 43, 74
Partridge, Anthony
See Oppenheim, E(dward) Phillips
Pascal, Blaise 1623-1662 .... **LC 35**
Pascoli, Giovanni 1855-1912 .... **TCLC 45**
See also CA 170
Pasolini, Pier Paolo 1922-1975 .. **CLC 20, 37, 106; PC 17**
See also CA 93-96; 61-64; CANR 63; DLB 128, 177; MTCW 1
Pasquini
See Silone, Ignazio
Pastan, Linda (Olenik) 1932- .... **CLC 27; DAM POET**
See also CA 61-64; CANR 18, 40, 61; DLB 5
Pasternak, Boris (Leonidovich)
1890-1960 .... **CLC 7, 10, 18, 63; DA; DAB; DAC; DAM MST, NOV, POET; PC 6; SSC 31; WLC**
See also CA 127; 116; DA3; MTCW 1, 2
Patchen, Kenneth 1911-1972 .. **CLC 1, 2, 18; DAM POET**
See also CA 1-4R; 33-36R; CANR 3, 35; DLB 16, 48; MTCW 1
Pater, Walter (Horatio) 1839-1894 . **NCLC 7, 90**
See also CDBLB 1832-1890; DLB 57, 156
Paterson, A(ndrew) B(arton)
1864-1941 .... **TCLC 32**
See also CA 155; SATA 97
Paterson, Katherine (Womeldorf)
1932- .... **CLC 12, 30**
See also AAYA 1, 31; CA 21-24R; CANR 28, 59; CLR 7, 50; DLB 52; JRDA; MAICYA; MTCW 1; SATA 13, 53, 92
Patmore, Coventry Kersey Dighton
1823-1896 .... **NCLC 9**
See also DLB 35, 98
Paton, Alan (Stewart) 1903-1988 ...... **CLC 4, 10, 25, 55, 106; DA; DAB; DAC; DAM MST, NOV; WLC**
See also AAYA 26; CA 13-16; 125; CANR 22; CAP 1; DA3; DLB 225; DLBD 17; MTCW 1, 2; SATA 11; SATA-Obit 56
Paton Walsh, Gillian 1937- .... **CLC 35**
See also Walsh, Jill Paton
See also AAYA 11; CANR 38, 83; CLR 2, 65; DLB 161; JRDA; MAICYA; SAAS 3; SATA 4, 72, 109
Paton Walsh, Jill
See Paton Walsh, Gillian
Patton, George S. 1885-1945 .... **TCLC 79**
Paulding, James Kirke 1778-1860 ... **NCLC 2**
See also DLB 3, 59, 74
Paulin, Thomas Neilson 1949-
See Paulin, Tom
See also CA 123; 128
Paulin, Tom CLC 37
See also Paulin, Thomas Neilson
See also DLB 40
Pausanias c. 1st cent. - .... **CMLC 36**
Paustovsky, Konstantin (Georgievich)
1892-1968 .... **CLC 40**
See also CA 93-96; 25-28R
Pavese, Cesare 1908-1950 .. **TCLC 3; PC 13; SSC 19**
See also CA 104; 169; DLB 128, 177
Pavic, Milorad 1929- .... **CLC 60**
See also CA 136; DLB 181
Pavlov, Ivan Petrovich 1849-1936 . **TCLC 91**
See also CA 118; 180
Payne, Alan
See Jakes, John (William)
Paz, Gil
See Lugones, Leopoldo

Paz, Octavio 1914-1998 . CLC 3, 4, 6, 10, 19,
51, 65, 119; DA; DAB; DAC; DAM
MST, MULT, POET; HLC 2; PC 1;
WLC
See also CA 73-76; 165; CANR 32, 65;
DA3; DLBY 90, 98; HW 1, 2; MTCW 1,
2

p'Bitek, Okot 1931-1982 .... CLC 96; BLC 3;
DAM MULT
See also BW 2, 3; CA 124; 107; CANR 82;
DLB 125; MTCW 1, 2

Peacock, Molly 1947- .... CLC 60
See also CA 103; CAAS 21; CANR 52, 84;
DLB 120

Peacock, Thomas Love
1785-1866 .... NCLC 22
See also DLB 96, 116

Peake, Mervyn 1911-1968 .... CLC 7, 54
See also CA 5-8R; 25-28R; CANR 3; DLB
15, 160; MTCW 1; SATA 23

Pearce, Philippa CLC 21
See also Christie, (Ann) Philippa
See also CLR 9; DLB 161; MAICYA;
SATA 1, 67

Pearl, Eric
See Elman, Richard (Martin)

Pearson, T(homas) R(eid) 1956- ...... CLC 39
See also CA 120; 130; INT 130

Peck, Dale 1967- .... CLC 81
See also CA 146; CANR 72

Peck, John 1941- .... CLC 3
See also CA 49-52; CANR 3

Peck, Richard (Wayne) 1934- .... CLC 21
See also AAYA 1, 24; CA 85-88; CANR
19, 38; CLR 15; INT CANR-19; JRDA;
MAICYA; SAAS 2; SATA 18, 55, 97;
SATA-Essay 110

Peck, Robert Newton 1928- .... CLC 17; DA;
DAC; DAM MST
See also AAYA 3; CA 81-84, 182; CAAE
182; CANR 31, 63; CLR 45; JRDA; MAI-
CYA; SAAS 1; SATA 21, 62, 111; SATA-
Essay 108

Peckinpah, (David) Sam(uel)
1925-1984 .... CLC 20
See also CA 109; 114; CANR 82

Pedersen, Knut 1859-1952
See Hamsun, Knut
See also CA 104; 119; CANR 63; MTCW
1, 2

Peeslake, Gaffer
See Durrell, Lawrence (George)

Peguy, Charles Pierre 1873-1914 ... TCLC 10
See also CA 107

Peirce, Charles Sanders
1839-1914 .... TCLC 81

Pellicer, Carlos 1900(?)-1977
See also CA 153; 69-72; HLCS 2; HW 1

Pena, Ramon del Valle y
See Valle-Inclan, Ramon (Maria) del

Pendennis, Arthur Esquir
See Thackeray, William Makepeace

Penn, William 1644-1718 .... LC 25
See also DLB 24

PEPECE
See Prado (Calvo), Pedro

Pepys, Samuel 1633-1703 ..... LC 11, 58; DA;
DAB; DAC; DAM MST; WLC
See also CDBLB 1660-1789; DA3; DLB
101

Percy, Walker 1916-1990 .... CLC 2, 3, 6, 8,
14, 18, 47, 65; DAM NOV, POP
See also CA 1-4R; 131; CANR 1, 23, 64;
DA3; DLB 2; DLBY 80, 90; MTCW 1, 2

Percy, William Alexander
1885-1942 .... TCLC 84
See also CA 163; MTCW 2

Perec, Georges 1936-1982 .... CLC 56, 116
See also CA 141; DLB 83

Pereda (y Sanchez de Porrua), Jose Maria
de 1833-1906 .... TCLC 16
See also CA 117

Pereda y Porrua, Jose Maria de
See Pereda (y Sanchez de Porrua), Jose
Maria de

Peregoy, George Weems
See Mencken, H(enry) L(ouis)

Perelman, S(idney) J(oseph)
1904-1979 .. CLC 3, 5, 9, 15, 23, 44, 49;
DAM DRAM; SSC 32
See also AITN 1, 2; CA 73-76; 89-92;
CANR 18; DLB 11, 44; MTCW 1, 2

Peret, Benjamin 1899-1959 .... TCLC 20
See also CA 117; 186

Peretz, Isaac Loeb 1851(?)-1915 ... TCLC 16;
SSC 26
See also CA 109

Peretz, Yitzkhok Leibush
See Peretz, Isaac Loeb

Perez Galdos, Benito 1843-1920 ... TCLC 27;
HLCS 2
See also CA 125; 153; HW 1

Peri Rossi, Cristina 1941-
See also CA 131; CANR 59, 81; DLB 145;
HLCS 2; HW 1, 2

Perlata
See Peret, Benjamin

Perrault, Charles 1628-1703 ... LC 3, 52; DC
12
See also MAICYA; SATA 25

Perry, Anne 1938- .... CLC 126
See also CA 101; CANR 22, 50, 84

Perry, Brighton
See Sherwood, Robert E(mmet)

Perse, St.-John
See Leger, (Marie-Rene Auguste) Alexis
Saint-Leger

Perutz, Leo(pold) 1882-1957 .... TCLC 60
See also CA 147; DLB 81

Peseenz, Tulio F.
See Lopez y Fuentes, Gregorio

Pesetsky, Bette 1932- .... CLC 28
See also CA 133; DLB 130

Peshkov, Alexei Maximovich 1868-1936
See Gorky, Maxim
See also CA 105; 141; CANR 83; DA;
DAC; DAM DRAM, MST, NOV; MTCW
2

Pessoa, Fernando (Antonio Nogueira)
1888-1935 .... TCLC 27; DAM MULT;
HLC 2; PC 20
See also CA 125; 183

Peterkin, Julia Mood 1880-1961 ...... CLC 31
See also CA 102; DLB 9

Peters, Joan K(aren) 1945- .... CLC 39
See also CA 158

Peters, Robert L(ouis) 1924- .... CLC 7
See also CA 13-16R; CAAS 8; DLB 105

Petofi, Sandor 1823-1849 .... NCLC 21

Petrakis, Harry Mark 1923- .... CLC 3
See also CA 9-12R; CANR 4, 30, 85

Petrarch 1304-1374 .... CMLC 20; DAM
POET; PC 8
See also DA3

Petronius c. 20-66 .... CMLC 34
See also DLB 211

Petrov, Evgeny TCLC 21
See also Kataev, Evgeny Petrovich

Petry, Ann (Lane) 1908-1997 ... CLC 1, 7, 18
See also BW 1, 3; CA 5-8R; 157; CAAS 6;
CANR 4, 46; CLR 12; DLB 76; JRDA;
MAICYA; MTCW 1; SATA 5; SATA-Obit
94

Petursson, Halligrimur 1614-1674 .... LC 8

Peychinovich
See Vazov, Ivan (Minchov)

Phaedrus c. 18B.C.-c. 50 .... CMLC 25
See also DLB 211

Philips, Katherine 1632-1664 .... LC 30
See also DLB 131

Philipson, Morris H. 1926- .... CLC 53
See also CA 1-4R; CANR 4

Phillips, Caryl 1958- . CLC 96; BLCS; DAM
MULT
See also BW 2; CA 141; CANR 63; DA3;
DLB 157; MTCW 2

Phillips, David Graham
1867-1911 .... TCLC 44
See also CA 108; 176; DLB 9, 12

Phillips, Jack
See Sandburg, Carl (August)

Phillips, Jayne Anne 1952- .... CLC 15, 33;
SSC 16
See also CA 101; CANR 24, 50; DLBY 80;
INT CANR-24; MTCW 1, 2

Phillips, Richard
See Dick, Philip K(indred)

Phillips, Robert (Schaeffer) 1938- .... CLC 28
See also CA 17-20R; CAAS 13; CANR 8;
DLB 105

Phillips, Ward
See Lovecraft, H(oward) P(hillips)

Piccolo, Lucio 1901-1969 .... CLC 13
See also CA 97-100; DLB 114

Pickthall, Marjorie L(owry) C(hristie)
1883-1922 .... TCLC 21
See also CA 107; DLB 92

Pico della Mirandola, Giovanni
1463-1494 .... LC 15

Piercy, Marge 1936- .... CLC 3, 6, 14, 18, 27,
62, 128; PC 29
See also CA 21-24R; CAAS 1; CANR 13,
43, 66; DLB 120, 227; MTCW 1, 2

Piers, Robert
See Anthony, Piers

Pieyre de Mandiargues, Andre 1909-1991
See Mandiargues, Andre Pieyre de
See also CA 103; 136; CANR 22, 82

Pilnyak, Boris TCLC 23
See also Vogau, Boris Andreyevich

Pincherle, Alberto 1907-1990 .... CLC 11, 18;
DAM NOV
See also Moravia, Alberto
See also CA 25-28R; 132; CANR 33, 63;
MTCW 1

Pinckney, Darryl 1953- .... CLC 76
See also BW 2, 3; CA 143; CANR 79

Pindar 518B.C.-446B.C. .... CMLC 12; PC 19
See also DLB 176

Pineda, Cecile 1942- .... CLC 39
See also CA 118

Pinero, Arthur Wing 1855-1934 ... TCLC 32;
DAM DRAM
See also CA 110; 153; DLB 10

Pinero, Miguel (Antonio Gomez)
1946-1988 .... CLC 4, 55
See also CA 61-64; 125; CANR 29, 90; HW
1

Pinget, Robert 1919-1997 .... CLC 7, 13, 37
See also CA 85-88; 160; DLB 83

Pink Floyd
See Barrett, (Roger) Syd; Gilmour, David;
Mason, Nick; Waters, Roger; Wright, Rick

Pinkney, Edward 1802-1828 .... NCLC 31

Pinkwater, Daniel Manus 1941- .... CLC 35
See also Pinkwater, Manus
See also AAYA 1; CA 29-32R; CANR 12,
38, 89; CLR 4; JRDA; MAICYA; SAAS
3; SATA 46, 76, 114

Pinkwater, Manus
See Pinkwater, Daniel Manus
See also SATA 8

Pinsky, Robert 1940- .... CLC 9, 19, 38, 94, 121; DAM POET; PC 27
See also CA 29-32R; CAAS 4; CANR 58; DA3; DLBY 82, 98; MTCW 2

Pinta, Harold
See Pinter, Harold

Pinter, Harold 1930- .. CLC 1, 3, 6, 9, 11, 15, 27, 58, 73; DA; DAB; DAC; DAM DRAM, MST; WLC
See also CA 5-8R; CANR 33, 65; CDBLB 1960 to Present; DA3; DLB 13; MTCW 1, 2

Piozzi, Hester Lynch (Thrale) 1741-1821 .... NCLC 57
See also DLB 104, 142

Pirandello, Luigi 1867-1936 ...... TCLC 4, 29; DA; DAB; DAC; DAM DRAM, MST; DC 5; SSC 22; WLC
See also CA 104; 153; DA3; MTCW 2

Pirsig, Robert M(aynard) 1928- ... CLC 4, 6, 73; DAM POP
See also CA 53-56; CANR 42, 74; DA3; MTCW 1, 2; SATA 39

Pisarev, Dmitry Ivanovich 1840-1868 .... NCLC 25

Pix, Mary (Griffith) 1666-1709 .... LC 8
See also DLB 80

Pixerecourt, (Rene Charles) Guilbert de 1773-1844 .... NCLC 39
See also DLB 192

Plaatje, Sol(omon) T(shekisho) 1876-1932 .... TCLC 73; BLCS
See also BW 2, 3; CA 141; CANR 79; DLB 225

Plaidy, Jean
See Hibbert, Eleanor Alice Burford

Planche, James Robinson 1796-1880 .... NCLC 42

Plant, Robert 1948- .... CLC 12

Plante, David (Robert) 1940- ...... CLC 7, 23, 38; DAM NOV
See also CA 37-40R; CANR 12, 36, 58, 82; DLBY 83; INT CANR-12; MTCW 1

Plath, Sylvia 1932-1963 ..... CLC 1, 2, 3, 5, 9, 11, 14, 17, 50, 51, 62, 111; DA; DAB; DAC; DAM MST, POET; PC 1; WLC
See also AAYA 13; CA 19-20; CANR 34; CAP 2; CDALB 1941-1968; DA3; DLB 5, 6, 152; MTCW 1, 2; SATA 96

Plato 428(?)B.C.-348(?)B.C. ... CMLC 8; DA; DAB; DAC; DAM MST; WLCS
See also DA3; DLB 176

Platonov, Andrei
See Klimentov, Andrei Platonovich

Platt, Kin 1911- .... CLC 26
See also AAYA 11; CA 17-20R; CANR 11; JRDA; SAAS 17; SATA 21, 86

Plautus c. 251B.C.-184B.C. ... CMLC 24; DC 6
See also DLB 211

Plick et Plock
See Simenon, Georges (Jacques Christian)

Plimpton, George (Ames) 1927- .... CLC 36
See also AITN 1; CA 21-24R; CANR 32, 70; DLB 185; MTCW 1, 2; SATA 10

Pliny the Elder c. 23-79 .... CMLC 23
See also DLB 211

Plomer, William Charles Franklin 1903-1973 .... CLC 4, 8
See also CA 21-22; CANR 34; CAP 2; DLB 20, 162, 191, 225; MTCW 1; SATA 24

Plowman, Piers
See Kavanagh, Patrick (Joseph)

Plum, J.
See Wodehouse, P(elham) G(renville)

Plumly, Stanley (Ross) 1939- .... CLC 33
See also CA 108; 110; DLB 5, 193; INT 110

Plumpe, Friedrich Wilhelm 1888-1931 .... TCLC 53
See also CA 112

Po Chu-i 772-846 .... CMLC 24

Poe, Edgar Allan 1809-1849 ..... NCLC 1, 16, 55, 78; DA; DAB; DAC; DAM MST, POET; PC 1; SSC 34; WLC
See also AAYA 14; CDALB 1640-1865; DA3; DLB 3, 59, 73, 74; SATA 23

Poet of Titchfield Street, The
See Pound, Ezra (Weston Loomis)

Pohl, Frederik 1919- .... CLC 18; SSC 25
See also AAYA 24; CA 61-64; CAAS 1; CANR 11, 37, 81; DLB 8; INT CANR-11; MTCW 1, 2; SATA 24

Poirier, Louis 1910-
See Gracq, Julien
See also CA 122; 126

Poitier, Sidney 1927- .... CLC 26
See also BW 1; CA 117

Polanski, Roman 1933- .... CLC 16
See also CA 77-80

Poliakoff, Stephen 1952- .... CLC 38
See also CA 106; DLB 13

Police, The
See Copeland, Stewart (Armstrong); Summers, Andrew James; Sumner, Gordon Matthew

Polidori, John William 1795-1821 . NCLC 51
See also DLB 116

Pollitt, Katha 1949- .... CLC 28, 122
See also CA 120; 122; CANR 66; MTCW 1, 2

Pollock, (Mary) Sharon 1936- .... CLC 50; DAC; DAM DRAM, MST
See also CA 141; DLB 60

Polo, Marco 1254-1324 .... CMLC 15

Polonsky, Abraham (Lincoln) 1910- .... CLC 92
See also CA 104; DLB 26; INT 104

Polybius c. 200B.C.-c. 118B.C. ...... CMLC 17
See also DLB 176

Pomerance, Bernard 1940- ... CLC 13; DAM DRAM
See also CA 101; CANR 49

Ponge, Francis 1899-1988 . CLC 6, 18; DAM POET
See also CA 85-88; 126; CANR 40, 86

Poniatowska, Elena 1933-
See also CA 101; CANR 32, 66; DAM MULT; DLB 113; HLC 2; HW 1, 2

Pontoppidan, Henrik 1857-1943 .... TCLC 29
See also CA 170

Poole, Josephine .... CLC 17
See Helyar, Jane Penelope Josephine
See also SAAS 2; SATA 5

Popa, Vasko 1922-1991 .... CLC 19
See also CA 112; 148; DLB 181

Pope, Alexander 1688-1744 ...... LC 3, 58, 60; DA; DAB; DAC; DAM MST, POET; PC 26; WLC
See also CDBLB 1660-1789; DA3; DLB 95, 101

Porter, Connie (Rose) 1959(?)- .... CLC 70
See also BW 2, 3; CA 142; CANR 90; SATA 81

Porter, Gene(va Grace) Stratton 1863(?)-1924 .... TCLC 21
See also CA 112

Porter, Katherine Anne 1890-1980 ... CLC 1, 3, 7, 10, 13, 15, 27, 101; DA; DAB; DAC; DAM MST, NOV; SSC 4, 31
See also AITN 2; CA 1-4R; 101; CANR 1, 65; CDALBS; DA3; DLB 4, 9, 102; DLBD 12; DLBY 80; MTCW 1, 2; SATA 39; SATA-Obit 23

Porter, Peter (Neville Frederick) 1929- .... CLC 5, 13, 33
See also CA 85-88; DLB 40

Porter, William Sydney 1862-1910
See Henry, O.
See also CA 104; 131; CDALB 1865-1917; DA; DAB; DAC; DAM MST; DA3; DLB 12, 78, 79; MTCW 1, 2; YABC 2

Portillo (y Pacheco), Jose Lopez
See Lopez Portillo (y Pacheco), Jose

Portillo Trambley, Estela 1927-1998
See also CANR 32; DAM MULT; DLB 209; HLC 2; HW 1

Post, Melville Davisson 1869-1930 .... TCLC 39
See also CA 110

Potok, Chaim 1929- ... CLC 2, 7, 14, 26, 112; DAM NOV
See also AAYA 15; AITN 1, 2; CA 17-20R; CANR 19, 35, 64; DA3; DLB 28, 152; INT CANR-19; MTCW 1, 2; SATA 33, 106

Potter, Dennis (Christopher George) 1935-1994 .... CLC 58, 86
See also CA 107; 145; CANR 33, 61; MTCW 1

Pound, Ezra (Weston Loomis) 1885-1972 .. CLC 1, 2, 3, 4, 5, 7, 10, 13, 18, 34, 48, 50, 112; DA; DAB; DAC; DAM MST, POET; PC 4; WLC
See also CA 5-8R; 37-40R; CANR 40; CDALB 1917-1929; DA3; DLB 4, 45, 63; DLBD 15; MTCW 1, 2

Povod, Reinaldo 1959-1994 .... CLC 44
See also CA 136; 146; CANR 83

Powell, Adam Clayton, Jr. 1908-1972 .... CLC 89; BLC 3; DAM MULT
See also BW 1, 3; CA 102; 33-36R; CANR 86

Powell, Anthony (Dymoke) 1905- . CLC 1, 3, 7, 9, 10, 31
See also CA 1-4R; CANR 1, 32, 62; CDBLB 1945-1960; DLB 15; MTCW 1, 2

Powell, Dawn 1897-1965 .... CLC 66
See also CA 5-8R; DLBY 97

Powell, Padgett 1952- .... CLC 34
See also CA 126; CANR 63

Power, Susan 1961- .... CLC 91
See also CA 145

Powers, J(ames) F(arl) 1917-1999 ..... CLC 1, 4, 8, 57; SSC 4
See also CA 1-4R; 181; CANR 2, 61; DLB 130; MTCW 1

Powers, John J(ames) 1945-
See Powers, John R.
See also CA 69-72

Powers, John R. .... CLC 66
See also Powers, John J(ames)

Powers, Richard (S.) 1957- .... CLC 93
See also CA 148; CANR 80

Pownall, David 1938- .... CLC 10
See also CA 89-92; 180; CAAS 18; CANR 49; DLB 14

Powys, John Cowper 1872-1963 ... CLC 7, 9, 15, 46, 125
See also CA 85-88; DLB 15; MTCW 1, 2

Powys, T(heodore) F(rancis) 1875-1953 .... TCLC 9
See also CA 106; DLB 36, 162

Prado (Calvo), Pedro 1886-1952 ... TCLC 75
See also CA 131; HW 1

Prager, Emily 1952- .... CLC 56

Pratt, E(dwin) J(ohn) 1883(?)-1964 .... CLC 19; DAC; DAM POET
See also CA 141; 93-96; CANR 77; DLB 92

Premchand .... TCLC 21
See also Srivastava, Dhanpat Rai

Preussler, Otfried 1923- .... CLC 17
See also CA 77-80; SATA 24

Prevert, Jacques (Henri Marie)
　　1900-1977 .... **CLC 15**
　　See also CA 77-80; 69-72; CANR 29, 61;
　　MTCW 1; SATA-Obit 30
Prevost, Abbe (Antoine Francois)
　　1697-1763 .... **LC 1**
Price, (Edward) Reynolds 1933- ... **CLC 3, 6,
　　13, 43, 50, 63; DAM NOV; SSC 22**
　　See also CA 1-4R; CANR 1, 37, 57, 87;
　　DLB 2; INT CANR-37
Price, Richard 1949- .... **CLC 6, 12**
　　See also CA 49-52; CANR 3; DLBY 81
Prichard, Katharine Susannah
　　1883-1969 .... **CLC 46**
　　See also CA 11-12; CANR 33; CAP 1;
　　MTCW 1; SATA 66
Priestley, J(ohn) B(oynton)
　　1894-1984 .... **CLC 2, 5, 9, 34; DAM
　　DRAM, NOV**
　　See also CA 9-12R; 113; CANR 33; CD-
　　BLB 1914-1945; DA3; DLB 10, 34, 77,
　　100, 139; DLBY 84; MTCW 1, 2
Prince 1958(?)- .... **CLC 35**
Prince, F(rank) T(empleton) 1912- .. **CLC 22**
　　See also CA 101; CANR 43, 79; DLB 20
Prince Kropotkin
　　See Kropotkin, Peter (Aleksieevich)
Prior, Matthew 1664-1721 .... **LC 4**
　　See also DLB 95
Prishvin, Mikhail 1873-1954 .... **TCLC 75**
Pritchard, William H(arrison)
　　1932- .... **CLC 34**
　　See also CA 65-68; CANR 23; DLB 111
Pritchett, V(ictor) S(awdon)
　　1900-1997 ...... **CLC 5, 13, 15, 41; DAM
　　NOV; SSC 14**
　　See also CA 61-64; 157; CANR 31, 63;
　　DA3; DLB 15, 139; MTCW 1, 2
Private 19022
　　See Manning, Frederic
Probst, Mark 1925- .... **CLC 59**
　　See also CA 130
Prokosch, Frederic 1908-1989 ...... **CLC 4, 48**
　　See also CA 73-76; 128; CANR 82; DLB
　　48; MTCW 2
Propertius, Sextus c. 50B.C.-c.
　　16B.C. .... **CMLC 32**
　　See also DLB 211
Prophet, The
　　See Dreiser, Theodore (Herman Albert)
Prose, Francine 1947- .... **CLC 45**
　　See also CA 109; 112; CANR 46; SATA
　　101
Proudhon
　　See Cunha, Euclides (Rodrigues Pimenta)
　　da
Proulx, Annie
　　See Proulx, E(dna) Annie
Proulx, E(dna) Annie 1935- .. **CLC 81; DAM
　　POP**
　　See also CA 145; CANR 65; DA3; MTCW
　　2
**Proust, (Valentin-Louis-George-Eugene-)
　　Marcel** 1871-1922 .... **TCLC 7, 13, 33;
　　DA; DAB; DAC; DAM MST, NOV;
　　WLC**
　　See also CA 104; 120; DA3; DLB 65;
　　MTCW 1, 2
Prowler, Harley
　　See Masters, Edgar Lee
Prus, Boleslaw 1845-1912 .... **TCLC 48**
Pryor, Richard (Franklin Lenox Thomas)
　　1940- .... **CLC 26**
　　See also CA 122; 152
Przybyszewski, Stanislaw
　　1868-1927 .... **TCLC 36**
　　See also CA 160; DLB 66

Pteleon
　　See Grieve, C(hristopher) M(urray)
　　See also DAM POET
Puckett, Lute
　　See Masters, Edgar Lee
Puig, Manuel 1932-1990 .... **CLC 3, 5, 10, 28,
　　65, 133; DAM MULT; HLC 2**
　　See also CA 45-48; CANR 2, 32, 63; DA3;
　　DLB 113; HW 1, 2; MTCW 1, 2
Pulitzer, Joseph 1847-1911 .... **TCLC 76**
　　See also CA 114; DLB 23
Purdy, A(lfred) W(ellington) 1918- ... **CLC 3,
　　6, 14, 50; DAC; DAM MST, POET**
　　See also CA 81-84; CAAS 17; CANR 42,
　　66; DLB 88
Purdy, James (Amos) 1923- .... **CLC 2, 4, 10,
　　28, 52**
　　See also CA 33-36R; CAAS 1; CANR 19,
　　51; DLB 2; INT CANR-19; MTCW 1
Pure, Simon
　　See Swinnerton, Frank Arthur
Pushkin, Alexander (Sergeyevich)
　　1799-1837 . **NCLC 3, 27, 83; DA; DAB;
　　DAC; DAM DRAM, MST, POET; PC
　　10; SSC 27; WLC**
　　See also DA3; DLB 205; SATA 61
P'u Sung-ling 1640-1715 .... **LC 49; SSC 31**
Putnam, Arthur Lee
　　See Alger, Horatio Jr., Jr.
Puzo, Mario 1920-1999 .... **CLC 1, 2, 6, 36,
　　107; DAM NOV, POP**
　　See also CA 65-68; 185; CANR 4, 42, 65;
　　DA3; DLB 6; MTCW 1, 2
Pygge, Edward
　　See Barnes, Julian (Patrick)
Pyle, Ernest Taylor 1900-1945
　　See Pyle, Ernie
　　See also CA 115; 160
Pyle, Ernie 1900-1945 .... **TCLC 75**
　　See also Pyle, Ernest Taylor
　　See also DLB 29; MTCW 2
Pyle, Howard 1853-1911 .... **TCLC 81**
　　See also CA 109; 137; CLR 22; DLB 42,
　　188; DLBD 13; MAICYA; SATA 16, 100
Pym, Barbara (Mary Crampton)
　　1913-1980 .... **CLC 13, 19, 37, 111**
　　See also CA 13-14; 97-100; CANR 13, 34;
　　CAP 1; DLB 14, 207; DLBY 87; MTCW
　　1, 2
Pynchon, Thomas (Ruggles, Jr.)
　　1937- ...... **CLC 2, 3, 6, 9, 11, 18, 33, 62,
　　72; DA; DAB; DAC; DAM MST, NOV,
　　POP; SSC 14; WLC**
　　See also BEST 90:2; CA 17-20R; CANR
　　22, 46, 73; DA3; DLB 2, 173; MTCW 1,
　　2
Pythagoras c. 570B.C.-c. 500B.C. . **CMLC 22**
　　See also DLB 176

Q
　　See Quiller-Couch, SirArthur (Thomas)
Qian Zhongshu
　　See Ch'ien Chung-shu
Qroll
　　See Dagerman, Stig (Halvard)
Quarrington, Paul (Lewis) 1953- ..... **CLC 65**
　　See also CA 129; CANR 62
Quasimodo, Salvatore 1901-1968 ..... **CLC 10**
　　See also CA 13-16; 25-28R; CAP 1; DLB
　　114; MTCW 1
Quay, Stephen 1947- .... **CLC 95**
Quay, Timothy 1947- .... **CLC 95**
Queen, Ellery **CLC 3, 11**
　　See also Dannay, Frederic; Davidson,
　　Avram (James); Lee, Manfred
　　B(ennington); Marlowe, Stephen; Stur-
　　geon, Theodore (Hamilton); Vance, John
　　Holbrook

Queen, Ellery, Jr.
　　See Dannay, Frederic; Lee, Manfred
　　B(ennington)
Queneau, Raymond 1903-1976 ..... **CLC 2, 5,
　　10, 42**
　　See also CA 77-80; 69-72; CANR 32; DLB
　　72; MTCW 1, 2
Quevedo, Francisco de 1580-1645 .... **LC 23**
Quiller-Couch, SirArthur (Thomas)
　　1863-1944 .... **TCLC 53**
　　See also CA 118; 166; DLB 135, 153, 190
Quin, Ann (Marie) 1936-1973 .... **CLC 6**
　　See also CA 9-12R; 45-48; DLB 14
Quinn, Martin
　　See Smith, Martin Cruz
Quinn, Peter 1947- .... **CLC 91**
Quinn, Simon
　　See Smith, Martin Cruz
Quintana, Leroy V. 1944-
　　See also CA 131; CANR 65; DAM MULT;
　　DLB 82; HLC 2; HW 1, 2
Quiroga, Horacio (Sylvestre)
　　1878-1937 .... **TCLC 20; DAM MULT;
　　HLC 2**
　　See also CA 117; 131; HW 1; MTCW 1
Quoirez, Francoise 1935- .... **CLC 9**
　　See also Sagan, Francoise
　　See also CA 49-52; CANR 6, 39, 73;
　　MTCW 1, 2
Raabe, Wilhelm (Karl) 1831-1910 . **TCLC 45**
　　See also CA 167; DLB 129
Rabe, David (William) 1940- .. **CLC 4, 8, 33;
　　DAM DRAM**
　　See also CA 85-88; CABS 3; CANR 59;
　　DLB 7, 228
Rabelais, Francois 1483-1553 .... **LC 5, 60;
　　DA; DAB; DAC; DAM MST; WLC**
Rabinovitch, Sholem 1859-1916
　　See Aleichem, Sholom
　　See also CA 104
Rabinyan, Dorit 1972- .... **CLC 119**
　　See also CA 170
Rachilde
　　See Vallette, Marguerite Eymery
Racine, Jean 1639-1699 . **LC 28; DAB; DAM
　　MST**
　　See also DA3
Radcliffe, Ann (Ward) 1764-1823 ... **NCLC 6,
　　55**
　　See also DLB 39, 178
Radiguet, Raymond 1903-1923 ...... **TCLC 29**
　　See also CA 162; DLB 65
Radnoti, Miklos 1909-1944 .... **TCLC 16**
　　See also CA 118
Rado, James 1939- .... **CLC 17**
　　See also CA 105
Radvanyi, Netty 1900-1983
　　See Seghers, Anna
　　See also CA 85-88; 110; CANR 82
Rae, Ben
　　See Griffiths, Trevor
Raeburn, John (Hay) 1941- .... **CLC 34**
　　See also CA 57-60
Ragni, Gerome 1942-1991 .... **CLC 17**
　　See also CA 105; 134
Rahv, Philip 1908-1973 .... **CLC 24**
　　See also Greenberg, Ivan
　　See also DLB 137
Raimund, Ferdinand Jakob
　　1790-1836 .... **NCLC 69**
　　See also DLB 90
Raine, Craig 1944- .... **CLC 32, 103**
　　See also CA 108; CANR 29, 51; DLB 40
Raine, Kathleen (Jessie) 1908- ..... **CLC 7, 45**
　　See also CA 85-88; CANR 46; DLB 20;
　　MTCW 1
Rainis, Janis 1865-1929 .... **TCLC 29**
　　See also CA 170; DLB 220

Rakosi, Carl 1903- .... **CLC 47**
See also Rawley, Callman
See also CAAS 5; DLB 193

Raleigh, Richard
See Lovecraft, H(oward) P(hillips)

Raleigh, Sir Walter 1554(?)-1618 .... **LC 31, 39; PC 31**
See also CDBLB Before 1660; DLB 172

Rallentando, H. P.
See Sayers, Dorothy L(eigh)

Ramal, Walter
See de la Mare, Walter (John)

Ramana Maharshi 1879-1950 .... **TCLC 84**

Ramoacn y Cajal, Santiago 1852-1934 .... **TCLC 93**

Ramon, Juan
See Jimenez (Mantecon), Juan Ramon

Ramos, Graciliano 1892-1953 .... **TCLC 32**
See also CA 167; HW 2

Rampersad, Arnold 1941- .... **CLC 44**
See also BW 2, 3; CA 127; 133; CANR 81; DLB 111; INT 133

Rampling, Anne
See Rice, Anne

Ramsay, Allan 1684(?)-1758 .... **LC 29**
See also DLB 95

Ramuz, Charles-Ferdinand 1878-1947 .... **TCLC 33**
See also CA 165

Rand, Ayn 1905-1982 ...... **CLC 3, 30, 44, 79; DA; DAC; DAM MST, NOV, POP; WLC**
See also AAYA 10; CA 13-16R; 105; CANR 27, 73; CDALBS; DA3; DLB 227; MTCW 1, 2

Randall, Dudley (Felker) 1914-2000 . **CLC 1; BLC 3; DAM MULT**
See also BW 1, 3; CA 25-28R; CANR 23, 82; DLB 41

Randall, Robert
See Silverberg, Robert

Ranger, Ken
See Creasey, John

Ransom, John Crowe 1888-1974 .. **CLC 2, 4, 5, 11, 24; DAM POET**
See also CA 5-8R; 49-52; CANR 6, 34; CDALBS; DA3; DLB 45, 63; MTCW 1, 2

Rao, Raja 1909- ..... **CLC 25, 56; DAM NOV**
See also CA 73-76; CANR 51; MTCW 1, 2

Raphael, Frederic (Michael) 1931- ... **CLC 2, 14**
See also CA 1-4R; CANR 1, 86; DLB 14

Ratcliffe, James P.
See Mencken, H(enry) L(ouis)

Rathbone, Julian 1935- .... **CLC 41**
See also CA 101; CANR 34, 73

Rattigan, Terence (Mervyn) 1911-1977 .... **CLC 7; DAM DRAM**
See also CA 85-88; 73-76; CDBLB 1945-1960; DLB 13; MTCW 1, 2

Ratushinskaya, Irina 1954- .... **CLC 54**
See also CA 129; CANR 68

Raven, Simon (Arthur Noel) 1927- .. **CLC 14**
See also CA 81-84; CANR 86

Ravenna, Michael
See Welty, Eudora

Rawley, Callman 1903-
See Rakosi, Carl
See also CA 21-24R; CANR 12, 32, 91

Rawlings, Marjorie Kinnan 1896-1953 .... **TCLC 4**
See also AAYA 20; CA 104; 137; CANR 74; CLR 63; DLB 9, 22, 102; DLBD 17; JRDA; MAICYA; MTCW 2; SATA 100; YABC 1

Ray, Satyajit 1921-1992 .. **CLC 16, 76; DAM MULT**
See also CA 114; 137

Read, Herbert Edward 1893-1968 ..... **CLC 4**
See also CA 85-88; 25-28R; DLB 20, 149

Read, Piers Paul 1941- .... **CLC 4, 10, 25**
See also CA 21-24R; CANR 38, 86; DLB 14; SATA 21

Reade, Charles 1814-1884 .... **NCLC 2, 74**
See also DLB 21

Reade, Hamish
See Gray, Simon (James Holliday)

Reading, Peter 1946- .... **CLC 47**
See also CA 103; CANR 46; DLB 40

Reaney, James 1926- .. **CLC 13; DAC; DAM MST**
See also CA 41-44R; CAAS 15; CANR 42; DLB 68; SATA 43

Rebreanu, Liviu 1885-1944 .... **TCLC 28**
See also CA 165; DLB 220

Rechy, John (Francisco) 1934- .... **CLC 1, 7, 14, 18, 107; DAM MULT; HLC 2**
See also CA 5-8R; CAAS 4; CANR 6, 32, 64; DLB 122; DLBY 82; HW 1, 2; INT CANR-6

Redcam, Tom 1870-1933 .... **TCLC 25**

Reddin, Keith CLC 67

Redgrove, Peter (William) 1932- . **CLC 6, 41**
See also CA 1-4R; CANR 3, 39, 77; DLB 40

Redmon, Anne CLC 22
See also Nightingale, Anne Redmon
See also DLBY 86

Reed, Eliot
See Ambler, Eric

Reed, Ishmael 1938- .. **CLC 2, 3, 5, 6, 13, 32, 60; BLC 3; DAM MULT**
See also BW 2, 3; CA 21-24R; CANR 25, 48, 74; DA3; DLB 2, 5, 33, 169, 227; DLBD 8; MTCW 1, 2

Reed, John (Silas) 1887-1920 .... **TCLC 9**
See also CA 106

Reed, Lou CLC 21
See also Firbank, Louis

Reese, Lizette Woodworth 1856-1935 . **PC 29**
See also CA 180; DLB 54

Reeve, Clara 1729-1807 .... **NCLC 19**
See also DLB 39

Reich, Wilhelm 1897-1957 .... **TCLC 57**

Reid, Christopher (John) 1949- .... **CLC 33**
See also CA 140; CANR 89; DLB 40

Reid, Desmond
See Moorcock, Michael (John)

Reid Banks, Lynne 1929-
See Banks, Lynne Reid
See also CA 1-4R; CANR 6, 22, 38, 87; CLR 24; JRDA; MAICYA; SATA 22, 75, 111

Reilly, William K.
See Creasey, John

Reiner, Max
See Caldwell, (Janet Miriam) Taylor (Holland)

Reis, Ricardo
See Pessoa, Fernando (Antonio Nogueira)

Remarque, Erich Maria 1898-1970 ... **CLC 21; DA; DAB; DAC; DAM MST, NOV**
See also AAYA 27; CA 77-80; 29-32R; DA3; DLB 56; MTCW 1, 2

Remington, Frederic 1861-1909 ..... **TCLC 89**
See also CA 108; 169; DLB 12, 186, 188; SATA 41

Remizov, A.
See Remizov, Aleksei (Mikhailovich)

Remizov, A. M.
See Remizov, Aleksei (Mikhailovich)

Remizov, Aleksei (Mikhailovich) 1877-1957 .... **TCLC 27**
See also CA 125; 133

Renan, Joseph Ernest 1823-1892 .. **NCLC 26**

Renard, Jules 1864-1910 .... **TCLC 17**
See also CA 117

Renault, Mary -1983 .... **CLC 3, 11, 17**
See also Challans, Mary
See also DLBY 83; MTCW 2

Rendell, Ruth (Barbara) 1930- . **CLC 28, 48; DAM POP**
See also Vine, Barbara
See also CA 109; CANR 32, 52, 74; DLB 87; INT CANR-32; MTCW 1, 2

Renoir, Jean 1894-1979 .... **CLC 20**
See also CA 129; 85-88

Resnais, Alain 1922- .... **CLC 16**

Reverdy, Pierre 1889-1960 .... **CLC 53**
See also CA 97-100; 89-92

Rexroth, Kenneth 1905-1982 .... **CLC 1, 2, 6, 11, 22, 49, 112; DAM POET; PC 20**
See also CA 5-8R; 107; CANR 14, 34, 63; CDALB 1941-1968; DLB 16, 48, 165, 212; DLBY 82; INT CANR-14; MTCW 1, 2

Reyes, Alfonso 1889-1959 .. **TCLC 33; HLCS 2**
See also CA 131; HW 1

Reyes y Basoalto, Ricardo Eliecer Neftali
See Neruda, Pablo

Reymont, Wladyslaw (Stanislaw) 1868(?)-1925 .... **TCLC 5**
See also CA 104

Reynolds, Jonathan 1942- .... **CLC 6, 38**
See also CA 65-68; CANR 28

Reynolds, Joshua 1723-1792 .... **LC 15**
See also DLB 104

Reynolds, Michael S(hane) 1937- ..... **CLC 44**
See also CA 65-68; CANR 9, 89

Reznikoff, Charles 1894-1976 .... **CLC 9**
See also CA 33-36; 61-64; CAP 2; DLB 28, 45

Rezzori (d'Arezzo), Gregor von 1914-1998 .... **CLC 25**
See also CA 122; 136; 167

Rhine, Richard
See Silverstein, Alvin

Rhodes, Eugene Manlove 1869-1934 .... **TCLC 53**

Rhodius, Apollonius c. 3rd cent. B.C.- .... **CMLC 28**
See also DLB 176

R'hoone
See Balzac, Honore de

Rhys, Jean 1890(?)-1979 ...... **CLC 2, 4, 6, 14, 19, 51, 124; DAM NOV; SSC 21**
See also CA 25-28R; 85-88; CANR 35, 62; CDBLB 1945-1960; DA3; DLB 36, 117, 162; MTCW 1, 2

Ribeiro, Darcy 1922-1997 .... **CLC 34**
See also CA 33-36R; 156

Ribeiro, Joao Ubaldo (Osorio Pimentel) 1941- .... **CLC 10, 67**
See also CA 81-84

Ribman, Ronald (Burt) 1932- .... **CLC 7**
See also CA 21-24R; CANR 46, 80

Ricci, Nino 1959- .... **CLC 70**
See also CA 137

Rice, Anne 1941- .. **CLC 41, 128; DAM POP**
See also AAYA 9; BEST 89:2; CA 65-68; CANR 12, 36, 53, 74; DA3; MTCW 2

Rice, Elmer (Leopold) 1892-1967 ...... **CLC 7, 49; DAM DRAM**
See also CA 21-22; 25-28R; CAP 2; DLB 4, 7; MTCW 1, 2

Rice, Tim(othy Miles Bindon) 1944- .... **CLC 21**
See also CA 103; CANR 46

Rich, Adrienne (Cecile) 1929- ... **CLC 3, 6, 7, 11, 18, 36, 73, 76, 125; DAM POET; PC 5**
See also CA 9-12R; CANR 20, 53, 74; CDALBS; DA3; DLB 5, 67; MTCW 1, 2

Rich, Barbara
See Graves, Robert (von Ranke)

Rich, Robert
See Trumbo, Dalton

Richard, Keith CLC 17
See also Richards, Keith

Richards, David Adams 1950- .... **CLC 59; DAC**
See also CA 93-96; CANR 60; DLB 53

Richards, I(vor) A(rmstrong) 1893-1979 .... **CLC 14, 24**
See also CA 41-44R; 89-92; CANR 34, 74; DLB 27; MTCW 2

Richards, Keith 1943-
See Richard, Keith
See also CA 107; CANR 77

Richardson, Anne
See Roiphe, Anne (Richardson)

Richardson, Dorothy Miller 1873-1957 .... **TCLC 3**
See also CA 104; DLB 36

Richardson, Ethel Florence (Lindesay) 1870-1946
See Richardson, Henry Handel
See also CA 105

Richardson, Henry Handel TCLC 4
See also Richardson, Ethel Florence (Lindesay)
See also DLB 197

Richardson, John 1796-1852 .... **NCLC 55; DAC**
See also DLB 99

Richardson, Samuel 1689-1761 ...... **LC 1, 44; DA; DAB; DAC; DAM MST, NOV; WLC**
See also CDBLB 1660-1789; DLB 39

Richler, Mordecai 1931- ...... **CLC 3, 5, 9, 13, 18, 46, 70; DAC; DAM MST, NOV**
See also AITN 1; CA 65-68; CANR 31, 62; CLR 17; DLB 53; MAICYA; MTCW 1, 2; SATA 44, 98; SATA-Brief 27

Richter, Conrad (Michael) 1890-1968 .... **CLC 30**
See also AAYA 21; CA 5-8R; 25-28R; CANR 23; DLB 9, 212; MTCW 1, 2; SATA 3

Ricostranza, Tom
See Ellis, Trey

Riddell, Charlotte 1832-1906 .... **TCLC 40**
See also CA 165; DLB 156

Ridge, John Rollin 1827-1867 ...... **NCLC 82; DAM MULT**
See also CA 144; DLB 175; NNAL

Ridgway, Keith 1965- .... **CLC 119**
See also CA 172

Riding, Laura CLC 3, 7
See also Jackson, Laura (Riding)

Riefenstahl, Berta Helene Amalia 1902-
See Riefenstahl, Leni
See also CA 108

Riefenstahl, Leni CLC 16
See also Riefenstahl, Berta Helene Amalia

Riffe, Ernest
See Bergman, (Ernst) Ingmar

Riggs, (Rolla) Lynn 1899-1954 ..... **TCLC 56; DAM MULT**
See also CA 144; DLB 175; NNAL

Riis, Jacob A(ugust) 1849-1914 ..... **TCLC 80**
See also CA 113; 168; DLB 23

Riley, James Whitcomb 1849-1916 .... **TCLC 51; DAM POET**
See also CA 118; 137; MAICYA; SATA 17

Riley, Tex
See Creasey, John

Rilke, Rainer Maria 1875-1926 .. **TCLC 1, 6, 19; DAM POET; PC 2**
See also CA 104; 132; CANR 62; DA3; DLB 81; MTCW 1, 2

Rimbaud, (Jean Nicolas) Arthur 1854-1891 . **NCLC 4, 35, 82; DA; DAB; DAC; DAM MST, POET; PC 3; WLC**
See also DA3

Rinehart, Mary Roberts 1876-1958 .... **TCLC 52**
See also CA 108; 166

Ringmaster, The
See Mencken, H(enry) L(ouis)

Ringwood, Gwen(dolyn Margaret) Pharis 1910-1984 .... **CLC 48**
See also CA 148; 112; DLB 88

Rio, Michel 19(?)- .... **CLC 43**

Ritsos, Giannes
See Ritsos, Yannis

Ritsos, Yannis 1909-1990 .... **CLC 6, 13, 31**
See also CA 77-80; 133; CANR 39, 61; MTCW 1

Ritter, Erika 1948(?)- .... **CLC 52**

Rivera, Jose Eustasio 1889-1928 ... **TCLC 35**
See also CA 162; HW 1, 2

Rivera, Tomas 1935-1984
See also CA 49-52; CANR 32; DLB 82; HLCS 2; HW 1

Rivers, Conrad Kent 1933-1968 .... **CLC 1**
See also BW 1; CA 85-88; DLB 41

Rivers, Elfrida
See Bradley, Marion Zimmer

Riverside, John
See Heinlein, Robert A(nson)

Rizal, Jose 1861-1896 .... **NCLC 27**

Roa Bastos, Augusto (Antonio) 1917- .... **CLC 45; DAM MULT; HLC 2**
See also CA 131; DLB 113; HW 1

Robbe-Grillet, Alain 1922- .... **CLC 1, 2, 4, 6, 8, 10, 14, 43, 128**
See also CA 9-12R; CANR 33, 65; DLB 83; MTCW 1, 2

Robbins, Harold 1916-1997 .... **CLC 5; DAM NOV**
See also CA 73-76; 162; CANR 26, 54; DA3; MTCW 1, 2

Robbins, Thomas Eugene 1936-
See Robbins, Tom
See also CA 81-84; CANR 29, 59; DAM NOV, POP; DA3; MTCW 1, 2

Robbins, Tom CLC 9, 32, 64
See also Robbins, Thomas Eugene
See also AAYA 32; BEST 90:3; DLBY 80; MTCW 2

Robbins, Trina 1938- .... **CLC 21**
See also CA 128

Roberts, Charles G(eorge) D(ouglas) 1860-1943 .... **TCLC 8**
See also CA 105; CLR 33; DLB 92; SATA 88; SATA-Brief 29

Roberts, Elizabeth Madox 1886-1941 .... **TCLC 68**
See also CA 111; 166; DLB 9, 54, 102; SATA 33; SATA-Brief 27

Roberts, Kate 1891-1985 .... **CLC 15**
See also CA 107; 116

Roberts, Keith (John Kingston) 1935- .... **CLC 14**
See also CA 25-28R; CANR 46

Roberts, Kenneth (Lewis) 1885-1957 .... **TCLC 23**
See also CA 109; DLB 9

Roberts, Michele (B.) 1949- .... **CLC 48**
See also CA 115; CANR 58

Robertson, Ellis
See Ellison, Harlan (Jay); Silverberg, Robert

Robertson, Thomas William 1829-1871 .... **NCLC 35; DAM DRAM**

Robeson, Kenneth
See Dent, Lester

Robinson, Edwin Arlington 1869-1935 ... **TCLC 5; DA; DAC; DAM MST, POET; PC 1**
See also CA 104; 133; CDALB 1865-1917; DLB 54; MTCW 1, 2

Robinson, Henry Crabb 1775-1867 .... **NCLC 15**
See also DLB 107

Robinson, Jill 1936- .... **CLC 10**
See also CA 102; INT 102

Robinson, Kim Stanley 1952- .... **CLC 34**
See also AAYA 26; CA 126; SATA 109

Robinson, Lloyd
See Silverberg, Robert

Robinson, Marilynne 1944- .... **CLC 25**
See also CA 116; CANR 80; DLB 206

Robinson, Smokey CLC 21
See also Robinson, William, Jr.

Robinson, William, Jr. 1940-
See Robinson, Smokey
See also CA 116

Robison, Mary 1949- .... **CLC 42, 98**
See also CA 113; 116; CANR 87; DLB 130; INT 116

Rod, Edouard 1857-1910 .... **TCLC 52**

Roddenberry, Eugene Wesley 1921-1991
See Roddenberry, Gene
See also CA 110; 135; CANR 37; SATA 45; SATA-Obit 69

Roddenberry, Gene CLC 17
See also Roddenberry, Eugene Wesley
See also AAYA 5; SATA-Obit 69

Rodgers, Mary 1931- .... **CLC 12**
See also CA 49-52; CANR 8, 55, 90; CLR 20; INT CANR-8; JRDA; MAICYA; SATA 8

Rodgers, W(illiam) R(obert) 1909-1969 .... **CLC 7**
See also CA 85-88; DLB 20

Rodman, Eric
See Silverberg, Robert

Rodman, Howard 1920(?)-1985 .... **CLC 65**
See also CA 118

Rodman, Maia
See Wojciechowska, Maia (Teresa)

Rodo, Jose Enrique 1872(?)-1917
See also CA 178; HLCS 2; HW 2

Rodriguez, Claudio 1934- .... **CLC 10**
See also DLB 134

Rodriguez, Richard 1944-
See also CA 110; CANR 66; DAM MULT; DLB 82; HLC 2; HW 1, 2

Roelvaag, O(le) E(dvart) 1876-1931 .... **TCLC 17**
See also Rolvaag, O(le) E(dvart)
See also CA 117; 171; DLB 9

Roethke, Theodore (Huebner) 1908-1963 .... **CLC 1, 3, 8, 11, 19, 46, 101; DAM POET; PC 15**
See also CA 81-84; CABS 2; CDALB 1941-1968; DA3; DLB 5, 206; MTCW 1, 2

Rogers, Samuel 1763-1855 .... **NCLC 69**
See also DLB 93

Rogers, Thomas Hunton 1927- .... **CLC 57**
See also CA 89-92; INT 89-92

Rogers, Will(iam Penn Adair) 1879-1935 ... **TCLC 8, 71; DAM MULT**
See also CA 105; 144; DA3; DLB 11; MTCW 2; NNAL

Rogin, Gilbert 1929- .... **CLC 18**
See also CA 65-68; CANR 15

Rohan, Koda
See Koda Shigeyuki

Author Index

Rohlfs, Anna Katharine Green
See Green, Anna Katharine
Rohmer, Eric CLC 16
See also Scherer, Jean-Marie Maurice
Rohmer, Sax TCLC 28
See also Ward, Arthur Henry Sarsfield
See also DLB 70
Roiphe, Anne (Richardson) 1935- .. CLC 3, 9
See also CA 89-92; CANR 45, 73; DLBY 80; INT 89-92
Rojas, Fernando de 1465-1541 .... LC 23; HLCS 1
Rojas, Gonzalo 1917-
See also HLCS 2; HW 2
Rojas, Gonzalo 1917-
See also CA 178; HLCS 2
Rolfe, Frederick (William Serafino Austin Lewis Mary) 1860-1913 .... TCLC 12
See also CA 107; DLB 34, 156
Rolland, Romain 1866-1944 .... TCLC 23
See also CA 118; DLB 65
Rolle, Richard c. 1300-c. 1349 ...... CMLC 21
See also DLB 146
Rolvaag, O(le) E(dvart)
See Roelvaag, O(le) E(dvart)
Romain Arnaud, Saint
See Aragon, Louis
Romains, Jules 1885-1972 .... CLC 7
See also CA 85-88; CANR 34; DLB 65; MTCW 1
Romero, Jose Ruben 1890-1952 .... TCLC 14
See also CA 114; 131; HW 1
Ronsard, Pierre de 1524-1585 . LC 6, 54; PC 11
Rooke, Leon 1934- . CLC 25, 34; DAM POP
See also CA 25-28R; CANR 23, 53
Roosevelt, Franklin Delano 1882-1945 .... TCLC 93
See also CA 116; 173
Roosevelt, Theodore 1858-1919 ..... TCLC 69
See also CA 115; 170; DLB 47, 186
Roper, William 1498-1578 .... LC 10
Roquelaure, A. N.
See Rice, Anne
Rosa, Joao Guimaraes 1908-1967 ... CLC 23; HLCS 1
See also CA 89-92; DLB 113
Rose, Wendy 1948- .. CLC 85; DAM MULT; PC 13
See also CA 53-56; CANR 5, 51; DLB 175; NNAL; SATA 12
Rosen, R. D.
See Rosen, Richard (Dean)
Rosen, Richard (Dean) 1949- .... CLC 39
See also CA 77-80; CANR 62; INT CANR-30
Rosenberg, Isaac 1890-1918 .... TCLC 12
See also CA 107; DLB 20
Rosenblatt, Joe CLC 15
See also Rosenblatt, Joseph
Rosenblatt, Joseph 1933-
See Rosenblatt, Joe
See also CA 89-92; INT 89-92
Rosenfeld, Samuel
See Tzara, Tristan
Rosenstock, Sami
See Tzara, Tristan
Rosenstock, Samuel
See Tzara, Tristan
Rosenthal, M(acha) L(ouis) 1917-1996 .... CLC 28
See also CA 1-4R; 152; CAAS 6; CANR 4, 51; DLB 5; SATA 59
Ross, Barnaby
See Dannay, Frederic
Ross, Bernard L.
See Follett, Ken(neth Martin)

Ross, J. H.
See Lawrence, T(homas) E(dward)
Ross, John Hume
See Lawrence, T(homas) E(dward)
Ross, Martin
See Martin, Violet Florence
See also DLB 135
Ross, (James) Sinclair 1908-1996 ... CLC 13; DAC; DAM MST; SSC 24
See also CA 73-76; CANR 81; DLB 88
Rossetti, Christina (Georgina) 1830-1894 . NCLC 2, 50, 66; DA; DAB; DAC; DAM MST, POET; PC 7; WLC
See also DA3; DLB 35, 163; MAICYA; SATA 20
Rossetti, Dante Gabriel 1828-1882 . NCLC 4, 77; DA; DAB; DAC; DAM MST, POET; WLC
See also CDBLB 1832-1890; DLB 35
Rossner, Judith (Perelman) 1935- . CLC 6, 9, 29
See also AITN 2; BEST 90:3; CA 17-20R; CANR 18, 51, 73; DLB 6; INT CANR-18; MTCW 1, 2
Rostand, Edmond (Eugene Alexis) 1868-1918 .... TCLC 6, 37; DA; DAB; DAC; DAM DRAM, MST; DC 10
See also CA 104; 126; DA3; DLB 192; MTCW 1
Roth, Henry 1906-1995 ..... CLC 2, 6, 11, 104
See also CA 11-12; 149; CANR 38, 63; CAP 1; DA3; DLB 28; MTCW 1, 2
Roth, Philip (Milton) 1933- ... CLC 1, 2, 3, 4, 6, 9, 15, 22, 31, 47, 66, 86, 119; DA; DAB; DAC; DAM MST, NOV, POP; SSC 26; WLC
See also BEST 90:3; CA 1-4R; CANR 1, 22, 36, 55, 89; CDALB 1968-1988; DA3; DLB 2, 28, 173; DLBY 82; MTCW 1, 2
Rothenberg, Jerome 1931- .... CLC 6, 57
See also CA 45-48; CANR 1; DLB 5, 193
Roumain, Jacques (Jean Baptiste) 1907-1944 ...... TCLC 19; BLC 3; DAM MULT
See also BW 1; CA 117; 125
Rourke, Constance (Mayfield) 1885-1941 .... TCLC 12
See also CA 107; YABC 1
Rousseau, Jean-Baptiste 1671-1741 ...... LC 9
Rousseau, Jean-Jacques 1712-1778 .... LC 14, 36; DA; DAB; DAC; DAM MST; WLC
See also DA3
Roussel, Raymond 1877-1933 .... TCLC 20
See also CA 117
Rovit, Earl (Herbert) 1927- .... CLC 7
See also CA 5-8R; CANR 12
Rowe, Elizabeth Singer 1674-1737 ..... LC 44
See also DLB 39, 95
Rowe, Nicholas 1674-1718 .... LC 8
See also DLB 84
Rowley, Ames Dorrance
See Lovecraft, H(oward) P(hillips)
Rowson, Susanna Haswell 1762(?)-1824 .... NCLC 5, 69
See also DLB 37, 200
Roy, Arundhati 1960(?)- .... CLC 109
See also CA 163; CANR 90; DLBY 97
Roy, Gabrielle 1909-1983 .... CLC 10, 14; DAB; DAC; DAM MST
See also CA 53-56; 110; CANR 5, 61; DLB 68; MTCW 1; SATA 104
Royko, Mike 1932-1997 .... CLC 109
See also CA 89-92; 157; CANR 26
Rozewicz, Tadeusz 1921- .. CLC 9, 23; DAM POET
See also CA 108; CANR 36, 66; DA3; MTCW 1, 2

Ruark, Gibbons 1941- .... CLC 3
See also CA 33-36R; CAAS 23; CANR 14, 31, 57; DLB 120
Rubens, Bernice (Ruth) 1923- ...: CLC 19, 31
See also CA 25-28R; CANR 33, 65; DLB 14, 207; MTCW 1
Rubin, Harold
See Robbins, Harold
Rudkin, (James) David 1936- .... CLC 14
See also CA 89-92; DLB 13
Rudnik, Raphael 1933- .... CLC 7
See also CA 29-32R
Ruffian, M.
See Hasek, Jaroslav (Matej Frantisek)
Ruiz, Jose Martinez CLC 11
See also Martinez Ruiz, Jose
Rukeyser, Muriel 1913-1980 . CLC 6, 10, 15, 27; DAM POET; PC 12
See also CA 5-8R; 93-96; CANR 26, 60; DA3; DLB 48; MTCW 1, 2; SATA-Obit 22
Rule, Jane (Vance) 1931- .... CLC 27
See also CA 25-28R; CAAS 18; CANR 12, 87; DLB 60
Rulfo, Juan 1918-1986 ...... CLC 8, 80; DAM MULT; HLC 2; SSC 25
See also CA 85-88; 118; CANR 26; DLB 113; HW 1, 2; MTCW 1, 2
Rumi, Jalal al-Din 1297-1373 .... CMLC 20
Runeberg, Johan 1804-1877 .... NCLC 41
Runyon, (Alfred) Damon 1884(?)-1946 .... TCLC 10
See also CA 107; 165; DLB 11, 86, 171; MTCW 2
Rush, Norman 1933- .... CLC 44
See also CA 121; 126; INT 126
Rushdie, (Ahmed) Salman 1947- .... CLC 23, 31, 55, 100; DAB; DAC; DAM MST, NOV, POP; WLCS
See also BEST 89:3; CA 108; 111; CANR 33, 56; DA3; DLB 194; INT 111; MTCW 1, 2
Rushforth, Peter (Scott) 1945- .... CLC 19
See also CA 101
Ruskin, John 1819-1900 .... TCLC 63
See also CA 114; 129; CDBLB 1832-1890; DLB 55, 163, 190; SATA 24
Russ, Joanna 1937- .... CLC 15
See also CA 5-28R; CANR 11, 31, 65; DLB 8; MTCW 1
Russell, George William 1867-1935
See Baker, Jean H.
See also CA 104; 153; CDBLB 1890-1914; DAM POET
Russell, (Henry) Ken(neth Alfred) 1927- .... CLC 16
See also CA 105
Russell, William Martin 1947- .... CLC 60
See also CA 164
Rutherford, Mark TCLC 25
See also White, William Hale
See also DLB 18
Ruyslinck, Ward 1929- .... CLC 14
See also Belser, Reimond Karel Maria de
Ryan, Cornelius (John) 1920-1974 ..... CLC 7
See also CA 69-72; 53-56; CANR 38
Ryan, Michael 1946- .... CLC 65
See also CA 49-52; DLBY 82
Ryan, Tim
See Dent, Lester
Rybakov, Anatoli (Naumovich) 1911-1998 .... CLC 23, 53
See also CA 126; 135; 172; SATA 79; SATA-Obit 108
Ryder, Jonathan
See Ludlum, Robert

Ryga, George 1932-1987 .... **CLC 14; DAC; DAM MST**
See also CA 101; 124; CANR 43, 90; DLB 60

S. H.
See Hartmann, Sadakichi

S. S.
See Sassoon, Siegfried (Lorraine)

Saba, Umberto 1883-1957 .... **TCLC 33**
See also CA 144; CANR 79; DLB 114

Sabatini, Rafael 1875-1950 .... **TCLC 47**
See also CA 162

Sabato, Ernesto (R.) 1911- .... **CLC 10, 23; DAM MULT; HLC 2**
See also CA 97-100; CANR 32, 65; DLB 145; HW 1, 2; MTCW 1, 2

Sa-Carniero, Mario de 1890-1916 . **TCLC 83**

Sacastru, Martin
See Bioy Casares, Adolfo

Sacastru, Martin
See Bioy Casares, Adolfo

Sacher-Masoch, Leopold von
1836(?)-1895 .... **NCLC 31**

Sachs, Marilyn (Stickle) 1927- .... **CLC 35**
See also AAYA 2; CA 17-20R; CANR 13, 47; CLR 2; JRDA; MAICYA; SAAS 2; SATA 3, 68; SATA-Essay 110

Sachs, Nelly 1891-1970 .... **CLC 14, 98**
See also CA 17-18; 25-28R; CANR 87; CAP 2; MTCW 2

Sackler, Howard (Oliver)
1929-1982 .... **CLC 14**
See also CA 61-64; 108; CANR 30; DLB 7

Sacks, Oliver (Wolf) 1933- .... **CLC 67**
See also CA 53-56; CANR 28, 50, 76; DA3; INT CANR-28; MTCW 1, 2

Sadakichi
See Hartmann, Sadakichi

Sade, Donatien Alphonse Francois, Comte de 1740-1814 .... **NCLC 47**

Sadoff, Ira 1945- .... **CLC 9**
See also CA 53-56; CANR 5, 21; DLB 120

Saetone
See Camus, Albert

Safire, William 1929- .... **CLC 10**
See also CA 17-20R; CANR 31, 54, 91

Sagan, Carl (Edward) 1934-1996 .... **CLC 30, 112**
See also AAYA 2; CA 25-28R; 155; CANR 11, 36, 74; DA3; MTCW 1, 2; SATA 58; SATA-Obit 94

Sagan, Francoise CLC 3, 6, 9, 17, 36
See also Quoirez, Francoise
See also DLB 83; MTCW 2

Sahgal, Nayantara (Pandit) 1927- .... **CLC 41**
See also CA 9-12R; CANR 11, 88

Saint, H(arry) F. 1941- .... **CLC 50**
See also CA 127

St. Aubin de Teran, Lisa 1953-
See Teran, Lisa St. Aubin de
See also CA 118; 126; INT 126

Saint Birgitta of Sweden c.
1303-1373 .... **CMLC 24**

Sainte-Beuve, Charles Augustin
1804-1869 .... **NCLC 5**

Saint-Exupery, Antoine (Jean Baptiste Marie Roger) de 1900-1944 .... **TCLC 2, 56; DAM NOV; WLC**
See also CA 108; 132; CLR 10; DA3; DLB 72; MAICYA; MTCW 1, 2; SATA 20

St. John, David
See Hunt, E(verette) Howard, (Jr.)

Saint-John Perse
See Leger, (Marie-Rene Auguste) Alexis Saint-Leger

Saintsbury, George (Edward Bateman)
1845-1933 .... **TCLC 31**
See also CA 160; DLB 57, 149

Sait Faik TCLC 23
See also Abasiyanik, Sait Faik

Saki TCLC 3; SSC 12
See also Munro, H(ector) H(ugh)
See also MTCW 2

Sala, George Augustus NCLC 46

Saladin 1138-1193 .... **CMLC 38**

Salama, Hannu 1936- .... **CLC 18**

Salamanca, J(ack) R(ichard) 1922- .. **CLC 4, 15**
See also CA 25-28R

Salas, Floyd Francis 1931-
See also CA 119; CAAS 27; CANR 44, 75; DAM MULT; DLB 82; HLC 2; HW 1, 2; MTCW 2

Sale, J. Kirkpatrick
See Sale, Kirkpatrick

Sale, Kirkpatrick 1937- .... **CLC 68**
See also CA 13-16R; CANR 10

Salinas, Luis Omar 1937- ..... **CLC 90; DAM MULT; HLC 2**
See also CA 131; CANR 81; DLB 82; HW 1, 2

Salinas (y Serrano), Pedro
1891(?)-1951 .... **TCLC 17**
See also CA 117; DLB 134

Salinger, J(erome) D(avid) 1919- .. **CLC 1, 3, 8, 12, 55, 56; DA; DAB; DAC; DAM MST, NOV, POP; SSC 2, 28; WLC**
See also AAYA 2; CA 5-8R; CANR 39; CDALB 1941-1968; CLR 18; DA3; DLB 2, 102, 173; MAICYA; MTCW 1, 2; SATA 67

Salisbury, John
See Caute, (John) David

Salter, James 1925- .... **CLC 7, 52, 59**
See also CA 73-76; DLB 130

Saltus, Edgar (Everton) 1855-1921 . **TCLC 8**
See also CA 105; DLB 202

Saltykov, Mikhail Evgrafovich
1826-1889 .... **NCLC 16**

Samarakis, Antonis 1919- .... **CLC 5**
See also CA 25-28R; CAAS 16; CANR 36

Sanchez, Florencio 1875-1910 .... **TCLC 37**
See also CA 153; HW 1

Sanchez, Luis Rafael 1936- .... **CLC 23**
See also CA 128; DLB 145; HW 1

Sanchez, Sonia 1934- .... **CLC 5, 116; BLC 3; DAM MULT; PC 9**
See also BW 2, 3; CA 33-36R; CANR 24, 49, 74; CLR 18; DA3; DLB 41; DLBD 8; MAICYA; MTCW 1, 2; SATA 22

Sand, George 1804-1876 ..... **NCLC 2, 42, 57; DA; DAB; DAC; DAM MST, NOV; WLC**
See also DA3; DLB 119, 192

Sandburg, Carl (August) 1878-1967 . **CLC 1, 4, 10, 15, 35; DA; DAB; DAC; DAM MST, POET; PC 2; WLC**
See also AAYA 24; CA 5-8R; 25-28R; CANR 35; CDALB 1865-1917; DA3; DLB 17, 54; MAICYA; MTCW 1, 2; SATA 8

Sandburg, Charles
See Sandburg, Carl (August)

Sandburg, Charles A.
See Sandburg, Carl (August)

Sanders, (James) Ed(ward) 1939- ... **CLC 53; DAM POET**
See also CA 13-16R; CAAS 21; CANR 13, 44, 78; DLB 16

Sanders, Lawrence 1920-1998 .... **CLC 41; DAM POP**
See also BEST 89:4; CA 81-84; 165; CANR 33, 62; DA3; MTCW 1

Sanders, Noah
See Blount, Roy (Alton), Jr.

Sanders, Winston P.
See Anderson, Poul (William)

Sandoz, Mari(e Susette) 1896-1966 .. **CLC 28**
See also CA 1-4R; 25-28R; CANR 17, 64; DLB 9, 212; MTCW 1, 2; SATA 5

Saner, Reg(inald Anthony) 1931- .... **CLC 9**
See also CA 65-68

Sankara 788-820 .... **CMLC 32**

Sannazaro, Jacopo 1456(?)-1530 .... **LC 8**

Sansom, William 1912-1976 .... **CLC 2, 6; DAM NOV; SSC 21**
See also CA 5-8R; 65-68; CANR 42; DLB 139; MTCW 1

Santayana, George 1863-1952 .... **TCLC 40**
See also CA 115; DLB 54, 71; DLBD 13

Santiago, Danny CLC 33
See also James, Daniel (Lewis)
See also DLB 122

Santmyer, Helen Hoover 1895-1986 . **CLC 33**
See also CA 1-4R; 118; CANR 15, 33; DLBY 84; MTCW 1

Santoka, Taneda 1882-1940 .... **TCLC 72**

Santos, Bienvenido N(uqui)
1911-1996 .... **CLC 22; DAM MULT**
See also CA 101; 151; CANR 19, 46

Sapper TCLC 44
See also McNeile, Herman Cyril

Sapphire
See Sapphire, Brenda

Sapphire, Brenda 1950- .... **CLC 99**

Sappho fl. 6th cent. B.C.- ..... **CMLC 3; DAM POET; PC 5**
See also DA3; DLB 176

Saramago, Jose 1922- ..... **CLC 119; HLCS 1**
See also CA 153

Sarduy, Severo 1937-1993 .... **CLC 6, 97; HLCS 1**
See also CA 89-92; 142; CANR 58, 81; DLB 113; HW 1, 2

Sargeson, Frank 1903-1982 .... **CLC 31**
See also CA 25-28R; 106; CANR 38, 79

Sarmiento, Domingo Faustino 1811-1888
See also HLCS 2

Sarmiento, Felix Ruben Garcia
See Dario, Ruben

Saro-Wiwa, Ken(ule Beeson)
1941-1995 .... **CLC 114**
See also BW 2; CA 142; 150; CANR 60; DLB 157

Saroyan, William 1908-1981 ... **CLC 1, 8, 10, 29, 34, 56; DA; DAB; DAC; DAM DRAM, MST, NOV; SSC 21; WLC**
See also CA 5-8R; 103; CANR 30; CDALBS; DA3; DLB 7, 9, 86; DLBY 81; MTCW 1, 2; SATA 23; SATA-Obit 24

Sarraute, Nathalie 1900- . **CLC 1, 2, 4, 8, 10, 31, 80**
See also CA 9-12R; CANR 23, 66; DLB 83; MTCW 1, 2

Sarton, (Eleanor) May 1912-1995 ..... **CLC 4, 14, 49, 91; DAM POET**
See also CA 1-4R; 149; CANR 1, 34, 55; DLB 48; DLBY 81; INT CANR-34; MTCW 1, 2; SATA 36; SATA-Obit 86

Sartre, Jean-Paul 1905-1980 . **CLC 1, 4, 7, 9, 13, 18, 24, 44, 50, 52; DA; DAB; DAC; DAM DRAM, MST, NOV; DC 3; SSC 32; WLC**
See also CA 9-12R; 97-100; CANR 21; DA3; DLB 72; MTCW 1, 2

Sassoon, Siegfried (Lorraine)
1886-1967 .... **CLC 36, 130; DAB; DAM MST, NOV, POET; PC 12**
See also CA 104; 25-28R; CANR 36; DLB 20, 191; DLBD 18; MTCW 1, 2

Satterfield, Charles
See Pohl, Frederik

Satyremont
  See Peret, Benjamin
Saul, John (W. III) 1942- ...... **CLC 46; DAM NOV, POP**
  See also AAYA 10; BEST 90:4; CA 81-84; CANR 16, 40, 81; SATA 98
Saunders, Caleb
  See Heinlein, Robert A(nson)
Saura (Atares), Carlos 1932- .... **CLC 20**
  See also CA 114; 131; CANR 79; HW 1
Sauser-Hall, Frederic 1887-1961 ...... **CLC 18**
  See also Cendrars, Blaise
  See also CA 102; 93-96; CANR 36, 62; MTCW 1
Saussure, Ferdinand de
  1857-1913 .... **TCLC 49**
Savage, Catharine
  See Brosman, Catharine Savage
Savage, Thomas 1915- .... **CLC 40**
  See also CA 126; 132; CAAS 15; INT 132
Savan, Glenn 19(?)- .... **CLC 50**
Sayers, Dorothy L(eigh)
  1893-1957 .... **TCLC 2, 15; DAM POP**
  See also CA 104; 119; CANR 60; CDBLB 1914-1945; DLB 10, 36, 77, 100; MTCW 1, 2
Sayers, Valerie 1952- .... **CLC 50, 122**
  See also CA 134; CANR 61
Sayles, John (Thomas) 1950- . **CLC 7, 10, 14**
  See also CA 57-60; CANR 41, 84; DLB 44
Scammell, Michael 1935- .... **CLC 34**
  See also CA 156
Scannell, Vernon 1922- .... **CLC 49**
  See also CA 5-8R; CANR 8, 24, 57; DLB 27; SATA 59
Scarlett, Susan
  See Streatfeild, (Mary) Noel
Scarron
  See Mikszath, Kalman
Schaeffer, Susan Fromberg 1941- ..... **CLC 6, 11, 22**
  See also CA 49-52; CANR 18, 65; DLB 28; MTCW 1, 2; SATA 22
Schary, Jill
  See Robinson, Jill
Schell, Jonathan 1943- .... **CLC 35**
  See also CA 73-76; CANR 12
Schelling, Friedrich Wilhelm Joseph von
  1775-1854 .... **NCLC 30**
  See also DLB 90
Schendel, Arthur van 1874-1946 ... **TCLC 56**
Scherer, Jean-Marie Maurice 1920-
  See Rohmer, Eric
  See also CA 110
Schevill, James (Erwin) 1920- .... **CLC 7**
  See also CA 5-8R; CAAS 12
Schiller, Friedrich 1759-1805 . **NCLC 39, 69; DAM DRAM; DC 12**
  See also DLB 94
Schisgal, Murray (Joseph) 1926- .... **CLC 6**
  See also CA 21-24R; CANR 48, 86
Schlee, Ann 1934- .... **CLC 35**
  See also CA 101; CANR 29, 88; SATA 44; SATA-Brief 36
Schlegel, August Wilhelm von
  1767-1845 .... **NCLC 15**
  See also DLB 94
Schlegel, Friedrich 1772-1829 .... **NCLC 45**
  See also DLB 90
Schlegel, Johann Elias (von)
  1719(?)-1749 .... **LC 5**
Schlesinger, Arthur M(eier), Jr.
  1917- .... **CLC 84**
  See also AITN 1; CA 1-4R; CANR 1, 28, 58; DLB 17; INT CANR-28; MTCW 1, 2; SATA 61
Schmidt, Arno (Otto) 1914-1979 ...... **CLC 56**
  See also CA 128; 109; DLB 69

Schmitz, Aron Hector 1861-1928
  See Svevo, Italo
  See also CA 104; 122; MTCW 1
Schnackenberg, Gjertrud 1953- .... **CLC 40**
  See also CA 116; DLB 120
Schneider, Leonard Alfred 1925-1966
  See Bruce, Lenny
  See also CA 89-92
Schnitzler, Arthur 1862-1931 . **TCLC 4; SSC 15**
  See also CA 104; DLB 81, 118
Schoenberg, Arnold 1874-1951 ...... **TCLC 75**
  See also CA 109
Schonberg, Arnold
  See Schoenberg, Arnold
Schopenhauer, Arthur 1788-1860 .. **NCLC 51**
  See also DLB 90
Schor, Sandra (M.) 1932(?)-1990 ..... **CLC 65**
  See also CA 132
Schorer, Mark 1908-1977 .... **CLC 9**
  See also CA 5-8R; 73-76; CANR 7; DLB 103
Schrader, Paul (Joseph) 1946- .... **CLC 26**
  See also CA 37-40R; CANR 41; DLB 44
Schreiner, Olive (Emilie Albertina)
  1855-1920 .... **TCLC 9**
  See also CA 105; 154; DLB 18, 156, 190, 225
Schulberg, Budd (Wilson) 1914- .. **CLC 7, 48**
  See also CA 25-28R; CANR 19, 87; DLB 6, 26, 28; DLBY 81
Schulz, Bruno 1892-1942 .. **TCLC 5, 51; SSC 13**
  See also CA 115; 123; CANR 86; MTCW 2
Schulz, Charles M(onroe)
  1922-2000 .... **CLC 12**
  See also CA 9-12R; CANR 6; INT CANR-6; SATA 10
Schumacher, E(rnst) F(riedrich)
  1911-1977 .... **CLC 80**
  See also CA 81-84; 73-76; CANR 34, 85
Schuyler, James Marcus 1923-1991 .. **CLC 5, 23; DAM POET**
  See also CA 101; 134; DLB 5, 169; INT 101
Schwartz, Delmore (David)
  1913-1966 ... **CLC 2, 4, 10, 45, 87; PC 8**
  See also CA 17-18; 25-28R; CANR 35; CAP 2; DLB 28, 48; MTCW 1, 2
Schwartz, Ernst
  See Ozu, Yasujiro
Schwartz, John Burnham 1965- .... **CLC 59**
  See also CA 132
Schwartz, Lynne Sharon 1939- .... **CLC 31**
  See also CA 103; CANR 44, 89; MTCW 2
Schwartz, Muriel A.
  See Eliot, T(homas) S(tearns)
Schwarz-Bart, Andre 1928- .... **CLC 2, 4**
  See also CA 89-92
Schwarz-Bart, Simone 1938- . **CLC 7; BLCS**
  See also BW 2; CA 97-100
Schwitters, Kurt (Hermann Edward Karl Julius) 1887-1948 .... **TCLC 95**
  See also CA 158
Schwob, Marcel (Mayer Andre)
  1867-1905 .... **TCLC 20**
  See also CA 117; 168; DLB 123
Sciascia, Leonardo 1921-1989 .. **CLC 8, 9, 41**
  See also CA 85-88; 130; CANR 35; DLB 177; MTCW 1
Scoppettone, Sandra 1936- .... **CLC 26**
  See also AAYA 11; CA 5-8R; CANR 41, 73; SATA 9, 92
Scorsese, Martin 1942- .... **CLC 20, 89**
  See also CA 110; 114; CANR 46, 85
Scotland, Jay
  See Jakes, John (William)

Scott, Duncan Campbell
  1862-1947 .... **TCLC 6; DAC**
  See also CA 104; 153; DLB 92
Scott, Evelyn 1893-1963 .... **CLC 43**
  See also CA 104; 112; CANR 64; DLB 9, 48
Scott, F(rancis) R(eginald)
  1899-1985 .... **CLC 22**
  See also CA 101; 114; CANR 87; DLB 88; INT 101
Scott, Frank
  See Scott, F(rancis) R(eginald)
Scott, Joanna 1960- .... **CLC 50**
  See also CA 126; CANR 53, 92
Scott, Paul (Mark) 1920-1978 ...... **CLC 9, 60**
  See also CA 81-84; 77-80; CANR 33; DLB 14, 207; MTCW 1
Scott, Sarah 1723-1795 .... **LC 44**
  See also DLB 39
Scott, Walter 1771-1832 . **NCLC 15, 69; DA; DAB; DAC; DAM MST, NOV, POET; PC 13; SSC 32; WLC**
  See also AAYA 22; CDBLB 1789-1832; DLB 93, 107, 116, 144, 159; YABC 2
Scribe, (Augustin) Eugene
  1791-1861 ..... **NCLC 16; DAM DRAM; DC 5**
  See also DLB 192
Scrum, R.
  See Crumb, R(obert)
Scudery, Madeleine de 1607-1701 .. **LC 2, 58**
Scum
  See Crumb, R(obert)
Scumbag, Little Bobby
  See Crumb, R(obert)
Seabrook, John
  See Hubbard, L(afayette) Ron(ald)
Sealy, I(rwin) Allan 1951- .... **CLC 55**
  See also CA 136
Search, Alexander
  See Pessoa, Fernando (Antonio Nogueira)
Sebastian, Lee
  See Silverberg, Robert
Sebastian Owl
  See Thompson, Hunter S(tockton)
Sebestyen, Ouida 1924- .... **CLC 30**
  See also AAYA 8; CA 107; CANR 40; CLR 17; JRDA; MAICYA; SAAS 10; SATA 39
Secundus, H. Scriblerus
  See Fielding, Henry
Sedges, John
  See Buck, Pearl S(ydenstricker)
Sedgwick, Catharine Maria
  1789-1867 .... **NCLC 19**
  See also DLB 1, 74
Seelye, John (Douglas) 1931- .... **CLC 7**
  See also CA 97-100; CANR 70; INT 97-100
Seferiades, Giorgos Stylianou 1900-1971
  See Seferis, George
  See also CA 5-8R; 33-36R; CANR 5, 36; MTCW 1
Seferis, George **CLC 5, 11**
  See also Seferiades, Giorgos Stylianou
Segal, Erich (Wolf) 1937- . **CLC 3, 10; DAM POP**
  See also BEST 89:1; CA 25-28R; CANR 20, 36, 65; DLBY 86; INT CANR-20; MTCW 1
Seger, Bob 1945- .... **CLC 35**
Seghers, Anna **CLC 7**
  See also Radvanyi, Netty
  See also DLB 69
Seidel, Frederick (Lewis) 1936- .... **CLC 18**
  See also CA 13-16R; CANR 8; DLBY 84
Seifert, Jaroslav 1901-1986 .. **CLC 34, 44, 93**
  See also CA 127; MTCW 1, 2

Sei Shonagon c. 966-1017(?) .... **CMLC 6**

Séjour, Victor 1817-1874 .... **DC 10**
See also DLB 50

Sejour Marcou et Ferrand, Juan Victor
See S

Selby, Hubert, Jr. 1928- .... **CLC 1, 2, 4, 8; SSC 20**
See also CA 13-16R; CANR 33, 85; DLB 2, 227

Selzer, Richard 1928- .... **CLC 74**
See also CA 65-68; CANR 14

Sembene, Ousmane
See Ousmane, Sembene

Senancour, Etienne Pivert de 1770-1846 .... **NCLC 16**
See also DLB 119

Sender, Ramon (Jose) 1902-1982 ...... **CLC 8; DAM MULT; HLC 2**
See also CA 5-8R; 105; CANR 8; HW 1; MTCW 1

Seneca, Lucius Annaeus c. 1-c. 65 .... **CMLC 6; DAM DRAM; DC 5**
See also DLB 211

Senghor, Leopold Sedar 1906- .... **CLC 54, 130; BLC 3; DAM MULT, POET; PC 25**
See also BW 2; CA 116; 125; CANR 47, 74; MTCW 1, 2

Senna, Danzy 1970- .... **CLC 119**
See also CA 169

Serling, (Edward) Rod(man) 1924-1975 .... **CLC 30**
See also AAYA 14; AITN 1; CA 162; 57-60; DLB 26

Serna, Ramon Gomez de la
See Gomez de la Serna, Ramon

Serpieres
See Guillevic, (Eugene)

Service, Robert
See Service, Robert W(illiam)
See also DAB; DLB 92

Service, Robert W(illiam) 1874(?)-1958 .... **TCLC 15; DA; DAC; DAM MST, POET; WLC**
See also Service, Robert
See also CA 115; 140; CANR 84; SATA 20

Seth, Vikram 1952- .... **CLC 43, 90; DAM MULT**
See also CA 121; 127; CANR 50, 74; DA3; DLB 120; INT 127; MTCW 2

Seton, Cynthia Propper 1926-1982 .. **CLC 27**
See also CA 5-8R; 108; CANR 7

Seton, Ernest (Evan) Thompson 1860-1946 .... **TCLC 31**
See also CA 109; CLR 59; DLB 92; DLBD 13; JRDA; SATA 18

Seton-Thompson, Ernest
See Seton, Ernest (Evan) Thompson

Settle, Mary Lee 1918- .... **CLC 19, 61**
See also CA 89-92; CAAS 1; CANR 44, 87; DLB 6; INT 89-92

Seuphor, Michel
See Arp, Jean

Sevigne, Marie (de Rabutin-Chantal) Marquise de 1626-1696 .... **LC 11**

Sewall, Samuel 1652-1730 .... **LC 38**
See also DLB 24

Sexton, Anne (Harvey) 1928-1974 ..... **CLC 2, 4, 6, 8, 10, 15, 53; DA; DAB; DAC; DAM MST, POET; PC 2; WLC**
See also CA 1-4R; 53-56; CABS 2; CANR 3, 36; CDALB 1941-1968; DA3; DLB 5, 169; MTCW 1, 2; SATA 10

Shaara, Jeff 1952- .... **CLC 119**
See also CA 163

Shaara, Michael (Joseph, Jr.) 1929-1988 .... **CLC 15; DAM POP**
See also AITN 1; CA 102; 125; CANR 52, 85; DLBY 83

Shackleton, C. C.
See Aldiss, Brian W(ilson)

Shacochis, Bob CLC 39
See also Shacochis, Robert G.

Shacochis, Robert G. 1951-
See Shacochis, Bob
See also CA 119; 124; INT 124

Shaffer, Anthony (Joshua) 1926- ..... **CLC 19; DAM DRAM**
See also CA 110; 116; DLB 13

Shaffer, Peter (Levin) 1926- .. **CLC 5, 14, 18, 37, 60; DAB; DAM DRAM, MST; DC 7**
See also CA 25-28R; CANR 25, 47, 74; CDBLB 1960 to Present; DA3; DLB 13; MTCW 1, 2

Shakey, Bernard
See Young, Neil

Shalamov, Varlam (Tikhonovich) 1907(?)-1982 .... **CLC 18**
See also CA 129; 105

Shamlu, Ahmad 1925- .... **CLC 10**

Shammas, Anton 1951- .... **CLC 55**

Shandling, Arline
See Berriault, Gina

Shange, Ntozake 1948- .... **CLC 8, 25, 38, 74, 126; BLC 3; DAM DRAM, MULT; DC 3**
See also AAYA 9; BW 2; CA 85-88; CABS 3; CANR 27, 48, 74; DA3; DLB 38; MTCW 1, 2

Shanley, John Patrick 1950- .... **CLC 75**
See also CA 128; 133; CANR 83

Shapcott, Thomas W(illiam) 1935- .. **CLC 38**
See also CA 69-72; CANR 49, 83

Shapiro, Jane CLC 76

Shapiro, Karl (Jay) 1913- . **CLC 4, 8, 15, 53; PC 25**
See also CA 1-4R; CAAS 6; CANR 1, 36, 66; DLB 48; MTCW 1, 2

Sharp, William 1855-1905 .... **TCLC 39**
See also CA 160; DLB 156

Sharpe, Thomas Ridley 1928-
See Sharpe, Tom
See also CA 114; 122; CANR 85; INT 122

Sharpe, Tom CLC 36
See also Sharpe, Thomas Ridley
See also DLB 14

Shaw, Bernard
See Shaw, George Bernard
See also BW 1; MTCW 2

Shaw, G. Bernard
See Shaw, George Bernard

Shaw, George Bernard 1856-1950 .. **TCLC 3, 9, 21, 45; DA; DAB; DAC; DAM DRAM, MST; WLC**
See also Shaw, Bernard
See also CA 104; 128; CDBLB 1914-1945; DA3; DLB 10, 57, 190; MTCW 1, 2

Shaw, Henry Wheeler 1818-1885 .. **NCLC 15**
See also DLB 11

Shaw, Irwin 1913-1984 .... **CLC 7, 23, 34; DAM DRAM, POP**
See also AITN 1; CA 13-16R; 112; CANR 21; CDALB 1941-1968; DLB 6, 102; DLBY 84; MTCW 1, 21

Shaw, Robert 1927-1978 .... **CLC 5**
See also AITN 1; CA 1-4R; 81-84; CANR 4; DLB 13, 14

Shaw, T. E.
See Lawrence, T(homas) E(dward)

Shawn, Wallace 1943- .... **CLC 41**
See also CA 112

Shea, Lisa 1953- .... **CLC 86**
See also CA 147

Sheed, Wilfrid (John Joseph) 1930- . **CLC 2, 4, 10, 53**
See also CA 65-68; CANR 30, 66; DLB 6; MTCW 1, 2

Sheldon, Alice Hastings Bradley 1915(?)-1987
See Tiptree, James, Jr.
See also CA 108; 122; CANR 34; INT 108; MTCW 1

Sheldon, John
See Bloch, Robert (Albert)

Shelley, Mary Wollstonecraft (Godwin) 1797-1851 ..... **NCLC 14, 59; DA; DAB; DAC; DAM MST, NOV; WLC**
See also AAYA 20; CDBLB 1789-1832; DA3; DLB 110, 116, 159, 178; SATA 29

Shelley, Percy Bysshe 1792-1822 .. **NCLC 18; DA; DAB; DAC; DAM MST, POET; PC 14; WLC**
See also CDBLB 1789-1832; DA3; DLB 96, 110, 158

Shepard, Jim 1956- .... **CLC 36**
See also CA 137; CANR 59; SATA 90

Shepard, Lucius 1947- .... **CLC 34**
See also CA 128; 141; CANR 81

Shepard, Sam 1943- .... **CLC 4, 6, 17, 34, 41, 44; DAM DRAM; DC 5**
See also AAYA 1; CA 69-72; CABS 3; CANR 22; DA3; DLB 7, 212; MTCW 1, 2

Shepherd, Michael
See Ludlum, Robert

Sherburne, Zoa (Lillian Morin) 1912-1995 .... **CLC 30**
See also AAYA 13; CA 1-4R; 176; CANR 3, 37; MAICYA; SAAS 18; SATA 3

Sheridan, Frances 1724-1766 .... **LC 7**
See also DLB 39, 84

Sheridan, Richard Brinsley 1751-1816 .... **NCLC 5, 91; DA; DAB; DAC; DAM DRAM, MST; DC 1; WLC**
See also CDBLB 1660-1789; DLB 89

Sherman, Jonathan Marc CLC 55

Sherman, Martin 1941(?)- .... **CLC 19**
See also CA 116; 123; CANR 86

Sherwin, Judith Johnson 1936-
See Johnson, Judith (Emlyn)
See also CANR 85

Sherwood, Frances 1940- .... **CLC 81**
See also CA 146

Sherwood, Robert E(mmet) 1896-1955 .... **TCLC 3; DAM DRAM**
See also CA 104; 153; CANR 86; DLB 7, 26

Shestov, Lev 1866-1938 .... **TCLC 56**

Shevchenko, Taras 1814-1861 .... **NCLC 54**

Shiel, M(atthew) P(hipps) 1865-1947 .... **TCLC 8**
See also Holmes, Gordon
See also CA 106; 160; DLB 153; MTCW 2

Shields, Carol 1935- .... **CLC 91, 113; DAC**
See also CA 81-84; CANR 51, 74; DA3; MTCW 2

Shields, David 1956- .... **CLC 97**
See also CA 124; CANR 48

Shiga, Naoya 1883-1971 ..... **CLC 33; SSC 23**
See also CA 101; 33-36R; DLB 180

Shikibu, Murasaki c. 978-c. 1014 .. **CMLC 1**

Shilts, Randy 1951-1994 .... **CLC 85**
See also AAYA 19; CA 115; 127; 144; CANR 45; DA3; INT 127; MTCW 2

Shimazaki, Haruki 1872-1943
See Shimazaki Toson
See also CA 105; 134; CANR 84

Shimazaki Toson 1872-1943 .... **TCLC 5**
See also Shimazaki, Haruki
See also DLB 180

Sholokhov, Mikhail (Aleksandrovich) 1905-1984 .... **CLC 7, 15**
See also CA 101; 112; MTCW 1, 2; SATA-Obit 36

Shone, Patric
See Hanley, James

Shreve, Susan Richards 1939- .... **CLC 23**
See also CA 49-52; CAAS 5; CANR 5, 38, 69; MAICYA; SATA 46, 95; SATA-Brief 41

Shue, Larry 1946-1985 .... **CLC 52; DAM DRAM**
See also CA 145; 117

Shu-Jen, Chou 1881-1936
See Lu Hsun
See also CA 104

Shulman, Alix Kates 1932- .... **CLC 2, 10**
See also CA 29-32R; CANR 43; SATA 7

Shuster, Joe 1914- .... **CLC 21**

Shute, Nevil CLC 30
See also Norway, Nevil Shute
See also MTCW 2

Shuttle, Penelope (Diane) 1947- .... **CLC 7**
See also CA 93-96; CANR 39, 84, 92; DLB 14, 40

Sidney, Mary 1561-1621 .... **LC 19, 39**

Sidney, Sir Philip 1554-1586 . **LC 19, 39; DA; DAB; DAC; DAM MST, POET**
See also CDBLB Before 1660; DA3; DLB 167

Siegel, Jerome 1914-1996 .... **CLC 21**
See also CA 116; 169; 151

Siegel, Jerry
See Siegel, Jerome

Sienkiewicz, Henryk (Adam Alexander Pius) 1846-1916 .... **TCLC 3**
See also CA 104; 134; CANR 84

Sierra, Gregorio Martinez
See Martinez Sierra, Gregorio

Sierra, Maria (de la O'LeJarraga) Martinez
See Martinez Sierra, Maria (de la O'LeJarraga)

Sigal, Clancy 1926- .... **CLC 7**
See also CA 1-4R; CANR 85

Sigourney, Lydia Howard (Huntley) 1791-1865 .... **NCLC 21, 87**
See also DLB 1, 42, 73

Siguenza y Gongora, Carlos de 1645-1700 .... **LC 8; HLCS 2**

Sigurjonsson, Johann 1880-1919 ... **TCLC 27**
See also CA 170

Sikelianos, Angelos 1884-1951 ...... **TCLC 39; PC 29**

Silkin, Jon 1930- .... **CLC 2, 6, 43**
See also CA 5-8R; CAAS 5; CANR 89; DLB 27

Silko, Leslie (Marmon) 1948- .... **CLC 23, 74, 114; DA; DAC; DAM MST, MULT, POP; SSC 37; WLCS**
See also AAYA 14; CA 115; 122; CANR 45, 65; DA3; DLB 143, 175; MTCW 2; NNAL

Sillanpaa, Frans Eemil 1888-1964 ... **CLC 19**
See also CA 129; 93-96; MTCW 1

Sillitoe, Alan 1928- ... **CLC 1, 3, 6, 10, 19, 57**
See also AITN 1; CA 9-12R; CAAS 2; CANR 8, 26, 55; CDBLB 1960 to Present; DLB 14, 139; MTCW 1, 2; SATA 61

Silone, Ignazio 1900-1978 .... **CLC 4**
See also CA 25-28; 81-84; CANR 34; CAP 2; MTCW 1

Silver, Joan Micklin 1935- .... **CLC 20**
See also CA 114; 121; INT 121

Silver, Nicholas
See Faust, Frederick (Schiller)

Silverberg, Robert 1935- .... **CLC 7; DAM POP**
See also AAYA 24; CA 1-4R; 186; CAAE 186; CAAS 3; CANR 1, 20, 36, 85; CLR 59; DLB 8; INT CANR-20; MAICYA; MTCW 1, 2; SATA 13, 91; SATA-Essay 104

Silverstein, Alvin 1933- .... **CLC 17**
See also CA 49-52; CANR 2; CLR 25; JRDA; MAICYA; SATA 8, 69

Silverstein, Virginia B(arbara Opshelor) 1937- .... **CLC 17**
See also CA 49-52; CANR 2; CLR 25; JRDA; MAICYA; SATA 8, 69

Sim, Georges
See Simenon, Georges (Jacques Christian)

Simak, Clifford D(onald) 1904-1988 . **CLC 1, 55**
See also CA 1-4R; 125; CANR 1, 35; DLB 8; MTCW 1; SATA-Obit 56

Simenon, Georges (Jacques Christian) 1903-1989 .... **CLC 1, 2, 3, 8, 18, 47; DAM POP**
See also CA 85-88; 129; CANR 35; DA3; DLB 72; DLBY 89; MTCW 1, 2

Simic, Charles 1938- .... **CLC 6, 9, 22, 49, 68, 130; DAM POET**
See also CA 29-32R; CAAS 4; CANR 12, 33, 52, 61; DA3; DLB 105; MTCW 2

Simmel, Georg 1858-1918 .... **TCLC 64**
See also CA 157

Simmons, Charles (Paul) 1924- .... **CLC 57**
See also CA 89-92; INT 89-92

Simmons, Dan 1948- .... **CLC 44; DAM POP**
See also AAYA 16; CA 138; CANR 53, 81

Simmons, James (Stewart Alexander) 1933- .... **CLC 43**
See also CA 105; CAAS 21; DLB 40

Simms, William Gilmore 1806-1870 .... **NCLC 3**
See also DLB 3, 30, 59, 73

Simon, Carly 1945- .... **CLC 26**
See also CA 105

Simon, Claude 1913- .... **CLC 4, 9, 15, 39; DAM NOV**
See also CA 89-92; CANR 33; DLB 83; MTCW 1

Simon, (Marvin) Neil 1927- ... **CLC 6, 11, 31, 39, 70; DAM DRAM**
See also AAYA 32; AITN 1; CA 21-24R; CANR 26, 54, 87; DA3; DLB 7; MTCW 1, 2

Simon, Paul (Frederick) 1941(?)- ..... **CLC 17**
See also CA 116; 153

Simonon, Paul 1956(?)- .... **CLC 30**

Simpson, Harriette
See Arnow, Harriette (Louisa) Simpson

Simpson, Louis (Aston Marantz) 1923- ...... **CLC 4, 7, 9, 32; DAM POET**
See also CA 1-4R; CAAS 4; CANR 1, 61; DLB 5; MTCW 1, 2

Simpson, Mona (Elizabeth) 1957- .... **CLC 44**
See also CA 122; 135; CANR 68

Simpson, N(orman) F(rederick) 1919- .... **CLC 29**
See also CA 13-16R; DLB 13

Sinclair, Andrew (Annandale) 1935- . **CLC 2, 14**
See also CA 9-12R; CAAS 5; CANR 14, 38, 91; DLB 14; MTCW 1

Sinclair, Emil
See Hesse, Hermann

Sinclair, Iain 1943- .... **CLC 76**
See also CA 132; CANR 81

Sinclair, Iain MacGregor
See Sinclair, Iain

Sinclair, Irene
See Griffith, D(avid Lewelyn) W(ark)

Sinclair, Mary Amelia St. Clair 1865(?)-1946
See Sinclair, May
See also CA 104

Sinclair, May 1863-1946 .... **TCLC 3, 11**
See also Sinclair, Mary Amelia St. Clair
See also CA 166; DLB 36, 135

Sinclair, Roy
See Griffith, D(avid Lewelyn) W(ark)

Sinclair, Upton (Beall) 1878-1968 ..... **CLC 1, 11, 15, 63; DA; DAB; DAC; DAM MST, NOV; WLC**
See also CA 5-8R; 25-28R; CANR 7; CDALB 1929-1941; DA3; DLB 9; INT CANR-7; MTCW 1, 2; SATA 9

Singer, Isaac
See Singer, Isaac Bashevis

Singer, Isaac Bashevis 1904-1991 .. **CLC 1, 3, 6, 9, 11, 15, 23, 38, 69, 111; DA; DAB; DAC; DAM MST, NOV; SSC 3; WLC**
See also AAYA 32; AITN 1, 2; CA 1-4R; 134; CANR 1, 39; CDALB 1941-1968; CLR 1; DA3; DLB 6, 28, 52; DLBY 91; JRDA; MAICYA; MTCW 1, 2; SATA 3, 27; SATA-Obit 68

Singer, Israel Joshua 1893-1944 .... **TCLC 33**
See also CA 169

Singh, Khushwant 1915- .... **CLC 11**
See also CA 9-12R; CAAS 9; CANR 6, 84

Singleton, Ann
See Benedict, Ruth (Fulton)

Sinjohn, John
See Galsworthy, John

Sinyavsky, Andrei (Donatevich) 1925-1997 .... **CLC 8**
See also CA 85-88; 159

Sirin, V.
See Nabokov, Vladimir (Vladimirovich)

Sissman, L(ouis) E(dward) 1928-1976 .... **CLC 9, 18**
See also CA 21-24R; 65-68; CANR 13; DLB 5

Sisson, C(harles) H(ubert) 1914- .... **CLC 8**
See also CA 1-4R; CAAS 3; CANR 3, 48, 84; DLB 27

Sitwell, Dame Edith 1887-1964 ..... **CLC 2, 9, 67; DAM POET; PC 3**
See also CA 9-12R; CANR 35; CDBLB 1945-1960; DLB 20; MTCW 1, 2

Siwaarmill, H. P.
See Sharp, William

Sjoewall, Maj 1935- .... **CLC 7**
See also Sjowall, Maj
See also CA 65-68; CANR 73

Sjowall, Maj
See Sjoewall, Maj

Skelton, John 1463-1529 .... **PC 25**

Skelton, Robin 1925-1997 .... **CLC 13**
See also AITN 2; CA 5-8R; 160; CAAS 5; CANR 28, 89; DLB 27, 53

Skolimowski, Jerzy 1938- .... **CLC 20**
See also CA 128

Skram, Amalie (Bertha) 1847-1905 .... **TCLC 25**
See also CA 165

Skvorecky, Josef (Vaclav) 1924- ...... **CLC 15, 39, 69; DAC; DAM NOV**
See also CA 61-64; CAAS 1; CANR 10, 34, 63; DA3; MTCW 1, 2

Slade, Bernard CLC 11, 46
See also Newbound, Bernard Slade
See also CAAS 9; DLB 53

Slaughter, Carolyn 1946- .... **CLC 56**
See also CA 85-88; CANR 85

Slaughter, Frank G(ill) 1908- .... **CLC 29**
See also AITN 2; CA 5-8R; CANR 5, 85; INT CANR-5

Slavitt, David R(ytman) 1935- ..... **CLC 5, 14**
See also CA 21-24R; CAAS 3; CANR 41, 83; DLB 5, 6

Slesinger, Tess 1905-1945 .... **TCLC 10**
See also CA 107; DLB 102

Slessor, Kenneth 1901-1971 .... **CLC 14**
See also CA 102; 89-92

Slowacki, Juliusz 1809-1849 .... **NCLC 15**

Smart, Christopher 1722-1771 .. **LC 3; DAM POET; PC 13**
See also DLB 109

Smart, Elizabeth 1913-1986 .... **CLC 54**
  See also CA 81-84; 118; DLB 88
Smiley, Jane (Graves) 1949- ...... **CLC 53, 76;**
  DAM POP
  See also CA 104; CANR 30, 50, 74; DA3;
  DLB 227; INT CANR-30
Smith, A(rthur) J(ames) M(arshall)
  1902-1980 .... **CLC 15; DAC**
  See also CA 1-4R; 102; CANR 4; DLB 88
Smith, Adam 1723-1790 .... **LC 36**
  See also DLB 104
Smith, Alexander 1829-1867 .... **NCLC 59**
  See also DLB 32, 55
Smith, Anna Deavere 1950- .... **CLC 86**
  See also CA 133
Smith, Betty (Wehner) 1896-1972 .... **CLC 19**
  See also CA 5-8R; 33-36R; DLBY 82;
  SATA 6
Smith, Charlotte (Turner)
  1749-1806 .... **NCLC 23**
  See also DLB 39, 109
Smith, Clark Ashton 1893-1961 .... **CLC 43**
  See also CA 143; CANR 81; MTCW 2
Smith, Dave CLC 22, 42
  See also Smith, David (Jeddie)
  See also CAAS 7; DLB 5
Smith, David (Jeddie) 1942-
  See Smith, Dave
  See also CA 49-52; CANR 1, 59; DAM
  POET
Smith, Florence Margaret 1902-1971
  See Smith, Stevie
  See also CA 17-18; 29-32R; CANR 35;
  CAP 2; DAM POET; MTCW 1, 2
Smith, Iain Crichton 1928-1998 .... **CLC 64**
  See also CA 21-24R; 171; DLB 40, 139
Smith, John 1580(?)-1631 .... **LC 9**
  See also DLB 24, 30
Smith, Johnston
  See Crane, Stephen (Townley)
Smith, Joseph, Jr. 1805-1844 .... **NCLC 53**
Smith, Lee 1944- .... **CLC 25, 73**
  See also CA 114; 119; CANR 46; DLB 143;
  DLBY 83; INT 119
Smith, Martin
  See Smith, Martin Cruz
Smith, Martin Cruz 1942- .... **CLC 25; DAM**
  MULT, POP
  See also BEST 89:4; CA 85-88; CANR 6,
  23, 43, 65; INT CANR-23; MTCW 2;
  NNAL
Smith, Mary-Ann Tirone 1944- .... **CLC 39**
  See also CA 118; 136
Smith, Patti 1946- .... **CLC 12**
  See also CA 93-96; CANR 63
Smith, Pauline (Urmson)
  1882-1959 .... **TCLC 25**
  See also DLB 225
Smith, Rosamond
  See Oates, Joyce Carol
Smith, Sheila Kaye
  See Kaye-Smith, Sheila
Smith, Stevie CLC 3, 8, 25, 44; PC 12
  See also Smith, Florence Margaret
  See also DLB 20; MTCW 2
Smith, Wilbur (Addison) 1933- .... **CLC 33**
  See also CA 13-16R; CANR 7, 46, 66;
  MTCW 1, 2
Smith, William Jay 1918- .... **CLC 6**
  See also CA 5-8R; CANR 44; DLB 5; MAI-
  CYA; SAAS 22; SATA 2, 68
Smith, Woodrow Wilson
  See Kuttner, Henry
Smolenskin, Peretz 1842-1885 .... **NCLC 30**
Smollett, Tobias (George) 1721-1771 ... **LC 2,**
  46
  See also CDBLB 1660-1789; DLB 39, 104

Snodgrass, W(illiam) D(e Witt)
  1926- .... **CLC 2, 6, 10, 18, 68; DAM**
  POET
  See also CA 1-4R; CANR 6, 36, 65, 85;
  DLB 5; MTCW 1, 2
Snow, C(harles) P(ercy) 1905-1980 ... **CLC 1,**
  4, 6, 9, 13, 19; DAM NOV
  See also CA 5-8R; 101; CANR 28; CDBLB
  1945-1960; DLB 15, 77; DLBD 17;
  MTCW 1, 2
Snow, Frances Compton
  See Adams, Henry (Brooks)
Snyder, Gary (Sherman) 1930- . **CLC 1, 2, 5,**
  9, 32, 120; DAM POET; PC 21
  See also CA 17-20R; CANR 30, 60; DA3;
  DLB 5, 16, 165, 212; MTCW 2
Snyder, Zilpha Keatley 1927- .... **CLC 17**
  See also AAYA 15; CA 9-12R; CANR 38;
  CLR 31; JRDA; MAICYA; SAAS 2;
  SATA 1, 28, 75, 110; SATA-Essay 112
Soares, Bernardo
  See Pessoa, Fernando (Antonio Nogueira)
Sobh, A.
  See Shamlu, Ahmad
Sobol, Joshua CLC 60
Socrates 469B.C.-399B.C. .... **CMLC 27**
Soderberg, Hjalmar 1869-1941 ...... **TCLC 39**
Sodergran, Edith (Irene)
  See Soedergran, Edith (Irene)
Soedergran, Edith (Irene)
  1892-1923 .... **TCLC 31**
Softly, Edgar
  See Lovecraft, H(oward) P(hillips)
Softly, Edward
  See Lovecraft, H(oward) P(hillips)
Sokolov, Raymond 1941- .... **CLC 7**
  See also CA 85-88
Solo, Jay
  See Ellison, Harlan (Jay)
Sologub, Fyodor TCLC 9
  See also Teternikov, Fyodor Kuzmich
Solomons, Ikey Esquir
  See Thackeray, William Makepeace
Solomos, Dionysios 1798-1857 .... **NCLC 15**
Solwoska, Mara
  See French, Marilyn
Solzhenitsyn, Aleksandr I(sayevich)
  1918- .. **CLC 1, 2, 4, 7, 9, 10, 18, 26, 34,**
  78, 134; DA; DAB; DAC; DAM MST,
  NOV; SSC 32; WLC
  See also AITN 1; CA 69-72; CANR 40, 65;
  DA3; MTCW 1, 2
Somers, Jane
  See Lessing, Doris (May)
Somerville, Edith 1858-1949 .... **TCLC 51**
  See also DLB 135
Somerville & Ross
  See Martin, Violet Florence; Somerville,
  Edith
Sommer, Scott 1951- .... **CLC 25**
  See also CA 106
Sondheim, Stephen (Joshua) 1930- . **CLC 30,**
  39; DAM DRAM
  See also AAYA 11; CA 103; CANR 47, 68
Song, Cathy 1955- .... **PC 21**
  See also CA 154; DLB 169
Sontag, Susan 1933- .... **CLC 1, 2, 10, 13, 31,**
  105; DAM POP
  See also CA 17-20R; CANR 25, 51, 74;
  DA3; DLB 2, 67; MTCW 1, 2
Sophocles 496(?)B.C.-406(?)B.C. .... **CMLC 2;**
  DA; DAB; DAC; DAM DRAM, MST;
  DC 1; WLCS
  See also DA3; DLB 176
Sordello 1189-1269 .... **CMLC 15**
Sorel, Georges 1847-1922 .... **TCLC 91**
  See also CA 118

Sorel, Julia
  See Drexler, Rosalyn
Sorrentino, Gilbert 1929- .. **CLC 3, 7, 14, 22,**
  40
  See also CA 77-80; CANR 14, 33; DLB 5,
  173; DLBY 80; INT CANR-14
Soto, Gary 1952- .... **CLC 32, 80; DAM**
  MULT; HLC 2; PC 28
  See also AAYA 10; CA 119; 125; CANR
  50, 74; CLR 38; DLB 82; HW 1, 2; INT
  125; JRDA; MTCW 2; SATA 80
Soupault, Philippe 1897-1990 .... **CLC 68**
  See also CA 116; 147; 131
Souster, (Holmes) Raymond 1921- .... **CLC 5,**
  14; DAC; DAM POET
  See also CA 13-16R; CAAS 14; CANR 13,
  29, 53; DA3; DLB 88; SATA 63
Southern, Terry 1924(?)-1995 .... **CLC 7**
  See also CA 1-4R; 150; CANR 1, 55; DLB
  2
Southey, Robert 1774-1843 .... **NCLC 8**
  See also DLB 93, 107, 142; SATA 54
Southworth, Emma Dorothy Eliza Nevitte
  1819-1899 .... **NCLC 26**
Souza, Ernest
  See Scott, Evelyn
Soyinka, Wole 1934- .... **CLC 3, 5, 14, 36, 44;**
  BLC 3; DA; DAB; DAC; DAM
  DRAM, MST, MULT; DC 2; WLC
  See also BW 2, 3; CA 13-16R; CANR 27,
  39, 82; DA3; DLB 125; MTCW 1, 2
Spackman, W(illiam) M(ode)
  1905-1990 .... **CLC 46**
  See also CA 81-84; 132
Spacks, Barry (Bernard) 1931- .... **CLC 14**
  See also CA 154; CANR 33; DLB 105
Spanidou, Irini 1946- .... **CLC 44**
  See also CA 185
Spark, Muriel (Sarah) 1918- ..... **CLC 2, 3, 5,**
  8, 13, 18, 40, 94; DAB; DAC; DAM
  MST, NOV; SSC 10
  See also CA 5-8R; CANR 12, 36, 76, 89;
  CDBLB 1945-1960; DA3; DLB 15, 139;
  INT CANR-12; MTCW 1, 2
Spaulding, Douglas
  See Bradbury, Ray (Douglas)
Spaulding, Leonard
  See Bradbury, Ray (Douglas)
Spence, J. A. D.
  See Eliot, T(homas) S(tearns)
Spencer, Elizabeth 1921- .... **CLC 22**
  See also CA 13-16R; CANR 32, 65, 87;
  DLB 6; MTCW 1; SATA 14
Spencer, Leonard G.
  See Silverberg, Robert
Spencer, Scott 1945- .... **CLC 30**
  See also CA 113; CANR 51; DLBY 86
Spender, Stephen (Harold)
  1909-1995 .... **CLC 1, 2, 5, 10, 41, 91;**
  DAM POET
  See also CA 9-12R; 149; CANR 31, 54;
  CDBLB 1945-1960; DA3; DLB 20;
  MTCW 1, 2
Spengler, Oswald (Arnold Gottfried)
  1880-1936 .... **TCLC 25**
  See also CA 118
Spenser, Edmund 1552(?)-1599 ..... **LC 5, 39;**
  DA; DAB; DAC; DAM MST, POET;
  PC 8; WLC
  See also CDBLB Before 1660; DA3; DLB
  167
Spicer, Jack 1925-1965 .... **CLC 8, 18, 72;**
  DAM POET
  See also CA 85-88; DLB 5, 16, 193
Spiegelman, Art 1948- .... **CLC 76**
  See also AAYA 10; CA 125; CANR 41, 55,
  74; MTCW 2; SATA 109
Spielberg, Peter 1929- .... **CLC 6**
  See also CA 5-8R; CANR 4, 48; DLBY 81

Spielberg, Steven 1947- .... **CLC 20**
See also AAYA 8, 24; CA 77-80; CANR
32; SATA 32

Spillane, Frank Morrison 1918-
See Spillane, Mickey
See also CA 25-28R; CANR 28, 63; DA3;
DLB 226; MTCW 1, 2; SATA 66

Spillane, Mickey CLC 3, 13
See also Spillane, Frank Morrison
See also MTCW 2

Spinoza, Benedictus de 1632-1677 .. **LC 9, 58**

Spinrad, Norman (Richard) 1940- ... **CLC 46**
See also CA 37-40R; CAAS 19; CANR 20,
91; DLB 8; INT CANR-20

Spitteler, Carl (Friedrich Georg)
1845-1924 .... **TCLC 12**
See also CA 109; DLB 129

Spivack, Kathleen (Romola Drucker)
1938- .... **CLC 6**
See also CA 49-52

Spoto, Donald 1941- .... **CLC 39**
See also CA 65-68; CANR 11, 57

Springsteen, Bruce (F.) 1949- .... **CLC 17**
See also CA 111

Spurling, Hilary 1940- .... **CLC 34**
See also CA 104; CANR 25, 52

Spyker, John Howland
See Elman, Richard (Martin)

Squires, (James) Radcliffe
1917-1993 .... **CLC 51**
See also CA 1-4R; 140; CANR 6, 21

Srivastava, Dhanpat Rai 1880(?)-1936
See Premchand
See also CA 118

Stacy, Donald
See Pohl, Frederik

Staël, Germaine de 1766-1817
See also Staël-Holstein, Anne Louise Germaine Necker Baronn de

**Staël-Holstein, Anne Louise Germaine
Necker Baronn de** 1766-1817 . **NCLC 3,
91**
See also DLB 192
See also Staël, Germaine de

Stafford, Jean 1915-1979 .. **CLC 4, 7, 19, 68;
SSC 26**
See also CA 1-4R; 85-88; CANR 3, 65;
DLB 2, 173; MTCW 1, 2; SATA-Obit 22

Stafford, William (Edgar)
1914-1993 .. **CLC 4, 7, 29; DAM POET**
See also CA 5-8R; 142; CAAS 3; CANR 5,
22; DLB 5, 206; INT CANR-22

Stagnelius, Eric Johan 1793-1823 . **NCLC 61**

Staines, Trevor
See Brunner, John (Kilian Houston)

Stairs, Gordon
See Austin, Mary (Hunter)

Stairs, Gordon
See Austin, Mary (Hunter)

Stalin, Joseph 1879-1953 .... **TCLC 92**

Stannard, Martin 1947- .... **CLC 44**
See also CA 142; DLB 155

Stanton, Elizabeth Cady
1815-1902 .... **TCLC 73**
See also CA 171; DLB 79

Stanton, Maura 1946- .... **CLC 9**
See also CA 89-92; CANR 15; DLB 120

Stanton, Schuyler
See Baum, L(yman) Frank

Stapledon, (William) Olaf
1886-1950 .... **TCLC 22**
See also CA 111; 162; DLB 15

Starbuck, George (Edwin)
1931-1996 .... **CLC 53; DAM POET**
See also CA 21-24R; 153; CANR 23

Stark, Richard
See Westlake, Donald E(dwin)

Staunton, Schuyler
See Baum, L(yman) Frank

Stead, Christina (Ellen) 1902-1983 ... **CLC 2,
5, 8, 32, 80**
See also CA 13-16R; 109; CANR 33, 40;
MTCW 1, 2

Stead, William Thomas
1849-1912 .... **TCLC 48**
See also CA 167

Steele, Richard 1672-1729 .... **LC 18**
See also CDBLB 1660-1789; DLB 84, 101

Steele, Timothy (Reid) 1948- .... **CLC 45**
See also CA 93-96; CANR 16, 50, 92; DLB
120

Steffens, (Joseph) Lincoln
1866-1936 .... **TCLC 20**
See also CA 117

Stegner, Wallace (Earle) 1909-1993 .. **CLC 9,
49, 81; DAM NOV; SSC 27**
See also AITN 1; BEST 90:3; CA 1-4R;
141; CAAS 9; CANR 1, 21, 46; DLB 9,
206; DLBY 93; MTCW 1, 2

Stein, Gertrude 1874-1946 .... **TCLC 1, 6, 28,
48; DA; DAB; DAC; DAM MST, NOV,
POET; PC 18; WLC**
See also CA 104; 132; CDALB 1917-1929;
DA3; DLB 4, 54, 86, 228; DLBD 15;
MTCW 1, 2

Steinbeck, John (Ernst) 1902-1968 ... **CLC 1,
5, 9, 13, 21, 34, 45, 75, 124; DA; DAB;
DAC; DAM DRAM, MST, NOV; SSC
11, 37; WLC**
See also AAYA 12; CA 1-4R; 25-28R;
CANR 1, 35; CDALB 1929-1941; DA3;
DLB 7, 9, 212; DLBD 2; MTCW 1, 2;
SATA 9

Steinem, Gloria 1934- .... **CLC 63**
See also CA 53-56; CANR 28, 51; MTCW
1, 2

Steiner, George 1929- .. **CLC 24; DAM NOV**
See also CA 73-76; CANR 31, 67; DLB 67;
MTCW 1, 2; SATA 62

Steiner, K. Leslie
See Delany, Samuel R(ay, Jr.)

Steiner, Rudolf 1861-1925 .... **TCLC 13**
See also CA 107

Stendhal 1783-1842 .... **NCLC 23, 46; DA;
DAB; DAC; DAM MST, NOV; SSC
27; WLC**
See also DA3; DLB 119

Stephen, Adeline Virginia
See Woolf, (Adeline) Virginia

Stephen, SirLeslie 1832-1904 .... **TCLC 23**
See also CA 123; DLB 57, 144, 190

Stephen, Sir Leslie
See Stephen, SirLeslie

Stephen, Virginia
See Woolf, (Adeline) Virginia

Stephens, James 1882(?)-1950 .... **TCLC 4**
See also CA 104; DLB 19, 153, 162

Stephens, Reed
See Donaldson, Stephen R.

Steptoe, Lydia
See Barnes, Djuna

Sterchi, Beat 1949- .... **CLC 65**

Sterling, Brett
See Bradbury, Ray (Douglas); Hamilton,
Edmond

Sterling, Bruce 1954- .... **CLC 72**
See also CA 119; CANR 44

Sterling, George 1869-1926 .... **TCLC 20**
See also CA 117; 165; DLB 54

Stern, Gerald 1925- .... **CLC 40, 100**
See also CA 81-84; CANR 28; DLB 105

Stern, Richard (Gustave) 1928- ... **CLC 4, 39**
See also CA 1-4R; CANR 1, 25, 52; DLBY
87; INT CANR-25

Sternberg, Josef von 1894-1969 .... **CLC 20**
See also CA 81-84

Sterne, Laurence 1713-1768 .. **LC 2, 48; DA;
DAB; DAC; DAM MST, NOV; WLC**
See also CDBLB 1660-1789; DLB 39

Sternheim, (William Adolf) Carl
1878-1942 .... **TCLC 8**
See also CA 105; DLB 56, 118

Stevens, Mark 1951- .... **CLC 34**
See also CA 122

Stevens, Wallace 1879-1955 ...... **TCLC 3, 12,
45; DA; DAB; DAC; DAM MST,
POET; PC 6; WLC**
See also CA 104; 124; CDALB 1929-1941;
DA3; DLB 54; MTCW 1, 2

Stevenson, Anne (Katharine) 1933- .. **CLC 7,
33**
See also CA 17-20R; CAAS 9; CANR 9,
33; DLB 40; MTCW 1

Stevenson, Robert Louis (Balfour)
1850-1894 . **NCLC 5, 14, 63; DA; DAB;
DAC; DAM MST, NOV; SSC 11; WLC**
See also AAYA 24; CDBLB 1890-1914;
CLR 10, 11; DA3; DLB 18, 57, 141, 156,
174; DLBD 13; JRDA; MAICYA; SATA
100; YABC 2

Stewart, J(ohn) I(nnes) M(ackintosh)
1906-1994 .... **CLC 7, 14, 32**
See also CA 85-88; 147; CAAS 3; CANR
47; MTCW 1, 2

Stewart, Mary (Florence Elinor)
1916- .... **CLC 7, 35, 117; DAB**
See also AAYA 29; CA 1-4R; CANR 1, 59;
SATA 12

Stewart, Mary Rainbow
See Stewart, Mary (Florence Elinor)

Stifle, June
See Campbell, Maria

Stifter, Adalbert 1805-1868 .. **NCLC 41; SSC
28**
See also DLB 133

Still, James 1906- .... **CLC 49**
See also CA 65-68; CAAS 17; CANR 10,
26; DLB 9; SATA 29

Sting 1951-
See Sumner, Gordon Matthew
See also CA 167

Stirling, Arthur
See Sinclair, Upton (Beall)

Stitt, Milan 1941- .... **CLC 29**
See also CA 69-72

Stockton, Francis Richard 1834-1902
See Stockton, Frank R.
See also CA 108; 137; MAICYA; SATA 44

Stockton, Frank R. TCLC 47
See also Stockton, Francis Richard
See also DLB 42, 74; DLBD 13; SATA-
Brief 32

Stoddard, Charles
See Kuttner, Henry

Stoker, Abraham 1847-1912
See Stoker, Bram
See also CA 105; 150; DA; DAC; DAM
MST, NOV; DA3; SATA 29

Stoker, Bram 1847-1912 .... **TCLC 8; DAB;
WLC**
See also Stoker, Abraham
See also AAYA 23; CDBLB 1890-1914;
DLB 36, 70, 178

Stolz, Mary (Slattery) 1920- .... **CLC 12**
See also AAYA 8; AITN 1; CA 5-8R;
CANR 13, 41; JRDA; MAICYA; SAAS
3; SATA 10, 71

Stone, Irving 1903-1989 . **CLC 7; DAM POP**
See also AITN 1; CA 1-4R; 129; CAAS 3;
CANR 1, 23; DA3; INT CANR-23;
MTCW 1, 2; SATA 3; SATA-Obit 64

Stone, Oliver (William) 1946- .... **CLC 73**
See also AAYA 15; CA 110; CANR 55

Stone, Robert (Anthony) 1937- ... **CLC 5, 23, 42**
　See also CA 85-88; CANR 23, 66; DLB 152; INT CANR-23; MTCW 1

Stone, Zachary
　See Follett, Ken(neth Martin)

Stoppard, Tom 1937- ... **CLC 1, 3, 4, 5, 8, 15, 29, 34, 63, 91; DA; DAB; DAC; DAM DRAM, MST; DC 6; WLC**
　See also CA 81-84; CANR 39, 67; CDBLB 1960 to Present; DA3; DLB 13; DLBY 85; MTCW 1, 2

Storey, David (Malcolm) 1933- . **CLC 2, 4, 5, 8; DAM DRAM**
　See also CA 81-84; CANR 36; DLB 13, 14, 207; MTCW 1

Storm, Hyemeyohsts 1935- ..... **CLC 3; DAM MULT**
　See also CA 81-84; CANR 45; NNAL

Storm, Theodor 1817-1888 .... **SSC 27**

Storm, (Hans) Theodor (Woldsen) 1817-1888 .... **NCLC 1; SSC 27**
　See also DLB 129

Storni, Alfonsina 1892-1938 . **TCLC 5; DAM MULT; HLC 2**
　See also CA 104; 131; HW 1

Stoughton, William 1631-1701 .... **LC 38**
　See also DLB 24

Stout, Rex (Todhunter) 1886-1975 ..... **CLC 3**
　See also AITN 2; CA 61-64; CANR 71

Stow, (Julian) Randolph 1935- ... **CLC 23, 48**
　See also CA 13-16R; CANR 33; MTCW 1

Stowe, Harriet (Elizabeth) Beecher 1811-1896 .... **NCLC 3, 50; DA; DAB; DAC; DAM MST, NOV; WLC**
　See also CDALB 1865-1917; DA3; DLB 1, 12, 42, 74, 189; JRDA; MAICYA; YABC 1

Strabo c. 64B.C.-c. 25 .... **CMLC 37**
　See also DLB 176

Strachey, (Giles) Lytton 1880-1932 .... **TCLC 12**
　See also CA 110; 178; DLB 149; DLBD 10; MTCW 2

Strand, Mark 1934- .... **CLC 6, 18, 41, 71; DAM POET**
　See also CA 21-24R; CANR 40, 65; DLB 5; SATA 41

Straub, Peter (Francis) 1943- . **CLC 28, 107; DAM POP**
　See also BEST 89:1; CA 85-88; CANR 28, 65; DLBY 84; MTCW 1, 2

Strauss, Botho 1944- .... **CLC 22**
　See also CA 157; DLB 124

Streatfeild, (Mary) Noel 1895(?)-1986 .... **CLC 21**
　See also CA 81-84; 120; CANR 31; CLR 17; DLB 160; MAICYA; SATA 20; SATA-Obit 48

Stribling, T(homas) S(igismund) 1881-1965 .... **CLC 23**
　See also CA 107; DLB 9

Strindberg, (Johan) August 1849-1912 .... **TCLC 1, 8, 21, 47; DA; DAB; DAC; DAM DRAM, MST; WLC**
　See also CA 104; 135; DA3; MTCW 2

Stringer, Arthur 1874-1950 .... **TCLC 37**
　See also CA 161; DLB 92

Stringer, David
　See Roberts, Keith (John Kingston)

Stroheim, Erich von 1885-1957 ..... **TCLC 71**

Strugatskii, Arkadii (Natanovich) 1925-1991 .... **CLC 27**
　See also CA 106; 135

Strugatskii, Boris (Natanovich) 1933- .... **CLC 27**
　See also CA 106

Strummer, Joe 1953(?)- .... **CLC 30**

Strunk, William, Jr. 1869-1946 ...... **TCLC 92**
　See also CA 118; 164

Stryk, Lucien 1924- .... **PC 27**
　See also CA 13-16R; CANR 10, 28, 55

Stuart, Don A.
　See Campbell, John W(ood, Jr.)

Stuart, Ian
　See MacLean, Alistair (Stuart)

Stuart, Jesse (Hilton) 1906-1984 ... **CLC 1, 8, 11, 14, 34; SSC 31**
　See also CA 5-8R; 112; CANR 31; DLB 9, 48, 102; DLBY 84; SATA 2; SATA-Obit 36

Sturgeon, Theodore (Hamilton) 1918-1985 .... **CLC 22, 39**
　See also Queen, Ellery
　See also CA 81-84; 116; CANR 32; DLB 8; DLBY 85; MTCW 1, 2

Sturges, Preston 1898-1959 .... **TCLC 48**
　See also CA 114; 149; DLB 26

Styron, William 1925- .... **CLC 1, 3, 5, 11, 15, 60; DAM NOV, POP; SSC 25**
　See also BEST 90:4; CA 5-8R; CANR 6, 33, 74; CDALB 1968-1988; DA3; DLB 2, 143; DLBY 80; INT CANR-6; MTCW 1, 2

Su, Chien 1884-1918
　See Su Man-shu
　See also CA 123

Suarez Lynch, B.
　See Bioy Casares, Adolfo; Borges, Jorge Luis

Suassuna, Ariano Vilar 1927-
　See also CA 178; HLCS 1; HW 2

Suckling, John 1609-1641 .... **PC 30**
　See also DAM POET; DLB 58, 126

Suckow, Ruth 1892-1960 .... **SSC 18**
　See also CA 113; DLB 9, 102

Sudermann, Hermann 1857-1928 .. **TCLC 15**
　See also CA 107; DLB 118

Sue, Eugene 1804-1857 .... **NCLC 1**
　See also DLB 119

Sueskind, Patrick 1949- .... **CLC 44**
　See Suskind, Patrick

Sukenick, Ronald 1932- .... **CLC 3, 4, 6, 48**
　See also CA 25-28R; CAAS 8; CANR 32, 89; DLB 173; DLBY 81

Suknaski, Andrew 1942- .... **CLC 19**
　See also CA 101; DLB 53

Sullivan, Vernon
　See Vian, Boris

Sully Prudhomme 1839-1907 .... **TCLC 31**

Su Man-shu TCLC 24
　See also Su, Chien

Summerforest, Ivy B.
　See Kirkup, James

Summers, Andrew James 1942- .... **CLC 26**

Summers, Andy
　See Summers, Andrew James

Summers, Hollis (Spurgeon, Jr.) 1916- .... **CLC 10**
　See also CA 5-8R; CANR 3; DLB 6

Summers, (Alphonsus Joseph-Mary Augustus) Montague 1880-1948 .... **TCLC 16**
　See also CA 118; 163

Sumner, Gordon Matthew CLC 26
　See also Sting

Surtees, Robert Smith 1803-1864 .. **NCLC 14**
　See also DLB 21

Susann, Jacqueline 1921-1974 .... **CLC 3**
　See also AITN 1; CA 65-68; 53-56; MTCW 1, 2

Su Shih 1036-1101 .... **CMLC 15**

Suskind, Patrick
　See Sueskind, Patrick
　See also CA 145

Sutcliff, Rosemary 1920-1992 .... **CLC 26; DAB; DAC; DAM MST, POP**
　See also AAYA 10; CA 5-8R; 139; CANR 37; CLR 1, 37; JRDA; MAICYA; SATA 6, 44, 78; SATA-Obit 73

Sutro, Alfred 1863-1933 .... **TCLC 6**
　See also CA 105; 185; DLB 10

Sutton, Henry
　See Slavitt, David R(ytman)

Svevo, Italo 1861-1928 ...... **TCLC 2, 35; SSC 25**
　See also Schmitz, Aron Hector

Swados, Elizabeth (A.) 1951- .... **CLC 12**
　See also CA 97-100; CANR 49; INT 97-100

Swados, Harvey 1920-1972 .... **CLC 5**
　See also CA 5-8R; 37-40R; CANR 6; DLB 2

Swan, Gladys 1934- .... **CLC 69**
　See also CA 101; CANR 17, 39

Swanson, Logan
　See Matheson, Richard Burton

Swarthout, Glendon (Fred) 1918-1992 .... **CLC 35**
　See also CA 1-4R; 139; CANR 1, 47; SATA 26

Sweet, Sarah C.
　See Jewett, (Theodora) Sarah Orne

Swenson, May 1919-1989 ...... **CLC 4, 14, 61, 106; DA; DAB; DAC; DAM MST, POET; PC 14**
　See also CA 5-8R; 130; CANR 36, 61; DLB 5; MTCW 1, 2; SATA 15

Swift, Augustus
　See Lovecraft, H(oward) P(hillips)

Swift, Graham (Colin) 1949- ...... **CLC 41, 88**
　See also CA 117; 122; CANR 46, 71; DLB 194; MTCW 2

Swift, Jonathan 1667-1745 ..... **LC 1, 42; DA; DAB; DAC; DAM MST, NOV, POET; PC 9; WLC**
　See also CDBLB 1660-1789; CLR 53; DA3; DLB 39, 95, 101; SATA 19

Swinburne, Algernon Charles 1837-1909 .... **TCLC 8, 36; DA; DAB; DAC; DAM MST, POET; PC 24; WLC**
　See also CA 105; 140; CDBLB 1832-1890; DA3; DLB 35, 57

Swinfen, Ann CLC 34

Swinnerton, Frank Arthur 1884-1982 .... **CLC 31**
　See also CA 108; DLB 34

Swithen, John
　See King, Stephen (Edwin)

Sylvia
　See Ashton-Warner, Sylvia (Constance)

Symmes, Robert Edward
　See Duncan, Robert (Edward)

Symonds, John Addington 1840-1893 .... **NCLC 34**
　See also DLB 57, 144

Symons, Arthur 1865-1945 .... **TCLC 11**
　See also CA 107; DLB 19, 57, 149

Symons, Julian (Gustave) 1912-1994 .... **CLC 2, 14, 32**
　See also CA 49-52; 147; CAAS 3; CANR 3, 33, 59; DLB 87, 155; DLBY 92; MTCW 1

Synge, (Edmund) J(ohn) M(illington) 1871-1909 . **TCLC 6, 37; DAM DRAM; DC 2**
　See also CA 104; 141; CDBLB 1890-1914; DLB 10, 19

Syruc, J.
　See Milosz, Czeslaw

Szirtes, George 1948- .... **CLC 46**
　See also CA 109; CANR 27, 61

Author Index

Szymborska, Wislawa 1923- .... **CLC 99**
See also CA 154; CANR 91; DA3; DLBY
96; MTCW 2

T. O., Nik
See Annensky, Innokenty (Fyodorovich)

Tabori, George 1914- .... **CLC 19**
See also CA 49-52; CANR 4, 69

Tagore, Rabindranath 1861-1941 ... **TCLC 3,
53; DAM DRAM, POET; PC 8**
See also CA 104; 120; DA3; MTCW 1, 2

Taine, Hippolyte Adolphe
1828-1893 .... **NCLC 15**

Talese, Gay 1932- .... **CLC 37**
See also AITN 1; CA 1-4R; CANR 9, 58;
DLB 185; INT CANR-9; MTCW 1, 2

Tallent, Elizabeth (Ann) 1954- .... **CLC 45**
See also CA 117; CANR 72; DLB 130

Tally, Ted 1952- .... **CLC 42**
See also CA 120; 124; INT 124

Talvik, Heiti 1904-1947 .... **TCLC 87**

Tamayo y Baus, Manuel
1829-1898 .... **NCLC 1**

Tammsaare, A(nton) H(ansen)
1878-1940 .... **TCLC 27**
See also CA 164; DLB 220

Tam'si, Tchicaya U
See Tchicaya, Gerald Felix

Tan, Amy (Ruth) 1952- . **CLC 59, 120; DAM
MULT, NOV, POP**
See also AAYA 9; BEST 89:3; CA 136;
CANR 54; CDALBS; DA3; DLB 173;
MTCW 2; SATA 75

Tandem, Felix
See Spitteler, Carl (Friedrich Georg)

Tanizaki, Jun'ichiro 1886-1965 ... **CLC 8, 14,
28; SSC 21**
See also CA 93-96; 25-28R; DLB 180;
MTCW 2

Tanner, William
See Amis, Kingsley (William)

Tao Lao
See Storni, Alfonsina

Tarantino, Quentin (Jerome)
1963- .... **CLC 125**
See also CA 171

Tarassoff, Lev
See Troyat, Henri

Tarbell, Ida M(inerva) 1857-1944 . **TCLC 40**
See also CA 122; 181; DLB 47

Tarkington, (Newton) Booth
1869-1946 .... **TCLC 9**
See also CA 110; 143; DLB 9, 102; MTCW
2; SATA 17

Tarkovsky, Andrei (Arsenyevich)
1932-1986 .... **CLC 75**
See also CA 127

Tartt, Donna 1964(?)- .... **CLC 76**
See also CA 142

Tasso, Torquato 1544-1595 .... **LC 5**

Tate, (John Orley) Allen 1899-1979 .. **CLC 2,
4, 6, 9, 11, 14, 24**
See also CA 5-8R; 85-88; CANR 32; DLB
4, 45, 63; DLBD 17; MTCW 1, 2

Tate, Ellalice
See Hibbert, Eleanor Alice Burford

Tate, James (Vincent) 1943- ..... **CLC 2, 6, 25**
See also CA 21-24R; CANR 29, 57; DLB
5, 169

Tauler, Johannes c. 1300-1361 ...... **CMLC 37**
See also DLB 179

Tavel, Ronald 1940- .... **CLC 6**
See also CA 21-24R; CANR 33

Taylor, Bayard 1825-1878 .... **NCLC 89**
See also DLB 3, 189

Taylor, C(ecil) P(hilip) 1929-1981 .... **CLC 27**
See also CA 25-28R; 105; CANR 47

Taylor, Edward 1642(?)-1729 ..... **LC 11; DA;
DAB; DAC; DAM MST, POET**
See also DLB 24

Taylor, Eleanor Ross 1920- .... **CLC 5**
See also CA 81-84; CANR 70

Taylor, Elizabeth 1912-1975 ..... **CLC 2, 4, 29**
See also CA 13-16R; CANR 9, 70; DLB
139; MTCW 1; SATA 13

Taylor, Frederick Winslow
1856-1915 .... **TCLC 76**

Taylor, Henry (Splawn) 1942- .... **CLC 44**
See also CA 33-36R; CAAS 7; CANR 31;
DLB 5

Taylor, Kamala (Purnaiya) 1924-
See Markandaya, Kamala
See also CA 77-80

Taylor, Mildred D. CLC 21
See also AAYA 10; BW 1; CA 85-88;
CANR 25; CLR 9, 59; DLB 52; JRDA;
MAICYA; SAAS 5; SATA 15, 70

Taylor, Peter (Hillsman) 1917-1994 .. **CLC 1,
4, 18, 37, 44, 50, 71; SSC 10**
See also CA 13-16R; 147; CANR 9, 50;
DLBY 81, 94; INT CANR-9; MTCW 1, 2

Taylor, Robert Lewis 1912-1998 .... **CLC 14**
See also CA 1-4R; 170; CANR 3, 64; SATA
10

Tchekhov, Anton
See Chekhov, Anton (Pavlovich)

Tchicaya, Gerald Felix 1931-1988 .. **CLC 101**
See also CA 129; 125; CANR 81

Tchicaya U Tam'si
See Tchicaya, Gerald Felix

Teasdale, Sara 1884-1933 .... **TCLC 4; PC 31**
See also CA 104; 163; DLB 45; SATA 32

Tegner, Esaias 1782-1846 .... **NCLC 2**

Teilhard de Chardin, (Marie Joseph) Pierre
1881-1955 .... **TCLC 9**
See also CA 105

Temple, Ann
See Mortimer, Penelope (Ruth)

Tennant, Emma (Christina) 1937- .. **CLC 13,
52**
See also CA 65-68; CAAS 9; CANR 10,
38, 59, 88; DLB 14

Tenneshaw, S. M.
See Silverberg, Robert

Tennyson, Alfred 1809-1892 ... **NCLC 30, 65;
DA; DAB; DAC; DAM MST, POET;
PC 6; WLC**
See also CDBLB 1832-1890; DA3; DLB
32

Teran, Lisa St. Aubin de CLC 36
See also St. Aubin de Teran, Lisa

Terence c. 184B.C.-c. 159B.C. ...... **CMLC 14;
DC 7**
See also DLB 211

Teresa de Jesus, St. 1515-1582 .... **LC 18**

Terkel, Louis 1912-
See Terkel, Studs
See also CA 57-60; CANR 18, 45, 67; DA3;
MTCW 1, 2

Terkel, Studs CLC 38
See also Terkel, Louis
See also AAYA 32; AITN 1; MTCW 2

Terry, C. V.
See Slaughter, Frank G(ill)

Terry, Megan 1932- .... **CLC 19; DC 13**
See also CA 77-80; CABS 3; CANR 43;
DLB 7

Tertullian c. 155-c. 245 .... **CMLC 29**

Tertz, Abram
See Sinyavsky, Andrei (Donatevich)

Tesich, Steve 1943(?)-1996 .... **CLC 40, 69**
See also CA 105; 152; DLBY 83

Tesla, Nikola 1856-1943 .... **TCLC 88**

Teternikov, Fyodor Kuzmich 1863-1927
See Sologub, Fyodor
See also CA 104

Tevis, Walter 1928-1984 .... **CLC 42**
See also CA 113

Tey, Josephine TCLC 14
See also Mackintosh, Elizabeth
See also DLB 77

Thackeray, William Makepeace
1811-1863 ...... **NCLC 5, 14, 22, 43; DA;
DAB; DAC; DAM MST, NOV; WLC**
See also CDBLB 1832-1890; DA3; DLB
21, 55, 159, 163; SATA 23

Thakura, Ravindranatha
See Tagore, Rabindranath

Tharoor, Shashi 1956- .... **CLC 70**
See also CA 141; CANR 91

Thelwell, Michael Miles 1939- .... **CLC 22**
See also BW 2; CA 101

Theobald, Lewis, Jr.
See Lovecraft, H(oward) P(hillips)

Theodorescu, Ion N. 1880-1967
See Arghezi, Tudor
See also CA 116; DLB 220

Theriault, Yves 1915-1983 .... **CLC 79; DAC;
DAM MST**
See also CA 102; DLB 88

Theroux, Alexander (Louis) 1939- .... **CLC 2,
25**
See also CA 85-88; CANR 20, 63

Theroux, Paul (Edward) 1941- ..... **CLC 5, 8,
11, 15, 28, 46; DAM POP**
See also AAYA 28; BEST 89:4; CA 33-36R;
CANR 20, 45, 74; CDALBS; DA3; DLB
2; MTCW 1, 2; SATA 44, 109

Thesen, Sharon 1946- .... **CLC 56**
See also CA 163

Thevenin, Denis
See Duhamel, Georges

Thibault, Jacques Anatole Francois
1844-1924
See France, Anatole
See also CA 106; 127; DAM NOV; DA3;
MTCW 1, 2

Thiele, Colin (Milton) 1920- .... **CLC 17**
See also CA 29-32R; CANR 12, 28, 53;
CLR 27; MAICYA; SAAS 2; SATA 14,
72

Thomas, Audrey (Callahan) 1935- .... **CLC 7,
13, 37, 107; SSC 20**
See also AITN 2; CA 21-24R; CAAS 19;
CANR 36, 58; DLB 60; MTCW 1

Thomas, Augustus 1857-1934 .... **TCLC 97**

Thomas, D(onald) M(ichael) 1935- . **CLC 13,
22, 31, 132**
See also CA 61-64; CAAS 11; CANR 17,
45, 75; CDBLB 1960 to Present; DA3;
DLB 40, 207; INT CANR-17; MTCW 1,
2

Thomas, Dylan (Marlais)
1914-1953 ... **TCLC 1, 8, 45; DA; DAB;
DAC; DAM DRAM, MST, POET; PC
2; SSC 3; WLC**
See also CA 104; 120; CANR 65; CDBLB
1945-1960; DA3; DLB 13, 20, 139;
MTCW 1, 2; SATA 60

Thomas, (Philip) Edward
1878-1917 .... **TCLC 10; DAM POET**
See also CA 106; 153; DLB 98

Thomas, Joyce Carol 1938- .... **CLC 35**
See also AAYA 12; BW 2, 3; CA 113; 116;
CANR 48; CLR 19; DLB 33; INT 116;
JRDA; MAICYA; MTCW 1, 2; SAAS 7;
SATA 40, 78

Thomas, Lewis 1913-1993 .... **CLC 35**
See also CA 85-88; 143; CANR 38, 60;
MTCW 1, 2

Thomas, M. Carey 1857-1935 .... **TCLC 89**
Thomas, Paul
    See Mann, (Paul) Thomas
Thomas, Piri 1928- .... **CLC 17; HLCS 2**
    See also CA 73-76; HW 1
Thomas, R(onald) S(tuart) 1913- ...... **CLC 6,**
    13, 48; DAB; DAM POET
    See also CA 89-92; CAAS 4; CANR 30;
    CDBLB 1960 to Present; DLB 27; MTCW
    1
Thomas, Ross (Elmore) 1926-1995 .. **CLC 39**
    See also CA 33-36R; 150; CANR 22, 63
Thompson, Francis Clegg
    See Mencken, H(enry) L(ouis)
Thompson, Francis Joseph
    1859-1907 .... **TCLC 4**
    See also CA 104; CDBLB 1890-1914; DLB
    19
Thompson, Hunter S(tockton)
    1939- ... **CLC 9, 17, 40, 104; DAM POP**
    See also BEST 89:1; CA 17-20R; CANR
    23, 46, 74, 77; DA3; DLB 185; MTCW
    1, 2
Thompson, James Myers
    See Thompson, Jim (Myers)
Thompson, Jim (Myers)
    1906-1977(?) .... **CLC 69**
    See also CA 140; DLB 226
Thompson, Judith CLC 39
Thomson, James 1700-1748 ... **LC 16, 29, 40;**
    DAM POET
    See also DLB 95
Thomson, James 1834-1882 .... **NCLC 18;**
    DAM POET
    See also DLB 35
Thoreau, Henry David 1817-1862 .. **NCLC 7,**
    21, 61; DA; DAB; DAC; DAM MST;
    PC 30; WLC
    See also CDALB 1640-1865; DA3; DLB 1,
    223
Thornton, Hall
    See Silverberg, Robert
Thucydides c. 455B.C.-399B.C. ..... **CMLC 17**
    See also DLB 176
Thumboo, Edwin 1933- .... **PC 30**
Thurber, James (Grover)
    1894-1961 .... **CLC 5, 11, 25, 125; DA;**
    DAB; DAC; DAM DRAM, MST, NOV;
    SSC 1
    See also CA 73-76; CANR 17, 39; CDALB
    1929-1941; DA3; DLB 4, 11, 22, 102;
    MAICYA; MTCW 1, 2; SATA 13
Thurman, Wallace (Henry)
    1902-1934 .... **TCLC 6; BLC 3; DAM**
    MULT
    See also BW 1, 3; CA 104; 124; CANR 81;
    DLB 51
Tibullus, Albius c. 54B.C.-c.
    19B.C. .... **CMLC 36**
    See also DLB 211
Ticheburn, Cheviot
    See Ainsworth, William Harrison
Tieck, (Johann) Ludwig
    1773-1853 .... **NCLC 5, 46; SSC 31**
    See also DLB 90
Tiger, Derry
    See Ellison, Harlan (Jay)
Tilghman, Christopher 1948(?)- .... **CLC 65**
    See also CA 159
Tillich, Paul (Johannes)
    1886-1965 .... **CLC 131**
    See also CA 5-8R; 25-28R; CANR 33;
    MTCW 1, 2
Tillinghast, Richard (Williford)
    1940- .... **CLC 29**
    See also CA 29-32R; CAAS 23; CANR 26,
    51
Timrod, Henry 1828-1867 .... **NCLC 25**
    See also DLB 3

Tindall, Gillian (Elizabeth) 1938- ...... **CLC 7**
    See also CA 21-24R; CANR 11, 65
Tiptree, James, Jr. CLC 48, 50
    See also Sheldon, Alice Hastings Bradley
    See also DLB 8
Titmarsh, Michael Angelo
    See Thackeray, William Makepeace
Tocqueville, Alexis (Charles Henri Maurice
    Clerel, Comte) de 1805-1859 . **NCLC 7,**
    63
Tolkien, J(ohn) R(onald) R(euel)
    1892-1973 .. **CLC 1, 2, 3, 8, 12, 38; DA;**
    DAB; DAC; DAM MST, NOV, POP;
    WLC
    See also AAYA 10; AITN 1; CA 17-18; 45-
    48; CANR 36; CAP 2; CDBLB 1914-
    1945; CLR 56; DA3; DLB 15, 160;
    JRDA; MAICYA; MTCW 1, 2; SATA 2,
    32, 100; SATA-Obit 24
Toller, Ernst 1893-1939 .... **TCLC 10**
    See also CA 107; 186; DLB 124
Tolson, M. B.
    See Tolson, Melvin B(eaunorus)
Tolson, Melvin B(eaunorus)
    1898(?)-1966 .... **CLC 36, 105; BLC 3;**
    DAM MULT, POET
    See also BW 1, 3; CA 124; 89-92; CANR
    80; DLB 48, 76
Tolstoi, Aleksei Nikolaevich
    See Tolstoy, Alexey Nikolaevich
Tolstoy, Alexey Nikolaevich
    1882-1945 .... **TCLC 18**
    See also CA 107; 158
Tolstoy, Count Leo
    See Tolstoy, Leo (Nikolaevich)
Tolstoy, Leo (Nikolaevich)
    1828-1910 .. **TCLC 4, 11, 17, 28, 44, 79;**
    DA; DAB; DAC; DAM MST, NOV;
    SSC 9, 30; WLC
    See also CA 104; 123; DA3; SATA 26
Tomasi di Lampedusa, Giuseppe 1896-1957
    See Lampedusa, Giuseppe (Tomasi) di
    See also CA 111
Tomlin, Lily CLC 17
    See also Tomlin, Mary Jean
Tomlin, Mary Jean 1939(?)-
    See Tomlin, Lily
    See also CA 117
Tomlinson, (Alfred) Charles 1927- .... **CLC 2,**
    4, 6, 13, 45; DAM POET; PC 17
    See also CA 5-8R; CANR 33; DLB 40
Tomlinson, H(enry) M(ajor)
    1873-1958 .... **TCLC 71**
    See also CA 118; 161; DLB 36, 100, 195
Tonson, Jacob
    See Bennett, (Enoch) Arnold
Toole, John Kennedy 1937-1969 ..... **CLC 19,**
    64
    See also CA 104; DLBY 81; MTCW 2
Toomer, Jean 1894-1967 .... **CLC 1, 4, 13, 22;**
    BLC 3; DAM MULT; PC 7; SSC 1;
    WLCS
    See also BW 1; CA 85-88; CDALB 1917-
    1929; DA3; DLB 45, 51; MTCW 1, 2
Torley, Luke
    See Blish, James (Benjamin)
Tornimparte, Alessandra
    See Ginzburg, Natalia
Torre, Raoul della
    See Mencken, H(enry) L(ouis)
Torrence, Ridgely 1874-1950 .... **TCLC 97**
    See also DLB 54
Torrey, E(dwin) Fuller 1937- .... **CLC 34**
    See also CA 119; CANR 71
Torsvan, Ben Traven
    See Traven, B.
Torsvan, Benno Traven
    See Traven, B.

Torsvan, Berick Traven
    See Traven, B.
Torsvan, Berwick Traven
    See Traven, B.
Torsvan, Bruno Traven
    See Traven, B.
Torsvan, Traven
    See Traven, B.
Tournier, Michel (Edouard) 1924- .... **CLC 6,**
    23, 36, 95
    See also CA 49-52; CANR 3, 36, 74; DLB
    83; MTCW 1, 2; SATA 23
Tournimparte, Alessandra
    See Ginzburg, Natalia
Towers, Ivar
    See Kornbluth, C(yril) M.
Towne, Robert (Burton) 1936(?)- ..... **CLC 87**
    See also CA 108; DLB 44
Townsend, Sue CLC 61
    See also Townsend, Susan Elaine
    See also AAYA 28; SATA 55, 93; SATA-
    Brief 48
Townsend, Susan Elaine 1946-
    See Townsend, Sue
    See also CA 119; 127; CANR 65; DAB;
    DAC; DAM MST
Townshend, Peter (Dennis Blandford)
    1945- .... **CLC 17, 42**
    See also CA 107
Tozzi, Federigo 1883-1920 .... **TCLC 31**
    See also CA 160
Traill, Catharine Parr 1802-1899 .. **NCLC 31**
    See also DLB 99
Trakl, Georg 1887-1914 .... **TCLC 5; PC 20**
    See also CA 104; 165; MTCW 2
Transtroemer, Tomas (Goesta)
    1931- .... **CLC 52, 65; DAM POET**
    See also CA 117; 129; CAAS 17
Transtromer, Tomas Gosta
    See Transtroemer, Tomas (Goesta)
Traven, B. (?)-1969 .... **CLC 8, 11**
    See also CA 19-20; 25-28R; CAP 2; DLB
    9, 56; MTCW 1
Treitel, Jonathan 1959- .... **CLC 70**
Trelawny, Edward John
    1792-1881 .... **NCLC 85**
    See also DLB 110, 116, 144
Tremain, Rose 1943- .... **CLC 42**
    See also CA 97-100; CANR 44; DLB 14
Tremblay, Michel 1942- .... **CLC 29, 102;**
    DAC; DAM MST
    See also CA 116; 128; DLB 60; MTCW 1,
    2
Trevanian CLC 29
    See also Whitaker, Rod(ney)
Trevor, Glen
    See Hilton, James
Trevor, William 1928- .. **CLC 7, 9, 14, 25, 71,**
    116; SSC 21
    See also Cox, William Trevor
    See also DLB 14, 139; MTCW 2
Trifonov, Yuri (Valentinovich)
    1925-1981 .... **CLC 45**
    See also CA 126; 103; MTCW 1
Trilling, Diana (Rubin) 1905-1996 . **CLC 129**
    See also CA 5-8R; 154; CANR 10, 46; INT
    CANR-10; MTCW 1, 2
Trilling, Lionel 1905-1975 .... **CLC 9, 11, 24**
    See also CA 9-12R; 61-64; CANR 10; DLB
    28, 63; INT CANR-10; MTCW 1, 2
Trimball, W. H.
    See Mencken, H(enry) L(ouis)
Tristan
    See Gomez de la Serna, Ramon
Tristram
    See Housman, A(lfred) E(dward)

Trogdon, William (Lewis) 1939-
See Heat-Moon, William Least
See also CA 115; 119; CANR 47, 89; INT 119

Trollope, Anthony 1815-1882 ... **NCLC 6, 33; DA; DAB; DAC; DAM MST, NOV; SSC 28; WLC**
See also CDBLB 1832-1890; DA3; DLB 21, 57, 159; SATA 22

Trollope, Frances 1779-1863 .... **NCLC 30**
See also DLB 21, 166

Trotsky, Leon 1879-1940 .... **TCLC 22**
See also CA 118; 167

Trotter (Cockburn), Catharine 1679-1749 .... **LC 8**
See also DLB 84

Trotter, Wilfred 1872-1939 .... **TCLC 97**

Trout, Kilgore
See Farmer, Philip Jose

Trow, George W. S. 1943- .... **CLC 52**
See also CA 126; CANR 91

Troyat, Henri 1911- .... **CLC 23**
See also CA 45-48; CANR 2, 33, 67; MTCW 1

Trudeau, G(arretson) B(eekman) 1948-
See Trudeau, Garry B.
See also CA 81-84; CANR 31; SATA 35

Trudeau, Garry B. CLC 12
See also Trudeau, G(arretson) B(eekman)
See also AAYA 10; AITN 2

Truffaut, Francois 1932-1984 ... **CLC 20, 101**
See also CA 81-84; 113; CANR 34

Trumbo, Dalton 1905-1976 .... **CLC 19**
See also CA 21-24R; 69-72; CANR 10; DLB 26

Trumbull, John 1750-1831 .... **NCLC 30**
See also DLB 31

Trundlett, Helen B.
See Eliot, T(homas) S(tearns)

Tryon, Thomas 1926-1991 .... **CLC 3, 11; DAM POP**
See also AITN 1; CA 29-32R; 135; CANR 32, 77; DA3; MTCW 1

Tryon, Tom
See Tryon, Thomas

Ts'ao Hsueh-ch'in 1715(?)-1763 .... **LC 1**

Tsushima, Shuji 1909-1948
See Dazai Osamu
See also CA 107

Tsvetaeva (Efron), Marina (Ivanovna) 1892-1941 .... **TCLC 7, 35; PC 14**
See also CA 104; 128; CANR 73; MTCW 1, 2

Tuck, Lily 1938- .... **CLC 70**
See also CA 139; CANR 90

Tu Fu 712-770 .... **PC 9**
See also DAM MULT

Tunis, John R(oberts) 1889-1975 ..... **CLC 12**
See also CA 61-64; CANR 62; DLB 22, 171; JRDA; MAICYA; SATA 37; SATA-Brief 30

Tuohy, Frank CLC 37
See also Tuohy, John Francis
See also DLB 14, 139

Tuohy, John Francis 1925-
See Tuohy, Frank
See also CA 5-8R; 178; CANR 3, 47

Turco, Lewis (Putnam) 1934- ... **CLC 11, 63**
See also CA 13-16R; CAAS 22; CANR 24, 51; DLBY 84

Turgenev, Ivan 1818-1883 .... **NCLC 21; DA; DAB; DAC; DAM MST, NOV; DC 7; SSC 7; WLC**

Turgot, Anne-Robert-Jacques 1727-1781 .... **LC 26**

Turner, Frederick 1943- .... **CLC 48**
See also CA 73-76; CAAS 10; CANR 12, 30, 56; DLB 40

Tutu, Desmond M(pilo) 1931- .... **CLC 80; BLC 3; DAM MULT**
See also BW 1, 3; CA 125; CANR 67, 81

Tutuola, Amos 1920-1997 ...... **CLC 5, 14, 29; BLC 3; DAM MULT**
See also BW 2, 3; CA 9-12R; 159; CANR 27, 66; DA3; DLB 125; MTCW 1, 2

Twain, Mark 1835-1910 ...... **TCLC 6, 12, 19, 36, 48, 59; SSC 34; WLC**
See also Clemens, Samuel Langhorne
See also AAYA 20; CLR 58, 60, 66; DLB 11, 12, 23, 64, 74

20/1631
See Upward, Allen

Tyler, Anne 1941- . **CLC 7, 11, 18, 28, 44, 59, 103; DAM NOV, POP**
See also AAYA 18; BEST 89:1; CA 9-12R; CANR 11, 33, 53; CDALBS; DLB 6, 143; DLBY 82; MTCW 1, 2; SATA 7, 90

Tyler, Royall 1757-1826 .... **NCLC 3**
See also DLB 37

Tynan, Katharine 1861-1931 .... **TCLC 3**
See also CA 104; 167; DLB 153

Tyutchev, Fyodor 1803-1873 .... **NCLC 34**

Tzara, Tristan 1896-1963 ...... **CLC 47; DAM POET; PC 27**
See also CA 153; 89-92; MTCW 2

Uhry, Alfred 1936- .. **CLC 55; DAM DRAM, POP**
See also CA 127; 133; DA3; INT 133

Ulf, Haerved
See Strindberg, (Johan) August

Ulf, Harved
See Strindberg, (Johan) August

Ulibarri, Sabine R(eyes) 1919- .... **CLC 83; DAM MULT; HLCS 2**
See also CA 131; CANR 81; DLB 82; HW 1, 2

Unamuno (y Jugo), Miguel de 1864-1936 ..... **TCLC 2, 9; DAM MULT, NOV; HLC 2; SSC 11**
See also CA 104; 131; CANR 81; DLB 108; HW 1, 2; MTCW 1, 2

Undercliffe, Errol
See Campbell, (John) Ramsey

Underwood, Miles
See Glassco, John

Undset, Sigrid 1882-1949 .... **TCLC 3; DA; DAB; DAC; DAM MST, NOV; WLC**
See also CA 104; 129; DA3; MTCW 1, 2

Ungaretti, Giuseppe 1888-1970 ... **CLC 7, 11, 15**
See also CA 19-20; 25-28R; CAP 2; DLB 114

Unger, Douglas 1952- .... **CLC 34**
See also CA 130

Unsworth, Barry (Forster) 1930- .... **CLC 76, 127**
See also CA 25-28R; CANR 30, 54; DLB 194

Updike, John (Hoyer) 1932- . **CLC 1, 2, 3, 5, 7, 9, 13, 15, 23, 34, 43, 70; DA; DAB; DAC; DAM MST, NOV, POET, POP; SSC 13, 27; WLC**
See also CA 1-4R; CABS 1; CANR 4, 33, 51; CDALB 1968-1988; DA3; DLB 2, 5, 143, 227; DLBD 3; DLBY 80, 82, 97; MTCW 1, 2

Upshaw, Margaret Mitchell
See Mitchell, Margaret (Munnerlyn)

Upton, Mark
See Sanders, Lawrence

Upward, Allen 1863-1926 .... **TCLC 85**
See also CA 117; DLB 36

Urdang, Constance (Henriette) 1922- .... **CLC 47**
See also CA 21-24R; CANR 9, 24

Uriel, Henry
See Faust, Frederick (Schiller)

Uris, Leon (Marcus) 1924- .... **CLC 7, 32; DAM NOV, POP**
See also AITN 1, 2; BEST 89:2; CA 1-4R; CANR 1, 40, 65; DA3; MTCW 1, 2; SATA 49

Urista, Alberto H. 1947-
See Alurista
See also CA 45-48, 182; CANR 2, 32; HLCS 1; HW 1

Urmuz
See Codrescu, Andrei

Urquhart, Guy
See McAlmon, Robert (Menzies)

Urquhart, Jane 1949- .... **CLC 90; DAC**
See also CA 113; CANR 32, 68

Usigli, Rodolfo 1905-1979
See also CA 131; HLCS 1; HW 1

Ustinov, Peter (Alexander) 1921- .... **CLC 1**
See also AITN 1; CA 13-16R; CANR 25, 51; DLB 13; MTCW 2

U Tam'si, Gerald Felix Tchicaya
See Tchicaya, Gerald Felix

U Tam'si, Tchicaya
See Tchicaya, Gerald Felix

Vachss, Andrew (Henry) 1942- .... **CLC 106**
See also CA 118; CANR 44

Vachss, Andrew H.
See Vachss, Andrew (Henry)

Vaculik, Ludvik 1926- .... **CLC 7**
See also CA 53-56; CANR 72

Vaihinger, Hans 1852-1933 .... **TCLC 71**
See also CA 116; 166

Valdez, Luis (Miguel) 1940- .. **CLC 84; DAM MULT; DC 10; HLC 2**
See also CA 101; CANR 32, 81; DLB 122; HW 1

Valenzuela, Luisa 1938- .... **CLC 31, 104; DAM MULT; HLCS 2; SSC 14**
See also CA 101; CANR 32, 65; DLB 113; HW 1, 2

Valera y Alcala-Galiano, Juan 1824-1905 .... **TCLC 10**
See also CA 106

Valery, (Ambroise) Paul (Toussaint Jules) 1871-1945 ... **TCLC 4, 15; DAM POET; PC 9**
See also CA 104; 122; DA3; MTCW 1, 2

Valle-Inclan, Ramon (Maria) del 1866-1936 .... **TCLC 5; DAM MULT; HLC 2**
See also CA 106; 153; CANR 80; DLB 134; HW 2

Vallejo, Antonio Buero
See Buero Vallejo, Antonio

Vallejo, Cesar (Abraham) 1892-1938 .. **TCLC 3, 56; DAM MULT; HLC 2**
See also CA 105; 153; HW 1

Valles, Jules 1832-1885 .... **NCLC 71**
See also DLB 123

Vallette, Marguerite Eymery 1860-1953 .... **TCLC 67**
See also CA 182; DLB 123, 192

Valle Y Pena, Ramon del
See Valle-Inclan, Ramon (Maria) del

Van Ash, Cay 1918- .... **CLC 34**

Vanbrugh, Sir John 1664-1726 .... **LC 21; DAM DRAM**
See also DLB 80

Van Campen, Karl
See Campbell, John W(ood, Jr.)

Vance, Gerald
See Silverberg, Robert

Vance, Jack CLC 35
See also Vance, John Holbrook
See also DLB 8**

Vance, John Holbrook 1916-
See Queen, Ellery; Vance, Jack
See also CA 29-32R; CANR 17, 65; MTCW 1

Van Den Bogarde, Derek Jules Gaspard Ulric Niven 1921-1999 .... **CLC 14**
See also CA 77-80; 179; DLB 19

Vandenburgh, Jane CLC 59
See also CA 168

Vanderhaeghe, Guy 1951- .... **CLC 41**
See also CA 113; CANR 72

van der Post, Laurens (Jan)
1906-1996 .... **CLC 5**
See also CA 5-8R; 155; CANR 35; DLB 204

van de Wetering, Janwillem 1931- ... **CLC 47**
See also CA 49-52; CANR 4, 62, 90

Van Dine, S. S. TCLC 23
See also Wright, Willard Huntington

Van Doren, Carl (Clinton)
1885-1950 .... **TCLC 18**
See also CA 111; 168

Van Doren, Mark 1894-1972 .... **CLC 6, 10**
See also CA 1-4R; 37-40R; CANR 3; DLB 45; MTCW 1, 2

Van Druten, John (William)
1901-1957 .... **TCLC 2**
See also CA 104; 161; DLB 10

Van Duyn, Mona (Jane) 1921- ...... **CLC 3, 7, 63, 116; DAM POET**
See also CA 9-12R; CANR 7, 38, 60; DLB 5

Van Dyne, Edith
See Baum, L(yman) Frank

van Itallie, Jean-Claude 1936- .... **CLC 3**
See also CA 45-48; CAAS 2; CANR 1, 48; DLB 7

van Ostaijen, Paul 1896-1928 .... **TCLC 33**
See also CA 163

Van Peebles, Melvin 1932- .... **CLC 2, 20; DAM MULT**
See also BW 2, 3; CA 85-88; CANR 27, 67, 82

Vansittart, Peter 1920- .... **CLC 42**
See also CA 1-4R; CANR 3, 49, 90

Van Vechten, Carl 1880-1964 .... **CLC 33**
See also CA 183; 89-92; DLB 4, 9, 51

Van Vogt, A(lfred) E(lton)
1912-2000 .... **CLC 1**
See also CA 21-24R; CANR 28; DLB 8; SATA 14

Varda, Agnes 1928- .... **CLC 16**
See also CA 116; 122

Vargas Llosa, (Jorge) Mario (Pedro)
1936- .... **CLC 3, 6, 9, 10, 15, 31, 42, 85; DA; DAB; DAC; DAM MST, MULT, NOV; HLC 2**
See also CA 73-76; CANR 18, 32, 42, 67; DA3; DLB 145; HW 1, 2; MTCW 1, 2

Vasiliu, Gheorghe 1881-1957
See Bacovia, George
See also CA 123; DLB 220

Vassa, Gustavus
See Equiano, Olaudah

Vassilikos, Vassilis 1933- .... **CLC 4, 8**
See also CA 81-84; CANR 75

Vaughan, Henry 1621-1695 .... **LC 27**
See also DLB 131

Vaughn, Stephanie CLC 62

Vazov, Ivan (Minchov) 1850-1921 . **TCLC 25**
See also CA 121; 167; DLB 147

Veblen, Thorstein B(unde)
1857-1929 .... **TCLC 31**
See also CA 115; 165

Vega, Lope de 1562-1635 .... **LC 23; HLCS 2**

Venison, Alfred
See Pound, Ezra (Weston Loomis)

Verdi, Marie de
See Mencken, H(enry) L(ouis)

Verdu, Matilde
See Cela, Camilo Jose

Verga, Giovanni (Carmelo)
1840-1922 .... **TCLC 3; SSC 21**
See also CA 104; 123

Vergil 70B.C.-19B.C. .... **CMLC 9, 40; DA; DAB; DAC; DAM MST, POET; PC 12; WLCS**
See also Virgil
See also DA3; DLB 211

Verhaeren, Emile (Adolphe Gustave)
1855-1916 .... **TCLC 12**
See also CA 109

Verlaine, Paul (Marie) 1844-1896 .. **NCLC 2, 51; DAM POET; PC 2**

Verne, Jules (Gabriel) 1828-1905 ... **TCLC 6, 52**
See also AAYA 16; CA 110; 131; DA3; DLB 123; JRDA; MAICYA; SATA 21

Very, Jones 1813-1880 .... **NCLC 9**
See also DLB 1

Vesaas, Tarjei 1897-1970 .... **CLC 48**
See also CA 29-32R

Vialis, Gaston
See Simenon, Georges (Jacques Christian)

Vian, Boris 1920-1959 .... **TCLC 9**
See also CA 106; 164; DLB 72; MTCW 2

Viaud, (Louis Marie) Julien 1850-1923
See Loti, Pierre
See also CA 107

Vicar, Henry
See Felsen, Henry Gregor

Vicker, Angus
See Felsen, Henry Gregor

Vidal, Gore 1925- ...... **CLC 2, 4, 6, 8, 10, 22, 33, 72; DAM NOV, POP**
See also AITN 1; BEST 90:2; CA 5-8R; CANR 13, 45, 65; CDALBS; DA3; DLB 6, 152; INT CANR-13; MTCW 1, 2

Viereck, Peter (Robert Edwin)
1916- .... **CLC 4; PC 27**
See also CA 1-4R; CANR 1, 47; DLB 5

Vigny, Alfred (Victor) de
1797-1863 .. **NCLC 7; DAM POET; PC 26**
See also DLB 119, 192

Vilakazi, Benedict Wallet
1906-1947 .... **TCLC 37**
See also CA 168

Villa, Jose Garcia 1904-1997 .... **PC 22**
See also CA 25-28R; CANR 12

Villarreal, Jose Antonio 1924-
See also CA 133; DAM MULT; DLB 82; HLC 2; HW 1

Villaurrutia, Xavier 1903-1950 ...... **TCLC 80**
See also HW 1

Villehardouin 1150(?)-1218(?) .... **CMLC 38**

Villiers de l'Isle Adam, Jean Marie Mathias Philippe Auguste, Comte de
1838-1889 .... **NCLC 3; SSC 14**
See also DLB 123

Villon, Francois 1431-1463(?) .... **PC 13**
See also DLB 208

Vine, Barbara CLC 50
See also Rendell, Ruth (Barbara)
See also BEST 90:4

Vinge, Joan (Carol) D(ennison)
1948- .... **CLC 30; SSC 24**
See also AAYA 32; CA 93-96; CANR 72; SATA 36, 113

Violis, G.
See Simenon, Georges (Jacques Christian)

Viramontes, Helena Maria 1954-
See also CA 159; DLB 122; HLCS 2; HW 2

Virgil 70B.C.-19B.C.
See Vergil

Visconti, Luchino 1906-1976 .... **CLC 16**
See also CA 81-84; 65-68; CANR 39

Vittorini, Elio 1908-1966 .... **CLC 6, 9, 14**
See also CA 133; 25-28R

Vivekananda, Swami 1863-1902 .... **TCLC 88**

Vizenor, Gerald Robert 1934- .... **CLC 103; DAM MULT**
See also CA 13-16R; CAAS 22; CANR 5, 21, 44, 67; DLB 175, 227; MTCW 2; NNAL

Vizinczey, Stephen 1933- .... **CLC 40**
See also CA 128; INT 128

Vliet, R(ussell) G(ordon)
1929-1984 .... **CLC 22**
See also CA 37-40R; 112; CANR 18

Vogau, Boris Andreyevich 1894-1937(?)
See Pilnyak, Boris
See also CA 123

Vogel, Paula A(nne) 1951- .... **CLC 76**
See also CA 108

Voigt, Cynthia 1942- .... **CLC 30**
See also AAYA 3, 30; CA 106; CANR 18, 37, 40; CLR 13, 48; INT CANR-18; JRDA; MAICYA; SATA 48, 79, 116; SATA-Brief 33

Voigt, Ellen Bryant 1943- .... **CLC 54**
See also CA 69-72; CANR 11, 29, 55; DLB 120

Voinovich, Vladimir (Nikolaevich)
1932- .... **CLC 10, 49**
See also CA 81-84; CAAS 12; CANR 33, 67; MTCW 1

Vollmann, William T. 1959- .. **CLC 89; DAM NOV, POP**
See also CA 134; CANR 67; DA3; MTCW 2

Voloshinov, V. N.
See Bakhtin, Mikhail Mikhailovich

Voltaire 1694-1778 .... **LC 14; DA; DAB; DAC; DAM DRAM, MST; SSC 12; WLC**
See also DA3

von Aschendrof, BaronIgnatz
See Ford, Ford Madox

von Daeniken, Erich 1935- .... **CLC 30**
See also AITN 1; CA 37-40R; CANR 17, 44

von Daniken, Erich
See von Daeniken, Erich

von Hartmann, Eduard
1842-1906 .... **TCLC 96**

von Heidenstam, (Carl Gustaf) Verner
See Heidenstam, (Carl Gustaf) Verner von

von Heyse, Paul (Johann Ludwig)
See Heyse, Paul (Johann Ludwig von)

von Hofmannsthal, Hugo
See Hofmannsthal, Hugo von

von Horvath, Odon
See Horvath, Oedoen von

von Horvath, Oedoen -1938
See Horvath, Oedoen von
See also CA 184

von Liliencron, (Friedrich Adolf Axel) Detlev
See Liliencron, (Friedrich Adolf Axel) Detlev von

Vonnegut, Kurt, Jr. 1922- . **CLC 1, 2, 3, 4, 5, 8, 12, 22, 40, 60, 111; DA; DAB; DAC; DAM MST, NOV, POP; SSC 8; WLC**
See also AAYA 6; AITN 1; BEST 90:4; CA 1-4R; CANR 1, 25, 49, 75, 92; CDALB 1968-1988; DA3; DLB 2, 8, 152; DLBD 3; DLBY 80; MTCW 1, 2

Von Rachen, Kurt
See Hubbard, L(afayette) Ron(ald)

von Rezzori (d'Arezzo), Gregor
See Rezzori (d'Arezzo), Gregor von

von Sternberg, Josef
See Sternberg, Josef von

Vorster, Gordon 1924- .... **CLC 34**
    See also CA 133
Vosce, Trudie
    See Ozick, Cynthia
Voznesensky, Andrei (Andreievich)
    1933- .... **CLC 1, 15, 57; DAM POET**
    See also CA 89-92; CANR 37; MTCW 1
Waddington, Miriam 1917- .... **CLC 28**
    See also CA 21-24R; CANR 12, 30; DLB
    68
Wagman, Fredrica 1937- .... **CLC 7**
    See also CA 97-100; INT 97-100
Wagner, Linda W.
    See Wagner-Martin, Linda (C.)
Wagner, Linda Welshimer
    See Wagner-Martin, Linda (C.)
Wagner, Richard 1813-1883 .... **NCLC 9**
    See also DLB 129
Wagner-Martin, Linda (C.) 1936- .... **CLC 50**
    See also CA 159
Wagoner, David (Russell) 1926- .... **CLC 3, 5,**
    15
    See also CA 1-4R; CAAS 3; CANR 2, 71;
    DLB 5; SATA 14
Wah, Fred(erick James) 1939- .... **CLC 44**
    See also CA 107; 141; DLB 60
Wahloo, Per 1926- .... **CLC 7**
    See also CA 61-64; CANR 73
Wahloo, Peter
    See Wahloo, Per
Wain, John (Barrington) 1925-1994 . **CLC 2,**
    11, 15, 46
    See also CA 5-8R; 145; CAAS 4; CANR
    23, 54; CDBLB 1960 to Present; DLB 15,
    27, 139, 155; MTCW 1, 2
Wajda, Andrzej 1926- .... **CLC 16**
    See also CA 102
Wakefield, Dan 1932- .... **CLC 7**
    See also CA 21-24R; CAAS 7
Wakoski, Diane 1937- ...... **CLC 2, 4, 7, 9, 11,**
    40; DAM POET; PC 15
    See also CA 13-16R; CAAS 1; CANR 9,
    60; DLB 5; INT CANR-9; MTCW 2
Wakoski-Sherbell, Diane
    See Wakoski, Diane
Walcott, Derek (Alton) 1930- .... **CLC 2, 4, 9,**
    14, 25, 42, 67, 76; BLC 3; DAB; DAC;
    DAM MST, MULT, POET; DC 7
    See also BW 2; CA 89-92; CANR 26, 47,
    75, 80; DA3; DLB 117; DLBY 81;
    MTCW 1, 2
Waldman, Anne (Lesley) 1945- .... **CLC 7**
    See also CA 37-40R; CAAS 17; CANR 34,
    69; DLB 16
Waldo, E. Hunter
    See Sturgeon, Theodore (Hamilton)
Waldo, Edward Hamilton
    See Sturgeon, Theodore (Hamilton)
Walker, Alice (Malsenior) 1944- ... **CLC 5, 6,**
    9, 19, 27, 46, 58, 103; BLC 3; DA;
    DAB; DAC; DAM MST, MULT, NOV,
    POET, POP; PC 30; SSC 5; WLCS
    See also AAYA 3, 33; BEST 89:4; BW 2, 3;
    CA 37-40R; CANR 9, 27, 49, 66, 82;
    CDALB 1968-1988; DA3; DLB 6, 33,
    143; INT CANR-27; MTCW 1, 2; SATA
    31
Walker, David Harry 1911-1992 ...... **CLC 14**
    See also CA 1-4R; 137; CANR 1; SATA 8;
    SATA-Obit 71
Walker, Edward Joseph 1934-
    See Walker, Ted
    See also CA 21-24R; CANR 12, 28, 53
Walker, George F. 1947- . **CLC 44, 61; DAB;**
    DAC; DAM MST
    See also CA 103; CANR 21, 43, 59; DLB
    60

Walker, Joseph A. 1935- .... **CLC 19; DAM**
    DRAM, MST
    See also BW 1, 3; CA 89-92; CANR 26;
    DLB 38
Walker, Margaret (Abigail)
    1915-1998 .... **CLC 1, 6; BLC; DAM**
    MULT; PC 20
    See also BW 2, 3; CA 73-76; 172; CANR
    26, 54, 76; DLB 76, 152; MTCW 1, 2
Walker, Ted **CLC 13**
    See also Walker, Edward Joseph
    See also DLB 40
Wallace, David Foster 1962- ..... **CLC 50, 114**
    See also CA 132; CANR 59; DA3; MTCW
    2
Wallace, Dexter
    See Masters, Edgar Lee
Wallace, (Richard Horatio) Edgar
    1875-1932 .... **TCLC 57**
    See also CA 115; DLB 70
Wallace, Irving 1916-1990 .... **CLC 7, 13;**
    DAM NOV, POP
    See also AITN 1; CA 1-4R; 132; CAAS 1;
    CANR 1, 27; INT CANR-27; MTCW 1,
    2
Wallant, Edward Lewis 1926-1962 ... **CLC 5,**
    10
    See also CA 1-4R; CANR 22; DLB 2, 28,
    143; MTCW 1, 2
Wallas, Graham 1858-1932 .... **TCLC 91**
Walley, Byron
    See Card, Orson Scott
Walpole, Horace 1717-1797 .... **LC 49**
    See also DLB 39, 104
Walpole, Hugh (Seymour)
    1884-1941 .... **TCLC 5**
    See also CA 104; 165; DLB 34; MTCW 2
Walser, Martin 1927- .... **CLC 27**
    See also CA 57-60; CANR 8, 46; DLB 75,
    124
Walser, Robert 1878-1956 .... **TCLC 18; SSC**
    20
    See also CA 118; 165; DLB 66
Walsh, Gillian Paton
    See Paton Walsh, Gillian
Walsh, Jill Paton **CLC 35**
    See Paton Walsh, Gillian
    See also CLR 2, 65
Walter, Villiam Christian
    See Andersen, Hans Christian
Wambaugh, Joseph (Aloysius, Jr.)
    1937- .... **CLC 3, 18; DAM NOV, POP**
    See also AITN 1; BEST 89:3; CA 33-36R;
    CANR 42, 65; DA3; DLB 6; DLBY 83;
    MTCW 1, 2
Wang Wei 699(?)-761(?) .... **PC 18**
Ward, Arthur Henry Sarsfield 1883-1959
    See Rohmer, Sax
    See also CA 108; 173
Ward, Douglas Turner 1930- .... **CLC 19**
    See also BW 1; CA 81-84; CANR 27; DLB
    7, 38
Ward, E. D.
    See Lucas, E(dward) V(errall)
Ward, Mary Augusta
    See Ward, Mrs. Humphry
Ward, Mrs. Humphry 1851-1920 .. **TCLC 55**
    See also DLB 18
Ward, Peter
    See Faust, Frederick (Schiller)
Warhol, Andy 1928(?)-1987 .... **CLC 20**
    See also AAYA 12; BEST 89:4; CA 89-92;
    121; CANR 34
Warner, Francis (Robert le Plastrier)
    1937- .... **CLC 14**
    See also CA 53-56; CANR 11
Warner, Marina 1946- .... **CLC 59**
    See also CA 65-68; CANR 21, 55; DLB
    194

Warner, Rex (Ernest) 1905-1986 ...... **CLC 45**
    See also CA 89-92; 119; DLB 15
Warner, Susan (Bogert)
    1819-1885 .... **NCLC 31**
    See also DLB 3, 42
Warner, Sylvia (Constance) Ashton
    See Ashton-Warner, Sylvia (Constance)
Warner, Sylvia Townsend
    1893-1978 .... **CLC 7, 19; SSC 23**
    See also CA 61-64; 77-80; CANR 16, 60;
    DLB 34, 139; MTCW 1, 2
Warren, Mercy Otis 1728-1814 ..... **NCLC 13**
    See also DLB 31, 200
Warren, Robert Penn 1905-1989 .. **CLC 1, 4,**
    6, 8, 10, 13, 18, 39, 53, 59; DA; DAB;
    DAC; DAM MST, NOV, POET; SSC 4;
    WLC
    See also AITN 1; CA 13-16R; 129; CANR
    10, 47; CDALB 1968-1988; DA3; DLB
    2, 48, 152; DLBY 80, 89; INT CANR-10;
    MTCW 1, 2; SATA 46; SATA-Obit 63
Warshofsky, Isaac
    See Singer, Isaac Bashevis
Warton, Thomas 1728-1790 ..... **LC 15; DAM**
    POET
    See also DLB 104, 109
Waruk, Kona
    See Harris, (Theodore) Wilson
Warung, Price 1855-1911 .... **TCLC 45**
Warwick, Jarvis
    See Garner, Hugh
Washington, Alex
    See Harris, Mark
Washington, Booker T(aliaferro)
    1856-1915 ...... **TCLC 10; BLC 3; DAM**
    MULT
    See also BW 1; CA 114; 125; DA3; SATA
    28
Washington, George 1732-1799 .... **LC 25**
    See also DLB 31
Wassermann, (Karl) Jakob
    1873-1934 .... **TCLC 6**
    See also CA 104; 163; DLB 66
Wasserstein, Wendy 1950- .. **CLC 32, 59, 90;**
    DAM DRAM; DC 4
    See also CA 121; 129; CABS 3; CANR 53,
    75; DA3; DLB 228; INT 129; MTCW 2;
    SATA 94
Waterhouse, Keith (Spencer) 1929- . **CLC 47**
    See also CA 5-8R; CANR 38, 67; DLB 13,
    15; MTCW 1, 2
Waters, Frank (Joseph) 1902-1995 .. **CLC 88**
    See also CA 5-8R; 149; CAAS 13; CANR
    3, 18, 63; DLB 212; DLBY 86
Waters, Roger 1944- .... **CLC 35**
Watkins, Frances Ellen
    See Harper, Frances Ellen Watkins
Watkins, Gerrold
    See Malzberg, Barry N(athaniel)
Watkins, Gloria Jean 1952(?)-
    See hooks, bell
    See also BW 2; CA 143; CANR 87; MTCW
    2; SATA 115
Watkins, Paul 1964- .... **CLC 55**
    See also CA 132; CANR 62
Watkins, Vernon Phillips
    1906-1967 .... **CLC 43**
    See also CA 9-10; 25-28R; CAP 1; DLB 20
Watson, Irving S.
    See Mencken, H(enry) L(ouis)
Watson, John H.
    See Farmer, Philip Jose
Watson, Richard F.
    See Silverberg, Robert
Waugh, Auberon (Alexander) 1939- .. **CLC 7**
    See also CA 45-48; CANR 6, 22, 92; DLB
    14, 194

Waugh, Evelyn (Arthur St. John)
1903-1966 .. CLC 1, 3, 8, 13, 19, 27, 44,
107; DA; DAB; DAC; DAM MST,
NOV, POP; SSC 41; WLC
See also CA 85-88; 25-28R; CANR 22; CD-
BLB 1914-1945; DA3; DLB 15, 162, 195;
MTCW 1, 2
Waugh, Harriet 1944- .... CLC 6
See also CA 85-88; CANR 22
Ways, C. R.
See Blount, Roy (Alton), Jr.
Waystaff, Simon
See Swift, Jonathan
Webb, Beatrice (Martha Potter)
1858-1943 .... TCLC 22
See also CA 117; 162; DLB 190
Webb, Charles (Richard) 1939- .... CLC 7
See also CA 25-28R
Webb, James H(enry), Jr. 1946- ...... CLC 22
See also CA 81-84
Webb, Mary Gladys (Meredith)
1881-1927 .... TCLC 24
See also CA 182; 123; DLB 34
Webb, Mrs. Sidney
See Webb, Beatrice (Martha Potter)
Webb, Phyllis 1927- .... CLC 18
See also CA 104; CANR 23; DLB 53
Webb, Sidney (James) 1859-1947 .. TCLC 22
See also CA 117; 163; DLB 190
Webber, Andrew Lloyd CLC 21
See also Lloyd Webber, Andrew
Weber, Lenora Mattingly
1895-1971 .... CLC 12
See also CA 19-20; 29-32R; CAP 1; SATA
2; SATA-Obit 26
Weber, Max 1864-1920 .... TCLC 69
See also CA 109
Webster, John 1579(?)-1634(?) ... LC 33; DA;
DAB; DAC; DAM DRAM, MST; DC
2; WLC
See also CDBLB Before 1660; DLB 58
Webster, Noah 1758-1843 .... NCLC 30
See also DLB 1, 37, 42, 43, 73
Wedekind, (Benjamin) Frank(lin)
1864-1918 .... TCLC 7; DAM DRAM
See also CA 104; 153; DLB 118
Weidman, Jerome 1913-1998 .... CLC 7
See also AITN 2; CA 1-4R; 171; CANR 1;
DLB 28
Weil, Simone (Adolphine)
1909-1943 .... TCLC 23
See also CA 117; 159; MTCW 2
Weininger, Otto 1880-1903 .... TCLC 84
Weinstein, Nathan
See West, Nathanael
Weinstein, Nathan von Wallenstein
See West, Nathanael
Weir, Peter (Lindsay) 1944- .... CLC 20
See also CA 113; 123
Weiss, Peter (Ulrich) 1916-1982 .. CLC 3, 15,
51; DAM DRAM
See also CA 45-48; 106; CANR 3; DLB 69,
124
Weiss, Theodore (Russell) 1916- ... CLC 3, 8,
14
See also CA 9-12R; CAAS 2; CANR 46;
DLB 5
Welch, (Maurice) Denton
1915-1948 .... TCLC 22
See also CA 121; 148
Welch, James 1940- ..... CLC 6, 14, 52; DAM
MULT, POP
See also CA 85-88; CANR 42, 66; DLB
175; NNAL
Weldon, Fay 1931- . CLC 6, 9, 11, 19, 36, 59,
122; DAM POP
See also CA 21-24R; CANR 16, 46, 63;
CDBLB 1960 to Present; DLB 14, 194;
INT CANR-16; MTCW 1, 2

Wellek, Rene 1903-1995 .... CLC 28
See also CA 5-8R; 150; CAAS 7; CANR 8;
DLB 63; INT CANR-8
Weller, Michael 1942- .... CLC 10, 53
See also CA 85-88
Weller, Paul 1958- .... CLC 26
Wellershoff, Dieter 1925- .... CLC 46
See also CA 89-92; CANR 16, 37
Welles, (George) Orson 1915-1985 .. CLC 20,
80
See also CA 93-96; 117
Wellman, John McDowell 1945-
See Wellman, Mac
See also CA 166
Wellman, Mac 1945- .... CLC 65
See also Wellman, John McDowell; Well-
man, John McDowell
Wellman, Manly Wade 1903-1986 ... CLC 49
See also CA 1-4R; 118; CANR 6, 16, 44;
SATA 6; SATA-Obit 47
Wells, Carolyn 1869(?)-1942 .... TCLC 35
See also CA 113; 185; DLB 11
Wells, H(erbert) G(eorge)
1866-1946 . TCLC 6, 12, 19; DA; DAB;
DAC; DAM MST, NOV; SSC 6; WLC
See also AAYA 18; CA 110; 121; CDBLB
1914-1945; CLR 64; DA3; DLB 34, 70,
156, 178; MTCW 1, 2; SATA 20
Wells, Rosemary 1943- .... CLC 12
See also AAYA 13; CA 85-88; CANR 48;
CLR 16; MAICYA; SAAS 1; SATA 18,
69, 114
Welty, Eudora 1909- ...... CLC 1, 2, 5, 14, 22,
33, 105; DA; DAB; DAC; DAM MST,
NOV; SSC 1, 27; WLC
See also CA 9-12R; CABS 1; CANR 32,
65; CDALB 1941-1968; DA3; DLB 2,
102, 143; DLBD 12; DLBY 87; MTCW
1, 2
Wen I-to 1899-1946 .... TCLC 28
Wentworth, Robert
See Hamilton, Edmond
Werfel, Franz (Viktor) 1890-1945 ... TCLC 8
See also CA 104; 161; DLB 81, 124
Wergeland, Henrik Arnold
1808-1845 .... NCLC 5
Wersba, Barbara 1932- .... CLC 30
See also AAYA 2, 30; CA 29-32R, 182;
CAAE 182; CANR 16, 38; CLR 3; DLB
52; JRDA; MAICYA; SAAS 2; SATA 1,
58; SATA-Essay 103
Wertmueller, Lina 1928- .... CLC 16
See also CA 97-100; CANR 39, 78
Wescott, Glenway 1901-1987 .. CLC 13; SSC
35
See also CA 13-16R; 121; CANR 23, 70;
DLB 4, 9, 102
Wesker, Arnold 1932- ... CLC 3, 5, 42; DAB;
DAM DRAM
See also CA 1-4R; CAAS 7; CANR 1, 33;
CDBLB 1960 to Present; DLB 13; MTCW
1
Wesley, Richard (Errol) 1945- .... CLC 7
See also BW 1; CA 57-60; CANR 27; DLB
38
Wessel, Johan Herman 1742-1785 .... LC 7
West, Anthony (Panther)
1914-1987 .... CLC 50
See also CA 45-48; 124; CANR 3, 19; DLB
15
West, C. P.
See Wodehouse, P(elham) G(renville)
West, Cornel (Ronald) 1953- .... CLC 134;
BLCS
See also CA 144; CANR 91
West, (Mary) Jessamyn 1902-1984 ... CLC 7,
17
See also CA 9-12R; 112; CANR 27; DLB
6; DLBY 84; MTCW 1, 2; SATA-Obit 37

West, Morris L(anglo) 1916-1999 ..... CLC 6,
33
See also CA 5-8R; CANR 24, 49, 64;
MTCW 1, 2
West, Nathanael 1903-1940 .... TCLC 1, 14,
44; SSC 16
See also CA 104; 125; CDALB 1929-1941;
DA3; DLB 4, 9, 28; MTCW 1, 2
West, Owen
See Koontz, Dean R(ay)
West, Paul 1930- .... CLC 7, 14, 96
See also CA 13-16R; CAAS 7; CANR 22,
53, 76, 89; DLB 14; INT CANR-22;
MTCW 2
West, Rebecca 1892-1983 ... CLC 7, 9, 31, 50
See also CA 5-8R; 109; CANR 19; DLB
36; DLBY 83; MTCW 1, 2
Westall, Robert (Atkinson)
1929-1993 .... CLC 17
See also AAYA 12; CA 69-72; 141; CANR
18, 68; CLR 13; JRDA; MAICYA; SAAS
2; SATA 23, 69; SATA-Obit 75
Westermarck, Edward 1862-1939 . TCLC 87
Westlake, Donald E(dwin) 1933- .... CLC 7,
33; DAM POP
See also CA 17-20R; CAAS 13; CANR 16,
44, 65; INT CANR-16; MTCW 2
Westmacott, Mary
See Christie, Agatha (Mary Clarissa)
Weston, Allen
See Norton, Andre
Wetcheek, J. L.
See Feuchtwanger, Lion
Wetering, Janwillem van de
See van de Wetering, Janwillem
Wetherald, Agnes Ethelwyn
1857-1940 .... TCLC 81
See also DLB 99
Wetherell, Elizabeth
See Warner, Susan (Bogert)
Whale, James 1889-1957 .... TCLC 63
Whalen, Philip 1923- .... CLC 6, 29
See also CA 9-12R; CANR 5, 39; DLB 16
Wharton, Edith (Newbold Jones)
1862-1937 .... TCLC 3, 9, 27, 53; DA;
DAB; DAC; DAM MST, NOV; SSC 6;
WLC
See also AAYA 25; CA 104; 132; CDALB
1865-1917; DA3; DLB 4, 9, 12, 78, 189;
DLBD 13; MTCW 1, 2
Wharton, James
See Mencken, H(enry) L(ouis)
Wharton, William (a pseudonym) CLC 18,
37
See also CA 93-96; DLBY 80; INT 93-96
Wheatley (Peters), Phillis
1754(?)-1784 ...... LC 3, 50; BLC 3; DA;
DAC; DAM MST, MULT, POET; PC
3; WLC
See also CDALB 1640-1865; DA3; DLB
31, 50
Wheelock, John Hall 1886-1978 .... CLC 14
See also CA 13-16R; 77-80; CANR 14;
DLB 45
White, E(lwyn) B(rooks)
1899-1985 . CLC 10, 34, 39; DAM POP
See also AITN 2; CA 13-16R; 116; CANR
16, 37; CDALBS; CLR 1, 21; DA3; DLB
11, 22; MAICYA; MTCW 1, 2; SATA 2,
29, 100; SATA-Obit 44
White, Edmund (Valentine III)
1940- .... CLC 27, 110; DAM POP
See also AAYA 7; CA 45-48; CANR 3, 19,
36, 62; DA3; DLB 227; MTCW 1, 2
White, Patrick (Victor Martindale)
1912-1990 ...... CLC 3, 4, 5, 7, 9, 18, 65,
69; SSC 39
See also CA 81-84; 132; CANR 43; MTCW
1

White, Phyllis Dorothy James 1920-
See James, P. D.
See also CA 21-24R; CANR 17, 43, 65;
DAM POP; DA3; MTCW 1, 2

White, T(erence) H(anbury)
1906-1964 .... **CLC 30**
See also AAYA 22; CA 73-76; CANR 37;
DLB 160; JRDA; MAICYA; SATA 12

White, Terence de Vere 1912-1994 ... **CLC 49**
See also CA 49-52; 145; CANR 3

White, Walter
See White, Walter F(rancis)
See also BLC; DAM MULT

White, Walter F(rancis)
1893-1955 .... **TCLC 15**
See also White, Walter
See also BW 1; CA 115; 124; DLB 51

White, William Hale 1831-1913
See Rutherford, Mark
See also CA 121

Whitehead, Alfred North
1861-1947 .... **TCLC 97**
See also CA 117; 165; DLB 100

Whitehead, E(dward) A(nthony)
1933- .... **CLC 5**
See also CA 65-68; CANR 58

Whitemore, Hugh (John) 1936- .... **CLC 37**
See also CA 132; CANR 77; INT 132

Whitman, Sarah Helen (Power)
1803-1878 .... **NCLC 19**
See also DLB 1

Whitman, Walt(er) 1819-1892 .. **NCLC 4, 31,**
81; DA; DAB; DAC; DAM MST,
POET; PC 3; WLC
See also CDALB 1640-1865; DA3; DLB 3,
64; SATA 20

Whitney, Phyllis A(yame) 1903- ...... **CLC 42;**
DAM POP
See also AITN 2; BEST 90:3; CA 1-4R;
CANR 3, 25, 38, 60; CLR 59; DA3;
JRDA; MAICYA; MTCW 2; SATA 1, 30

Whittemore, (Edward) Reed (Jr.)
1919- .... **CLC 4**
See also CA 9-12R; CAAS 8; CANR 4;
DLB 5

Whittier, John Greenleaf
1807-1892 .... **NCLC 8, 59**
See also DLB 1

Whittlebot, Hernia
See Coward, Noel (Peirce)

Wicker, Thomas Grey 1926-
See Wicker, Tom
See also CA 65-68; CANR 21, 46

Wicker, Tom CLC 7
See also Wicker, Thomas Grey

Wideman, John Edgar 1941- ...... **CLC 5, 34,**
36, 67, 122; BLC 3; DAM MULT
See also BW 2, 3; CA 85-88; CANR 14,
42, 67; DLB 33, 143; MTCW 2

Wiebe, Rudy (Henry) 1934- .. **CLC 6, 11, 14;**
DAC; DAM MST
See also CA 37-40R; CANR 42, 67; DLB
60

Wieland, Christoph Martin
1733-1813 .... **NCLC 17**
See also DLB 97

Wiene, Robert 1881-1938 .... **TCLC 56**

Wieners, John 1934- .... **CLC 7**
See also CA 13-16R; DLB 16

Wiesel, Elie(zer) 1928- .... **CLC 3, 5, 11, 37;**
DA; DAB; DAC; DAM MST, NOV;
WLCS
See also AAYA 7; AITN 1; CA 5-8R; CAAS
4; CANR 8, 40, 65; CDALBS; DA3; DLB
83; DLBY 87; INT CANR-8; MTCW 1,
2; SATA 56

Wiggins, Marianne 1947- .... **CLC 57**
See also BEST 89:3; CA 130; CANR 60

Wight, James Alfred 1916-1995
See Herriot, James
See also CA 77-80; SATA 55; SATA-Brief
44

Wilbur, Richard (Purdy) 1921- ..... **CLC 3, 6,**
9, 14, 53, 110; DA; DAB; DAC; DAM
MST, POET
See also CA 1-4R; CABS 2; CANR 2, 29,
76; CDALBS; DLB 5, 169; INT CANR-
29; MTCW 1, 2; SATA 9, 108

Wild, Peter 1940- .... **CLC 14**
See also CA 37-40R; DLB 5

Wilde, Oscar (Fingal O'Flahertie Wills)
1854(?)-1900 .... **TCLC 1, 8, 23, 41; DA;**
DAB; DAC; DAM DRAM, MST, NOV;
SSC 11; WLC
See also CA 104; 119; CDBLB 1890-1914;
DA3; DLB 10, 19, 34, 57, 141, 156, 190;
SATA 24

Wilder, Billy CLC 20
See also Wilder, Samuel
See also DLB 26

Wilder, Samuel 1906-
See Wilder, Billy
See also CA 89-92

Wilder, Thornton (Niven)
1897-1975 .. **CLC 1, 5, 6, 10, 15, 35, 82;**
DA; DAB; DAC; DAM DRAM, MST,
NOV; DC 1; WLC
See also AAYA 29; AITN 2; CA 13-16R;
61-64; CANR 40; CDALBS; DA3; DLB
4, 7, 9, 228; DLBY 97; MTCW 1, 2

Wilding, Michael 1942- .... **CLC 73**
See also CA 104; CANR 24, 49

Wiley, Richard 1944- .... **CLC 44**
See also CA 121; 129; CANR 71

Wilhelm, Kate CLC 7
See also Wilhelm, Katie Gertrude
See also AAYA 20; CAAS 5; DLB 8; INT
CANR-17

Wilhelm, Katie Gertrude 1928-
See Wilhelm, Kate
See also CA 37-40R; CANR 17, 36, 60;
MTCW 1

Wilkins, Mary
See Freeman, Mary E(leanor) Wilkins

Willard, Nancy 1936- .... **CLC 7, 37**
See also CA 89-92; CANR 10, 39, 68; CLR
5; DLB 5, 52; MAICYA; MTCW 1; SATA
37, 71; SATA-Brief 30

William of Ockham 1285-1347 ..... **CMLC 32**

Williams, Ben Ames 1889-1953 ..... **TCLC 89**
See also CA 183; DLB 102

Williams, C(harles) K(enneth)
1936- .... **CLC 33, 56; DAM POET**
See also CA 37-40R; CAAS 26; CANR 57;
DLB 5

Williams, Charles
See Collier, James L(incoln)

Williams, Charles (Walter Stansby)
1886-1945 .... **TCLC 1, 11**
See also CA 104; 163; DLB 100, 153

Williams, (George) Emlyn
1905-1987 .... **CLC 15; DAM DRAM**
See also CA 104; 123; CANR 36; DLB 10,
77; MTCW 1

Williams, Hank 1923-1953 .... **TCLC 81**

Williams, Hugo 1942- .... **CLC 42**
See also CA 17-20R; CANR 45; DLB 40

Williams, J. Walker
See Wodehouse, P(elham) G(renville)

Williams, John A(lfred) 1925- ..... **CLC 5, 13;**
BLC 3; DAM MULT
See also BW 2, 3; CA 53-56; CAAS 3;
CANR 6, 26, 51; DLB 2, 33; INT
CANR-6

Williams, Jonathan (Chamberlain)
1929- .... **CLC 13**
See also CA 9-12R; CAAS 12; CANR 8;
DLB 5

Williams, Joy 1944- .... **CLC 31**
See also CA 41-44R; CANR 22, 48

Williams, Norman 1952- .... **CLC 39**
See also CA 118

Williams, Sherley Anne 1944-1999 . **CLC 89;**
BLC 3; DAM MULT, POET
See also BW 2, 3; CA 73-76; 185; CANR
25, 82; DLB 41; INT CANR-25; SATA
78; SATA-Obit 116

Williams, Shirley
See Williams, Sherley Anne

Williams, Tennessee 1911-1983 . **CLC 1, 2, 5,**
7, 8, 11, 15, 19, 30, 39, 45, 71, 111; DA;
DAB; DAC; DAM DRAM, MST; DC
4; WLC
See also AAYA 31; AITN 1, 2; CA 5-8R;
108; CABS 3; CANR 31; CDALB 1941-
1968; DA3; DLB 7; DLBD 4; DLBY 83;
MTCW 1, 2

Williams, Thomas (Alonzo)
1926-1990 .... **CLC 14**
See also CA 1-4R; 132; CANR 2

Williams, William C.
See Williams, William Carlos

Williams, William Carlos
1883-1963 .... **CLC 1, 2, 5, 9, 13, 22, 42,**
67; DA; DAB; DAC; DAM MST,
POET; PC 7; SSC 31
See also CA 89-92; CANR 34; CDALB
1917-1929; DA3; DLB 4, 16, 54, 86;
MTCW 1, 2

Williamson, David (Keith) 1942- ..... **CLC 56**
See also CA 103; CANR 41

Williamson, Ellen Douglas 1905-1984
See Douglas, Ellen
See also CA 17-20R; 114; CANR 39

Williamson, Jack CLC 29
See also Williamson, John Stewart
See also CAAS 8; DLB 8

Williamson, John Stewart 1908-
See Williamson, Jack
See also CA 17-20R; CANR 23, 70

Willie, Frederick
See Lovecraft, H(oward) P(hillips)

Willingham, Calder (Baynard, Jr.)
1922-1995 .... **CLC 5, 51**
See also CA 5-8R; 147; CANR 3; DLB 2,
44; MTCW 1

Willis, Charles
See Clarke, Arthur C(harles)

Willy
See Colette, (Sidonie-Gabrielle)

Willy, Colette
See Colette, (Sidonie-Gabrielle)

Wilson, A(ndrew) N(orman) 1950- .. **CLC 33**
See also CA 112; 122; DLB 14, 155, 194;
MTCW 2

Wilson, Angus (Frank Johnstone)
1913-1991 . **CLC 2, 3, 5, 25, 34; SSC 21**
See also CA 5-8R; 134; CANR 21; DLB
15, 139, 155; MTCW 1, 2

Wilson, August 1945- ... **CLC 39, 50, 63, 118;**
BLC 3; DA; DAB; DAC; DAM
DRAM, MST, MULT; DC 2; WLCS
See also AAYA 16; BW 2, 3; CA 115; 122;
CANR 42, 54, 76; DA3; DLB 228;
MTCW 1, 2

Wilson, Brian 1942- .... **CLC 12**

Wilson, Colin 1931- .... **CLC 3, 14**
See also CA 1-4R; CAAS 5; CANR 1, 22,
33, 77; DLB 14, 194; MTCW 1

Wilson, Dirk
See Pohl, Frederik

Wilson, Edmund 1895-1972 .. **CLC 1, 2, 3, 8, 24**
See also CA 1-4R; 37-40R; CANR 1, 46; DLB 63; MTCW 1, 2

Wilson, Ethel Davis (Bryant) 1888(?)-1980 .... **CLC 13; DAC; DAM POET**
See also CA 102; DLB 68; MTCW 1

Wilson, John 1785-1854 .... **NCLC 5**

Wilson, John (Anthony) Burgess 1917-1993
See Burgess, Anthony
See also CA 1-4R; 143; CANR 2, 46; DAC; DAM NOV; DA3; MTCW 1, 2

Wilson, Lanford 1937- .... **CLC 7, 14, 36; DAM DRAM**
See also CA 17-20R; CABS 3; CANR 45; DLB 7

Wilson, Robert M. 1944- .... **CLC 7, 9**
See also CA 49-52; CANR 2, 41; MTCW 1

Wilson, Robert McLiam 1964- .... **CLC 59**
See also CA 132

Wilson, Sloan 1920- .... **CLC 32**
See also CA 1-4R; CANR 1, 44

Wilson, Snoo 1948- .... **CLC 33**
See also CA 69-72

Wilson, William S(mith) 1932- .... **CLC 49**
See also CA 81-84

Wilson, (Thomas) Woodrow 1856-1924 .... **TCLC 79**
See also CA 166; DLB 47

Winchilsea, Anne (Kingsmill) Finch Counte 1661-1720
See Finch, Anne

Windham, Basil
See Wodehouse, P(elham) G(renville)

Wingrove, David (John) 1954- .... **CLC 68**
See also CA 133

Winnemucca, Sarah 1844-1891 ..... **NCLC 79**

Winstanley, Gerrard 1609-1676 .... **LC 52**

Wintergreen, Jane
See Duncan, Sara Jeannette

Winters, Janet Lewis CLC 41
See also Lewis, Janet
See also DLBY 87

Winters, (Arthur) Yvor 1900-1968 .... **CLC 4, 8, 32**
See also CA 11-12; 25-28R; CAP 1; DLB 48; MTCW 1

Winterson, Jeanette 1959- .... **CLC 64; DAM POP**
See also CA 136; CANR 58; DA3; DLB 207; MTCW 2

Winthrop, John 1588-1649 .... **LC 31**
See also DLB 24, 30

Wirth, Louis 1897-1952 .... **TCLC 92**

Wiseman, Frederick 1930- .... **CLC 20**
See also CA 159

Wister, Owen 1860-1938 .... **TCLC 21**
See also CA 108; 162; DLB 9, 78, 186; SATA 62

Witkacy
See Witkiewicz, Stanislaw Ignacy

Witkiewicz, Stanislaw Ignacy 1885-1939 .... **TCLC 8**
See also CA 105; 162

Wittgenstein, Ludwig (Josef Johann) 1889-1951 .... **TCLC 59**
See also CA 113; 164; MTCW 2

Wittig, Monique 1935(?)- .... **CLC 22**
See also CA 116; 135; DLB 83

Wittlin, Jozef 1896-1976 .... **CLC 25**
See also CA 49-52; 65-68; CANR 3

Wodehouse, P(elham) G(renville) 1881-1975 .... **CLC 1, 2, 5, 10, 22; DAB; DAC; DAM NOV; SSC 2**
See also AITN 2; CA 45-48; 57-60; CANR 3, 33; CDBLB 1914-1945; DA3; DLB 34, 162; MTCW 1, 2; SATA 22

Woiwode, L.
See Woiwode, Larry (Alfred)

Woiwode, Larry (Alfred) 1941- ... **CLC 6, 10**
See also CA 73-76; CANR 16; DLB 6; INT CANR-16

Wojciechowska, Maia (Teresa) 1927- .... **CLC 26**
See also AAYA 8; CA 9-12R, 183; CAAE 183; CANR 4, 41; CLR 1; JRDA; MAICYA; SAAS 1; SATA 1, 28, 83; SATA-Essay 104

Wojtyla, Karol
See John Paul II, Pope

Wolf, Christa 1929- .... **CLC 14, 29, 58**
See also CA 85-88; CANR 45; DLB 75; MTCW 1

Wolfe, Gene (Rodman) 1931- .... **CLC 25; DAM POP**
See also CA 57-60; CAAS 9; CANR 6, 32, 60; DLB 8; MTCW 2

Wolfe, George C. 1954- .... **CLC 49; BLCS**
See also CA 149

Wolfe, Thomas (Clayton) 1900-1938 ...... **TCLC 4, 13, 29, 61; DA; DAB; DAC; DAM MST, NOV; SSC 33; WLC**
See also CA 104; 132; CDALB 1929-1941; DA3; DLB 9, 102; DLBD 2, 16; DLBY 85, 97; MTCW 1, 2

Wolfe, Thomas Kennerly, Jr. 1930-
See Wolfe, Tom
See also CA 13-16R; CANR 9, 33, 70; DAM POP; DA3; DLB 185; INT CANR-9; MTCW 1, 2

Wolfe, Tom CLC 1, 2, 9, 15, 35, 51
See also Wolfe, Thomas Kennerly, Jr.
See also AAYA 8; AITN 2; BEST 89:1; DLB 152

Wolff, Geoffrey (Ansell) 1937- .... **CLC 41**
See also CA 29-32R; CANR 29, 43, 78

Wolff, Sonia
See Levitin, Sonia (Wolff)

Wolff, Tobias (Jonathan Ansell) 1945- .... **CLC 39, 64**
See also AAYA 16; BEST 90:2; CA 114; 117; CAAS 22; CANR 54, 76; DA3; DLB 130; INT 117; MTCW 2

Wolfram von Eschenbach c. 1170-c. 1220 .... **CMLC 5**
See also DLB 138

Wolitzer, Hilma 1930- .... **CLC 17**
See also CA 65-68; CANR 18, 40; INT CANR-18; SATA 31

Wollstonecraft, Mary 1759-1797 ..... **LC 5, 50**
See also CDBLB 1789-1832; DLB 39, 104, 158

Wonder, Stevie CLC 12
See also Morris, Steveland Judkins

Wong, Jade Snow 1922- .... **CLC 17**
See also CA 109; CANR 91; SATA 112

Woodberry, George Edward 1855-1930 .... **TCLC 73**
See also CA 165; DLB 71, 103

Woodcott, Keith
See Brunner, John (Kilian Houston)

Woodruff, Robert W.
See Mencken, H(enry) L(ouis)

Woolf, (Adeline) Virginia 1882-1941 .. **TCLC 1, 5, 20, 43, 56; DA; DAB; DAC; DAM MST, NOV; SSC 7; WLC**
See also Woolf, Virginia Adeline
See also CA 104; 130; CANR 64; CDBLB 1914-1945; DA3; DLB 36, 100, 162; DLBD 10; MTCW 1

Woolf, Virginia Adeline
See Woolf, (Adeline) Virginia
See also MTCW 2

Woollcott, Alexander (Humphreys) 1887-1943 .... **TCLC 5**
See also CA 105; 161; DLB 29

Woolrich, Cornell 1903-1968 .... **CLC 77**
See also Hopley-Woolrich, Cornell George

Woolson, Constance Fenimore 1840-1894 .... **NCLC 82**
See also DLB 12, 74, 189, 221

Wordsworth, Dorothy 1771-1855 .. **NCLC 25**
See also DLB 107

Wordsworth, William 1770-1850 .. **NCLC 12, 38; DA; DAB; DAC; DAM MST, POET; PC 4; WLC**
See also CDBLB 1789-1832; DA3; DLB 93, 107

Wouk, Herman 1915- ... **CLC 1, 9, 38; DAM NOV, POP**
See also CA 5-8R; CANR 6, 33, 67; CDALBS; DA3; DLBY 82; INT CANR-6; MTCW 1, 2

Wright, Charles (Penzel, Jr.) 1935- .. **CLC 6, 13, 28, 119**
See also CA 29-32R; CAAS 7; CANR 23, 36, 62, 88; DLB 165; DLBY 82; MTCW 1, 2

Wright, Charles Stevenson 1932- ... **CLC 49; BLC 3; DAM MULT, POET**
See also BW 1; CA 9-12R; CANR 26; DLB 33

Wright, Frances 1795-1852 .... **NCLC 74**
See also DLB 73

Wright, Frank Lloyd 1867-1959 .... **TCLC 95**
See also AAYA 33; CA 174

Wright, Jack R.
See Harris, Mark

Wright, James (Arlington) 1927-1980 .... **CLC 3, 5, 10, 28; DAM POET**
See also AITN 2; CA 49-52; 97-100; CANR 4, 34, 64; CDALBS; DLB 5, 169; MTCW 1, 2

Wright, Judith (Arundell) 1915-2000 .... **CLC 11, 53; PC 14**
See also CA 13-16R; CANR 31, 76; MTCW 1, 2; SATA 14

Wright, L(aurali) R. 1939- .... **CLC 44**
See also CA 138

Wright, Richard (Nathaniel) 1908-1960 .... **CLC 1, 3, 4, 9, 14, 21, 48, 74; BLC 3; DA; DAB; DAC; DAM MST, MULT, NOV; SSC 2; WLC**
See also AAYA 5; BW 1; CA 108; CANR 64; CDALB 1929-1941; DA3; DLB 76, 102; DLBD 2; MTCW 1, 2

Wright, Richard B(ruce) 1937- .... **CLC 6**
See also CA 85-88; DLB 53

Wright, Rick 1945- .... **CLC 35**

Wright, Rowland
See Wells, Carolyn

Wright, Stephen 1946- .... **CLC 33**

Wright, Willard Huntington 1888-1939
See Van Dine, S. S.
See also CA 115; DLBD 16

Wright, William 1930- .... **CLC 44**
See also CA 53-56; CANR 7, 23

Wroth, LadyMary 1587-1653(?) .... **LC 30**
See also DLB 121

Wu Ch'eng-en 1500(?)-1582(?) .... **LC 7**

Wu Ching-tzu 1701-1754 .... **LC 2**

Wurlitzer, Rudolph 1938(?)- .... **CLC 2, 4, 15**
See also CA 85-88; DLB 173

Wyatt, Thomas c. 1503-1542 .... **PC 27**
See also DLB 132

Wycherley, William 1641-1715 ...... **LC 8, 21; DAM DRAM**
See also CDBLB 1660-1789; DLB 80

Wylie, Elinor (Morton Hoyt) 1885-1928 .... **TCLC 8; PC 23**
See also CA 105; 162; DLB 9, 45

Wylie, Philip (Gordon) 1902-1971 ... **CLC 43**
See also CA 21-22; 33-36R; CAP 2; DLB 9
Wyndham, John CLC 19
See also Harris, John (Wyndham Parkes Lucas) Beynon
Wyss, Johann David Von
1743-1818 .... **NCLC 10**
See also JRDA; MAICYA; SATA 29; SATA-Brief 27
Xenophon c. 430B.C.-c. 354B.C. ... **CMLC 17**
See also DLB 176
Yakumo Koizumi
See Hearn, (Patricio) Lafcadio (Tessima Carlos)
Yamamoto, Hisaye 1921- .... **SSC 34; DAM MULT**
Yanez, Jose Donoso
See Donoso (Yanez), Jose
Yanovsky, Basile S.
See Yanovsky, V(assily) S(emenovich)
Yanovsky, V(assily) S(emenovich)
1906-1989 .... **CLC 2, 18**
See also CA 97-100; 129
Yates, Richard 1926-1992 .... **CLC 7, 8, 23**
See also CA 5-8R; 139; CANR 10, 43; DLB 2; DLBY 81, 92; INT CANR-10
Yeats, W. B.
See Yeats, William Butler
Yeats, William Butler 1865-1939 .... **TCLC 1, 11, 18, 31, 93; DA; DAB; DAC; DAM DRAM, MST, POET; PC 20; WLC**
See also CA 104; 127; CANR 45; CDBLB 1890-1914; DA3; DLB 10, 19, 98, 156; MTCW 1, 2
Yehoshua, A(braham) B. 1936- .. **CLC 13, 31**
See also CA 33-36R; CANR 43, 90
Yellow Bird
See Ridge, John Rollin
Yep, Laurence Michael 1948- .... **CLC 35**
See also AAYA 5, 31; CA 49-52; CANR 1, 46, 92; CLR 3, 17, 54; DLB 52; JRDA; MAICYA; SATA 7, 69
Yerby, Frank G(arvin) 1916-1991 . **CLC 1, 7, 22; BLC 3; DAM MULT**
See also BW 1, 3; CA 9-12R; 136; CANR 16, 52; DLB 76; INT CANR-16; MTCW 1
Yesenin, Sergei Alexandrovich
See Esenin, Sergei (Alexandrovich)
Yevtushenko, Yevgeny (Alexandrovich)
1933- .. **CLC 1, 3, 13, 26, 51, 126; DAM POET**
See also CA 81-84; CANR 33, 54; MTCW 1
Yezierska, Anzia 1885(?)-1970 .... **CLC 46**
See also CA 126; 89-92; DLB 28, 221; MTCW 1
Yglesias, Helen 1915- .... **CLC 7, 22**
See also CA 37-40R; CAAS 20; CANR 15, 65; INT CANR-15; MTCW 1
Yokomitsu, Riichi 1898-1947 .... **TCLC 47**
See also CA 170

Yonge, Charlotte (Mary)
1823-1901 .... **TCLC 48**
See also CA 109; 163; DLB 18, 163; SATA 17
York, Jeremy
See Creasey, John
York, Simon
See Heinlein, Robert A(nson)
Yorke, Henry Vincent 1905-1974 ..... **CLC 13**
See also Green, Henry
See also CA 85-88; 49-52
Yosano Akiko 1878-1942 .... **TCLC 59; PC 11**
See also CA 161
Yoshimoto, Banana CLC 84
See also Yoshimoto, Mahoko
Yoshimoto, Mahoko 1964-
See Yoshimoto, Banana
See also CA 144
Young, Al(bert James) 1939- . **CLC 19; BLC 3; DAM MULT**
See also BW 2, 3; CA 29-32R; CANR 26, 65; DLB 33
Young, Andrew (John) 1885-1971 ...... **CLC 5**
See also CA 5-8R; CANR 7, 29
Young, Collier
See Bloch, Robert (Albert)
Young, Edward 1683-1765 .... **LC 3, 40**
See also DLB 95
Young, Marguerite (Vivian)
1909-1995 .... **CLC 82**
See also CA 13-16; 150; CAP 1
Young, Neil 1945- .... **CLC 17**
See also CA 110
Young Bear, Ray A. 1950- ..... **CLC 94; DAM MULT**
See also CA 146; DLB 175; NNAL
Yourcenar, Marguerite 1903-1987 ... **CLC 19, 38, 50, 87; DAM NOV**
See also CA 69-72; CANR 23, 60; DLB 72; DLBY 88; MTCW 1, 2
Yuan, Chu 340(?)B.C.-278(?)B.C. . **CMLC 36**
Yurick, Sol 1925- .... **CLC 6**
See also CA 13-16R; CANR 25
Zabolotsky, Nikolai Alekseevich
1903-1958 .... **TCLC 52**
See also CA 116; 164
Zagajewski, Adam 1945- .... **PC 27**
See also CA 186
Zamiatin, Yevgenii
See Zamyatin, Evgeny Ivanovich
Zamora, Bernice (B. Ortiz) 1938- .. **CLC 89; DAM MULT; HLC 2**
See also CA 151; CANR 80; DLB 82; HW 1, 2
Zamyatin, Evgeny Ivanovich
1884-1937 .... **TCLC 8, 37**
See also CA 105; 166
Zangwill, Israel 1864-1926 .... **TCLC 16**
See also CA 109; 167; DLB 10, 135, 197

Zappa, Francis Vincent, Jr. 1940-1993
See Zappa, Frank
See also CA 108; 143; CANR 57
Zappa, Frank CLC 17
See also Zappa, Francis Vincent, Jr.
Zaturenska, Marya 1902-1982 ..... **CLC 6, 11**
See also CA 13-16R; 105; CANR 22
Zeami 1363-1443 .... **DC 7**
Zelazny, Roger (Joseph) 1937-1995 . **CLC 21**
See also AAYA 7; CA 21-24R; 148; CANR 26, 60; DLB 8; MTCW 1, 2; SATA 57; SATA-Brief 39
Zhdanov, Andrei Alexandrovich
1896-1948 .... **TCLC 18**
See also CA 117; 167
Zhukovsky, Vasily (Andreevich)
1783-1852 .... **NCLC 35**
See also DLB 205
Ziegenhagen, Eric CLC 55
Zimmer, Jill Schary
See Robinson, Jill
Zimmerman, Robert
See Dylan, Bob
Zindel, Paul 1936- ..... **CLC 6, 26; DA; DAB; DAC; DAM DRAM, MST, NOV; DC 5**
See also AAYA 2; CA 73-76; CANR 31, 65; CDALBS; CLR 3, 45; DA3; DLB 7, 52; JRDA; MAICYA; MTCW 1, 2; SATA 16, 58, 102
Zinov'Ev, A. A.
See Zinoviev, Alexander (Aleksandrovich)
Zinoviev, Alexander (Aleksandrovich)
1922- .... **CLC 19**
See also CA 116; 133; CAAS 10
Zoilus
See Lovecraft, H(oward) P(hillips)
Zola, Emile (Edouard Charles Antoine)
1840-1902 .... **TCLC 1, 6, 21, 41; DA; DAB; DAC; DAM MST, NOV; WLC**
See also CA 104; 138; DA3; DLB 123
Zoline, Pamela 1941- .... **CLC 62**
See also CA 161
Zoroaster 628(?)B.C.-551(?)B.C. ... **CMLC 40**
Zorrilla y Moral, Jose 1817-1893 .... **NCLC 6**
Zoshchenko, Mikhail (Mikhailovich)
1895-1958 .... **TCLC 15; SSC 15**
See also CA 115; 160
Zuckmayer, Carl 1896-1977 .... **CLC 18**
See also CA 69-72; DLB 56, 124
Zuk, Georges
See Skelton, Robin
Zukofsky, Louis 1904-1978 ... **CLC 1, 2, 4, 7, 11, 18; DAM POET; PC 11**
See also CA 9-12R; 77-80; CANR 39; DLB 5, 165; MTCW 1
Zweig, Paul 1935-1984 .... **CLC 34, 42**
See also CA 85-88; 113
Zweig, Stefan 1881-1942 .... **TCLC 17**
See also CA 112; 170; DLB 81, 118
Zwingli, Huldreich 1484-1531 .... **LC 37**
See also DLB 179

Literary Criticism Series
Cumulative Topic Index

This index lists all topic entries in Gale's *Classical and Medieval Literature Criticism, Contemporary Literary Criticism, Literature Criticism from 1400 to 1800, Nineteenth-Century Literature Criticism,* and *Twentieth-Century Literary Criticism.*

The Aesopic Fable LC 51: 1-100
    The British Aesopic Fable, 1-54
    The Aesopic Tradition in Non-English-Speaking Cultures, 55-66
    Political Uses of the Aesopic Fable, 67-88
    The Evolution of the Aesopic Fable, 89-99

Age of Johnson LC 15: 1-87
    Johnson's London, 3-15
    aesthetics of neoclassicism, 15-36
    "age of prose and reason," 36-45
    clubmen and bluestockings, 45-56
    printing technology, 56-62
    periodicals: "a map of busy life," 62-74
    transition, 74-86

Age of Spenser LC 39: 1-70
    Overviews, 2-21
    Literary Style, 22-34
    Poets and the Crown, 34-70

AIDS in Literature CLC 81: 365-416

Alcohol and Literature TCLC 70: 1-58
    overview, 2-8
    fiction, 8-48
    poetry and drama, 48-58

American Abolitionism NCLC 44: 1-73
    overviews, 2-26
    abolitionist ideals, 26-46
    the literature of abolitionism, 46-72

American Autobiography TCLC 86: 1-115
    overviews, 3-36
    American authors and autobiography, 36-82
    African-American autobiography, 82-114

American Black Humor Fiction TCLC 54: 1-85
    characteristics of black humor, 2-13
    origins and development, 13-38
    black humor distinguished from related literary trends, 38-60
    black humor and society, 60-75
    black humor reconsidered, 75-83

American Civil War in Literature NCLC 32: 1-109
    overviews, 2-20
    regional perspectives, 20-54
    fiction popular during the war, 54-79
    the historical novel, 79-108

American Frontier in Literature NCLC 28: 1-103
    definitions, 2-12
    development, 12-17
    nonfiction writing about the frontier, 17-30

    frontier fiction, 30-45
    frontier protagonists, 45-66
    portrayals of Native Americans, 66-86
    feminist readings, 86-98
    twentieth-century reaction against frontier literature, 98-100

American Humor Writing NCLC 52: 1-59
    overviews, 2-12
    the Old Southwest, 12-42
    broader impacts, 42-5
    women humorists, 45-58

American Mercury, **The** TCLC 74: 1-80

American Popular Song, Golden Age of TCLC 42: 1-49
    background and major figures, 2-34
    the lyrics of popular songs, 34-47

American Proletarian Literature TCLC 54: 86-175
    overviews, 87-95
    American proletarian literature and the American Communist Party, 95-111
    ideology and literary merit, 111-7
    novels, 117-36
    Gastonia, 136-48
    drama, 148-54
    journalism, 154-9
    proletarian literature in the United States, 159-74

American Romanticism NCLC 44: 74-138
    overviews, 74-84
    sociopolitical influences, 84-104
    Romanticism and the American frontier, 104-15
    thematic concerns, 115-37

American Western Literature TCLC 46: 1-100
    definition and development of American Western literature, 2-7
    characteristics of the Western novel, 8-23
    Westerns as history and fiction, 23-34
    critical reception of American Western literature, 34-41
    the Western hero, 41-73
    women in Western fiction, 73-91
    later Western fiction, 91-9

American Writers in Paris TCLC 98: 1-156
    overviews and general studies, 2-155

Anarchism NCLC 84: 1-97
    overviews and general studies, 2-23
    the French anarchist tradition, 23-56

    Anglo-American anarchism, 56-68
    anarchism: incidents and issues, 68-97

Aristotle CMLC 31:1-397
    introduction, 1
    philosophy, 3-100
    poetics, 101-219
    rhetoric, 220-301
    science, 302-397

Art and Literature TCLC 54: 176-248
    overviews, 176-93
    definitions, 193-219
    influence of visual arts on literature, 219-31
    spatial form in literature, 231-47

Arthurian Literature CMLC 10: 1-127
    historical context and literary beginnings, 2-27
    development of the legend through Malory, 27-64
    development of the legend from Malory to the Victorian Age, 65-81
    themes and motifs, 81-95
    principal characters, 95-125

Arthurian Revival NCLC 36: 1-77
    overviews, 2-12
    Tennyson and his influence, 12-43
    other leading figures, 43-73
    the Arthurian legend in the visual arts, 73-6

Australian Literature TCLC 50: 1-94
    origins and development, 2-21
    characteristics of Australian literature, 21-33
    historical and critical perspectives, 33-41
    poetry, 41-58
    fiction, 58-76
    drama, 76-82
    Aboriginal literature, 82-91

Beat Generation, Literature of the TCLC 42: 50-102
    overviews, 51-9
    the Beat generation as a social phenomenon, 59-62
    development, 62-5
    Beat literature, 66-96
    influence, 97-100

The Bell Curve Controversy CLC 91: 281-330

Bildungsroman **in Nineteenth-Century Literature** NCLC 20: 92-168
    surveys, 93-113
    in Germany, 113-40

in England, 140-56
female *Bildungsroman,* 156-67

Bloomsbury Group TCLC 34: 1-73
history and major figures, 2-13
definitions, 13-7
influences, 17-27
thought, 27-40
prose, 40-52
and literary criticism, 52-4
political ideals, 54-61
response to, 61-71

The Blues in Literature TCLC 82: 1-71

Bly, Robert, *Iron John: A Book about Men and Men's Work* CLC 70: 414-62

The Book of J CLC 65: 289-311

British Ephemeral Literature LC 59: 1-70
overviews, 1-9
broadside ballads, 10-40
chapbooks, jestbooks, pamphlets, and newspapers, 40-69

Buddhism and Literature TCLC 70: 59-164
eastern literature, 60-113
western literature, 113-63

Businessman in American Literature TCLC 26: 1-48
portrayal of the businessman, 1-32
themes and techniques in business fiction, 32-47

The Calendar LC 55: 1-92
overviews, 2-19
measuring time, 19-28
calendars and culture, 28-60
calendar reform, 60-92

Catholicism in Nineteenth-Century American Literature NCLC 64: 1-58
overviews, 3-14
polemical literature, 14-46
Catholicism in literature, 47-57

Celtic Mythology CMLC 26: 1-111
overviews, 2-22
Celtic myth as literature and history, 22-48
Celtic religion: Druids and divinities, 48-80
Fionn MacCuhaill and the Fenian cycle, 80-111

Celtic Twilight See Irish Literary Renaissance

Chartist Movement and Literature, The NCLC 60: 1-84
overview: nineteenth-century working-class fiction, 2-19
Chartist fiction and poetry, 19-73
the Chartist press, 73-84

Children's Literature, Nineteenth-Century NCLC 52: 60-135
overviews, 61-72
moral tales, 72-89
fairy tales and fantasy, 90-119
making men/making women, 119-34

The City and Literature TCLC 90: 1-124
Overviews, 2-9
The City in American Literature, 9-86
The City in European Literature, 86-124

Civic Critics, Russian NCLC 20: 402-46
principal figures and background, 402-9
and Russian Nihilism, 410-6
aesthetic and critical views, 416-45

The Cockney School NCLC 68: 1-64
overview, 2-7
Blackwood's Magazine and the contemporary critical response, 7-24
the political and social import of the Cockneys and their critics, 24-63

Colonial America: The Intellectual Background LC 25: 1-98
overviews, 2-17

philosophy and politics, 17-31
early religious influences in Colonial America, 31-60
consequences of the Revolution, 60-78
religious influences in post-revolutionary America, 78-87
colonial literary genres, 87-97

Colonialism in Victorian English Literature NCLC 56: 1-77
overviews, 2-34
colonialism and gender, 34-51
monsters and the occult, 51-76

Columbus, Christopher, Books on the Quincentennial of His Arrival in the New World CLC 70: 329-60

Comic Books TCLC 66: 1-139
historical and critical perspectives, 2-48
superheroes, 48-67
underground comix, 67-88
comic books and society, 88-122
adult comics and graphic novels, 122-36

Connecticut Wits NCLC 48: 1-95
general overviews, 2-40
major works, 40-76
intellectual context, 76-95

Crime in Literature TCLC 54: 249-307
evolution of the criminal figure in literature, 250-61
crime and society, 261-77
literary perspectives on crime and punishment, 277-88
writings by criminals, 288-306

The Crusades CMLC 38: 1-144
history of the Crusades, 3-60
literature of the Crusades, 60-116
the Crusades and the people: attitudes and influences, 116-44

Czechoslovakian Literature of the Twentieth Century TCLC 42:103-96
through World War II, 104-35
de-Stalinization, the Prague Spring, and contemporary literature, 135-72
Slovak literature, 172-85
Czech science fiction, 185-93

Dadaism TCLC 46: 101-71
background and major figures, 102-16
definitions, 116-26
manifestos and commentary by Dadaists, 126-40
theater and film, 140-58
nature and characteristics of Dadaist writing, 158-70

Darwinism and Literature NCLC 32: 110-206
background, 110-31
direct responses to Darwin, 131-71
collateral effects of Darwinism, 171-205

Death in Nineteenth-Century British Literature NCLC 68: 65-142
overviews, 66-92
responses to death, 92-102
feminist perspectives, 103-17
striving for immortality, 117-41

Death in Literature TCLC 78:1-183
fiction, 2-115
poetry, 115-46
drama, 146-81

de Man, Paul, Wartime Journalism of CLC 55: 382-424

Detective Fiction, Nineteenth-Century NCLC 36: 78-148
origins of the genre, 79-100
history of nineteenth-century detective fiction, 101-33
significance of nineteenth-century detective fiction, 133-46

Detective Fiction, Twentieth-Century TCLC 38: 1-96
genesis and history of the detective story, 3-22
defining detective fiction, 22-32
evolution and varieties, 32-77
the appeal of detective fiction, 77-90

Dime Novels NCLC 84: 98-168
overviews and general studies, 99-123
popular characters, 123-39
major figures and influences, 139-52
socio-political concerns, 152-167

Disease and Literature TCLC 66: 140-283
overviews, 141-65
disease in nineteenth-century literature, 165-81
tuberculosis and literature, 181-94
women and disease in literature, 194-221
plague literature, 221-53
AIDS in literature, 253-82

The Double in Nineteenth-Century Literature NCLC 40: 1-95
genesis and development of the theme, 2-15
the double and Romanticism, 16-27
sociological views, 27-52
psychological interpretations, 52-87
philosophical considerations, 87-95

Dramatic Realism NCLC 44: 139-202
overviews, 140-50
origins and definitions, 150-66
impact and influence, 166-93
realist drama and tragedy, 193-201

Drugs and Literature TCLC 78: 184-282
overviews, 185-201
pre-twentieth-century literature, 201-42
twentieth-century literature, 242-82

Eastern Mythology CMLC 26: 112-92
heroes and kings, 113-51
cross-cultural perspective, 151-69
relations to history and society, 169-92

Electronic "Books": Hypertext and Hyperfiction CLC 86: 367-404
books vs. CD-ROMS, 367-76
hypertext and hyperfiction, 376-95
implications for publishing, libraries, and the public, 395-403

Eliot, T. S., Centenary of Birth CLC 55: 345-75

Elizabethan Drama LC 22: 140-240
origins and influences, 142-67
characteristics and conventions, 167-83
theatrical production, 184-200
histories, 200-12
comedy, 213-20
tragedy, 220-30

Elizabethan Prose Fiction LC 41: 1-70
overviews, 1-15
origins and influences, 15-43
style and structure, 43-69

Enclosure of the English Common NCLC 88: 1-57
overviews, 1-12
early reaction to enclosure, 12-23
nineteenth-century reaction to enclosure, 23-56

The Encyclopedists LC 26: 172-253
overviews, 173-210
intellectual background, 210-32
views on esthetics, 232-41
views on women, 241-52

English Caroline Literature LC 13: 221-307
background, 222-41
evolution and varieties, 241-62
the Cavalier mode, 262-75
court and society, 275-91
politics and religion, 291-306

English Decadent Literature of the 1890s
NCLC 28: 104-200
  fin de siècle: the Decadent period, 105-19
  definitions, 120-37
  major figures: "the tragic generation,"
    137-50
  French literature and English literary Deca-
    dence, 150-7
  themes, 157-61
  poetry, 161-82
  periodicals, 182-96

English Essay, Rise of the LC 18: 238-308
  definitions and origins, 236-54
  influence on the essay, 254-69
  historical background, 269-78
  the essay in the seventeenth century, 279-93
  the essay in the eighteenth century, 293-
    307

English Mystery Cycle Dramas LC 34: 1-88
  overviews, 1-27
  the nature of dramatic performances, 27-42
  the medieval worldview and the mystery
    cycles, 43-67
  the doctrine of repentance and the mystery
    cycles, 67-76
  the fall from grace in the mystery cycles,
    76-88

The English Realist Novel, 1740-1771 LC 51:
102-98
  Overviews, 103-22
  From Romanticism to Realism, 123-58
  Women and the Novel, 159-175
  The Novel and Other Literary Forms, 176-
    197

English Revolution, Literature of the LC 43:
1-58
  overviews, 2-24
  pamphlets of the English Revolution, 24-38
  political Sermons of the English Revolu-
    tion, 38-48
  poetry of the English Revolution, 48-57

English Romantic Hellenism NCLC 68: 143-
250
  overviews, 144-69
  historical development of English Roman-
    tic Hellenism, 169-91
  influence of Greek mythology on the Ro-
    mantics, 191-229
  influence of Greek literature, art, and cul-
    ture on the Romantics, 229-50

English Romantic Poetry NCLC 28: 201-327
  overviews and reputation, 202-37
  major subjects and themes, 237-67
  forms of Romantic poetry, 267-78
  politics, society, and Romantic poetry,
    278-99
  philosophy, religion, and Romantic poetry,
    299-324

The Epistolary Novel LC 59: 71-170
  overviews, 72-96
  women and the Epistolary novel, 96-138
  principal figures: Britain, 138-53
  principal figures: France, 153-69

Espionage Literature TCLC 50: 95-159
  overviews, 96-113
  espionage fiction/formula fiction, 113-26
  spies in fact and fiction, 126-38
  the female spy, 138-44
  social and psychological perspectives,
    144-58

European Romanticism NCLC 36: 149-284
  definitions, 149-77
  origins of the movement, 177-82
  Romantic theory, 182-200
  themes and techniques, 200-23
  Romanticism in Germany, 223-39
  Romanticism in France, 240-61
  Romanticism in Italy, 261-4

  Romanticism in Spain, 264-8
  impact and legacy, 268-82

Existentialism and Literature TCLC 42: 197-
268
  overviews and definitions, 198-209
  history and influences, 209-19
  Existentialism critiqued and defended,
    220-35
  philosophical and religious perspectives,
    235-41
  Existentialist fiction and drama, 241-67

Familiar Essay NCLC 48: 96-211
  definitions and origins, 97-130
  overview of the genre, 130-43
  elements of form and style, 143-59
  elements of content, 159-73
  the Cockneys: Hazlitt, Lamb, and Hunt,
    173-91
  status of the genre, 191-210

The Faust Legend LC 47: 1-117

Fear in Literature TCLC 74: 81-258
  overviews, 81
  pre-twentieth-century literature, 123
  twentieth-century literature, 182

**Feminism in the 1990s: Commentary on
Works by Naomi Wolf, Susan Faludi, and
Camille Paglia** CLC 76: 377-415

Feminist Criticism in 1990 CLC 65: 312-60

Fifteenth-Century English Literature LC 17:
248-334
  background, 249-72
  poetry, 272-315
  drama, 315-23
  prose, 323-33

Film and Literature TCLC 38: 97-226
  overviews, 97-119
  film and theater, 119-34
  film and the novel, 134-45
  the art of the screenplay, 145-66
  genre literature/genre film, 167-79
  the writer and the film industry, 179-90
  authors on film adaptations of their works,
    190-200
  fiction into film: comparative essays,
    200-23

**Finance and Money as Represented in
Nineteenth-Century Literature** NCLC 76:
1-69
  historical perspectives, 2-20
  the image of money, 20-37
  the dangers of money, 37-50
  women and money, 50-69

Folklore and Literature TCLC 86: 116-293
  overviews, 118-144
  Native American literature, 144-67
  African-American literature, 167-238
  Folklore and the American West, 238-57
  Modern and postmodern literature, 257-91

French Drama in the Age of Louis XIV LC
28: 94-185
  overview, 95-127
  tragedy, 127-46
  comedy, 146-66
  tragicomedy, 166-84

French Enlightenment LC 14: 81-145
  the question of definition, 82-9
  Le siècle des lumières, 89-94
  women and the salons, 94-105
  censorship, 105-15
  the philosophy of reason, 115-31
  influence and legacy, 131-44

French New Novel TCLC 98: 158-234
  overviews and general studies, 158-92
  influences, 192-213
  themes, 213-33

French Realism NCLC 52: 136-216
  origins and definitions, 137-70
  issues and influence, 170-98
  realism and representation, 198-215

French Revolution and English Literature
NCLC 40: 96-195
  history and theory, 96-123
  romantic poetry, 123-50
  the novel, 150-81
  drama, 181-92
  children's literature, 192-5

Futurism, Italian TCLC 42: 269-354
  principles and formative influences, 271-9
  manifestos, 279-88
  literature, 288-303
  theater, 303-19
  art, 320-30
  music, 330-6
  architecture, 336-9
  and politics, 339-46
  reputation and significance, 346-51

**Gaelic Revival See Irish Literary Renais-
sance**

**Gates, Henry Louis, Jr., and African-
American Literary Criticism** CLC 65: 361-
405

Gay and Lesbian Literature CLC 76: 416-39

German Exile Literature TCLC 30: 1-58
  the writer and the Nazi state, 1-10
  definition of, 10-4
  life in exile, 14-32
  surveys, 32-50
  Austrian literature in exile, 50-2
  German publishing in the United States,
    52-7

German Expressionism TCLC 34: 74-160
  history and major figures, 76-85
  aesthetic theories, 85-109
  drama, 109-26
  poetry, 126-38
  film, 138-42
  painting, 142-7
  music, 147-53
  and politics, 153-8

The Gilded Age NCLC 84: 169-271
  popular themes, 170-90
  Realism, 190-208
  Aestheticism, 208-26
  socio-political concerns, 226-70

***Glasnost* and Contemporary Soviet Litera-
ture** CLC 59: 355-97

Gothic Novel NCLC 28: 328-402
  development and major works, 328-34
  definitions, 334-50
  themes and techniques, 350-78
  in America, 378-85
  in Scotland, 385-91
  influence and legacy, 391-400

Graphic Narratives CLC 86: 405-32
  history and overviews, 406-21
  the "Classics Illustrated" series, 421-2
  reviews of recent works, 422-32

Greek Historiography CMLC 17: 1-49

Greek Mythology CMLC 26: 193-320
  overviews, 194-209
  origins and development of Greek mythol-
    ogy, 209-29
  cosmogonies and divinities in Greek my-
    thology, 229-54
  heroes and heroines in Greek mythology,
    254-80
  women in Greek mythology, 280-320

Harlem Renaissance TCLC 26: 49-125
  principal issues and figures, 50-67
  the literature and its audience, 67-74

theme and technique in poetry, fiction, and drama, 74-115
and American society, 115-21
achievement and influence, 121-2

Havel, Václav, Playwright and President CLC 65: 406-63

Historical Fiction, Nineteenth-Century NCLC 48: 212-307
definitions and characteristics, 213-36
Victorian historical fiction, 236-65
American historical fiction, 265-88
realism in historical fiction, 288-306

Holocaust and the Atomic Bomb: Fifty Years Later CLC 91: 331-82
the Holocaust remembered, 333-52
Anne Frank revisited, 352-62
the atomic bomb and American memory, 362-81

Holocaust Denial Literature TCLC 58: 1-110
overviews, 1-30
Robert Faurisson and Noam Chomsky, 30-52
Holocaust denial literature in America, 52-71
library access to Holocaust denial literature, 72-5
the authenticity of Anne Frank's diary, 76-90
David Irving and the "normalization" of Hitler, 90-109

Holocaust, Literature of the TCLC 42: 355-450
historical overview, 357-61
critical overview, 361-70
diaries and memoirs, 370-95
novels and short stories, 395-425
poetry, 425-41
drama, 441-8

Homosexuality in Nineteenth-Century Literature NCLC 56: 78-182
defining homosexuality, 80-111
Greek love, 111-44
trial and danger, 144-81

Hungarian Literature of the Twentieth Century TCLC 26: 126-88
surveys of, 126-47
Nyugat and early twentieth-century literature, 147-56
mid-century literature, 156-68
and politics, 168-78
since the 1956 revolt, 178-87

Hysteria in Nineteenth-Century Literature NCLC 64: 59-184
the history of hysteria, 60-75
the gender of hysteria, 75-103
hysteria and women's narratives, 103-57
hysteria in nineteenth-century poetry, 157-83

Imagism TCLC 74: 259-454
history and development, 260
major figures, 288
sources and influences, 352
Imagism and other movements, 397
influence and legacy, 431

Incest in Nineteenth-Century American Literature NCLC 76: 70-141
overview, 71-88
the concern for social order, 88-117
authority and authorship, 117-40

Indian Literature in English TCLC 54: 308-406
overview, 309-13
origins and major figures, 313-25
the Indo-English novel, 325-55
Indo-English poetry, 355-67
Indo-English drama, 367-72

critical perspectives on Indo-English literature, 372-80
modern Indo-English literature, 380-9
Indo-English authors on their work, 389-404

The Industrial Revolution in Literature NCLC 56: 183-273
historical and cultural perspectives, 184-201
contemporary reactions to the machine, 201-21
themes and symbols in literature, 221-73

The Irish Famine as Represented in Nineteenth-Century Literature NCLC 64: 185-261
overviews, 187-98
historical background, 198-212
famine novels, 212-34
famine poetry, 234-44
famine letters and eye-witness accounts, 245-61

Irish Literary Renaissance TCLC 46: 172-287
overview, 173-83
development and major figures, 184-202
influence of Irish folklore and mythology, 202-22
Irish poetry, 222-34
Irish drama and the Abbey Theatre, 234-56
Irish fiction, 256-86

Irish Nationalism and Literature NCLC 44: 203-73
the Celtic element in literature, 203-19
anti-Irish sentiment and the Celtic response, 219-34
literary ideals in Ireland, 234-45
literary expressions, 245-73

Irish Novel, The NCLC 80: 1-130
overviews, 3-9
principal figures, 9-22
peasant and middle class Irish novelists, aristocratic Irish and Anglo-Irish novelists, 76-129

Israeli Literature TCLC 94: 1-137
overviews, 2-18
Israeli fiction, 18-33
Israeli poetry, 33-62
Israeli drama, 62-91
women and Israeli literature, 91-112
Arab characters in Israeli literature, 112-36

Italian Futurism See See Futurism, Italian

Italian Humanism LC 12: 205-77
origins and early development, 206-18
revival of classical letters, 218-23
humanism and other philosophies, 224-39
humanism and humanists, 239-46
the plastic arts, 246-57
achievement and significance, 258-76

Italian Romanticism NCLC 60: 85-145
origins and overviews, 86-101
Italian Romantic theory, 101-25
the language of Romanticism, 125-45

Jacobean Drama LC 33: 1-37
the Jacobean worldview: an era of transition, 2-14
the moral vision of Jacobean drama, 14-22
Jacobean tragedy, 22-3
the Jacobean masque, 23-36

Jewish-American Fiction TCLC 62: 1-181
overviews, 2-24
major figures, 24-48
Jewish writers and American life, 48-78
Jewish characters in American fiction, 78-108
themes in Jewish-American fiction, 108-43
Jewish-American women writers, 143-59

the Holocaust and Jewish-American fiction, 159-81

Knickerbocker Group, The NCLC 56: 274-341
overviews, 276-314
Knickerbocker periodicals, 314-26
writers and artists, 326-40

Lake Poets, The NCLC 52: 217-304
characteristics of the Lake Poets and their works, 218-27
literary influences and collaborations, 227-66
defining and developing Romantic ideals, 266-84
embracing Conservatism, 284-303

Larkin, Philip, Controversy CLC 81: 417-64

Latin American Literature, Twentieth-Century TCLC 58: 111-98
historical and critical perspectives, 112-36
the novel, 136-45
the short story, 145-9
drama, 149-60
poetry, 160-7
the writer and society, 167-86
Native Americans in Latin American literature, 186-97

The Levellers LC 51: 200-312
Overviews, 201-29
Principal Figures, 230-86
Religion, Political Philosophy, and Pamphleteering, 287-311

Literature and Millenial Lists CLC 119: 431-67
criticism, 434-67
introduction, 431-33
The Modern Library list, 433
The Waterstone list, 438-439

Madness in Nineteenth-Century Literature NCLC 76: 142-284
overview, 143-54
autobiography, 154-68
poetry, 168-215
fiction, 215-83

Madness in Twentieth-Century Literature TCLC 50: 160-225
overviews, 161-71
madness and the creative process, 171-86
suicide, 186-91
madness in American literature, 191-207
madness in German literature, 207-13
madness and feminist artists, 213-24

Medical Writing LC 55: 93-195
colonial America, 94-110
enlightenment, 110-24
medieval writing, 124-40
sexuality, 140-83
vernacular, 185-95

Memoirs of Trauma CLC 109: 419-466
overview, 420
criticism, 429

Metaphysical Poets LC 24: 356-439
early definitions, 358-67
surveys and overviews, 367-92
cultural and social influences, 392-406
stylistic and thematic variations, 407-38

Modern Essay, The TCLC 58: 199-273
overview, 200-7
the essay in the early twentieth century, 207-19
characteristics of the modern essay, 219-32
modern essayists, 232-45
the essay as a literary genre, 245-73

Modern Japanese Literature TCLC 66: 284-389
poetry, 285-305
drama, 305-29

fiction, 329-61
western influences, 361-87

Modernism TCLC 70: 165-275
definitions, 166-184
Modernism and earlier influences, 184-200
stylistic and thematic traits, 200-229
poetry and drama, 229-242
redefining Modernism, 242-275

Muckraking Movement in American Journalism TCLC 34: 161-242
development, principles, and major figures, 162-70
publications, 170-9
social and political ideas, 179-86
targets, 186-208
fiction, 208-19
decline, 219-29
impact and accomplishments, 229-40

Multiculturalism in Literature and Education CLC 70: 361-413

Music and Modern Literature TCLC 62: 182-329
overviews, 182-211
musical form/literary form, 211-32
music in literature, 232-50
the influence of music on literature, 250-73
literature and popular music, 273-303
jazz and poetry, 303-28

Native American Literature CLC 76: 440-76

Natural School, Russian NCLC 24: 205-40
history and characteristics, 205-25
contemporary criticism, 225-40

Naturalism NCLC 36: 285-382
definitions and theories, 286-305
critical debates on Naturalism, 305-16
Naturalism in theater, 316-32
European Naturalism, 332-61
American Naturalism, 361-72
the legacy of Naturalism, 372-81

Negritude TCLC 50: 226-361
origins and evolution, 227-56
definitions, 256-91
Negritude in literature, 291-343
Negritude reconsidered, 343-58

New Criticism TCLC 34: 243-318
development and ideas, 244-70
debate and defense, 270-99
influence and legacy, 299-315

The New World in Renaissance Literature LC 31: 1-51
overview, 1-18
utopia vs. terror, 18-31
explorers and Native Americans, 31-51

New York Intellectuals and *Partisan Review* TCLC 30: 117-98
development and major figures, 118-28
influence of Judaism, 128-39
Partisan Review, 139-57
literary philosophy and practice, 157-75
political philosophy, 175-87
achievement and significance, 187-97

The New Yorker TCLC 58: 274-357
overviews, 274-95
major figures, 295-304
New Yorker style, 304-33
fiction, journalism, and humor at *The New Yorker,* 333-48
the new *New Yorker,* 348-56

Newgate Novel NCLC 24: 166-204
development of Newgate literature, 166-73
Newgate Calendar, 173-7
Newgate fiction, 177-95
Newgate drama, 195-204

Nigerian Literature of the Twentieth Century TCLC 30: 199-265
surveys of, 199-227

English language and African life, 227-45
politics and the Nigerian writer, 245-54
Nigerian writers and society, 255-62

Nineteenth-Century Captivity Narratives NCLC 80:131-218
overview, 132-37
the political significance of captivity narratives, 137-67
images of gender, 167-96
moral instruction, 197-217

Nineteenth-Century Native American Autobiography NCLC 64: 262-389
overview, 263-8
problems of authorship, 268-81
the evolution of Native American autobiography, 281-304
political issues, 304-15
gender and autobiography, 316-62
autobiographical works during the turn of the century, 362-88

Norse Mythology CMLC 26: 321-85
history and mythological tradition, 322-44
Eddic poetry, 344-74
Norse mythology and other traditions, 374-85

Northern Humanism LC 16: 281-356
background, 282-305
precursor of the Reformation, 305-14
the Brethren of the Common Life, the Devotio Moderna, and education, 314-40
the impact of printing, 340-56

Novel of Manners, The NCLC 56: 342-96
social and political order, 343-53
domestic order, 353-73
depictions of gender, 373-83
the American novel of manners, 383-95

Nuclear Literature: Writings and Criticism in the Nuclear Age TCLC 46: 288-390
overviews, 290-301
fiction, 301-35
poetry, 335-8
nuclear war in Russo-Japanese literature, 338-55
nuclear war and women writers, 355-67
the nuclear referent and literary criticism, 367-88

Occultism in Modern Literature TCLC 50: 362-406
influence of occultism on literature, 363-72
occultism, literature, and society, 372-87
fiction, 387-96
drama, 396-405

Opium and the Nineteenth-Century Literary Imagination NCLC 20:250-301
original sources, 250-62
historical background, 262-71
and literary society, 271-9
and literary creativity, 279-300

The Oxford Movement NCLC 72: 1-197
overviews, 2-24
background, 24-59
and education, 59-69
religious responses, 69-128
literary aspects, 128-178
political implications, 178-196

The Parnassian Movement NCLC 72: 198-241
overviews, 199-231
and epic form, 231-38
and positivism, 238-41

Pastoral Literature of the English Renaissance LC 59: 171-282
overviews, 172-214
principal figures of the Elizabethan period, 214-33

principal figures of the later Renaissance, 233-50
pastoral drama, 250-81

Periodicals, Nineteenth-Century British NCLC 24: 100-65
overviews, 100-30
in the Romantic Age, 130-41
in the Victorian era, 142-54
and the reviewer, 154-64

Plath, Sylvia, and the Nature of Biography CLC 86: 433-62
the nature of biography, 433-52
reviews of *The Silent Woman,* 452-61

Political Theory from the 15th to the 18th Century LC 36: 1-55
Overview, 1-26
Natural Law, 26-42
Empiricism, 42-55

Polish Romanticism NCLC 52: 305-71
overviews, 306-26
major figures, 326-40
Polish Romantic drama, 340-62
influences, 362-71

Politics and Literature TCLC 94: 138-61
overviews, 139-96
Europe, 196-226
Latin America, 226-48
Africa and the Caribbean, 248-60

Popular Literature TCLC 70: 279-382
overviews, 280-324
"formula" fiction, 324-336
readers of popular literature, 336-351
evolution of popular literature, 351-382

The Portrayal of Jews in Nineteenth-Century English Literature NCLC 72: 242-368
overviews, 244-77
Anglo-Jewish novels, 277-303
depictions by non-Jewish writers, 303-44
Hebraism versus Hellenism, 344-67

Postmodernism TCLC 90:125-307
Overview, 126-166
Criticism , 166-224
Fiction, 224-282
Poetry, 282-300
Drama, 300-307

Pre-Raphaelite Movement NCLC 20: 302-401
overview, 302-4
genesis, 304-12
Germ and *Oxford and Cambridge Magazine,* 312-20
Robert Buchanan and the "Fleshly School of Poetry," 320-31
satires and parodies, 331-4
surveys, 334-51
aesthetics, 351-75
sister arts of poetry and painting, 375-94
influence, 394-9

Pre-romanticism LC 40: 1-56
overviews, 2-14
defining the period, 14-23
new directions in poetry and prose, 23-45
the focus on the self, 45-56

Pre-Socratic Philosophy CMLC 22: 1-56
overviews, 3-24
the Ionians and the Pythagoreans, 25-35
Heraclitus, the Eleatics, and the Atomists, 36-47
the Sophists, 47-55

Protestant Reformation, Literature of the LC 37: 1-83
overviews, 1-49
humanism and scholasticism, 49-69
the reformation and literature, 69-82

Psychoanalysis and Literature TCLC 38: 227-338
overviews, 227-46
Freud on literature, 246-51
psychoanalytic views of the literary process, 251-61
psychoanalytic theories of response to literature, 261-88
psychoanalysis and literary criticism, 288-312
psychoanalysis as literature/literature as psychoanalysis, 313-34

Rap Music CLC 76: 477-50

Renaissance Natural Philosophy LC 27: 201-87
cosmology, 201-28
astrology, 228-54
magic, 254-86

Restoration Drama LC 21: 184-275
general overviews, 185-230
Jeremy Collier stage controversy, 230-9
other critical interpretations, 240-75

Revising the Literary Canon CLC 81: 465-509

Revolutionary Astronomers LC 51: 314-65
Overviews, 316-25
Principal Figures, 325-51
Revolutionary Astronomical Models, 352-64

Robin Hood, Legend of LC 19: 205-58
origins and development of the Robin Hood legend, 206-20
representations of Robin Hood, 220-44
Robin Hood as hero, 244-56

Rushdie, Salman, *Satanic Verses* Controversy CLC 55 214-63; 59:404-56

Russian Nihilism NCLC 28: 403-47
definitions and overviews, 404-17
women and Nihilism, 417-27
literature as reform: the Civic Critics, 427-33
Nihilism and the Russian novel: Turgenev and Dostoevsky, 433-47

Russian Thaw TCLC 26: 189-247
literary history of the period, 190-206
theoretical debate of socialist realism, 206-11
Novy Mir, 211-7
Literary Moscow, 217-24
Pasternak, *Zhivago,* and the Nobel Prize, 224-7
poetry of liberation, 228-31
Brodsky trial and the end of the Thaw, 231-6
achievement and influence, 236-46

Salem Witch Trials LC 38: 1-145
overviews, 2-30
historical background, 30-65
judicial background, 65-78
the search for causes, 78-115
the role of women in the trials, 115-44

Salinger, J. D., Controversy Surrounding *In Search of J. D. Salinger* CLC 55: 325-44

Science and Modern Literature TCLC 90: 308-419
Overviews, 295-333
Fiction, 333-395
Poetry, 395-405
Drama, 405-419

Science Fiction, Nineteenth-Century NCLC 24: 241-306
background, 242-50
definitions of the genre, 251-6
representative works and writers, 256-75
themes and conventions, 276-305

Scottish Chaucerians LC 20: 363-412

Scottish Poetry, Eighteenth-Century LC 29: 95-167
overviews, 96-114
the Scottish Augustans, 114-28
the Scots Vernacular Revival, 132-63
Scottish poetry after Burns, 163-6

Sea in Literature, The TCLC 82: 72-191
drama, 73-79
poetry, 79-119
fiction, 119-191

Sensation Novel, The NCLC 80: 219-330
overviews, 221-46
principal figures, 246-62
nineteenth-century reaction, 262-91
feminist criticism, 291-329

Sentimental Novel, The NCLC 60: 146-245
overviews, 147-58
the politics of domestic fiction, 158-79
a literature of resistance and repression, 179-212
the reception of sentimental fiction, 213-44

Sex and Literature TCLC 82: 192-434
overviews, 193-216
drama, 216-263
poetry, 263-287
fiction, 287-431

Sherlock Holmes Centenary TCLC 26: 248-310
Doyle's life and the composition of the Holmes stories, 248-59
life and character of Holmes, 259-78
method, 278-9
Holmes and the Victorian world, 279-92
Sherlockian scholarship, 292-301
Doyle and the development of the detective story, 301-7
Holmes's continuing popularity, 307-9

The Silver Fork Novel NCLC 88: 58-140
criticism, 59-139

Slave Narratives, American NCLC 20: 1-91
background, 2-9
overviews, 9-24
contemporary responses, 24-7
language, theme, and technique, 27-70
historical authenticity, 70-5
antecedents, 75-83
role in development of Black American literature, 83-8

The Slave Trade in British and American Literature LC 59: 283-369
overviews, 284-91
depictions by white writers, 291-331
depictions by former slaves, 331-67

Social Conduct Literature LC 55: 196-298
overviews, 196-223
prescriptive ideology in other literary forms, 223-38
role of the press, 238-63
impact of conduct literature, 263-87
conduct literature and the perception of women, 287-96
women writing for women, 296-98

Socialism NCLC 88: 141-237
origins, 142-54
French socialism, 154-83
Anglo-American socialism, 183-205
Socialist-Feminism, 205-36

Spanish Civil War Literature TCLC 26: 311-85
topics in, 312-33
British and American literature, 333-59
French literature, 359-62
Spanish literature, 362-73
German literature, 373-5
political idealism and war literature, 375-83

Spanish Golden Age Literature LC 23: 262-332
overviews, 263-81
verse drama, 281-304
prose fiction, 304-19
lyric poetry, 319-31

Spasmodic School of Poetry NCLC 24: 307-52
history and major figures, 307-21
the Spasmodics on poetry, 321-7
Firmilian and critical disfavor, 327-39
theme and technique, 339-47
influence, 347-51

Sports in Literature TCLC 86: 294-445
overviews, 295-324
major writers and works, 324-402
sports, literature, and social issues, 402-45

Steinbeck, John, Fiftieth Anniversary of *The Grapes of Wrath* CLC 59: 311-54

Sturm und Drang NCLC 40: 196-276
definitions, 197-238
poetry and poetics, 238-58
drama, 258-75

Supernatural Fiction in the Nineteenth Century NCLC 32: 207-87
major figures and influences, 208-35
the Victorian ghost story, 236-54
the influence of science and occultism, 254-66
supernatural fiction and society, 266-86

Supernatural Fiction, Modern TCLC 30: 59-116
evolution and varieties, 60-74
"decline" of the ghost story, 74-86
as a literary genre, 86-92
technique, 92-101
nature and appeal, 101-15

Surrealism TCLC 30: 334-406
history and formative influences, 335-43
manifestos, 343-54
philosophic, aesthetic, and political principles, 354-75
poetry, 375-81
novel, 381-6
drama, 386-92
film, 392-8
painting and sculpture, 398-403
achievement, 403-5

Symbolism, Russian TCLC 30: 266-333
doctrines and major figures, 267-92
theories, 293-8
and French Symbolism, 298-310
themes in poetry, 310-4
theater, 314-20
and the fine arts, 320-32

Symbolist Movement, French NCLC 20: 169-249
background and characteristics, 170-86
principles, 186-91
attacked and defended, 191-7
influences and predecessors, 197-211
and Decadence, 211-6
theater, 216-26
prose, 226-33
decline and influence, 233-47

Television and Literature TCLC 78: 283-426
television and literacy, 283-98
reading vs. watching, 298-341
adaptations, 341-62
literary genres and television, 362-90
television genres and literature, 390-410
children's literature/children's television, 410-25

Theater of the Absurd TCLC 38: 339-415
"The Theater of the Absurd," 340-7
major plays and playwrights, 347-58
and the concept of the absurd, 358-86
theatrical techniques, 386-94

predecessors of, 394-402
influence of, 402-13

Tin Pan Alley See American Popular Song, Golden Age of

Tobacco Culture LC 55: 299-366
social and economic attitudes toward tobacco, 299-344
tobacco trade between the old world and
the new world, 344-55
tobacco smuggling in Great Britain, 355-66

Transcendentalism, American NCLC 24: 1-99
overviews, 3-23
contemporary documents, 23-41
theological aspects of, 42-52
and social issues, 52-74
literature of, 74-96

Travel Writing in the Nineteenth Century
NCLC 44: 274-392
the European grand tour, 275-303
the Orient, 303-47
North America, 347-91

Travel Writing in the Twentieth Century
TCLC 30: 407-56
conventions and traditions, 407-27
and fiction writing, 427-43
comparative essays on travel writers,
443-54

True-Crime Literature CLC 99: 333-433
history and analysis, 334-407
reviews of true-crime publications, 407-23
writing instruction, 424-29
author profiles, 429-33

***Ulysses* and the Process of Textual Recon-
struction** TCLC 26:386-416
evaluations of the new *Ulysses,* 386-94
editorial principles and procedures, 394-
401
theoretical issues, 401-16

Utilitarianism NCLC 84: 272-340
J. S. Mill's Utilitarianism: liberty, equality,
justice, 273-313
Jeremy Bentham's Utilitarianism: the science of happiness, 313-39

Utopianism NCLC 88: 238-346
overviews: Utopian literature, 239-59
Utopianism in American literature, 259-99
Utopianism in British literature, 299-311
Utopianism and Feminism, 311-45

Utopian Literature, Nineteenth-Century
NCLC 24: 353-473
definitions, 354-74
overviews, 374-88
theory, 388-408
communities, 409-26
fiction, 426-53
women and fiction, 454-71

Utopian Literature, Renaissance LC 32: 1-63
overviews, 2-25
classical background, 25-33
utopia and the social contract, 33-9
origins in mythology, 39-48
utopia and the Renaissance country house,
48-52
influence of millenarianism, 52-62

Vampire in Literature TCLC 46: 391-454
origins and evolution, 392-412
social and psychological perspectives,
413-44
vampire fiction and science fiction, 445-53

Victorian Autobiography NCLC 40: 277-363
development and major characteristics,
278-88
themes and techniques, 289-313
the autobiographical tendency in Victorian
prose and poetry, 313-47
Victorian women's autobiographies, 347-62

Victorian Fantasy Literature NCLC 60: 246-
384
overviews, 247-91
major figures, 292-366
women in Victorian fantasy literature,
366-83

Victorian Hellenism NCLC 68: 251-376
overviews, 252-78
the meanings of Hellenism, 278-335
the literary influence, 335-75

Victorian Novel NCLC 32: 288-454
development and major characteristics,
290-310
themes and techniques, 310-58
social criticism in the Victorian novel,
359-97
urban and rural life in the Victorian novel,
397-406
women in the Victorian novel, 406-25
Mudie's Circulating Library, 425-34
the late-Victorian novel, 434-51

Vietnam War in Literature and Film CLC
91: 383-437
overview, 384-8
prose, 388-412
film and drama, 412-24
poetry, 424-35

Violence in Literature TCLC 98: 235-358
overviews and general studies, 236-74
violence in the works of modern authors,
274-358

Vorticism TCLC 62: 330-426
Wyndham Lewis and Vorticism, 330-8
characteristics and principles of Vorticism,
338-65

Lewis and Pound, 365-82
Vorticist writing, 382-416
Vorticist painting, 416-26

Well-Made Play, The NCLC 80: 331-370
overviews, 332-45
Scribe's style, 345-56
the influence of the well-made play, 356-69

**Women's Autobiography, Nineteenth Cen-
tury** NCLC 76: 285-368
overviews, 287-300
autobiographies concerned with religious
and political issues, 300-15
autobiographies by women of color, 315-38
autobiographies by women pioneers,
338-51
autobiographies by women of letters,
351-68

Women's Diaries, Nineteenth-Century NCLC
48: 308-54
overview, 308-13
diary as history, 314-25
sociology of diaries, 325-34
diaries as psychological scholarship, 334-43
diary as autobiography, 343-8
diary as literature, 348-53

Women in Modern Literature TCLC 94: 262-
425
overviews, 263-86
American literature, 286-304
other national literatures, 304-33
fiction, 333-94
poetry, 394-407
drama, 407-24

Women Writers, Seventeenth-Century LC 30:
2-58
overview, 2-15
women and education, 15-9
women and autobiography, 19-31
women's diaries, 31-9
early feminists, 39-58

World War I Literature TCLC 34: 392-486
overview, 393-403
English, 403-27
German, 427-50
American, 450-66
French, 466-74
and modern history, 474-82

Yellow Journalism NCLC 36: 383-456
overviews, 384-96
major figures, 396-413

Young Playwrights Festival
1988 CLC 55: 376-81
1989 CLC 59: 398-403
1990 CLC 65: 444-8

NCLC Cumulative Nationality Index

AMERICAN

Alcott, Amos Bronson **1**
Alcott, Louisa May **6, 58, 83**
Alger, Horatio Jr. Jr. **8, 83**
Allston, Washington **2**
Apess, William **73**
Audubon, John James **47**
Barlow, Joel **23**
Beecher, Catharine Esther **30**
Bellamy, Edward **4, 86**
Bird, Robert Montgomery **1**
Brackenridge, Hugh Henry **7**
Brentano, Clemens (Maria) **1**
Brown, Charles Brockden **22, 74**
Brown, William Wells **2, 89**
Brownson, Orestes Augustus **50**
Bryant, William Cullen **6, 46**
Burney, Fanny **12, 54, 81**
Calhoun, John Caldwell **15**
Channing, William Ellery **17**
Child, Lydia Maria **6, 73**
Chivers, Thomas Holley **49**
Cooke, John Esten **5**
Cooper, James Fenimore **1, 27, 54**
Crockett, David **8**
Dana, Richard Henry Sr. **53**
Dickinson, Emily (Elizabeth) **21, 77**
Douglass, Frederick **7, 55**
Dunlap, William **2**
Dwight, Timothy **13**
Emerson, Mary Moody **66**
Emerson, Ralph Waldo **1, 38**
Field, Eugene **3**
Foster, Stephen Collins **26**
Frederic, Harold **10**
Freneau, Philip Morin **1**
Fuller, Margaret **5, 50**
Hale, Sarah Josepha (Buell) **75**
Halleck, Fitz-Greene **47**
Hamilton, Alexander **49**
Hammon, Jupiter **5**
Harris, George Washington **23**
Hawthorne, Nathaniel **2, 10, 17, 23, 39, 79**
Holmes, Oliver Wendell **14, 81**
Horton, George Moses **87**
Irving, Washington **2, 19**
Jackson, Helen Hunt **90**
Jacobs, Harriet A(nn) **67**
James, Henry Sr. **53**
Jefferson, Thomas **11**
Kennedy, John Pendleton **2**
Kirkland, Caroline M. **85**
Lanier, Sidney **6**
Lazarus, Emma **8**
Lincoln, Abraham **18**
Longfellow, Henry Wadsworth **2, 45**
Lowell, James Russell **2, 90**
Melville, Herman **3, 12, 29, 45, 49, 91**
Mowatt, Anna Cora **74**
Murray, Judith Sargent **63**
Parkman, Francis Jr. Jr. **12**
Parton, Sara Payson Willis **86**

Paulding, James Kirke **2**
Pinkney, Edward **31**
Poe, Edgar Allan **1, 16, 55, 78**
Rowson, Susanna Haswell **5, 69**
Sand, George **2, 42, 57**
Sedgwick, Catharine Maria **19**
Shaw, Henry Wheeler **15**
Sigourney, Lydia Howard (Huntley) **21, 87**
Simms, William Gilmore **3**
Smith, Joseph Jr. **53**
Southworth, Emma Dorothy Eliza Nevitte **26**
Stowe, Harriet (Elizabeth) Beecher **3, 50**
Taylor, Bayard **89**
Thoreau, Henry David **7, 21, 61**
Timrod, Henry **25**
Trumbull, John **30**
Tyler, Royall **3**
Very, Jones **9**
Warner, Susan (Bogert) **31**
Warren, Mercy Otis **13**
Webster, Noah **30**
Whitman, Sarah Helen (Power) **19**
Whitman, Walt(er) **4, 31, 81**
Whittier, John Greenleaf **8, 59**
Winnemucca, Sarah **79**

ARGENTINIAN

Echeverria, (Jose) Esteban (Antonino) **18**
Hernandez, Jose **17**

AUSTRALIAN

Adams, Francis **33**
Clarke, Marcus (Andrew Hislop) **19**
Gordon, Adam Lindsay **21**
Kendall, Henry **12**

AUSTRIAN

Grillparzer, Franz **1**
Lenau, Nikolaus **16**
Nestroy, Johann **42**
Raimund, Ferdinand Jakob **69**
Sacher-Masoch, Leopold von **31**
Stifter, Adalbert **41**

CANADIAN

Crawford, Isabella Valancy **12**
Haliburton, Thomas Chandler **15**
Lampman, Archibald **25**
Moodie, Susanna (Strickland) **14**
Richardson, John **55**
Traill, Catharine Parr **31**

COLOMBIAN

Isaacs, Jorge Ricardo **70**

CUBAN

Marti (y Perez), Jose (Julian) **63**

CZECH

Macha, Karel Hynek **46**

DANISH

Andersen, Hans Christian **7, 79**
Grundtvig, Nicolai Frederik Severin **1**
Jacobsen, Jens Peter **34**
Kierkegaard, Soren **34, 78**

ENGLISH

Ainsworth, William Harrison **13**
Arnold, Matthew **6, 29, 89**
Arnold, Thomas **18**
Austen, Jane **1, 13, 19, 33, 51, 81**
Bagehot, Walter **10**
Barbauld, Anna Laetitia **50**
Barham, Richard Harris **77**
Barnes, William **75**
Beardsley, Aubrey **6**
Beckford, William **16**
Beddoes, Thomas Lovell **3**
Bentham, Jeremy **38**
Blake, William **13, 37, 57**
Borrow, George (Henry) **9**
Bronte, Anne **4, 71**
Bronte, Charlotte **3, 8, 33, 58**
Bronte, Emily (Jane) **16, 35**
Browning, Elizabeth Barrett **1, 16, 61, 66**
Browning, Robert **19, 79**
Bulwer-Lytton, Edward (George Earle Lytton) **1, 45**
Burton, Richard F(rancis) **42**
Byron, George Gordon (Noel) **2, 12**
Carlyle, Thomas **22**
Carroll, Lewis **2, 53**
Clare, John **9, 86**
Clough, Arthur Hugh **27**
Cobbett, William **49**
Coleridge, Hartley **90**
Coleridge, Samuel Taylor **9, 54**
Coleridge, Sara **31**
Collins, (William) Wilkie **1, 18**
Cowper, William **8**
Crabbe, George **26**
Craik, Dinah Maria (Mulock) **38**
Darwin, Charles **57**
De Quincey, Thomas **4, 87**
Dickens, Charles (John Huffam) **3, 8, 18, 26, 37, 50, 86**
Disraeli, Benjamin **2, 39, 79**
Dobell, Sydney Thompson **43**
Du Maurier, George **86**
Eden, Emily **10**
Eliot, George **4, 13, 23, 41, 49, 89**
FitzGerald, Edward **9**
Forster, John **11**
Froude, James Anthony **43**
Gaskell, Elizabeth Cleghorn **5, 70**
Gilpin, William **30**
Godwin, William **14**
Gore, Catherine **65**
Hazlitt, William **29, 82**

Hemans, Felicia **29, 71**
Holcroft, Thomas **85**
Hood, Thomas **16**
Hopkins, Gerard Manley **17**
Hunt, (James Henry) Leigh **1, 70**
Huxley, T(homas) H(enry) **67**
Inchbald, Elizabeth **62**
Ingelow, Jean **39**
Jefferies, (John) Richard **47**
Jerrold, Douglas William **2**
Jewsbury, Geraldine (Endsor) **22**
Keats, John **8, 73**
Keble, John **87**
Kemble, Fanny **18**
Kingsley, Charles **35**
Lamb, Charles **10**
Lamb, Lady Caroline **38**
Landon, Letitia Elizabeth **15**
Landor, Walter Savage **14**
Lear, Edward **3**
Lennox, Charlotte Ramsay **23**
Lewes, George Henry **25**
Lewis, Matthew Gregory **11, 62**
Linton, Eliza Lynn **41**
Macaulay, Thomas Babington **42**
Marryat, Frederick **3**
Martineau, Harriet **26**
Mayhew, Henry **31**
Mill, John Stuart **11, 58**
Mitford, Mary Russell **4**
Montagu, Elizabeth **7**
More, Hannah **27**
Morris, William **4**
Newman, John Henry **38**
Norton, Caroline **47**
Oliphant, Laurence **47**
Opie, Amelia **65**
Paine, Thomas **62**
Pater, Walter (Horatio) **7, 90**
Patmore, Coventry Kersey Dighton **9**
Peacock, Thomas Love **22**
Piozzi, Hester Lynch (Thrale) **57**
Planche, James Robinson **42**
Polidori, John William **51**
Radcliffe, Ann (Ward) **6, 55**
Reade, Charles **2, 74**
Reeve, Clara **19**
Robertson, Thomas William **35**
Robinson, Henry Crabb **15**
Rogers, Samuel **69**
Rossetti, Christina (Georgina) **2, 50, 66**
Rossetti, Dante Gabriel **4, 77**
Sala, George Augustus **46**
Shelley, Mary Wollstonecraft (Godwin) **14, 59**
Shelley, Percy Bysshe **18**
Smith, Charlotte (Turner) **23**
Southey, Robert **8**
Surtees, Robert Smith **14**
Symonds, John Addington **34**
Tennyson, Alfred **30, 65**
Thackeray, William Makepeace **5, 14, 22, 43**
Trelawny, Edward John **85**
Trollope, Anthony **6, 33**
Trollope, Frances **30**
Wordsworth, Dorothy **25**
Wordsworth, William **12, 38**

FILIPINO

Rizal, Jose **27**

FINNISH

Kivi, Aleksis **30**
Lonnrot, Elias **53**
Runeberg, Johan **41**

FRENCH

Augier, Emile **31**
Balzac, Honore de **5, 35, 53**
Banville, Theodore (Faullain) de **9**

Barbey d'Aurevilly, Jules Amedee **1**
Baudelaire, Charles **6, 29, 55**
Becque, Henri **3**
Beranger, Pierre Jean de **34**
Bertrand, Aloysius **31**
Borel, Petrus **41**
Chateaubriand, Francois Rene de **3**
Comte, Auguste **54**
Constant (de Rebecque), (Henri) Benjamin **6**
Corbiere, Tristan **43**
Daudet, (Louis Marie) Alphonse **1**
Dumas, Alexandre (fils) **9**
Dumas, Alexandre (Davy de la Pailleterie) **11, 71**
Feuillet, Octave **45**
Flaubert, Gustave **2, 10, 19, 62, 66**
Fourier, Charles **51**
Fromentin, Eugene (Samuel Auguste) **10**
Gaboriau, Emile **14**
Gautier, Theophile **1, 59**
Gobineau, Joseph Arthur (Comte) de **17**
Goncourt, Edmond (Louis Antoine Huot) de **7**
Goncourt, Jules (Alfred Huot) de **7**
Hugo, Victor (Marie) **3, 10, 21**
Joubert, Joseph **9**
Kock, Charles Paul de **16**
Laclos, Pierre Ambroise Francois Choderlos de **4, 87**
Laforgue, Jules **5, 53**
Lamartine, Alphonse (Marie Louis Prat) de **11**
Lautreamont, Comte de **12**
Leconte de Lisle, Charles-Marie-Rene **29**
Maistre, Joseph de **37**
Mallarme, Stephane **4, 41**
Maupassant, (Henri Rene Albert) Guy de **1, 42, 83**
Merimee, Prosper **6, 65**
Michelet, Jules **31**
Musset, (Louis Charles) Alfred de **7**
Nerval, Gerard de **1, 67**
Nodier, (Jean) Charles (Emmanuel) **19**
Pixerecourt, (Rene Charles) Guilbert de **39**
Renan, Joseph Ernest **26**
Rimbaud, (Jean Nicolas) Arthur **4, 35, 82**
Sade, Donatien Alphonse Francois, Comte de **3, 47**
Sainte-Beuve, Charles Augustin **5**
Sand, George **2, 42, 57**
Scribe, (Augustin) Eugene **16**
Senancour, Etienne Pivert de **16**
Staël-Holstein, Anne Louise Germaine Necker Baronn de **3, 91**
Stendhal **23, 46**
Sue, Eugene **1**
Taine, Hippolyte Adolphe **15**
Tocqueville, Alexis (Charles Henri Maurice Clerel, Comte) de **7, 63**
Valles, Jules **71**
Verlaine, Paul (Marie) **2, 51**
Vigny, Alfred (Victor) de **7**
Villiers de l'Isle Adam, Jean Marie Mathias Philippe Auguste, Comte de **3**

GERMAN

Arnim, Achim von (Ludwig Joachim von Arnim) **5**
Arnim, Bettina von **38**
Bonaventura **35**
Buchner, (Karl) Georg **26**
Claudius, Matthias **75**
Droste-Hulshoff, Annette Freiin von **3**
Eichendorff, Joseph Freiherr von **8**
Engels, Friedrich **85**
Fichte, Johann Gottlieb **62**
Fontane, Theodor **26**
Fouque, Friedrich (Heinrich Karl) de la Motte **2**
Goethe, Johann Wolfgang von **4, 22, 34, 90**
Grabbe, Christian Dietrich **2**

Grimm, Jacob Ludwig Karl **3, 77**
Grimm, Wilhelm Karl **3, 77**
Hebbel, Friedrich **43**
Hegel, Georg Wilhelm Friedrich **46**
Heine, Heinrich **4, 54**
Hoffmann, E(rnst) T(heodor) A(madeus) **2**
Holderlin, (Johann Christian) Friedrich **16**
Immermann, Karl (Lebrecht) **4, 49**
Jean Paul **7**
Kant, Immanuel **27, 67**
Kleist, Heinrich von **2, 37**
Klinger, Friedrich Maximilian von **1**
Klopstock, Friedrich Gottlieb **11**
Kotzebue, August (Friedrich Ferdinand) von **25**
Ludwig, Otto **4**
Marx, Karl (Heinrich) **17**
Meyer, Conrad Ferdinand **81**
Morike, Eduard (Friedrich) **10**
Novalis **13**
Schelling, Friedrich Wilhelm Joseph von **30**
Schiller, Friedrich **39, 69**
Schlegel, August Wilhelm von **15**
Schlegel, Friedrich **45**
Schopenhauer, Arthur **51**
Storm, (Hans) Theodor (Woldsen) **1**
Tieck, (Johann) Ludwig **5, 46**
Wagner, Richard **9**
Wieland, Christoph Martin **17**

GREEK

Solomos, Dionysios **15**

HUNGARIAN

Arany, Janos **34**
Madach, Imre **19**
Petofi, Sandor **21**

INDIAN

Chatterji, Bankim Chandra **19**
Dutt, Toru **29**
Ghalib **39, 78**

IRISH

Allingham, William **25**
Banim, John **13**
Banim, Michael **13**
Boucicault, Dion **41**
Carleton, William **3**
Croker, John Wilson **10**
Darley, George **2**
Edgeworth, Maria **1, 51**
Ferguson, Samuel **33**
Griffin, Gerald **7**
Jameson, Anna **43**
Le Fanu, Joseph Sheridan **9, 58**
Lever, Charles (James) **23**
Maginn, William **8**
Mangan, James Clarence **27**
Maturin, Charles Robert **6**
Merriman, Brian **70**
Moore, Thomas **6**
Morgan, Lady **29**
O'Brien, Fitz-James **21**
Sheridan, Richard Brinsley **5, 91**

ITALIAN

Collodi, Carlo **54**
Foscolo, Ugo **8**
Gozzi, (Conte) Carlo **23**
Leopardi, (Conte) Giacomo **22**
Manzoni, Alessandro **29**
Mazzini, Guiseppe **34**
Nievo, Ippolito **22**

JAPANESE

Higuchi, Ichiyo **49**
Motoori, Norinaga **45**

LITHUANIAN

Mapu, Abraham (ben Jekutiel) **18**

MEXICAN

Lizardi, Jose Joaquin Fernandez de **30**

NORWEGIAN

Collett, (Jacobine) Camilla (Wergeland) **22**
Wergeland, Henrik Arnold **5**

POLISH

Fredro, Aleksander **8**
Krasicki, Ignacy **8**
Krasinski, Zygmunt **4**
Mickiewicz, Adam **3**
Norwid, Cyprian Kamil **17**
Slowacki, Juliusz **15**

ROMANIAN

Eminescu, Mihail **33**

RUSSIAN

Aksakov, Sergei Timofeyvich **2**
Bakunin, Mikhail (Alexandrovich) **25, 58**
Bashkirtseff, Marie **27**
Belinski, Vissarion Grigoryevich **5**
Chernyshevsky, Nikolay Gavrilovich **1**
Dobrolyubov, Nikolai Alexandrovich **5**
Dostoevsky, Fedor Mikhailovich **2, 7, 21,
    33, 43**

Gogol, Nikolai (Vasilyevich) **5, 15, 31**
Goncharov, Ivan Alexandrovich **1, 63**
Granovsky, Timofei Nikolaevich **75**
Herzen, Aleksandr Ivanovich **10, 61**
Karamzin, Nikolai Mikhailovich **3**
Krylov, Ivan Andreevich **1**
Lermontov, Mikhail Yuryevich **5**
Leskov, Nikolai (Semyonovich) **25**
Nekrasov, Nikolai Alekseevich **11**
Ostrovsky, Alexander **30, 57**
Pisarev, Dmitry Ivanovich **25**
Pushkin, Alexander (Sergeyevich) **3, 27, 83**
Saltykov, Mikhail Evgrafovich **16**
Smolenskin, Peretz **30**
Turgenev, Ivan **21**
Tyutchev, Fyodor **34**
Zhukovsky, Vasily (Andreevich) **35**

SCOTTISH

Baillie, Joanna **2**
Beattie, James **25**
Blair, Hugh **75**
Campbell, Thomas **19**
Carlyle, Thomas **22**
Ferrier, Susan (Edmonstone) **8**
Galt, John **1**
Hogg, James **4**
Jeffrey, Francis **33**
Lockhart, John Gibson **6**
Mackenzie, Henry **41**
Oliphant, Margaret (Oliphant Wilson) **11,
    61**

Scott, Walter **15, 69**
Stevenson, Robert Louis (Balfour) **5, 14, 63**
Thomson, James **18**
Wilson, John **5**
Wright, Frances **74**

SPANISH

Alarcon, Pedro Antonio de **1**
Caballero, Fernan **10**
Castro, Rosalia de **3, 78**
Espronceda, Jose de **39**
Larra (y Sanchez de Castro), Mariano Jose
    de **17**
Tamayo y Baus, Manuel **1**
Zorrilla y Moral, Jose **6**

SWEDISH

Almqvist, Carl Jonas Love **42**
Bremer, Fredrika **11**
Stagnelius, Eric Johan **61**
Tegner, Esaias **2**

SWISS

Amiel, Henri Frederic **4**
Burckhardt, Jacob (Christoph) **49**
Charriere, Isabelle de **66**
Keller, Gottfried **2**
Meyer, Conrad Ferdinand **81**
Wyss, Johann David Von **10**

UKRAINIAN

Shevchenko, Taras **54**

Nationality Index

NCLC-91 Title Index

Adelaide and Theodore (de Staël)
  See *Adélaïde et Théodore*
Adélaïde et Théodore (de Staël) **91**:322, 339
Affectation (Sheridan) **91**:243
"After the Pleasure Party" (Melville) **91**:184
Agar (de Staël) **91**:359
The Ambiguities (Melville)
  See *Pierre; or, The Ambiguities*
"Appel aux Soverains" (de Staël) **91**:340, 342
Benito Cereno (Melville) **91**:204
Billy Budd, Sailor: An Inside Narrative
  (Melville) **91**:53, 193
Cahier staëlien (de Staël) **91**:359-60
The Camp (Sheridan) **91**:242
Des circonstances actuelles qui peuvent
  terminer la Révolution et des principes
  qui doi vent fonder la république en
  France (de Staël) **91**:291
Circumstances (de Staël)
  See *Des circonstances actuelles qui peuvent*
  terminer la Révolution et des principes
  qui doi vent fonder la république en
  France
Clarel: A Poem and Pilgrimage in the Holy
  Land (Melville) **91**:9, 184
"Clio's Protest" (Sheridan) **91**:231, 233
A Comparative Statement of the Two Bills for
  the Better Government of the British
  Possessions in India (Sheridan) **91**:273
Concerning the Influence of the Passions upon
  the Happiness of Individuals and of
  Nations (de Staël)
  See *De l'influence des passions sur le*
  bonheur des individus et des nations
The Confidence-Man: His Masquerade
  (Melville) **91**:84, 121, 175, 177, 180, 204
Considerations (de Staël)
  See *Considérations sur la Révolution*
  française
Considérations sur la Révolution française (de
  Staël) **91**:323, 360
Corinne ou l'Italie (de Staël) **91**:292-92, 303,
  314-15, 318, 320, 327-31, 337-38, 340-42,
  344-56, 359–60, 365
Correspondence (Melville) **91**:218, 220, 222
The Critic; or, Tragedy Rehearsed (Sheridan)
  91:242, 244-45, 255-58, 260, 262-64
Delphine (de Staël) **91**:291-92, 297-98, 304-05,
  308-10, 312, 323-26, 331-32, 335-37, 340,
  351, 353-55, 359-60, 365
Dix années d'exil (de Staël) **91**:325, 350-51,
  360, 363, 365
"Dry Be That Tear" (Sheridan) **91**:232
The Duenna; or, The Doubling Elopement
  (Sheridan) **91**:241-42, 251
"Elegy on the Death of a British Officer"
  (Sheridan) **91**:233
"Epitaph on Brooks" (Sheridan) **91**:233
"L'Epître au malheur" (de Staël) **91**:335, 358
Essai sur les fictions (de Staël) **91**:299-301,
  303-04, 311, 332, 339-40
Essay (de Staël)
  See *Essai sur les fictions*

Essay on Fiction (de Staël)
  See *Essai sur les fictions*
"A Familiar Epistle" (Sheridan) **91**:231
Fictions (de Staël)
  See *Essai sur les fictions*
Folle (de Staël) **91**:360
Geneviève de Brabant (de Staël) **91**:359
Génie du christianisme (de Staël) **91**:332, 359
"Grave Comedy" (Sheridan) **91**:245
"The Grotto" (Sheridan) **91**:232
"Hawthorne and his Mosses" (Melville)
  91:33-4, 140, 209, 212, 219
Histoire de Pauline (de Staël) **91**:324, 339-40,
  358, 360
"Hymen and Hirco: A Vision" (Sheridan)
  91:230
Les Inconvénients de la vie de Paris (de Staël)
  91:358
Ixion (Sheridan) **91**:257
Jane Gray (de Staël) **91**:323, 326, 335, 340,
  358
Jean de Witt (de Stael) **91**:358
De la littérature (de Staël)
  See *De la littérature considérée dans ses*
  rapports avec les institutions sociales
De la littérature considérée dans ses rapports
  avec les institutions sociales (de Staël)
  91:298, 304-06, 310-12, 323-24, 326, 332,
  340, 359
De l'Allemagne (de Staël) **91**:338, 340, 350-51,
  359-60, 365
De l'esprit des traductions (de Staël) **91**:340
The Letters of Herman Melville (Melville)
  91:30, 32-3
Lettres (de Staël)
  See *Lettres sur les ouvrages et le caractère*
  de Jean-Jacques Rousseau
Lettres sur les ouvrages et le caractère de
  Jean-Jacques Rousseau (de Staël) **91**:339,
  358
Lettres sur Rousseau (de Staël)
  See *Lettres sur les ouvrages et le caractère*
  de Jean-Jacques Rousseau
"Lines By a Lady on the Loss of Her Trunk"
  (Sheridan) **91**:233
De l'influence des passions sur le bonheur des
  individus et des nations (de Staël) **91**:298-
  305, 311, 332-36, 340
The Mannequin (de Stael)
  See *Le Mannequin*
Le Mannequin (de Stael) **91**:326, 360
Mardi: And a Voyage Thither (Melville) **91**:4,
  7, 10, 18, 30-2, 42-3, 45-6, 55, 88, 121,
  204, 212
Mirza, ou lettre d'un voyageur (de Staël)
  91:339-42, 358, 360
Moby-Dick; or, The Whale (Melville) **91**:3-6,
  9-10, 18, 21, 24, 28-34, 41-7, 50-1, 53-6,
  68, 74, 81, 88-90, 93, 111, 113, 115, 121,
  134, 180-81, 193, 198, 204, 206, 212-13,
  217-20
Montmorency (de Staël) **91**:358

"Mosses" (Melville)
  See "Hawthorne and his Mosses"
Oeuvres complètes (de Staël) **91**:332-36
Omoo: A Narrative of Adventures in the South
  Seas (Melville) **91**:10, 42, 45, 55, 212
On Germany (de Staël) **91**:326-27
On Literature (de Stael)
  See *De la littérature considérée dans ses*
  rapports avec les institutions sociales
On Literature Considered in Its Relationship
  with Social Institutions
  See *De la littérature considérée dans ses*
  rapports avec les institutions sociales
"On the Death of Elizabeth Linley" (Sheridan)
  91:232
"On Women Who Cultivate Letters" (de Staël)
  91:311
Passions (de Staël)
  See *De l'influence des passions sur le*
  bonheur des individus et des nations
Pierre; or, The Ambiguities (Melville) **91**:1-228
Pizarro (Sheridan) **91**:274, 279-87
"A Portrait for Amoret" (Sheridan) **91**:233-34
Recueil de morceaux détachés (de Staël) **91**:339,
  358
Redburn: His First Voyage (Melville) **91**:42,
  45, 54-5, 218
"Réflexions sur la paix" (de Staël) **91**:340
"Réflexions sur le procès de la reine" (de
  Stael) **91**:340
"Réflexions sur le suicide" (de Staël) **91**:360
"The Ridotto" (Sheridan)
  See "The Ridotto of Bath, a Panegyrick,
  Being an Epistle from Timothy Screw,
  Under Server to Messrs. Kuhf and
  Fitzwater, to his brother Heny, Waiter at
  Almack's"
"Ridotto of Bath" (Sheridan)
  See "The Ridotto of Bath, a Panegyrick,
  Being an Epistle from Timothy Screw,
  Under Server to Messrs. Kuhf and
  Fitzwater, to his brother Heny, Waiter at
  Almack's"
"The Ridotto of Bath" (Sheridan)
  See "The Ridotto of Bath, a Panegyrick,
  Being an Epistle from Timothy Screw,
  Under Server to Messrs. Kuhf and
  Fitzwater, to his brother Heny, Waiter at
  Almack's"
"The Ridotto of Bath, a Panegyrick, Being an
  Epistle from Timothy Screw, Under
  Server to Messrs. Kuhf and Fitzwater, to
  his brother Heny, Waiter at Almack's"
  (Sheridan) **91**:230-31, 239
The Rivals (Sheridan) **91**:236-37, 239-41, 245-
  48, 251-54, 256-64, 266-70
Sapho (de Staël)
  See *Sappho*
Sappho (de Staël) **91**:326, 359
The School for Scandal (Sheridan) **91**:233-34,
  242-43, 251, 253-54, 256, 258, 260-64, 266-
  70, 272
La Signora Fantastici (de Staël) **91**:360

Sophie ou les sintiments setrcts (de Staël)
    91:326-27, 340, 358
Story of Pauline (de Staël)
    See *Histoire de Pauline*
St. Patrick's Day; or, The Scheming Lieutenant
    (Sheridan) **91**:240-41
La Sunamite (de Staël) **91**:359-60
Ten Years of Exile (de Staël)
    See *Dix années d'exil*
Timoleon (Melville) **91**:184
"To Elizabeth Linley" (Sheridan) **91**:232

"To Laura" (Sheridan) **91**:232
"To the Recording Angel" (Sheridan) **91**:232
A Treatise on the Influence of the Passions
    upon the Happiness of Individuals and
    Nations (de Staël)
    See *De l'influence des passions sur le*
    bonheur des individus et des nations
A Trip to Scarborough (Sheridan) **91**:242
Typee: A Peep at Polynesian Life (Melville)
    91:9, 33, 44-5, 55, 63, 122, 212
"Verses Addressed to Laura" (Sheridan) **91**:233

"Verses to the Memory of Garrick" (Sheridan)
    91:234
"The Walse" (Sheridan) **91**:233
"We Two, Each Other's Only Pride"
    (Sheridan) **91**:232
The Whale (Melville)
    See *Moby-Dick; or, The Whale*
White-Jacket; or, The World in a Man-of-War
    (Melville) **91**:42-3, 45, 55, 186
Zulma (de Staël) **91**:340, 358

ISBN 0-7876-4546-X

90000

9 780787 645465